THE OXFORD HANDBOOK OF CRIMINOLOGY

Sixth edition

Edited by

ALISON LIEBLING
SHADD MARUNA
LESLEY McARA

OXFORD
UNIVERSITY PRESS

OXFORD
UNIVERSITY PRESS

Great Clarendon Street, Oxford, OX2 6DP,
United Kingdom

Oxford University Press is a department of the University of Oxford.
It furthers the University's objective of excellence in research, scholarship,
and education by publishing worldwide. Oxford is a registered trade mark of
Oxford University Press in the UK and in certain other countries

Third edition published in 2002
Fourth edition published in 2007
Fifth edition published in 2012

Impression: 2

Published in the United States of America by Oxford University Press
198 Madison Avenue, New York, NY 10016, United States of America

British Library Cataloguing in Publication Data
Data available

Library of Congress Control Number: 2016963288

ISBN 978–0–19–871944–1

Printed in Great Britain by
Bell and Bain Ltd, Glasgow

OUTLINE CONTENTS

PART III DYNAMICS OF CRIME AND VIOLENCE

PART IV RESPONSES TO CRIME

DETAILED CONTENTS

PART III DYNAMICS OF CRIME AND VIOLENCE

PART IV RESPONSES TO CRIME

NOTES ON CONTRIBUTORS

ANDREW ASHWORTH is Vinerian Professor of English Law Emeritus, University of Oxford.

JON BANNISTER is Professor of Criminology at Manchester Metropolitan University, where he directs the Crime and Well-Being Big Data Centre.

MARY BOSWORTH is Professor of Criminology and Fellow of St Cross College, University of Oxford, as well as Professor of Criminology at Monash University, Australia.

SIR ANTHONY BOTTOMS is Emeritus Wolfson Professor of Criminology, Life Fellow of Fitzwilliam College, and Director of the Centre for Penal Theory and Penal Ethics in the Institute of Criminology, University of Cambridge, as well as Honorary Professor of Criminology at the University of Sheffield.

BEN BOWLING is Professor of Criminology and Criminal Justice and Acting Dean of the Dickson Poon School of Law at King's College London.

AVI BRISMAN is Associate Professor in the School of Justice Studies, Eastern Kentucky University, and Adjunct Associate Professor in the School of Justice, Queensland University of Technology, Australia.

MICHELE BURMAN is Professor of Criminology and Head of the School of Social and Political Sciences at the University of Glasgow.

SIMON COTTEE is Senior Lecturer in Criminology at the University of Kent.

ADAM CRAWFORD is Professor of Criminology and Criminal Justice, and Director of the Leeds Social Sciences Institute at the University of Leeds. He is also Director of the N8 Policing Research Partnership.

BEN CREWE is Deputy Director of the Prisons Research Centre and Reader in Penology at the Institute of Criminology, University of Cambridge.

RON DUDAI is Martin Buber Postdoctoral Fellow and Project Manager at the Hebrew University of Jerusalem.

MANUEL EISNER is Professor of Comparative and Developmental Criminology at the University of Cambridge.

KAREN EVANS is Senior Lecturer in Sociology, Social Policy, and Criminology at the University of Liverpool.

JOHN FLINT is Professor of Town and Regional Planning and Head of Department of Geography at the University of Sheffield.

KATJA FRANKO is Professor of Criminology at the University of Oslo.

ALISTAIR FRASER is Lecturer in Criminology and Sociology at the University of Glasgow.

DAVID GADD is Professor of Criminology and Director of the Centre for Criminology and Criminal Justice at the University of Manchester.

DAVID GARLAND is the Arthur T. Vanderbilt Professor of Law and Professor of Sociology at New York University.

LORAINE GELSTHORPE is Professor of Criminology and Criminal Justice, Director of the Centre for Community, Gender and Social Justice, Deputy Director of the Institute of Criminology, and a Fellow of Pembroke College, University of Cambridge.

PENNY GREEN is Professor of Law and Globalisation at Queen Mary University of London.

CHRIS GREER is Professor of Criminology and Head of Department of Sociology at City, University of London.

KEITH HAYWARD is Professor of Criminology at the University of Copenhagen.

PADDY HILLYARD is Professor Emeritus of Sociology at Queen's University Belfast.

DICK HOBBS is Emeritus Professor, University of Essex, and Professor of Sociology, University of Western Sydney and Associate Fellow at the Royal United Services Institute (RUSI).

MIKE HOUGH is a Visiting Professor at the School of Law, Birkbeck, University of London.

MARTIN INNES is Director of the Crime and Security Research Institute, Professor in the School of Social Sciences, and Director of the Police Science Institute at Cardiff University.

YVONNE JEWKES is Research Professor in Criminology at the University of Brighton.

TREVOR JONES is Professor in the School of Social Sciences at Cardiff University.

NICOLA LACEY is School Professor of Law, Gender, and Social Policy at the London School of Economics and Political Science.

CHERYL LAWTHER is Lecturer in Criminology at Queen's University Belfast.

MICHAEL LEVI is Professor of Criminology at Cardiff University.

ALISON LIEBLING is Professor of Criminology and Criminal Justice, and Director of the Prisons Research Centre at the University of Cambridge.

IAN LOADER is Professor of Criminology and Professorial Fellow of All Souls College at the University of Oxford.

NICHOLAS LORD is Senior Lecturer in Criminology at the University of Manchester.

AMY LUDLOW is a Fellow and College Lecturer in Law at Gonville and Caius College and an Affiliated Lecturer at the Faculty of Law at the University of Cambridge.

MIKE MAGUIRE is Professor of Criminology at the University of South Wales and Professor Emeritus, Cardiff University.

SHADD MARUNA is Professor of Criminology at the University of Manchester.

LESLEY McARA is Chair of Penology in the School of Law and Co-Director of the Edinburgh Study of Youth Transitions and Crime at the University of Edinburgh, and is an Associate Director of the Scottish Centre for Crime and Justice Research.

KIERAN McEVOY is Professor of Law and Transitional Justice and Senior Research Fellow at the Institute of Conflict Transformation and Social Justice at Queen's University Belfast.

EUGENE McLAUGHLIN is Professor of Criminology and Associate Dean at City, University of London.

FERGUS McNEILL is Professor of Criminology and Social Work and Head of Sociology at the University of Glasgow.

SUSAN McVIE is Professor of Quantitative Criminology, Director of the Applied Quantitative Methods Network, Co-Director of the Edinburgh Study of Youth Transitions and Crime, and associate member of the Scottish Centre for Crime and Justice Research, at the University of Edinburgh.

DOMINIQUE MORAN is Reader in Carceral Geography at the University of Birmingham.

ROD MORGAN is Emeritus Professor of Criminal Justice at the University of Bristol.

DAVID NELKEN is Professor of Comparative and Transnational Law in Context, Vice Dean, and Head of Research at the Dickson Poon School of Law, King's College London.

TIM NEWBURN is Professor of Criminology and Social Policy at the London School of Economics and Political Science.

JILL PEAY is Professor of Law at the London School of Economics and Political Science.

CORETTA PHILLIPS is Associate Professor (Reader) in the Department of Social Policy and the Mannheim Centre for Criminology at the London School of Economics and Political Science.

JO PHOENIX is Professor of Criminology at the Open University.

ROBERT REINER is Emeritus Professor of Criminology at the London School of Economics and Political Science.

JULIAN V. ROBERTS is Professor of Criminology at the University of Oxford, member of the Sentencing Council of England and Wales, and Visiting Research Professor at the University of Minnesota.

GWEN ROBINSON is Reader in Criminal Justice at the University of Sheffield.

PAUL ROCK is Emeritus Professor of Sociology at the London School of Economics and Political Science.

MEREDITH ROSSNER is Assistant Professor of Criminology at the London School of Economics and Political Science.

BETHANY E. SCHMIDT is Ph.D. Student and Research Associate at the University of Cambridge.

TOBY SEDDON is Professor of Criminology and Head of the School of Law at the University of Manchester.

JOANNA SHAPLAND is Edward Bramley Professor of Criminal Justice and Director of the Centre for Criminological Research at the University of Sheffield.

DAVID J. SMITH is Visiting Professor in the Mannheim Centre for Criminology, London School of Economics and Political Science, and Honorary Professor of Criminology, University of Edinburgh.

OLIVER SMITH is Associate Professor (Reader) in Criminology at the University of Plymouth.

NIGEL SOUTH is Professor, Department of Sociology, University of Essex and Adjunct Professor, School of Justice, Queensland University of Technology.

RICHARD SPARKS is Professor of Criminology and Head of the School of Law at the University of Edinburgh.

ALEX STEVENS is Professor in Criminal Justice and Deputy Head of the School of Social Policy, Sociology, and Social Research at the University of Kent.

STEVE TOMBS is Professor of Criminology at the Open University.

TONY WARD is Professor of Law at Northumbria University.

PER-OLOF H. WIKSTRÖM is Professor of Ecological and Developmental Criminology and Director of the PADS+ Research Centre at the University of Cambridge.

LUCIA ZEDNER is Senior Research Fellow at All Souls College and Professor of Criminal Justice at the University of Oxford, as well as Conjoint Professor at the University of New South Wales.

GUIDED TOUR OF THE ONLINE RESOURCE CENTRE

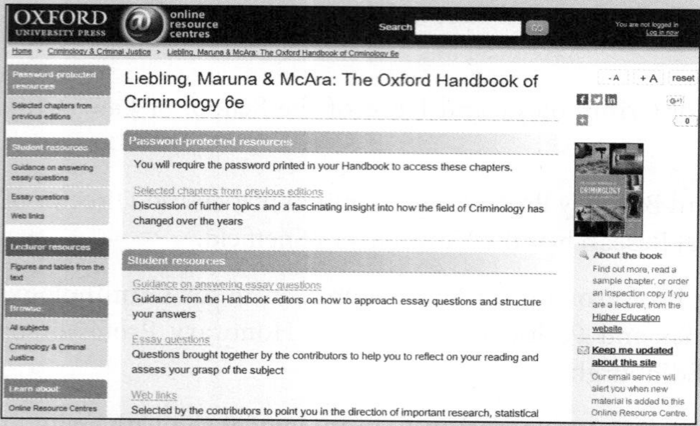

www.oxfordtextbooks.co.uk/orc/liebling6e/

The Online Resource Centre that accompanies this book provides students and lecturers with ready-to-use teaching and learning materials. These resources are free of charge and are designed to maximize the learning experience.

STUDENT RESOURCES

SELECTED CHAPTERS FROM PREVIOUS EDITIONS

In-depth material on topics, including the development of criminology as a discipline, and key issues, such as punishment and control, and crime reduction, have been taken from previous editions of this text and provided in electronic format for those interested in a more thorough discussion of these topics.

This resource is password protected. The login details to enter this part of the Online Resource Centre are:

Username: liebling6e
Password: Chapters

WEB LINKS

A selection of annotated web links, chosen by the contributors, have been provided to point you in the direction of important research, statistical data, and classic texts to keep you informed of the developments in criminology both past and present.

ESSAY QUESTIONS

To encourage you to fully consider the key criminological issues, the contributors have written essay questions to accompany each chapter. These essay questions will help you to reflect on your reading and provide an opportunity to assess your understanding of the subject.

ADVICE ON ANSWERING ESSAY QUESTIONS

Advice from the Handbook editors has been included on how to approach essay questions and structure your answers to ensure you are successful in demonstrating your knowledge and critical understanding of criminology.

LECTURER RESOURCES

FIGURES AND TABLES FROM THE TEXT

A selection of figures and tables from the text have been provided in high resolution format for downloading into presentation software for use in assignments and exam material.

INTRODUCTION: THE NEW VISION

Alison Liebling, Shadd Maruna, and Lesley McAra

The three of us are deeply honoured to open this sixth edition of the *Oxford Handbook of Criminology*, the first new edition in the series to be edited by anyone besides the founding editors Mike Maguire, Rod Morgan, and Robert Reiner. Their path-breaking editorship lasted 18 years, with editions appearing in 1994 (the first), 1997 (the second), 2002 (the third), 2007 (the fourth), and 2012 (the fifth). We clearly owe them a huge debt for what they have achieved, and they should be congratulated on their dedication and perseverance, but especially their vision.

The first appearance of the *Oxford Handbook* on the market substantially altered and enhanced the field, so much so that one can easily forget what a radical and risky undertaking the *Handbook* was in 1994. Indeed, in an insightful early book review, Tony Jefferson (1995: 372) worried that the 1259-page first edition of the *Handbook* might become 'the longest single suicide note in history, a compendious demonstration of the inherent incoherence of the criminological project'. Instead, over its many subsequent editions, the *Handbook* has become an indispensable archive of the evolving state of criminology. Even more importantly, it has played a constitutive and agenda-setting role in the field: not least in shaping core criminological curricula and functioning as an important touchstone for research scholarship. The first five editions have sold a total of around 100,000 copies, with sales increasing over time (unusually, for a handbook) and peaking as new editions were published. Indeed, one indication of the success of Maguire, Morgan, and Reiner's immense undertaking is that since 1994, the field has become awash with handbooks, on everything from youth justice to prison ethnography, to organized crime, and the criminology of war.[1]

[1] A short and incomplete list includes the *Handbook on Crime, The International Handbook of Rural Criminology, Handbook of Youth and Justice, A Handbook of Policing, Student Handbook of Criminal Justice and Criminology, Handbook of Transnational Crime and Justice, Handbook of Probation, Handbook of Criminal Investigation, Handbook of Victims and Victimology, International Handbook of Juvenile Justice, Youth Justice Handbook, Handbook of Quantitative Criminology, Sage Handbook of Punishment and Society, The Oxford Handbook of Juvenile Crime and Juvenile Justice, The Oxford Handbook of Crime Prevention,*

We take up guardianship of the *Handbook* as it reaches the key age of 18. The first editors—its real parents—stewarded it from gestation to the beginning of what is now known as 'emerging adulthood' (Arnett 2000). Our role then is less authoritative—our protégée has a certain independence and autonomy these days, and is perfectly capable of thriving without us. That said, the emergent adult is still trying to 'find itself' and its place in the world. Our task is therefore both less—and more—ambitious than that of the founding editors. Since 1994, criminology has become a crowded and unwieldy field, growing in multiple directions with competing sub-fields and specialisms emerging (variously described as 'harm-ology', 'security-ology', and 'victim-ology'; see Shearing 2015). With this new edition we hope to help the field achieve a semblance of coherence, an understanding of its distinctive history, and a clear sense of direction for its future. To round off our metaphor, we hope to nurture criminology into a mature self-identity capable of sustainable growth and vitality.

Of course, we approached this challenge with no shortage of trepidation. Beyond the obvious fears of being able to fill the enormous shoes of our predecessors, we also were fully aware of the ultimately political nature of this undertaking. David Downes (1983) famously described criminology as a 'rendezvous' discipline, characterized by an eclectic set of methodological concerns, theoretical perspectives, and normative frameworks. This eclecticism means that any attempt to define its contours or capture its core is at best going to fail and at worst might be understood as an 'imperialistic' (Jefferson 1995) enterprise of the worst sort.

When we first agreed to take on the project collectively, we felt reasonably confident that we could 'represent' (or use our presence and contacts to good effect in) England and Wales, Scotland, and Northern Ireland respectively (during the preparing of this edition, Shadd has lived and worked in three different countries). Where relevant, we asked authors to make mention of the four nations which make up the United Kingdom in their contributions (particularly in the context of criminal justice responses to crime).

But inevitably, criminology continues to be politically and methodologically contested. It is inter-disciplinary and applied—characteristics that may help explain, but cannot justify, its lack of representation as an independent subject within the UK's Research Excellence Framework. The core objects of our study (e.g. 'crime' and 'justice') are still topics of considerable debate with no agreed upon definitions. Criminology is surely unique in that many of the leading scholars in our field do not describe themselves as criminologists at all (Hayward and Smith, this volume) with many actively eschewing the label entirely (see Tombs and Hillyard, this volume). Indeed, it must be some indication of the level of identity crisis the subject still faces when, as recently as 2009, Oxford University's 50-year-old Centre for Criminology hosted a conference and published an edited book with the title *What is Criminology?*

The Sage Handbook of Criminological Theory, Handbook of Policing, Ethics and Professional Standards, The Oxford Handbook of Organized Crime, The Palgrave Handbook of Prison Ethnography, Handbook of Forensic Sociology and Psychology, The Wiley Handbook to the Criminology of Terrorism, The Handbook of Measurement Issues in Criminology and Criminal Justice, The Palgrave Handbook of Criminology and War, The Oxford Handbook of the History of Crime and Criminal Justice, The Routledge Handbook of Technology, Crime and Justice, and The Handbook of Restorative Justice.

(see Bosworth and Hoyle 2011). Clearly, our subject is an 'oddity' with delinquent tendencies.

Criminology has been, from its origins, an admirably self-critical field, forever questioning its role and value. Critics worry loudly about the popularity of criminology as a subject among young people, and indeed some of the expansion of the subject (combined with the decline and diminishment of more traditional disciplines in the humanities and social sciences) concerns us too (see Tombs and Hillyard, this volume). Yet, there is a reason for this widespread appeal. Young people are drawn to criminology because it feels relevant—significant, even. The topic speaks to broad issues of social justice and societal transformation in concrete and tangible ways. What other field could claim the sort of transformational social impact evident in Phil Scraton's (2013) research on the Hillsborough tragedy, to take just one example? At its best, criminology does something no other discipline does: bringing inter-disciplinary insight to bear on both empirical and normative questions of individual behaviour, social order, and justice in a way that is meaningful and relevant to the 'real world'. By its nature, criminological knowledge goes to the heart of debates on citizenship, good governance, or 'the right way to organize authority in a society' (Roberts 2010; see also Loader and Sparks, this volume). We have tried to highlight and nurture some of these unique strengths in this sixth edition.

In this Introduction we review the state of the field, set out our vision for the *Handbook*, and introduce some its core themes. We begin by taking stock. Where is criminology today? Who does it? What key developments are shaping knowledge production? How has the organizational context in which we work changed since the publication of the first edition? We show why, in our view, the *Oxford Handbook of Criminology* retains major relevance today.

PASSING OF THE TORCH: ENTER THIRD GENERATION CRIMINOLOGY

In parallel with our own transition as an editorial team, a generational shift of much importance is clearly taking place in British criminology after decades of striking consistency. The introduction of criminology in the UK largely resulted from the pioneering efforts of three post-Second World War émigrés Hermann Mannheim, Max Grunhut, and Leon Radzinowicz around the middle of the last century (see Garland 2002). This first generation of British criminologists laid the groundwork and established the institutional foundations in elite English universities like the LSE, Oxford, and Cambridge, respectively, yet the field remained largely on the fringes of intellectual life. Criminology did not grow into a proper academic subject until a second group, described by Paul Rock (1988: 190) as the 'fortunate generation' of British criminologists 'appointed in and around the single decade of the 1970s' burst on to the scene promising to overthrow the emerging orthodoxy with a 'new criminology' (Taylor, Walton, and Young 1973). Rock, this volume, writes:

> In that take-off phase, urged on by publishers, made discontinuous with the past by a thrusting generation of newly appointed young Turks, criminology became striving, expansive, quarrelsome, factious, and open, its practitioners jostling with one another for *Lebensraum*.

As long ago as 1988, in what can only seem like a cruel irony today, Rock pointed out that these young Turks would not be young forever and would instead rapidly become 'the establishment' themselves:

> The stock of sociologists is not being fully replenished and it is ageing. In late 1986, the average age of a criminologist in a law department was 40, in a sociology department 42, and in a department of social administration 43. Since that Golden Age of the 1970s, no comparable body of young criminologists has been allowed to rise up to make their own mark on the world of theory (Rock 1988: 192).

Although this situation did change somewhat in the decades subsequent to Rock's assessment, there is no question that the (no-longer young) Turks of the 'fortunate generation' remained towering figures in criminology for at least 40 years, dominating the journals, conferences, and wider 'criminological imagination'.

In recent years, however, the torch lit by the 'fortunate generation' is at last being passed to a new generation. Indeed, the past few years alone have seen the sad passing of some of the chief architects of twentieth-century criminology, including: John Benyon (1951–2016), Jason Ditton (1949–2015), Stuart Hall (1932–2014), Barbara Hudson (1945–2013), Mary McIntosh (1936–2013), Terence Morris (1931–2013), Geoff Pearson (1943–2013), Keith Soothill (1941–2014), and Nigel Walker (1917–2014). Two recent losses in particular stand out, however, even among this incredible list of luminaries: Jock Young (1942–2013) and Stanley Cohen (1942–2013). Such was their influence on criminological teaching and research that to much of the international criminology community, British criminology *was* Jock and Stan (for an entertaining discussion of their relationship, see Cohen and Young 2004).

These tragic losses and the retirement of so many other criminological pioneers has created an opening (indeed a necessity) for new voices to emerge. As editors we are representatives of this 'distinct new cohort' (Platt 2004) or third generation in criminology, recruited during the 1990s following the virtual cessation of academic hiring during the 1980s. We were too young to attend the formative National Deviancy Symposium in York in 1968, but some of us did witness the inaugural (then biennial) British Criminology Conference (in 1987 at Sheffield University), and we all grew up excited by critical and radical criminology. Yet, we were also carefully trained in multiple methodologies and understood the requirements of and opportunities presented by funded research.

As the field has expanded into a wider range of universities, criminology has become more socially diverse and democratized. Ironically, although the field has therefore become less clubby and more informal, third generation criminology has also become less quarrelsome than the previous generation (see Young 1988; Taylor, Walton, and Young 1973). This might be related to the fact that the field has become less exclusively male. The 'rather tumultuous jostling for space' (Rock 1988) that characterized 1970s and 1980s criminology—with intellectual battles between Marxists and 'bourgeois' criminology, empiricists versus criticals, feminists against patriarchal criminology, quantitatives versus qualitatives, left realists against left romanticists, and so forth—was a necessary aspect of the development of the subject area. It left a powerful legacy of self-critique, humility, and awareness of the contexts of knowledge production among contemporary criminologists. Yet, third gen criminologists have largely moved on from such internal wrangling to carrying out the business of criminological research.

Indeed, for better or for worse, there has never been so much criminological research in terms of sheer quantity of output—on violence, gang membership, drug use, victimization, illegal trade, self-narratives, policing and surveillance, prison sociology, identity and desistance, penal reform, community penalties, punishment and political culture, and the politics of crime—nor so much publishing. If the state of our field is represented by the health of its journals (accepting reservations about 'bibliometry' as a measure of quality (Collini 2012)), then we are indeed flourishing.

British criminology has long been represented by two founding journals: the *British Journal of Criminology* (BJC) and *The Howard Journal of Criminal Justice*. Originally named the *British Journal of Delinquency* when first published in 1950, the *British Journal of Criminology* remains one of the world's most prestigious criminology journals by most measures. *The Howard Journal*, which first appeared in 1921 and has been published annually since 1951, was relaunched in 2016, with a new editor (Oxford's Ian Loader), a new direction (to be 'an influential international journal at the forefront of thinking about ideas and issues that impact on crime and justice globally'), and a new title: *The Howard Journal of Crime and Justice*. This is a fitting development and one that takes the journal formally from its early origins campaigning for penal policy reform to its evolving status as a fully independent academic criminology journal. That the original journals in our field had distinct identities and origins—one with psychiatry/practitioner and the other with pressure group roots—symbolizes the history of British criminology as an academic subject steeped in practice.

Other journals have appeared on the scene in the past two decades, including the increasingly popular *Theoretical Criminology* (established in 1997), as well as numerous specialist journals, such as *Crime, Media, Culture* (2005) and *Youth Justice* (2000). The British Society of Criminology developed its own affiliated journal *Criminology and Criminal Justice* (*CCJ*) in 2000, and it has rapidly become a central outlet for new research in the field. The tender process for *CCJ* was won in 2014 by a team from a consortia of Scottish universities led by Michele Burman and Sarah Armstrong at Glasgow University and Laura Piacentini of Strathclyde University. Notably, one of the *CCJ*'s previous editorial teams had been based at the University of Cardiff consisting of Gordon Hughes, Trevor Jones, Michael Levi, Matthew Williams, and Kirsty Hudson.

This editorial leadership is one of latest indicators of the shifting centre of gravity in British criminology that began in the 1970s, away from a monopoly among a small number of universities in southern England (especially Oxbridge and the LSE) to a more geographically dispersed criminological field. Within Scotland the first Chair of Criminology was established in the University of Edinburgh in 1970 (only the second such chair after Cambridge in the UK). Since that time, Scottish criminology has experienced exponential growth across the wider university sector. In recent years this has been given particular momentum with the successful establishment of the Scottish Centre for Crime and Justice Research, a collaboration of four Scottish universities. This Centre has contributed to major increases in the number of doctoral students studying criminology across Scotland and advances in doctoral training. It has also resulted in a growing body of critical policy research and has embedded Scottish criminology more firmly within international networks. A parallel development in Wales, The Welsh Centre for Crime and Social Justice, has likewise sought to bring together criminologists from eight Welsh universities to encourage inter-institutional collaboration. Northern Ireland has strong criminological traditions at both of its universities, but this work has grown in importance with the development of the 'North-South' Irish Criminology Research Network, which recently hosted its 10th annual conference in Maynooth, Ireland. Irish criminology even has a new handbook (!) (Healy *et al.* 2015) with contributions and leadership from across both the Republic of Ireland and Northern Ireland.

Finally, the *content* of third gen criminological research has shifted distinctly as well. The traditional criminological focus on aetiology of delinquency has somewhat dwindled outside of a small number of departments (such as those in the universities of Cambridge, Sheffield, and Edinburgh; see Sarnecki 2014). Several prominent departments of criminology do not even have the capacity to teach more than one basic course in delinquency theories. Today, it is far more common to find new PhDs with interests in subjects like 'stop and search' police practices, the death penalty, restorative justice, or alternatives to incarceration, than in self-control research or patterns of differential association. Whilst we do not subscribe to Colin Sumner's rather pessimistic prediction (1994) that we are witnessing the death of the sociology of deviance, the balance of attention is clearly shifting from what was once understood as the basic ingredient of criminology (the causes of crime) to a more applied focus on criminal justice (or indeed social justice) practices (see also Burman and Gelsthorpe, this volume) and their relationship with, or contribution to, offending life narratives. This shift is underpinned by patterns in research and student funding (discussed in more detail below), and evolving epistemological and methodological debates.

Histories of British criminology (see, e.g., the chapters by Garland and Rock in the first edition of the *Handbook*), have highlighted an epistemological divide between 'administrative' criminology (predominant in the first few decades after the Second World War) and more critical approaches (gaining ascendance in the 1970s with the establishment of the National Deviancy Conference). The so-called 'Big Bang' in criminology (heralded by the establishment of critical criminology) was accompanied by a gradual decoupling of the study of crime from the study of punishment (Hamilton 2014, Tonry 2007). This development gained momentum during the 1980s with the invocation of 'penality' in the sociology of punishment by scholars who aimed to set an academic as well as political agenda by critically engaging with social theory as the principal lens through which to 'read' contemporary penal systems (Garland and Young 1983, Cohen and Scull 1983, Blomberg and Cohen 1995). The decoupling is mirrored by (sometimes overplayed) methodological differences within British criminology, as seen between, *inter alia*: those who research crime control and penal practice in late modernity, whose principal analytical focus lies in understanding institutional dynamics or the contribution of state level actors; grounded accounts of penal practices or transformations based on critical policy analysis;

cultural criminologists and ethnographers who highlight the significance of 'edge-work' and lived cultural practices; but also still an enduring body of developmental and life-course criminology, predicated on traditional social-scientific rationalism (McAra and McVie 2015). Increasingly, third gen criminologists are bridging these categories as well, connecting their interests in penal practices with those of traditional criminologists interested in individual life trajectories.

In this sense, it seems to us that of the original post-War criminological theories, the labelling perspective appears to be surviving particularly well within the UK (see Tannenbaum 1938, Farrington and Murray 2013, and Liberman, Kirk, and Kim 2014). This is not to say labelling theory is considered the 'best' supported explanatory theory of criminal behaviour in any empirical sense. (Indeed, fortunately, the era of the sport-like competition of theories in head-to-head comparisons like 'self-control theory vs. strain theory' appears to have largely conceded to the impulse to combine insights from across different theoretical traditions into integrative theories, for example, Braithwaite 1989, see also McAra and McVie, this volume). Rather, we would argue that the labelling perspective has emerged as an enduring paradigm because it assigns a central role to penality, the state and societal reaction in the social construction of criminality, recognizing both the structural and the phenomenological dynamics involved in the development of deviant behaviours. Even among contemporary criminologists who would not consider themselves labelling theorists (or among its vocal critics) such frameworks have become part of the furniture in the contemporary study of crime and justice—another of the many positive legacies of the debates of the 1970s and 1980s.

THE NEW WORLD WE LIVE IN

Some of the changes in the nature of third generation criminology have been driven not by ideology but rather by major structural changes in the way in which criminology is organized as a discipline within British universities. Staff employment within universities, the diverse nature and growing scale of student education, the increasingly competitive ways in which research is funded and evaluated, and the way power flows in the relationship between knowledge and its political and policy contexts, have each changed the way our discipline functions. We offer some reflections on each of these developments.

PATTERNS OF EMPLOYMENT

Perhaps we are succumbing to nostalgic fantasies, but academic life for those who came before us now really does seem 'rarified', contemplative, and intellectually creative (if also more lonely) compared to the current more frantic academic scene. During the past two decades, curiosity-driven research appears to have largely given way somewhat to more instrumental concerns.

For our generation of criminologists, the boundaries between government and the academy have become more porous, bringing welcome dialogue. In-house researchers in both the Scottish Office and the Home Office undertook original research and there was a much greater transfer of personnel from government into universities and vice versa than is apparent today (on Scotland, see McAra 2008). Many of the leading criminologists of our generation were at some stage policy-makers or government research staff.

Rapid expansion, and more rapid promotion, has led to an opening up of the discipline, but also greater specialization, and perhaps, methodological fragmentation. As argued in A.H. Halsey's *History of Sociology in Britain*, employment patterns impact on 'the relative chances of institutionalisation of different intellectual currents' (Halsey 2004: 218) and shape the character and direction of departments. There are more secure jobs overall, with better remuneration (if less equality), but there is also huge pressure on tenured academic staff to 'bring in research money', and considerable uncertainty and insecurity for increasing numbers of young scholars yet to find their way into tenured positions. As post-doctoral funding has diminished, living on competitive, short-term research contracts has become a way of life for a larger new generation of criminologists. These patterns: growth, 'success' for our discipline, and yet precarious living, create anxiety, over-productivity, and a 'culture of speed' (Berg and Seeber 2016) which poses, we think, a threat to intellectual enquiry. We shall consider the effects of the 'corporatization' of our universities, and the linking of research to 'economic growth', on the shape of our discipline later.

THE EDUCATIONAL LANDSCAPE

Higher and therefore criminological education has been transformed, with changing patterns of student funding (increased costs, the withdrawal of grants, and increased emphasis on 'satisfaction' surveys) within the UK reflecting the commodification of knowledge. There is a huge demand for criminology degrees (in contrast to sociology and social policy which have seen major drops in student numbers), with some 800 degree programmes on offer across 111 universities which include criminology as a core component (WhatUni 2016). This expansion has been accompanied by a market-led shift from full-time postgraduate to undergraduate and part-time professional educational provision. Whilst this is testimony to the relevance and appeal of criminology, there are concerns that this shift may threaten some of the strengths arising from inter-disciplinarity. First, second and third generation criminologists generally pursued a core undergraduate discipline (e.g. sociology, psychology, law, or political science). The postgraduate experience enabled a genuine fusion of intellectual interests to emerge: from mastery of one discipline to a field that required synthesis. We firmly believe that knowledge from different disciplines brings insight to complex social problems and that criminology should retain its grounding in other major disciplines.

The demand for professional education has also increased: the search for 'greater research literacy' and 'better familiarity with the evidence base' is coming from senior managers and other practitioners within the criminal justice system as well as from policy-makers and politicians (albeit in selective ways). The Master of Studies Programme at Cambridge, first established in 1998, has been strongly supported by the National Offender Management Service as well as by the Scottish Prison Service (and prison and probation services in other jurisdictions) and is, we are assured, very highly regarded. Other courses are appearing in several other universities committed to engagement with operational staff and leaders. Within Scotland, criminologists have been involved in the Justice Leaders Network, which brings together senior leaders across all dimensions of criminal justice, including the Scottish government, the judiciary, statutory services, and third sector organizations, supporting collaborative leadership development for many years. Such trends have shaped thinking and practice, and the relationship between research and criminal justice. There are risks in such close collaborations, but increasing the critical faculties of those operating in criminal justice worlds, and engaging in mutual challenge, can lead to enhanced standards and practices in both worlds: a point to which we return below.

RESEARCH GOVERNANCE AND FUNDING

The ways in which the quality of research is assessed through the Research Excellence Framework (REF, formerly the Research Assessment Exercise (RAE)) has had significant implications for academic criminology. Criminology does not have its own REF panel—criminological research typically is assigned to panels dependent upon its home department: sociology, social policy, or law. A project undertaken by Maruna and colleagues (2009) after the last RAE found that the total number of criminology publications submitted to these different panels was greater than some of the returns in fields that had their own unique panels. Questions remain as to whether a separate panel would benefit, or might undermine, our multi-disciplinary foundations, but the politics of excluding such a large field of study are blatant.

On the other hand, criminologists have, arguably, gained greater esteem within universities as a consequence of REF requirements. As a field, we raise significant amounts of grant income and are well positioned to provide 'impact case studies' as our subject matter is by its nature applied to policy issues. A less welcome consequence of REF has been the demise of the research monograph. The need to produce four publications of the 'highest international quality', coupled with uncertainty about how monographs are 'weighed', has meant that investment in large-scale intellectual writing projects has been displaced, to some extent, by increased emphasis on the peer reviewed journal article. Key-note texts from the past—the real game changers in terms of discipline development (e.g. Stan Cohen's *Visions of Social Control* [1985] or David Garland's *Punishment and Welfare* [1985])—may become fewer in number as a consequence.

REF results have consequences for the funding of Higher Education, but there are other concerns about the patterns of research funding. The Economic and Social Research Council (ESRC) increasingly funds a smaller number of larger scale or existing enterprises. The demise of small grants has the potential to create a stasis in knowledge advancement if universities become risk averse when required to 'demand manage' grant applications, with the consequence that narrower tranches of established expertise may be consistently reproduced. Devolution across the United Kingdom has seen the emergence of co-funded centres of research excellence, including the cross institutional Scottish Crime and Justice Research Centre, mentioned earlier, (funded by the Scottish government and the Scottish Funding Council from 2006, but now required to be self-sustaining) aimed at building capacity, developing new knowledge, and promoting research led policy advice. WISERD (the Wales Institute of Social & Economic Research, Data & Methods, co-funded by the Welsh government and the ESRC), although not primarily criminological in orientation, researches issues of core salience to the discipline, such as poverty and inequalities. Research leaders within such resource intensive centres have a key role to play in shaping the wider discipline in the future. Whilst the transfer of resources to particular sites of excellence presents opportunities, critics have warned of how funding decisions create new cadres of insiders and outsiders and will determine the contours of knowledge production for years to come.

A PRECARIOUS POLITICAL LANDSCAPE

Finally, the political and institutional landscape of crime and punishment has undergone radical change over the past 18 years, driven by a changing social mood, the dynamics of devolution across the UK, and a number of critical events including the terrorists attacks of 9/11 and 7/7, the global economic crash in 2008, and the referendum on EU membership in 2016 (see McAra, this volume). The expansion of criminology as a field of inquiry has been accompanied by a growing harshness in political rhetoric internationally—for example with the US election of Donald Trump on a platform of 'making America safe again' and authoritarian fear-mongering—as well as in England and Wales (see Morgan and Smith, this volume). In this second decade of the twenty-first century, we may be witnessing a further repeat of what Hall (1979) termed the great moving right show, with populism predominating at both a civic and political level, and xenophobic and Europhobic impulses becoming a source of both identity and pride for certain key demographic groups. We are entering a new era of austerity and 'revolution': high aspirations, bold claims, increased use of all disposals, and fewer resources. The impact of these factors on criminal justice practices, and individual life narratives, remain to be seen (on their effects on prisons; see Crewe and Liebling, this volume).

Indeed, the first edition of the *Handbook* was published at a time that, in retrospect, was a watershed moment for crime and justice in the UK as well as for British criminology. The tragic murder of the toddler James Bulger by two children in Liverpool in February 1993—prompting the remarkable quote from then Prime Minister John Major that 'Society needs to condemn a little more and understand a little less'—is often seen as a turning point in criminal justice policy (in England especially; see Morgan and Smith, this volume). The tragedy's legacy included Home Secretary Michael Howard's infamous 'Prison Works' speech to the Conservative Party Conference in October of 1993, and the 'tough on crime' policies of the Blair Administration that ultimately led to a doubling of the prison population and the privileging of a specific type of criminological evidence (known variously as 'what works' or a new strand of 'administrative criminology'). Within England, the period most characterized by 'evidence-led' policy (the new Labour years from 1997 to 2010), was one in which risk management (derived from psychological–criminological knowledge) served a youth justice agenda which undermined the rights of children and young people who came into conflict with the law (see Goldson 2011 for a critical overview). This was mirrored in Scotland by the first of the post-devolutionary governments (a coalition between new Labour and the Liberal Democrats; see McAra, this volume).

Paradoxically, the relationship between criminology (academic life in the social sciences and humanities) and political life has, in England and Wales at least, become both more distant and more 'servile' since the *Handbook* was first published, as autonomy is challenged and research funding becomes more closely tied to national or government 'priorities' (see Collini 2012). Some aspects of 'authoritarian neo-liberalism's ascendance' (Westergaard 2004) has seeped into the organization and funding of our field—threatening the arts and social sciences in higher education, and strengthening the 'control' orientation or components within our discipline.

Elsewhere in the UK, things currently look quite different. In Scotland, in particular, the now ruling pro-independence Scottish National Party (SNP), has exerted a significantly progressive effect on criminal justice and social policy (see McAra, this volume). The SNP's tone and language of penal policy ('unlocking potential', 'transforming lives', 'building a safer Scotland', and a symposium in 2016 on 'Re-Imagining Custody, Community and Citizenship for 21st Century Scotland') are noticeably social. Scotland is set on a more symbiotic or evidence-friendly relationship between research and policy. As a small jurisdiction, there has always been greater access to politicians, policy-makers and other justice leaders. Criminologists living and working in England can only look north of the border with envy.

These discussions are of particular importance in a context where, as noted above, the quality of research is increasingly measured by its impact (narrowly defined), with financial rewards in the form of REF generated income or access to research funding (with Research Council UK (RUK) grant applications now requiring pathways to impact statements). Importantly research has shown that the politics of knowledge production confound a linear conception of the movement of research into policy and practice (see Liebling *et al.*, this volume). Pathways to impact are not always under the control of researchers—once knowledge is taken up by policy, researchers often lose control of the ways in which it is deployed. As McAra (2016) has argued, impact often occurs most where research findings accord with dominant political narratives. Governments seek out research to support a view already taken, rather than critically engaging with a wider field of knowledge (some of which may contradict or confound political perception). Under these circumstances criminologists must argue for greater critical understanding and political realism on the part of funders and research assessors about the limited capacity for impact in the narrow sense in which it is conceived, and for a broader and more subtle concept of 'benefit' (Collini 2012). We should resist the temptation to sacrifice integrity for influence.

CRIMINOLOGY WITH AND WITHOUT BORDERS

Perhaps the most fundamental feature of contemporary British criminology, however, is just how decreasingly British it is—'Brexit' politics aside. That is to say, like nearly every aspect of society, the field of criminology has become more globalized with researchers, research projects, and scholarship easily travelling across borders—as does crime (see Franko, this volume). Of course, this was ever the case in criminology. The resource *Fifty Key Thinkers in Criminology* (Hayward *et al.* 2010) lists among the earliest pioneers of our field: Cesare Beccaria (Italy), Adophe Quetelet (Belgium), Cesare Lomroso (Italy), Peter Kropotkin (Russia), Emile Durkheim (France), W.E.B. Du Bois (USA), and Willem Bonger (Netherlands). As noted above, criminology in Britain was born as a result of post-Second World War immigration. With the rise of the internet, budget airline travel, and translation software, these kinds of border crossings are now common in academic life. Students taking classes in criminology and security at the University of Liverpool's Singapore campus can view a podcast of a lecture by a Dutch criminologist filmed in Kentucky discussing her research in Brazil, then discuss the work with a Brazilian prison official via an online forum.

Criminology is expanding its borders, necessarily, and seeking new answers to questions of citizenship and democratic living. Whilst British criminology often focuses on issues of crime and punishment of particular relevance to UK jurisdictions, it includes state crime, the impacts of globalization, and comparative research. Some of the newest areas of study in criminology include migration, asylum, and the management and integration of global populations as a consequence of wars and famines; the governance of 'big data', the internet, the questions they raise for privacy, surveillance and security; and the nature of global and sub-state dynamics and their implications for justice, citizenship, and belonging.

Contemporary scholarship is far less introspective than in earlier decades, and many UK-based researchers work closely with international networks, linking with work being carried out in Europe, the Americas, Australasia, and Africa. Criminology's reach is increasingly global. Of course, the British Society of Criminology continues to develop along with its associated annual conference, attracting participants from all over the world. However, British criminology may be increasingly influenced by international organizations like the European Group (founded in 1974) which recently developed its own journal, *Justice, Power & Resistance*, and the European Society of Criminology (ESC), with its linked journal, the *European Journal of Criminology*, established in 2004.

In such a world, what is the point of a handbook like this that—although more international in scope than previous editions (see, e.g., McEvoy *et al.*, this volume)—highlights the 'Best of British' criminology? Most of the sales to date have been in the UK, but high numbers have also been sold in the US, Australia, Canada, Germany, the Netherlands, and India (and elsewhere). This tells us something about the relationship of British criminology to the rest of the world—a relationship we value and would like to develop further. What do we even mean by British criminology, in the modern world? How many 'British Criminologists' live and work outside Britain? How many university positions in our field are filled by British citizens? How many of our students are British? Is 'British criminology' a meaningful concept in 2016?

At the time of writing, the UK is facing a major period of uncertainty following the referendum on EU membership (so-called 'Brexit'), with a government committed to abolishing the Human Rights Act, and severing our ties with the Council of Europe. As already noted, there is increased xenophobia in political discourse, increased reporting of hate crime, and major challenges ahead with regard to transnational policing, border controls, and the capacity to tackle trafficking in pernicious forms. At the same time, authoritarian forms of ultra nationalism are emerging around the globe. So, the very idea of a British criminology can feel like an anachronism. This is most certainly not a 'Brexit' handbook. None of us wants to work (or live) in isolation from the rest of Europe, or the rest of the world. We hope this is a work of connection and dialogue.

Yet, despite these very real changes brought on by globalization, most criminal behaviours retain a strong element of localism. A Polish-born drug dealer on a street corner in Portsmouth might be selling heroin manufactured in Kyrgystan with opium produced in Afganistan, smuggled into Europe by Belgian traffickers. Yet the street dealer will be subject to the laws of the United Kingdom, processed by the police and courts of Portsmouth, with their own specific, contingent practices and cultures, and likely serve his (or her) punishment in a British prison. In other words, as argued by Girling *et al.* (1999) in *Crime and Social Change in Middle England*, crime is also distinctly local as in the field of criminal justice, 'the particular and the local perpetually intersect with wider national and global forces'. As a social construction, crime is deeply influenced by cultural, political, economic, and historical factors specific to a locality (see Hillyard and Tombs, this volume). Criminal justice agencies have learned this lesson in unsuccessful attempts to import interventions from one context into another. Whilst an intervention may have successfully reduced crime patterns in Pittsburgh in 1989, it may have completely the opposite effects when imported into Cardiff in 2017.

Just as criminal justice is local in important ways, then, so is criminology. British criminology, although deeply influenced by global trends since its origins, has developed a unique character of its own, shaped both by the backgrounds and proclivities of individual scholars, but also by the history, culture, and organization of British universities and wider society. We have tried to capture the nuance and nature of this unique brand of criminology, but do so, by necessity, in snapshot form as the character of the field continues to grow and evolve. This volume constitutes a living archive—a marked step in the life narrative of our field, and a celebration of its growing strengths and popularity as a subject.

WHAT IS NEW IN THE NEW EDITION?

According to Rock, those wishing to understand the history and significance of criminology should recognize that criminology is:

> a structure of power and politics searching for the gatekeepers to the institutions and the men and women who have the influence to determine who and what will thrive in the discipline. They should look for ensuing patterns of inclusion and exclusion that shape who is invited to attend colloquia give broadcasts or write papers—who in effect is allowed to be seen, heard and known. (Rock 1994: 123–4)

We are conscious that the very process of selecting authors and themes for inclusion in a handbook (and especially this one) is a core element of the politics Rock describes. Indeed, the *Handbook*'s significance in the field can be deduced from the fact that every potential author we approached took up their invitation to participate in the new edition (not a common occurrence when assembling edited collections, in our experience). Clearly being a contributing author to the *Oxford Handbook* is regarded as an honour, an opportunity, and a mark of esteem. We take particular pride in the fact that the founding editors of the *Handbook* still wanted to contribute to this new volume, authoring or co-authoring chapters on: crime statistics (Maguire); the politics of crime (Morgan); and political economy and policing (Reiner).

Whilst we take some pride in our selections in that regard, we can also live with some critique of our own values and practices. If this collection displays a little more of the intellectual and methodological conflict inherent in our discipline than the earliest editions did, then we have done our job. As stated previously, we believe that British criminology speaks to some of the most challenging social issues of our time, and we hope that the collection we have gathered together in this edition demonstrates that, and inspires more of it.

We have resisted compiling this collection 'for the market', although we are confident that it will have wide appeal. Instead, we have compiled it 'for criminology'. We have been led by the topics, questions, and outstanding scholars or research agendas known to, or found by, us collectively. We did seek to broaden the field of vision, inviting a wider range of (especially younger, fourth generation) scholars on board, taking account of new developments in the field such as zemiology and green criminology, and including whole chapters on previously neglected themes such as domestic violence and sex work. Additionally we commissioned a series of 'thought pieces', such as Ian Loader and Richard Sparks' critical account of penal populism and technocracy as ideological artifacts, David Garland's reappraisal of the relationship between punishment and welfare, and Katya Franko's analysis of the meaning and significance of globalization for the scope and development of criminology.

By shortening the chapters to around 10,000 words each, we aimed to make them more likely to be read fully, and to make room for greater inclusiveness and diversity. Our own locations, and orientations, are varied, and it is not insignificant (indeed, it is a sign of progress in our field) that two of us are women. Almost half of our contributors are women. That more of them are co-authors than sole authors reflects, we propose, a flair for collaboration rather than a lack of status (although we are aware of persisting differences in opportunity and remuneration for women in academic life). Among our female authors are very many with strong voices and identities in our field. This is a welcome development since the *Handbook* was launched, and it may reflect a difference between American and European criminology (see Chancer 2016). The same cannot be said of race or ethnicity. Our field, like our *Handbook*, is impoverished in this respect, but we hope that future editions might represent more of the growing number of younger scholars from more diverse backgrounds who are establishing themselves within our universities.

There are 44 chapters (including this one) and we have organized them into four sections: constructions of crime and justice, borders, boundaries, and beliefs; dynamics of crime and violence; and responses to crime. These imposed divisions are imperfect—so some chapters could have been placed in other sections, or ordered differently within them. We deliberated carefully over the structure and flow of chapters and sections as if any reader might read the whole *Handbook* from start to finish. Perhaps some readers will. In any event, we hope that we have given this collection a shape that makes sense, that shows what criminology is, and that reflects its depth, richness, and relevance to the modern world, as a discipline. Like the original editors, we have not attempted any overarching perspective or manifesto, and we have welcomed contentious argument (e.g. Cottee, this volume; Hayward and Smith, this volume). We share a passion for synthesis between the empirical, the normative, and the theoretical. This is what excites us as scholars. We admire our colleagues at many positions in the political and methodological spectrum.

Of course, there are always risks and limitations in any attempt to select and 'showcase' (a very small number of our efforts to solicit finished chapters on time were, in the end, unsuccessful). But we have attempted a volume that holds together a great deal of what is interesting, important, and intellectually and methodologically rich, in our field.

Some of the omissions in this edition are deliberate, many due to space, one or two because authors could not, in the end, deliver their chapters to the timescale, and others reflecting our flaws and blind spots as editors. One deliberate omission is a lower emphasis placed on what has appeared in past editions as the 'What Works' literature. Our evaluations and understandings of criminal justice practices are more circumspect and context-specific (less individualistic–psychological) than those evaluations belonging to this era were, on the whole. Other omissions (such as the study of sex offending, the growing field of experimental criminology, and research on cybercrime) have existing or recent volumes dedicated to their methods and findings (see Beech *et al.*, 2009; Piquero and Weisberg 2010; Levi 2017 respectively).

We will of course expect to hear about other omissions from readers and reviewers, and we look forward to responding to such helpful feedback. Like our predecessors, we see our role as partly delineative and partly responsive: we are keen to get our description of the state of British criminology as close to an authentic account as we can manage. Yet, this can only happen in a genuine dialogue with researchers and scholars in the field. So let us hear from you.

The *Handbook* is a living research project and its various editions are testimony to its function as an archive of some of the best and most influential scholarship within British criminology (however loosely defined). In our review of the contexts of academic criminology, we note a paradox that although criminological research has flourished and expanded in recent decades, those years have also witnessed repeated political crises in the systems of criminal justice, including dangerously increasing rates of imprisonment. The collective essays which make up this new edition of the *Handbook*, demonstrate, however, the continued salience of criminological knowledge to an understanding of the problems and challenges facing late modern societies, such as changing norms and trajectories of crime and violence, threats to security, to human rights, to the planetary eco-system, and to state legitimacy. Criminal justice policy is not always responsive to best forms of evidence, even when practitioners try to be. Criminology is, nonetheless, working to provide better understandings as well as potential solutions—useful knowledge in Radzinowicz's terms (1961). After 18 years, the *Handbook* may have reached adulthood, but we may still have our best years ahead of us.

REFERENCES

Arnett, J. J. (2000), 'Emerging adulthood: A theory of development from the late teens through the twenties', *American psychologist*, 55(5): 469.

Beech, A., Craig, L., and Browne, K. (2009), *Assessment and Treatment of Sex Offenders: A Handbook*, London: Wiley and Sons Ltd.

Berg, M. and Seeber, B. (2016), *The Slow Professor: Challenging the Culture of Speed in the Academy*, Toronto: University of Toronto Press.

Blomberg, T. G. and Cohen, S. (eds) (1995), *Punishment and Social Control*, New York: Altine de Gruyer.

Bosworth, M. and Hoyle, C. (eds) (2011), *What is Criminology?* Oxford: Oxford University Press.

Braithwaite, J. (1989), *Crime, Shame and Reintegration*, Cambridge: Cambridge University Press.

Chancer, L. (2016), 'Introduction to Special 10th Anniversary Issue of Feminist Criminology: Is Criminology Still Male Dominated?', *Feminist Criminology*, 11(4): 307–10.

Cohen, S. (1985), *Visions of Social Control*, Cambridge: Polity.

Cohen, S. and Scull, A. (eds) (1983), *Social Control and the State*, Oxford: Blackwell.

Cohen, S. and Young, J. (2004), 'Comments on Simon Cottee's 'Folk Devils and Moral Panics: "Left Idealism" Reconsidered', in Theoretical Criminology 6 (4)', *Theoretical Criminology*, 8(1): 93–7.

Collini, S. (2012), *What are Universities For?*, London: Penguin.

Downes, D. (1983), *Law and order: theft of an issue*, London: Fabian Society.

Farrington, D. P., and Murray, J. (eds) (2013), *Labeling theory: Empirical tests* (Vol. 1), New Brunswick, NJ: Transaction.

Garland, D. (1985), *Punishment and Welfare: A History of Penal Strategies*, Aldershot: Gower.

Garland, D. (2002), *The Culture of Control: Crime and Social Order in Contemporary Society*, Chicago: University of Chicago Press.

Garland, D. and Young, P. (eds) (1983), *The Power to Punish: Contemporary Penality and Social Analysis*, London: Heinemann.

Girling, E., Loader, I., and Sparks, R. (1999), *Crime and Social Change in Middle England: Questions of Order in an English Town*, London: Routledge.

Goldson, B. (ed.) (2011), *Youth in Crisis? Gangs, Territoriality and Violence*, London: Routledge.

Hall, S. (1979), 'The great moving right show', *Marxism Today*, January 1979: 14–20.

Halsey, A. H. (2004), *A History of Sociology in Britain*, Oxford: Oxford University Press.

Hamilton, C. (2014), *Reconceptualising Penality: A comparative perspective on punitiveness in Ireland, Scotland and New Zealand*, Farnham: Ashgate.

Hayward, K. J., Maruna, S., and Mooney, J. (eds) (2010), *Fifty Key Thinkers in Criminology*, Abingdon: Routledge.

Healy, D., Hamilton, C., Daly, Y., and Butler, M. (eds) (2015), *The Routledge Handbook of Irish Criminology*, Abingdon: Routledge.

Jefferson, T. (1995), 'Book Review: *The Oxford Handbook of Criminology* by Mike Maguire, Rod Morgan, Robert Reiner', *Sociology*, 29: 372–4.

Levi, M. (2017), 'Assessing the Trends, Scale and Nature of Economic Cybercrimes: Overview and Issues', *Crime, Law and Social Change*, 67(1): 3–20.

Liberman, A. M., Kirk, D. S., and Kim, K. (2014), 'Labelling effects of first juvenile arrests: Secondary deviance and secondary sanctioning', *Criminology*, 52(3): 345–70.

Maruna, S., and RAE/REF Sub-Committee of the British Society of Criminology (2009), BSC Response to RAE/REF Consultation. Unpublished Document.

McAra, L. (2008), 'Crime, Criminology and Criminal Justice in Scotland', *European Journal of Criminology*, 5(4): 481–504.

McAra, L. (2016), 'Criminological knowledge and the politics of impact: implications for juvenile justice', in S. Armstrong, J. Blaustein, and A. Henry (eds), *Impact and the Reflexive Imperative in Criminal Justice Policy, Practice and Research*, London: Palgrave MacMillan.

McAra, L. and McVie, S. (2015), 'The Case for Diversion and Minimum Necessary Intervention', in B. Goldson and J. Muncie (eds), *Youth Crime and Justice*, London: Sage Publications.

Piquero, A. and Weisburd, D. (eds) (2010), *The Handbook of Quantitative Criminology*, New York: Springer.

Platt, J. (2004), 'Epilogue in Eight Essays', in A. H. Halsey (ed.), *A History of Sociology in Britain: Science, Literature, and Society*, Oxford: Oxford University Press.

Radzinowicz, L. (1961), *In Search of Criminology*, London: Heinemann.

Roberts, A. (2010), *The Logic of Discipline: Global Capitalism and the Architecture of Government*, Oxford: Oxford University Press.

Rock, P. (ed.) (1988), *A History of British Criminology*, Oxford: Oxford University Press.

Rock, P. (ed.) (1994), *The History of Criminology*, Aldershot: Dartmouth.

Sarnecki, J. (2014), 'Should criminologists shift their focus away from juvenile delinquency?', *International Journal of Offender Therapy and Comparative Criminology*, 58(5): 519–21.

Scraton, P. (2013), 'The legacy of Hillsborough: Liberating truth, challenging power', *Race & Class*, 55(2): 1–27.

Shearing, C. (2015), 'Criminology and the Anthropocene', *Criminology and Criminal Justice*, 15(3): 255–69.

Sumner, C. (1994), *The Sociology of Deviance: An Obituary*, Buckingham: Open University Press.

Tannenbaum, F. (1938), *Crime and the Community*, Boston: Ginn.

Taylor, I., Walton, P. and Young, J. (1973), *The New Criminology: For a Social Theory of Deviance*, London: Routledge & Kegan Paul.

Tonry, M. (ed.) (2007), *Crime, Punishment, and Politics in Comparative Perspective*, Chicago: University of Chicago Press.

Westergaard, J. (2004), 'Epilogue in Eight Essays', in A. H. Halsey (ed.), *A History of Sociology in Britain: Science, Literature, and Society*, Oxford: Oxford University Press.

WhatUni (2016), Available at: https://www.whatuni.com/.

Young, J. (1988), 'Radical Criminology in Britain: The Emergence of a Competing Paradigm', *British Journal of Criminology*, 28(2): 159–83.

PART I

CONSTRUCTIONS OF CRIME AND JUSTICE

1

THE FOUNDATIONS OF SOCIOLOGICAL THEORIES OF CRIME

Paul Rock

INTRODUCTION

Criminology emerged so fitfully, discontinuously, and indecisively in Britain that its history does not lend itself to easy description. Even the core definition of the discipline has been contested, scholars having raised doubts about whether there can ever be professional agreement about its identity. So it was that, more than 150 years after it was first named, Mary Bosworth and Carolyn Hoyle felt it necessary to invite contributors, in the words of the title of their edited book, to examine the question of 'what is criminology?' (Bosworth and Hoyle 2011: 530–41). There are, after all, no professional associations controlling what it is and who can practise it. *Anyone* can be a criminologist, and *anyone* can decide what that means. Criminology is what David Downes once called a *rendez-vous* subject where different disciplines and people converge around a common subject area. It has been stocked, *inter alia*, by psychiatrists, psychologists, sociologists, historians, social and physical anthropologists, lawyers, statisticians, journalists, and documentary film makers, and they have tended to talk about rather different things and share rather different traditions, audiences, styles, and preoccupations. The result has been something of a cacophony in which they have not always been able to listen to, or understand, one another.

Yet what they *would* all probably agree upon is the broad content of their chosen terrain. Criminology has been defined (or undefined) chiefly by its association with an area marked, in Irvin Waller's alliterative words, by cops, crimes, courts, and corrections (and, he would add, victims); or, as Edwin Sutherland and Donald Cressey put it, by the study of 'making laws, breaking laws, and of reacting towards the breaking of laws' (1955: 3). That is an unambiguously empirical set of bearings and it is not hard to appreciate why theorizing has remained relatively underdeveloped. Take the contents of two journals that were current just as this passage was being drafted. The April 2015 issue of *Criminology and Criminal Justice,* the journal of the British

Society of Criminology, and the May 2015 issue of its counterpart, *Criminology*, published by the American Society of Criminology, contained no article at all that was recognizably theoretical.

There are added difficulties. There has never been a simple progression over time from one distinct criminological era to another—from an age distinguished at the outset, say, by classical theorizing in the eighteenth century and culminating in conflict theory in the twentieth, as one trio of authors, Taylor, Walton, and Young (1973), conceived it. No such template fits the facts There has been such a welter of voices and currents flowing from such different disciplines and institutions, and such a propensity of old theories to linger on, co-existing and merging with newer ideas in a variety of combinations, that any simple evolutionary scheme of that kind is quite impossible (Rock 2011). And scholars on both sides of the Atlantic have tended to confuse matters further by continually forgetting their own past (Rafter 2013, Rock 2005), offering what can only be described as muddled assertions about the originality and provenance of what they have done. Rather than look at a succession of discrete theoretical eras, then, it may be more useful to begin by treating criminology as a *practical* activity deeply immersed in an exploration of the empirical world.

THE ORIGINS OF BRITISH CRIMINOLOGY

Although it is now some 50 years old, Hermann Mannheim's model of criminology's loosely connected evolutionary stages remains as serviceable as any (1965: Vol. 1, 79). First, he said, there were private individuals working alone, citing as examples John Howard and Jeremy Bentham. One might add that these were men working in a newly established tradition of social, juridical, and political improvement, often lawyers by training and nonconformists or utilitarians by inclination, who believed in the possibility of reform through the application of reason to confusing and apparently illogical laws, institutions, and practices that composed the English and Welsh *ancien régime*. Jeremy Bentham, said John Stuart Mill in a biographical essay, 'found the philosophy of law a chaos, he left it a science . . . ' (1838, republished 1950: 75).

It was a group that was tenuously united at the end of the eighteenth and the beginning of the nineteenth centuries by a copious correspondence; an independence of thought; an independence of wealth; the holding of pivotal positions as magistrates, sheriffs, and Members of Parliament; and a common membership of philanthropic societies and religious organizations (see Whitten 2011). They learned at first or second hand about conditions in Britain and elsewhere, and they cultivated in their turn the beginnings of a systematic, comparative, and investigative stance towards problems of crime, policing, and punishment. John Howard's *The State of the Prisons* of 1784, Patrick Colquhoun's *A Treatise on the Police of the Metropolis* of 1797, Samuel Romilly's *Observations on the Criminal Law of England* of 1811, and Jeremy Bentham's *Draught for the Organization of Judicial Establishments* of 1838 are prime examples of their method. But, being largely self-sufficient men of private means they did not lay much of a foundation for an enduring tradition of collective research and teaching.

Second and third in Mannheim's chronology was what he described as the work of public officials acting first in a private and then in a public capacity, and he cited as examples André-Michel Guerry and Cesare Lombroso. One might again add that that second era was marked by the activity of embryonic criminologists who made use of the copious data and institutions that the newly reformed, expanding, interventionist, and increasingly wealthy state of the nineteenth century—the state that the Enlightenment reformers had built—had created in the service of public administration. The very word 'statistic' refers to a fact bearing on the condition of the state, and it first came into use in the late 1780s, to be joined by the word 'statistician' in 1825, and together they heralded the arrival of a new kind of blue book knowledge. The first population census in Britain was conducted in 1801; the new police, judicial, and penal authorities began to produce their own statistical returns after the 1830s; and a great mass of numerical data began to flood into the public realm. Louis Chevalier remarked of that period in France that there was 'a determination to obtain figures for everything, to measure everything, to know everything, but to know it by numbers, [it was an] encyclopedic hunger' (1973: 43).

The new statistics were eagerly explored by those who sought to discover patterns and trends in the social world: Joseph Fletcher (1850), André-Michel Guerry (1864), and Adolphe Quetelet (1848), above all, sought to devise a new social physics that could reveal law-like regularities of behaviour in space and time. One of the three, the Belgian, Adolphe Quetelet, boldly claimed in 1831, for instance, that 'we can count in advance how many individuals will soil their hands with the blood of their fellows, how many will be swindlers, how many poisoners, almost as we can number in advance the births and deaths that will take place' (Quetelet 1831: 80–1).

A second concomitant of the emergence of the new penitentiaries, police forces, and asylums was the creation of new *cadres* of administrators who managed, diagnosed, and ministered to the populations they oversaw, and they claimed new mandates and fostered new intellectual disciplines to shore up their infant and somewhat fragile professional authority. There was W. D. Morrison, a prison chaplain, the author of *Crime and its Causes*, published in 1891, and *Juvenile Offenders*, published in 1896, and the editor of the criminology series in which Lombroso's *The Criminal Woman* first appeared in English translation in 1895. There was S. A. Strahan, a doctor and lawyer, a physician at the Northampton County Asylum, and author of writings on 'instinctive criminality', criminal insanity, suicide, and morphine habituation. These men established new professional associations to promote and defend their expertise—for instance, the Association of Medical Officers of Asylums and Hospitals for the Insane that was founded in 1841; and the Medico-Legal Association that was founded in 1901. The new associations founded new journals and new forms of knowledge to support their activities. The word 'professional' appeared for the first time in 1848, to be followed by 'professionalism' eight years later, and they signify the emergence of a new kind of expert. The novel disciplines of criminal anthropology, criminal psychiatry, criminology, and medico-legal science gave their members a capacity to control and speak about new problems, and they conferred a tenuous legitimacy. It was almost inevitable that it was to be medicine, the established science of bodily pathology, that became the principal prototype for their fledgling science of social pathology. British criminology took much of its form at that time, remaining for a long while a statistically driven, administratively-bent form of knowledge copying the forms of applied medicine and borrowing the language of diagnosis, prognosis, epidemiology, treatment, and rehabilitation. Garland would argue that it was a project which came to embody contradictions that have yet fully to be resolved: the quest, on the one hand, for a criminology as the science of the causes of crime and, on the other, for a practical discipline subordinate to the administrative demands of the state (2002).

It is that medical model, established in the nineteenth century, which has long framed much of how we think about crime, and it has had a renaissance as its offshoots of genetics, anatomy, and the science of the brain, of 'neuro-criminology' and 'bio-criminology', have recently resurfaced to engage the popular, journalistic and criminological imagination (Rafter 2008; Raine 2014).

The penultimate phase was identified by Mannheim as work undertaken by university departments or individual teachers. By the end of the nineteenth century, enough had been accomplished by the pioneers to entice people to view an infant criminology as a discrete discipline that could be detached from its anchorage in the working practices of state institutions to be pursued as an academic project in its own right. The word 'criminology' was devised first in the 1850s and came into more general currency in the 1890s when it began to be taught in universities in Italy, Austria, Germany, and France. It was to be associated with a cluster of European thinkers, and particularly with Cesare Lombroso and his followers (see Rafter 2009)—although Lombroso tended to be regarded as too fanciful, too extravagant in his mannerisms, too lackadaisical in his methods, to warrant serious consideration by the largely pragmatic, statistically minded and empirical researchers of the United Kingdom (see Goring 1919; Kenny 1909: 220).

British criminology is not and never has been significantly Lombrosian in its affections (see Rock 2007), and, when it did come tentatively to establish itself in England in the early 1920s, it was not as an offshoot of the new criminal anthropology. Rather, the first university post in the discipline was established in Birmingham University in 1921 for Maurice Hamblin Smith, the author of *The Psychology of the Criminal* (1922), and he was a Freudian-leaning psychologist (see Garland 1988: 8).

Yet what came in time decisively to spur British criminology's growth was the flight of intellectuals from Nazi Europe in the 1930s. Three legally trained *emigré* criminologists transplanted the discipline to three universities: Leon Radzinowicz to the University of Cambridge in 1941; Max Grünhut, first to the London School of Economics in 1934, and then to the University of Oxford in 1940, where he was appointed to the university's first lectureship in the field in 1947; and Hermann Mannheim to the London School of Economics in 1935—and it was in that year of 1935, David Garland said, that criminology was established as a professional academic discipline in Britain (1988: 1). Injected into English universities, virtually at a stroke, was the criminology which had been maturing apart in the universities of Western Europe, although it did not necessarily receive a ready acceptance (see Hood 2004).

Mannheim's course on the Principles of Criminology at the LSE in the 1930s was eclectic, comprehensive, and multi-disciplinary, and that was to be the vein in which

British criminology long remained: catholic and multi-causal; averse to a reliance on single theories and disciplines; grounded in medicine and medical metaphor; quantitative, reformist, applied, and tied to the penal politics of the day. Its very heterogeneity meant that successive generations of students were able routinely to receive instruction in a broad range of ideas and conduct research across a wide landscape. Sociologists like Terence Morris and Roger Hood could study under Hermann Mannheim or Leon Radzinowicz, and their students, like David Downes, Stan Cohen, Paul Wiles, and Jock Young, and their students' students, like Dick Hobbs, Nigel Fielding, Ken Plummer, and Ian Taylor, were to advance, refine, and extend criminology along a protracted chain of begats.

When the great wave of university expansion was launched in England and Wales in the 1960s, when the number of universities grew from 30 to 52 in twenty years, criminology could come freely into its own, blossoming with the rest of the academy, and colonizing departments of psychology, law, social policy, and, above all, sociology. The 1970s were especially propitious: a survey conducted in 1986 revealed that nearly 60 per cent of the criminologists then teaching in British universities had been appointed in that decade, and 30 per cent in the years between 1973 and 1976 alone (Rock 1988). In that take-off phase, urged on by publishers, made discontinuous with the past by a thrusting generation of newly appointed young Turks, criminology became striving, expansive, quarrelsome, factious, and open, its practitioners jostling with one another for *Lebensraum*.

One camp established the National Deviancy Symposium in 1968 in open confrontation with what were regarded as the old orthodoxies represented by the Institute of Criminology at the University of Cambridge and the Home Office Research Unit in London (Cohen 1971; Downes 1988: 177). Their defection rankled. The director of the Cambridge Institute, Leon Radzinowicz, called them a 'group of naughty schoolboys playing a nasty game on their stern headmaster' (1999: 229). But they too soon splintered along the confrontational fault-lines of sociology proper, importing into criminology the larger quarrels of Marxist and post-Marxist theory, the new phenomenologies and ethnomethodologies of social life, feminism, and an emerging sociology of deviance. And then, after a while and inevitably—in the 1980s and beyond—most, but not all (see Hillyard *et al.* 2004; Sumner 1994, 2004)—were to become progressively reconciled to one another as new facts became available through instruments such as crime surveys, battle fatigue set in, scholars mellowed with age, and the pragmatics of having to work together continually in departments, committees, and journals began to supersede the earlier, heady excitement of intellectual struggle.

SOCIOLOGICAL CRIMINOLOGY

Criminology in Britain is largely an adjunct of sociology, and the wide-reaching character of its parent discipline has permeated its treatment of crime. It extends, for example, from an examination of the smallest detail of dyadic interaction chain rituals locking victims and offenders together in violent relations and restorative encounters (Collins 2008; Rossner 2014), through long-term changes in public and official conceptions of organized crime (Hobbs 2013) to comparative analyses of large movements in nations' aggregate rates of violent crime over centuries; see (Eisner 2003 and Spierenburg 2008), and it is sometimes difficult to determine where its boundaries should be drawn.

Although there is no one, royal way to lay out the contemporary sociology of crime, as useful a procedure as any is to identify and describe a number of families of theories that share some big idea or ideas in common.

The organization of the remainder of this chapter will dwell on a group of themes which convey some of the intellectual concerns and environment of sociological criminology as it has come to be known in Britain, drawing both on native work and on other, largely American, ideas that inspired it.

It will, in particular, attend to the key issues of control, signification, and order. Crime, after all, is centrally bound up with the state's attempts to impose its will through law; with the meanings of those attempts to lawbreaker, law-enforcer, observer, and victim; and with concomitant patterns of social order and disorder. Those themes are prominent features of the discipline's landscape, and I shall employ them to steer a more or less straight route through Durkheimian and Mertonian theories of anomie; control theories; rational choice theory; routine activities theory; the work of the 'Chicago School'; studies of the relations between control and space, including Newman's 'defensible space', and more recent ideas of risk and the marshalling of dangerous populations; radical criminology and Left Realism; functionalist criminology; and 'labelling theory' and cultural and subcultural analyses of crime as meaningful behaviour. Such a grand tour should encompass most of the major landmarks which criminologists would now consider central to their field.

CRIME AND CONTROL

ANOMIE AND THE CONTRADICTIONS OF SOCIAL ORDER

I shall begin by describing anomie theory, one of the most enduring and, for a while, hard-researched of all criminological ideas, and one that still persists, albeit in occasionally disguised form.

At heart, many theories take it that crime is a consequence of defective social regulation. People are said to deviate because the disciplines and authority of society are so flawed that they offer few restraints or moral direction. The idea is an old one, antedating the emergence of sociology itself, but its formal birth into theory is linked indissolubly with anomie and the French sociologist, Émile Durkheim.

Durkheim awarded two rather different meanings to anomie, or normlessness. In *The Division of Labour in Society*, published in 1893, and in *Suicide*, published in 1897, he asserted that French society was in uneasy transition from one state of solidarity or social integration to another. A society without an elaborate division of labour rested on what he called (perhaps misleadingly) the mechanical solidarity of people who not only reacted much alike to problems, but also saw that everyone about them reacted alike to those problems, thereby lending objectivity, scale, authority, unanimity, and solidity to moral response, and bringing a potential for massive disapproval and repression to bear down on the deviant. Such a social order was conceived to lie in the simpler past of a less differentiated pre-industrial society.

The future of industrial society would eventually be distinguished by a state of organic solidarity, the cohesion appropriate to a complex division of labour. People would then be allocated by merit and effort to diverse social positions, and they would not only recognize the legitimacy of the manner in which rewards were distributed, but also acknowledge the indispensability of what each did in his or her work for the other and for the common good. Organic solidarity would thus have controls peculiar to itself. People might no longer think wholly in unison, their moral response might not be undifferentiated, they might not be so punitive, but they could acknowledge the fairness of disparities in wealth and should be able to resolve their conflicts peaceably by means of a system of restitutive justice that made amends for losses suffered.

Durkheim's distinction between the two forms of solidarity and their accompanying modes of control was anthropologically suspect (see, e.g., Llewellyn and Hoebel 1941), but criminologists were most interested in his analysis of the liminal state between them. In that transition, where capitalism was thought to impose a 'forced division of labour', people acquiesced neither in the apportionment of rewards nor in the moral authority of the economy or state. They were obliged to work and act in a society that not only enjoyed little legitimacy but also exercised an incomplete control over their desires. Moral regulation was relatively deficient and people were correspondingly free to deviate. That is the first meaning Durkheim gave to anomie. His second will be visited below.

Given another, distinctively American, complexion by Robert Merton, the first version of anomie became a socially fostered state of discontent and deregulation that generated crime and deviance as part of the routine functioning of a society which promised much to everyone but actually denied them equal access to its attainment (Merton 1938). People might have been motivated to achieve success in the United States, the society on which Merton focused, but they confronted class, race, and other barriers that manifestly contradicted the myth of openness. It was not easy for a poor, inner-city adolescent to receive sponsorship for jobs, achieve academic awards, or acquire capital. In a society where failure is still interpreted as a sign of personal rather than social weakness, where it can lead to individual guilt rather than political or collective anger (Newman 2006), the pressure to succeed can be so powerful that it impels people thus disadvantaged to bypass legitimate careers and take to illegitimate routes instead (Merton 1957).

Merton's anomie theory was to be modified progressively. In the work of Richard Cloward and Lloyd Ohlin, for example, it was elaborated to include *illegitimate* routes to success. *Delinquency and Opportunity* (1960) described the consequences of young American men (in the 1950s and 1960s the criminological gaze was almost wholly on the doings of young American *men*) not only being pushed into crime by the difficulties of acquiring money and position in conventional ways, but also being pulled by the lure of lucrative and unconventional criminal careers. There would be those who were offered an unorthodox path in professional or organized crime, and they could become thieves, robbers, or racketeers. There would be those for whom no path was available, and they could become members of conflict gangs. And there were those who failed to attain admission to either a law-abiding or a law-violating group, the 'double failures', who would, it was conjectured, give up and become drug-users and hustlers. Each of those modes of adaptation was, in effect, a way of life, supported by a system of meanings or a subculture, and Cloward and Ohlin provided one of the bridges between the structural and the interpretive models of crime which will be discussed towards the end of this chapter.

In Albert Cohen's *Delinquent Boys* (1957), anomie was to be synthesized with the Freudian idea of 'reaction formation' in an attempt to explain the manifestly expressive and 'non-rational' nature of much delinquency. Many young men did not and could not succeed in a patently unequal society, and the prospect of *failure* was depicted as bringing about a major psychological rejection of what had formerly been sought, so that the once-aspiring working-class adolescent emphatically turned his back on the middle-class world that spurned him and adopted a style of behaviour that was its systematic inversion. The practical and utilitarian in middle-class life was transformed into non-utilitarian delinquency; respectability became malicious negativism; and the deferment of gratification became short-run hedonism. Paul Willis would argue that a perverse consequence of such an embrace of a rejectionist lifestyle (in his case, the emphasis was on an assertive, rough masculinity which dismissed the academic ambitions of the so-called 'earoles') was that working-class males were eased smoothly into an acceptance of subordination (1977).

Again, in the work of David Downes (1966), conducted in London in the early 1960s to explore how far beyond America anomie theory might be generalized, the ambitions of working-class English adolescents were found to have been so depressed by the presence of relatively abundant, albeit low-paid, jobs and what was then a stable and legitimated system of social stratification, that they did not seem to undergo a taxing guilt, shame, or frustration in their failure to accomplish middle-class goals. They neither hankered after the middle-class world nor repudiated it. Rather, their response was 'dissociation'. Where they *did* experience a strong dissatisfaction, however, was in their thwarted attempts to enjoy leisure in the somewhat grey world of post-war England, and their delinquencies were principally hedonistic, focused on drinking, fighting, and malicious damage to property, rather than instrumentally turned towards the accumulation of wealth.

And that theme—of the part played by the adolescent 'manufacture of excitement' and the courting of risk—came to be echoed repeatedly in the empirical and theoretical work of later criminologists. Having 'mad ideas' and making 'something happen' in a dreary world without significant cultural or material resources could easily bring about a drift into delinquency (see Corrigan 1979; Cusson 1983; Katz 1988; Presdee 2000). Indeed, it was to be distinctive of much delinquency. Ferrell *et al.*, for example, talk about how many young people 'push themselves to "the edge", and engage there in "edgework", in search of "the adrenalin rush", authentic identity, and existential certainty. In effect, it was said, "they lose control to take control"' (2008, p. 72.).

An incarnation of anomie theory is thus to be found in a muted form in 'Left Realism' and its successor, 'cultural criminology' where the idea of structural tension is integrated with that of the social meanings of the act to produce a conception of delinquency as a giddy, motivated response to the inequalities of capitalism (Young 2004: 553). I shall return to that theme too.

Another application of the model has recently been produced by Densley and Stevens (2015) who have written about how perceived inequalities of race and class in England have infused a vocabulary of motive for Black urban delinquents: where material aspirations are high, what is seen as oppressive social control is ever-present and life-chances are poor, crime may be defined as a justifiable response. Their representation of a vocabulary of delinquent motives resonates well with Sherman's defiance theory which talks about the criminogenic impact of deep wellsprings of anger and resentment towards existing political and social arrangements, particularly in young African-Americans and Aboriginal Australians (Sherman 1993, 2010; Bouffard and Piquero 2010).

And there was to be yet another, rather different twist to the theory. Anomie is palpably not tied only to absolute or relative deprivation. It may be found wherever institutions are temporarily or permanently out of joint with one another, controls are weakened, and the lure of the economic sector is more dominant than, say, that of religious, communal, or educational organizations (Rosenfeld and Messner 2013). The ensuing functional dislocation, echoing an idea of systemic malintegration originally to be found in the writings of Talcott Parsons and his followers (see Mills 1959), has been christened 'institutional anomie'. It has a wide range. In the upper strata of society, for example, some people may feel relatively privileged, unfettered, and normless, able to conduct themselves freely in the pursuit of excess, and they too may take illegitimate paths and commit crime (see Jackall 1988; Punch 1996, Tett 2009). Think of the fall of Baring Brothers (Gordoni 1997), Lehmann Brothers (Mishkin 2011), the Royal Bank of Scotland (Board 2010), and Enron (Rapoport *et al.* 2009).

ANOMIE AND SOCIAL DISORGANIZATION

The second reading of anomie stemming from Durkheim touched on moral regulation that was not so much flawed as in a state of near collapse. People, he argued, are not endowed at birth with fixed appetites and ambitions. On the contrary, their purposes and aspirations are shaped by the opinions and reactions of others, by a collective conscience, that can appear through social ritual and routine to be externally derived, solid, and objective. When society is disturbed by rapid change or major disorder, however, that semblance of solidity, authority, and objectivity can founder, and people may no longer find their ambitions subject to effective social discipline. It is hard to live outside the reassuring structures of social life, and the condition of anomie can be experienced as a 'malady of infinite aspiration' that is accompanied by 'weariness', 'disillusionment', 'disturbance, agitation and discontent'.

Durkheim conceived such anomic deregulation to be a matter of crisis, innately unstable and short-lived. Disorganization could not be tolerated for long before a society collapsed or order of a sort was restored. Indeed, sociologists are generally ill-disposed towards the term, believing that it connotes a want of understanding and perception on the part of the observer (see Anderson 1976). Yet there are clear examples of people living in conditions where informal control and cooperativeness are only vestigial; where formal control is either absent or erratic; where others are, or are seen to be, predatory and dangerous; where life is unpredictable; and where, as cause and consequence, there is little personal safety, much anxiety, and abundant crime. On some housing estates in St Louis (Rainwater 1970), Nottingham (Davies 1998), and Paris (Wacquant 2008), social groupings have been portrayed as so lacking in cohesion that they enjoyed no shared trust, neighbour preyed on neighbour, and joint defensive action (or what has been called 'collective efficacy') was virtually impossible.

Rampant anomie, a state where life is solitary, poor, nasty, brutish, and short, has been widely documented (see Erikson 1994; Worsley 1968). Consider Colin Turnbull's description of the condition of the Ik of northern Uganda, a tribe that had been moved to a mountainous area after their traditional hunting grounds had been designated a national park. They could no longer live, cooperate, and work as they had done before; familiar patterns of social organization had become obsolete; and the Ik were portrayed as having become beset by 'acrimony, envy and suspicion' (1973: 239), 'excessive individualism, coupled with solitude and boredom' (ibid.: 238), and the victimization of the weak: 'without killing, it is difficult to get closer to disposal than by taking the food out of an old person's mouth . . .' (ibid.: 252).

In the 1990s a number of political scientists and others began to prophesy a new apocalypse in which anomie would flourish to such an extent that entire societies would dissolve into confusion and lawlessness. There are, they said, parts of the world, commonly called 'failed states', whose political structures have become so radically disordered that it is difficult to talk about legitimate governments operating effectively within secure national boundaries (see Bayart *et al.* 1999). So it was that Kaplan (1994) wrote graphically about the road-warrior culture of Somalia, the anarchic implosion of criminal violence in the Ivory Coast, and Sierra Leone, which he depicted at the time as a lawless state that had lost control over its cities at night, whose national army was a 'rabble', and which was reverting to tribalism. So, too, Martin van Creveld analysed what he called the ubiquitous growth of 'low-intensity conflict' waged by guerrillas and terrorists who threatened the state's conventional monopoly of violence.

The trends they foretold seem to have been fully realized in the havoc of societies where ISIS, Boko Haram, and Al Shabbab are at work (see Maiangwa *et al.* 2012). In the midst of that mayhem, without a viable state legislature, laws, and law enforcement, without adequate state control over the distribution of violence, how can one write intelligently about a discrete realm of crime at all? Crime, after all, is contingent on a state's ability clearly to define, ratify, and execute the law. Stan Cohen remarked that in many places there has been a widespread decline of the belief that the sovereign state can provide security, law, and order; a decline in the authority of the state through corruption scandals; a growth of international crime and a rise of criminal states such as Chechnya; and, in Africa particularly, the emergence of barbarism, horror, and atrocity. In many such places, Cohen said, 'lawlessness and crime have so destroyed the social fabric that the state itself has withdrawn' (1996: 9).

CONTROL THEORY

A second, linked cluster of theories centres loosely around the contention that people—almost all people—seek to commit crime because it is profitable, useful, or enjoyable for them to do so, and that they will almost certainly break the law if they can. Even if that contention, with its covert imagery of feral, predatory men (and women), is not strictly valid, control theorists would argue that it certainly directs enquiry in a helpful direction. They profess to be interested less in the fidelity of description than in its yield for policy intervention and prediction in concrete situations. Theirs is a theory of heuristic rather than of empirical truths, and the heuristic is thought to suggest that more will be learned by exploring a few, uncomplicated factors that seem to *prevent* people from offending than by investigating all the complicated motives, meanings, and antecedents of their actions. Travis Hirschi put the issue baldly: 'The question "Why do they do it?" is simply not the question the theory is designed to answer. The question is, "Why don't we do it?"' (1969: 34).

Such a doctrine is a recognizably close neighbour of anomie theories in its focus on the regulation of potentially unbridled appetites; and, indeed, it is occasionally difficult to distinguish one set of ideas from the other. Earlier variants of control theory, compiled in the 1960s and 1970s, proceeded by drafting lists of the constraints which could check the would-be offender, an offender who, it was assumed for analytic purposes, could be much like you, me, or anyone.

Four chief elements were held by Hirschi to induce people to comply with rules: attachment, commitment, involvement, and belief. Attachment reflected a person's sensitivity to the opinions of others; commitment flowed from an investment of time, energy, and reputation in conformity; involvement stemmed from engrossment in conventional activity; and belief mirrored a person's conviction that he or she should obey legal rules. There is tautology and repetition in that formulation, and it is clearly closer to subcultural and anomie theory than Hirschi would have cared to admit, but he nevertheless usefully directed the criminological mind towards answering his one big question, 'Why *don't* we do it?'

Later, with Gottfredson, Hirschi developed his thesis by turning to self-control and impulsivity. Crime, they claimed, flows from low self-control: it provides a direct and simple gratification of desires that is attractive to those who cannot or will not postpone pleasure. In the main, it requires little skill or planning. It can be intrinsically enjoyable because it involves the exercise of cunning, agility, deception, or power. It requires a lack of sympathy for the victim. But it does not provide medium- or long-term benefits equivalent to those that can flow from more orthodox careers (1990).

David Matza almost certainly would not have called himself a control theorist, but in *Delinquency and Drift* (1964) he effectively straddled theories of control, anomie, and signification, and he portrayed delinquents and delinquency in a manner that many control theorists would find persuasive. Delinquents are not very different from us, he argued. Most of the time they are conventional enough in belief and conduct (and see Matza 1971), and it is difficult to predict who will conform and who will not. But there are occasions when the grip of control loosens, adolescents fatalistically experience themselves (perhaps for opportunistic or rhetorical reasons) as if they were object and effect rather than as subject and cause, as if they were no longer morally responsible for their actions, and they will then find themselves released to drift in and out of delinquency. What eases that process of disengagement are widely circulating accounts or 'techniques of neutralization' (a massively influential idea that he had developed earlier with Gresham Sykes (Sykes and Matza 1957)) which enable people methodically to counter the guilt and offset the censure they might experience when offending (see Maruna and Copes 2005). Delinquents can draw on commonplace morality and be fortified in their resolve by an ability to condemn their condemners (by asserting that police and judges were themselves corrupt and illegitimate critics, for instance); deny injury (by asserting that no significant harm was done); deny the victim (by asserting that the victim was of no consequence, or deserved what happened); or appeal to higher loyalties (a noble motive, such as the protection of family or friends).

Steven Box took analysis yet further by reconciling Hirschi's emphasis on social bonds with Matza's conception of drift. He compiled his own list of variables that were held to affect control: secrecy (the delinquent's chances of concealment); skills (a mastery of knowledge and techniques needed for the deviant act); supply (access to appropriate equipment); social support (the endorsement offered by peers and others); and symbolic support (the endorsement offered by accounts available in the wider culture) (1971: 150). The greater the access to requisite skills, secrecy, supplies, and social and symbolic support, he argued, the greater would be the likelihood of offending.

Perhaps one of the most telling and economical contributions to control theory was supplied by Harriet Wilson. Examining 'socially deprived' families in Birmingham, England, she was to conclude that what most sharply differentiated families with delinquent children from those with none was simply what she called the exercise of 'chaperonage' (1980). Parents who acted as chaperons effectively prevented their children from offending: they were so convinced that the neighbourhood in which they lived was dangerous and contaminating that they sought to protect their children by keeping them indoors or under close supervision, escorting them to school, and prohibiting them from playing with others defined as undesirable (and see Reckless 1957).

Control theory has been applied with effect to the problem of gender differences in offending. Apart from age, no other demographic feature so powerfully discriminates between offenders and non-offenders. At one time, however, scant criminological attention was paid to female crime because there was so very little of it (see Innes 2003: 54). By contrast, what made male offending appear so interesting was its sheer seriousness and scale.

Feminist criminologists and others tacitly adopting a control perspective retorted that that was *precisely* what made women so important analytically (Heidensohn 1968), and they inverted the problem by asking Hirschi's central question (without citing Hirschi himself) about why women did *not* offend. There was the criminologically new and intriguing riddle of the conforming woman, and the riddle was answered, in part, by reference to the effects of differentials in control. John Hagan and his colleagues put it that deviation as a form of fun and excitement in public space was more commonly open to males than to females because daughters, sisters, wives, and partners are more frequently risk-averse and more frequently subject to intense, continual, and diffuse family control in the private, domestic sphere. That control, by extension, not only removed girls and women from the purview of agents of formal social control, the criminal justice system, and the possibility of public identification as criminal; it also worked more effectively because it rested on the manipulation of emotional sanctions rather than the imposition of physical or custodial controls. Shaming strategies and the withdrawal of affection are seemingly more potent than fines, probation, or prison. It followed that the more firmly structured and hierarchical the family, the sharper the distinction drawn between male and female roles, the more women were confined to private space, the greater would be the disparity between rates of male and female offending (see Hagan *et al.* 1979, 1985, and 1988).

The converse was also true. Pat Carlen observed that female criminals were most likely to emerge when what she called the 'gender deal' was broken, young women left home or were taken into the care of the state, and were thereby exposed to controls characteristically experienced by men (1988). The answer to the 'crime problem', Frances Heidensohn once concluded, tongue in cheek, would have to lie in the feminization of control.

Control theory is now greatly in vogue, particularly in the United States, where it is linked with theories of the 'life-course' in the work of authors such as Sampson and Laub, whose *Crime in the Making* of 1993 was to be succeeded by their *Shared Beginnings, Divergent Lives* of 2003. Both works explore the genesis of, and desistance from, delinquency in the lives of men studied over decades: and they devoted especial attention to the manner in which the social bonds of family, friends, employment, and military service work as informal controls that filter influences emanating from the wider social structure. Marriage or the onset of work, they argue, may act as critical turning points which induce discontinuities in a life history; create new sets of social relations, dependencies, and responsibilities; introduce new disciplines into social life; and invite stock-taking and reflection. Conversely, involvement with the criminal justice system and imprisonment may interrupt or undermine participation in stabilizing social environments; stigmatize the offender and prevent re-entry into the 'straight' world; encourage cynicism about criminal justice through a close acquaintance with its game-like and seedier features; and introduce the offender to other lawbreakers who help to amplify deviance through differential association. Throughout, and following Matza, Katz, and others, Laub and Sampson portray the process not as a grim and ineluctable descent into criminality, but as a sequence of events and actions which is influenced by the capacity of people to interpret and *choose* how they will respond. The part played by human agency and contingency is repeatedly underscored, leading them to observe how impossible it is to predict future criminality from present circumstances.

The interplay between structure, subjectivity, and voluntarism in the shaping of deviant careers is also the pivot of a Scottish longitudinal study that explores how, over time, men and women acquire situated identities and motives (Henry and McAra 2012) as they undergo a succession of fateful experiences of what are called 'regulatory mechanisms' (McAra and McVie 2012). It is yet another theme to which I shall return.

RATIONAL CHOICE THEORY

An increasingly important, but not indispensable, foundation for control theories is 'rational choice theory', a resuscitation of old utilitarian theories that preceded sociology. It was reintroduced to criminology through the medium of a revived economics of crime, and it brought with it the convenient fiction of economic man (see Becker 1968), a fiction which has an immediate affinity with the criminal man (or woman) of control theory. Economic man, deemed to be continually looking about him for opportunities, making amoral and asocial choices to maximize his personal utility, may not be a wholly credible entity, but, it is argued, he does help to simplify model-making, strip away what rational choice theorists conceive to be 'unessential theoretical and descriptive clutter', and aim directly at what are conceived to be practically useful policy questions (see Clarke and Cornish 1985). Economic man in his (or her) criminal guise does not have a past, complex motives, a rich social life, or, indeed, a recognizable social identity (a 'disposition' is how Ron Clarke put it; 1992). He or she may not be perfectly rational, muddling through or 'satisficing', as we all do, on the basis of imperfect information and in the presence of risks and uncertainty. He or she needs no such complexity, because what weighs in control theory is the piecemeal theoretical analysis of discrete episodes of disembodied offending behaviour conducted by people making decisions around the issues of risk, effort, and reward (Clarke and Cornish 2000: 7) in the settings in which they take place (see introduction to Clarke and Felson 1993).

In Ron Clarke's particularly significant formulation, the rate of crime was held to vary in response to three broad configurations of factors. The first revolved around increasing the effort Everyman would have to expend in committing a crime, and that entailed 'target hardening' (by defending objects and people by physical shields and other devices); 'access control' (and that involved making it difficult for predators to approach targets); deflecting offenders (e.g. by encouraging them to act in a legitimate rather than an illegitimate manner through the provision of graffiti boards, litter bins, and spittoons); and 'controlling facilitators' (through gun control or checks on the sales of spray cans, for instance). The second revolved around increasing the risks of offending through the screening of people (e.g. by means of border searches); formal surveillance by police, security guards, and others; informal surveillance by employees such as bus conductors, train guards, concierges, and janitors; and 'natural surveillance' (aided by lowering or removing obstacles such as hedges around private dwellings (see Bennett and Wright 1984)), installing closed circuit television cameras, lighting the interiors of stores, and enhanced street lighting (Painter 1996). The final grouping was 'reducing the rewards' of crime, itself composed of 'target removal' (using electronic transactions and 'oyster' cards to reduce the number of monetary payments, and thus the accumulation of cash in single places, for instance); property identification; removal of inducements (by the rapid cleaning of graffiti or repair of vandalized property); and rule-setting (through income tax returns, customs declarations, and the like) (Clarke 1992: 13). A pursuit of those common-sense, sometimes indistinguishable, but nevertheless practical ideas allowed research officers at Clarke's Home Office Research Unit in the 1970s and early 1980s to undertake a succession of illustrative studies, discovering, for example, that compact, old school buildings on small urban sites were a third as likely to be burgled as large, sprawling, modern buildings with their many points of access and weak possibilities of surveillance (see Hope 1982); or that there was some 20 times as much malicious damage on the upper than on the lower decks of 'one man', double-decker buses whose drivers' powers of surveillance were confined to one level only (Mayhew *et al.* 1976: 26). The measures they introduced have been invoked as one of the only convincing explanations of the decline in crime rates since the mid-1990s (see van Dijk 2008).

None of those variables touched on conventional sociological questions about who offenders might be, how they reason, and how they act (and for that rational choice theorists have been criticized; see Wright and Decker 1997; and Haggerty, who remarked astringently that control theorists are more akin to 'Wal-Mart security consultants than research criminologists'; 2004: 218). Control theorists concentrated instead on the imagined impact of different forms of control on Everyman or Everywoman, and from that it was but a short step to extend control theory to an analysis of the disciplines that are built into everyday social practices, on the one hand, and into the social uses of space, on the other.

ROUTINE ACTIVITIES THEORY

Ron Clarke, the situational control theorist, and Marcus Felson, the routine activities theorist, agreed that they shared ideas in common (see Clarke and Felson 1993) as well as ideas apart (thus situational control theory is microscopic, routine activities theory largely macroscopic in its application; Clarke and Cornish undated: 25). Clarke and his colleagues had asked what prevented specific criminal incidents from occurring in specific situations. Felson asked how such incidents originate or are checked in the structures of mundane social life (1994). Just as Clarke and others had emphasized how, for explanatory purposes, it was convenient to assume that offenders were little different from anyone else, so Felson and his colleagues argued that most criminals are very ordinary people. Just as control theorists made use of a tacit version of original sin, so routine activities theory adopted a series of presuppositions about basic human frailty, the importance of temptation and provocation, and the part played by idleness (1994: 20).

The routine activities criminologist would argue that the explanation of predatory crime does not necessarily require weighty causes. Neither does it demand that the theorist commit the 'like-causes-like' fallacy which implicitly insists that a 'pathological' phenomenon such as crime must be explained by a pathological condition such as alienation, poverty, family dysfunction, or class or racial oppression. Crime was taken to be built into the very architecture of everyday life. More precisely, it was to be found in the convergence in space and time of motivated offenders, suitable targets, and capable guardians (see Cohen and Felson 1979), being affected by such matters as the weight, value, incidence, and distribution of stealable goods (the growth in the quantity of portable, high-cost goods such as lap-top computers, DVD-recorders and mobile (or 'cell') telephones will encourage more theft, for instance); the impact of motor cars (they aid rapid flight, permit the discreet transportation of objects, and give rise to a geographical dispersal of the population which dilutes surveillance); habits of leisure (adolescents now have larger swathes of empty time than did their predecessors); habits of work (when all members of a household are in outside employment, there will be no capable guardians to protect a home); habits of residence (single people are less effective guardians of property than are larger households); the growth of technology (modern mobile telephones, for instance, amplify the public's ability to report and record crime); and so on. A recent illustration of the argument about the habits of leisure has been the contention that delinquency rates may have been falling simply because boys and young men are now increasingly playing computer games at home instead of misbehaving in public space (Morris and Johnson 2014). Overall, routine activities is an uncomplicated enough theory but again, like its near relative, control theory, it does ask empirically rewarding questions.

CRIME, CONTROL, AND SPACE

THE CHICAGO SCHOOL

Routine activities theory and control theory both talk about convergence in space, and space has always been analytically prominent in criminology. Indeed, one of the earliest and most fruitful of the research traditions laid down in criminology was the social ecology and urban mapping practised by the sociology department of the University of Chicago in the 1920s and beyond (see Park 1915, 1925; Thrasher 1927; and Landesco 1968).

As cities grow, it was held, so there would be a progressive, 'organic' and largely spontaneous differentiation of space, population, and function that concentrated different groupings in different areas. The main organizing structure was the *zone*, and the Chicago sociologists discerned five principal concentric zones shaping the city: the central business district around the 'Loop' at the core; the 'zone in transition' about that centre; an area of stable working-class housing; middle-class housing; and outer suburbia.

The zone in transition was marked by the greatest volatility. It was an area of comparatively cheap rents, weak social control, internal social differentiation, and rapid physical and demographic change. It was to the zone in transition that new immigrants most frequently came, and it was there that they settled into what were called 'natural areas', small, 'spontaneously'-generated, communal enclaves that were said to be relatively homogeneous in composition and culture. Chicago sociologists plotted the incidence of social problems on to census maps of the city, and it was the zone in transition that was found repeatedly to house the largest visible proportions of the poor, the illegitimate, the illiterate, the mentally ill (see Faris and Dunham 1939), juvenile delinquents (Shaw and McKay 1942), and prostitutes (Reckless 1933). The zone in transition was, in effect, virtually co-extensive with what was then described as social pathology. Not only were formal social controls held to be at their weakest there (the zone in transition was, as it were, socially dislocated from the formal institutions and main body of American society (see Whyte 1942); but informal social controls were eroded by moral and social diversity, continual population movement, insecurity of tenure (see Desmond 2016), and a lack of strong and pervasive local institutions (Wirth 1964: 236)).

A number of the early Chicago sociologists united social ecology, the study of the patterns formed by different groups living together in the same space, with the fieldwork methods of social anthropology, to explore the traditions, customs, and practices of the residents of natural areas. They found that, while there may well have been a measure of social and moral dislocation between the zone in transition and the wider society, as well as within the zone in transition itself, those natural areas could also manifest a remarkable inner coherence and persistence of culture and behaviour from generation to generation and immigrant group to immigrant group within the same terrain over time. Delinquency was, in effect, not disorganized at all, but a stable attribute of social life, an example of continuity in change (Shaw and McKay 1942: 260). Cultural transmission was to be the focus of the work pursued by a small group of the so-called second-generation Chicago sociologists. Sometimes under the name of 'differential association', it was studied as a normal process of learning motives, skills, and meanings in the company of others who bore criminal traditions (see Sutherland and Cressey 1955).

That urban research was to prepare a diverse legacy for criminology: the spatial analysis of crime and the enduring moral differentiation of neighbourhoods (see Sampson 2012); the study of subcultures; the epidemiology of crime; crime as an interpretive practice; what came to be known as 'collective efficacy'—the informal controls mobilized by communities (see Sampson *et al.* 1997), and much else. Let me turn first to some examples of spatial analysis.

CONTROL AND SPACE: BEYOND THE CHICAGO SCHOOL

The Chicago sociologists' preoccupation with the cultural and symbolic correlates of spatial congregations of people was to be steadily elaborated. For instance, Paul Wiles, Tony Bottoms, and their colleagues, then working at the University of Sheffield, added two important observations. They argued first that, in a then more closely administered Britain, social segregation did not emerge, as it were, organically with unplanned city growth (although Chicago was never quite as unplanned as some of the early social ecologists had alleged (see Suttles 1972)), but with the intended and unintended consequences of policy decisions taken by local government departments responsible for housing a large proportion of the population in municipal rented accommodation. Housing allocation was an indirect and sometimes unwitting reflection of moral judgements about tenants that resulted, or were assumed to result, in the spatial concentration of criminal populations (see Bottoms *et al.* 1989). Further, and partly in accord with that argument, the reputations of natural areas themselves became a criminological issue: how was it, these criminologists asked, that the moral meanings attached to space by residents and outsiders affected people's reputations, choices, and action? One's address and an historical memory of 'dreadful enclosures' (see Damer 1974) could become a constraining moral fact that shaped not only how one would be treated by others in and about the criminal justice system but also how one would come to rate oneself as a potential deviant or conformist (see Gill 1977; Sampson 2012).

Secondly, Bottoms and his colleagues argued, while the Chicago sociologists may have examined the geographical distribution of offenders, it was instructive also to scrutinize how *offending* itself could be plotted, because the two measures need not correspond (Baldwin and Bottoms 1976 and see Morris 1957). Offending has its maps. Indeed, it appears to be densely concentrated, clustered around offenders' homes, areas of work and recreation, and the pathways in between (Brantingham and Brantingham 1981–2; Wikström 2007). So it was that, pursuing routine activities theory, Sherman and his colleagues surveyed all calls made to the police in Minneapolis in one year; and discovered that a few 'hot spots' had exceptional densities of crime: only 3 per cent of all places produced 50 per cent of the calls; all robberies took place in only 2.2 per cent of places, all rapes in 1.2 per cent of places, and all car thefts in 2.7 per cent of places (Sherman *et al.* 1989).

DEFENSIBLE SPACE

If offending has its maps, so does social control; and criminologists and others have become ever more interested in the fashion in which space, conduct, and control intersect. One forerunner was Jane Jacobs, who speculated about the relations between city landscapes and informal controls, arguing, for example, that dense, busy thoroughfares with their *habitués* have many more 'eyes on the street' and opportunities for witness reporting and bystander intervention than the sterile pedestrian precinct or 'confused' mixed space (Jacobs 1965).

The idea of 'defensible space', in particular, has been borrowed from social anthropology and architecture, coupled with the concept of surveillance, and put to work in analysing formal and informal responses to different kinds of terrain. 'Defensible space' itself leans on the psychological notion of 'territoriality', the sense of property and symbolic attachment that people can acquire in a place. Territoriality is held by some to be a human universal, an imperative that leads people to wish to protect what is their own. Those who have a stake in a physical area, it is argued, will care for it, police it, and report strangers and others who have no apparent good purpose to be there.

What is quite critical is how space is marked out and bounded. The prime author of the idea, Oscar Newman (1972), claimed that, other things being equal, what induces territorial sentiments is a clear demarcation between private and public areas, even if the demarcation is only token. The private will be protected in ways that the public is not, and the fault of much domestic and institutional space is that separations and segregations are not clearly enough inscribed in design. The geographer, Alice Coleman, and others took it that improvements to the structure of the built environment could then achieve a significant impact on crime. Above all, she insisted on restricting access to sites; reducing the interconnections or 'walkways' between buildings; and emphasizing the distinction between public and private areas and minimizing what Oscar Newman called 'confused space', the space that was neither one thing nor the other (Coleman 1985). She has been roundly faulted, both methodologically and analytically, for her neglect of dimensions other than the physical (see Hillier 1973, 1986), but she and Newman succeeded in introducing an analytic focus on the interrelations between space and informal control that was largely absent before. Only rarely have others, such as Campbell (1993), Duneier (2001), Power (1997), and Shapland and Vagg (1988), enquired into the informal controlling practices of people as they observe, interpret, and respond to the ambiguous, deviant, and non-deviant conduct in the spaces around them.

It was Shapland and Vagg's contention, for instance, that there is a continuous, active process of informal surveillance and intervention conducted by people on the ground; a process which is so discreet and taken for granted that it has escaped much formal notice, and which meshes only haphazardly with the work of the police. And similarly Duneier laid bare the complex webs of informal control practised by homeless entrepreneurs selling books and magazines from stalls on New York's streets. Far from creating a problem of social disorder, they acted as palpable but subtle agents of order, looking after and protecting one another, and preserving public stability.

CRIME, POWER, AND SPACE

Surveillance has not always been construed as neutral or benign, and there are current debates about what its newer forms might portend. It began to be argued, especially by those who followed Michel Foucault, that a so-called 'punitive city' was in the making, that, in Stan Cohen's words, there was 'a deeper penetration of social control into the social body' (1979a: 356).

Some came to claim not only that there has been a move progressively to differentiate and elaborate the distribution of controls in space, but also that there has been a proliferating surveillance of dangerous areas, often conducted obliquely and with an increasingly advanced technology. Michel Foucault's (1977) dramatic simile of Jeremy Bentham's model prison, the Panopticon, was to be put to massive use in criminology. Just as the Panopticon, or inspection house, was supposed to have permitted the unobserved observation of many inmates around the bright, illuminated rim of a circular prison by the few guards in its obscured centre, just as the uncertainty of unobserved observation worked to make the controlled control themselves, so, Foucault and those who followed him wished to argue, modern society is coming to exemplify the perfection of the automatic exercise of power through generalized surveillance. The carceral society was a machine in which everyone was supposed to be caught: it relied on diffuse control through unseen monitoring and the individualization and 'interiorization' of control (Gordon 1972). Public space, it has been said, was becoming exposed to ever more perfunctory, distant, and technologically driven policing by formal state agencies; while control in private and semi-private space (the space of the shopping malls, university campus and theme park (Shearing and Stenning 1985: 347)) was itself becoming more dense, privatized, and widespread, placed in the hands of security guards and store detectives, and reliant on a new electronic surveillance (Davis 1992b: 233).

What also underlies much of that vision is a companion stress on the sociology of risk, a stress linked importantly with the work of Ulrich Beck (1992). It has been argued that people and groups are becoming significantly stratified by their exposure to risk and their power to neutralize harm (but see O'Malley 2010). The rich can afford private protection, the poor cannot, and a new landscape emerges (Simon 1987). Phrased only slightly differently, and merged with newly burgeoning ideas about the pervasiveness of surveillance by machine and person (Gordon 1986–7 and Lyon 1994), those theories of risk suggest that controls are being applied by state and private organizations, not on the basis of some moralistic conception of individual wrongdoing, but on a foundation of the mass identification, classification, and management of groups categorized by their perceived dangerousness (Feeley and Simon 1992; Simon 2007). Groups are becoming ever more rigidly segregated in space: some (members of the new dangerous classes or underclass) being confined to prison, semi-freedom under police surveillance, or probation or parole in the community (see Goffman 2014); others (the more affluent) retreating into their locked and gated communities, secure zones, and 'mass private' spaces. There are new bifurcations of city space into a relatively uncontrolled 'badlands' occupied by the poor and highly controlled 'security bubbles' inhabited by the rich (Davis 1992a; Bottoms and Wiles 1997). Geographical and social exclusion thereby conspires to corral together populations of the unprotected, victimized, and victimizing—the mentally disordered, the young, and the homeless—reinforcing both their vulnerability and their propensities to offend (Carlen 1996; Hagan and McCarthy 1998; Rock and Newburn 2006).

RADICAL CRIMINOLOGY

So far, control has been treated without much direct allusion to the power, politics, and inequalities that are its bedfellows. There was to be a relatively short-lived but active challenge to such quiescence from the radical, new or critical criminologies of the late 1960s and 1970s, criminologies that claimed their mandate in Marxism (Taylor, Walton, and Young 1973), libertarianism (Douglas 1971), anarchism (Kittrie 1971; Cohen 1985), or American populism (Quinney 1970), and whose ambitions pointed to the need for political activism or 'praxis' (Mathiesen 1974).

Crime control was said to be an oppressive and mystifying process that worked through legislation, law-enforcement, and stereotyping to preserve unequal class relations (Chambliss 1976; Box 1983). The radical political economy of crime sought chiefly to expose what were thought to be the hegemonic ideologies that masked the 'real' nature of crime and repression in capitalist society. Most mundane offending, it was argued, was less politically or socially consequential than other evils such as alienation, exploitation, industrial safety (Carson 1981), pollution, or racism (Schwendinger and Schwendinger 1974; Scraton 1987). Much proletarian crime should be redefined as a form of redistributive class justice, or as a sign of the possessive individualism which resided in the core values of capitalist society. Criminal justice itself was engineered to create visible crowds of working-class and black scapegoats who could divert the public gaze away from the more serious delicts of the rich and the more serious ills of a capitalism that was usually said to be in terminal crisis. If the working class reacted in hostile fashion to the crime in their midst then they were, in effect, little more than the victims of a false consciousness which turned proletarian against proletarian, black against black, inflated the importance of petty problems, defused class conflict, and concealed the true nature of bourgeois society.

So construed, signification, the act of giving meaning to crime and criminals, was either manipulative or misconceived, a matter of giving and receiving incorrect and deformed interpretations of reality. Indeed, it was in the nature of subordination in a capitalist society that most people must be politically unenlightened about crime, control, and much else, and the task of the radical criminologist was to expose, denounce, and demystify. It was concluded variously that crime was not a problem which the poor and their academic and political allies should actually address (there were more important matters for Marxists to think about: Hirst 1975); that the behaviour which *should* be analysed was the abundant harms of capitalist society that had successfully resisted criminalization (Hillyard *et al.* 2004), the crimes of the powerful that were too lightly suppressed (Slapper and Tombs 1999), or those exceptional examples of law-breaking that seemed to represent an incipient revolt against the state (Hobsbawm 1959). Black prisoners, in particular, were sometimes depicted, and depicted themselves (Cleaver 1969), as prisoners of class or race wars. Prisons were the point of greatest state repression, and prison riots a possible spearhead of revolution.

In that early guise, radical criminology withered somewhat under a quadruple-barrelled assault. In America (where it had never been firmly implanted), it went against the intellectual and, in one instance, the political grain—the radical criminology department at the University of California at Berkeley (Platt 1974; Schauffler 1974) being closed down. More often, radical criminology did not lend itself to the government-funded, policy-driven, 'soft money', empiricist research that began to dominate schools of criminology in North America in the 1970s and 1980s.

Second was the effect of the publication of mass victim surveys in the 1970s and 1980s (Hough and Mayhew 1983) which disclosed both the extent of working-class victimization and the manner in which it revolved around intra-class, rather than inter-class, criminality. It was evident that crime *was* a manifest problem for the proletariat, adding immeasurably to their burdens, and difficult to dismiss as an ideological distraction. Two prominent radical criminologists came to concede that they had believed that 'property offences [were] directed solely against the bourgeoisie and that violence against the person [was] carried out by amateur Robin Hoods in the course of their righteous attempts to redistribute wealth. All of this [was], alas, untrue' (Lea and Young 1984: 262).

Third was the critique launched from within the left by a new generation of feminist scholars, who asserted that the victimization of women was no slight affair or ideological diversion, and that rape, sexual assault, child abuse, and domestic violence should be taken very seriously indeed (Smart 1977). Not only had the female criminal been neglected, they said, but so had the female victim, and it would not do to wait until the revolution for matters to be put right. Once more, a number of radical criminologists gave ground (Jones *et al.* 1986: 3).

Finally, there was the critique launched belatedly from mainstream criminologists who resisted the imperious claims of radical criminology to be the only fully social theory of crime (Downes and Rock 1979; Inciardi 1980). Marxist and radical theories of crime, it was argued, lacked a comparative emphasis, not only treating all capitalist societies as if they were the same; but also neglecting crime in 'non-capitalist', 'pre-capitalist' societies and 'socialist' societies. There was a naivety about the expectation that crime would wither away as the state itself disappeared after the revolution. There was a trust in socialist justice which could actually be very repressive (Cohen 1979b: 44). There was an irresponsibility and callousness about radical arguments that 'reformism' would only strengthen the grip of the capitalist system.

The radicals gave ground and 'Left Realism' was to be the outcome, represented by Jock Young, one of its revisionist parents, as a novel fusion of analyses of crime in the vein of anomie theory and symbolic interactionist analyses of the reactions which crime evokes (Young 1997: 484). It was 'realist' because, newly refusing to accept the so-called 'left idealists,' dismissal of anxiety about crime as an ideological trick, it acknowledged the practical force of crime in society and its especially heavy impact on the poor, minority ethnic people, and women. It was 'left' because it focused descriptively and politically on the structural inequalities of class, race, and gender. Its project was to examine patterns of crime and control as they emerged out of what Young came to call the 'square of crime', a field of forces dominated by the state, the victim, the offender, and the public.

Left Realism was to follow the earlier radical criminologists' injunction to act, but action was now as much in the service of more effective and practical policing and crime reduction strategies as in the cause of radical social change. Left Realists joined the formerly disparaged 'administrative criminologists' working in and for the (usually local) state to work on situationally based projects to prevent crime and the fear of crime (see Matthews and Young 1992). Were it not for their theoretical preambles, it was at times difficult to distinguish between the programmes of the Home Office or other state criminal justice ministries, on the one hand, and of Left Realism, on the other.

If Left Realism was radical criminology's *praxis*, its more scholarly current continued to evolve in diverse directions. A number of criminologists began to turn away from analyses of crime causation towards studies of contemporary (Cohen 1985; Simon 1993) and historical forms of social control (see Scull 1979). Others responded to the wider theories that began to permeate sociology proper in the 1980s and 1990s, incorporating them to write about crime, postmodernism (or late modernity), risk and globalization, and producing what were, in effect, examples of the 'fully social theory' promised by the new criminologists back in 1973. Above all, that promise was fulfilled by books published in 1999 by two of the original troika of new criminologists: Ian Taylor's *Crime in Context* and Jock Young's *The Exclusive Society*; and one in 2007 by Jock Young, *The Vertigo of Late Modernity*.

Crime in Context catalogues a series of crises flowing from transitions in the political and economic structures of society, and the manner in which they impinge upon poverty, class, gender, race, and the family to affect the national and transnational environments of crime and control. *The Exclusive Society* is subtitled 'Social Exclusion, Crime and Difference in Late Modernity', and its focus is more narrow but nevertheless intense, concentrating upon the social and political consequences of what then seemed to be the inexorable and vast increases in crime in the West. Crime was held by Young to be no longer regarded as abnormal, the property of a pathological few who can be restored therapeutically to the security of a moral community at one with itself, but *normal*, the actions of a significant, obdurate minority of Others who were excluded and demonized in a world newly insecure, fractured, and preoccupied with problems of risk and danger. More recently, late modernity was portrayed in Young's *The Vertigo of Late Modernity* as an epoch of flux, mobility, and shifting boundaries; where selves, careers, and histories are unstable, marked by social hybridization and a constant traffic of ideas across the frontiers of groups; where reward appears arbitrary and chaotic, community is weakened, class identity and biographical narratives are splintered; and the prosperity of a seemingly contented middle class is dependent on the work of a largely unacknowledged, undervalued, humiliated, and underpaid service class labouring at home and overseas to form a new 'underclass', an underclass which becomes publicly visible only through a stigmatizing process of 'othering' and demonization as deviant, shiftless, and dependent. Crime itself is then presented, not so much as the work of a reasoning criminal, but as an angry, expressive *riposte* launched by the impoverished, dishonoured, powerless, and dispossessed, and it works through an answering language of control, selfhood, and violence, an 'othering', Jock Young says, of the 'otherers' who so devalue the poor. Crime's new companion, terrorism, is but a radical extension of such a project of existential affirmation.

What perhaps these accounts do not accommodate with any success is the resilience of community (Boyce 2006; Foster 1990; Sampson 2012) and, mirroring the comparable myopia of Durkheim and Marx in the nineteenth century (Macdonald 1982), the persistent *decline* in crime rates across the western world since the mid-1990s. One wonders whether 'othering', 'hybridity', 'globalization', the decline of community, and the 'vertigo' of late modernity itself have moved into reverse, and, if they have, what the reason might be. No one seems able to say (see Zimring 2007).

FUNCTIONALIST CRIMINOLOGY

Another, apparently dissimilar but substantially complementary, theory presented deviance and control as forces that worked discreetly to maintain social order. Functionalism was a theory of social systems or wholes, developed at the beginning of the twentieth century within a social anthropology growing tired of speculative accounts of the origins and evolution of societies which lacked a written history to support them, and dedicated to what was seen to be the scientific pursuit of intellectual problems. It was argued that the business of a social science necessitated moving enquiry beyond the reach of common sense or lay knowledge to an examination of the unintended, objective consequences of action that were visible only to the trained eye.

There were three clear implications. First, what ordinary people thought they were doing could be very different from what they actually achieved. The functionalist was preoccupied only with what were held to be objective outcomes, and people's own accounts of action afforded little interest. Secondly, the functionalist looked at the impact made by institution upon institution, structure upon structure, in societies that were remarkable for their capacity to persist over time and beyond the lives of the individuals who composed them. Thirdly, those interactions, viewed as a totality, constituted a system in which, it was thought, not only did the parts affect one another and the whole, but also, the whole affected them in return. To be sure, some institutions were relatively detached, but functionalists argued that the alternative proposition—that social phenomena lack influence upon one another, that there was no functional reciprocity between them—was conceptually insupportable.

There have been very few dedicated functionalist criminologists (see Gottfredson and Hirschi 1990: 78). Functionalists tend to deal with global systems. But crime and deviance did supply a particularly intriguing laboratory for thought-experiments about social order. It was easy enough to contend that religion or education shaped social integration, but how much harder it would be to show that *crime* succeeded in doing so. After all, 'everyone knew' that crime undermined society. It followed that functionalists occasionally found it tempting to try to confound lay knowledge by showing that, to the contrary, the seemingly recalcitrant case of crime could be shown scientifically to contribute to the effective working of the social system. From time to time, therefore, they wrote about crime as if to demonstrate the potency of their theory. Only one functionalist, its grand master, Talcott Parsons, ever made the obvious, and therefore intellectually unsatisfying, point that crime could be what was called 'dysfunctional' or injurious to the social system as it was then constituted (Parsons 1951). Everyone else asserted that crime actually worked mysteriously to support it.

The outcome was a somewhat miscellaneous collection of papers documenting the multiple functions of deviance: Kingsley Davis showed that prostitution bolstered monogamy by providing an unemotional, impersonal, and unthreatening release for the sexual energy of the promiscuous married male (Davis 1937); Ned Polsky made much the same claim for pornography (Polsky 1967); Daniel Bell showed that racketeering provided 'queer ladders of success' and political and social stability in the New York dockside (1960); Émile Durkheim (1964) and George Herbert Mead (1918) contended that the formal rituals of trial and punishment enhanced social solidarity and consolidated moral boundaries; and, more complexly, Mary Douglas (1966), Kai Erikson (1966), Robert Scott (1972), and others argued that deviance offered social systems a dialectical or educational tool for the clarification and management of threats, ambiguities, and anomalies in moral classification systems. The list could be expanded, but all the arguments tended to one end: what appeared, on the surface, to weaken social order accomplished the very reverse. A criminological counterpart of the invisible hand transmuted deviance into a force for the cohesion and permanence of community.

Functionalism was to be dismissed by many criminologists in time: it smacked too much of teleology (the doctrine that effects work retrospectively to act as the causes of events); it defied rigorous empirical investigation (see Cotterrell 1999: 75); and, for some, more politically driven criminologists, it represented a form of reaction that championed the *status quo*. But its ghost lingers on. Any who would argue that, contrary to appearances, crime and deviance buttress social order; any who argue for the fully social study of seamless systems; any who argue that the sociologist should mistrust people's own accounts of their actions; any who insist that social science is the study of unintended consequences; must share something of the functionalist's standpoint. Anomie theories that represented crime as the system-stabilizing, unintended consequence of strains in the social order are one example (see Merton 1995). But so, less explicitly, are some versions of radical criminology. More than one such criminologist has argued that crime, deviance, and control were necessary for the survival of capitalism (Stinchcombe 1968). Although they did not talk explicitly of '*function*', the neo-Marxists, Hall *et al.* (1978), Pearce (1976), and Reiman (1990), *were* recognizably functionalist in their treatment of the criminal justice system's production of visible and scapegoated roles for the proletarian criminal, roles that attracted public anxiety and outrage, deflected anger away from the state, emasculated political opposition, and preserved capitalism (Pearce and Tombs 1998; Ferrell and Sanders 1995: 10). What could be more functionalist than that?

SIGNIFICATION

LABELLING THEORY

Perhaps the only other outstanding big criminological idea is signification, the interpretive practice that orders social life. There has been an enduring strain of analysis, linked most particularly to symbolic interactionism, ethnomethodology, and phenomenology, which insists that people do not, and cannot, respond immediately, uncritically, and passively to the world 'as it is'. Rather they respond to their *ideas* of the world, and the business of sociology is to capture, understand, and reproduce those ideas; examine their interaction with one another; and analyse the processes and structures that generated them. Sociology becomes the study of people, relations, and practices as symbolic and symbolizing processes.

Central to that idea is reflexivity, the capacity of consciousness to turn back on and translate itself into its own object. People are able to think about themselves, define themselves in various ways, toy with different identities, and position themselves imaginatively into different situations. They can view themselves vicariously by reading the reactions of 'significant others', and, in so 'taking the role of the other', move symbolically to a distance outside themselves to inspect how they might appear. Elaborating action through 'significant gestures', the symbolic projection of acts and identities, they can anticipate the likely responses of others, and tailor their own prospective acts to accommodate them (Mead 1934). In all this, social worlds are compacted symbolically into the phrasing of action, and the medium that makes that possible is language.

Conferring names enables people to impart moral and social meanings to their own and others' motives (Mills 1940; Scott and Lyman 1970), intentions, and identities. It will matter a great deal if someone is defined as eccentric, erratic, or mad; a drinker, a drunk, or an alcoholic; a lovelorn admirer, sexual predator, or stalker; a freedom fighter or a terrorist; a 'bit of a lad' or a delinquent. Consequences flow from naming, consequences that affect not only how one regards oneself and one's position in the world, but also how one may be treated by others. Naming creates a self.

Transposed to the study of crime and deviance, symbolic interactionism and phenomenology gave prominence to the processes by which over time deviant acts and identities are constructed, interpreted, judged, and controlled (Katz 1988). Deviance itself became more generally likened to a moral career consisting of interlocking phases, each of which feeds into and shapes the next; each of which presents different existential problems and opportunities; each of which is populated by different constellations of significant others; and each of which can distinctively mould the self of the deviant. The process is contingent rather than inexorable. Not every phase is inevitable or irreversible, and deviants can often choose to change direction (Luckenbill and Best 1981: 201).

What punctuates such a career is acts of naming, the deployment of language to confer, anticipate, and fix the meanings of behaviour, and symbolic interactionism and phenomenology became known within criminology as 'labelling theory'. One of the most frequently cited of all passages in sociological criminology was Becker's seemingly simple dictum that 'deviance is not a quality of the act the person commits, but rather a consequence of the application by others of rules and sanctions to an "offender". The deviant is one to whom that label has successfully been applied; deviant behavior is behavior that people so label' (1963: 9).

Labelling itself is contingent and there are special occasions when the ability of the self to resist definition is circumscribed. Most fateful of all may be an encounter with agents of the criminal justice system, because they can work with the often seemingly irresistible force and authority of the state. In such meetings, criminals and deviants are obliged to confront not only their own and others' possibly defensive, fleeting, and insubstantial reactions to what they have done, their 'primary deviation', but also contend publicly with the formal reactions of others, and their deviation can then become a response to responses—'secondary deviation' (Lemert 1951: 76).

What is important about secondary deviation is that it may be a symbolic synthesis of more than just the meanings and activities of primary deviation. It incorporates the myths, professional knowledge, stereotypes, experience, and working assumptions of lay people, police officers, judges, medical practitioners, prison officers, prisoners, policy-makers, and politicians. And it also entails confrontations with new obstacles that foreclose future choice. Once a person is publicly identified as a deviant, it may become difficult for him or her to slip back into the conventional world.

Quite deliberately in response to such dangerously amplified problems of the outlawed deviant is the increasing adoption by states of strategies of restorative justice, discussed elsewhere in this handbook. Restorative justice, based largely on the work of Braithwaite (1989), attempts to unite the informal control of shaming by significant others with rituals of reintegration that work against the alienating consequences of secondary deviation. It sits remarkably well with a series of studies of reoffending after prison that argue that the critical variable in desistance from crime is the capacity of offenders to construct a new narrative or story about their lives to frame a new self now going 'straight' (Maruna 2001) and then of successfully conveying to themselves (Maruna, Lebel, and Mitchell 2004) and others (Maruna 2012) that that narrative is actually authentic.

CULTURE AND SUBCULTURE

Meanings and motives are not established and confirmed by the self in isolation. They are a social accomplishment, and criminology has paid sustained attention to signification as a collaborative, subcultural process. Subcultures themselves are taken to be exaggerations, accentuations, or editings of cultural themes prevalent in the wider society. Any social group which has permanence, a common pursuit, and, perhaps, common problems is likely to engender, inherit, or modify a subculture; but the criminologist's particular interest is in those subcultures that ignore, condone, promote, or otherwise make possible the commission of delinquent acts. A subculture was not conceived to be utterly distinct from the beliefs held by people at large. Neither was it necessarily oppositional. It was a *sub*culture, not a discrete culture or a counterculture, and the descriptive stress has tended to be on dependency, 'hybridization', and synthesis rather than on conflict or symbolic autonomy.

The materials for subcultural theory are to be found across the broad swathe of criminology, and they have been combined in various proportions. Anomie theory supplied the supposition that social inequalities generate problems that may have delinquent solutions, and that those solutions, in their turn, could be shared and transmitted by people thrown together by their common disadvantage. The social anthropology of the Chicago School, channelled for a while into differential association theory, supplied an emphasis upon the enduring, intelligible, and locally adapted cultural traditions shared both by professional criminals and by boys living, working, and playing together on the crowded streets of morally differentiated areas. David Matza and a number of control theorists pointed to the manner in which moral proscriptions could be neutralized by invoking commonly available and culturally transmitted motivational accounts. And symbolic interactionism supplied a focus on the negotiated, collective, and processual character of meaning. In all this, an argument ran that deviance might emerge as young men (it was almost always urban young men), growing up in the city, banded together in groups or 'near-groups' in the crowded and dangerous public life of the streets, encountered common problems, were exposed to common stereotypes and stigmas, were subjected to similar formal controls, flirted with transgressive excitement, and set themselves against common others who might 'disrespect' or attack them (Anderson 1990, 1999). Subcultural theory and research were to dominate explanations of delinquency until they exhausted themselves for a while in the 1960s, only to be revived in a new guise a decade later.

Subcultural theory lent itself to amalgamation with radical criminology in the 1970s, and particularly the criminology which was preoccupied with the reproduction of class inequalities. In Britain, there was to be a renaissance of anomie-derived subcultural theory as a group of young sociologists, clustered around Stuart Hall at the Centre for Contemporary Cultural Studies at the University of Birmingham, gave special attention to the existential plight of young working-class men about to enter the labour market. Deviance became a form of symbolic resistance to tensions perceived through the mists of false consciousness. It was doomed to disappoint because it did not address the root causes of discontent, but it *did* offer a fleeting release. There was a contradiction within that version of subcultural theory because it was not easy to reconcile a structural Marxism which depicted adolescent culture as illusory with a commitment to the appreciation of meaning (Willis 1977). But it was a spirited and vivid revival of a theory that had declined in significance in the 1960s, and it continues to influence theorizing (see Ferrell 1993), culminating in the creation of the new theoretical hybrid to which I have already alluded, cultural criminology (see Ferrell *et al.* 2004), a hybrid which re-emphasizes how transgression attains meaning in what is called a fluid, pluralistic, contested, hedonistic, 'edgy', consumerist, and 'media-saturated world' (Ferrell *et al.* 2008: 5–6; Hallsworth 2005).

THE FUTURE OF SOCIOLOGICAL CRIMINOLOGY

What of the future? It is not as hospitable to theory and free enquiry as it once was. Many academics in Britain will undoubtedly be constrained by ever tighter regulatory regimes which restrict what they can do and the frameworks in which they can do it. There was a time when they could work relatively unhindered in what was a rather poorly funded research environment that was spared the blunter impact of market forces. Then came what Tank Waddington called the Faustian compact in which English and Welsh universities embarked on radical expansion supported by substantial government funds. Commentators at the time worried about the effects of recruiting larger numbers of weak students (see Little 1961). But they did not consider the problems that would arise from the universities' obligation to give a continual financial accounting to their paymasters. Quite extraordinarily, the universities of England and Wales have now fallen under the alien *aegis* of the Department for Business, Innovation and Skills which requires them chiefly to service the economy and foster social mobility; to 'encourage diversity' and 'pursue priorities for supporting high quality science, technology, engineering and maths (STEM) provision, widening participation in higher education and recognising the needs of small and specialist institutions'.[1] Scotland is not so different: its government's research strategy for universities talks about 'Inform[ing] policy making (at national and institutional levels); . . . provid[ing] an analysis of current trends in higher education (and their social and economic consequences); . . . [and] generat[ing] income'.[2] Where, one may wonder, are academic criminologists supposed to find a home there?

What criminologists are now required to do is produce a steady volume of policy-relevant research publications and maximize income as if those were laudable ends in their own right, the securing of funding having been defined as 'a strategic goal' by the organizers of the REF (the *soi-disant* Research Excellence Framework that underpins the state's funding of universities[3]), and importance having been attached to the reach and significance of impacts on the economy, society 'and/or culture'. Other state and private sponsors have become equally prescriptive (see McAra 2008). So it was that, in 2015, the government's Economic and Social Research Council (ESRC), favoured research supporting its 'strategic priorities' of 'Economic Performance and Sustainable Growth', 'Influencing Behaviour and Informing Interventions' ('to help rethink the delivery of public services, influence consumer and corporate behaviour, and enhance wellbeing'), and a 'Vibrant and Fair Society' ('to deepen the evidence base that can inform policy and practice in the UK and internationally, around social cohesion, civil and civic engagement, and democratic renewal'). The ESRC does *not* entertain proposals for what it calls 'unspecified research work'. It imposes controls

[1] https://www.gov.uk/government/news/government-outlines-higher-education-funding-priorities-for-2015-to-2016, accessed 9 December 2016.

[2] http://www.qaa.ac.uk/en/AboutUs/Documents/QAA-Research-Strategy.pdf, accessed 9 December 2016.

[3] http://www.ref.ac.uk/, accessed 9 December 2016.

on 'ethical considerations' (controls which the eminent sociologist, Jack Katz (2007), described as based on the imperfect precedent of protecting human subjects in clinical research which is quite inimical to qualitative social research). The once academically liberal Nuffield Foundation is now bent on fostering quantitative methods and applied research. 'We do not', it declares, 'fund . . . research that simply advances knowledge'.[4] And yet another institutional patron, the Ministry of Justice, stipulated in 2015 that research funding must 'be spent on activities, processes and interventions that provide the greatest possible economic and social return'.[5] There is not much room here for scholars who wish to work on time-consuming, open-ended and theoretically driven projects propelled chiefly by a sense of intellectual curiosity.

A decline in funding has been accompanied—a little perversely one might think—by the decision of the ESRC to foster ever-more expensive individual projects. The minimum award made by the Council in 2015 was £200,000, but it is to rise to £350,000. Such a conception of academic work is quite incompatible with the kind of criminology which requires little more than a modest expenditure and a reasonable amount of time set aside for thinking, discussion, and reading.

The practitioners of an empirically driven discipline committed to 'impact', criminologists will undoubtedly respond to new kinds of *data* as they emerge (the self-report offending studies such as the Offending, Crime and Justice Survey[6] and crime victim surveys,[7] are instances). They will respond to significant *events* as they arise: changes in the architecture, policies, and programmes of the criminal justice system, including those prompted by continuing economic cuts and the shrinking and remodelling of institutions; and politically salient changes in the *forms* of crime, including child sexual abuse, human trafficking, terrorism,[8] and cybercrime.[9]

The ideas mustered to describe those events will almost certainly draw on the discipline's existing bank of theories to produce new combinations, permutations and variants of what has been called criminological *bricollage* (Fleisher 1995: 5). And possibly the most ambitious *bricollage* of all may be found in the work of P-O. Wikström who has constructed a criminological version of a theory of everything. Wikström pieced together 'situational action theory' out of the stock of ideas touching on people's life histories; their ability to exercise self-control; what he calls their 'moral propensity' (the way in which they define, filter, and choose particular courses of action); the selection of settings which they visit; and the history, content, structure, and enforcement of those settings' 'moral norms' (see Wikström 2006, 2010, 2014 and his chapter in this volume). His undoubted achievement is probably the closest the discipline will ever come to grand theory.

There is, one fears, the very real risk that what has been a surprisingly lively and creative discipline seems to be journeying in Britain and America (see Bernard

[4] http://www.nuffieldfoundation.org/grants-research-and-innovation-projects, accessed 9 December 2016.

[5] http://www.justice.gov.uk/search?&collection=moj-matrix-dev-web&form=simple&profile=_default&query=research+funding&start_rank=11, accessed 9 December 2016.

[6] https://www.gov.uk/government/publications/the-offending-crime-and-justice-survey-longitudinal-analysis-2003-to-06, accessed 9 December 2016.

[7] See http://www.crimesurvey.co.uk/previous-research.html, accessed 3 January 2017.

[8] https://www.gov.uk/government/organisations/home-office, accessed 9 December 2016.

[9] See http://www.crimeandjustice.org.uk/resources/curious-case-fall-crime, accessed 9 December 2016.

1990: 325) to a future distinguished, not so much by paradigmatic revolution, but by abstracted empiricism, the manipulation of large data sets and a mushrooming of repetitive, profitable, quantitative, and readily assessable work in the service of the state (see Wacquant 2011). It is perhaps all the more remarkable that an appreciable segment has yet managed to retain some independence, interest, and vitality. May it long continue to do so.

SELECTED FURTHER READING

There is no substitute for the original works, some of the more important of which are Becker's *Outsiders* (1963); Braithwaite's *Crime, Shame and Reintegration* (1989); Cloward and Ohlin's *Delinquency and Opportunity* (1960); Matza's *Delinquency and Drift* (1964); Taylor, Walton, and Young's *The New Criminology* (1973); and Young's *The Exclusive Society* (1999). Among the secondary texts are Downes and Rock's *Understanding Deviance* (2003, 2007 and, with the co-authorship of Mclaughlan, 2016), Tierney's *Criminology: Theory and Context* (1996 and 2005), and Newburn's *Criminology* (2013).

REFERENCES

ANDERSON, E. (1976), *A Place on the Corner*, Chicago: University of Chicago Press.

ANDERSON, E. (1990), *Streetwise*, Chicago: University of Chicago Press.

ANDERSON, E. (1999), *Code of the Street*, New York: W. W. Norton.

BALDWIN, J. and BOTTOMS, A. (1976), *The Urban Criminal*, London: Tavistock.

BAYART, J.-F., ELLIS, S., and HIBOU, B. (1999), *The Criminalization of the State in Africa*, Bloomington: Indiana University Press.

BECK, U. (1992), *Risk Society*, London: Sage.

BECKER, G. (1968), 'Crime and Punishment: An Economic Approach', *The Journal of Political Economy*, 76(2): 169–217.

BECKER, H. (1963), *Outsiders*, New York: Free Press.

BELL, D. (1960), 'The Racket-Ridden Longshoremen', in D. Bell (ed.), *The End of Ideology*, New York: Collier.

BENNETT, T. and WRIGHT, R. (1984), *Burglars on Burglary: Prevention and the Offender*, Aldershot: Gower.

BERNARD, T. (1990), 'Twenty Years of Testing Theories', *Journal of Research in Crime and Delinquency*, 27.

BOARD, D. (2010), 'Leadership: The ghost at the trillion dollar crash?', *European Management Journal*, 28(4): 269–77.

BOSWORTH, M. and HOYLE, C. (eds) (2011), Introduction to *What is Criminology?*, Oxford: Oxford University Press.

BOTTOMS, A., Mawby, R.I., and Xanthos, P. (1989), 'A Tale of Two Estates', in D. Downes (ed.), *Crime and the City*, Macmillan: Basingstoke.

BOTTOMS, A. and WILES, P. (1997), 'Environmental Criminology', in M. Maguire, R. Morgan, and R. Reiner (eds), *The Oxford Handbook of Criminology*, Oxford: Oxford University Press.

BOUFFARD, L. and PIQUERO, N. (2010), 'Defiance Theory and Life Course Explanations of Persistent Offending', *Crime & Delinquency*, 56(2): 227–52.

BOX, S. (1971), *Deviance, Reality and Society*, London: Holt, Rinehart, and Winston.

BOX, S. (1983), *Power, Crime and Mystification*, London: Tavistock.

BOYCE, I. (2006), *Communal Responses to Paedophilia: An Ethnographic Case Study*, PhD (London) thesis, LSE.

BRAITHWAITE, J. (1989), *Crime, Shame and Reintegration*, Cambridge: Cambridge University Press.

BRANTINGHAM, P. and BRANTINGHAM, P. (1981–2), 'Mobility, Notoriety, and Crime', *Journal of Environmental Systems*, 11(1): 89–99.

CAMPBELL, B. (1993), *Goliath: Britain's Dangerous Places*, London: Methuen.

CARLEN, P. (1988), *Women, Crime and Poverty*, Milton Keynes: Open University Press.

CARLEN, P. (1996), *Jigsaw: A Political Criminology of Youth Homelessness*, Buckingham: Open University Press.

CARSON, W. (1981), *The other Price of Britain's Oil: Safety and Control in the North Sea*, Oxford: Martin Robertson.

CHAMBLISS, W. (1976), 'The State and Criminal Law', in W. Chambliss and M. Mankoff (eds), *Whose Law, What Order?*, New York: Wiley.

CHEVALIER, L. (1973), *Labouring Classes and Dangerous Classes in Paris During the First Half of the Nineteenth Century*, London: Routledge & Kegan Paul.

CLARKE, R. (1992), *Situational Crime Prevention*, New York: Harrow and Heston.

CLARKE, R. and CORNISH, D. (undated), 'Rational Choice', unpublished.

CLARKE, R. and CORNISH, D. (1985), 'Modeling Offenders' Decisions', in M. Tonry and N. Morris (eds), *Crime and Justice*, 6, Chicago: University of Chicago Press.

CLARKE, R. and CORNISH, D. (2000), 'Analyzing Organized Crime', unpublished.

CLARKE, R. and FELSON, M. (eds) (1993), *Routine Activity and Rational Choice*, New Brunswick: Transaction.

CLEAVER, E. (1969), *Post-Prison Writings and Speeches*, London: Cape.

CLOWARD, R. and OHLIN, L. (1960), *Delinquency and Opportunity*, New York: Free Press.

COHEN, A. (1957), *Delinquent Boys*, Glencoe: Free Press.

COHEN, L. and FELSON, M. (1979), 'Social Change and Crime Rate Trends', *American Sociological Review*, 44.

COHEN, S. (1971), *Images of Deviance*, London: Penguin.

COHEN, S. (1979a), 'The Punitive City: Notes on the Dispersal of Social Control', *Contemporary Crises*, 3(4): 339–63.

COHEN, S. (1979b), 'Guilt, Justice and Tolerance', in D. Downes and P. Rock (eds), *Deviant Interpretations*, Oxford: Martin Robertson.

COHEN, S. (1985), *Visions of Social Control*, Cambridge: Polity.

COHEN, S. (1996), 'Crime and Politics: Spot the Difference', *British Journal of Sociology*, 47(1): 1–21.

COLEMAN, A. (1985), *Utopia on Trial*, London: Hilary Shipman.

COLLINS, R. (2008), *Violence: A Micro-Sociological Theory*, Princeton: Princeton University Press.

COLQUHOUN, P. (1797), *A Treatise on the Police of the Metropolis*, London: H. Fr.

CORRIGAN, P. (1979), *Schooling the Smash Street Kids*, London: Macmillan.

COTTERRELL, R. (1999), *Émile Durkheim: Law in a Moral Domain*, Stanford: Stanford University Press.

CUSSON, M. (1983), *Why Delinquency?*, Toronto: University of Toronto Press.

DAMER, S. (1974), 'Wine Alley: The Sociology of a Dreadful Enclosure', *Sociological Review*, 22(2): 221–48.

DAVIES, N. (1998), *Dark Heart: The Shocking Truth about Hidden Britain*, London: Vintage.

DAVIS, K. (1937), 'The Sociology of Prostitution', *American Sociological Review*, 2(5): 744–55.

DAVIS, M. (1992a), 'Beyond Blade Runner', *Open Magazine Pamphlet*, New Jersey.

DAVIS, M. (1992b), *City of Quartz*, New York: Vintage.

DENSLEY, J. and STEVENS, A. (2015), '"We'll show you gang": The subterranean structuration of gang life in London', *Criminology and Criminal Justice* 15(1): 102–20.

DESMOND, M. (2016), *Evicted: Poverty and Profit in the American City*, London: Penguin.

DOUGLAS, J. (1971), *American Social Order*, London: Collier-Macmillan.

DOUGLAS, M. (1966), *Purity and Danger*, London: Pelican.

DOWNES, D. (1966), *The Delinquent Solution*, London: Routledge & Kegan Paul.

DOWNES, D. (1988), 'The Sociology of Crime and Social Control in Britain, 1960–1987', in P. Rock (ed.), *A History of British Criminology*, Oxford: Clarendon.

DOWNES, D. and ROCK, P. (eds) (1979), *Deviant Interpretations*, Oxford: Martin Robertson.

DOWNES, D. and ROCK, P. (2003), *Understanding Deviance*, 7th edn (with Eugene McLachlan, 2016), Oxford: Oxford University Press.

DUNEIER, M. (2001), *Sidewalk*, New York: Farrar, Straus and Giroux.

DURKHEIM, É. (1952), *Suicide*, London: Routledge & Kegan Paul.

DURKHEIM, É. (1964), *The Division of Labour in Society*, New York: Free Press.

EISNER, M. (2003), 'Long-Term Historical Trends in Violent Crime', in M. Tonry (ed.), *Crime and Justice*, University of Chicago Press, Chicago.

ERIKSON, K. (1966), *Wayward Puritans*, New York: Wiley.

ERIKSON, K. (1994), *A New Species of Trouble*, New York: Norton.

FARIS, R. and DUNHAM, H. (1939), *Mental Disorders in Urban Areas*, Chicago: University of Chicago Press.

FEELEY, M. and SIMON, J. (1992), 'The New Penology', *Criminology*, 30(4): 449–74.

FELSON, M. (1994), *Crime and Everyday Life*, California: Pine Forge.

FERRELL, J. (1993), *Crimes of Style*, Boston, MA: Northeastern University Press.

FERRELL, J. and SANDERS, C. (1995), *Cultural Criminology*, Boston, MA: Northeastern University Press.

FERRELL, J., HAYWARD, K., MORRISON, W., and PRESDEE, M. (eds) (2004), *Cultural Criminology Unleashed*, London: Glasshouse.

FERRELL, J., HAYWARD, K., and YOUNG, J. (2008), *Cultural Criminology*, London: Sage.

FLEISHER, M. (1995), *Beggars and Thieves*, Madison, Wis.: University of Wisconsin Press.

FLETCHER, J. (1850), *Summary of the Moral (and Educational) Statistics of England and Wales*, London: privately printed.

FOSTER, J. (1990), *Villains: Crime and Community in the Inner City*, London: Routledge.

FOUCAULT, M. (1977), *Discipline and Punish*, Harmondsworth: Penguin.

GARLAND, D. (1988), 'British Criminology before 1935', in P. Rock (ed.), *A History of British Criminology*, Oxford: Clarendon.

GARLAND, D. (2002), 'Of Crimes and Criminals: The Development of Criminology in Britain', in M. Maguire, R. Morgan, and R. Reiner (eds), *The Oxford Handbook of Criminology*, 3rd edn, Oxford: Oxford University Press.

GILL, O. (1977), *Luke Street: Housing Policy, Conflict and the Creation of the Delinquent Area*, London: Macmillan.

GOFFMAN, A. (2014), *On the Run: Fugitive Life in an American City*, Chicago: University of Chicago Press.

GORDON, C. (ed.) (1972), *Power/Knowledge*, Brighton: Harvester Press.

GORDON, D. (1986–7), 'The Electronic Panopticon', *Politics and Society*, 15(4): 483–511.

GORDONI, C. (1997), 'Rogues and Regulation in Global Finance: Maxwell, Leeson and the City of London', *Regional Studies*, 31(3): 221–36.

GORING, C. (1919), 'The English Convict: A Statistical Study, London: HMSO.

GOTTFREDSON, M. and HIRSCHI, T. (1990), *A General Theory of Crime*, Stanford: Stanford University Press.

GUERRY, A. (1864), *Statistique morale de l'Angleterre comparée avec la statistique morale de la France*, Paris: J. B. Bailliere et Fils.

HAGAN, J. (1985), 'The Class Structure of Gender and Delinquency: Toward a Power-Control Theory of Common Delinquent Behavior', *American Journal of Sociology*, 90(6): 1151–78.

HAGAN, J. (1988), *Structural Criminology*, Cambridge: Polity.

HAGAN, J. and MCCARTHY, B. (1998), *Mean Streets: Youth Crime and Homelessness*, Cambridge: Cambridge University Press.

HAGAN, J., SIMPSON, J. H., and GILLIS, A. R. (1979), 'The Sexual Stratification of Social Control', *British Journal of Sociology*, 30(1): 25–38.

HAGGERTY, K. (2004), 'Displaced Expertise', *Theoretical Criminology*, 8(2): 211–31.

HALL, S., CRITCHER, C., JEFFERSON, T., CLARKE, J., and ROBERTS, B. (1978), *Policing the Crisis*, London: Macmillan.

HALLSWORTH, S. (2005), *Street Crime*, Cullompton: Willan.

HEIDENSOHN, F. (1968), 'The Deviance of Women: A Critique and an Enquiry', *British Journal of Sociology*, 19(2): 160–75.

HENRY, A. and MCARA, L. (2012), 'Negotiated order: implications for theory and practice in criminology', *Criminology and Criminal Justice*, 12(4): 341–6.

HILLIER, W. (1973), 'In Defence of Space', *RIBA Journal*, November.

HILLIER, W. (1986), 'City of Alice's Dreams', *Architecture Journal*, 9: 39–41.

HILLYARD, P., PANTAZIS, C., TOMBS, S., and GORDON, D. (eds) (2004), *Beyond Criminology: Taking Harms Seriously*, London: Pluto Press.

HILLYARD, P., SIM, J., TOMBS, S., and WHYTE, D. (2004), 'Leaving a "Stain upon the Silence": Contemporary Criminology and the Politics of Dissent', *British Journal of Criminology*, 44(3): 369–90.

HIRSCHI, T. (1969), *The Causes of Delinquency*, Berkeley, Cal.: University of California Press.

HIRST, P. (1975), 'Marx and Engels on Law, Crime and Morality', in I. Taylor *et al.* (eds), *Critical Criminology*, London: Routledge & Kegan Paul.

HOBBS, D. (2013), *Lush Life: Constructing Organized Crime in the UK*, Oxford: Clarendon.

HOBSBAWM, E. (1959), *Primitive Rebels: Studies in Archaic Forms of Social Movement in the 19th and 20th Centuries*, Manchester: Manchester University Press.

HOOD, R. (2004), 'Hermann Mannheim and Max Grünhut: Criminological Pioneers in London and Oxford', *British Journal of Criminology*, 44(4): 469–95.

HOPE, T. (1982), *Burglary in Schools*, London: Home Office.

HOUGH, M. and MAYHEW, P. (1983), *The British Crime Survey*, London: HMSO.

HOWARD, J. (1784), *The State of the Prisons*, London: Cadell, Johnson, and Dilly.

INCIARDI, J. (ed.) (1980), *Radical Criminology: the Coming Crises*, Beverly Hills, Cal.: Sage.

INNES, M. (2003), *Understanding Social Control: Deviance, Crime And Social Order*, Maidenhead: Open University Press.

JACOBS, J. (1965), *The Death and Life of Great American Cities*, Harmondsworth: Penguin.

JACKALL, R. (1988), *Moral Mazes: The World of Corporate Managers*, Oxford: Oxford University Press.

JONES, T., MACLEAN, B., and YOUNG, J. (1986), *The Islington Crime Survey*, Aldershot: Gower.

KAPLAN, R. (1994), 'The Coming Anarchy', *The Atlantic Monthly*, February.

KATZ, J. (1988), *Seductions of Crime*, New York: Basic Books.

KATZ, J. (2007), 'Toward a Natural History of Ethical Censorship', *Law and Society Review*, 41(4): 797–810.

KENNY, C. (1909), 'The Death of Lombroso', *Journal of the Society of Comparative Legislation*, 9(2): 220–8.

KITTRIE, N. (1971), *The Right to be Different*, Baltimore: Johns Hopkins University Press.

LANDESCO, J. (rep. 1968), *Organized Crime in Chicago*, Chicago: University of Chicago Press.

LAUB, J. and SAMPSON, R. (2003), *Shared Beginnings: Divergent Lives: Delinquent Boys to Age 70*, Cambridge, MA: Harvard University Press.

LEA, J. and YOUNG, J. (1984), *What is to be Done about Law and Order?*, London: Penguin Books.

LEMERT, E. (1951), *Social Pathology*, New York: McGraw-Hill.

LITTLE, A. (1961), '" Will More Mean Worse?": An Inquiry into the Effects of University Expansion', *The British Journal of Sociology*, 12(4): 351–62.

LLEWELLYN, K. and HOEBEL, A. (1941), *The Cheyenne Way: Conflict and Case Law in Primitive Jurisprudence*, Norman, Okla.: University of Oklahoma Press.

LOMBROSO, C. (1895), *The Female Offender*, London: T. Fisher Unwin.

LUCKENBILL, D. and BEST, J. (1981), 'Careers in Deviance and Respectability', *Social Problems*, 29(2): 197–206.

LYON, D. (1994), *The Electronic Eye*, Cambridge: Polity.

MACDONALD, L. (1982), 'Theory and Evidence of Rising Crime in the Nineteenth Century', *The British Journal of Sociology*, 33(3): 404–20.

MAIANGWA, B., UZODIKE, U., WHETHO, A., and ONAPAJO, H. (2012), '"Baptism by Fire": Boko Haram and the Reign of Terror in Nigeria', *Africa Today*, 59(2): 109–10.

MANNHEIM, H. (1965), *Comparative Criminology*, London: Routledge & Kegan Paul.

MARUNA, S. (2001), *Making Good: How Ex-Convicts Reform and Rebuild their Lives*, Washington, DC: American Psychological Association.

MARUNA, S. (2012), 'Elements of Successful Desistance Signaling', *Criminology and Public Policy*, 11(1): 73–86.

MARUNA, S. and COPES, H. (2004), 'What Have We Learned from Five Decades of Neutralization Research?', *Crime and Justice* 32, January: 221–320.

MARUNA, S., LEBEL, T., and MITCHELL, N. (2004), 'Pygmalion in the reintegration process: Desistance from crime through the looking glass', *Psychology, Crime and Law*, 10(3): 271–81.

MATHIESEN, T. (1974), *The Politics of Abolition*, London: Martin Robertson.

MATTHEWS, R. and YOUNG, J. (eds) (1992), *Rethinking Criminology: The Realist Debate*, London: Sage.

MATZA, D. (1964), *Delinquency and Drift*, New York: Wiley.

MATZA, D. (1969), *Becoming Deviant*, New Jersey: Prentice-Hall.

MATZA, D. (1971), 'Subterranean Traditions of Youth', *Annals of the American Academy of Political and Social Science*, 338, November: 102–18.

MAYHEW, P., CLARKE, R. V. G., SHURMAN, A., and HOUGH, J. M. (1976), *Crime as Opportunity*, Home Office Research Study No. 34, London: Home Office.

MCARA, L. (2008), 'Crime, Criminology and Criminal Justice in Scotland', *European Journal of Criminology*, 5(4): 481–504.

MCARA, L. and MCVIE, S. (2012), 'Negotiated order: The groundwork for a theory of offending pathways', *Criminology and Criminal Justice*, 12(4): 347–75.

MEAD, G. (1918), 'The Psychology of Punitive Justice', *American Journal of Sociology*, 23(5): 577–602.

MEAD, G. (1934), *Mind Self and Society*, Chicago: University of Chicago Press.

MERTON, R. (1938), 'Social Structure and Anomie', *American Sociological Review*, 3(5): 672–82.

MERTON, R. (1957), *Social Theory and Social Structure*, Glencoe, Ill.: Free Press.

MERTON, R. (1995), 'Opportunity Structure: The Emergence, Diffusion and Differentiation of a Sociological Concept, 1930s–1950s', in F. Adler and W. Laufer (eds), *The Legacy of Anomie Theory*, New Brunswick: Transaction.

MILL, J. (originally published 1838, republished 1950), *Bentham and Coleridge*, London: Chatto and Windus.

MILLS, C. W. (1940), 'Situated Actions and Vocabularies of Motive', *American Sociological Review*, 5(6): 904–13.

MILLS, T. (1959), 'Equilibrium and the Processes of Deviance and Control', *American Sociological Review*, 24(5): 671–79.

MISHKIN, F. (2011), 'Over the Cliff: From the Subprime to the Global Financial Crisis', *Journal of Economic Perspectives*, 25(1): 49–70.

MORRIS, R. and JOHNSON, M. (2014), 'Sedentary Activities, Peer Behavior, and Delinquency among American Youth', *Crime and Delinquency*, 60(6): 939–68.

MORRIS, T. (1957), *The Criminal Area*, London: Routledge & Kegan Paul.

MORRISON, W. (1891), *Crime and its Causes*, London: Swan Sonnenschein.

MORRISON, W. (1896), *Juvenile Offenders*, London: Swan Sonnenschein.

NEWBURN, T. (2007), *Criminology*, Cullompton: Willan.

NEWMAN, K. (2006), *Chutes and Ladders: Navigating the Low-Wage Labor Market*, New York: Russell Sage Foundation.

NEWMAN, O. (1972), *Defensible Space: People and Design in the Violent City*, London: Architectural Press.

O'MALLEY, P. (1992), 'Risk, Power and Crime Prevention', *Economy and Society*, August, 21.

O'MALLEY, P. (2010), *Crime and Risk*, London: Sage.

PAINTER, K. (1996) 'The influence of street lighting improvements on crime, fear and pedestrian street use, after dark', *Landscape and Urban Planning*, 35(2): 193–201.

PARK, R. (1915), 'The City: Suggestions for the Investigation of Human Behavior in the City Environment', *American Journal of Sociology*, 20(5): 577–612.

PARK, R. (1925), 'Community Organization and Juvenile Delinquency', in R. Park and R. Burgess (eds), *The City*, Chicago: University of Chicago Press.

PARSONS, T. (1951), *The Social System*, London: Routledge & Kegan Paul.

PEARCE, F. (1976), *Crimes of the Powerful*, London: Pluto.

PEARCE, F. and TOMBS, S. (1998), *Toxic Capitalism: Corporate Crime and the Chemical Industry*, Aldershot: Dartmouth.

PLATT, T. (1974), 'Prospects for a Radical Criminology in the United States', *Crime and Social Justice*, 1 (Spring–Summer): 2–10.

POLSKY, N. (1967), *Hustlers, Beats and Others*, Chicago: Aldine.

POWER, A. (1997), *Estates on the Edge: The Social Consequences of Mass Housing in Northern Europe*, New York: St. Martin's Press.

PRESDEE, M. (2000), *Cultural Criminology and the Carnival of Crime*, London: Routledge.

PUNCH, M. (1996), *Dirty Business: Exploring Corporate Misconduct*, London: Sage.

QUETELET, L. (1831), 'Recherches sur le Penchant au Crime aux Différens Ages', *Nouveaux Mémoires de L'Academie 1*, Brussels: Belgian Academy of Sciences.

QUETELET, L. (1848), *Du système social et des lois qui le régissent*, Paris: np.

QUINNEY, R. (1970), *The Social Reality of Crime*, Boston, MA: Little Brown.

RADZINOWICZ, L. (1999), *Adventures in Criminology*, London: Routledge.

RAFTER, N. (2008), *The Criminal Brain: Understanding Biological Theories of Crime*, New York: New York University Press.

RAFTER, N. (2009), (ed.), *The Origins of Criminology*, Abingdon: Routledge.

RAFTER, N. (2010), 'Silence and Memory in Criminology—The American Society of Criminology 2009 Sutherland Address', *Criminology*, 48(2): 339–55.

RAINE, A. (2014), *The Anatomy of Violence: The Biological Roots of Crime*, London: Vintage.

RAINWATER, L. (1970), *Behind Ghetto Walls*, Chicago: Aldine.

RAPOPORT, N., VAN NIEL, J., and DHARAN, B (eds) (2009), *Enron and other corporate fiascos*, New York: Thomson Reuters/Foundation Press.

RECKLESS, W. (1933), *Vice in Chicago*, Chicago: University of Chicago Press.

RECKLESS, W., DINITZ, S., and MURRAY, E. (1957), 'The Good Boy in a High Delinquency Area', *Journal of Criminal Law, Criminology, and Police Science*, 48(1): 18–25.

REIMAN, J. (1990), *The Rich Get Richer and the Poor Get Prison*, New York: Macmillan.

REINER, R. (2000), 'Crime and Control in Britain', *Sociology*, 34(1): 71–94.

ROCK, P. (1988), 'The Present State of British Criminology', in P. Rock (ed.), *A History of British Criminology*, Oxford: Clarendon.

ROCK, P. (2005) 'Chronocentrism and British Criminology', *The British Journal of Sociology*, 56(3): 473–91.

ROCK, P. (2007), 'Caesare Lombroso as a Signal Criminologist', *Criminology and Criminal Justice*, 7(2): 117–33.

ROCK, P. (2010), 'Comment on "Public Criminologies" ', *Criminology & Public Policy*, 9(4): 751–68.

ROCK, P. (2011), 'What have we done? Trends in criminological theorising', *Acta Criminologica*, 24(1): 19–43.

ROCK, P. and NEWBURN, T. (2006), 'Urban Homelessness, Crime and Victimisation in England', *International Review of Victimology*, 13(2): 121–56.

ROMILLY, S. (1811), *Observations on the Criminal Law of England*, London.

ROSENFELD, R. and MESSNER, S. (2013), *Crime and the Economy*, London: Sage.

ROSSNER, M. (2014), *Just Emotions*, Oxford: Clarendon.

SAMPSON, R. (2012), *Great American City: Chicago and the Enduring Neighborhood Effect*, Chicago: University of Chicago Press.

SAMPSON, R. and LAUB, J. (1993), *Crime in the Making: Pathways and Turning Points Through Life*, Cambridge, MA: Harvard University Press.

SAMPSON, R., RAUDENBUSH, S., and EARLS, F. (1997), 'Neighborhoods and violent crime: A multilevel study of collective efficacy', *Science*, 277(5328): 918–24.

SCHWENDINGER, H. and SCHWENDINGER, J. (1974), 'Defenders of Order or Guardians of Human Rights.' *Issues in Criminology*, 5(2): 123–57.

SCOTT, M. and LYMAN, S. (1970), 'Accounts, Deviance and Social Order', in J. Douglas (ed.), *Deviance and Respectability*, New York: Basic Books.

SCOTT, R. (1972), 'A Proposed Framework for Analyzing Deviance as a Property of Social Order', in R. Scott and J. Douglas (eds), *Theoretical Perspectives on Deviance*, New York: Basic Books.

SCRATON, P. (ed.) (1987), *Law, Order, and the Authoritarian State: Readings in Critical Criminology*, Milton Keynes: Open University Press.

SHAPLAND, J. and VAGG, J. (1988), *Policing by the Public*, Oxford: Clarendon.

SCHAUFFLER, R. (1974), 'Criminology at Berkeley: Resisting Academic Repression', *Crime and Social Justice*, 1: 58–61.

SHAW, C. (1971), 'Male Juvenile Delinquency and Group Behavior', in J. Short (ed.), *The Social Fabric of the Metropolis*, Chicago: University of Chicago Press.

SHAW, C. and MCKAY, H. (1942), *Juvenile Delinquency and Urban Areas*, Chicago: University of Chicago Press.

SHEARING, C. and STENNING, P. (1985), 'From the Panopticon to Disney World: The Development of Discipline', in A. Doob and E. Greenspan (eds), *Perspectives in Criminal Law*, Aurora: Canada Law Book.

SHERMAN, L. (1993), 'Defiance, deterrence, and irrelevance: A theory of the criminal sanction', *Journal of Research in Crime and Delinquency*, 30(4): 445–73.

SHERMAN, L. (2010), 'Defiance, Compliance and Consilience: A General Theory of Criminology', in E. McLaughlin and T. Newburn (eds), *The Sage Handbook of Criminological Theory*, London: Sage.

SHERMAN, L., GARTIN, P., and BUERGER, M. (1989), 'Hot Spots of Predatory Crime: Routine Activities and the Criminology of Place', *Criminology*, 27(1): 27–56.

SHORT, J. and STRODBECK, F. (1967), *Group Process and Gang Delinquency*, Chicago: University of Chicago Press.

SIMON, J. (1987), 'The Emergence of a Risk Society', *Socialist Review*, 95: 60–89.

SIMON, J. (1993), *Poor Discipline: Parole and the Social Control of the Underclass*, Chicago: University of Chicago Press.

SIMON, J. (2007), *Governing Through Crime: How the War on Crime Transformed American Democracy and Created a Culture of Fear*, New York: Oxford University Press.

SLAPPER, G. and TOMBS, S. (1999), *Corporate Crime*, London: Longman.

SMART, C. (1977), *Women, Crime and Criminology*, London: Routledge & Kegan Paul.

SMITH, M. (1922), *The Psychology of the Criminal*, New York: Methuen.

SPIERENBURG, P. (2008), *A History of Murder*, Cambridge: Polity.

STINCHCOMBE, A. (1968), *Constructing Social Theories*, New York: Harcourt Brace and World.

SUMNER, C. (1994), *The Sociology of Deviance: An Obituary*, Buckingham: Open University Press.

SUMNER, C. (ed.) (2004), Introduction to *The Blackwell Companion to Criminology*, Oxford: Blackwell.

SUTHERLAND, E. and CRESSEY, D. (1955), *Principles of Criminology*, Chicago: Lippincott.

SUTTLES, G. (1972), *The Social Construction of Communities*, Chicago: University of Chicago Press.

SYKES, G. and MATZA, D. (1957), 'Techniques of Neutralization', *American Sociological Review*, 22(6): 664–70.

TAYLOR, I. (1999), *Crime in Context: A Critical Criminology of Market Societies*, Cambridge: Polity.

TAYLOR, I., WALTON, P., and YOUNG, J. (1973), *The New Criminology*, London: Routledge & Kegan Paul.

TETT, G. (2009), *Fool's gold: How Unrestrained Greed Corrupted a Dream, Shattered Global Markets and Unleashed a Catastrophe*, London: Little, Brown.

THRASHER, F. (1927), *The Gang*, Chicago: University of Chicago Press.

TIERNEY, J. (1996), *Criminology: Theory and Context*, 2nd edn 2005, London: Prentice-Hall.

TURNBULL, C. (1973), *The Mountain People*, London: Paladin.

VAN CREVELD, M. (1991), *The Transformation of War*, New York: Free Press.

VAN DIJK, J. (2008), *The World of Crime: Breaking the Silence on Problems of Security, Justice, and Development Across the World*, Thousand Oaks, Cal.: Sage.

WACQUANT, L., (2008), *Urban Outcasts: A Comparative Sociology of Advanced Marginality*, Cambridge; Polity.

WACQUANT, L., (2011), 'From "Public Criminology" to the Reflexive Sociology of Criminological Production and Consumption: A Review of *Public Criminology?* by Ian Loader and Richard Sparks', *British Journal of Criminology*, 51(2): 438–48.

WHITTEN, M. (2002), 'Protection, Prevention, Reformation: A History of the Philanthropic Society', PhD dissertation, London School of Economics.

WHYTE, W. (1942), *Street Corner Society*, Chicago: University of Chicago Press.

WIKSTRÖM, P-O. (2006), 'Individuals, Settings and Acts of Crime: Situational Mechanisms and the Explanation of Crime', in P-O. Wikström and R. Sampson (eds), *The Explanation of Crime: Context, Mechanisms and Development. Cambridge*, Cambridge University Press.

WIKSTRÖM, P-O. (2007), 'The Social Ecology of Crime: The Role of the Environment in Crime Causation', in H. Schneider (ed.), *Internationales Handbuch der Kriminologie*, Berlin: de Gruyter.

WIKSTRÖM, P-O. (2010), 'Explaining Crime as Moral Action', in S. Hitlin and S. Vaysey (eds), *Handbook of the Sociology of Morality*, New York: Springer Verlag.

WIKSTRÖM, P-O. (2014), 'Why Crime Happens', in G. Manzo (ed.), *Analytical Sociology: Norms, Actions and Networks*, Chichester: Wiley and Sons.

WILLIS, P. (1977), *Learning to Labour*, Farnborough, Hants: Gower.

WILSON, H. (1980), 'Parental Supervision: A Neglected Aspect of Delinquency', *British Journal of Criminology*, 20(3): 203–35.

WILSON, W. (1996), *When Work Disappears: The World of the New Urban Poor*, New York: Alfred Knopf.

WIRTH, L. (1964), 'Culture Conflict and Misconduct', in L. Wirth, *On Cities and Social Life*, Chicago: University of Chicago Press.

WORSLEY, P. (1968), *The Trumpet Shall Sound: A Study of 'Cargo' Cults in Melanesia*, London: MacGibbon and Kee.

WRIGHT, R. and DECKER, S. (1997), *Armed Robbers in Action: Stickups and Street Culture*, Boston: Northeastern University Press.

YOUNG, J. (1971), *The Drugtakers*, London: Paladin.

YOUNG, J. (1997), 'Left Realist Criminology', in M. Maguire, R. Morgan, and R. Reiner (eds), *The Oxford Handbook of Criminology*, 2nd edn, Oxford: Oxford University Press.

YOUNG, J. (1998), 'From Inclusive to Exclusive Society: Nightmares in the European Dream', in V. Ruggiero, N. South, and I. Taylor (eds), *The New European Criminology*, London: Routledge.

YOUNG, J. (1999), *The Exclusive Society*, London: Sage.

YOUNG, J. (2004), 'Crime and the Dialectics of Inclusion/ Exclusion', *British Journal of Criminology*, 44(4): 550–61.

YOUNG, J. (2007), *The Vertigo of Late Modernity*, London: Sage.

ZIMRING, F. (2007), *The Great American Crime Decline*, New York: Oxford University Press.

■ CHAPTER ACKNOWLEDGEMENTS

The author is grateful to Rachel Condry, Janet Foster, Gordon Hughes, Alison Liebling, Lesley McAra, Tim Newburn, Elaine Player, Nicky Rafter, Meredith Rossner, and Tank Waddington for their help and advice in revising this chapter.

2

CRIMINALIZATON: HISTORICAL, LEGAL, AND CRIMINOLOGICAL PERSPECTIVES

Nicola Lacey and Lucia Zedner

INTRODUCTION

Criminology and criminal law share crime as a common object of enquiry and intellectual challenge. Yet the professional autonomy and technical nature of legal scholarship have historically created rigid boundaries between the two disciplines. Although the status of criminology as a discrete discipline has always been contested and criminological research is informed mainly by the methods and insights of the wider social sciences, criminological interest in and interaction with criminal law is limited. It is rare to find a criminology text that concerns itself with the scope and nature of criminal law, even though criminal law texts now more readily engage with criminological questions and literature (see Wells and Quick 2010; Bronitt and McSherry 2010; Farmer 2016).

In this chapter, we examine the relationship between legal and criminological constructions of crime and explore how these have changed over time. The chapter falls into five sections. In the first section, we sketch a conceptual framework—criminalization—within which we situate the relationship between legal and criminological constructions of crime (Lacey 1995, 2009). Criminalization keeps the close relationship between criminal law and criminal justice practices in view, without losing sight of their specific contributions. In the second section, we use the framework of criminalization to consider the way in which the boundaries of crime have developed in England over the last 300 years, demonstrating their historical contingency. The third section sketches law's formal construction of crime in England and Wales today and teases out its implicit normative vision of criminal law. In the fourth section, we consider some of the most important developments in formal criminalization in England and Wales over recent decades. And in the final section, we consider the contribution of criminology to our understanding of the scope of, and limits on, criminalization.

CRIMINAL LAW, CRIMINOLOGY, AND CRIMINALIZATION

The study of criminalization is divided broadly into two areas—the social and legal construction of crime.[1] Study of the social construction of crime divides into two broad fields—criminology and criminal justice—brought together in this *Handbook*. Criminal law scholarship, by contrast, concerns itself with the formally established norms according to which individuals or groups are adjudged guilty or innocent of criminal offences. Criminal law articulates substantive rules of conduct addressed to citizens. It also sets out rules determining how liability should be attributed and how breaches of criminal norms should be graded; rules which are addressed primarily to officials rather than to potential offenders (Robinson 1997). Historically, criminal lawyers tended to be concerned not so much with the development and scope of these norms as with their conceptual structure, content, and judicial interpretation in particular cases. Lawyers are also concerned with the framework of principles within which legislation is made and legal judgments are reached (Horder 2016; Williams 1953, 1983). Rules of evidence and procedure are marginal to criminal law studies in Britain, and are often dealt with in specialist courses, or criminal justice or legal methods courses. While the organization of research conforms less rigidly to this division between criminal law and procedure, it nonetheless closely reflects the different areas of expertise of scholars within their respective fields. Although a superficially similar division characterized the English approach for much of the twentieth century, criminal law treatise writers of the nineteenth century saw offence definitions, procedure, and punishment as equally central to their terrain (Stephen 1893). From the perspective of countries like France and Germany, where the very language of *droit pénal* and *Strafrecht* make clear the close relationship between criminal law and punishment and where sentencing decisions are closely integrated with decisions about criminal liability, the Anglo-American separation of criminal law and criminal procedure, and of criminal law and sentencing, appears extraordinary (Fletcher 1978). Moves in recent scholarship (Duff *et al.* 2004b, 2005, 2007) to explore the implications of criminal procedure for criminal law are much to be welcomed.

The contemporary division of labour between lawyers and criminologists is based on their respective expertise and the distinctive roles of legal and social factors in the construction of crime (Zedner 2004: ch. 2). Yet, this division obscures the fact that the making, interpretation, and enforcement of criminal law occur in a social context and as a result of political processes (Reiner 2006, 2016). Moreover the boundaries of

[1] Legal constructions of crime are, of course, also social phenomena.

criminalization are porous: criminal justice practices are affected by political, economic, moral, psychiatric, religious, educational, and family structures (Wells and Quick 2010: ch. 1). Nonetheless, legal rules set the formal boundaries by defining offences and constituting the key institutions (the police, criminal process, courts, and so on) through which criminalization takes place. So it is important for criminologists to understand how these boundaries are set, where they lie, and how they shape criminalization. Within this broad concept of criminalization, we need to make three distinctions.

First, we can draw a distinction between criminalization as an outcome and criminalization as a practice. Criminalization as an outcome refers to the *results* of legislative, judicial, prosecutorial, or other processes; as in, 'the new terrorism legislation has expanded the scope of criminalization'. Criminalization as a practice refers to the creative, interpretive, or enforcement *activities* of actors such as legislators, judges, police, lawyers, and the public. Official practices of criminalization are nested within criminal justice institutions and shaped by the norms peculiar to particular roles and professions: they coalesce over time to produce the outcomes to which criminalization in the first sense refers. Thinking about criminalization as outcome and as practice cuts across the distinction between legal and social constructions of crime: both outcomes and practices are shaped by law and by broader social dynamics. But while the legal contribution to criminalization outcomes is made primarily by criminal law, practices of criminalization are structured primarily by rules of criminal procedure, constitutional law, and public law rules defining the responsibilities and powers of criminal justice officials.

Second, we need to distinguish between formal and substantive criminalization. When terrorism legislation expands the boundaries of criminal law by creating a new offence proscribing acts preparatory to terrorist offences, this marks a shift in formal criminalization. However, substantive criminalization remains unchanged until police, prosecutors, and courts act on that new law. This distinction between formal and substantive criminalization is more than a conceptual distinction. Heightened anxiety about terrorism might prompt an increase in terrorist prosecutions and convictions irrespective of changes in law or levels of terrorist activity. Conversely, the creation of new terrorism offences may not lead to greater substantive criminalization in practice unless certain other conditions—notably an increase in the resources available to enforcement agencies or a change in their incentives—are met. Formal criminalization sets parameters within which substantive criminalization proceeds; but substantive enforcement depends on many factors beyond law. Criminology comes in here to explain why criminalization occurs as it does. Factors such as penal politics, media coverage, and the extensive discretion exercised by criminal justice officials have a powerful impact on the scope of what is actually criminalized (Stuntz 2001).

Thirdly, the distinction between formal and substantive criminalization also applies to criminalization as a social practice. Constitutionally, the various processes which combine to produce criminalization outcomes—legislation, policing, prosecution, and trial—are the responsibility of different actors. Legislators are not supposed to pre-empt prosecutorial, let alone judicial, decisions. Police and prosecutors are supposed to exercise their distinctive enforcement roles within the contours of legal norms. And while the distinction between judicial interpretation and judicial creativity is contested, judges are not entitled to create new criminal offences. But when we move from formal to substantive practices of criminalization, the boundaries between law-creation, interpretation, and enforcement are fluid, with the reporting decisions of ordinary citizens influencing when and how the criminal process is set in train. Practices like plea-bargaining accord prosecutors quasi-adjudicative authority and give judges quasi-legislative power, shaping the outcome of the criminalization process. Civil preventive orders like the former Anti-Social Behaviour Order (ASBO) or current orders such as the Serious Crime Prevention Order and Sexual Harm Prevention Order permit judges to determine the individualized conditions of the order, breach of which can result in a criminal sanction of up to five years' imprisonment. In so doing, civil preventive orders effectively delegate legislative power to criminalize to the civil court (Ashworth and Zedner 2014: 86–7). Moreover criminal justice officials on occasion exceed or abuse their legal powers, for example by using undue pressure to elicit confessions. Where such abuses go undetected, substantive criminalization may stray far beyond the formal boundaries of the criminal law.

Note that, unlike the distinction between criminalization as outcome and as practice, the distinction between formal and substantive criminalization tracks that between legal and social constructions of crime. Criminal law, the law of evidence and procedure, constitutional law, public law, and human rights law combine to define the formal boundaries of criminalization, while substantive practices can only be understood by appreciating the interaction between legal and social processes. A focus on formal criminalization would be unsatisfactory because it says nothing about the relationship between legal and social constructions of crime. A historical grasp of how criminal law changes over time and space, as well as the changing balance between different kinds of legal regulation and between legal and informal social modes of governance, are essential to a full understanding of criminalization.

In what follows, we continue to draw distinctions between formal and substantive criminalization in the sense of outcomes and practices, while considering the contribution of different scholarly approaches to our understanding of legal constructions of crime and their significance for criminology. How is formal criminalization organized? What is its content? How does it influence substantive criminalization? What values does it purport to embody or respect, and how far does it do so? Are those values coherent or otherwise appealing? Do the answers to these questions change over time, and if so, why?

CRIMINALIZATION IN HISTORICAL PERSPECTIVE

For answers to these questions, an obvious starting point is to seek an overall conception of what criminal law 'is': a conception of the formal features of criminal law and of its substantive aims and functions. There have been fundamental changes in the nature and intensity of law's involvement in criminalization over the course of modern English history, themselves premised on radical changes in the form and content of criminal law, the structure of the criminal trial, and the composition of the agencies empowered to interpret and enforce the law. History reveals that the categories of criminal offence are contingent upon time and place, prevailing social mores, cultural sensibilities, and religious and moral precepts (Lacey 1995; Farmer 1996). Reiner notes the 'huge cultural variation across space and time in what is counted by the law as criminal' (Reiner 2007: 25) and observes how many seventeenth-century offences no longer exist today, including: witchcraft, failing to attend church, adultery, fornication, bridal pregnancy, scolding, disrupting the Sabbath, and 'wearing felt hats' (ibid.). Property-related offences predominated historically, as they do today, but before the establishment of the formal police in the early nineteenth century, 'thief-taking' was a private enterprise pursued for profit and driven by a complex system of rewards and protection arrangements (McMullen 1996). Until the mid-eighteenth century the office of constable was held voluntarily by members of the community backed up by the ancient institutions of 'hue and cry' and the Posse Comitatus, an arrangement that required able men to join in pursuit of a felon (Zedner 2006: 88). However, voluntary systems of policing worked less well in the growing towns and cities whose larger populations were more mobile and social relations were weaker. Those unwilling to serve voluntarily as constables often paid deputies instead, creating a profitable market in private policing and protection. In the eighteenth century, the wealthy formed mutually beneficial 'prosecution associations' to share the financial burden of bringing offenders to trial by private prosecution (King 2000: 53–7). The protection ostensibly provided by the criminal law was far from universally enjoyed since prosecution depended at least partially on financial means. The claim that eighteenth-century criminal law was a product of the English class system or a tool of ruling class oppression (Hay 1975: 52) has, however, been challenged by evidence of widespread recourse to the criminal law by non-elite groups and by the labouring poor (Langbein 1983; King 2000). Blackstone, in his influential *Commentaries on the Laws of England* (Blackstone 1765–9), felt able vigorously to assert a notion of crime as public wrong, organized in terms of groups of offences threatening distinctively public or shared interests: offences against God and religion; offences against the state; offences against the person; and offences against property.

In the second half of the eighteenth century the growing pressures of industrialization and urbanization necessitated a criminal law capable of effective deterrence. A growing sense of the ungovernability of urban society, spawned by riots in London in the 1780s, resulted in propertied citizens forming 'Voluntary Associations for Defence' which undertook to detect and apprehend criminals, as well as to prosecute (Radzinowicz 1956: 100). The development of new economic relations resulted in the rapid growth of capital sentences, particularly for property crimes and offences involving the exploitation of trust, such as forgery. Deterrence was important as there was no general police force under government control in London until 1829: the setting up of formal police forces in the rest of the country came even later. The form of the modern adversarial criminal trial emerged only during the close of the eighteenth and early nineteenth century. Lawyers came to dominate trials only gradually and felony defendants did not gain the right to full legal representation until 1836. Prosecutions were initiated by private individuals, who might or might not have legal representation at trial. Cases were selected for trial by a grand jury composed of local landowners sitting as Justices of the Peace (the precursors to modern day magistrates). These Justices also heard the vast majority of criminal cases, with a mere dozen judges travelling the assize circuit even in the later eighteenth century. Even assize hearings were relatively speedy and non-technical affairs: it has been estimated that the average length of a criminal trial in the late eighteenth century was between 20 and 30 minutes (Langbein 2003: 16–18, 21–5; Beattie 1986: 378; 1991: 222; 2001: 260). Other than in very serious cases, such as homicide, the criminal trial up to the early nineteenth century was a lay-dominated rather than a lawyer-dominated affair.[2]

The institutional conditions favourable to the gradual development, refinement, and systematic application of general legal doctrines were gradually constructed over a period of almost 200 years. In the mid-eighteenth century, the process of criminalization operated more or less on the basis of a presumption of guilt, which the trial gave the defendant an opportunity to rebut, generally on the basis of character evidence (Langbein 2003: 263; see also King 2000; Beattie 1986, 1991; Emsley 2007). The law of evidence was developed gradually over the next 150 years through systematic reporting of criminal cases, a system of criminal appeals, legal education, and legal representation. Together these fostered the formalization and professionalization of criminal law.

The abolition of many of the capital statutes in the 1820s and the expansion of the penitentiary system to accommodate long-term prisoners replaced an *ancien régime* criminal law organized around draconian threats of death—tempered by extensive discretion and exercise of mercy (King 2000)—with a system of calibrated and regularly administered penalties (Hay 1975; Wiener 1990). These changes can be ascribed partly to civilizing processes that fed a growing revulsion against public execution and partly to the development of modern police and prisons that reduced the need for spectacular deterrent penalties (Spierenburg 1984).

What explains these changes over time, and what can they tell the criminologist about the nature of criminal law? Like any system of social norms, criminal law has to specify the practical conditions for its own operation and to legitimate its activities *in respect of* those who are subject to them. Over the eighteenth and nineteenth centuries, fundamental social, political, and economic developments underpinned significant changes in the relationship between legal and social constructions of crime. The extension of the franchise gradually changed the legitimation conditions for criminal law, with the decisive expansion of suffrage in the Reform Act of 1867 strengthening the popular mandate for formal criminalization. The development of the police, and the emergence of medical science and psychology and other forms of specialist knowledge and technology further changed the conditions under which criminal law had to operate. At the same time, urbanization, greater mobility, and social anonymity deprived the criminal justice system of reliable sources of local knowledge on which the eighteenth century criminal process had relied. In the

[2] Lay magistrates' courts, of course, continue to predominate in the criminal process to the present day, hearing no fewer than 95 per cent of cases: https://www.cps.gov.uk/victims_witnesses/going_to_court/court_case.html, accessed 18 January 2016. But magistrates today operate within a clear legal framework and are advised by legally trained clerks.

hands of an increasingly ambitious government, the expansion of criminal law's role in the regulatory field, along with increasing social diversity and moral pluralism in the growing urban areas, further complicated criminal law's core tasks. Later in the nineteenth century, the position was further complicated by the emergence of new scientific notions of crime as atavism, reflected in laws instituting distinctive criminalization regimes for categories of offender such as the 'habitual criminal' and the 'feeble-minded' (Radzinowicz and Hood 1990).

Blackstone's notion of crime as public wrong had worked well enough for the eighteenth century. But as the scope and functions of criminal law increased dramatically in the nineteenth, it could no longer bear the weight placed upon it. Many continental European countries avoided such an expansion through the creation of a separate legal edifice of regulatory law, as well as by constitutional constraints on the content of criminal law, which were absent in England (Whitman 2003: ch. 4). Hence in England expansion of the criminal law entailed a fragmentation of criminal law's rationale and an intensified focus in legal commentaries on criminal procedure as what defined crime as crime in law.

NORMATIVE ACCOUNTS: RATIONALIZING AND LEGITIMATING CRIMINAL LAW THROUGH 'GENERAL PRINCIPLES'

Whereas 300 hundred years ago English criminal law was far less extensive and more readily rationalized in terms of core interests and values, rapid urbanization, industrialization, and the growth of regulatory government significantly altered and made more complex the operating conditions and the roles of criminal law (Lacey 2008, 2016). Reforms of the policing, prosecution, trial, and the prison in the nineteenth century (Langbein 2003; Lacey 2008, 2016) led to the professionalization of law enforcement and penal practice, a spectacular reduction in capital offences, and rapid expansion of the prison system, in line with an emerging, rationalist, modern, and, potentially, liberal conception of criminal law (Dubber 2005). While the criminal law was never fully codified, efforts to modernize it resulted in the consolidating legislation of the mid-nineteenth century, for example, the Offences Against the Person Act 1861, which still defines crimes of violence today. But these legislative reforms left criminal law diverse, extensive, and divided between a vaguely differentiated terrain of 'real crime' and 'regulatory offences'.

Yet the impulse to rationalize criminal law, to make general statements about its aims, functions, underlying values, and operation persisted. In the first half of the twentieth century, they assumed the form of a gradual construction of a 'general part' of criminal law: the principles governing the conditions of liability across the offences (Kenny 1902; Radzinowicz and Turner 1945), culminating in Glanville Williams' magisterial *Criminal Law: The General Part*, first published in 1953. These 'general principles' have little bearing on the substance of criminal offences: the so-called 'special part' of criminal law that defines individual crimes.[3]

[3] It is significant that Williams never followed up his original plan to publish a second volume on the 'special part'. For this implies that it had now become unnecessary to rationalize the substance of offences

In English texts today, two rather different visions of the defining features of criminal law still predominate. These visions have competed for dominance since the expansion of formal criminalization and the diversification of criminal law's functions prompted by the growth of the regulatory state in the nineteenth century (Horder 2016; Wells and Quick 2010). On one view, criminal law is concerned with wrongdoing in a quasi-moral sense. Crime is conduct judged to be a sufficiently seriously violation of core social interests or shared values that it is appropriate for the state to proscribe and punish it.[4] On another view, criminal law is understood in more neutrally instrumental terms as a regulatory system: attaching costs, through sanctions, to kinds of conduct which it is in the public interest to reduce.[5] How are these competing views to be reconciled as rationalizations of criminal law?

In the twentieth century the most influential approaches attempted to incorporate both quasi-moral and regulatory aspects of criminal law. Building on the liberal utilitarianism of J. S. Mill (1859), H. L. A. Hart (1963, 1968) argued that, while the general justifying aim of criminal law is a utilitarian one of crime reduction through deterrence, the state is only justified in criminalizing conduct for which an individual is responsible and which is harmful to others. This is a less moralistic account of the nature of crime than the quasi-moral, retributive conception, while nonetheless explaining why criminal law is of special ethical significance. It has difficulty, however, in generating an adequately clear concept of harm: for example, does the offence felt by people who disapprove of public nudity count as 'harm' (Feinberg 1984–8, von Hirsh and Simester 2006)? If not, should it be criminalized? If the concept of 'harm' is neither fixed nor analytically robust, how are socio-cultural notions of harm constructed and how do they influence legal constructions of harm (Harcourt 1999; Hillyard *et al.* 2004)?

In legal scholarship, the most common approach to making sense of these different aspects is to divide the terrain of criminal law between the moral core of 'real' crime (such as theft, homicide, assault, and rape) and quasi-criminal regulatory offences (such as health and safety, licensing, driving, tax, and pollution offences) (Quirk *et al.* 2010). This approach accepts that criminal law has not one, but two main rationales: to define and punish wrongdoing and to regulate social life. However, this leaves many questions unaddressed. How is the division between 'quasi-moral' and 'regulatory' crimes defined, and is the boundary a clear one, in practice or law? How does it change over time? Under what conditions does a bifurcated criminal law system emerge, and what broader governmental purposes does it serve? These are questions in which contemporary criminal lawyers are relatively uninterested.

The historic shift to a formal conception of criminal law was itself a function of the modernization process already described (Norrie 2001). Successive attempts to codify the law, alongside the modernization of the trial process, produced a more

in criminal law in anything like the substantive terms which had come naturally to Blackstone (1765–9) 200 years earlier, or indeed to James Fitzjames Stephen (1893) 100 years before. Rather, it was the distinctive *modus operandi* of criminal law, with its edifice of general principles, which supplied its rationale.

[4] This is a view that sits naturally with a retributive approach to punishment and an emphasis on the expressive dimensions of criminal justice (Duff 2001, Bennett 2012).

[5] This second view sits naturally with a utilitarian view of punishment, justified by its beneficial consequences.

sophisticated institutional basis for working out a conceptual framework for offence definitions and legal argument (Williams 1953; Smith 1998). In a world in which the substance of criminal law is fragmented, diverse, and hence hard to rationalize in a coherent way, it has become tempting for lawyers to regard the identity of criminal law as residing in formal features such as the presumption of innocence, the principle of legality,[6] and the requirements of conduct and responsibility that apply irrespective of the content of offences. Formalizing the criminal law has helped to address the problems of gathering and validating evidence in an increasingly centralized system in which it is no longer feasible to rely on the local knowledge of jurors and justices of the peace.

Today, contemporary codes and commentaries on criminal law in both the common law and civil law systems tend to be organized around a core framework that sets out the general conditions under which criminal liability may be established. One striking development is the gradual formalization of principles of criminal responsibility around mental concepts such as intention, knowledge, belief, and recklessness, replacing the overtly evaluative concepts such as malice and wilfulness which had characterized the common law for centuries (Binder 2002; Horder 1997). This shift from older ideas of fault to a more empirically based conception of responsibility was made possible by the growth of psychology and psychiatry, premised on a certain understanding of the mind–body distinction and of mental capacity as a discrete object of social knowledge. But this legal development could not have occurred had it not been accepted that the factual question of what is going on in someone's mind can be an object of investigation and proof in a criminal court (Smith 1981; Loughnan 2012). This in turn depended on advances such as the professionalization of the trial process and the development of the law of evidence already considered (Lacey 2001a, 2001b).

Today, the foundations of criminal liability are generally thought to consist in four distinct elements: those relating to capacity, to conduct, to responsibility or fault, and to defence. We deal with each of these in turn:

1. *Capacity*: Individuals may only be held criminal liable if they have sufficient mental capacity. Defences such as insanity define certain kinds of people as lacking capacity under criminal law. Since law operates in terms of general standards, the line between criminal capacity and criminal incapacity is relatively crude. Almost every criminal law system exempts from criminal liability people under a certain age, whatever their actual capacities, though the age at which the line between capacity and incapacity is drawn varies significantly by country and over time. Yet again, this underlines the interplay between legal and social constructions of crime. In England and Wales, the abolition of the presumption of incapacity for 10–14 year olds by the Crime and Disorder Act 1998 reduced the age of criminal liability to 10, as compared to 13 in France and 15 in the Nordic countries. Since it cannot plausibly be claimed that children

[6] The principle of legality requires that there should be no penalty without law and that criminal law must be announced clearly to citizens in advance of its imposition so that they have a fair opportunity to conform to it.

mature at such widely differing rates in neighbouring countries, capacity must be understood as a legal construct contingent on local culture and politics.

2. *Conduct*: criminal law defines the conduct necessary for an offence: appropriating another person's property in the case of theft; causing a person's death in the case of homicide; having sexual intercourse with a person without their consent in the case of rape; driving with a certain level of alcohol in one's blood in the case of driving while intoxicated. Though there are exceptions in English criminal law, it is generally asserted that the law does not criminalize mere thoughts, status, or omissions. To take some illustrative examples: if I simply fantasize about committing a sophisticated fraud, without taking any steps towards it, I am guilty of no crime. Similarly, my failure to rescue a drowning child will only attract criminal liability if my relationship with the child or my professional responsibility imposes a special duty to act. This last example is a further reminder of the contingency of legal constructions of crime on local values. In France, laws impose a relatively wide-ranging duty of rescue so that, unlike in England and Wales, failing to rescue a drowning child could render me criminally liable.

3. *Responsibility/fault*: criminal liability is generally said to depend on a person with capacity being responsible for or at fault in committing the conduct specified in the offence. To put it simply, we do not hold people liable for accidents. Responsibility or fault conditions generally consist of mental states or attitudes such as intention, recklessness, knowledge, belief, dishonesty, or negligence. In the examples above, the relevant conditions are: for theft 'a dishonest intention permanently to deprive'; for homicide 'an intention to kill or cause serious bodily harm' or 'gross negligence'; for rape 'recklessness' or 'negligence' as to the victim's lack of consent. The fourth example—driving while intoxicated—is an exception to the general principle that fault must be proven by the prosecution: only the driving and the blood alcohol level need be established. Notwithstanding their supposedly 'exceptional' status, however, these offences of strict liability substantially outnumber offences that require a mental element (*mens rea*) in English criminal law today (though it is difficult to count). Ashworth and Blake estimated (1996: 309) that even of the more serious criminal offences about half featured either 'strict' no-fault liability or only a partial fault requirement, and 40 per cent include a reverse burden of proof, placing the burden on the defendant to disprove liability. Most strict liability offences are said to be regulatory rather than condemnatory, whereas offences requiring proof of fault are said to correspond to the quasi-moral terrain of criminal law doctrine. However, as the example of driving while intoxicated illustrates, the line between the two is neither clear nor static: 30 years ago drunk driving was regarded as a regulatory offence; today it attracts strong condemnation. Changing moral and social values influence the meaning, as well as the practice, of criminal law and, as we shall see, point to the importance of criminological and sociological knowledge in understanding how and why crime is defined as it is.

4. *Defences*: Even where a person with criminal capacity has committed the relevant conduct with the requisite degree of fault, a range of defences may preclude

or mitigate liability (Duff 2007: ch. 11). If the defendant has committed a theft while under a threat of violence, she may plead a defence of duress. If a person kills, intentionally, in order to defend himself against an immediate attack, he may plead self-defence. General defences apply not only to crimes requiring proof of responsibility but also to strict liability offences. A person who drives while intoxicated under duress or threat, or in circumstances of necessity, may escape liability. So if you threaten to shoot me if I fail to drive you home, I may be acquitted even if I do so while intoxicated.

Defences are often grouped under the headings of exemptions, justifications and excuses. Each relates to the other three components of liability already mentioned, that is, capacity, conduct, and fault. The defence of insanity recognizes that the defendant's incapacity *exempts* her from criminal liability. If I kill while suffering a mental illness, which causes me to misunderstand entirely the nature of my own action, I am considered to lack capacity. Even before trial I may be deemed unfit to plead; or I may be found not guilty by reason of insanity. If I kill while defending myself from attack, I may plead self-defence to claim that my conduct was, in the circumstances, *justified* and hence not criminal. And if I plead that I assaulted someone because a third party had threatened me or my family with violence if I did not do so, my defence of duress may *excuse* me because the conditions under which I formed the relevant fault condition mitigate my guilt. The defences may thus be seen as fine-tuning liability to take account of excusatory and justificatory factors.

This conceptual framework provides building blocks with which legislators and lawyers construct criminal liability. As the reference to general principles suggests, it contains an implicit set of normative assumptions about what makes the imposition of criminal liability justifiable. The law does not criminalize mere thoughts, or under circumstances in which internal incapacity or external circumstance deprived a defendant of a fair opportunity to conform to the law. It does not convict unless a defendant is responsible for their conduct. The criminal law is not merely an institutionalized system of coercion but a system which purports to address its subjects as responsible for their conduct, which is structured around broadly liberal principles of justice (Ashworth and Zedner 2008).

Acknowledging the individual as independent, rational, and free-willed requires that those who commit wrongdoing are identified, held to account, and punished proportionately. To do otherwise would constitute a failure to acknowledge individuals as moral agents who can justly be held responsible for their actions (von Hirsch 1993: 11). Individual autonomy and dignity are also protected, in theory at least, by procedural safeguards relating to investigation, prosecution, and the criminal trial, by the principles of legality and the presumption of innocence, and the values and principles pertaining to the criminal process (Ashworth and Redmayne 2010, ch. 2). These are intended to safeguard individuals against unwarranted state interference and uphold fundamental human rights enshrined in the European Convention of Human Rights. This paradigmatic liberal account of criminal law emphasizes respect for the rights and dignity of the individual in the criminal process (Roberts 2006). This said, as criminological research reveals, formal protections are often ignored, subverted, or breached. Some suggest that the liberal rhetoric of respect for the individual masks and makes possible a legal process that has more to do with efficiency than procedural protections (McBarnet 1981: 156).

The various assumptions underlying the conceptual framework within which criminal liability is constructed provide insights into the processes of interpretation in the court room—a key site in the process of criminalization. They also raise interesting questions about the coherence of the criminal process. Are the assumptions of rationality, understanding, and self-control which lie at the heart of criminal law's conception of (normal) defendants the same as, or even consistent with, those that underpin policing strategy, sentencing, probation, or prison regimes? Are the assumptions of moral autonomy, free will, and rationality consistent with criminological knowledge about factors closely associated with offending such as drug and alcohol abuse, mental disorder, and the constraints on choice imposed by social and economic deprivation (Delgado 1985; Peay, this volume; Rock, this volume)?

THE SHIFTING BOUNDARIES OF CONTEMPORARY CRIMINAL LAW

It is estimated that over 3,200 new offences were added to the statute books in the decade following 1997.[7] Some resulted from new legislation against particular areas of activity such as serious and organized crime, immigration, and terrorism. About two-thirds were created by the growing number of regulatory agencies, which have the power to introduce secondary legislation. In addition to powers already held by local authorities and trading standards authorities, over 60 national regulatory bodies now have the power to create criminal law in support of their work. For example, in the year to May 2014 alone, 280 new offences were created of which a quarter were created by the Department for Business, Innovation and Skills.[8]

Untrammeled expansion of the criminal law is a cause for concern not least because it has the potential to limit individual choice and expand the power of the state to exercise its most coercive powers over more and more aspects of daily life. Recent developments have seen liability extend downwards (to regulatory offences), back in time (inchoate offences, preparatory offences, possession, risk-creation, and other precursor offences), and outwards (associative crimes—especially in respect of fraud, organized crime, proscribed organizations and terrorism) (Ramsay 2012, Ashworth and Zedner 2014; Lacey 2016: chs 3 and 5). This expansion of criminal liability adds considerably to the discretionary powers of prosecutors and the police; yet many new

[7] 1,169 in primary legislation and 1,854 in subordinate legislation. Halsbury's Statutes of England and Wales has four volumes devoted to criminal laws: strikingly, more than two and a half times as many pages were needed in Halsbury's Statutes to cover offences created in the 19 years between 1989 and 2008 than were needed to cover the offences created in the preceding 637 years (The Law Commission 2010: 5).

[8] Ministry of Justice *New criminal offences England and Wales 1st June 2009–31st May 2014*, available at: https://www.gov.uk/government/statistics/new-criminal-offences-statistics-in-england-and-wales-may-2014 p. 6, accessed 17 December 2016. On the question of quantification, see Chalmers and Leverick 2015.

criminal offences, especially those created by regulatory agencies, are rarely used. For example, section 8 of the Asylum and Immigration Act 1996, which prohibits the employment of illegal migrant workers, resulted in, on average, only one prosecution a year between 1998 and 2004. Nor has the increase in criminal offences on the statute books since 1997 led to a corresponding increase in prosecutions and convictions. Indeed from 2007, the numbers dealt with formally by the criminal process in England and Wales began to decline. Prosecutions in magistrates' courts fell from 2 million in 1997 to 1.6 million in 2008 and to 1.47 million in 2015. The total number of people found guilty in both magistrates' and Crown Courts fell from 1.49 million to 1.36 million and then to 1.2 million over the same period.[9] And despite a 1 per cent increase in total prosecutions in the year to June 2016, prompted by an increase in summary prosecutions, the overall level now appears to have stabilized at a lower level than a decade ago, with the numbers prosecuted at magistrates' courts for indictable offences seeing an overall decline since the 12 months ending June 2011, from 470,000 to 340,000 in the year ending June 2016.[10] Thus the expansion of criminal law appears to have coincided with a growth in the gap between formal and substantive criminalization.

Part of the reason may be that the criminal trial is often regarded as unduly expensive, time-consuming, ineffective, inappropriate, or unnecessary as a means of dealing with low-level offending (Ashworth and Zedner 2010: 23). This view has encouraged greater recourse to mechanisms for diversion; fixed penalties (e.g. the Penalty Notice for Disorder or PND); and a growing range of civil and hybrid civil–criminal measures that reduce reliance upon the criminal law (of which the ASBO—now replaced by a civil injunction under the Anti-Social Behaviour, Crime and Policing Act 2014—is the best known) (Ramsay 2012; Ashworth and Zedner 2014, ch. 4).[11] Criminalization becomes just one tool in a growing array of administrative and regulatory measures (Ashworth and Zedner 2014: 396; Horder 2014). It would be a mistake, however, to assume that these measures are necessarily less intrusive or less burdensome than the criminal law. The Penalty Notice for Disorder imposes a fixed penalty that may be significantly more onerous than a court fine (which must be set in accordance with the offender's means). Similarly, the new civil injunction may target low levels of nuisance well below the normal threshold of the criminal law.

Whether the response to low-level or regulatory offences ought to lie with the criminal law, or be replaced by administrative measures or civil orders of the sort just described, is a matter of lively debate. On the one hand it is suggested that where appropriate levels of punishment or deterrence can be secured by lesser civil means these should be preferred over stigmatizing and potentially overly punitive criminalization (Law Commission 2010). On the other hand, to the extent that civil measures impose burdens equivalent to punishment, placing these measures within civil

[9] https://www.gov.uk/government/uploads/system/uploads/attachment_data/file/478037/criminal-justice-statistics-quarterly-june-2015.pdf, accessed 18 January 2016.

[10] https://www.gov.uk/government/uploads/system/uploads/attachment_data/file/570022/criminal-justice-statistics-quarterly-update-to-june-2016.pdf, accessed 5 January 2017, p. 13.

[11] The focus on low-level offensive behaviour as an appropriate object of early intervention built on Wilson and Kelling's (controversial) broken windows thesis (1982): that broken windows, litter, and graffiti lead to increased crime (Crawford 2009: 816).

procedure denies individuals the protections of the criminal process and may constitute an instance of under-criminalization (Ashworth and Zedner 2010, 2014; Horder 2011). Yet as Crawford observed, '[i]t is a supreme irony that whilst many of the new technologies of control have sought to circumvent criminal procedures due to their apparent ineffectiveness, this has not diminished the appetite for more criminal laws' (2009: 826).[12]

Two dominant and divergent trends characterize practices of criminalization over the past two decades. On the one hand there has been recourse to diversion, through fixed penalties and civil–criminal preventive measures, and downgrading, through greater use of summary trials, stronger incentives to plead guilty, and an increase in offences of strict liability (mostly, though not all, carrying low penalties) (Crown Prosecution Service 2015, Ward 2015). On the other hand, over the last 40 years there has been a steep increase in the number of criminal offences and in the severity of penal measures, notably in the use of imprisonment (the prison population is now nearly 85,000).[13] The 1970s and 1980s saw a well-documented growing public concern about the scale and extent of crime.[14] No surprise then that determining the proper limits of criminalization became a matter of academic and political interest to criminal lawyers anxious to restrain the tendency to 'over-criminalization' in countries such as England and the United States (Husak 2008: ch. 1; Stuntz 2011). Although criminological accounts of the 'new punitiveness' prompted legal interest in the appropriate boundaries of the criminal law (Duff *et al.* 2010), that interest has hardly been shared by criminology. While lawyers are alert to the sociological drivers of over-criminalization, the criminological focus has been on penal populism rather than on the legitimate scope of criminalization (Annison 2015; *Theoretical Criminology Special Issue* 2010). As a result, lawyers, philosophers, and political theorists seek to determine the proper limits of criminalization largely unaided by criminology, despite the obvious contribution that criminology might make to a fully social and political account of why and to what ends conduct is criminalized (Zedner 2011).

LIMITS ON CRIMINALIZATION: THE CONTRIBUTION OF CRIMINOLOGY

Prevailing theories of criminal law are closely tied to theories of the state and the dominant political order (Duff *et al.* 2004a; Brudner 2009): the liberal account of

[12] In a bid to cap the proliferation of new criminal offences, the Ministry of Justice announced in 2010 the creation of a 'gateway' designed to scrutinize all new proposals for legislation containing criminal offences 'to ensure that they are justified and proportionate', http://www.justice.gov.uk/downloads/legislation/criminal-offences-gateway-guidance.pdf/, accessed 4 January 2017.

Nonetheless, 280 new criminal offences were created in 2014.

[13] There were 84,857 people in prisons on 4 January 2017: http://howardleague.org/prisons-information/prison-watch/, accessed 4 January 2017.

[14] Although a significant decline in serious crime since the mid-1990s has somewhat modified this trend.

crime as a means of holding individuals to account for wrongful conduct has come to prevail as the dominant model of criminal law. Yet this account has been subject to criticism from many quarters. Christie famously characterized crimes as private disputes between victims and offenders whose interests were 'stolen' by state criminalization (Christie 1977). Understanding crime not as an infraction of the law deserving of punishment but as a dispute to be resolved by those party to it was one factor contributing to the development of Restorative Justice, an alternative to the criminal justice paradigm, that proposes dialogue in place of prosecution, dispute resolution in place of the trial, and 'reintegrative shaming' in place of punishment (Braithwaite 1989, see Rossner, this volume). Such has been the power and influence of this advocacy that liberal legal theorists have been moved to take up the challenge of trying to determine how the claims of Restorative Justice might be reconciled with more conventional accounts of crime and criminal justice (von Hirsch *et al.* 2003).

Perhaps the most trenchant criticism of liberal accounts of criminal liability has come from communitarian thinkers who argue that they are premised on an atomized view of the individual that overplays autonomy and fails to recognize that we are social beings inseparable from our personal and social relations (Lacey 1988: ch. 8). Recognizing the importance of community to individuals and the choices they make has profound implications for thinking about wrongdoing and places in question the assumption of individual responsibility upon which the criminal law is predicated. Significant efforts have been made to combine the insights of liberal and communitarian traditions (Duff 2001). These balance the liberal strengths of respect for human agency and rights with an acknowledgement that the social antecedents of crime should inform the definition of defences and of responsibility more generally (Duff 2001, 2007; Tonry 2014).

A more radical critique still comes from the attempt by some criminologists to move 'beyond crime' (Hillyard *et al.* 2004) on the grounds that crime is too restrictive a concept to capture the full extent of harmful behaviour that causes most loss and suffering. Hillyard and colleagues claim that criminal liability is attributed by questionable means and that focusing on the liability of the individual fails to address serious social harms inflicted by groups, organizations, and states (ibid.). Significantly, this attack on the category of crime is motivated partly by the observation that 'criminology has largely failed to be self-reflective regarding the dominant, state defined notion of "crime" ... The issue of what crime is, is rarely stated, but rather simply assumed' (Hillyard and Tombs 2007: 11; see also Hillyard and Tombs, this volume). Yet this insight might equally suggest that criminology should make good this failure by engaging with the scope and nature of crime, the principles upon which it is defined, and the legal structures in which it is inscribed (Zedner 2011; Reiner 2016: chs 1 and 2).

Although this chapter has as its focus legal constructions of crime, its argument shows that criminology has much to contribute to the ongoing and often heated debates around criminalization. Criminology has a vital role to play in ensuring that the normative questions with which criminal lawyers grapple are neither framed nor answered as purely normative or legal issues. These questions cannot be divorced from the political, economic, and social factors underpinning the ways that offences are identified as criminal wrongs (rather than matters subject to other kinds of regulation) and criminal categories are defined, framed, and structured. It is commonly asserted that there is a core of offences universally accepted as criminal wrongs around which exists a penumbra of lesser, disputed categories. Yet even the most serious of offences pose challenges. The core offence of murder poses interpretive difficulty in cases such as mercy killing. And even the most serious offences may escape criminalization if they do not easily supply the paradigmatic individual offender who can be held to account. Take two examples from either end of the scale of criminalization as currently constructed: crimes of the state often appear to be above or too big for criminalization (Cohen 2001), while workplace injuries are often dealt with as regulatory matters by Health and Safety authorities rather than prosecuting employers and factory owners (Hawkins 2002). Identifying the contextual and structural conditions which favour or impede criminalization is a task that has long eluded criminal lawyers but one which criminology is well equipped to tackle.

As we have seen, for lawyers the construction of crime proceeds by reference to concepts of culpability, wrongfulness, harm, and offence; by delineating the boundary between civil and criminal liability; by seeking to determine which harms are too remote and which offences too trivial to merit criminalization (Simester and von Hirsch 2011). But lawyerly attention to these normative questions risks overlooking practical, structural, and policy considerations that criminologists are arguably better placed to address. Should crimes be defined and enforced in response to the relative prevalence of conduct in a particular area or at a given time and the level of public concern about it? What weight should be given to the enforceability of a prohibition or the costs of enforcement? Should the financial burdens of policing an activity or the intrusions entailed by enforcement measures be a factor in determining what is and what is not criminalized? What role should public opinion play? Given the difficulty of ensuring compliance if there is widespread dissent, should public consensus play any part in determining what is criminalized and, if so, in what circumstances? Should the danger that a law will be widely flouted or otherwise prove impossible to enforce (as was the case in respect of the much derided ban on fox-hunting) be considered a valid policy consideration or not?

To these policy questions one might add research into the ways in which political processes, and not least party political interests, influence the construction and application of legal categories. Consider too the administrative pressures and constraints upon implementing laws, training criminal justice officials, and influencing professional culture. These extra-legal factors play an important part in determining how crime is actually policed and prosecuted through the criminal justice process. Criminological knowledge is no less central to understanding how, in practice, legal categories are applied, to whom, in what circumstances, and with what consequences. Criminology examines the relations of class, race, and gender, the cultural assumptions and prejudices, and the political considerations that inform and influence the practice of law. It explains how and why the formal equality and universality of the criminal law may be undermined by the partial, targeted, and often discriminatory ways in which it is applied. No less important is the larger *Realpolitik* of inter-governmental and international politics that frames the construction and implementation of international criminal law, and of supranational offences like organized crime, the smuggling of peoples, arms and drugs, and terrorism.

Criminology is alert to the volatile and contradictory character of modern penal politics (O'Malley 1999; Garland 2001). It has observed the normalization of crime as a fact of everyday life to be managed and regulated. This routinization of crime licenses 'defining deviance down', the removal of lesser offences from the criminal process to the less onerous channels of civil and administrative law, and resort to other regulatory mechanisms, not least the 'contractual governance' of deviance (Crawford 2003). But it is far from clear that these managerial, regulatory, and contractual developments have resulted in less commitment to the control of crime through the criminal law. Indeed, as we have seen, the latter part of the twentieth century witnessed an extraordinary and unprecedented programme of criminalization encompassing serious offences in areas such as terrorism and sexual conduct as well as the proliferation of regulatory offences. Criminalization has decelerated in the last decade but arguably not in proportion to the marked decline in serious crime since the mid-1990s. Yet, the legal construction of crime is one part of the picture of contemporary penal politics that criminology has yet to engage with in any sustained fashion. It should by now be clear that criminalization is not just a matter of legal principle but 'a politically charged set of decisions that result in a complex set of individual laws by which the state seeks to govern its subjects' (Ashworth and Zedner 2008: 44). Recognizing that criminal law is an engine of governance renders it impossible to separate its study not only from that of political theory and political economy but also, and not least, from criminology.

SELECTED FURTHER READING

The relationship between questions of criminal law and criminal justice is explored extensively in Farmer's *Making the Modern Criminal Law: Criminalization and Civil Order* (2016) and Lacey's *In Search of Criminal Responsibility: Ideas, Interests and Institutions* (2016). For further discussion of legal constructions of crime, see Reiner's *Crime: The Mystery of the Common-Sense Concept* (2016).

On recent developments in the changing scope, exercise, and aims of criminal law and criminal justice, see Ashworth and Zedner's *Preventive Justice* (2014). For a legal–philosophical treatment of criminalization, see Duff and Green's (eds) *Philosophical Foundations of the Criminal Law* (2011) and Simester and von Hirsch's *Crimes, Harms, and Wrongs: on the Principles of Criminalisation* (2011). Finally, see the volumes arising from the Criminalization project led by Duff, Farmer, Marshall, Renzo, and Tadros (eds) *Criminalization: The Boundaries of the Criminal Law; The Structures of the Criminal Law; The Constitution of the Criminal Law; The Political Morality of the Criminal Law* (2010, 2011, 2013, 2015). This project, involving criminal lawyers, philosophers, and criminologists, has done much to bridge the gulf between disciplines described in this chapter.

REFERENCES

Annison, H. (2015), *Dangerous Politics: Risk, Political Vulnerability, and Penal Policy*, Oxford: Oxford University Press.

Ashworth, A. and Zedner, L. (2008), 'Defending the Criminal Law', *Criminal Law and Philosophy*, 2(1): 21–51.

ASHWORTH, A. and ZEDNER, L. (2010), 'Preventive Orders: a case of undercriminalization', in R. A. Duff, *et al.* (eds), *The Boundaries of the Criminal Law*, Oxford: Oxford University Press.

ASHWORTH, A. and ZEDNER, L. (2014), *Preventive Justice*, Oxford: Oxford University Press.

ASHWORTH, A. and BLAKE, M. (1996), 'The Presumption of Innocence in English Criminal Law', *Criminal Law Review*, 306.

ASHWORTH, A. and REDMAYNE, M. (2010), *The Criminal Process: An Evaluative Study*, 4th edn, Oxford: Oxford University Press.

BEATTIE, J. M. (1986), *Crime and the Courts in England 1660–1800*, Princeton: Princeton University Press.

BEATTIE, J. M. (1991), 'Scales of Justice', *Law and History Review*, 9(2): 221.

BEATTIE, J. M. (2001), *Policing and Punishment in London 1660–1750: Urban Crime and the Limits of Terror*, Oxford: Oxford University Press.

BENNETT, C. (2012), 'Expressive Punishment and State Authority', *Ohio State Journal of Criminal Law*, 8(2): 285–318.

BINDER, G. (2002), 'The Rhetoric of Motive and Intent', *Buffalo Criminal Law Review*, 1–96.

BLACKSTONE, W. (1765–9), *Commentaries on the Laws of England* (1979), Chicago: University of Chicago Press.

BRAITHWAITE, J. (1989), *Crime, Shame and Reintegration*, Cambridge: Cambridge University Press.

BRONITT, S. and MCSHERRY, B. (2010), *Principles of Criminal Law*, 3rd edn, Pyrmont, N.S.W.: Law Book Company.

BRUDNER, A. (2009), *Punishment and Freedom*, Oxford: Oxford University Press.

CHALMERS, J. and LEVERICK, F. (2015), 'Quantifying Criminalization', in R. A. Duff *et al.* (eds), *Criminalization: The Political Morality of the Criminal Law*, Oxford: Oxford University Press.

CHRISTIE, N. (1977), 'Conflicts as Property', *British Journal of Criminology*, 17: 1–15.

COHEN, S. (2001), *States of Denial: Knowing about Atrocities and Suffering*, Cambridge: Polity.

CRAWFORD, A. (2003), '"Contractual Governance" of Deviant Behaviour', *Journal of Law and Society*, 30(4): 479–505.

CRAWFORD, A. (2009), 'Governing through Anti-Social Behaviour: Regulatory Challenges to Criminal Justice', *British Journal of Criminology*, 49: 810–31.

CROWN PROSECUTION SERVICE (2015), *Transforming Summary Justice: A Criminal Justice System-wide initiative*, London: HMSO.

DELGADO, R. (1985), '"Rotten Social Background": Should the Criminal Law Recognize a Defence of Severe Environmental Deprivation?', *Law and Inequality*, 3: 9–90.

DUBBER, M. D. (2005), *The Police Power*, New York: Columbia University Press.

DUFF, R. A. (2001), *Punishment, Communication and Community*, Oxford: Oxford University Press.

DUFF, R. A. (2007), *Answering for Crime: Responsibility and Liability in the Criminal Law*, Oxford: Hart.

DUFF, R. A. *et al.* (2004a), 'Introduction: Towards a Normative Theory of the Criminal Trial', in R. A. Duff, L. Farmer, S. E. Marshall, and V. Tadros (eds), *The Trial on Trial, Volume 1*, Oxford: Hart.

DUFF, R. A., FARMER, L., MARSHALL, S. E., and TADROS, V. (eds) (2004b, 2005, 2007), *The Trial on Trial: Volumes I: Truth and Due Process; II: Judgment and Calling to Account; III: Towards a Normative Theory of the Criminal Trial*, Oxford: Hart.

DUFF, R. A., FARMER, L., MARSHALL, S. E., RENZO, M., and TADROS, V. (eds) (2010), *Criminalization: The Boundaries of the Criminal Law*, Oxford: Oxford University Press.

DUFF, R. A., FARMER, L., MARSHALL, S. E., RENZO, M., and TADROS, V. (2011), *The Structures of the Criminal Law*, Oxford: Oxford University Press.

DUFF, R. A. FARMER, L., MARSHALL, S. E., RENZO, M., and TADROS, V. (eds) (2013), *The Constitution of the Criminal Law*, Oxford: Oxford University Press.

DUFF, R. A., FARMER, L., MARSHALL, S. E., RENZO, M., and TADROS, V. (eds) (2015), *The Political Morality of the Criminal Law* Oxford: Oxford University Press.

DUFF, R. A. and GREEN, S., (2011), *Philosophical Foundations of the Criminal Law* Oxford: Oxford University Press.

EMSLEY, C. (2007), 'Historical Perspectives on Crime', in M. Maguire, R. Morgan, and R. Reiner (eds), *The Oxford Handbook of Criminology*, 4th edn, Oxford: Oxford University Press.

FARMER, L. (1996), *Criminal Law, Tradition and Legal Order*, Cambridge: Cambridge University Press.

FARMER, L. (2016), *Making the Modern Criminal Law: Criminalization and Civil Order*, Oxford: Oxford University Press.

FEINBERG, J. (1984–8), *The Moral Limits of the Criminal Law*, Oxford and New York: Oxford University Press.

FLETCHER, G. (1978), *Rethinking Criminal Law*, Boston and Toronto: Little, Brown & Co.

GARLAND, D. (2001), *The Culture of Control: Crime and Social Order in Contemporary Society*, Oxford, Oxford University Press.

HARCOURT, B. (1999), 'The Collapse of the Harm Principle', *Journal of Criminal Law and Criminology*, 90(1): 109.

HART, H. L. A. (1963), *Law, Liberty and Morality*, Oxford: Oxford University Press.

HART, H. L. A. (1968), *Punishment and Responsibility*, Oxford: Clarendon.

HAWKINS, K. (2002), *Law as Last Resort: Prosecution Decision-Making in a Regulatory Agency*, Oxford, Oxford University Press.

HAY, D. (1975), 'Property, Authority and Criminal Law', in D. Hay, P. Linebaugh, and E. P. Thompson (eds), *Albion's Fatal Tree*, Harmondsworth: Penguin.

HILLYARD, P., PANTAZIS, C., TOMBS, S., and GORDON, D. (eds) (2004), *Beyond Criminology: Taking Harm Seriously*, London: Pluto Press.

HILLYARD, P. and TOMBS S. (2007), 'From "crime" to social harm?', *Crime, Law and Social Change*, 48: 9–25.

HORDER, J. (1997), 'Two Histories and Four Hidden Principles of Mens Rea', 113, *Law Quarterly Review*, 95.

HORDER, J. (2011), 'Harmless Wrongdoing and the Anticipatory Perspective on Criminalisation', in I. Dennis and G. R. Sullivan (eds), *Seeking Security: Pre-empting the Commission of Criminal Harms*, Oxford: Hart.

HORDER, J. (2014), 'Bureaucratic "Criminal" Law: Too Much of a Bad Thing?', in R. A. Duff, L. Farmer, S. E. Marshall, M. Renzo, and V. Tadros (eds), *Criminalization: The Aims and Limits of the Criminal Law*. Oxford University Press.

HORDER, J. (2016), *Ashworth's Principles of Criminal Law*, 8th edn, Oxford: Clarendon.

HUSAK, D. N. (2008), *Overcriminalization*, New York: Oxford University Press.

KENNY, C. S. (1902), *Outlines of Criminal Law*, 1st edn, Cambridge: Cambridge University Press.

KING, P. (2000), *Crime, Justice and Discretion in England 1740–1820*, Oxford: Oxford University Press.

LACEY, N. (1988), *State Punishment*, Oxford: Oxford University Press.

LACEY, N. (1995), 'Contingency and Criminalization', in I. Loveland (ed.), *Frontiers of Criminality*, London: Sweet and Maxwell.

LACEY, N. (2001a), 'In Search of the Responsible Subject', *Modern Law Review*, 64(3): 350–71.

LACEY, N. (2001b), 'Responsibility and Modernity in Criminal Law', *Journal of Political Philosophy*, 9(3): 249–77.

LACEY, N. (2008), *Women, Crime and Character: from Moll Flanders to Tess of the d'Urbervilles*, Oxford: Oxford University Press.

LACEY, N. (2009), 'Historicising Criminalization: Conceptual and Empirical Issues', *Modern Law Review*, 72(6): 936–61.

LACEY, N. (2016), *In Search of Criminal Responsibility: Ideas, Interests and Institutions*, Oxford: Oxford University Press.

LANGBEIN, J. (1983), 'Albion's Fatal Flaws', *Past and Present*, 98: 96–120.

LANGBEIN, J. (2003), *The Origins of Adversary Criminal Trial*, Oxford: Oxford University Press.

THE LAW COMMISSION (2010), *Criminal Liability in Regulatory Contexts. Consultation Paper No 195*, London: Law Commission.

LOUGHNAN, A. (2012), *Manifest Madness: Mental Incapacity in Criminal Law*, Oxford: Oxford University Press.

MCBARNET, D. (1981), *Conviction: Law, the State and the Construction of Justice*, London: Macmillan.

MCMULLEN, J. (1996), 'The New Improved Monied Police: Reform, Crime Control, and the Commodification of Policing in London', *British Journal of Criminology*, 36(1): 85–108.

MILL, J. S. (1859), *On Liberty*, Harmondsworth: Penguin 1974.

NORRIE, A. (2001), *Crime, Reason and History*, 2nd edn, London: Butterworths.

O'MALLEY, P. (1999), 'Volatile and Contradictory Punishment', *Theoretical Criminology*, 3: 175–96.

QUIRK, H, SEDDON, T., and SMITH, G. (eds) (2010), *Regulation and Criminal Justice*, Cambridge: Cambridge University Press.

RADZINOWICZ, L. (1956), *A History of English Criminal Law and its Administration from 1750* (Vol. 3), London: Steven & Sons Limited.

RADZINOWICZ, L. and HOOD, R. (1990), *The Emergence of Penal Policy in Victorian and Edwardian England*, Oxford: Oxford University Press.

RADZINOWICZ, L. and TURNER, J. W. C. (1945), *The Modern Approach to Criminal Law*, London: Macmillan.

REINER, R. (2006), *Beyond Risk: A Lament for a Social Democratic Criminology*, in T. Newburn and P. Rock (eds), *The Politics of Crime Control*, Oxford: Oxford University Press.

REINER, R. (2007), *Law and Order: An Honest Citizen's Guide to Crime and Control*, Cambridge: Polity.

REINER, R. (2016), *Crime: The Mystery of the Common-Sense Concept*, Cambridge: Polity.

RAMSAY, P. (2012), *The Insecurity State: Vulnerable Autonomy and the Right to Security in the Criminal Law*, Oxford: Oxford University Press.

ROBERTS, P. (2006), 'Theorising Procedural Tradition: Subjects, Objects and Values in Criminal Adjudication', in R. A. Duff *et al.* (eds), *The Trial on Trial, Volume 2*, Oxford: Hart.

ROBINSON, P.H. (1997), *Structure and Function in Criminal Law*, Oxford: Clarendon.

SIMESTER, A. P. and VON HIRSCH, A. (2006), 'Regulating offensive conduct through two-step prohibitions', in von Hirsch and Simester (eds), *Incivilities: Regulating offensive behaviour*, Oxford: Hart.

SIMESTER, A. P. and VON HIRSCH, A. (2011), *Crimes, Harms, and Wrongs: on the Principles of Criminalisation*, Oxford: Hart.

SMITH, K. J. M. (1998), *Lawyers, Legislators and Theorists*, Oxford: Clarendon.

SMITH, R. (1981), *Trial by Medicine*, Edinburgh: Edinburgh University Press.

SPIERENBURG, P. (1984) *The Spectacle of Suffering: Executions and the Evolution of Repression*, Cambridge: Cambridge University Press.

STEPHEN, J. F. (1893), *A History of the Criminal Law of England*, London: Macmillan.

STUNTZ, W. J. (2001), 'The Pathological Politics of Criminal Law', *Michigan Law Review*, 100, 505–600.

STUNTZ, W. J. (2011), *The Collapse of American Criminal Justice*, Cambridge: Harvard University Press.

THEORETICAL CRIMINOLOGY (2010), *Special Issue—Penal Parsimony*, 14(3).

TONRY, M. (2014), 'Can Deserts be Just in an Unjust World?', in , A. Simester *et al.* (eds) *Liberal Criminal Theory*, Oxford: Oxford University Press.

VON HIRSCH, A. (1993), *Censure and Sanctions*, Oxford: Oxford University Press.

Von Hirsch, A. *et al.* (eds) (2003), *Restorative Justice and Criminal Justice*, Oxford: Hart.

Von Hirsch, A. and Simester, A. (eds) (2006), *Incivilities: Regulating Offensive Behaviour*, Oxford: Hart.

Ward, J. (2015), 'Transforming "Summary Justice" Through Police-Led Prosecution and "Virtual Courts" Is "Procedural Due Process" Being Undermined?', *British Journal of Criminology*, 55(2): 341–58.

Wells, C. and Quick, O. (2010), *Lacey, Wells and Quick's Reconstructing Criminal Law: Critical Perspectives on Crime and the Criminal Process*, 4th edn, Cambridge: Cambridge University Press.

Whitman, J. (2003), *Harsh Justice: Criminal Punishment and the Widening Divide between America and Europe*, New York: Oxford University Press.

Wiener, M. (1990), *Reconstructing the Criminal: Culture, Law and Policy in England, 1830–1914*, Cambridge: Cambridge University Press.

Williams, G. (1953, (2nd edn, 1961)), *Criminal Law: The General Part*, London: Stevens.

Williams, G. (1983, 2nd edn), *A Textbook of Criminal Law*, London: Stevens.

Wilson, J. Q. and Kelling, G. L. (1982), 'Broken Windows: the police and neighbourhood safety', *Atlantic Monthly*, March Issue: 29–38.

Zedner, L. (2004), *Criminal Justice*, Oxford: Oxford University Press.

Zedner, L. (2006), 'Policing before and after the Police: the historical antecedents of contemporary crime control', *British Journal of Criminology*, 46(1): 78–96.

Zedner, L. (2011), 'Putting Crime back on the Criminological Agenda', in M. Bosworth and C. Hoyle (eds), *What is Criminology?* Oxford: Oxford University Press.

CHAPTER ACKNOWLEDGEMENTS

The authors are grateful to Vandana Venkatesh for her insightful comments on previous drafts of this chapter.

3

PUNISHMENT AND WELFARE: SOCIAL PROBLEMS AND SOCIAL STRUCTURES

David Garland

INTRODUCTION

In the sociology of punishment and comparative penology it has become common to observe significant connections between 'punishment' and 'welfare'—or more precisely, between a jurisdiction's penal practices and its institutions of public assistance. In this chapter I discuss these connections and ask how they might best be understood. After reviewing the existing literature, I argue that future research ought to view the relationship between penal and welfare policy in relation to the social problems these policies purportedly address (usually thought of as 'crime' and 'poverty' respectively) and also in relation to the larger social and economic processes that shape these policies and generate these problems. These relationships are neither straightforward nor well understood, and one aim of this chapter is to introduce greater clarity into our discussions of these issues.

I begin by discussing the relationship between punishment and welfare as it features in current research and the scholarly literature. I then turn to the less-discussed question of how penal and welfare policies relate to the social problems that they purport to address and to the political and socio-economic structures within which they operate.

The punishment–welfare connection is currently conceptualized in two rather different ways—as a *historical* relationship and as a *comparative* correlation—and I discuss each of these in turn.

HISTORICAL STUDIES

One well established account of the punishment–welfare relationship takes the form of a historical thesis about the rise and subsequent retrenchment of welfare states and the impact of these welfare state developments on penal policy and criminal justice. Historical monographs such as *Punishment and Welfare* (Garland 1985) and *City of Courts* (Willrich 2003) describe how the emergence of welfare states in the UK and the US at the start of the twentieth century reshaped ideas of crime causation and criminal responsibility and prompted the development of an array of 'penal-welfare' practices, the most important of which were the juvenile court, probation, social inquiry reports, social work with offenders, indeterminate sentencing, rehabilitative prison regimes, and parole. In France, works by Michel Foucault and his collaborators Jacques Donzelot and Francois Ewald—most notably *Discipline and Punish* (1977), *The Policing of Families* (1980), and *L'Etat Providence* (1986)—drew attention to similar shifts in the nature of legal judgment and penal control: shifts that these authors associated with the emergence of the 'human sciences' (medicine, psychiatry, criminology, psychoanalysis, etc.) and the rise of 'the social' with its new forms of tutelage, supervision, and expert-led relations of power-knowledge.[1]

In recent years it has been the retrenchment of the welfare state and the impact of that retrenchment on criminal justice that has drawn renewed attention to the penal-welfare nexus. Simon's *Poor Discipline* (1993) and Garland's *Culture of Control* (2001) analyse how the penal-welfare practices of mid-twentieth-century America and Britain were revised or replaced in the 1980s and 1990s as the political forces of the New Right harnessed the effects of economic and cultural change to attack the welfare state and its associated practices. In the penal sphere, this rightward movement resulted in a shift of emphasis from social causation to individual blame; a downgrading of offender-centered welfarism; and a renewed stress on more traditional penal purposes such as retribution and incapacitation. Recent studies of neoliberalism and penality—notably Wacquant's *Punishing the Poor* (2009) and Harcourt's *The Illusion of Free Markets* (2011)—make much the same claim, viewing the emergence of punitive sentencing and mass incarceration as one aspect of a hegemonic neoliberalism that seeks to reinforce a precarious, low-wage labour market by restricting welfare benefits and extending penal controls.

We can summarize the central finding of the historical literature as the claim that a certain style of penal practice—variously described as correctionalism, rehabilitation, the treatment approach, or penal-welfarism—is a concomitant of welfare state government and that the penal-welfare aspects of criminal justice tend to rise and fall in tandem with the broader social policies of the welfare state. Stated in these bald terms, the punishment-welfare connection seems like an obvious one but it has often been overlooked nevertheless—probably because of the disciplinary division between the 'social policy' literature (which generally omits any mention of crime policy and

[1] In the Foucauldian literature, the concept of 'the social' refers to the powers and practices of welfare state agencies but also to philanthropic and private forms of social support and intervention (see Curtis 2002 for a discussion).

criminal justice) and 'criminology' (which neglects other areas of social policy and social control). If we were to ignore this artificial division between academic specialisms, we could begin to integrate criminal justice history into the broader history of social policy and the welfare state. So for instance, the analysis of post-1960s socio-economic change and its criminological impacts set out in Garland (2001) could be viewed as a specific instance of a more general social phenomenon that has been extensively analysed in recent social policy scholarship: namely, the emergence of 'New Social Risks' brought about by deindustrialization, labour market transformations, and changes in family form and household structure together with the development of adaptive policy responses designed to deal with them.[2] If this is indeed the case, then criminological researchers ought to consider whether the structural transformations that are currently remaking welfare state regimes—that is, the ongoing shift from the *neoliberalized* welfare regimes of the 1990s (with their emphasis on marketization, privatization, and restricted benefits) to the *social investment* welfare states of the twenty-first century (with their emphasis on labour market activation and investment in human capital)—are resonating in the penal domain and if so, precisely how these wider changes are beginning to affect the ideology and operation of criminal justice systems.[3]

A rather different connection between punishment and welfare has been suggested by Elizabeth Hinton in her recent historical monograph, *From the War on Poverty to the War on Crime* (2016). Hinton's provocative, revisionist thesis argues that the 'War on Poverty'—the large-scale social reform project launched by President Johnson's administration in 1960s America—led more or less directly to President Nixon's subsequent 'War on Crime' and later to the mass incarceration of the 1980s and 1990s.[4] It is unclear whether Hinton's claim is that the 'seeds' of mass incarceration were already present in the poverty-fighting initiatives of Johnson's liberal administration—in which case, a certain form of welfarism somehow entails a hidden, incipient punitiveness—or is the less provocative (and more plausible) idea that the perceived failure of Johnson's social welfare approach prompted the subsequent build-up of policing and punishment as an alternative means of dealing with urban unrest and rising crime. In either case, Hinton's thesis concerns a particular episode in American urban politics and the generalizability of her thesis remains to be shown.

Hinton's book also describes how the War on Poverty's subsequent focus on crime-control led to the involvement of police departments in community agencies, welfare centres and youth service bureaus. This on-the-ground blending of welfare

[2] See for example Bonoli (2005) and Taylor-Gooby (2004). The term 'New Social Risks' refers to newly emerging social and economic problems that were not effectively addressed by post-war welfare states: the working poor; single parent families; long-term unemployment, the life–work balance of two-income families, poorly integrated immigrant groups, and so on (Garland 2016).

[3] For details of this transformation, see Garland (2016) and Morel *et al.* (2012). Researchers in the sociology of punishment have traced neoliberalism's impact on penal policy but so far, with the important exception of migration issues (Melossi 2015), they have had little to say about the rise of the New Social Risks and the adaptive social policy responses that they have prompted.

[4] For a different account of this relationship, see Kohler-Hausmann (2015: 89 and 91) who writes: 'Instead of stepping into the welfare state's void or representing its antithesis, the growing carceral apparatus often built upon the welfare state.... In many settings, responsibility for handling specific social problems was transferred from welfare programs to law enforcement.'

and policing functions is a theme that has become prominent again today as neo-liberal governments seek to scale back public assistance and discourage individuals from applying for welfare support. In both America and Britain there has been a pronounced tendency for means-tested welfare benefits to become more conditional and more disciplinary; for a greater emphasis to be placed on the pursuit of welfare fraud; and for welfare recipients to become increasingly subject to sanctions (such as loss or suspension of benefits) for the violation of benefit conditions and procedures (Gustavson 2011; Soss *et al.* 2011; Goddard 2012; Kohler-Hausmann 2015, and Adler 2016).

This process of blending and blurring reminds us that the distinction between punishment and welfare is more easily drawn in the abstract than in practice. Long before the rise of the modern welfare state, penal sanctions such as imprisonment provided some minimal forms of welfare—a basic diet, a modicum of healthcare, evangelical prison visits, help with resettlement, etc.—especially for 'deserving' inmates such as juveniles or female offenders (Morris and Rothman 1995).[5] And even capital punishment will generally provide some minimal care for the condemned in the form of medical supervision, an elaborate final meal, a pastor to administer the last rites, and so on (Garland 2010). Perhaps only monetary penalties appear altogether devoid of welfare elements, though courts often permit instalment payment which help ensure compliance by limiting hardship.

If we turn to welfare measures—and particularly to practices of public assistance and welfare for the poor (as opposed to insurance-based entitlements or corporate welfare)—we find, conversely, that welfare provision is often accompanied by restrictions, conditions, and disciplinary elements of various kinds. Whether we consider nineteenth- century workhouses, twentieth-century Aid to Families with Dependent Children (AFDC), or twenty-first-century 'workfare', in each case the provision of aid to the poor—and the application procedures required to access such aid—generally involves some penal measure of stigma, humiliation, and hard treatment.

Penal practices flow into, overlap with, and merge together with welfare practices—and vice versa. Distinctions between the two are nominal rather than substantive. This hybridity is born of the fact that both penal and welfare practices are forms of remedial social control that target a suspect population—offenders, delinquents, claimants, etc.—whose dependency upon the public purse is at once a fact to be recognized and a cost to be minimized.[6]

This hybridity is encapsulated in conceptual terms such as 'penal-welfare' and 'penal-welfarism' that have grown out of research in this field. Penal-welfarism and penal-welfare refer to the adoption of welfarist goals *in the criminal justice context* and to *penal* practices designed to promote these welfarist ends. Penal-welfare measures are penal sanctions that contain 'welfarist' (i.e. educational, or therapeutic, or social work) elements. A penal-welfare regime is thus a hybrid criminal justice system involving welfare as well as punishment—with penal-welfare measures operating

[5] Whitman (2003) points out that in nineteenth-century France and Germany, upper class prisoners and those incarcerated for political offences enjoyed quite extensive amenities. The same is true of inmates in debtors' prisons in the UK prior to the reforms of the early nineteenth century (Morris and Rothman 1995).

[6] On the concept of 'dependency' see Fraser and Gordon (1994).

alongside straightforwardly penal forms of sentencing and punishment. Moreover, in penal-welfare systems the rehabilitative treatment of needy, reformable, deserving offenders is generally accompanied by the control and incapacitation of the incorrigible or the dangerous—both modes being facilitated by indeterminate sentencing, classification processes, and the reduced concern for 'proportionality' that are essential elements of penal-welfarism.

'Penal-welfarism' should be distinguished from a purely *welfarist* approach to crime control. In contrast to penal-welfare, a properly welfarist approach would not operate primarily in the context of criminal justice or the penal system. Rather than intervene in the process of punishment, welfarist policies would seek to prevent crime and head off criminal involvement by means of policies such as family support, education and training, employment, and social inclusion that support at-risk families and communities and generally promote social and economic integration.[7]

Public assistance and penal control frequently encounter the same underlying problems—mental illness, addiction, and drug abuse, joblessness, destitution, and homelessness—though they address these problems in different ways and with different effects.[8] And similar debates and dilemmas tend to emerge in both domains. Practices of punishment and welfare always raise questions of culpability and responsibility. Are individual offenders and claimants to blame for their personal circumstances? Are they helpless victims of large-scale social forces or responsible agents who chose their own fates? And in both domains, these moral questions of desert are mixed up with practical problems such as ensuring deterrence and minimizing dependency.

Punishment and welfare both raise issues of reciprocity—giving people what they deserve and ensuring *quid pro quo*—and they each entertain the possibility of compassion in the form of charity, forgiveness, and mercy. They both involve elements of stigma and humiliation that can make individuals feel outcast and degraded, and thereby intensify their deviance or dependency (Matza 1966). They utilize common techniques such as incentives and disincentives, normalization and discipline, reporting and responsibilization and they draw upon similar discourses of personal responsibility, dependency, and desistance (Seeds 2012; Haney 2004). And in both domains, opinion is sharply divided between progressives who blame the social system and seek to maximize the welfare and minimize punishment and conservatives who hold individuals responsible for their own fate and treat them accordingly. Debates about freedom versus determinism and desert versus deterrence are recurring features in both areas, and over time they tend to display parallel histories that shift from individualism to collectivism and back again (Garland 2001).

[7] An example of a welfarist approach to crime control is the Mobilization for Youth projects of the early 1960s that aimed to address crime and delinquency by expanding economic opportunity and providing remedial education, job training, and social services (Kohler-Hausmann 2015; Hinton 2016). As the 1967 President's Crime Commission put it, 'Warring on poverty, inadequate housing, and unemployment, is warring on crime'.

[8] Lappi Seppala (2017) notes that 'welfare states . . . provide workable alternatives to imprisonment' (p. 20) and 'extensive and generous social service networks often function. . .. as effective crime prevention measures'. Gottschalk (2006) notes that extensive welfare states provide important criminal policy options—such as victim compensation and support, criminal injuries compensation, etc.—that are not available in more market-oriented nations such as the US.

There is a final point about the penal-welfare connection that we might draw from the historical literature. In his comparative historical study of correctional criminology and its influence in America and Europe, Michele Pifferi (2016) presents evidence that suggests that a jurisdiction's commitment to penal-welfare practices need not co-vary with its broader commitment to welfare policies and a particular welfare state regime. According to Pifferi, American states such as California had, by the 1960s, established indeterminate sentencing regimes that went much further than those of any European nation. At the same time, America's welfare state institutions were, in general, much less extensive and much less generous than those of the Western Europeans (Garland 2016). The implication is that penal-welfare institutions can, in practice, be disaggregated and one element (such as indeterminate sentencing) can be effectively and extensively established while others (such as social provision for offenders) remain under-developed. Precisely because welfare and social services were—and are—much less developed in America than in Western European nations, it is not surprising that America's commitment to the caring, supportive aspects of penal-welfarism—such as the provision of social services, education, training, and treatment to offenders—has been less extensive (Whitman 2003; Subramanian and Shames 2013) while its embrace of penal-welfarism's risk-management aspects has been much more thoroughgoing. The component elements of penal-welfarism can, it seems, be implemented to differing degrees: such regimes are not a matter of all or nothing.

COMPARATIVE STUDIES

The punishment–welfare link has also, and more recently, been a recurring finding in a developing research literature on comparative penology, though here the connection is a slightly different one. The association being observed is not between penal and welfare modes of governmental thinking and acting, nor is the focus on the emergence of hybrid penal-welfare measures. Instead, comparative inquiry has centred on an observed relationship between the size and generosity of welfare states and the size and severity of penal systems. A growing body of work has converged around a negative correlation thesis in which nations (or sub-national states) with more generous welfare states tend to exhibit lower *per capita* imprisonment rates and more lenient and humane penal systems, while jurisdictions with smaller, meaner welfare states are prone to higher rates of imprisonment and more severe sentencing.[9] It should be said that this punishment–welfare correlation, while frequently observed, is by no means unvarying: results vary across time periods (Beckett and Western 2001) and the association is more significant with respect to extreme cases (such as

[9] See for example Cavadino and Dignan (2006), Lappi-Seppala (2017), Pratt and Eriksson (2013), Lacey and Soskice (2017), Sutton (2004), Downes and Hansen (2006), Beckett and Western (2001), Stucky *et al.* (2005), and Shannon (2013).

the US and Norway) than it is in the middle range (Cavadino and Dignan 2006). But on the basis of what we currently know, the correlation seems empirically robust and conceptually plausible.

These comparative studies are important and will form the basis for significant research in the future. But there are some issues in this literature that merit further attention, particularly the data and metrics used in comparative studies; the conceptions of 'welfare state' and 'penal system' that these studies employ; and the causal mechanisms that are assumed to underpin the empirical correlations of punishment and welfare. In what follows I examine these three topics with the aim of revealing what is at stake and suggesting some possible routes forward. Thereafter, I proceed to discuss the relationship of penal and welfare policies to the problems they purportedly address and the relationship of these policies and problems to larger structures of social and economic organization.

DATA AND METRICS

The first issue to consider is the question of the appropriate data and metrics to be used in comparative studies of punishment and welfare. Most commentators acknowledge that single dimension metrics such as 'rates of imprisonment per 100,000 population', or 'levels of social expenditure as a proportion of GDP' are too crude to get at the character of a penal system or a welfare state, but these easy-to-access metrics nevertheless continue to form the basis for many analyses in comparative penology.

One reason why comparison by reference to a single one-dimensional metric is inadequate has to do with the complexity of penal systems. If the penal systems being compared are internally heterogeneous—and all of them are—then any single metric will tend to gloss over important variation. In the early 1970s, Scottish criminal justice was characterized *both* by a radically welfarist, community-based, non-custodial approach to juvenile offenders—the Children's Hearing System—*and* also by the notorious Segregation Unit in Inverness Prison—'the Cages'—where unruly inmates were subjected to shockingly harsh and degrading conditions (Boyle 1984). A comparison that focused exclusively on the system's rate of imprisonment would miss both of these aspects, and hence much that was significant about the system. And if small systems are mixed in this way, how much more heterogeneous are larger, federated systems such as that of the US, where the imprisonment rates of some states are four times as high as others?

Another reason why such measures are inadequate—to be discussed later in this chapter—has to do with the problem environment in which penal policy develops. Comparisons between penal systems are decontextualized and distorted if penal measures are discussed without reference to the nature and extent of the patterns of crime and violence that trigger penal processes and (indirectly, to some extent) shape penal policy. This is particularly the case when commentators equate higher levels of penal sanctioning with greater 'punitiveness' without discussing the underlying conduct being addressed by penal measures.

The same problem of non-uniformity applies to the analysis of trends and patterns of change. For instance, a recent Sentencing Project report (2015) noted that the recent, widely discussed trend towards reduced rates of imprisonment in the US is, in fact, an aggregation of several more varied state-level trends, with two thirds of the states showing modest reductions and the other third continuing to increase their prison populations. Moreover, as Christopher Seeds (forthcoming) has pointed out, the recent trends towards decarceration in American states are themselves complex, since the reforms that reduce incarceration for 'shallow-end' offenders are often offset by new laws that increase the tariff for more serious offenders—a bifurcation that decreases the overall numbers in prison while increasing the time that some offenders spend there.

Reductive, single-dimension comparisons will consequently be of limited use, providing little more than a starting point for analysis. On the other hand, more in-depth, qualitative measures such as the ten-dimensional analysis of penal 'harshness' developed by Whitman (2003) in his comparative study of the US, France, and Germany are difficult to operationalize for large-scale international comparisons. What then are the appropriate research strategies?

One approach is to adopt the method of in-depth, small-N comparison along the lines of Downes (1988), Barker (2009), Whitman (2003), and Pratt and Eriksson (2013), though these are most effective when strategically related to patterns and puzzles suggested by large-N comparisons (and vice versa).[10] Alternatively, one might persist with the examination of a large number of cases while expanding the set of variables that forms the basis of comparison, as in the important work of Sutton (2004) and Lacey and Soskice (2017).

The issues raised here are problems that most fields of comparative analysis encounter in the early stages of their development. Similar problems characterized early work in comparative social policy. Like the sociology of punishment, comparative social policy (the comparative sociology of welfare states) began with single-factor explanations, pointing to processes of industrialization (Wilensky 1965) or of modernization (Flora and Alber 1976) as the causes of welfare state growth, and using single-metric data—typically government social expenditure as a percentage of GDP—as a basis for comparison. It then entered a phase of theoretical divergence and dispute, notably the contest between functionalist theory—which assumed that welfare states were pragmatic responses to the new economic and social needs of modern society—and theories of class action or power resources—which viewed welfare policies as the outcome of struggles between social classes or political groups (Korpi 1983; Myles and Quadagno 2002). Eventually, a more sophisticated, multi-dimensional, comparative approach emerged, using multiple methods, large-N and small-N studies, and comparative, historical and quantitative data (Baldwin 1990). At the same time, welfare states came to be viewed as an aspect of larger production systems and political economies and were studied within that larger framework (Hall and Soskice 2001). There is every reason to expect that the sociology of punishment will develop in similar ways, with work becoming more comparative, historical, and quantitative, situating penal practice in relation to its underlying problem environment as well as

[10] Small-N studies examine a small number of theoretically selected cases, using thick description and qualitative methods. They enable in-depth understanding but their results are of limited generalizability. Large-N studies examine a large number of cases and use inferential statistics to identify generalizable patterns. See Kohn (1987).

to the larger political process and overarching socio-economic structures that shape its development and functioning.

The methodological limitations that initially affected comparative social policy were eventually mitigated by better theorizations of the core features of welfare regimes and by the development of multi-dimensional metrics designed to measure these characteristics. At the level of welfare state theory, the influential work of Esping-Andersen (1990) shifted attention away from public spending (or 'welfare effort') towards an analysis of the operation and effects of welfare institutions, focusing on the extent to which they de-commodified social relations and redistributed resources; their impact on stratification and solidarity; the relation of state welfare to other sources of welfare; defamilialization effects, and so on. These theoretical advances were subsequently supported by the generation of more extensive and more detailed data-gathering by the Organization for Economic Co-operation and Development (OECD) and later by the development of advanced data sets such as Korpi's Social Citizenship Indicator Program (SCIP) which supplied empirical material for the new questions that comparative scholars were pursuing.[11]

There is reason to hope for similar improvements in comparative penology as the field develops, particularly if its proponents can develop improved theorizations of penal systems and gather more detailed, systematic international data.

CONCEPTIONS OF THE WELFARE STATE

Current work being done in the sociology of punishment and comparative penology does not exhibit a clear or consistent view of what exactly we mean when we talk about 'welfare' or 'the welfare state'. And while there is no need for all scholarship in this field to work with the same conception, a greater level of precision and consistency in the use of key terms and concepts would improve analysis and help avoid confusion.

As a proxy for welfare state spending, some penal-welfare researchers use data on means-tested benefits for the poor even though these benefits constitute a very small part of overall welfare state effort and expenditure. That this is often done without acknowledging that the place of means-tested assistance in the welfare state as a whole runs the risk of reproducing a narrow and somewhat ideological conception of 'welfare'. So for example, when Wacquant (2009) and Beckett and Western (2001) discuss 'welfare' levels and correlate these with rates of imprisonment, the welfare policies they refer to are AFDC, Medicaid, Supplementary Security Income (SSI), and food stamps—all of them means-tested benefits as opposed to social insurance entitlements.[12] As a consequence, the associations they discover are between punishment and public assistance rather than between punishment and 'welfare' more broadly defined. (In most welfare states, the primary beneficiaries of welfare state transfers and social insurance entitlements are middle-class and upper-class employees and their families—see Garland 2016.)

[11] https://snd.gu.se/en/catalogue/series/55, accessed 10 December 2016.

[12] Downes and Hansen (2006) measure welfare by reference to a nation's social spending as a proportion of its GDP.

The overlapping impact of punishment and welfare—and their shared function of governing the poor—has prompted the observation that the 'welfare population' and the 'penal population' are, particularly in neoliberal America, drawn from the same socio-economic groups—that is, poor, urban communities of colour, with the men in prison, the women on welfare.[13] However, one needs to take care not to conflate welfare clients and prison inmates. In the US system (and elsewhere) it is the elderly, women, children, whites, and low-earning working people who are the chief recipients of means-tested benefits recipients—and these are not the demographic groups that compose the majority of the prison population. By contrast, the working age, able-bodied men who are typically sent to American jails and prisons are generally ineligible for social welfare benefits—and were not eligible even prior to the recent neoliberal reforms (Shannon 2013).[14] And of course being in need of welfare support and being convicted of a criminal offence are not equivalent statuses, however much the two categories may, in practice, overlap.

Some writers also give the impression that the 1960s *social* state has become the 1990s *penal* state, the implication being that neoliberalism has effectively abolished the welfare state (Wacquant 2009). In fact, however, even in neoliberal America the welfare state has sustained its primary commitments to the major insurance-based programmes such as Social Security and Medicare as well as its corporate welfare transfers, most of which are hidden in the tax code (Pierson 2010; Garland 2016; Mettler 2011). It is welfare for the poor—above all, social services and support for families with dependent children—that has been most thoroughly recast and retrenched by neoliberal policies: the core institutions of the welfare state have remained firmly in place (Soss *et al.* 2011; Shannon 2013; Garland 2016).

Other writers in comparative penology, notably Cavadino and Dignan (2006), utilize a broader conception of welfare regimes that encompasses the institutions of social insurance, social welfare, and labour market regulation, and distinguish between 'neoliberal', 'conservative corporatist', 'social democratic corporatist', and 'oriental corporatist' regime types. Here the emphasis is on regime variation and on mapping national variations in rates of imprisonment and severity of sentencing on to the various 'worlds of welfare' that have been identified in comparative social policy research (Esping-Andersen 1990). And scholars such as Sutton (2004), De Giorgi (2006), Lacey (2007), and Lacey and Soskice (2017) work with a yet broader conception, focusing on forms of 'political economy' and 'varieties of capitalism' within

[13] See for example Wacquant (2009: 98–9): '[T]he social silhouette of AFDC beneficiaries turns out to be a near-exact replica of the profile of jail inmates save for the gender inversion. . .. the primary clients of the assistantial and carceral wings of the neoliberal state are essentially the two gender sides of the postindustrial working class'. While there is reason to suppose that, at the state and local levels, there is a trade-off between welfare spending and correctional spending, it is unlikely that there is a transfer of people from one institutional setting to another because penal and welfare institutions by and large deal with different age and gender demographics (Guetzkow 2006; Shannon 2013). For important discussions of the gender issues raised by research on punishment and welfare, see Haney (2004; 2010) and McCorkel (2004).

[14] Able-bodied working age men without child dependents in the US are ineligible for the main form of US welfare support—Temporary Assistance to Needy Families (similarly, before 1996 they were ineligible for AFDC). They may be eligible for food stamps and for general assistance but these are discretionary, means-tested, locally administered, and not available in every state. In the US there is no equivalent of the UK Jobseekers' Allowance and associated forms of income support for which such men would be eligible in Britain.

which welfare regimes operate as one institutional complex within a larger socio-economic structure. Here the concept of 'welfare state' includes not just welfare for the poor and social insurance but also the institutions of economic management, collective agreements, corporatist processes, labour relations, and vocational training.

This broader analytic frame has been used to great effect in comparative research on economics, labour relations, and government, but it remains to be seen whether it can be effectively deployed in respect to penal policy—not least because it begs the question of how well integrated (or relatively autonomous) penal systems are with respect to mainstream economic processes. A focus on political economy takes us quite far away from the most important and most proximate determinants of penal outcomes—such as sentencing law and practice; prosecution policy, etc.—making it all the more important to specify the linkages between these two realms. The 'varieties of capitalism' literature was developed to explain the impact of production regimes and styles of economic management on outcomes such as growth, GDP, employment levels, and inequality. But these processes and relationships are not necessarily so illuminating for understanding the fates of those who are mostly outside the labour market, as individuals sent to prison tend to be (Western 2006). The analysis of economic and social stratification—particularly the systematic exclusion from job markets, housing, higher education, and marriage—is undoubtedly important for understanding patterns of crime and poverty and their concentration within specific demographic groups (Wilson 2011; Sampson 1987; 2012; Western 2006). What remains to be discovered is whether these production regimes and styles of economic management also shape punishment and welfare policy.

CAUSAL MECHANISMS

The recent turn to political economy as a framework for explaining penal policy leads me to the final issue I want to discuss: the question of causal mechanisms. We currently lack a clear and settled conception of the mechanisms and processes that produce the observed correlations between welfare states and penal outcomes. What exactly is it about generous welfare states that promotes low rates of imprisonment and more humane penal practices? Are generous welfare systems and lenient penal systems a joint expression of an underlying culture of inclusion and solidarity, as Pratt and Eriksson (2013) suggest? Are generous welfare states a corollary of solidaristic civil society institutions—families, communities, unions, and churches—that serve to prevent crime, thus reducing the need for penal controls (Garland 2017)? Do extensive welfare states—such as Sweden or the Netherlands—empower public sector professionals and pro-social ideologies that in turn inhibit or resist punitive policies (Pratt and Eriksson 2013; Downes 1988)? And why are residual, market-oriented welfare states—such as the US and the UK—associated with high levels of imprisonment and harsh sentencing? Is it because market individualism is associated with low levels of trust and solidarity; because economic and social insecurity generate higher crime levels and more punishment; or for some other reason? Does expenditure on corrections crowd out public spending on welfare (Ellwood and Guetskow 2017)? These are all questions that remain unanswered. If we are to move beyond the intuitive sense that harshness or generosity in one policy sphere is likely to be replicated in others, we will have to discover more about the causal processes that underlie the observed associations.

Some analysts, most notably Loic Wacquant (2009), view punishment and welfare as conjoined aspects of a single governmental strategy, designed to shore up a low-wage labour market by removing alternatives to employment such as living off criminal activities or claiming welfare benefits.[15] This analysis answers the causal question of how welfare policy determines penal outcomes by positing a single strategy that directs *both* penal *and* welfare policy in coordinated ways; thereby viewing both punishment and public assistance primarily as modes of governing the poor. Instead of explaining how penal policy, with its multiple determinants and intrinsic purposes (Garland 1990) comes to be aligned with welfare policy—which is similarly complex in its aims and dynamics (Garland 2016)—this approach eliminates the causal question by assuming that there is a single intelligence, a single strategy, directing both penal and welfare policy in a coordinated manner. The two policy domains co-vary because they are not in fact separate: they are two aspects of a single governmental undertaking—the government of neoliberal insecurity.

The problem with this approach is that there is little empirical evidence to support its central thesis. Wacquant insists that the same political actors who pressed for free-market, small state, 'neoliberal' policies were responsible for the movement towards 'hyper-incarceration' but he is unable to provide empirical evidence of this joint authorship or to explain away the fact that neoliberal principles are implacably opposed to the build-up of a large, expensive state sector, whether devoted to punishment or to anything else.[16] Harcourt (2011) is similarly vague in respect of the causal processes that explain the link between 'free market' economics and 'despotic' forms of punishment such as mass incarceration—a link that he believes to be a historically recurring one.

Problems in specifying causal mechanisms also affect the important work of Lacey and Soskice (2017) who theorize penal practice as a corollary of the varieties of political economy, production regime, and electoral system that characterize the nations in question. Drawing on the 'varieties of capitalism' literature—developed by David Soskice and his colleagues—they hypothesize that countries with 'coordinated market economies' (such as Germany or Sweden) will be less inclined than uncoordinated 'liberal market economies' (such as the US or the UK) to deal with offenders by means of exclusionary penal measures and more inclined to create pathways to employment, education, or training. In keeping with their political economy approach, Lacey and Soskice suggest that the key variable in the relationship between welfare states and penal outcomes is the level of public investment in human capital and that the causal process at work is the patterned action of decision-makers who seek to protect that

[15] Here Wacquant is following in the wake of Rusche and Kirchheimer (1969) and Piven and Cloward (1993). For critical discussions of his thesis, see Abbott (2011) and Lacey (2010).

[16] To say, as some writers do, that 'real-world neoliberalism' disregards these fundamental principles and produces policy outcomes at odds with them is to negate the value of 'neoliberal' as an analytical category. In any case, the (real world) emergence of the campaigning group 'Right on Crime' and its neoliberal critique of big penal government confirms the implausibility of viewing the build-up of a penal state as an aim of neoliberal strategy, properly so-called. See Garland (2001) and Western (2009) on the role of *neoconservative* forces in driving the build-up of the penal state; and on the alliance between neoconservatives and neoliberals within the US Republican and UK Conservative Party coalitions.

social investment.[17] The causal inference is that coordinated market economies—in which educational pathways and employment outcomes are closely coordinated by corporatist agreements—will be less inclined than liberal market economies to use exclusionary penal measures and more inclined to deal with offenders by creating opportunities for 're-entry' or 're-insertion' via employment, education, or training. On this account, America's mass incarceration is an effect of the paucity of governmental policies that invest in human capital and promote integration.

There is much to be said for this way of framing the issues. Both welfare states and criminal justice institutions are nested within political economies and are structured by them to some extent. And it is certainly plausible to suppose that governments that invest heavily in human capital will be disinclined to waste that investment by consigning masses of citizens to penal institutions—particularly since prisons are known to de-skill and de-socialize inmates and reduce their potential for gainful employment (Western *et al.* 2004; Clear and Rose 1998). But even in this more developed account the identification of causal mechanisms remains problematic. Most of the people who end up in the criminal courts—even in relatively integrative societies such as Germany and Sweden—are not those who have benefited from human capital investments but instead those who have dropped out of school and out of lawful employment. So if the authorities hesitate to imprison and exclude these people, this may not be because of the considerations that Lacey and Soskice identify—that is, sunk costs and preserving public investments—but instead because of other factors such as a cultural disposition to value human worth and potential; a negative view of the effectiveness of prisons; or a wish to minimize social divisions and marginalized groups.[18] And if that is the case, the causal processes have more to do with culture than with political economy.

This last point leads me to a final explanatory approach that might be described as a cultural causation thesis. In several studies (Downes 1988; Whitman 2003; Pratt and Eriksson 2013) the correlation between high levels of welfare and low levels of punishment is understood as a cultural effect, brought about by the prevalence of a culture of tolerance, respect for dignity, or by theories of individual causality and responsibility. On these accounts it is the underlying culture and the shaping of official action by culturally embedded values that explains the distinctive character of welfare and punishment in any specific nation. Like the 'conjoined strategy' approach, this cultural account relocates the causal question away from welfare-penal relations to a more basic, third factor—national culture—that causes both. A similar analytical move is involved when welfare and penal policies are explained by underlying social or demographic conditions such as ethnic and religious homogeneity or solidaristic, egalitarian social relations (Sorokin 1957).

[17] 'Human capital' is a measure of the economic value of an employee's skill set. The term is used more generally to describe the stock of skills, knowledge, and experience accumulated by individuals in a population. Human capital investments are resources spent by governments, employers, families, etc. to improve these individual capacities and enable individuals to produce greater economic value for themselves and others. See Becker (2008).

[18] On this basis, one might see American mass imprisonment as an expression of the low social and political value placed on the lives of poor people of colour, above all young black males who lack a high school degree (cf. Western 2006).

The extent to which public authorities deliver punishment or welfare to people, and the harshness or the generosity of these policies, are a measure of the relationship between citizens and the state and between social groups one with another—a measure of the range and depth of social solidarity and respect for human dignity. But as well as being expressive institutions, punishment and welfare have an instrumental aspect, focused on resources, effectiveness, and externalities. Is it more efficient and effective for markets, or families, or employers to provide welfare than for the state to do so? Does it promote crime if we treat offenders instead of punishing them? Do generous welfare systems reduce crime and poverty? Would other arrangements do so more effectively? These are instrumental, means-ends issues and are necessarily involved in the shaping of penal and welfare policies.

It is certainly plausible to suppose that in societies where communal sentiment, fellow-feeling, ethnic identification, or shared citizenship extend to the poor and the marginal, these sentiments will make for a more lenient penal system and more generous welfare. And it also seems plausible to suppose that societies with deep racial, religious, or class divisions—or divisions between nationals and immigrants—will tend to treat outsiders more harshly and minimize their receipt of public resources. The fact that increased immigration to Western European nations has coincided with increasingly severe penal policies may be viewed as evidence of just this tendency (Downes and Swaaningen 2007). So cultural and social accounts are certainly plausible—and we await the detailed historical and ethnographic studies that will allow us to specify these causal processes with more precision.

Cultural processes may, however, be insufficient by themselves to explain temporal or cross-national variations in penal (or welfare) law and practice. Cultural values and legal policy are not always in close alignment. What the public believes and what state officials do are not necessarily consistent; especially in complex multicultural societies. Cultural currents and social values have an impact on official action only to the extent that they are translated into law and policy by means of political and institutional processes. And, depending on the structure of the relevant political institutions, the impact of specific cultures and values may be muted or amplified, thereby enhancing or minimizing their effect on penal and welfare outcomes. Explanations of policy that are phrased in terms of 'culture' or 'public attitudes' are therefore obliged to describe how these social attitudes are, in fact, translated—or not translated—into laws and penal practices.

To this end, writers such as Barker (2009) and Garland (2013) have pointed to the structures and capacities of state institutions as shaping forces in the exercise of penal power, focusing on the nature of 'the penal state' and its relation to other sectors and characteristics of state government. In contemporary societies, penal policy is enacted and administered by specialist governmental institutions that together form the penal state—just as welfare policy is enacted and administered by the complex of agencies that make up the welfare state. And these penal state institutions vary along a number dimensions such as their levels of autonomy; their control of the power to punish; their preferred modes of penal power; and the capacities and resources available to them. In considering the causal processes shaping penal or welfare policy—and, therefore, the relations, affinities and alignments that connect these two domains—we ought to give due attention to the proximate, system-specific causes that enact and enforce policy, as well as the social background causes that shape these actions.

It also seems plausible to suppose that choices about the use of penal measures are shaped by 'supply side' factors as well as 'demand side' ones—by what the penal state is capable of doing, and in the habit of doing, as well as what the public wants it to do. So, for example, penal states in nations with extensive welfare systems are likely to have more forms of soft power (i.e. non-penal forms of influence, management and social control) available to them than do penal states in nations with minimalist forms of welfare provision. In other words, a jurisdiction's penal capacities may be conditioned, in part, by the character and capacities of the welfare state institutions alongside which its penal system operates. The fact that American city and county jails contain large populations of mentally ill, addicted, and homeless persons who, in northern European nations, would be the recipients of social services rather than prison inmates (Gottschalk 2015) is a case in point. And recall that the penal institutions of nations such as Norway are able to utilize the resources of an extensive welfare state infrastructure of social assistance when they choose to manage offenders in the community or resettle them following a period of confinement (Pratt and Eriksson 2013; Lappi Sepalla 2017).

The existence of a dense network of social agencies and welfare practices can provide a platform for the exercise of positive control by the state, acting through schools, community centers, welfare bureaus, social work departments, and so on. An extensive welfare state provides criminal justice authorities with ways of acting at a distance, with forms of soft power, and with an infrastructure of normative controls that they can deploy for control or reform purposes. In nations with a poorly developed social state these methods of extending, projecting, and softening penal power do not exist to the same extent. To deal with problems of crime and violence such nations rely more exclusively on prisons and penal control (Garland 2017). Welfare states shape penal policy ideologically—by establishing conceptions, aims, and values—and also substantively—by providing an operational infrastructure and an array of controls.

PUNISHMENT, WELFARE, AND THE PROBLEMS THEY ADDRESS

In thinking about 'punishment' and 'welfare' it is important to locate them in the context of their societal operation and functioning. The punishment of offenders is not a stand-alone enterprise: it operates as one element within a larger set of ordering practices that also includes policing, crime control, and the maintenance of security. In the same way, public assistance is a constituent element of a larger world of welfare provision that includes not just social insurance and public services but also non-state sources of welfare such as employment, family, and community. And while the institutions of punishment and public assistance each have their own distinctive policies and practices, their overall direction and dynamics are necessarily shaped by the larger systems of which they form a part.

Welfare policy operates alongside and in coordination with the apparatuses of social insurance and social security that form the welfare state. Penal policy is one aspect—together with policing, prosecution, courts, etc.—of criminal justice and social control. Viewing the punishment of offenders as one aspect, among others, of criminal justice; and viewing social welfare as one aspect, among others of economic and social security, helps locate these policies in their proper frameworks and connect them with more mainstream processes. These mainstream social and economic processes are, in fact, doubly determinative of punishment and welfare. In the first instance, they generate the rates and patterns of crime and poverty that form the problem environments addressed by punishment and welfare. And in the second instance, these same social and political processes shape the policies that animate the activities of penal and welfare agencies.

Viewing matters more broadly also reminds us that large shifts in the nature of social governance—such as the shift from the laissez-faire capitalism of the nineteenth century to the welfare states of the twentieth, the rise of neoliberalism, or the emergence of social investment policies in the early twenty-first century—will impact the character and conduct of penal and welfare policy. Punishment and welfare are, in vital respects, practices of governing, even if this aspect of their functioning is cast into shadow by ideologies of 'doing justice' or 'meeting need'. Transformations in the nature of political economy, class relations, and modes of social and economic governance will impact the status of the poor and the forms of government to which they are subjected—including the treatment they receive from penal and welfare agencies (Garland 1985; Piven and Cloward 1993; Wacquant 2009).

If penal and welfare policy are modes of governing individuals, they are also, in some measure, problem-solving policies. But it is vital to bear in mind that problems of crime and poverty are not reducible to 'problem individuals'. Penal sanctions and public assistance target those who fall through the cracks of the mainstream processes of social ordering and social provision. Public assistance addresses problems of indigence and hardship created by the unequal distribution of employment, resources, and life chances. And although individual-level factors play a part in the incidence of poverty, its prevalence is a consequence of labour market processes and the redistributive effects of the state's employment regulations, tax system, and social provision. In much the same way, although criminal involvement is influenced by individual characteristics and choices, a society's rates and patterns of crime and violence result from the operation of social institutions such as families, neighbourhoods, schools, and the labour market, as modified by the effects of policing and punishment.

Most studies of punishment and welfare connect the two policy realms directly, interpreting their commonalities as a matter of policy congruence or elective affinity. On this account, penal and welfare policies exhibit common characteristics and recurring relations because the same policy ideas or political strategies are being applied in different policy domains. And these ideational affinities are, no doubt, part of the story. But neither penal policy nor welfare policy operates independently of socio-economic structures or of the problems of physical and economic insecurity to which these structures give rise. Policy-makers are not free to design any policy they choose. They are instead constrained by the need to address the social problems (primarily criminal offending and poverty) that penal and welfare institutions are expected to ameliorate and control. Policies that fail to manage these problems in ways that are regarded as tolerably effective by political and public audiences will, sooner or later, be subject to demands for change. Ideologies of crime-control and poverty-reduction are, in that sense, real constraints on the institutions that claim to be operating in accordance with them.

Of course the phenomena of crime, poverty, and insecurity become 'social problems'—or not—in ways that are partly determined by the policy-making agencies that define, measure, classify, and address them. And these definitional interactions (between policy and problem) are ongoing and contested. But the phenomena of crime and poverty have external, objective correlates and real world effects that are relatively independent of the policy response, assuming some minimal level of agreement about what is to count as a crime or an instance of poverty. So we can, at least in principle, know on the basis of independent empirical evidence when a policy is failing (because more people experience criminal victimization or impoverishment) and when it is succeeding (because fewer people become crime victims or fall below the poverty line). Data on these issues will always be subject to dispute and all sorts of reporting and recording mediations will affect the numbers. But the point I want to stress is that policy-makers cannot define the issues as they please. Nor can they persuasively claim to be effectively dealing with perceived problems in the face of widespread public experience and evidence to the contrary. The upshot is that any analysis of punishment or welfare needs to pay attention to the problem environment in which these policies operate and to the structural processes that generate the social problems of crime and poverty that punishment and welfare institutions purport to address.

It follows from this that both punishment and welfare ought to be viewed as being, in some part, *remedial*: each one exists to manage a set of problems, variously conceived as crime, violence, and law-breaking or poverty, insecurity, and exclusion. But it also follows that these underlying problems can never be fully controlled by the practices of punishment and welfare because the economic and social processes that generate crime and insecurity are barely addressed by their after-the-fact remediations. The prevalence of economic insecurity is an effect of labour markets, property laws, and the distribution of life chances created by the larger political economy. The prevalence of crime and violence is an effect of the functioning of families, schools, and communities, and the mainstream processes of socialization, social integration, and social control.[19] Penal sanctions and public assistance are post hoc remediations that manage the fall-out of these structures without tackling the generative processes that continue to create the problems. Precisely for that reason, they are always destined to fail to some extent (Hirst 1986; Garland 2016).

[19] For example, in the US more than 60 per cent of black males who fail to graduate from high school spend a period of their lives in prison. The failure of America's public schools to retain and educate poor black men is thus a major factor in the generation of mass incarceration. So too is the failure of the US labour market to find employment for so many inner city black youths. Social failures generate criminal involvement which in turn feeds the growth of penal populations.

To understand the policy options clearly, and to set our expectations for their implications and effects, we ought to view penal policy and welfare policy in their structural context, as remedial practices nested within broader sets of social and economic institutions. And in thinking about punishment and welfare, we ought also to be considering a more fundamental set of interrelated questions—about the relationships between punishment and crime and between welfare and poverty; about the relationship between crime and poverty; and about the social and economic causes of crime and poverty. We tend to think of punishment as being affected by the welfare state whenever social workers get involved or rehabilitative programmes are rolled out. But the biggest impact that welfare states have on penal policy is unseen. It is the tendency of effective welfare state policies to reduce social conflict and to make punishment less central to the repertoires of state control. Welfare states that ensure work, limit inequality, secure families, and support communities are less prone to high levels of crime or extensive use of punishment.[20]

CONCLUSION

Penal systems are shaped by, change with, and flow into systems of social welfare provision and the analysis of these relations has proven to be interesting and important. But a more fundamental question we have to ask is how the overarching political economy works to shape the labour market, the distribution of life chances, and recurring patterns of crime and poverty—while simultaneously shaping the policy responses to these problems that go by the name of punishment and welfare. To the extent that we begin to address these more basic questions, we will succeed in reconnecting the sociology of punishment with the most fundamental issues of social and economic analysis.

The original insight that drives the study of the penal-welfare connection is a recognition that both punishment and welfare are modes of control that are intimately and jointly involved in governing the poor (Rusche and Kirchheimer 1969; Garland 1985). But the institutions of punishment and welfare are merely the front-line, street-level modes of governing. A more fundamental form of governing the poor—and everyone else—operates at the level of political economy and the political decisions that shape labour markets, property laws, tax codes, redistributive policies, and the collective rights of workers and corporations (Hacker and Pierson 2010; Gilens 2012). In our concern to appreciate the fate of those caught up in penal and welfare processes, we ought not to forget the larger processes that shape and manage that collective experience.

[20] See Johnson *et al.* (2007) for an analysis of the crime prevention effects of welfare spending during the Great Depression of the 1930s; and Shannon (2013) for an analysis of the effects of public assistance on crime levels.

SELECTED FURTHER READING

As an antidote to the ideological distortions that often characterize contemporary discussions of 'welfare' and the 'welfare state', readers should consult Garland's *The Welfare State: A Very Short Introduction* (2016). On the rise of welfare states and their implications for punishment and criminal justice, see Donzelot's *The Policing of Families* (1980) and Garland's *Punishment and Welfare* (1985). For comparative surveys, see Downes and Hansen's 'Welfare and Punishment in Comparative Perspective' (2006) and also Beckett and Western's 'Governing Social Marginality' (2001). Garland's *Culture of Control* (2001) traces how (and why) these two domains were simultaneously transformed in the late twentieth century; as does Wacquant's *Punishing the Poor* (2009)—a critical account that owes much to the classic work Piven and Cloward's *Regulating the Poor* (1993). Haney highlights the gendered aspects of penal and welfare policies in 'Gender, Welfare, and States of Punishment' (2004) and Fraser and Gordon, in their classic article 'A Genealogy of Dependency' (1994), trace how gendered power relations suffuse the surface of welfare state practices.

REFERENCES

ABBOTT, A. (2011), 'Review of L. Wacquant, "Punishing the Poor" ', *American Journal of Sociology*, 116(4): 1356–60.

ADLER, M. (2016), 'A New Leviathan? Benefits Sanctions in the 21st Century', *Journal of Law and Society*, 43(2): 195–227.

BALDWIN, P. (1990), *The Politics of Social Solidarity*, New York: Cambridge University Press.

BARKER, V. (2009), *The Politics of Imprisonment*, New York: Oxford University Press.

BECKER, G. (2008), 'Human Capital', in D. R. Henderson (ed.), *The Concise Encyclopedia of Economics*, Indianapolis: The Liberty Fund.

BECKETT, K. and WESTERN, B. (2001), 'Governing Social Marginality: Welfare, Incarceration and the Transformation of State Policy', *Punishment and Society*, 3(1): 43–59.

BONOLI, G. (2005), 'The Politics of the New Social Policies: Providing Coverage Against New Social Risks in Mature Welfare States', *Policy and Politics*, 33(3): 431–49.

BOYLE, J. (1984), *The Pain of Confinement: Prison Diaries*, London: Pan Books.

CAVADINO, M. and DIGNAN, J. (2006), *Penal Systems: A Comparative Approach*, London: Sage.

CLEAR, T. and ROSE, D. (1998), 'Social Capital and Crime: Explaining the Unintended Consequences of Incarceration', *Criminology*, 36: 441–79.

CURTIS, B. (2002), 'Surveying the Social: Techniques, Practices, Power', *Social History*, 35(69): 83–108.

DE GIORGI, A. (2006), *Rethinking the Political Economy of Punishment: Perspectives on Post-Fordism and Penal Politics*, Aldershot: Ashgate.

DONZELOT, J. (1980), *The Policing of Families*, London: Hutchinson.

DOWNES, D. (1988), *Contrasts in Tolerance: Post-War Penal Policies in the Netherlands and England and Wales*, Oxford: Oxford University Press.

DOWNES, D. and HANSEN, K. (2006), 'Welfare and Punishment in Comparative Perspective', in L. McAra and S. Armstrong (eds), *Perspectives on Punishment*, Oxford: Oxford University Press.

DOWNES, D. and SWAANINGEN, R. (2007) 'The Road to Dystopia?: Changes in the Penal Climate of the Netherlands', *Crime and Justice*, 35: 31–71.

ELLWOOD, J. and GUETZKOW, J. (2017), 'Footing the Bill: Causes and Consequences of State Spending on Corrections', in S. Raphael and M. Stoll (eds), *The Increasing Prison Population in the United States*, New York: Russell Sage.

EWALD, F. (1986), *L'Etat providence*, Paris: Bernard Grasset.

ESPING-ANDERSEN, G. (1990), *The Three Worlds of Welfare Capitalism*, Princeton: Princeton University Press.

FLORA, P. and ALBER J. (1976), 'Modernization, Democratization and the Development of Welfare States in Western Europe', in P. Flora and A. Heidenheimer (eds), *The Development of Welfare States in Europe and America*, Boston: Little, Brown & Co.

FOUCAULT, M. (1977), *Discipline and Punish: The Birth of the Prison*, London: Allen Lane.

FRASER, N. and GORDON, L. (1994), 'A Genealogy of Dependency: Tracing a Keyword of the US Welfare State', *Signs*, 19(2): 309–36.

GARLAND, D. (1985), *Punishment and Welfare: A History of Penal Strategies*, Gower: Aldershot.

GARLAND, D. (1990), *Punishment and Modern Society: A Study in Social Theory*, Oxford: Oxford University Press.

GARLAND, D. (2001), *The Culture of Control: Crime and Social Order in Contemporary Society*, Oxford: Oxford University Press.

GARLAND, D. (2010), *Peculiar Institution: America's Death Penalty in an Age of Abolition*, Cambridge, MA: Harvard University Press.

GARLAND, D. (2013), 'Penality and the Penal State', *Criminology*, 51(3): 475–517.

GARLAND, D. (2016), *The Welfare State: A Very Short Introduction*, Oxford: Oxford University Press.

GARLAND, D. (2017), 'Penal power in the US: Forms, functions and social foundations', *Journal of the British Academy*, 5: 1–35.

GILENS, M. (2012), *Affluence and Influence: Economic Inequality and Political Power in America*, Princeton: Princeton University Press.

GODDARD, T. (2012), 'Post-welfare risk managers? Risk, crime prevention and the responsibilization of community-based organizations', *Theoretical Criminology*, 16(3): 347–63.

GOTTSCHALK, M. (2006), *The Prison and the Gallows: The Politics of Mass Incarceration in America*, New York: Cambridge University Press.

GOTTSCHALK, M. (2015), *Caught: The Prison State and the Lockdown of America*, Princeton: Princeton University Press.

GUETZKOW, J. (2006), 'Bars or Butter: Understanding the Prison-Welfare Tradeoff', http://citation.allacademic.com/meta/p_mla_apa_research_citation/1/1/0/4/5/p110455_index.html, accessed 9 December 2016.

GUSTAVSON, K. (2011), *Cheating Welfare: Public Assistance and the Criminalization of Welfare*, New York: New York University Press.

HACKER, J. and PIERSON, P. (2010), *Winner Take All Politics: How Washington Made the Rich Richer and Turned its Back on the Middle Class*, New York: Simon and Schuster.

HALL, P. and SOSKICE, D. (eds) (2001), *Varieties of Capitalism: The Institutional Foundations of Comparative Advantage*, Oxford; Oxford University Press.

HANEY, L. (2004), 'Gender, Welfare, and States of Punishment', *Social Politics*, 11(3): 333–62.

HANEY, L. (2010), *Offending Women: Power, Punishment and the Regulation of Desire*, Chicago: University of Chicago Press.

HARCOURT, B. (2011), *The Illusion of Free Markets: Punishment and the Myth of Natural Order*, Cambridge, MA: Harvard University Press.

HINTON, E. (2016), *From the War on Poverty to the War on Crime: The Making of Mass Incarceration in America*, Cambridge MA: Harvard University Press.

HIRST, P. Q. (1986), 'On the Concept of Punishment', in P. Q. Hirst, *Law, Socialism and Democracy*, London: Routledge.

JOHNSON, R., KANTOR, S., and FISHBACK, P. (2007), 'Striking at the Roots of Crime: The Impact of Social Welfare Spending on Crime During the Great Depression', NBER Working Paper 12825.

KOHLER-HAUSMANN, J. (2015), 'Guns and Butter: The Welfare State, the Carceral State and the Politics of Exclusion in the Postwar United States', *The Journal of American History*, 101(1): 87–99.

KOHN, M. (1987), 'Cross National Research as a Research Strategy', *American Sociological Review*, 52(6): 713–31.

KORPI, W. (1983), *The Democratic Class Struggle*, London: Routledge.

LACEY, N. (2007), *The Prisoners' Dilemma: Political Economy and Punishment in Contemporary Democracies*, Cambridge: Cambridge University Press.

LACEY, N. (2010), 'Differentiating between Penal States', *British Journal of Sociology*, 61(4): 778–94.

LACEY, N. and SOSKICE, D. (2017), 'American Exceptionalism in Crime, Punishment and Disadvantage', in K. Reitz (ed.), *American Exceptionalism in Crime and Punishment*, New York: Oxford University Press.

LAPPI SEPPALA, T. (2017), 'American Penal Exceptionalism in Comparative Perspective', in K. Reitz (ed.), *American Exceptionalism in Crime and Punishment*, New York: Oxford University Press.

MATZA, D. (1966), 'Poverty and Disrepute', in Merton and Nisbet (eds), *Contemporary Social Problems*, 4th edn, New York: Houghton, Miffin, Harcourt.

MCARA, L. (2006), 'Welfare in Crisis? Key Developments in Scottish Youth Justice', in J. Muncie and B. Goldson (eds), *Comparative Youth Justice*, London: Sage.

MCCORKEL, J. (2004), 'Criminally Dependent? Gender, Punishment and the Rhetoric of Welfare Reform', *Social Politics* 11(3): 386–410.

MELOSSI, D. (2015), *Crime, Punishment and Migration*, London: Sage.

METTLER, S. (2011), *The Submerged State: How Invisible Government Policies Undermine American Democracy*, Chicago: University of Chicago Press.

MOREL, N., PALIER, B., and PALME J. (2012), *Towards a Social Investment Welfare State*, London: Policy Press.

MORRIS, N. and ROTHMAN, D. (eds) (1995), *The Oxford History of the Prison*, New York: Oxford University Press.

MYLES, J. and QUADAGNO, J. (2002), 'Political Theories of the Welfare State', *Social Service Review*, March, 34–57.

PIERSON, P (2010), 'Welfare State Reform over the (Very) Long Term', https://www.youtube.com/watch?v=ST7IxbNjrJQ, accessed 9 December 2016.

PIFFERI, M. (2016), *Reinventing Punishment: A Comparative History of Criminology and Penology*, Oxford: Oxford University Press.

PIVEN, F. and CLOWARD, R. (1993), *Regulating the Poor: The Functions of Public Welfare, updated edition*, New York: Vintage.

PRATT, J. and ERIKSSON, A. (2013), *Contrasts in Punishment: An Explanation of Anglophone Excess and Nordic Exceptionalism*, London: Routledge.

President's Commission on Law Enforcement and the Administration of Justice (1967), *The Challenge of Crime in a Free Society*, Washington, DC: Government Printing Office.

Rusche, G. and Kirchheimer, O. (1969), *Punishment and Social Structure*, New York: Columbia University Press.

Sampson, R. (1987), 'Urban black violence: The effects of male joblessness and family disruption', *American Journal of Sociology*, 93(2), 348–83.

Sampson, R. (2012), *Great American City: Chicago and the Enduring Neighborhood Effect*, Chicago: University of Chicago Press.

Seeds, C. (2012), 'The Three Levels of Welfare and Punishment Analysis' (unpublished paper).

Seeds, C. (forthcoming), 'Bifurcation Nation: American Penal Policy in Late Mass Incarceration', *Punishment & Society*.

Sentencing Project (2015), *US Prison Population Trends*, http://www.sentencingproject.org/publications/u-s-prison-population-trends-1999-2013-broad-variation-among-states-in-recent-years/, accessed 9 December 2016.

Shannon, S. K. S. (2013), 'Does the Right Hand Know What the Left Hand is Doing? General Assistance Welfare, Crime and Punishment in the United States', PhD dissertation, University of Minnesota.

Simon, J. (1993), *Poor Discipline: Parole and the Social Control of the Underclass*, Chicago: University of Chicago Press.

Sorokin, P. (1957), *Social and Cultural Dynamics*, Boston: Porter Sargent.

Soss, J., Fording, R., and Schram, S. (2011), *Disciplining the Poor: Neoliberal Paternalism and the Persistent Power of Race*, Chicago: University of Chicago Press.

Stucky, T., Heimer, K., and Lang, J. (2005), 'Partisan Politics, Electoral Competition and Imprisonment: Analysis of States over Time', *Criminology*, 43(1): 211–48.

Subramanian, R. and Shames A. (2013), *Sentencing and Prison Practice in Germany and the Netherlands*, New York: Vera Institute.

Sutton, J. (2004), 'The Political Economy of Imprisonment in Affluent Western Democracies, 1960-1990', *American Sociological Review*, 69(2): 170–89.

Taylor-Gooby, P. (2004), *New Social Risks and New Welfare States*, Oxford: Oxford University Press.

Wacquant, L. (2009), *Punishing the Poor: The Neoliberal Governance of Social Insecurity*, Durham, NC: Duke University Press.

Western, B. (2006), *Punishment and Inequality in America*, New York: Russell Sage.

Western, B. (2011), 'Poverty Politics and Crime Control in Europe and America', *Contemporary Sociology*, 40(3): 283–6.

Western, B., Weiman, D. and Patillo, M. (eds) (2004), *The Impacts of Incarceration on Families and Communities*, New York: Russell Sage.

Whitman, J. Q. (2003), *Harsh Justice: The Growing Divergence between America and Europe*, New York: Oxford University Press.

Wilensky, H. (1965), *Industrial Society and Social Welfare*, New York: Russell Sage.

Willrich, M. (2003), *City of Courts: Socializing Justice in Progressive Era Chicago*, New York: Cambridge University Press.

Wilson, W. J. (2011), 'Being Poor, Black and American: The Impact of Political, Economic and Cultural Forces', *American Educator*, Spring, 35(1): 10–23.

CHAPTER ACKNOWLEDGEMENTS

I am grateful to Mike Adler, Christopher Seeds, and Lesley McAra for helpful comments and to the Filomen D'Agostino and Max E. Greenberg Research Fund of NYU School of Law for its support.

4

PENAL POPULISM AND EPISTEMIC CRIME CONTROL

Ian Loader and Richard Sparks

INTRODUCTION

The debate about crime and its control has in recent years featured regular appearances by actors voicing public demands for greater security and punishment on the one hand and those seeking to prevent crime by means of some kind of technical or expert intervention on the other. These positions—which are often termed populism and technocracy—appear to press conflicting claims. Populists purport to speak for 'victims', or 'law-abiding citizens' who have been ill-served by 'out-of-touch' elites—whether they be remote government officials, high-minded lawyers, unworldly academics, or unaccountable criminal justice professionals. They demand that the sturdy common sense of 'ordinary people', or the 'silent majority', be reintroduced to the criminal justice system. Proponents of technocracy conversely worry that crime policy risks being unduly influenced by vote-chasing politicians and mass media demonization and driven by an emotive irrationalism concerned more with symbolic display than effective performance in tackling crime. They seek to counter the claims of populism by supporting, or creating, insulated institutions that enhance the power and influence of experts/knowers thereby generating rational crime policy and evidence-based practice. Often today, discussions about how to respond to crime appear to be a contest between these two seemingly diametrically opposed positions.

These ways of thinking about and acting upon crime have of late received considerable attention in criminology. In the case of populism, research has generally sought to identify the social conditions that have led to the emergence of penal populism as a force (such as declining deference and loss of trust in authority) or has tried to explain the role of populism in generating the penal excess experienced across the USA and the Anglophone world in recent decades (e.g. Bottoms 1995; Pratt 2007). With few exceptions (Garland 2017), such analysis has been conducted with critical intent: in fact, the very use of the label 'populism' typically carries a strong whiff of disapproval. By contrast, accounts of technocratic or evidence-based thinking more commonly hail from its proponents. These have generally taken the form of reports of research on 'what works, what doesn't work, and what is promising' in crime prevention; stipulations of how evaluation in criminology should be done, or proposals for designing institutions that can assemble, assess, and disseminate evidence and thereby inform the making of rational crime policy (e.g. Sherman *et al.* 2002; Sherman 2009; Weisburd and Neyroud 2011).

Our purpose in this chapter is not of this kind: we aim neither to trash populism and technocracy as approaches to crime control, nor to champion them. Nor are we primarily interested in discovering the causes of populism and technocracy or assessing their respective influence over penal policy in different jurisdictions. Instead, we want to examine populism and technocracy as political ideologies in the sense outlined in the work of Michael Freeden (1998, 2003, 2013). For Freeden a political ideology is a form of 'thought-behaviour' that shapes how individuals and groups respond to and act in the world. As such, ideologies function as 'a set of ideas, beliefs, opinions and values' that 'compete over providing and controlling plans for public policy . . . with the aim of justifying, contesting or changing the social and political arrangements and processes of a political community' (Freeden 2003: 32). We propose to treat populism and technocracy as ideologies in this sense. In so doing, we want to subject them to a 'political evaluation' that reconstructs and reappraises their claims as candidate answers to the question of how to build a 'better politics of crime' (Loader and Sparks 2010: ch. 5). This reconstructive element of this task entails that we ask of populism and technocracy the following questions: What are the constitutive concepts and central claims of each position? To what visions of good crime governance (and the good society) are their proponents committed? How do they understand—and what resources can they offer to—the project of developing democratically legitimate practices of crime control? In sum, what is the 'normative character' of populism and technocracy (Urbaniti 2014: 135)?[1]

The task of providing a best case interpretation of the visions of crime control to be found in populist and technocratic ideologies takes up most of the ensuing chapter. We embark, in the next section, on an assessment of populism as a general mode of political intervention and especially its offspring penal populism. In the subsequent section, we describe and appraise the claims pressed on behalf of technocracy—or what we prefer to call 'epistemic crime control'. This clarification of what is at stake in disputes between populism and technocracy underpins our principal evaluative claim, to which we turn in conclusion. We dispute the assumption that they are competing alternatives. We argue, instead, that populism and technocracy are connected pathologies of our contemporary anti-political malaise, both of which 'disfigure' (Urbaniti 2014) the ideal and practice of democracy by neglecting the normative force of democratic procedures in the making of legitimate crime control.

[1] A fuller elaboration and defence of subjecting crime control practices to a 'political mode of evaluation' can be found in Loader and Sparks (2016). The present chapter forms part of a wider project on which we are embarking that investigates how competing political traditions think about what is involved in making and imagining a better politics of crime and its regulation. Our guiding assumption is that such a politics does not simply need reliable evidence about what works in crime control; it also needs new ideas. We have to journey into political thought.

POPULISM AND PENAL POPULISM

To secure a better handle on *penal* populism it is helpful to begin outside of criminology, with populism proper. What is populism? What kind of ideology is it? To what political family does it properly belong? These are not easy questions to answer. Unlike other political ideologies (e.g. conservatism, liberalism, feminism, environmentalism), populism has no founding figures or classic texts: one cannot isolate and consult a body of avowedly populist political thought. Its concerns, moreover, tend to be local and particular rather than global or universal, as do its heroes (Stanley 2008). Populism also carries divergent historical resonances and contemporary meanings across different parts of the globe—it has, for example, in both North and South America, a connection to progressive politics that is almost entirely absent in Europe where it is associated with right-wing, xenophobic political movements. Additional difficulties flow from what Canovan (2005: 81) describes as the 'seldom comfortable' relations that exist between populists and the academy. Political actors rarely self-identify as 'populists'. Rather, populism is a label fixed on politicians or political parties by external observers, usually as a term of abuse. It is also a censure applied by members of a social group—intellectuals—who are themselves a prime target of populists' vitriol.[2] Finally, it is sometimes claimed that populism possesses insufficient heft to warrant being called an ideology at all; it can simply be understood as a style of political communication (Taggart 2000), a mode of discursive framing that offers alluringly simple solutions to complex problems couched in a language that people understand (Aslanidis 2015).

Yet there is more to populism than that. It is possible to detect in the political movements and figures to whom the label populist is commonly applied—the Front National in France, the Austrian Freedom Party, the United Kingdom Independence Party, the Tea Party, Donald Trump, and so on—a recurring cluster of claims that express an underlying ideology. In Freeden's terms populism is a 'thin' ideology (Freeden 2003: 98–100; see also Canovan 2002; Stanley 2008). It is 'thin' in so far as it offers no overarching vision of society and lacks the ambition and conceptual capacity to address the full gamut of political problems—it has what Freeden (2003: 98) calls a 'restricted morphology'. Populism is an ideology because it 'gives precise meaning and priority to certain key concepts of political discourse' (Abts and Rummens 2007: 408) in ways that render it distinctive and coherent as an approach to political life. In particular, populism can be understood as a 'moralistic imagination of politics' (Müller 2014: 485) constituted by three principal claims.

First, populists speak for 'the people' imagined and depicted as a homogeneous entity. Their core claim, as Müller (2015) puts it, is that 'they—and only they—properly represent the authentic, proper and morally pure people'. As such, 'the people' is

[2] Populist movements—or perhaps more precisely, political movement that deploy populist tropes—do sometimes have their house intellectuals. For example, pro-death penalty lobbies, or pro-gun groups, or those arguing in favour of more severe prison sentences, often claim in aid statistics or research produced by various think-tanks, of differing degrees of respectability (Wacquant 2009). Populist rhetoric is not immune to the attraction of the 'killer fact'. In general, however, populists and intellectuals stand in tension and often in open conflict.

a fiction, an 'empty signifier' (Laclau 2005) which is filled out across different contexts in more substantive ways: leftist populists may identify the people as the working-class exploited by a property-owning elite; right-wing populists tend to characterize the people in ethno-racial terms and defend their interests against minorities or migrants. Defending the people tends therefore to involve affirming the correctness and rights of majorities over those of minorities. 'Nevertheless, what all populisms have in common is an appeal to the notion of "the people" as ultimate source of legitimacy' (Canovan 2005: 80).

Secondly, the people are understood to be in a mutually antagonistic relation to a malign, self-interested elite. The defining distinction populism makes is moral: the 'pure' people are set against a 'corrupt' (or at any rate privileged) elite (Mudde and Kaltwasser 2013). Elites can be constituted by election (politicians) or selection (government officials) or can be 'opinion-formers in the academy and the media' (Canovan 1999: 3). In all cases, they are depicted as a remote, 'out-of-touch', politically correct 'establishment', working for themselves or else championing the claims of unpopular minorities, sometimes through benign but misguided and unworldly motives. The core claim is that elites seek to narrow the limits of what, politically, can be said and done in ways that are contemptuous of the concerns of ordinary people and unable to advance their aspirations. Hence, Nigel Farage's speech claiming victory for the 'Brexit' side in the recent UK referendum on membership of the European Union, in which he proclaimed that this was a victory 'for the real people, for the ordinary people, for the decent people', was a classic piece of populist rhetoric.

Thirdly, populism is committed to the ideal of popular sovereignty. The purpose of politics is to express and enact the general will which populists hold to be unified and transparent. The will of the people is capable of being advanced by strong, charismatic leadership—by leaders unafraid to say out loud what people are really thinking. Populists object to the grubby process of bargaining and accommodation in which politicians routinely engage. They exude impatience with human rights, institutional checks and balances, and unelected bodies—all of which obstruct the will of the people.[3] But, although populist politicians sometimes support direct democratic mechanisms such as referenda, populism need not involve a principled commitment to public participation. Rather, the people who are invoked are often a passive audience—the ordinary, decent people 'at home', as Mrs Thatcher was wont to say. This leads to the charge that the people of populist discourse are a 'reactive mass of followers' (Urbaniti 2014: 157), whose interests and concerns can be organically discerned and directly represented by a charismatic leader (Wolkenstein 2015). Populism is, in this regard, frequently a politics of personality.

Populism can, then, be understood as an ideology that appeals to, and mobilizes, 'the people' versus 'elites'. It tends to favour a binary worldview. It is an ideology that sets the 'pure many' against the 'corrupt few', one that conceives politics as matter of 'us' versus 'them', a practice constituted—in Schmittian (2007) terms—by the naming of 'friends' and 'enemies'. Populism is, we might provisionally observe, a force for

[3] As Canovan (1999: 6) puts it: 'populists love transparency and distrust mystification: they denounce backroom deals, shady compromises, complicated procedures, secret treaties, and technicalities that only experts can understand'.

'simplification and polarization' (Urbaniti 2014: 131). What though can this distillation of the conceptual architecture of populism tell us about the more local phenomenon that has come to be known as 'penal populism'?

The first thing to say is that it should come as little surprise that 'crime' (and a cluster of connected issues to do with security, terrorism, migration, and border control) figures often and prominently among the issues around which populist actors and movements agitate. Indeed, the rise of the 'new populism' across Europe over the last two decades has been centrally animated by impassioned demands to defend 'us', and 'our society', from 'outsiders' who threaten 'our way of life'—demands whose rhetoric tends wilfully to conflate categories such as criminal, terrorist, migrant, and Muslim (e.g. Berezin 2009). As Durkheim taught us over a century ago, crime is an inescapably emotive, symbolically charged issue, a vehicle through which a political community's (moral) boundaries are challenged, negotiated, and affirmed. This helps to account for why crime is never very far from the mobilizing rhetoric of xenophobic populist movements. A large part of the appeal of penal populism also lies in the fact that it acknowledges and embraces crime's affectivity.

It is nonetheless the case that 'penal populism' (as it has come to be understood within criminology) has not simply entailed a situated application of populist logic to questions of crime and punishment. Rather, what one finds in the penal field are 'partial embodiments' (Abts and Rummens 2007: 420) of that wider logic, what one might call intimations of the populist ideology just described. To be sure, penal populism has involved new social actors (notably victims' movements) demanding that the voice of ordinary people are listened to by penal elites. But this local variant has also—and arguably mainly—assumed the form of what Canovan (2005) calls 'politicians' populism', by which she means the deployment by political insiders (those who are typically the object of populist ire) of claims to defend the people against 'the establishment' with a view to sustaining coalitions of support and shoring-up their legitimacy as leaders, or more commonly perhaps, as challengers. Our diagnosis of penal populism must remain attentive to these dynamics. For these reasons crime and punishment are favoured topics for those politicians whose strategy involves depicting themselves as atypical of the ruling group and thus more intuitively connected to real people's real concerns and as sharing their common sense about the world.

The analysis of penal populism has—as with populism proper—largely been conducted by criminologists with a commitment to the sorts of rational policy-making and liberal crime policy that populism has assailed—criminologists, as Garland (2017) has observed, who typically feel little obligation to justify their own preferences or to explain why the public *ought* to defer to experts. Such analysis has in the main deemed penal populism as a pathology and remained rather tone-deaf to the character of its appeal. The literature on penal populism has sought to identify its conditions of emergence, assess its contribution to punitive excess, and figure out what needs to be done to counter it (e.g. Roberts *et al.* 2002; Pratt 2007; Green 2008; Tonry 2010). Rather less attention has been devoted to studying it 'in the first instance as a rhetoric expressing an ideology, without yet making any further claims as to its wider influence' (Jones 2010: 332). It is to that latter task that we turn here.

In the first place, penal populism denigrates liberal-minded, expert-led criminal justice and its remote rationality. Pressed by the tabloid media, by assorted groups of victims, and by politicians from the 1990s onwards, populist ideology railed against the organizing assumptions and working methods of what in England and Wales was a hitherto dominant group of 'Platonic guardians' (Loader 2006)—what one former Conservative Home Secretary, Michael Howard, called 'the criminal justice establishment'. It also took issue with what it represented as the vested interests and complacency of criminal justice professionals. Penal populism challenged the substantive concerns of penal elites with due process rights and rehabilitation; their failure to recognize, still less stem, the relentless rise in volume crime; their behind closed doors, we-know-best methods of administering justice, and their inability to empathize with, or attend to, the anxieties of the public and experiences of victims. In all these ways, penal populism casts aspersions upon the claims of penal experts. More radically, it takes issue with the very idea that there is something (valuable) called 'expertise' in criminal justice, refusing to accept that the issues at stake are that complex, especially in respect of sentencing.[4]

Secondly, penal populism presses the claims of those groups excluded from influencing criminal justice by bureaucratic and professional elites. This is done in a number of idioms. It most often takes the form of a demand that victims' voices are heard—that they are involved more fully in the criminal justice process (e.g. by making impact statements about the harm caused by 'their' offender) or given prominent roles in the making of relevant law and policy.[5] It can also give rise to objections to the 'wrong' people being prosecuted, notably 'law-abiding' citizens 'defending' their own property (see Farmer 2006). This element of penal populism more generally takes the form of demands that the experience and plain-speaking wisdom of 'hard-working' or 'law-abiding' citizens is listened to. Or it can simply be a demand to give 'public opinion' a much larger place in determining crime and penal policy: on the assumption that this can be read-off from newspaper headlines, or located in the inboxes of parliamentarians, or captured in opinion polls. It has been a common complaint of criminologists that such instruments fail to capture the complexity of what different 'publics' really think about crime (Hough and Roberts 2005; Turner 2016).

Penal populism has, thirdly, insisted upon the properly emotive nature of crime (making crime control affective rather than effective, or preferring to assume that these will coincide) and the inherently moral quality of punishment. In respect of the former, populism seeks to counter-pose the 'cool', sanitized discourse of 'the system' with one that recognizes crime control as an expressive practice—a field where outbursts of anger, resentment, blame, censure, demonization and the like are not merely to be expected, but to be treated as legitimate. In respect of the latter, populism not only evinces 'a strong belief in the propriety of penal power' (Jones 2010: 342); it tends to weigh up the effectiveness of police and penal actions in terms of delivering

[4] Although in so far as penal populism entails strong imaginative identification with the idea of policing and punishment this on occasion entails some kind of deferral to the 'knowledge' that criminal justice professionals have about criminal threats and how to respond to them, especially that possessed by police officers 'on the ground'. On the other hand if very senior police officers are seen as having 'lost touch' they may lose much of this credit.

[5] In England and Wales, this has given rise to the appointment of some high-profile crime victims to positions as government advisors, or to a place in the House of Lords.

pain to criminal others and offering symbolic reassurance to the 'law-abiding majority'.[6] David Garland (2017) may be right to argue that there is a contingent rather than internal relation between populism and punitiveness. But these dimensions of penal populist ideology (not least an 'us' v. 'them', zero-sum conception of relations between offenders and victims) indicate that there is an affinity between its core commitments and representational style and certain kinds of transparent and symbolic modes of control—visible patrolling, zero-tolerance, truth-in-sentencing, mandatory minimum sentences, sexual offender notification statutes, and so on. It is no accident that populists tend not to lobby for rehabilitation and parole.[7]

How then is one to assess the conception of good (crime) governance found in populist ideology? What resources, if any, does it bring to the building of a better politics of crime? We return to this issue in the conclusion. But for now two broad interpretations can helpfully be introduced. The first appraises populism positively as a force with potential to expose and make good the failings of democracy, while fretting about its anti-liberal commitments. This judgement rests on a 'two-strand' theory of constitutional democracy (Canovan 2005: 83-90; Abts and Rummens 2007) viewed as a delicate balance between processes of public will formation, expression, and consent (the 'democratic pillar') and rule of law constraints on the exercise of power and protections for minorities (the 'liberal pillar'). The affirmative view of populism sees it as a vehicle for giving voice to anger and resentments from below, for including new groups in the democratic process, for mobilizing the 'disruptive noise' of the powerless in ways that demand access to the political system (e.g. Arditi 2003; Laclau 2005). In so doing, populism arguably recognizes that democratic legitimacy today depends at least in part on what Rosanvallon (2011: chs 10–11) calls the 'politics of proximity'—the capacity of politicians to display solidarity with the suffering of ordinary citizens. In its demand to make politics accessible and transparent populism offers a critique of the way in which actually existing democracy operates to keep the people at a distance from government (Müller 2014: 490). In this regard, populism presents as a resource of hope. As Canovan (1999) argues, populism refuses to accept that democracy can only be a 'pragmatic' mechanism for handling social conflicts without resort to violence, but commits itself instead to democracy's 'redemptive' promise: to a conception of democratic politics as a conduit for delivering a better world.

Faint echoes of this political evaluation can be found here and there in the literature on penal populism. Mick Ryan (2003) offered an early appreciation of how populism opened up penal policy to the 'voice of the people' in ways that countered the condescension towards 'the public' found among metropolitan penal elites. More recently, Albert Dzur (2012: ch. 2) has made a distinction between 'thin' populism of the kind that has dominated US penal politics over recent decades, and a more promising 'thick' populism concerned with deepening civic action and public participation

[6] Though in a recent analysis of 'populist leniency', Richard Jones (2010) describes how this affective and largely unconditional attachment to penal power is called into question when such power is directed against members or representatives of that majority, at which point populist politics can suddenly rediscover the value of rights and due process (see also Farmer 2006).

[7] For this reason it remains one of the more testing puzzles for liberal and progressive penal strategies to wonder how, and under what conditions, it may be possible to build popular support for less punitive or more radical interventions.

in the justice sphere. Even David Garland's (2017) sceptical recent treatment of penal populism reminds us that it sharply forces onto the agenda a question that penal elites have been trained to overlook: that of the proper relation in the making of crime policy between professional expertise and community sentiment.

The worry about populism expressed in this interpretation is not, then, about its democratic credentials. Rather, it concerns the threat that populism explicitly poses to constitutional democracy's 'liberal pillar'. It highlights the impatience that populist politics evinces towards the rule of law, minority rights, the dispersal of power, indeed to a whole range of mechanisms viewed as obstructions to the people's will. This anti-liberalism has also long underpinned the dismay expressed by criminologists in the face of penal populism (e.g. Freiberg and Gelb 2013), along with the view that populism's demotic mobilization of opinion 'generates policies that have little relation to penological wisdom and decency' (Garland 2017: 24).

A critique of populism's anti-liberalism is shared by the second appraisal we want to introduce. But this second appraisal calls sharply into question the idea that (penal) populism is a friend of democracy. This account of populism departs from the 'two-strand' theory of democracy that underpins the first. Instead, it theorizes democratic procedures and individual rights as 'co-original' foundations of constitutional democracy (Habermas 1998), 'both aspects of which are essential because they allow a political community to remain open and to realize the freedom of its citizens' (Abts and Rummens 2007: 413). From this starting point, what is striking about populism—in crime policy as elsewhere—is its drive to close down spaces of active political deliberation. By seeking to mobilize 'the people' around leaders, rather than actively engage citizens in democratic dialogue, populism replaces the revisable discursive construction of democratic opinion with the effort to concentrate power in the name of the 'unified' masses (Urbaniti 2014). Rather than promoting an extension of democracy, populism seeks to occupy the 'empty space' of politics (Lefort 1988) and fill it with an anti-pluralist decisionism. It is this claim—that populism is not a force for democratizing the politics of crime, but an agent of democratic degeneration—that we develop in conclusion.

EPISTEMIC CRIME CONTROL

Technocracy appears to have a relatively poor claim to be considered as an ideology. For a start, it lacks the trademark 'ism'. It barely if ever features in textbook overviews of the ideological landscape. It rarely mobilizes social groups or the support of political movements. It is also—along with populism—one of the most 'loosely defined' terms in political sociology (Centano 1993: 309; for a review, see Gunnell 1982). Technocracy can nonetheless be interpreted in ways that bring it within shouting distance of Freeden's (2003: 32) definition of an ideology discussed at the outset of the chapter. It can be characterized as a set of beliefs—or at least a 'shared mentality or cognitive framework' (Centano 1993: 312)—that compete over public policy and justify or contest the social and political arrangements of a political community. In this respect, technocracy is an ideology that disavows ideology, making use instead 'of value-free, objective criteria for making decisions' and creating 'depoliticized' solutions to public problems (ibid.: 311). Central to these solutions is what Centano calls 'an ideology of method' (ibid.: 312). Technocracy claims that public policy outcomes will be improved under systems of rule in which experts take decisions in place of politicians (Pastorella 2015), or at least in conditions where political actors scrupulously follow the best available advice deriving from expert evidence. This can take the form of technocratic government (in which experts are invited to become government ministers), or it can entail the delegation of policy fields to selected groups of specialists—as has happened in several jurisdictions in recent years in respect of the transfer of monetary policy to independent central banks.

The idea of rule by knowers, of preferring expert calculation to the 'vices' of partisanship and political competition, has a lineage that can be traced back to Plato's republic of philosopher guardians. Over the course of the twentieth century it either resurfaced within, or possessed a close affinity with, various renditions of elitist democracy, from Lippmann (1922), to Schumpeter (1942), to Sartori (1962). The delegation of political authority to experts has, moreover, undergone something of a renaissance in recent years. We have witnessed both the construction of a new architecture of outsourced and delegated governance designed to make markets 'safe' from intrusion by democratic publics (Roberts 2010), as well as renewed attention to the idea that technocratic government is necessary to rebuild economic order following the global financial crisis of 2008. The promotion of expert calculation and technique as ways of delivering better crime prevention and penal policy outcomes can helpfully be understood in this larger historical and intellectual frame.

This approach to crime has gained renewed traction in recent years in criminology and related policy sciences, as well as among police and criminal justice practitioners. It has done so often in response and overt opposition to the populist penal politics we have just described. It has, as we shall see, come in several variants each offering different diagnoses and policy prescriptions. But these variants have enough in common to warrant terming this general approach to thinking about and acting upon crime 'epistemic crime control'. So what are the principal contentions and aspirations of the epistemic worldview? To what vision of good crime governance are its proponents committed? How are we to judge its conception of a better politics of crime? In this section, we reconstruct the claims found in three variants of epistemic crime control, before offering an overall appraisal of epistemic ideology.

The first variant of epistemic crime control aims to find ways to improve the quality of social information about crime and justice; to create, if you like, a better public opinion. On this view, the key issue that contemporary criminal justice confronts is that people are poorly informed about crime and justice (Indermaur and Hough 2002). This ignorance, the argument runs, underpins low levels of public confidence in criminal justice and drives demands for greater punitivity. It is a cognitive deficit upon which populism thrives. Proponents of this position recognize that 'public opinion' matters to the legitimacy of crime control. They also do not demur from the idea that such opinion should have some, albeit limited, role in shaping penal policy and practice (Roberts 2014). What is lacking—and urgently needed—are the following things:

more accurate calibrations of existing 'public opinion'; mechanisms to ensure that people are more reliably informed about crime and justice; and procedures for generating more considered forms of 'public judgement' about crime matters (Green 2006).

In respect of the first of these items, it is claimed that a sober assessment of existing opinion poll evidence reveals that popular attitudes towards, for example, sentencing or the aims of punishment are far more nuanced than the rendition of 'public opinion' that typically finds expression in tabloid headlines or the utterances of politicians. Public attitudes to justice have also been found to become milder and less punitive the more detail people are given about the concrete circumstances of cases and situations (Hough and Roberts 2005). The lesson drawn from this is that effort needs to be expended on communicating this complexity in the public domain. In response to the second problem, experiments have been conducted to measure the impact of disseminating factual information on public confidence (e.g. Mirrlees-Black 2002). Proposals also abound for creating 'information resource centres' (Indermaur and Hough 2002) or cognate institutions able to supply reliable data about crime and its control and rebut ill-informed policy proposals on a systematic basis (Roberts *et al.* 2002: ch. 10). At one end of the spectrum such methods of enhancing the 'quality' of public opinion are vulnerable to the criticism that they are top-down and monological. That is, they involve the imparting of wisdom by knowers to the ill-informed populace (though more often their advocates would argue that their aim is a democratization of access to the best available information). The third ambition—that of nurturing a more engaged public opinion—is more dialogical. This orientation has found expression in recent criminological enthusiasm for deliberative polling (Green 2006; Turner 2016; see, generally, Fishkin and Luskin 2006). Deliberative polls involve assembling a sample of citizens and measuring their attitudes before and after they have participated in discussion of penal matters with a range of experts and interest groups, and among one another. The hope—and there is a some evidence to support this claim (Hough and Park 2002)—is that such engagement and argumentation produces more informed and measured opinions.

It is hard to object to the idea that one should seek to underpin public sensibilities towards crime with more reliable information. But this variant of epistemic crime control prompts certain hard questions—questions that warrant more sustained attention than they have received in the literature. The worry here is that this approach assumes, naively, that political actors are going to attend to the complexity of public opinion without some alteration in the incentive structures within which they operate—structures which mean they have little to gain and much to lose from acknowledging the contradictory, ambivalent condition of lay attitudes towards crime and punishment (Lacey 2008). A related charge is that the epistemic approach rests on the 'scholastic fallacy' (Bourdieu 2000) that public sensibilities can be altered by exposure to the 'facts-of-the-matter' rather than being shot through with affect and crime's symbolically charged capacity to 'condense' wider social fears and fantasies (Turner 1970).[8] Similar problems surround the case for deliberative polling. Does

[8] To be fair, proponents of this view often appear to acknowledge this: 'the real battle is not over facts or details but over morals and emotions' (Indermaur and Hough 2002: 210). It is not altogether clear however that this recognition ever escapes from the margins of this overall approach to studying—and changing—public opinion.

this case rest on the complacent assumption that more informed citizens will think and act, well, like liberal criminologists, and are such polls supported mainly in the expectation that they will generate penal moderation, not because an informed, active citizenry has intrinsic democratic value? Does deliberative polling risk becoming a form of deliberation without democracy—a mechanism for mobilizing and creating a selected, competent few while leaving the many in their role as passive spectators (Urbaniti 2014: 115)?

The second variant of epistemic crime control we want to consider claims that one needs to defend or create insulated institutions of policy formation that empower agents of reason and expertise. It aims not to change the quality of public opinion but to privilege knowers in respect of such opinion. This approach to crime control has been explicitly forged in contexts of penal populism. Zimring and Johnson, for example, couch their call for a return to expertise as a much needed corrective to the adverse effects of direct democracy on penal matters—notably, the publicly initiated referenda that brought 'three strikes' sentencing laws to California (Zimring and Johnson 2006; see also Barker 2009: ch. 3).[9] Lacey (2008) argues that reinvesting authority in penal experts is necessary to moderate the harsh, expansive penal systems that have been created by the exclusionary dynamics of liberal market societies with first-past-the-post electoral systems and weak counter-majoritarian constitutional constraints. Pettit (2001) detects what he calls an 'outrage spiral' that tends to be activated when punishment becomes a topic of partisan politics—a spiral that sees politicians demonstrate how 'in touch' they are with popular anger in a manner that ratchets up criminal sentences 'towards the cultural maximum' (ibid.: 437). Punishment, Pettit concludes, is a policy realm uniquely and stubbornly resistant to public reason.

The proposed solution—for all these authors—lies in restraining the 'politics of passion' that imbues 'sensitive issues' like crime (Urbaniti 2014: 118). This calls, first, for a defence of those existing institutions of impartial/professional judgement that stand between criminal justice practice and unmediated public opinion, such as unelected judges, sentencing commissions, parole boards, the doctrine of police operational responsibility, and regimes of independent inspection. Second, it requires the creation of institutions—Lacey endorses calls for a Royal Commission, Pettit proposes what he calls a 'penal policy board'—that can assemble experts and interest groups to deliberate on how to produce effective, humane penal outcomes that do not chip away at the 'liberal pillar' of constitutional democracies. The preferred model from which these authors explicitly borrow is the delegation of monetary policy to independent central banks—another area of policy where it is alleged that elected politicians are incentivized to take myopic, self-interested decisions.

In making these recommendations, these advocates of epistemic crime control accept that governments and legislatures will remain the 'ultimate arbiter' of policy choices (Pettit 2001: 448). This is no crude attempt to replace politics with calculation. The aim, rather, is to create a buffer between partisan politics and the operation of criminal justice systems, an insulated space in which experts can determine how

[9] It needs to be noted that in November 2014 this 'inflammatory' democratic procedure was successfully used to pass Proposition 47, curtailing the operation of California's three strikes laws.

to implement broad strategic choices, or generate effective outcomes, away from the media spotlight and the heat of political competition. Yet here too some tricky questions arise—and are not fully answered. The first is sociological. How in democratic societies where crime has become a contested political topic can one create the conditions of possibility for new 'insulated' institutions and what are the prospects for such institutions fostering and sustaining public legitimacy? The second speaks to the normative character of these proposals. Does this idea—like that of deliberative polls—seek to extend forms of 'unpolitical democracy' (Urbaniti 2014) that elevate competence over consent as the key ingredient of a better crime politics and assume that what such politics most pressingly calls for is the expansion of forensic, quasi-judicial judgement not deeper democratic deliberation? Deliberative polling at least has the merit of engaging with public opinion. This variant of epistemic crime control seeks to marginalize it.

Proponents of the third variant of epistemic crime control are explicitly concerned to elevate the role that knowledge plays in shaping responses to crime. Their claim is that the effectiveness and legitimacy of crime control requires discovering 'what works' and grounding policy and practice in the evidence base. The starting point is that 'experimental criminology' and 'crime science' have over recent decades generated a body of reliable evidence on what works, what doesn't work, and what is promising in policing and crime reduction (Sherman 2013; Welsh *et al.* 2013; cf. Smith and Tilley 2005).[10] That knowledge is, however, at best sporadically used to inform crime prevention policy and practice—a situation, it is claimed, that would be intolerable if found in, say, the licensing and funding of medicines. In policy terms a range of 'political barriers' (Welsh and Farrington 2002: 419) are said to stand in the way of arriving at effective, evidence-based outcomes. Practitioners, it is claimed, remain largely ignorant, or poor consumers, of available knowledge and are locked into professional habits and working methods that do not routinely include consulting what is known before acting—for example, in relation to strategies to reduce domestic violence or knife crime.

The proposed solution to this situation is threefold. First, to invest in and spread the use of methodologies that can most readily extend the reach of valid knowledge about what works—namely, randomized controlled trials and systematic reviews. The Campbell Collaboration—modelled on the Cochrane Collaboration in the health field—exists to do precisely this.[11] Second, to build much closer working relations between evaluators and police and criminal justice practitioners. Minimally, this is to be done with a view to making the latter more informed, critical consumers of research evidence. More ambitiously, the aim is to break down fixed barriers between the two—producing clinical professors with a foot in police and criminal justice practice and a cadre of skilled practitioner-researchers. This has been the focus of much policy attention in England and Wales of late, much of it instigated by the College of Policing. The third response is to create expert institutions whose purpose is to

[10] The differences between experimental criminology and crime science need not concern us here. They turn mainly on the centrality one affords to randomized controlled trials as *the* route to knowledge in evaluation research and the significance one affords to police and penal interventions as means to prevent crime. For a fuller account see Loader and Sparks (2010: ch. 4).

[11] See http://www.campbellcollaboration.org/, accessed 9 February 2016).

assemble, assess, and disseminate reliable evidence about what works. This can be done with the aim of distilling that evidence into best practice guidance for citizens, stakeholders, and practitioners or, more ambitiously, with a view to making that evidence count in determining policy priorities and targeting limited public safety budgets. The preferred model to aspire to and borrow from across these three domains is that of medicine (Weisburd and Neyroud 2011). In respect of this final ambition, the hope is to create an equivalent agency in the justice field to the National Institute for Health and Clinical Excellence, or NICE (Sherman 2009; for an alternative reading see Loader 2010).

The evidence-based variant of epistemic crime control aims to perform two civic functions. Its critical purpose is to be a counterweight to populist folly: to pinpoint policies high on alluring rhetoric but low in practical effectiveness (e.g. 'scared straight' programmes) and thereby reduce the waste of tax-payers money and the perpetuation of preventable harm. The dissemination of knowledge becomes an ally of citizens wanting to call populist posturing on crime to account. The constructive purpose is to raise the epistemic quality of government decisions and to produce police and criminal justice practices rooted in good evidence—evidence that its proponents trust will reduce harm while promoting liberty (Sherman 2009). At first blush these seem like perfectly reasonable aspirations. Few candidates for a better politics of crime will depart from the view that government and criminal justice agencies ought to take knowledge more seriously and use it more extensively—though, as we have seen, populism is one such candidate.[12] That though is not the question. Rather, we need to ask: in what wider account of the governance of crime are these epistemic claims situated? What should we make of that political vision?

Distilling these wider governance claims is not a straightforward task. Epistemic criminologists tend to devote their time and energy to producing the knowledge they claim ought to be addressed more seriously rather than to articulating and defending their vision of 'the right way to organize authority in a society' (Roberts 2010: 136). That vision of authority therefore tends to be implicit, or expressed *sotto voce,* in these more 'practical' endeavours. It is nonetheless possible to discern in epistemic criminology a conception of good crime governance: one that side-lines partisanship and untutored opinion in the determination of crime policy in favour of the claims of knowledge producers and other competent authorities. Herein lies the attraction of (new) institutions that bring reason and expertise much closer to the centre of policy formation. This, the argument runs, will produce more effective outcomes and by this means legitimate crime control among spectating citizens (Sherman 2013). The organizing claim is that truth is the motor of a better politics of crime—cleansing error and promoting virtue. Sometimes this is pressed in a defensive vain—as a means of successfully regulating crime while protecting the liberal commitments that populism threatens. But the promotion of episteme can also take on a redemptive quality; part and parcel of a vision of government engaged in a recurring process of innovation, experimental testing, and collective learning (Sherman 2009).

[12] As prominent Brexit campaigner and former Justice Secretary Michael Gove MP put it during Britain's EU referendum: 'people in this country have had enough of experts'.

Two evaluative points can be made about this vision of governance. The first concerns its status and cogency as a response to penal populism. It is not at all clear in this regard how, in societies in which crime has become an emotive, highly-charged political question, it is possible to generate the support needed to create and sustain novel institutions of evidence-based policy formation, whether a penal policy board or a NICE for criminal justice. It seems premature to assume that such institutions will be adequate to the task of countering the appeals of populism. Indeed, epistemic crime control faces the problem that it responds to the 'dangers' of populism by reasserting the very practices of elite governance that fuel populist resentment in the first place.[13] It even sometimes appears to reproduce in reverse populism's depiction of political life as a struggle between elites and the masses, truth versus opinion.

We can observe, secondly, that epistemic crime control rests upon a radically under-developed account of the relationship between its preferred model of expert policy development and processes of democratic will formation—a silence in respect of how or where practices of democratic dialogue fit into its vision of good governance. The worry here is that its preference for expertise and evidence has defining properties—it raises barriers for entry to policy discussion, it privileges competence over consent as the arbiter of crime policy, and it locates the criteria for making 'good' decisions outside of the process of reaching those decisions—that neglect the normative force of democratic procedures. In this respect, epistemic crime control risks becoming a form of technocratic governance that shuts down the space of public deliberation around crime by turning it into a terrain of competent knowledge, one which prioritizes the search for order over the uncertainties of democratic freedom. As Urbaniti warns: 'Once *episteme* enters the domain of politics, the possibility that political equality gets questioned is in the air because the criterion of competence is intrinsically inegalitarian' (2014: 83; emphasis in original).

CONCLUSION: PARTNERS IN CRIME?

We have in this chapter sought to reconstruct the claims of two perspectives on crime that have over recent decades commanded renewed attention and vied for influence: penal populism and what we have termed 'epistemic crime control'. Our aim has been to understand these perspectives as ideologies—that is, as clusters of belief that justify or contest the arrangements for responding to crime found in a given political community. We have set out to appraise these ideologies as candidate answers to the question of how to build a better politics of crime and its regulation (Loader and Sparks 2010: ch. 5). As answers to that question penal populism and epistemic crime control present—and are usually understood—as competing alternatives, not least in respect of the role that public opinion and expertise should ideally play in shaping responses

[13] As Wolkenstein (2015: 112) puts it: 'the standard story of condemnation'—and epistemic crime control's story is pretty standard—'in fact seems to fan the flames and reinforce populism's appeal'.

to crime and the prevention of harm. Our analysis calls into doubt this conventional portrait of penal populism as a critique of elite governance, and epistemic crime control as a bulwark against populism. It turns out, rather, that these two ideologies of crime control have some unexpected affinities.

The first thing to note in this regard is that populism and epistemic crime control have shared conditions of emergence as actors in the penal field. They have co-developed in social contexts marked by a collective loss of faith in political ideologies and reduced expectations of democratic politics as an effective vehicle of social betterment (Crouch 2004; Mair 2011). Having emerged as symptoms of an 'anti-political' malaise (Rosanvallon 2008), populism and epistocracy press claims that recycle and reinforce the idea that democratic politics is unable to respond effectively to public anxieties about crime, security and related problems, or find a way towards effective and legitimate solutions. They become unlikely partners in questioning the claims and doubting the promise of democratic politics.

In our earlier discussion of some similar dilemmas (Loader and Sparks 2010: ch. 2) we pointed to some connections between the (as we interpreted them, rather stuck) condition of debates and oppositions in criminology and some wider themes in the sociology of science. It is a wide and deep contemporary problem that world-changing advances in science (e.g. in bio-technology, energy, and climate change) whose technical aspects far exceed the capacity of non-specialists to fully absorb, must also strive to explicate themselves to wider public audiences. In some of these fields, however, novel and potentially radical ways of stimulating public engagement and fostering deliberation have begun to emerge, and the boundaries between expertise strictly so-called and various levels of user-involvement become more porous and complicated. There too, the recognition of the importance of public communication is more evident—a discipline and a savoir in its own right, increasingly, not to mention the source of a prolific publishing industry of popular science. Yet, in respect of crime control, the gap between the populists and the epistocrats seems especially resistant to mediation.

It is with this in mind that we can return to the normative character of penal populism and epistemic crime control. We have argued that for all their sharp differences, these ideologies share in common a focus on outcomes that overlooks the value, and closes down the 'open space', of political deliberation (Lefort 1988). Populists colonize that space with a claim to be speaking for a unified people (or 'crime victims' or the 'law-abiding majority') and proposing simple solutions that 'everyone' knows to be common sense. Epistemic crime control evacuates that space in preference for insipid, partisan-free governance where the arbiter of what is to be done is 'truth', or at least the best available evidence. As Müller (2014: 490) puts it: 'in a curious way, the two mirror each other: technocracy holds there is only one correct policy solution; populism claims there is only one authentic will of the people'. Both lend credence to the belief 'that there is no real room for debate and disagreement' (ibid.). In this regard, populism and epistemic crime control are, in the end, best understood as forces for depoliticizing democracy.

What gets lost in the 'contest' between them is a recognition of the normative force of democratic procedures, of the importance of politics as a common space in which all-affected can voice their opinions, publically debate, and give or withhold their approval to, competing proposals for responding to crime and insecurity. In the absence of such recognition, penal populism and epistemic crime control are trapped in what they hold to be a must-win struggle between opinion and knowledge. They are, as such, prevented from attending to the question of the role knowledge can best play in practices of crime control that should, in a democracy, be grounded in discursively produced, always revisable, public consent (Estlund 2008).

SELECTED FURTHER READING

In our view, Margaret Canovan's writings on populism are among the most astute and can still be helpfully consulted. The best introduction to penal populism remains Pratt's (2007) book of that title. A good empirical assessment of public opinion measured against the backdrop of penal populism is Roberts *et al.*'s, *Penal Populism and Public Opinion* (2002). This volume also remains worth a read for the liberal rationalist response to populism that it articulates. A lively debate on the normative significance of public opinion for sentencing and punishment can be found in the collection edited by Ryberg and Roberts, *Popular Punishment: On the Normative Significance of Public Opinion* (2014).

On the application of deliberative polling to crime issues, see Green's 'Public Opinion versus Public Judgment about Crime: Correcting the "Comedy of Errors"' (2006). Pettit's 'Is Criminal Justice Politically Feasible?' (2001) offers a thoughtful articulation of the case for insulating criminal justice from partisan politics, written not by a criminologist but by a political theorist. Sherman's (2009) article on 'Evidence and Liberty' is the best account we know of the claims and governance implications of experimental criminology.

Readers who want to know more about the concept of ideology are advised to begin with Freeden's *Ideology: A Very Short Introduction. The Oxford Handbook of Political Ideologies*, Freeden and Stears (eds) (2013) is also a helpful guide, and includes a very good chapter on populism. Our own efforts to use Freeden's work to develop a 'political mode of evaluation' for crime control are contained in Loader and Sparks' 'Ideologies and Crime: Political Ideas and the Dynamics of Crime Control' (2016).

REFERENCES

Abts, K. and Rummens, S. (2007), 'Populism versus Democracy', *Political Studies*, 55(4): 405–24.

Arditi, B. (2003), 'Populism, or Politics at the Edge of Democracy', *Contemporary Politics*, 9(1): 17–31.

Aslanidis, P. (2015), 'Is Populism an Ideology? A Refutation and a New Perspective', *Political Studies*, DOI: 10.1111/1467-9248.12224.

Barker, V. (2009), The Politics of Imprisonment, Oxford: Oxford University Press.

Berezin, M. (2009), *Illiberal Politics in Neoliberal Times: Culture, Security and Populism in the New Europe*, Cambridge: Cambridge University Press.

Bottoms, A. E. (1995), 'The Philosophy and Politics of Punishment and Sentencing', in C. Clarkson and R. Morgan (eds), *The Politics of Sentencing Reform*, Oxford: Oxford University Press.

Bourdieu, P. (2000), *Pascalian Meditations*, Cambridge: Polity.

Canovan, M. (1999), 'Trust the People! Populism and the Two Faces of Democracy', *Political Studies*, 47(1): 2–16.

Canovan, M. (2002), 'Taking politics to the people: populism as the ideology of democracy', in Y. Mény and Y. Surel (eds), *Democracies and the Populist Challenge*, Basingstoke: Palgrave.

Canovan, M. (2005), *The People*, Cambridge: Polity.

Centano, M. A. (1993), 'The New Leviathan: The Dynamics and Limits of Technocracy', *Theory and Society*, 22: 307–35.

Crouch, C. (2004), *Post-Democracy*, Cambridge: Polity.

Dzur, A. (2012), *Punishment, Participatory Democracy, and the Jury*, New York: Oxford University Press.

Estlund, D. (2008), *Democratic Authority: A Philosophical Framework*, Princeton: Princeton University Press.

FARMER, L. (2006), 'Tony Martin and the nightbreakers: on criminal law in late modern society', in S. Armstrong and L. McAra (eds), *Perspectives on Punishment: The Contours of Control*, Oxford: Oxford University Press.

FISHKIN, J. S. and LUSKIN, R. C. (2006), 'Experimenting with a Democratic Ideal: Deliberating Polling and Public Opinion', *Acta Politica*, 40: 248–98.

FREEDEN, M. (1998), *Ideologies and Political Theory: A Conceptual Approach*, Oxford: Oxford University Press.

FREEDEN, M. (2003), *Ideology: A Very Short Introduction*, Oxford: Oxford University Press.

FREEDEN, M. (2013), 'The morphological analysis of ideology', in M. Freeden and M. Stears (eds), *The Oxford Handbook of Political Ideologies*, Oxford: Oxford University Press.

FREIBERG, A. and GELB, K. (eds) (2013), *Penal Populism, Sentencing Councils and Sentencing Policy*, Abingdon: Routledge.

GARLAND, D. (2017), 'What is penal populism?', in A. Liebling, J, Shapland, and J. Tankebe (eds), *Crime, Justice and Social Order: Essays in Honour of A. E. Bottoms*, Oxford: Oxford University Press.

GREEN, D. (2006), 'Public Opinion versus Public Judgment about Crime: Correcting the "Comedy of Errors"', *British Journal of Criminology*, 46: 131–54.

GREEN, D. (2008), *When Children Kill Children: Penal Populism and Political Culture*, Oxford: Oxford University Press.

GUNNELL, J. G. (1982), 'The Technocratic Image and the Theory of Technocracy', *Technology and Culture*, 23(3): 392–416.

HABERMAS, J. (1998), *The Inclusion of the Other: Studies in Political Theory*, Cambridge, MA: MIT Press.

HOUGH, M. and PARK, A. (2002), 'How malleable are public attitudes to crime and punishment?: findings from a British deliberative poll', in J. Roberts and M. Hough (eds), *Changing Attitudes to Punishment: Public Opinion, Crime and Justice*, Cullompton: Willan.

HOUGH, M. and ROBERTS, J. (2005), *Understanding Public Attitudes to Criminal Justice*, Buckingham: Open University Press.

INDERMAUR, D. and HOUGH, M. (2002), 'Strategies for changing public attitudes to punishment', in J. Roberts and M. Hough (eds), *Changing Attitudes to Punishment: Public Opinion, Crime and Justice*, Cullompton: Willan.

JONES, R. (2010), 'Populist Leniency, Crime Control and Due Process', *Theoretical Criminology*, 14(3): 331–47.

LACEY, N. (2008), *The Prisoners' Dilemma: Political Economy and Punishment in Contemporary Democracies*, Oxford: Oxford University Press.

LACLAU, E. (2005), *On Populist Reason*, London: Verso.

LEFORT, C. (1988), *Democracy and Political Theory*, Cambridge: Polity.

LIPPMANN, W. (1922), *Public Opinion*, New York: Free Press.

LOADER, I. (2006), 'Fall of the "Platonic Guardians": Liberalism, Criminology and Political Responses to Crime in England and Wales', *British Journal of Criminology*, 46(4): 561–86.

LOADER, I. (2010), 'Is it NICE?: The Appeal, Limits and Promise of Translating a Health Innovation into Criminal Justice', *Current Legal Problems*, 63(1): 72–91.

LOADER, I. and SPARKS, R. (2010), *Public Criminology?*, London: Routledge.

LOADER, I. and SPARKS, R. (2016), 'Ideologies and Crime: Political Ideas and the Dynamics of Crime Control', *Global Crime*, 17(3–4): 314–30.

MAIR, P. (2011), *Ruling the Void: The Hollowing out of Western Democracy*, London: Verso.

MIRRLESS-BLACK, C. (2002), 'Improving public knowledge about crime and punishment', in J. Roberts and M. Hough (eds), *Changing Attitudes to Punishment: Public Opinion, Crime and Justice*, Cullompton: Willan.

MUDDE, C. and KATLWASSER, C. R. (2013), 'Populism', in M. Freeden and M. Stears (eds), *The Oxford Handbook of Political Ideologies*, Oxford: Oxford University Press.

MÜLLER, J.-W. (2014), '"The People Must be Extracted from the People": Reflections on Populism', *Constellations*, 21(4): 483–94.

MÜLLER, J.-W. (2015), 'Parsing Populism: Who is and Who is Not a Populist these Days?', Juncture, available at: http://www.ippr.org/juncture/parsing-populism-who-is-and-who-is-not-a-populist-these-days, accessed 5 January 2017.

PASTORELLA, G. (2015), 'Technocratic Governments in Europe: Getting the Critique Right', *Political Studies*, doi: 10.1111/1467-9248.12217.

PETTIT, P. (2001), 'Is Criminal Justice Politically Feasible?', *Buffalo Criminal Law Review*, 5(2): 427–50.

PRATT, J. (2007), *Penal Populism*, Abingdon: Routledge.

ROBERTS, A. (2010), *The Logic of Discipline: Global Capitalism and the Architecture of Government*, Oxford: Oxford University Press.

ROBERTS, J. (2014), 'Clarifying the significance of public opinion for sentencing policy and practice', in J. Ryberg and J. Roberts (eds), *Popular Punishment: On the Normative Significance of Public Opinion*, Oxford: Oxford University Press.

ROBERTS, J., STALANS, L., INDERMAUR, D., and HOUGH, M. (2002), *Penal Populism and Public Opinion*, Oxford: Oxford University Press.

ROSANVALLON, P. (2008), *Counter-Democracy: Politics in an Age of Distrust*, Cambridge: Cambridge University Press.

ROSANVALLON, P. (2011), *Democratic Legitimacy: Impartiality, Reflexivity, Proximity*, Princeton: Princeton University Press.

RYAN, M. (2003), *Penal Policy and Political Culture in England and Wales*, Winchester: Waterside Press.

SARTORI, G. (1962), *Democratic Theory*, Detroit: Wayne State University Press.

SCHMITT, C. (2007), *The Concept of the Political*, Chicago: University of Chicago Press.

SCHUMPETER, J. (1942), *Capitalism, Socialism and Democracy*, Floyd, Virginia: Impact Books.

SHERMAN, L. (2009), 'Evidence and Liberty: The Promise of Experimental Criminology', *Criminology & Criminal Justice*, 9(1): 5–28.

SHERMAN, L. (2013), 'The rise of evidence-based policing: targeting, testing and tracking', in M. Tonry (ed.), *Crime and Justice: An Annual Review of Research—Volume 42*, Chicago: University of Chicago Press.

SHERMAN, L., FARRINGTON, D., WELSH, B., and MACKENZIE, D. (eds) (2002), *Evidence-Based Crime Prevention: Revised Edition*, Abingdon: Routledge.

SMITH, M. and TILLEY, N. (eds) (2005), *Crime Science: New Approaches to Preventing and Detecting Crime*, Cullompton: Willan.

STANLEY, B. (2008), 'The Thin Ideology of Populism', *Journal of Political Ideologies*, 13(1): 95–110.

TAGGART, P. (2000), *Populism*, Buckingham: Open University Press.

TONRY, M. (2010), 'The Costly Consequences of Populist Posturing: ASBOs, Victims, "Rebalancing" and Diminution in Support for Civil Liberties', *Punishment & Society*, 12(4): 387–413.

TURNER, E. (2016) 'Mass Incarceration and Public Opinion on Crime and Justice: From Democratic Theory to Method and Reality' in A. Dzur, I. Loader, and R. Sparks (eds), *Democratic Theory and Mass Incarceration*, New York: Oxford University Press.

TURNER, V. (1970), *The Forest of Symbols*, Cornell: Cornell University Press.

URBANITI, N. (2014), *Democracy Disfigured: Opinion, Truth, and the People*, Cambridge, MA: Harvard University Press.

WACQUANT, L. (2009), *Prisons of Poverty*, Minneapolis: University of Minnesota Press.

WEISBURD, D. and NEYROUD, P. (2011), *Police Science: Towards a New Paradigm*, Washington: Department of Justice; available at: https://www.ncjrs.gov/pdffiles1/nij/228922.pdf, accessed 5 January 2017.

WELSH, B. and FARRINGTON, D. (2002), 'Conclusion: what works, what doesn't, what's promising and future directions', in L. Sherman, D. Farrington, B. Welsh, and D. MacKenzie (eds), *Evidence-Based Crime Prevention: Revised Edition*, Abingdon: Routledge.

WELSH, B., BRAGA, A., and BRUINSMA, G. (eds) (2013), *Experimental Criminology: Prospects for Advancing Science and Public Policy*, Cambridge: Cambridge University Press.

WOLKENSTEIN, F. (2015), 'What can we Hold Against Populism?', *Philosophy and Social Criticism*, 41(2): 111–29.

ZIMRING, F. and JOHNSON, D. (2006), 'Public Opinion and the Governance of Punishment in Democratic Political Systems', *The ANNALS of the American Academy of Political and Social Science*, 605/1: 265–80.

5

POLITICAL ECONOMY, CRIME, AND CRIMINAL JUSTICE

Robert Reiner

INTRODUCTION: POLITICAL ECONOMY AND CRIMINOLOGY

Criminology was rooted in political economy, which has been a largely taken for granted foundation of thinking about crime and its control since the eighteenth century. However, political economy was largely expelled from criminology after the mid-1970s, by a combination of cultural shifts that will be explored. In the last decade it has undergone a limited revival, primarily in punishment theory. Political economy remains little used nowadays in attempts to explain crime, or to analyse other aspects of criminal justice such as policing.

This chapter will first discuss what political economy means, and how it may be delineated as a criminological perspective. It will go on to analyse its fluctuating salience within criminology. The empirical evidence about the role of political economy in understanding crime and criminal justice will be reviewed. Finally the chapter will consider how political economy is needed to make sense of contemporary trends in crime and control.

The notion that there exists some connection between crime and economic circumstances is ancient and deeply ingrained, as the etymology of the terms 'villain', 'rogue'—or 'propriety' for that matter—indicates. However, what is labelled the 'economic' is part of a complex set of interdependent individual, moral, cultural, and social dimensions of human action. It is this dialectical interplay of levels of analysis that the label 'political economy' conveys.

WHAT IS POLITICAL ECONOMY?

'Over its long lifetime, the phrase "political economy" has had many different meanings' (Weingast and Wittman 2008: 3). Although it most frequently signifies a perspective that is distinct from 'economics', it is also sometimes treated as synonymous with it. *The Journal of Political Economy*, for instance, is the house journal of the Chicago School, most famously associated with Milton Friedman and other exponents of the neo-classical economics that now dominates the academic discipline. This perspective is rather different from the 'political economy' that was its origin. The most famous work of eighteenth-century political economy, Adam Smith's *The Wealth of Nations*, 'was part of a much broader inquiry into the foundations of society. It was inseparable from moral philosophy' (Haakonsen 2006). Over time it fed into what is now referred to as 'classical political economy', the leading exponents of which were Malthus, Ricardo, James Mill, and his son John Stuart Mill (Ruggiero 2013). Marx saw himself as heir to this tradition, synthesizing it with the dialectical philosophy of Hegel and with French St Simonian socialism, and 'political economy' is sometimes virtually a synonym for Marxism.

'Economics' grew out of political economy in the late nineteenth century as a distinct discipline, focusing on the economic in abstraction from wider social dimensions, and now refers primarily to a supposedly apolitical, value-free, 'scientific' enterprise. As succinctly summarized by *The Oxford Handbook of Political Economy*, 'The unit of analysis is typically the individual. The individual is motivated to achieve goals (usually preference maximization . . .), the theory is based in mathematics . . . and the empirics . . . involve sophisticated statistical techniques' (Weingast and Wittman 2008: 4). A common contemporary usage of 'political economy' is the application of this methodology to the analysis of political institutions and processes (op. cit.). In criminology, it is the progenitor of the economics of crime (Becker 1968; Albertson and Fox 2012), and 'rational choice' theories, which have had a huge impact on crime control policy and practice (Albertson and Fox 2012: 4).

There was a parallel emergence of other social science disciplines out of the broad discourses of political economy and philosophy: political science, sociology, psychology—and indeed criminology. They constituted and studied what came to be seen as different institutional fields: the 'private' and 'public'; 'civil society' and 'the state'; 'the economy' and 'the polity'; 'criminal' and 'civil' law (Neocleous 2000: 13–14; Lea 2002: chs 1–3).

The conception of 'political economy' adopted here questions these intellectual and institutional separations, suggesting that whilst particular studies may focus on specific levels, the dialectical interdependence of macro, meso, and micro processes, and of the different dimensions of social existence, must always be recognized. The most explicit exposition of this in criminology is the sketch of 'a fully social theory of deviance' in *The New Criminology* (Taylor, Walton, and Young 1973: 268–80). This was explicitly intended as 'a political economy of criminal action, and of the reaction it excites', together with 'a politically informed social psychology of these ongoing social dynamics' (ibid.: 279).

The closest attempt to incorporate all these elements into one study was the magisterial analysis of 'mugging', *Policing the Crisis* (Hall *et al.* 1978). Starting from a particular robbery in Birmingham, this dissected the construction by the mass media, police, and courts of a 'moral panic' about 'mugging'. It then proceeded to a wide-ranging account of British economic, political, social, and cultural history since the Second World War, explaining the deeper concerns that 'mugging' condensed. The later chapters analysed the impact of transformations in the political economy on young black men in particular, and how this structured specific subcultures in which robbery became more likely.

Most research studies inevitably focus more narrowly, but the checklist of elements for a 'fully social theory' is a constant reminder of the wider contexts in which particular aspects of deviance and control are embedded. Even so the framework has been criticized for not including enough, not least by some of its creators. It has been claimed that its fundamentally structuralist perspective precludes adequate exploration of the psychodynamics of crime and control (Jefferson 2008). It is possible, however, to synthesize psychoanalytic and political economy analyses, as pioneered in the 1930s by Erich Fromm and other members of the Frankfurt School (Anderson and Quinney 2000; Cheliotis 2013). Others have claimed that political economy brackets off existentialist appreciation of 'the seductions of crime' from the perspective of offenders (Katz 1988), and suggest a synthesis with the cultural, interpretive, and symbolic dimensions that are foregrounded in cultural criminology (Young 2011).

In the political arena, Conservative and New Labour leaders have criticized structural explanations of crime for absolving offenders of moral responsibility for their acts, implicitly condoning them (Reiner 2007: 125). An especially egregious example is a memo on the 1980s riots by Oliver Letwin that came to light in 2015, which stated that 'riots, criminality and social disintegration are caused solely by individual character and attitudes' (Harker 2015).

Such critiques, however, have encouraged an unjustifiable neglect of structural and macro-social dimensions of crime and control. This chapter is not intended to encourage a reverse accentuation, but it seeks to show that without the holistic sensibility of political economy it is impossible to explain patterns and trends in crime and control.

POLITICAL ECONOMY AND CRIMINOLOGICAL THEORY

This section briefly reviews the fluctuating influence of political economy in the history of criminological theory (fuller accounts are in previous editions of this *Handbook*).

POLITICAL ECONOMY AND THE DAWN OF CRIMINOLOGY

The standard account of the history of criminology places its origins in the 'classical' perspective pioneered by Beccaria's 1764 *Dei Delitti e Delle Pene*. Beccaria held a Chair of 'Political Economy and Science of Police', and Enlightenment discussions of crime and criminal justice were embedded in political economy. This was most evident in the 'science of police', which flourished in the eighteenth and early nineteenth centuries, but was overlooked by criminologists (apart from Radzinowicz 1956) until rediscovered by Foucault and some of his followers in the late 1970s (Foucault 1977; Pasquino 1978). In his 1763 *Lectures on Justice, Police, Revenue and Arms* Adam Smith defined 'police' as 'the second general division of jurisprudence. The name . . . is originally derived from the Greek "politeia" which properly signified the policy of civil government, but now it only means the regulation of the inferior parts of government, viz: cleanliness, security and cheapness of plenty' (cited in Radzinowicz 1956: 421).

In England the leading exponent of the 'science of police' was the magistrate Patrick Colquhoun. His proposals for the prevention and control of crime were rooted in political economy. Colquhoun located the ultimate causes of crime in the overall structure of economy and society, but traced down the social and cultural mediations generating criminality and conformity. Crime (mainly theft) was attributable to the poor (Neocleous 2000: 49–56), but poverty did not determine crime. Poverty was inevitable and indeed beneficial (as the crucial incentive for labour); the 'evil' was indigence—unwillingness to labour. Structural sources of indigence included variations in the opportunities for training available to different ethnic groups, and downturns in the economic cycle. But cultural and informal moral controls (such as religion and uplifting rather than 'bawdy' forms of popular pastimes) were also important to encourage 'virtuous manners'.

Deterrence by regular police patrol was more effective than harsh punishment. But the beneficial effects of police patrol were more to encourage moral discipline than to deter or catch perpetrators. Its terrain was to be 'upon the broad scale of General Prevention—mild in its operations—effective in its results; having justice and humanity for its basis, and the general security of the State and Individuals for its ultimate object' (Colquhoun 1800: 38).

Overall the analysis of security, order, crime, and policing advanced by the 'science of police' was more sensitive to the interplay of politics, law, and justice with criminality than the later nineteenth-century 'science of the criminal'. As with the contemporaneous displacement of political economy by economics, the apparent gain in 'scientific' rigour was bought at a high price in terms of the obscuring of the political, economic, and ethical dimensions of crime and welfare.

POLITICAL ECONOMY AND POSITIVIST CRIMINOLOGY

The term 'positivism' in histories of criminology refers to the project of seeking causal explanations of crime, on the methodological model attributed to the natural sciences. As a self-conscious movement, positivism was associated with the late nineteenth-century Lombrosian school, which emphasized individual constitutional factors. But significant pioneers of the socio-economic explanation of crime predated Lombroso: the 'moral statisticians' of the early nineteenth century, notably Quetelet and Guerry (Beirne 1993: chs 3–4). They used the new French national crime statistics to explore the contours of criminality, anticipating many patterns subsequently charted by econometric studies. They found, for example, that crime was a function both of social pressures stemming from inequality *and* of the distribution of targets and temptations. Overall the explorations of the 'moral statisticians' paved the way for subsequent sociological criminology, above all the theory of anomie.

Anomie theory is the most influential formulation of a political economy of crime outside the Marxist tradition, originating in Durkheim's 1897 book *Suicide*. Durkheim suggested that healthy societies require effective cultural regulation of people's aspirations. Rapid social change dislocated such controls, producing anomie, characterized by restlessness, dissatisfaction, agitation, and other maladies conducive to deviance. Economic downturns *and* upturns disrupted the regulation of aspirations.

Merton picked up on this analysis in a brief but seminal article, offering a framework for explaining variations in deviance between and within societies (Merton 1938) that remains a cogent paradigm for a structural criminological theory (Messner and Rosenfeld 2012). Most accounts of Merton's analysis represent it as 'strain' theory, focusing on one aspect of his paper: the argument that a society combining *cultural* encouragement of common material aspirations through a meritocratic mythology, with a *structural* reality of unequal opportunities, generates anomic pressures. This is frequently reduced to a social psychology of deviance, probing psychic gaps between individual aspirations and achievement. But Merton's analysis was only partly directed at explaining the individual or subcultural sources of deviance *within* a society, although his typology of possible reactions to anomic pressure is the most frequently reproduced section of his paper (Merton 1957: 140). This aspect was also most influential in policy terms, leading—via the concept of opportunity structures—to some of the 'Great Society' programmes of the early 1960s (Cloward and Ohlin 1960).

Merton's analysis of intra-societal variations in crime was part of a broader account aimed at understanding differences *between* societies. Anomie was at root a consequence of the nature of the goals encouraged by particular cultures. A materialistic culture is prone to anomie, and hence to crime, at *all* levels, and not just among the relatively deprived lower classes.

Merton is a paradigm for a political economy of crime, suggesting links between a materialistic culture, overall problems of moral regulation, and the structural distribution of legitimate opportunities. But it is not an economically determinist account. It is not inequality or deprivation *per se* that generate anomie and deviance. The cultural significance these material factors have in different social settings is crucial to how they are experienced, mediating between structural pressure and human action. For all its strengths, however, Merton's theory has been rather out of fashion in recent decades. Its social democratic critique of unbridled capitalism made him too 'cautious' a rebel for the radical criminology of the 1960s/1970s, too radical for post-1980s neoliberal triumphalism, and too structuralist for postmodernists.

Since the mid-1970s mainstream criminology has been increasingly dominated by pragmatic realism, concerned with 'what works?' This was predicated on an explicit rejection of 'root cause' theories such as Merton's (Wilson 1975: xv). Causal explanation was not eschewed altogether, but pursued at individual, situational, or community levels, which are more amenable to policy interventions that do not raise questions of wider social justice or reform.

POLITICAL ECONOMY AND RADICAL CRIMINOLOGY

Until the flowering of radical criminology in the 1960s and 1970s little systematic attention was given by Marxists or others on the Left to crime or criminal justice. It is of course possible to construct several alternative readings of Marx's voluminous corpus of work, all highly contested. Many claim that in his mature theoretical work Marx did not systematically address issues of law, crime, or criminal justice. Chapter 10 of *Capital*, however, is a lengthy historical analysis of the emergence of the Factory Acts in early nineteenth-century England (Marx 1867/1976: ch. 10). It constitutes a pioneering case study of criminalization, and corporate crime. Marx's account is very far from the economic determinism attributed to him, and gives weight to both structure and action, in complex interaction (Reiner 2016: 73–7).

The Factory Acts presented something of a puzzle to Marx. How could legislation that restricted the autonomy of manufacturers be passed by a state that was (not only rhetorically but in fact, in an era before working class enfranchisement) 'a committee for managing the common affairs of the whole bourgeoisie' (Marx and Engels 1848/1998: 37)?

Marx starts his explanation with structural factors. Without external regulation, competitive pressures constrained factory-owners to increase the hours and intensity of work by their employees to the maximum, threatening the long-term viability of the system of production. Legislation required effective human action, however. Marx shows the role of progressive factory-owners, workers themselves, and (once they were established) the Factory Inspectors in the formulation and enforcement of the new laws. Altogether, this long chapter is a significant early example of a political economy of crime and control, that gives due weight to the human actions and conflicts that mediate between macro structures and specific events.

Willem Bonger, a Dutch professor, made the first attempt to develop a systematic Marxist analysis of crime (Bonger 1916/1969). Bonger argued the structure of capitalism generated particular criminogenic pressures and conflicts. In common with Marxism in general he has been accused of economic determinism, but his attempt to spell out the mediating links between structural roots and criminal acts is complex, and allowed scope for individual autonomy and moral responsibility. To Bonger the main way in which capitalism was related to crime was through the stimulation of a culture of egoism, at all levels of society. In terms that anticipated Merton's analysis of anomie, Bonger talked of the stimulation of material desires by modern marketing and retail methods, so that 'the cupidity of the crowd is highly excited' (Bonger 1916/1969: 108). This explained not only proletarian crime but also crimes of the powerful (ibid.: 138).

Bonger recognized a complex multiplicity of linkages between the structural conflicts of capitalism, with its general egoism, and particular forms of crime. The root causes of crime in the larger immorality and injustices of capitalism did not remove the moral accountability of offenders (Bonger 1935: 23). Individual psychology as well as contingent factors, such as unpredictable temptations, had also to be considered (Bonger 1916/1969: 36).

Bonger introduced many ideas that were explored in later critical criminology. He recognized that legal conceptions of crime reflected disproportionately the interests of the powerful (Bonger 1916/1969: 24). But whilst acknowledging that class and power influenced the content and operation of the legal system, he nonetheless saw that it contributed to the maintenance of order in general, which benefited all classes. Some aspects of law were controversial, and enforcement might sometimes be biased, but most criminal law had the moral approval of the population. Not only did Bonger acknowledge the harm done by much conventional crime, he also saw it as inflicting pain particularly on the least powerful. He was also sensitive to the oppression of women, and to the prevalent persecution of gay people and ethnic minorities (Bemmelen 1960). Bonger was in many ways an ethically inspiring figure, pioneering many themes of subsequent radical (and indeed liberal) criminology (Moxon 2014).

The other significant contribution to political economy by early twentieth-century radical criminology was Rusche and Kirchheimer's historical study of punishment (Rusche and Kirchheimer 1939/2009). Two Frankfurt School refugees from Nazism, Rusche and Kirchheimer, published *Punishment and Social Structure* in 1939. Its long-term historical analysis of trends in punishment since the early medieval period demonstrated that the development of penal measures was shaped by changes in the mode of production, in particular fluctuations in the supply of and demand for labour power. Although Rusche and Kirchheimer recognized the role of cultural, political, and other factors, it was left to later studies to spell these out in much more elaborate detail, qualifying the economism of their account (de Giorgi 2006; Lacey 2008).

'Labelling theory' and other critical perspectives that developed in the early 1960s owed more to symbolic interactionism and other micro-sociologies than to political economy, but they began exploring how the structurally patterned play of power and advantage shaped the emergence and enforcement of definitions of deviance. Political economy assumed a central position with the Marxist-influenced radical criminologies that became prominent in the early 1970s, above all the conception of a 'fully social' theory of crime discussed above (Taylor, Walton, and Young, op. cit.).

The 'Left Realist' auto-critique that some of these radical criminologists mounted in the 1980s distanced itself from straightforward economic analyses of crime. Economic models were associated with a supposed 'aetiological crisis' of radical criminology, as the reductions in poverty and unemployment associated with the post-war Keynesian welfare state failed to stop crime from rising. The Left Realist emphasis was on the need for immediate steps to control crime through more effective policing and penality, not the 'root causes' approach attributed to earlier 'left idealism'. Nonetheless, Left Realist analysis of crime causation incorporated earlier political economy perspectives such as relative deprivation and anomie (e.g. Lea and Young 1984: ch. 6; Webber 2007).

Since the turn of the Millennium there has been some revival of macro-analyses of the relationship between crime, criminal justice, and political economy, in combination with cultural analyses of late modernity (starting with Taylor 1999; Young 1999; and Garland 2001), synthesized in a proposed 'ultra-realism' (Hall and Winlow 2015). Such attempts to develop a political economy of contemporary trends in crime and control will be considered in the fourth section of this chapter. First, however, the next section will review the empirical evidence about the role of economic factors in explaining crime.

ECONOMIC FACTORS AND CRIME: A COMPLEX CONNECTION

The idea of an association between economic conditions and crime is embedded deeply in our culture. At a straightforward empirical level it is indicated by official statistics on patterns of formally labelled offending and victimization, which disproportionately bear down on the poor and economically excluded, summed-up in the title of a classic critical text—*The Rich Get Richer and the Poor Get Prison* (Reiman and Leighton 2012).

Although political economy has been played down in criminology since the 1970s. *a priori* economic factors might be expected to impact on crime in a variety of ways. For a crime to occur there are several logically necessary preconditions: labelling, motive, means, opportunity, and the absence of control (Reiner 2007: ch. 4; 2016: ch. 7). Economic factors are relevant to all of these.

1. *Labelling.* Economic factors shape labelling processes at all levels: the emergence of criminal laws, the propensity of victims to report crimes, and/or the police to record them. The application of criminal labels to individuals is patterned by police deployment and enforcement decisions. These are influenced by perceptions of particular (usually poorer) areas as high crime hotspots, or stereotypes of specific groups (usually low in power) as likely offenders—'police property'.

2. *Motive.* Most criminological theories have sought to understand the motivations tempting, seducing, or driving people to commit crimes. Many identify economic variables such as poverty, unemployment, and relative deprivation as risk factors precipitating individuals towards criminal motivations, in conjunction with other aspects of family context and socialization.

Although in the 1980s conservatives such as Mrs Thatcher denied a link between economic conditions and crime, it is a straightforward inference of neo-classical economics that economic fluctuations affect the perceived costs and benefits of legitimate compared with illegitimate actions (Becker 1968; Albertson and Fox 2012). Although in economic theory (as in classical 'criminology') offenders are presumed to have the same fundamental motivations as the law-abiding, changing economic circumstances, such as the buoyancy of labour markets, shape whether the utility-maximizing rational actor will be likely to commit crimes.

3. *Means.* The availability of illegal markets for stolen goods, and the shifting price of different items on them, structures crime patterns (Sutton *et al.* 2001). Unemployment may provide the Devil with the opportunity to make work for idle hands. Prosperity increases the means to purchase and consume socially the intoxicating drink and drugs that fuel fights (Field 1990). The Internet has vastly expanded the means of crime (Yar 2013).

4. *Opportunity.* The proliferation of valuable, easily stolen consumer goods (cars, videos, mobile phones, etc) was a key factor in the growth of crime since the mid-1950s. 'Thefts and burglaries are linked to the stock of crime opportunities, represented by the sum of real consumer expenditure . . . For every 1 per cent increase in this stock, burglary and theft have increased by about 2%' (Field 1999: 7). Economic

development changes the 'routine activities' of different groups, shifting their vulnerability to victimization, for example by leaving houses unguarded when owners go to work (Felson and Eckert 2015), so that 'opportunity makes the thief' (Felson and Clarke 1998).

5. *Absence of controls.* The occurrence of a crime requires the absence of effective controls, whether the 'inner police' of conscience (Eysenck 1965: 261), or the threat of external policing and punishment. Economic factors affect the functioning of both informal and formal controls. Employment is amongst other things a direct and indirect form of discipline. The availability, resourcing, deployment, and management of the formal controls of policing and punishment are also heavily influenced by economic factors, such as changes in the politics of public expenditure.

ECONOMETRIC EVIDENCE

There are crucial limitations of all econometric studies from a criminological perspective. One is that the variables measured by econometricians have at best a rough correspondence to criminological concepts. Unemployment or inequality rates, for example, may be related to anomie, but they are not direct measures of it. The social and psychological meaning of economic variables such as employment or income will vary according to different economic, cultural, and individual circumstances. At best econometrics can establish correlations between economic indicators and official crime measures (with all the pitfalls of these statistical indices), not causal relationships. In addition the relationships have to be 'adequate at the level of meaning' (Weber 1947/1964: 99–100). There have to be plausible narratives linking the variables as sequences of comprehensible human action.

In the mid-1980s a comprehensive literature search found that 64 per cent of econometric studies indicated that higher unemployment was associated with more crime (Box 1987). This was the result that would be predicted by anomie theory, radical criminology, and neo-classical economics. But the score-line was far from overwhelming! Nearly half the studies supported the opposite prediction, that recession *reduces* crime by decreasing the available targets and increasing the number of unemployed 'guardians' staying at home.

Box also reviewed econometric studies probing links between income inequality and crime levels. Theoretically it would be expected that these variables were closely associated, because inequality would be likely to produce a sense of relative deprivation. All studies reported a positive relationship between inequality and property crime (but not violence).

It is important to note that the studies reviewed by Box were all carried out before the mid-1980s. The social character, meaning, and impact of such variables as unemployment and inequality changed fundamentally during the 1980s. Data for the studies Box reviewed were gathered mainly in the post-Second World War decades of virtual full employment, when unemployment would have been mainly transitional and voluntary. There would be little reason to expect such unemployment to be associated with crime.

After 1973, however, monetarism resulted in long-term, sometimes permanent, exclusion from legitimate livelihoods of growing numbers of young men. Unemployment in an increasingly insecure and competitive consumerist culture signified a fatal combination of enhanced anomie, and an erosion of the controls represented by work, marriage, and family responsibilities (Currie 1998).

Although most studies conducted since the 1980s find positive relationships between higher unemployment and crime rates (especially property crime), the strength of the association remains fairly modest (e.g. Fielding *et al.* 2000: Pt. II; Lin 2008; Hooghe *et al.* 2011; Jennings *et al.* 2012; Albertson and Fox 2012: ch. 5; Hale 2013; Levy *et al.* 2014). In part this may be because official measures include both voluntary and involuntary unemployment. An attempt to estimate the significance of this, by assuming that unemployment rates below 4 per cent mainly involve transitional unemployment, found very strong associations between burglary and *involuntary* unemployment (Marris 2000: 73–4).

Transformations in the labour market, associated with the change from Keynesian economic management to neoliberalism, have made unemployment statistics a less adequate measure of economic exclusion. Chris Hale has demonstrated the criminogenic significance of the emergence of a 'dual labour market' (Hale 2013). There is a growing contrast between a *primary* sector of skilled workers, enjoying relative security, buoyant earnings, benefits, and employment rights, and a *secondary* sector of low-skilled, insecure, poorly paid, 'zero-hours' 'McJobs'. The latter are much less likely to reduce crime in the way that employment traditionally did.

Deindustrialization in the wake of neoliberalism during the 1980s expanded the peripheral relative to the primary sector. This was associated with increasing crime rates, especially in economic downturns when earnings in the secondary sector are particularly squeezed. Declining wages for unskilled workers has been associated with increasing property crime (Machin and Meghir 2004). Conversely, the introduction of the minimum wage was followed by greater decreases in crime in areas that gained most from it (Hansen and Machin 2003).

Since the 1980s there has been a sharp increase in economic inequality (Dorling 2015). Recent studies, in Britain and the USA, have confirmed a strong association between inequality, economic exclusion, and crime overall (Gilligan 2011; Healy *et al.* 2013; Rufrancos *et al.* 2013; Hale 2013; McAra and McVie 2016). A significant change, however, is that homicide is no longer an apparent exception. Studies in several countries show associations between greater inequality and more homicide (Wilkinson and Pickett 2009: ch. 10).

The downplaying of economic factors in criminal justice policy discourse since the 1970s was due to shifts in dominant political and intellectual perspectives, not evidence that there are no significant economic correlates of crime. Even in the Chicago School papers that pioneered the revival of interest in the economics of crime, for example, the data clearly showed strong associations between poverty, inequality, unemployment, and crime levels (Ehrlich 1973, 1975: 409–13). The emphasis on the significance of deterrence variables (probability and severity of sanctions) by neoliberals was because they saw policing and punishment as desirable and available policy levers, whilst the economic factors either could not or should not be reversed by government action.

POLITICAL ECONOMIES, CRIME, AND CRIMINAL JUSTICE

The econometric evidence reviewed above focuses on the relationships between economic factors and crime, *within* particular social orders. Political economy is more concerned to analyse how 'the routine functioning of economies organised around the capital-labour relation or around individual self-interest may in itself be a factor in crime' (Taylor 1997: 266). In this section comparative and historical evidence will be reviewed, showing that the overall character of different political economies is related to variations in their patterns of crime and criminal justice.

COMPARATIVE CRIMINOLOGY AND PUNISHMENT

In the last few years there has been some resurgence of interest in the political economy of penality. The seminal text has been David Garland's *The Culture of Control* (Garland 2001), a magisterial analysis of the epochal shift from penal welfarism to more punitive and pervasive penal and prevention policies (for critical discussions and elaborations see Zedner 2002; Pratt 2006; Matravers 2009; Nelken 2010: ch. 4; De Giorgi 2006, 2012; Lacey 2008, 2012, 2013; Wacquant 2009).

The most wide-ranging book explicitly utilizing a political economy framework has been Cavadino and Dignan's influential *Penal Systems: A Comparative Approach* (Cavadino and Dignan 2006), a comparative study of 12 industrial, liberal-democratic countries. The analysis recognizes the force of globalization (op. cit.: 10–12), involving massively heightened flows of information, global commodity and financial markets, with increasing economic and cultural domination by the USA. But whilst this shapes common international pressures and trends, it does not entail homogenization. There remain 'varieties of capitalism' (Hall and Soskice 2003), despite a shared trajectory of globalization under neoliberal, 'Washington consensus' auspices. Cavadino and Dignan develop the seminal typology formulated by Esping-Anderson 1990, distinguishing four ideal-type political economies:

1. *Neoliberalism*—minimal welfare state; extreme income and wealth differences; formal status egalitarianism; individualism with limited social rights; increasing social exclusion; right-wing political dominance (the USA being the closest exemplar).
2. *Conservative corporatism*—status-related welfare state; pronounced but not extreme income differentials; moderately hierarchical status rankings; moderate social rights; some social exclusion; centrist politics (e.g. Germany).
3. *Social democratic corporatism*—universalistic, generous welfare state; limited income differentials; egalitarian status system; relatively unconditional generous social rights; limited social exclusion; left political dominance (e.g. Scandinavian states).
4. *Oriental corporatism*—private sector-based paternalistic welfare; limited income differentials; traditional status hierarchy; quasi-feudal corporatist duties; little social exclusion but alienation of 'outsiders'; centre-right politics (e.g. Japan).

Cavadino and Dignan's analysis shows that this typology of political economies corresponds to clear differences in the punitiveness of penal policy and culture. The chapters on individual countries, and on particular aspects of policy, detail the complexity that any summary must over-simplify. Nonetheless, the four models of political economy appear to differ qualitatively in penal practice and culture. In terms of punitiveness, as measured by the (admittedly crude and problematic) data on official imprisonment rates, four fundamentally different groups can be discerned: neoliberal countries are the most punitive; conservative corporatist next; social democracies considerably lower; with the oriental corporatism of Japan having the lowest imprisonment rate.

These differences correspond also to variations in styles of penal policy. Neoliberal regimes are much more receptive than social democracies to prison privatization, for example. They also differ in their modes of punishment, with social democracies and Japan more inclined to inclusionary rather than exclusionary methods. The penal ideologies of these regimes differ fundamentally. Neoliberalism is associated with a dominant politics of 'law and order', whilst conservative corporatism emphasizes rehabilitation, and social democracies a rights-based approach. Several other comparative studies confirm the broad pattern of a positive relationship between welfarism and lower punitiveness (Beckett and Western 2001; Western 2006; Downes and Hansen 2006; Pratt and Eriksson 2014).

The explanatory variable in these studies is *political economy*, not economics, and Cavadino and Dignan explicitly reject economic determinism. They deploy a pluralist framework that gives weight to the interaction between material and cultural dimensions, as well as to political conflicts and the practices of individual actors and groups. Other studies have developed the analysis of the *political* in political economy, demonstrating that differences in political institutions and culture help explain variations in penality (Sutton 2004, 2010; Simon 2007; Lacey 2008; Koster *et al.* 2008; Barker 2009; Miller 2010, 2016; Bell 2011, 2014; Ruggiero and Ryan 2013; Scott 2013; Enns 2014; Annison 2015; Gottschalk 2015). The broad shift towards more punitive penality has also been related to changing modalities of control of the labour force and of the marginal 'precariat', dubbed the 'new dangerous class' (Standing 2011), as neoliberalism became hegemonic (de Giorgi 2006, 2012; Wacquant 2009; Cheliotis and Xanakis 2010).

COMPARATIVE CRIMINOLOGY AND CRIME

There is no systematic comparative study of the relationship between crime and political economy, analogous to those on punishment. The well-known hazards of interpreting national crime statistics are amplified by international variations in legal definitions, police practices, and cultural conceptions of crime, order, and morality, bedevilling comparative analysis.

Since 1989 criminologists in several countries have conducted several sweeps of an 'International Crime Victims Survey' (ICVS), seeking to overcome some of these issues (van Kesteren *et al.* 2014). The survey is a state-of-the-art attempt to provide data on comparative crime patterns and trends. Nonetheless, the ICVS ordering of different countries is equally mysterious to liberals, political economists, or deterrence theorists, possibly owing more to cross-cultural vicissitudes in perceptions of order than to crime patterns. The league tables of different societies run so counter to expectation that higher-ranked societies may paradoxically be ones where the relative *absence* of serious violence makes respondents more sensitive to low-level incivility, and thus more likely to report incidents to interviewers (Young 2011: 36–7, 46).

There are fewer problems of international comparison of homicide statistics, because there is less diversity in legal definitions and recording practices. The international pattern of homicide rates fits the Cavadino and Dignan typology of political economies closely (Reiner 2007: 106), with lethal violence highest in neoliberal political economies, and lowest in social democracies.

There are several mediating links between neoliberal political economy and greater pressures towards violent crime (James 1995; Currie 1997, 1998, 2009; Dorling 2004; Winlow and Hall 2006; Hall *et al.* 2008; Hall and McLean 2009; Pridemore 2011; Gilligan 2011; Hall 2012; Hall and Wilson 2014). These include 'the withdrawal of public services and supports, especially for women and children; the erosion of informal and communal networks of mutual support, supervision, and care; the spread of a materialistic, neglectful, and "hard" culture; the unregulated marketing of the technology of violence; and . . . the weakening of social and political alternatives' (Currie 1997: 154). The link between neoliberal political economies and propensities towards serious crime is further supported by historical evidence.

CRIME, JUSTICE, AND POLITICAL ECONOMY: HISTORICAL

Since the Middle Ages, a broad 'civilising process' (Elias 1939/1994), including growing state monopolization of the means of legitimate violence, and the incorporation of the mass of the population into a common status of citizenship, was associated with a secular decline in violence and disorder (Eisner 2001; 2014; cf. also Spierenburg 2008; Roth 2010; Pinker 2011). The long-term trajectory from the medieval period can be summarized roughly as a J-curve (Eisner 2001: 629). Homicide rates fall sharply up to the late eighteenth century. There was then an increase up to the middle of the nineteenth century, but much smaller than the earlier fall. The decline subsequently is resumed until the last quarter of the twentieth century, when there is a return to the levels of the mid-Victorian period. This has again reversed since the mid-1990s, with recorded violent crime falling in Western societies, along with a much debated fall in crime overall (Tonry 2014; Reiner 2016: 125–7, 165–85).

Focusing on the trend since the early nineteenth century in greater detail suggests a U-shape pattern in homicide and other serious crime for most of this period. Crime rates increased between the late eighteenth and mid-nineteenth century, declined in the later nineteenth century, and were fairly stable until the mid-1950s, when there was a return to rising recorded crime (Gatrell 1980; Gurr 1981: 325). The rising recorded crime rates of the second half of the twentieth century have been reversed since the mid-1990s.

Historical studies show a similar U-shaped pattern of violence in political and industrial disorders: secular decline from the mid-nineteenth to the last quarter of the twentieth century, with an increase thereafter. This has gone hand in hand with a similar trend in the militarism of policing tactics (Reiner 2010: 72–4, 85–8, 85–101, 101–3).

Recent econometric evidence further underlines an association between economic fluctuations and political unrest and violence (Bohlken and Sergeant 2010; Ponticelli and Voth 2011).

Attempts to explain these long-term trends must involve a complex mix of interdependent considerations. Eisner, Pinker, and others primarily invoke Elias' analysis of a broader 'civilising process' (Elias 1939/1994). This depicted a secular cultural, social, and psychic tendency of greater sensitization towards control of bodily processes, including violence, during modernization. Whilst the emphasis in Elias' analysis is on cultural and psychic sensibilities, these are intertwined with developments in state formation, together with disciplinary and stabilization processes associated with the emergence of markets and factories (Fletcher 1997: 36, 64). The state came to monopolize the means of violence, as part of a process of pacification of social and economic life, with the police emerging as the institutional locus for this (Bittner 1970; Brodeur 2010).

The changes in cultural sensibilities analysed in Elias' account of the civilizing process were bound up with broad shifts in political economy. A sharpening of social conflicts, crime, and disorder during the early stages of industrial capitalism was succeeded by a long-term process of inclusion of the majority of the population in legal, political, and (to a lesser extent) economic and social citizenship (Marshall 1950). This was the precondition for the mix of mass seduction and discipline represented by 'penal welfarism' during the first three-quarters of the twentieth century (Garland 2001: ch. 2), and 'policing by consent' (Reiner 2010: ch. 3).

Of course the profound changes in social order, crime, and control since the 1970s have complex, multiple, interacting sources. However, a pivotal role was played by the shift from Keynesian political economy and a growing Welfare State (Garland 2016), to 'Washington Consensus' neoliberalism. The main alternative 'grand narrative' is the conservative account that places the primary if not sole explanatory weight on 'permissiveness', the undermining of social controls by liberalism. As Currie has argued most cogently, however, an either/or approach

> begins to get in the way of understanding both the multiplicity and the interconnectedness of the forces that operate to increase the risks of violent crime in specific, real world social circumstances. When we examine patterns of youth violence in, say, South Chicago or South London, we . . . are likely to see great structural inequalities *and* community fragmentation and weakened ability of parents to monitor and supervise their children—and a great many other things, all going on at once, all entwined with each other, and all affecting the crime rate—with the combination having an impact that is much greater than the sum of its parts [Currie 1997: 150].

The emergence of a globalized neoliberal political economy has been associated with social and cultural changes that are likely to aggravate crime, and to displace all frameworks for crime control policy apart from 'law and order' (Reiner 2007). The spread of consumerist culture, especially when coupled with increasing social inequality and exclusion, involves a heightening of what Merton called anomie (Messner and Rosenfeld 2012), to a degree that Jock Young aptly characterized as social 'bulimia' (Young 1999). It generates a broader culture of narcissistic aspiration for more consumer goods that are perpetually out of reach of the legitimate means of many, the seductive edge for crime and disorder (Hayward 2004; Hallsworth 2005; Hall *et al.* 2008; Winlow *et al.* 2015).

At the same time the egoistic culture of a 'market society', with its zero-sum, 'winner–loser', survival of the fittest ethos, erodes conceptions of ethical means of success being preferable, or of concern for others limiting ruthlessness, and ushers in a 'new barbarism' across the social spectrum (Reiner 2016: chs 3, 4). This is indicated by research exploring 'The Moral Maze of the Middle Class' in the UK and Germany, documenting the growth of fraud and unethical business practices, and the techniques of neutralization facilitating this (Karstedt and Farrall 2004). The corruption of the commanding heights of economic power is indicated by the growth of corporate malpractice, whether illegal, on the borderline, or tolerated by a criminal law that has increasingly defined down such egregious activities as tax avoidance by the use of offshore havens (Shaxson 2011; Tombs and Whyte 2015). Informal social controls, the inculcation of a 'stake in conformity', through family, education, and work, become forlorn dreams. The eclipse of social democratic hopes shuts off prospects of alleviating deprivation (absolute or relative) by legitimate collective industrial or political action, leaving the 'responsibilized' individual to sink or swim. Sometimes, as neoclassical economics would predict, offending is the 'rational choice' in adverse labour market conditions. The reversal of the 'solidarity project' (Garland 2001: 199), the long-term incorporation of the mass of the population into a common status of citizenship, which underpinned the 'civilizing process' of declining violence and crime, formed a dark couple of rising crime and harsher control efforts (Reiner 2007, 2011: Part III).

In the 1990s recorded crime figures and victimization survey rates began to fall, first in the USA, but then in most Western countries, including the UK (Blumstein and Wallman 2000; Zimring 2007, 2012; Tonry 2014; Farrell *et al.* 2014; Roeder *et al.* 2015; Reiner 2016: 125–7, 165–85). The dramatic fall in New York City, formerly seen as a world crime capital, attracted particular media attention. This has caused a reverse 'aetiological crisis' to that associated with the 1950s crime rise. No 'grand narrative' seems satisfactory. Neo-liberalism, the Left's prime suspect, retains its global economic hegemony. But conversely there has not been any reversal of 'permissiveness', the Right's dominating bête noire. The favourite criminal justice accounts all have some plausibility, but not as complete explanations.

The zero-tolerance policing explanation, celebrated by many promoters of the supposed New York miracle, fails to survive close analyses. The precise timing of the crime changes in New York does not fit the zero-tolerance account, and many US cities showed similar falls in crime without the same policing changes (Bowling 1999; Karmen 2000; Jones and Newburn 2006: ch. 6; Punch 2007; Young 2011: ch. 6). In so far as policing changes contributed to the fall, it was the 'smart' rather than the 'tough' aspects of the NYPD reforms that were crucial—the managerial and intelligence-analysing reforms referred to as 'Compstat' (Zimring 2012).

Nor has the enormous expansion of punitiveness, above all the staggering and gross levels of imprisonment, contributed more than marginally (Roeder *et al.* 2015). More mundane improvements in the effectiveness of crime prevention have played the largest part in the reduction of 'volume crimes' such as burglary and car theft (Farrell *et al.* 2014).

Within the array of explanations, economic factors are certainly significant, if peculiarly unheralded by governments wishing to appear 'tough on crime' (Reiner 2016: 173–80). But they cannot provide more than part of the explanation. Unemployment has certainly been at much lower levels than during the crime explosion of the 1980s. This has been achieved, however, largely by the expansion of secondary labour market jobs. In the USA there has been no reduction in poverty or inequality. In the UK, the minimum wage had a significant crime reduction effect in some areas. But overall there has not been any significant change in the level of economic inequality and insecurity, which has grown since the 1970s. The crime drop remains something of a mystery, defying any simple account. The Conservative-led governments' austerity policy of cuts since 2010 was predicted to exacerbate the drivers of crime and disorder. However, despite the return of some protests—and riots in 2011—they are nothing like the uprisings of the 1980s, and the officially recorded crime statistics continue to fall. Nonetheless, it would be premature to conclude that the falling official crime statistics are due to conquest of the causes of criminality. There is strong evidence that serious crimes not included in these statistics have increased, in cyberspace (Travis 2015), violence against women hidden behind domestic walls (Walby *et al.* 2015), and crimes of the powerful (Tombs and Whyte 2015).

CONCLUSION: MARKETS, MEANINGS, MORALS

Primarily structural perspectives have been sidelined in the last 30 years, by a number of 'turns' in intellectual, cultural, and political life, a pincer movement from right and left, denying the reality or adequacy of structural causes and grand narratives. This chapter has sought to rehabilitate political economy approaches from these various critiques, restating their importance for understanding patterns and trends in crime and criminal justice. As argued earlier, political economy stands for a holistic approach, but one that recognizes the dialectical complexity of mediations and interactions between macro-structures and individual actions. As Weber put it long ago, explanation has to be both 'causally adequate' and 'adequate at the level of meaning' (Weber 1947/1964: 99–100). *Verstehen* and structural pressures are *both* necessary elements of explanation, complementary not contradictory. Nor (again following Weber's venerable lead) are understanding or explanation incompatible with ethical judgements or policies (Reiner 2011: Introduction).

Contrary to the critiques of 'Realists' of the Left, Right, or centre, recognition of the existence of 'root causes' does not mean that it is unnecessary or undesirable to explore all possible avenues of immediate crime reduction, victim support, or penal reform. However, this should not deny the causal importance of macro-political economy too. This is supported by empirical evidence of relationships between types of political economy and patterns of crime and punishment.

Neoliberal political economies have a 'dark heart' (Davies 1998) of serious crime and cruel punishment compared to social democracies. Short-term pain and symptom relief are helpful and ethical, but only provided they do not become 'liddism' (Rogers 2010), a futile struggle to hold down the lid on what remain 'root causes'. The discourse and practices of law and order that have become increasingly dominant since the late 1970s have exacerbated criminality, 'the tendency of our society to produce criminals' (Currie 2000). During the 1980s and early 90s, when crime rates exploded, this was evident in official statistics. The decline in recorded crime since then was not due to getting tough on crime, let alone on its causes. It is primarily because enhanced security has held the lid down, and because the very mild and *sotto voce* social democratic policies implemented by many Western governments (now largely reversed by Conservative 'austerity') afforded some hope of justice and progress to the socially excluded.

The crime control discourse and policies associated with neoliberalism embody an image of people as necessarily selfishly egoistic and asocial, requiring tough, exclusionary forms of discipline to maintain order and security. This is quite different from the social democratic conception of criminals as people who have acted wrongly, often because of economic and cultural pressures that are themselves targets of reform, but who remain capable of rehabilitation and reintegration. New Labour's espousal of law and order in the early 1990s was a Faustian pact to secure election, but which (together with its broader embrace of neoliberalism) has threatened its political extinction.

The paradox is that social democratic policies—coupled with smarter crime prevention, policing, and penal policy as first-aid responses to crime—*can* deliver lower crime rates. Periods of Labour government have generally been associated with lower crime (Downes and Young 1987; Reiner 2007: chs 3, 4), and the same is true of Democratic presidencies in the USA (Gilligan 2011). Neoliberalism fanned the flames of social breakdown and crime, stimulating an ever more insatiable popular lust for harsher punishments.

Social peace requires getting tough on the 'root causes' of crime that realism scorned. Whilst this perspective has for the time being lost the political battle, it does not follow it has lost the argument. There are still mysteries in explaining the sudden rise of neoliberalism to dominance in the 1970s, sweeping away so rapidly the post-Second World War social democratic consensus that had delivered so much in terms of widely shared growth in material prosperity and security, as well as relatively low crime and benign control strategies by historical standards. Many of the standard accounts assume that the success of neoliberalism is attributable to fatal rather than contingent flaws in the social democratic or Keynesian models it supplanted. Whilst in economics and political philosophy this conclusion is vigorously contested (e.g. Harvey 2005, 2014; Judt 2010; Streeck 2014; Gamble 2014), criminology has largely accepted neoliberal hegemony as inevitable.

Even more important, and at least as mysterious: where are we going now? For a brief moment when credit crunched in late 2007 the neoliberal model seemed discomfited if not totally discredited. Even Alan Greenspan, former Chair of the Fed and high priest of neoliberalism in its heyday, confessed his free market faith had been refuted ('Greenspan: I Was Wrong About the Economy' *The Guardian,* 24 October 2008). But within a couple of years, neoliberalism's savagely deflationary prescriptions for dealing with the sovereign debt crisis (resulting from governmental support for banking to cope with the 2007 banking debacle) became the new 'austerity' orthodoxy, a zombie neoliberalism literally fatal in its consequences (Stuckler and Basu 2013; Reiner 2016: 99–101). John Pilger succinctly nails this 'fraud called "austerity", which demands that ordinary people pay for the crimes of the financial elite' https://profile.theguardian.com/user/id/15931548.

Neoliberalism inevitably fans social injustice, and feeds the barbarisms of disorder and repression (Hall *et al.* 2008; Winlow *et al.* 2015). An alternative narrative to neoliberal instrumentalism and egoistic aspiration is needed, evoking the mutualism of Buber's ideal of 'I-thou' (as argued by Benjamin 2010 in relation to financial markets). This echoes the ethics of the Golden Rule that underpinned social democracy (Reiner 2011: Introduction). Criminology must help chart a way forward to reviving the conditions for security and peace, which social democratic political economies had begun gradually to deliver. This will entail new economic, social, and criminal justice policies that may again advance the security and liberty of the majority of people. The signs are not propitious, but the alternative (as Rosa Luxemburg put it a century ago) is barbarism.

SELECTED FURTHER READING

For analyses of recent crime and criminal justice trends incorporating political economy, see Currie's *Crime and Punishment in America* (1998); Taylor's *Crime in Context* (1999); Garland's *The Culture of Control* (2001); Reiner's *Law and Order: An Honest Citizen's Guide to Crime and Control* (2007) and *Crime* (2016); Hall, Winlow, and Ancrum's *Criminal Identities and Consumer Culture* (2008). Cavadino, and Dignan's, *Penal Systems: A Comparative Approach* (2006), Lacey's *The Prisoners' Dilemma: Political Economy and Punishment in Contemporary Democracies* (2008), and Bell's *Criminal Justice and Neoliberalism* (2011) offer pioneering comparative analyses of the political economy of penal systems.

REFERENCES

Albertson, K. and Fox, C. (2012), *Crime and Economics*, London: Routledge.

Anderson, K. and Quinney, R. (2000), *Erich Fromm and Critical Criminology*, Urbana: University of Illinois Press.

Annison, H. (2015), *Dangerous Politics: Risk, Political Vulnerability, and Penal Policy*, Oxford: Oxford University Press.

Barker, V. (2009), *The Politics of Imprisonment*, Oxford: Oxford University Press.

Becker, G. (1968), 'Crime and Punishment: An Economic Approach', *Journal of Political Economy*, 76(1): 175–209.

Beckett, K. and Western, B. (2001), 'Governing Social Marginality: Welfare, Incarceration and the Transformation of State Policy', *Punishment and Society*, 3(1): 43–59.

Beirne, P. (1993), *Inventing Criminology*, Albany, NY: State University of New York Press.

Bell, E. (2011), *Criminal Justice and Neoliberalism*, London: Sage.

Bell, E. (2014), 'There Is An Alternative: Challenging the Logic of Neoliberal Penality', *Theoretical Criminology*, 18(4): 489–505.

Bemmelen, J. M. (1960), 'Willem Adrian Bonger', in H. Mannheim (ed.), *Pioneers in Criminology*, London: Stevens.

Benjamin, J. (2010), 'The Narratives of Financial Law', *Oxford Journal of Legal Studies*, 30(4): 787–814.

Bittner, E. (1970), *The Functions of the Police in Modern Society*, Maryland: National Institute of Mental Health.

Blumstein, A. and Wallman, J. (eds) (2000), *The Crime Drop in America*, Cambridge: Cambridge University Press.

Bohlken, A. T. and Sergeant, E. J. (2010), 'Economic growth and ethnic violence: An empirical investigation of Hindu-Muslim riots in India', *Journal of Peace Research*, 47(5): 589–600.

Bonger, W. (1916/1969), *Criminality and Economic Conditions*, Bloomington: Indiana University Press.

BONGER, W. (1935), *An Introduction to Criminology*, London: Methuen.

BOWLING, B. (1999), 'The Rise and Fall of New York Murder', *British Journal of Criminology*, 39(4): 531–54.

BOX, S. (1987), *Recession, Crime and Punishment*, London: Macmillan.

CAVADINO, M. and DIGNAN, J. (2006), *Penal Systems: A Comparative Approach*, London: Sage.

CHELIOTIS, L. (2013), 'Neoliberal Capitalism and Middle-class Punitiveness: Bringing Erich Fromm's "Materialistic Psychoanalysis" to Penology', *Punishment and Society*, 15(3): 247–73.

CHELIOTIS, L. and XENAKIS, S. (2010), 'What's Neoliberalism Got to Do With It? Towards a Political Economy of Punishment in Greece', *Criminology and Criminal Justice*, 10(4): 353–73.

CLOWARD, R. and OHLIN, L. (1960), *Delinquency and Opportunity*, New York: Free Press.

COLQUHOUN, P. (1800), *Treatise on the Commerce and Police of the River Thames*, London: J. Mowman.

CURRIE, E. (1997), 'Market, Crime and Community: Toward a Mid-range Theory of Post-industrial Violence', *Theoretical Criminology*, 1(1): 147–72.

CURRIE, E. (1998), *Crime and Punishment in America*, New York: Holt.

CURRIE, E. (2000) 'Reflections on Crime and Criminology at the Millennium', *Western Criminology Review*, 21(1): 1–15.

CURRIE, E. (2009), *The Roots of Danger: Violent Crime in Global Perspective*, Harlow: Prentice-Hall.

DAVIES, N. (1998), *Dark Heart*, London: Verso.

De GIORGI, A. (2006), *Rethinking the Political Economy of Punishment*, Aldershot: Ashgate.

De GIORGI, A. (2012), 'Punishment and Political Economy', in J. Simon and R. Sparks (eds), *Handbook of Punishment and Society*, London: Sage.

DORLING, D. (2004), 'Prime Suspect: Murder in Britain', in P. Hillyard, C. Pantazis, S. Tombs, and D. Gordon (eds), *Beyond Criminology*, London: Pluto.

DORLING, D. (2015), *Injustice*, Bristol: Policy.

DOWNES, D. and HANSEN, K. (2006), 'Welfare and Punishment in Comparative Perspective', in S. Armstrong and L. McAra (eds), *Perspectives on Punishment*, Oxford: Oxford University Press.

DOWNES, D. and YOUNG, J. (1987), 'A Criminal Failure: The Tories' Law and Order Record', *New Society*, 13 May.

EHRLICH, I. (1973), 'Participation in Illegal Activities: A Theoretical and Empirical Investigation', *Journal of Political Economy*, 81(3): 521–63.

EHRLICH, I. (1975), 'The Deterrent Effect of Capital Punishment', *American Economic Review*, 65(3): 397–447.

EISNER, M. (2001), 'Modernisation, Self-control and Lethal Violence: The Long-term Dynamics of European Homicide Rates in Theoretical Perspective', *British Journal of Criminology*, 41(4): 618–38.

EISNER, M. (2014), 'From Swords to Words: Does Macro-Level Change in Self-Control Predict Long-Term Variation in Levels of Homicide?', in M. Tonry (ed.), *Why Crime Rates Fall and Why They Don't*, Chicago: University of Chicago Press.

ELIAS, N. (1939/1994), *The Civilising Process*, Oxford: Blackwell.

ENNS, P. (2014), 'The Public's Increasing Punitiveness and Its Influence on Mass Incarceration in the United States', *American Journal of Political Science*, 58(4): 857–72.

ESPING-ANDERSON, G. (1990), *The Three Worlds of Welfare Capitalism*, Cambridge: Polity.

EYSENCK, H. (1965), *Fact and Fiction in Psychology*, London: Penguin.

FARRELL, G., TILLEY, N., and TSELONI, A. (2014), 'Why the Crime Drop?', in M. Tonry (ed.), *Why Crime Rates Fall and Why They Don't*, Chicago: University of Chicago Press.

FELSON, M. and ECKERT, M. (2015), *Crime and Everyday Life*, 5th edn, California: Sage.

FELSON, M. and CLARKE, R. (1998), *Opportunity Makes the Thief*, London: Home Office.

FIELD, S. (1990), *Trends in Crime and Their Interpretation: A Study of recorded Crime in Post-war England and Wales*, London: Home Office.

FIELD, S. (1999), *Trends in Crime Revisited*, London: Home Office.

FIELDING, N., CLARKE, A., and WITT, R. (eds) (2000), *The Economic Dimensions of Crime*, London: Palgrave.

FLETCHER, J. (1997), *Violence and Civilization*, Cambridge: Polity.

FOUCAULT, M. (1977), *Discipline and Punish*, London: Penguin.

GAMBLE, A. (2014), *Crisis Without End?*, London: Palgrave.

GARLAND, D. (2001), *The Culture of Control*, Oxford: Oxford University Press.

GARLAND, D. (2016), *The Welfare State*, Oxford: Oxford University Press.

GATRELL, V. (1980), 'The Decline of Theft and Violence in Victorian and Edwardian England', in V. Gatrell, B. Lenman, and G. Parker (eds), *Crime and the Law*, London: Europa.

GILLIGAN, J. (2011), *Why Some Politicians are More Dangerous Than Others*, Cambridge: Polity.

GOTTSCHALK, M. (2015), *Caught: The Prison State and the Lockdown of American Politics*, Princeton: Princeton University Press.

GURR, T. R. (1981), 'Historical Trends In Violent Crime', in M. Tonry and N. Morris (eds), *Crime and Justice 3*, Chicago: Chicago University Press.

HAAKONSEN K. (ed.) (2006), *The Cambridge Companion to Adam Smith*, Cambridge: Cambridge University Press.

HALE, C. (2013), 'Economic Marginalization and Social Exclusion', in C. Hale, K. Hayward, A. Wahidin, and E. Wincup (eds), *Criminology*, 3rd edn, Oxford: Oxford University Press.

HALL, P. and SOSKICE, D. (eds) (2003), *Varieties of Capitalism*, Oxford: Oxford University Press.

HALL, S. (2012), *Theorising Crime and Deviance*, London: Sage.

HALL, S., WINLOW, S., and ANCRUM, C. (2008), *Criminal Identities and Consumer Culture: Crime, Exclusion and the New Culture of Narcissism*, Cullompton: Willan.

HALL S. and MCLEAN, C. (2009), 'A tale of two capitalisms: Preliminary Spatial and Historical Comparisons of Homicide', *Theoretical Criminology*, 13(3): 313–39.

HALL, S. and WILSON, D. (2014), 'New Foundations: Pseudopacification and Special Liberty as Potential Cornerstones of a Multi-Level Theory of Homicide and Serial Murder', *European Journal of Criminology*, 11(5): 635–55.

HALL, S. and WINLOW, S. (2015), *Revitalizing Criminological Theory*, Abingdon: Routledge.

HALL, S., CRITCHER, C., JEFFERSON, T., CLARKE, J., and ROBERTS, B. (1978), *Policing the Crisis*, London: Macmillan.

HALLSWORTH, S. (2005), *Street Crime*, Cullompton, Devon: Willan.

HANSEN, K. and MACHIN, S. (2003), 'Spatial Crime Patterns and the Introduction of the UK Minimum Wage', *Oxford Bulletin of Economics and Statistics*, 64: 677–97.

HARKER, J. (2015), 'Oliver Letwin's memo on race is not ancient history. It's current Tory policy', http://www.theguardian.com/commentisfree/2015/dec/30/oliver-letwin-memo-race-1985-riots-david-cameron-2011-race-equality, accessed 16 January 2016.

HARVEY, D. (2005), *A Brief History of Neoliberalism*, Oxford: Oxford University Press.

HARVEY, D. (2014), *Seventeen Contradictions and the End of Capitalism*, London: Profile.

HAYWARD, K. (2004), *City Limits*, London: Glasshouse.

HEALY, D., MULCAHY, A., and O'DONNELL, I. (2013), 'Crime, Punishment and Inequality in Ireland', GINI Discussion Paper 93, Amsterdam: Institute for Advanced Labour Studies.

HOOGHE, M., VANHOUTTE, B., HARDYNS, W., and BIRCAN, T. (2011), 'Unemployment, Inequality, Poverty and Crime: Spatial Distribution Patterns of Criminal Acts in Belgium 2001–6', *British Journal of Criminology*, 51(1): 1–20.

JAMES, O. (1995), *Juvenile Violence in a Winner-Loser Society*, London: Free Association Books.

JEFFERSON, T. (2008), 'Policing the Crisis Revisited: The State, Masculinity, Fear of Crime and Racism', *Crime Media Culture*, 4(1): 113–21.

JENNINGS, W., FARRALL, S., and BEVAN, S. (2012), 'The Economy, Crime and Time: an analysis of recorded property crime in England & Wales 1961-2006', *International Journal of Law, Crime and Justice*, 40(3): 192–210.

JONES, T. and NEWBURN, T. (2006), *Policy Transfer and Criminal Justice*, Maidenhead: Open University Press.

JUDT, T. (2010), *Ill Fares the Land*, London: Allen Lane.

KARMEN, A. (2000), *New York Murder Mystery*, New York: New York University Press.

KARSTEDT, S. and FARRALL, S. (2004), 'The Moral Maze of the Middle Class: The Predatory Society and its Emerging Regulatory Order', in H.-J. Albrecht, T. Serassis, and H. Kania (eds), *Images of Crime II*, Freiburg: Max Planck Institute.

KATZ, J. (1988), *Seductions of Crime*, New York: Basic Books.

KOSTER, DE W., WAAL, VAN DER, J., ACHTERBERG, P., and HOUTMAN, D. (2008), 'The Rise of the Penal State', *British Journal of Criminology*, 48(6): 720–34.

LACEY, N. (2008), *The Prisoners' Dilemma: Political Economy and Punishment in Contemporary Democracies*, Cambridge: Cambridge University Press.

LACEY, N. (2012), 'Punishment, (Neo)Liberalism and Social Democracy', in J. Simon and R. Sparks (eds), *Handbook of Punishment and Society*, London: Sage.

LACEY, N. (2013), 'The Rule of Law and the Political Economy of Criminalisation: An Agenda for Research', *Punishment and Society*, 15(4): 349–66.

LEA, J. (2002), *Crime and Modernity*, London: Sage.

LEA, J. and YOUNG, J. (1984), *What is to be Done about Law and Order?*, London: Penguin.

LEVY, L., SANTHAKUMURAN, D., and WHITECROSS, R. (2014), *What Works to Reduce Crime?: A Summary of the Evidence*, Edinburgh: Scottish Government, http://www.gov.scot/Resource/0046/00460517.pdf, accessed 12 December 2016.

LIN, M-J. (2008), 'Does Unemployment Increase Crime? Evidence From US Data 1974-2000', *Journal of Human Resources*, 43(3): 413–36.

MACHIN, S. and MEGHIR, C. (2004), 'Crime and Economic Incentives', *Journal of Human Resources*, 39: 958–79.

MARRIS, R. (2000), *Survey of the Research Literature on the Economic and Criminological Factors Influencing Crime Trends*, London: Volterra Consulting.

MARSHALL, T. H. (1950), *Citizenship and Social Class*, Cambridge: Cambridge University Press.

MARX, K. (1867/1976), *Capital Vol. 1*, London: Penguin.

MARX, K. and ENGELS, F. (1848/1998), *The Communist Manifesto*, London: Verso.

MATRAVERS, M. (ed.) (2009), *Managing Modernity*, London: Routledge.

MERTON, R. (1938), 'Social Structure and Anomie', *American Sociological Review*, 3(5): 672–82 (revised in R. Merton (1957), *Social Theory and Social Structure*, London: Free Press).

MCARA, L. and MCVIE, S. (2016), 'Understanding youth violence: The mediating effects of gender, poverty and vulnerability', *Journal of Criminal Justice*, http://www.sciencedirect.com/science/article/pii/S0047235216300125, accessed 2 March 2016.

MESSNER, S. and ROSENFELD, R. (2012), *Crime and the American Dream*, 5th edn, Belmont, Cal.: Wadsworth.

MILLER, L. L. (2010), *The Perils Of Federalism: Race, Poverty, and the Politics of Crime Control*, Oxford: Oxford University Press.

MILLER, L. L. (2016), *The Myth of Mob Rule*, Oxford: Oxford University Press.

MOXON, D. (2014), 'Willem Bonger', in J. M. Miller (ed.), *The Encyclopedia of Theoretical Criminology*, Chichester: Wiley Blackwell.

NELKEN, D. (2010), *Comparative Criminal Justice*, London: Sage.

NEOCLEOUS, M. (2000), *The Fabrication of Social Order*, London: Pluto.

PASQUINO, P. (1978), 'Theatrum Politicum: The Genealogy of Capital—Police and the State of Prosperity', *Ideology and Consciousness*, 4(1): 41–54.

PINKER, S. (2011), *The Better Angels of Our Nature: Why Violence Has Declined*, London: Allen Lane.

PONTICELLI, J. and VOTH, H-J. (2011), *Austerity and Anarchy: Budget Cuts and Social Unrest in Europe 1919-2009*, Discussion Paper 8513, London: Centre for Economic Policy Research.

PRATT, J. (2006), *Penal Populism*, London: Routledge.

PRATT, J. and ERIKSSON, A. (2014), *Contrasts in Punishment*, London: Routledge.

PRIDEMORE, W. A. (2011), 'Poverty matters: A reassessment of the inequality-homicide relationship in cross-national studies', *British Journal of Criminology*, 51(5): 739–72.

RADZINOWICZ, L. (1956), *A History of the English Criminal Law Vol. 3*, London: Stevens.

REIMAN, J. and LEIGHTON (2012), *The Rich Get Richer and the Poor Get Prison*, 9th edn, Boston: Allyn and Bacon.

REINER, R. (2007), *Law and Order: An Honest Citizen's Guide to Crime and Control*, Cambridge: Polity.

REINER, R. (2010), *The Politics of the Police*, 4th edn, Oxford: Oxford University Press.

REINER, R. (2011), *Policing, Popular Culture and Political Economy: Towards A Social Democratic Criminology*, Farnham: Ashgate.

REINER, R. (2016), *Crime*, Cambridge: Polity.

ROEDER, O., EISEN, L-B., and BOWLING, J. (2015), *What Caused the Crime Decline?*, New York: Brennan Center for Justice, NYU Law School.

ROGERS, P. (2010), *Losing Control: Global Security in the Twenty-first Century*, 3rd edn, London: Pluto.

ROTH, R. (2010), *American Homicide*, Cambridge: Harvard University Press.

RUFRANCOS, H., POWER, M., PICKETT, K., and WILKINSON, R. (2013), 'Income Inequality and Crime: A Review and Explanation of the Time–series Evidence', *Sociology and Criminology-Open Access*, 1(1): 1–9, available at: https://www.equalitytrust.org.uk/income-inequality-and-crime-review-and-explanation-time%E2%80%93series-evidence-october-2013, accessed 9 January 2017.

RUGGIERO, V. (2013), *The Crimes of the Economy*, London: Routledge.

RUGGIERO, V. and RYAN, M. (eds) (2013), *Punishment in Europe*, London: Palgrave.

RUSCHE, G. and KIRCHHEIMER, O. (1939/2003), *Punishment and Social Structure*, New Jersey: Transaction.

SCOTT, D. (ed.) (2013), *Why Prison?*, Cambridge: Cambridge University Press.

SHAXSON, N. (2011), *Treasure Islands: Tax Havens and the Men Who Stole the World*, London: Bodley Head.

SIMON, J. (2007), *Governing Through Crime*, New York: Oxford University Press.

SPIERENBURG, P. (2008), *A History of Murder*, Cambridge: Polity.

STANDING, G. (2011), *The Precariat: The New Dangerous Class*, London: Bloomsbury.

STREECK, W. (2014), *Buying Time: The Delayed Crisis of Democratic Capitalism*, London: Verso.

STUCKLER, D. and BASU, S. (2013), *The Body Economic: Why Austerity Kills*, New York: Basic Books.

SUTTON, J. R. (2004), 'The Political Economy of Imprisonment in Affluent Western Democracies, 1960-1990', *American Sociological Review*, 69(1): 170–89.

SUTTON, J. R. (2010), 'Imprisonment and Opportunity Structures', *European Sociological Review*, advance access, 11 August, 1–16.

SUTTON, M., SCHNEIDER, J., and HETHERINGTON, S. (2001), *Tackling Theft With the Market Reduction Approach*, London: Home Office.

TAYLOR, I. (1997), 'The Political Economy of Crime', in M. Maguire, R. Morgan, and R. Reiner (eds), *The Oxford Handbook of Criminology*, 2nd edn, Oxford: Oxford University Press.

TAYLOR, I. (1999), *Crime in Context*, Cambridge: Polity.

TAYLOR, I., WALTON, P., and YOUNG, J. (1973), *The New Criminology*, London: Routledge.

TOMBS, S. and WHYTE, D. (2015), *The Corporate Criminal*, London: Routledge.

TONRY, M. (ed.) (2014), *Crime and Punishment in Western Countries 1980-1999*, Chicago: Chicago University Press.

TRAVIS, A. (2015), 'Crime rate to rise by 40% after inclusion of cyber-offences', *The Guardian*, 15 October.

VAN KESTEREN, J., VAN DIJK, J., and MAYHEW, P. (2014), 'The international crime victim surveys: A retrospective', *International Review of Victimology*, 20(1): 49–69.

WACQUANT, L. (2009), *Punishing the Poor: The Neoliberal Government of Social Insecurity*, Durham, N.C.: Duke University Press.

WALBY, S., TOWERS, J., and FRANCIS, B. (2015), 'Is Violent Crime Increasing or Decreasing? A New Methodology to Measure Repeat Attacks Making Visible the Significance of Gender and Domestic Relations', *British Journal of Criminology*, 56(6): 1023–234, available at: http://bjc.oxfordjournals.org/content/early/2015/12/31/bjc.azv131.full, accessed 12 December 2016.

WEBER, M. (1947/1964), *The Theory of Social and Economic Organisation*, Glencoe, Ill.: Free Press.

WEBBER, C. (2007), 'Revaluating Relative Deprivation Theory', *Theoretical Criminology*, 11(1): 97–120.

WEINGAST, B. and WITTMAN, D. (eds) (2008), *The Oxford Handbook of Political Economy*, Oxford: Oxford University Press.

WESTERN, B. (2006), *Punishment and Inequality in America*, New York: Russell Sage.

WILKINSON, R. and PICKETT, K. (2009), *The Spirit Level: Why More Equal Societies Almost Always Do Better*, London: Allen Lane.

WILSON, J. Q. (1975), *Thinking About Crime*, New York: Vintage.

WINLOW, S., HALL, S., TREADWELL, J., and BRIGGS, D. (2015), *Riots and Political Protest*, London: Routledge.

YAR, M. (2013), *Cybercrime and Society*, 2nd edn, London: Sage.

YOUNG, J. (1999), *The Exclusive Society*, London: Sage.

YOUNG, J. (2011), *The Criminological Imagination*, Cambridge: Polity.

ZEDNER, L. (2002), 'The Dangers of Dystopias in Penal Theory', *Oxford Journal of Legal Studies*, 22(2): 341–66.

ZIMRING, F. (2007), *The Great American Crime Decline*, New York: Oxford University Press.

ZIMRING, F. (2012), *The City That Became Safe: New York's Lessons for Urban Crime and Its Control*, New York: Oxford University Press.

6

DELIVERING MORE WITH LESS: AUSTERITY AND THE POLITICS OF LAW AND ORDER

Rod Morgan and David J. Smith

A STARTNOTE

We are writing this startnote in August 2016, four months after completing the main text of the chapter in April. There is seldom a good time to write an essay on the politics of policy-making. There is always a degree of flux. But spring/early summer 2016 proved particularly calamitous. Most analysts confidently anticipated that the referendum which took place on June 23 on whether the United Kingdom should 'leave' or 'remain' a member of the European Community would result in 'remain'. It did not. Brexit prevailed by 52 to 48 per cent. The shock waves felt both nationally and internationally continue to reverberate and the accompanying uncertainties will persist for years. The immediate party political ramifications were seismic. Prime Minister Cameron resigned and his successor, Theresa May, formerly Home Secretary, thereupon purged the Cameron Cabinet, those sacked including Michael Gove, formerly Justice Secretary. Shortly thereafter, a majority of Labour Party MPs supported a vote of no confidence in the leader of the Labour Party, Jeremy Corbyn, and two thirds of his colleagues resigned from the Shadow Cabinet. A leadership battle ensued. Which means that all the key decision-makers cited in what follows are either no longer in post or have a precarious tenure or have responsibilities different from those that prompted us to cite their words. Moreover, because the constituent parts of the United Kingdom voted differently in the referendum, a serious question mark hangs over the future of the United Kingdom. Finally, the prospects of the British economy have been cast fundamentally in doubt which makes the shape of every aspect of short- and medium-term government policy, including justice policy, particularly difficult to assess. Profound uncertainty prevailed in the summer of 2016. It seemed as if Britain had collectively painted itself into a corner from which no one was able confidently to identify an escape route. Trust was in very short supply and the absence of trust provides a poor basis for stable 'law and order' policy formation.

PARADOXICAL POSTURES

In recent years, statements by senior political figures have often contradicted folk knowledge about what their parties stand for.

It [prison] is an extremely expensive way of accommodating people for a time and making no progress whatever in stopping them being criminals. The prison population has soared pointlessly. I would like to stabilize the situation. [Kenneth Clarke, Conservative Minister of State for Justice, BBC television *Newsnight*, 16 September 2011]

Prison DOES Work—and I helped prove it

A key factor in reducing crime has been the increased number of offenders sentenced to prison. From January 1995 to January 2009, in tandem with the fall in crime, the prison population increased in size by 65 per cent. Today, there are 85,000 prisoners in English and Welsh jails—nearly an all-time high . . . The fact that there were 75 per cent more serious and violent offenders in prison in June 2009 than in June 1997, and that they are staying inside for longer, means there are fewer of them on the streets committing crime. . . . Mr Cameron's broad approach was right before the election. Indeed, so was his consistent criticism in his years in opposition that Labour was not being tough enough. Which makes it all the more remarkable that he has allowed his government's penal policy to be dictated not by his own common sense but by Justice Secretary Kenneth Clarke in alliance with 57 Liberal Democrat MPs. The Lib Dems are using the need to cut the deficit to pursue what they have always wanted, which is going back to a more weak penal policy. [Jack Straw, Labour Home Secretary 1997–2001, *Mail Online*, 30 June 2010]

Societies that obsess solely about punishment often end up with large prison populations and a very high rate of reoffending. Countries that go in for a combination approach, including a rehabilitation process, often end up with smaller prison populations, less reoffending and less crime. [Jeremy Corbyn, then a backbench Labour Member of Parliament, during a Parliamentary debate 16 January 2014 (*Hansard* col 381WH), before his election as leader of the Labour Party in September of the following year]

If we are to protect ourselves—and the most vulnerable in society—from brutality, from violence, from exploitation, then we need to ensure that we turn criminals away from crime. And that means a new and unremitting emphasis in our prisons on reform, rehabilitation and redemption. . . . no moral society can tolerate law—breaking without punishment. But we should never define individuals by their worst moments. . . . Committing an offence should not mean that society always sees you as an offender. Because that means we deny individuals the chance to improve their lives, provide for their families and give back to their communities. And as we reflect on the fate and the future of those individuals who have made terrible mistakes we should acknowledge that many will have grown up in terrible circumstances. [Michael Gove, Conservative Minister of State for Justice, speaking to his party's Conference, 5 October 2015]

Politicians from all sides of the political spectrum are starting to realize the diminishing returns from ever higher levels of incarceration. . . . the truth is that simply warehousing ever more prisoners is not financially sustainable, nor is it necessarily the most cost-effective way of cutting crime. . . . being tough on criminals is not always the same thing as being tough on crime. [Conservative Prime Minister David Cameron in a speech at Policy Exchange, a right-leaning 'think-tank', on 8 February 2016]

These quotations illustrate the contradictory, paradoxical ways in which political discourse deals with crime and justice. Conflicting ideas about the appropriate response to crime jostle for attention. No party rejects any of these ideas completely. But attention switches from one to another in response to immediate pressures. Reform and rehabilitation are at best in tension with retribution and deterrence and at worst in outright conflict with them. But an emphasis on one or other does not neatly map onto the territory of political parties. The parties devote sustained attention to developing coherent and consistent programmes on economic policy, whereas crime, justice, and law enforcement have received relatively little attention in political programmes or campaigns since 2005. Thus the policies of two successive Conservative Ministers for Justice—Chris Grayling and Michael Gove—can appear almost diametrically opposed.

THE FRAMEWORK OF THE POLITICS OF CRIME

THE LONGER HISTORY

These paradoxes emerge out of a longer history, as set out in David Garland's classic study *Punishment and Welfare* (1985). Until the middle of the nineteenth century, the usual response to crime was pain, degradation, the destruction of the offender, or exclusion by transportation or imprisonment in harsh conditions. The impact of these practices was greatly softened by the widespread use of fines for many minor offences and the haphazard inefficiency of the system, which meant that only a tiny fraction of offences were prosecuted. The target of enforcement was very largely the working classes, whereas the middle classes were more lightly policed and illegal business activities were dealt with by regulation and civil process. As the century progressed, all areas were required to establish modern police forces on a common pattern, a centrally administered prison system was established, and imprisonment rather than corporal or capital punishment became the usual penalty for most crimes. The policing and prison system was complemented by the efforts of a network of charitable organizations and a system for controlling and managing the destitute in workhouses managed by local authorities. However, by the end of the nineteenth century there was a widespread recognition of a 'social crisis' that began to place intolerable strains on this control system. Some of the factors underlying this perceived crisis were the growth of education, the extension of the franchise, the need for efficiency in business and the military, and the spread of socialism, trade unions, and agitation. There was growing recognition that 'discipline could no longer function through repression and exclusion' (Garland 1985: 247). The response was a deep and wide-ranging reconfiguration of both the penal and the welfare realms which became closely interrelated in a 'penal-welfare complex'. A system of social security was introduced on the insurance principle, although heavily financed by the state, which protected people from the direst poverty but preserved an ideology of individual responsibility. A range of charitable organizations and public officials (probation officers, district nurses, school attendance officers, agencies for the protection of cruelty to children, etc.) came to regulate and support people and families in various ways. In the penal realm there were efforts to provide useful instruction and moral development and to help prisoners find their feet on release. In both welfare and penal realms, the new official functions were intricately meshed with the pre-existing services of charitable organizations.

By the 1920s, the Victorian penal and welfare system had been transformed. Although the Liberal Party was the main political force behind this transformation, it involved Conservatives and the rising Labour Party as well. The reconfigured system provided a minimum level of welfare for the poor, but imposed a whole range of new controls as the price for this security. Prison remained a threat for those inclined to resist these inducements, and as an institution for containing and managing the incorrigible. This transformation brilliantly addressed some of the causes of crime without breaching the ideology of individual responsibility and it marshalled the resources and evangelical zeal of voluntary organizations: it spoke the language of Christian charity rather than coercion by the state. These developments expressed power relationships, but they were so well camouflaged that they were 'depoliticized' (Garland 1985: 250).

After the Second World War, under a Labour government, the penal-welfare system established earlier in the century became the basis for a new settlement within the framework of a strengthened 'welfare state' established on principles laid out by William Beveridge, a leading Liberal, and all major parties bought into what became known as the Butskellite[1] settlement in the post-war period until Margaret Thatcher became leader of the Conservative party in 1975 (Downes and Morgan 1994). By then the steep rise in crime that had started in the early 1950s and was set to continue for 40 years had become impossible to ignore. The Conservatives in opposition spotted the opportunity to attack the Labour government. They fused the rise in crime with the plethora of industrial disputes that characterized the late 1970s attributing both to government policy. So the period of competition between political parties on penal and criminal justice issues began. Thus the post-war consensus, during which policy was substantially left to advisory bodies mainly consisting of experts (Downes and Morgan 1994), was really a development of the penal/welfare complex reshaped between 1880 and 1920. This longer history helps to explain the nature of political discourse about crime and justice after 1975, when the consensus between the major political parties broke down. The penal-welfare settlement combined disparate and contrasting ideas and practices: it incorporated punishment and retribution, but also evangelical moralization, reform and rehabilitation; individual choice and insistence on personal responsibility, but also recognition that poverty, poor living conditions, lack of education and skills, and family breakdown could be causes of crime and were sometimes remediable; an expanding role for the state in control and regulation, but also for voluntary organizations. When politicians after 1975 emphasized some of these elements more than others, they were generally not rejecting the whole penal-welfare settlement, but just trimming the boat.

[1] 'Butskellism' was a term coined in the 1950s to convey the continuity in economic policy between the outgoing Labour Chancellor of the Exchequer, Hugh Gaitskell, and the new Conservative Chancellor, R. A. Butler. See Marwick 1990: ch. 6.

PERCEPTIONS OF CRIME AND PUBLIC DEMANDS

A number of social and economic changes in the post-war period formed a framework within which the politics of crime had to evolve. The very large rise in crime from 1953 to 1994 can be demonstrated by combining data from victim surveys and recorded crime statistics (Smith 1995; Maguire 2012; Maguire and McVie, this volume). In Figure 6.1 the lines show survey data from 1981 (the first year they became available) for five selected crime categories, illustrating the turning point in 1994, when the upward trends reversed. The bars show the percentage of respondents in the same surveys who believed there is 'a little more' or 'a lot more' crime than two years ago ('in the past few years' from 2012–13). Over the whole period, but with apparently random fluctuations from year to year, a solid majority of respondents (generally around 70 per cent) thought crime was rising in the country at large, and this continued even 20 years after the upward trend in crime had reversed. By contrast, perceptions of the crime trend in the local area began to reflect the trend in the actual crime rate about two years after the reversal. These findings constitute the backcloth—not the determinant—to the politics of crime over the period. Politicians have agency. They can, if they choose, play on a vague perception that rising crime is a national problem—a perception that is not generally grounded in lived experience—and they can continue to appeal to such fears even when crime is going down. Alternatively, they can draw attention to conditions on the ground in support of practical and moderate measures to deal with crime, because people notice local improvements.

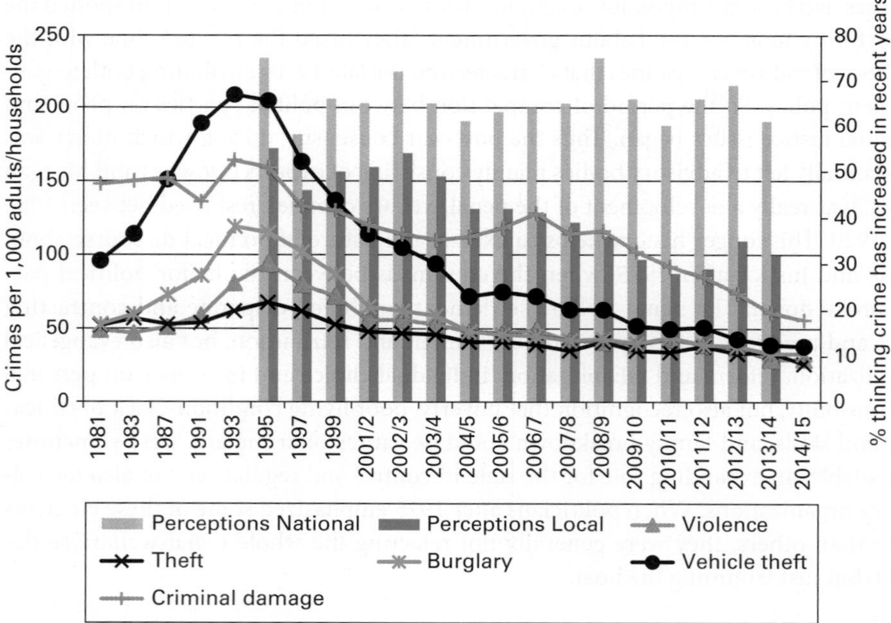

Figure 6.1 Trends in crime and perceptions of crime trends
Source: Crime Survey England and Wales.

Political discourse has also been set free by the exclusion of social scientists from government policy-making forums, for the most part, since the 1970s and their failure to agree about explanations for the dramatic rise in crime in the forty years from 1953, and for the reversal since 1994. The field is left open for politicians to emphasize whichever story best fits their personal or party brand and sales pitch at any particular time. What can be established from social science is that there were too many explanations for rising crime rather than too few: in sociological jargon, the problem was one of 'over-determination'. Most of the plausible explanations had to do with complex social and economic changes such as the rise of consumerism, a feature outside the field of criminal justice and penal policy and largely beyond the control of government. Yet few social scientists would want to exclude the possibility that penal and criminal justice policy played some part in shaping crime trends. When Jack Straw claimed in the article quoted at the head of this chapter that Labour had reduced crime by putting more people in prison, he was placing an emphasis on deterrence and incapacitation that few criminologists would share (Smith 1999; Tonry and Farrington 2005; Tonry 2008). But he was not spouting arrant nonsense: most informed commentators would accept that a functioning penal system is a necessary foundation for crime control in modern societies, and that increases in the probability that offenders will be punished have some (probably rather small) effect in reducing crime. The complexity of causes, and the great difficulty in establishing the relative importance of each, means that politicians are relatively free to place the emphasis where they like. It was Michael Howard who was lucky enough to be Conservative Home Secretary in 1994 when the tide of rising crime finally turned, but also astute enough to coin the slogan 'prison works' (a claim endorsed above by a later Labour Home Secretary, Jack Straw). The slogan is resonant not just because it arrogates all the credit for crime reduction to hard line criminal justice policy, but more because it plays on the multiple meanings of punishment. 'Prison works' because it reinforces social solidarity, satisfies potential and actual victims, ensures bad people get their deserts, and even because it moralizes, reforms and re-educates offenders (Garland 2001).

Because the crime rate is driven by complex causes mostly outwith the field of criminal justice and penal policy, the rising then falling crime rate has been part of the framework within which Home Office and Justice ministers *had* to work rather than the *product* of their policies. It is important to ask, therefore, whether that framework has imposed tight constraints on government action, or whether public concerns and demands have been largely created by politics and media representations. The question cannot be answered conclusively. But there are useful indications from a long series of surveys by Ipsos-MORI on the issues that people consider important.

In surveys of the adult population carried out from 1974 (though, note, there were sparse data points before 1983) up to the present time Ipsos-MORI asked people to name 'the most important issue facing Britain' and then to name any other important issues (Ipsos-MORI 2016). The answers to these open questions were coded by the survey analysts: 'crime, law and order, violence, vandalism' was a coding category from the beginning and throughout. Figure 6.2 shows that the percentage naming crime as an important issue has been highly volatile. There is some evidence that concern about crime can be a direct response to political campaigns. For example, the percentage finding the issue important rose from 14 to 41 between February and April

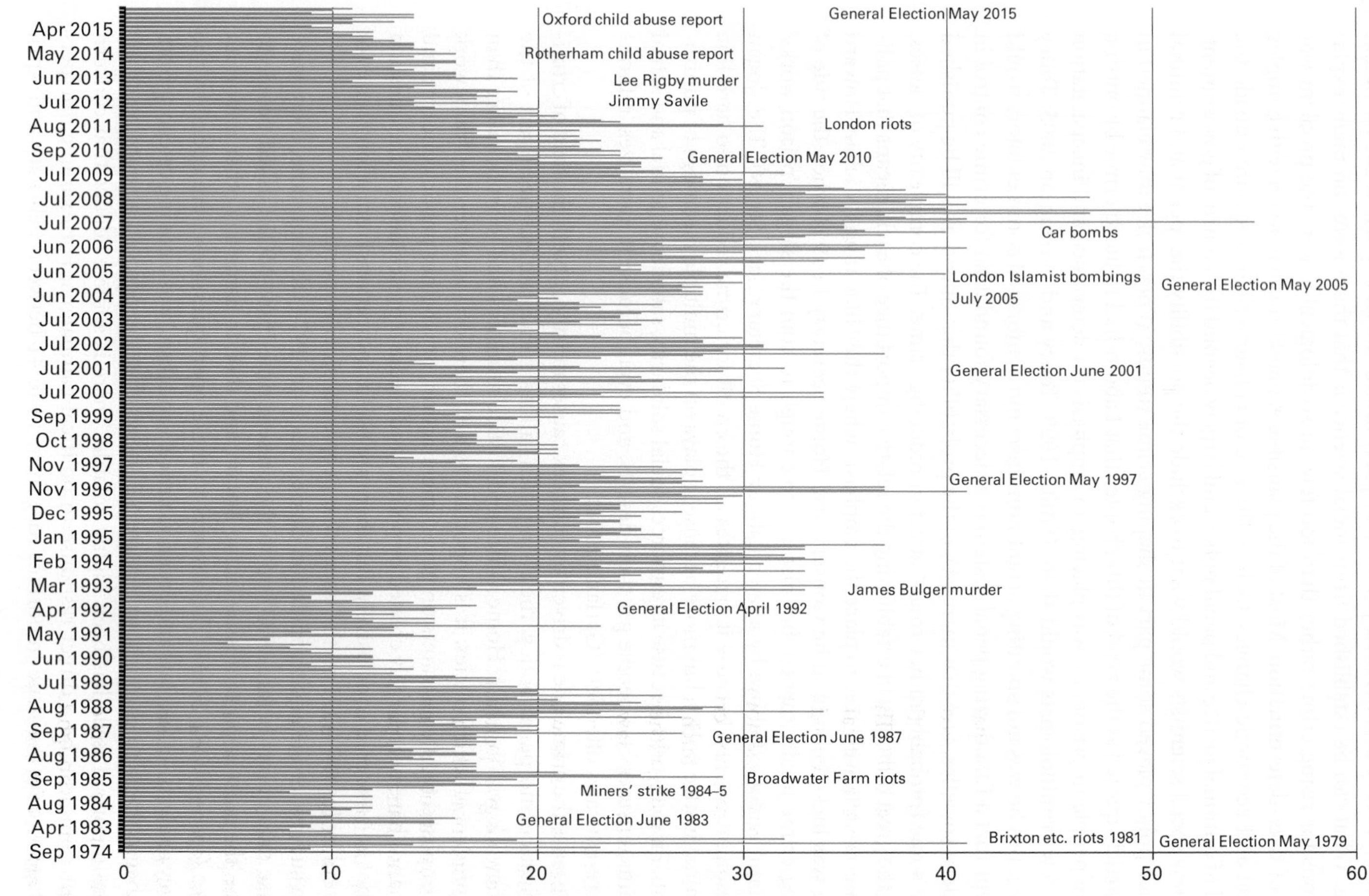

Figure 6.2 Percentage of adults naming crime etc. as one of the most important issues facing Britain

Source: Ipsos-MORI 1974–2006

1979, the month in which the Conservatives won an election on an assertive law and order platform. Serious events may also result in a spike. There was a notable jump in the statistic (up to 29 per cent) at the time of the Broadwater Farm riots in October 1985 and another jump at the time of the murder of two-year old James Bulger in February 1993 (from 17 to 33 per cent). In 1992, when Tony Blair became Shadow Home Secretary, concern about crime according to the Ipsos measure was at a low level (between 9 and 12 per cent). Blair took a calculated, much harder line approach than his Labour predecessors, particularly after the murder of James Bulger— see his own account (Blair 2010)— and concern about crime remained at a relatively high level until the 1997 Labour electoral landslide. It remained fairly high for most of the next decade of Labour government, rising to a particularly high level in 2007 and 2008 coinciding with terrorist incidents and growing concerns about child sexual abuse. However, from 2009 concern about crime gradually declined (apart from a blip corresponding to the riots of 2011) to reach in 2015 some of the lowest levels seen since 1974 when the survey started.

It seems clear from these patterns that public concern about crime (on this measure) is more related to particular events than to trends in the overall level of crime. Some of the highest levels of concern were recorded in 2007 and 2008 when crime had been declining for more than ten years but there had been Islamic bombings in London in 2005 and 2007. There are also times when the trend appears to be closely related to increased political competition on law and order issues. The current low level of concern is confirmed by surveys using closed questions. For example, a YouGov poll carried out in April 2015, two weeks before the General Election, found that only 7 per cent of the electorate thought crime was among the three most important issues facing the country: crime was ranked equal 11th in a list of 13 issues (YouGov 2010; YouGov 2015). Such a low level of concern would probably not be possible if crime had been rising rather than falling for many years. Nevertheless, the patterns support the view that on law and order issues politicians play a leading role in making the weather.

There are other ways, too, in which politicians shape the environment they have to deal with in the field of criminal justice and penal policy. Politicians of all parties present tougher policies as a response to public demand for condign punishment: this phenomenon, which some analysts (following Bottoms 1995) have termed 'penal populism', undoubtedly grew during the 1980s and 1990s. Yet, as a large body of research has demonstrated, public attitudes to crime and punishment are complex and far from being uniformly or increasingly punitive (see, e.g., Jones 2010; Hough and Roberts, this volume). The more that respondents are drawn in to consider case scenarios in detail, the more nuanced and liberal are the responses to crime they consider appropriate. Such findings show that the context in which people consider these matters is all-important, and this context is set as much by politics and mass media representations as by personal experience. The various competing ideas that form part of the penal-welfare settlement are embedded in the public consciousness while the ebb and flow of political discourse and media representations brings one or another set of ideas to the surface at any one time.

In sum, although law and order discourse is necessarily bounded by the nature and extent of crime, it is not determined by it. Party politicians have an attentive ear to crime events which strike the public consciousness (child abuse outrages, acts of racial intolerance, terrorist attacks, urban riots, youth gang-related violence, etc.). In an age of 24-hour media they are regularly called upon, and seek, to demonstrate that they have answers to crime concerns and are capable of managing them more effectively than their opponents. They compete to find an elevator to the high ground of public confidence and system legitimacy. Like the makers of consumer goods they do not create new desires but search out partly hidden needs and satisfactions which have been suppressed for a time by competing priorities. In all this they have agency. They make policy choices. But they do so in the light of what is now a good deal of evidence, assembled by researchers and professional practitioners, as to what will or will not— probably— make a significant difference. Because the politics of law and order are about appearance as well as substance, they pivot on slogans ('prison works', 'tough on crime, tough on the causes of crime', 'zero tolerance', 'truth in sentencing', etc.) as much as on what the system actually delivers. In the early 1980s, for example, Willie Whitelaw as Home Secretary privately admitted that the 'short, sharp, shock' detention centres he introduced but soon abandoned were 'red meat for the blue-rinse mob' (although not in exactly those words) and in reality the treatment of young offenders became less punitive during the 1980s (Graham 2010: 106, fig. 4.1). An ideologically opposite example from the 2010s has been the commitment to 'restorative justice' that is more symbolic than real, except in Northern Ireland: in England, Wales, and Scotland there has been a great deal of talk about doing it but remarkably little action (Collins 2015). Some of these policy disjunctions arise because law and order policies have to be packaged with the rest of the government's programme and wrapped in the ideological commitments of the day— privatization, freedom of choice, individual responsibility, devolution of management, regulation of standards, national identity, sovereignty, and whatever else that may seem to bind the bundle together. At the same time, spending priorities have played a crucial role in shaping law and order policies, to the extent that we need to ask whether fiscal constraints are driving ideology or the other way about. Policing and justice budgets have to compete with other spheres of policy (welfare, education, health, employment, housing, etc.) which arguably have at least as much impact on the incidence of crime and public order as anything done by the police or the judiciary. Explaining the politics of criminal justice and penal policy requires an appreciation of the shifting sands of constitutional change and the interplay of economic, managerial, and ideological forces.

KEY POINTS ABOUT THE POLITICS OF CRIME BEFORE 2010

The post-war story of the politics of law and order up to the period before the 2010 election has been recounted in the corresponding chapter of five previous editions of this *Handbook*. Before continuing the story from 2010, we should recall some features of the earlier trajectory of law and order discourse as described in previous editions.

- After a victorious Conservative party in 1979 initiated a law and order arms race, and after New Labour learnt to compete successfully on these issues, even overtaking the Conservatives in 1997, the contest cooled during the early Noughties, and the financial crash of 2008 put an end to it because of the huge expense of maintaining and—up to then— expanding the criminal justice system.

- Admissions that crime and disorder ills lie to a degree beyond the effective control of government policy can be found as far back as the Conservative Manifestos of 1983 and 1987 (Downes and Morgan 1994: 192). When the economic weather changed, governments therefore had reasoned arguments and an ideology to justify a move away from penal populism.
- After 1997, elections were no longer fought on law and order issues. Although election manifestos still included whole chapters on crime and justice, these were resources to be called on should questions arise, which generally they did not, and they comprised commitments very similar to those of political opponents. Law and order was no longer what the argument was about. It was more about health and employment. Crime was falling. The Labour government, justifiably or not, claimed credit for that fall and the opposition parties did not seek to out-tough them.
- The Labour Administrations from 1997–2010 outdid the expansion of spending on police and justice services of their Conservative predecessors. Whereas spending on the police, for example, had in real terms increased by 33 per cent in the decade 1988/89–1998/99 it rose by 46 per cent in real terms between 1998/9 and 2008/9 (Barclay and Tavares 1999; Mills, Silvestri, and Grimshaw 2010a). The total number of police personnel (officers and civilians) had remained much the same for the last ten years of Conservative government. But during the first ten years under Labour the number rose by 30 per cent. The same pattern emerges from an analysis of probation and prisons expenditure. In 2009 the Labour Party boasted that since it had come to power spending on the prison and probation services had increased by 37 and 70 per cent in real terms compared to a 7 per cent increase and a 5 per cent decrease respectively during the last four years under the Conservatives (Straw 2009; Mills, Silvestri and Grimshaw 2010b). Youth justice expenditure was also up by 45 per cent over the first ten years of Labour government (Solomon and Garside 2008).
- The major part of this substantial growth in expenditure was explained by the record numbers of juveniles and adults in custody, something which the Labour Party was subsequently to claim an achievement in their 2010 Election Manifesto— 26,000 additional prison places since 1997, offenders going to prison for longer, and yet more places, 96,000 overall, to be provided by 2014 (Labour Party 2010), but about which questions were increasingly being asked. The House of Commons Home Affairs Committee (2006/7: 3) for example, noted that the reduction in the incidence of crime had started well before the rise in police numbers. In which case what had justified the increase? These questions, which in the case of the criminalization of juveniles and the increasing use of custody had always been critically posed by the academic research community, could no longer be resisted after the banking crisis and the government's looming budget deficit.

CRIMINAL JUSTICE POLITICS 2010–16

THE 2010 ELECTION AND THE COALITION AGREEMENT

The 2010 General Election will likely go down as a political turning-point comparable in importance to the elections of 1945, 1979, and 1997. During the campaign it was widely predicted that the outcome would be a hung Parliament. So it proved. The Labour Party, uncomfortably led by Gordon Brown following his long and fratricidal partnership with Tony Blair, was compromised by what was widely seen as the disgrace of the Iraq invasion, the likely pointless loss of life arising from the Afghanistan excursion, and the regulatory failure of the state leading up to the banking crisis of 2007–8. The Conservative Party was unable to show clean hands on any of these fronts: it had argued for even greater deregulation of the financial markets, had supported Labour's foreign policies, and was led by the young, untested David Cameron. It seemed possible that the Liberal Democrats might make an electoral breakthrough but, despite the success of their Leader, Nick Clegg, in the innovative television leadership debates, their vote faded and they lost seats. No party commanded an overall majority in the House of Commons and, for the first time since the war-time cabinet of 1940–5, a Coalition government was formed. The Conservatives and Liberal Democrats formed an alliance in which ministerial responsibilities were shared, the Liberal Democrats playing the junior partner.

Forging the Coalition required a compact which superseded and to some extent cut across the parties' election manifestos. The *coalition agreement* dealt mostly with specific policy propositions rather than policy values. But its foreword spoke of redistributing power 'from Westminster and Whitehall to councils, communities and homes' so that 'wherever possible' people could 'call the shots over the decisions that affect their lives' (HM Government 2010:7, an objective which chimed with traditional Liberal values. Likewise the *Comprehensive Spending Review* published in October (HM Treasury 2010) emphasized that the government's spending priorities and departmental budgetary settlements were underpinned by the aim of radically reforming public services to build what the Conservatives had trailed in their Manifesto as the Big Society, 'where everyone plays their part. . . . shifting power away from central government to the local level, as well as getting the best possible value for taxpayers' money'. (HM Treasury 2010: 6). This meant, *inter alia*:

- 'Localizing power and funding', the removal of resourcing ring fences, and 'extending use of personal budgets for service users';
- 'Cutting the burdens on frontline staff, including policing';
- 'Increased diversity of provision in public services through further use of payment by results, removing barriers to greater independent provision, and supporting communities, citizens and volunteers to play a greater role in shaping and providing services'; and
- 'improving the transparency, efficiency and accountability of public services'. (Ibid.: 8)

In the same way that New Labour had in 1997 successfully distanced itself from its Old Labour 'skeletons in the cupboard' (as champions of trade unionism, libertarian causes and, when necessary, civil disobedience: see Downes and Morgan 2002) and captured the electoral centre ground with a promise of being 'tough on crime, tough on the causes of crime', the emphasis being firmly on the former, so the Conservative Party now sought to distance itself from aspects of the Thatcherite heritage. There *was* 'such a thing as society': but it was 'not the same thing as the state' (Conservative Party 2010). The 'Big Society' would replace Labour's 'Big Government'. This meant dismantling New Labour's Whitehall-based, top-down, micro-managerial framework for the delivery of public services and refreshing all sectors with elements of localization, democratization. and diversification. The Prime Minister's Delivery Unit (PMDU) was disbanded and departmental Public Service Agreements (PSAs) with their associated targets, such as the Home Office's 'offences brought to justice' numerical pledge, were abolished. The government would henceforth commit to inputs, not outputs, and departments would be assessed in terms of how well they coped with reduced budgets.

Much of the Coalition rhetoric was broadly in accord with a book—*The Hidden Wealth of Nations*—written by a former Labour Party adviser (Halpern 2010), which argued that though the causal relationship between subjective well being and wealth creation is complex, a strong sense of social well being is important for economic success (see also Stiglitz 1998). Politicians, Halpern suggested, should pay more attention to policies that might enhance public well being. He illustrated his contention by considering the relationship between the incidence of crime and the public's sense of security. Most of the variation between nations regarding fear of burglary is explained, he argued, not by the actual rate of burglary but by the general level of social trust between people. The incidence of crime had to be tackled. But fear of crime and public confidence in the police and criminal justice system should be the focus of policy.

What was needed, Halpern argued, was a shift away from 'squeezing vice' towards 'rewarding virtue', rebuilding what he called the 'gift' or 'regard' economy, the mutually positive way in which people look after each other. 'Regard' had not been sufficiently encouraged or rewarded: for example there were many ASBOs punishing bad behaviour but few individual support orders. This punitive approach carried the danger that people generally treated like rogues tend to become so. What model of government and public services did this imply? Halpern argued that:

> effective government rests heavily on the 'virtue' of citizens, and the strength of social capital and norms in society. These webs of interconnection, everyday habits and institutional habits are what do most of the heavy lifting to keep our societies, economies and governments going. Viewed from this perspective, the state is only a part-player in good government. . .. the paternalistic model. . .. is one rooted in co-production and partnership. . .. agency is not a zero-sum game. More collective responsibility does not necessarily imply less personal responsibility.

Cameron's 'Big Society' rhetoric surfed and sought to capture the communitarian pleadings being canvassed by a range of writers, all of whom spelt out the socially dysfunctional consequences of greater economic inequality, social fragmentation, and political disengagement (see, e.g., Putnam 2001; Putnam and Feldstein 2003; Stiglitz 1998; Wilkinson and Pickett 2009).

The Big Society, however, was backed by precious little operational substance and was seen by many observers as fraudulent cover for sharply reduced, 'austerity' public service budgets and privatization, albeit proposals for more 'contracting out' ostensibly gave equal opportunity to local state and voluntary sector bidders as well as the commercial sector. Further, as we shall see, the commitment to democratization, diversification, and localization was less than consistently applied, nor were Whitehall priorities pursued equally throughout the United Kingdom. Devolution gave rise to variable geometry.

THE COALITION RECORD 2010–15

The Coalition government operated against the background of a global financial crisis and followed 13 years of Labour government during which, as we have seen, there had appeared to be relative plenty and an expectation of rising departmental budgets. It was widely predicted that the strains would see the Coalition's early demise. There were fundamental disagreements and compromises. But the provision for fixed term parliaments (the Fixed Term Parliaments Act 2011 provided for general elections every five years, fixed in advance, as opposed to being called by the government at a time of their choosing) was fulfilled and the half decade was characterized by remarkable political stability. The backcloth was an aimed-for elimination of the deficit and 'austerity'. Spending on some services, health, for example, was to be safeguarded. But public order and safety spending, which largely comprises criminal justice, was among the hardest hit. Whereas expenditure on public order and safety had risen by 17 per cent in the four years to 2010, it fell by 12 per cent in the four years to 2014.

The police, once described by Prime Minister Cameron as the 'last great unreformed public service', received the most political attention and experienced the greatest change. While in Opposition the Conservatives had prepared reform plans (Conservative Party 2007) and moved swiftly to implement them (Home Office 2010). Directly elected Police and Crime Commissioners were to provide greater democratic accountability, though their election in 2012 (following the 2011 Police Reform and Social Responsibility Act) attracted a voter turnout of only 15 per cent, 'the lowest recorded level of participation at a peacetime non-local government election in the UK' (Electoral Commission 2013). Their subsequent operation was anything but smooth: disputes arose between some PCCs and Chief Constables, resignations occurred and it was observed that there were insufficient checks and balances to prevent 'maverick behaviour' (Home Affairs Committee 2013). At the same time the Association of Chief Police Officers (ACPO) had its Home Office funding withdrawn and following a review of police leadership (Neyroud 2011), a College of Policing was established. Further, having completed his highly controversial (as far as the police associations were concerned) review of police pay and conditions (Winsor 2011), Tom Winsor, formerly the rail regulator, was appointed HM Chief Inspector of Constabulary, the first civilian ever to hold the post. Part of the deal for the new Chief Inspector was that the inspectorate should henceforward play no part in the appointment of chief officers (Shute 2013). It was a root and branch assault on the traditional bastions of police occupational power whose reception was marked by the stony silence with which Home Secretary Theresa May was received when she addressed the Police Federation conference in May 2011.

One outcome of the severe cuts to police budgets during the period 2010–15 was a reduction, to 127,110 or 12 per cent, of 17,000 police officers in England and Wales while the Inspectorate of Constabulary, in a series of incisive reports, maintained that many forces had demonstrated that the police were capable of doing as much or more with less (see, e.g., HMIC 2014). The evidence suggested that the incidence of crime continued to fall (with the possible exception of cybercrime) and if there were fewer police officers on the streets, it appeared that the public had generally not noticed (HMIC 2012: 46).

Scandal and irruption is often the trigger for policy change. Two events in particular galvanized politicians' attention. The first was the four days of destructive rioting that convulsed London, and to a degree spread to other urban areas, in the wake of the police shooting of Mark Duggan in Tottenham in August 2011. Thousands of offences were recorded and almost 4000 people arrested of whom over 1200 were convicted and sentenced to immediate custody. The disturbances gave rise to a raft of questions ranging from the quality of police relations with ethnic minority young people to the adequacy of police equipment in the age of social media (see *Guardian*/LSE 2012). They also provoked a government White Paper the title of which, *Swift and Sure Justice* (Ministry of Justice 2012), emphasized that lessons had been learnt which the government intended to weave into a court reform programme on which they had already embarked. The scandal was the publication in 2014 of an independent inquiry report into the sexual exploitation of children in Rotherham (Jay 2014) which came hard on the heels of parallel evidence of child sexual abuse in other cities and the ongoing revelations regarding the abuses perpetrated by Jimmy Savile and other celebrities. The report on Rotherham concluded that the police and senior managers in children's services had for years disbelieved and ignored a litany of reports of abuse and that an estimated 1400 children in that city alone had been victims.

The disjunctions in Whitehall policy were well exhibited by the Courts and Tribunals Service which was stripped of all semblance of local accountability. In 2010 HM Inspectorate of Courts Administration was abolished, scores of local courthouses were closed, magistrate benches were merged, and additional district judges appointed. Unpaid, lay magistrates, arguably the epitome of the 'Big Society', felt marginalized, the admittedly questionable concept of 'local justice' was undermined, and the administration of courts wholly centralized (Magistrates Association 2012; Morgan 2013). Major financial reforms followed. Language services for the whole of the England and Wales justice sector were commissioned and the contract awarded to Applied Language Services, almost immediately acquired by Capita. The service delivered fell woefully short and resulted in a highly critical parliamentary report of the lack of consultation in the commissioning process (Public Accounts Committee 2012). Even more controversial were the cuts to legal aid for both civil and criminal court cases. By 2015 it was no longer an amusing novelty to see bewigged lawyers protesting with placards outside Parliament or on the pavement before the Royal Courts of Justice. Access to legal aid was restricted and competitive price tendering introduced for the provision of legal services to clients with neither the knowledge nor the resources to select their own representatives.

More fundamental was the marketization of penal services. After 24 years of contracting out the management of a few prisons (and, much earlier, that of immigration detention centres), the prison service was relatively well prepared for the decision to market test nine further prisons, all of them establishments said to deliver poor value for money when benchmarked against their peers. In the event, however, the market testing plans fell apart and only two prisons, Birmingham and Northumberland, underwent the process, which proved too slow and unlikely to deliver the cost reductions the government was intent on achieving (le Vay 2016; Ludlow 2015). However, the breaking up of the probation service in order that it be *delivered* to the market represented a full frontal assault on a national service exhibiting low morale and lacking effective leadership. The probation trusts, the legacy from the pre-millennium days when probation services were genuinely local, were abolished, core court and high risk supervision services were retained by a National Probation Service, itself part, alongside the Prison Service, of the National Offender Management Service (NOMS) within the Ministry of Justice, and all other work with low and medium risk offenders taken on by 22 Community Rehabilitation Companies dominated by the private sector. Early performance reviews by the Inspectorate of Probation are identifying all the liaison shortcomings that one might expect from this fracturing of what had previously been a unified service and it is not without significance that one previously senior NOMS insider has described the exercise as 'like watching people doing their best to organize the perfect train crash' (Le Vay 2016: 251). For while these budgetary cuts and fundamental organizational changes were taking place the caseloads remained steady, in the case of prisons at a near record high of 86,000.

Yet Justice Minister Grayling was simultaneously presiding over the continuation of a revolution in youth justice started by the previous Labour government. Since 2007–8, both the number entering the youth justice system and the number in custody has fallen by about three quarters (Ministry of Justice/Youth Justice Board 2015), a truly dramatic reduction achieved by a mix of initiatives (abandonment of police targets for 'offences brought to justice', charging local authorities for the costs of custodial remands, incentivizing diversion initiatives, and generally raising awareness in high custody areas—see Allen 2011) about which no government politician has boasted and which has attracted virtually no media attention. It has been done by stealth with, as far as can be gauged, no adverse consequences for youth crime rates or the safety of the public at large. And the shift has hugely reduced expenditure by permitting the closure or reassignment of several youth justice custodial establishments. Grayling quietly allowed these initiatives in youth penal policy to continue while at the same time acting tough on treatment of adult offenders.

On one interpretation, the 'Big Society' agenda was about decentralizing, giving power back to local communities and institutions, and reducing the dominance of 'Big Government'. Yet clearly the thrust of criminal justice policy in the Coalition years was the opposite. The police reforms were about reducing the power of local police chiefs and imposing centrally prescribed standards through the Inspectorate and the College of Policing. The new Police and Crime Commissioners were represented as a gain in local democracy, but were really another attack on the power of local councils, a long-established, legitimately democratic institution (Jones *et al.* 2011). Courts and tribunals were stripped of local accountability. Probation for serious offenders was more strongly centralized than before, whereas probation for minor offenders was privatized, with two giant transnational companies, Sodexo and Interserve, gaining more than half of the contracts. Whereas privatization of probation and prisons was represented as devolution of power, it actually places that power in the hands of very large and unaccountable transnational companies that legitimize their activities through partnerships with British 'voluntary' organizations, such as NACRO. One result is that this new, capitalist stakeholder has an obvious interest in expanding the market for penal services (Christie 1993).

WALES, SCOTLAND, AND NORTHERN IRELAND

Longstanding political differences between England and Wales, Scotland, and Northern Ireland have been given greater scope for differentiation in recent years as a result of devolution. The Centre for Crime and Justice Studies, which routinely monitors and reports on UK crime and justice policy developments, has suggested that the principal driver of policy across the UK has been austerity, but that beneath that leitmotif there have been important distinctive differences in each of the four countries (Garside and Silvestri 2015: 26–9). We concur. Public order and safety spending declined throughout the UK during the Coalition years and the fall was greatest (over 20 per cent) in both England and Wales, this area of spending not being devolved to the Welsh Assembly. In Northern Ireland and Scotland, where decision-making lay with the Northern Ireland Assembly and the Scottish government, the cuts were tempered, though they were nonetheless significant (13 and 9 per cent respectively). In England and Wales austerity was combined with the vigorous development of the market, procuring competitive bids from the commercial and voluntary sectors and from state agencies for the contracted out management of former state services. The appetite for contracting out services was much smaller in Scotland and Northern Ireland (and would have been in Wales, had the devolution settlement for the Welsh Assembly been extended to cover policing and justice, as the Assembly wished). In Scotland the emphasis was on the central and local state taking direct responsibility for the challenges posed by austerity. Whereas Labour Home Secretary Charles Clarke had sought and failed in 2005–6 to merge the 43 police forces in England and Wales into eight to twelve regional forces, in 2013 the Scottish government merged eight mostly small Scottish police forces to form Police Scotland. In Scotland the management of two prisons was early contracted out (as a result of which the proportion of Scottish prisoners held in contracted out institutions is ironically higher than in England) but devolution and the opposition of the ascendant Scottish Nationalist Party has for the foreseeable future put an end to further commercial management (Taylor and Cooper 2002). In England and Wales 14 institutions are privately managed including several so-called DCMF (designed, constructed, managed, and financed) establishments the contracts for which run for 25 years. Though the debate in Scotland regarding what constitutes effective supervision and programming for offenders best to achieve desistance from offending (see McNeill 2015) is similar to that in England and Wales, there is no probation service as such in Scotland, the supervision of offenders being undertaken by local authority social work departments with 100 per cent funding by the Scottish government.

Policing and justice services were devolved to the Northern Ireland Assembly in 2010 following the Good Friday Agreement. From 1968 onwards, the 'troubles' had bequeathed a 'pumped up' level of spending on law and order, and the power sharing arrangements meant that maintaining the peace was more important than scaling down expenditure to a level comparable to the rest of the UK. It has also meant that far greater engagement with civil society in the delivery of law and order services has continued. Thus, for example, whereas in England and Wales there has been a good deal of rhetoric but remarkably little implementation, in Northern Ireland restorative justice is embedded in law and penal practice. For much the same reason the probation service in Northern Ireland has a strong 'Big Society' commitment to community engagement (see Carr and Maruna 2012).

Though criminal justice services are not yet devolved to the Welsh Assembly, services that arguably have as great an impact on crime and the response to crime—health, education, housing, employment, etc.—are devolved, and the Assembly has from the outset been dominated by a Labour Party with a distinctly Old rather than New Labour tendency. Wales' distinctly 'welfarist' approach has meant that Welsh youth justice policy has been in the vanguard of the trend away from criminalization and incarceration (Drakeford 2010; Haines *et al.* 2013).

THE 2015 ELECTION

At no point in the 2015 Election campaign did 'law and order' figure as an issue. With the exception of the Scottish Nationalists the main political parties did what was by now customary: they each devoted at least a whole chapter in their substantial manifestos to 'crime and punishment' or 'community safety' issues. They prepared for the unexpected: they sought comprehensive policy coverage. But the focus of their leaders' pitches in the high profile television debates, their daily press releases, and their proxy news stories all lay elsewhere. This was an election quintessentially about the 'economy, stupid'. The party political battle was about how and over what period of time to reduce the national debt and balance the budget. Almost all specific policy issues—which public services should be protected and which cut, welfare reform, at what level to set the minimum or living wage, and so on—were ultimately resolved with reference to the core issues and claims to 'fiscal responsibility'. The closest the debate came to 'law and order' issues was with reference to immigration—safety issues arising out of the growing numbers of migrants entering the country and whether the government controlled our border. Even here, however, the focus was on economics—on whether public services were able to cope with the influx and whether wage rates were being driven down.

This is not to suggest, however, that manifesto details are unimportant. Analysis of the records of government administrations over the last half century suggests that manifesto statements are rather a good guide to policies subsequently enacted (see previous versions of this chapter in earlier editions). Furthermore, major reversals of manifesto undertakings can result in profound losses of legitimacy. The failure of the Liberal Democrats to honour their 2010 promise to abolish university undergraduate fees was highlighted by Labour in the 2015 campaign and probably had a crucial influence on the outcome (see the next section of this chapter). And the Conservatives' major reorganization of the health service after 2010, a restructuring disavowed beforehand, subsequently undermined their claim that the National Health Service was 'safe in their hands'.

How much agreement, then, was there between the major parties' manifestos about 'law and order' policy?

With regard to immigration there was a good deal of common ground. Both the Conservatives and Labour promised to get tougher on illegal migrants and foreign offenders resident in the UK. The Conservatives would adopt a 'deport first, appeal later' policy (Conservative Party 2015: para 31). The Liberal Democrats emphasized that the Coalition had already 'begun to tackle abuse in our immigration system . . . closing colleges that break the rules, cracking down on illegal working and human trafficking, and reintroducing border checks' (Liberal Democratic Party 2015: 118). Labour would strengthen the Border Force, 'introduce stronger controls to prevent those who have committed serious crimes coming to Britain', and deport more (Labour Party 2015: paras 48–9).

Regarding policing and penal policy, the competing claims circled around the government's record and the direction of policy travel: just below the surface lurked the issue of 'fiscal responsibility'. Both the Conservatives and the Liberal Democrats unsurprisingly took credit for the continuing fall in the incidence of crime and the Conservatives vowed to push forward the police reform programme on which they had embarked: with the introduction of Police and Crime Commissioners the police were now more accountable; red tape had been reduced (thereby ensuring that more officers were engaged in front line duties); the police and penal services would be given the latest technological aids; fighting cybercrime, female genital mutilation, and child sexual abuse would be given a higher priority; a new Victims Charter had been introduced (Conservative Party 2015). Labour by contrast pointed out that the incidence of certain crimes had risen and undertook to scrap Police and Crime Commissioners. They would also safeguard neighbourhood policing, which the government's expenditure cuts were threatening. The Liberal Democrats sought to distance themselves from aspects of the Coalition record. They would replace Police and Crime Commissioners with Police Boards, and reduce the prison population by placing more emphasis on community-based rehabilitative programmes. They would also conduct an 'impact assessment' of the new legal aid arrangements and amend where the evidence demonstrated that justice was being denied (Liberal Democratic Party 2015). All three major parties would somehow make prisons more rehabilitative.

THE ELECTION OUTCOME

Though it was widely predicted that stalemate and coalition government would be the outcome in May 2015, the Conservatives secured an outright majority, the Liberal Democrats were reduced to a rump while Labour was almost wiped out in Scotland and failed badly to make headway elsewhere. South of the Border the Conservatives were judged by the electorate to have the safest pair of hands for running the economy and in Scotland the Nationalists, despite their failure to secure independence in the 2014 referendum, swept the board.

Other than filling government posts formerly occupied by Liberal Democrats, the Prime Minister, David Cameron, introduced very few new faces to senior posts. Theresa May remained Home Secretary, though Michael Gove replaced Chris Grayling as Minister of Justice, while Grayling became Chief Whip. Mr Gove, it was thought, might be as much the harbinger of change as Kenneth Clarke had promised to be in 2010–1, until he was shortly moved to the backbenches.

From the outset Theresa May made it clear that reform of the police and reductions in expenditure were to continue unabated. The police were to do yet more with less, with Chief Inspector of Constabulary Tom Winsor as the effective monitor of what was possible. Only when, in late autumn 2015, it became apparent that the Home Office had miscalculated their new police funding formulae did the dire warnings of chief constables and police and crime commissioners begin to get an attentive hearing. Was it really sensible to close as many police stations, lay off as many Community Police Support Officers and constables and effectively abandon the neighbourhood policing framework which had previously been said to be so vital a part of community confidence and safety? And could the police really give more attention to the running sore of child sexual abuse (previously neglected), the growing problem of cybercrime and the increased risks of terrorism, if their numbers were depleted as the inevitable outcome of the cuts to their budgets? In late 2015 Theresa May wisely announced that the introduction of the new funding formulae would be got right and delayed it. But she emphasized that whatever the new method for determining the distribution of expenditure between areas, overall spending on policing would be reduced over the period 2015–19, meaning that police forces would have to make do with fewer buildings, fewer officers in senior ranks, more imaginative use of police civilian staff, and improved collaboration between forces in providing specialist and back-office services. This warning was reiterated by the Association of Police and Crime Commissioners after the 2016 Budget announcement in March 2016: the Association anticipated that the number of police officers in England and Wales might fall to 100,000.[2]

Meanwhile Michael Gove delivered a distinctive speech to the 2015 Conservative Party Conference (see quote at the head of this chapter) and in February 2016 the Prime Minister himself devoted a lengthy speech to prisons policy, a virtually unprecedented event. The key point to note in these two coordinated speeches is that the aim of reducing the size of the prison population was implicitly disavowed. The government believed in punishment. Most prisoners deserved to be in prison. And judges needed the increased sentencing powers they had been given. But behind this disavowal was an agenda with substantial reductionist potential. The mentally ill and women with small children could be 'dealt with in a different way'. 'Foreign national offenders' could be deported more speedily. The American specialist drugs court model with its 'tough-love', repeated drug testing in the community approach could be emulated. Satellite tracking of offenders in the community offered great opportunities. These possibilities were to be explored because 'politicians from all sides of the political spectrum are starting to realize the diminishing returns from ever higher levels of incarceration' (Cameron 2016).

The reductionist imperative was urgent for, as the outgoing Chief Inspector of Prisons, Nick Hardwick, had emphasized, a declining number of prisons (18 prisons providing roughly 6000 places had been closed since 2010 and slightly fewer beds provided in either new prisons or new cell blocks on existing sites (see Le Vay

[2] http://www.apccs.police.uk/press_release/budget-cuts-will-radically-change-policing/, accessed 13 December 2016.

2016: 37) were increasingly overcrowded and poorly staffed. Prisoner suicides were up as was the incidence of prisoner-on-prisoner and prisoner-on-staff violence. Drug use was prevalent and tensions were said to be running high (HM Inspectorate of Prisons 2015). Were a serious prison disturbance to occur or a prison officer to die, the consequences would inevitably be laid squarely at the door of the government.

It remains to be seen whether Justice Secretary Gove can shift the centre of policy gravity away from incarceration for adult offenders towards punishment and control in the community. All the signs are that he intends to allow the striking decline in incarceration of young people to continue, and he may or may not decide to take that as an example for the adult system. In early 2016 an interim review of the youth justice system conducted for the government by Charlie Taylor, an ex-head of a special school, was published, which pushed the youth justice reductionist/reformist agenda further. On the strength of the report, the Minister asked the Lord Chief Justice 'to develop proposals for greater use of problem-solving approaches in our courts' (Ministry of Justice 2016). Taylor concluded that most staff in youth custodial institutions did not have the requisite skills to deal with their charges, 'rather than preparing children for life outside, too often these establishments seem to be teaching children how to survive in prison'. He recommended that what was required was rather the creation of small, local schools for young offenders 'in which we overlay the necessary security arrangements', a proposal which 'presents financial and operational challenges'. Challenges indeed, and a far cry from Chris Grayling's 2013 proposal that there be built a 1000-bed youth prison in the East Midlands capable of housing the overwhelming majority of young prisoners in England and Wales, a plan which Michael Gove scrapped shortly after taking office as Justice Secretary in 2015.

Should he wish to carry over the youth justice transformation to adult offenders, Michael Gove may wish to take up the proposal by the Institute for Public Police Research (IPPR), a left-leaning think-tank, that local authorities be incentivized to develop community programmes, thereby persuading the courts to send fewer offenders from their areas to prison (Clifton 2016). Directly elected mayors and Police and Crime Commissioners could be given, IPPR suggests, a 'custody budget' representing the current cost of imprisoning low level offenders from their areas, a budget which they would retain if offenders were in future dealt with in the community but charged against if they were imprisoned. This 'justice re-investment' concept lay at the heart of the successful reduction in the criminalization and incarceration of children and young persons by the Youth Justice Board and was commended as an approach by the House of Commons Justice Committee under a Labour government (House of Commons Justice Committee 2009: see also Fox, Albertson, and Wong 2013). It seems probable that it will find favour with a Conservative government needing further severe cuts in the costs of a prisons system whose population still stands, at 86,000, at a near all-time record high. It is certainly an approach which will chime well with Michael Gove's announced intentions of giving prison governors greater autonomy to commission services locally, a policy he is carrying over from the 'academization' of schools which he pursued as Education Secretary.

However, the scope that each Justice Secretary has to change penal culture, institutions, law, and practice, is limited by the consequences of actions taken by earlier Justice Secretaries, and whenever a Justice Secretary takes decisions in response to the pressure of events, such decisions have often unintended consequences that will frustrate future attempts at reform. For example, a number of events and decisions, some of them progressive in intention, have led to increased sentence lengths and the rise of the prison population. It was a reformist 'guidelines movement' which, with the aim of promoting consistency in sentencing, advocated the Sentencing Advisory Board established in 1998 and the Sentencing Council in 2010. This Council, dominated by its judicial members, now issues sentencing guidelines which every court is statutorily obliged to follow (see Ashworth and Roberts, this volume). Within this framework of sentencing guidelines, New Labour's Criminal Justice Act 2003 introduced the concept of the 'dangerous offender' and prescribed increased and in certain cases indeterminate sentences for such offenders (described as a 'penological disaster' by Ashworth and Roberts 2012: 889). Furthermore, past Home Secretaries have ratcheted up sentencing minima for murder. In combination, these past decisions and the institutional cultures they have engendered have locked sentencing practice into greatly increased tariffs that could only be unscrambled by a Justice Secretary determined to beat off the brickbats of political opponents accusing him of being soft on serious crime. Diversion of juvenile offenders from being criminalized is one thing: getting the sentencing tariff down for recidivist burglars or street robbers carrying knives is a different matter altogether. Penal politics in the UK are not subject to the highly devolved, democratic populist pressures which characterize the United States (see Garland 2013). But they are nonetheless hemmed in institutionally. Various observers have canvassed the return of some form of independent advisory or executive body comprising experts or representative practitioners from the key criminal justice agencies, the equivalent of the National Institute for Clinical Excellence or the Office for Budget Responsibility in the fields of health and fiscal policy (see Lacey 2008; Jones 2010) but there seems little immediate prospect of our elected politicians giving up power which is useful in gaining votes, as long as the public are convinced that they are exercising it legitimately.

CONCLUSION

Keeping the peace and controlling crime are core tasks that define what is meant by government, and consequently they are essential to politics. Yet there is a disjunction between the symbolic significance of law and order and the means available to achieve results. There is no shortage of social and economic policies that have an influence on crime and security, but law and order remains a core area of policy where outcomes are hard to identify and the tools labelled for the job can seldom be shown to be effective. These are circumstances ripe for symbolic politics used to boost government legitimacy, and both rising and falling crime provide opportunities for grandstanding. Yet political leaders have not always grasped such opportunities. For 30 years there was cross-party consensus, with little attempt to question the penal-welfare settlement that had emerged in the early part of the twentieth century. Then in the Thatcher and Blair years, the parties took to marketing fear and competed to out-tough each other, before returning from the late-1990s to something closer to the earlier consensus. The polling data show that political leaders in Britain have not been obliged by the pressure of public opinion to adopt tougher (or for that matter, more compassionate) policies. Instead, they have made choices in response to the opportunities they saw, and they could have chosen otherwise.

The story of the politics of crime over the past 50 years leads to some surprising conclusions. One is that amid the ebb and flow of political competition, the penal-welfare settlement lives: the twists and turns have never meant a radical departure from the complex balancing act achieved early in the twentieth century. Many or most important changes of policy take place under cover of political rhetoric that contradicts them—most notably, the reductions in youth custody during the Thatcher years and most strikingly under the Coalition government with a stridently right-wing minister, Chris Grayling, in charge. The need to cut expenditure can lead to radical change of policy that may be of a broadly progressive kind. It is therefore possible that, with the appointment of Michael Gove as Minister of Justice, a Conservative Party government, traditionally the high church of law and order, may turn out to be more confident than any previous post-war government about challenging the police and radically reshaping penal policy.

SELECTED FURTHER READING

The grand theorizing range of Garland's *The Culture of Control* (2001) has been followed by several comparative empirical studies considering aspects of law and order policy. These include: Stenson and Sullivan's *Crime, Risk and Justice: The Politics of Crime Control in Liberal Democracies* (2001); Newburn and Sparks', *Criminal Justice and Political Cultures—National and international dimensions of crime control* (2004); Cavadino and Dignan's *Penal Systems: A Comparative Approach* (2006); Killias' article on 'crime waves, law creation and crime prevention' (2006); the collection of essays edited by Tonry on *Crime, Punishment, and Politics in Comparative Perspective* (2007); Lappi-Seppälä's essay on 'Imprisonment in Europe' (2011); and Jones and Newburn's monograph *Policy Transfer and Criminal Justice* (2006).

Readers looking for detailed analyses of the part played by 'law and order' issues in British general elections since 1945 should consult the essays on this topic by Downes and Morgan in earlier editions of this *Handbook*. Norton's *Law and Order and British Politics* (1984) and Brake and Hale's *Public Order and Private Lives: the Politics of Law and Order* (1992), the latter a highly critical account of the Thatcher years, are among the few British studies of the topic. Downes' edited collection, *Unravelling Criminal Justice* (1992), contains relevant essays, particularly those by Bottoms and Stevenson on the extent and difficulties of the liberal consensus, and McBarnet on the burgeoning field of tax avoidance and evasion. Hood's collection, *Crime, Criminology and Public Policy: Essays in Honour of Leon Radzinowicz* (1974), provides detailed scrutiny of the public policy issues of the mid-period, and Morris' *Crime and Criminal Justice in Britain Since 1945* (1989) covers the entire period with shrewd political insight. The criminal justice record in the government of early New Labour is critically scrutinized by Tonry in *Confronting Crime* (2003) and the manner in which unforeseen events and the media shaped policy under New Labour up to 2010 is insightfully analysed by Silverman in *Crime, Policy and the Media* (2012). Finally, Ryan's *Penal Policy and*

Political Culture in England and Wales (2003) documents the micro-politics of penal reform in the wider political economy of Britain.

REFERENCES

Allen, R. (2011), *Last Resort?: Exploring the reduction in child imprisonment 2008-11*, London: Prison Reform Trust.

Ashworth, A. and Roberts, J. (2012), 'Sentencing Theory, Principle and Practice', in M. Maguire, R. Morgan, and R. Reiner (eds), *The Oxford Handbook of Criminology*, 5th edn, Oxford: Oxford University Press.

Barclay, G. and Tavares, C. (eds) (1999), *Information on the Criminal Justice System England and Wales*, London: Home Office Research, Statistics and Development Directorate.

Blair, A. (2010), *Tony Blair: A Journey*, London: Random House.

Bottoms, A. E. (1995), 'The Philosophy and Politics of Punishment and Sentencing', in C. Clarkson and R. Morgan (eds), *The Politics of Sentencing Reform*, Oxford: Oxford University Press.

Brake, M. and Hale, C. (1992), *Public Order and Private Lives*, London: Routledge.

Cameron, D. (2016), 'Prison Reform—speech delivered to Policy Exchange', Westminster, 8 February 2016, https://www.gov.uk/government/speeches/prison-reform-prime-ministers-speech, accessed 12 December 2016.

Carr, N. and Maruna, S. (2012), 'Legitimacy through Neutrality: probation and conflict in Northern Ireland', *Howard Journal*, 51(5): 474–87.

Cavadino, M. and Dignan, J. (2006), *Penal Systems: A Comparative Approach*, London: Sage.

Christie, N. (1993), *Crime Control as Industry*, 2nd enlarged edn, London and New York: Routledge.

Clifton J. (2016), *Prisons and Prevention: giving local areas the power to reduce offending*, London: IPPR.

Collins, J. (2015), 'Restorative Justice in England and Wales: From the Margins to the Mainstream', *Restorative Justice, an International Journal*, 3(1): 129–34.

Conservative Party (2007), *Policing for the People: Interim report of the police reform taskforce*, London: Conservative Party.

Conservative Party (2010), *Invitation to Join the Government of Britain: the Conservative Manifesto 2010*, London: Conservative Party.

Conservative Party (2015), *Conservative Manifesto: Strong Leadership, A Clear Economic Plan, A Brighter More Secure Future*, London: Conservative Party.

Downes, D. (ed.) (1992), *Unravelling Criminal Justice: Eleven British Studies*, Basingtoke: Macmillan.

Downes, D. and Morgan, R. (1994), '"Hostages to Fortune"? The Politics of Law and Order in Post-War Britain', in M. Maguire, R. Morgan, and R. Reiner (eds) *The Oxford Handbook of Criminology*, 1st edn, Oxford: Oxford University Press.

Downes, D. and Morgan, R. (2002), 'The Skeletons in the Cupboard: The Politics of Law and Order at the Turn of the Millenium', in M. Maguire, R. Morgan, and R. Reiner (eds), *The Oxford Handbook of Criminology*, 3rd edn, Oxford: Oxford University Press.

Drakeford, M. (2010), 'Devolution and Youth Justice in Wales', *Criminology and Criminal Justice*, 10(2): 137–54.

Electoral Commission (2013), *Police and Crime Commissioner Elections in England and Wales: Report on the administration of the elections held on 15 November 2012*, London: Electoral Commission.

Fox, C., Albertson, K., and Wong, K. (2013), *Justice Reinvestment: Can the Criminal Justice System Deliver More for Less?*, London: Routledge.

Garland, D. (1985), *Punishment and Welfare: A History of Penal Strategies*, Aldershot: Gower.

Garland, D. (2001), *The Culture of Control: Crime and Social Order in Contemporary Society*, Oxford: Oxford University Press.

Garland, D. (2013), 'Penality and the Penal State', *Criminology*, 51(3): 475–517.

Garside, R. and Silvestri, A. (2015), *The Coalition Years: Criminal justice in the United Kingdom: 2010 to 2015*, London: Centre for Crime and Justice Studies.

Graham, J. (2010), 'Responding To Youth Crime', in D. J. Smith (ed.) *A New Response to Youth Crime*, Cullompton: Willan.

The Guardian/LSE (2012), *Reading the Riots: Investigating England's Summer of Disorder*, London: *The Guardian*/London School of Economics.

Haines, K., Case, S., Davies, K., and Charles, A. (2013), 'The Swansea Bureau: a Model of Diversion from the Youth Justice System', *International Journal of Law, Crime and Justice*, 41(2): 212–18.

Halpern, D. (2010), *The Hidden Wealth of Nations*, Cambridge: Polity.

HM Government (2010), *The Coalition: our Programme for Government*, London: Stationery Office.

HM Inspectorate of Constabulary (2012), *Policing in Austerity: One Year On*, London: HMIC.

HM Inspectorate of Constabulary (2014), *Policing in Austerity: Meeting the Challenge*, London: HMIC.

HM Inspectorate of Prisons (2015), *Annual Report 2014–15*, London: HM Inspectorate of Prisons.

HM Treasury (2010), *Spending Review 2010*, Cm 7492, London: Stationery Office.

HOME AFFAIRS COMMITTEE (2013), *Police and Crime Commissioners: Power to Remove Chief Constables*, 20 July 2013, HC 487, 2013–16.

HOME OFFICE (2010), *Policing in the 21st Century: Reconnecting Police and Public*, Cm 7925, London: Stationery Office.

HOOD, R. (ed.) (1974), *Crime, Criminology and Public Policy: Essays in Honour of Sir Leon Radzinovicz*, London: Heinemann Educational Books.

HOUSE OF COMMONS HOME AFFAIRS COMMITTEE (2007), *Police Funding*, Fourth Report of Session 2006/7. London: Stationery Office.

HOUSE OF COMMONS JUSTICE COMMITTEE (2009), *Cutting Crime: The Case for Justice Reinvestment*, First Report of Session 2009-10, London: Stationery Office.

IPSOS-Mori (2016), *Important Issues Facing Britain* in Political and Social Trends Archive at https://www.ipsos-mori.com/researchspecialisms/socialresearch/specareas/politics/trends.aspx#issues, accessed 12 December 2016.

JAY, A. (2014), *Independent Inquiry into Child Sexual Exploitation in Rotherham (1997-2013)*, Rotherham: Rotherham Metropolitan Borough Council.

JONES, T. (2010), 'Public Opinion, Politics and the Response to Youth Crime', in D. J. Smith (ed.), *A New Response to Youth Crime*, Cullompton: Willan.

JONES, T., NEWBURN, T., and SMITH, D. J. (2011), 'Democracy and Police and Crime Commissioners', in T. Newburn and J. Peay (eds), *Policing, Politics, Culture and Control*, Oxford and Portland, Oregon: Hart.

KILLIAS, M. (2006), 'The Opening and Closing of Breaches: A Theory on Crime Waves, Law Creation and Crime Prevention', *European Journal of Criminology*, 3(1): 11–32.

LABOUR PARTY (2015), *Britain Can Be Better: the Labour Manifesto 2015*, London: Labour Party.

LACEY, N. (2008), *The Prisoners' Dilemma: Political Economy and Punishment in Contemporary Democracies*, Cambridge: Cambridge University Press.

LAPPI-SEPPÄLÄ, T. (2011), 'Explaining Imprisonment in Europe', *European Journal of Criminology*, 8(4): 303–28.

LE VAY, J. (2016), *Competition for Prisons: Public or Private?*, Bristol: Policy.

LIBERAL DEMOCRATIC PARTY (2015), *Manifesto 2015: Stronger Economy. Fairer Society. Opportunity for Everyone*, London: Liberal Democratic Party.

LUDLOW, A. (2015), *Privatising Public Prisons: Labour Law and the Public Procurement Process*, Oxford: Hart.

MAGISTRATES' ASSOCIATION (2012), *Active, Accessible, Engaged: the Magistracy in the 21st Century*, London: London Magistrates Association.

MAGUIRE, M. (2012), 'Criminal Statistics and the Construction of Crime', in M. Maguire, R. Morgan, and R. Reiner (eds), *The Oxford Handbook of Criminology*, 5th edn, Oxford: Oxford University Press.

MARWICK, A (1990), *British Society Since 1945*, London: Penguin.

MCNEILL F. (2015), 'Desistance and Criminal Justice in Scotland', in H. Croall, G. Mooney, and M. Munro (eds), *Crime, Justice and Society in Scotland*, London: Routledge.

MILLS, H., SILVESTRI, A., and GRIMSHAW, R. (2010a), *Police Expenditure 1999-2009*, London: Centre for Crime and Justice Studies.

MILLS, H., SILVESTRI, A., and GRIMSHAW, R. (2010b), *Prison and Probation Expenditure 1999-2009*, London: Centre for Crime and Justice Studies.

MINISTRY OF JUSTICE (2012) Swift and Sure Justice: the Government's Plans for Reform of the Criminal Justice System, Cm 8388, London: The Stationery Office.

MINISTRY OF JUSTICE (2016), *Review of the Youth Justice System: An Interim Report of Emerging Findings* (the Taylor Review), London: Ministry of Justice.

MINISTRY OF JUSTICE/YOUTH JUSTICE BOARD (2015), *Youth Justice Statistics 2014-15 England and Wales*, London: National Statistics.

MORGAN, R. (2013), 'The Magistracy: Secure Epitome of the Big Society?', *Criminal Justice Matters*, 91(1): 8–9.

MORRIS, T. (1989), *Crime and Criminal Justice since 1945*, Oxford: Basil Blackwell.

NEWBURN, T. and SPARKS, R. (2004), *Criminal Justice and Political Cultures: National and International Dimensions of Crime Control*, Cullompton: Willan.

NEYROUD, P. (2011), *Review of Police Leadership and Training*, London: Home Office.

NORTON, P. (1984), *Law and Order and British Politics*, Aldershot: Gower.

PUBLIC ACCOUNTS COMMITTEE (2012), *The Ministry of Justice's Language Service Contract: Twenty First Report of the Select Committee of Public Accounts*, HC 620, London: Stationery Office.

PUTNAM, R. (2001), *Bowling Alone: Making Democracy Work*, New York: Simon and Schuster.

PUTNAM, R. and FELDSTEIN, L. (2003), *Better Together*, New York: Simon and Schuster.

RYAN, M. (2003), *Penal Policy and Political Culture in England and Wales: Four Essays on Policy and Process*, Winchester: Waterside.

SHUTE, S. (2013), 'Serving Their Political Masters: the Development of Criminal Justice Inspection in England and Wales – Prisons and Police', *Criminal Law Review*, 11: 869–943.

SILVERMAN, J. (2012), *Crime, Policy and the Media: The Shaping of Criminal Justice, 1989-2010*, London: Routledge.

SMITH, D. J. (1995), 'Youth Crime and Conduct Disorders: Trends, Patterns, and Causal Explanations', in M. Rutter and D. J. Smith, *Psychosocial Disorders in Young People: Time Trends and Their Causes*, Chichester: Wiley.

SMITH, D. J. (1999), 'Less Crime Without More Punishment', *Edinburgh Law Review*, 3(3): 295–316.

Solomon, E. and Garside, R. (2008), *Ten Years of Labour's Youth Justice Reforms: An Independent Audit*, London: Centre for Crime and Justice Studies.

Stenson, K. and Sullivan, R. R. (2001), *Crime, Risk and Justice: The Politics of Crime Control in Liberal Democracies*, Cullompton: Willan.

Stiglitz, J. E. (1998), *Towards a New Paradigm of Development: Strategies, Polices and Processes*, in H. Chang (ed.), *The Rebel Within*, London: Wimbledon Publishing.

Straw, J. (2009), Speech to the National Offender Management Service Annual Conference, 5 February 2009: http://www.justice.gov.uk?news/speeches.Oct08htm, accessed 12 December 2016.

Taylor, P. and Cooper, C. (2002), 'Privatised Prisons and Detention Centres in Scotland: An Independent Report', Glasgow: Rowan Tree Press.

Tonry, M. (2004), *Confronting Crime: Crime Control Policy Under New Labour*, Cullompton: Willan.

Tonry, M. (ed.) (2007), *Crime, Punishment, and Politics in Comparative Perspective: Crime and Justice, a Review of Research vol. 36*, Chicago: University of Chicago Press.

Tonry, M. (2008), 'Learning from the Limitations of Deterrence Research', in M. Tonry (ed.), *Crime and Justice, A Review of Research vol. 37*, Chicago: University of Chicago Press.

Tonry, M. and Farringon, D. (2005), *Crime and Punishment in Western Countries 1980-1999: Crime and Justice, A Review of Research vol. 33*, Chicago: University of Chicago Press.

Wilkinson, R. and Pickett, K. (2009), *The Spirit Level: Why More Equal Societies Almost Always Do Better*, London: Allen Lane.

Winsor, T. (2011), *Independent Review of Police Officer and Staff Remuneration and Conditions, Part 1 Report*, Cm 8024, London: Stationery Office.

YouGov (2010), The Sun Survey Results, 23rd February, (important issues in deciding party to support) at: https://d25d2506sfb94s.cloudfront.net/today_uk_import/YG-Archives-Pol-Suntopical-100223.pdf, accessed 12 December 2016.

YouGov (2015), The Sun Survey Results, 29th April (important issues facing the country) at: https://d25d2506sfb94s.cloudfront.net/cumulus_uploads/document/b2yp0zm7p9/YG-Archive-Pol-Sun-results-280415.pdf, accessed 12 December 2016.

7

CRIME DATA AND CRIMINAL STATISTICS: A CRITICAL REFLECTION

Mike Maguire and Susan McVie

INTRODUCTION

This chapter explores a number of interrelated questions about 'crime levels', 'crime patterns', and 'crime trends' and how they are measured. These range from what may sound like (but are not) straightforward empirical and methodological questions, such as 'how much crime is there?', 'how is it changing?' and 'how do we know?', to broader questions about the relationships between, on the one hand, the kinds of crime data which are collected and published and, on the other, changing perceptions of the nature of 'the crime problem' and policy demands arising from developments in the politics of crime control. The chapter considers the steep falls in crime rates that have been apparent globally over the past two decades (following a long period of increases) and questions whether it is possible to determine that there has been a real 'crime drop' given the problems inherent in measuring crime both consistently and reliably over time. It also identifies a decline in public trust in official crime statistics, and charts attempts to regain this trust through changes in how they are collated and presented.

The chapter is divided into three sections. The first provides an overview of the development of the 'official' crime statistics in England and Wales, derived originally from police records and more recently from the Crime Survey for England and Wales (CSEW). It also looks at what the data from each appear to tell us about the scale of crime and trends over time, and to what extent they give similar, complementary, or contradictory messages. In doing so, it highlights some of the key decisions that are made about how to present statistics to the public, such as whether to pursue comprehensiveness or to focus only on selected offences (the more serious, or those more easily measured); and how to respond to legal changes, new sources of data, and the emergence of new kinds of criminal behaviour.

The second section examines, and explores the reasons behind, a rapid growth in demand for new kinds of information about crime which has been evident since the 1970s, fuelling (and being fuelled by) a massive expansion in data collection and analysis, and a 'pluralization' of sources, methodologies, and providers. Particular attention is paid to types of crime that are especially difficult to 'count', such as domestic violence, cybercrime, crimes within closed institutions, corporate fraud, cross-border and organized crime, and crimes by governments. While noting that the growth in information in these areas has served to highlight the limitations of the official statistics, it is argued that the overall state of knowledge about them remains patchy and contradictory, owing to the serious methodological challenges they present. The final section summarizes challenges, dilemmas, and recent debates about the future of national crime statistics, which have been prompted by continuing concerns about comprehensibility, coverage, integrity, and 'relevance'. These include questions about how to maintain public trust, and whether the aim should be to strive for 'comprehensiveness' or to provide an 'index' based on weighting crimes by seriousness or on a 'basket' of selected offences.

THE 'OFFICIAL STATISTICS'

HISTORICAL OVERVIEW

The idea of 'measuring' crime in a systematic way—for example, attempting to count the numbers of offences committed, or to determine where and when they most often occur—first came to prominence in France in the 1830s, where it was promoted by the so-called 'moral statisticians', Quetelet and Guerry, as part of a scientific vision of discovering laws and regularities in the social world akin to those that had been identified in the natural world (see, e.g., Beirne 1993). However, the idea was also highly compatible with the aims and practices of the centralized bureaucracies that were expanding across Europe. As theorists such as Foucault (1977) have argued, the compilation of detailed information about many aspects of social life was a crucial factor in the development of modernity, and closely tied up with the consolidation of central government control. It was unsurprising, therefore, that the collection and analysis of crime data soon became part of the standard work of government statisticians.

There is no overarching set of official crime statistics for the United Kingdom. Following the Act of Union in 1707, the constitutional settlement allowed Scotland and Northern Ireland to retain separate legal systems to that of England and Wales (see McVie 2017); therefore, crime data are collated separately by each government administration. This chapter will focus on England and Wales, as trends in crime have been broadly similar and developments here have largely influenced practice and policy around crime counting and statistical monitoring in the rest of the UK, although it is worth noting that there are some differences between jurisdictions (further resources to explore these are provided at the end of the chapter).

The Home Office began in 1857 to produce a regular series of national statistics for England and Wales based on annual returns from the police and the courts in local areas. This provided a new window for central administrators on what was happening in different parts of the country, and was later used to assist them in allocating police resources. The data were presented in an annual Command Paper which continued to be published in broadly the same format until 2001, latterly under the title *Criminal Statistics England and Wales*. This was divided into two main sections, one covering offences recorded by the police and the other 'offenders cautioned or found guilty'. Most of the tables on recorded crime comprised counts of legally defined offence categories, broken down by, for example, police force area. They also showed both long- and short-term trends in these counts and in the overall total. Innovation in presentation or analysis was rare, as the statisticians attached higher priority to the accurate measurement of trends through consistency in definitions and methodology, than to collecting new kinds of data or presenting them in formats more relevant to current policy concerns. For example, as violent offences were categorized according to their legal status ('wounding' etc.) rather than their social context, domestic violence could not be distinguished from other kinds of assaults.

For much of their history, the reliability of police figures as a vehicle for measuring patterns and trends in crime was accepted without serious challenge, although periodically they became caught up in fierce political battles in which accusations were made that the police were manipulating statistical returns to bolster demands for increased pay or manpower. This occurred in the early 1920s, which saw the level of recorded crime surpass 100,000 for the first time; and again in the period following the Second World War, when protracted negotiations on pay coincided with a series of exceptionally large rises and falls, leading Radzinowicz (1977: 6) to speculate that the latter might be attributable to a 'police go-slow'. In less turbulent times, however, few questions were asked about the validity of the data or the lack of external scrutiny of how they were collected and analysed, nor was serious attention paid to the fundamental issue of how closely the picture of crime derived from police records reflects the reality of crime as experienced by the public. This remained true even in the 1980s, when 'rising crime' became a major political issue (Morgan and Smith, this volume): although the statistics received greater publicity, the 'truth' of the picture they presented was not subject to any sustained challenge.

In the 1990s things began to change with the establishment of regular 'sweeps' of the British Crime Survey (BCS)—later renamed the Crime Survey for England and Wales (CSEW)[1]—in which respondents from randomly sampled households were asked whether they had experienced victimization within the previous year.[2] This provided a valuable alternative source of information about crime levels as it allowed estimates to be made of the incidence of selected kinds of personal and household crime, whether or not they had come to police notice. At this stage, the BCS results were generally seen as complementing and enhancing, rather than 'rivalling', police recorded crime statistics, the latter still being regarded as the 'official' figures. Nevertheless, confidence in the reliability of survey data grew rapidly and, in 2002, the decision was taken to replace the standard volumes of *Criminal Statistics* with a series of new publications

[1] Early sweeps of the BCS included Scotland, but Scottish surveys were run independently from 1993. Northern Ireland began its own series of crime surveys in 1998. Despite the misnomer, BCS was not renamed as CSEW until 2012.

[2] The BCS was undertaken at intervals from 1982, biennially from 1991, and on a continuous basis from 2000–1. The size of the sample increased from 11,000 households in the early years to over 45,000 in 2004–5, before reducing to 35,000. For details on the methodology of the survey, see ONS (2016a).

entitled *Crime in England and Wales*, in which BCS findings were presented alongside the police figures. This resulted not only in a rapid rise in the status and prominence of survey data, but over the longer term fuelled a perception of two competing 'official' pictures of crime levels and trends: this was particularly the case in years when one set of figures suggested an overall increase in crime rates and the other a fall.

To the extent that the two data sources compete, there is little doubt that the survey results are winning the battle for credibility. The rising confidence in crime survey data has been matched by growing distrust of statistics based on police records, with concerns re-emerging about both the consistency and the integrity of police recording practices. Such concerns led to the introduction of a National Crime Recording Standard in 2002, closer auditing of recording decisions, a number of high level inquiries and eventually a decision by the UK Statistics Authority (2014) that data based on police records did not meet the required standard for designation as National Statistics. Temporarily at least, this has left the CSEW as the only 'official' source of national crime statistics, although both sets of figures continue to be published together. These developments will be discussed in more detail later.

'COUNTS' AND 'TRENDS': POLICE RECORDED CRIME AND THE CSEW

Figures produced by both police records and CSEW interviews are designed to provide two key types of information: 'counts' of and 'trends' in criminal offences. We discuss each in turn.

Counting offences

Table 7.1 shows (a) counts of offences recorded by the police in England and Wales in the financial year April 2015 to March 2016;[3] and (b) estimates of incidents experienced by victims over the same period from CSEW interview responses. For both, the figures are broken down by broad offence type and an overall total is given.

The first important point to make about these tables is that, although there are overlaps, the two sets of figures relate to considerably different groups of offences. The CSEW covers only selected kinds of 'personal' and 'household' crimes: it does not include, for example, crimes against organizations, drug-related offences, sexual offences, or fraud (although some information on the latter two categories is gathered and presented separately, as discussed later in the chapter). The police figures are much more comprehensive in scope, encompassing all types of crime that appear on the Home Office 'notifiable offences list',[4] but they still omit many minor motoring, public order, and other kinds of summary offences.[5] They also include only those incidents that come to the notice of, and are recorded as crimes by, the police (ONS 2016b: 7).

[3] For most of their history, annual crime statistics were presented on a calendar year basis (January to December), but since 1998 they have been aligned with the financial year (April to March).

[4] This includes all 'indictable' and 'triable either way' offences (i.e. those which must or may be tried in a Crown Court), as well as some of the more serious summary offences (i.e. offences triable only in magistrates' courts).

[5] This is mainly to avoid excessive bureaucratic burdens on the police and to provide a picture of crime above a certain level of seriousness, rather than one dominated by a multitude of minor infractions.

These differences mean that one cannot simply look at the two overall totals (6.3 million estimated CSEW crimes and 4.5 million police recorded crimes) and conclude that the CSEW shows that about 40 per cent of crime goes unrecorded by the police: this would not be comparing like with like. Plainly, neither set of figures can be regarded as providing a measure of 'all crime'. Rather, they each offer their own limited picture through a different kind of lens. The main strength of the police recorded data is their breadth of coverage of crime types. However, the CSEW captures incidents not reported to, or recorded by, the police, which not only tells us something about the extent of 'hidden' crime (albeit within limited categories), but helps to make the CSEW

Table 7.1 Offences recorded by the police and CSEW estimates, England and Wales, 2015–16

(a) Offences recorded by the police

Offence group	N to nearest 1,000	Per cent
Theft	1,360,000	31
(Theft from the person	83,000)	(2)
(Vehicle related	367,000)	(8)
(Bicycle theft	87,000)	(2)
(Shoplifting	337,000)	(8)
(All other theft	487,000)	(11)
Burglary	400,000	9
(Domestic	194,000)	(4)
(Non-domestic	206,000)	(5)
Criminal damage/arson	540,000	12
Fraud and forgery	621,000	14
Violence against the person	994,000	22
Robbery	51,000	1
Sexual offences	106,000	2
Drug offences	147,000	3
Public order	205,000	5
Other	89,000	2
Total	**4,514,000**	**100**

(continued)

Table 7.1 Continued

(b) Estimated totals of CSEW incidents ('main crime count')

Offence group	N to nearest 1,000	Per cent
Theft	3,004,000	47
(Theft from the person	363,000)	(6)
(Other theft of personal property	764,000)	(12)
(Other household theft	672,000)	(11)
(Vehicle-related theft	878,000)	(14)
(Bicycle theft	327,000)	(5)
Domestic burglary	701,000	11
Criminal damage	1,209,000	19
Violence	1,268,000	20
(With injury	575,000)	(9)
(Without injury	693,000)	(11)
Robbery	154,000	2
Total	**6,334,000**	**100**

Source: Adapted from ONS (2016b) *Crime in England and Wales, Year Ending March 2016.*

figures more reliable measures both of the relative frequency of individual crime types and of trends over time.

Relative frequency of offence types

Police figures are not a good indicator of the relative frequency of different kinds of offences. Crime surveys consistently demonstrate that the propensity of the public to report crime to the police varies by crime type: serious forms of crime and those which typically trigger insurance claims are more likely to be reported than crimes perceived as trivial or causing little harm. Therefore, police figures tend to distort the frequency of certain types of crime compared to others. This distortion is exacerbated by subsequent differences in police recording behaviour, particularly in relation to violent and sexual offences (see HMIC 2009).

CSEW results are not subject to these problems, so we can place more confidence in the relative frequencies shown by the CSEW figures in Table 7.1(b) than in those indicated by the police figures in Table 7.1(a). However, this does not mean that the CSEW figures are invulnerable to distortions. For example, while they indicate that property related offences are much more common than violent offences, it is possible that the scale of this difference is exaggerated by the survey's failure to capture large numbers of incidents of domestic violence. It has been known for many years that respondents are reluctant to mention such assaults in an interview situation (see Walby and Allen 2004).

The 'comparable subset'

Although direct comparisons cannot be made between the overall totals derived from police records and the CSEW, the survey is designed to enable meaningful comparisons for some specific offence categories. Known collectively as the *comparable subset* of crime (ONS 2016a), this allows fair comparisons to be made between around three-quarters of the estimated CSEW crimes and equivalent offences recorded by the police.[6] The results consistently indicate that victims experience between three to four times more offences of these particular kinds than appear in the police recorded statistics. This ratio contrasts starkly with the estimate by Sparks *et al.* (1977) from their pioneering victim survey in London, where the volume of unrecorded crime (the so-called 'dark figure') was *eleven* times higher than the police figure. The discrepancy seems to be explained by differences both in the nature of the areas surveyed and in the methodologies used. The London survey, carried out mainly in deprived areas, uncovered large volumes of relatively minor thefts and assaults which residents were not inclined to report to the police (and the police often did not record even if they were reported); and comparisons with police figures were not made on the basis of a carefully constructed 'comparable dataset'. As will be discussed below, other local surveys carried out in inner city areas in the 1980s also found much larger proportions of unrecorded crime (including 'harassment' and sexual and domestic assault) than the national surveys.

Trends in crime and the 'crime drop'

Both datasets also provide indications of trends in crime, as shown in Figure 7.1. The headline message of both is that crime in England and Wales has declined strikingly since the mid-1990s, although police figures show a more fluctuating pattern than those derived from the CSEW. This pattern is very much in line with that observed in many other countries over the same period—a phenomenon commonly referred to as the 'crime drop'. Comparative analysis by van Dijk and Tseloni (2012) of both crime surveys and recorded crime figures led to the conclusion that there had been a dramatic and continued fall since the early to mid-1990s across Europe, the US, and beyond. Their analysis indicates, however, that there has been far greater consistency across jurisdictions in falling rates of household crime, such as burglary and vehicle theft, than personal crimes, such as violence. While there is a burgeoning literature on this apparently global crime drop and its causes (see Zimring 2007; van Dijk *et al.* 2012; Rosenfeld and Weisburd 2016), there is no consensus as to its 'true' shape and scale, how consistent it has been across countries, or what the main drivers behind it might have been (Aebi and Linde 2010; McVie 2017). Moreover, claims of a global effect have largely been made at the expense of ignoring significant local differences. The question of how methods of, and changes in, crime counting and trend measurement within

[6] The main exclusions are 'other household thefts' and 'other thefts of personal property', many of which are very minor and do not map sufficiently well on to police definitions of crime for direct comparisons to be made.

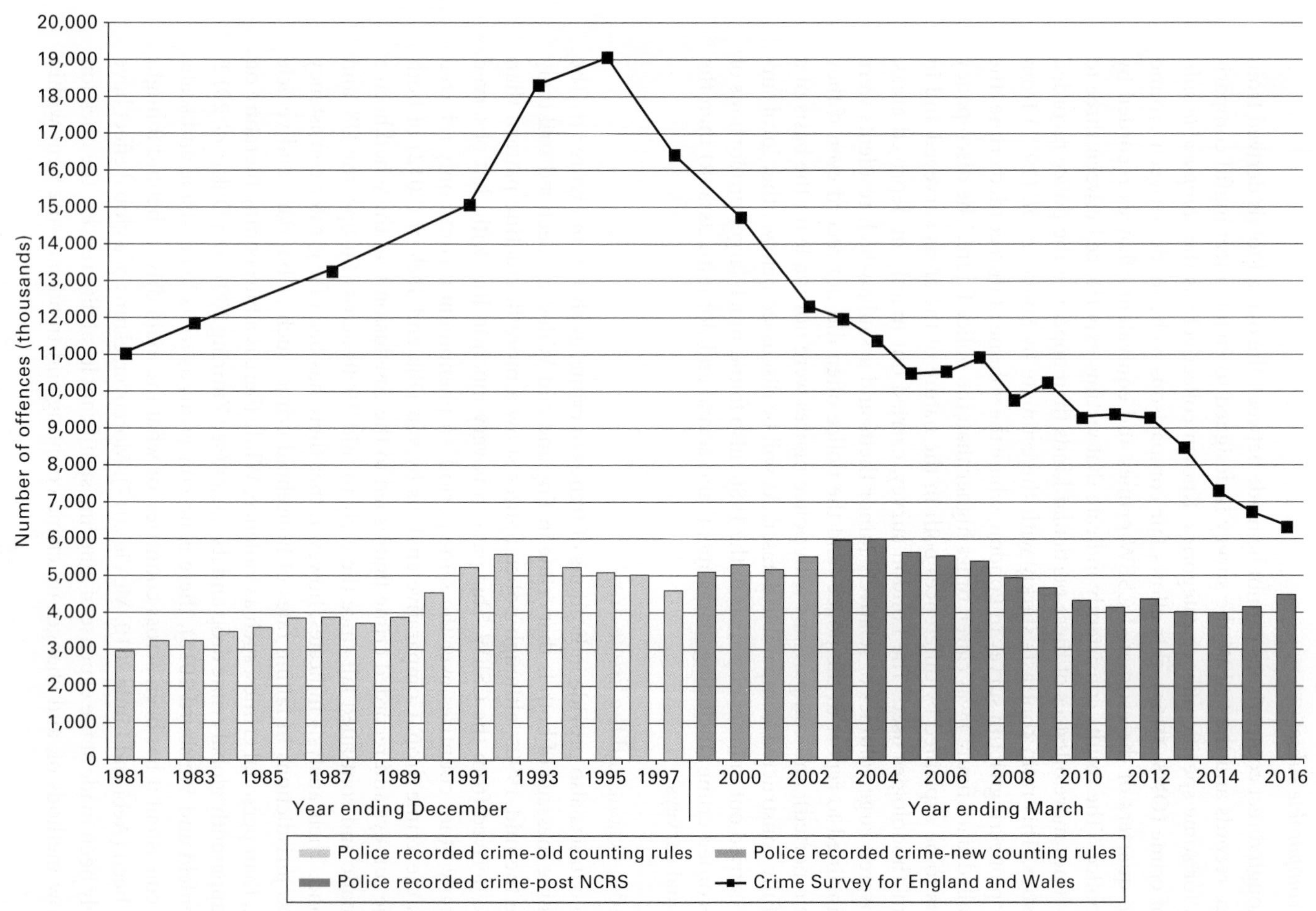

Figure 7.1 Trends in Crime Survey for England and Wales and police recorded crime, year ending December 1981 to year ending March 2016

Source: Crime Survey for England and Wales, Office for National Statistics/Police recorded crime, Home Office recorded crime, Home Office (ONS 2016b: 7).

particular jurisdictions have impacted on conceptions of the crime drop is, therefore, an important one.

Attempts to measure trends in crime over time face a fundamental dilemma. It is important to maintain *comparability* of what is being measured year to year (i.e. as far as possible to collect and present data on the same phenomena in the same way), in order to maintain a robust 'statistical series'. However, laws change and new kinds of criminal behaviour (and new sources of information about them) emerge, so that if one sticks rigidly to the same approach every year, the statistical series will lose both *comprehensiveness* and *relevance to current crime problems*.

These issues have bedevilled the compilation of police recorded crime figures for over 20 years, and the trend data in Figure 7.1 have to be interpreted in the light of consequent changes in policy and practice. As noted earlier, for much of their history police recorded data were presented every year in the same way, and (despite occasional statutory or practice changes which interrupted the series[7]) the measurement of trends was relatively straightforward. Since the late 1990s, however, the pursuit of year-on-year comparability has been overridden by demands to increase the integrity, comprehensiveness, and relevance of crime statistics (which will be discussed later). This has led to a series of changes that have rendered the identification of trends highly problematic. In 1998–9, on the grounds of producing a 'more accurate and comprehensive' picture of violent crime, it was decided to promote the summary offences of common assault, harassment, and assault on a constable to the status of notifiable offences, and hence include them in the recorded crime figures. This added at a stroke over 250,000 extra offences of 'violence against the person' to the official recorded crime count. In 2002, in response to concerns that a high proportion of reports initially logged by the police as 'crime incidents' failed to end up as recorded offences, a new National Crime Recording Standard (NCRS) was introduced. Based on the so-called *prima facie* principle (Simmons 2000), this stipulated that any incident log containing a report of a crime should be taken at face value and *automatically* recorded as an offence; thereafter, it could be removed from the crime records, with a supervisor's agreement (and subject to later audit), only if there was clear evidence that no offence had actually taken place.[8]

Calculations from BCS data indicate that the NCRS had a significant effect on police recording behaviour, as the percentage of crimes reported to the police that were recorded rose from 62 per cent in 2000–1 to 75 per cent in 2003–4 (Simmons *et al.* 2003). The effects of both the above policies can be seen in Figure 7.1 in the rises in raw totals of recorded crime (and the narrowing of the gap between these and BCS totals) between 1999 and 2005. Clearly, these rises were artificial, making it difficult to identify 'real' trends through year-on-year comparisons. Similar problems have persisted as compliance with the NCRS appears to have declined between 2008 and

[7] For example, under the 1968 Theft Act the definition of burglary, which had previously been restricted to 'breaking and entering' at night, was extended to include 'entering as a trespasser with intent' at any time, while offences such as 'housebreaking' and 'shopbreaking' disappeared (Maguire and Bennett 1982: 8–9).

[8] This can be contrasted with the traditional 'evidential' approach, whereby reports of crimes were added to the official records only if officers decided that there was clear evidence that an offence had actually been committed (Simmons 2000).

2013, then risen again as new pressures were put on the police by HM Inspectorate of Constabulary and others to improve the quality of crime recording (HMIC 2014; ONS 2016a: 38).

By contrast, the CSEW has so far avoided such problems, great care having been taken to ensure that the estimated totals are directly comparable year to year. Indeed, the Office for National Statistics makes it clear that '*the key aim of the CSEW is to provide robust trends for the crime types and population it covers*; the survey does not aim to provide an absolute count of crime and has notable exclusions' (ONS 2016a: 5, emphasis added). It is for this reason that the CSEW's 'headline' crime count—on which the figures reproduced in Table 7.1 and Figure 7.1 are based—still includes only those offences that are captured in the 'core victimization module', which has remained unchanged since the survey began. As the survey has matured, information on other offences has become available: it has developed supplementary and experimental modules to gather data on sexual crime, stalking, fraud, and cybercrime, and crimes against victims aged 10 to 15. However, owing to the overriding importance attached to maintaining a consistent statistical series, figures for these other offences are published separately from the main count.[9]

The downside of this approach is that omitting other—especially 'new'—kinds of criminal behaviour from the headline count may create a misleading impression of patterns and trends in *crime as a whole*. For example, responses to an experimental module in the most recent CSEW estimated that there were *5.8 million* 'fraud and computer misuse' offences committed during 2015–16 (ONS 2016a: 38). This is not far short of the estimated total of all other CSEW offences combined! If these offences were included in the main count, a very different overall picture of crime would be produced. What their inclusion would do to crime trends (beyond creating a huge artificial 'spike' initially) is unclear, as there are as yet no long-term data. However, given that cybercrime is a relatively new kind of offence that is thought to be growing in frequency, it is quite possible that if such data had been available and included in the main count over the past few years, the 'overall trend in crime' would have appeared either stable or upward rather than downward, calling into question the widely accepted view that we have been experiencing a 'crime drop'.

Broader critiques of national crime statistics: hidden and 'serial' crimes

There is broader criticism of both police and survey based methods of producing national crime statistics, based around the argument that, while one or both may be quite good at 'counting' particular types of offence, there are other types of crime whose incidence is not meaningfully captured by either method. Particular doubts have been raised about the capacity of both sources to capture adequate data on crimes that tend to be hidden from public view: for example, domestic violence, sexual abuse, and drug dealing. Such crimes are less likely to be reported to the police, and victims are more reluctant to mention them to survey interviewers. This helps to explain why both police and CSEW statistics are dominated by offences committed by *strangers*: for

[9] It should also be noted that the results from some of these extra modules are considered less reliable than those from the core module, but the reluctance to include any of them in the main count derives principally from the desire to maintain a consistent statistical series to measure trends.

example, both contain many fewer cases of domestic violence than of stranger or acquaintance violence.[10]

These concerns date back to the 1980s, when criminologists writing from a left realist and/or a feminist perspective argued that the BCS did not sufficiently reflect the lived experiences of women or the very poor (Matthews and Young 1986; Stanko 1988; Genn 1988; Dobash and Dobash 1992). In particular, they observed that a large proportion of assaults on women were committed by people known to them, including their partners, but they were unlikely to report these to an interviewer on the doorstep. A series of local surveys were developed in which emphasis was placed on gaining respondents' confidence through careful selection and training of interviewers and sensitively worded questions (Kinsey 1984; Jones *et al.* 1986, 1987; Crawford *et al.* 1990).

The results of the local surveys contrasted starkly with the BCS findings. For example, the Islington survey (Jones *et al.* 1986) found significantly higher levels of sexual assault, and higher proportions of reported violent assaults were classified as 'domestic'.[11] Questions were also asked about incidents which would not necessarily be classified by the police as 'crime', but may be experienced as serious by victims, namely sexual and racial 'harassment'; it was found that over two-thirds of women under the age of 24 had been 'upset by harassment' in the previous 12 months. More generally, such surveys (unlike the BCS) indicated that crime was heavily concentrated in areas blighted by poverty and disproportionately experienced by certain social groups and individuals within such areas. Thus, the Islington survey not only found that as many as a third of local households had been touched by burglary, robbery, or assault within the previous 12 months, but that young, black females in the area were 29 times more likely to be assaulted than white females over 45. Using this methodology, some people's risk of victimization was found to be many times higher than that of the notional 'statistically average' person referred to in a reassuring tone in the first BCS (see Hough and Mayhew 1983).

Related debates have surrounded the issue of multiple or '*serial*' offences against the same victim. Most incidents reported to the CSEW are discrete events that occur suddenly and unexpectedly—an almost random event that could strike anyone at any time. However, for some people, victimization occurs on a frequent, almost continuous, basis. Genn (1988) revisited female respondents to the first large-scale

[10] The Office for National Statistic regularly advises that domestic violence is significantly undercounted by the CSEW and that findings on this kind of offence should be treated with caution (ONS 2016a: 42). Police statistical returns do not routinely distinguish between domestic and other assaults, but since April 2015 the Home Office has been collecting information from the police on the proportion of offences which are flagged as 'domestic abuse related': only around one third of 'violence against the person' offences are flagged in this way (ONSb 2016: 26).

[11] Similarly, a survey by Hanmer and Saunders (1984) focused on domestic violence found that 59 per cent of 129 women surveyed in Leeds had suffered some form of threat, violence, or sexual harassment within the previous year; while Painter (1991) found in a survey of married women that 14 per cent had been raped by their husbands at some time during their marriage. Such findings are starkly different to BCS/CSEW findings, even those from the supplementary self-completion modules introduced in the late 1990s, which allow interviewees to enter sensitive data directly into a computer without it being seen by the interviewer (Percy and Mayhew 1997; Mirrlees-Black 1999). For example, the latter indicated in 2013–14 that only 8.5 per cent of women and 4.4 per cent of men had experienced domestic abuse in the past year (ONS 2015a:110).

victim survey in London (Sparks *et al.* 1977) who claimed to have been victimized many times, and found that their lives were blighted by frequent sexual and physical assaults, thefts, burglaries, and other forms of mistreatment, often by people with whom they had a continuing relationship. Yet the frequency of this kind of crime is not captured in national surveys, partly because they limit the number of crimes that are counted for any one victim. In the CSEW, the number of offences of any one kind that is recorded per victim is 'capped' at five; otherwise, it is argued, a small number of victims could seriously 'skew' the estimated totals. The ONS User Guide (ONS 2016a: 15) quotes an example of an American survey of violence against women, in which one victim reported having been raped 24 times; when weighted to the population, this victim accounted for 34 per cent of the total number of rapes estimated to have occurred. Nevertheless, capping has been criticized for systematically under-representing the number of violent crimes, especially those committed repeatedly against women by partners and acquaintances, by 60 per cent on average (Walby *et al.* 2014). Of course, this raises fundamental questions about how meaningful it is to conceptualize certain types of crime as a set of discrete incidents that can simply be counted. As Genn (1988: 91) notes: 'It is clear that violent victimization may often be better conceptualized as a process rather than as a series of discrete events'.

Finally, examination of the differential risks of victimization between social groups should be complemented with an understanding of the differential *impact* of crime on these groups. A debate about this arose when the first BCS reported that younger males, and people who frequently went out drinking, faced the highest risks of being assaulted. The Home Office authors concluded that the fears of street violence expressed by both women and the elderly (which were greater than those of young men) were to some extent 'irrational' (Hough and Mayhew 1983). Young (1988: 173–5) responded robustly that such a conclusion, like their argument that fears are exaggerated because much crime is 'trivial' in terms of loss or injury, obscures the fact that what are 'objectively' similar events can have enormously different meanings and consequences for different people: 'The relatively powerless situation of women—economically, socially and physically—makes them more unequal victims than men.'

THE EXPANSION AND 'PLURALIZATION' OF CRIME DATA

Despite the critiques outlined above, the BCS/CSEW has played a major part over the last 30 years in the move away from over-reliance on police recorded statistics and the opening up of new windows on crime. Although they have not changed their 'main count', the designers of the CSEW have responded in a variety of ways to calls for attention to previously unexplored areas of crime and victimization. For example, 'booster' samples have been used to explore victimization amongst ethnic minorities (Clancy *et al.* 2001); separate analysis has been undertaken of crimes against older people

(Chivite-Matthews and Maggs 2002); computer aided self-interviewing has produced better data on the prevalence of sexual assault, domestic violence, and 'stalking' (Percy and Mayhew 1997; Mirrlees-Black 1999; Budd and Mattinson 2000; Walby and Allen 2004); and, more recently, the survey has collected new data on fraud and cybercrime and included samples of 10 to 15 year olds (ONS 2016b).

Many other new sources of data about crime have played an equally important part, however. In this section we outline a much broader process of expansion and 'pluralization' that has taken place over this period in the production of knowledge about crime levels, patterns, and trends. This includes a wide range of innovative and creative efforts, by a variety of individuals and organizations for a variety of purposes, to find out more about the nature and scale of previously under-explored forms of criminal activity, especially those which were largely hidden from external scrutiny.

NEW THINKING AND NEW DATA DEMANDS

Before the 1970s, analysis of crime patterns was based on limited sources (mainly the regular statistical returns from criminal justice agencies) and carried out within a narrow frame of reference. Much criminological research was aimed at understanding why some individuals engage in crime and how to 'treat' them, and hence data collection focused mainly on the characteristics of offenders. By contrast, little attention was paid to the physical and social circumstances or geographical distribution of offences.

All this has since changed as the demand for information about crime has grown enormously. Crime has become a major focus of public concern and a core issue in party politics (Morgan and Smith, this volume). Governments have increasingly set out to 'manage' crime problems, and the crime prevention and control industry has responded by expanding rapidly. This has involved new theoretical and practical approaches, many of them based around detailed assessment and risk management, and around measuring and improving the effectiveness of crime reduction initiatives. Advances in information technology, including the capacity to collect, store, and analyse massive electronic datasets, have facilitated and encouraged such developments. In trying to make sense of these advances, it is important to look not just at technological change, but at changes in ways of *thinking about* and *responding to* crime. These form a dynamic relationship with the production of crime data, both driving demands for new kinds of information and, in turn, being influenced by the new knowledge they generate. Key developments of note here include:

- 'Situational crime prevention' policies focused on identifying and reducing opportunities for crime (Clarke 1980; Crawford and Evans 2012).
- 'Intelligence-led' and 'problem-oriented' forms of policing which aim to identify, analyse, and tackle existing or emerging crime problems (Bullock and Tilley 2003; Maguire 2008).
- Crime control activities developed by agencies outside the criminal justice field, particularly through their incorporation into formal partnerships (e.g. Integrated Offender Management, and Community Safety Partnerships).
- Promotion of 'evidence-based policy' using research and evaluation to identify effective interventions (e.g. Sherman *et al.* 2006).

- Managerialist attempts to improve the effectiveness of crime control agencies through performance measurement and targets (Hough 2007; Senior *et al.* 2007).

All of these factors have contributed to the continuing demand for more information about crime, including detailed analysis of patterns in specific types of offence that can directly inform policy-making and operational practice, and data that can be processed and disseminated quickly. They have also fuelled the development of increasingly sophisticated methodologies for analysing data (including mapping techniques and 'hot spot' analysis—see Bannister and Flint, this volume), as well as intelligence products such as the 'strategic assessments' and 'problem profiles' built into the National Intelligence Model (John and Maguire 2007).

Importantly, the field of interest has extended far beyond 'conventional' forms of crime (such as theft, burglary, and criminal damage) which make up the bulk of recorded offences, to many kinds of criminal behaviour that previously remained largely hidden from official view. This has been strongly influenced by campaigns to get particular forms of behaviour taken more seriously by the police and justice agencies, notably the pioneering efforts of feminist groups in the 1970s in relation to domestic violence and sexual assault, and the persistent demands of organizations such as Childline (set up in 1986) for more action in relation to child sexual abuse. Recently, more attention has been paid to new and often highly organized forms of crime with international dimensions such as internet fraud, people trafficking, and money laundering (Brookman *et al.* 2010; Levi and Lord, this volume). Again, all these developments have created major new data needs at local, national, and international level.

This continuing surge in demand for crime-related information, combined with the prominence of crime on the national political agenda, has resulted in a huge increase in data collection and research, as well as the opening up of numerous new fields of inquiry—in short, a veritable 'data explosion' in the field. This is evident within government itself, where Home Office and Ministry of Justice research teams have played major roles in the development of new ways of measuring crime and analysing reoffending. At the same time, criminology in universities has grown from a minor subsidiary subject to a flourishing specialist discipline employing several hundred academics, many of them engaged in empirical research. Many public, private, and voluntary sector organizations with a role in crime reduction or security employ researchers to analyse records or conduct surveys to produce new data about crime. Organizations outside the criminal justice system have also been persuaded to collect and share crime data—as seen, for example, in the use of records of assault victims attending Accident and Emergency departments to measure trends in violence (Maguire and Hopkins 2003; Sivarajasingam *et al.* 2009; Centre for Public Health 2014).

NEW KNOWLEDGE: ACHIEVEMENTS, AND CHALLENGES

In essence, then, we have moved from a situation in which there was only one 'official picture' of crime, to one in which not only are the official crime statistics based on more than one kind of data (CSEW and police figures), but data from many other sources provide a new set of windows on to a much broader range of criminal activity. However, some important areas of criminal activity remain relatively unexplored, while others are characterized by conflicting findings. Brief illustrative examples are given below of attempts that have been made to produce new knowledge about the incidence and prevalence of specific types of criminal activity, together with comments on their strengths and limitations.

Child abuse

As with domestic violence against adults (discussed earlier in the chapter), child abuse often involves an ongoing series of assaults within a particular household, so it makes little sense to attempt to count the number of individual 'offences' (*incidence*). Estimates are therefore usually expressed in terms of the proportion of children experiencing it over a given period (*prevalence*). However, this too can be misleading, especially in 'lifetime prevalence' studies, if no effort is made to distinguish those who have been assaulted only once or twice from those who have been victimized repeatedly over many years. Moreover, definitions of what is being measured can make a critical difference to the results. For example, in the 1970s the first US National Incidence Study of Child Abuse and Neglect, a major survey of health service and other professionals, initially defined 'child maltreatment' as harmful parental conduct and estimated that 30 per cent of all children had been victims of maltreatment over the previous year. When the definition was restricted to conduct resulting in a specified minimum degree of harm (e.g. marks on the skin lasting at least 48 hours), the estimate dropped to one per cent (Besharov 1981).

Some evidence on the incidence of physical abuse has been gleaned from hospital data on 'non-accidental injuries', although records vary depending on whether children are injured seriously enough to go to hospital and whether hospital staff define their injuries as non-accidental. Most evidence about the prevalence of child abuse comes from asking adults to recall events from childhood, with predictably conflicting results arising from varying methodologies (see Straus *et al.* 1980; Baker and Duncan 1985; Morgan and Zedner 1992). Perhaps the most reliable results come from a UK survey of over 6,000 parents or guardians of children under 11, young people aged 11 to 17, and young adults aged 18 to 24 years (Radford *et al.* 2011). It found that between 5 and 14.5 per cent of young people had experienced 'severe maltreatment' by a parent or guardian at some point during their childhood (predominantly severe neglect or physical violence—few referred to contact sexual abuse); and that 2.5 per cent of under 11s and six per cent of 11 to 17s had experienced such mistreatment in the past year.

Crimes against businesses

Crimes against businesses—chiefly theft or fraud—pose considerable difficulties for measurement for a variety of reasons (see Hopkins 2002). Nevertheless, the Home Office has developed the *Commercial Victimisation Survey* (CVS), first piloted in 2002 and carried out annually since 2012. This estimates the prevalence and incidence of crimes against businesses in selected sectors. In 2015, it surveyed wholesale/retail, agriculture, construction, and information/communication businesses (Williams 2016) and found that the wholesale/retail sector was the most victimized, with 40 per cent of premises reporting crimes against them. The incidence rate of over 12,000 offences per 1,000 premises was dominated by shoplifting, which accounted for 71 per cent of the total. However, the overall estimated total of business crimes had fallen from over 21 million in 2002 to about 8 million in 2015 (Williams 2016). While this echoes CSEW findings on personal and household crimes, it has to be treated with caution as its findings are very different to those of another survey, the British Retail Consortium's Retail Crime Survey, which found a 14 per cent *increase* in the incidence of shoplifting between 2008–9 and 2014–15 (BRC 2016).[12] Police recorded offences of shoplifting, meanwhile, have remained fairly stable for a long period.

Fraud has received increasing attention in recent years, particularly online fraud which is widely agreed to have increased. The BRC survey found a 55 per cent increase in reported fraud between 2013–14 and 2014–15, while the CVS found that over a fifth of retailers/wholesalers had lost money to 'phishing'. Other information comes from reports to fraud prevention bodies such Action Fraud and the National Fraud Intelligence Bureau, although it is difficult to distinguish offences against businesses from those against individuals.

The overall picture of crimes against businesses remains unclear, and estimates of losses to organizations through theft and fraud—especially of the global costs to international companies (e.g. Pricewaterhouse Coopers 2005)—tend to be highly speculative. It could be argued that a clearer understanding of the problem of theft within various types of workplace might be obtained through qualitative research, such as that undertaken many years ago by Ditton (1977) and Mars (1982), who spent time with people working in warehouses and docks, and came to understand the informal cultural rules among employees about pilfering.

Corporate crime

Crime committed *by* organizations is even harder to measure in any meaningful way. It may include crimes against an organization's employees (e.g. health and safety breaches leading to death or injury), against other organizations (e.g. failures to pay for orders, and the operation of illegal cartels), or against customers or the general public (e.g. the sale of sub-standard or stolen goods, deliberate frauds, and environmental pollution). Some of the best insights into such offences—which can involve millions of pounds—have come from reconstructions of large-scale cases through analysis of investigation files, court records, or newspaper stories (see Passas and Groskin 2001 on the BCCI swindle). There have been some attempts to gather data on corporate criminal behaviour by investigative journalists or through interviews with business people or auditors, but systematic studies are rare and the overall level of knowledge in the field remains limited. (For useful overviews, see Levi and Lord, this volume; Minkes 2010; Tombs 2010.)

Crime in closed institutions

Criminal activity which takes place in closed institutions (such as prisons, army barracks, mental institutions, children's homes, old people's homes, and boarding schools) rarely comes to police notice and often goes unrecorded internally. It is also not captured by the CSEW, which only interviews people in private households. Cultures of secrecy, and sometimes intimidation, make collection of reliable data in institutions

[12] It should be noted that the surveys are not directly comparable: they cover different periods and the BRC survey focuses disproportionately on larger retailers.

very difficult. Although some surveys have been conducted, this is another area that may be better researched through qualitative methodologies such as in-depth interviews with ex-residents or participant observation. Innovative examples include studies of bullying among prisoners (Ireland 2005) and in children's homes (Barter *et al.* 2004; Evans 2010). Research on other institutions is less well developed, despite recent high profile cases involving deaths in army barracks and maltreatment of old people.

Online fraud and cybercrime

Arguably the fastest growing 'new' type of crime is online fraud, more commonly known as 'cybercrime' (see Tcherni *et al.* 2016). Like other forms of fraud, failure to reflect its scale and growth adequately in police recorded crime statistics or the CSEW main count risks giving a false picture of current patterns of crime in the UK (a comment that applies to many other countries). As already mentioned, a supplementary module on fraud and cybercrime introduced in the CSEW estimated that 5.8 million such offences were committed in 2015–16 (ONS 2016a: 37–9). A particular example of online fraud, identity theft, has also been highlighted by Cifas (2016), which collects fraud data from over 250 organizations in the UK, as the fastest growing type of cybercrime. In 2015, nearly 170,000 cases of identity fraud were reported, making up 53 per cent of all frauds reported to Cifas and a rise of 49 per cent compared with the previous year. These are very large numbers and, given that much of the so-called 'crime drop' is thought to be attributable to falls in property crime, it could be argued that this has simply been replaced by different ways of stealing property online.

Organized and cross-border crime

A form of criminal behaviour which continues to pose daunting challenges for information gathering and research is that of 'organized' crime, especially when this involves activities that cross international borders (such as EU subsidy fraud, money laundering, smuggling, and drug or people trafficking). The rapidly changing and well-concealed nature of such crimes mean that conventional methods of gathering data are inadequate. At present, regular 'threat assessments' are made as part of a National Strategic Assessment, led by the National Crime Agency and a range of international partners, based on a wide variety of data from both closed and open sources and published in sanitized form (see NCA 2015). Otherwise, much of the available information is based on newspaper reports, court cases, investigation files, and interviews with convicted organized criminals. Generally speaking, empirical investigations have tended to focus on charting the numbers, size, and ethnic connections of organized criminal groups, rather than attempting to measure the scale of 'organized crime' in terms of offences committed. A key problem is distinguishing among recorded offences between those that have been committed by individuals and those by organized groups—with the further complication of defining 'organized' (see Levi and Lord, this volume; Levi and Maguire 2004).

Crimes by governments and in war

Green and Ward, this volume, draw attention to a plethora of horrific state-sanctioned crimes, including crimes against humanity, that have to a large extent remained off the radar of most criminological work (see also Cohen 2001; Aitchison 2010).

Unsurprisingly, figures on war crimes, torture, or killings sanctioned by governments are not usually gathered or published by state officials, but by external bodies such as Amnesty International and Human Rights Watch. Such data are occasionally used in analysis by small numbers of criminologists (see the Special Issue of the *British Journal of Criminology* edited by Green and Ward in 2005) but are still too rarely thought of as 'criminal statistics'—which, of course, they are.

International and comparative perspectives

Finally, a growing need for international comparisons in crime data has been recognized through the development of major surveys that collect information across several countries at once. Most notable is the International Crime Victims Survey (ICVS) (van Dijk 2013). This has suffered from methodological problems and shortages of resources, but offers rich datasets for comparative analysis. The ICVS has been undertaken six times since 1989, most recently in 2010. It has covered 80 countries in all, although few more than three times. The results provide valuable international comparisons in terms of levels of crime, reporting rates, and attitudes to crime and justice. It has been used extensively to examine the scale and nature of the 'crime drop' across many different countries (see van Dijk and Tseloni 2012). Importantly, too a 39-country analysis found no correlation between survey and police figures, leading van Kesteren *et al.* (2014: 53) to conclude that: 'Police figures are nothing but a source of misinformation on the levels of crime across countries'.

KEY DILEMMAS AND CHALLENGES

In recent years, national crime statistics in the UK have come under increasing scrutiny, as evidenced by a series of critical reports reflecting a growing sense of uncertainty about their legitimacy and core purpose. In this section we briefly discuss some of the recurring themes from these reports and subsequent debates: in particular, dilemmas and challenges around public mistrust; the pursuit of 'relevance' and 'comprehensiveness'; and how to deal with 'distortions' caused by large differences in seriousness between offences.

THE PROBLEM OF TRUST

Since the turn of this century, a plethora of official inquiries and reports have highlighted concern about public distrust in the production and dissemination of crime statistics (Simmons 2000; Statistics Commission 2006; UK Statistics Authority 2010; Matheson 2011; Public Administration Select Committee 2014). In a broad review of 'user perspectives', the Statistics Commission (2005) identified public trust in the crime figures as one of its top five priorities. Specifically addressing the problem of political 'spin', it concluded that the Home Office and other official bodies were exerting such a high degree of control over the publication of crime data (often in the face of a cynical and antagonistic press) that it was severely undermining public confidence in the figures—leading to a perception that people were receiving 'a filtered, government friendly, version of the truth' (Statistics Commission 2005: 4). An independent review for the Home Office identified a further set of problems:

> Public trust in crime statistics can be undermined by any or all of the following: presentations of statistics that are perceived to be in conflict with—or of no relevance to—the direct individual experiences of members of the public; presentations of statistics using categories or definitions that do not accord with public commonsense interpretations; presentation of conflicting statistics apparently open to widely differing interpretations; lack of coverage of significant areas of criminal activity and victims; perceived potential for police or ministerial interference in the production and presentation of the statistics. (Smith 2006: iii)

Ironically, this suggests that some of the changes to systems for recording and presenting crime statistics discussed earlier (such as the inclusion of common assault in the Notifiable Offence List, introduction of the NCRS, and the publication of CSEW findings alongside police figures), which were intended to improve the reliability and 'truth' of the official statistics, had the perverse effect of *increasing* distrust. They made the statistics more difficult for casual observers to interpret and opened up more opportunities for politicians to exploit contradictions in the data and 'cherry pick' figures to their advantage, or to sow general mistrust in the integrity of the data. Media responses to the release of statistics tend to look no further than the raw figures, and show little interest in 'technical' arguments about how to interpret them.

Such distrust is further fuelled by a mismatch between the picture of falling crime offered by the official crime statistics and a perception among large sections of the public that it has continued to rise. In every sweep of the BCS/CSEW since 1996—a period in which both survey-derived and police recorded crime totals have fallen sharply—between 58 and 75 per cent of respondents have been found to believe that crime is rising (see Chaplin *et al.* 2011; ONS 2015b). While often attributed to the publication of mistruths in the popular media (e.g. Gash 2016), this perception is also partly formed by people's own observations and experiences, discussions with friends and neighbours, and so on. An important factor may be the fact that people tend to make little distinction between 'crime' and 'anti-social behaviour'. There is a widespread impression (which may or may not be correct) that levels of, for example, 'loutish' behaviour in the street, late night drunkenness in town centres, and littering, have increased significantly (Wikström 2009; Mackenzie *et al.* 2010). Whilst this contributes to a general belief that 'crime is rising', most such acts do not constitute notifiable criminal offences and consequently their existence is not reflected in the recorded crime statistics.

Almost unanimously, the various reviews of crime statistics recommended that overcoming the problem of public mistrust required greater transparency and more independent oversight and control of the process of collecting, analysing, and presenting data. Therefore, in 2010 the Home Secretary decided that, while responsibility for the collection and validation of recorded crime data would remain with the Home Office, responsibility for analysis, interpretation, and publication of the results would transfer to an independent body, the Office for National Statistics (ONS). Nevertheless, concerns around the consistency and integrity of police recording practices persisted and in 2014 the UK Statistics Authority decided that crime statistics based on police data did not meet the required standard for designation as National Statistics and it stripped them of this official label.

It is too early to conclude whether these changes have reduced levels of public mistrust. A recent survey (Simpson *et al.* 2015) found that the ONS as an organization was accorded high levels of trust and a majority of respondents (66 per cent) thought that the publication of crime statistics was 'free of government interference'; however, only 28 per cent agreed that 'the government presents official figures honestly when talking about its policies'. Therefore, the question of whether or not public trust in UK crime statistics is likely to increase rests not only on the independence, robustness, and validity of the data collection and analysis, but also on the way in which the results are used and presented by politicians.

'MODERNIZATION', 'RELEVANCE', AND THE SEARCH FOR THE 'FULL JIGSAW'

Another key set of challenges facing those responsible for national statistics concerns the problem of how to balance competing demands for 'relevance', 'comprehensiveness', and robust measurement of trends. The case for relevance and comprehensiveness was made forcefully in 2000 in a radical report which advocated a fundamental shift away from the outmoded practices and philosophies underpinning the production of crime statistics, towards:

> a more flexible view of information—one where we first define the problems requiring solution and then develop the information needed to better understand those problems . . . rather than rely on the routine statistics supplied in summary form by the police. (Simmons 2000: ii).

Simmons recommended replacing the traditional *Criminal Statistics* with an annual 'Picture of Crime in England and Wales' which incorporated information from a range of sources, including the BCS, police incident data, research studies, other kinds of surveys, and administrative data from other agencies and institutions. If information was to be useful, he argued, it had to be as comprehensive, timely, reliable, and context-rich as possible. Accordingly, he maintained that police officers should be encouraged or compelled to formally record *every* incident of crime or disorder, even if merely alleged, in order to provide a victim-centred approach to crime recording. The subsequent changes which took place fell well short of Simmons' ambitions, but the decision to publish survey results alongside police data in the annual publication *Crime in England and Wales* was clearly in line with his thinking.

Decisions about how to collect and present crime data have not occurred in a vacuum: they have responded to the changing demands of 'consumers' and the dominant preoccupations of the day. Moreover, modern government needs malleable and contextualized forms of information with which to assess and respond quickly to the highly specific and fast-changing 'crime problems' which have emerged at frequent intervals to preoccupy the public, politicians, and media. The Smith review recognized the need for reliable data of relevance to the needs of policy-makers and practitioners, and identified 'serious and growing gaps in the national figures', accepting the need to 'extend the coverage of national statistics' (Smith 2006: 7–11). Similarly, the National Statistician used the analogy of a 'jigsaw puzzle' with missing pieces to make the case for the gradual incorporation of a much wider range of data sources into the published national crime statistics (Matheson 2011). Describing victim survey and police data as major pieces in the jigsaw, she advocated the publication of additional contextual data on crime (such as counts of non-notifiable summary offences, police records of incidents of 'antisocial behaviour', and estimates of the extent of cybercrime) in order to improve transparency and public understanding.

Many of these recommendations have been followed and ONS Statistical Bulletins now regularly present survey data on a range of crime-related topics (such as business crime and internet fraud)—although it is important to emphasize that these additional data have not yet been included in the main ('headline') crime count. Moves in this direction raise the fundamental question of whether it is a sensible ambition to work towards the production of an 'overall' or 'total' measure of crime—to use Matheson's analogy, to try to complete the full jigsaw. Clearly, if this was understood in terms of adding together every 'crime' known to have been committed in a given year (through any reliable source available), and coming up with a total figure, the task would be made almost impossibly difficult by problems of definition, double counting, serial victimization, and so on. More importantly, one would have to question whether the resulting figure would have any real meaning, having been arrived at by adding together a range of very different types of behaviour, (the proverbial 'apples and pears'), some of them inherently more 'countable' than others. They would inevitably be dominated, too, by a vast number of minor offences, many of them on the fuzzy borderline between criminal and antisocial (but non-criminal) behaviour.

TAKING ACCOUNT OF DIFFERENCES IN SERIOUSNESS AND HARM

Inevitably some kinds of offence are significantly more serious than others, and the most serious and damaging are vastly outnumbered by the relatively minor. The problem of minor offences 'counting' the same as major offences was recognized many years ago by Sellin and Wolfgang (1964), who devised a weighted index for measuring crime levels, based on the notional gravity of each recorded offence. They argued that weighting would allow more realistic comparisons of the seriousness of the crime problem, either over time or in different cities, states, or countries. They attached a score to each crime category, based upon ratings of seriousness derived from interviews with random samples of the population: the range of the index was very wide, the gravest offences being given over 300 times more weight than the least serious. Various comparisons were carried out in the USA between trends in officially recorded crime rates and annual scores on the Sellin–Wolfgang index. Some interesting results emerged—for example, Normandeau (1969) found that in Philadelphia the index indicated a contrary trend to that shown by the official Uniform Crime Rates—but eventually most criminologists and statisticians of the time abandoned it as of dubious validity and utility.

Similar ideas have been revived more recently, however. The reviews by Simmons (2000), Smith (2006), the Statistics Commission (2006), and Matheson (2011) all discussed the possibility of using either a 'basket' of serious offences[13] or a weighted index of all crime to overcome the problem of crime figures being dominated by minor offences, although all noted the daunting difficulties involved in achieving either. Sherman *et al.* (2016) have recently created such a weighted index in the form of the 'Cambridge Crime Harm Index (CHI)'. Rather than treating all crimes equally and summing them into a single total, they argue that each crime type should be classified according to how *harmful* it is and weighted accordingly. Moreover, they include only crimes reported by victims or witnesses, omitting those proactively generated by the police or other organizations (e.g. drug arrests or shoplifting), whose incidence and harms they argue cannot be reliably measured. Their suggested method for calculating the relative harm of a crime type is the number of days in prison which the Sentencing Guidelines Council recommends as the 'starting point' of punishment for that offence. The weighted data are then summed, and the total index score for any given year is expressed in terms of 'total CHI sentence days'. The authors argue that this represents a 'barometer of the total impact of harm from crimes committed by other citizens, as reported by witnesses and victims' and will potentially allow the measurement of 'national trends in public safety'. The overall picture of crime that emerges from this methodology is very different to that produced from traditional crime counts. For example, robbery (26 per cent of total 'harms'), grievous bodily harm (17 per cent), and rape (15 per cent) dominate the picture, while theft from vehicles, other theft, and criminal damage make up only 1 per cent each. Trends, too are different: for example, the reduction in the index between 2002–3 and 2011–12 emerges as 21 per cent, compared with a 37 per cent fall in the total count of police recorded offences over the same period.

Interesting as such approaches are, they come up against the obvious problem that not everyone would agree on how best to assess seriousness and harm. While the architects of sentencing guidelines take into account harm to victims, they also consider many other factors when recommending tariffs. Moreover, as Young (1988) argued, a minor crime to some may be experienced very differently by others. Some may also find unconvincing the very low proportion of total harm that the CHI attributes to 'volume crime' such as theft and criminal damage. There is an argument that although such offences may be relatively minor at the individual level, the whole is greater than the sum of the parts: in other words, harm (in the form of fear, worry, or anger) is caused as much by awareness of their overall frequency as by their impact on an individual. Finally, it should be emphasized that the index is based only on offences reported to and recorded by the police. Hence it inevitably under-represents offences such as domestic abuse that tend to remain hidden from police view but cause relatively high harm to victims.

[13] The thinking behind this is that, rather like the Footsie index in relation to all company shares, it would act as a proxy for the overall state of crime. It should be based only on *serious offences* which can be *relatively reliably counted* and *change little in nature year to year*, allowing relatively robust measurement of trends.

CONCLUDING COMMENTS

This chapter has considered a range of key issues in the development and expansion of both crime data and criminal statistics. From a historical perspective, the systematic measurement of crime is not new—police records have existed for over 150 years; however, it is only in recent years that we have come to rely upon multiple sources of data to build up a bigger picture of how crime levels, patterns, and trends are changing. CSEW data provide a valuable alternative to police recorded crime, and have rapidly risen in prominence, taking the lead in the battle for credibility. Even so, neither source can be said to present a 'true' picture of crime, in terms of either raw counts or relative frequency. The apparent 'crime drop' that has swept many western countries seems to reflect a real underlying change in crime levels; and yet, it raises important questions about the extent to which our methods of measurement, in an effort to balance consistency and accuracy, have evolved sufficiently to keep up with modern transformations in the crime phenomenon.

Over the past three decades, advances in information technology have not only opened up many new avenues for criminal behaviour, they have expanded the sources of data that can be used to 'measure' crime, and the ownership and control of systems of data collection and analysis. As a consequence, the messages about the shape of the 'crime problem' that are conveyed to the outside world have become more complex and, often, contradictory. The previously static, monochrome picture of crime provided by police records alone has given way to a kaleidoscope of new images produced by a variety of alternative ways of exploring the nature and scale of crime, undertaken by a wide range of individuals and organizations. In short, neither the government nor the ONS (to which responsibility for official crime and justice data has transferred) retains anything like a 'monopoly on truth' where statements about the extent of crime are concerned.

Crime figures now occupy a contested space in which knowledge claims are often challenged and both data and data providers are under intense scrutiny. A series of inquiries and reviews into the UK crime statistics highlighted high levels of mistrust in both the production and dissemination of crime statistics. The public find the conflicting data sources about crime confusing, and attempts to increase public confidence by changing systems for recording and presenting data have been perceived as nothing more than government 'spin'. Distrust is further fuelled by apparent discrepancies in the official picture of falling crime that does not accord with a public perception that crime and antisocial behaviour continue to blight communities. Government responses, such as bringing the data together under an independent body and presenting a unified picture of crime in one single report, have tried to reinstall confidence in the figures. However, removal of the accreditation status of the official, police recorded, crime statistics as a 'national statistic' in 2014 called into serious question the legitimacy of this form of crime measurement. Alternative approaches, such as creating a weighted index based on seriousness or harm, offer a new way of conceptualizing the crime problem. But it seems unlikely that such approaches will readily replace the tried and tested mechanisms of crime measurement that have come to dominate our official statistics, however problematic these might be.

SELECTED FURTHER READING

There are relatively few recent textbooks on criminal statistics, especially in the UK. Although obviously out of date in some respects, Coleman and Moynihan's *Understanding Crime Data* (1996) is still one of the best British textbooks on the subject, and covers in more depth several of the main issues discussed in this chapter. It has the added advantage of accessibility and a light and humorous touch. We also recommend that you review previous chapters of Maguire, *The Oxford Handbook of Criminology* (2007, 2012) as these provide important contextual background to, and greater detail on, some of the issues contained in this chapter.

The ONS now publishes most of the 'official' data relating to crime and justice in England and Wales. This includes quarterly statistical bulletins containing the latest crime figures—the most recent at the time of writing being *Crime in England and Wales: Year Ending June 2016* (2016c). The ONS website is highly recommended as the primary resource for national statistics as it includes a wealth of downloadable reports, data, and tables (http://www.ons.gov.uk/peoplepopulationandcommunity/crimeandjustice). For those interested in methodological issues related to recorded crime and the Crime Survey for England and Wales, the *User Guide to Crime Statistics for England and Wales* (2016a) is informative and readily comprehensible. A rich archive of Home Office research and statistics reports published prior to 2013 (including statistical bulletins and analyses of data from police and other agency records, the BCS and other crime related surveys) can also be accessed at: http://webarchive.nationalarchives.gov.uk/20130128103514/http://www.homeoffice.gov.uk/publications/science-research-statistics/research-statistics/crime-research/.

For those interested in reviewing crime and justice statistics from the other parts of the UK, we recommend the highly accessible and detailed pages of the Scottish government's crime and justice website (http://www.gov.scot/Topics/Statistics/Browse/Crime-Justice). This provides a 'high level summary' of statistical trends across many areas of crime and justice, and links to a wide range of published reports, statistical bulletins, and downloadable tables. For the most up-to-date information on police recorded crime you should refer to the *Recorded crime in Scotland, 2015-16* statistical bulletin; and for the most recent published data from the Scottish Crime and Justice Survey (Scotland's equivalent to the CSEW) the *2014-15 Scottish Crime and Justice Survey: Main Findings*. For details of crime and justice statistics in Northern Ireland, we refer you to the Northern Ireland Statistics and Research Agency (http://www.nisra.gov.uk/publications/default.asp4.htm). The most recently published reports of relevance here are *Trends in Police Recorded Crime in Northern Ireland 1998/99 to 2015/16*; and *Experience of Crime: Findings from the 2014/15 Northern Ireland Crime Survey*.

There are also several compilations of data and statistics providing international comparisons of crime rates and patterns. Among the most comprehensive is the *European Sourcebook of Crime and Criminal Justice Statistics* which is collated by a panel of experts from across Europe (http://www.europeansourcebook.org/). The fifth edition (HEUNI, 2014) covers the five years from 2007 to 2011 and includes police, prosecution, conviction, and correctional statistics, as well as data from the victimization surveys (http://www.heuni.fi/en/index/tiedotteet/2014/09/europeansourcebookofcrimeandcriminaljusticestatistics2014published.html). Interesting cross-national surveys include the International Crime Victim Survey (see van Dijk's *The International Crime Victims Survey 1988-2010* (2013) and Del Frate's 'International Crime Business Survey' (2004). Statistical and other kinds of research data on the nature and extent of over 40 separate types of crime (together with data on their history and social context) are presented and analysed in Brookman *et al.*'s comprehensive *Handbook on Crime* (2010).

REFERENCES

Aebi, M. F. and Linde, A. (2010), 'Is there a crime drop in Western Europe?', *European Journal of Criminal Policy Research*, 16(4): 251–77.

Aitchison, A. (2010), 'Genocide and "ethnic cleansing" ', in F. Brookman, M. Maguire, H. Pierpoint, and T. Bennett (eds), *Handbook on Crime*. Devon: Willan.

Alvazzi Del Frate, A. (2004), 'The International Crime Business Survey: Findings from Nine Central–Eastern European Cities', *European Journal on Criminal Policy and Research*, 10(2): 137–61.

Baker, A. and Duncan, S. (1985), 'Child Sexual Abuse: A Study of Prevalence in Great Britain', *Child Abuse and Neglect*, 9(4): 457–67.

Barter, C., Renold, E., Berridge, D., and Cawson, P. (2004), *Peer Violence in Children's Residential Care*, Basingstoke: Palgrave Macmillan.

Beirne, P. (1993), *Inventing Criminology: Essays on the Rise of 'Homo Criminalis'*, Albany, NY: State University of New York Press.

Besharov, D. (1981), 'Toward better research on child abuse and neglect: Making definitional issues an explicit methodological concern', *Child Abuse and Neglect*, 5(4): 383–90.

BRC (2016), *Retail Crime Survey, 2015*, London: British Retail Consortium.

Brookman, F., Maguire, M., Pierpoint, H., and Bennett, T. (eds) (2010), *Handbook on Crime*, Devon: Willan.

Budd, T. and Mattinson, J. (2000), *The Extent and Nature of Stalking: Finding from the 1998 British Crime Survey*, Research Study No. 210, London: Home Office.

Bullock, K. and Tilley, N. (ed.) (2003), *Crime Reduction and Problem-oriented Policing*, Devon: Willan.

Centre for Public Health (2014), *A Guide to Using Health Data to Inform Local Violence Prevention*, Liverpool John Moores University: Centre for Public Health.

Chaplin, R., Flatley, J., and Smith, K. (2011), *Crime in England and Wales, 2010/11*, Statistical Bulletin 10/11. London: Home Office.

Chivite-Matthews, N. and Maggs, P. (2002), *Crime, Policing and Justice: The Experience of Older People. Findings from the British Crime Survey, England and Wales*, Online Report 08/02. London: Home Office.

CIFAS (2016), *Fraudscape 2016*, London: Cifas.

Clancy, A., Hough, M., Aust, R., and Kershaw, C. (2001), *Crime, Policing and Justice: The Experience of Ethnic Minorities. Findings from the 2000 British Crime Survey*, Home Office Research Study No. 223, London: Home Office.

Clarke, R. V. G. (1980), 'Situational Crime Prevention: Theory and Practice', *British Journal of Criminology*, 20(2): 136–47.

Cohen, S. (2001), *States of Denial: Knowing about Atrocities and Suffering*, Cambridge: Polity.

Coleman, C. and Moynihan, J. (1996), *Understanding Crime Data*. Buckingham and Philadelphia, Penn.: Open University Press.

Crawford, A. and Evans, K. (2012), 'Crime prevention and community prevention', in M. Maguire, R. Morgan, and R. Reiner (eds), *The Oxford Handbook of Criminology*, 5th edn, Oxford: Oxford University Press.

Crawford, A., Jones, T., Woodhouse, T., and Young, J. (1990), *Second Islington Crime Survey*, London: Middlesex Polytechnic.

Ditton, J. (1977), *Part-time Crime*, London: Macmillan.

Dobash, R. E. and Dobash, R. P. (1992), *Women, Violence and Social Change*, London: Routledge.

Evans, J. (2010), 'Institutional abuse and children's homes', in F. Brookman, M. Maguire, H. Pierpoint, and T. Bennett (eds), *Handbook on Crime*, Devon: Willan.

Foucault. M. (1977), *Discipline and Punish: The Birth of the Prison*, London: Allen Lane.

Gash, T. (2016), *Criminal: The Truth about why People do Bad Things*, London: Penguin.

Genn, H. (1988), 'Multiple Victimization', in M. Maguire and J. Pointing (eds), *Victims of Crime: A New Deal?*, Milton Keynes: Open University Press.

Green, P. and Ward, T. (2005), 'Introduction', Special Issue, *British Journal of Criminology*, 45(4): 431–3.

Hanmer, J. and Saunders, S. (1984), *Well-founded Fear*, London: Hutchinson.

HMIC (2009), *Crime Counts: A review of data quality for offences of the most serious violence*, London: Her Majesty's Inspectorate of Constabulary.

HMIC (2014), *Crime Recording: Making the Victim Count*. London: Her Majesty's Inspectorate of Constabulary.

Hopkins, M. (2002), 'Crimes against businesses: The way forward for future research', *British Journal of Criminology*, 42(4): 782–97.

Hough, M. (2007), 'Policing, New Public Management and Legitimacy', in T. Tyler (ed.), *Legitimacy and Criminal Justice*, New York: Russell Sage Foundation.

Hough, M. and Mayhew, P. (1983), *The British Crime Survey*, Home Office Research Study No. 76, London: HMSO.

Ireland, J. (ed.) (2005), *Bullying Among Prisoners: Innovations in Research and Theory*, Devon: Willan.

John. T. and Maguire, M. (2007), 'Criminal Intelligence and the National Intelligence Model', in T. Newburn (ed.), *Handbook of Criminal Investigation*, Devon: Willan.

Jones, T., Maclean, B., and Young, J. (1986), *The Islington Crime Survey: Crime, Victimization and Policing in Inner City London*. Aldershot: Gower.

Jones, T., Lea, J., and Young, J. (1987), *Saving the Inner City: The First Report of the Broadwater Farm Survey*, London: Middlesex Polytechnic.

Kinsey, R. (1984), *Merseyside Crime Survey: First Report*, Liverpool: Merseyside Metropolitan Council.

Levi, M. and Maguire, M. (2004), 'Reducing and preventing organised crime: An evidence-based critique', *Crime, Law and Social Change*, 41(5), 397–469.

MACKENZIE, S., BANNISTER, J., FLINT, J., PARR, S., MILLIE, A., and FLEETWOOD, J. (2010), *The drivers of perceptions of anti-social behaviour*. Research Report 34. London: Home Office.

MAGUIRE, M. (2007), 'Crime data and statistics', in M. Maguire, R. Morgan, and R. Reiner (eds), *The Oxford Handbook of Criminology*, 4th edn, Oxford: Oxford University Press.

MAGUIRE, M. (2008) 'Criminal Investigation and Crime Control', in T. Newburn (ed.), *Handbook of Policing*, 2nd edn, Devon: Willan.

MAGUIRE, M. (2012), 'Criminal statistics and the construction of crime', in M. Maguire, R. Morgan, and R. Reiner (eds), *The Oxford Handbook of Criminology*, 5th edn, Oxford: Oxford University Press.

MAGUIRE, M. and BENNETT, T. (1982), *Burglary in a Dwelling: The Offence, the Offender and the Victim*, London: Heinemann Educational Books.

MAGUIRE, M. and HOPKINS, M. (2003), 'Data and analysis for problem-solving: alcohol-related crime in pubs, clubs and the street', in K. Bullock and N. Tilley (eds), *Crime Reduction and Problem-oriented Policing*, Devon: Willan.

MARS, G. (1982), *Cheats at Work*, London: Allen and Unwin.

MATHESON, J. (2011), *National Statistician's Review of Crime Statistics: England and Wales*, London: Government Statistical Service.

MATTHEWS, R., and YOUNG, J. (eds) (1986), *Confronting Crime*, London: Sage.

MCVIE, S. (2017), 'Social order: crime and justice in Scotland', in D. McCrone (ed.), *The New Sociology of Scotland*, London: Sage.

MINKES, J. (2010), 'Corporate financial crimes', in F. Brookman, M. Maguire, H. Pierpoint, and T. Bennett (eds), *Handbook on Crime*, Devon: Willan.

MIRRLEES-BLACK, C. (1999), *Domestic Violence: Findings from a new British Crime Survey Self-Completion Questionnaire*. Home Office Research Study No. 191. London: Home Office.

MORGAN, J. and ZEDNER, L. (1992), *Child Victims: Crime, Impact and Criminal Justice*, Oxford: Oxford University Press.

NCA (2015), *National Strategic Assessment of Serious and Organised Crime 2015*, London: National Crime Agency.

NORMANDEAU (1969), 'Trends in Robbery as Reflected by Different Indexes', in T. Sellin and M. Wolfgang (eds), *Delinquency: Selected Studies*, New York: Wiley.

ONS (2015a), *Focus on Violent Crime and Sexual Offences: Year ending March 2015*, Newport: Office for National Statistics.

ONS (2015b), *Focus on Perceptions of Crime and the Police, and the Personal Well-being of Victims: 2013 to 2014*, Newport: Office for National Statistics.

ONS (2016a), *User Guide to Crime Statistics for England and Wales*, Newport: Office for National Statistics.

ONS (2016b), *Crime in England and Wales: Year ending March 2016*, Statistical Bulletin, Newport: Office for National Statistics.

ONS (2016c), *Crime in England and Wales: Year ending June 2016*, Statistical Bulletin, Newport: Office for National Statistics.

PAINTER, K. (1991), *Wife Rape, Marriage and the Law: Survey Report*, Manchester: Faculty of Economic and Social Science, University of Manchester.

PASSAS, N. and GROSKIN, R. (2001), 'Overseeing and overlooking: The US federal authorities' response to money laundering and other misconduct at BCCI', *Crime Law and Social Change*, 35(1–2): 141–75.

PERCY, A. and MAYHEW, P. (1997), 'Estimating sexual victimisation in a national crime survey: a new approach', *Studies in Crime and Crime Prevention*, 6(2): 125–50.

PRICEWATERHOUSE COOPERS (2005), '*Global Economic Crime Survey 2005*', available at: http://www.pwc.com/hu/en/publications/assets/pwc_2005_global-crimesurvey.pdf, accessed 8 January 2017.

PUBLIC ADMINISTRATION SELECT COMMITTEE (2014), *Caught red-handed: Why we can't count on Police Recorded Crime Statistics*. Thirteenth Report, HC 760, 9 April 2014, London: House of Commons.

RADFORD, L., CORRAL, S., BRADLEY, C., FISHER, H., BASSETT, C., HOWAT, N., and COLLISHAW, S. (2011), *Child abuse and neglect in the UK today*, London: NSPCC.

RADZINOWICZ, L. (1977), *The Growth of Crime*, London: Hamish Hamilton.

ROSENFELD, R. and WEISBURD, D. (2016), 'Explaining Recent Crime Trends: Introduction to the Special Issue', *Journal of Quantitative Criminology*, 32(3): 329–34.

SELLIN, T. and WOLFGANG, M. (1964), *The Measurement of Delinquency*, New York: Wiley.

SENIOR, P., CROWTHER-DOVEY, C., and LONG, M. (2007), *Understanding the Modernisation of Criminal Justice*, Milton Keynes: Open University Press.

SHERMAN, L., FARRINGTON, D., WELSH, B., and MACKENZIE, D. (2006), *Evidence-Based Crime Prevention*, Abingdon: Routledge.

SHERMAN, L., NEYROUD, P., and NEYROUD, E. (2016), 'The Cambridge Crime Harm Index: Measuring Total Harm from Crime Based on Sentencing Guidelines', *Policing*, doi:10.1093/police/paw003.

SIMMONS, J. (2000), *Review of Crime Statistics: A Discussion Document*, London: Home Office.

SIMMONS, J., LEGG, C., and HOSKING, R. (2003), *National Crime Recording Standard (NCRS): an Analysis of the Impact on Recorded Crime*, Home Office Online Report 31/03. London: Home Office.

SIMPSON, I., BENINGER, K., and ORMSTON, R. (2015), *Public confidence in official statistics*, London: Natcen.

SIVARAJASINGAM, V., MORGAN, P., MATTHEWS, K., SHEPHERD, J., and WALKER, R. (2009), 'Trends in violence in England and Wales 2000–2004: an accident and emergency perspective', *Injury*, 40(8): 820–5.

SMITH, A. (2006), *Crime Statistics: An Independent Review*, London: Home Office.

SPARKS, R., GENN, H., and DODD, D. (1977), *Surveying Victims*, Chichester: John Wiley.

STANKO, E. (1988), 'Hidden Violence against Women', in M. Maguire and J. Pointing (eds), *Victims of Crime: A New Deal?*, Milton Keynes: Open University Press.

STATISTICS COMMISSION (2005), *Crime Statistics: User Perspectives: Interim Report*, London: Statistics Commission.

STATISTICS COMMISSION (2006), *Crime Statistics: User Perspectives: Report No. 30*, London: Statistics Commission.

STRAUS, M., GELLES, R., and STEINMETZ, S. (1980), *Behind Closed Doors*, New York: Anchor Press.

TCHERNI, M., DAVIES, A., LOPES, G. and LIZOTTE, A. (2016), 'The dark figure of online property crime: Is cyberspace hiding a crime wave?', *Justice Quarterly*, 33(5): 890–911.

TOMBS, S. (2010), 'Corporate Violence and Harm', in F. Brookman, M. Maguire, H. Pierpoint, and T. Bennett (eds), *Handbook on Crime*, Devon: Willan.

UK STATISTICS AUTHORITY (2010), *Overcoming Barriers to Trust in Crime Statistics: England and Wales*, Monitoring Report 5, London: UK Statistics Authority.

UK STATISTICS AUTHORITY (2014), *Code of Practice for Official Statistics: Statistics on Crime in England and Wales*, Assessment Report 268, London: UK Statistics Authority.

VAN DIJK, J. (2013), *The International Crime Victims Survey 1988-2010; latest results and prospects*, Lausanne: ICVS, http://wp.unil.ch/icvs/category/uncategorized/, accessed 13 December 2016.

VAN DIJK, J. and TSELONI, A. (2012), 'Global overview: International trends in victimization and recorded crime', in J. van Dijk, A. Tseloni, and G. Farrell (eds), *The International Crime Drop: New Directions in Research*, London: Palgrave Macmillan.

VAN DIJK, J., TSELONI, A., and FARRELL, G. (2012), *The International Crime Drop: New Directions in Research*, London: Palgrave Macmillan.

VAN KESTEREN, J., VAN DIJK, J., and MAYHEW, P. (2014), 'The International Crime Victim Surveys: A Retrospective', *International Review of Victimology*, 20(1): 49–69.

WALBY, S. and ALLEN, J. (2004), *Domestic violence, sexual assault and stalking: Findings from the British Crime Survey*, Home Office Research Study 276, London Home Office Development and Statistics Directorate.

WALBY, S., TOWERS, J., and FRANCIS, B. (2014), *The decline in the rate of domestic violence has stopped: removing the cap on repeat victimisation reveals more violence*, Lancaster University, http://eprints.lancs.ac.uk/id/eprint/72272, accessed 13 December 2016.

WIKSTRÖM, P.-O. H. (2009), 'Questions of Perception and Reality', *British Journal of Sociology*, 60(1), 59–63.

WILLIAMS, L. (ed.) (2016), *Crime against Businesses: Findings from the 2015 Commercial Victimisation Survey*, Statistical Bulletin 03/16, London: Home Office.

YOUNG, J. (1988), 'Risk of Crime and Fear of Crime: a Realist Critique of Survey-based Assumptions', in M. Maguire and J. Pointing (eds), *Victims of Crime: A New Deal?*, Milton Keynes: Open University Press.

ZIMRING, F. E. (2007), *The Great American Crime Decline*, Oxford: Oxford University Press.

8

ETHNICITIES, RACISM, CRIME, AND CRIMINAL JUSTICE

Coretta Phillips and Ben Bowling

INTRODUCTION

The fatal shooting of Mark Duggan by police officers in August 2011 sparked riots in the London borough of Tottenham and other urban areas across the country, most with large minority ethnic populations. The private security officers involved in the deportation of Jimmy Mubenga in 2014 were not convicted of manslaughter despite a coroner's verdict of unlawful killing. In the same year, black people in England and Wales were five times as likely as white people to be stopped and searched by the police. The Prime Minister, announcing an investigation into racial bias in the criminal justice system in 2016 said 'If you're black, you're more likely to be in a prison cell than studying at a top university. And if you're black, it seems you're more likely to be sentenced to custody for a crime than if you're white'. People from minority ethnic groups remain vulnerable to violent racism, and the spike in hate crimes in the wake of the Brexit EU referendum result is a chilling reminder of this; other recent illustrations include the murder of 75-year old Muslim, Mohammed Saleem, in April 2013 and regular attacks on Jewish schools and synagogues. Police use of force, riots, deaths in custody, stop and search, and racist violence are common themes in the vexed relationship between minority ethnic groups and the criminal justice system in the UK and beyond. And while the chapter has a primary focus on England and Wales, the recent solidarity shown between the #blacklivesmatter movement in the US and similar coalitions in the UK and elsewhere, underlines the common experiences of state violence against minorities across the globe.

The study of 'race' and crime has a long and troubling history. Cesare Lombroso (1871), the founding father of criminology, developed a science of 'the criminal' based on the anthropometric study of the physical and psychological traits of racial types. In the second edition of *Criminal Man*, Lombroso (1884/2006: 115, 119) wrote that 'some tribes have no morality at all' and that Gypsies 'epitomise a thoroughly criminal race'. Later, Lombroso (1897) recognized that black people in the United States faced discrimination in the justice system but thought that their very high homicide rates was due to their primitivism, brutalism, shiftlessness, and indifference to the lives of others. The contention that certain minority ethnic groups have a greater propensity to commit crime than the white majority ethnic group has been at the heart of the 'race and crime debate' for decades. Yet, more recent criminological scholarship has shifted its focus to new manifestations of the problematic relationship between minorities and the criminal justice system, particularly in relation to migration control and Islamist terrorism.

This chapter explores both old and new dimensions of the 'race and crime debate' beginning with a discussion of the emergence of the modern idea of race, before contextualizing the current picture by examining patterns of migration and settlement, and the demographic and socio-economic profiles of ethnic groups in England and Wales.[1] This sets the scene for an analysis of criminal statistics, contemporary empirical and theoretical work on patterns of crime of victims and offenders, before moving onto the functioning of the criminal justice system from policing to prisons. The chapter ends with a critical look within our own discipline for the ways in which race and ethnicity inform the development of criminological scholarship.

HISTORICAL AND CONTEMPORARY CONTEXTS

MAPPING THE CONCEPTUAL TERRAIN

The pseudo-scientific notion that humanity could be divided into innate, distinct, and hierarchically arranged racial groups originated in the European Enlightenment. For philosophers and physical scientists such as Hume, Kant, de Gobineau, Linne, and Blumenbach, reason and civilization were synonymous with the white or Caucasian race, while other, supposedly primitive racial groups, and especially the 'Negro' were regarded as naturally inferior in terms of their moral, intellectual, and behavioural capacities (Banton 1998). Hume's (1754/1997: 33) claim that '[t]here never was a civilised nation of any other complexion than white' and Kant's (1754/1997: 55) assertion that Africans 'have by nature no feeling that rises above the trifling' epitomize this perspective. These racist ideas— comprising what Gilroy (2000) refers to as 'raciology'— legitimized practices of slavery and indentured labour and became embedded in British colonial policies. Racial science was also integral to the policies pursued in Nazi Germany and the ideological root of the genocide of Jews and Gypsies in the Holocaust.

[1] There are valid reasons, in addition to space constraints, for the almost exclusive focus on England and Wales in this chapter. The minority ethnic population of the United Kingdom is largest in England and Wales (14 per cent), compared with Scotland (4 per cent) and Northern Ireland (2 per cent). It is also the case that the bulk of empirical and theoretical work in the field of race and crime has centred on the experiences of the largest minority ethnic groups of black and Asian origin who reside in England and (to a lesser extent) Wales.

Scholars in the post-war period roundly rejected such ideas. Montagu (1943), for example, regarded the idea of 'race' itself as 'man's most dangerous myth' and, with many others, argued that race is a social construction rather than an objective analytical category (Mason 2000). Nonetheless, race has persisted in the public (and criminological) imagination and has yet to be eclipsed by the more politically neutral term 'ethnicity' preferred by some social scientists. Eschewing the biological basis of racial differences, and notions of superiority and inferiority, ethnicity refers to self-defined collectivities of people of common origin with a shared culture linked to language, religion, nationality, and ancestral traditions (Fenton 2003). Unlike race, which fixes human difference as an unchanging ahistorical essence, the analysis of ethnicity allows us to understand variation according to local socio-cultural practices (Barth 1969).

While the idea of race has been discredited in academic circles, as Anne Phillips (2007: 15) has observed, 'simply denying its validity is never enough to combat the hierarchies of power'. Thus, social scientists are left to find the least problematic means by which they can enumerate and assess whether different ethnic groups have distinctive experiences of power and (in)justice. Criminologists have reluctantly turned to the administrative categories used in the UK census; these carry the risk of reifying an essentialist notion of race, as well as obscuring the internal heterogeneity of the groups they are supposed to describe. 'Critical whiteness studies', which is only just beginning to percolate into criminology, also underlines the need to reject monolithic notions of white ethnicity, and this issue has come to the fore in the context of post-2004 EU migration from Central and Eastern Europe (see also Webster 2008; Phillips and Webster 2013; Smith 2014). Similarly, we are now seeing the value of looking at criminological issues through the lens of intersectionality, recognizing that individual identities straddle race, ethnicity, gender, social class, sexual orientation, and so on (Henne and Troshynski 2013).

EARLY MIGRANT SETTLEMENT, SOCIO-ECONOMIC INEQUALITIES, AND THE SOCIAL CONSTRUCTION OF ETHNIC CRIMINALITIES

Britain became an ethnically diverse society by virtue of its imperial past. Everyone born in the empire had, in theory at least, the right to a British passport and to settle in the 'mother country'. Thus those experiencing crime and justice in the twenty-first century include the children, grandchildren, and great-grandchildren of post-war settlers from Britain's former colonial territories, including those from the Caribbean, Africa, and Asia. At the time of the 2011 census, Britain was home to nearly 8 million people of minority ethnic backgrounds. Of the general population, 3 per cent were black, 8 per cent Asian, 2 per cent 'mixed race', and 1 per cent of 'other ethnic origins'. There were a further 3 million people of 'other white' backgrounds, comprising 5 per cent of the population, including the Irish, Travellers, and Gypsies. However, the vast majority of the population—around 80 per cent—identified as white British.

Migrant settlement into urban areas during the 1950s, 1960s, and 1970s was shaped by the availability of jobs and homes that the indigenous community did not want, so minority ethnic communities were (and still are) geographically concentrated in London, the South East, the Midlands, and the North West of England (Lupton and

Power 2004). Early research found that migrants were employed in occupations far below those for which they were qualified and skilled and they were excluded from public and private sector housing. This research showed that exclusion from jobs, homes, and other aspects of British life was largely explained by patterns of formal and informal discrimination known as the 'colour bar' (Daniel 1968). The structural effects of deindustrialization further entrenched disadvantage, particularly for those of Indian and Pakistani origin, while Travellers and Gypsies have been adversely affected by the disappearance of itinerant employment opportunities, particularly in agriculture (Smith and Greenfields 2012).

The legacy of overt and covert racial discrimination in the middle and later years of the twentieth century has contemporary resonance as economic and social inequalities among Britain's minority ethnic groups have been sustained over time, although with increasing differentiation. Today, poor levels of GCSE attainment in 2013–14 is most striking for the lowest cluster of Irish Traveller, Gypsy, and Roma pupils followed by the next cluster of black Caribbean, Pakistani, and white pupils from disadvantaged areas (Exley 2016). School exclusions are highest among boys of Irish Traveller, Gypsy, Roma, black Caribbean, and mixed race origins (DfE 2015; Gillborn 2008). Looked-after status is more common among black and mixed race children (Zaye and Harker 2015). High unemployment and low pay are particularly marked for black men, Pakistani, Bangladeshi, and black African women, and the economic returns from education are still not being fully realized even among the more successful Indian and Chinese communities (Phillips and Platt 2016). Research on 'ethnic penalties' points to racial discrimination playing a significant part in this disadvantage (Heath and Cheung 2006), accentuating household and neighbourhood deprivation (Phillips and Harrison 2010). For those of Traveller and Gypsy origin the picture in relation to illiteracy, unemployment, and poor physical and mental health, is particularly bleak (Smith & Greenfields, 2012).

These markers of material disadvantage, in which racism is implicated, have consequences for criminal victimization and offending. Yet while a House of Commons Select Committee in 1972 reported that the white and 'West Indian' populations offended at similar rates, with lower rates for Asians, by the mid-1970s and into the 1980s, this image had changed dramatically. Sensationalist media reports about mugging and robbery, with headlines such as 'black crime shock' along with images of street disorders in the 1980s promoted in the public imagination views of black people as innately violent, drug-abusing, and disorderly (Hall *et al.* 1978; Gilroy 1982). In contrast, Asian communities were for many years portrayed as conformist, passive, inward-looking, and self-regulating (Webster 1997). More recently the 'Asian gang' (Alexander 2000) has been identified as culturally separatist and a source of 'home-grown' Islamist terrorism (McGhee 2008), reinforcing the shift in perceptions of people of Asian origin from 'saint' to 'sinner'. The identification of Pakistani men collectively involved in racialized sexual violence against vulnerable young white women has proved another powerful motif in which criminality is fused, this time with patriarchal Asian cultural practices. It is rather similar to the earlier mugging moral panic, but further tinged with the alleged gendered failures of state protection, resulting from so-called 'misguided political correctness' (Cockbain 2013). It is a salutary reminder that the 'whiteness' of white collar crime, football violence, and alcohol-fuelled disorder has not produced the same essentialized notions of a 'white criminality' in either public or political consciousness.

The postcolonial generations have been joined by newer migrants from countries across the globe as diverse as Poland, Latvia, Germany, Romania, China, Sri Lanka, Somalia, and Kenya. In a political climate hostile to migration, particularly of low-skilled workers, migrants of the twenty-first century face many of the same barriers as those settling in Britain in the post-war period. Non-EU citizens, in particular, are more likely to experience unemployment, labour market insecurity, and poverty than national or EU citizens (Shutes 2016). However, far less is known about the victimization and offending experiences of newer migrants, many of whom are white, and to a degree the same can be said about people from Traveller and Gypsy communities (James 2013).

VICTIMIZATION AND FEAR OF CRIME

The Crime Survey England and Wales (CSEW) estimates that the risk of being a victim of a 'personal crime' in 2015 was highest for those describing themselves as mixed race (11 per cent) compared with black (6 per cent), white (4 per cent), or Asian (5 per cent) (MoJ 2015a). The comparative victimization rate between white and black respondents has widened since 2010, but long before this the British Crime Survey (the predecessor of the CSEW) found victimization rates for burglary and vehicle theft, as well as anxieties about crime, highest among minority ethnic respondents. People of mixed race have also consistently experienced substantially higher levels of household crimes (Clancy *et al.* 2001). Multivariate analyses of survey data found that factors such as age, low income, unemployment, urban residence, and a lack of academic qualifications, were more important than ethnic origin *per se* in explaining minority ethnic groups' higher levels of victimization (Clancy *et al.* 2001; Salisbury and Upson 2004). Nevertheless, some of these factors, such as urban residence and unemployment, are themselves partly explained by discrimination in housing and employment. Questions remain as to why victimization risks are significantly higher for mixed race people, over and above their younger age strcuture (Salisbury and Upson 2004).

RACIST, ANTISEMITIC, AND ANTI-IMMIGRANT VICTIMIZATION

As well as being generally more likely to be victimized, people from minority ethnic groups are also the targets of racist violence and other forms of hate crime (Bowling 1999). There were around 46,000 notifiable hate crimes in 2014–15, of which 93 per cent were racially motivated and 7 per cent religiously motivated, with the latter showing the far larger year-on-year increase. There has also been a 4 per cent increase in racist incidents between 2010–11 and 2014–15, totalling just short of 54,000 incidents (MoJ 2015a).[2] There is now a very extensive literature on hate crimes in general and violent racism in particular.

[2] Statistical data on hate crimes in Scotland (Scottish Government 2015) also finds recent increases for racist and religious incidents and offences, with a study by Moody and Clark (2004) similarly pointing to problems of under-protection for victims. In Northern Ireland, hate crime statistics highlight a disproportionately high number of victims of white ethnicity, particularly of Irish Traveller origin, but also with those of black and Asian origins affected too (PSNI 2016). McKeever *et al.* (2013) have looked at violent racist discourse directed at the Chinese community.

A relatively new and increasingly recognized problem is the subtle and pervasive ways in which racist victimization occurs in the virtual or cyber sphere. Awan and Zempi (2015), using information from the self-report service TellMAMA (Measuring Anti-Muslim Attacks), found that victims were most likely to be 'visible Muslims' wearing religious clothing, such as the hijab, and could include white converts to Islam. More than 20 per cent of victims reported repeated incidents; such repetition is characteristic of racist victimization, often leading to feelings of vulnerability, fear, insecurity, and frustration (Bowling 1999), which can encompass the wider British Muslim population too.

Data on anti-Semitic incidents numbered 1,179 in 2014 and 924 in 2015, according to reports to the Community Security Trust (CST), while the Department for Communites and Local (DCLG 2014) recently reported a rise in anti-semitic comments on social media and a rise in anti-semitic daubings on private and public property (DCLG 2014). Anti-immigrant sentiments, more generally, particularly after the EU referendum decision, have been blamed for the rise in migrant victimization, with the Home Secretary announcing a review into police practices in this area in July 2016 (Home Office 2016). The absence of centrally recorded data on this, coupled with low reporting rates, particularly where victims' insecure immigration status means they may feel threatened by state scrutiny into their lives, makes this an area where little reliable data is available (Spenkuch 2014).

STREET CRIME: CRIMINOLOGICAL STATISTICS AND RESEARCH

Comparing patterns of crime among different ethnic groups is an inherently flawed exercise, limited by weaknesses in official 'ethnic monitoring' data and other potential sources of information. We must be cautious in any attempt to use official statistics to discover the 'real' rate of crime or to compare crime rates between groups. It is also important to note that self-report offending surveys, which rely on the honesty of interviewees to disclose criminal behaviour, typically find lower reported rates of offending and drug use among those of Asian ethnicities, with higher rates for the mixed race group, and with black offending rates a little lower than or similar to the white majority (Sharp and Budd 2005; see also Bowling and Phillips 2002 for a detailed examination of the data).

OFFICIAL STATISTICS

Arrest, prosecution, conviction, and sentencing data are relatively robust 'head counts' which assume sufficient evidence of wrongdoing to justify official action and that the ethnic origin of the suspect has been accurately recorded. The major weakness of these data for this purpose is that they are accounts of decisions taken by criminal justice officials rather than evidence of offending *per se*. Biases in the administration of criminal justice will therefore create a skewed picture (see Lacey and Zedner, this volume).

Table 8.1 Criminal justice statistics per 1,000 population, by ethnicity

	White	Black	Mixed	Asian	Chinese/Other	Black/White Ratio
Police searches	15	65	28	23	14	**4.3**
Arrests	19	56	38	20	18	**3.0**
Cautions	3	7	–	2	–	***0.4***
Prosecutions[1]	6	18	11	5	4	**3.0**
Convictions[1]	5	14	9	4	3	**2.8**
Prison population (British)[2]	182	603	462	151	6	**3.3**

Notes:

1. For indictable only offences tried at the magistrates' court.
2. Per 100,000 of the population aged 15 years+.

Source: Ministry of Justice (2016) Freedom of Information request.

At the crucial entry point to the criminal justice system, around 80 per cent of the people arrested by the police for criminal offences are recorded as being of white ethnicity. However, as Table 8.1 shows, there are higher arrest *rates* (calculated as the number per 100,000 people in the general population) for those of black and mixed ethnic origins. These statistics vary markedly by *type of offence*; black people are overrepresented in robbery, fraud/forgery, and drug arrests; the mixed race group for drugs; while Asians are overrepresented in arrests for fraud/forgery and sexual offences. The way different offences come to police attention is crucial for interpreting these data. Robbery arrests, discussed below, typically follow a report from a victim. Arrests for drug offences commonly result from proactive police practices and are therefore more vulnerable to discrimination than other offences. The degree to which 'ethnic specialization' in different types of offending, such as fraud and forgery, occurs is unknown and must await future research.

The pattern of a higher black to white ratio at each stage of the criminal justice process from arrest to imprisonment is stark and consistent. Cautioning practices are an exception in that the black minority ethnic group appears to be at an advantage compared with other groups. The reason for this is unclear although it might reflect the higher number of first-time entrants to the criminal justice system among the black group (MoJ 2015a). Statistics on the ethnic origin of prisoners have consistently shown a higher rate of imprisonment for black people since they were first published in the mid-1980s (Home Office 1986). This is true for male and female prisoners and people of both British and foreign nationality.

VICTIMS' DESCRIPTIONS OF OFFENDERS

Police statistics on the ethnicity of offenders for particular offences—most often street robbery— have long been used selectively to justify the police targeting of minority ethnic communities (Hall *et al.* 1978; Gilroy 1987; Bowling and Phillips 2002). Yet victims' descriptions may be inaccurate because eyewitness identification is not always reliable (Coleman and Moynihan 1996) and there is often, particularly in property crimes, no victim–offender interaction. Clancy *et al.* (2001) found only about 40 per cent of surveyed victims could describe an assailant, although among 203 victims of 'mugging', 30 per cent described their assailant as black. While street robbery accounts for less than 2 per cent of recorded crime it has been the focus of public concerns and media panics since the early 1970s (Hall *et al.* 1978). Smith (2003: 26) found that the majority of robbery suspects were black in six out of the nine police areas he studied. The exceptions were Stockport, Preston, and Blackpool where 99 per cent of the suspected offenders were white (see also Harrington and Mayhew 2001 for similar findings).

Homicide and weapon data

The police recorded 1,571 victims of murder, manslaughter, or infanticide in England and Wales in the two years to November 2014. Around three-quarters of homicide victims in this period were white. Black people are about four times as likely to be murdered by comparison with their white counterparts and people of Asian origin are one and half times as likely (MoJ 2015a). Where a suspect was identified, 94 per cent of white victims were killed by white assailants, while almost two-thirds (60 per cent) of Asian victims and over half (53 per cent) of black victims were murdered by someone from the same ethnic group (MoJ 2015a). Recent years have seen high levels of public anxiety about gun and knife crime within minority ethnic communities. In the two-year period to November 2014, an average of 19 black people were victims of gun murder each year compared with around 28 white people and 2 Asians (MoJ 2015a). Black murder victims are much more likely to have been shot (26 per cent) than white (4 per cent) or Asian (3 per cent) victims. There is only limited research on this topic, perhaps because gun homicide remains relatively rare in the UK (Bullock and Tilley 2002; Hales 2006; Pitts 2008; Gunther 2010).

Black people are also disproportionately cautioned or convicted of weapon possession (MoJ 2015a) which could be a feature of police disproportionate use of stop and search powers under PACE 1984 and the Firearms Act 1968. However, there is also a rich literature suggesting that carrying weapon results from peer influences, status, and as a form of social capital, especially among young people (Dijkstra *et al.* 2010; Taylor *et al.* 2015). This can be coupled with the consistent finding that minority ethnic groups have higher levels of fear of crime.

Gangs

Traditionally thought of as an American problem, increasing media and political attention has been paid to the problem of street gangs in Britain. As Williams and Clarke (2016: 10) observe, 'the gang construct is racialised to Black and Brown men' (see also Alexander 2000; Smithson *et al.* 2013; Hallsworth and Young 2008). Estimating the extent and nature of gang membership is plagued by definitional and methodological issues and consequently no meaningful official data are available (Hallsworth and Young 2008; Goldson 2011). For Hagedorn (2007) gang membership reflects those disadvantaged by economic restructuring, the neoliberal retrenchment of welfare, and social exclusion, a view echoed by Pitts' (2008) study of London gangs. Hagedorn suggests that gang members assert their oppositional religious, ethnic, or cultural identities in urban areas, although Hales *et al.* (2006) and Aldridge and Medina (2008) show that gangs exist also in predominantly 'white areas' of England. Gangs can be loosely structured, bound by territorial identification by 'postcode' or 'housing estate' (see Fraser and Hobbs, this volume). Many engage in drug-dealing and other illicit activities, often segmented along class and ethnic lines (Ruggiero 2000).

Domestic Violence: honour crimes and forced marriage

For activists such as Hannana Siddiqui from the NGO, Southall Black Sisters, honour punishments and killings—where male family members violently discipline, control, or ostracize female relatives—should be seen conceptually and legally as domestic violence (Siddiqui 2005: see also Reddy 2008). Fundamental to such crimes is men's patriarchal reactions to perceived violations of women's chastity and autonomy (Cooney 2014). The neglect of such violent social control, possibly out of misguided respect for cultural difference, has endangered many minority ethnic women. The worry that media and political discourses uphold singular views of minority ethnic groups as routinely engaging in extremes of violence against women *is* nevertheless real. Such perspectives display cultural determinism, ignoring within-group heterogeneity, and risking cultural or religious essentialism (Dustin and Phillips 2008). The Home Office's Forced Marriage Unit provides statistics (there were reported cases 1,267 in 2014), and their own research by Hester and colleagues (2007) recognizes the wide reach of forced marriages among groups whose origins were as diverse as South Asian, Central European, Chinese, African, African Caribbean, as well as Irish Traveller and orthodox religious UK communities. Poverty, bride price, social control, and immigration were motivating factors for forced marriages. These were made illegal in the Anti-social Behaviour, Crime and Policing Act 2014.

THE POLICE AND POLICING MINORITY COMMUNITIES

The relationship between police and minority ethnic communities has long been fractious. Early research showed how the role of the police in immigration control during the postcolonial years shaped their relationship with black and Asian communities and led to the infusion of racism, stereotyping, and discrimination into everyday police practice (Hall *et al.* 1978; Gordon 1983; Gilroy 1987). This had the twin effects of focusing police suspicion on minority communities and undermining the response to their victimization, so that they were 'over policed, but under-protected'.

Deaths following police contact is the most controversial of all issues and came to the fore in recent years again following the international publicity around the police shootings of more than 1000 black people in the US in 2015 (see *The Guardian's* 'The Counted' police killings database), and the filmed killings by police of Alton

Sterling (Louisiana 2016), Philando Castille (Minnesota 2016), Walter Scott (South Carolina 2015), following Mike Brown (Missouri 2014). The groundswell of anger within minority communities connected the US #blacklivesmatter movement and the UK United Families and Friends campaign. Despite the contrast between the USA and the UK, where a total of 23 people in the UK were shot dead by the police in the decade to 2014, police violence remains a highly contentious issue in Britain. Police brutality is also evident in contact with the police involving the use of restraints, Tasers, vehicle collisions, and the neglect of the duty of care to people in custody. The Black Lives Matter movement seems likely to continue to build and grow on both sides of the Atlantic in the foreseeable future.

After deaths in police custody, stop and search has been the most contentious issue in the relationship between the police and minority ethnic communities since the 1970s, with sharp rises in the use of police powers during the 1980s, 1990s, and 2000s. Searches under section 1 of the Police and Criminal Evidence Act 1984—which require 'reasonable suspicion' that a person has committed an offence—hit a peak of 1.2 million per year in 2011 but fell to just over 0.5 million in 2015.[3] Suspicionless searches, carried out for counter-terrorism and special operations against knife crime also rose dramatically to 360,000 in 2009 after which they reduced sharply to fewer than 1,000 in 2015. The use of suspicionless searches were particularly controversial because they were used very extensively against minority ethnic communities; for example in 2002, compared with the white population, Asians were more than six times more frequently stopped and searched using 'suspicionless powers' and black people 27 times more frequently. The evidence indicates that ethnic disproportionality in the use of stop and search powers results from direct and indirect discrimination (Bowling and Phillips 2007).

After decades of attempts by police policy-makers to address this issue, people from black and minority ethnic groups are still more likely to be stopped than their white counterparts, but racial disproportionality has fallen from 7.5 in 2011 to 4 in 2015 for black people and from 2:1 to 1.5:1 for Asians (see Table 8.1) and many fewer people from minority ethnic backgrounds are being stopped overall. The reasons for the reduction in the use of stop and search powers are a complex mix of legal, political, procedural, and cultural changes. The key legal change was the 2010 European Court of Human Rights ruling that led to the abolition of section 44 of the Terrorism Act. Pressure from community organizations, the Equality and Human Rights Commission, Inspectorate of Constabulary, and the Home Office was for police officers to use these suspicionless powers less frequently and more discerningly (Bowling and Marks 2017).

Traveller communities are also disproportionately affected by spatial regulation by enforcement agents. Their 'nomadism', which some police officers see as a cloak for criminality, means that traditional approaches to improve trust and police-community relations, using consultation and recruitment, seem likely to fail (Mulcahy 2012).

[3] Scottish research by Murray and Harkin (2016) has highlighted the far greater use of stop and search powers in Scotland compared with England and Wales, often conducted on a non-statutory basis. The focus has been primarily on young working-class men, with a view to reducing knife-carrying and violence.

This leaves Traveller communities significantly 'underprotected' by the police as most experience policing largely through enforcement rather than community engagement (James 2004, 2013).

THE STEPHEN LAWRENCE INQUIRY

The racist murder of Stephen Lawrence in London in 1993 and the public inquiry which followed in 1999 into the failed Metropolitan Police investigation brought the issues of racist violence, stop and search, and racism to the top of the political agenda (Bowling 1999; Hall *et al.* 2009). The Inquiry concluded that the initial investigation into the murder was 'marred by a combination of professional incompetence, institutional racism, and a failure of leadership by senior officers' (Macpherson 1999: 46.1). Institutional racism—the 'collective failure of an organization to provide an appropriate and professional service to people because of their colour, culture, or ethnic origin'—could be 'seen or detected in processes, attitudes and behaviour which amount to discrimination through unwitting prejudice, ignorance, thoughtlessness and racist stereotyping which disadvantage minority ethnic people' (Macpherson 1999: 34). The report criticized the police for denying the racist motive for the murder, stereotyping Stephen's friend, Duwayne Brooks at the scene (Hall *et al.* 1998), using inappropriate and offensive language, and insensitive and patronizing handling of the Lawrence family throughout the investigation. It confirmed research and community accounts revealing dissatisfaction with the police failure to investigate reported racist violence. Having an 'explosive impact on the workings of the criminal justice system' (Rock 2004: 481), the government established a Ministerial Priority 'to increase trust and confidence in policing amongst minority ethnic communities', as well as a range of other measures (Home Office 1999a). It was to take 18 years, new DNA evidence, and legislative change to the 'double jeopardy' rule, before Gary Dobson and David Norris were convicted of Stephen Lawrence's racist murder (Stone 2015).

Post-Lawrence research indicates an absence of the overt racism prevalent in the occupational cultures of the 1970s and 1980s and officers feel less able to carry out unjustified stop and search 'fishing trips' (Foster *et al.* 2005: 30). However, minority ethnic police officers have expressed concern about more subtle forms of discrimination leading to unequal treatment (Holdaway and O'Neill 2007; Loftus 2008). It is possible that racist attitudes and behaviour may simply have gone 'underground' (Foster *et al.* 2005). And while the Home Office (1999) set targets to increase recruitment, retention, career progression, and senior level representation of the police, this was only partially successful. There is continued under-representation with minority ethnic police officers making up only 6 per cent of the total in 2014 (MoJ 2015a). There remains little ethnic diversity in the senior ranks of the police service while recruitment efforts have been hampered by high profile employment tribunals alleging racial discrimination by managers and colleagues. Such experiences may be further compounded by sexism and harassment for women officers (Holder *et al.* 2000). The Morris Inquiry (2004) in London documented 'management by retreat' as managers' anxiety about handling poor performance by minority ethnic officers meant they failed to tackle this early enough using supervision and training, instead subjecting minority ethnic officers more often to formal investigations and suspensions (see also Butts 2010).

POLICING, LEGITIMACY, AND GLOBALIZATION

The question of trust and police legitimacy, particularly among young people, was central to explanations of the riots of August 2011 which erupted following the fatal shooting of Mark Duggan, by the police in London. Just as the disorders in Ferguson, Missouri spread to other parts of the USA, unrest broke out in several urban areas in Britain, mostly with large minority populations. Many of the rioters interviewed in the LSE/Guardian study, mentioned earlier black deaths in custody, such as those of Cherry Groce in the 1980s (Lewis *et al.* 2011). Amid widespread feelings of hostility and a sense of injustice caused by negative and humiliating treatment by police lacking accountability, particularly in relation to stop and search, similar views were found in areas like Salford with small minority ethnic communities. The riots, young people told Newburn and colleagues, were 'payback'. Kawalerowicz and Biggs' (2015) study based on interviews with 1,674 people charged with riot-related offences, found that many rioters lived in postcodes experiencing socio-economic deprivation in terms of family structures, housing, education, and employment. This did not prevent a punitive stance being advocated by then Prime Minister David Cameron as he recalled Parliament, seeing the rioting as 'criminality, pure and simple', urging sentencers to ensure that 'anyone convicted should expect to go to jail' (*Hansard*, 11 August 2011, cols 1051–2).

Perhaps surprisingly, Bradford *et al.* (2015), using crime survey data for 2008–11, found immigrants displayed higher levels of trust towards the police than those born in the UK. This was in all likelihood a reflection on policing in their countries of origin. Similarly, while some Muslims have been critical of their being 'over-policed' particularly with regard to counter-terrorism measures like 'suspicionless searches' discussed above (Parmar 2011; Mythen 2012), as well as their under-protection from victimization, crime survey data show that Muslim respondents appear to express approximately the same level of positive attitudes towards the police as other socio-demographic groups. Possible explanations include the political pressure Muslims face to condemn acts of terrorism and support the police (Innes *et al.* 2011), but more research is needed on this.

Coalescing in the global policing of Western borders are traditional anxieties expressed in the political discourse and the media about migrants polluting superior national identities and cultures, familiar concerns about welfare scrounging, and newer fears of the threat of Islamist terrorism. The latter is seen as an *internal risk* from those 'home grown' in alienated and radicalized minority ethnic communities in Britain and as an *external risk* from a disparate but technologically connected Isis-affiliated diaspora. For Goldberg (2009), the twenty-first century 'racial state' acts as a kind of traffic cop, that facilitates the mobility of the global elite while coercively regulating the excluded masses from low-income countries through mechanisms of surveillance and containment. This is facilitated through the merging of criminal and immigration laws creating a system of 'crimmigration' control managed increasingly as an integral part of transnational law enforcement (Bowling 2013).

Despite the portrayal of the borders of nation states as increasingly irrelevant in the globalized digital age, given the increased mobility of goods, workers, services, and capital, the number of countries that an individual can travel to depends on the origin of their passport—a holder of the least restricted passport, from Finland or the UK, is able to travel to 173 countries freely, whereas the holder of the most restricted passport, from 'countries of colour' like Afghanistan, may only travel to 28 countries without visas which are typically prohibitively expensive and often refused. The most restricted countries tend to be those with a particularly exploitative colonial history or who have recently been subject to Western military intervention. Western states are increasingly reconfiguring the border in order to control the movement of individuals with a 'perceived low-economic or production value' within global markets (Weber and Bowling 2008: 367). Those deemed economically weak or racially disreputable may experience criminalization through punitive detention and face a heightened risk of deportation. Claiming asylum, an inalienable human right, or seeking economic migration is commonly obstructed by border control measures, heralding what some have called a new 'global apartheid', benefiting Western states at the expense of minorities from low-income countries (Richmond 1985; Bowling 2013).

THE CRIMINAL JUSTICE PROCESS

By the end point of the criminal justice process, the cumulative effects of social exclusion, direct and indirect racial discrimination, and restrictive border controls can be seen in disproportionate rates of imprisonment. In 2014, minority ethnic men and women comprise 11 per cent and 6 per cent respectively of the British male and female prison populations, despite the fact that they comprise only 3 per cent of the general population. Among foreign national prisoners the figures were 58 per cent and 49 per cent (MoJ 2015a). This is not unique to prisons in England and Wales. What Alexander (2010: 191) refers to as 'racial caste-making' and Wacquant (2009: 197) damningly calls 'carceral affirmative action' in the US can be seen in other Western states. Minority ethnic groups are all too frequently subject to the coercive powers of the state when unemployment resulting from deindustrialization and welfare retrenchment fosters criminality. Regarded as each nation state's internal 'suitable enemies', foreign nationals, often of minority ethnic origin, make up an average of 20 per cent of prisoners across Europe with countries like Greece, Luxembourg, and Switzerland having exceptionally high proportions (Wacquant 1999).

There remains some grounds for optimism in political responses to disproportionality in the UK and the US. In January 2016 the prominent black MP, David Lammy, was invited by the UK Prime Minister, with cross-party support, to examine claims of racial bias in the criminal justice system and to make recommendations to tackle prejudice and discrimination. In 2015 US President Barack Obama, acknowledged in a speech to the National Association for the Advancement of Coloured People that '[t]he bottom line is that in too many places, black boys and black men, Latino boys and Latino men experience being treated differently under the law'.[4] Under his

[4] https://www.whitehouse.gov/the-press-office/2015/07/14/remarks-president-naacp-conference, accessed 16 December 2016.

presidency, drug sentencing laws that were widely condemned as institutionally racist were amended. The mandatory minimum sentencing for trafficking crack cocaine (more common among African Americans) at a gram disparity of 100:1 compared with powder cocaine (more common among white Americans) was brought closer to 18:1 in the Fair Sentencing Act 2010. Whether such political interventions will be able to fully incorporate an understanding of the historical ideologies of imperialism and slavery, which scholars such as Agozino (2003) and Hudson (2006) have argued plague contemporary practices of over-penalizing and criminalizing racialized subjects, remains to be seen. It is to the empirical research examining the particularities of police detention, court, and sentencing processes, that the chapter now turns.

INDIRECT RACIAL DISCRIMINATION

Minority ethnic suspects and defendants can be cumulatively disadvantaged by long-established rituals of the criminal justice process, such as those that rely on cooperation with police and prosecutors. At the police station, minority ethnic suspects have been found more likely to offer no-comment interviews and less likely to admit offences during interview or before trial, rendering them ineligible for a caution or sentencing discount (Bucke and Brown 1997). Whilst such decisions are formally 'racially neutral', minority ethnic individuals are effectively denied the benefits of cooperation because of long-standing mistrust of the police.

In 2014, more defendants of black and mixed race origin than average received custodial remands (MoJ 2015a), reflecting the evidence that minority ethnic groups are more likely than average to be remanded in police and prison custody at least partly because of socio-economic and demographic factors. Housing inequalities and an alleged lack of 'community ties' for black defendants in particular, may increase the perceived risk that they will abscond or interfere with witnesses. Being held in prison awaiting trial is in itself a burden, but also increases the likelihood of imprisonment on conviction (MoJ 2015a). Hudson (1993: 164) observed the irony that the 'characteristics of the penalized population are so often the very characteristics we are building into various formalised decision-making criteria, adherence to which we take as evidence that we are dispensing impartial criminal justice'. This can be seen as indirect racial discrimination but is defended on the grounds of system efficiency; deciding 'which decision-making criteria are justifiable or legitimate raises deep and difficult problems in the philosophy of law' (Smith 1997: 753).

DIRECT RACIAL DISCRIMINATION

Evidence of direct racial discrimination comes from studies employing multivariate analysis to tease out the independent effects of ethnicity as a predictor of a more severe outcome in the criminal justice process. Such studies problematically uphold individualizing notions of race and ethnicity, rather than seeing it as a dynamic social relation (Cuneen 2011), but they do present persuasive evidence of discriminatory practices by criminal justice agents. Such approaches have found that, once legally relevant factors had been controlled, black suspects were twice as likely to be strip-searched at the police station (Newburn *et al.* 2004) and being from a minority ethnic group predicted an increased chance of case termination by the CPS indicating likely police bias at charging

(Phillips *et al.* 1998; Mhlanga 1997). Likewise, Hood's (1992) pioneering, but now dated, study of racial bias in Crown Court sentencing practices in the West Midlands estimated that black defendants had a 5 per cent greater probability of custody compared with white defendants. In guilty plea cases, Asian defendants received nine months and black defendants three months longer than white defendants. Recent analysis by Hopkins (2015) found 40 per cent and 30 per cent higher odds of custodial sentencing for minority ethnic male and female defendants, respectively, compared with white defendants, regardless of criminal history, although the study did not include the potentially explanatory variables of offence seriousness, mitigating, and aggravating factors.

Qualitative studies, including on pre-sentence reports in one North-West probation area observed judgemental comments and distancing language in Asian offenders' reports which portrayed them as less remorseful than white offenders (Hudson and Bramhall 2005). Lower conviction ratios for black, mixed, and Asian offenders in 2009–14 are also suggestive of discrimination (MoJ 2015a).

YOUTH JUSTICE

The House of Commons Home Affairs Committee on *Young Black People and the Criminal Justice System* (2007) concluded that social exclusion was the main determinant of black over-representation in the criminal justice system. Linked to greater lone female parenting and the absence of prosocial male role models were central to many of the accounts given by minority ethnic witnesses to the Committee's inquiry. Notwithstanding, based on a multivariate analysis of 17,054 case decisions, Feilzer and Hood (2004) found indications of discriminatory treatment variously across the criminal justice process, and this was most marked for black and mixed race young men, and on occasion for Asian men too. May *et al.* (2010) examined 18,083 case decisions, and similarly found even with offence type, seriousness, and suspects' criminal histories, black and mixed race young people had worse outcomes across stages of youth justice process including pre-court disposals, case termination, custodial remand, acquittals, committals to Crown court, PSR sentence recommendations, and sentencing.

Significant racial bias has emerged in the use of 'joint enterprise' laws. This is a particular form of secondary liability where individuals can be held culpable for the actions of another individual if they continue with an agreed common criminal venture knowing that the other individual is intending to commit a criminal offence. Williams and Clarke (2016) have convincingly argued that this is a collective mode of punishment that relies on the use of linguistic cues and dehumanizing signifiers by prosecutors in court who use a gang discourse, even when the people convicted are not gang members. Given that 'the gang is always seen to wear a black or brown face' (Hallsworth and Young 2008: 185), joint enterprise bears particularly heavily on minority ethnic men; it leads to long custodial sentences, significantly undermines the legitimacy of the criminal law, the operation of the police and courts, and presents challenging social relations in prison environments (Crewe *et al.* 2015). This law provides a good example of Phillips' (2011) notion of meso-level institutional discrimination, which links together the racialized material deprivation experienced in the neighbourhoods where many of the individuals prosecuted live, the political and media discourse which sensationalizes 'gang violence', alongside the institutional practices of the criminal law which permit ambiguity and severity in application.

RACE AND RACISM IN PRISONS AND IMMIGRATION DETENTION CENTRES

Discriminatory treatment against minority ethnic prisoners in accessing jobs and receiving harsh discipline was identified in Genders and Player's (1989) classic study despite the fact that 'race relations' policies were introduced into prisons in the early 1980s, and allegations of prison officer racism have resurfaced ever since. The Commission for Racial Equality's (2003) formal investigation laid 17 counts of unlawful racial discrimination against the Prison Service including: failure to protect prisoners and staff from racist abuse; violence and intimidation; failure to meet the religious needs of Muslim prisoners; denying some black prisoners access to jobs and earned privileges; and in disproportionate disciplinary action (see also Cheliotis and Liebling 2006; Edgar and Martin 2004; Beckford *et al.* 2005). The role of discretion in unequal outcomes was underlined in the NOMS (2008) *Race Review*, which found that black prisoners were 30 per cent more likely than white prisoners to be on the basic regime without privileges, 50 per cent more likely to be held in a segregation unit, and 60 per cent more likely to have physical force used against them by prison officers. NOMS data for 2014–15 present similar patterns, but with mixed race prisoners experiencing similar outcomes to black prisoners (MoJ, 2015b). Amidst concerns about Islamist radicalization and security risks, Muslim prisoners have characterized relations with staff as suspicious and distant (HMIP 2010).

The failure of protection of prisoners highlighted by the CRE was brought tragically to light in 2000 by the murder of Asian prisoner Zahid Mubarek by his cellmate Robert Stewart. The public inquiry into Mubarek's death criticized officers for not fully taking account of Stewart's previously disturbed, violent, and overtly racist behaviour (Keith 2006). Likewise, the death of Sarah Reed, a young black woman, in Holloway Prison in January 2016, who had suffered police brutality in 2012, raised concerns that black prisoners and patients are perceived as less likely to have symptoms of ill health and therefore less likely to be afforded effective treatment than their white counterparts (Gushue 2004; Independent Commission on Mental Health and Policing 2013).

Notwithstanding the Mubarek case, Phillips' (2012) research suggested a complex picture of wary and ambivalent relations among white and minority ethnic prisoners in medium security prisons. Potent undercurrents of racist sentiment sometimes surfaced amidst a professed 'multicultural conviviality'. White prisoners often struggled to navigate their encounters with culturally assertive black prisoners, causing anxiety, envy, and resentment, that sometimes erupted into confrontation. Contemporary understandings of prison life must consider the complex intersections between identities forged around masculinity, ethnicity, class, and neighbourhood. In the high security estate, these features appear to have been compounded by an influx of young minority ethnic prisoners, from violent street worlds, serving long sentences, often under joint enterprise legislation (Liebling *et al.* 2012).

Understanding the affective elements and political implications of foreign national prisoners' experience of punishment was centre-stage in Kaufman's (2015) study. Her powerful account documents how foreign national prisoners express their bewilderment at the actions of the postcolonial British state, institutionalized through policies of detention and deportation. The long-lasting hypocrisy and ramifications of British colonialism are present in prisoners' narratives; as one prisoner told Kaufman (2015: 189), '[T]he mentality of England is they go to your country and take you over. But when you come here they don't like you'. Such sentiments were absent from the rousing political statements asserting state authority in response to the 'foreign national prisoner crisis' of 2006. Inside, xenophobia led some prisoners to perceive their lesser access to goods and services within prisons as their being punished for their citizenship rather than their criminality. Similar findings have been reported in Bosworth's (2014) study of immigration detention (see Bosworth, this volume). Finally, the controversy surrounding the 11 deaths in immigration detention centres or during the process of deportation which have been characterized as from non-natural or unknown causes (INQUEST, 2016), further underline the vulnerabilities of minority ethnic individuals. And some, like Jimmy Mubenga, the Angolan unlawfully killed by private security officers, serve as a reminder that border control, like crime control, operates through a racialized lens, where minority ethnic lives can be endangered and lost (Bowling *et al.* 2012).

PROBATION

Despite the imperialist roots of probation with religious missionaries seeking to save intemperate souls, the needs of minority ethnic groups only came to be recognized in probation policies from the 1980s and since then policy development has been somewhat uneven. Concerns have centred on the quality of supervision of minority ethnic individuals and whether probation officers have given sufficient weight to racism contributing to offending behaviour (HMIP 2000; Lewis *et al.* 2006). Black empowerment programmes seeking individual change within a collective learning context of black history offer promise but evaluative evidence on effectiveness is scarce (Cuneen 2011; Williams 2005). Glynn's (2014) 'black criminology of desistance', developed from critical race theory, studying black men from Baltimore, Birmingham, and HMP Grendon, emphasized the need to acknowledge the trauma associated with racialization, criminalization, father absence, neighbourhood deprivation, and negative conceptions of blackness. Calverley's (2012) research suggests desistance may be more easily facilitated through family networks in Indian and Bangladeshi communities compared with black and mixed race communities, but little is known about the resettlement needs of minority ethnic girls and women (Gelsthorpe 2005).

THE DISCIPLINE OF CRIMINOLOGY

Looking inwards at the subfield of race, ethnicity, and crime, criminology's origins can hardly be considered auspicious. Mired in the racism of the day, Lombroso's work embodied a pseudo-scientific discourse that has not been entirely laid to rest.

The intellectual work of black scholars such as Du Bois (Gabbidon 2007; Back and Tate 2015) has been neglected, although critical questions of the influence of race on epistemology, methodology, and reflexivity have recently come to the fore (Phillips and Bowling 2003; Garland *et al.* 2006; Lumsden and Winter 2014). The absence of engagement with colonialization in 'bourgeois' criminology scholarship has also been highlighted by Agozino (2003). In his call for postcolonial perspectives, Cuneen (2011) argues against the myopia of Western criminology, for intellectual development in work on human rights abuses by states targeting racialized and indigenous groups, which serves to uphold notions of who can belong to Western nation states and who is to be excluded. Going further, Cunneen reproaches criminology for having an embedded racialized discourse in which race is constitutively constructed through processes of policing and punishment.

While the grand narratives in criminology, by the likes of Cohen, Garland, Simon, and others, can be said to partially obscure the significance of race, a refreshing theoretical intervention, in the work of Unnever and Gabbison (2011), on African American offending may have wider applicability. Historically rooted and contemporarily experienced collective memories of racialized humiliation, pejorative stereotyping, unfair treatment, and inhumanity, it is argued, produces a distinctive worldview as African Americans (and other minorities) 'experience their present in light of their past' (Unnever and Gabbidon, 2011: 27, see also Glynn 2014). These stresses result in weak bonds to educational and workplace institutions which increases the likelihood of offending. Regarding teaching, a present and future challenge for academia as a whole is the *Why is my curriculum white?* agenda. Engaging with this challenge offers the possibility of enhancing criminological curricula to reflect more fully on postcolonial intellectual developments that recognize the exclusion and criminalization of all minority ethnic groups, including forgotten ones such as Travellers and Gypsy/Roma communities.

CONCLUSION

British criminology has gradually incorporated analysis of racism and ethnicity into the study of crime and criminal justice and, in so doing, has moved well beyond the narrow 'race and crime debate' that preoccupied some earlier criminologists. Researchers interested in this field of study can now draw upon an extensive library of theoretical, empirical, and policy studies of the various ways in which crime, victimization, criminal justice, and punishment are shaped by racism and ethnicity. As the remarks in the introduction make clear, there are some obvious continuities in the criminological agenda over time, but as the field has matured, new and more nuanced questions, with a more global, transnational frame have emerged.

Over the past thirty years the overrepresentation of black people, and to a lesser extent of those of other minority ethnic groups, has persisted in stop and search, arrest, criminal convictions, and imprisonment. It is well established that victimization tends to occur between people from the same ethnic group and this is most obvious in personal violence including homicide. Moreover, researchers are increasingly observing that patterns of crime are shaped by capital and markets like other aspects of society; unsurprisingly, the poorest tend not to be involved in bank fraud or offshore tax evasion while the richest rarely engage in street robbery. Patterns of crime reflect the fact that the economy is also stratified on the basis of ethnicity.

Racism and discrimination in the operation of the criminal justice system also remain very much on the research agenda, but here too the field has shifted. Exploring the extent to which direct discrimination explains why particular groups are more frequently in contact with the police, become enmeshed in the criminal justice system, and end up in prison is still an important and troubling topic. Influential studies on decision-making in the courts are now dated and the changes that have occurred in recent years demand fresh research on old topics. Researchers have also come to focus on more indirect and subtle ways that disadvantage shapes criminal justice outcomes.

There are grounds for both pessimism and optimism at this moment in time. The prison population doubled from around 40,000 in the late 1980s to 80,000 in 2010 and has now hit a plateau; yet the disproportionate imprisonment of people from black and minority ethnic backgrounds persists. Placed in a global and postcolonial context, however, it is striking that the largest single group of foreign national prisoners in British jails is from Poland, with Ireland, Romania, Jamaica, Albania, Lithuania, Pakistan, Somalia, India, and Nigeria making up the 'top ten' (Allen and Dempsey 2016). The most recent developments in policing also indicate a nuanced picture with both continuity and change in patterns of policing. While stop and search has fallen sharply, ethnic disproportionality persists. Deaths in custody, use of force, and the use of spies to infiltrate black family protest campaigns have each led to allegations of malign neglect, racism, and discrimination.

At the same time, entirely new issues have emerged either through research or media reporting of phenomena that have hitherto been subject to limited empirical scrutiny. We have attempted to provide some pointers on such topics as gangs, 'honour violence' and domestic violence within minority ethnic communities, anti-semitic and Islamaphobic violence. We have touched on reaction and resistance to state violence, surveillance, and criminalization. On these topics, academic research lags behind the changes in the real world. Moreover, criminology has been slow to recognize demographic changes in ethnic diversity and to document the experiences of crime and justice among new migrant communities, white minorities, and people of Arabic, Middle Eastern and mixed heritage. For the energetic criminology student and scholar of the future, there is much work that remains to be done in developing the subfield of racism, ethnicity, crime, and justice.

■ SELECTED FURTHER READING

This chapter develops the ideas explored in the authors' *Racism, Crime and Justice* (2002); a more recent volume is Phillips and Webster's (eds) *New Directions in Race, Ethnicity and Crime* (2014) and Phillips' four volume *Race and Crime* (2014). Other useful texts include Webster's *Understanding Race and Crime* (2007), and Patel and Tyrer's *Race, Crime and Resistance* (2011).

On ethnicity and victimization, look at the special issue on hate crime in the *Journal of Interpersonal Violence* (2015), Gadd and Dixon's *Losing the Race* (2011) and for how hate crime came onto the political agenda, see Bowling's *Violent Racism*, (1999). Rowe's *Policing, Race and Racism* (2005) provides an overview and a historical perspective is provided by Whitfield, in *Unhappy Dialogue: the Metropolitan Police and London's West Indian Community* (2004). For the other key areas of criminal justice, see May and colleagues, *Differential Treatment in the Youth Justice System* (2010), Lewis *et al.*, *Race and Probation* (2005), Phillip's *The Multicultural Prison* (2012), Kaufman's *Punish and Expel* (2015), and Bosworth's *Inside Immigration Detention* (2014). The starting point for a critical perspective on these issues is Hall and colleagues, *Policing the Crisis* (1978) and Agozino's *Counter-Colonial Criminology* (2003). Aas and Bosworth's *The Borders of Punishment* (2013) is an excellent resource on border control.

REFERENCES

AGOZINO, B. (2003), *Counter-Colonial Criminology: A Critique of Imperialist Reason*, London: Pluto Press.

ALDRIDGE, J. and MEDINA, J. (2008), *Youth Gangs in an English City: Social Exclusion, Drugs and Violence. End of Award Report (Res-000-23-0615)*, Swindon: Economic and Social Research Council.

ALEXANDER, C. (2000), *The Asian Gang: Ethnicity, Identity, Masculinity*, Oxford: Berg.

ALEXANDER, M. (2010), *The New Jim Crow: Mass Incarceration in the Age of Colorblindness*, New York, NY: The New Press.

ALLEN, G. and DEMPSEY, N. (2016), *Prison Population Statistics. House Of Commons Library Briefing Paper SN/SG/04334*, London: House Of Commons.

AWAN, I. and ZEMPI, I. (2015), '"I Will Blow Your Face Off"—Virtual and Physical World Anti-Muslim Hate Crime', *British Journal of Criminology*, 57(2): 362–80.

BACK, L. and TATE, M. (2015), 'For a Sociological Reconstruction: W.E.B. Du Bois, Stuart Hall and Segregated Sociology', *Sociological Research Online*, 20(3): 15.

BANTON, M. (1998), *Racial Theories*, Cambridge: Cambridge University Press.

BARTH, F. (1969), *Ethnic Groups and Boundaries: The Social Organisation of Cultural Difference*, London: George Allen and Unwin.

BECKFORD, J. A., JOLY, D., and KHOSROKHAVAR, F. (2005), *Muslims in Prison—Challenge and Change in Britain and France*, Basingstoke: Palgrave.

BOSWORTH, M. (2014), *Inside Immigration Detention: Foreigners in a Carceral Age*, Oxford: Oxford University Press.

BOWLING, B. (1999), *Violent Racism: Victimization, Policing And Social Context*, New York, NY: Oxford University Press.

BOWLING, B. (2013), 'Epilogue, "The Borders Of Punishment: Towards A Criminology Of Mobility"', in K. Aas, and M. Bosworth, (eds), *The Borders Of Punishment*, Oxford: Oxford University Press.

BOWLING, B. and MARKS, E. (2017), 'The Rise And Fall Of Suspicionless Searches', *Kings Law Journal* (forthcoming).

BOWLING, B. and PHILLIPS, C. (2002), *Racism, Crime And Justice*, Harlow: Pearson Education.

BOWLING, B., PHILLIPS, C., and SHEPTYCKI, J. (2012), '"Race", Political Economy And The Coercive State', in T. Newburn and J. Peay (eds), *Policing: Politics, Culture and Control*, Oxford: Hart.

BUCKE, T. and BROWN, D. (1997), *In Police Custody: Police Powers and Suspects' Rights under the Revised Pace Codes of Practice*, Home Office Research Study 174, London: Home Office.

BUTTS, C. (2010), *Race and Faith Inquiry Report*, London: MPA.

CALVERLEY, A. (2012), *Cultures of Desistance: Rehabilitation, Reintegration and Ethnic Minorities*, London: Routledge.

CHELIOTIS, L. and LIEBLING, A. (2006), 'Race Matters in British Prisons: Towards a Research Agenda', *British Journal of Criminology*, 46(2): 286–317.

CLANCY, A., HOUGH, M., AUST, R., and KERSHAW, C. (2001), *Crime, Policing and Justice: The Experience Of Ethnic Minorities; Findings From The 2000 British Crime Survey*, Home Office Research Study 223, London: Home Office.

COCKBAIN, E. (2013), 'Grooming and the "Asian Sex Gang Predator": The Construction of a Racial Crime Threat', *Race & Class*, 54(4): 22–32.

COMMISSION FOR RACIAL EQUALITY (2003), *A Formal Investigation by the Commission for Racial Equality into HM Prison Service of England and Wales—Part 2: Racial Equality in Prisons*, London: Commission for Racial Equality.

COONEY, M. (2014), 'Death by Family: Honor Violence as Punishment', *Punishment and Society*, 16(4): 406–27.

CREWE, B., LIEBLING, A., PADFIELD, N., and VIRGO, G. (2015), 'Joint Enterprise: The Implications of an Unfair and Unclear Law', *Criminal Law Review*, (4): 252–69.

CUNEEN, C. (2011), 'Postcolonial Perspectives for Criminology', in M. Bosworth, and C. Hoyle (eds), *What Is Criminology?*, Oxford: Oxford University Press.

DANIEL, W. W. (1968), *Racial Discrimination in England*, Harmondsworth: Penguin.

DCLG (2014), 'Government Action on Antisemitism', London: Department of Communities and Local Government.

DFE (2015), *Permanent and Fixed Period Exclusions in England: 2013 to 2014*, London: DfE.

DUSTIN, M. and PHILLIPS, A. (2008), 'Whose Agenda Is It?: Abuses of Women and Abuses of "Culture" in Britain', *Ethnicities*, 8(3): 405–24.

EDGAR, K. and MARTIN, C. (2004), *Perceptions of Race and Conflict: Perspectives of Minority Ethnic Prisoners and of Prison Officers*, RDS Online Report 11/04, London: Home Office.

EXLEY, S. (2016), 'Education and Learning', in H. Dean, and L. Platt (eds), *Social Advantage and Disadvantage*, Oxford: Oxford University Press.

FEILZER, M. and HOOD, R. (2004), *Differences or Discrimination?*, London: Youth Justice Board.

FENTON, S. (2003), *Ethnicity*, Cambridge: Polity.

FOSTER, J., NEWBURN, T., and SOUHAMI, A. (2005), *Assessing the Impact of the Stephen Lawrence Inquiry*, Home Office Research Study 294, London: Home Office.

GABBIDON, S. L. (2007), *W.E.B. Du Bois on Crime and Justice: Laying the Foundations of Sociological Criminology*, Aldershot: Ashgate.

GADD, D. and DIXON, B. (2011), *Losing the Race: Thinking Psychosocially About Racially Motivated Crime*, London: Karnac.

GARLAND, J., SPALEK, B., and CHAKRABORTI, N. (2006), 'Hearing Lost Voices: Issues in Researching "Hidden" Minority Ethnic Communities', *British Journal of Criminology*, 46(3): 423–37.

GELSTHORPE, L. (2005), 'The Experiences of Female Minority Ethnic Offenders: The Other "Other" ', in S. Lewis, P. Raynor, D. Smith, and A. Wardak (eds), *Race and Probation*, Cullompton: Willan.

GENDERS, E. and PLAYER, E. (1989), *Race Relations in Prison*, Oxford: Clarendon.

GILLBORN, D. (2008), *Racism and Education: Coincidence or Conspiracy*, London: Routledge.

GILROY, P. (1982), 'The Myth of Black Criminality', *Socialist Register*, 19: 46–56.

GILROY, P. (2000), *Between Camps; Nations, Cultures and the Allure of Race*, London: Penguin Books.

GLYNN, M. (2014), *Black Men, Invisibility, and Desistance from Crime: Towards a Critical Race Theory of Desistance*, London: Routledge.

GOLDBERG, D. T. (2009), *The Threat of Race: Reflections on Racial Neoliberalism*, Oxford: Wiley-Blackwell.

GOLDSON, B. (2011), *Youth in Crisis?: 'Gangs', Territoriality and Violence*, London: Routledge.

HAGEDORN, J. (2007), 'Gangs, Institutions, Race and Space: The Chicago School Revisited', in J. Hagedorn (ed.), *Gangs in the Global City: Alternatives to Traditional Criminology*, Urbana, IL: University of Illinois Press.

HALES, G., LEWIS, C., and SILVERSTONE, D. (2006), *Gun Crime: The Market in and Use of Illegal Firearms*, Home Office Research Study 298, London: Home Office.

HALL, S., CRITCHER, C., JEFFERSON, T., CLARKE, J., and ROBERTS, B. (1978), *Policing the Crisis: Mugging, the State and Law and Order*, London: Macmillan.

HALLSWORTH, S. and YOUNG, T. (2008), 'Gang Talk and Gang Talkers: A Critique', *Crime, Media, Culture*, 4(2): 175–95.

HARRINGTON, V. and MAYHEW, P. (2001), *Mobile Phone Theft*, Home Office Research Study 235, London: Home Office.

HEATH, A. and CHEUNG, S. Y. (2006), *Ethnic Penalties in the Labour Market: Employers and Discrimination*, Research Report No. 341, London: Department for Work and Pensions.

HENNE, K. and TROSHYNSKI, E. (2013), 'Mapping the Margins of Intersectionality: Criminological Possibilities in a Transnational World', *Theoretical Criminology*, 17(4): 455–73.

HESTER, M., CHANTLER, K., GANGOLI, G., DEVGON, J., SHARMA, S. S., and SINGLETON, A. (2007), *Forced Marriage: The Risk Factors and the Effect of Raising the Minimum Age for a Sponsor, and of Leave to Enter the UK as a Spouse or Fiancé*, London: Home Office.

HMIP (2000), *Towards Race Equality: A Thematic Inspection*, London: Her Majesty's Inspectorate of Probation.

HMIP (2010), *Muslim Prisoners' Experiences: A Thematic Review*, London: Her Majesty's Inspectorate of Prisons.

HOLDAWAY, S. and O'NEILL, M. (2007), 'Where Has All the Racism Gone? Views of Racism within Constabularies after Macpherson', *Ethnic and Racial Studies*, 30(3): 397–415.

HOLDER, K. A., NEE, C., and ELLIS, T. (2000), 'Triple Jeopardy? Black and Asian Women Police Officers' Experiences of Discrimination', *International Journal of Police Science and Management*, 3(1): 68–87.

HOME OFFICE (1999), *Staff Targets for the Home Office, the Prison, the Police, the Fire and the Probation Services*, London: Home Office.

HOME OFFICE (2016) *Action Against Hate: The UK Government's Plan For Tackling Hate Crime*, London: Home Office.

HOOD, R. (1992), *Race and Sentencing*, Oxford: Oxford University Press.

HOPKINS, K. (2015), *Associations between Police-Recorded Ethnic Background and Being Sentenced to Prison in England and Wales*, London: MoJ.

HOUSE OF COMMONS (1972), Select Committee on Race Relations and Immigration Session 1971–2, *Police/Immigrant Relations*, 1, 147, London: House of Commons.

HOUSE OF COMMONS (2007), Home Affairs Select Committee, *Young Black People and the Criminal Justice System*, London: The Stationery Office.

Hudson, B. (1993), *Penal Policy and Social Justice*, Basingstoke: Macmillan.

Hudson, B. (2006), 'Beyond White Man's Justice: Race, Gender and Justice in Late Modernity', *Theoretical Criminology*, 10(1): 29–47.

Hudson, B. and Bramhall, G. (2005), 'Assessing the Other: Constructions of "Asianness" in Risk Assessments by Probation Officers', *British Journal of Criminology*, 45(5): 721–40.

Hume, D. (1754/1997), '"Negroes ... Naturally Inferior to the Whites"', in E. C. Eze, (ed.), *Race and the Enlightenment: A Reader*, Malden, MA: Blackwell Publishers Ltd.

Innes, M., Roberts, C., Innes, H., Lowe, T., and Lakhani, S. (2011), *Assessing the Effects of Prevent Policing: A Report to the Association of Chief Police Officers*, Cardiff: Universities' Police Science Institute.

James, Z. (2013), 'Offenders or Victims?: An Exploration of Gypsies and Travellers as a Policing Paradox', in C. Phillips and C. Webster (eds), *New Directions in Race, Ethnicity and Crime*, London: Routledge.

Journal of Interpersonal Violence (2015), Special Section: 'The Philosophy of Hate Crime', D. Brax and C. Munthe (guest eds), June 2015, 30(10): 1687–802.

Kawalerowicz, J. and Biggs, M. (2015), 'Anarchy in the UK: Economic Deprivation, Social Disorganization, and Political Grievances in the London Riot of 2011', *Social Forces*, 94(2): 673-98.

Kant, I. (1754/1997), '"The Fellow Was Quite Black ... A Clear Proof That What He Said Was Stupid"', in E. C. Eze (ed.), *Race and the Enlightenment: A Reader*, Malden, MA: Blackwell Publishers Ltd.

Kaufman, E. (2015), *Punish and Expel: Border Control, Nationalism, and the New Purpose of the Prison*, Oxford: Oxford University Press.

Keith, B. (2006), *Report of the Zahid Mubarek Inquiry*, HC 1082-I, London: HMSO.

Lewis, S., Raynor, P., Smith, D. A., and Wardak, A. (2006), *Race and Probation*, Cullompton: Willan.

Lewis, P., Newburn, T., Taylor, M., Macgillivray, C., Greenhill, A., Frayman, H., and Proctor R. (2011), 'Reading the Riots: Investigating England's Summer of Disorder', London: *The Guardian*.

Liebling, A., Arnold, H., and Straub, C. (2012), *An Exploration of Staff-Prisoner Relationships at HMP Whitemoor: Twelve Years On*, London: NOMS.

Loftus, B. (2008), 'Dominant Culture Interrupted: Recognition, Resentment and the Politics of Change in an English Police Force', *British Journal of Criminology*, 48(6): 756–77.

Lombroso, C. (1871), *White Man and Colored Man: Lectures on the Origin and Variety of the Human Races*, Padua: F. Sacchetto.

Lombroso, C. (1884/2006), *Criminal Man. Translated and with a New Introduction by Mary Gibson and Nicole Hahn Rafter*, Durham, NC: Duke University Press.

Lombroso, C. (1897), 'Why Homicide Has Increased in the United States', *The North American Review*, 165(493): 641–8.

Lumsden, K. and Winter, A. (2014), *Reflexivity in Criminological Research: Experiences with the Powerful and the Powerless*, Basingstoke: Palgrave Macmillan.

Lupton, R. and Power, A. (2004), *Minority Ethnic Groups in Britain*, London: Centre for the Analysis of Social Exclusion.

Macpherson, W. (1999), *The Stephen Lawrence Inquiry, Report of an Inquiry by Sir William Macpherson of Cluny*. Cm 4262-1, London: Home Office.

Mason, D. (2000), *Race and Ethnicity in Modern Britain*, Oxford: Oxford University Press.

May, T., Gyateng, T., and Hough, M. (2010), *Differential Treatment in the Youth Justice System*, EHRC Research Report 50, London: EHRC.

McGhee, D. (2008), *The End of Multiculturalism: Terrorism, Integration and Human Rights*, Maidenhead: Open University Press.

Mhlanga, B. (1997), *The Colour of English Justice: A Multivariate Analysis*, Aldershot: Avebury.

Mckeever, E. R., Reed, R., Pehrson, S., Storey, L., and Cohrs, J. C. (2013), 'How Racist Violence Becomes A Virtue: An Application Of Discourse Analysis', *International Journal Of Conflict & Violence*, 7(1): 108–20.

MoJ (2015a), *Statistics on Race and the Criminal Justice System 2014*, London: Ministry of Justice.

MoJ (2015b), *Offender Equalities Annual Report 2014/15*, London: Minstry of Justice.

Montagu, A. (1943), Man's Most Dangerous Myth: The Fallacy of Race, London: AltaMira Press.

Moody, S. R. and Clark, I. (2004), 'Dealing With Racist Victimisation: Racially Aggravated Offences In Scotland', *International Review Of Victimology*, 10(3): 261–80.

Morris, W. (2004), *The Report of the Morris Inquiry the Case for Change: People in the Metropolitan Police Service*, London: Metropolitan Police Authority.

Mulcahy, A. (2012), '"Alright in Their Own Place": Policing and the Spatial Regulation of Irish Travellers', *Criminology and Criminal Justice*, 12(3): 307-327.

Murray, K. and Harkin, D. (2016), 'Policing In Cool And Hot Climates: Legitimacy, Power And The Rise And Fall Of Mass Stop And Search In Scotland', *British Journal Of Criminology*, doi: 10.1093/bjc/azw007.

Mythen, G. (2012), '"No One Speaks for Us": Security Policy, Suspected Communities and the Problem of Voice', *Critical Studies on Terrorism*, 5(3): 409–424.

Newburn, T., Shiner, M., and Hayman, S. (2004), 'Race, Crime and Injustice? Strip Search and the Treatment of Suspects in Custody', *British Journal of Criminology*, 44(5): 677–94.

NOMS (2008), *Race Review 2008: Implementing Race Equality in Prisons—Five Years On*, London: NOMS.

Parmar, A. (2011), 'Stop and Search in London: Counter-Terrorist or Counter-Productive?', *Policing and Society*, 21(4): 369–82.

Patel, T. G. and Tyrer, D. (2011), *Race, Crime and Resistance*, London: Sage.

Phillips, A. (2007), *Multiculturalism without Culture*, Princeton, NJ: Princeton University Press.

Phillips, C. (2011), 'Institutional Racism and Ethnic Inequalities: An Expanded Multilevel Framework', *Journal of Social Policy*, 40(1): 173–92.

Phillips, C. (2012), *The Multicultural Prison: Ethnicity, Masculinity, and Social Relations among Prisoners*, Oxford: Oxford University Press.

Phillips, C. (2014) (ed.), *Race and Crime*, London: Routledge.

Phillips, C. and Bowling, B. (2003), 'Racisim, Race and Ethnicity: Developing Minority Perspectives in Criminology', *British Journal of Criminology*, 43(2): 269–90.

Phillips, C., Brown, D., James, Z., and Goodrich, P. (1998) *Entry into the Criminal Justice System: A Survey of Police Arrests and Their Outcomes*, London: Home Office.

Phillips, C. and Platt, L. (2016), '"Race" and Ethnicity', in H. Dean, and L. Platt, (eds), *Social Advantage and Disadvantage*, Oxford: Oxford University Press.

Phillips, C. and Webster, C. (2013), 'Introduction: Bending the Paradigm—New Directions and New Generations', in C. Phillips and C. Webster (eds), *New Directions in Race, Ethnicity and Crime*, London: Routledge.

Phillips, D. and Harrison, M. (2010), 'Constructing an Integrated Society: Historical Lessons for Tackling Black and Minority Ethnic Housing Segregation in Britain', *Housing Studies*, 25(2): 221–35.

Pitts, J. (2008), *Reluctant Gangsters: The Changing Face of Youth Crime*, Cullompton: Willan.

PSNI (2016), *Incidents And Crimes With A Hate Motivation Recorded By The Police In Northern Ireland: Quarterly Update to 31 March 2016*, Belfast: PSNI.

Reddy, R. (2008), 'Gender, Culture and the Law: Approaches to 'Honour Crimes' in the UK', *Feminist Legal Studies*, 16(3): 305–21.

Rock, P. (2004), *Constructing Victims' Rights: The Home Office, New Labour, and Victims*, Oxford: Oxford University Press.

Scottish Government (2015), *Racist Incidents Recorded by the Police in Scotland, 2013–14*, Edinburgh: Scottish Government.

Sharp, C. and Budd, T. (2005), *Minority Ethnic Groups and Crime. Home Office Online Report 33/05*, London: Home Office.

Shutes, I. (2016), 'Citizenship and Migration', in H. Dean and L. Platt (eds), *Social Advantage and Disadvantage*, Oxford: Oxford University Press.

Siddiqui, H. (2005), '"There is No 'Honour' in Domestic Violence, Only Shame!": Women's Struggles against "Honour" Crimes in the UK', in L. Welchman and S. Hossain (eds), *'Honour': Crimes, Paradigms, and Violence against Women*, London: Zed Books.

Smith, D. and Greenfields, M. (2012), 'Housed Gypsies and Travellers in the UK: Work, Exclusion and Adaptation', *Race & Class*, 53(3): 48–64.

Richmond, A. H. (1985), *Global Apartheid: Refugees, Racism and the New World Order*, Oxford: Oxford University Press.

Salisbury, H. and Upson, A. (2004), *Ethnicity, Victimisation and Worry About Crime: Findings from the 2001/2002 and 2002/3 British Crime Surveys. Findings 237*, London: Home Office.

Smith, D. J. (1997), 'Ethnic Origins, Crime, and Criminal Justice', in M. Maguire, R. Morgan, and R. Reiner (eds), *The Oxford Handbook of Criminology*, Oxford: Clarendon.

Smith, J. M. (2014), 'Interrogating Whiteness within Criminology', *Sociology Compass*, 8(2): 107–18.

Smithson, H., Ralphs, R., and Williams, P. (2013), 'Used and Abused: The Problematic Usage of Gang Terminology in the United Kingdom and Its Implications for Ethnic Minority Youth', *British Journal of Criminology*, 53(1): 113–28.

Spenkuch, J. (2014), 'Understanding the Impact of Immigration on Crime', *American Law and Economics Review*, 16(1): 177–219.

Unnever, J. D. and Gabbidon, S. L. (2011), *A Theory of African American Offending: Race, Racism, and Crime*, London: Routledge.

Wacquant, L. (1999), '"Suitable Enemies": Foreigners and Immigrants in the Prisons of Europe', *Punishment & Society*, 1(2): 215–22.

Wacquant, L. (2009), *Prisons of Poverty*, Minneapolis, MN: University of Minnesota Press.

Weber, L. and Bowling, B. (2008), 'Valiant Beggars and Global Vagabonds : Select, Eject, Immobilize', *Theoretical Criminology*, 12(3): 355–75.

Webster, C. (1997), 'The Construction of British "Asian" Criminality', *International Journal of the Sociology of Law*, 25(1): 65–86.

Webster, C. (2008), 'Marginalized White Ethnicity, Race and Crime', *Theoretical Criminology*, 12(3): 293–312.

Whitfield, J. (2004), Unhappy Dialogue: the Metropolitan Police and London's West Indian Community, Cullompton: Willan.

Williams, P. (2005), 'Designing and Delivering Programmes for Minority Ethnic Offenders', in S. Lewis, P. Raynor, D. Smith, and A. Wardak (eds), *Race and Probation*, Cullompton: Willan.

Williams, P. and Clarke, B. (2016), *Dangerous Associations: Joint Enterprise, Gangs and Racism*, London: Centre for Crime and Justice Studies.

Zaye, Y. and Harker, R. (2015), *Children in Care in England:Statistics, Briefing Paper No 04470*, London: House of Commons Library.

9

FEMINIST CRIMINOLOGY: INEQUALITIES, POWERLESSNESS, AND JUSTICE

Michele Burman and Loraine Gelsthorpe

INTRODUCTION

A distinctive feminist Criminology emerged from the 1960s onwards amidst what is widely recognized as a second wave of feminism.[1] It set out to challenge some of the gender-blind assumptions inherent within criminology at that time and to create a space for women's experiences and voices.

This chapter charts the history of feminist contributions to criminology, dwelling in particular on a range of paradigmatic shifts, which have extended both the terrain of feminist criminological theorizing and understanding of knowledge forms. A key theme for this chapter is 'inequality before the law' and what this means in terms of promoting and delivering justice on the ground.

The chapter begins with a review of the ways in which early feminist scholarship reshaped the contours of criminology, including understandings of victimization and offending, and ways of evolving a praxis. It then examines feminist debates on methodology and modes of knowledge production. This is followed by an exploration of new and emerging research agendas focused on issues of powerlessness, justice, and inequality (exemplified here by research on human trafficking, migration, and criminal justice). The chapter concludes by considering the future prospects for feminism in criminology as it transitions towards a more humanist stance in relation to crime and justice.

[1] First-wave feminism might be described as a period of feminist activity and thought which occurred within the time period of the nineteenth and early twentieth century. Occurring in several western countries in particular, it focused on legal issues and on gaining women's suffrage (the right to vote).

FEMINIST CONTRIBUTIONS IN THE PAST: RESHAPING THE CONTOURS OF CRIMINOLOGY

The publication of Carol Smart's *Women, Crime and Criminology* (1976) had a resounding impact on new generations of criminologists and established a ground-breaking agenda. Thereafter, almost every textbook contained an obligatory reference to women, if not a chapter on women in their own right. In a percipient conclusion to the text, Carol Smart wrote at the time:

> Criminology and the sociology of deviance must become more than the study of men and crime if it is to play any significant part in the development of our understanding of crime, law, and the criminal process and play any role in the transformation of existing social practices. (Smart 1976: 185)

Of course, the relationship between 'feminism' and 'criminology' is a complex one, for there is no one 'feminism' and no one 'criminology', and at best we might argue that we can speak only of feminist criminologies or feminist perspectives. Criminology itself has changed over time and is much more diverse than hitherto, although whether it is sufficiently diverse or open enough to accommodate some of the critical precepts of feminism, remains a matter for contemporary debate. Certainly, there are feminist critics who have made a strong case for abandoning criminology or who, because of resistance to a feminist transformation of the discipline, see fundamental incompatibilities between feminism and criminology (Smart 1990; Stanko 1993; Young 1994). Smart's original concern was that criminology, even in radical form would be 'unmoved' by feminist critiques (bearing in mind that she was writing in the mid 1970s when 'radical' and critical perspectives in criminology were emerging with some force but took little note of the power of patriarchy and gendered discourses).

The range of feminist work in criminology has been extraordinarily wide—from empirical studies to theoretical developments of gender and crime and indeed, some of the most important critiques—and insights—of feminist criminology have emerged from spirited debates waged amongst feminist scholars themselves (see, e.g., Delmar 2001; Gelsthorpe and Morris 1990; Rafter and Heidensohn 1995; Daly and Maher 1998). A core tranche of early work questioned the neglect of women in criminology and the dominant unreflective thinking about gender-role stereotypes. Feminist scholarship also began to draw attention to women and girls as victims and offenders, and explained more systematically how women's and girls' experiences were similar to, and different from, those of the men and boys who had been the focus of most research. Early phases of work can be termed: *Doing Gender* which involved an early critique of criminological theory and which, by the 1990s, developed into a consideration of how gender shaped crime and the responses to it; and then *Doing Difference* which drew attention to women and girls as victims and offenders, and how this was reflected in criminal justice practices in what we might describe, respectively, as a *substantive* and a *political* project. We review each in turn.

DOING GENDER

As was noted, attention to gender in criminology emerged from second wave feminist responses to the far-reaching social changes of the 1960s and 1970s. Questioning the amnesia or neglect within criminology in relation to women offenders and victims, this work drew attention to the continuance of sexist assumptions from Lombroso to Pollak and beyond. The focus of this critique was limited, however. Although this was a substantive venture, some writers assumed that a remedy to 'male-centred' criminological theories and criminal justice deficiencies could be achieved by 'inserting' women, whether this be discovering 'girl gangs' (Velimesis 1975) or considering girls in relation to subcultural theory (Shacklady-Smith 1978; McRobbie 1980). This soon came to be questioned. Later work called for a close consideration of masculinity and the social construction of 'maleness' (Cain 1990) and the development of more critical conceptions of gender and its relationship to crime (Daly 1997; Walklate 2004). Such that, according to Chesney-Lind (2006)

> contemporary approaches to gender and crime . . . tend to avoid the problems of reductionism and determinism that characterise early discussions of gender and gender relations, stressing instead the complexity, tentativeness, and variability with which individuals, particularly youth, negotiate (and resist) gender identity. (2006: 8)

West and Zimmerman (1987) first proposed that women and men engage in gendered practices (i.e. 'do gender') in response to situated social hierarchies and expectations about masculinity and femininity, thus contributing to the reproduction of social structure (1987: 147). Within Criminology, 'doing gender' became an influential perspective following arguments that for many men, crime serves as a 'resource' for doing gender' (Messerschmidt 1993: 84), and that different crimes are useful for demonstrating masculinity depending on men's social structural positions across axes of race and class. Of central importance is the idea that masculinity can be seen as a crucial point of intersection of different forms of power, stratification, and identity formation. Together with Connell's recognition of gender as a configuration of practices within a system of gender relations (Connell 1995: 84), this work has been particularly significant in articulating an account of gender as a dynamic and shifting system of social practices. Conceptualizing gender as 'situated action' recognizes the existence of multiple masculinities and femininities constructed across different situational contexts and social/structural positions (revealing different hierarchies) rather than one fixed and determined set of gender roles (Connell 1995).

Feminist theoretical work on the social construction of gender and that on concepts and practices of gender converged with this work to (re)assert the crucial role and enactment of (male) power, leading to a paradigm shift in thinking about gender and gender inequality. Perhaps most importantly, drawing attention to the contingent nature of gender and the social processes through which it is enacted, mediated, and accomplished, gender as social practice also allowed for a theorization of the relationship between agency and structural inequalities such as race, class, and age and, the role of agency in resistance and social change (McNay 2000).

A continuing challenge for researchers who employ 'doing gender 'is investigating adequately the intersections of gender with other dimensions of inequality (Collins

1990, 1995; Collins and Bilge 2016) so as to comprehend the ways in which cross-cutting systems of oppression (of race, class, gender, nation, sexuality, and age) intersect to mutually shape each other and mediate experience (Crenshaw 1991; see also Gadd, this volume). Consideration of the interlocking systems of oppression is now a crucial part of third wave feminist theorization. Indeed, Burgess (2006) argues that the future of feminist criminology lies in its willingness to embrace a theoretical framework that recognizes such multiple, intersecting inequalities, and specifically the linkages between inequality and crime. How well feminist criminologists have achieved this though remains open to question. Whilst there is a growing body of criminological research informed by the intersectionality paradigm, exploring the multiplicative (rather than simply additive) effects of varying (and messy) systems of oppression in the lives of both victims and offenders (Balfour and Comack 2006; Malloch and McIvor 2013; Annison *et al.* 2015), most criminological work has yet to accomplish fully an integration of gender with other axes of oppression, not least because feminist criminologists tend to afford gender primacy in their analyses.

DOING DIFFERENCE

Turning then to 'doing difference', early feminist scholars also introduced a substantive *political* project into criminology which involved striving for formal 'equality' (i.e. for women to be treated as equals to men), although this early, limited liberal feminist position gradually also came to be challenged by those who questioned the meaning and nature of equality (MacKinnon 1987a, 1987b; Smart 1990). Dominant strands in feminist thinking and research here, nevertheless, displayed and illuminated discriminatory practices. Explicit and informal controls over women and girls were exposed in the home, at school, and at work. Feminist writers drew attention to correspondences between the policing of everyday life and policing through more formal mechanisms of social control and produced nuanced research on the different ways in which 'conformity' was being reproduced (Hutter and Williams 1981; Allen 1987; Cain 1989; Gelsthorpe 1989; Howe 1994).

Brown and Heidensohn (2000) gave particular attention to gender and policing and the ways in which female police officers survive in a predominantly masculine occupation. The treatment of women in the courts also drew attention with the conclusion that the widely assumed concept of 'chivalry' was misplaced and that women who did not occupy an appropriate gender role were seen as 'doubly deviant' (Edwards 1984; Eaton 1986; Gelsthorpe and Loucks 1997; Worrall 1990). A focus on women's prisons revealed outdated, outmoded, and gender-insensitive discourses and practices. Although Pat Carlen has disavowed the label of 'feminist', her skilled analysis of regimes in women's prisons produced the memorable phrase that 'women's prisons infantalize, feminize, medicalize, and domesticize their occupants' (1985: 182). Women and girls' confinement was revealed to be shaped by powerful and pervasive ideologies about femininity and the 'proper place of women' (Gelsthorpe 1989; Worrall 1990).

More recently, volumes of research have emerged to indicate a broad consensus regarding the complexity of women's experiences within the criminal justice system. Indeed, there is much evidence to suggest that women are subject to gendered organizational logics and gendered agents of power at all levels of the system (Carlen and

Worrall 1987; Worrall and Carlen 2004). Within this research we can discern a shift in the pursuit of justice, from formal equality for women, to substantive equality. In sympathy with this tranche of work, Baroness Corston coined the phrase 'equality means difference', in her review of vulnerable women in the criminal justice system (2007), and called for a 'distinct, radically different, visibly-led, strategic, proportionate, holistic and women centred, integrated approach' for both women who offend and those at risk of offending (2007: 79). This thematic was echoed in a subsequent Probation-led report (Criminal Justice Joint Inspection 2011).

The push for broader gender-specific understandings of women's experiences and needs in the criminal justice system has prompted a range of policy and practice developments over time, with a specific focus on community-based provision. Examples within England and Wales include the Home Office's *Women's Offending Reduction Programme* (2004) and the creation of community centres for women (the *Together Women Project).* In Scotland too, there have been calls for community-based provision, most recently in the Report of the Commission on Female Offenders (2012). Notwithstanding some methodological problems (Hedderman *et al.* 2008; Jolliffe *et al.* 2011), evaluations of such community-based activity thus far, gives cause for optimism, as can be seen in evaluations of the *218 Centre* in Glasgow (Loucks *et al.* 2006; Easton and Matthews 2010; Beglan 2013), the *Inspire* project in Belfast (Easton and Matthews 2011), and the *Turnaround* project in Wales (Holloway and Brookman 2008).

Feminist criminologists, with practitioners, have been at the core of campaigns for a better understanding of women and girl's needs and concerns, attempts to reduce women's imprisonment, and attempts to explain that women offenders are often the victims of domestic circumstance and structural oppressions (see Annison *et al.* 2015). Together they have played a key part in the quest for 'better justice'—social justice, not simply formal criminal justice. The creation of international protocols have also assisted these endeavours, from the Convention on the Elimination of all Forms of Discrimination Against Women (CEDAW)—adopted in 1979 by the United Nations General Assembly, to the Bangkok Rules (United Nations Rules for the Treatment of Women Prisoners and Non-custodial Measures for Women Offenders) focused on the needs of women offenders and prisoners—adopted by the United Nations General Assembly in 2010.

ONE STEP FORWARDS, TWO STEPS BACK?

But there is a need to question developments too. There is no overarching success story in the feminist quest for substantive justice. There is evidence that, in attempts to 'make women count' (Beveridge *et al.* 2000) there are unintended consequences. For example, there are concerns that women's vulnerability and high levels of 'welfare needs' are transmogrified into 'risks' (Hannah-Moffat and O'Malley 2007); there are unintended consequences of creating community services for women, and encouraging the police and courts to utilize those services insofar as what was once voluntary involvement has now become 'required'. Malloch and McIvor (2013) remind us of the need to consider human rights both in prisons and in relation to community penalties, noting that women very often receive additional requirements concerning medical, psychiatric, or drug treatments. Moreover, despite appearances that community-based centres are entirely women-friendly, some women engaged with the support services have indicated that there is a coercive element too (Hedderman *et al.* 2008). Pollack's (2010) research in the USA on women prisoners echoes the need for caution here as she explains how women are expected to 'perform empowerment' in order to gain access to parole. Barton and Cooper (2013) suggest that women's centres and approved premises become sites for the construction and perpetuation of idealized forms of femininity and domesticity. Commenting on Canadian prisons, Pollack also observes that women are encouraged to reveal their vulnerability and dependency only to find that the 'dependency discourse leads to social control' (2000). Recent activity in the criminal justice system in regard to 'personality disorder' amongst women (NOMS and NHS 2015a, 2015b) and 'trauma informed' work also runs the risk of returning to a pathologization of women's behaviour. Transformations in the structure of the criminal justice system in England and Wales also suggest that seeming progress may have unintended consequences.

The Rehabilitation Revolution which has reshaped probation and community support for offenders, creating a market for provision from private, commercial, and third sector suppliers has a clear focus on payment by results, but this reflects a crime reduction goal rather than a welfare-oriented goal; women are not attractive to suppliers in this context (Gelsthorpe and Hedderman 2012). Moreover, the Howard League's (2015) *Inquiry into Preventing Unnecessary Criminalisation of Women* suggests that the companies who are now supplying community-based support and supervision, lack both knowledge and experience in relation to women and their gender-specific needs.

AWARENESS OF AND RESPONSIVENESS TO VIOLENCE AGAINST WOMEN

Without doubt, one of the most significant and influential contributions of feminist scholarship to criminology has been the generation of a large and multi-disciplinary body of theoretical, methodological, and empirical literature on violence against women (see, e.g., Morris 1987; Kelly 1988; Hester 2013; Hoyle 1998; Walby *et al.* 2015; Walklate 2004). Feminist work has been pivotal in expanding the gaze and the domains of criminology to encompass the diverse yet interlinked forms of violence against women (Kelly 1988; Belknap 1996; Westmarland 2015), challenging its hidden and privatized nature (Gelsthorpe and Morris 1990) and positioning it as a public matter. From early work conceptualizing such violence as a continuum (Kelly 1988) and conveying its 'everyday' nature (Stanko 1990), and that which revealed domestic violence as a crime that requires systematic examination (Dobash and Dobash 1979) (discussed in more detail by Gadd, this volume) through to more contemporary work on state rape (Lenning and Brightman 2009), honour killing (Gill *et al.* 2014; Begikhani *et al.* 2015), and rape as a 'weapon in war' and technique of domination directed at entire communities (Diken and Laustsen 2005; Mullins 2009), this significant body of scholarship has exposed some of the most prevalent and devastating forms of harmful behaviour committed against women and girls, whilst also broadening and deepening understandings and definitions of what counts as 'crime'.

From the early 1970 onwards, most of this work has had an activist character. Alongside the rise of radical feminism, feminist researchers and activists aligned to call for attention to the gendered nature of crime and challenge the state and the criminal justice system to develop better responses to women's violent victimization, a trajectory which continues in contemporary work combining activism, advocacy, and action research (e.g. Brooks and Burman 2016; Howarth and Robinson 2016; Kelly and Westmarland 2016).

A raft of influential studies 'gendering' the victim, simultaneously and fundamentally expanded the study of victimology and broadened the focus of criminology (Dobash and Dobash 1979; Walklate 2003, 2007; Hoyle 1998) A key strand of critical feminist development here related to awareness of women's experiences as victims, subject to different forms of violence (emotional as well as physical) both within the home, at work, and in the street. The acceptance of 'rape myths', defined by Burt (1980: 217) as '. . . prejudicial, stereotyped, or false beliefs about rape, rape victims, and rapists' was systematically challenged (Gray 2006), and more nuanced questions posed around factors which inhibit women's opportunity to leave violent men. Internationally, the use of rape as a 'weapon of war' highlighted the strategic and political use of violence by men against women (Askin 1997). Thus the hegemonic masculinity of criminological work and criminal justice agencies came under critical scrutiny once more and feminist criminologists pointed the way to future gender-conscious research and practice.

VICTIMIZATION, AGENCY, AND RESISTANCE

Whilst recognizing the reality and impact of women's experiences of victimization, debates centring around questions and conceptualizations of women's agency and power have been particularly productive in challenging perceptions of women as passive and powerless and contributing more nuanced understandings of the dimensions of power. In the 1970s and 1980s when feminists were raising awareness of the extent of violence against women and analysing it as an act of male power, it was strategically important to construct women as victims of male violence (Estrich 1988). An unintended consequence was to reinforce a homogenizing connection between 'women' and 'victim', depicting women as inherently vulnerable to victimization and simultaneously underplaying women's capacity or agency (Mahoney 1994). This plays out in a dichotomous discourse which denies women's agency if she experiences victimization, and denies victimization if she experiences agency (Pollack 2000; Mahoney 1994).

Kelly's (1988) book *Surviving Sexual Violence* was pivotal in recasting women 'victims' into 'survivors from the recognition that 'the term victim . . . makes invisible the other side of women's victimisation: the active and positive ways in which women resist, cope and survive' (1988: 163). With its focus on women's mechanisms for managing and surviving the aftermath of male violence, it shifted the emphasis from passive victims to active survivors reconstructing their lives. The dual themes of survival and resistance have characterized more recent work which, whilst recognizing the trauma of sexual violence, reveals the resilience of those who experience it. For example, Jordan's (2013) research with women who were attacked by a serial rapist shows how they not only endured the attack itself—becoming simultaneously a victim and a survivor—but also survived the ensuing investigative, prosecution, and court processes and the various ways in which others around them responded. Relatedly, recent work on domestic violence demonstrates that, whilst overwhelmingly it is women that continue to be victims, they draw on and utilize their agency in responding to, resisting, and surviving such violence in complex ways (Johnson 2011).

The ways in which women who have broken the law have been characterized and responded to have long been the subject of controversy and debate. Female offenders have been variously ignored, vilified, stigmatized, medicalized and pathologized (Allen 1987; Eaton 1986) and managed, disciplined, and punished in ways that call attention to their gender (Hutter and Williams 1981; Cain 1989; Carlen 1985). Empirical research documenting the characteristics of such women has revealed backgrounds of abuse and victimization, unmet needs, and interrelated problems; we know that women lawbreakers tend to have a history of violent and sexual victimization (Chesney-Lind and Pasko 2013; Burman and Batchelor 2009); poor physical and mental health (Plugge *et al.* 2006); addiction problems (Loucks 1998; Malloch 2000); backgrounds of poverty (Carlen 1988; Gelsthorpe 2011), and housing and employment difficulties (Sheehan *et al.* 2007). Whilst there may well be 'psychological sequelae' (Hollin and Palmer 2006) linking victimization to women's pathways into crime, there has been a tendency in some work to focus on women's responses to victimization as a *sole* explanation for their law-breaking (Gilfus 1992). Situating women as multiple victims propelled into offending through the actions of others or by circumstances beyond their control circumscribes the range of women's experiences, overlooking other important aspects of their lives that may contribute to their offending (Miller 2001). The emphasis on dependence and vulnerability results in accounts that leave 'little agency, responsibility or meaning to women's law breaking' (Daly 1992: 150) and 'tend[s] to create the false impression that women have only been victims . . . [and] cannot be effective social agents on behalf of themselves or others' (Harding 1987: 5).

However, a new generation of feminist criminological scholars, informed by broader currents in feminist theory (see, e.g., Archer 2001; McNay 2000, 2004) have been producing empirically informed critical analyses of women's power, agency, and choice which recognize and acknowledge the duality between victimization and agency. Through research on women's involvement in sex work and street drug markets (Maher 1997), gang-involved girls (Miller 2001), violent young women (Batchelor 2005), shoplifters (Caputo and King 2011), and women drug 'mules' (Fleetwood 2014), this work shows that 'agency' is key to understanding both women's law-breaking behaviour and their response to victimization, even when social structures constrict individual motivations, choices, and decisions.

Much of this work employs ethnographic methods, where questions of agency and resistance are explored as 'lived experiences' in the specific contexts of drug use, prostitution, trafficking, and violence in order to reveal how the women's lives are influenced by socio-economic and cultural factors and, in turn, how these shape the opportunities that they have and the choices that they make. Far from seeing gender as irrelevant for understanding women's crime (Baskin, Sommers, and Fagan 1993), this body of work pays very close attention to the ways in which gender inequalities function as basic organizing principles of social life which shape opportunities for crime (Bottcher 2001).

Whilst there is a large body of work addressing women's and girls pathways into crime, with some notable exceptions, (Baldry 2010) there has been relatively little work theorizing processes of desistance for women. Desistance work has tended to be androcentric in character (Farrall *et al.* 2007) and limited in what it says about the relationships between women, their criminogenic (and non-criminogenic) needs, and (re)offending. Yet work which has paid attention to the 'marginal spaces' (Baldry 2010) occupied by criminalized women is instructive for understanding women's pathways out of crime, specifically by drawing attention to both *structural* and *personal* barriers that inhibit women's desistance (Gelsthorpe and Wright 2015) and the role of agency within that.

INFLUENCING POLITICS AND PRACTICE: TOWARDS A PRAXIS

Transversing all feminist perspectives has been a strong commitment to social change, manifest within feminist work in criminology in the use of research to transform or influence legislation, policy, and practice within formal institutions. Yet there has been a lack of consensus amongst scholars and shifting priorities with regard to the focus, direction, or nature of change required in relation to women as victims or as offenders.

Operating from the belief that a clear punitive state response was required to combat violence against women, some second wave feminists highlighted the importance of a robust legal response—advocating mandatory arrests, 'no drop' prosecution policies, and harsher punishment of offenders. Yet limitations of the criminal law and the criminal justice structures within which it operates has forced reconsideration of the appropriateness of recourse to criminal law and justice institutions (Larcombe 2011). Empirical work on women's experiences revealed the extent and negative effects of secondary victimization by the criminal justice system, particularly for victims of rape (Brown *et al.* 1993; Temkin 2002; Burman 2009), and problematized the relationship between coercive responses and victims' needs and interests (Hoyle 1998). Moreover, Bumiller (2008) highlights how, in the US, awareness raising around the distinctiveness of violence against women as a prevalent social problem, and lobbying around sexual violence in particular, has coincided with an expansion of tougher state control and higher imprisonment rates. Calls for increased criminalization and sanctioning of perpetrators therefore found a counterpoint in feminist critiques pointing to the problematic nature of mandatory approaches (Hoyle 1998) and state-based punishment of offenders (Snider 1998a), creating seams of uncertainty and tension about the appropriateness of law and criminal justice within an already intensely politicized landscape.

Feminist theory and activism has undoubtedly been essential both to developing an understanding of violence against women and to pioneering reforms to the legal system. But work which reveals the contextualized and gendered features of the principles and practices of criminal law (Smart 1989; Edwards 1984; Lacey 2002) to that documenting the ways in which legal and criminal justice responses might pose risks, especially to socio-economically marginalized groups (Gelsthorpe and Morris 2002; Hoyle 2007; Snider 1998b), has fed into ongoing debates amongst feminist scholars of the importance and worth of a reliance on criminal law and the criminal justice system to address violence against women and achieve feminist goals. With regard to rape in particular, researchers internationally have pointed to the ways in which the organizational context within which the criminal justice response to rape occurs, can mitigate against rape victims being treated in a responsive and supportive way and can compound their sense of victimization (Lees 1996; Jordan 2004; Martin 2005). Moreover, decades of legislative and policy reform have resulted in limited success, due to a set of interconnected problems that concern: the implementation gap between policy intent and practice (Westmarland and Gangoli 2012); the oft-encountered problem of unintended consequences of law reform (Burman 2009; Snider 1998b); the performance of legal practice (Brown *et al.* 1993), and; a set of entrenched and problematic attitudes which together contribute to the 'justice gap' (Temkin and Krahe 2008). Feminist reformers have been confronted with hard—and painful—questions as to whether the kind of actions that have resulted from feminist activism at policy and practice levels are really achieving what is best for those women whose lives are affected.

By drawing attention to inequalities in the criminal justice process and the potential harms of excessive criminalization and harsh penal sanctions, especially for marginalized/minority groups, several theorists have grappled with the thorny question of the scope for 'doing justice' in relation to what Daly (2006) terms 'gendered harms'. In an attempt to navigate alternatives, a body of work has explored the potential, relevance, and value of restorative justice to violence against women and sexual assault in particular (see, e.g., Daly 2006; Daly and Curtis-Fawley 2005; Hudson 2002; Ptacek 2010; Strang and Braithwaite 2002). This is highly contested ground however; many feminist researchers and those delivering front-line women's services are openly antagonistic towards restorative justice. Suggestions that it might offer a way of validating victim accounts and reduce victim-blaming as well as afford a degree of victim satisfaction (Daly 2006; McGlynn *et al.* 2012) have been met with fierce opposition, and counter-claims that restorative justice diminishes the seriousness of violence against women and compromises women's safety, whilst also constituting a form of (re)victimization (see, e.g., Lewis *et al.* 2001). In their review of feminist engagement with restorative justice, Daly and Stubbs (2006) call for greater recognition of the complexities and different meanings and practices within restorative justice, so that feminist principles and ideals are not constrained, shaped, or compromised by restorative justice ideals. However, whilst restorative justice is pursued less contentiously in youth justice settings, when applied to violence against (adult) women the debate often tends to dead-end in the oppositional contrasting of restorative justice and conventional criminal justice (Stubbs 2007) rather than in a more expansive acknowledgement of the limitations of the criminal justice system and an opening up to the potential of new ways of thinking.

There is little question that violence against women remains a pressing issue globally, that its prevalence is unacceptably high, that safer communities have not been created for women and there are still significant problems with the way victims are treated by criminal justice agencies and systems, however there is some evidence of a shift away from a predominant focus on criminal justice outcomes to broader questions about the relationships between violence against women and gender equality. A process of re-evaluation of feminist goals in relation to violence against women has broadened the lens somewhat. Here, 'success' is not entirely defined by conviction or attrition rates and harsh punishment of perpetrators, but increasingly by the extent to which the criminal justice system might afford women access to procedural and substantive justice (Konradi 2007; Martin, 2005), whilst also assuming responsibility for treating victims with dignity and respect (see, e.g., Larcombe 2011; McGlynn *et al.* 2012), and on addressing the ways that violence against women is tolerated in wider society.

In relation to women drawn into the criminal justice system as offenders, there has been a long-standing reform movement to reduce the incarceration of women, alongside more recent calls for a reassessment of the punishment of women (Malloch and McIvor 2013) which allows for an assessment of women's needs and what might 'work' in a holistic way to ameliorate problems and thus help reduce women's offending (Annison *et al.* 2015). Researchers have emphasized the crucial importance of the social, structural, and personal factors that together impact upon women's pathways into and out of the criminal justice system and how these are crucial for informing responses to women's offending. Feminists have lobbied for more available services within communities, mentoring schemes, and innovative provision to address these issues and provide support and appropriate assistance to those women who need it. Yet the ways in which these insights into the lived experiences of women's lives have been incorporated into prison programmes and initiatives tailored for women to 'help' them with their criminogenic need, have sometimes had the undesired effect of more women being sent to prison. Carlen (2002) warned some years ago that improvements to prison regimes may inadvertently legitimate the sending of more women to prison and, whilst Corston (2007: 9) specifically warned against using prisons as 'places of safety', concerns remain.

There is an increasingly vociferous debate played out amongst researchers, practitioners, and prison reform organizations around the need or otherwise of distinctive provision for women and girls, whether in prison or the community. Currently, gender-specific provision and 'gender-sensitive' approaches and resources characterize the landscape. However, as experience internationally has shown, 'ostensibly well-intentioned initiatives can be subverted by wider institutional imperatives' (Burman *et al.* 2015: 74) and by overarching preoccupations with security and control (Malloch 2000; Hannah-Moffat, 2000) limiting the ability of prison reforms to achieve meaningful change.

Third wave feminism, largely seen as emerging from the mid–late 1990s, signals an opening up of feminism—beyond the academy, beyond activist spheres—to engage more publicly in a refreshing celebration of the multiplicity of ways of 'doing feminism' (Snyder 2008). Less constrained by earlier feminist ideals, and more embracing of diversity and individuality, third wave feminist praxis is informed by iconoclastic inter-disciplinary thinking. Whilst second wave feminism dominated early feminist criminology, the influence of the third wave can now be discerned in relation to work on gendered violence for example, and, through an emphasis on intersectionality, on the impact of criminal justice on those who cross identities.

BEYOND CRITIQUE: METHODOLOGICAL ADVENTURES

As the above section has demonstrated, feminist contributions to criminology have gone well beyond critique. In this section we develop this argument further by reviewing the important contribution that feminism has made to understandings of methodology and variant modes of knowledge production.

Daly and Chesney-Lind (1988) raised two questions in relation to criminology, the 'generalizability problem' and 'gender ratio problem'. In essence, they expressed concern about 'gender', the implication being that theories of crime must be able to take account of both men's and women's (criminal) behaviour, and that they must be able to highlight factors which operate differently on men and women. Moreover, they must be able to account for differences in crime rates (why women commit less crime than men) and, in terms of 'gendered' control, examine gendered codes in social, political, and cultural contexts. Thus there was encouragement to listen to women's voices directly rather than relying on distorted received wisdom about them, and to recognize the ethnocentric nature of accounts. Smart's (1990) distinctive contribution was to draw attention to the very wide variety of feminist scholarship—going beyond the traditional boundaries of positivist paradigms inherent in traditional criminology and elsewhere. Feminist theorists and methodologists Harding (1986), Weedon (1987), Fraser and Nicolson (1990), Gunew (1990), and Oakley (2000) all questioned the notion of universal 'truths' and engaged feminist criminologists in the task of reappraising knowledge forms and scientific approaches to knowledge (Gelsthorpe, 2002). Feminist writers in criminology thus came to focus on 'women's experiences' as an important knowledge form. As Maureen Cain (1990) put it, strategies for the transformation of criminology needed to involve reflexivity, deconstruction and reconstruction, and a clear focus on women. This was not envisaged as a corrective to the omission of women, but rather 'for women's 'experiences' to be captured, experienced, named and tamed' (1990: 9) without using men and their experiences as a yardstick against which women's experiences must be compared. Such thinking not only made women more visible through research studies, but brought to the fore feminist epistemology (beliefs about what counts as appropriate knowledge) and feminist ontology (beliefs about the nature of the world). According to feminist scholars, appropriate knowledge is that which allows women to speak for themselves, rather than knowledge about men's worlds presuming to be about women's worlds too. Some critics and commentators argued that women's knowledge was 'better knowledge', and that 'feminist standpointism' (which captures this) is unique because there is commitment to seeing the world through the perspective of the socially subjugated (Cain 1986; Harding 1987; Naffine 1997).

If we characterize the first two developments in feminist criminology as *feminist empiricism* (as evidenced in the wide-ranging criminological research on women, crime, control, and justice—to counterbalance the absence of women in conventional criminology), and *feminist standpointism* (drawing attention to the need to place women's experiences at the centre of knowledge), the third is best described as *feminist deconstructionism*, since it draws on postmodern insights. Deconstructionism revolves around the problematizing of concepts and language (following the influence of Foucault (1972) and Derrida (1978, 1981) for instance. This kind of thinking is evident in the work of Alison Young (1994) for example—where she encourages resistance in relation to the 'master narratives' of criminology as a pre-eminent modernist science. Naffine (1997) illustrates the challenges very clearly in discussing how images, meaning, and interpretation *can* change. Writing about feminist crime fiction, she notes how the influence of postmodernist thinking can change the usual plot involving a hard-boiled male detective as the central character in plots which involve women as vulnerable sexual sirens or sexual victims is transposed into something quite different, with an overtly feminine expert who solves corporate crimes and not just crimes against women.

There have been a number of attempts to summarize the impact of such feminist activity on criminology (see, e.g., Gelsthorpe and Morris 1988; Daly and Chesney-Lind 1988; Heidensohn 2002). It has drawn criticism; black women were noticeably missing from early discourse for example (Rice 1990). Moreover, the 'theoreticist, libertarian, separatist, and gender-centric tendencies' in feminist writings came under attack (Carlen 1992). So too, what has been described as 'mistaken glorification' in 'allowing women to speak for themselves' (Carlen 1992: 63), though it could be that what Carlen sees as a distinctly feminist pursuit is merely 'good social science' (Gelsthorpe 1990). Other criticisms find their mark in relation to feminist jurisprudence (MacKinnon 1987b) or in relation to ideas about wholly separate criminal justice systems for women. One key question, of course, is 'was anyone listening?' Another is whether more recent feminist contributions learned lessons from the earlier ones. We return to this point in our conclusion.

Moving forward from the argument that methodology is gendered (Oakley 1998), and beyond the once rather entrenched and overly simplistic dichotomization between quantitative (positivist, objective, statistical, masculinist) and qualitative methods (interpretive, textual, subjective, feminist), contemporary feminist research in all disciplines tends now to be much more methodologically pluralist, with many researchers recognizing the value and salience of different research methods, if applied from a feminist perspective. This signals a retreat from earlier entrenched positions which viewed quantitative methods as being in direct conflict with the aims of feminist research (Graham 1983; Pugh 1990) and qualitative methods more appropriate for feminist research by allowing for subjective knowledge and a more equal relationship between the researcher and the researched (Oakley 1974; Stanley and Wise 1983). However, the feminist qualitative/quantitative debates have deep roots and despite methodological advances yielding new insights (Walby *et al.* 2010), the (old) argument, that the positivist nature of the majority of research does not capture the realities of women's lives, resurfaces in debates about the emphasis on 'measurement' in research on violence against women, and the ways in which a quantitative approach overshadows, decontextualizes, and acts as a barrier to capturing the myriad aspects of women's experiences.

Feminist researchers in all disciplines are highly cognizant of the need for research to be able to 'speak' directly to policy-makers and practitioners in order to contribute to legislative, policy, and material change on both national and international levels

(Beetham and Demetriades 2007; Walby *et al.* 2010). Alongside this runs an astute awareness (though not necessarily wholehearted acceptance) that sound measurement and robust quantification of data is strategically important for gaining policy attention and crucial for gaining any traction thereafter. In the current policy and political climate where the relevance and utility of academic research is uncertain/under scrutiny, being able to play the 'numbers game' is perhaps even more important but so is being able to show, through robust methodological means, the value of qualitative research for revealing the nuances and complexities of women's (and men's) lives and the subtleties of gender and its intersections with class, race, age, and sexuality.

Within contemporary feminism, more broadly, it is now contended that 'there is not one method . . . that necessarily makes research feminist', rather a feminist 'research approach, or framework, is critical' (Beetham and Demetriades 2007: 199–200). From a feminist criminological perspective, Mason and Stubbs (2010) argue similarly that there is no standard methodology in feminist criminology but rather a set of methodological preferences that feminists adopt as a means of pursuing particular research questions. Specifically this means an attentiveness to the insights of gender theory; a motivation towards the need for change; a privileging of the importance of experience in understanding crime and justice and; a commitment to breaking down the power relations inherent in research through processes of reflexivity (Mason and Stubbs 2010).

Adopting a reflexive approach entails the rejection of an ontological positioning of the social world as independent of the researcher and the research process; rather the researcher is acknowledged as a subjective resource within the research (see, e.g. Oakley 1998; Stanley and Wise 1983). Essentially this means acknowledging the ways in which the knowledge, experience, values, and identity of the researcher influence and affect the research process, but also points to the ways in which knowledge is produced—not solely by the researcher but in conjunction with the researched, as well as facilitators of the research (gatekeepers, funders). Feminist commitments to reflexivity throughout the research process have had salience for broader criminological thinking and echo through contemporary reflexive criminological accounts of research with the powerful and powerless (Lumsden and Winter 2014).

NEW RESEARCH AGENDAS

Much feminist research on women and justice has focused on governance in the penal sphere, importantly exposing the injustices experienced by women who break the law and their differential treatment within the criminal justice system. Whilst this has formed the bedrock of much feminist criminological scholarship it has, somewhat paradoxically, led to what Hannah-Moffat (2011) describes as a 'narrowing' of perspective focused on women's experiences within the criminal justice system in isolation from other institutional forms and theorizations about the regulations of gender, sexuality, race, and marginality' (2011: 444). Similarly, through her work on the governance of young women, Sharpe (2016) argues that their interactions with education and welfare institutions and specifically their experiences of governance and control across institutional boundaries have received relatively little attention. In some ways, this takes us back to earlier claims about 'policing the boundaries of social life' (Cain 1989) and despite the rapid growth and proliferation of feminist criminology, there remains a need for a more expansive feminist research agenda, one which demands a reconceptualization of 'justice' and which aims to extend feminist criminological knowledge beyond penality to engage with forms of governance and control within and across agency/institutional boundaries (Sharpe 2016).

Both the feminization and criminalization of poverty come into play here. Diana Pearce (1978) who coined the term 'feminization of poverty' makes clear the pattern that women have always experienced more poverty than men; Pat Carlen (1988), Chunn and Gavigan (2006), and Loïc Wacquant (2009) are amongst those who indicate that poverty is increasingly penalized. In a broad reconstruction of the state restricted 'workfare' and expansive 'prisonfare' are linked as the poor are 'brought to heel', with state assistance bringing obligations regarding employment. Other examples of work which has gone beyond the traditional tramlines of criminology include Bosworth *et al.*'s (2016) work on punishment, citizenship, and identity, arguing that when considered through the lens of citizenship, our understanding of imprisonment is enlarged to include the prison's connections with other geographical sites and legal frameworks, and race, gender, and class (see also, Bosworth and Kellezi 2014). There is recognition of 'new victims' of domestic violence amongst women who are disabled (Thiara *et al.* 2012), violence against older women (Bows and Westmarland 2015), as well as increased recognition of violence in 'care' homes. Contributors to Malloch and McIvor (2013) push a new agenda of social justice and human rights as the core of contemporary concerns about women and punishment, with attempts to promote a paradigm shift—away from imprisonment and towards community responses to women in conflict with the law. And as the contours of 'crime' change there is a need for attention to gendered dimensions of terrorism (Silvestri and Crowther-Dowey 2016), and cybercrime (Hutchings and Ting Chua 2017).

HUMAN TRAFFICKING, MIGRATION, AND CRIMINAL JUSTICE

One new area of interest which both fuels feminist perspectives in criminology and the quest to look beyond the traditional boundaries of criminal justice systems to all forms of social regulation (since women are very often victims) and challenges feminist criminologists (because women are sometimes perpetrators too), concerns human trafficking, migration, and criminal justice, with clear implications for understandings of inequalities, powerlessness, and justice. Mary Bosworth addresses some of the broad issues relating to immigration control and penal power in chapter 16 of this volume; our focus here is on gender dimensions of the issues.

Recognizing that there are contested definitional issues (Lee 2011; Troshynski 2012) and difficulties in measurement (Smith and Kangaspunta 2012), part of the problem is that popular conceptualizations of trafficking (as one element of migration) suggest that it is primarily an organized crime and illegal immigration problem—requiring criminal justice and immigration control interventions (Weitzer 2007).[2] It is also assumed to be a predominantly male activity. The United Nations Office on Drugs and Crime Global Report on Trafficking (UNODC 2014) suggests that some 64 per cent of convicted traffickers are men, nearly 30 per cent are women, but approximately half of all detected trafficking victims are adult women and, although this number has seemingly declined in recent years, the number of victims who are girls has increased. Interestingly, while the majority of trafficking victims are subjected to sexual exploitation, trafficking for forced labour (including manufacturing cannabis, cleaning work, catering and catering services, domestic work, and textile production) has expanded in recent years. Trafficking for exploitation that is neither sexual nor forced labour is also increasing, including forced begging, baby selling, forced marriages, benefit fraud, and armed combat (UNODC 2014). The recruitment of victims is often via feigned romantic interest, with exploiters entering into a relationship with the victim to gain her trust, and then manipulating or otherwise coercing the victim into sexual exploitation (including internet pornography); this is sometimes by men operating alone, sometimes in groups. Siegel (2012) observes that girls from Northern Romania, and as young as 13 idealize the Western sex industry, thanks to the popularity of the MTV channel. In their interpretation, prostitution offers the opportunity for foreign travel and a 'handsome' boss (pimp); these girls equate prostitution with 'gifts'. The rationalization begins so young and presents such an idealized view of prostitution, that simple education or advocacy programmes may not be strong enough to counteract them. Insofar as we can trust the data, there are regional differences, showing that in Africa and the Middle East, as well as in South Asia, East Asia, and the Pacific, women account for the majority of the detected victims trafficked for the purpose of forced labour (domestic labour very often). Women are also frequently detected as victims of trafficking for forced labour in Europe and Central Asia and in the Americas, although not as frequently as males.

But one of the main problems here concerns the difficulty in detecting victimization, even in the UK where there are seemingly sophisticated mechanisms for identifying victims. For example, Hales and Gelsthorpe (2012) reveal that between 1999 and 2009, the number of foreign nationals in women's prisons in England and Wales doubled; they had mainly come from countries like Nigeria and Vietnam, and were usually imprisoned as a result of crimes relating to theft, drugs, or false documentation. However, the distinction between 'victim' and 'offender' in many of the cases was blurred. Closer investigation via research interviews indicated that some of the women

[2] An internationally agreed definition of human trafficking emerged relatively recently in the UN Convention Against Transnational Organised Crime and its accompanying Trafficking Protocol (The Palermo Agreement) and other relevant protocols in the early 2000s. Essentially, 'Trafficking in persons' means—' the recruitment, transportation, transfer, harbouring or receipt of persons, by means of the threat or use of force or other forms of coercion, of abduction, of fraud, of deception, of the abuse of power or of a position of vulnerability or of the giving or receiving of payments or benefits to achieve the consent of a person having control over another person, for the purpose of exploitation' (UN Convention 2000, Article 3). 'Smuggling' on the other hand involves a business transaction between willing parties and usually includes movement across borders by illegal means. It occurs with the consent of individuals and the transaction usually ends upon arrival. And for completeness, migration is a general term that refers to the movements of refugees and internally displaced people (e.g. those displaced by conflicts within their country of origin) as well as people displaced by natural or environmental disasters, famine, or development projects. Migration can be forced or voluntary.

had been held captive in slavery-like conditions, forced to work as prostitutes or in drug factories—sometimes for years. Some had been raped and beaten, and their documents withheld by criminal gangs. Maria De Angelis (2016) who collected 'stories' of women's narratives of human trafficking, similarly explores the lived experiences of human trafficking. As De Angelis puts it, 'In response to the 3-P anti-trafficking paradigm—to prevent and protect victims and prosecute traffickers—official discourse constructs agency in singular opposition to victimhood. The "true" victim of trafficking is reified in attributes of passivity and worthiness, whereas signs of women's agency are read as consent in their own predicament or as culpability in criminal justice and immigration rule-breaking' (De Angelis 2016: book cover).

Notwithstanding the existence of a National Referral Mechanism (NRM) for the identification and support of 'victims' of trafficking introduced in 2009, some women escape the protective net and find themselves in prison as offenders. During the course of the development of the Modern Slavery Act 2015 the government reviewed the NRM (Home Office 2014), recommending major reforms so as to ensure better safeguarding; this is clearly important in relation to conceptions of justice.

A further example comes from the USA. Drawing on research with prosecutors, attorneys, victim advocates, social service providers, and police in an urban Midwestern city, Nichols and Heil (2015) identify challenges to identifying and prosecuting sex trafficking cases. Trafficking techniques such as coercion, online solicitation, hidden venues, and interstate movement, as well as issues with police reporting and investigation, alongside police reporting errors and the limits of evidentiary requirements, the statute of limitations, overlapping jurisdictions, and issues with victim testimony, all played a part here. Indeed, both examples serve to demonstrate how the dynamics may contribute to lowered numbers of identified and prosecuted cases, and consequent underestimation of the prevalence of sex trafficking.

There are other critical points to raise. Gozdziak (2014) amongst others, has highlighted that there is a relative empirical vacuum with regard to gendered dimensions of human trafficking. Firstly, as indicated, the usual lens of men as 'perpetrators' and women as 'victims' means that men who are victims are sometimes rendered invisible; their exploitation and vulnerability is not readily recognized. Secondly, a feminist focus on the sexual exploitation of women and girls in trafficking discourse means that we know relatively little about other forms of labour exploitation (Anker and Liempt 2012). Mahdavi (2011) suggests that this is due to a chasm 'between the broad legal definition that embraces any worker who experienced force, fraud, or coercion, and the narrow latitude of activist and policy discussions that focuses on sex work' (2011: 13). Indeed, it is arguable that the focus on women and inequality, and the exploitation of women in this realm, leads to lack of sensitivity to race and class (Kempadoo 2012). Thirdly, whilst human trafficking is often conceived as a 'security threat' to the state with the need to better control borders, emerging feminist analyses of human trafficking pose challenges by prioritizing the security of trafficked persons and recognizing the manner in which victims are made subject to control via traffickers and the state itself (Lobasz 2009).

We can add to this a number of critical observations with regard to the gendered dimension of migration. Here too, women are perceived to be victims with media attention to 'rape epidemics' (Kern 2016; News.Com.Au 2016) performed by male migrants leading to a 'convergence' of controls on immigration and crime (Melossi 2015). Marmo and Smith (2012), Lee (2014), Pickering and Ham (2014), and Bosworth *et al.* (2015) all draw attention to the 'gendering of borders'. Indeed, Bosworth *et al.* observe that gender serves to 'delegitimize' women as transnational migrants, especially in the face of increasing border control; the sorting of desirable from undesirable migrants at the border is heavily invested in 'civilizing' tropes and 'gendered moralities' (2015).

Alongside forced migration (for arranged marriages, and asylum seeking, for instance), the reasons for migration include the wish to seek work to support families back home. But the exercise of agency and efforts to meet changing gender expectations in countries of origin (being a good mother by wanting to ensure financial security) are denied; women's narratives of providing for children and aged parents do not impact on 'failed scripts of women at the border' (Bosworth *et al.* 2015). Unauthorized mobility thus fosters gendered disapproval and criminalization.

Much of the debate in recent years regarding trade in human beings and migration has been conducted within feminist frameworks of analysis and advocacy, noting in particular, the importance of the 'the body' as an instrument (for the purposes of prostitution, reproductive care, commercial surrogacy, and domestic services). Indeed, we have witnessed an intrusion of market relations in the domain of sexuality and social reproduction which is global, international, and transnational. As Truong (2015) notes, there are competing interpretations. Global feminism views human trafficking as a form of violence against women, reflecting patriarchal culture as a 'single mould'. International feminism emphasizes the politics between nation states and views gender as a structure and process that together inform the global political economy of cross-border prostitution, sex trafficking, and reproductive care services (Truong 2015: 2). Transnational feminism focuses on the complexity regarding intersections of national identity, race, and sexuality with regard to economic exploitation within an emergent global capitalism. But there is need to add another perspective, that of transfeminism which aims to understand the nexus of identity formation and the meanings of agency as produced by the interrelationships and interactions among individuals and groups. Indeed, under the forces of globalization there is need for innovative ways for rethinking the relationship between 'sex', 'gender', and 'power'. Laura Augustin (2007) demonstrates this most eloquently in her book on 'sex at the margins' which shows that what happens to poor immigrant women from the Global South when they 'leave home for sex' is neither a tragedy nor the panacea of finding the promised land. According to Agustin (2005, 2007), the moralizing bent of government and non-government organizations alike (as part of a rescue industry) is remote from the women's wishes and experiences.

Finally, the wider context of closed borders in Europe (Askola 2010), the feminization of poverty, and the feminization of the care industry (see Ehrenreich and Russell 2002; Agustin 2005) all suggest that there are more questions to ask. Are the women who become perpetrators of human trafficking one-time victims? Are the women subject to duress or blackmail in participating (in the same way that women who engage in drug trafficking as 'drug mules' might be seen to be) for instance? It is arguably simplistic to categorize women as either 'offenders' *or* 'victims'. Indeed, what is required is a sociologically informed analysis of the trafficking–migration nexus and the underlying factors which contribute to the exploitation of women (and men) in trafficking and other forms of migration. As Sassen (2000) has suggested, there is arguably a 'feminisation of survival'—as households and sometimes whole communities are increasingly reliant on the labour efforts of migrant women to make their living and send financial support home. There is need for more research here, including investigations of the social constructions of human trafficking and migration which address the limitations of sexist and racist stereotypes in constructing categories. Feminist contributions thus far have connected the newly emerging body of work on the criminalization of mobility with feminist theorizations and methodologies for an empirical understanding of the lived experiences of those subject to practices of border control, but there is further to go.

CONCLUDING REFLECTIONS: WHITHER FEMINISM AND CRIMINOLOGY?

In reviewing the prospects for a criminology that would fully understand and embrace the precepts of feminist perspectives and address the quest for gender equality, Carol Smart (1990) chose to turn away from criminology towards sociology, seeing criminology as 'atavistic' and beyond redemption.

Counter to Smart's claims, this chapter has demonstrated that feminist contributions to criminology have challenged theory and method within criminology and had some wider influence on policy and practice. We have seen major paradigm shifts within feminist scholarship, moving beyond an exclusive focus on gender to recognize the need for intersectionality and the ways in which social contexts and mobilities shape human relations. We have witnessed political commitment to social change and equality as a critical part of feminist scholarship and practice, and we have seen epistemological questioning and creative thinking about the processes of knowledge production. We have also witnessed some positive policy developments in the criminal justice system, though often with unintended negative consequences. Whether these developments amount to transformation of the discipline remains open to question.

For some, feminist criminology is but one step towards a humanistic criminology: one that would be oriented towards human betterment and fulfilment rather than 'crime control' and 'offender management' (Hartjen 2015). It is also a criminology which would reflect the diversity and intersectionality that third wave feminism has prompted, and it is potentially a critical criminology which would turn attention to the state as oppressor as much as defender of individuals. Whatever the futures, the legacies of feminism remind us of the need to adopt inclusive and non-judgemental approaches to scholarship and to ensure that the lives and experiences of women remain a central focus of the criminological gaze.

SELECTED FURTHER READING

Annison, Brayford, and Deering's *Women and Criminal Justice: From the Corston Report to Transforming Rehabilitation* (2015) outlines key developments since the publication of Baroness Jean Corston's Report into vulnerable women in the criminal justice system in 2007. Looking forwards more than backwards to the report, although using the report as a springboard to examine how far things have changed, the contributors describe new developments in regard to the meaning of 'transforming rehabilitation' for women.

Barbaret's *Women, Crime and Criminal Justice: A Global Enquiry* (2014) uses an interdisciplinary and feminist gendered perspective to explore global ideas relating to women's offending and victimization, and as criminal justice professionals. The book fills a gap in relation to the internationalization of analysis, and includes a wide range of voices; importantly, voices from non-Anglophone as well as Anglophone societies.

Gartner and McCarthy's *The Oxford Handbook on Gender, Sex, and Crime* (2015) is an edited collection of essays that captures wide ranging multidisciplinary debates about men and women's involvement in crime, as well as biological, psychological, and social science perspectives on gender, sex, and criminal activity. The contributors press the case for considerations of intersectionality, viewing sex and gender as they interact with ethnicity, class, age, peer groups, and community, for instance. The contributors explore new topics such as human trafficking, honour killing, state rape, gender violence during war, and genocide, as well as more traditional topics such as sexual violence and domestic violence.

The contributors to Malloch and McIvor's *Women, Punishment and Social Justice: Human Rights and Penal Practice* (2013) provide a critical analysis of approaches and experiences of penal sanctions, human rights, and social justice as shown in practice in different jurisdictions within and beyond the UK. Combined, the chapters question the efficacy of gender-responsive interventions by examining issues which are known to impact on women drawn into the criminal justice system, including mental health, age, and ethnicity. A key theme in this book concerns human rights and the paradox of trying to implement rights within a largely punishment-oriented system.

Smart's *Women, Crime, and Criminology: A Feminist Critique* (1976) was one of the first feminist critiques of conventional criminology. It reviews the early literature on women's crime, challenges the 'received wisdom' and altogether provides a searching agenda for new considerations of women, crime, and criminal justice. The book had a huge impact when it was first published; it marked a turning point in critical thinking about women, crime, and criminal justice, and it remains a classic, much read text.

Westmarland's *Violence against Women. Criminological Perspectives on Men's Violences* (2015) is a hugely important text which addresses significant forms of violence against women, from research, policy, and practice perspectives. The book includes a focus on forms of violence which hitherto have attracted little attention as well as well-known forms of violence. The author brings together work on violence against women committed by partners, family members, strangers, acquaintances, institutions and businesses, and thus widens the lens through which we view men's violences against women.

REFERENCES

AGUSTIN, L. (2007), *Sex at the Margins. Migration, Labour Markets and the Rescue industry*, London: Zed.

ALLEN, H. (1987), *Justice Unbalanced: Gender, Psychiatry and Judicial Decisions*, Milton Keynes: Open University Press.

ANNISON, J., BRAYFORD, J., and DEERING, J. (eds) (2015), *Women and Criminal Justice: From the Corston Report to Transforming Rehabilitation*, Bristol: Policy Press.

ANKER, C. and VAN LIEMPT, I. (2012), *Human rights and Migration: Trafficking for Forced Labour*, Basingstoke: Palgrave Macmillan.

ARCHER, M. (2001), *Being Human: The Problem with Agency*, Cambridge: Cambridge University Press.

ASKIN, K. (1997), *War Crimes Against Women*, Boston: Martinus Nijhoft Publishers.

ASKOLA, H. (2010), '"Illegal immigrants", gender and vulnerability: the case of the EU's returns directive', *Feminist Legal Studies*, 18 (2):159–78.

BALDRY, E. (2010), 'Women in transition: from prison to . . .', *Current Issues in Criminal Justice*, 22(2): 253–67.

BALFOUR, G. and COMACK, E. (eds) (2006), *Criminalising Women*, Halifax: Fernwood Publishing.

BARBARET, R. (2014), *Women, Crime and Criminal Justice: A Global Enquiry*, Abingdon: Routledge.

BARTON, A. and COOPER, V. (2013), 'Hostels and community justice for women': The semi-penal paradox', in M. Malloch and G. McIvor (eds), *Women, Punishment and Social Justice*, Abingdon: Routledge.

BATCHELOR, S. (2005), '"Prove me the bam . . ." victimization and agency in the lives of young women who commit violent offences', *Probation Journal*, 52(4): 358–75.

BASKIN, D., SOMMERS, I., FAGAN, J. (1993), 'The Political Economy of Violent Female Street Crime', *Fordham Urban Law Journal*, 20(3): 401–7.

BEETHAM, G. and DEMETRIADES, J. (2007), 'Feminist research methodologies and development: overview and practical application', *Gender and Development*, 15(2): 199–216.

BEGIKHANI, N., GILL, A., and HAGUE, G. (2015), *Honour-based Violence: Experiences and Counter Strategies in Iraqi Kurdistan and the UK Kurdish Diaspora*, Aldershot: Ashgate.

BEGLAN, M. (2013), '*The 218 experience*', in M. Malloch and G. McIvor (eds), *Women, Punishment and Social Justice*. Human rights and penal practices, London: Routledge.

BELKNAP. J. (1996), *The Invisible Woman: Gender, Crime, and Justice*, Belmont, CA: Thomson Wadsworth Publishing Company.

BEVERIDGE, F., NOTT, S., and STEPHEN, K. (2000), *Making Women Count: Integrating Gender into Law and Policy-making*, Aldershot: Ashgate.

BOSWORTH, M., HOYLE, C., and DEMPSEY, M. (2011), 'Researching Trafficked Women: On Institutional Resistance and the Limits to Feminist Reflexivity', *Qualitative Inquiry*, 17(9): 769–79.

BOSWORTH, M., HASSELBERG, I., and TURNBULL, S. (2016), 'Punishment, Citizenship and Identity: An Introduction', *Criminology and Criminal Justice*, 16(3): 257–66.

BOSWORTH, M. and KELLEZI, B. (2014), 'Citizenship and belonging in a women's immigration detention centre', in C. Phillips and C. Webster, *New Directions in Race, Ethnicity and Crime*, Abingdon: Routledge.

BOSWORTH, M., PICKERING, S., and FILI, A. (2015), *Border Crossings and Gender in the Greek Detention System*, http://bordercriminologies.law.ox.ac.uk/border-crossings-and-gender-in-the-greek-detention-system/, accessed 28 August 2016.

BOTTCHER, J. (2001), 'Social Practices of Gender: How Gender Relates to Delinquency in the Everyday Lives of High Risk Youths', *Criminology*, 39(4): 893–932.

BOWS, H. and WESTMARLAND, N. (2015), 'Rape of Older People in the United Kingdom: Challenging the "Real Rape" Stereotype', *British Journal of Criminology* (published online November 2015).

BROOKS, O. and BURMAN, M. (2016), 'Reporting rape: victim perspectives on advocacy support in the criminal justice process', *Criminology and Criminal Justice* (published online September 2016).

BROWN, J. and HEIDENSOHN, F. (2000), *Gender and Policing*, Basingstoke: Palgrave.

BROWN, B., BURMAN, M., and JAMIESON, L. (1993), *Sex Crimes on Trial*, Edinburgh: Edinburgh University Press.

BUMILLER, K. (2008), *In An Abusive State: How Neoliberalism Appropriated the Feminist Movement against Sexual Violence*, Durham and London: Duke University Press.

BURGESS-PROCTOR, A. (2006), 'Intersections of Race, Class, Gender, and Crime: Future Directions for Feminist Criminology', *Feminist Criminology*, 1(1): 27–47.

BURMAN, M. (2009), 'Evidencing sexual assault: women in the witness box', *Probation Journal*, 56(4): 379–98.

BURMAN, M. and BATCHELOR, S. (2009), 'Between two stools: responding to young women who offend', *Youth Justice*, 9(3): 270–85.

BURMAN, M., MALLOCH, M., and MCIVOR, G. (2015), 'A comparison: criminalised women in Scotland', in J. Annison, J. Brayford, and J. Deering (eds), *Women and Criminal Justice: From the Corston Report to Transforming Rehabilitation*, Bristol: Policy Press.

BURT, M. (1980), 'Cultural myths and supports for rape', *Journal of Personality and Social Psychology*, 38(2): 217–30.

CAIN, M. (1986), 'Realism, Feminism, Methodology and Law', *International Journal of the Sociology of Law*, 14(3): 255–67.

CAIN, M. (1989), *Growing Up Good: Policing the Behaviour of Girls in Europe*, London: Sage.

CAIN, M. (1990), 'Towards Transgression: New Directions in Feminist Criminology', *International Journal of Sociology*, 18(1): 1–18.

CAPUTO, G. and KING, A. (2011), 'Shoplifting: Work, Agency, and Gender', *Feminist Criminology*, 6(3): 159–77.

CARLEN, P. (1988), *Women, Crime and Poverty*, Milton Keynes: Open University Press.

CARLEN, P. (1992) 'Criminal women and criminal justice: the limits to, and potential of, feminist and left realist perspectives', in R. Matthews and J. Young (eds), *Issues in Realist Criminology*. London: Sage.

CARLEN, P. (ed.) (2002), *Women and Punishment. The Struggle for Justice*, Cullompton: Willan.

CARLEN, P. and WORRALL, A. (1987), *Gender, Crime and Justice*, Milton Keynes: Open University Press.

CARLEN, P., HICKS, J., O'DWYER, J., CHRISTINA, D., and TCHAIKOVSKY, C. (1985), *Criminal Women*, Cambridge: Polity.

CHESNEY-LIND, M. (2006), 'Patriarchy, Crime and Justice: Feminist Criminology in an Age of Backlash', *Feminist Criminology*, 1(1): 6–26.

CHESNEY-LIND, M. and PASKO, L. (2013), *The Female Offender: Girls, Women and Crime*, 3rd edn, London: Sage.

CHUNN, D. and GAVIGAN, S. (2006), 'From welfare fraud to welfare as fraud: the criminalization of poverty', in G. Balfour and E. Comack (eds), *Criminalizing Women*, Halifax: Fernwood Publishing.

COLLINS, P. (1990), *Black Feminist Thought: Knowledge, Consciousness, and the Politics of Empowerment*, Boston: Unwin Hyman.

COLLINS, P. (1995), 'Symposium: On West and Fenstermaker's "Doing Difference" ', *Gender & Society*, 9: 491–4.

COLLINS, P. and BILGE, S. (2016), *Intersectionality*, Oxford: Polity.

Commission on Women Offenders (2012), *Report of the Commission on Women Offenders Edinburgh: Scottish Government*, http://www.gov.scot/resource/0039/00391588.pdf, accessed 15 August 2016.

CONNELL, R. (1995), *Masculinities*, California: University of California Press.

CORSTON, J. (2007), *The Corston Report: A Report by Baroness Jean Corston of a Review of Women with Particular Vulnerabilities in the Criminal Justice System*, London: Home Office.

CRENSHAW, K. (1991), 'Mapping the Margins: Intersectionality, Identity Politics, and Violence against Women of Color', *Stanford Law Review*, 43(6): 1241–99.

CRIMINAL JUSTICE JOINT INSPECTION (2011), *Thematic Inspection Report: Equal but Different? An Inspection of the use of alternatives to custody for women*, A Joint Inspection by HMI Probation, HMCPSI and HMI Prisons, https://www.justiceinspectorates.gov.uk/hmiprisons/inspections/equal-but-different-an-inspection-of-the-use-of-alternatives-to-custody-for-women-offenders/, accessed 4 September 2016.

DALY, K. (1992), 'Women's Pathways to Felony Court: Feminist Theories of Lawbreaking and Problems of Representation', *Review of Law and Women's Studies*, 2: 11–52.

DALY, K. (1997), 'Different ways of conceptualizing sex/gender in feminist theory and their implications for criminology', *Theoretical Criminology*, 1(1): 25–51.

DALY, K. (2006), 'Restorative Justice and Sexual assault: An Archival Study of Court and Conference Cases', *British Journal of Criminology*, 46(2): 334–56.

DALY, K. and CHESNEY-LIND, M. (1988), 'Feminism and Criminology', *Justice Quarterly*, 5: 497–538.

DALY, K. and CURTIS-FAWLEY, S. (2005), 'Restorative Justice for Victim-survivors of Sexual Assault', in K. Heimer and C. Kruttschnitt (eds), *Gender and Crime: Patterns of Victimization and Offending*.

DALY, K. and MAHER, L. (1998), *Criminology at the Crossroads: Feminist Readings in Crime and Justice*, Oxford: Oxford University Press.

DALY, K. and STUBBS, J. (2006), 'Feminist Engagement with Restorative Justice', *Theoretical Criminology*, 10(1): 9–28.

DE ANGELIS, M. (2016), *Human Trafficking: Women's Stories of Agency*, Lady Stephenson Library, Newcastle Upon Tyne: Cambridge Scholars Publishing.

DELMAR, R. (2001) 'What is Feminism?' In A. C. Hermann and A. Stewart (eds), *Theorizing Feminism*, Boulder, CO: Westview Press.

DERRIDA, J. (1978), *Writing and Difference*, London: Routledge.

DIKEN, B. and LAUSTSEN, C. B. (2005), 'Becoming Abject: Rape as a Weapon of War', *Body and Society*, 11(1): 111–28.

DOBASH, R. and DOBASH, R. (1979), *Violence against Wives: A Case Against the Patriarchy*, New York: Free Press.

DRAGIEWICZ (2012), 'Anti-feminist backlash and critical criminology', in W. Dekeseredy and M. Dragiewicz (eds), *Routledge Handbook of Critical Criminology*, Abingdon: Routledge.

EASTON, H. and MATTHEWS, R. (2010), *Evaluation of the 218 Service: Examining Implementation and Outcomes*, Scottish Government Social Research.

EASTON, H. and MATTHEWS, R. (2011), *Evaluation of the Inspire Women's Project*, Belfast: DOJ.

EATON, M. (1986), *Justice for Women?*, Milton Keynes: Open University Press.

EDWARDS, S. (1984), *Women on Trial*, Manchester: Manchester University Press.

EHRENREICH, B. and RUSSELL, A. (2002), *Global Woman*, New York: Henry Holt and Company.

ESTRICH, S. (1988), *Real Rape*, Cambridge, MA: Harvard University Press.

FARRALL, S., MAWBY, R. C., and WORRALL, A. (2007), 'Prolific/Persistent Offenders and Desistance', in L. Gelsthorpe and R. Morgan (eds), *Handbook of Probation*, Cullompton: Willan.

FLEETWOOD, J. (2014), *Drug Mules: Women in the International Cocaine Trade*, London: Palgrave MacMillan.

FOUCAULT, M. (1972), *The Archaeology of Knowledge and the Discourse of Language* (trans from French by A. M. Sheridan Smith), New York: Pantheon Books.

FRASER, N. and NICOLSON L. (1990), 'Social Criticism without Philosophy', in L. Nicholson (ed.), *Feminism/Postmodernism*, London: Routledge.

GARTNER, R. and MCCARTHY, B. (eds) (2015), *The Oxford Handbook on Gender, Sex, and Crime*, London: Oxford University Press.

GELSTHORPE, L. (1989), *Sexism and the Female Offender: An Organisational Analysis*, Aldershot: Gower.

GELSTHORPE (1990), 'Feminist Methodologies in Criminology: A New Approach or Old Wine in New Bottles?', in L. Gelsthorpe and A. Morris (eds), *Feminist Perspectives in Criminology*, Buckingham: Open University Press.

GELSTHORPE, L. (2002), 'Feminism and Criminology', in M. Maguire, R. Morgan, and R. Reiner (eds), *The Oxford Handbook of Criminology*, 3rd edn, Oxford: Oxford University Press.

GELSTHORPE, L. (2011), 'Women, Crime and Control: A Response to "Punishing the Poor: The Neoliberal Government of Social Insecurity and

Prisons of Poverty" ' by Loic Wacquant, *Special Issue of Criminology and Criminal Justice*, 10(4): 375–86.

Gelsthorpe, L. and Hedderman, C. (2012), 'Providing for women offenders: the risks of adopting a payment by results', *Probation Journal*, 59(4): 374–90.

Gelsthorpe, L. and Loucks, N. (1997), 'Magistrates Explanations of Sentencing Decisions', in C. Hedderman and L. Gelsthorpe (eds), *Understanding the Sentencing of Women*, Home Office Research Study 130, London: Home Office.

Gelsthorpe, L. and Morris, A. (1988), 'Feminism and Criminology in Britain', *British Journal of Criminology*, 28(2): 93-110

Gelsthorpe, L. and Morris, A. (1990), *Feminist Perspectives in Criminology*, Buckingham: Open University Press.

Gelsthorpe, L. and Morris, A. (2002) 'Women's Imprisonment in England and Wales: A Penal Paradox', *Criminology and Criminal Justice*, 2(3): 277–301.

Gelsthorpe, L. and Wright, S. (2015), 'The context: women as lawbreakers', in J. Annison, J. Brayford, and J. Deering (eds), *Women and Criminal Justice: From the Corston Report to Transforming Rehabilitation*, Bristol: Policy Press.

Gilfus, M. (1992), 'From Victims to Survivors to Offenders: Women's Routes of Entry and Immersion in to Street Crime', *Women and Criminal Justice*, 4(1); 63–89.

Gill, A., Strange, C., and Roberts, K. (eds) (2014), *Honour Killing and Violence*, London: Palgrave Macmillan.

Gill, A. (2011) 'Reconfiguring "honour"-based violence as a form of gendered violence', in M. Idriss and T. Abbas (eds), *Honour, Violence, Women and Islam*, London and New York: Routledge-Cavendish.

Gozdziak, E. (2014), 'In search of research on human trafficking', in R. Gartner and B. McCarthy (eds), *The Oxford Handbook of Gender, Sex, and Crime*, New York: Oxford University Press.

Gray, J. M. (2006), 'Rape Myth Beliefs and Prejudiced Instructions: Effects on Decisions of Guilt in a Case of Date Rape', *Legal and Criminological Psychology*, 11: 75–80.

Gunew, S. (1990), *Feminist Knowledge: Critique and Construct*, London and New York: Routledge.

Graham, H.(1983), 'Do her answers fit his questions? Women and the survey method', in E. Gamarnikow, D. Morgan, J. Purvis, and D. Taylorson (eds), *The Public and the Private*, London: Heinemann.

Hales, L. and Gelsthorpe, L. (2012), *The Criminalisation of Migrant Women*, Cambridge: Institute of Criminology, University of Cambridge.

Hannah-Moffat, K. (2000), 'Prisons that Empower: Neoliberal Governance and in Canadian Women's Prisons', *British Journal of Criminology*, 40(3): 510–31.

Hannah-Moffat K (2011), 'Criminological cliques: Narrowing dialogues, institutional protectionism, and the next generation', in M. Bosworth and C. Hoyle (eds), *What Is Criminology?*, Oxford: Oxford University Press.

Hannah-Moffat, K. and O'Malley P. (eds) (2007), *Gendered Risks*, Abingdon: Routledge-Cavendish.

Harding, S. (1986), *The Science Question in Feminism*, Ithaca and London: Cornell University Press.

Harding, S. (1987), 'Introduction: Is There a Feminist Method?', in S. Harding (ed.), *Feminism and Methodology*, Bloomington: Indiana University Press.

Hartjen, C. (2015), 'Humanistic Criminology: Is it possible?', *The Journal of Sociology & Social Welfare*, 12(3): 444–68.

Hedderman, C., Palmer, E., and Hollin, C. (2008), *Implementing services for women offenders and those 'at risk' of offending: action research with Together Women*, Ministry of Justice Research Series 12/08, London: Ministry of Justice.

Heidensohn, F. (2002), 'Gender and Crime', in M. Maguire, R. Morgan, and R. Reiner (eds), *The Oxford Handbook of Criminology*, 3rd edn, Oxford: Oxford University Press.

Hester, M. (2013), 'Who does what to whom? Gender and domestic violence perpetrators in English police records', *European Journal of Criminology*, 10(5): 623–37.

Hollin, C. and Palmer, E. (2006), 'Criminogenic need and women offenders: A critique of the literature', *Legal and Criminological Psychology*, 11: 17–195.

Holloway, K. and Brookman, F. (2008), *An Evaluation of the Women's Turnaround Project*, Report prepared for NOMS Cymru, http://criminology.research.southwales.ac.uk/media/files/documents/2009-01-29/WTP_Final_Version_Report_of_Phase_1_201008.pdf, accessed 4 September 2016.

Home Office (2004), *Women's Offending Reduction Programme (WORP), Action Plan*, London: Home Office.

Home Office (2014), *Review of the National Referral Mechanism for victims of human trafficking*, London: Home Office, https://www.gov.uk/government/uploads/system/uploads/attachment_data/file/467434/Review_of_the_National_Referral_Mechanism_for_victims_of_human_trafficking.pdf, accessed 4 September 2016.

Howe, A. (1994), *Punish and Critique: Towards a feminist analysis of penality*, London: Routledge.

Howard League (2015), *Report on the Inquiry into Preventing Unnecessary Criminalisation of Women*, London: The Howard League for Penal Reform.

Howarth, E. and Robinson, A. (2016), 'Responding effectively to women experiencing severe abuse: identifying key components of a British advocacy intervention', *Violence Against Women*, 22(1): 41–63.

Hoyle, C. (1998), *Negotiating Domestic Violence: Police, Criminal Justice and Victims*, Clarendon Studies in Criminology, Oxford: Clarendon.

Hoyle, C. (2007), 'Feminism, Victimology and Domestic Violence', in S. Walklate (ed.), *Handbook of Victims and Victimology*, Devon, UK: Willan.

Hudson, B. (2002), 'Restorative Justice and Gendered Violence—Diversion or Effective Justice', *British Journal of Criminology*, 42(3): 616–34.

HUTCHINGS, A. and TING CHUA, Y. (2017), 'Gendering Cybercrime', in T. Holt (ed.), *Cybercrime Through an Interdisciplinary Lens*, Abingdon: Routledge (forthcoming).

HUTTER, B. and WILLIAMS, G. (1981), *Controlling Women: The Normal and the Deviant*, Oxford: Croom Helm.

JOHNSON, M. (2011), 'Gender and Types of Intimate Partner Violence: A Response to an Anti-feminist Literature Review', *Aggression and Violent Behaviour*, 16: 289–96.

JOLLIFFE, D., HEDDERMAN, C., PALMER, E., and HOLLIN, C. (2011), *Re-offending analysis of women offenders referred to Together Women (TW) and the scope to divert from custody*, Ministry of Justice Research Series. London: Ministry of Justice.

JORDAN, J. (2004), *The Word of A Woman? Police, Rape and Belief*, London: Palgrave MacMillan.

JORDAN, J. (2013), 'From Victim to Survivor—And from Survivor to Victim: Reconceptualising the Survivor Journey', *Sexual Abuse in Australia and New Zealand*, 5(2):48–57.

KELLY, L. (1988), *Surviving Sexual Violence (Feminist Perspectives)*, Cambridge: Polity.

KELLY, L. and WESTMARLAND, N. (2016), 'Naming and defining "domestic violence": lessons from research with violent men', *Feminist Review*, 112(1): 113–27.

KEMPADOO, K., SANGHERA, J., and PATTANAIK, B. (eds) (2012), *Trafficking and Prostitution Reconsidered: New Perspectives on Migration, Sex Work and Human Rights*, 2nd edn, Abingdon, Oxford: Routledge.

KERN, S. (2016), 'Migrant rape epidemic reaches Austria', https://www.gatestoneinstitute.org/7995/migrants-rape-austria, accessed 28 August 2016.

KONRADI, A. (2007), *Taking the Stand: Rape Survivors and the Prosecution of Rape*, Westport, Connecticut: Praeger.

LACEY, N. (2002), 'Violence, ethics and law: feminist reflections on a familiar dilemma', in S. James and S. Palmer (eds), *Visible Women: Essays on Feminist Legal Theory and Political Philosophy*, Oxford: Hart.

LARCOMBE, W. (2011), 'Falling conviction rates: (Some) feminist aims and measures for rape law', *Feminist Legal Studies*, 19(1): 27–45.

LEE, M. (2011), *Human Trafficking*, Collumpton: Willan.

LEES, S. (1996), *Carnal Knowledge: Rape on Trial*, London: Hamish Hamilton.

LENNING, E. and BRIGHTMAN, S. (2009), 'Oil, Rape and State Crime in Nigeria', *Critical Criminology*, 17(1): 35–48.

LEWIS, R., DOBASH, R., DOBASH, R., and CAVANAGH, K. (2001), 'Law's progressive potential: the value of engagement with the law for domestic violence', *Social and Legal Studies*, 10(1): 105–30.

LOBASZ, J. (2009), 'Beyond Border Security: Feminist Approaches to Human Trafficking', *Security Studies*, 18(2): 319–44.

LOUCKS, N. (1998), *HMPI Cornton Vale: Research into drugs and alcohol, violence and bullying, suicide and self-injury and backgrounds of abuse*, Scottish Prison Service Occasional Papers No. 1/98, Edinburgh: Scottish Prison Service.

LOUCKS, N., MALLOCH, M., MCIVOR, G., and GELSTHORPE, L. (2006), *Evaluation of the 218 Centre*, Edinburgh: Scottish Executive.

LUMSDEN, K. and WINTERS, A. (eds) (2014), *Reflexivity in Criminological Research: Experiences with the Powerful and the Powerless*, London: Palgrave Macmillan.

MACKINNON, C. (1987a), *Feminism Unmodified: Discourses on Life and Law*, Cambridge, MA: Harvard University Press.

MACKINNON, C. (1987b), 'Feminism, Marxism, Method and the State: Towards Feminist Jurisprudence', in S. Harding (ed.), *Feminism and Methodology*, Milton Keynes: Open University Press.

MAHDAVI, P. (2011), *Gridlock: Labor, Migration, and Human Trafficking in Dubai*, Stanford: Stanford University Press.

MAHER, L. (1997), *Sexed Work: Gender, Race, and Resistance in a Brooklyn Drug Market*, Clarendon Studies in Criminology, Oxford: Clarendon.

MAHONEY, M. R. (1994), 'Victimization or Oppression? Women's Lives, Violence and Agency', in M. Fineman, and R. Mykitiuk, (eds), *The Public Nature of Private Violence*, New York: Routledge.

MALLOCH, M. (2000), *Women, Drugs and Custody*, Winchester: Waterside Press.

MALLOCH, M. and MCIVOR, G. (eds) (2013), *Women, Punishment and Social Justice: Human Rights and Penal Practice*, Abingdon: Routledge.

MARMO, M. and SMITH, E. (2012), 'Female Migrants: Sex, Value and Credibility in Immigration Control', in S. Pickering and J. McCulloch (eds), *Borders and Transnational Crime: Pre-Crime, Mobility and Serious Harm in an Age of Globalisation*, London: Palgrave Macmillan.

MARTIN, P. (2005), *Rape Work: Victims, Gender and Community Context*, New York: Routledge.

MASON, G. and STUBBS, J. (2010), 'Feminist Approaches to Criminological Research', in S. Gadd, S. Karstedt, and S. Messner (eds), *Doing Criminological Research*, London: Sage.

MCGLYNN, C., WESTMARLAND, N., and GODDEN, N. (2012), '"I just wanted him to hear me": sexual violence and the possibilities of restorative justice', *Journal of Law and Society*, 39(2): 213–40.

MCNAY, L. (2000), *Gender and Agency: Reconfiguring the Subject in Feminist and Social Theory*, Cambridge: Polity.

MCNAY, L. (2004), 'Agency and Experience: Gender as a Lived Relation', in *The Sociological Review*, 2(2): 173–90. (Issue reprinted as L. Adkins (ed.) *Feminists After Bourdieu: International Perspectives*, London: Blackwell.)

MCROBBIE, A. (1980), 'Settling accounts with subculture: a feminist critique', *Screen Education*, 39(Spring): 37-49 (reprinted in *Feminism and Youth Culture*), Basingstoke: Macmillan.

MELOSSI, D. (2015), *Crime, Punishment and Migration*, London: Sage.

Messerschmidt, J. (1993), *Masculinities and Crime: Critique and Reconceptualisation of Theory*, Lanham, MD: Rowman and Littlefield.

Miller, J. (2001), *One of the Guys: Girls, Gang and Gender*, New York: Oxford University Press.

Morris, A. (1987), *Women, Crime and Criminal Justice*, Oxford: Basil Blackwell.

Mullins C. (2009), '"We are going to rape you and taste Tutsi women": Rape during the 1994 Rwandan genocide', *British Journal of Criminology*, 49(6): 719–35.

Naffine. N. (1997), *Feminism and Criminology*, Cambridge: Polity Press.

National Offender Management Service (NOMS) and NHS England (2015a), *The Offender Personality Disorder Pathway Strategy 2015*, Gateway reference 04272, https://www.england.nhs.uk/commissioning/wp-content/uploads/sites/12/2016/02/opd-strategy-nov-15.pdf, accessed 6 September 2016.

National Offender Management Service (NOMS) and NHS England (2015b), *Brochure of Offender Personality Disorder Services for women*, http://www.academyforjusticecommissioning.org.uk/wp-content/uploads/2015/03/Brochure-of-Womens-OPD-services-Feb-2015.pdf, accessed 10 January 2017.

News.com.au (2016), http://www.news.com.au/finance/economy/world-economy/cologne-is-everyday-europes-rape-epidemic/news-story/e2e618e17ad4400b5ed65045e65e141d, accessed 28 August 2016.

Nichols, A. and Heil, E. (2015), 'Challenges to Identifying and Prosecuting Sex Trafficking Cases in the Midwest United States', *Feminist Criminology*, 10(1): 7–35.

Oakley, A. (1974), *The Sociology of Housework*, London: Martin Robertson.

Oakley, A. (1998), 'Science, gender and women's liberation: An argument against postmodernism', *Women's Studies International Forum*, 21(2):133–46.

Oakley, A. (2000), *Experiments in Knowing: Gender and Method in the Social Sciences*, Cambridge: Polity.

Pearce, D. (1978), 'The Feminization of Poverty: Women, Work and Welfare', *The Urban and Social Change Review*, 11(1–2): 28–36.

Pickering, S. and Ham, J. (2014), 'Hot Pants at the Border: Sorting Sex Work from Sex Trafficking', *British Journal of Criminology*, 54(1): 2–19.

Plugge, E., Douglas, N., and Fitzpatrick, R. (2006), *The Health of Women in Prison Study Findings*, Department of Public Health, University of Oxford.

Pollack, S. (2000), 'Dependency discourse as social control', in K. Hannah-Moffat and M. Shaw (eds), *An Ideal Prison? Critical Essays on Women's Imprisonment in Canada*, Halifax: Fernwood Press.

Pollack, S. (2010), 'Labelling clients "risky": Social work and the neo-liberal welfare state', *British Journal of Social Work*, 40(4): 1263–78.

Ptacek, J. (ed.) (2010), *Restorative Justice and Violence Against Women*, Oxford: Oxford University Press.

Pugh, A. (1990), 'My statistics and feminism', in L. Stanley (ed.), *Feminist Praxis*, London: Routledge.

Rafter, N. H. and Heidensohn, F. (eds) (1995), *International Feminist. Perspectives in Criminology: Engendering a Discipline*, Buckingham: Open University Press.

Rice, M. (1990), 'Challenging Orthodoxies in Feminist Theory: A Black Feminist Critiques', in L. Gelsthorpe and A. Morris (eds), *Feminist Perspectives in Criminology*, Buckingham: Open University Press.

Sassen, S. (2000) '"Women's burden": counter-geographies of globalization and feminisation of survival', *Journal of International Affairs*, 53(2): 503–24.

Shacklady Smith, L. (1978), 'Sexist assumptions and female delinquency', in C. Smart and B. Smart (eds), *Women, Sexuality and Social Control*, London: Routledge.

Sharpe, G. (2016), 'Re-Imagining Justice for Girls: A New Agenda for Research', *Youth Justice*, 16(1): 3–17.

Sheehan, R., McIvor, G., and Trotter, C. (2007), *What Works with Women Offenders*, Cullompton: Willan.

Siegel, D. (2012), 'The Mobility of Sex Workers in European Cities', *European Journal of Criminal Policy Research*, 18(3): 255–68.

Silvestri, M. and Crowther-Dowey, C. (2016), *Gender & Crime: A Human Rights Approach*, London: Sage.

Smart, C. (1976), *Women, Crime, and Criminology: A Feminist Critique*, London: Routledge & Kegan Paul.

Smart, C. (1989), *Feminism and the Power of Law*, London: Routledge.

Smart, C. (1990), 'Feminist approaches to criminology, or postmodern woman meets atavistic man', in L. Gelsthorpe and A. Morris (eds), *Feminist Perspectives in Criminology*, Buckingham: Open University Press.

Smith, C.J. and Kangaspunta, K. (2012), 'Defining Human Trafficking and Its Nuances in a Cultural Context', in J. Winterdyk, B. Perrin, and P. Reichel (eds), *Human Trafficking: Exploring the International Nature, Concerns, and Complexities*, Boca Raton: CRC Press, Taylor & Francis Group.

Snider, L. (1998a), 'Feminism, Punishment, and the Potential of Empowerment', in K. Daly and L. Maher (eds), *Criminology at the Crossroads: Feminist Readings in Crime and Justice*, Oxford: Oxford University Press.

Snider, L. (1998b), 'Towards Safer Societies: Punishment, Masculinities and Violence Against Women', *British Journal of Criminology*, 38(1): 1–39.

Snyder, R. (2008), 'What Is Third-Wave Feminism? A New Directions Essay', *Signs*, 34(1): 175–96.

Stanko, E. (1990), *Everyday Violence: How Men and Women Experience Sexual and Physical Danger*, London: Pandora.

Stanko, E. (1993), 'Ordinary fear: women, violence and personal safety', in P. Bart and E. Moran (eds), *Violence Against Women: The Bloody Footprints*, London: Sage.

Stanley, L. and Wise, S. (1983), *Breaking Out: Feminist Consciousness and Feminist Research*, London: Routledge & Kegan Paul.

Strang, H. and Braithwaite, J. (2002) (eds), *Restorative Justice and Family Violence*, Cambridge: Cambridge University Press.

Stubbs, J. (2007), 'Beyond Apology? Domestic Violence and Critical Questions for Restorative Justice', *Criminology and Criminal Justice*, 7(2): 169–87.

Temkin, J. (2002), *Rape and the Legal Process*, 2nd edn, Oxford: Oxford University Press.

Temkin, J. and Krahe, B. (2008), *Sexual Assault and the Justice Gap: A Question of Attitude*, Oxford: Hart.

Thiara, R., Hague, G., Bashall, R., Ellis, B., and Mullender, A. (2012), *Disabled Women and Domestic Violence: Responding to the Experience of Survivors*, London: Jessica Kingsley Publishers.

Troshynski, E. (2012), 'Human Trafficking', in W. DeKeseredy and M. Dragiewicz (eds), *Routledge Handbook of Critical Criminology*, London: Routledge.

Truong, T-D. (2015), 'Human Trafficking, Globalization, and Transnational Feminist Responses', in R. Baksh and W. Harcourt (eds), *The Oxford Handbook of Transnational Feminist Movements*, Oxford Handbooks Online.

United Nations Office on Drugs and Crime (UNODC) (2014), *Global Report on Trafficking in Persons* (United Nations publication), Vienna, https://www.unodc.org/documents/data-and-analysis/glotip/GLOTIP_2014_full_report.pdf, accessed 6 September 2016.

Velimesis, M. (1975), 'The Female Offender', *Crime and Delinquency Literature*, 7(1): 94–112.

Wacquant, L. (2009), *Punishing the Poor: The Neoliberal Government of Social Insecurity*, Durham, NC: Duke University Press.

Walby, S., Towers, J., and Francis, B. (2015), 'Is Violent Crime Increasing or Decreasing? A New Methodology to Measure Repeat Attacks Making Visible the Significance of Gender and Domestic Relations', *British Journal of Criminology* (published online 31 December 2015).

Walklate, S. (2003), 'Can there be a Feminist Victimology?', in P. Davies, P. Francis, and V. Jupp (eds), *Victimization: Theory, Research and Policy*, London: Palgrave Policy and Practice.

Walklate, S. (2004), *Gender, Crime and Criminal Justice*, Cullompton: Willan.

Walklate, S. (2007), *Imagining the Victim of Crime*, Milton Keynes: Open University Press.

Weedon, C. (1987), *Feminist Practice and Poststructuralist Theory*, London: Basil Blackwell.

Weitzer, R. (2007), 'The Social Construction of Sex Trafficking: Ideology and Institutionalization of a Moral Crusade', *Politics and Society*, 35(3): 447–75.

West, C. and Zimmerman, D. (1987), 'Doing Gender', *Gender & Society*, 1(2): 125–51.

Westmarland, N. (2015), *Violence against Women, Criminological Perspectives on Men's Violences*, London: Routledge.

Westmarland, N. and Gangoli, G. (2012), *International Approaches to Rape*, Bristol: Policy Press.

Worrall, A. (1990), *Offending Women*, London: Routledge.

Worrall, A. and Carlen, P. (2004), *Analysing Women's Imprisonment*, Cullompton: Willan.

Young, A. (1994), 'Feminism and the body of criminology', in D. Farrington and S. Walklate (eds), *Offender and Victims: Theory and Policy*, London: British Society of Criminology and ISTD British Criminology Conference Selected Papers, vol. 1.

10

PUBLIC OPINION, CRIME, AND CRIMINAL JUSTICE

Mike Hough and Julian V. Roberts

INTRODUCTION

Public opinion affects every stage of criminal justice. Legislators contemplate the public's reaction when they propose legislation. A policy perceived to be deeply unpopular is unlikely to be enacted, however principled or effective it may be. The police consider community views when deciding where to allocate their resources; public concern about a local issue such as the sex or drug trade may determine where or how often the police conduct patrols. Prosecutors apply a 'public interest' test when deciding whether to launch a prosecution. The evidence against a suspect may be very strong, but if the prosecutor believes it would not be in the public interest, a prosecution will not proceed.

Courts are affected indirectly by public opinion; research has demonstrated increases in sentence severity as a response to increasing public concern about crime. Enns (2016) has recently argued that changes in public punitiveness have contributed to the rise of mass incarceration in the US. The evidence of a link between public punitiveness and sentencing practice is less convincing elsewhere, but public opinion may have influenced sentencing policies and practice in other countries. For example, it has been argued that the severe sentences imposed for of offences during the English riots of 2011 was a reflection of public anger, rather than a reasoned response to mass offending (see Lightowler and Quirk 2015). Sentencing Commissions consider public views too, for example in determining the sentence ranges for various crimes. Most parole boards include members of the community to help decide whether (and when) prisoners should be released on licence or parole and release decisions may well be affected by likely community reaction.

There is no doubt then, that the public—or in some cases, what is assumed to be public opinion—influences the direction and nature of criminal justice. Whether and to what extent this is appropriate is less clear. Scholars are divided on the issue. Some argue that criminal justice would benefit from more (and more direct) public involvement (see essays in Ryberg and Roberts (2014) for contrasting views). For better or worse, however, criminal justice has become more responsive to public opinion. For example, there has been a resurgence of interest in the jury; several countries have introduced or re-introduced the jury system. In England and Wales, citizens now elect Police and Crime Commissioners who work with and provide civilian oversight for police forces. Some people refer to this as the *democratization* of criminal justice, and see it as a good thing. Others regard it as a dangerous move towards mere populism.

Deciding how to accommodate public opinion in criminal justice policy provokes fundamental questions about the way in which democracies should function. For most of the last century, politicians have tended to assume that public opinion about crime and punishment was something to be *managed*. The death penalty in Britain provides the clearest example of this: for 50 years a majority of the public has been in favour of bringing back hanging—and Parliament has repeatedly voted against reinstatement.[1] In the last two decades, however, we have witnessed signs of increasing political responsiveness to public opinion. Whether this trend should be seen as mere 'populism' or as a long-overdue sensitivity to the public depends partly on one's reading of political motives and partly on whether public opinion can be regarded as sufficiently informed to justify consideration in penal policy-making. Whatever the case, no system of justice can ignore community views entirely.

Public opinion has long been, and remains, a challenge for politicians and criminal justice practitioners. The former must devise policies that are not radically inconsistent with community views. This requires them to first determine the nature of public opinion towards criminal justice, and to recognize the limits on public knowledge of crime and the response to crime. Practitioners—whether prosecutors, judges, or parole board members—need to ensure that their decisions promote or at least do not undermine public trust and confidence. The role of scholars is to determine, using the appropriate methodologies, the true nature of public opinion and its place in the criminal justice system. Their challenge is twofold. First, to articulate the relationship that should exist between public opinion and criminal justice policies. Second, to determine the true character of public opinion. The first challenge is conceptual; the second methodological.

A large body of research has by now accumulated on public attitudes to crime and criminal justice. Much of this work consists of polls which pose short (and simple) questions about justice policies; but there is also a substantial scholarly literature drawing upon a range of methodologies, both quantitative and qualitative (see Roberts, Feilzer, and Hough 2011; Tendayi Viki and Bohner 2009). Of all the topics included in this *Handbook*, public opinion is possibly of widest relevance to other jurisdictions and within the limits of a single chapter we illustrate the discussion with examples from around the world.

This chapter is structured in four parts. Part I summarizes research on public knowledge of crime and criminal justice. We demonstrate that most people are misinformed about trends in crime and justice; for example, the majority of the public assume that crime rates are constantly rising, and people underestimate the severity of the criminal justice system. Part II moves from public *knowledge* to public *attitudes*. Unsurprisingly,

[1] We do not discuss the death penalty any further here as only a small number of western jurisdictions retain this punishment. It remains an issue in the east, however (e.g. Sato 2014).

given the misperceptions, most people are critical of the justice system. Part III links these two domains by investigating the link between levels of knowledge and attitudes to justice. Part IV explores issues of public trust, confidence, and perceived legitimacy; these have become particularly important in recent years.

PUBLIC KNOWLEDGE OF CRIME AND CRIMINAL JUSTICE

This section first examines knowledge of crime trends—about which people have both at least some direct knowledge, and rather more indirect knowledge. We then consider their—generally even shakier—knowledge of the operation of the justice system.

KNOWLEDGE OF CRIME TRENDS

Surveys of the public in many countries have for decades asked people to answer factual questions about crime and justice and the results have revealed widespread misperceptions.[2] For example, although crime rates in most Western nations have been declining steadily since the mid-1990s, the public appear unaware of this important trend. According to the Crime Survey of England and Wales (CSEW) crime rates have been falling or steady since 1995, yet the CSEW has consistently shown that most people think that crime rates have risen, at least on a national level. In the most recent year for which data are available (2013–14), almost two-thirds of the public held this view (ONS 2015a). People have a more realistic sense of crime in their own neighbourhood. Thus in the same year less than one-third of respondents thought that crime had risen in their local area.[3] This is an important finding since the same research showed that level of fear depends more upon perceptions of the local rather than national trends (ONS 2015a).

These misperceptions should not be surprising. In the first place, the measurement of crime is far from straightforward, even if the evidence is clear that crime has fallen in many Western countries.[4] Second, crime rose in most industrialized nations for most of the second half of the twentieth century, leading people to assume that crime always rises. Third, the fact that claims about crime trends are contestable inevitably means that politicians *do* contest them. For example, there was no political consensus

[2] Crime and criminal justice are not the only areas of public policy where the public are misinformed. Ipsos-MORI surveys reveal low levels of public knowledge in the field of a range of fiscal issues, including the scale of welfare cuts (see Ipsos-MORI 2015).

[3] Media coverage of crime appears responsible for misperceptions of crime trends on the national level; people are more likely to draw upon personal experience when responding to questions about local crime rates. The CSEW found that when asked to identify their source of information about national trends, over two-thirds of the sample cited TV or radio news (ONS 2015a).

[4] For example, crimes measured by the CSEW have fallen from a peak of 19 million in 1995 to just over 6 million at the end of 2015–16. This fall has been offset to some extent by new—and less well measured—crimes, especially cybercrimes (ONS 2016).

about crime trends over the first decade of this century in Britain, even if criminologists and statisticians agreed that crime had fallen. Politicians took every opportunity to attack their opponents if and when they claimed that crime was falling. Finally, the news values of the mass media, and the priority placed on dramatic stories, ensure that reports of rising crime attract much more coverage in newspapers, television, and radio than declining crime rates. In other words, there are many factors that lead people to think that crime 'out there' is still rising, even if they do not think that this is true for their own neighbourhoods.

The public in other countries also misperceive crime trends. Research in Scotland has found the same widely held belief that crime is increasing and has been doing so for many years (Scottish Executive Social Research 2007). Between 1992 and 2008, the property crime rate in the US declined by 59 per cent and reported incidents of violent crime fell by almost two-thirds (Sourcebook of Criminal Justice Statistics 2012). Yet when asked about crime trends most Americans continued to believe that there was more crime than the previous year. Over the period 1992–2011, the percentage of respondents believing that crime was rising averaged 65 per cent (Sourcebook of Criminal Justice Statistics 2012).[5] Similar distortions exist with respect to serious crimes of violence. When samples of the public were surveyed about murder trends in 2010 most people believed the murder rate had been increasing, when in fact it had been declining (Mitchell and Roberts 2010). Other misperceptions have been documented. Over three-quarters of the public in many countries including Northern Ireland, the US, Canada, Australia, New Zealand, and Barbados overestimated the proportion of crime involving violence (Doob and Roberts 1988; Amelin *et al.* 2000; Nuttall *et al.* 2003; Halstead 2015). People around the world also have overly pessimistic perceptions of the crime rates of offenders on licence or recently released from prison, and recidivism rates in general (Paulin *et al.* 2003; Roberts and White 1986; Redondo *et al.* 1996).[6]

Misperceptions also exist with respect to the workings of the justice system. Researchers in several countries have asked people to estimate the imprisonment rate for various crimes and most people underestimate the severity of the courts. This has been repeatedly documented in Britain using the CSEW. In 2010–11, almost all (99 per cent) of convicted rapists were sentenced to custody. However, when people were asked to estimate the imprisonment rate for rape, almost half (48 per cent) estimated that less than 60 per cent of all those convicted were imprisoned; another quarter (23 per cent) estimated between 60 per cent and 85 per cent. As many as 90 per cent of CSEW respondents underestimated the custody rate for domestic burglary in 2010–11 (Hough *et al.* 2013a).[7] Table 10.1 summarizes trends across four administrations of the survey.

[5] Similar trends are observed elsewhere including Australia (Roberts and Indermaur 2009; Butler and McFarlane 2009) and Canada (Doob and Roberts 1988).

[6] Beyond statistical trends, most people also have unrealistic views of institutions such as prisons. A common perception is that prisons are relatively benign (see e.g. Roberts and Hough 2005b). Criminal justice professionals who work in prison have a more realistic perception.

[7] Similar trends have been found in several other countries including Australia (Halstead 2015), Norway (Olaussen 2014), and Canada (Doob and Roberts 1988).

Table 10.1 Comparison of public estimates of the custody rate for rape, 1996 to 2011

	1996	1998	2007	2011
Roughly accurate estimate of custody rate	17%	19%	31%	29%
Small underestimate of custody rate	26%	25%	34%	23%
Large underestimate of custody rate	57%	56%	34%	48%
	100%	*100%*	*100%*	*100%*

Sources: CSEW; Hough and Roberts (1998); Mattinson and Mirrlees-Black (2000)

People recognize the limits on their own knowledge. People report knowing most about the police—presumably because they are the most visible criminal justice professionals and the ones people are most likely to encounter. Approximately three-quarters of the sample reported knowing a great deal or a fair amount about the police; self-reported levels of knowledge are much lower for other parts of the justice system. Thus well over half the sample admitted knowing 'hardly anything' about youth offending teams, and between a third and a half knowing hardly anything about the probation service, the Crown Prosecution Service, or youth courts. These branches of criminal justice are generally invisible to most people, unless they become involved in the system as a victim or witness.

The factors that shape public knowledge—or lack of knowledge—about the criminal justice system are very probably linked to knowledge about crime itself. Those people—perhaps the majority—who think that crime trends are a function of the deterrent capacity of the justice system may assume that sentencing *must* be too soft given that they believe that crime is rising. In addition, media coverage of the courts tends to focus on dramatically unusual sentences—especially where judges appear to have been unreasonably lenient.

PUBLIC ATTITUDES TO CRIMINAL JUSTICE

This section moves from consideration of public knowledge to an examination of public attitudes. We cover views on the purposes of the criminal justice system, before moving on to examine perceptions of fairness and in particular whether sentencing is adequate.

PURPOSES OF THE CRIMINAL JUSTICE SYSTEM

The criminal justice system serves multiple purposes, seeking to prevent crime before it occurs as well as to punish convicted offenders. Criminal policies—and media coverage—generally pay more attention to punishment rather than prevention. Crime prevention programs such as *Neighbourhood Watch* are less newsworthy than sentencing laws such as the 'three strikes' mandatory penalties. It is often suggested that the public are more interested in punishment than prevention; indeed the public are often described as being more punitive than the courts—a description we will contest later in this chapter.

The public believe that crime is caused by more than individual decision-making, and that crime reduction is therefore not a task exclusively for the criminal justice system. As long ago as 1947, Americans identified 'lack of parental control and supervision' as the principal cause of youth crime (see Erskine 1974). This finding is echoed in polls conducted in many other countries (see Roberts and Hastings 2011). Over the decade 2000–2009, MORI asked the British public to identify the most effective ways to reduce crime. On every occasion better parenting and better discipline were chosen most often and by over two-thirds in the most recent administration (2009). The 'get tough' option—'put more offenders in prison'—attracted least support (MORI 2010). Most recently a UK survey found that people believed rewards for good behaviour rather than punishment for bad behaviour was more effective (Onepoll 2015).

Politicians often believe that getting tough with offenders carries political benefits. The consequence is punitive populism (e.g. Pratt 2007; Roberts *et al.* 2003). Politicians in a number of Western jurisdictions have promoted punitive criminal justice policies such as mandatory sentencing more with an eye to winning votes than to actually reducing crime.[8] The emergence of penal populism raises a number of questions. The first is whether politicians are sufficiently good at 'reading' the popular mood to enable them to craft their policies to respond to this mood. The right answer, in all probability, is that they are, at least if the public mood is taken to be the 'top of the head' opinions that people offer in response to dramatic newspaper headlines or claims made at the hustings. They are certainly more exposed to, and sensitive to opinion of this sort than academic criminologists. Being seen to be soft on crime is a vote-loser—and being tough on crime can be electorally decisive (see Downes and Morgan 2012, for a discussion). Behind this question is a more complex one, about the political legitimacy of responding to public preferences that are poorly informed. We shall return to this question, but first, let us review the evidence about public support for 'tough on crime' penal policies, as reflected by well-conducted survey research.

When a national sample of the UK public was asked to identify the best response to crime they were far more likely to support prevention than punishment. Thus, two thirds of the polled public favoured addressing the causes of crime, less than one third supported tougher punishment (Roberts and Hastings 2011). Given a choice between punishment and crime prevention through social development, the US public has repeatedly chosen the former, as can be seen in Table 10.2. On the face of it, this message appears lost on politicians who perceive the public to be very supportive of punitive responses to crime. US research also suggests that there are electoral benefits to be gained by promoting crime prevention: a poll found that over four-fifths of

[8] Few politicians are likely to admit to this publicly, of course, so the evidence about populist motives is almost always circumstantial.

Table 10.2 Public attitudes toward approaches to lower the crime rate (US)

	Address social problems	More law enforcement
1989	61%	32%
1990	57%	36%
1992	67%	25%
1994	57%	39%
2000	68%	27%
2003	69%	29%
2006	65%	31%
2010	64%	32%
Average	64%	31%

Source: Adapted from *Sourcebook of Criminal Justice Statistics* (2011)

respondents stated that they would be much *more* likely to vote for a political candidate who endorsed investing in crime prevention programs (e.g. Cooper and Sechrest 2008). In comparison, a much lower proportion of respondents said they would be more likely to support a candidate who endorsed tougher sentencing. Public support for non-punitive responses to crime is not limited to the issue of crime reduction. When asked to identify the best way to prevent reoffending, there was much more support for rehabilitation than punishment (MORI 2010).

At the time of writing (in 2016), there are some signs that the intensive competition between the political parties to be 'tough on crime' may be waning in the UK and the US. Certainly there have been marked falls in levels of public anxiety about crime since 1995 (ONS 2015a), and crime is much less salient as a social issue than it was in the period from the early 1990s to the mid-2000s (MORI 2016a)—perhaps because these worries have been displaced by concerns about the economy since 2007. This may have opened up possibilities for more level-headed politics on law and order. It remains to be seen whether the temperature of penal debate is genuinely cooling, or whether we shall see a return to the overheated climate of the last two decades if economic concerns wane.

PERCEPTIONS OF LENIENCY BIAS

Reviewing polls conducted over the past 40 years, it is clear that people believe that the justice system goes to excessive lengths to protect the rights of defendants. People believe that the scales of justice are skewed in favour of the suspect, accused, or offender, at the expense of the victim. According to the public, 'criminals' are treated better, and have more rights than crime victims. Thus 70 per cent of Americans agreed that the laws and the courts are more concerned with protecting the rights of defendants than they are with protecting the rights of victims while three-quarters of respondents to a poll in Britain agreeing that: 'the law works to the advantage of the criminal and not victims' (MORI 2000). In Australia, 81 per cent of the public believed the criminal justice system did a good job of respecting the rights of accused persons, but less than half felt the system met the needs of victims (Halstead 2015).

Sentencing represents the apex of the criminal process and the element of the justice system which attracts most media attention and public interest. This stage has also accounted for more research on public opinion than all the other components of the justice system.

Public views—or rather views ascribed to the public—appear to have fueled a more punitive response to offending on the part of sentencers. For example, penal policies in England and Wales over the period 1992–2007 became tougher in part because successive administrations cited the need to respond to public views: a Conservative Home Secretary in the mid-1990s justified proposals for tougher sentencing by reference to the need to maintain public confidence (see Ashworth and Hough 1996). The subsequent Labour government expressed a desire to align policies more closely with its perception that the public demanded more punitive responses to crime and anti-social behaviour (Allen and Hough 2008). Research in several jurisdictions (including England and New Zealand) has identified sentencers' responsiveness to public pressure as a probable cause of harsher sentencing (e.g. Millie *et al.* 2005; Pratt 2007). Many punitive and ineffective sentencing policies of recent years such as 'three strikes' sentencing laws have arisen in response to public concern about serious crime (Roberts *et al.* 2003). The historical record is therefore not especially encouraging for advocates of greater public consultation. Seen from this perspective the public represent a source of pressure towards more punitive sentencing.

A great deal of research going back 50 years has assessed the degree of 'fit' between public sentencing preferences and court practice. The overall picture to emerge, especially in common law countries, is as follows. If general questions are asked such as: 'Are the courts too lenient, too harsh or about right?', the weight of opinion will always be that they are too lenient. Thus the CSEW routinely finds that three quarters of the population consistently say that the courts are too lenient, and the percentage saying 'much too lenient' grew by 10 per cent in the first decade of this century (Hough *et al.* 2013a). The reasons for this can be found in the previous discussion of public knowledge. When people think of the typical crime, the typical image of an offender that comes to mind is of a violent crime committed by a recidivist (Indermaur 1987). Similarly, when people think about sentences they have read about, they are likely to recall some sentence that appeared so lenient that it attracted media coverage. In short, people's 'top of the head' reactions to sentencing are likely to draw upon an unrepresentative archetype of crimes and punishments.

This finding on attitudes to sentencing has been replicated over time, using different methodologies and across disparate jurisdictions. For example, 74 per cent in Scotland (Justice 1 Committee 2007) and 85 per cent of respondents in South Africa expressed the view that sentences were too lenient (Schonteich 1999). US polls also reveal little variation over time in the percentage perceiving sentences to be too lenient. This did not vary outside a narrow range from 79 per cent in 1975 to 67 per cent in 2002

(*Sourcebook of Criminal Justice Statistics* 2012) and the same pattern emerges from Australia and Canada[9] (see Roberts and Indermaur 2009).[10]

Such findings led many politicians to assume that the public are much more punitive than the courts. However, a poll using a simple and very general question asking if sentences are tough enough is an inappropriate method of seeing whether opinion and sentencing practice are in step, if only because it takes no account of respondents' level of knowledge. Researchers have therefore given people summaries of actual or realistic cases and asked them to impose a hypothetical sentence. In this way participants are more informed, having been given the details of the crime and the offender. Public 'sentences' emerging from this method are then compared to the sentences that were actually imposed in these cases. The advantage of this approach is that it sidesteps problems of ignorance about actual practice. Assessed in this way, public sentencing preferences and judicial practice are usually closer together—the 'punitiveness gap' diminishes (see Roth 2014).

One example of this in England and Wales comes from the CSEW, which has since 1996 asked a sub-sample to 'sentence' a 23-year-old burglar with previous convictions who broke into an old man's home and stole electrical goods. The case on which the vignette was modelled had attracted a sentence of three years, reduced on appeal to two (Hough and Roberts 1998). However, when the public were asked to sentence this case, only 54 per cent of the sample favoured imprisonment at all. Clearly, the attitudes of the public and the practice of the courts are closer than polls would suggest. This general finding has been replicated on numerous occasions in Britain and elsewhere (e.g. Balvig *et al.* 2015; see Roberts and Hough 2005a, for a review).

The argument that public punitiveness is a myth should not be overstated, however (see de Keijser, van Koppen, and Elffers 2007). Crime raises strong emotions of anger and anxiety in people, not only when it involves serious harm but also in more mundane crimes. Being the victim of crime is at the very least a significant irritant, and at worst a life-deforming experience. It is not surprising that people expect politicians to find an effective response to it. Whether this response should be simply punitive turns partly on questions of effectiveness—but it also depends in part on what a *properly informed* public would support.

ATTITUDES TO INCARCERATION: A SEA CHANGE IN PUBLIC OPINION?

The findings discussed so far, both in the area of knowledge and opinion, suggest that little has changed over the past few decades: knowledge has generally been poor, and opinions stable. In this section, we highlight an exception to this picture of stability.

One of the most significant recent trends in public opinion is a swing away from support for imprisonment. Even in the US, where the public has traditionally been more

[9] Comparable findings emerge from other countries, including Belgium (Parmentier *et al.* 2004), Germany (Kury *et al.* 2002), and Barbados (Nuttall *et al.* 2003).

[10] The perception of leniency is only part of the story; courts are also criticized for being out of touch with 'what ordinary people think'. Thus 82 per cent held this view of judges in England and Wales (Hough and Roberts 1998).

punitive in its attitudes to offenders, members of the public appear to be growing more sceptical of the use of custody. One survey found that half the US voters expressed the view that there were too many people in prison (Lake, Gotoff, and Pultorak 2013). In a California referendum held in 2012 (Proposition 36) voters overwhelmingly approved reforms to reduce the lengths of prison sentences. This change in public attitudes probably reflects the grass roots movement to amend or repeal mandatory sentences for drug offenders and a growing public awareness of the striking racial disparities of prison populations in the US (The Opportunity Agenda 2015). A further factor in the US is almost certainly the growing public and political awareness of the very heavy tax burden imposed by the high levels of imprisonment in that country. Signs of a similar sea-change in opinion can be seen elsewhere: Approximately three-quarters of the British public endorsed measures to reduce crime other than imprisonment (Onepoll 2015).

We live in an era of austerity, in which governments around the world have been reducing the budgets of all public services, including the criminal justice system. The UK government has cut drastically the amount it spends on legal aid, the court system, and prisons. The public appear very sensitive to the issue, even without knowing how much the system actually costs. For example, in 2013–14 the average cost of providing a prison place was approximately £35,000, yet when asked to estimate the costs of a prison place, approximately half the public underestimated the figure. Yet almost three-quarters of the public agreed that the government should use cheaper punishments (Onepoll 2015). Similarly, when people are informed about the true costs of custody, support for imprisonment declines. Roberts and Hough (2011) found evidence that majorities thought that sentencers should take costs into account in sentencing—especially for less serious cases. The public in the US also overwhelmingly support increasing the use of less expensive alternatives to prison (Pew Centre on the States 2012).

To summarize this set of findings, there is now a large body of research that qualifies the conventional view that the public are deeply punitive towards those convicted of crimes. Simple questions yield simple—and largely negative—answers. However, when people are asked to deliberate about particular cases, a different and more nuanced picture emerges, where many people are less tough-minded than sentencers. We would not want to overstate this point, however: some crimes—especially those with very vulnerable victims—elicit anger and revulsion, and for these, there is little public tolerance for lenient sentencing.

THE RELATIONSHIP BETWEEN KNOWLEDGE AND OPINION

How malleable are public attitudes to criminal justice? A considerable literature has arisen around attempts to change public attitudes—to improve the public image of criminal justice—by providing information about the system. The hypothesis being tested is that if knowledge levels improve, attitudes will become more accepting of current practice. One approach to changing attitudes or to increase confidence might simply be to dispel the most persistent and prevalent misperceptions. The general research strategy in this field has been to provide some members of the public with information about a particular issue—such as the death penalty, community sentencing, or parole—and then to measure attitudes to the issue in question. These peoples' attitudes are then compared to those held by the general public or by other participants who have not been provided with information. Since many of these studies have used an experimental approach—involving random assignment to condition—differences in attitudes or changes in opinions can be attributed to the role of information.

Several studies are illustrative. The first involved a 'deliberative poll' carried out in England in 1994, in which almost 300 people spent a weekend together, hearing lectures, receiving information on crime and punishment, and being given opportunities to 'deliberate' on the issues. The idea was to see to what extent public views differed from their 'top of the head' opinions, and to see if any change was durable over time. Analysis of 'before and after' surveys—including a follow-up survey 10 months after the event—showed significant and lasting change, at least on some issues (Hough and Park 2002). On balance, attitudes shifted in a liberal direction. More recently, Marteache (2012) conducted a similar study and found that attitudes were less punitive compared to opinions expressed in polls. The importance of these studies lies in their demonstration that considered views *are* genuinely different from those charted by straightforward polls, and that attitude change following deliberation can be lasting.

Mitchell and Roberts (2011) explored the effects of information on public attitudes to sentencing for murder. These authors tested the hypothesis that providing information about sentencing for this most serious crime would change opinions. Most people believe that offenders sentenced to life imprisonment are free once they leave prison on licence; in fact, these offenders are subject to recall to prison for the rest of their life. Half the respondents to a nation-wide survey were given a brief factual description of what actually happens to offenders convicted of murder; the other half of the sample received no such information. All respondents were then asked a series of questions about sentencing in cases of murder. Participants who were given the additional information were less critical of sentencing, and less punitive in the sentences that they imposed in case histories.[11]

Finally, two deliberative polls in Japan (Sato 2014; Sato and Bacon 2015) offer a more nuanced view of the impact of providing information and opportunities for deliberation, in the context of support for the death penalty in Japan. When provided with information about hangings, some participants changed their position on the death penalty; of these, some shifting towards abolition, others towards retention. The more striking finding was that exposure to information and deliberation tended to increase people's uncertainty about their position, even if they did not change their views, and to increase their tolerance of the views of others. The implication is that those who factor public opinion into their decisions should not construe strongly expressed opinions to be strongly held and unamenable to change.

[11] Hough and Roberts (ibid) report similar findings for England and Wales. (For comparable findings in Australia and Canada, see Jones and Weatherburn (2010) and Sanders and Roberts (2000).)

These studies demonstrate that it is possible to change attitudes through the provision of information. This is not to say that public cynicism about justice can be traced exclusively to misinformation about crime and punishment. As discussed above, it would be naïve to ignore the deep-seated anger with which some people respond to crime, and even more naïve to think that this could be effectively countered by public education initiatives (see Loader and Sparks 2011). Increasing public levels of knowledge is not easy and attitude change does not always occur; the challenge is to attract peoples' attention and to counter news media misrepresentations of justice (see Feilzer 2007). At the same time, the evidence is overwhelming that public misunderstanding is at least a contributory factor to the overheated nature of political debate about crime and punishment.

TRUST, CONFIDENCE, AND PERCEIVED LEGITIMACY

Public trust or confidence has become one of the most researched issues in the field of public opinion and justice. Recognizing the importance of maintaining public faith in justice, almost all Western nations have measured levels of public confidence in criminal justice (see Hough *et al.* 2013a and for reviews, Hough and Roberts 2004; Maffei and Markopolou 2014). Polls and surveys have revealed low levels of public confidence in justice across many countries. As a result, a number of jurisdictions have also launched initiatives to promote public trust in the administration of justice.

EFFECT OF MANDATE OF THE JUSTICE SYSTEM ON PUBLIC TRUST IN JUSTICE

Confidence and trust are often used as synonyms—and indeed, in many European languages, both terms are translated into the same word. Anglophone scholars have nevertheless regarded confidence as a backward-looking concept, assessing past performance, and trust as a forward-looking one, relating to expectations (e.g. Skogan 2006). We think that 'trust' is the more accurate term, having connotations of something that has to be *earned*. Arguably, too, the justice system has features that differentiate it clearly from other public services and this makes trust a more appropriate term than confidence. Public services and utilities typically provide *personal* services that are financed *publicly*. Health, schooling, and refuse collection, for example, are services that can be bought in the market place, but in some jurisdictions they are publicly funded, through taxes. As taxpayers we can reasonably expect to have confidence in the quality of the work they do. Criminal justice is, by contrast, a public good from which we all benefit, but we often have no choice about being the object of *regulation*. Our behaviour—or, perhaps, our misbehaviour—falls within the ambit of the justice system whether we like it or not. Given that it is not our choice to be regulated, it is, for reasons to be discussed, especially important that we can invest our trust in the fairness of the process.

Even where we choose to involve the justice system—through reporting a crime to the police, for example—this is often a reluctant or coerced choice that may embroil us in processes that are unwelcome. Explaining the lack of public confidence in the courts, Kritzer and Voelker (1998) wrote that: 'It is not surprising that courts generate dissatisfaction; they are associated with unpleasant things such as criminals, injuries, divorces and the like. Many, perhaps most, people are probably as likely to choose voluntarily to go to court as they are to choose to have their wisdom teeth extracted' (p. 59). Comparison with the National Health Service is instructive. The patient's well-being is the foremost concern of the NHS, and of the professionals who work in the system. However, the justice system has many functions besides responding to crime victims' needs. For many victims, the protracted nature of legal proceedings, the experience of being cross-examined in court, or their inability to influence sentencing may all create frustration. This helps to explain the negative views of the justice system expressed by many victims of crime.

TRUST IN THE LOCAL AND NATIONAL RESPONSE TO CRIME

In 2003, British respondents were asked: *Overall, how confident are you about the way crime is dealt with*? The question was posed with respect to the respondent's area, and the country as a whole, with very different outcomes—as was the case when people were asked about local and national crime trends. When the question asked about confidence in the *local* response, significantly more people were confident than not—with almost two-thirds (63 per cent) reporting confidence, and 34 per cent lacking confidence. At the *national* level, 47 per cent expressed confidence, 51 per cent lacked confidence (MORI 2003). More recently, a survey asked people whether they were confident that the criminal justice service 'works to bring criminals to justice', and less than one third expressed confidence (YouGov 2011). Conclusions about levels of trust in criminal justice can therefore only be drawn having first made a distinction between the local and national levels. At the local level, a strong majority of the public has trust in the criminal justice response to crime. At the national level, a slim majority *lacks* trust. Which evaluation reflects the true state of public trust in criminal justice? Public attitudes to the local response are probably more important. Knowledge about crime across the country, and the nature of the criminal justice response, comes from the news media, and is indirect in nature. Public trust in the response of their local police and other authorities is far more likely to reflect direct experience.

TRUST IN FAIRNESS AND TRUST IN EFFECTIVENESS

Trust in justice has many dimensions. Survey respondents make clear distinctions between their judgements about the fairness of the criminal justice system and its effectiveness (Jackson *et al.* 2012; Hough *et al.* 2013a; Hough *et al.* 2013b). The CSEW has found that people's levels of trust in the fairness of the criminal justice system are consistently higher than trust in effectiveness. In the 2013–14 CSEW, 64 per cent of respondents said they were very or fairly confident the justice system was fair and 48 per cent said they were very or fairly confident the it was effective (Jansson 2015). Similar trends have recently been found in Australia (Jones and Weatherburn 2010). Since 2007–08 both indices show that trust is growing. Although it is often said that UK institutions face a crisis of trust, long-run trends since 1983 show that in common with most other occupations—with the exception of politicians—trust in both judges and the police have increased (MORI 2016b). Since 2007–08, trust in both the fairness and effectiveness of the criminal justice system in England and Wales has increased (Jansson 2015).

CONFIDENCE IN SPECIFIC FUNCTIONS OF JUSTICE

Considerable variability exists in public levels of confidence with respect to specific functions of the criminal justice system. A MORI poll in 2009 found that confidence levels are much higher for some functions than for others. Over three-quarters of the public have confidence that the system respects the rights of accused persons and treats them fairly, but less than one quarter of the polled public are confident that the system is effective in dealing with young people accused of a crime. A more detailed picture of the functions that attract the lowest levels of public confidence may be derived from a MORI survey. There is a clear discrepancy between public perceptions of the importance of different objectives of criminal justice, and the extent to which people are confident that these objectives are being achieved. Specifically, people were asked (a) to rate the importance of specific functions such as 'bringing people who commit crimes to justice' and (b) to express their level of confidence that these objectives were being realized. Respondents were asked about more than 20 criminal justice objectives.

As can be seen in Table 10.3, the objectives people rated as being most important tended to be ones that attracted the least amount of confidence. Thus 'creating a safe society' was ranked second in importance, but tenth in the level of confidence that

Table 10.3 Public rankings of importance and confidence in criminal justice system functions

	Importance Ranking (based on % rating function as 'absolutely essential')	Confidence ranking (based on % responding 'very' or 'fairly' confident)
Treating all people fairly, regardless of race	1. 72%	2. 61%
Creating a society where people feel safe	2. 69%	14. 41%
Bringing people who commit crimes to justice	3. 68%	10. 50%
Dealing effectively with sex offenders	4. 68%	11. 51%
Dealing effectively with violent crime	5. 67%	6. 53%
Reducing the level of crime	6. 63%	17. 40%
Stopping offenders from committing more crimes	7. 60%	20. 24%

Source: MORI (2003); Questions: 1. 'How important, if at all, do you regard each of the following aspects of the criminal justice system? For each, please give me a number from 1–10, where 1 is not at all important and 10 is absolutely essential'; 2. How confident are you that the system is performing this function?'.

Table 10.4 Public confidence in branches of criminal justice

	% Confident that:
Police are effective at catching criminals	69%
Crown Prosecution Service is effective at prosecuting people accused of committing a crime	55%
The courts are effective in dealing with cases promptly	45%
The courts are effective at giving punishments which fit the crime	31%
Prisons are effective at punishing offenders who have been convicted of a crime	32%
Prisons are effective at rehabilitating offenders who have been convicted of a crime	22%
The probation service is effective at preventing criminals from reoffending	26%
The Criminal Justice System as a whole is fair	48%

Source: adapted from Jansson (2015). Contains public sector information licensed under the Open Government Licence v3.0.

this objective was being achieved. Similarly, 'reducing the level of crime' was one of the highest ranked in importance (sixth) but attracted a very low confidence ranking (17th). In general, people gave high confidence scores to functions such as protecting the rights of offenders, and lower scores to effectiveness in terms of preventing crime or protecting the public. The nature of the functions on the list is also revelatory. It suggests that much of the public's lack of confidence springs from concern about personal safety. People have the least amount of confidence that the system is dealing with crimes of high visibility: mugging, burglary, and drug dealing, for example. It is also interesting that the lowest confidence rating occurs for the issue of preventing reoffending. This finding is consistent with a number of other polls that have found that people believe reoffending rates are high, and that the system is generally incapable of addressing the problem. In this respect, people are right on both counts.

COMPARISONS WITHIN AND ACROSS CRIMINAL JUSTICE SYSTEMS

The CSEW has repeatedly measured public ratings of the various elements of the criminal justice system. When asked to rate the performance of the police and other professions a clear hierarchy emerges. Table 10.4 draws upon the CSEW to summarize levels of public confidence in various branches of criminal justice. As can be seen, the levels are very variable with the police attracting the highest levels of confidence. The public expressed significantly less confidence in the ability of the probation service (Table 10.4, and see Jansson 2015).[12]

[12] The hierarchy of trust—with the police at the top and the courts at the bottom—is found in other countries. For example, three-quarters of the New Zealand public gave the police excellent or good ratings, only 45 per cent were as positive about the courts (Paulin *et al.* 2003; Roberts 2007).

The 2010 European Social Survey (ESS) is the most up-to-date and reliable guide to variations in trust in justice across Europe, as this included a 45-question module on the topic (Jackson *et al.* 2012). Earlier findings from a wider range of countries are also available from the 2005 World Values Survey (Lappi-Seppälä 2011). The picture to emerge from the ESS is consistent with surveys that measure other aspects of social trust and well-being. The Scandinavian countries score highest on various measures of trust in the police and courts, and ex-communist countries tend to score lowest. The UK generally tends to fall in the second quartile, depending on which measure is being examined (Hough *et al.* 2013b).

TRUST IN JUSTICE, LEGITIMACY, AND COMPLIANCE WITH THE LAW

As the discussion in the first part of this chapter shows, research on public opinion in this field has aimed to identify the penal policies that the public will or will not tolerate. It has been conducted in a somewhat a-theoretical way; insofar as any hypotheses were made explicit, these tested and challenged the prevailing political assumptions about public punitivity. To the extent that research measured trust in justice, it did so largely because public trust in any public service was reckoned to be of self-evident value, and thus worth monitoring. Alongside this research, however, there is an important body of work tracing the linkages between trust in justice, perceptions of legitimacy, and public compliance and cooperation with the law.

These 'compliance theories' can be located within broader theories of normative compliance tracing back to Durkheimian and Weberian thinking about the roots of social order. On the one hand, there has been increasing (or perhaps, more accurately, rediscovered) interest over the last two decades in the relationship between 'political economy', which trace the connections between the social distribution of wealth and attachment to—or detachment from—social norms; such theories well fall outside of the scope of this chapter. On the other hand, there are also compliance theories about the impact on societal norms of the institutions of formal social control. Thus Robinson (2013) argues that if the law's potential for building a moral consensus is to be exploited, sentences must be aligned at least to some degree with public sentiments. Tyler (e.g. 2011) emphasizes the need for justice institutions to pursue fair and respectful *processes*—in contrast to *outcomes*—as the surest strategies for building trust in justice, and thus institutional legitimacy and compliance with the law. This is the central hypothesis in procedural justice theory. Procedural justice theories offer the possibility of resolving the tension that is often thought to exist between effective crime control and the respecting of people's rights. They suggest that fair, respectful, and legal behaviour on the part of justice officials is not only ethically desirable, but is a prerequisite for effective justice.

Studies in the US, the UK, and elsewhere (e.g. Kochel 2012; Gau *et al.* 2012; Bradford *et al.* 2013; Mazerolle *et al.* 2013) have consistently found that in general terms, the expected relationships are found between fairness, trust, perceptions of legitimacy, cooperation with the law, and compliance with the law. In other words, there is evidence that the way in which the institutions of justice treat people can support or erode their consent to the rule of law. There is an emerging consensus amongst legitimacy theorists that the quality of treatment that justice officials mete out to citizens is a key determinant of citizen perceptions of legitimacy. The key elements of procedurally just treatment appear to be: treating people respectfully; explaining the reasons for decisions and action; allowing people 'voice'; and 'playing by the rules'—whether these are organizational standards or legal requirements. Whilst these conclusions may appear little more than common sense, providing the foundation of policing by consent over generations, it is less obvious that public trust in procedural justice emerges as a stronger predictor of institutional legitimacy than public trust in institutional effectiveness. However, this is a consistent finding in the studies cited above, and one that has obvious and important policy implications.

It should be stressed, however, that there are limits to the ability of survey research to capture such subtle processes accurately (see Hough 2012; Jackson *et al.* 2012). There are problems of measurement—for example in devising sensitive measures of trust and perceptions of legitimacy, and in measuring people's compliance with the law through self-report measures. There is continuing debate about the different dimensions of fairness in justice (see, e.g., Bottoms and Tankebe 2012; Jackson *et al.* 2012; Tankebe 2013.) Scholars usually distinguish between procedural fairness, distributive fairness, and outcome fairness, and it seems likely that different dimensions may play a greater or lesser role at different points in the criminal process. For example, whilst it is very well established that procedural fairness is critically important in *policing*, qualitative work indicates that in the *courts,* sentencing outcomes are what really matter to the defendant, to the victim and (cf. Jacobson, Hunter, and Kirby 2015). Further, it seems highly likely that in jurisdictions where relations between police and policed are strained, distributive justice—treating different groups in the same way—may be a key factor.

Difficulties arise in establishing the direction of causal relationships, especially in cross-sectional (snapshot) surveys: does distrust in the police reduce obedience to the law, for example, or does law-breaking prompt distrust? There is an emerging body of experimental research involving randomized controlled trials (notably Mazerolle *et al.* 2013) which has begun to address these issues of causality. There are also problems of 'reach' in survey research of this sort, in that the most important groups to research—marginalized young men, for example—are least likely to take part in survey interviews.

Despite the limitations, research of this kind is important; deriving a better understanding of the relationships between people's moral norms, their consent to the rule of law, and their perceptions and experience of the justice system is a major enterprise—and one which in our view goes to the heart of the criminological enterprise. There are signs, too, that this body of research is beginning to affect policy. One example is the report commissioned by President Obama in the wake of several highly contentious shootings by police of Black suspects. That report's main recommendation was that 'Law enforcement agencies should adopt procedural justice as the guiding principle for internal and external policies and practices to guide their interactions with rank and file officers and with the citizens they serve.' (President's Task Force 2015: 1). A significant development in the UK has been a series of 'legitimacy inspections' by Her Majesty's Inspectorate of Constabulary (HMIC 2015).

CONCLUSION

This chapter has reviewed empirical research into attitudes to crime and punishment which now spans more than half a century. Several conclusions can be drawn. First, the public in most developed countries tend towards cynicism about their justice systems, thinking that the police and the courts are ineffective and overly lenient towards offenders. Second, these attitudes are grounded in part on misinformation. We have not reviewed the relationship between media portrayals of crime and justice and public trust in justice, but there is a *prima facie* case for believing that the media provide little accurate information and have a corrosive impact on public trust in criminal justice. There is good evidence to show that public trust in the police, the courts, and other criminal justice agencies is of critical importance to the effective operation of justice. People obey the law as much out of normative considerations as they do out of instrumental (or self-interested) ones. A lack of trust in justice is likely to damage the mechanisms that promote compliance with the law, because it corrodes perceptions of the legitimacy of the institutions of justice. So governments need to attend more closely to research that identifies the drivers of trust and that can provide early warnings of any crisis in public trust in criminal justice.

■ SELECTED FURTHER READING

A summary of British polling on criminal justice topics can be found in Duffy *et al.*, *Closing the Gaps: Crime and Public Perceptions* (2008). For reviews of the literature, see Roberts and Hough, *Understanding Public Attitudes to Criminal Justice* (2005a); Cullen, Fisher, and Applegate, 'Public Opinion about Punishment and Corrections' (2000); and Van de Walle and Raine, *Explaining Attitudes Towards the Justice System in the UK and Europe* (2008). A good discussion of the psychology of punitiveness can be found in Maruna, Matravers, and King, 'Disowning our shadow: A psychoanalytic approach to understanding punitive public attitudes' (2004). For readings on a diversity of issues, see Wood and Gannon, *Public Opinion and Criminal Justice* (2009).

■ REFERENCES

ALLEN, R. and HOUGH, M. (2008), 'Does it matter? Reflections on the effectiveness of institutionalised public participation in the development of sentencing policy', in K. Gelb and A. Freiberg (eds), *Penal Populism: Sentencing Councils and Sentencing Policy*, Cullompton: Willan.

AMELIN, K., WILLIS, M., BLAIR, C., and DONNELLY, D. (2000), *Attitudes to Crime, Crime Reduction and Community Safety in Northern Ireland. Review of the Criminal Justice System in Northern Ireland*, Research Report No. 1, Belfast: Northern Ireland Office.

ASHWORTH, A. and HOUGH, M. (1996), 'Sentencing and the Climate of Opinion', *Criminal Law Review*, November, 776–87.

BALVIG, F., GUNNLAUGSSON, H., JERRE, K., THAM, H., and KINNUNEN, A. (2015), 'The public sense of justice in Scandinavia: A study of attitudes towards punishments', *European Journal of Criminology*, 12(3): 342–61.

BOTTOMS, A. and TANKEBE, J. (2012), 'Beyond procedural justice: A dialogic approach to legitimacy in criminal justice', *Journal of Criminal Law and Criminology*, 102(1): 119–70.

BRADFORD, B., HUQ, A., JACKSON, J., and ROBERTS, B. (2013), 'What Price Fairness When Security is at Stake? Police Legitimacy in South Africa', *Regulation and Governance*, doi: 10.1111/rego.12012.

BUTLER, A. and MCFARLANE, K. (2009), Public Confidence in the NSW Criminal Justice System, available at: http://www.lawlink.nsw.gov.au/sentencingcouncil, accessed 29 July 2016.

Cooper and Sechrest Associates (2008), *Third Way Crime Poll Highlights*, Washington: Cooper and Sechrest Associates.

Cullen, F., Fisher, B., and Applegate, B. (2000), 'Public Opinion about Punishment and Corrections', in M. Tonry (ed.), *Crime and Justice*, Chicago: University of Chicago Press.

De Keijser, J., Van Koppen, P., and Elffers, H. (2007), 'Bridging the gap between judges and the public? A multi-method study', *Journal of Experimental Criminology*, 3(2): 131–61.

Doob, A. N. and Roberts, J. V. (1988), 'Public Punitiveness and Public Knowledge of the Facts: Some Canadian Surveys', in N. Walker and M. Hough (eds), *Public Attitudes to Sentencing*, Aldershot: Gower.

Downes, D. and Morgan, R. (2012), 'Overtaking on the Left: the politics of law and order in the 'Big Society', in M. Maguire, R. Morgan, and R. Reiner (eds), *The Oxford Handbook of Criminology*, 5th edn, Oxford: Oxford University Press.

Duffy, B., Wake, R., Burrows, T., and Bremner, P. (2008), *Closing the Gaps: Crime and Public Perceptions*, London: MORI.

Enns, P. (2016), *Incarceration Nation*, Cambridge: Cambridge University Press.

Erskine, H. (1974), 'The Polls: Causes of Crime', *Public Opinion Quarterly*, 38(2): 288–98.

Feilzer, M. (2007), 'The Magic Bullet', *Prison Service Journal*, 170: 39–44.

Gau, J. M., Corsaro, N., Stewart, E. A., and Brunson, R. K. (2012), 'Examining Macro-Level Impacts on Procedural Justice and Police Legitimacy', *Journal of Criminal Justice*, 40(4): 333–43.

Halstead, I. (2015), 'Public Confidence in the New South Wales Criminal Justice System: 2014 update', *Crime and Justice Bulletin*, Number 182, New South Wales Bureau of Crime Statistics and Research.

HMIC (2015), PEEL: Police legitimacy 2015. A national overview, London: Her Majesty's Inspectorate of Constabulary, available at: https://www.justiceinspectorates.gov.uk/hmic/wp-content/uploads/peel-police-legitimacy-2015.pdf, accessed 29 July 2016.

Hough, M. (2012), 'Researching trust in the police and trust in justice: A UK perspective', *Policing and Society*, 22(3): 332–45.

Hough, M., Bradford, B., Jackson, J., and Roberts, J. V. (2013a), 'Attitudes to Crime and Trust in Justice: Findings from the Crime Survey for England and Wales', London: Ministry of Justice.

Hough, M., Jackson, J., and Bradford, B. (2013b), 'Trust in justice and the legitimacy of legal authorities: topline findings from a European comparative study', in S. Body-Gendrot, M. Hough, R. Levy, K. Kerezsi, and S. Snacken (eds), *European Handbook of Criminology*, London: Routledge.

Hough, M. and Park, A. (2002), 'How Malleable are Public Attitudes to Crime and Punishment?' in J. V. Roberts and M. Hough (eds), *Changing Attitudes to Punishment: Public Opinion, Crime and Justice*, Cullompton, Willan.

Hough, M. and Roberts, J. V. (1998), *Attitudes to Punishment: Findings from the British Crime Survey*, Home Office Research Study No. 179, London: Home Office.

Hough, M. and Roberts, J. V. (2004), *Confidence in Justice: An International Review*, London: Home Office.

Indermaur, D. (1987), 'Public Perception of Sentencing in Perth', *Australian and New Zealand Journal of Criminology*, 20(3): 163–83.

Ipsos-Mori (2015), *The Ipsos-MORI Almanac*, London: MORI.

Jackson, J., Bradford, B., Hough, M., Myhill, A., Quinton, P., and Tyler, T. (2012), 'Why do People Comply with the Law? Legitimacy and the Influence of Legal Institutions', *British Journal of Criminology*, 52(6): 1051–71.

Jacobson, J., Hunter, G., and Kirby, A. (2015), *Inside Crown Court: Personal Experiences and Questions of Legitimacy*, Bristol: Policy Press.

Jansson, K. (2015), *Public Confidence in the Criminal Justice System—findings from the Crime Survey for England and Wales (2013/14)*, London: Ministry of Justice.

Jones, C. and Weatherburn, D. (2010), 'Public Confidence in the NSW Criminal Justice System: A Survey of the NSW Public', *Australian and New Zealand Journal of Criminology*, 43(3): 506–25.

Justice 1 Committee (2007), Public attitudes towards sentencing and alternatives to imprisonment, available at: http://archive.scottish.parliament.uk/business/committees/historic/justice1/reports-02/j1r02-pats-02.htm, accessed 29 July 2016.

Kochel, T. R. (2012), 'Can Police Legitimacy Promote Collective Efficacy?' *Justice Quarterly*, 29(3): 384–419.

Kritzer, H. and Voelker, J. (1998), 'Familiarity Breeds Respect: How Wisconsin Citizens View Their Courts', *Judicature*, 82(2): 58–64.

Kury, H. (2002), 'Introduction to special issue: International Comparison of Crime and Victimization: The ICVS', *International Journal of Comparative Criminology*, 2(1):, 22–37.

Lake, C., Gotoff, D., and Pultorak, K. (2013), *Reducing Incarceration Levels in the U.S.: Opportunities for Reform*, New York: Open Society Foundations.

Lappi-Seppälä. T. (2011), 'Explaining Imprisonment in Europe', *European Journal of Criminology*, 8(4): 303–28.

Lightowler, C. and Quirk, H. (2015), 'The 2011 English "Riots": Prosecutorial Zeal and Judicial Abandon', *British Journal of Criminology*, 55(1): 65–85.

Loader, I. and Sparks, R. (2011), *Public Criminology?*, London: Routledge.

Maffei, S. and Markopolou, L. (2014), *FIDUCIA New European Crimes and Trust-based Policy*, V[illegible]me 2, Parma: University of Parma, available a[illegible]ww.fiduciaproject.eu/publication/12/r[illegible]for-new-european-crimes-and[illegible]l-ume-2, accessed 29 J[illegible]

MARTEACHE, N. (2012), 'Deliberative processes and attitudes towards sex offenders in Spain', *European Journal of Criminology*, 9(2): 159–75.

MARUNA, S., MATRAVERS, A., and KING, A. (2004), 'Disowning our shadow: A psychoanalytic approach to understanding punitive public attitudes', *Deviant Behavior*, 25(3): 277–9.

MATTINSON, J. and MIRLEES-BLACK, C. (2000), *Attitudes to Crime and Criminal Justice: Findings from the 1998 British Crime Survey*, Home Office Research Study No.200, London: Home Office.

MAZEROLLE, L., ANTROBUS, E., BENNETT, S., and TYLER, T. (2013), 'Shaping citizen perceptions of police legitimacy: a randomised field trial of procedural justice', *Criminology*, 51(1): 33–63.

MILLIE, A., JACOBSON, J., and HOUGH, M. (2005), 'Understanding the Growth in the Prison Population in England and Wales', in C. Emsley (ed.), *The Persistent Prison*, London: Francis Boutle Publishers.

MITCHELL, B. and ROBERTS, J. V. (2010), *Public Opinion and the Law of Murder*, London: Nuffield Foundation.

MITCHELL, B. and ROBERTS, J. V. (2011), 'Public Attitudes Towards the Mandatory Life Sentence for Murder: Putting Received Wisdom to the Empirical Test', *Criminal Law Review*, 6 (June): 454–65.

MORI (2000), *Crime and Punishment Poll. MORI poll 16 July 2000*, London: MORI, available at: https://www.ipsos-mori.com/researchpublications/researcharchive/1593/Crime-And-Punishment-Poll.aspx, accessed 29 July 2016.

MORI (2003), *Public Confidence in Criminal Justice*, London: MORI

MORI (2009), *Sentencing—Public Attitudes Survey*, London: MORI.

MORI (2010), *Where are the public on crime and punishment?* London: MORI.

MORI (2016a), *MORI Issues Archive*. London: MORI, available at: https://www.ipsos-mori.com/researchpublications/researcharchive/2420/Issues-Index-Archive.aspx, accessed 29 July 2016.

MORI (2016b), *Would you generally trust them to tell the truth or not?* London: MORI, available at: https://www.ipsos-mori.com/Assets/Docs/Polls/Veracity%202014%20trend.pdf, accessed 29 July 2016.

NUTTALL, C., EVERSLEY, D., RUDDER, I., and RAMSAY, J. (2003), *Views and Beliefs about Crime and Criminal Justice*, Bridgetown, Barbados: Barbados Statistical Department.

OLAUSSEN, L. (2014), 'Concordance between Actual Level of Punishment and Punishments suggested by Lay People—but with less use of Imprisonment', *Bergen Journal of Criminal Law and Criminal Justice*, 2(1): 69–99.

ONEPOLL (2015), *Public attitudes towards criminal punishment, rehabilitation and reform*, London: Onepoll, available at: http://www.onepoll.com/public-attitudes-towards-criminal-punishment-reh[illegible]bilitation-and-reform/, accessed 29 July 2016.

ONS [illegible]2015a), *Crime Statistics, Focus on Public F[illegible]ptions of Crime and the Police, and the Personal [illegible]ing of Victims, 2013 to 2014*, London: Office [illegible]nal Statistics, available at: http://www.ons.gov.uk/ons/rel/crime-stats/crime-statistics/focus-on-public-perceptions-of-crime-and-the-police--and-the-personal-well-being-of-victims--2013-to-2014/index.html, accessed 29 July 2016.

ONS (2015b), *Crime in England and Wales, Year Ending March 2015. Statistical Bulletin*, London: Office of National Statistics, available at: http://www.ons.gov.uk/ons/rel/crime-stats/crime-statistics/year-ending-march-2015/index.html, accessed 29 July 2016.

ONS (2016), *Crime in England and Wales, Year Ending March 2016. Statistical Bulletin*, London: Office of National Statistics, available at: http://www.ons.gov.uk/peoplepopulationandcommunity/crimeandjustice/bulletins/crimeinenglandandwales/yearendingmar2016, accessed 29 July 2016.

PARMENTIER, S., VERVAEKE, G., DOUTRELEPONT, R., and KELLENS, G. (eds) (2004), *Public Opinion and the Administration of Justice. Popular perceptions and their implications for policy-making in western countries*, Brussels: Politeia Press.

PAULIN, J., SEARLE, W., and KNAGGS, T. (2003), *Attitudes to Crime and Punishment: A New Zealand Study*, Wellington: Ministry of Justice.

Pew Centre on the States (2012), *Public Opinion on Sentencing and Corrections Policy in America*, available at: http://www.pewtrusts.org/~/media/assets/2012/03/30/pew_nationalsurveyresearchpaper_final.pdf, accessed 29 July 2016.

PRATT, J. (2007), *Penal Populism*, London: Routledge.

PRESIDENT'S TASK FORCE (2015), *Final Report of the President's Task Force on 21st Century Policing*, Washington, DC: Office of Community Oriented Policing Services, available at: http://www.cops.usdoj.gov/pdf/taskforce/taskforce_finalreport.pdf, accessed 29 July 2016.

REDONDO, S., LUQUE, E., and FUNES, J. (1996), 'Social Beliefs about Recidivism in Crime', in G. Davies, S. Lloyd-Bostock, M. McMurran, and C. Wilson (eds), *Psychology, Law, and Criminal Justice*, New York: Walter de Gruyter.

ROBERTS, J. V., FEILZER, M., and HOUGH, M. (2011), 'Measuring Public Attitudes to Criminal Justice', in D. Gadd, S. Karstedt, and S. Messner (eds), *Handbook of Criminological Research Methods*, London: Sage Publications.

ROBERTS, J. V. and HASTINGS, R. (2011), 'Public Opinion and Crime Prevention', in D. Farrington and B. Welsh (eds), *The Oxford Handbook of Crime Prevention*, New York: Oxford University Press.

ROBERTS, J. V. and HOUGH, M. (2005a), *Understanding Public Attitudes to Criminal Justice*, Maidenhead: Open University Press.

ROBERTS, J. V. and HOUGH, M. (2005b), 'The State of the Prison: Exploring Public Knowledge and Opinion', *The Howard Journal of Criminal Justice*, 44(3): 286–307.

ROBERTS, J. V. and HOUGH, M. (2011), 'Custody or Community? Exploring the Boundaries of Public Punitiveness in England and Wales', *Criminology and Criminal Justice*, 11(2): 181–97.

ROBERTS, J. V., STALANS, L. S., INDERMAUR, D., and HOUGH, M. (2003), *Penal Populism and Public Opinion: Lessons from Five Countries*, Oxford: Oxford University Press.

ROBERTS, J. V. and WHITE, N. (1986), 'Public Estimates of Recidivism Rates: Consequences of a Criminal Stereotype', *Canadian Journal of Criminology*, 28(3): 229–41.

ROBERTS, L. and INDERMAUR, D. (2009), *What Australians Think About Crime and Justice*, Canberra: Australian Institute of Criminology.

ROBINSON, P. H. (2013), *Intuitions of Justice and the Utility of Desert*, New York: Oxford University Press.

ROTH, L. (2014), *Public Opinion on Sentencing: Recent Research in Australia*, New South Wales Parliamentary Research Service.

RYBERG, J. and ROBERTS, J. V. (eds) (2014), *Popular Punishment*, New York: Oxford University Press.

SANDERS, T. and ROBERTS, J. V. (2000), 'Public Attitudes toward Conditional Sentencing: Results of a National Survey', *Canadian Journal of Behavioural Science*, 32(4): 199–207.

SATO, M. (2014), *The Death Penalty in Japan*, London: Springer.

SATO, M. and BACON, P. (2015), *The Public Opinion Myth: Why Japan Retains the Death Penalty*, London: The Death Penalty Project.

SCHONTEICH, M. (1999), *Sentencing in South Africa, Public Perception and Judicial Practice*, Occasional Paper No. 43, Institute for Security Studies.

SCOTTISH EXECUTIVE SOCIAL RESEARCH (2007), *Community Sentencing: Public Perceptions and Attitudes*, Edinburgh: Scottish Executive.

SKOGAN, W. (2006), 'Asymmetry in the impact of encounters with the police', *Policing and Society*, 16(2): 99–126.

SOURCEBOOK OF CRIMINAL JUSTICE STATISTICS (2012), *New York: The State University of New York at Albany*, available at: http://www.albany.edu/sourcebook/, accessed 29 July 2016.

TANKEBE, J. (2013), 'Viewing things differently: the dimensions of public perceptions of legitimacy', *Criminology*, 51(1): 103–35.

TENDAYI VIKI, G. and BOHNER, G. (2009), 'Achieving accurate assessment of attitudes toward the criminal justice system: methodological issues', in J. Wood and T. Gannon (eds), *Public Opinion and Criminal Justice*, Cullompton: Willan.

THE OPPORTUNITY AGENDA (2015), *An Overview of Public Opinion and Discourses on Criminal Justice Issues*, New York: The Opportunity Agenda.

TYLER, T. R. (2011), *Why People Cooperate: The Role of Social Motivations*, Princeton: Princeton University Press.

VAN DE WALLE, S. and RAINE, J. (2008), *Explaining Attitudes Towards the Justice System in the UK and Europe*, London: Ministry of Justice.

WOOD, J. and Gannon, T. (eds) (2009), *Public Opinion and Criminal Justice*, Cullompton: Willan.

YOUGOV (2011), *Cambridge Survey Results*, fieldwork, June.

11

NEWS POWER, CRIME AND MEDIA JUSTICE

Chris Greer and Eugene McLaughlin

INTRODUCTION

If 100 criminologists were gathered in a room, they would struggle to find consensus over most issues of crime and criminal justice. The definition of crime; its causes, nature, and distribution; its impact on society; the most appropriate or effective responses to criminal behaviour—all these issues remain sources of heated debate and trenchant disagreement. And yet, irrespective of their theoretical or methodological perspective, all would probably agree on two seemingly incontestable criminological 'facts'. First, the news media distort the 'true' picture of crime and criminal justice. And second, this distortion matters because it is somehow detrimental to society. Perspectives on the negative outcomes of this distortion will vary across a diversity of concerns, including: the generation of public misunderstanding of the problem of crime and the functioning and effectiveness of the criminal justice system; the politicization of law and order; the criminalization of marginalized groups; and the formation of punitive crime control policies. These 'bad news' criminological 'facts' lie at the heart of most crime news research.

Steve Chibnall's (1977: 1) observation 40 years ago that crime news remained 'a curiosity of no more than marginal interest' for mainstream media researchers and criminologists still applies today. Back then, the principal media-crime research interest was in evaluating the possible behavioural effects, usually upon children, of media portrayals of sex and violence (Cohen and Young 1973). The lack of interest was incomprehensible to Chibnall, given that news is one of the central repositories for and creators of public knowledge. The news media:

> exert a considerable influence over our perceptions of groups and lifestyles of which we have little first-hand experience. They have the power to create issues and define the boundaries of debates and, while they may not be able to manipulate our opinions in any direct sense—creating attitudes to replace old ones—they can organise opinion and develop world views by providing structures of understanding into which isolated and unarticulated attitudes and beliefs may be fitted. They provide interpretations, symbols of identification, collective values and myths which are able to transcend the moral boundaries within a society like Britain. (Chibnall 1977: 226)

It is our position that, despite widespread consensus that crime news distorts and that this distortion has negative consequences for society, the dynamic relations between news power, crime, and criminal justice remain under-researched and under-conceptualized. In this chapter it is not our intention to present a comprehensive overview of the existing research on crime news. Such overviews can be found elsewhere (Greer 2010a, b, 2013; Greer and Reiner 2012; Jewkes 2015). Our aims are more specific. First, we revisit two key concepts that continue to dominate UK crime news research, but tend to do so in caricatured form: news values and moral panic. Although these concepts are still important for understanding news power, their institutionalization and taxonomical application in criminological research has marginalized analysis of dramatic shifts in the nature of crime news, the markets in which it circulates, and its power to shape crime consciousness and criminal justice rhetoric and practice. Second, we consider the work of penologists who in the 1990s resituated crime news within a context of wider social change by identifying 'the media' as a key driver of the punitive turn. Third, we set out our own position on developments that currently are transforming the relations between news power, crime, and criminal justice. While these developments have global significance, our empirical focus remains in the UK because its news media system is in important respects unique (Tunstall 1996). Most important is the existence of an overwhelmingly conservative tabloidized national newspaper market, run by powerful corporations that resource fully integrated 24-7 hard copy and online operations. Amidst ongoing debate about the death of print news and the contemporary crisis of professional journalism (Alexander *et al.* 2016; Rusbridger 2008), we propose that UK newspaper corporations are in fact fighting to increase their agenda-setting power. In response to the emergence of an ultra-competitive digital information market they continue to develop a distinctive brand of adversarial journalism that is working at the edges of what is legally permissible in order to extend their influence (Brock 2013). Because of tighter legal restrictions around objectivity and impartiality, the UK's broadcast news media routinely follow the national press agenda (Bromley 1998). Consequently, newspapers remain pivotal in setting the public and policy agendas around crime and criminal justice.

The technological, cultural, and economic transformation of the news market has increased corporate power to define *what is news* and, in the context of this chapter, *what is crime news*. Potential crime news stories circulate endlessly, intermediatized across and between different platforms as ever-repeating, ever-proliferating circuits beyond the control of any one group or institution. In this context of informational chaos and contestation, UK newspaper corporations are reasserting their authority as powerful filters and legitimators, revalidating the distinction between 'information' and 'news' and imposing their own brand of interpretive order. We identify the emergence of 'trial by media' and 'scandal hunting' as illustrative of the shifting balance of news power in this digital market. These news practices are capable simultaneously of providing an alternative forum for delivering 'justice' to victims failed by the state and inflicting potentially devastating reputational damage on convicted and alleged offenders, criminal justice authorities, politicians, policy elites, and 'failing' institutions. We propose that in-depth crime news research has fallen off the criminological radar at a time when news corporations have reconstituted and dramatically extended their power to shape crime consciousness and influence official rhetoric and practice. It is in this intermediatized context that we situate the shift from criminal justice to media justice.

NEWS POWER, NEWS VALUES, AND MORAL PANIC

The 1970s and 1980s represented a high point of crime news research. Scholars were motivated by an interdisciplinary concern to move beyond psychological positivism's preoccupations with direct media effects in order to develop a deeper and more nuanced understanding of news power at a time of radical social change. Of the numerous crime news studies produced in this period (Halloran *et al.* 1970; Chibnall 1977; Cohen 1972; Cohen and Young 1973; Hall *et al.* 1978; Katz 1987; Ericson *et al.* 1987, 1989, 1991), three stand out as having defined the field: Cohen's (1972) *Folk Devils and Moral Panics: The Creation of Mods and Rockers*, Chibnall's (1977) *Law and Order News: An Analysis of Crime Reporting in the British Press*, and Hall *et al.*'s (1978) *Policing the Crisis: Mugging, the State and Law and Order.* These studies, produced in dialogue with each other, have maintained their influence largely because of the two organizing concepts they collectively developed: news values and moral panic.

NEWS VALUES

Chibnall (1977: x–xi) identified crime as the news category that allows news organizations to act as barometers of the public temper at any given moment:

> Crime news may serve as a focus for the articulation of shared morality and communal sentiments. A chance not simply to speak to the community but to speak for the community, against all that the criminal outsider represents, to delineate the shape of the threat, to advocate a response, to eulogise on conformity to established norms and values, and to warn of the consequences of deviance. In short, crime news provides a chance for a newspaper to appropriate the moral conscience of its readership.

Chibnall's Marxist framework built on Halloran *et al.*'s (1970) classic analysis of press and television reporting of the 1968 Vietnam demonstrations in London's Grosvenor Square. He argued that news power resides in the ability of journalists, working within the constraints of professional conventions, source relationships, and legal limitations, to select and construct what *is* and what *is not* crime news. In selecting and constructing events as newsworthy journalists are guided by eight professional 'news values'. These news values are seldom written down and many journalists struggle to articulate them when asked. Nevertheless, all to some extent internalize a 'sense' of 'news', which provides a stock of professional knowledge enabling the informed assessment of 'newsworthiness'. The eight universal news values Chibnall identifies are: immediacy, dramatization, personalization, simplification, titillation, conventionalism, structured access, and novelty. These news values can be refined, inflected, and augmented by other criteria to add greater insight or gravity in the reporting of particular 'types' of crime. For example, at least five informal rules of relevance guide journalists' treatment of violence by asserting the importance of: visible and spectacular acts, sexual and political connotations, graphic description and presentation, individual pathology, and deterrence and repression (Chibnall 1977: 776). Understanding news values helps to make sense of crime news selection and content. For example, it explains why violence in public places between strangers tends to be newsworthy, whilst violence in private residences between intimates does not. It also helps explain why news tends to focus on dramatic criminal incidents, rather than abstract and complex debates around criminal justice policy.

MORAL PANIC

For Cohen (1972) the most dramatic demonstration of the news media's power to shape crime consciousness is the creation of 'moral panics'. This power is most productive at moments of cultural strain and ambiguity that challenge existing moral boundaries. First used by Young (1971) in his study of drug-takers, the concept was developed and extended by Cohen (1972) in his interactionist analysis of the simultaneous construction and demonization of Mods and Rockers in 1960s Britain. Cohen traces the spiralling social reaction to these youth subcultures through initial intolerance, media stereotyping, moral outrage, increased surveillance, labelling and marginalization, and deviancy amplification that seemed to justify the initial concerns. The defiant misbehaviour of sexually and economically liberated youth affronted the post-War values of hard work, sobriety, and deferred gratification. For Cohen, at a time of rapid social change these subcultures were the visible manifestation of a world that was slipping away—'folk devils' who provided a crystallizing focus for social anxiety and 'respectable fears' and an agenda for journalists, politicians, and moral entrepreneurs.

Hall *et al.* (1978) provided a Marxist explanation of news power in their analysis of a 'mugging' moral panic—with the 'black mugger' as 'folk devil'—which they read as an ideological intervention to address an escalating crisis in state hegemony. Building on Cohen (1972) and Chibnall (1977), they argue that the news media play a critical role in defining 'for the majority of the population *what* significant events are taking place, but, also, they offer powerful interpretations of *how* to understand these events' (Hall *et al.* 1978: 57). Crime news functions as a morality play 'in which the 'devil' is both symbolically and physically cast out from the society by its guardians—the police and the judiciary' (1978: 66). For Hall *et al.* (1978: 42) the news media orchestrate moral panics as a key ideological means through which 'the 'silent majority' is won over to the support of increasingly coercive measures by the state, and lends its legitimacy to a 'more than normal' exercise of control.

Though both Chibnall (1977) and Hall *et al.* (1978) were writing from a Marxist perspective, they arrive at different understandings of news power. Chibnall (1977: 9–10) seeks to expose 'the deficiencies in most Marxist approaches' that 'simply assert the function of the news media in reproducing a dominant ideology without explaining how it is achieved beyond referring to the media structure of ownership and control'. News values are central to the freedom of the press and the 'craft of journalism'. Chibnall's bottom line is that journalistic 'common sense' will place 'news values' above other interests, including state interests, in selecting and constructing 'news'. For Hall *et al.* (1978), the notion of journalistic autonomy is illusory. The news media function as part of a wider ideological state apparatus within which journalists have limited autonomy: in the final instance, they sit in a position of 'structured subordination' to the powerful sources upon whom they rely for newsworthy information. From Cohen's interactionist perspective, everyone involved in a moral panic, including the news media, the authorities, and the folk devils, is in a state of panic. Each of these studies is concerned to illustrate how crime news stigmatizes and criminalizes the powerless. For Chibnall (1977) news power is understood primarily as professional practice. For Hall *et al.* (1978) it is ideological practice. For Cohen (1972) it is social practice.

These two concepts—news values and moral panic—have provided generations of crime news researchers with all they need to examine the selection, production, distribution, and 'effects' of crime news. But the studies in which these concepts were developed were in depth analyses of social change that situated crime news within the wider contexts of generational conflict, the politics of law and order, or the transition to an authoritarian state. It is their more immediately reproducible elements that have survived, caricatured and detached from wider contextual considerations. Thus crime news is researched in order to demonstrate taxonomically that 'news values' retain their explanatory value—reflecting Rock's (1973) notion of news as 'eternal recurrence'—and that the news media are still biased on the basis of gender, class, ethnicity, age, or sexuality. Or the news media and wider reaction to a putative social problem is examined in order to evaluate whether or not it constitutes a moral panic (see Jewkes 2015 for an overview). While these concepts still have much to offer the analysis of crime news, we would propose that their taxonomical application does not do them justice, and has diverted research attention from the radical changes that have transformed the relations between news power, crime, and criminal justice in the past 40 years (for important exceptions see Ericson *et al.* 1987, 1989, 1991; Schlesinger and Tumber 1994).

Useful insights into these changes came from penologists, who were only peripherally interested in media. Analysts of the punitive turn, whose main concern was the rise of mass incarceration, noted the dominance of crime in public discourse and the extent to which its increasing everyday salience was reshaping electoral politics and reorienting crime control policy towards quick fix solutions (Beckett 1997; Bottoms 1995; Garland 2001a, b; Pratt 2007; Roberts *et al.* 2003; Sasson 1995). Perhaps because their starting point was attempting to understand the socio-economic and cultural transformations that were driving penal expansion, media were situated within that wider context. It is to this body of research that we turn next.

NEWS POWER AND THE PUNITIVE TURN

Hall (1979, 1980) used the term 'authoritarian populism' to explain how Thatcherism had harnessed public fears and anxieties to popularize neoliberal solutions to economic and political problems, including law and order. Building on *Policing the Crisis* (Hall *et al.* 1978), he argued that authoritarian populism represented a fundamental ideological shift in which the UK conservative news media's role was pivotal in criminalizing marginalized groups and legitimating punitive law and order policies. This shift would be difficult to reverse because it was intimately connected to the New Right's attempt to create an authoritarian state and a free market. In the mid-1990s, following decades of rising crime rates, penologists identified the punitive turn—the adoption across many Anglophone jurisdictions of both the rhetoric and practice of ever-harsher punishments, including the extension of criminal law and criminalization, tougher policing and sentencing, and increased imprisonment. Bottoms (1995) argued that the rise of what he termed 'populist punitiveness' signalled a departure from the post-War consensus that curtailed the expression of excessively punitive sentiments and the politicization of criminal justice policy. Unlike Hall, for Bottoms this shift was unsustainable and would pass. Yet despite choosing the term 'populist', at no point does he consider the significance of news media in shaping public opinion. Though they were both interested in the law and order implications of the collapsing social democratic consensus, Hall's cultural studies approach was sensitized to an appreciation of news power. From Bottoms' policy-centric perspective, news power remained either invisible or insignificant.

More recent penological work has given greater recognition to the role of mass media in driving the punitive turn. In Garland's (2001: 158) analysis of the UK and US, television has 'tapped into, then dramatized and reinforced, a new public experience—an experience with profound psychological resonance—and in doing so it has *institutionalised* that experience'. By heightening consciousness, most significantly among the previously well-insulated middle classes, of the increasing risks of criminal victimization and the ineffectual and uncaring nature of criminal justice, it has provided 'everyday opportunities to play out the emotions of fear, anger, resentment, and fascination that our experience of crime provokes' (Garland 2001: 158). Roberts *et al*.'s (2003) comparative research on penal populism and public opinion highlights 'the dynamic and powerfully co-ordinating force of the media—framing not only reality to feed late modern anxieties but also telling stories about how to think about the remedies to the anxieties and what political actors are doing or failing to do in "making things better"' (Roberts *et al.* 2003: 87). Their account of media influence draws heavily on Garland, but also identifies what they see as the malign outcomes of tabloid law and order campaigns. Pratt (2007) also acknowledges the importance of tabloid campaigning. His analysis offers a deeper understanding of a transforming media environment characterized by market deregulation, technological change, increased competition, and globalization. For Pratt (2007), the core media message is clear: citizens can no longer rely for public protection on a criminal justice system that seems more interested in protecting the rights of criminals.

Across this body of work, a consistent bad news view emerges. 'The media' feed into the punitive turn by: over-concentrating on the threat posed by violent predatory offenders; emphasizing exceptional or aberrant crimes; identifying 'new' crimes requiring 'new' forms of punishment; employing simplified frames of right and wrong; highlighting injustices perpetrated against victims by a soft, ineffectual, and uncaring criminal justice system; attacking politicians, authority figures, and experts deemed to be soft on crime; questioning official explanations; and lending editorial support for retributive policies. The most significant development in the context of this chapter is the recognition of a more antagonistic relationship between the news media and state authority. Nevertheless, the consensus is that the punitive turn is reversible and that sections of the news media—a clear distinction is maintained between tabloid and broadsheet—are manageable. For Roberts *et al.* (2003), the UK tabloids are a lost cause. The challenge is keeping broadsheet journalists on-message through education by academic experts and policy elites. Specifically, more accurate coverage of crime and criminal justice could be achieved by 'pointing out the unintended consequences of irresponsible, sensationalised reporting' and 'improving access to specialist staff such as statisticians and academics' (Roberts *et al.* 2003: 175–6). We would suggest that this view underestimates and under-conceptualizes contemporary news power. In what follows, we develop this position through reference to two key processes: tabloidization and digitalization. These processes—central theoretical and empirical concerns within journalism and communication studies, but largely absent from criminological analysis—are key to understanding the dynamic and rapidly transforming relations between UK news power, crime and criminal justice.

RECONSTITUTING UK NEWS POWER: TABLOIDIZATION AND DIGITALIZATION

In 1986 Rupert Murdoch relocated production of his UK national newspapers from the historic but technologically and spatially inadequate Fleet Street to new computerized, full-colour printing facilities in Wapping. His success was such that tabloid formats, techniques, and logics rapidly spread across the industry, and by 1989 the last newspaper had left Fleet Street for upgraded premises (Lang and Dodkins 2011). New computer and printing technologies enabled newspapers to rationalize their workforces, while reformatting and sharpening their design, style, content, and competitive edge. But tabloidization was more than technological. It transformed journalistic practice and the nature of news itself by prioritizing scandal, sensation, and infotainment over in-depth political and economic coverage, and redefining the criteria that should be used in judging a person's fitness for public office (Bird 1992; Conboy 2006; Franklin 1997; Sparks and Tulloch 2000). The tabloidization of the UK press also fundamentally transformed newspapers' sense of their own power. As Tunstall puts it (1996: 30):

> . . . the national newspaper industry massively cut its costs and boosted its profits. The national press owners, managers and editors also boosted their own financial and political confidence. Rupert Murdoch's success seemed to indicate that industrial power, political influence, and profitability were all consistent goals. All three could be pursued, and put in evidence, at the same time.

Crime news was ideally suited to this new environment. As we have already shown, crime has always been a news staple, but tabloidization transformed newspapers' capacity to produce stories that could seize the public imagination. For the first time, full-colour images formed the centrepieces of increasingly graphic and emotionally charged crime and justice stories, adding a new dimension of dramatic realism that elevated the potential to invoke consumer empathy, shock and anger. Melodramatic headlines, moralistic interpretive frameworks and streamlined explanations—standard practice for decades—were augmented by a growing readiness to challenge official explanations and institutional authority (Turner 1999; Reiner *et al.* 2000; Brock 2013).

As tabloidization was taking hold, newspapers were also experimenting with the Internet. Early attempts to go online enjoyed mixed success, with some being likened to a 'dumping ground' for news content. 'Digital convergence'—the combination within a single portable device of, most significantly, Internet access, camera functionality, and messaging services—created the technological conditions in which the mass production and use of news-related content and services could flourish (Westlund 2013). As with tabloidization, however, digital convergence is more than just a technological shift. It 'alters the relationship between existing technologies, industries, markets genres, and audiences. Convergence refers to a process, but not an endpoint' (Jenkins 2004: 34). It has further transformed the nature and content of crime news and the cultural and regulatory environments in which it circulates. Three interconnected dynamics, at once fostered and intensified by digital convergence, are key: proliferation, interactivity, and adversarialism.

News media proliferation has resulted in countless platforms disseminating 24-7 breaking news globally. The main challenge facing news-hungry consumers has shifted from finding and accessing to choosing and filtering. Two decades after Wapping, Rupert Murdoch (2006) heralded a second revolution that would require further radical adaptation from newspapers if they were to retain their power:

> Power is moving away from those who own and manage the media to a new and demanding generation of consumers—consumers who are better educated, unwilling to be led, and who know that in a competitive world they can get what they want, when they want it. The challenge for us in the traditional media is how to engage with this new audience . . . There is only one way. That is by using our skills to create and distribute dynamic, exciting content . . . Content is being repurposed to suit the needs of a contemporary audience . . . The words, pictures and graphics that are the stuff of journalism have to be brilliantly packaged: they must feed the mind and move the heart [as] must read, must have content.

National newspapers have responded to declining print readerships and the proliferation of online news platforms by developing digital operations with global reach, in the process transforming themselves into corporate news brands. A snapshot from August 2016 reveals that *The Guardian* newspaper sold fewer than 160,000 print copies per day, yet its mobile compatible website attracted more than 8 million daily unique browsers. Daily print sales of the *Daily Mail*, whilst eclipsing those of *The Guardian* ten-to-one, were still only 1.6 million. *MailOnline* averaged over 15 million daily unique browsers (ABC, http://www.abc.org.uk/). Corporate newspaper websites are constantly updated, rendering obsolete the physical, temporal, and geographical constraints of the printed format. In an increasingly crowded and competitive market, newspaper corporations are under ever-greater pressure to attract and retain fickle consumers. One effective way of achieving this is increased interactivity.

Boczkowski (2004: 21) notes that news has moved from being 'mostly journalist-centred, communicated as a monologue, and primarily local, to also being increasingly audience-centred, part of multiple conversations and micro-local'. The integration of video-streaming and podcasting, real-time comments threads, and discussion groups, means that consumers are woven into the news process, submitting their views or, more importantly, sending or uploading their photographs and footage of crime and justice events. The transformation of this producer-source-consumer relationship was exemplified during and after the London bombings of 7 July 2005. The BBC's Richard Sambrook (2005) recalled:

> Within 6 hours [of 7/7] we received more 1,000 photos, 20 pieces of amateur video, 4000 text messages, and 21,000 emails. People were participating in our coverage in a way we had never seen before. By the next day, our main evening television newscast began with a package edited entirely from video sent in by viewers. Our audiences had become involved like they never had before. By day's end, the BBC's newsgathering had crossed a Rubicon . . . Of course the BBC has used phone-ins, amateur video, and email in its programmes for years, but what was happening now was moving us way beyond where we'd been before.

There was further movement during the 2011 London riots, when journalists, police officers, bystanders, rioters, and victims all contributed in real time to the creation of an intermediatized news story (Lewis and Newburn 2011). The increased interactivity fostered by digital convergence means that consumers can become producers, 'watchers' can become 'doers', and everyone can be a 'citizen reporter'. It is the interactive experience of crime news that matters. The nature of this interactivity can in turn be shaped by a third major transformation brought about by the mutually reinforcing processes of tabloidization and digitalization—increased adversarialism.

Within a proliferating news market, one of the main ways in which newspaper corporations have sought to achieve distinction has been through the development of an increasingly adversarial style (Lloyd 2004; Milne 2005; Protess *et al.* 1991; Sabato 1991). The growth of press adversarialism results from a range of interconnected factors. Some of these, as discussed above, are particular to rapidly transforming communications markets. Others, like the widely reported decline in deference to authority and a deterioration of public trust in official or elite institutions, reflect wider changes in values and culture (Fukuyama 2000; Seldon 2009; Mishra 2017). As McNair (2006: 71) notes, a prominent characteristic of contemporary news coverage is its 'negativism and wilfully destructive attitude towards authority' (McNair 2006: 71). We propose that this adversarialism—unprecedented in scope and ambition—lies at the heart of a new business model for newspaper corporations. Energized by tabloidization and digitalization, and committed to challenging establishment authority by investigating and exposing institutional failure, this business model is reconstituting news power in the UK. In the next section we illustrate the evolution of this business model by analysing the interconnected processes of trial by media, victim-centred news campaigning, and scandal hunting.

NEWS POWER, TRIAL BY MEDIA, AND INSTITUTIONAL FAILURE

Trial by media (TBM) is a form of populist justice in which individuals and institutions are judged in the intermediatized 'court of public opinion' (Greer and McLaughlin 2010, 2011, 2012a, b, 2013). This digital 'court' can be attended by media users across the globe, and anyone with an Internet connection can participate in the trial proceedings.

The allegations underpinning TBM range across three overlapping categories of infraction: criminality, immorality, and incompetence. The disruptive power of TBM resides in its capacity to generate an intense emotional public reaction that can redefine cultural, political, and policy agendas. The nature and targets of these trials are diverse, and include (Greer and McLaughlin 2016):

- naming and shaming public figures and institutions accused of:
  - acting as if they are above the law
  - offending against an assumed moral consensus
  - failing to deliver on obligations and responsibilities
- pre-judging the outcome of criminal investigations involving 'unknowns'
- 'retrying' those considered to have evaded criminal justice.

Active participation—which may vary from posting speculation and opinion to submitting hard evidence to sharing 'one-click' judgement on the guilt or innocence of the accused—is integral to the immersive experience. Through this interactivity, TBM reclaims aspects of 'justice' from the courts and returns them to a networked citizenry. The extra-legal news media investigation that forms a core part of TBM may uncover sufficient evidence to activate formal due process. TBM thus has the power to initiate legal proceedings that otherwise may not have occurred. But it also challenges and subverts due process. Inverting its defining principle, TBM cases are premised on a presumption of guilt. This presumption of guilt precipitates an intermediatized search for further 'evidence' that contributes to consolidating a public image of the accused as 'guilty as charged'. While opinion and hearsay are generally regarded as inadmissible in a court of law, 'evidence' in TBM ranges from that which might be legally admissible to conjecture and insinuation. Newspaper corporations must only be convinced that it is sufficiently compelling to justify the risk of libel action. Those who deny the charges and attempt to fight back through public statements or legal retaliation risk intensified scrutiny aimed at uncovering further evidence of their guilt. Through the naming and shaming of alleged individual and institutional 'wrongdoers', TBM orchestrates status degradation ceremonies that dramatize moral and ideological boundaries. TBM ritually transforms the public identity of individual and institutional actors. Its outcomes range from varying degrees of reputational damage, to criminal prosecution, the introduction of new regulatory frameworks, the transformation of institutional practice, and the reconfiguration of collective memory.

The development of TBM as a criminal justice intervention played a key role in the investigative campaign, which was re-energized and restructured in the 1990s to establish market distinction and demonstrate newspapers' growing sense of power. The shift at this time to campaigning across a range of hard and soft news issues emboldened UK newspapers in claiming to represent the 'public interest', and extended their traditional agenda setting role to one of overt advocacy and activism (Birks 2010). Through a series of high-profile campaigns, different newspapers began pressurizing governments in the name of the public to take responsibility for a succession of institutional failures in the criminal justice system. Below we identify and analyse five exemplars that for us personify essential characteristics of this process, namely: failure through convicting the innocent; failure to convict the guilty; failure to protect children from paedophiles; failure to find missing children; and failure to provide competent criminal justice leadership. The development of TBM through victim-centred campaigns allowed newspaper corporations to test the legal limits and consumer appeal of an evolving business model focused on the exposure of institutional failure.

INSTITUTIONAL FAILURE THROUGH CONVICTING THE INNOCENT

In the aftermath of successful 'miscarriages of justice' campaigns, most notably the Guildford Four and Birmingham Six, some liberal newspapers continued to investigate and campaign on behalf of individuals who it was claimed had been the subject of wrongful conviction and imprisonment (Greer and McLaughlin 2014). Logistically these 'traditional' campaigns are difficult to run as they are premised on the assumption that the criminal justice system is not only incompetent and ineffective, but almost certainly institutionally corrupt. In addition, it was difficult to generate public sympathy for individuals who had been convicted of high-profile murders. Nevertheless, there were notable successes, including overturned convictions in the cases of the Bridgewater Three in 1997, Derek Bentley in 1998, and Stephen Downing in 2002 (Huff and Killias 2008). These campaigns were damaging to public confidence in criminal justice because they highlighted systemic incompetence or corruption in the wrongful conviction of innocent citizens and, in so doing, signalled that the real killer(s) were still at large.

Other newspapers initiated campaigns on behalf of crime victims who had been failed by the criminal justice system. These campaigns were grounded in intense coverage of murders where the victims' families proclaimed that 'justice had not been done' because a killer or killers had not been apprehended or prosecuted, or had received a light sentence or early release from prison. Two unprecedented 'trial by media' campaigns marked a watershed in UK newspaper corporations' agenda-setting capacities.

INSTITUTIONAL FAILURE TO CONVICT THE GUILTY

In February 1997 the inquest into the killing of Stephen Lawrence resumed. Despite various prosecution attempts, no-one had been convicted for the murder of the young black Londoner in a racially motivated attack in April 1993. During this inquest the five primary suspects refused to cooperate, claiming privilege against self-incrimination (Cottle 2004). The verdict of unlawful killing 'in a completely unprovoked racist attack by five white youths' was already newsworthy because it exceeded the bounds of the jury's instructions (Hall *et al.* 2013). Outraged by what was seen as the state's inability to secure a conviction in the face of overwhelming evidence of guilt, the *Daily Mail* took matters into its own hands. Its unprecedented front page on 14 February 1997 displayed full-colour photographs of the five suspects beneath the headline, 'MURDERERS: The Mail accuses these men of killing. If we are wrong, let them sue us' (see Figure 11.1).

In publishing this front page the newspaper was in contempt of court, but no legal action was taken by the accused and the *Daily Mail*'s campaign for a public inquiry gathered momentum. That this newspaper championed the case was remarkable

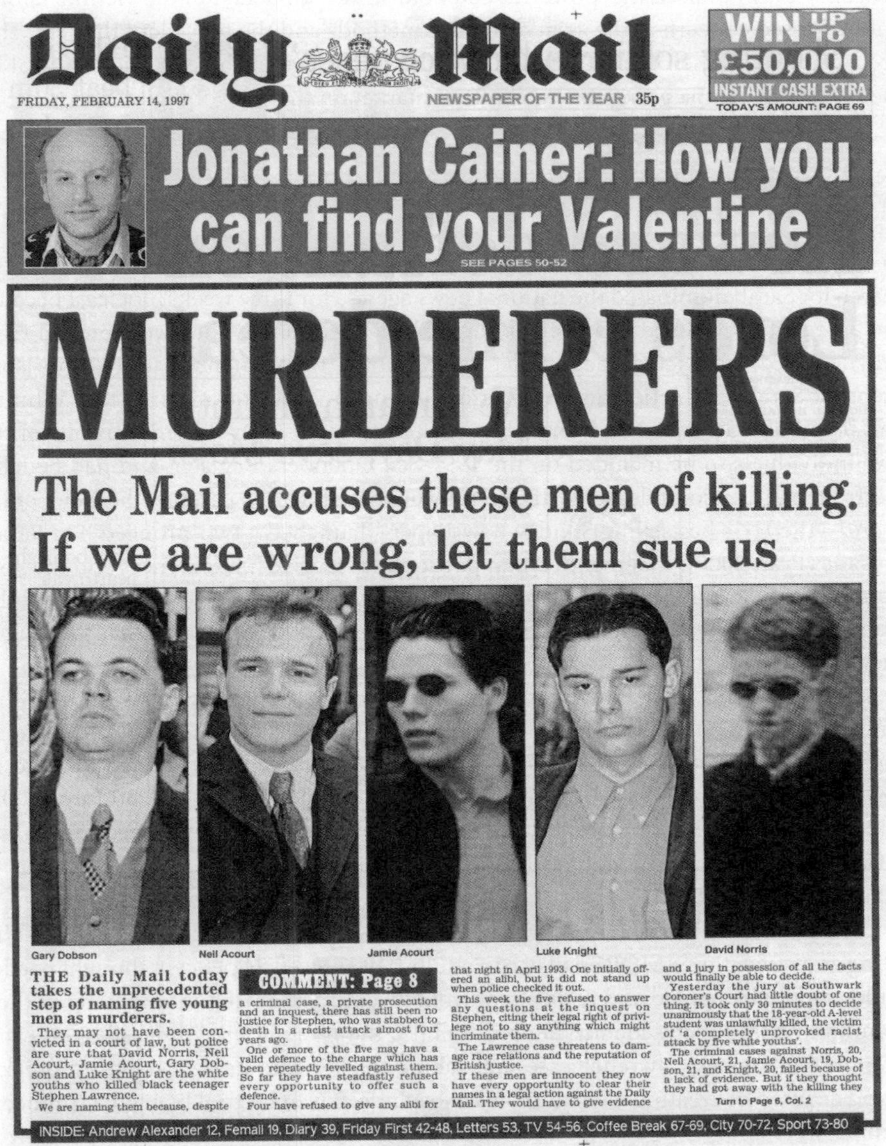

Daily Mail

FRIDAY, FEBRUARY 14, 1997 NEWSPAPER OF THE YEAR 35p

WIN UP TO £50,000 INSTANT CASH EXTRA

TODAY'S AMOUNT: PAGE 69

Jonathan Cainer: How you can find your Valentine

SEE PAGES 50-52

MURDERERS

The Mail accuses these men of killing. If we are wrong, let them sue us

Gary Dobson | Neil Acourt | Jamie Acourt | Luke Knight | David Norris

THE Daily Mail today takes the unprecedented step of naming five young men as murderers.

They may not have been convicted in a court of law, but police are sure that David Norris, Neil Acourt, Jamie Acourt, Gary Dobson and Luke Knight are the white youths who killed black teenager Stephen Lawrence.

We are naming them because, despite

COMMENT: Page 8

a criminal case, a private prosecution and an inquest, there has still been no justice for Stephen, who was stabbed to death in a racist attack almost four years ago.

One or more of the five may have a valid defence to the charge which has been repeatedly levelled against them. So far they have steadfastly refused every opportunity to offer such a defence.

Four have refused to give any alibi for that night in April 1993. One initially offered an alibi, but it did not stand up when police checked it out.

This week the five refused to answer any questions at the inquest on Stephen, citing their legal right of privilege not to say anything which might incriminate them.

The Lawrence case threatens to damage race relations and the reputation of British justice.

If these men are innocent they now have every opportunity to clear their names in a legal action against the Daily Mail. They would have to give evidence and a jury in possession of all the facts would finally be able to decide.

Yesterday the jury at Southwark Coroner's Court had little doubt of one thing. It took only 30 minutes to decide unanimously that the 18-year-old A-level student was unlawfully killed, the victim of 'a completely unprovoked racist attack by five white youths'.

The criminal cases against Norris, 20, Neil Acourt, 21, Jamie Acourt, 19, Dobson, 21, and Knight, 20, failed because of a lack of evidence. But if they thought they had got away with the killing they

Turn to Page 6, Col. 2

INSIDE: Andrew Alexander 12, Femail 19, Diary 39, Friday First 42-48, Letters 53, TV 54-56, Coffee Break 67-69, City 70-72, Sport 73-80

Figure 11.1 *Daily Mail* front page
Source: Daily Mail, 14 February 1997

given its long history of overt hostility to campaigns around racial discrimination (McLaughlin 2005). The Macpherson Inquiry Report, released in February 1999, reached the historic conclusion that the Metropolitan Police was 'institutionally racist'. It also implied institutional corruption by castigating police officers of all ranks for 'fundamental errors' that fatally undermined the investigation. The *Daily Mail*'s stark demonstration of news power sent shock waves across the criminal justice system, and sat uneasily with other sections of the British news media. A *Guardian* editorial (15

February 1997) praised the 'powerful and bold stroke' on behalf of the victim's family, but expressed concern at the 'trial by media' methods and the precedent they set. This precedent established the foundations for the next stage in the evolution of trial by media-driven campaigning in a tabloidized market on the cusp of digitalization.

INSTITUTIONAL FAILURE TO PROTECT CHILDREN FROM PAEDOPHILES

In July 2000 eight-year-old Sarah Payne disappeared from her home in Sussex. The search for Sarah dominated the national news agenda for three weeks, not least because the parents believed she had been abducted by a paedophile. They were proved right (Payne 2005). Convicted paedophile, Roy Whiting, was sentenced to life imprisonment for Sarah's abduction and murder in December 2001. It transpired that Whiting had previously abducted and sexually assaulted an eight-year-old girl, was one of the first individuals to be included on the 1997 Sex Offenders Register, and had benefitted from early prison release. With the full support of Sarah's parents, the *News of the World*—the UK's bestselling Sunday newspaper—launched a two-pronged 'For Sarah' crusade (Pratt 2007). It demanded that paedophiles receive life sentences and the government pass a 'Sarah's Law' giving parents the right to know whether paedophiles were living in their community. The *News of the World*'s position was that the lack of such a law had cost Sarah's life.

Sarah's mother, Sara Payne, quickly became the campaign's most high-profile ambassador and a tireless advocate of Sarah's Law. The *News of the World* adopted an unprecedented 'naming and shaming' strategy, having already threatened to build its own online public database of convicted UK paedophiles. On 23 and 30 July 2000 it published the names, photographs, and locations of 82 alleged known paedophiles and set up a telephone hotline for readers to provide information on the whereabouts of others (see Figure 11.2).

The *News of the World* vowed to identify all 110,000 known paedophiles in the UK, citing as justification a MORI poll of 614 adults that showed 84 per cent thought paedophiles should be named and 88 per cent would want to know if one was living in their community. In directly identifying paedophiles the *News of the World*, like the *Daily Mail* in the Stephen Lawrence case, was taking the law into its own hands. It quickly stood accused of creating a lynch mob atmosphere driven by trial by media. Innocent people were indeed attacked (Silverman and Wilson 2002). After well-publicized meetings with the Home Office and criminal justice agencies the *News of the World* suspended its 'naming and shaming' campaign on 6 August 2000. The campaign did not succeed in establishing all its proposed reforms, but the government was forced to tighten up controls over paedophiles. After more than a decade of pressure, a child sex offender disclosure scheme known as 'Sarah's Law' became operational in England and Wales in April 2011 (Jones and Newburn 2013). This scheme allows members of the public to ask the police if individuals in contact with their children pose a risk.

Newspaper campaigning in the UK changed as a result of the Stephen Lawrence and Sarah Payne murders. The *Daily Mail* and *News of the World* campaigns were potent demonstrations of news power, dominating the news agenda, imposing interpretive order, galvanizing public opinion, triggering national debates, and pressurizing

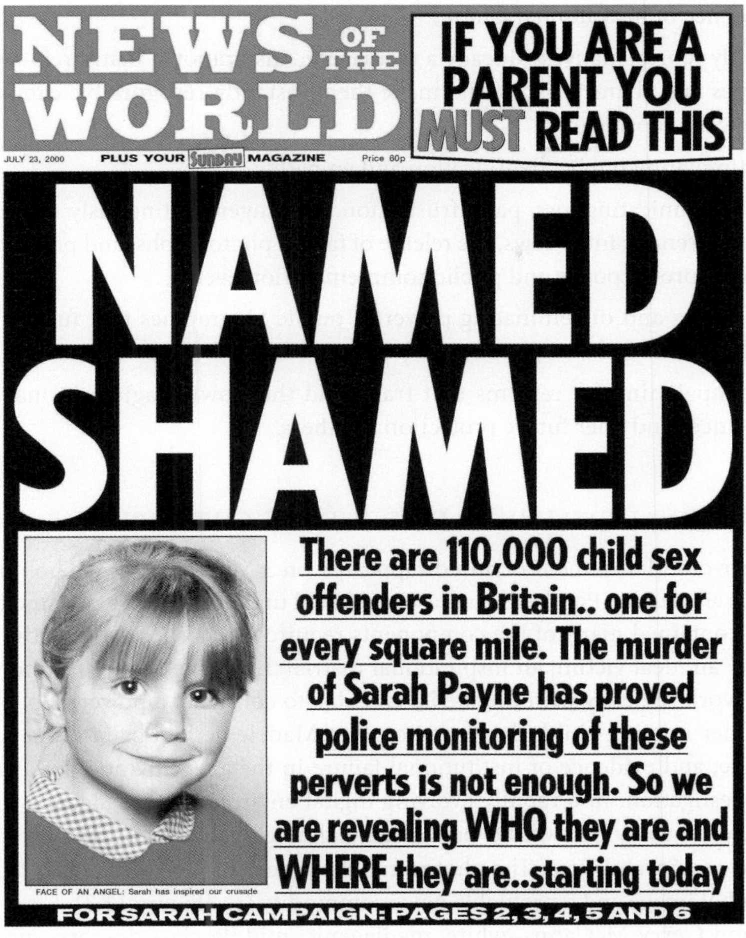
NEWS OF THE WORLD

IF YOU ARE A PARENT YOU MUST READ THIS

JULY 23, 2000 PLUS YOUR SUNDAY MAGAZINE Price 60p

NAMED SHAMED

There are 110,000 child sex offenders in Britain.. one for every square mile. The murder of Sarah Payne has proved police monitoring of these perverts is not enough. So we are revealing WHO they are and WHERE they are..starting today

FACE OF AN ANGEL: Sarah has inspired our crusade

FOR SARAH CAMPAIGN: PAGES 2, 3, 4, 5 AND 6

Figure 11.2 *News of the World* front page
Source: © *News of the World.* News Syndication, 23 July 2000

politicians, policy-makers, and criminal justice professionals to acknowledge systemic failures. Doreen Lawrence and Sara Payne personified how the violent actions of dangerous criminals, aided and abetted by a malfunctioning criminal justice system, could destroy innocent lives and families (Charman and Savage 2009). Both women acquired celebrity status and political prominence, and were officially recognized by the state for their efforts as inspirational mothers who had produced significant transformations in criminal law, professional practice, and social attitudes. After a succession of public awards, Doreen Lawrence was elevated to the House of Lords as a Baroness in 2013. Sara Payne became the Government's first Victims' Champion in 2009. We would argue that the Stephen Lawrence and Sarah Payne cases established a new template containing all the components necessary to run a successful victim-centred campaign in a tabloidized and digitalized news market. These components include:

1. ideal victims murdered in horrific circumstances;
2. suspected or convicted killers who can be demonized;

3. evidence of institutional failure;
4. family representatives—ideally a mediagenic inspirational matriarch—with core values and characteristics that make them instantly recognizable campaign figureheads capable of:
   - stimulating public identification and empathy;
   - communicating loss, pain, frustration, and anger continuously through news conferences, interviews, the release of family photographs, and participation in high-profile police and public commemoration events;
   - crafting and disseminating powerful public biographies that further idealize the victims, who might become posthumous celebrities;
   - campaigning for reforms that transcend their own tragic personal circumstances and offer future protection to others.

INSTITUTIONAL FAILURE TO FIND MISSING CHILDREN

Three-year-old Madeleine McCann disappeared on 3 May 2007 from a holiday apartment in Praia da Luz, Portugal. The case generated unprecedented global media attention and contained many of the components required for a successful victim-centred campaign: an ideal victim; an inspirational matriarch in Kate McCann, who was prepared to work tirelessly with the media and able to construct a powerful public biography of her missing child; the suspicion that Madeleine had been kidnapped by a paedophile; and evidence of institutional failure in the allegedly bungled Portuguese police investigation. In a rapidly evolving digital environment, Madeleine was intermediatized in a way that would have been technologically impossible with Stephen Lawrence and Sarah Payne. The photogenic three-year-old girl was converted into an iconic global image and a profitable news commodity (see Figure 11.3).

Kate and Gerry McCann—white, mediagenic, middle-class doctors—proactively engaged with journalists to try and maximize the news visibility of the case and manage the news agenda. For a period several UK newspapers offered the McCanns unequivocal support by throwing their weight behind the Find Madeleine campaign. Unlike in the UK, however, there was no culture of formalized dialogue between the Portuguese police and the news media, so when the investigation failed to produce a breakthrough the news vacuum needed to be filled. Seemingly unrestrained by UK contempt and libel laws, several UK newspaper corporations demonstrated the destructive capacity of news power. Over several months, a succession of stories based on unofficial sources, police leaks, speculation, and rumour insinuated that Kate and Gerry McCann were responsible for their daughter's death, had disposed of her body, and had conspired to cover up their actions by deliberately diverting police attention from evidence that would expose their guilt (Statement in Open Court, available at http://www.carter-ruck.com; Greer and McLaughlin 2012; Greer 2017).

The McCanns began a legal action that resulted in several newspaper corporations making public apologies and substantial donations to the Find Madeline fund. Their libellous treatment figured prominently in the Leveson Inquiry into UK press abuses ranging from industrial scale phone hacking and paying corrupt police officers for

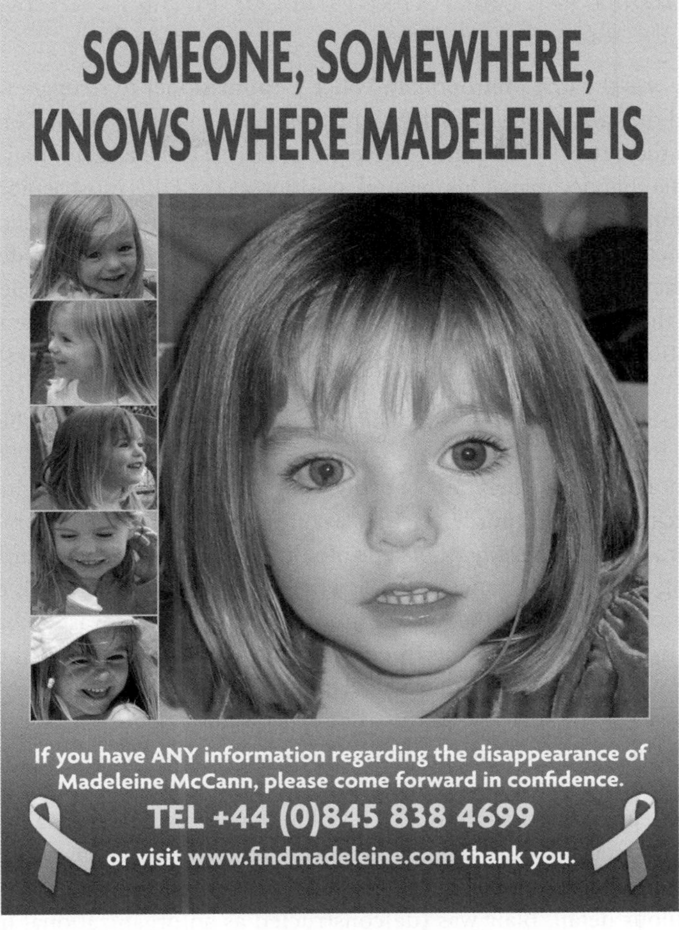

Figure 11.3 'Find Madeleine' poster

Source: http://findmadeleine.com/support/light/download_materials/english/english_poster1_0.pdf

tip-offs to harassing celebrities and crime victims (http://www.levesoninquiry.org.uk/). In their evidence to the inquiry the McCanns described how false and malicious news coverage had undermined the search for their daughter and subjected them to attempted blackmail and sustained trial by media (ibid.). Kate McCann explained how she felt 'worthless' and 'mentally raped' after extracts from a private diary were reprinted in a tabloid newspaper without her permission (*Daily Telegraph*, 17 November, 2011: 2).

This case illustrates a period in the evolution of UK newspaper corporations' new business model when the convergence of tabloidization and digitalization produced a remarkable state of anomie within sections of the market. What began as a story of the institutional failure of the Portuguese police ended as a story of the institutional failure of the British press. The McCanns' evidence played an important role in the Leveson inquiry's attempt to redraw ethical boundaries around journalistic practice and, in so doing, to set limits on trial by media.

INSTITUTIONAL FAILURE TO PROVIDE COMPETENT CRIMINAL JUSTICE LEADERSHIP

Sir Ian Blair was the first Metropolitan Police Commissioner to struggle with the tabloidized and digitalized news developments described in this chapter. Considered too liberal from the outset by the conservative press, Blair was the target for an unrelenting trial by media that decimated his 'natural' position as the UK's most senior police officer. The tipping point in Blair's trial by media came at a Metropolitan Police Authority monthly meeting. When challenged on the unequal resourcing of murder investigations, he stated that the Metropolitan Police allocated resources to murders in accordance with the difficulty of the investigation. He then asserted that the news media were institutionally racist in how they reported murders. Blair further questioned news media selectivity by asking why the disappearance and murder of two ten-year-old Soham girls, Holly Wells and Jessica Chapman—which precipitated the biggest police manhunt in British history, received so much news attention in August 2002.

The reaction was overwhelmingly hostile. Newspapers reproduced high-profile coverage of black and Asian murder victims as 'proof' that they were not racist in their reporting practices. The *Daily Mail* reprinted its ground-breaking 'Murderers' front page naming Stephen Lawrence's alleged killers. But Blair attracted an entirely different order of criticism for the Soham murders comment. He was lambasted across newspaper front pages for daring to question the newsworthiness of the abduction and murder of Holly Wells and Jessica Chapman. The following morning Blair made an unreserved 'on air' apology on BBC Radio 4 for any offence his comments might have caused the murdered girls' families (Blair 2009). But the fallout of the Soham remarks coalesced with a hostile political environment to make his Commissionership untenable (Greer and McLaughlin 2011). Calling the press institutionally racist was a provocation for certain journalists, who quickly rebutted the claim. Questioning the newsworthiness of the murder of two ten-year-old girls was inexcusable.

In meticulous detail, Blair was (de)constructed as an organizational liability who had lost his grip on Scotland Yard, forfeited the respect of the rank-and-file, and exhausted political support. Over time, the words and images that came to constitute Blair's news media identity were those of a 'politicized', 'operationally compromised', and 'gaffe-prone' Commissioner. As columnist and former *Times* editor Simon Jenkins (2006) put it:

> London's police chief, Sir Ian Blair, is being dragged into the street by a mob of journalists and politicians, blood-stained but still twitching. He is taunted, spat at, kicked and beaten. The editor of the Sun is looking for a gibbet, and of the Mail for a rope. Politicians are queuing to thwack the horse from under the gallows.

After three years of unyielding trial by media, Sir Ian Blair resigned from post on 2 October 2008. He was the first Commissioner to do so since Sir Charles Warren in 1888, who resigned for failing to catch Jack the Ripper. Sir Ian Blair's trial by media did more than delegitimize one particular Commissioner. It clarified what 'type' of Commissioner and policing philosophy would be acceptable to the UK conservative national press. Further, it set a precedent for police–media relations and established a new set of reputational risks that would have to be managed by anyone seeking to become the UK's most senior police officer (Greer and McLaughlin 2011). Sir Ian Blair's successor, Sir Paul Stephenson, became the second Metropolitan Police Commissioner since 1888 to resign before term, as a result of the *News of the World* phone hacking scandal of 2011. The favourite to succeed him, Sir Hugh Orde, withdrew from the contest in the midst of his own publicly humiliating trial by media (Greer and McLaughlin 2012c). The successful candidate, Sir Bernard Hogan-Howe, became the third Metropolitan Police Commissioner since 1888 to resign before term. The same conservative newspapers that had initially offered qualified support undermined Hogan-Howe's Commissionership through trial by media following a botched police investigation into historical child sexual abuse in which Field Marshall Lord Brammall was publicly named as a suspected paedophile in the absence of any credible evidence (Henriques 2016).

NEWS POWER, SCANDAL HUNTING AND MEDIA JUSTICE

Newspaper corporations are still learning how to maximize the impact of trial by media. The ethically questionable tactics used by certain journalists to gather information in the past, such as industrial-scale phone hacking, were finally outlawed by the Leveson inquiry. One of the most remarkable periods in the history of British journalism resulted in the closure of the 168-year-old flagship tabloid, the *News of the World*, journalists being prosecuted, and newspaper corporations settling substantial civil claims (Keeble and Mair 2012). This anomic moment appears to have precipitated a recalibration and refocusing of the relations between news power, crime, and criminal justice. As UK newspaper corporations continue to learn from their mistakes, and their successes, there has emerged an even more ambitious form of news campaigning, directed not just at powerful public figures but at Britain's core institutions and government. In a digitally-led news environment characterized by ever-increasing proliferation, interactivity, and adversarialism, newspaper corporations have taken their business model to the next level: from portraying individual institutional failures to exposing systemic institutional scandal.

The overlapping categories of infraction that underpin scandals are the same as those that drive trial by media; criminality, immorality, and incompetence. However, while anyone can potentially become a target for TBM, scandals implicate the institutionally powerful—high-profile individuals or institutions whose official position carries the expectation of upholding clearly defined moral or ethical principles. The infractions are sufficiently shocking that their public revelation triggers a powerful negative social reaction that can have life-changing reputational consequences for the protagonists (Greer and McLaughlin 2013, 2015). Though diverse, we would argue that scandals progress through consistent phases—hunting, latency, activation, reaction, amplification, and accountability. These phases are illustrated in Figure 11.4. (see also Greer

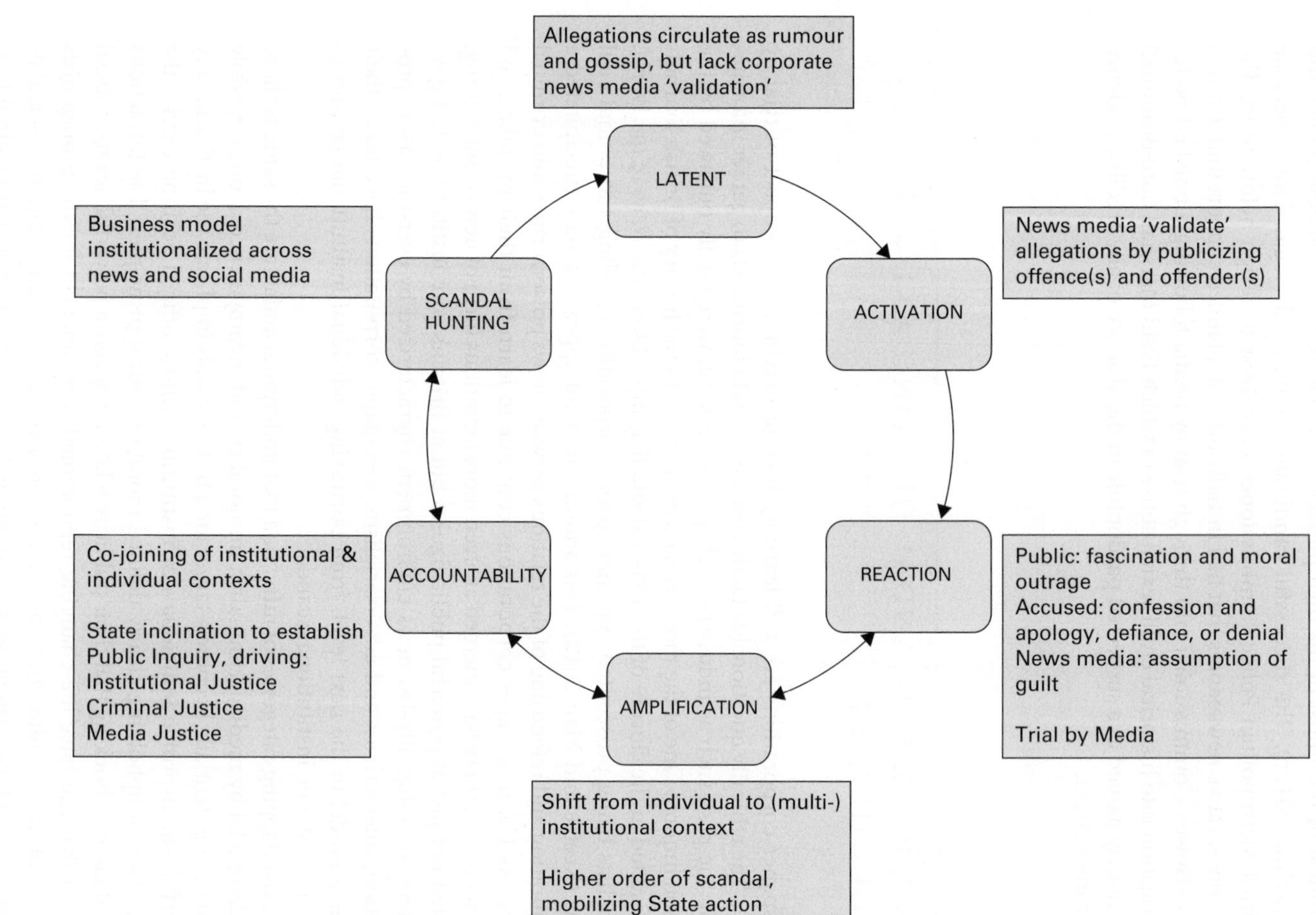

Figure 11.4 Institutional scandal model

and McLaughlin 2016). Scandal hunting in the UK has traditionally been viewed as the archetypal tabloid news practice: cheap, sensationalist, salacious, exploitative, and a distraction from 'real' news. However, institutional scandal hunting is now practiced by all of the UK's newspaper corporations and a multitude of online news and social media sites. Scandal hunting involves:

- sting operations to catch public figures engaging in scandalous behaviours;
- investigating rumours and allegations that might in turn result in a new scandal scoop;
- inviting members of the public and whistleblowers to share scandalous information.

While scandals may be activated—or claimed—and subsequently 'owned' by particular newspaper corporations, they will become intermediatized across digital platforms and inflected in accordance with ideological position. In addition to being commercially valuable, scandal hunting is inherently political. There is no shortage of high-profile examples: the politicians' expenses scandal (*Daily Telegraph* 2009); the WikiLeaks' scandal triggered by the release of confidential US national security and diplomatic documents (*Guardian, New York Times, Der Spiegel* 2010); the phone-hacking scandal that resulted in the closure of the *News of the World* (*Guardian* 2011); the mass surveillance scandal resulting from the document leak by National Security Agency whistleblower Edward Snowden (*Guardian* 2013); the Panama Papers scandal revealing the offshore tax avoidance behaviours of the world's rich and powerful (*Guardian* 2016); international sports scandals resulting from the exposure of institutionalized corruption at the highest levels (*Times* and *Sunday Times* 2016); the UK Football Association scandal resulting from the exposure of corruption in the transfer market (*Daily Telegraph* 2016); historical child sex abuse scandals implicating dozens of UK football clubs (*Guardian* and *Daily Mirror* 2016). However, if the Stephen Lawrence and Sarah Payne cases established a template to guide UK newspapers' orchestration of victim-centred campaigns, the Sir Jimmy Savile case has established a template for the activation and amplification of institutional scandal.

Sir Jimmy Savile (1926–2011) was a BBC celebrity, philanthropist, and friend of the establishment. One year after his death, in October 2012, a television documentary claimed that Savile was also a sexual predator who for decades had used his celebrity status to abuse teenage girls. This documentary activated an intermediatized trial by media that destroyed Savile's reputation and implicated the BBC—the institution that catapulted him to superstardom—into an extraordinary institutional child sex abuse scandal. The BBC's initial reaction—denial of knowledge and responsibility—triggered another trial by media that amplified the scandal from the individual problem of Savile's offending to the institutional problem of the BBC's failure, denial, and cover-up. As police and, crucially, news media investigations uncovered more alleged victims and offenders, the scandal escalated and amplified across numerous public institutions (Greer and McLaughlin 2016). Police investigations resulted in the questioning, and in some cases high-profile arrest and prosecution, of aging celebrities and public figures accused of historical sexual assaults. All of those accused publicly denied their guilt. Only some were convicted, but all were subjected to a shaming intermediatized trial by media. Child protection organizations reported that the 'Savile effect' had led to a dramatic increase in reports of child sexual abuse. The Independent Inquiry into Child Sexual Abuse (IICSA) was established in 2015 to investigate the extent to which 'institutions have failed in their duty of care to protect children from sexual abuse and exploitation' (https://www.iicsa.org.uk/about-us/terms-of-reference). In addition to being the UK's most large-scale and wide-ranging public inquiry, the IICSA is also its most intermediatized to date. The inquiry's remit, the credibility of those appointed as chair, the appointment process itself, and the character and competence of inquiry members have all been scrutinized across news and social media forums. Trial by media remains an ever-present risk for anyone deemed unacceptable. As we illustrated above, the charge of institutional failure to provide competent criminal justice leadership has become a particular focus for newspaper corporations' moral outrage. The first three Chairs of the IICSA, Baroness Elizabeth Butler-Sloss, Fiona Woolf, and Justice Lowell Goddard, were all subjected to trial by media. All resigned in humiliating circumstances. In the context of UK newspaper corporations' reconstituted sense of adversarial power, most dramatically evidenced through trial by media and institutional scandal hunting, even public inquiries now run the risk of becoming part of the scandal they have been established to manage.

CONCLUSION

In this chapter we have set out our position on the transformation of news power that is reshaping crime consciousness and criminal justice rhetoric, practice and policy in the UK. Crime will always be newsworthy, and therefore profitable as a news category, because it works across the emotional registers of fear, anger, and fascination. Criminologists will continue to research the processes through which crime news is selectively produced and the emotional social reactions it generates. This programme of research will of course include continued analysis of the functioning of crime news values and of the conditions under which we might justifiably say that the social reaction to crime constitutes a moral panic. But for such concept-testing analyses to be meaningful—for them to move beyond their taxonomical application—requires a broader and deeper appreciation of a rapidly transforming tabloidized and digitalized news market. We have argued that, as a result of criminology's failure to keep pace with recent transformations, the reconstitution of contemporary news power remains under-researched and under-conceptualized.

The news media have always been a key site where justice is seen to be done. Today, however, UK newspaper corporations are redefining what justice is, and how it can and should be achieved. Victim-centred campaigns are exposing the scandalous institutional failure of the UK criminal justice system to provide public protection. In a context of declining confidence in the effectiveness of contemporary governance, trial by media is creating and delivering an alternative and highly distinctive form of justice. Media justice is a parallel and, at times, more visible, easily intelligible, and immediately impactful justice paradigm than that represented by the increasingly dysfunctional criminal justice process. Digital news sites have become platforms not only for the generation of intermediatized crime and justice debates and campaigns, but also for immersive participation in the naming and shaming of individuals and institutions. Though the criminal justice system retains the executive power to prosecute and sentence offenders, newspaper corporations are pre-empting and circumventing due process by pronouncing on guilt or innocence and, if the judgment is guilty, administering their own form of retribution. Media justice at once invokes, channels, and expresses moral outrage. Its unique form of extra-judicial punishment is administered through destroying the credibility and reputation of 'guilty' individuals or institutions. Its core mechanisms—trial by media and scandal hunting—form the basis of a business model that has been adopted by all UK newspaper corporations. Scandal hunting, activation and amplification, premised on maximum exposure and maximum moral outrage, is further complicating the state's capacity for governance by reconfiguring the power relations between newspaper corporations, a networked citizenry, and a scandal-ridden criminal justice system.

SELECTED FURTHER READING

Greer's *Crime and Media: A Reader* (2010) is an annotated collection of key contributions covering many of the issues discussed in this chapter. Illuminating studies of the production of crime news are Chibnall's *Law and Order News: An Analysis of Crime Reporting* (1977) and the trilogy by Ericson, Baranek, and Chan, *Visualising Deviance, Negotiating Control, and Representing Order* (1987, 1989, 1991 respectively); Schlesinger and Tumber's *Reporting Crime* (1994); Greer's *Sex Crime and the Media* (2012/2003) and 'News Media Criminology' (2010). The most important studies of moral panic remain Cohen's *Folk Devils and Moral Panics* (1972/2002) and Hall *et al.*'s, *Policing the Crisis* (1978). Overview texts on crime and media are Carrabine's *Crime, Culture, and the Media* (2008) and Jewkes, *Media and Crime* (2015). Key articles on trial by media and scandal hunting are Greer and McLaughlin's 'The Sir Jimmy Savile scandal: Child sexual abuse and institutional denial at the BBC' (2013) and 'Theorizing institutional scandal and the regulatory state' (2016). The journal *Crime Media Culture: An International Journal* (London: Sage) is a key source for current and relevant articles.

REFERENCES

Alexander, J., Breese, E., and Luengo, M. (eds) (2016), *The Crisis of Journalism Reconsidered: Democratic Culture, Professional Codes, Digital Future*, Cambridge: Cambridge University Press.

Beckett, K. (1997), *Making Crime Pay: Law and Order in Contemporary American Politics*, Oxford: Oxford University Press.

Bird, E. (1992), *For Enquiring Minds: A Cultural Study Supermarket Tabloids*, Tennessee: University of Tennessee Press.

Birks, J. (2010), 'Press protest and publics: the agency of publics in newspaper campaigns', *Discourse and Communication*, 4(1): 56–67.

Blair, I. (2009), *Policing Controversy*, London: Profile.

Boczkowski, P. J. (2004), *Digitizing the News: Innovation in Online Newspapers*, Cambridge, MA: MIT Press.

Bottoms, A. E. (1995), 'The Philosophy and Politics of Punishment and Sentencing', in C. Clarkson and R. Morgan (eds), *The Politics of Sentencing Reform*, Oxford: Clarendon.

Brock, G. (2013), *Out of Print: Newspapers, Journalism and the Business of News in the Digital Age*, London: Kogan Page.

Bromley, M. (1998), 'The "Tabloiding" of Britain: "Quality" Newspapers in the 1990s', in M. Bromley and H. Stephenson (eds), *Sex, Lies and Democracy: The Press and the Public*, Harrow, Addison Wesley Longman.

Carrabine, E. (2008) *Crime, Culture, and the Media*, Cambridge: Polity.

Charman, S. and Savage, S. P. (2009), 'Mothers for Justice?', *British Journal of Criminology*, 49(6): 900–15.

Chibnall, S. (1977), *Law and Order News: An Analysis of Crime Reporting in the British Press*, London: Tavistock.

Cohen, S. (1972/2002), *Folk Devils and Moral Panics: The Creation of the Mods and Rockers*, London: MacGibbon and Kee (3rd edn, Routledge, 2002).

Cohen, S. and Young, J. (eds) (1973), *The Manufacture of News: Social Problems, Deviance and Mass Media*, London: Constable (revised edn 1981).

Conboy, M. (2006), *Tabloid Britain: Constructing a Community Through Language*, London: Routledge.

Cottle, S. (2004), *The Racist Murder of Stephen Lawrence: Media Performance and Public Transformation*, Westport, CT: Praeger.

Ericson, R., Baranek, P., and Chan, J. (1987), *Visualising Deviance: A Study of News Organisation*, Milton Keynes: Open University Press.

Ericson, R., Baranek, P., and Chan, J. (1989), *Negotiating Control: A Study of News Sources*, Milton Keynes: Open University Press.

Ericson, R., Baranek, P., and Chan, J. (1991), *Representing Order: Crime, Law and Justice in the News Media*, Milton Keynes: Open University Press.

Franklin, B. (1997), *Newszak and News Media*, London: Arnold.

Fukuyama, F. (2000), *Trust: the Social Virtues and the Creation of Prosperity*, New York: Diane.

Garland, D. (2001a), *The Culture of Control: Crime and Social Order in Contemporary Society*, Oxford: Oxford University Press.

Garland, D. (ed.) (2001b), *Mass Imprisonment: Social Causes and Consequences*, Los Angeles: Sage.

Greer, C. (2003/2012), *Sex Crime and the Media: Sex Offending and the Press in a Divided Society*, London: Routledge.

Greer, C. and McLaughlin, E. (2010), 'We Predict a Riot: Public Order Policing, New Media Environments and the Rise of the Citizen Journalist', in *British Journal of Criminology*, 50(6): 1041–59.

Greer, C. (ed.) (2010a), *Crime and Media: A Reader*, London: Routledge.

Greer, C. (2010b), 'News Media Criminology' in E. McLaughlin and T. Newburn (eds), *The Sage Handbook of Criminological Theory*, London: Sage.

Greer, C. and McLaughlin, E. (2011), 'Trial by media: Policing, the News 24-7 News Mediasphere, and the Politics of Outrage', *Theoretical Criminology*, 15(1): 23–46.

Greer, C. and Reiner, R. (2012), 'Mediated Mayhem: Media, Crime and Criminal Justice', in M. Maguire, R. Morgan, and R. Reiner (eds), *The Oxford Handbook of Criminology*, 5th edn, Oxford: Oxford University Press.

Greer, C. and McLaughlin, E. (2012a), 'This is not Justice: Ian Tomlinson, Institutional Failure and the Press Politics of Outrage', *British Journal of Criminology*, 52(2): 274–93.

Greer, C. and McLaughlin, E. (2012b), 'Media Justice: Madeleine McCann, Intermediatization and "Trial by Media" in the British press', *Theoretical Criminology*, 16(4): 395–416.

Greer, C. and McLaughlin, E. (2012c), 'Trial by Media: Riots, Looting, Gangs and Mediatised Police Chiefs', in J. Peay and T. Newburn (eds), *Policing, Politics, Culture and Control: Essays in Honour of Robert Reiner* (Festschrift), London: Hart.

Greer, C. (2013), 'Crime and Media: Understanding the Connections', in C. Hale, K. Hayward, A. Wahadin, and E. Wincup (eds), *Criminology*, 3rd edn, Oxford: Oxford University Press.

Greer, C. and McLaughlin, E. (2013), 'The Sir Jimmy Savile scandal: Child sexual abuse and institutional denial at the BBC', *Crime, Media, Culture*, 9(3): 243–63.

Greer, C. and McLaughlin, E. (2014), 'Righting Wrongs: Citizen Journalism and Miscarriages of Justice', in S. Allan and E. Thorsen (eds), *Citizen Journalism: Global Perspectives, Volume Two*, London: Peter Lang.

Greer, C. and McLaughlin, E. (2015), 'The Return of the Repressed: Secrets, Lies, Denial and "Historical" Institutional Child Sexual Abuse Scandals', in D. Whyte (ed.), *How Corrupt is Britain?*, London: Pluto.

Greer, C. and McLaughlin, E. (2016), 'Theorizing Institutional Scandal and the Regulatory State', *Theoretical Criminology*: doi: 10.1177/1362480616645648.

Greer, C. (2017), 'News Media, Victims and Crime', in P. Davies, P. Francis, and C. Greer (eds), *Victims, Crime and Society*, 2nd edn, London: Sage.

Hall, S. (1980), 'Popular Democratic vs. Authoritarian Populism: Two Ways of Taking *Democracy* Seriously', in A. Hunt (ed.), *Marxism and Democracy*, London: Lawrence and Wishart.

Hall, S. (1979), 'The Great Moving Right Show', *Marxism Today*, January, 14–20.

Hall, N., Grieve, J., and Savage, S. (eds) (2013), *Policing and the Legacy of Lawrence*, Cullompton: Willan.

Hall, S., Critcher, C., Jefferson, T., Clarke, J., and Roberts, B. (1978), *Policing the Crisis: Mugging, the State and Law and Order*, London: Macmillan.

Halloran, J., Elliott, P., and Murdock, G. (1970), *Demonstrations and Communication. A Case Study*, Harmondsworth: Penguin.

Henriques, Sir R. (2016), *Independent Review of Metropolitan Police Service's Handling of Non-Recent Sexual Offences Investigations*, London: Metropolitan Police Service.

Huff, C. R. and Killias, M. (2008), *Wrongful Conviction International Perspectives on Miscarriages of Justice*, Philadelphia: Temple University Press.

Jenkins, H. (2004), The Cultural Logic of Media Convergence, *International Journal of Cultural Studies*, 7(1): 33–43.

JENKINS, S. (2006), 'Only Livingstone Emerges from all this with any Credit', *The Guardian*, 14 June: https://www.theguardian.com/commentisfree/2006/jun/14/comment.july7, accessed 14 December 2016.

JEWKES, Y. (2015), *Media and Crime*, 3rd edn, London: Sage.

JONES, T. and NEWBURN, T. (2013), 'Policy convergence, politics and comparative penal reform: Sex offender notification schemes in the USA and UK', *Punishment & Society*, 15(5): 439–67.

KATZ, J. (1987), 'What Makes Crime News', in *Media, Culture and Society*, 9(1): 47–76.

KEEBLE, R. and MAIR, J. (eds) (2012), *The Phone Hacking Scandal: Journalism on Trial*, London: Abramis.

LANG, J. and DODKINS, G. (2011), *Bad News: The Wapping Dispute*, London: Spokesman.

LEWIS, P. and NEWBURN, T. (2011), *Reading the Riots: Investigating England's Summer of Disorder*, London: Guardian Books.

LLOYD, J. (2004), *What the Media are Doing to our Politics*, London: Constable.

MCLAUGHLIN, E. (2005), 'Recovering Blackness - Repudiating Whiteness: The Daily Mail's Construction of the Five White Suspects Accused of the Racist Murder of Stephen Lawrence', in K. Murji and J. Solomos (eds), *Racialization: Studies in Theory and Practice*, Oxford: Oxford University Press.

MCNAIR, B. (2006), *Cultural Chaos: Journalism, News and Power in a Globalised World*, London: Routledge.

MILNE, K. (2005), *Manufacturing Dissent: Single-Issue Protest, the Public and the Press*, London: Demos.

MISHRA, P. (2017), *Age of Anger: A History of the Present*, London: Allen Lane.

MURDOCH, R. (2006), *Newspapers will change, not die*. Paper presented at the Worshipful Company of Stationers And Newspaper Makers Annual Livery Lecture London: http://business.timesonline.co.uk/tol/business/industry_sectors/media/article740587.ece.

PAYNE, S. (2005), *Sara Payne: A Mother's Story*, London: Hodder and Stoughton.

PRATT, J. (2007), *Penal Populism*, London: Routledge.

PROTESS, D. L., COOK, F., DOPPELT, J., ETERMA, J., GORDON, M., LEFF, D., and MILLER, P. (1991), *The Journalism of Outrage: Investigative Reporting and Agenda Building in America*, New York; London: Guilford Press.

REINER, R., LIVINGSTONE, S., and ALLEN, J. (2000), 'Casino Culture: Media and Crime in a Winner-Loser Society', in K. Stenson and D. Cowell (eds), *Crime, Risk and Justice*, Cullompton: Willan.

ROBERTS, J., STALANS, L., INDERMAUR, D., and HOUGH, M. (2003), *Penal Populism and Public Opinion: Lessons from Five Countries*, New York: Oxford University Press.

ROCK, P. (1973), 'News as Eternal Recurrence', in S. Cohen and J. Young (eds), *The Manufacture of News: Social Problems, Deviance and Mass Media*, London: Constable.

RUSBRIDGER, A. (2008), 'Can Newspapers Survive and Serve the Public Interest?': Intelligence 2: The World of Debate, available at: https://www.youtube.com/watch?v=2wO2Ags30_8

SABATO, L. (1991), *Feeding Frenzy: How Attack Journalism Has Transformed American Politics*, New York: Free Press.

SAMBROOK, R. (2005), 'Citizen Journalism and the BBC', in *Nieman Reports*, available at: http://www.nieman.harvard.edu/reportsitem.aspx?id=100542, accessed 14 December 2016.

SASSON, T. (1995), *Crime Talk: How Citizens Construct A Social Problem*, New York: Aldine De Gruyter.

SCHLESINGER, P. and TUMBER, H. (1994), *Reporting Crime: The Media Politics of Criminal Justice*, Oxford: Clarendon Press.

SELDON, A. (2009), *Trust: How we Lost it and How to Get it Back*, London: Biteback.

SILVERMAN, J. and WILSON, D. (2002), *Innocence Betrayed: Paedophilia, the Media and Society*, Cambridge: Polity.

SPARKS, C. and TULLOCK, J. (eds) (2000), *Tabloid Tales: Global Debates Over Media Standards*, Maryland: Rowman and Littlefield Publishers.

TUNSTALL, J. (1996), *Newspaper Power: The New National Press in Britain*, Oxford, Oxford University Press.

TURNER, G. (1999), 'Tabloidization, Journalism and the Possibility of Critique', *International Journal of Cultural Studies*, 2(1): 59–76.

WESTLUND, O. (2013), Mobile News, *Digital Journalism*, 1(1): 6–26.

YOUNG, J. (1971), 'The Role of the Police as Amplifiers of Deviancy, Negotiators of Reality, and Translators of Fantasy: Some Consequences of our Present System of Drug Control as Seen in Notting Hill', in S. Cohen and J. Young (eds), *Images of Deviance*, Harmondsworth: Penguin.

12

SOCIAL HARM AND ZEMIOLOGY

Paddy Hillyard and Steve Tombs

INTRODUCTION

We all grow up with a story of crime—of what crime and who the criminal is. This, at the same time, entails stories of what is *not* crime and who is *not* the criminal. These stories constitute a part of the common sense of crime although these dominant constructions of common sense can change over time and place.

Within the story of crime with which British readers will be most familiar, the criminal will likely look like a young, male adult, disproportionately of black and minority ethnic (BME origin), dressed in one of several stereotypical ways, to be particularly feared in certain places at certain times. Such stereotypes are easily contradicted, but are still recognizable. As teachers and students we all learn very quickly to laugh at first-year representations of Lombroso's claims around the physical manifestations of atavism, but at the same time we recognize it and act upon it in our daily lives. Who has not heard, said, or thought the phrase, 'he doesn't look the type'? Who has not made assumptions about a group of young people based upon their being gathered in a public place, dressed in certain manner? For us, as important as those whom our stories of crime identify as actual or potential offenders, are those excluded. Our ingrained, common-sense tropes regarding the criminal do not include the restaurant or factory owner, nor the directors of road transport or food-processing companies. It won't include senior managers at one of the 'Big Four' supermarkets, or petrol companies. It is even unlikely to include the company itself, represented by a headquarters, a corporate logo, an organogram, or a memorandum of incorporation, each of which would more accurately identify the origins of corporate-produced harm.

Of course, criminologists engage with and produce much more sophisticated stories of crime and criminals than these popular versions. But, as we shall argue here, criminology is neither immune to this general common sense, nor is it in control of it. Indeed, much criminological research is produced and maintained by very powerful interests, not least the state, which produces definitions of crime through criminal law, around which the whole edifice of the criminal justice system and its onlookers in the media, public, and political spheres are then mobilized. In short, criminologists, like other criminal justice actors, have largely accepted a definition of crime as a violation of the criminal law, hence leaving the discipline hostage to a system that has criminalized individual behaviours like homosexuality and abortion, but largely not harms generated through corporate activities such as tax avoidance nor state atrocities such as genocide.

Now, many criminologists long recognized, and struggled with, the inherent limitations of a state-based definition of crime. Sellin (1938), for example, suggested the alternative notion of 'conduct norms'. Sutherland (1945) famously extended the label crime to those acts prohibited by bodies of law beyond the criminal law, illustrating 'divergence between legal, social and political definitions of criminality' and thus reminding us 'of the artificiality of all definitions of crime' (Nelken 1994: 366). Using a human rights framework, Schwendinger and Schwendinger (1970) proposed that the harms arising from racism, sexism, and economic exploitation should be central to the study of criminology. For Michalowski (1985: 317), illegal or harmful acts that arise from the ownership or management of capital, which he calls 'crimes of capital', should also be studied within the discipline. More recently, Tifft and Sullivan (2001: 191) sought to extend the definition of crime to include, 'social conditions, social arrangements, or actions of intent or indifference that interfere with the fulfilment of fundamental needs and obstruct the spontaneous unfolding of human potential'. Notwithstanding these, and other efforts, by the turn of this century, 'the concept of social harm' had 'never seriously been incorporated into criminology' (Muncie 2000: 3).

In the late 1990s a group of academics began to think in a more concentrated way about how a concept of social harm could be more progressively developed as an alternative to crime. The motivations, or routes, via which individuals joined this conversation, were various. Some were pursuing the conceptual struggles of Sellin, Sutherland, and others to operationalize a concept of crime in their respective areas of work, where a lack of definitional and legal clarity, and indeed relative *non*-criminalization, were the norm—notably those working on corporate, state, and white-collar crime. Others approached this enterprise on the basis of a concern with the marked expansion of criminology as a discipline and the concomitant increase in the number of degree courses in British and Irish universities, while older subjects, such as social policy and sociology, were declining. Some of this group felt that the notion of social harm could be developed at the margins of criminology, through challenging the discursive power of concepts of crime, criminal and criminal justice. For others, given the integral nature of these latter concepts to the discipline of criminology itself, any sustained focus on social harm could only be achieved within a new and separate discipline.

An outcome of these discussions was a speculative consideration of a sustained focus on the study of social harm, or the development of an alternative discipline, zemiology. The word was adopted in 1998 from the Greek word for harm, Zemia, during the Annual Conference of the European Group for the Study of Deviance and Social Control on the Greek island of Spetses. Months later, a conference, *Zemiology: Beyond criminology?*, was held in Dartington, England. It included a diverse range of contributions from academics, policy-makers, and practitioners, from a range of disciplines, including criminal justice, development economics and development studies, geosciences, law, poverty studies, public health, social policy, and sociology, with criminology being a decidedly minority presence.[1] Subsequently, some of these papers, along with commissioned essays, were published as *Beyond Criminology: Taking Harm Seriously* (Hillyard *et al.* 2004).

Beyond criminology was an eclectic, somewhat contradictory work reflecting a wide variety of contributors, theoretical positions, and levels and objects of analysis. The first section of this chapter reviews some of the central arguments in the challenge entailed in that book's title. In a subsequent section, we seek to elaborate on some of those arguments, first through illustrating the kinds of harms we believe to be more significant a focus than crime and, following that, to consider how these might take peculiar forms under neoliberalism. The chapter then turns to consider responses to our arguments—both at the level of the discipline as a set of institutions, and then via analyses of some of the more critical, intellectual responses. Our final substantive section explores the relationship between critical criminology, social harm, and zemiology.

BEYOND CRIMINOLOGY?

The starting point of *Beyond Criminology* was an elaboration upon nine fundamental criticisms of the discipline of criminology (Hillyard and Tombs 2004). These were fundamental in two senses: first, we believed them to be significant; second, they were the basis for the considerations that followed throughout the book about the relative merits of social harm and zemiology, as a development of or an alternative to criminology. These nine criticisms can be briefly summarized.

Crime has no ontological reality. There is nothing intrinsic in any behaviour that allows us to know that it is a crime without reference to an external index—namely, criminal law. It is in fact difficult if not impossible to conceive of any act that in all circumstances, in all places, at all times, appears as a crime. The taking of life, the expropriation of another's property, and the deprivation of liberty all take legal forms. Crime is thus a 'myth' of everyday life, albeit a highly salient one. To be clear, to say that crime has no ontological reality (Becker 1963; Box 1983; Christie 2004; De Hann 1996; Hulsman 1986; Mathiesen 1974; Steinert 1986) is not 'a dismissal of crime as a "fictive event" '—it is simply to recognise that its status as a reality is one that is constructed (and indeed can only be understood) within any given set of social relations, a "social complex" which is always "contingent rather than necessary" ' (Lasslett, 2010: 1–3).

Criminology perpetuates the myth of crime. In the large and growing criminological literature, with a few notable exceptions, criminologists typically take crime as an unproblematic concept and there is little or no attempt to offer a definition. For example, it was not until its third edition that *The Oxford Handbook* contained a dedicated chapter discussing the definition of crime (Lacey 2002). Criminology texts continue to offer theories about why people commit crime, about how crime should be measured,

[1] On the conference, see http://www.radstats.org.uk/no070/conference2.htm, accessed 16 December 2016.

about how crime might be prevented or responded to without any discussion of the concept.

Crime consists of many petty events. Most crimes in popular consciousness are perceived as very harmful events. Yet most behaviours which are defined as crimes are relatively harmless. They would not, as Hulsman (1986) has noted, score particularly highly on a scale of personal hardship. Reiman argues in his 'pyrrhic defeat theory' of criminal justice policy and system, that 'the definitions of crime in the criminal law do not reflect the only or the most dangerous of antisocial behaviours' (1998: 61). He goes on to argue that neither do the decisions of whom to arrest or charge or the resulting convictions reflect the only or the most dangerous behaviours.

Crime excludes many serious harms. By contrast, the criminal law often fails to embrace many serious harmful behaviours or if it does, they are ignored or handled without resort to it. The two most obvious examples are corporate crime and state crime. The focus on events that are defined as crimes clearly distract attention away from the more serious harmful behaviours. As Tifft and Sullivan (1980: 6) argue, 'by insisting on legal assumptions as sacred, criminologists comply in the concealment and distortion of the reality of social harms', particularly those harms inflicted by persons with power.

Constructing crimes. The construction of a crime involves a number of complex and elaborate processes. For example, central to determining guilt is the concept of '*mens rea*' (the guilty mind) which applies principally, but not exclusively, to the individual. This involves a series of legal processes, artificial, proxy measures whereby intention has to be judged by examining a person's words and deeds, then speculatively assessing these against the standard: a fictitious ordinary person. This fixation with the guilty mind also reflects the individualistic basis upon which bourgeois law has been constructed; this bias is evident in the difficulties of ascribing criminal liability upon collective entities such as the corporation, in turn underpinning the effective decriminalization of many of the socially destructive effects of corporate activity.

Criminalization and punishment. Once a behaviour or incident has been categorized as a possible crime, the whole process of criminalization begins: arrest, prosecution, conviction, punishment. The state, as Christie (1977) has pointed out, appropriates the conflict and imposes punishment. To categorize and respond to harmful behaviours as criminal sets in train a process which is managed by state institutions, focusing on the offender not the victim nor the underlying conditions which may have produced the crime (Macnaughton-Smith 1970). In so doing, the state tends to reproduce pain, harm, and indeed the likelihood of further crime, while such processes of criminalization foreclose any other form of response to harmful behaviour other than more criminalization.

'Crime control' is ineffective. Ironically, perhaps the greatest contribution of criminology has been to show that 'crime control' is ineffective. Recent Ministry of Justice data, for 2012–13, indicates that 26.4 per cent of adult and juvenile 'offenders' who have been cautioned, convicted, or were released from custody were 'proven reoffenders' within 12 months of that sentence. But within this cohort, custodial sentences were much more likely to produce reoffending: the 'proven reoffending rate for adult offenders released from custody was 45.4 per cent' (a figure which had remained static, between 45–49 per cent, for a decade), while this 'proven reoffending rate for juvenile offenders

released from custody in 2013 was 66.5 per cent' (MoJ 2015: 6–7). Given that the MoJ's figures refer to 'proven reoffending', actual recidivism rates are likely to be considerably higher; for example, the MoJ also notes[2] that some 59 per cent of people sentenced to sentences of less than 12 months reoffend within the year following release. Thus, the starkest evidence of failure is in relation to prison—the ultimate sanction in England and Wales. Mathiesen in his classic text *Prison on Trial* (1990) describes the prison as a 'fiasco' with no theoretical rationale for its existence.

The category of crime, and therefore criminology which is largely organized around it, gives legitimacy to the expansion of 'crime control'. Crime control is now a large industry solving two major problems, as Christie (1993) has noted: differential access to paid work and the uneven distribution of wealth. The industry provides profit and work while producing control of those who would otherwise cause trouble. It can expand effortlessly because crime dominates all social harm concerns. For Henry and Milovanovic conventional 'crime control' efforts fuel the engine of crime: 'control interventions take criminal activity to new levels on investment and self-enclosed innovation' (1996, x–xi). Much of the criminalization process is autopoietic: the system itself produces crimes, such as resisting arrest, assisting an offender, defaulting on a fine or a civil order, or jumping bail, as a direct consequence of the initial intervention. The system therefore reproduces and maintains itself. Second, the state creates and perpetuates harm, harms to the individual and to her/his family which often far exceed the harm done by the alleged behaviour.

The category of crime serves to maintain power relations. Crime plays a fundamental role in modern societies in maintaining existing power relations: it facilitates the ignoring of the collective harmful behaviours of those in power through privileging individual acts; it disallows reference to structural determinants of harmful individual behaviour such as poverty or inequality; and it maintains and sustains the powerful corporate bodies in the crime control industry. Since its inception, criminology has enjoyed an intimate relationship with the powerful, a relationship determined largely by its failure to subject to critique the category of crime—and disciplinary agendas set by this—which has been handed down by the state, and around which the criminal justice system has been organized (Foucault 1980; Cohen 1981; Garland 1992).

In the light of these nine fundamental criticisms, we argue that criminology is a distorting discipline—one incapable, because of a framework delimited by an existing body of criminal law, of understanding and analysing a whole range of harmful events and activities.

Many criminologists would recognize and even agree with some or many of the above observations. Yet, just as we can all be subject to critique crime stories and crime talk, exposing their myths, fallacies, even pure falsehoods, this does not in and of itself undermine them. In other words, a key issue for us is *the power of crime discourse*. Such is its power that it is naturalizes the idea that crime captures the most important and most dangerous of all social harms that will affect us from the cradle to the grave, as well as our belief that the only or most effective response to social harm is 'criminal justice'. These beliefs about crime constitute what Gramsci (1971: 419–25) called 'common sense'—constructed and reconstructed through pro-hegemonic forces, albeit that

[2] MoJ, *Open Justice*, http://open.justice.gov.uk/reoffending/, accessed 16 December 2016.

they are not, of course, immune from challenge. 'Social harm' and 'zemiology' represent a challenge to common sense about crime.

A social harm approach, or zemiology as a separate discipline focusing on harm, may provide a number of advantages over criminology and a focus on crime. First, it has the potential to be more coherent theoretically, as well as more comprehensive, encompassing a far wider range of the deleterious harms to peoples' welfare throughout their life. Second, the focus of such a discipline could be much broader than the specific harms experienced by individuals where the perpetuator had a 'guilty mind'. Zemiology would also include the harms experienced by individuals, households, family units, and indeed communities from whatever source, even encompassing mass harms. As a starting point, we suggested a fourfold typology of harm: physical, financial, psychological, and cultural/environmental. Third, a focus on harm allows a much wider investigation into who might be responsible unrestricted by individualistic notions of responsibility. Finally, it creates the opportunity to consider a range of policy responses to reduce harm beyond the dominant, relatively easy, but ineffective response of criminalization.

DIMENSIONS OF HARM PRODUCTION

In this section, we wish to introduce some indicative data in order to illustrate the levels of harm which a social harm or zemiological approach might document and seek to explain, harms which for the most part fall entirely beyond the ambit of criminal justice systems as well as academic criminology.

We have quite deliberately selected three forms of harm for our focus. One of these emphasizes the need for a social harm approach to encompass harms across the life cycle through a focus upon a form of harm experienced by older people. The other two categories of harm considered are occupational injury and illness—potentially affecting all of the working-age population—and exposure to unfit food, affecting all of the population but which may have differential effects, for example on those with other poor-health conditions, pregnant women, infants, and older people. These two categories cover workers and consumers; they are areas potentially but in fact very rarely subject to criminalization; and they are both phenomena at the margins of the discipline of criminology, analysed within the work of a handful of scholars. Following a brief, discursive overview of the data, we address why this matters and what place such data has in the context of a social harm or zemiology approach.

Excess Winter Deaths. Each year, the UK's Office for National Statistics calculates the number of 'excess winter deaths'—deaths from December to March compared with the average number of deaths occurring in the preceding and following four-month periods—in England and Wales. The most recently (November 2015) published figure estimates 43,900 such deaths occurred in England and Wales in 2014–15, the highest number since 1999–2000. Most of these (36,000), occurred among those 75 and over, with 7,700 deaths of people aged under 75. More than one-third of these deaths are caused by respiratory diseases. These are not people killed by the cold *per se*. In fact, countries with very low winter temperatures in Scandinavia and Northern Europe have very low rates of such deaths. Instead, most die of illnesses brought on by lack of access to affordable heating, or suitably insulated, warm and dry accommodation, or most likely both (Office for National Statistics 2015).

Fatal Workplace Injuries. Each year, the Health and Safety Exective (HSE) press releases the numbers of 'fatal injuries' to workers, which, in 2014–15, was 142. But this headline figure omits vast swathes of occupational deaths. Its *Health and Safety Statistics 2014–15* reveals 'Around 13,000 deaths each year from occupational lung disease and cancer are estimated to have been caused by past exposure, primarily to chemicals and dust at work'. (Health and Safety Executive, 2015: 2) This data still remains a gross underestimate. For example, researchers from the European Agency for Safety and Health at Work calculated, in 2009, 21,000 deaths per year in the UK from work-related fatal diseases, though such data 'might still be an under-estimation' (Hämäläinen *et al.* 2009: 127). And long-term research by the Hazards campaign,[3] drawing on a range of studies of occupational and environmental cancers, the number of heart-disease deaths with a work-related cause, as well as estimates of other diseases to which work can be a contributory cause, showed a lower-end estimate of 50,000 deaths from work-related illness in the UK each year (See Tombs 2014).

Food Poisoning. Finally, what is most commonly referred to as 'food poisoning' is a major source of death and illness in the UK. According to the most recent report from the Chief Scientist, 'Our best estimate suggests that there are around a million cases of foodborne illness in the UK each year, resulting in 20,000 hospital admissions and 500 deaths' (Food Standards Agency 2012: 11). Even these estimates of food related illness are likely to understate the scale of the problem. (Food Standards Agency, nd). More recently, Food Standards Agency sampling of chickens bought from large UK retail outlets and smaller independent stores and butchers between February 2014 and February 2015 found that about three-quarters (73 per cent) of these tested positive for the presence of campylobacter (Food Standards Agency 2015).

There are several observations to be made on such data.

First, in each area are significant numbers of deaths, life-shortening and life-threatening illnesses. Moreover, as with all forms of physical harms, these harms are associated with a wider series of harms generated by each death, injury, or illness. These might be financial, entailing a loss of income or additional costs incurred by the stricken person or his/her family members, or economic, in the sense that all of these harms entail various layers of costs for the state. Where the harms are generated in profit-making settings, these costs are socialized, while profits remain privatized—so there are harmful wealth-distribution effects, also. Moreover, associated with these harms are various emotional and psychological harms, many of which may be short-lived, others of which may endure over long periods.

Second, while statistics can be viewed as a collation of a series of isolated cases or incidents or harms, the harms captured in the above categories are much more usefully

[3] The Hazards Campaign 'supports those organising and campaigning for justice and safety at work'; see http://www.hazardscampaign.org.uk/?page_id=16, accessed 16 December 2016.

thought of not as incidents *per se*, but as processes, or effects of processes, indeed processes which arise in organizational settings, through forms of economic and social organization, and in structures. So although these may *manifest* themselves at the level of individuals, they are not *explicable* at the level of individuals. Relatedly, effective responses to them cannot be achieved through systems of accountability developed on the basis of individual categories such as those upon which criminal law is based (see earlier).

Third, the reference to structures in the previous paragraph should highlight to us the fact that these and other forms of harms are not distributed randomly but indeed differentially. In this respect it is often reasonable to emphasize the cumulative as opposed to the isolated experience of harm. This point is well made by Pemberton (2015), and developed below.

Let us finally reiterate the rationale for highlighting data such as that presented at the beginning of this section, not least in the context of Loader and Sparks' dismissal of zemiology as 'harm science' (2011: 24), 'at times surprisingly positivistic', attempting to produce 'objective measures' of harm via experiences and data which are believed 'to be free of state contamination' (Loader and Sparks 2011: 151).

First, it is clear that the data which we have presented here is socially constructed, and cannot be free of 'state' nor indeed other sources of contamination. To accept this simply means that all data, official or otherwise must be subjected to rigorous academic scepticism and interrogation rather than simply accepting or rejecting it.

Second, to identify the relative scale of deaths, injuries, and illnesses, for example, linked to a specific social activity or process, is not merely a 'numbers game'; it seems sensible for such considerations to inform debates on priorities in social or public policy.

Third, critical social scientists, including critical criminologists, often spend a great deal of their time uncovering hidden harm or crimes—and often this involves not simply using, reconstructing, or generating statistical data, but also comparing this with other statistical indices of social or crime problems. Thus, the 'numbers game' seems to be pretty integral to much academic work.

The production of social harm, which the above 'numbers' illustrate, is not a random phenomenon. Capitalist forms of economic *and harm* production may be organized in a series of quite distinct ways, but for us neoliberal forms of capitalism are qualitatively and quantitatively more harmful than other forms (Tombs and Hillyard 2004). Moreover, the very processes of globalization—the internationalization of neoliberalism—have created a new set of economic and political realities with significant harm-producing effects within and beyond nation states (ibid.).

Garside (2013: 248) has suggested that for a social harm approach to be truly progressive it must consider more carefully the underlying structural and historical causes of social harm both within varieties of existing capitalism, but also how harm might be mitigated in alternative, that is, non-capitalistic, forms of social organization.

Relatedly, then, for Garside, reducing harm is not *simply* a matter of states pursuing different policies, such as increased regulation. It will require much more profound material political and ideological transformations to reduce harm. There is little here with which to disagree. But it is worth emphasizing that in the past decade, searing harms have been associated with the dominant fiscal and political response to the economic crises which followed 2007, responses institutionalized in government programmes of austerity since 2010 in the UK. For example, the Poverty and Social Exclusion surveys show clearly the rise in acute deprivation between 1999 and 2012 in the UK. A significant proportion of children are missing out on the most basic of contemporary needs. Twenty-five per cent had no annual holiday away from home and 20 per cent live in a house that is cold or damp. While more families are falling into poverty, many more are struggling financially with nearly a fifth of households in arrears on at least one of the household bills and are close to becoming defined as poor (Lansley and Mack 2015; see also http://www.poverty.ac.uk).

All of this is occurring against a backdrop of increasing levels of income and wealth inequality, which, as Tombs (2016: 216) has noted, are most pronounced in those nation states 'where neoliberalism has been embraced most thoroughly; and that these levels of widening inequalities are associated with a wide-ranging cluster of economic, physical and social harms' (see, notably, Dorling 2014; Lansley 2011; Lansley and Mack 2015; Pemberton 2015; Sayer 2015; Therborn 2013; Wilkinson and Pickett 2009).

In other words, these are harms not of capitalism in general, but of a specific form of UK neoliberalism, turbo-charged by a combination of economic and political factors. This is not to say that other forms of more or less regulated capitalism are not harmful; Pemberton demonstrates powerfully, through cross-national analyses, how harm generation is a feature of all existing varieties of capitalism, while varying in extent according to the specific forms of societies. Crucially, he notes, 'these analyses demonstrate how the extraction of surplus value, the experience of alienation and the relentless commodification of human relations serve to compromise human flourishing in many harmful ways'. (Pemberton 2015: 139). Thus his focus on capitalist harm production is also a focus on the differential existence of harm reduction infrastructures, including forms of regulation, infrastructures which are won (and lost) through political struggle, and reflect compromises reached as regards the nature and level of the social wage. What Pemberton refers to as the 'social state', and which Tombs has recently (2016) discussed in terms of the 'social protection state', has been systematically dismantled under rampant neoliberalism. Therein, the twin processes of marketization—characterized by Whitfield (2006: 4) as 'the process by which market forces are imposed in public services' and financialization—the increasing pre-eminence of finance capital, coupled with the hard-wiring into civil, economic, political, and cultural institutions of our lives—have generated greater as well as new forms of harm production (Tombs 2016: 37–43, passim).

We are clear that neoliberalism cannot be effectively regulated (Tombs and Whyte 2015), while also recognizing that there are some forms of capitalism where regulation can have more progressive effects. Finally, we would argue that the chances in the UK of a return to, for example, even the (what now appear to be) halcyon days of the post-1945 social-democratic settlement are past. With specific reference to the UK, while the state has withdrawn from a raft of areas in which it had hitherto provided social protection (however inadequately), these have either been abandoned or handed over to private providers; in either case, the conditions under which these can be revived and returned to state hands appear less and less obvious. Thus a smaller state is providing fewer goods and services, and offering diminished levels of social protection. If the current cuts trajectory continues, UK public spending will fall below that of the US (Taylor-Gooby 2013: 5). At the same time, this does not equate to any necessary diminution of state power (Tombs 2016). Certainly, in the context of regulating populations, it can be argued that the state is becoming bigger, a central set of actors in seemingly-endlessly proliferating forms of social control, through processes of both panopticism and synopticism.

AFTER *BEYOND CRIMINOLOGY*: INSTITUTIONAL AND INTELLECTUAL RESPONSES

In this section, we focus first, briefly, on some dimensions of what we call the 'institutional' response to arguments for social harm and zemiology, before discussing the substance of some of the 'intellectual' response. That is, we examine the effects of such arguments upon criminology and then on criminologists. But first it is important to consider the broader impacts of *Beyond Criminology* and why it has put social harm onto a criminological agenda in ways in which previous struggles over the limitations of working within a legal definition of crime have failed to do.

First, *Beyond Criminology* was a collection of some sixteen chapters, in the context of one book, all of which sought in some way to address an issue—crime or social harm?—which had hitherto been covered sporadically and, to some extent, in relative isolation. Second, the range of areas covered in, and the diversity of disciplines contributing to, the edited collection was unique in this enterprise. Third, the content—and indeed title—of the book was deliberately provocative, as well as indicating arguments which were bold (far too bold, as some might say, on which more, below): in other words, the book's contributions were couched within the frame not simply of taking social harm seriously, but in terms of abandoning criminology for a new discipline, zemiology. We were clear within the book that the shift to social harm from criminology was not one endorsed by all of the authors nor indeed editors. Yet, the book was *designed to generate debate*—and in this and the subsequent section, we discuss how it has done so.

Criminology, as with any other discipline, is organized as a profession via a set of institutions, spanning associations and societies, conferences, symposia, and seminars, a range of written publications, processes of formal accreditation, and associated higher education provision, and so on. While we cannot quantify at all the various institutional responses, it is clear that social harm and/or zemiology have very quickly become an element of what constitutes the discipline, in a number of ways and at various levels. It is worth adding that this observation holds internationally, at least in the English-speaking academic world, and is not confined to the UK.

In the UK, the scope and content of criminology as a discipline is, as with every other discipline taught at Higher Education Institutions, set out by the Quality Assurance

Agency (QAA) in its Subject Benchmark Statement. The two most recent versions of such a statement for criminology were produced in 2007 and 2014 respectively. While the 2007 statement had several references to harms, including to 'crime and harm' and to 'social harm', the 2014 statement referred to post-2007 'new directions within the subject', providing three examples of such 'new directions', one of which was 'Zemiology' (Quality Assurance Agency 2014: 6). This is reflected in course and module content across undergraduate and postgraduate provision in UK universities. For example, Birmingham City University runs a module in 'Crime, Social Harm and Social Justice', the descriptor for which notes that, 'Specifically the module draws from what could broadly be termed Zemiology, the study of social harms', while the University of Lincoln offers 'Harm, Agency and Regulation', which 'makes substantial use of the literature on social harm theory; organisational and corporate crime; white-collar crime/professional wrongdoing; international/transnational crime; and harmful activities—or neglect—by the state.' [4] Numerous universities describe their criminology degrees as focusing also on social harm and provide social harm input at various stages throughout their respective programmes. This includes those institutions which offer criminology 'with' another discipline; indeed, where criminology meets social policy, there is clear evidence of an increasing focus on social harm. Bristol, for example, offers a BSc in social policy with criminology in which social harm figures prominently—perhaps not surprising, since located in the school which offers the programme, is a 'Reader in Zemiology'.

The 'institutional' response of criminology has operated at other levels—not least in the form of criminological outputs, such as books and articles. Of the former, there is now small but growing literature on aspects of social harm and zemiology. Rob White's (2014) *Environmental Harm. An Eco-Justice Perspective*, was the first book to appear in a new series by Policy Press, entitled Studies in Social Harm. This was quickly followed by the ground-breaking *Harmful Societies. Understanding social harm* (Pemberton 2015), on which more, below. Several further books are in production in this series, including Allen (2018), Copson (2018), Corteen *et al.* (2016), Payne (2017), and Scott (2017), while two further texts have taken or will take their central focus as social harm or zemiology—Davies *et al.* (2014) and Boukli and Kotzé (forthcoming), respectively.

Core undergraduate texts aimed at a mass student audience have latterly begun to include discussions of social harm, or zemiology, or both. The very fact that this contribution is appearing in the sixth edition of this *Handbook* is one testimony to that observation. McLaughlin and Muncie's first and second editions of *The Sage Dictionary of Criminology* (2001, 2006) both had entries for 'social harm', albeit neither contained any reference to the work associated with editors nor contributors to *Beyond Criminology*, a fact which changed in the third edition with an expanded definition of 'social harm' which appeared therein (McLaughlin and Muncie 2013). That most recent edition also contained an entry for 'zemiology', which we cite in full: 'See: Social harm' (McLaughlin and Muncie 2013: 496). Tim Newburn's *Criminology* includes

[4] See, respectively, http://www.birmingham.ac.uk/schools/law/courses/llb/modules/Criminology-modules/llb-crime-social-harm-and-social-justice.aspx and http://www.lincoln.ac.uk/home/course/cricriub/, accessed 16 January 2017.

'zemiology' as a short sub-section within a chapter constituting a whistle stop tour of 'radical and critical criminology' (Newburn 2007: 258).

Recent years have seen special issues of journals devoted to the topic, notably *Crime, Law and Social Change*, 48, 1–2, September 2007 and two special issues of *Revista Crítica Penal y Poder* [Critical Review of Criminal Critique and Power][5] (2014: 6, and 2013: 5, respectively), while others have featured social harm centrally (*The Howard Journal of Criminal Justice*, 54(1), and *State Crime*, Autumn, 3(2)). Finally, as well as there also being individual articles too numerous to cite which deal either centrally or at least tangentially with aspects of 'social harm', it is also worth closing this section with the observation that the suffix 'and harm' when speaking of crime, notably but not exclusively by those who would see themselves as critical criminologists, is now ubiquitous—on which more, below. In addition, it is now commonplace to see streams, panels, and papers on social harm/zemiology at UK and international conferences and symposia.

A number of scholars working under the rubric 'beyond criminology' have, either explicitly or implicitly, promisingly adopted a social harm perspective to study an instructive variety of social phenomena. For example, work has been undertaken on the production of social harm in social care (Brogden and Nijhar 2006; Phillips 2007); in old age (Machniewski 2010), the cut-flower industry (McGill 2012), in the provision of new technology (Hope 2013), in learning care settings (Feeley 2014), and by corporations (Freudenberg 2014; Passas and Goodwin 2004). Somewhat differently, but in our view significantly, Presser (2013) has sought to develop a first attempt at a general theory of harm, based on four cases studies—genocide, meat eating, intimate partner violence, and penal harm.

Here, however, our concerns are with the reception of our claims within criminology. Therein, and as indicated in the previous section, an increasing number of criminological texts make explicit reference to the term 'zemiology'. Typically, it is seen as another word for 'social harm'—a concept which has long been part of criminology but which is receiving greater attention (McLaughlin and Muncie 2013). Hence, the term zemiology has been happily embraced by some in the discipline as a 'The branch of criminology studying the social harm caused by actions' (Gooch and Williams 2007: 391) rather than the impetus for a separate discipline. In general, this embrace has been identified in the context of 'critical' criminology. For example, the second edition of *Introduction to Criminological Theory* by Richard Hopkins Burke contains a section titled 'Critical Criminology and the Challenge of Zemiology', which makes no references to the origins of or debates around the term, but simply begins, 'A significant and fast expanding contemporary variant of critical criminology has been Zemiology or the study of social harm' (Burke 2005: 179, see also Hil and Robertson 2003).

Others have subjected our arguments to more or less sustained criticism, and it is with these critical responses that the rest of this section is concerned. In so doing, we shall use as reference points work by Hughes (2006, 2007); Loader and Sparks (2011); Maruna (2013); Muncie (2005); and Reiman (2006). We do so not to engage in a point-by-point response to these criticisms, nor to engage directly with specific authors and

[5] Available at: http://revistes.ub.edu/index.php/CriticaPenalPoder/issue/archive, accessed 16 December 2016.

their disagreements with us—the latter are the stuff of healthy academic life, and these responses all entail genuine engagements with our work. Indeed, these texts are chosen not least because they reflect the most common critical responses to our claims regarding social harm and zemiology—those published as well as those made in response to versions of our arguments being presented at conferences, seminars, and symposia. Thus, we focus upon the *types* of criticisms levelled at *Beyond Criminology* and the arguments therein, focusing upon their key points of substance and also upon their omissions. For us, the latter are particularly telling.

One broad form of response is to emphasize the pluralistic nature of criminology, so that many of the concerns with the discipline to which we point are poorly made, since criminology is an increasingly rich, diverse discipline within which many of the objects of study to which our arguments point are indeed already the stuff of the discipline. Thus, for example, Hughes (2007: 197) defends criminology, on the grounds that: 'State and corporate crimes, as well as the ills bought by an unequal and divided world, are, indeed, key concerns of criminology'. He further suggests that we have set up a 'straw(wo)man' of a singular criminology which he argues parodies much of the actually existing, plural forms of contemporary criminological work today (2006: 158). Similarly, Loader and Sparks comment that we produce 'a scarcely recognisable caricature of the fragmented and diverse field that is being trashed and left behind' (Loader and Sparks 2011: 25). Relatedly, Hughes denies the originality of many of the claims set out in *Beyond Criminology*, arguing that many of the objects of focus therein are already recognizable criminological concerns, evidenced in 'best-selling recent introductory texts', (Hughes 2006: 158) reflected in the awards for best criminology books made by the British Society of criminology (ibid.) and characteristic of the work of radical scholars in critical criminology and socio-legal studies for at least 30 years (ibid.: 157). Thus, as Pemberton (2015: 5) observed:

> For critics of *Beyond Criminology*, the social harm critique presented a caricature of criminology that failed to acknowledge the contributions of 'critical criminology' or 'sociological criminologists', and in reality, the much needed reformulation of the notion of crime to include wider social harms or 'deepenings' in criminological knowledge have been part of the disciplinary enterprise for some time (Muncie 2005: 2000; Hughes 2006). Indeed, for some within criminology, there was a sense that *Beyond Criminology* represented the 'emperor's new clothes'.

There is no doubt that the focus of criminology has continued to expand—and that there is a significant body of critical criminological work with a healthy diversity of concerns. This may, of course, simply be an effect of the growth of the discipline *per se*, so that while there is more 'critical' work undertaken, its relative size compared to criminological output is no greater. In any case, the claim regarding pluralism ultimately misses the point: work conducted within the boundaries of criminology must ultimately confront the inherent limitations of working within the discipline—a point that is rarely, if ever, addressed in critical responses to the claims made in *Beyond Criminology*. It is, however, an issue raised by others. For example, drawing on the work of Pavlich (1999) and Foucault (1997), Reece Walters has noted that, 'some radical departures' within criminology find themselves 'drawn back by the magnet of pragmatism in an attempt to be seen as "useful" in preference to an idealistic and academic knowledge of little practical utility' (Walters, 2003: 39). Thus, he continues, 'critical genres fail to question their historical and internal logics and thus continually run the risk of becoming fractured, fluid and susceptible to domination by conservative ideologies' (ibid.). It was precisely such 'historical and internal logics' which we sought to address through the work of Foucault (1977, 1979, 1980) on discursive formations, and this is precisely the issue that seems to be avoided by our critics.

A somewhat distinct, broad response has been to question the political project entailed in *Beyond Criminology*, in at least two senses: first, to advocate a continued commitment to reformism within and of criminology, and second to reject any exigence to abandon the discipline.

On the former, Maruna (2013) is clear: for him, criminal justice matters. It matters, for example, to those who are incarcerated—so the more criminologists studying prisons and proffering progressive reform, the better. Similar arguments were made regarding other criminal justice institutions, such as police, with the explicit statement that powerful institutions need to be studied. We agree wholeheartedly with this point (Tombs and Whyte 2003), but ultimately it takes us back full circle to our starting place: it matters from where one studies these, or other, organizations. In any case, for Maruna (2013), were criminology to be 'abolished' and zemiology established in its place, there would be considerable pleasure among those critical of the 'left-wing' nature of the discipline (Maruna 2013). Such a claim rather begs the question of what it means to describe the discipline as 'left-wing', and then what being a 'left-wing' criminologist can or does achieve. Further, and again, it fails to address the construction and limits of the discipline.

Criminology, then, needs to be defended (Maruna 2013). It is wrong to blame criminology for the failure of the criminal justice system, just as it is illogical to blame historians for growing inequality in society. As Hughes (2007: 197) elaborates, 'Zemiologists' have taken 'Foucault's typically magisterial' and 'radical totalitarian' critique of criminology as proof of 'criminology's sins, past and present'. He goes on to suggest we argue that criminology, as the 'handmaiden of the State', has a role in the 'socially destructive trends of "mass criminalization"'.

On this basis, abandoning the discipline is a mistake. Better, says Hughes, to engage in 'progressive alliance building' in order 'to govern the soul of the criminological beast' (Hughes 2006: 159, 158). Similarly, for Maruna, offering a thoroughgoing rejection of what counts for criminology, alongside an exigence to simply sign up to an alternative position, is a poor way to generate change. While there may be apparent plausibility to these observations, we are clear that, ultimately, criminology cannot change enough given the way in which it has been historically constructed, as a particular discursive formation, on which more, below.

For Maruna, then, critics have a choice—either to exit the discipline, or to remain within criminology and express their criticisms from therein. The former, he claimed, was all too common within criminology and not very helpful because it was often the Left that exited leaving a more conservative group behind. This is not an unreasonable point to make, but it seems to us that it simply points to a political dilemma facing many who are members of organizations, be they political parties or academic disciplines. Carol Smart and Stan Cohen are well-known examples of key figures who explicitly abandoned the discipline—Smart with the later, reflective verdict that 'the thing that criminology cannot do is deconstruct crime' (Smart 1990: 77)—but anecdotally, many of us know colleagues who have done so also. As Muncie observes, 'the abandonment of crime in favour of "harm" is ultimately a political project' (Muncie 2005: 201). On this point, with which we agree, we are taken back to our starting point, one aptly noted by Reiman, thus:

> Criminology, alone among recognized social sciences, bears the burden of having the object of its study determined by the state. We are accustomed to hearing about the politics of research, but this is the politicization of research with a vengeance. The result of it is that criminology bears a special responsibility: it must either declare its independence of the state or serve as an arm of the state. (Reiman 2006: 362)

Thus we had proposed at least the consideration of abandoning the discipline in favour of zemiology—even though, as we noted, as two authors we took different positions on this consideration. It is certainly the case that while we set out some of the epistemological, theoretical, and substantive commitments of zemiology as an alternative discipline, we certainly did not attempt to set out in detail what that discipline might look like—a point rehearsed in critical commentaries. And this constitutes the essence of the third, broad critical response to *Beyond Criminology*. Thus Loader and Sparks (2011) argue that we spend too long critiquing criminology and not enough time describing what will replace it. Hughes (2007:198) concludes that we fail to offer 'a viable critical project for criminology, intellectually or politically'. Reiman, in particular, notes that taking 'the next step . . . from a provocative kaleidoscope to a coherent disciplinary perspective', entails at least two tasks: first, being 'clear on the harm perspective's relationship to criminology' (Reiman 2006: 363); and, second, since 'so much of the harm discussed in *Beyond Criminology* is attributed to social groups or structures, the harm perspective will need to spell out a plausible doctrine of social or structural responsibility' (ibid.: 364). These points are well made, and represent a significant challenge to those who would either develop a social harm perspective or an alternative discipline of zemiology. It is to these and their relationship that we now turn.

CRITICAL CRIMINOLOGY, SOCIAL HARM, AND ZEMIOLOGY

In this final substantive section, we argue that there are a number of fundamental theoretical differences between social harm, critical criminology, and zemiology which help clarify the on-going debates on whether zemiology should be considered as a separate discipline or simply a branch of critical criminology.

As we have indicated, criminology, and in particular critical criminology, has long struggled over the boundaries of the discipline in an attempt to shake off the limitations of the straightjacket of the legal definitions of crime and in order to expand the discipline to study a whole range of harms not captured by the criminal law. And within these efforts, a significant body of literature has emerged which encompasses a range of criminalizeable harms, from ethnic and religious intolerance to ecocide and genocide.

Conceptually within the vast terrain of critical criminological work, conduct norms, social aberrance, social deviance, social harm, and social injury are just a few of the intellectual attempts to mark out a more inclusive set of harmful behaviours. Kramer (2013) provides a comprehensive overview of these attempts and argues that 'international law in all of its forms can still provide a rhetorical touchstone for criminologists to frame judgments about what is and is not criminal. It can allow us to "expand the core" of the discipline to better take into account corporate and state crimes' (Kramer 2013: 33). This is a very similar to the stance taken by the Schwendingers (1975) but opposed by Green and Ward (2000) not only because many inequalities are widely accepted as legitimate but also because this conceptualization breaks the link between crime and the notion of deviance.

Somewhat differently, Yar (2012), in a thoughtful analysis of the potential of zemiology, argues that 'the lack of specificity in our analysis leaves the concept of harm lacking the very same ontological reality that is postulated as grounds for rejecting the concept of crime' (2012: 59). In short, we fail to define what makes something 'a harm' or harmful and how harmful acts differ from non-harmful ones. He suggests that the concept of 'recognition' can deal with this deficit in our theorization and that it is possible to establish the basic needs that form human integrity and well-being. Harm occurs when there is no recognition of these basic needs. Harms, in this sense, reflect disrespect. While acknowledging that the criminal law can be conceived as 'a coercive instrument legitimated by the power of the capitalist state', Yar argues that it is possible to adopt a different view of the law using a recognition theoretical standpoint. From this position, the law's attempt, however 'partial, flawed or misguided', to enshrine formal codes and prohibitions to protect people from harm assists in securing their basic rights.

Yar, then, concludes with a clear appeal to the law in defining harm. On this basis he considers zemiology to be a promising orientation but within critical criminology. Similarly, much critical criminology, for all of its significance, originality, and sophistication, ends up in attempts to redefine the legitimate area of criminology and is based in an implicit or explicit call for law, not least criminal law, to be more effectively developed or enforced, in ways that promote greater social justice through criminal justice, and in ways that uphold or extend various rights.

In short, much of this work proceeds at least implicitly on the basis of a rights-based framework. But for us this is ultimately problematic, notwithstanding that some people may secure their basic rights through the criminal law and many more will buy into the notion of this possibility of justice, the majority of those affected by social harms will have little or no recognition by the formal system, particularly those victims of harms which are not captured by the criminal law. In other words, for many of the social harms upon which we and others have focused, law and rights are likely to be of very little relevance at all.

This is one of the key ways in which we can locate the relationships between critical criminology, social harm, and zemiology. It is only the latter which essentially breaks from (actual or potential) legal definitions of harm, not least those linked to apparently progressive—but ultimately flawed (Fudge and Glasbeek 1992)—rights-based frameworks. Thus, notwithstanding the need for its substance, contours, and commitments to be much more fully developed, as indicated in the previous section, in recent years zemiology is increasingly being grounded in a theory of human needs—a framework not linked to nor reliant upon law, jurisprudence, or some other legal framework. Of particular significance here is the work of Pemberton (2004, 2007) and Pantazis and Pemberton (2009) who use Doyal and Gough's (1991) theory of human need to develop the concept of harm arguing that harm is perpetuated when specified needs are not fulfilled. Subsequently, Pemberton (2015) in *Harmful Societies* attempts to operationalize a needs approach to harm. He admits, however, at the outset that while much has been written about the potential of 'social harm', such an approach

> remains a relatively empty space, insofar as few studies have actually sought to develop the conceptual lens and to operationalize it through empirical study. It is hoped that this book will contribute to how we may begin to collectively imagine an alternative approach to the study of harm. (Pemberton 2015: 11)

He provides an excellent overview of the origins and debates around the concept of social harm both within and outside of criminology before analysing the performance of a number of selected states and regimes in relation to a range of harms. It is a highly original work, illustrating the potential as well as the pitfalls of a social harm approach. There is no doubt that he advances our understanding of social harm considerably, but at the same time he has underscored the fact that a social harm approach is very much a work in progress (Tombs 2015).

The fundamental differences which now exist between the conceptualization of harm within criminology, critical criminology, and zemiology, reflecting different ideas and assumptions around issues of justice and liberty in the context of the fulfilment of human need, have been extensively analysed by Copson (2011, 2012). Criminology, she argues, deploys a liberal individualistic notion of harm as embraced by conventional jurisprudence. In contrast, zemiology situates harm in the context of human needs. Harm occurs when people are prevented by either the social structures or individual actions to meet their needs. Harm, in this sense, is linked to positive liberty in contrast to the negative liberties which law claims to protect and to which all forms of criminology are inevitably drawn. Critical criminology's notion of harm, she suggests, falls somewhere between the two positions. While increasingly recognizing socially structured harm, nevertheless it continues to embrace individualistic notions of harms articulated in rights or conventional jurisprudence.

We began this chapter by discussing the 'story of crime', with which we all familiar, and which permeates popular, political, and even academic consciousness. There is a further aspect to that story here, and this can be captured by the term 'proximity'. In many forms of harm upon which criminal justice systems overwhelmingly focus—that is, some version of crime—there is, or must at some point be, a degree of proximity between an offender and victim. This is most obviously the case with regard to personal assaults, robberies, and so on. Yet, it also applies to non-contact theft and burglary, in the sense of the victim's proximity as owners or residents. By contrast, in the case of the kinds of harms which we illustrated above, there are frequently enormous distances between the source and object of the harm, the 'offender' and 'victim', in terms of both space and time. So, for example, origins of the conditions which lead to excess winter deaths, or produce routine, large-scale food poisoning, worker deaths, or environmental pollution are likely to involve collections of disparate individuals or groups of individuals engaged in actions, decisions, or omissions separated from consequent deaths and illnesses in question by significant distance in terms of time and geography. These dimensions of lack of proximity run entirely contrary to our stories of crime—and also to the ways in which criminal law is constructed. Thus, distances of time and space make even awareness of, but certainly proving, victimization difficult if not impossible. Proximity, *mens rea*, and thus the possibilities of the kinds of accountability which the criminal justice system claims to be able to offer, are missing.

In short, a focus on crime points us towards a focus on the inter-personal; by contrast, a social harm or zemiological approach leads us more inevitably, or at least more easily, towards structures. This distinction has important epistemological and indeed political dimensions—yet nowhere are these they addressed in the critical responses to zemiology nor indeed social harm arguments. But a further point needs to be made here which follows on from the power of the crime discourse. For to remain within this means remaining in the realm of criminal justice responses to acts and omissions defined actually or potentially as crimes—responses which, as we have indicated, are overwhelmingly inefficient if not counter-productive, themselves often harm-producing and contrary to social justice on virtually any criterion. Copson (2016) shares our view that we must change the discourse and think differently about crime. In discussing alternatives to imprisonment, she argues that it is necessary to go beyond contemporary and conceptual frameworks and adopt a 'replacement discourse' of harm in order to build realistic utopias and meaningful alternatives to imprisonment.

It is in these ways, then, that we argued previously (Hillyard and Tombs 2004), and have sought to elaborate here, that legal, as well as dominant social constructions of crime, criminal justice practices, processes and systems, including processes of non-criminalization, *and the discipline of criminology itself* are inextricably linked. This does not make all criminologists 'handmaidens of the state', nor is it to deny that there have been numerous examples of progressive interventions in criminal justice based upon criminological work—but it does mean that criminology is inevitably, as a discipline (as opposed to the work of individual or groups of criminologists), drawn to focus upon crime and criminality, within a discursive regime which itself is characterized by a particular power-knowledge nexus, one in which very powerful political, social, and economic interests are intensely imbricated. Zemiology offers the potential to develop a new discourse (Copson 2016). This is not to deny that over time, it too will be characterized by its own power-knowledge nexus, but for the time being it is free of those very powerful social interests which underpin criminology.

CONCLUSION

We began this chapter by identifying some of the motivations which led us to propose both a social harm perspective and a discipline of zemiology as alternatives to the discipline of criminology. In so doing, we have never wished, and do not wish, to deny: that criminology has been eclectic, and is perhaps increasingly so; nor that criminology has produced theoretical, conceptual, methodological, and empirical insight; nor that the work of criminologists has certainly been associated with progressive social change. What we have sought to argue, however, for reasons we have set out here, is that there are *necessary* limitations on the extent to which criminology can be progressive. Ultimately, criminology is tied to and limited by necessary relationships to crime, criminal justice, and criminalization, defined in relation to power, law, and state, constituting a disciplinary regime of power-knowledge which is ultimately conservative.

We have also considered some of the impacts of, and responses to, such arguments over the past 15 years. For sure, as reference points, both social harm and zemiology have an increasing salience within and around criminology. This is not to say that there have not been critical responses to our claims, some of which we have set out above, within which there are certainly very powerful claims to which we cannot entirely credibly respond. But part of that inability to respond credibly and fully is a product of the youthfulness of work around both social harm and zemiology. As we indicated in *Beyond Criminology* (Hillyard and Tombs 2004: 29), and as John Muncie highlighted in 2005:

> Over 100 years of criminological inquiry have ushered in less social justice and more criminalisation and an expansion of criminal justice systems. It is difficult to disagree . . . that the construction of an alternative discipline based on social harm could barely be less successful. (Muncie 2005: 201)

Muncie qualified this immediately: 'But harm is far from a unified and uncontested concept' (ibid.). Quite so. As we have indicated above, there is a great deal to be done. There is theoretical, conceptual, methodological, and empirical work to be taken on. And the relationships between social harm and zemiology on the one hand, and then between these and (critical) criminology on the other, need to be more thoroughly explored and established. Much of this work is being taken up by social scientists. It remains our view that both a social harm perspective and zemiology, based within a fully developed theory of human needs, offers the basis for more progressive academic and indeed political activity, one where criminal justice might genuinely be challenged and replaced by social justice.

■ SELECTED FURTHER READING

Hillyard *et al.*'s *Beyond Criminology: Taking Harm Seriously* (2004) explores the potential of a new discipline—zemiology—outside of criminology, and presents a number of case studies using a social harm perspective. This work owes much to many criminologists who, over the years, have been concerned with the state's straightjacket on criminology. Two key texts in this tradition are Box's *Power, Crime and Mystification* (1983) and Reiman's *The Rich get Richer and the Poor get Prison* (1998). Muncie's 'Decriminalising Criminology' (2000) succinctly explored the implications for criminology when its key referent—'crime'—is subject to deconstruction. For an excellent overview of attempts to expand the legitimate core of criminology, see Kramer's 'Expanding the Core: Blameworthy Harms, International Law and State-Corporate Crimes' (2013).

In the first book-length study using a social harm perspective, Pemberton's, *Harmful Societies* (2015) provides a detailed analysis of the concept of social harm and demonstrates powerfully how harm is a feature of all existing varieties of capitalism. Presser's *Why We Harm* (2013) presents a general theory of harm based on four case studies—genocide, meat eating, intimate partner violence, and penal harm. Other work which coheres with a zemiological perspective are Freudenberg's *Lethal but Legal* (2014), which exposes the way the food, tobacco, alcohol, pharmaceutical, gun, and auto industries ignore public health in their pursuit of profit and thereby create widespread harm, and the edited collection by Passas and Goodwin, *It's Legal but it ain't Right: Harmful Social Consequences of Legal Industries* (2004).

REFERENCES

Allen, C. (2018, forthcoming), *New Perspectives on Islamophobia and Social Harm*, Bristol: Policy.

Becker, H. (1963), *Outsiders*, New York: Free Press.

Boukli, A. and Kotzé, J. (eds) (forthcoming), *Just Harm? Rethinking Zemiology and the Broader Context of Social Harm*, London: Palgrave Macmillan.

Box, S. (1983), *Power, Crime, and Mystification*, London: Tavistock.

Brogden, M. and Nijhar, P. (2006), 'Crime, abuse and social harm: Towards an integrated approach', in A. Wahidin and M. Cain (eds), *Aging, Crime and Society*, London: Routledge.

Burke, R. H. (2005), *An Introduction to Criminological Theory*, Cullompton: Willan.

Christie, N. (1977), 'Conflicts as Property', *British Journal of Criminology*, 17(1): 1–15.

Christie, N. (1993), *Crime Control as Industry: Towards Gulags, Western Style?*, London: Routledge.

Christie, N. (2004), *A Suitable amount of Crime*, London: Routledge.

Cohen, S. (1981), 'Footprints in the Sand: A further Report on Criminology and Sociology of Deviance in Britain', in M. Fitzgerald, G. McLennan, and J. Pawson (eds), *Crime and Society*, London: Routledge and Open University Press.

Copson, L. (2011), *Archaeologies of Harm: Criminology, Critical Criminology, Zemiology*, A dissertation submitted to the University of Bristol in accordance with the requirements for the award of the degree of Doctor of Philosophy in the Faculty of Social Sciences and Law. School of Sociology.

Copson, L. (2012), 'Zemiology: at the Edge of Criminology or Beyond its Borders?' Paper presented at the British Society of Criminology Annual Conference, University of Portsmouth.

Copson, L. (2016), 'Realistic Utopianism and Alternatives to Imprisonment: The Ideology of Crime and the Utopia of Harm', *Justice, Power and Resistance*, Foundation Volume, 79–104.

Copson, L. (2018, forthcoming), *A Sociology of Harm*, Bristol: Policy.

Corteen, K., Morley, S., Taylor, P., and Turner, J. (eds) (2016), *A Companion to Crime, Harm and Victimisation*, Bristol: Policy.

Davies, P., Francis, P., and Wyatt, T. (2014), *Invisible Crimes and Social Harms*, London: Palgrave Macmillan.

De Hann, W. (1996), 'Abolitionism and Crime Control', in J. Muncie, E. McLaughlin, and M. Langan (eds), *Criminological Perspectives: A Reader*, London: Sage.

Dorling, D. (2014), *Inequality and the 1%*, London: Verso.

Doyal, L. and Gough, I. (1991), *A Theory of Human Need*. Basingstoke: Palgrave Macmillan.

Feeley, M. (2014), *Learning care lessons: Literacy, love, care and solidarity*. London: Tufnell Press.

Food Standards Agency (2012), *Annual report of the Chief Scientist, Food Standards Agency*, www.food.gov.uk/multimedia/pdfs/publication/csar1112.pdf, accessed 15 December 2016.

Food Standards Agency (2015), *Campylobacter survey: Cumulative results from the full 12 months (Q1–Q4)*, https://www.food.gov.uk/news-updates/news/2015/14003/campylobacter-survey-results-12months, accessed 15 December 2016.

Food Standards Agency (nd), *The second study of infectious intestinal disease in the community (IID2 Study)*, https://www.food.gov.uk/science/research/foodborneillness/b14programme/b14projlist/b18021, accessed 6 January 2017.

Foucault, M. (1977), *Discipline and Punish*, London: Allen Lane.

Foucault, M. (1979), *The History of Sexuality, Vol. 1: An Introduction*, London: Allen Lane, Penguin Press.

Foucault, M. (1980), 'Truth and Power', in C. Gordon (ed), *Michel Foucault: Power/Knowledge: Selected Interviews and other writings, 1972-1977*, Brighton: Harvester Press.

Freudenberg, N. (2014), *Lethal but Legal: Corporations, Consumption, and Protecting Public Health*, Oxford: Oxford University Press.

Fudge, J. and Glasbeek, H. (1992), 'The politics of rights: a politics with little class', *Social & Legal Studies*, 1(1): 45–70.

Garland, D. (1992), 'Criminological Knowledge and its Relation to Power; Foucault's Genealogy and Criminology Today', *British Journal of Criminology*, 32(4): 403–22.

GARSIDE, R. (2013), 'Addressing Social Harm: Better Regulation versus Social Transformation', *Revista Crítica Penal y Poder*, 5: 247–65.

GOOCH, G. and WILLIAMS, M. (2007), *A Dictionary of Law Enforcement*, Oxford: Oxford University Press.

GRAMSCI, A. (1971), *Selections from the Prison Notebooks of Antonio Gramsci*, in Q. Hoare and G. Nowell Smith (eds, trans), London: Lawrence and Wishart.

GREEN, P. J. and WARD, T.C. (2000), 'State Crime, Human Rights, and the Limits of Criminology', *Social Justice*, 27(1): 101–15.

HÄMÄLÄINEN, P., SAARELA, K., and TAKALA, J. (2009), 'Global trend according to estimated number of occupational accidents and fatal work-related diseases at region and country level', *Journal of Safety Research*, 40(2): 125–39.

HENRY, S. and MILOVANOVIC, D. (1996), *Constitutive Criminology. Beyond Postmodernism*, London: Sage.

HIL, R. and ROBERTSON, R. (2003), 'What sort of Future for Critical Criminology', *Crime, Law and Social Change*, 39(1): 91–115.

HILLYARD, P., PANTAZIS, C., TOMBS, S., and GORDON, D. (eds) (2004), *Beyond Criminology: Taking Harm Seriously*, London: Pluto.

HILLYARD, P. and TOMBS, S. (2004), 'Beyond Criminology?', in P. Hillyard, C. Pantazis, S. Tombs, and D. Gordon (eds), *Beyond Criminology: Taking Harm Seriously*, London: Pluto.

HEALTH AND SAFETY EXECUTIVE (2015), *Health and Safety Statistics, Annual Report for Great Britain 2014-15*, London: Health and Safety Executive.

HOPE, A. (2013), 'The shackled school internet: zemiological solutions to the problem of over-blocking', *Learning, Media and Technology*, 38(3): 270–81.

HUGHES, G. (2006), 'Book review of *Beyond Criminology: Taking Harm Seriously*', *Social & Legal Studies: An International Journal*, 15(1): 157–9.

HUGHES, G. (2007), *The Politics of Crime and Community*, London: Palgrave Macmillan.

HULSMAN, L. (1986), 'Critical Criminology and the Concept of Crime', in H. Bianchi and R. van Swaaningen (eds), *Abolitionism, Towards a Non-Repressive Approach to Crime*, Amsterdam: Free University Press.

KRAMER, R. C. (2013), 'Expanding the Core: Blameworthy Harms, International Law and State-Corporate Crimes', paper presented at the Presidential Panel, 'Reconsidering the Legal Definition of Crime', at the annual meeting of the American Society of Criminology, 21 November 2013, Atlanta.

LACEY, N. (2002), 'Legal Construction of Crime', in M. Maguire, R. Morgan, and R. Reiner (eds), *The Oxford Handbook of Criminology*, Oxford: Oxford University Press.

LANSLEY, S. (2011), *The Cost of Inequality*, London: Gibson Square.

LANSLEY, S. and MACK, J. (2015), *Breadline Britain: The Rise of Mass Poverty*, London: Oneworld Publications.

LASSLETT, K. (2010), 'Crime or Social Harm? A Dialectical Perspective', *Crime, Law and Social Change*, 54(1): 1–19.

LOADER, I. and SPARKS, R. (2011), *Public Criminology?*, London: Routledge.

MACNAUGHTON-SMITH, P. (1970), 'What is Crime and why do we fight it', paper delivered to the Centre of Criminology, University of Toronto, Canada, 14 January 1970.

MARUNA, S. (2013), 'Expert witness for the Defence in the Mock Trial of Criminology', British Society of Criminology, Wolverhampton.

MATHIESEN, T. (1974), *The Politics of Abolition*, London: Martin Robertson.

MATHIESEN, T. (1990), *Prison on Trial*, Hampshire: Waterside Press.

MCGILL, C. H. (2012), 'The hidden environmental harms of the cut-flower industry', *Neo: A Journal of Student Research*, 2(1), http://eprints.lincoln.ac.uk/16180/, accessed 15 December 2016.

MCLAUGHLIN, E. and MUNCIE, J. (eds) (2001), *The SAGE Dictionary of Criminology* 1st edn, London: Sage.

MCLAUGHLIN, E. and MUNCIE, J. (eds) (2006), *The SAGE Dictionary of Criminology*, 2nd edn, London: Sage.

MCLAUGHLIN, E. and MUNCIE, J. (eds) (2013), *The SAGE Dictionary of Criminology*, 3rd edn, London: Sage.

MACHNIEWSKI, S. (2010), *Social Harm and Older People in Northern Ireland*. A dissertation submitted to Queen's University Belfast in accordance with the requirements for the award of the degree of Doctor of Philosophy in the Faculty of Arts, Humanities and Social Sciences.

MICHALOWSKI, R. (1985), *Order, Law and Crime*, New York: Random House.

MOJ (2015), *Proven Re-offending. Statistics Quarterly Bulletin October 2012 to September 2013, England and Wales Ministry of Justice Statistics Bulletin*, London: Ministry of Justice.

MUNCIE, J. (2000), 'Decriminalising Criminology', British Criminology Conference: Selected Proceedings. Volume 3, http://britsoccrim.org/volume3/010.pdf, accessed 15 December 2016.

MUNCIE, J. (2005), 'Book review of *Beyond Criminology: Taking Harm Seriously*', *Crime, Law and Social Change*, 43(2): 199–201.

NELKEN, D. (1994) 'White Collar Crime', in M. Maguire, R. Morgan, and R. Reiner (eds), *The Oxford Handbook of Criminology*, Oxford: Clarendon.

NEWBURN, T. (2007), *Criminology*, Abingdon: Willan.

OFFICE FOR NATIONAL STATISTICS (2015), *Excess Winter Mortality in England and Wales 2014/15 (Provisional) and 2013/14 (Final)*, London: Office for National Statistics.

PANTAZIS, C. and PEMBERTON, S. (2009), 'Nation States and the Production of Social Harm: Resisting the Hegemony of "TINA"', in R. Coleman, J. Sim, S. Tombs, and D. Whyte (eds), *State, Crime, Power*, London: Sage.

PASSAS, N. and GOODWIN, N. R. (2004), *It's Legal but it ain't Right: harmful social consequences of legal industries*, Michigan: University of Michigan Press.

PAVLICH, G. (1999), 'Criticism and Criminology: In Search of Legitimacy', *Theoretical Criminology*, 3(1): 136–52.

Payne, S. (2018, forthcoming), *Pharmaceuticals and Social Harm*, Bristol: Policy.

Pemberton, S. (2004), *The Production of Harm in the United Kingdom: A Social Harm Perspective.* A dissertation submitted to the University of Bristol in accordance with the requirements for the award of the degree of Doctor of Philosophy in the Faculty of Social Sciences and Law, Bristol: School of Policy Studies.

Pemberton, S. (2007), 'Social Harm Future(s): Exploring the Potential of the Social Harm Approach', *Crime, Law and Social Change*, 48(1): 27–41.

Pemberton, S. (2015), *Harmful Societies*, Bristol: Policy.

Phillips, J. (2007), *Care*, London: Polity.

Presser, L. (2013), *Why We Harm*, New Brunswick, NJ: Rutgers University Press.

Quality Assurance Agency (2014), *Subject Benchmark Statement. Criminology*, http://www.qaa.ac.uk/en/Publications/Documents/SBS-criminology-14.pdf, accessed 15 December 2016.

Reiman, J. (1998), *The Rich Get Richer and the Poor Get Prison: Ideologies, Class and Criminal Justice*, 5th edn, Boston, MA: Allyn and Bacon.

Reiman, J. (2006), 'Book Review of Beyond Criminology: Taking Harm Seriously', *British Journal of Criminology*, 46(2): 362–4.

Sayer, A. (2015), *Why We Can't Afford the Rich*, London: Policy.

Schwendinger, H. and Schwendinger, J. (1970), 'Defenders of Order and Guardians of Human Rights?', *Issues in Criminology*, 5(2): 123–57.

Scott, S. (2017), *Labour Exploitation and Work Based Harm*, Bristol: Policy.

Sellin, T. (1938), *Culture Conflict and Crime*, New York: Social Science Research Council.

Smart, C. (1990), 'Feminist Approaches to Criminology, or Postmodern Woman meets Atavistic Man', in L. Gelsthorpe and A. Morris (eds), *Feminist Perspectives in Criminology*, Milton Keynes: Open University Press.

Steinert, H. (1986), 'Beyond Crime and Punishment', *Contemporary Crises*, 10(1): 21–38.

Sutherland, E. (1945), 'Is "White-Collar Crime" Crime?', *American Sociological Review*, 10(2): 132–9.

Taylor-Gooby, P. (2013), *The Double Crisis of the Welfare State*, London: Palgrave Macmillan.

Therborn, G. (2013), *The Killing Fields of Inequality*, Cambridge: Polity.

Tifft, L. and Sullivan, D. C. (1980), *The Struggle to Be Human: Crime, Criminology and Anarchism*, Sanday, Orkney UK: Cienfuegos Press.

Tifft, L. and Sullivan, D. C. (2001), 'A Needs Based Social Harm Definition of Crime', in S. Henry and M. Lanier (eds), *What is Crime? Controversies over the Nature of Crime and What to Do about It*, Lanham, MD: Rowman & Littlefield.

Tombs, S. (2014), 'Hard Evidence: are work-related deaths in decline?', *The Conversation*, 29 October, https://theconversation.com/hard-evidence-are-work-related-deaths-in-decline-33553, accessed 15 December 2016.

Tombs, S. (2015) 'Harmful Societies', *Criminal Justice Matters*, 101(1): 36–7.

Tombs, S. (2016), *Social Protection after the Crisis: Regulation without Enforcement*, Bristol: Policy.

Tombs, S. and Hillyard, P. (2004), 'Towards a Political Economy of Harm: States, Corporations and the Production of Inequality', in P. Hillyard, C. Pantazis, S. Tombs, and D. Gordon (eds), *Beyond Criminology: Taking Harm Seriously*, London: Pluto.

Tombs, S. and Whyte, D. (2003), 'Unmasking the Crimes of the Powerful', *Critical Criminology*, 11(3): 217–36.

Tombs, S. and Whyte, D. (2015), *The Corporate Criminal: Why Corporations Must be Abolished*, London: Routledge.

Walters, R. (2003), *Deviant knowledge: Criminology, Politics and Policy*, London: Taylor & Francis.

White, R. (2014), *Environmental Harm: An Eco-Justice Perspective*, Bristol: Policy.

Whitfield, D. (2006), 'A Typology of Privatisation and Marketisation', Tralee: European Services Strategy Unit.

Wilkinson, R. G. and Pickett, K. (2009), *The Spirit Level: Why Equality is Better for Everyone*, London: Penguin.

Yar, M. (2012), 'Critical Criminology, Critical Theory and Social Harm', in S. Hall and S. Winlow (eds), *New Directions in Criminological Theory*, London: Routledge.

13

CRIME AND CONSUMER CULTURE

Keith Hayward and Oliver Smith

> The institution of a leisure class has an effect not only upon social structure but also upon the individual character of the members of society . . . It will to some extent shape their habits of thought and will exercise a selective surveillance over the deployment of men's aptitudes and inclinations.
>
> (Thorstein Veblen, *The Theory of the Leisure Class*, [1899] 1970:145)

INTRODUCTION

If we substitute 'consumer culture' for 'leisure class' in the above quotation by Thorstein Veblen, we get a clear sense of exactly what it means to live in a society predicated on consumption. Veblen's 'metaphysic' (Mills 1970: vi) suggests that to live in a consumer society is to inhabit a culture in which the practice of consumption influences everything from economic practice and political discourse to micro-level concerns about self-worth and self-identity. Veblen, of course, was writing at the end of the nineteenth century and describing an elite stratum of affluent American society. Yet his work on the symbolic practice of consumption was so perspicacious that it foreshadowed the era of mass consumption that started in the first decades of the twentieth century and has continued almost unabated ever since. That said, even Veblen, who originated the term 'conspicuous consumption', could not have predicted the rapid global expansion of the consumer society.

Today, over a quarter of all humanity—1.7 billion people—are now said to belong to 'the global consumer class', 'having adopted the diets, transportation systems, and lifestyles that were once mostly limited to the rich nations of Europe, North America, and Japan' (Gardner *et al.* 2004). In terms of annual expenditure, private consumption now exceeds $20 trillion—a fourfold increase over 1960 levels (ibid.). But this is not simply a matter of demographic expansion. Consumerism has changed qualitatively as well as quantitatively. To start with, the contemporary individual's consumption patterns are now far less constrained by social class than was the case only a couple of generations ago. Today, goods and services function not simply as markers of social class (as in Veblen's analysis), but as symbolic props for 'storying the self' (Baudrillard 1968; Featherstone 1994). Indeed, so encompassing is the ethos of consumption that, for many individuals, self-identity and self-actualization can now *only* be accomplished through material means. In other words, we have arrived at a point in human history where the process and practice of consumption now subsumes virtually all other more traditional modes of self-expression (Lasch 1979; Campbell 1989; Featherstone 1994).

That the vast majority of contemporary Western individuals now derive their values and subjectivities from activities associated with consumption is a given in social theory and across the social sciences (Slater 1997; Miller 1995). Yet the field of criminology has mostly ignored this situation, despite the obvious implications for criminalized consumption. This chapter aims to address this oversight by providing a general introduction to the small but growing body of criminological literature that is committed to understanding and developing what has been described helpfully elsewhere as the 'crime-consumerism nexus' (Hayward 2004a: 157–79; 2004b: 147). The chapter starts with a short review section that looks back over criminology's past in a bid to identify some of the moments when criminology did engage with issues relating to consumption and crime. It then returns to the present and a series of ongoing developments within theoretical criminology that collectively suggest our discipline is finally starting to take consumer culture, and in particular the seemingly unchecked growth of global consumption, seriously.

CRIMINOLOGY AND CONSUMER CULTURE

Although the changing sensibilities and subjectivities associated with consumerism have seldom been at the forefront of the criminological enterprise, it would be wrong to suggest that criminologists have never engaged with questions about market culture or the destructive emotional states, feelings, and desires associated with capitalist materialism. For example, in the early decades of the twentieth century, the oft-forgotten Dutch criminologist Willem Bonger was employing terms like 'covetousness' in his writings on the human pains of industrial capitalism, stating: 'As long as humanity has been divided into rich and poor . . . the desires of the masses have been awakened by the display of wealth; only to be repressed again by the moral teaching impressed upon them, that this was a sinful thing' (1936: 93). Occupying a far more prominent position in the discipline is the classic strain theory of Robert Merton (1938). Strain theory argues that crime and deviance occur when there is a discrepancy between what the social structure makes possible (i.e. the means and opportunities for obtaining success), and what the dominant culture extols (i.e. the social value of the glittering prizes associated with material success). While Merton stopped well short of evoking any such thing as a 'consumer society', he nonetheless recognized the growing importance of *mass consumption*, peppering his writing with terms such as 'success symbols' and 'differential class symbols of achievement' (Merton 1938: 680–1). But despite the monumental impact of Merton's theory on criminology, this particular element of his work seldom features in the countless retests of strain theory that have taken place in the subsequent decades (cf. Passas 1997).

Given these important early precursors, why then did twentieth-century criminology largely shy away from further investigations into the relationship between crime and consumption? The answer lies in the fact that, for the most part, mainstream criminology has proceeded from the position that capitalist consumerism is an essentially positive development and thus not something a discipline preoccupied with crime and deviance should be concerned with. The main deviation from this position came in the 1960s, with the emergence of critical and radical criminology. Even here, though, despite the focus very much being on the various harms associated with capitalist accumulation (white collar crime, the growth of the prison-industrial complex, the abuses of the Western state, etc.), the specific question of whether or not consumerism itself might be criminogenic remained largely unexplored. Instead, what interest there was in the consumption practices associated with a burgeoning consumer society tended to coalesce around issues of *class and culture*. It is to these (surprisingly few) examples that we now turn.

The obvious starting point here is the work of the broadly Marxist-inspired 'Birmingham School'. One of the original premises of the various scholars who gravitated to the University of Birmingham's Centre for Cultural Studies in the 1960s and 70s was that working-class youth delinquency should be understood as a form of 'symbolic rebellion' against the dominant values and social inequalities associated with capitalist society (Hall and Jefferson 1976). From this starting position, members of the Birmingham School saw something potentially liberating in consumerism. In particular, they believed that, by mobilizing and appropriating a new set of cultural signifiers drawn from the expanding world of mass consumption, young people could enhance their self-identity and use this heightened sense of autonomy to challenge convention and subvert the 'repressive social order'. Consequently, members of the Birmingham School took great pains elucidating the alleged transformative potential of seemingly innocuous or prosaic consumer items like Dr. Martin's boots, motor scooters, donkey jackets, and a host of other eclectic products associated with, *inter alia*, the mod, punk, and 'rude boy' subcultures.

The strength of the Birmingham approach was twofold. First, it trained the spotlight on the important (and previously neglected) relationship between deviance and subcultural style (Hebdige 1979). Second, and more significantly, it demonstrated sociologically the 'magical' quality of commodities, both in terms of their ability to mediate human relationships and shape individual and group identities. At the time, these were important breakthroughs. However, it is important to stress that the Birmingham School's analysis of consumerism, like Veblen's, was one that turned almost entirely around the issue of class—in this case the particular values and mores of working-class youth subcultures. As such, little attention was paid to the more complex question of whether or not the feelings and emotions engendered by consumerism might ultimately find expression in certain forms of criminal activity. A second problem with the Birmingham School's approach to consumerism was that it massively exaggerated the transformative political potential of subcultural consumption (Hayward and

Schuilenburg 2013). Put differently, not only did Birmingham School researchers fail to grasp the inherent paradox of attempting to resist capitalism at the point of consumption, but they also dramatically underestimated capitalism's ability to absorb so-called 'inventive consumer resistance' and then (re)market it in the form of depoliticized items of dull conformity (Frank 1997; Heath and Potter 2006).

Despite these failings, critical criminology of the 1970s and 80s largely accepted Birmingham School claims regarding the oppositional potential of consumerism. It was only after a full two decades of monetarism, neoliberalism and the onward march of consumer markets into more and more spheres of social and private life that critical criminologists started to take consumer culture seriously. The mood of the times was summed up succinctly by Ian Taylor (1999: 54) in a passage that speaks volumes about criminology's growing awareness of the ever-expanding scope of the late modern consumer society:

> 'the market' is now a *fundamental* motor force in contemporary social and political discourse and practice, in a way that it was not in the 1970s. 'The market' is *hegemonic* in the realm of discourse, and in very many practices (including some domains of that most resistant area of all, the public sector).

In short, Taylor had recognized that, by the end of the twentieth century, there was no longer any meaningful 'oppositional culture' strong enough to challenge the inexorable rise of 'market culture'. He evidenced this point in his 1999 book, *Crime in Context*, by stressing the prominence of values such as 'entrepreneurship' and 'self-interest' in end-of-the-century youth culture and how these new and fast-developing 'strategies of negotiation' would likely bring about the demise of classic subcultural adaptations (Taylor 1999: 75–7). Taylor's analysis was important in that it highlighted the evolution of critical criminology's position with regard to consumerism. However, it stopped well short of linking the forms of subjectivity engendered by a fast-paced consumer society to criminal motivation. For early criminological forays in this direction we must look elsewhere.

Developing a mid-range theory of post-industrial violence at around the same time, the US-based English criminologist, Elliott Currie, also called attention to 'the increasing potency and primacy of consumer values' (1997: 162). Ultimately Currie outlined seven 'mechanisms' that he believed were contributing to violence in 'materialistic US cities', but one mechanism in particular warrants attention here. Influenced by Bonger and Merton's thinking on relative deprivation, Currie shared with Taylor a concern that young people were rejecting 'productive community life' in favour of 'the valorization of consumption for its own sake—and of getting what you want, or getting ahead of others, by whatever means will suffice' (Currie 1997: 163). But unlike Taylor and other critical criminologists before him, what makes Currie's analysis stand out is that he also trained attention (albeit somewhat obliquely) on the actual 'psychological distortions' that were bring engendered within individuals by what he described as a 'dog-eat-dog', 'frantically consumerist culture' (ibid.). Consider, for example the following passage:

> One of the most chilling features of much violent street crime in America today, and also in some developing countries, is how directly it expresses the logic of immediate gratification in the pursuit of consumer goods, or of instant status and recognition . . . People who study crime, perhaps especially from a 'progressive' perspective, sometimes shy away

> from looking hard at these less tangible 'moral' aspects . . . A full analysis of these connections would need to consider, for example, the impact on crime of the specifically psychological distortions of market society, its tendencies to produce personalities less and less capable of relating to others except as consumer items or as trophies in a quest for recognition among one's peers. (Currie 1996: 348)

As Currie infers, this was not the first time that instant gratification and impulsivity had featured as foci of concern within criminological theory.[1] Famously, James Q. Wilson and Richard Herrnstein (1985) claimed that personality differences in traits such as impulsivity were often strongly correlated with the development of frequent and long-term antisocial behavior. Central to their argument, and frequently forgotten by many due to the controversy surrounding their work, was the concept of 'present orientation': the idea that a 'rapid cognitive tempo' and 'shortened time horizons' are responsible for impulsive and disinhibited behaviour.

This is a line of thinking common in conservative 'right realist' criminology more generally. For example, in his earlier work, *Thinking About Crime* (1985 [1975]), Wilson had already identified a set of emotions that he believed acted on and effected 'internalized commitment to self-control'. More specifically, he claimed that, as a result of the erosion of the modernist moral order, two modes of self-expression were taking hold: first, a growing sense of personal liberty and individual rights; and, second, a more radical individualism linked to immediate gratification and greed (Wilson 1985: 237–8). In some ways, these claims are not entirely out of step with the line of argument that would later be developed by Taylor, Currie, and others (e.g. Hall 1997; Young 1999; Fenwick and Hayward 2000). Yet, despite general agreement about the importance of subjectivities like individualism and instantaneity in the commission of certain types of predatory crime, the right realist respective explanations for the cause of the problem differed greatly, as one of us has commented previously:

> The problem is that Wilson's critique of immediate gratification, the rise of nouveau fully fledged individualism, and the concept of self-control (and thus his theory of crime more generally) remains one-dimensional. Wilson can only frame his analysis in terms of a perceived loss of 'traditional' (i.e. modern, or, more accurately, a mix of modern and traditional) forms—the erosion of the 'Protestant work ethic' and, more importantly, the demise of community values (remember the centre piece of Wilson's argument is that crime begets crime at a community level). By placing the concepts of impulsivity and immediate gratification so squarely within the context of a lack of social cohesion and disinvestment in society, Wilson presents us with a reading of these important aspects of criminality that is ultimately rooted in a set of conservative morals. By the same token, he chooses to ignore the fact that, in reality, these 'impulsive', 'disinvested' urbanites are simply the obvious end-products of an unmediated system of consumer capitalism. (Hayward 2004a:178)

One scholar who recognized the need for a more sophisticated analysis of impulsivity and the various other emotional states associated with late modern consumerism

[1] Most obviously, psychological criminologists have conducted a mass of research into the way in which supposed deficits in impulse control can bring about delinquent behaviour by interfering with children's ability to control their behaviour and to think of the future consequences of deviant acts (e.g. Farrington *et al.* 1990; White *et al.* 1994).

was the New Zealand criminologist Wayne Morrison. Writing in 1995, not only did Morrison provide a more sophisticated social theoretical context for Wilson and Herrnstein's ideas about 'differential time appreciation' (Morrison 1995: 309–10), but more importantly he also recognized the need to augment traditional Mertonian strain models so that they could more effectively incorporate the profound changes—both cultural and ontological—that consumerism was wreaking:

> Criminology not only operates with underdeveloped models of desire, but also largely restricts itself to narrow interpretations of strain theories; wherein crime is the result of frustration by the social structure of the needs which culture identifies for the individual. Today, even in the most contemporary of mainstream criminological theory, ideas of positionality and status are underdeveloped. Instead ideas of needs and greed predominate. (ibid.: 317)

Morrison's theoretical insights on the relationship between crime and consumerism are complex and manifold and at times get lost amidst his numerous other often overlapping arguments. However, if one were to summarize his thinking in this area, the following quote is particularly insightful:

> To become self-defining is the fate that the social structure of late-modernity imposes upon its socially created individuality. The individual is called into action; actions which are meant to express his/her self and enable the individual's destiny to be created out of the contingencies of his/her past . . . And while resources differ, all are subjected to variations of a similar pressure . . . namely that of the overburdening of the self as the self becomes the ultimate source of security. The tasks asked of the late-modern person require high degrees of social and technical skills. To control the self and guide it through the disequilibrium of the journeys of late modernity is the task imposed upon the late-modern person, but what if the life experiences of the individual have not fitted him/her with this power? . . . much crime is an attempt of the self to create sacred moments of control, to find ways in which the self can exercise control and power in situations where power and control are all too clearly lodged outside the self. (ibid.: iv)

Using social theory to make sense of the changing nature of the self within the open social terrain of late modernity is not something that has featured to any great degree in the criminological enterprise (Garland and Sparks 2000). The ascendency of consumer culture, however, meant this had to change. Following the line of travel set down by the likes of Currie and Morrison, other criminologists started to show a marked interest in the growing place of consumerism in everyday life. Echoing Morrison's 'dilemmas of transition' thesis, and drawing on Anthony Giddens' notion of 'ontological insecurity', Jock Young, for example, urged criminologists to rethink Mertonian strain theory for a contemporary world characterized by 'precariousness', 'a chaotic reward system', the 'rise of individualism', and 'a sense of unfairness and a feeling of the arbitrary' (1999: 8–9). Consider, for example, the following quote in which Young moves beyond a structural or class analysis to suggest that consumerism itself might now be criminogenic:

> The market . . . creates the practical basis of comparison: it renders visible inequalities of race, class age and gender. It elevates a universal citizenship of consumption yet excludes a significant minority from membership. It encourages an ideal of diversity, a marketplace of self-discovery yet provides for the vast majority a narrow, unrewarding individualism in practice. It creates 'uninterrupted disturbances of all social conditions, everlasting

> uncertainty and agitation' yet depends on a relatively uncritical acceptance of the given order. The market flourishes, expands, beckons yet undercuts itself. It does all this but is not a mere transmission belt: the mores of the market may be the dominant ethos of the age but this ether of aspiration is shaped, developed and given force by the human actors involved. It is in this light that the problems in the two spheres of order, relative deprivation and individuation, must be viewed. For these are the key to the crime wave in the post-war period. (Young 1999: 47)

Young made good on his promise of extending the concept of strain by augmenting notions of relative deprivation in two ways. First, he argued that relative deprivation should no longer be thought of simply as a 'gaze upwards', but also *as a troubled and anxious look downwards toward the excluded of society* ('it is dismay at the relative well-being of those who although below one on the social hierarchy are perceived as unfairly advantaged: they make too easy a living even if it's not as good as one's own', ibid.: 9). Second, and drawing on developments in cultural criminology, he sought to 'energize' the Mertonian position by showing that crime was not only about bridging a material or structural gap, but that the acquisition and display of consumer products often functioned to alleviate emotional or existential deficits (e.g. 'the structural predicament of the ghetto poor is not simply a deficit of goods—as Merton would have had it—it is a state of humiliation', Young 2003: 408). As ever, Young's work was thoughtful and provocative, but while it challenged researchers to update certain established criminological theories in light of the changing nature of late modern society, it fell some way short of developing a fully fledged theoretical framework for understanding the criminogenic tendencies inherent in consumer societies. Two other books, however, would do precisely that.

Although different in their approach, Keith Hayward's *City Limits: Crime, Consumer Culture and the Urban Experience* (2004a) and Steve Hall, Simon Winlow, and Craig Ancrum's *Criminal Identities and Consumer Culture* (2008) both focused attention on the specific question: how does consumer culture cause crime? For Hayward, the answer was to be found in the emotions and subjectivities engendered by consumerism. In particular, he argued that, with its emphasis on the 'new' and the 'now', consumer culture separates (especially young) people from the consequences of their actions and makes them more likely to pursue exciting or risk-laden activities without regard for conventional normative restraints. Hence his analysis focused primarily on crimes with a strong expressive dimension, such as gang violence, vandalism, joy riding, and drug use—transgressive activities that are most likely to involve playing with new forms of concomitant subjectivity based around desire, simultaneity, individualism, and impulsivity (2004a: 157).

Differing in their approach, Hall *et al.* focused on more problematic forms of narcissistic subjectivity in which individuals were willing to engage in harmful careers of acquisitive and entrepreneurial criminality in order to benefit the self. Their crucial insight was to reverse the conflation of norms and values which have perpetuated the notion that such forms of criminality 'deviate' from mainstream culture. Instead, Hall *et al.* suggest that their subjects' steadfast adherence to the values of consumerism, in addition to their methods of competitive entrepreneurialism within criminal marketplaces, was in many ways a perfect reflection of mainstream consumer and neoliberal values.

Therefore, in different but overlapping ways, these books were the first in the discipline to train attention specifically on the 'crime-consumerism nexus'. *City Limits* focused upon expressive and risk-taking forms of transgression within consumerism's 'culture of now'; while *Criminal Identities* focused upon entrepreneurial criminals' embodiment of ruthless neoliberal competitiveness and their fetishistic attachment to consumer commodities and associated lifestyles. However, both texts speak to consumerism's criminogenic qualities and in doing so set the tone for a new wave of criminological studies concerned with the psychological, social, economic, and environmental impacts of late modern consumerism. It is to this fast-developing body of work that we now turn.

CULTURAL CRIMINOLOGY

Cultural criminology is concerned with the convergence of cultural, criminal, and crime control processes; as such, it situates criminality and its control in the context of cultural dynamics and the contested production of meaning. Attentive to the realities of a deeply unequal world, cultural criminology strives to highlight how power affects the upwards and downwards construction of criminological phenomena: how rules are made, why they are broken, and the deeper implications of these processes.[2] Because of its focus on the lived experience of crime, cultural criminologists have always trained attention on those little situations, circumstances and crimes that make up everyday life. For cultural criminology's critics, this interest in micro-level analysis is a problem (O'Brien 2006; Hall and Winlow 2007). These critics suggest that, by focusing on everyday people and everyday crimes, cultural criminology has foregone macro-economic analyses of crime in the interests of a romantically subjectivist or narrowly cultural focus. But such criticism misses the point. In reality, cultural criminology's focus on the everyday is a strategic choice (Ferrell *et al.* 2015: 87–91; Ferrell and Ilan 2013). For it is here in the everyday world that it is possible to overcome the dualism of structure and agency, and to unearth the connections that frequently link petty transgressions with large-scale criminal markets or organized corporate crime networks. Put another way, while cultural criminologists continue to trace the damage caused by late capitalism at the macro level, they are equally committed to documenting the wide sweep of transcontinental capitalism amidst the most local of situations and common everyday transgressions.

This multilayered, multifaceted approach is especially useful when it comes to outlining the relationships that exist between consumerism and crime—not least because today consumer culture itself is transmitted and inculcated across *all* levels of late modern society. Not only is it operational at a grand or civic level, eroding informal networks of mutual support by converting collectivities into markets, public services into privatized corporate opportunities, and people into consumers, but the pervasive

[2] For general introductions to cultural criminology see Hayward and Young (2012), Ferrell *et al.* (2015).

logic of market society and its attendant consumer values also function psychologically; shaping individual consciousness by propagating insatiable wants and desires and promoting a culture that exalts atomized individual competition and consumption over other social considerations. In light of this situation, cultural criminology looks to analyse and highlight the criminogenic nature of consumerist discourses wherever they may feature within contemporary society.

Now in its third decade, cultural criminology has, since its emergence, trained considerable attention on consumer culture. It even featured in Ferrell and Sanders inaugurating publication, *Cultural Criminology,* in the guise of Lyng and Bracey's (1995) chapter on the dynamic by which consumerism transforms experiential opposition, and even overt criminal activity, into commodified product. Tracing the history of 'outlaw biker style', Lyng and Bracey show how early attempts to criminalize biker culture only served to amplify its illicit meanings, while later marketing schemes to incorporate the signifiers of biker style (most notably the Harley Davison motorcycle brand) into mass production effectively evacuated its original subversive potential. This process through which criminal or illicit practices are co-opted and then used to sell product is described by cultural criminologists as 'the commodification of crime', and has been identified in everything from the steady dilution of rap music's violent origins (Ferrell *et al.* 2015: ch. 6), to the way that fetishized S&M sexual practices became integrated into high-street shopping culture (Presdee 2000). Relatedly, cultural criminologists also talk about the 'marketing of transgression', a process by which everyday products such as soft drinks (Ferrell *et al.* 2015: 110), automobiles (Muzzatti 2010), and training shoes (Ferrell and Ilan 2013: 372) are made 'cool' by employing branding strategies associated with deviant themes or criminal imagery. Various other aspects of consumer culture have also featured prominently in cultural criminology, including work that traces the origins of everyday commodities to the grim sweatshop factories of China or the illegally-exploited rainforests of the Global South (Boekhout van Solinge 2008; Redmond 2015), and studies that show how particular consumption choices can function as 'tools of classification and identification by which agencies of social control construct profiles of potential criminal protagonists' (Hayward and Yar 2006: 23; Treadwell 2008).

Perhaps cultural criminology's main achievement in this area, though, is the clustering of ideas known as the 'crime-consumerism nexus' (Hayward 2004a, 2004b). The crime-consumerism nexus is a theoretical concept used by (cultural) criminologists to understand the relationships that exist within consumer societies between the values and emotions associated with consumerism and various forms of expressive and acquisitive criminality. The crime-consumerism nexus asserts that consumerism cultivates—especially among young people—new forms of subjectivity based around desire, individualism, hedonism, and impulsivity, which, in many instances, can find expression in transgressive and even criminal behaviour, from gang activity to drug use, mugging to rioting. Importantly, this is not to suggest that consumer culture is criminogenic in any simplistic sense of direct correlation/causation; nor is it an attempt to integrate consumerism into a general theory of crime. Rather, the crime-consumerism nexus should be understood simply as an attempt to outline the striking convergence between novel forms of subjectivity propagated by consumerism, and many of the characteristics identified within the criminological literature as being constitutive of criminality. Interdisciplinary in nature, drawing as it does on criminology, behavioural economics, consumer research, and the sociology of risk and identity, it is not an easy concept to define. However, four main themes can be identified:

1. *Insatiability of desire (and its concomitant, perpetual dissatisfaction)*: A unique feature of contemporary consumer culture is that insatiable desire is now not only normalized but essential to the very survival of the current socio-economic order. Far from an unintended or unwanted 'side effect', insatiable desire is actively cultivated in a consumer culture. Of relevance to any criminological analysis of consumerism is the flip side of such a situation: namely, *a constant sense of unfulfillment, dissatisfaction, and disillusionment*. The criminogenic consequences of this 'strange combination of perpetual dissatisfaction and a longing for the new' hardly need spelling out. At the most obvious level, a lot of crime—from shoplifting to street robbery—can be understood not as a desperate act of poverty or a defiant gesture against the system, but as an attempt to bridge a perceived 'consumer deficit', and as a form of identity construction.

2. *New forms of 'hyper strain'*: Such thinking is reminiscent of Merton's classic 'strain theory'. However, contemporary hyper-consumerism is contributing to the crime problem in ways that are qualitatively different from those expressed by strain theorists. Today, what people are feeling deprived of is no longer simply the material product itself, but, rather, the sense of identity that products have come to bestow on the individual. Such a situation demands a move away from the *instrumentality* inherent in Merton's strain theory towards a concept predicated more on the *expressivity* associated with new forms of desire.

3. *Engagement with risk*: A further source of tension exists between the desire for excitement that is so prominent a feature of consumer culture and the mundane/over-controlled nature of much modern life—from the encroachment of surveillance to the drudgery of low-wage employment. One way in which individuals attempt to escape this paradox is by exerting a sense of personal control—or more accurately, a 'controlled loss of control'—through engaging with risk. For example, many forms of street crime frequently perpetrated within urban areas such as peer group fighting or graffiti writing should be seen for exactly what they are, attempts to construct an enhanced sense of self or a semblance of control by engaging in risk-laden practices on the metaphorical edge.

4. *Instant gratification/impulsivity*: In addition to being insatiable, consumer culture cultivates a desire for *immediate, rather than delayed, gratification*. We are, at a societal level, increasingly encouraged to eschew long-term conservatism in favour of instant gratification as evidenced by the massive expansion of credit facilities and the constant emphasis on immediacy in the 'buy now' language of advertising. The bombardment of stimuli associated with consumer culture fundamentally distorts our experience of temporality, now reduced to 'a series of pure and unrelated presents'. With its particular emphasis on the 'new' and the 'now', consumer culture separates people from the consequences of their actions and makes them more likely to pursue excitement without regard for conventional normative constraints.

(Republished with permission of SAGE Reference, from the Encyclopaedia of Street Crime in America, Jeffrey Ian Ross (ed.), 2013; permission conveyed through Copyright Clearance Center, Inc.).

Since this model was developed other elements of the crime-consumerism nexus have started to emerge. First, a growing body of work has exposed the 'infantilizing' nature of late-capitalist culture (Hayward 2012, 2013; Smith 2013). This work explores how 'consumerism as a cultural ethos' is contributing to *both* the depreciation of mature adulthood (and the roles and responsibilities typically associated with that stage of people's lives), and importantly, the 'adultification' of very young teenagers (in terms of lifestyle choices and activities involving sexual activity, drugs, criminality, etc.) (Hayward 2012: 226). Although, the criminological implications of younger and younger people making adult decisions (or inversely, young adults acting like children) have yet to be fully developed, research is beginning to appear that outlines clear links between the narcissistic aspects of infantilization and the hedonistic excesses of the night-time economy (Smith 2013, 2014), forms of 'anti-social consumption' that impede efforts to limit environmental harms (Brisman and South 2015), and the selfish motivations behind inner-city predatory criminality (Hall *et al.* 2008).

A second additional element that one could now include in the crime-consumerism nexus is the relationship between circuits of wasteful consumption and environmental harm, something that is now being developed under the rubric 'green-cultural criminology' (Brisman and South 2014, this volume; Ferrell 2013). Drawing together the thoughtful green criminological scholarship of Avi Brisman and Nigel South with Jeff Ferrell's (2006) decade-long ethnographic investigations into trash picking, 'dumpster diving', and environmental activism, green-cultural criminology exposes the exploitative ecological practices associated with the globalized consumerist way of life. From the material consequences of the commodification of nature to 'greenwashing' campaigns by which deleterious corporate practices are recast as supposedly pro-environmental activism, green-cultural criminology not only adds an important component to the (green) crime-consumerism nexus, but also illustrates cultural criminology's more general goal of constantly enlivening and expanding the criminological imagination. With this same ambition in mind, two other recent criminological strands have emerged that share a fundamental interest in the relationship between consumer culture and crime: the overlapping theoretical perspectives known as 'ultra realism' and 'deviant leisure'.

ULTRA REALISM

'Ultra realism' represents a development of some of the more critical strains of criminological theory that have emerged since the 1970s. Through engagement with ethnographic methods, underpinned by a complex theoretical framework, ultra realism pushes beyond both left realism (Lea and Young 1984) and critical realism (Bhaskar 1997) to offer incisive and penetrative analysis of the realities of life in a world shaped in no small part by global consumer culture and neoliberal ideology.

Ultra realism's central claim is that the empirical world exists suspended above a maelstrom of deeper forces, processes, and structures which contribute to and influence our interaction with the social. In this sense, events such as crime, disorder, or the commission of harm are best described as symptoms—that is, they are visible and even measurable, but not in themselves causative. To fully understand the origins of crime and harm, we must uncover the deep-rooted human drives and actions that help perpetuate the dominant social order.

Taking this position as a starting point, ultra realism seeks to identify fundamental flaws in many of the building blocks of contemporary criminology's theoretical frameworks. More specifically, it criticizes both mainstream and critical criminological perspectives not simply on minor points of difference, but at the root of their fundamental domain assumptions. To illustrate this, consider the way in which 'human nature' is conceived within criminological literature. Although critical to understanding the causes of crime, assumptions about human nature are rooted in political philosophies that inform the most dominant mainstream and critical perspectives of right realist and left liberal paradigms. If these assumptions are questioned or problematized, then the edifice of criminological theory built upon these 'truths' begins to crumble.

This is precisely the aim of Hall and Winlow's thoughtful and provocative *Revitalizing Criminology* (2015). Within this book, the authors carefully explain that right realist and left liberal perspectives are, at their most fundamental level, mirror images of one another in their approach to individual agency and subjectivity. For ultra realists, both these positions are problematic in that they overstate the autonomy of rational and conscious individual agency and thus fail to pay sufficient attention to issues of the unconscious in shaping subjectivity. In a claim that bears some resemblance to the earlier work of Zygmunt Bauman, ultra realists argue that the individual is not inherently good or immoral. Morality is manipulated by social structures and systems as the individual subconsciously seeks to actively identify with what the French psychoanalyst Jacques Lacan refers to as a *symbolic order*—the set of signs, symbols, rules, and values by which individuals make cogent sense of their lives.[3]

However, in contemporary late modern society, identification with a coherent symbolic order appears increasingly difficult. Our current socio-symbolic system is now overwhelmingly predicated on the principles of neoliberal consumer-capitalism, ideologically supported and reproduced through a corporatized mass media. Identity and a semblance of ontological security are therefore only attainable through full immersion in consumer capitalism. Such a situation has inevitable implications when it comes to thinking about how one might resist or challenge consumer capitalism's hegemonic position. Despite an increase in critical perspectives on global consumerism, many scholars remain attached to the possibility of consumerism as a tool of resistance (Riley *et al.* 2013; Maffesoli 1996). For ultra realists, as well as proponents of cultural criminology and deviant leisure perspectives, resistance is impossible at the point of consumption. Rather, consumerism appears to have a tendency to engender a perpetual state of anxiety, fear of cultural irrelevance, and an enduring sense of lack, which in

[3] A coherent symbolic order provides a level of organization which is shared with other members of society in order to navigate everyday life. Importantly, incorporation into a symbolic order is not achieved through inculcation or coercion on behalf of some ideological state apparatus. Nor is it inflicted through the manufacture of consent by hegemonic power structures. It is a necessary and inescapable part of identity formation that ought to, under the right conditions, provide the individual with a level of stability and ontological security.

turn serves to perpetuate desire. Consumer capitalism therefore relies upon a culture of competitive interpersonal relations to cultivate envy and a pervasive, deep-rooted sense of dissatisfaction. Temporary relief is promised through consumption and the creation of consumer identities. In this way people actively seek out their own incorporation into consumer culture as a means of addressing their underlying individual anxieties.

Ultra realist theory has been utilized to develop a number of stringent critiques of contemporary issues that highlight the link between consumerism and crime. For example, consider Treadwell *et al.*'s (2013) examination of the 2011 UK riots. Initial criminological reactions were quick to fashion a narrative around the disorder that positioned those taking part as rising up in protest against swingeing economic cuts, few job prospects, and an increasing sense of injustice characterized by their interactions with state agencies. The data presented by Treadwell *et al.* however, tells a different story. Initially, the breakdown of law and order and the unpreparedness of the police response opened up a space in which rioters *could* have seized a political initiative. However, for many of the rioters the overwhelming response to this opportunity was to accumulate as many of consumerism's symbolic objects as possible. Thus, from an ultra-realist perspective, the 2011 London riots should be understood primarily as 'consumer riots'—that is, rather than seeking to challenge the established political orthodoxy, the rioters (in the main) illustrated a deep commitment to the ideology of consumer capitalism. Despite many participants' precarious socio-economic position, those who participated in the riots did not want grand socio-political change but simply more of what already existed: the commoditized markers of a life well-lived and the opportunity to correct their marginalized image of what Zygmunt Bauman (1998) might once have described as a 'flawed consumer' (i.e. individuals who are no longer capable of functioning effectively within consumer markets).

For ultra realists, competitive consumerism has infiltrated the core of Western society, impacting upon social relations among young people, driving desire across a broad demographic, and opening up the motivational capacity to commit crime and inflict harm on others in the process.[4] While anti-capitalist movements appear to offer a salve to the dominance of consumer capitalism, ultra realists indicate that even positions of anti-consumerism can be depoliticized and commodified (Frank 1997). At the same time, new criminal markets made possible by advances in technology are increasingly embedded into everyday life. This in turn provides the backdrop to what Steve Redhead (2015) describes as 'claustropolitanism'—the desire of those with the wealth and means to do so to secede from the reality of what constitutes the social today.

This is complex terrain for criminology, and thus one must be clear about some of the key terms utilized within ultra realism. In particular, it is important to recognize

[4] This willingness to inflict harm is achieved through a mechanism that ultra realists (see Hall 2012) refer to as 'special liberty'. Put simply, this is the individual belief that one is no longer constrained by ethical codes, and thus has the right to freely express their own unique desires and drives. Those in possession of special liberty are exonerated from the need to acknowledge their harm toward others. Instead, individuals are able to operate under the auspices of a fantasy that elevates them to the status of the most transcendent free individuals in which their harm is negated due to their powers of wealth creation, and their ability to drive new cultural trends.

what ultra realists mean by the 'return to motivation' (Hall *et al.* 2008: 1). Stated simply, and irrespective of whether they are analysing the privatization of public space or the intellectual wastelands of mainstream media, the primary goal of ultra realism is to explore below the *symptoms* of the crime-consumerism nexus and explain *why* individuals seek out the symbolism of consumer capitalism. Here, these complex forces and processes are linked to a social order that compels the individual to consume, and invokes what the philosopher Slavoj Žižek (2000) refers to as a reversal of the cultural superego. Under different socio-economic conditions, giving into desire would invoke a sense of guilt, as the superego brought to bear shame at an inability to defer gratification. However, today, shame is invoked at failure to take every consumer opportunity and experience that passes within reach of the individual. As Winlow and Hall (2013: 121) note:

> A good life is a life in which we have tasted extreme indulgence, a life in which we have denied ourselves nothing and exposed ourselves constantly to the thrill of the new; a life of sexual adventure, global travel and committed consumerism, in which we forge our own path and blithely ignore decaying conservative accounts of frugality, commitment, obligation and work.

In other words, success, or the 'good life', is measured entirely by competent and sustained engagement within the circuits of consumption, through knowing what to buy and how to flaunt it. However, within a post-crash, post-Brexit economic environment, it seems reasonable to question how, despite stagnating or falling incomes and increasing precarity, consumerism is still playing such an integral role within the capitalist project.

For ultra realists, the answer is found in the debt economy (Horsley 2015). Because economic growth depends to a large degree on the willingness of individuals to take on consumer debt, the consumer marketplace needs to ensure we remain committed to spending money in order to remain culturally relevant and connected. Today, largely as a result of the emergence of the so-called 'cashless economy' (Graeber 2014), British household debt stands at an estimated £1.5 trillion, a staggering increase from £400 billion in the mid-1990s (The Money Charity 2017). Within this new 'culture of indebtedness' (Horsley 2015), access to consumer credit is facilitated and expedited by companies operating (often with impunity) at the predatory end of the loan market. These doorstep credit companies, payday lenders, and rent-to-buy companies often disguise their exploitative practices as a form of community service, but in reality they exemplify the toxicity of debt as it relates to individuals, families, and communities.[5]

As this chapter has illustrated, it is now possible to link consumerism to a range of harms, many of which strengthen and perpetuate the existing socio-economic system. However, elsewhere, we can see a more direct connection between consumerism

[5] Importantly, consumers, while being marketed to at increasingly young ages (see Hayward 2012, 2013; Bakan 2011) are being inculcated into cultures of debt while still in their teenage years. Students attending university in England today can expect to take out sizeable loans to pay for tuition. This induction into debt peonage has far reaching implications. Put simply, immersion in a debt society negates any potential for dissent, rebellion, or resistance to the dominant social order. Rather, as some commentators have observed, debt obligations subjugate and depoliticize populations, binding the individual to the neoliberal socio-economic order, without removing the desire to acquire and display consumer symbolism (Lazzarato 2015).

and crime. In the effort to cultivate consumer identities, many have no choice but to immerse themselves in the circuits of consumption. Of course, most are able to acquire the necessary consumer symbolism within the legitimate market place, but for some, illegal methods are increasingly becoming a first resort, particularly in post-crash locales of permanent recession (see Hall *et al.* 2008; Contreras 2012). Intimidation and a capacity for violence allow determined criminals a direct, albeit brutal shortcut to consumer markets (Contreras 2012; Ellis 2015). Like the tax-avoiding economic elite of the corporate boardroom (Platt 2015), committed and opportunistic criminals are able to simply take the symbolic objects they need to raise themselves up above those to whom they feel no moral or ethical obligation (Hall *et al.* 2008). Hayward (2016) is perhaps right to suggest that not all crime stories are stories about capitalism, but the long-term effects on individuals of immersion in competitive cultures of acquisition and ornamental display should not be overlooked. In this sense, we can see the value of ultra realism's response to unfolding events and criminological issues that defy simplistic interpretation.

In the following section, our attention turns to commodified forms of leisure and their attendant harms. The development of a 'deviant leisure' perspective as outlined below allows us to draw on the advances in cultural criminology discussed above, while also incorporating the role of deep structures and processes relating to the competitive individualism and the normalized harm outlined in ultra realism.

DEVIANT LEISURE

Commodified leisure markets are perhaps one of the most rapidly evolving examples of global consumer capitalism. As both cultural and ultra realist criminologists have indicated, consumerism and identity are irreversibly connected, with much identity creation and maintenance carried out in the spheres of marketized leisure. Surprisingly, criminology to date has appeared interested only in instances where leisure contravenes legal definitions of crime, or where youthful leisure practices hint at transgression, rebellion, and excitement (see Smith and Raymen 2016). More recently, however, criminologists have begun to engage with the relationship between leisure and social harm in a more sophisticated and coherent fashion (ibid.; Kindynis 2016). This new 'deviant leisure' perspective draws upon advances in both cultural criminology (see Hayward 2016) and ultra-realist criminology (Hall and Winlow 2015) in order to illustrate the role of commodified and marketized forms of leisure in the commission of harm. As explained above, ultra realist criminology utilizes a broadly harm-based analysis of the systemic corrosiveness of global capitalism as its focus, whereas cultural criminology's traditional interest in crime, leisure, and subcultures has continuously evolved over the last decade to include an increasingly materialist critique of liberal capitalism, harm, and consumer culture (Ferrell *et al.* 2008/2015; Ferrell 2006; Hayward and Yar 2006). Through a careful synthesis of these two strands of criminological theory, alongside a reconceptualization of social deviance, deviant leisure perspectives illustrate how individual, social, economic, and environmental harms are structurally and culturally embedded within many accepted and normalized forms of leisure. As Oliver Smith and Tom Raymen (2016) have suggested in a recent article that outlines the parameters of this perspective:

> When the underlying violence of shopping explodes into realised physical violence in time-bound consumption events (Raymen and Smith, 2015); when sexual assault and violence is a normal, expected, and even desired feature of the ubiquitous night-time economy (Smith, 2014; Winlow and Hall, 2006); and when the humiliation and degradation of revenge porn and torture become forms of entertainment to be consumed through pornography and video games (Atkinson and Rodgers, 2015; Sherlock, 2016), criminology must look beyond what is socially-defined and culturally accepted as affirming leisure culture and instead interrogate the nature of leisure itself and its relationship with an increasingly liberalised consumer capitalism.

Defining deviant leisure is not an easy task—indeed the term itself is constructed from two of the broadest concepts in the social sciences. However, what is clear from the outset is that the deviant leisure perspective requires criminologists to travel beyond the boundaries associated with traditional socio-legal constructs of crime and criminality, and into the realm of harm and zemiology. Put differently, underlying the deviant leisure perspective is a fundamental rereading of the concept of social deviance. 'Deviance' is generally applied throughout the social sciences to describe behaviours that contravene socially accepted norms, values, and ethical standards (Downes and Rock 2007). However, a deviant leisure perspective seeks to invert this traditional interpretation. In an era characterized by the pursuit of 'cool individualism', and where the primary cultural imperative is to simultaneously fit in while standing out (Miles 1998), the cultivation of many contemporary 'deviant identities' can today be viewed as steadfastly conformist (Hall *et al.* 2008; Hayward and Schuilenburg 2014; Smith 2014). Expressed differently, what could within a more ethical social order be conceptualized as *deviant* behaviour is today being harnessed, pacified, and repositioned as a very specific form of creative dynamism that serves to propel desire for symbolic objects and experiences—desires which are then translated into demand within the circuits of consumption dominated by the leisure economy.

From a criminal justice perspective, the relationship between crime control and leisure is inconsistent. Marketized, taxable forms of leisure such as the gambling industry, or the development of an alcohol-based night-time economy are regulated relatively lightly, despite clear links to violent crime, debt, and mental health issues (see Smith and Raymen 2016). Other leisure pursuits however, appear to be regulated, criminalized, and controlled to an extent that appears disproportionate to the perceived harms that such pursuits pose. In these cases, capital has the privilege of defining and redefining the legitimacy of a particular space, thus continuously reclassifying the status of these activities as illegitimate 'deviance' or legitimate 'leisure'. Cultural lifestyle sports or forms of 'serious leisure' (Stebbins 2015) such as skateboarding, parkour, and urban exploration (Atkinson 2009; Garrett 2013) occupy a curious position at the interface between deviance and leisure. On the one hand, they are legitimate leisure activities, with their own competitive sporting events and official governing bodies. Moreover, the spectacular imagery of their practice is frequently utilized for the commercial purposes of feature films and advertisements. In these and other ways, then, sports like skateboarding and certain forms of graffiti should be conceptualized not as 'deviant' but entirely conformist; part of the injunction to discover one's true self and construct a persona of 'cool individualism' (Heath and Potter 2006). However, on the other hand, these activities are also policed and controlled, with those participating often facing fines and other sanctions for engaging in these leisure pursuits outside of the specific spaces of indoor gyms and skate parks. In this sense, as 'right' and 'wrong', 'deviant' or 'legitimate' have become increasingly synonymous with what is 'right' and 'wrong' for the *market,* there has also been a move towards a spatial and, by extension, political and economic definition of what constitutes harmful deviance and legitimate leisure.

While deviant leisure perspectives provide an explanation for the increased regulation, legitimation, and commodification of leisure forms, they are also used to examine the cultural dominance of the leisure industries. It is here at the interface of leisure and consumer culture that we can see harmful outcomes emanating from the commodification and marketization of a range of activities and behaviours. The night-time high street of bars, pubs, casinos, and strip-clubs, ubiquitous to cities across the UK and beyond, provides us with a clear example. The night-time economy (NTE) is not only culturally embedded within consumer society, but is a valuable source of employment and taxation. In this sense it is integral to the cultural and economic aspirations of city councils (see Smith 2014; Chatterton and Hollands 2003). However, it is also a site in which social harms are written into the same urban scripts that position alcohol-based leisure as indicative of a vibrant, 24-hour city (Roberts *et al.* 2006; Bianchini 1995). These harms tend to be concentrated around fault lines of gender and race (see Smith and Raymen 2016), and in many cases are so ubiquitous as to be accepted as an unfortunate by-product of a night out or employment in the NTE. More familiar to criminology, is the alcohol related violence reported regularly in the media, or served up as the subject of fly-on-the-wall documentaries (see Hayward and Hobbs 2007). These incidents of violence and disorder have been well documented within academic literature, with many commentators explaining the million hospital visits a year attributed to the NTE and the innumerable sexual assaults and violent encounters (IAS 2013) as the pathology of a minority of working class men whose actions taint an otherwise unproblematic site of creativity and identity construction (Newburn and Shiner 2001; Richardson and Budd 2003). The reality, of course, is much more complex.

If our night-time city centres really are loci of violence and exclusion, then how can we explain their enduring popularity for large numbers of consumers? The answer appears to be tied to the problem of identity within late modern society. Outside of social media, night-time leisure constitutes perhaps the most important arena for identity creation linked to conspicuous and ostentatious consumption in this period of consumer capitalism. Perhaps their appeal lies in the excitement of hedonism alongside the suspension of the moral regulation and behavioural norms associated with day-time comportment. However, central to the deviant leisure perspective is the assertion that these environments rarely generate resistance or political solidarity. For the most part, these drinkers are not kicking back against the system; they are entirely conformist in their dedication to the values dictated by the market. This claim is substantiated by the indication that this model of alcohol consumption is central to the continued viability of the industry, with committed consumers (or binge drinkers to use the common term) accounting for 60 per cent of profits accrued by the alcohol industry (Boseley 2016). By focusing on the range of harms engendered by legitimized and normalized forms of leisure, such as the NTE, the deviant leisure perspective opens up a space for reappraising our understanding of consumer capitalism and its deleterious effects. Of course, social harm approaches are not new, having been used for some time within the development of a green criminology (see Hillyard and Tombs 2004; Tombs and Hillyard, this volume; White 2013). As our attention now turns to environmental degradation associated with the democratization of tourism, it comes as no surprise that there is a degree of convergence between deviant leisure and green criminological perspectives.

Over the past two decades, the emergence of a distinct 'green' criminology has successfully directed criminological attention toward the harms inflicted upon the environment as a result of non-criminalized activities (see South 1998; White 2013) and from interaction with the global economy (Ruggierro and South 2013). Deviant leisure perspectives build upon this work, and interrogate not only the environmental harms that result from engaging with leisure cultures, but the role of consumerism in the creation of individual desire and the cultivation of competitive individualism. For example, as commodified forms of leisure became democratized through the rise of the budget airline, all-inclusive deals, and online booking-agents, leisure activities began to come into conflict with the natural environment on a global scale. Even beyond the 705 million tonnes of annual CO2 emissions from the 100,000 flights per day (ATAG 2014), the democratization of tourism places unsustainable strains upon the global commons in the pursuit of private gain. Moreover, the environmental harms and waste associated with leisure are not restricted to the far-off tourist idylls of the Maldives, but are simultaneously experienced in multiple locations globally.

As leisure markets evolve and grow in order to circumvent the limits to capital (Harvey 2007), the deviant leisure perspective describes a culturally symbiotic relationship between harmful leisure and consumerism. Here, participation in particular forms of leisure promises the creation of new, cool identities. While some of these may be relatively benign, deviant leisure scholars draw upon examples such as the rapid growth and cultural ubiquity of the gambling industry, which represents a market worth of £7.1 billion in the UK alone (GCUK 2015). With an increasing array of gambling opportunities quite literally at the fingertips of internet users, it is likely that 'social' gambling, fiercely defended by gambling industry lobbyists as non-problematic, masks a range of damaging social and individual effects. Existing criminological analyses have looked at gambling within a paradigm of 'edgework' (Banks 2013), yet only rarely do criminologists acknowledge the attendant harms of social gambling. By using a deviant leisure perspective, it is possible to emphasize how an identity-based culture of sports betting, combined with relentless promises of 'easy wins' encourages chasing losses and impulsive betting (Binde 2010). By embedding 'sociable' gambling within existing leisure markets, the cost of an afternoon watching football in the pub can quickly spiral; and for some individuals these losses are likely to manifest as stress, financial uncertainty, emotional volatility, depression, and anxiety.

The deviant leisure perspective undoubtedly stands in contrast to many of the more celebratory accounts of leisure and its associated activities. For some critics, then, it may present a rather dour or pessimistic outlook on something that for most people is a source of fun and enjoyment. However, there is some room for optimism, through identification of and engagement with so-called *prosocial* forms of leisure. However, as Smith and Raymen (2016: 5) point out, this will require disconnection of commodified leisure from the hypercompetitive consumer ideology propagated by the current social order:

> In short, *prosocial* forms of leisure are possible, but lie beyond what we term a *hedonic realism*, the inability to see beyond the horizon of a social order where leisure identity is synonymous with the hyper-competitive and individualized arena of consumer capitalism.

In sum, the deviant leisure perspective has the potential to allow us to think more critically about the crime-consumerism nexus. More specifically, the synthesis of ultra realist and critical cultural criminologies enables criminologists to illustrate and understand how individual, social, economic, and environmental harms are structurally embedded within many accepted and normalized forms of leisure.

CONCLUSION

Consumer culture pervades every aspect of our lives. The marketization, privatization, and commodification that is perhaps the defining feature of our late modern landscape underpins the global economy and provides us with the consumer symbolism of goods, experiences, and services that are utilized to create new hierarchies of social significance, cultivating envy and desire. In this sense, Anthony Giddens (1991) was right to suggest that we have 'no choice but to choose'; the alternative to immersion in the hypercompetitive individualistic environs of consumer markets is cultural obsolescence, a life not worth living.

The premise of our chapter has been to explore and explain the relationship between crime and consumerism. Here, it would be useful to point to some assiduously prepared statistics, a graph which neatly illustrates the correlation between the growth and dominance of consumer capitalism, and steadily rising crime rates. Unfortunately for us and indeed all criminologists, this is simply not possible. On the surface, the last two decades appear to have been an unremitting success for crime preventionists and other proponents of administrative criminology. Much if not all of the global North appears to be experiencing steadily declining rates of crime across the majority of volume crimes (Parker 2010). However, the so-called 'crime decline' masks both a host of new and expanding crime markets, and a huge number of non-criminal harms, some of which have been discussed above, that emanate from a socio-economic system working within neoliberal ideology. As Hall and Winlow (2015) argue:

> Beneath the superficial empirical level, in the realms of the actual and the real, we have seen profound developments in the neoliberal era. We have seen the normalisation and sociocultural integration of 'hybridized' illegal and legal economic activities in a shadow-economy that operates beneath governments' statistical radar.

While some crimes are certainly declining, it is unlikely that this is as much a result of greater sociability or enhanced societal well-being (Pinker 2012), as it is to increased securitization and implementation of pragmatic crime control measures. As we have suggested above, criminal markets are mutating, at a pace and into environments that collators of crime statistics are simply unable to keep up with. As scholars writing from all three of the perspectives outlined above have repeatedly observed, while there has been a statistical drop in 'crime', many harms are now simply normalized and embedded within deeply entrenched circuits of consumption (Raymen and Smith 2015).

When social scientists dare to problematize or critique something that tends to be held in high regard, such as consumer culture, there is a danger that they might be accused of a moralizing conservatism. Indeed, this view is widely held and fiercely protected. Even esteemed critical criminological voices such as Roger Matthews have positioned consumerism as 'one of the positive achievements of capitalism' (2014: 100). However, these arguments tend to conflate consumerism and consumption. As we have seen, consumerism involves significantly more than the simple purchase of material goods. Fundamentally, consumer culture relies on the velocity of fashion (Appadurai 1986)—the constant renewal of consumer goods within a marketplace—in tandem with a perpetual creation and re-creation of desire. As such it is vital for clothing, music, electronic items, and so on to rapidly fall from fashion and be identified by the anxious consumer as in need of immediate replacement. It is this cyclical process which we can link to global inequalities, ecological destruction, social disintegration, and a proliferation of harmful subjectivities.

Returning to where we started, and the work of Thorstein Veblen on leisure and consumption, many of the connections we have drawn between crime and consumerism echo Veblen's observations made over a century ago. Specifically, Veblen wrote about the emerging culture of barbarism that cultivates envy, harmful forms of competition, and narcissistic tendencies that are reflected in the perspectives outlined above. Contemporary cultures of consumption solicit consumers at increasingly early ages with cultural tropes that dismiss deferred gratification as being for 'losers'. At the same time they urge immediate and conspicuous forms of consumption which are not only tied to cultures of debt, but promote cultures of narcissism, infantilization, and individualized hypercompetitiveness. In this sense, the relationship between crime and consumerism is far from straightforward. Yet, within the criminological frameworks explored above, we are at least equipped to properly explore beneath the socio-legal constructions of criminality and examine the complex structural processes and drives underpinning the crime-consumerism nexus.

SELECTED FURTHER READING

Perhaps one of the most prescient and remarkably relevant explorations of consumerism is Veblen's *The Theory of the Leisure Class* [1899] (1970). For a more up-to-date overview of consumerism, Smart's *Consumer Society: Critical Issues and Environmental Consequences* (2010) is a useful starting point. The authors of this chapter have made a number of contributions to key discussions in this area. Specifically, Hayward's *City Limits: Crime, Consumer Culture and the Urban Experience* (2004a) explores the core issue of how consumer culture is linked to crime, and discusses how consumerism weakens some forms of social control, driving impulsive, individualistic actions. Published a decade later, Smith's *Contemporary Adulthood and the Night-Time Economy* (2014) examines the erosion of traditional adult identities, framing the cultural attachment to alcohol and its attendant harms as a form of deviant leisure. Hall and Winlow's *Revitalizing Criminology: Towards a New Ultra-Realism* (2015) provides readers with a cogent and persuasive argument for the adoption of an ultra-realist criminology. Hall, Winlow, and Ancrum's exploration of criminal motivation *Criminal Identities and Consumer Culture* (2008), is a similarly important contribution, while the best introduction to cultural criminology is still undoubtedly Ferrell, Hayward, and Young's *Cultural Criminology* (2015), now in its second edition. The significance of commodified forms of leisure for criminology is outlined in Oliver Smith and Thomas Raymen's 'Deviant Leisure, A criminological perspective' (2016).

REFERENCES

AIR TRANSPORT ACTION GROUP (2014), *Facts and Figures*, available at: http://www.atag.org/facts-and-figures.html, accessed 18 December 2016.

APPADURAI, A. (1986), *The Social Life of Things*, Cambridge: Cambridge University Press.

ATKINSON, M. (2009), 'Parkour, Anarcho-Environmentalism, and Poiesis', *Journal of Sport and Social Issues*, 33(2): 169–94.

ATKINSON, R. and RODGERS, T. (2015), 'Pleasure Zones and Murder Boxes: Online Pornography and Violent Video Games and Zones of Cultural Exception', *British Journal of Criminology*, available at: https://bjc.oxfordjournals.org/content/early/2015/10/27/bjc.azv113.full, accessed 18 December 2016.

BANKS, J. (2013), 'Edging your bets: Advantage play, gambling, crime and victimisation', *Crime, Media, Culture*, 9(2): 171–87.

BAUDRILLARD, J. (1968), *Les système des objects*, Paris: Denoel-Gonthier.

BAUDRILLARD, J. (1998), *The Consumer Society*, London: Sage.

BAUMAN, Z. (1998), *Work, Consumerism and the New Poor*, Buckingham: Open University Press.

BHASKAR, R. (1997[1975]), *A Realist Theory of Science*. London: Verso.

BIANCHINI, F. (1995), 'Night cultures, night economies', *Planning Practice and Research*, 10(2): 121–6.

BINDE P. (2010), '"You could become a millionaire": Truth, deception, and imagination in gambling advertising', in S. Kingma (ed.), *Global Gambling*, New York: Routledge.

BONGER, W. A. (1936), *An Introduction to Criminology*, London: Methuen and Co.

BOEKHOUT VAN SOLINGE, T. (2008), 'Eco-crime: the tropical timber trade', in D. Siegel and H. Nelen (eds), *Organized Crime*, Dordrecht: Springer.

BOSELEY, S. (2016), 'Problem drinkers account for most of alcohol industry's sales, figures reveal', *The Guardian*. 22 January.

BRISMAN, A. and SOUTH, N. (2014), *Green Cultural Criminology*, London: Routledge.

BRISMAN, A. and SOUTH, N. (2015), '"Life-stage dissolution", infantilization and anti-social consumption', *Young: Nordic Journal of Youth Research*, 23(3): 209–21.

CAMPBELL, C. (1989), *The Romantic Ethic and the Spirit of Modern Consumerism*, London: Blackwell.

CHATTERTON, P. and HOLLANDS, R. (2003), *Urban Nightscapes*, London: Routledge.

CONTRERAS, R. (2012), *The Stickup Kids: Race, Drugs, Violence, and the American Dream*, Berkeley: University of California Press.

CURRIE, E. (1996), 'Social crime prevention strategies in a market society', in J. Muncie, E. McLaughlin, and M. Langan (eds), *Criminological Perspectives*, London: Sage.

CURRIE, E. (1997), 'Market, crime and community: toward a mid-range theory of post-industrial violence', *Theoretical Criminology*, 1(2): 147–72.

DOWNES, D. and ROCK, P. (2007), *Understanding Deviance*, Oxford: Oxford University Press.

ELLIS, A. (2015), *Men, Masculinities and Violence: An Ethnographic Study*, London: Routledge.

FARRINGTON, D. LOBER, R., and VAN KAMMEN, W. (1990), 'Long-term criminal outcomes of hyperactivity-impulsivity-attention deficit and conduct problems in childhood', in L. N. Robins and M. Rutter (eds), *Straight and Devious Pathways From Childhood to Adulthood*, Cambridge: Cambridge University Press.

FEATHERSTONE, M. (1994), *Consumer Culture and Postmodernity*, London: Sage.

FENWICK, M. and HAYWARD, K. J. (2000), 'Youth crime, excitement and consumer culture: the reconstruction of aetiology in contemporary criminological theory', in J. Pickford (ed.), *Youth Justice*, London: Cavendish.

FERRELL, J. (2006), *Empire of Scrounge*, New York: New York University Press.

FERRELL, J. (2013), 'Tangled up in green: cultural criminology and green criminology', in N. South and A. Brisman (eds), *Routledge International Handbook of Green Criminology*, London: Routledge.

FERRELL, J., HAYWARD, K., and YOUNG, J. (2008/2015), *Cultural Criminology: An Invitation*, London: Sage.

FERRELL, J., HAYWARD, K., and YOUNG, J. (2015), *Cultural Criminology*, London: Sage.

FERRELL, J. and ILAN, J. (2013), 'Crime, culture and everyday life', in K. Hayward, C. Hale, A. Wahidin, and E. Wincup (eds), *Criminology*, Oxford: Oxford University Press.

FRANK, T. (1997), *The Conquest of Cool*, Chicago: Chicago University Press.

GARLAND, D. and SPARKS, R. (2000), *Criminology and Social Theory*, Oxford: Oxford University Press.

GARDNER, G., ASSADOURIAN, E., and SARIN, R. (2004), 'The state of consumption today', in B. Halweil and L. Mastny (eds), *State of the World, 2004*, New York: W. W. Norton.

GARRETT, B. (2013), *Explore Everything*, London: Verso.

GCUK (2015), *Industry Statistics*, London: GCUK.

GIDDENS, A. (1991), *Modernity and self-identity*, Cambridge: Polity.

GRAEBER, D. (2014), *Debt-Updated and Expanded: The First 5,000 Years*, New York: Melville House.

HALL, S. (1997), 'Visceral cultures and criminal practices', *Theoretical Criminology*, 1(4): 453–78.

HALL, S. (2012), *Theorizing Crime and Deviance: A New Perspective*, London: Sage.

HALL, S. and WINLOW, S. (2007), 'Cultural criminology and primitive accumulation', *Crime, Media, Culture*, 3(1): 82–90.

HALL, S. WINLOW, S., and ANCRUM, C. (2008), *Criminal Identities and Consumer Culture*, Cullompton: Willan.

HALL, S. and WINLOW, S. (2015), *Revitalizing Criminological Theory: Towards a New Ultra-Realism*, London: Routledge.

HALL, S. and JEFFERSON, T. (1976), *Resistance through Rituals*, London: Harper-Collins.

HARVEY, D. (2007), *The Limits to Capital*, London: Verso.

HAYWARD, K. J. (2004a), *City Limits: Crime, Consumer Culture and the Urban Experience*, London: GlassHouse.

HAYWARD, K. J. (2004b), 'Consumer culture and crime in late modernity', in C. Sumner (ed.), *The Blackwell Companion to Criminology*, Oxford: Blackwell.

HAYWARD, K. J. (2012), '"Pantomime Justice": a cultural criminological analysis of "life stage dissolution"', *Crime, Media, Culture*, 8(2): 213–29.

HAYWARD, K. J. (2013), '"Life stage dissolution" in Anglo-American advertising and popular culture: "Kidults", "Lil' Britneys" and "Middle Youths"', *Sociological Review*, 61(3): 525–48.

HAYWARD K. J. (2016), 'Cultural criminology: script rewrites', *Theoretical Criminology*, 20(3): 297–321.

HAYWARD, K. and HOBBS, D. (2007), 'Beyond the binge in "Booze Britain": market-led liminalization and the spectacle of binge drinking', *The British Journal of Sociology*, 58(3): 437–56.

HAYWARD, K. J. and KINDYNIS, T. (2013), 'Crime-Consumerism nexus', in J. Ross (ed.), *Encyclopedia of Street Crime in America*, Thousand Oaks: Sage.

HAYWARD, K. J. and SCHUILENBURG, M. (2014), 'To resist = to create?: Some thoughts on the concept of resistance in cultural criminology', *Tijdschrift over Cultuur & Criminaliteit*, (4)1: 22–36.

HAYWARD, K. J. and YAR, M. (2006), 'The "chav" phenomenon: consumption, media and the construction of a new underclass', *Crime, Media Culture*, 2(1): 9–28.

HAYWARD, K. J. and YOUNG, J. (2012), 'Cultural criminology', in M. Maguire, R. Reiner, and R. Morgan (eds), *The Oxford Handbook of Criminology*, Oxford: Oxford University Press.

HEATH, J. and POTTER, A. (2006), *Rebel Sell*, Toronto: Harper Collins.

HEBDIGE, D. (1979), *Subculture*, London: Methuen and Co.

HILLYARD, P. and TOMBS, S. (eds) (2004), *Beyond Criminology*, London: Pluto.

HORSLEY, M. (2015), *The Dark Side of Prosperity*, Farnham: Ashgate.

INSTITUTE OF ALCOHOL STUDIES (2015), *Alcohol's Impact on Emergency Services*, available at: http://www.ias.org.uk/uploads/IAS%20report%20low%20res.pdf, accessed 18 December 2016.

KINDYNIS, T. (2016), 'Urban Exploration: From Subterranea to Spectacle', *British Journal of Criminology*, available at: https://academic.oup.com/bjc/article/doi/10.1093/bjc/azw045/2624029/Urban-Exploration-From-Subterranea-to-Spectacle azw045, accessed 16 January 2017.

LASCH, C. (1979), *The Culture of Narcissism*, New York: W. W. Norton.

LAZZARATO, M. (2015), *Governing by Debt*, Intervention Series, South Pasadena: Semiotext(e).

LEA, J. (2016), *Revitalizing Criminological Theory*, by S. Hall and S. Winlow, reviewed in *British Journal of Criminology*, available at: https://academic.oup.com/bjc/article-lookup/doi/10.1093/bjc/azw004, accessed 16 January 2017.

LEA, J. and YOUNG, J. (1984), *What is to be Done about Law and Order*, Harmondsworth, Penguin.

LYNG, S. and BRACEY, M. (1995), 'Squaring the one percent: biker style and the selling of cultural resistance', in J. Ferrell and C. Sanders (eds), *Cultural Criminology*, Boston: Northeastern University Press.

MATTHEWS, R. (2014), *Realist Criminology*, London: Routledge.

MAFFESOLI, M. (1996), *The Time of the Tribes*, London: Sage.

Mills, C. W. (1970), 'Introduction', in T. Veblen, *The Theory of the Leisure Class*, London: Unwin.

MERTON, R. K. (1938), 'Social structure and anomie', *American Sociological Review*, 3: 672–82.

MILES, S. (1998), *Consumerism: As a Way of Life*, London: Sage.

MILES, S. (2012), 'The neoliberal city and the pro-active complicity of the citizen consumer', *Journal of Consumer Culture*, 12(2): 216–30.

MILLER, D. (1995), *Acknowledging Consumption*, London: Routledge.

MONEY CHARITY (THE) (2017), *The Money Statistics December 2016*, available at: http://themoneycharity.org.uk/money-statistics, accessed 12 January 2017.

MORRISON, W. (1995), *Theoretical Criminology: From Modernity to Post-Modernism*, London: Cavendish.

MUZZATTI, S. (2010), '"Driveit Like You Stole It": a cultural criminology of car commercials', in K. Hayward and M. Presdee (eds), *Framing Crime*, London: Routledge.

NEWBURN, T. and SHINER, M. (2001), *Teenage Kicks?: Young People and Alcohol*, York: Joseph Rowntree Foundation.

O'BRIEN, M. (2006), 'What is *cultural* about cultural criminology?', *British Journal of Criminology*, 45(5): 599–612.

PARKER, K. F. (2010), *Unequal Crime Decline*, New York: New York University Press.

PASSAS, N. (1997), 'Anomie and relative deprivation', in N. Passas and R. Agnew (eds), *The Future of Anomie Theory*, Boston: Northeastern University Press.

PINKER, S. (2012), *The Better Angels of our Nature*, London: Penguin.

PLATT, S. (2015), *Criminal Capital: How the Finance Industry Facilitates Crime*, London: Springer.

PRESDEE, M. (2000), *Cultural Criminology and the Carnival of Crime*, London: Routledge.

RAYMEN, T. and SMITH, O. (2015), 'What's Deviance Got to Do With It? Black Friday Sales, Violence and Hyper-conformity', *British Journal of Criminology*, 56(2): 389–405.

REDHEAD, S. (2015), *Football and Accelerated Culture*, London: Routledge.

REDMON, D. (2015), *Beads, Bodies, and Trash*, New York: Routledge.

RICHARDSON, A. and BUDD, T. (2003), 'Alcohol, Crime and Disorder: A Study of Young Adults', *Home Office Research Study 263*, London: Home Office.

ROBERTS, M., TURNER, C., GREENFIELD, S., and OSBORN, G. (2006), 'Continental ambience? Lessons in managing alcohol related evening and night-time entertainment from four European capitals', *Urban Studies*, 43(7): 1105–25.

RILEY, S., GRIFFIN, C., and MOREY, Y. (2013), 'The rise of the "Pleasure Citizen": how leisure can be a site for alternative forms of political participation', in K. N. Demetriou (ed.), *Democracy in Transition*, Springer: Berlin/Heidelberg.

RUGGIERO, V. and SOUTH, N. (2013), 'Green Criminology and the Crimes of the Economy: Theory, Research and Praxis', *Critical Criminology*, 21(3): 359–73.

SHERLOCK, P. (2016), 'Revenge pornography victims as young as 11, investigation finds', *BBC News*, available at: http://www.bbc.co.uk/news/uk-england-36054273, accessed 28 April 2016.

SLATER, D. (1997), *Consumer Culture and Modernity*, Cambridge: Polity.

SMART, B. (2010), *Consumer Society: Critical Issues & Environmental Consequences*, London: Sage.

SMITH, O. (2013), 'Holding back the beers: maintaining "youth" identity within the British night-time leisure economy', *Journal of Youth Studies*, 16(8): 1069–83.

SMITH, O. (2014), *Contemporary Adulthood and the Night-Time Economy*, London: Palgrave.

SMITH O. and RAYMEN, T. (2016), 'Deviant Leisure: A Criminological Perspective', *Theoretical Criminology*, forthcoming.

SOUTH, N. (1998), 'A green field for criminology? A proposal for a perspective', *Theoretical Criminology*, 2(2): 211–33.

STEBBINS, R. (2015), *Serious Leisure*, Piscataway: Transaction.

TAYLOR, I. (1999), *Crime in Context: a Critical Criminology of Market Societies*, Cambridge: Polity.

TREADWELL, J. (2008), 'Call the (fashion) police: how fashion becomes criminalized', *Papers from the British Criminology Conference*, 8(1): 117–33.

TREADWELL, J., BRIGGS, D., WINLOW, S., and HALL, S. (2013), 'Shopocalypse Now: Consumer Culture and the English Riots of 2011', *British Journal of Criminology*, 53(1): 1–17.

VEBLEN, T. (1970), *The Theory of the Leisure Class*, London: Unwin.

WHITE, R. D. (2013), *Environmental Harm*, Bristol. Policy Press.

WHITE, J., MOFFITT, T., AVSHALOM, C., BARTUSCH, D., NEEDLES, D., and STOUTHAMER-LOEVER, T. (1994), 'Measuring impulsivity and examining its relationships to delinquency', *Journal of Abnormal Psychology*, 103(2): 192–205.

WILSON, J. Q. (1985), *Thinking About Crime*, New York: Vintage Books.

WILSON, J. Q. and HERRNSTEIN, R. (1985), *Crime and Human Nature*, New York: Simon and Schuster.

WINLOW, S. and HALL, S. (2006), *Violent Night*, Oxford: Berg.

WINLOW, S. and HALL, S. (2013), *Rethinking Social Exclusion: The End of the Social?*, London: Sage.

YOUNG, J. (1999), *The Exclusive Society*, London: Sage.

YOUNG, J. (2003), '"Merton with energy, Katz with structure": the sociology of vindictiveness and the criminology of transgression', *Theoretical Criminology*, 7(3): 389–414.

ŽIŽEK, S. (2000), *The Ticklish Subject*, London: Verso.

14

GREEN CRIMINOLOGY

Avi Brisman and Nigel South

INTRODUCTION

If, as the song has it, 'money makes the world go around', it is well past time to consider the costs incurred.[1] The present global financial system depends on the exploitation of resources in order to maintain growth in production and consumption, producing levels of pollution and waste that are noticeably damaging ecosystems and even changing the climate of the planet.

This is not a new observation. Almost 50 years ago, Jerry Mander (1970: 253–4) asserted,

> The idea of an infinitely expanding Gross National Product on an isolated sphere, a finite system, an island in space, is complete nonsense [and] may be . . . the most dangerous tendency in the world today.
>
> You simply may not have a continually expanding economy within a finite system: Earth.

While awareness regarding threats to Earth's ecosystems and to the health and well-being of humans and all other species has increased, it still sits uncomfortably with a human inclination to deny that much—or anything—needs to be done. As Klein (2014: 3) puts it, at this 'jarring moment in history, when a crisis we have been studiously ignoring is hitting us in the face . . . we are doubling down on the stuff that is causing the crisis in the first place'—and engaging in 'cognitive dissonance' on a planetary scale. Criminology has much to contribute to the need for analysis and debate that follows from this but has only very recently begun to consider these matters in any substantial way.

To some extent, this may be understandable and predictable and yet, while a green criminology asks new questions and has led to innovation in theory and methods, it also shares some of the classic characteristics and challenges that have defined the criminological task more generally. Most significantly perhaps, it asks 'How can we capture the significance of actions that cause harm yet are not criminal?'

[1] Depending on your generation, this might be familiar as a song by 'I Fight Dragons' or from the musical 'Cabaret'—or phrased differently as 'Cash Rules Everything Around Me' in the song 'C.R.E.A.M.' by the American hip hop group, Wu-Tang Clan.

Environmental harms can be difficult to capture in a traditional criminological framework, as conceptions of "harm" and definitions of 'crime' frequently do not correspond or overlap. As White (2003: 485) has observed, 'in discipline specific terms, debates still occur about the proper object of criminological attention: how and under what conditions should an act or omission be conceived as environmental "crime" per se? A strictly legalistic response focuses on the central place of criminal law in defining criminality. . . . However, other writers propose that . . . the concept of "harm" ought to encapsulate activities that may be legal and "legitimate" but nonetheless have detrimental impacts on people and environments'. Lynch and colleagues (2013: 998) expand upon this point, making the provocative argument that 'green harm and crime are more widespread, have more victims and produce more damage than crimes that "occur on the streets"' (Jarrell *et al.* 2013; Lynch 2013) and that documenting such harm helps to make the case 'that these harms have substantively significant social and economic consequences and therefore deserve serious study within criminology'.

It has been acknowledged from its earliest statements that various criminologists have previously examined examples of environmental hazards and crimes (Lynch 1990: 3). The development of an explicitly 'green' perspective in criminology has built upon this past work (South and Beirne 2006; White 2009) while, at the same time, achieving a new and original profile, as well as formulating an expansive research agenda. 'Green criminology' thus serves as a convenient shorthand term for a fertile field, from which a wide range of research interests and theoretical orientations have grown (see Further Reading, below).

At the same time, green criminology is still evolving, offering a flexible and inclusive framework orientated toward particular problems (harms, offences, and crimes related to the environment, different species, and the planet) and often borrowing from and seeking connections with other disciplines. It is an important development because it enables criminology to examine crimes and harms that are often overlooked or excluded from its more traditional concerns and to illustrate how significant, wide-ranging and widespread these are.

This chapter begins by exploring the development of a green perspective within criminology and by reviewing some of the theoretical influences that have led to innovative ways of thinking about environmental issues of relevance to criminology. This background serves as an introduction to a discussion of key terms and typologies. The chapter then draws attention to some particular methodological issues that arise in the study of environmental crimes and harms. The section which follows illustrates the breadth and range of the different forms of environmental crime and harm, discussing: (1) climate change; (2) economy, consumption, and waste (further subdivided into state-corporate crime, organized crime, food crimes, and e-waste); (3) nonhuman animal abuse; and (4) poaching, trafficking, and trading. The next section examines responses to environmental crime and harm, including the articulation of calls for environmental justice and the development of an environmental victimology. This is followed by an overview of three areas of work that illustrate different aspects of the global relevance of a green criminology: (1) political economy and the treadmill of production; (2) linkages between environment and conflict; and (3) mechanisms of law enforcement and legal protections for the benefit of the planet. The chapter concludes by suggesting that much of the work to date in green criminology has centred on illuminating different types of environmental harm and describing their frequency across time and space, as well as analysing critically the causes and consequences of such harms to populations of humans and nonhuman animals today and in the future. Regulatory bodies and criminal justice systems have inadequately and insufficiently responded to such harms and this requires further research. The ambit of green criminology will continue to expand and will include themes of rights and protections, representations and denials (e.g. in relation to climate change debates), and the politics of food, migration, and security. Overall, we argue that green criminology can enhance and enrich mainstream criminology by emphasizing the ways in which environmental harms, just like other topics of study, 'can be regarded as a generalized form of behaviour, routinely produced by the normal patterns of social and economic life in contemporary society' (Garland 2001: 128). At the same time, green criminology is not coterminous with mainstream criminology, in that it is concerned with activities, behaviours, and practices that may indeed be part of normal conduct but which are frequently deviant and damaging from a larger ecological perspective (Brisman 2015). Thus, green criminology is in a position where it can both endeavour to improve upon and strengthen existing mainstream theory, while seeking new ways to understand the ordinary and extra-ordinary acts that contribute to ecocide.

TERMINOLOGY AND TYPOLOGIES

Concerns regarding environmental damage are centuries old. Thus, awareness of, and attention to, environmental destruction and despoliation is not the result of a recent social epiphany; what is relatively new is *criminological* regard for the causes and consequences—and possible responses to—environmental degradation. Within criminology, past studies have examined environmental damage, crime, and victimization (South 1998: 214). The sociology of deviance provides many descriptions of activities, such as hunting and poaching, that may be everyday behaviours in the lives of some, socially deviant in the eyes of others, or actually illegal but socially approved of or ignored (see generally Brisman 2015). In terms of the theoretical shaping of a green agenda, the principles of 'new deviancy theories' of the 1960s and 1970s, concerned with labelling, stigmatization, and the need for sensitivity to the plight of the powerless and voiceless, has informed thinking about speciesism, the treatment of indigenous peoples, and environmental injustice, while Marxist/critical criminological analysis of crimes of the powerful and the bias of dominant frameworks of law has influenced studies of environmental exploitation and injustice. The emphasis of feminist criminology on the crimes of men and victimization of women has connected with concerns about the violation of the environment and of other species (Gaarder 2011, 2013; Lane 1998; Sollund 2013; Wonders and Danner 2015). Other innovative directions, such as peacemaking criminology (Pepinsky and Quinney 1991; see also McClanahan and Brisman 2015) were path-breaking in calling for criminology to see the power of respect, conflict mediation, and reconciliation, and this underscores the need to recognize the intertwining of human rights with environmental rights (Brisman 2014a; South and Brisman 2013a). A green criminology has acknowledged, synthesized, built upon, and reinterpreted elements of these and other innovations in criminological theory and then contributed its own. Before turning to such developments, a word about definitions is in order.

TERMINOLOGY

Although this chapter uses the term 'green criminology', there is no universal agreement on the appropriate name for this sub-field or perspective. White (2008) has argued that the term 'environmental criminology' should be reclaimed from what might more properly be called 'place-based criminology' (see Bottoms (2012: 451) on acknowledgement of this point).

The term, 'green criminology', was first used by Lynch (1990) in an essay, 'The Greening of Criminology', which proposed its scope and aims in a way that can still stand as both an agenda and a 'manifesto' statement—a commitment to creating a 'humanistic society' based on environmentalism and a radical (Marxian) framework. Although its original place of publication—a newsletter of the American Society of Criminology's Division on Critical Criminology—meant it did not reach a wide audience, once 'rediscovered', it proved highly influential. Pečar (1981) put forward an even earlier statement about environmentally damaging forms of criminality in Slovenia and the role of criminology and sciences related to this (Eman, Meško, and Fields 2009: 584) but with no English-language translation, Pečar's article made no international impact. Other expressions of criminological interest in environmental problems can be found in the international literature from the 1970s to the 1990s (see Rodriguez-Goyes and South, forthcoming). Indeed, given the rise of interest in the natural sciences, and the growth in political attention and activism regarding environmental and conservation matters, some emergence of explicit green interests within criminology was inevitable, with teachers, researchers, and writers, in different ways in various places, expressing parallel concerns (see, e.g. Clifford 1998; Edwards *et al.* 1996; Halsey and White 1998; Koser Wilson 1999; Lynch and Stretesky 2001, 2003; Sollund 2008; South 1998; Walters 2004, 2006).

Other terminology has included White's (2010b: 6) notion of an 'eco-global criminology', while Walters (2010a) has suggested 'eco-crime' as helpful for encapsulating 'existing legal definitions of environmental crime, as well as sociological analyses of those environmental harms not necessarily specified by law'. Other formulations include 'conservation criminology' (Gibbs *et al.* 2010a) to describe an approach that integrates criminology, criminal justice, conservation. and natural resource management, alongside risk and decision science to examine environmental problems on a broad basis (see also Herbig and Joubert 2006).

Notwithstanding these terminological debates, at this stage in its development, it seems that criminologists most frequently employ the term 'green criminology' to describe the study of ecological, environmental, or green crime or harm, and related matters of speciesism and of environmental (in)justice. As suggested above, 'green criminology' is perhaps most usefully thought of as a 'perspective' or 'umbrella' category, but it is not subscribed to by all engaged in similar work. Moreover, use of the word 'green' has proven problematic: Lynch and Stretesky (2003) have articulated the competing definitions of 'green' provided by environmental justice movements and corporate redefinition, while Halsey (2004) has offered an exploration of the 'green' framework that effectively problematizes common conceptualizations within the field, challenging criminologists to rethink how they engage theoretically with environmental issues.

To some extent, the terminology does not matter greatly. It is simply descriptive of research and debate concerning actions and processes that are destroying our shared environment. Criminology, every once in a while, expands its conceptions of crime, deviance, and harm, driven by theory and events (Zahn 1999). In the case of green trends in criminology, this occurred slowly in different places from the late 1970s to the early 1990s and subsequently expanded (Rodriguez-Goyes and South, forthcoming). The term or concept is useful but it is only a signal, symbol, or expression regarding a perspective or orientation toward certain central concerns. It might well be called something else. What matters is the subject.

TYPOLOGIES

Whether 'green criminology' constitutes a 'theory' depends largely on how one conceptualizes the term 'theory' (Brisman 2014b). Early on, South (1998) proposed the idea of a green *perspective* rather than 'theory' in the same way that Plummer (1979: 90) had responded to critiques of labelling 'theories', with the argument that, in fact, such concept categories 'should not be equated with a theory or a proposition but should be seen as a perspective ... [able to] harbour several diverse theoretical positions'. This should apply to the idea of a 'green' conceptual category for use within criminology and, indeed, the idea of green criminology as a *perspective* or *orientation* has proven uncontroversial; arguably, the treatment and acceptance of green criminology as a 'perspective' has contributed to its growth, allowing for dialogue and collaboration between researchers and scholars associated with any number of theoretical positions and schools.

Various typologies have been offered to deepen our understanding of such crimes and harms. These categorizations can be important to help identify and organize clusters of issues and problems in ways that would be useful for research, policy, and methodological purposes, differentiating between a very wide range of possible topics of interest and investigation.

For example, one typology derives from a distinction between 'primary' and 'secondary' green crimes (Carrabine *et al.* 2014). This is a simple but suggestive way of differentiating clusters of harms and crimes by classifying some as resulting directly from the destruction and degradation of the earth's resources ('primary'), and others as those crimes or harms that are symbiotic with or dependent upon such destruction and efforts made to regulate or prevent it ('secondary'). Table 14.1 shows what four possible sets of 'primary' green crimes and harms might be.

'Secondary' (or symbiotic) green harms and crimes can arise from the exploitation of conditions that follow environmental damage or crisis (e.g. illegal markets for food, medicine, water) and/or from the violation of rules that attempt to regulate environmental harm and to respond to disaster. These can include numerous major and minor

Table 14.1 'Primary' green crimes and harms

1. Crimes / harms of air pollution	2. Crimes / harms of deforestation
3. Crimes / harms against nonhuman species	4. Crimes / harms of water and ground pollution

practices whereby states violate their own regulations (either by commission or omission) and in so doing contribute to environmental harms. Potter (2014: 11) has taken this scheme of categorization 'beyond secondary green crimes' to identify what—'in the spirit of consistency'—he calls 'tertiary green crimes', defined as those 'committed by environmental victims or as a result of environmental victimization . . . [e.g.] committed as a deliberate or direct response to environmental harm . . . [or] exacerbated by the experience of environmental victimisation'. These might include crimes committed by those forced to migrate in response to environmental harms (e.g. Hall and Farrall 2013), increasing crime rates as environmental harm and changing environments impact social and economic conditions that relate to crime (e.g. Agnew 2012), and crimes relating to exposure to environmental pollutants, such as lead or other heavy metals, which can have behavioural effects (e.g. aggression, learning difficulties) that some criminological theories posit as causes of crime (e.g. Lynch and Stretesky 2014).

White (2008: 98–9) has developed a threefold typology of 'brown', 'green', and 'white' issues: 'brown' issues tend to be defined in terms of urban life and pollution—air and water pollution, disposal of toxic/hazardous waste, oil spills, pesticides; 'green' issues refer to conservation matters and 'wilderness' areas, e.g. acid rain, biodiversity loss, habitat destruction, invasive species introduced via human transport, logging practices, ozone depletion; and 'white' issues, which refer to the impact of new technologies and various laboratory practices, for example, animal testing and experimentation; cloning; environmentally-related communicable diseases; food irradiation; genetically modified organisms.

Other typologies have been proposed (see South *et al.* 2013 for a discussion) but rather than rehearse them here, it may be more instructive to examine some of the substantive topics and themes that green criminologists have explored. Before doing so, however, we consider some of the methods by which green criminologists have undertaken their research.

METHODOLOGICAL ISSUES

As with any social scientific inquiry, the *methodology* that a criminologist studying environmental crime and harm employs—'the overall approach to the research process including the theoretical approach that influences the way the research is designed and conducted, and the lens through which the researcher views the social world' (White and Heckenberg 2014: 79)—and the *method* or *technique* used to gather and analyse the research data—all depend on the types of questions and issues to be explored.

A green criminological study is usually concerned with an environmental disaster or event that has occurred or is transpiring, an emerging or anticipated environmental crime or harm, or a pattern and practice of individual- and group-level acts, behaviours, customs, and omissions degrading to or destructive of, ecosystems and biotic life, in order to argue about its significance. Green criminologists employ a variety of research designs to collect their data, including surveys, observation, experiments (although this is uncommon), and secondary analysis of existing sources (see, e.g., Lynch and Stretesky 2001; Stretesky and Lynch 2001, 2004; White and Heckenberg 2014). Scientific data, whether relating to global climate change or derived from forensic analysis of toxic chemical spillage, is important and, with due regard to methodological cautions about the limits and construction of such data, it is as valuable for critical as for positivist criminologies. As Lynch and Stretesky (2014: 68) argue 'drawing on the scientific knowledge base of . . . [natural sciences concerned with environmental matters] to enhance the examination of green crime and justice issues . . . is important because it illustrates the extent to which green criminology can be linked to scientific values and principles'.

Not all research questions and issues of interest yield readily accessible or easily observable data, of course. In many cases, environmental crimes or harms are 'invisible' (Brisman 2014c; Wyatt 2014) and present challenges related to access, examination, and health and safety. The task of researching sensitive and/or hidden forms of harm, which may, for example, be so legal and pervasive as to be overlooked, or illegal and therefore likely to be clandestine, may require adoption of particular research methods. Ethnographic and other qualitative methods are most frequently chosen in such cases and can generate rich and deep information, although the task of analysis, interpretation, and representation is then not without its own challenges. Immersion in the field can generate numerous well-known methodological and ethical dilemmas, such as when researchers are given the 'choice' between violating promises of confidentiality to research participants or imprisonment for 'contempt of court' for refusing to cooperate with the authorities (see, e.g., Scarce 1994, 2006). Qualitative approaches can include visual analysis (Natali 2010), in-depth ethnography (Cianchi 2015; Kane 2012) and grounded theory as used in human ecology (Wilding 2012: 375).

With such methodological considerations in mind, we turn now to some of the substantive topics and themes addressed by the breadth of scholarship in green criminology, including crimes and harms to the environment, to humans, and to nonhuman animals.

TOPICS OF STUDY IN GREEN CRIMINOLOGY

The environmental harms and crimes perpetrated by humans, individually and collectively, whether out of necessity, hubris, or greed, are numerous in kind and far-reaching in impact. Green criminology has sought to expose and analyse many of these. For purposes of this chapter, we find it helpful to highlight some of the more common subjects and topics: (1) climate change; (2) economy, consumption, food, and waste; (3) nonhuman animal abuse; and (4) poaching, trafficking, and trading.

CLIMATE CHANGE

Climate change and its causes remain contested by some (see Brisman and South (2015b) for discussion), but the evidence that energy consumption is the principal cause is overwhelming. Rich consumer societies disproportionately contribute to a problem that will impose particularly high social and economic burdens on already poor and newly developing nations. Both international and domestic inequalities will follow, and a number of criminologists have suggested that climate change will stimulate a number of deeply criminogenic forces (South, 2012). Whereas Agnew (2012) applies micro- and mezzo-level criminological theories, such as strain and social control, to examine the relationship of climate change and crime, Kramer (2013) argues for the conceptualization of climate change as macro-level state-corporate crime. In other words, while the focus of Agnew (2012) is on how climate change will create 'new' reasons for individuals to commit crime(s)—or will exacerbate 'old' ones (e.g. strains and stressors)—Kramer (2013) contends that climate change denial and regulatory failure *constitute* state-corporate crime. Other explorations of current and anticipated connections between climate change and crime include Farrall and colleagues (2012) and White (2012).

ECONOMY, CONSUMPTION, AND WASTE

Current economic systems and processes facilitate or otherwise contribute to environmental harm. Here, it is useful to subdivide green criminological research into four categories: (a) state-corporate crime; (b) organized crime; (c) food crimes; and (d) e-waste.

State-corporate crime

As noted above, green criminology is concerned with the perpetrators, patterns, practices, and processes of environmental harm. States and corporations have been particularly blameworthy, and green criminologists have illuminated a range of their acts and omissions that have resulted in ecological degradation and environmental harm and disaster. Influential work by Pearce and Tombs (1998) described and analysed the environmental crimes of the chemical industry, conceptualizing it as 'toxic capitalism', as well as problematizing and exploring the differential distribution of both the benefits and harms associated with the chemical industry and the focus traditional criminology places on street and financial crimes. This is a similar argument to that made by Lynch and Stretesky (2014: 8–9), who assert that '[b]y reinforcing the common perception that street crimes are dangerous and require extraordinary resources and energy to control, the discipline of criminology aids in directing attention to those issues and, as a result, neglecting the other serious forms of harm that damage the world around us and promote a wide array of victimizations that make the world an unsafe place for human and nonhuman species'.

Lynch and colleagues (2002) present a definition and examples of 'toxic crime', while White (2002) attributes regulatory limitations and environmental harm to the needs of capitalist political economy. Friedrichs and Friedrichs (2002) offer a brief history of the criminogenic role of the World Bank in the developing world, including a case study of the practices of the World Bank in Thailand, and consider strategies and actions available as a response to environmental harms caused by globalization. More recently, Ruggiero and South (2010, 2013a, 2013b) consider environmental crimes and harms associated with crimes of the economy—in particular, those associated with the oil industry, such as the 2010 BP disaster in the Gulf of Mexico. Katz (2010) deals primarily with environmental crime caused by corporate actors and the ways that state agencies fail to properly mitigate the environmental crimes of the corporate state, examining the failure of the Environmental Protection Agency to address environmental harms caused by Dow Chemical, which, she argues, has created a criminogenic corporate-state. Similarly, Barrett (2013) offers a case study of the complicity between New York's Bethlehem Steel and the US Atomic Energy Commission, emphasizing the role of political economy in state-corporate environmental crimes.

Organized crime

The involvement of organized crime reaches into many aspects of public services, from waste disposal to building construction and maintenance, often resulting in corruption and pollution (Sergi and South 2016). Ruggiero and South (2010b) have described such illegal services as 'dirty collar crime' and Walters (2013: 281) observes that this kind of criminal enterprise has flourished as a result of 'lax implementation and enforcement' of rules and law. Where there is a legal market, there is often an illegal one and various commentators have explored the role of organized crime in waste disposal. Szasz (1986) investigates relationships between legal industries that produce toxic waste and organized crime enterprises that offer illegal disposal, arguing that corporate actors benefit, knowingly or otherwise, from their relationships with organized crime, refuting common claims of 'ignorance' and 'powerlessness'. Block (2002) uses routine activity theory to examine the involvement of organized crime in illegal waste disposal in New York and Haiti facilitated by failures of regulation. Dorn and colleagues (2007) consider vulnerabilities caused by harmful waste management practices in Europe and, more specifically, Ruggiero and South (2010a) examine the Naples garbage crisis of summer 2008 and describe the opportunities found by both corporate and criminal entrepreneurs when civil mechanisms and consumer society fail to manage waste.

Food crimes

Like air and water, food is an essential for life and, like other precious goods, has value in illegal, as well as legal, markets. The ways in which food is grown, manufactured, processed, and produced, as well as marketed and sold, attract different types of crime and harmful activity, such as food fraud, food poisoning, violations of food labelling laws, illegal trade and pricing practices, food labour exploitation, and financial crime (Croall 2007, 2013). Walters (2004, 2006, 2011) employs case-study approaches, examining the social, economic, and ecological risks of genetically modified foods and considering issues of potential exploitation of the developing world relating to genetic modification, as well as monopolies within the biotechnology industries, state-corporate collusion in food market control schemes, and the potential harms stemming from corporate control of food. Similar themes, as well as bio-piracy, are discussed in a case study of laws governing the use of seeds in Colombia (Rodríguez-Goyes and South 2016). A case study by Leighton (2015) examines how salmonella-contaminated peanuts caused nine deaths in the US in 2008–09, 11,000–20,000 illnesses, and the recall of 4000 products as a result of production in filthy, sometimes unregistered, plants, and demonstrates how regulatory failure led to this state-facilitated corporate crime. Criminological dimensions of food and agriculture, as well as the intersection of rural and green criminologies, are explored in Donnermeyer (2016).

E-waste

Almost 50 years ago, De Bell (1970: 153) observed that '[t]he production, use and disposal of technologically sophisticated gadgets is a big part of our ecological problem'. While human lives and livelihoods have continued to be enhanced in many ways through various electronic technologies, the disposal of these nondurable electronic goods can generate environmental harms. Gibbs and colleagues (2010b) consider white-collar crimes stemming from the global trade in electronic waste disposal and argue for the development of responsive regulation, including prevention, third-party, and self-regulation, and the potential for strong state intervention. Similarly, Rothe (2010) argues that responsive regulatory schemes will be successful only if they address individuals as well as organizational culture, while Snider (2010) concludes that differential relations of power will ultimately work to impede responsive regulation. Van Erp and Huisman (2010) explore the idea of 'smart' regulation and consider the promise of recycling markets, while Bisschop (2012, 2015) examines the transnational disposal of by-products of consumer waste in European markets and the legality of e-waste disposal in transnational legal environments. In this respect, a major development of the past few decades has been not simply removing and relocating waste from the developed world to the developing world to dump there as worthless disposables, but now relocating it as *resource-rich disposables* to be de-manufactured and recycled. Recycling is obviously 'good' but 'de-manufacturing' means that paradoxical problems arise. For example, these electronic goods do not need to be disposed of and replaced so rapidly, new ones do not have to be produced and marketed with such urgency and intensity, and the environmentally positive strategy of recycling should not hide the exploitation of low-paid workers in China and India, employed in recycling processes that release hazardous chemicals from e-waste, polluting air and land, and affecting the health of workers and communities, with links to serious diseases, including cancer (South 2015; see also Brisman and South, forthcoming).

NONHUMAN ANIMAL ABUSE

Criminology tends to be anthropocentric in its approach and orientation, 'emphasiz[ing] the biological, mental and moral superiority of *humans* over all other living and non-living entities', and viewing nonhuman nature '*instrumentally*—as something to be appropriated, processed, consumed, and disposed of in a manner which best suits the immediate interests of human beings' (Halsey and White 1998: 349) (emphases in original). One central theme in the development of a green perspective for criminology has been the call for greater awareness of harms and criminal acts committed against nonhuman species (e.g. Nurse 2013). This echoes work on crimes and harms against the powerless, and gender and feminist politics have informed important analyses of social movements concerned with animal rights (Gaarder 2011, 2013), and of trafficking in women, children, and animals (Sollund 2013).

The concept of 'speciesism' has been developed to describe human devaluation and prejudicial treatment of nonhuman species, as well as human perception of nonhuman animals as less worthy of concern, compassion, or justice. Beirne (1995, 2009) has explored several dimensions of criminological and philosophical engagement with animals and speciesism, and, more recently, has proposed the concept of 'theriocide' to refer to 'those diverse human actions that cause the deaths of animals' (2014: 55). In other pieces, Beirne (1997, 1999) has focused attention on developing criminological conceptualizations of interspecies sexual assault (see also Cazaux 1999).

POACHING, TRAFFICKING, AND TRADING

While poaching has long been a subject of study in criminology and the sociology of deviance, the emphasis has usually been on it as a form of rule-breaking in the context of hunting and other leisure activities, rather than in terms of conservation or environmental concerns. In law enforcement, as Moreto and colleagues (2015: 360) explain, '[w]ildlife offences are generally considered low priority when compared to other crimes (Cook *et al.* 2002)'. And until recently, the international trade in wildlife as 'live bodies' or as harvested 'parts and products' was largely overlooked. As the scope, extent, and geographical range of illegal trade in wildlife has grown and expanded, however—and as links between wildlife trafficking and terrorism have been suggested and raised national and international security concerns—criminological attention to poaching, trafficking, and related animal abuse has increased. For example, McMullan and Perrier (2002) explore regulatory failure in the lobster industry in Canada using a mixed-methods approach, while Tailby and Gant (2002) examine illegal abalone markets in Australia using case studies and market analysis. Petrossian and Clarke (2014), using the CRAVED model of theft (Concealable, Removable, Available, Valuable, Enjoyable, and Disposable), consider which fish are preferred by illegal commercial fishers, and Lemieux (2014) has investigated opportunity structures that favour poaching in a variety of contexts. Responses, such as market-reduction regulatory schemes to curb illicit trading in wildlife, the effect of international ivory bans on elephant poaching in Africa, and the principles of situational crime prevention have also been studied (Schneider 2008; Lemieux and Clarke 2009; Wellsmith 2010). Wyatt (2012, 2013) has made significant contributions to the study of wildlife trafficking, examining markets in Russia and elsewhere, as well as law enforcement efforts to curb illegal trafficking and trade in animals (which, interestingly, can overlap with other prohibited or controlled trades (see South and Wyatt 2011)).

RESPONSES TO ENVIRONMENTAL HARM

Important work has addressed the limitations of criminal justice responses to environmental crimes. Not all of the contributors to this literature would characterize themselves as 'green criminologists' but they would recognize shared interests and commitments. In one such early contribution, de Prez (2000) considered the creation of specialist courts to deal with environmental crimes and the ways in which prosecution of environmental crime may be trivialized by various courtroom factors. Situ and Emmons (2000) examined the role of criminal justice systems in protecting the environment, while du Rées (2001) questioned the efficacy of criminal law and courts in protecting the environment. Brack (2002) explored various practices used to combat transnational environmental crime, while Hayman and Brack (2002) offered definitions and typologies regarding the categorization of transboundary environmental crime.

Studies of law enforcement agencies and actors in preventing and prosecuting environmental crime and harm are not as common as might be expected, perhaps related to difficulties of gaining funding or access. The literature does, however, offer some insights into agencies and operations (e.g. Tompkins 2005; Gibbs *et al.* 2015).

Employing different frameworks, green criminologists have expanded their exploration of social, legal, and illegal responses to environmental crime and harm (e.g. Stretesky 2006; Elliott 2007; Green *et al.* 2007; Mares 2010; Walters 2010b; Brisman 2011; Cianchi 2015). An overarching theme emerging from all of this work is that law and justice are frequently biased and that powerful offenders will seek to reject criminal definitions that might be applied to them and will also pass on the costs of being found in breach of environmental regulations (including safety standards for products and workers) to others (Ruggiero and South 2010b: 246). Such corporate interests will also seek to influence and dilute environmental protection legislation and (re)construct the public and social meaning of 'green' (see, e.g., Brisman 2009; Lynch and Stretesky 2003). The impact of environmental harm is also skewed, imposing most damage and hardship on the living conditions and lives of the least powerful.

ENVIRONMENTAL JUSTICE AND ENVIRONMENTAL VICTIMS/ VICTIMIZATION

The differential impacts on the environment—and hence, environmental, nonhuman, and human victims—has led to a wide range of reaction, responses, and protest. Here, we highlight: (a) environmental justice and resistance to environmental harms affecting poor communities and communities of colour; and (b) environmental victims and victimization. A green victimology has also developed, incorporating critiques of the environmental justice framework.

Environmental justice and resistance to disproportionate impacts of environmental harms

Environmental justice has a lengthy history and literature outside of criminology. Bullard's (1990: 9) path-breaking study illustrated how environmental discrimination is 'a fact of life' for many black communities in the United States: 'The struggle for social justice by black Americans has been and continues to be rooted in white racism [which] has made it easier for black residential areas to become the dumping grounds for all types of health-threatening toxins and industrial pollution'. Bullard's (1990: xiv) analysis was one of the first to examine the pattern of how:

> Limited housing and residential options combined with discriminatory facility practices ... contributed to the imposition of all types of toxins on black communities

> through the siting of garbage dumps, hazardous-waste landfills, incinerators, . . . and a host of other polluting industries. These industries have generally followed the path of least resistance, which has been in economically poor and politically powerless black communities.

Calls for social and environmental activism and justice followed (Hofrichter 1993).

A number of discussions of environmental justice are relevant to and have been incorporated into the green criminological canon. For example, Simon (2000) emphasizes the importance of class power in his exploration of patterns of environmental crime among large multinational corporations, while Pinderhughes (1996) investigates race and class-related environmental inequality and differential toxic siting. Brook (1998) argues that the disparate impact of environmental harms borne by Native American populations constitutes a form of physical and cultural genocide, and describes growing environmental resistance movements within the Native American community. This resonates with Santana's (2002) case study of resistance to military operations on the Puerto Rican island of Vieques and the difficulties inherent in opposing military practices and militarism. Pellow's (2004) case study of illegal dumping in Chicago demonstrates how complex decisions underpin environmental inequity and racism, echoing Santana (2002), and adding to our understanding of the role of power.

While much research on environmental (in)justice focuses on communities of colour, some of it pays particular attention to the disproportionate impact of environmental harms on low-income communities. Saha and Mohai (2005) analyse the ways that waste facilities are disparately sited in low-income areas. Taking a similar approach to Pellow, the authors explore the legality and timing of NIMBY-driven waste-siting schemes. Finally, Brisman (2008) explores competing social and legal conceptualizations of environmental harm and crime, making a case for a broader understanding of environmental justice.

Environmental victims, victimization, and victimology

The environmental justice movement has provided a 'conceptual starting point' for the exploration of environmental victimization and an 'environmental victimology'. In a pioneering article on these topics, Williams (1996) identified a discrete area of study distinct from an environmental justice approach, pointing to the limitations of the environmental justice movement—particularly its subjective definitions of victimization, its assumptions about power, and its taken-for-granted notions of group identity (see also Stephens (1996) on the absence of children and children's narratives in the environmental justice movement).

Subsequent works have demonstrated the range of research that can be conducted on environmental victimization: Lynch and Stretesky (2001) studied the impact of corporate and industrial practices on minority health through an examination of medical and epidemiological evidence, while Jarrell and Ozymy (2012) considered the United States' Crime Victims' Rights Act and its use in providing legal redress for victims of environmental crimes. Finally, Hall (2013) considers the question 'who are the victims of environmental crimes and harms?', and discusses the unequal distribution of victimization among the world's populations.

CURRENT DEVELOPMENTS AND FUTURE DIRECTIONS

Research in green criminology will continue to broaden and deepen our understanding of the causes and consequences of, as well as possible responses to, environmental harms and crimes. In this section, we highlight several areas where we expect to see further work in the future. In so doing, we are cognizant of the fact that media images and representations are the windows through which most people see the planet they live on, and this also applies to their knowledge of their more immediate environments, nationally and locally. The role of media in presenting, reporting, and imagining environmental harms and crimes is therefore hugely important—not only as a reflection of and prediction for salient environmental issues, but as an inquiry unto itself (see, e.g., Brisman and South 2013b, 2014).

POLITICAL ECONOMY AND THE TREADMILL OF PRODUCTION

Lynch and Stretesky (2014: 139) argue that many environmental 'problems' are perpetuated by modes of production that underpin contemporary 'local and global political economies'. For these authors (and others, such as Ruggiero and South 2013a), taken-for-granted assumptions that relentless economic growth is necessary for social and global sustainability must be challenged. Stretesky and colleagues (2014) draw on Schnaiberg's (1980) ideas regarding ecological Marxism and the 'treadmill of production' to argue that market-oriented, advanced neoliberal societies are responsible for considerable environmental destruction as a result of the extraction of natural resources, the deforestation of woodlands and habitats, and the exploitation of flora and fauna. This process leads to 'ecological disorganization'—to 'the ways in which human preferences for organizing economic production consistent with the objectives of capitalism are an inherent contradiction with the health of the ecological system' (Lynch *et al.* 2013: 998). The treadmill generates supply to meet continuing demand from consumer society, stimulated by expanding markets and neoliberal international trade agreements (on the latter, see South, forthcoming). Commercialization and commodification are processes that diminish global resources but entrap consumers in visions of what they should be buying, drinking, eating, wearing, and so on (Brisman and South 2014). Indeed, as O'Brien (2011: 36–7) explains, 'the impoverishment of African and Asian populations', for example, 'and the over-exploitation of their natural resources are, in part at least, consequential on the paths to industrialization and consumerism taken by developed nations. In turn, these processes fuel the demand for more exploitable land and resources which . . . is responsible for global climate change. In turn again, such change alters the patterns of rainfall and desertification and intensifies the struggle for arable land and water, a key factor in many civil wars and driver of economic migration and people trafficking'. This linkage between environmental degradation and conflict is discussed next.

ENVIRONMENT AND CONFLICT

A wide variety of 'high value' natural resources can be subject to legal and illegal transactions, which can transform social stability into conditions of insecurity, unrest, and violence fraught with violations of human rights and environmental degradation (see Brisman *et al.* 2015). Such transactions can also generate profits that 'directly finance' various groups engaging in conflict. As Bergenas and Knight (2015: 123–5) report, 'the Islamic State's largest revenue stream comes from the terrorist organization illegally trading oil', and there are direct links between wildlife trafficking and terrorism in the cases of Sudanese groups, militias in the DRC and the Central African Republic, and the Lord's Resistance Army, with 'annual income to militias in all of Sub-Saharan Africa' from the ivory trade alone estimated at 'approximately US $4–12 million'.

South and Brisman (2013a) have argued that in current global economic conditions, democratic development in resource-producer nations is hindered by Western production practices and exploitative patterns of consumption. Monitoring these connections is one task for green criminology in the future.

MECHANISMS OF REGULATION AND ENFORCEMENT IN AN UNCERTAIN WORLD

The two principal 'models' that regulatory laws and mechanisms of enforcement follow are generally referred to as the *compliance* and *deterrence* models. The compliance approach seeks conformity with law or regulations without need for policing and punishment of infringements: behaviour is influenced by offering inducements and incentives, or by establishing administrative procedures designed to avoid non-compliance opportunities. Deterrence strategies, in turn, work by aiming to enforce the law, detecting violation and prosecuting and penalizing offenders. Punishment serves as a warning to others. In practice, elements of the two approaches may be combined. Some criticize compliance systems because they impose penalties only *after* an offence has actually been committed even though there may have been prior indications or even hard evidence that precautions and prevention were not adequately attended to. When penalties are applied, they may be quite limited in scope—usually economic measures in the form of a fine which is then typically absorbed by an organization, with customers and taxpayers ultimately paying out. Others therefore argue that more punitive measures should be taken and that where deterrent punishments have been used in the past these have had an impact especially where imprisonment and negative publicity follow (see Shelley and Hogan 2013).

A further view, however, might support the mixing of the voluntarism assumed by a compliance approach with tougher enforcement and restorative justice interventions as an effective strategy. As Higgins (2010: 143) puts it, 'Restorative justice is built on an understanding of our relationship with nature and the duty to remedy the harm caused'—addressing 'the needs of the beleaguered party to restore that which has been harmed rather than simply fixating on the punishment of the perpetrator'. This kind of approach to the administration of environmental regulation and justice, invoking methods and principles of mutual engagement, is both practical as well as consonant with ambitions to protect the planet (Higgins *et al.* 2013).

Higgins (2012; Higgins *et al.* 2013) argues for an international Law of Ecocide on the grounds that nations need to do more to prevent environmental destruction and ecosystem collapse. This proposal coincides with interest in the extension of existing environmental courts and tribunals which number over 350 now in operation in 41 jurisdictions, as well as arguments for the establishment of an International Environmental Court (Pring and Pring 2009). Proposals such as these may not yet be perfectly formed but at the very least they deserve contemplation and debate. The future may be uncertain but it could surely benefit from more effective and appropriate regulatory tools as well as more environmentally responsible and sensitive human instincts and behaviours.

CONCLUSION

The contribution of green criminology has been to illuminate different types of environmental harm and describe their temporal and geographic prevalence, analysing the causes and consequences of such harms, and the ways in which regulatory bodies and criminal justice systems, individuals and groups are, or should be, responding to such harms (Brisman and South 2015a; White and Graham 2015). Future concerns of green criminology will include themes of rights and protections, representations and denials (e.g. in relation to climate change debates), and the politics of food, migration, and security. The state of the environment affects populations of humans and nonhuman animals today and into the future. A green criminology can help to identify some of the central challenges facing all species and the planet. It can highlight questions of social and environmental justice and draw attention to failures and the need for remedies. Crucially, a 'green' perspective means that criminology is not silent on these issues.

■ SELECTED FURTHER READING

South and Brisman's 'A green-cultural criminology: An exploratory outline' (2013b) provides an overview of recent directions and international perspectives on a wide range of historical, methodological, and theoretical issues relevant to green criminology. Early introductions and overviews include essays in Beirne and South's *Issues in Green Criminology: Confronting Harms Against Environments, Humanity and Other Animals* (2007), which introduce readers to various topics in green criminology, and in Sollund's *Global harms: Ecological Crime and Speciesism* (2008) on animal abuse, speciesism, and ecological harm. White's *Crimes Against Nature: Environmental Criminology and Ecological justice* (2008) examines some of the underlying conceptual issues surrounding environmental crime and harm, and subsequently offered an argument for the development of an 'eco-global' criminology (White, *Transnational Environmental Crime: Toward an Eco-Global Criminology* (2011)). South and Beirne's *Green Criminology* (2006) and White, *Environmental Crime: A Reader* (2009) reprint contributions that provide theoretical, methodological, and substantive insights into the nature and dynamics of environmental harm. Ellefsen and colleagues' *Eco-global Crimes: Contemporary Problems and Future Challenges* (2012) focus on speciesism, animal abuse, and social movements, biodiversity and environmental and species justice. Walters and colleagues' *Emerging Issues in Green Criminology: Exploring Power, Justice and Harm* (2013) explore issues such as animal trafficking and abuse, organized crime in the carbon trading sector, e-waste disposal, and resource wealth and conflict. White and Heckenberg's *Green Criminology: An Introduction to the Study of Environmental Harm* (2014) offers the first introductory text for green criminology.

REFERENCES

Agnew, R. (2012), 'Dire forecast: A theoretical model of the impact of climate change on crime', *Theoretical Criminology*, 16(1): 21–42.

Barrett, K. (2013), 'Bethlehem Steel at Lackawanna: The state-corporate crimes that continue to victimize the residents and environment of western New York', *Journal of Crime and Justice*, 36(2): 262–82.

Bergenas, J. and Knight, A. (2015), 'Green terror: Environmental crime and illicit financing', *SAIS Review of International Affairs*, 35(1): 119–31.

Beirne, P. (1995), 'The use and abuse of animals in criminology: A brief history and current review', *Social Justice*, 22(1): 5–31.

Beirne, P. (1997), 'Rethinking bestiality: Towards a concept of interspecies sexual assault', *Theoretical Criminology*, 1(3): 317–40.

Beirne, P. (1999), 'For a nonspeciesist criminology: Animal abuse as an object of study', *Criminology*, 37(1): 117–47.

Beirne, P. (2009), *Confronting Animal Abuse: Law, Criminology, and Human-Animal Relationships*, Lanham, MD: Rowman & Littlefield.

Beirne, P. (2014), 'Theriocide: Naming Animal Killing', *International Journal for Crime, Justice and Social Democracy*, 3(2): 49–66.

Beirne, P. and South, N. (eds) (2007), *Issues in Green Criminology: Confronting Harms Against Environments, Humanity and Other Animals*, Cullompton: Willan.

Bisschop, L. (2012), 'Is it all going to waste? Illegal transports of e-waste in a European hub', *Crime, Law and Social Change*, 58(3): 221–49.

Bisschop, L. (2015), *Governance of the Illegal Trade in E-Waste and Tropical Timber: Case Studies on Transnational Environmental Crime*, Farnham: Ashgate.

Bottoms, A. (2012), 'Developing Socio-spatial Criminology', in R. Maguire, R. Morgan, and R. Reiner (eds), *The Oxford Handbook of Criminology*, Oxford: Oxford University Press.

Block, A (2002), 'Environmental crime and pollution: Wasteful reflections, *Social Justice*, 29(1–2): 61–81.

Brack, D. (2002), 'Combatting international environmental crime', *Global Environmental Change*, 12: 142–7.

Brisman, A. (2008), 'Crime-environment relationships and environmental justice', *Seattle Journal for Social Justice*, 6(2): 727–817.

Brisman, A. (2009), 'It Takes Green to Be Green: Environmental Elitism, "Ritual Displays," and Conspicuous Non-Consumption', *North Dakota Law Review*, 85(2): 329–70.

Brisman, A. (2011). '"Green harms" as art crime, art criticism as environmental dissent', *Journal of Contemporary Criminal Justice*, 27(4): 465–99.

Brisman, A. (2014a), 'Environmental and human rights' in G. Bruinsma and D. Weisburd (eds), *Encyclopedia of Criminology and Criminal Justice*, Vol. 3, New York: Springer Verlag.

Brisman, A. (2014b), 'Of Theory and Meaning in Green Criminology', *International Journal of Crime, Justice and Social Democracy*, 3(2): 22–35.

Brisman, A. (2014c), 'The Visual Acuity of Climate Change', in P. Davies, P. Francis, and T. Wyatt (eds), *Invisible Crimes and Social Harms*, Basingstoke: Palgrave.

Brisman, A. (2015), 'Environmental Harm as Deviance and Crime', in E. Goode (ed.), *Wiley Handbook on Deviance*, Hoboken, NJ: Wiley.

Brisman, A. and South, N. (2013a), 'Conclusion: The planned obsolescence of planet earth? How green criminology can help us learn from experience and contribute to our future', in N. South and A. Brisman (eds), *Routledge International Handbook of Green Criminology*, London: Routledge.

Brisman, A. and South, N. (2013b), 'A green-cultural criminology: An exploratory outline', *Crime Media Culture*, 9(2): 115–35.

Brisman, Avi, and South, N. (2014), *Green Cultural Criminology: Constructions of Environmental Harm, Consumerism, and Resistance to Ecocide*, London: Routledge.

Brisman, A. and South, N. (2015a), 'An Assessment of Tonry and Farrington's Four Major Crime Prevention Strategies as Applied to Environmental Crime and Harm', *Varstvoslovje: Journal of Criminal Justice and Security*, 17(2): 127–50.

Brisman, A. and South, N. (2015b), 'New "folk devils", denials and climate change: Applying the work of Stanley Cohen to green criminology and environmental harm', *Critical Criminology*, 23(4): 449–60.

Brisman, A. and South, N. (forthcoming), 'Consumer Technologies, Crime and Environmental Implications', in M. R. Maguire and T. J. Holt (eds), *The Routledge Handbook of Technology, Crime and Justice*, London and New York: Routledge.

Brook, D. (1998), 'Environmental genocide: Native Americans and toxic waste', *American Journal of Economics and Sociology*, 57(1): 105–13.

Bullard, R. D. (1990), *Dumping in Dixie: Race, class, and environmental quality*, Boulder, CO: Westview.

Carrabine, E., Cox, P., Fussey, P., Hobbs, D., South, N. Thiel, D., and Turton, J. (2014), *Criminology: A Sociological Introduction*, Abingdon: Routledge.

Cazaux, G. (1999), 'Beauty and the beast: Animal abuse from a non-speciesist criminological perspective', *Crime, Law and Social Change*, 31(2): 105–26.

Cianchi, J. (2015), *Radical Environmentalism: Nature, Identity and More-than-human Agency*, Basingstoke: Palgrave.

Clifford, M. (ed.) (1998), *Environmental crime: Enforcement, policy, and social responsibility*, Gaithersburg, MD: Aspen.

Cook, D., Roberts, M., and Lowther, J. (2002), 'The International Wildlife Trade and Organised Crime: A Review of the Evidence and the Role of the UK', WWF-UK.

Croall, H. (2007), 'Food crime', in P. Beirne and N. South (eds), *Issues in Green Criminology: Confronting Harms Against Environments, Humanity and Other Animals*, Cullompton: Willan.

Croall, H. (2013), 'Food crime: A green criminology perspective', in N. South and A. Brisman, *Routledge International Handbook of Green Criminology*, London: Routledge.

De Bell, G. (1970), 'A Future That Makes Ecological Sense', in G. De Bell (ed.), *The Environmental Handbook*, New York: Ballantine Books.

de Prez, P. (2000), 'Excuses, excuses: The ritual trivialization of environmental prosecutions', *Journal of Environmental Law*, 12(1): 65–77.

Donnermeyer, J. F. (ed.) (2016), *The Routledge International Handbook of Rural Criminology*, London: Routledge.

Dorn, N., Van Daele, S., and Vander Beken, T. (2007), 'Reducing vulnerabilities to crime of the European waste management industry', *European Journal of Crime, Criminal Law and Criminal Justice*, 15(1): 23–36.

Du Rées, H. (2001), 'Can criminal law protect the environment?', *Journal of Scandinavian Studies in Criminology and Crime Prevention*, 2(2): 109–26.

Edwards, S., Edwards, T., and Fields, C. (eds) (1996), *Environmental Crime and Criminality: Theoretical and practical issues*, New York: Garland.

Eman, K., Meško, G., and Fields, C. B. (2009), 'Crimes against the Environment: Green Criminology and Research Challenges in Slovenia', *Varstvoslovje: Journal of Criminal Justice and Security*, 11(4): 574–92.

Elliott, L. (2007), 'Transnational environmental crime in the Asia Pacific: An "un(der)securitized" security problem?', *Pacific Review*, 20(4): 499–522.

Ellefsen, R., Sollund, R., and Larsen, G. (eds) (2012), *Eco-global Crimes: Contemporary Problems and Future Challenges*, Farnham: Ashgate.

Farrall, S., Ahmed, T., and French, D. (eds) (2012), *Criminological and Legal Consequences of Climate Change*, Oxford: Hart.

Friedrichs, D. O. and Friedrichs, J. (2002), 'The World Bank and crimes of globalization: A case study', *Social Justice*, 29(1–2): 13–36.

Gaarder, E. (2011), *Women and the Animal Rights Movement*, New Brunswick, NJ: Rutgers University Press.

Gaarder, E. (2013), 'Evading responsibility for green harm: State-corporate exploitation of race, class, and gender inequality', in N. South and A. Brisman (eds), *Routledge International Handbook of Green Criminology*, Abingdon: Routledge.

Garland, D. (2001), *The Culture of Control*, Oxford: Oxford University Press.

Gibbs, C., Gore, M. L., McCarrell, E. F., and Rivers III, L. (2010a), 'Introducing conservation criminology: Towards interdisciplinary scholarship on environmental crimes and risk', *British Journal of Criminology*, 50(1): 124–44.

Gibbs, C., McGarrell, E. F., and Axelrod, M. (2010b), 'Transnational white-collar crime and risk: Lessons from the global trade in electronic waste', *Criminology and Public Policy*, 9(3): 543–60.

Gibbs, C., McGarrell, E. F., and Sullivan, B. (2015), 'Intelligence-led policing and transnational environmental crime: A process evaluation', *European Journal of Criminology*, 12(2): 242–59.

Green, P., Ward, T., and McConnachie, K. (2007), 'Logging and legality: Environmental crime, civil society and the state', *Social Justice*, 34(2): 94–110.

Hall, M. (2013), *Victims of Environmental Harm: Rights, Recognition and Redress under National and International Law*, London: Routledge.

Hall, M. and Farrall, S. (2013), 'The criminogenic consequences of climate change: Blurring the boundaries between offenders and victims', in N. South and A. Brisman (eds), *Routledge International Handbook of Green Criminology*, London and New York: Routledge.

Halsey, M. (2004), 'Against "green" criminology', *British Journal of Criminology*, 44(4): 833–53.

Halsey, M. and White, R. (1998), 'Crime, ecophilosophy and environmental harm', *Theoretical Criminology*, 2(3): 345–71.

Hayman, G., and Brack, D. (2002), *International Environmental Crime: The Nature and Control of Environmental Black Markets*, London: Chatham House.

Herbig, F. J. W. and Joubert, S. J. (2006), 'Criminological semantics: conservation criminology—vision or vagary?', *Acta Criminologica*, 19(3): 88–103.

Higgins, P. (2010), *Eradicating Ecocide*, London: Shepheard-Walwyn.

Higgins, P (2012), 'Closing the Door to Dangerous Industrial Activity: Concept paper for all Governments on the Law of Ecocide', available at: http://www.eradicatingecocide.com, accessed 16 January 2017.

HIGGINS, P., SHORT, D., and SOUTH, N. (2013), 'Protecting the planet: a proposal for a law of Ecocide', *Crime, Law and Social Change*, 59(3): 251–66.

HOFRICHTER, R. (1993), *Toxic Struggles: The Theory and Practice of Environmental Justice*, Philadelphia: New Society Publisher.

JARRELL, M. L. and OZYMY, J. (2012), 'Real crime, real victims: Environmental crime victims and the Crime Victims' Rights Act (CVRA)', *Crime, Law and Social Change*, 58(4): 373–89.

JARRELL, M. L., LYNCH, M. J., and STRETESKY, P. B. (2013), 'Green Criminology and Green Victimization', in B. Arrigo and H. Bersot (eds), *The Routledge Handbook of International Crime and Justice Studies*. London: Routledge.

KANE, S. C. (2012), *Where Rivers Meet the Sea: The Political Ecology of Water*, Philadelphia: Temple University Press.

KATZ, R. S. (2010), 'The Corporate Crimes of Dow Chemical and the Failure to Regulate Environmental Pollution', *Critical Criminology*, 18(4): 295–306.

KLEIN, N. (2014), *This Changes Everything: Capitalism vs. The Climate*, New York: Simon & Schuster.

KOSER WILSON, N. (1999), 'Eco-Critical Criminology—An Introduction', *Criminal Justice Policy Review*, 10(2): 155–60.

KRAMER, R. C. (2013), 'Carbon in the atmosphere and power in America: Climate change as state-corporate crime', *Journal of Crime and Justice*, 36(2): 153–70.

LEIGHTON, P. (2015), 'Mass Salmonella Poisoning by the Peanut Corporation of America: State-Corporate Crime Involving Food Safety', *Critical Criminology*, doi 10.1007/s10612-015-9284-5.

LANE, P. (1998), 'Ecofeminism Meets Criminology', *Theoretical Criminology*, 2(2): 235–48.

LEMIEUX, A. M. (ed.) (2014), *Situational Prevention of Poaching*, London: Routledge.

LEMIEUX, A. M., and CLARKE, R. V. (2009), 'The international ban on ivory sales and its effects on elephant poaching in Africa', *British Journal of Criminology*, 49(4): 451–71.

LYNCH, M. J. (1990), 'The greening of criminology: A perspective on the 1990s', *Critical Criminologist*, 2(3): 1–4; 11–12.

LYNCH, M. J. (2013), 'Reflecting on Green Criminology and its Boundaries: Comparing Environmental and Criminal Victimization and Considering Crime from an Eco-city Perspective', in N. South and A. Brisman (eds), *Routledge International Handbook of Green Criminology*, London: Routledge.

LYNCH, M. J. and STRETESKY, P. (2001), 'Toxic crimes: Examining corporate victimization of the general public employing medical and epidemiological evidence', *Critical Criminology*, 10(3): 153–72.

LYNCH, M. J. and STRETESKY, P. B. (2003), 'The meaning of green: Contrasting criminological perspectives', *Theoretical Criminology*, 7(2): 217–38.

LYNCH, M. J. and STRETESKY, P. B. (2014), *Exploring Green Criminology: Toward a Green Criminological Revolution*, Farnham: Ashgate.

LYNCH, M. J., STRETESKY, P. B., and MCGURRIN, D. (2002), 'Toxic crimes and environmental justice: Examining the hidden dangers of hazardous waste', in G. W. Potter (ed.), *Controversies in White-Collar Crime*, Cincinnati: Anderson.

LYNCH, M. J., LONG, M. A., BARRETT, K. L., and STRETESKY, P. B. (2013), 'Matter in the Analysis of Global Ecological Harms', *British Journal of Criminology*, 53(6): 997–1016.

MANDER, J. (1970), 'The Media and Environmental Awareness', in G. De Bell (ed.), *The Environmental Handbook*, New York: Ballantine Books.

MARES, D. (2010), 'Criminalizing ecological harm: Crimes against carrying capacity and the criminalization of eco-sinners', *Critical Criminology*, 18(4): 279–93.

MCCLANAHAN, B. and BRISMAN, A. (2015), 'Climate Change and Peacemaking Criminology', *Critical Criminology*, 23(4): 417–31.

MCMULLAN, J. L. and PERRIER, D. C. (2002), 'Lobster poaching and the ironies of law enforcement', *Law and Society Review*, 36(4): 679–720.

MORETO, W. D., BRUNSON, R. K., and BRAGA, A. A. (2015), '"Such Misconducts Don't Make a Good Ranger": Examining Law Enforcement Ranger Wrongdoing in Uganda', *British Journal of Criminology*, 55(2): 359–80.

NATALI, L. (2010), 'The big grey elephants in the backyard of Huelva, Spain', in R. White (ed.), *Global Environmental Harm: Criminological perspectives*, Cullompton: Willan.

NURSE, A. (2013), *Animal Harm: Perspectives on Why People Harm and Kill Animals*, Farnham: Ashgate.

O'BRIEN, M. (2011), 'Criminal Degradations of Consumer Culture', in R. Sollund (ed.), *Global Harms: Ecological Crime and Speciesism*, New York: Nova Science.

O'CONNOR, S. J. and HOGAN, M. J. (2013), 'Public perceptions of corporate environmental crime: Assessing the impact of economic insecurity on willingness to impose punishment for pollution', in N. South and A. Brisman (eds), *Routledge International Handbook of Green Criminology*, London: Routledge.

PEARCE, F. and TOMBS, S. (1998), *Toxic Capitalism: Corporate Crime and the Chemical Industry*, Aldershot: Ashgate.

PEČAR, J. (1981), 'Ekološka kriminaliteta in kriminologija', *Revija za kriminalistiko in kriminologijo*, 34(1): 33–45.

PELLOW, D. N. (2004), 'The politics of illegal dumping: An environmental justice framework', *Qualitative Sociology*, 27(4): 511–25.

PEPINSKY, H. and QUINNEY, R. (eds) (1991), *Criminology as Peacemaking*, Bloomington, IN: Indiana University Press.

PETROSSIAN, G. A. and CLARKE, R. V. (2014), 'Explaining and Controlling Illegal Commercial Fishing: An Application of the CRAVED Theft Model', *British Journal of Criminology*, 54(1): 73–90.

PINDERHUGHES, R. (1996), 'The impact of race on environmental quality: An empirical and theoretical discussion, *Sociological Perspectives*, 39(2): 231–48.

PLUMMER, K. (1979), 'Misunderstanding labelling perspectives', in D. Downes and P. Rock (eds), *Deviant Interpretations: Problems in Criminological Theory*, Oxford: Martin Robertson.

POTTER, G. (2014), 'The criminogenic effects of environmental harm: bringing a "green" perspective to mainstream criminology', in T. Spapens, R. White, and M. Kluin (eds), *Environmental Crime and its Victims: Perspectives within Green Criminology*, Farnham: Ashgate.

PRING, G. and PRING, C. (2009), *Greening Justice: Creating and Improving Environmental Courts and Tribunals*, The Access Initiative: http://www.law.du.edu/documents/ect-study/greening-justice-book.pdf, accessed 11 January 2017.

RODRIGUEZ-GOYES, D. and SOUTH, N. (2016), 'Land grabs, bio-piracy and the inversion of justice in Colombia', *British Journal of Criminology*, 56(3): 558–77.

RODRIGUEZ-GOYES, D. and SOUTH, N. (forthcoming), '"Green criminology before green criminology": Amnesia and absences', *Critical Criminology*, 25(2).

ROTHE, D. L. (2010), 'Global e-waste trade: The need for formal regulation and accountability beyond the organization', *Criminology and Public Policy*, 9(3): 561–7.

RUGGIERO, V. and SOUTH, N. (2010a), 'Critical criminology and crimes against the environment', *Critical Criminology*, 18(4): 245–50.

RUGGIERO, V. and SOUTH, N. (2010b), 'Green criminology and dirty-collar crime', *Critical Criminology*, 18(4): 251–62.

RUGGIERO, V. and SOUTH, N. (2013a), 'Green criminology and crimes of the economy: Theory, research and praxis', *Critical Criminology*, 21(3): 359–73.

RUGGIERO, V. and SOUTH, N. (2013b), 'Toxic state-corporate crimes, neo-liberalism and green criminology: The hazards and legacies of the oil, chemical and mineral industries', *International Journal for Crime, Justice and Social Democracy*, 2(2): 12–26.

SAHA, R. and MOHAI, P. (2005), 'Historical context and hazardous waste facility siting: Understanding temporal patterns in Michigan', *Social Problems*, 52(4): 618–48.

SANTANA, D. B. (2002), 'Resisting toxic militarism', *Social Justice*, 29(2): 37–47.

SCARCE, R. (1994), '(No) Trial (But) Tribulations: When Courts and Ethnography Conflict', *Journal of Contemporary Ethnography*, 23(2): 123–49.

SCARCE, R. (2006), *Eco-Warriors: Understanding the Radical Environmental Movement*, updated edn, Walnut Creek, California: Left Coast Press.

SCHNAIBERG, A. (1980), *The Environment: From Surplus to Scarcity*, New York: Oxford University Press.

SCHNEIDER, J. L. (2008), 'Reducing the illicit trade in endangered wildlife: the market reduction approach', *Journal of Contemporary Criminal Justice*, 24(3): 274–95.

SERGI, A. and SOUTH, N. (2016), '"Earth, Water, Air, and Fire": environmental crimes, Mafia power and political negligence in Calabria', in G. Antonopoulos (ed.), *Illegal Entrepreneurship, Organised Crime and Social Control*, New York: Springer.

SIMON, D. R. (2000), 'Corporate environmental crimes and social inequality: New directions for environmental justice research', *American Behavioral Scientist*, 43(4): 633–45.

SITU, Y. and EMMONS, D. (2000), *Environmental Crime: The Criminal Justice System's Role in Protecting the Environment*, Thousand Oaks, CA: Sage.

SNIDER, L. (2010), 'Framing e-waste regulation: The obfuscating role of power', *Criminology and Public Policy*, 9(3): 569–77.

SOLLUND, R. (ed.) (2008), *Global harms: Ecological Crime and Speciesism*, New York: Nova Science.

SOLLUND, R. (2013), 'The victimization of women, children and non-human species through trafficking and trade: Crimes understood through an eco-feminist perspective', in N. South and A. Brisman (eds), *Routledge International Handbook of Green Criminology*, London: Routledge.

SOUTH, N. (1998), 'A green field for criminology? A proposal for a perspective', *Theoretical Criminology*, 2(2): 211–33.

SOUTH, N. (2012), 'Climate change, environmental (in) security, conflict and crime', in S. Farrall, D. French, and T. Ahmed (eds), *Climate Change: Legal and Criminological Implications*, Oxford: Hart.

SOUTH, N. (2015), 'Green criminology, brown crime and problems of despoiling, disposal and de-manufacturing in global resource industries', in T. Wyatt (ed.), *Hazardous Waste and Pollution: Detecting and Preventing Green Crimes*, London: Springer.

SOUTH, N. (forthcoming), 'Free trade agreements, private courts and environmental exploitation: disconnected policies, denials and moral disengagement', *International Journal for Crime, Justice and Social Democracy*, 5(4): 45–59.

SOUTH, N. and BEIRNE, P. (eds) (2006), *Green Criminology*, Aldershot, Ashgate.

SOUTH, N. and BRISMAN, A. (2013a), 'Critical green criminology, environmental rights and crimes of exploitation', in S. Winlow and R. Atkinson (eds), *New Directions in Crime and Deviance*, London: Routledge.

SOUTH, N. and A. BRISMAN (eds) (2013b), *Routledge International Handbook of Green Criminology*, London: Routledge.

SOUTH, N. and WYATT, T. (2011), 'Comparing illicit trades in wildlife and drugs: an exploratory study', *Deviant Behavior*, 32(1): 1–24.

SOUTH, N., BRISMAN, A., and BEIRNE, P. (2013), 'A Guide to a Green Criminology', in N. South and A. Brisman (eds), *Routledge International Handbook of Green Criminology*, London: Routledge.

STEPHENS, S. (1996), 'Reflections on environmental justice: Children as victims and actors', *Social Justice*, 23(4): 62–86.

STRETESKY, P. B. (2006), 'Corporate self-policing and the environment', *Criminology*, 44(3): 671–708.

STRETESKY, P. and LYNCH, M. (2001), 'The relationship between lead and homicide', *Archives of Pediatric and Adolescent Medicine*, 155(5): 579–82.

STRETESKY, P. and LYNCH, M. (2004), 'The relationship between lead and crime', *Journal of Health and Social Behavior*, 45(2): 214–29.

STRETESKY P. B., LONG, M. A., and LYNCH, M. J. (2014), *The Treadmill of Crime: Political Economy and Green Criminology*, London: Routledge.

SZASZ, A. (1986), 'Corporations, organized crime, and the disposal of hazardous waste: An examination of the making of a criminogenic regulatory structure', *Criminology*, 24(1): 1–27.

TAILBY, R. and GANT, F. (2002), *The illegal market in Australian abalone*, Trends & Issues in Crime and Criminal Justice 225, Canberra: Australian Institute of Criminology.

TOMPKINS, K. (2005), 'Police, law enforcement and the environment', *Current Issues in Criminal Justice*, 16(3): 294–306.

VAN ERP, J. and HUISMAN, W. (2010), 'Smart regulation and enforcement of illegal disposal of electronic waste', *Criminology and Public Policy*, 9(3): 579–90.

WALTERS, R. (2004), 'Criminology and genetically modified food', *British Journal of Criminology*, 44(2): 151–67.

WALTERS, R. (2006), 'Crime, bio-agriculture and the exploitation of hunger', *British Journal of Criminology*, 46(1): 26–45.

WALTERS, R. (2010a), 'Eco crime' in J. Muncie, D. Talbot, and R. Walters (eds), *Crime: Local and Global*, Cullompton: Willan.

WALTERS, R. (2010b), 'Toxic atmospheres air pollution, trade and the politics of regulation', *Critical Criminology*, 18(4): 307–23.

WALTERS, R. (2011), *Eco crime and Genetically Modified Food*, Abingdon: Routledge.

WALTERS, R. (2013), 'Eco mafia and environmental crime', in K. Carrington, M. Ball, E. O'Brien, and J. Marcellus Tauri (eds), *Crime, Justice and Social Democracy*, Basingstoke: Palgrave.

WALTERS, R., WESTERHUIS, D., and WYATT, T. (eds) (2013), *Emerging Issues in Green Criminology: Exploring Power, Justice and Harm*, Basingstoke: Palgrave Macmillan.

WELLSMITH, M. (2010), 'The applicability of crime prevention to problems of environmental harm: a consideration of illicit trade in endangered species', in R. White (ed.), *Global Environmental Harm: Criminological Perspectives*, Cullompton: Willan.

WHITE, R. (2002), 'Environmental harm and the political economy of consumption', *Social Justice*, 29(1–2): 82–102.

WHITE, R. (2003), 'Environmental issues and the criminological imagination', *Theoretical Criminology*, 7(4): 483–506.

WHITE, R. (2008), *Crimes against Nature: Environmental Criminology and Ecological Justice*, Cullompton: Willan.

WHITE, R. (ed.) (2009), *Environmental Crime: A Reader*, Cullompton: Willan.

WHITE, R. (ed.) (2010a), *Global environmental harm: Criminological perspectives*, Cullompton: Willan.

WHITE, R. (2011), *Transnational Environmental Crime: Toward an Eco-Global Criminology*, London: Routledge.

WHITE, R. (ed.) (2012), *Climate Change From a Criminological Perspective*, New York: Springer.

WHITE, R. and GRAHAM, H. (2015), 'Greening Justice: Examining the Interfaces of Criminal, Social and Ecological Justice', *British Journal of Criminology*, 55(5): 845–65.

WHITE, R. and HECKENBERG, D. (2014), *Green Criminology: An Introduction to the Study of Environmental Harm*, London: Routledge.

WILDING, N. (2012), 'Experiments in action-research and human ecology: Developing a community of practice for rural resilience pioneers', in L. Williams, R. Roberts, and A. McIntosh (eds), *Radical Human Ecology: Intercultural and indigenous approaches*, Farnham: Ashgate.

WILLIAMS, C. (1996), 'An environmental victimology', *Social Justice*, 23(4): 16–40.

WONDERS, N. A. and DANNER, M. J. E. (2015), 'Gendering Climate Change: A Feminist Criminological Perspective', *Critical Criminology*, 23(4): 401–16.

WYATT, T. (2012), *Green Criminology & Wildlife Trafficking: The Illegal Fur and Falcon Trades in Russia Far East*, Saarbrücken, Germany: Lambert.

WYATT, T. (2013), *Wildlife Trafficking: A Deconstruction of the Crime, the Victims, and the Offenders*, Basingstoke: Palgrave Macmillan.

WYATT, T. (2014), 'Invisible Pillaging: The Hidden Harm of Corporate Biopiracy', in P. Davies, P. Francis, and T. Wyatt (eds), *Invisible Crimes and Social Harms*, Basingstoke: Palgrave Macmillan.

ZAHN, M. (1999), 'Thoughts on the Future of Criminology—The American Society of Criminology 1998 Presidential Address', *Criminology*, 37(1): 1–16.

PART II

BORDERS, BOUNDARIES, AND BELIEFS

15

CRIMINOLOGY, PUNISHMENT, AND THE STATE IN A GLOBALIZED SOCIETY

Katja Franko

INTRODUCTION

We live in a world marked by profound social transformations, instability, and crisis—of humanitarian, economic, ecological, security, and other kinds. Many of the social and political issues that capture contemporary research imagination are transnational, rather than simply local and national in nature, from terrorism, organized crime, sex trafficking to environmental degradation and irregular migration, to name a few. Contemporary societies are, as Zygmunt Bauman observes, 'faced with a need to seek (in vain, it seems) *local* solutions to *globally* produced problems' (2004: 6; italics original). What has been criminology's contribution to addressing these pressing questions?

Through much of their history, criminal justice and criminal law have been inherently territorial and tied to individual national states. Criminal justice has been conceived and imagined as what Nancy Fraser (2008) terms 'normal justice'; a type of justice which is practiced territorially, as a domestic relation among fellow citizens where 'parties frame their disputes as matters internal to territorial states, thereby equating the "who of justice" with the citizenry of a bounded polity' (Fraser 2008: 54). This chapter charts and analyses the processes through which this predicament has come to be profoundly challenged. Today, questions of criminal law and criminal justice are increasingly becoming international, overcoming the confines of traditional jurisdictional constraints. Issues such as the death penalty and the combating of terrorism, are not simply a question of how individual states use power over their citizens, but have become issues of world-wide politics and engage a global audience. Today, terms of imprisonment in Europe are not determined solely by individual states, but also by an expending body of European prison law and related monitoring institutional arrangements (Van Zyl Smit and Snacken 2009). Moreover, we live, as Paul Knepper observes, 'in the age of international crime' (2010: 1), where the social parameters of crime, social harm, and their regulation are increasingly gaining a transborder reach. Nor can it be any longer assumed that the 'who of criminal justice' today are only citizens of a given state. Numbers of foreign prisoners in most Western European countries are well above 20 per cent, reaching a staggering 73.8 per cent in Switzerland and 60.4 per cent in Greece.[1] Contemporary penal regimes process not only nationally marginalized populations, but increasingly also populations of what might be termed global outcasts (Bauman 2004), and are engaging in a series of strategies to control globally marginalized populations.

In order to be able to address and study these developments criminology needs to be able to engage with issues of global interconnectedness and expand the geographical reach of its research topics and imagination. However, like criminal law and criminal justice, criminology has also been, traditionally, in numerous and subtle ways, implicitly tied to the national state. Throughout the discipline's history these ties have often been supportive (in terms of sharing the state's objectives of crime reduction, rehabilitation, and the like), or highly critical (of its punitive and oppressive nature, class bias, and democratic deficits). Nevertheless, the national state—with its prerogatives of criminalization, punishment, policing, and the use of force, as well as its extensive data and knowledge production—has been the essential precondition for thinking about modern crime and punishment and a backdrop without which criminology, as a discipline, would hardly have been thinkable.

The growing body of studies on contemporary global connectivity has pointed out the need to challenge this natural and self-evident framing of previous scholarship. It has suggested that to fully understand the dynamics of crime, criminalization, and punishment in a global perspective, we need to challenge the established habits of thought, methodological pathways, and theoretical and conceptual assumptions, which have made the national frame of understanding 'the normal' also within criminology (see, *inter alia*, Morrison 2006; Findlay 2008; Nelken 2011; Pakes 2012; Aas 2013). This chapter traces the arguments of this line of scholarship in order to examine what relevance criminology has had, and may hold, for understanding contemporary global issues. By doing so, the chapter does not simply chart a demise of the state, as is sometimes assumed within studies of globalization. Instead it proposes a more subtle analytical and imaginary disconnection between crime, penality, and the nation state. It suggests that in order to be able to capture and address contemporary global interconnectedness, we need to take a step back and critically examine one of the most basic frames and powerful and defining assumptions for the understanding of modern penality, namely the idea of a functioning, sovereign national state. In other words, the state needs to be relieved of what David Held (2010) terms its ontological privilege in order to enable criminology to become a globally oriented discipline, particularly if its scholarship is to hold relevance for understanding developments beyond the confines of the relatively pacified global North.

[1] World Prison Brief available at: http://www.prisonstudies.org/map/europe, accessed 29 December 2016.

In the reminder of this chapter we shall examine how global perspectives challenge the national frame of understanding of issues of crime and punishment. In particular, we shall focus on the question of the changing nature of state sovereignty and its components—territory, authority, and rights.

DESTABILIZING THE NATIONAL FRAME

The global, as Ana Tsing (2005) observes, 'needs to be imagined in order to exist'. However, traditional imaginations of globalization have often been marked by two misleading and unproductive assumptions. The first is that we are dealing with a historically new phenomenon and that we are, due to the profoundness of technological and social change, even seeing a dawn of a new era. The focus has been on novelty and change. The second is a belief that engagement with the global involves researching phenomena which are somehow spanning the globe, or at least inhabiting a space which is clearly above local and national contexts. Consequently, globalization has had a fair share of critical observers, who have doubted both its usefulness as an analytical concept as well as the profoundness of its impact.

With regard to the first assumption, the growing body of knowledge within historical criminology has in recent years brought to attention the long historic roots through which crime and its control came to be seen as international issues (Knepper 2010, 2011). Particularly since the second half of the nineteenth century, concerns about white slavery, international migration, alien criminality, and the international underworld that stretches 'across every city of the world' came to dominate the public agenda, and coincided with intensified international scientific and police cooperation on these issues (Deflem 2002; Knepper 2010). Spurred on by innovations in the means of transport and communication, the internationalist view of crime was also encouraged by the growth of the British Empire (Knepper 2010). Contemporary global processes and concerns are therefore by no means novel, but are happening through institutional and conceptual architectures that are already in place and are also 'profoundly linked to the histories of colonialism and post-colonial aspirations' (Kenway and Fahey 2009: 20).

The second assumption has, on the other hand, promoted a view of globalization as a process towards creation of planetary uniformity, be it in terms of cultural similarity, the spread of neoliberalism, policy transfers, and the like. These approaches have often operated at high levels of generalization and abstraction and have conceptualized global interconnectedness primarily as a trend towards universality and convergence. The focus has been, for example, on the mobility of criminal networks and the speed with which they take advantage of the fragility of global economic systems and of new modes of communication (Miklaucic and Brewer 2013). Particularly the early stages of globalization research were marked by a tendency to 'zoom out' to the planetary level and to conceive of the global as a scale which is distinct and above the local and the national (Aas 2011). This conceptual and methodological dichotomy has been often supported by an accompanying normative view of the local as 'good' (and invested with 'real and earthy' attributes) and global as 'bad' (Kenway and Fahey 2009: 73).

More recent scholarship has pointed out, however, the heterogeneity of forms through which contemporary globalization is taking shape. Mafias and organized crime groups do not seamlessly operate across national borders, but are still deeply entrenched in local contexts, even when having a transborder reach (Varese 2011; Hobbs 2013). While involving formation of clearly global and transnational phenomena, such as for example the establishment of the International Criminal Court, many, and often most profound impacts of global interconnections, are to be found in national and local contexts. 'These constellations and networks do not engender planetary social uniformity unfolding to some inherent logic, but form particular milieus that vary historically and geographically' (Ong in Kenway and Fahey 2009: 89). Global policing today involves not only working with transnational formations, such as Interpol and Europol, or participation in UN missions and international networks of liaison officers (Goldsmith and Sheptycki 2007; Bowling and Sheptycki 2012), but also radically transforms the nature of local policing. Police officers in Oslo, for example, cooperate with their Romanian counterparts in efforts to control poor migrant populations in their local environments (Gundhus and Franko 2016). Contemporary local policing is in numerous contexts a deeply globalized phenomenon, addressing issues and populations which, although locally and nationally marginalized, are fused with transnational connectivity and shaped by global inequality and conflict.

Researching globalization therefore demands not only attention to overarching global structures and phenomena, but also 'faith in single sites with an attention to motion' (Appadurai in Kenway and Fahey 2009: 48). While sometimes requiring methodological innovation, such sites are nevertheless often still accessible through traditional criminological approaches and knowledge which is grounded and embodied. Prison ethnography has thus offered a wealth of insights into the nature of imprisonment in a globalized world (Ugelvik 2013; Bosworth 2014; Kaufman 2015). Although by their nature territorially separate and local, contemporary sites of confinement are marked by increasing diversity and are being profoundly reshaped by the regimes of global mobility and exclusion. Studying such phenomena demands that we transcend the ubiquitous opposition between the local, national, and global, and are able to detect 'the presence of globalizing dynamics in thick social environments that mix national and non-national elements' (Sassen 2007: 5).

Globalization therefore demands an eye for the less visible and involves a process of destabilization and breaking down of what, earlier, seemed to be stable categories. Certain assumptions and habits of academic thinking thus become unproductive, particularly the privilege which had traditionally been accorded to the national frame of understanding. As suggested earlier, for most of modernity the national frame has been the natural category of practice of domestic criminal justice systems, underpinning the imagery of homogenous, territorially bonded nation states. Globally aware approaches, on the other hand, challenge the national order of things as the normal or natural order of things (Aas 2013). They build on a critique of so-called methodological nationalism which, as Ulrich Beck (2002: 51) describes:

> equates societies with nation-state societies, and sees states and their governments as the cornerstones of a social science analysis. It assumes that humanity is naturally divided into

a limited number of nations, which on the inside, organize themselves as nation-states, and, on the outside, set boundaries to distinguish themselves from other nation-states.

As we shall see later, methodological nationalism builds its world view on a perception of social phenomena as bordered, and issues of governance as tied primarily to the nation state. There is, moreover, a clear distinction between inside and outside of the state—an understanding which is commonly described as the Westphalian order. This order—named after the 1648 treaty of Westphalia—was based on clear delineation between international and internal affairs of the state and was marked by adherence to as a fundamental principle of modern world order.

In the following sections, we shall see how contemporary dynamics of criminalization, crime, and harm production challenge this predicament. Phenomena such as transnational terrorism, migration control, and global prohibition regimes have in the past decades destabilized the established boundaries between internal and external security, between policing and soldiering, warfare and crime control (Andreas and Price 2002; Aas 2013). These developments demand that we, as Loader and Percy (2012) suggest, bring the 'outside' in and the 'inside' out and, ultimately, also bridge the academic divides between the domains of criminology, criminal law, international criminal law, security studies, and international relations. In what follows, we shall look more closely into these dynamics, particularly as they pertain to issues of state sovereignty and our understanding of statehood in a globalized society.

(ILLICIT) GLOBALIZATION AND STATE SOVEREIGNTY

A much rehearsed argument in popular debates about globalization is the idea of weakening of state sovereignty, partly due to the spread of international regulations and transnational governing bodies, as well as growing influence of licit and illicit, non-state actors. Their activities, such as various forms of smuggling, piracy, counterfeiting, and exploitation, create social conditions of violence and lawlessness, and mark an inherent demise of state power and create large spaces of private authority, particularly in the global South. Estimated by some to account for as much as a fifth of the global gross domestic product (Glenny 2008), illicit activities have been described as the dark underside which is undermining the global economy and is a source of permanent and growing security instability (Miklaucic and Brewer 2013; Shelley 2014). Also, developments within the field of international law, finance, and global governance have invited claims that global interdependence inevitably saps state sovereignty. Nation states are seen as losing control and authority to the supranational level, as well as to private corporate actors. While often uncritical and alarmist,[2] such prognoses nevertheless invite an examination of transformations of state sovereignty under

[2] For a discussion of measurement issues related to the global illicit trade, see Andreas and Greenhill (2010) and Picard (2013).

conditions of globalization as an issue of central criminological interest. This debate shall therefore form the backbone of this chapter.

Although of central importance to issues of punishment, the concept of state sovereignty has received relatively scarce criminological attention. This may be partly due to a more general trend in which the concept, as Kalmo and Skinner observe (2010: 1), brings up 'connotations of absolutist forms of government that a more moderate age, committed to international law and increasingly enmeshed in a web of global interdependence, simply has no use for it'. More importantly, criminology has been heavily indebted to Michel Foucault's invitation to 'cut off the King's head' in the social sciences (1980) and to focus on forms of power and governance, which are capillary and dispersed throughout society, rather than centred in the state. Due to this 'theoretical anti-statism' (Dean 2013: 52), much attention has been paid to the institutional production of docile, disciplined bodies and prudent, self-governing individuals, far less to the nature of state authority and its defining elements (although see Wacquant 2010; Loader and Walker 2007; Garland 2013). Nevertheless, Foucault, in his later work (2009: 11), distinguished between discipline, bio-politics, and sovereignty as distinct modalities of control: while the former is exercised over bodies of individuals, the latter is both marked by the ability to decide on issues of life and death as well as focused on controlling the territory. Sovereignty is preoccupied with management of circulation, including international circulation, and about distinguishing between desirable and undesirable mobility (Salter 2015). There is a growing body of criminological scholarship which demonstrates how this this type of control is increasingly relevant for understanding contemporary penal regimes (Aas and Bosworth 2013).

Globalization, with its perceived threat of erosion of state power, therefore demands that we examine the concept of state sovereignty as it pertains to issues of punishment, crime control, and criminalization and, importantly, that we do so with an international perspective. In such a context, having an international perspective implies not simply an analytical 'jump' to the global level, but also attention to the level of inter-state relations and the positions of states within the international order. Which states have the power to define the international agenda of crime prohibition and function as moral entrepreneurs[3] in the international arena (Jakobi 2013)? Which states have the power to engage in extra-territorial interventions in other states, be it in the name of controlling drugs, terror, or migration (Ryan and Mitsilegas 2010)? An understanding of contemporary transformations of state power requires a conceptual apparatus about what a state is (which allows us to describe the qualities that are supposed to be under threat or at least in retreat), as well as a language about relations between states (which allows us to analyse how states and other actors influence each other in terms of global crime governance).

Much of existing criminological scholarship has been marked by a tendency towards examining the 'inside' of the state, its internal organs, so to speak. It has been particularly centred on two archetypical models of statehood: the carceral state and the welfare state (Gottschalk 2006; Garland 2016). Several influential accounts (Wacquant 2009, 2010; Harcourt 2011) have suggested that we have been seeing, under the influence of

[3] Moral entrepreneur is a term popularized by Howard S. Becker's (1963) *Outsiders: Studies in the Sociology of Deviance*. The term denotes individuals or groups who create rules in a society (i.e. rule creators) or who take on a responsibility to enforce them (i.e. rule enforcers).

neoliberal policies, a process of expansion of the carceral state and mass imprisonment at the expense of the welfare state. While this trend has been particularly pronounced in the United States, some countries—most notably Scandinavian—have been able to retain the less punitive and more inclusive welfare penality (Pratt and Eriksson 2013). However, despite essentially standing at the opposite ends of the punitive spectrum and having different economic and institutional contexts (Cavadino and Dignan 2006; Lacey 2008), both the welfare and the carceral state have in common that they represent what might be described as examples of 'strong statehood'. While it is open to debate whether excessive use of carceral power can be understood as a sign of state strength, both the carceral and the welfare state are nevertheless built on a premise of effective legal sovereignty, where the state exerts control over a given territory and a population in the name of the will of the people.

Critics have pointed out though that from a global perspective these forms of statehood are, in fact, an anomaly rather than the rule (Hansen and Stepputat 2006). As Müller (2012: 11) suggests, unlike in the West, 'states in "most of the world" are—and have always been—characterized by the existence of areas of limited statehood' and have been crucially marked by processes of political negotiation, bargaining, and accommodation between the central state power holders and strong (licit and illicit) regional and local actors. These constellations have their origins in early colonial times, which were characterized by a top-down process of state building and co-option of local strongmen into the colonial rule, while leaving them considerable autonomy. In much literature on the global illicit economy such arrangements tend to be described as symptoms of state failure, while criminological scholarship has been conspicuously silent on the subject. Yet, if we are to grasp the nature of the darker sides of contemporary global interconnectedness—and move beyond the simplistic predictions of state demise—we need to gain a more nuanced understanding of the historically and geographically varied nature of state sovereignty. Seeing the state through a historically aware and international lens opens an insight into the global varieties of statehood, as well as the unequal power relations between them (Aas 2013). Some states are, as Dauvergne (2008) observes, more sovereign than others.

Moreover, while for some states combating illicit flows may be a great challenge, for others it may do quite the opposite and offer an opportunity for expansion of state power. As Peter Andreas' illuminating study *Smuggler Nation* reveals, historically, illicit trade has greatly empowered the American state by expanding the policing authority and reach of the federal government as well as its transformation into a global policing superpower. Smuggling, Andreas (2013: xi) contends, 'has been as much about building up the American state as about subverting it'. The relationship between (illicit) cross-border flows and state power is therefore far more complex than may appear at first glance. It is not a zero sum game where one is losing at the expense of the other (Sassen 2007; Aas 2013), instead some states (or parts of the state) may in fact be strengthened and reasserting their authority, while others come under challenge. The quality of the debate about the impact of global interdependence on state sovereignty would be therefore, as Kalmo and Skinner (2010: 6) observe, enhanced if sovereignty was not simply equated with independence and we, instead, developed a more discriminating vocabulary to describe the 'deepening of its complexity'. For this purpose, Saskia Sassen (2007: 51) suggests that we examine specific components of national states—namely, territory, authority, and rights (see also Sassen 2006). Rather than assessing the faith of the state as a whole, each of these categories is undergoing context-specific transformations under conditions of global interconnectedness. For analytical purposes, these three categories shall also form the frame for our further analysis in the remaining parts of this chapter, where we shall examine how each is being transformed in the field of crime control and criminal justice.

TERRITORY, CRIME, AND JUSTICE

While Anthony Giddens notably described the state as a 'bordered power container' (1995), much of globalization scholarship has stressed the challenges that globalization presents to the idea of a bordered nation state. Global processes destabilize 'the scalar hierarchy centered in the national state' (Sassen 2007: 14). Cross-border mobility becomes a central feature of social relations, including those pertaining to issues of crime and justice (Aas 2013). While the modern state has been marked by a territorial logic, globalization strengthens, and even privileges, non-territorial formations (Strandsbjerg 2010), particularly those of the network.

The development was influentially articulated in Manuel Castells' trilogy on the information age (2000). Castells applied the imagery of transnational networks to the field of organized crime by claiming that national and local organized crime groups have gone through a process of internationalization. Resembling business networks, these groups are now able to link up with criminal groups in other countries and establish international networks for the production, management, financing, and distribution of their products and services. The usefulness of the concept of the social network lies in its flexibility and has been applied to a variety of diverse social phenomena, such as terrorist associations, street gangs, and drug trafficking syndicates (Morseli 2009; Grabosky and Stohl 2010). Networks are seen as flatter and less hierarchical than traditional organizations, as well as capable of—with the help of modern communication technologies—achieving a transnational, even global reach and representing a serious security threat (Miklaucic and Brewer 2013). They have, allegedly, the ability not only to escape prosecution on the national level, but also to infiltrate the law enforcement, judicial, and political systems of several countries, as well as to penetrate the global financial systems (Shelley 2014).

The changing spatial dynamics of risk and harm has been particularly clear when it comes to debates about international terrorism. Alluding to Castells' space of flows, Bauman (2002) described 9/11 and the fallen Manhattan towers as the most potent symbolic reminder of the end of the era of space and the annihilation of the protective capacity of space. Violence and devastation, that before seemed to be banished to the outskirts of the prosperous West (or at least to the hidden pockets of its poverty-stricken ghettos), now moved inside and attacked its very symbols of power and prosperity. Foreign policy is thus no longer properly 'foreign', as external conflicts often have an almost immediate impact on national and local security strategies (Aas 2013). It is important to stress though that such dynamics do not necessarily indicate an objective growth in risk, but rather its changing spatial aspects and expose the relationship between globalization and systematic risk (Goldin and Mariathasan 2014). This is particularly evident when it comes to issues of environmental crime, an understanding of which, as White (2012: 15) observes, 'leads the analytical gaze to acknowledge the fusion of the local and the global, and to ponder the ways in which such harms transcend the normal boundaries of jurisdiction, geography and social divide' (see also Ellefsen *et al.* 2012; White 2009, 2011). Global interconnectedness is contributing to the growing complexity of social relations as well as increasing mutual vulnerability and fading boundaries between the global North and South.

When it comes to terrorism, trying to control this complexity and interconnectedness has led states in the global North to vastly expand their surveillance powers, as well as lowering the thresholds of engagement against emerging threats, whether through the means of preventive criminalization (Ashworth and Zedner 2015) and military and technological intervention, most notably drone attacks (Wall and Monahan 2011). The latter are also a symptomatic example of the growing scope of extra-territorial interventions and security strategies through which states in the global North are expanding their law-enforcement activities and their sphere of influence.[4] However, the 'exceptional' nature of international terrorism can easily be overstated due to extensive media and political attention. There are, moreover, sharp geographical divisions in terms of actual exposure to risk. While there has been, according to some estimates, over a ninefold increase in the number of deaths from terrorism in recent years, rising from 3,329 in 2000 to 32,685 in 2014, the majority of those did not occur in the West. Excluding 9/11, only 0.5 per cent of all deaths have occurred in Western countries (Institute for Economics and Peace 2015b). This *security inequality* between the global North and South relates not only to terrorism but also to other types of risk and harm and is a pervasive feature of contemporary societies, which shall be addressed further in the next section.

The above discussion indicates the changing spatial dynamics of contemporary risk and the growing transborder reach of illicit activities. This is not to suggest that borders have become irrelevant, quite the opposite. There has been an unprecedented investment in border control in the post-9/11 era, particularly by the states in the global North. Moreover, the increasing networked connectivity has been also a salient trait of activities of state agencies and actors. The past two decades have been marked by an increasingly transborder reach of crime control agencies, when it comes to transnational police cooperation (Bowling and Sheptycki 2012), judicial cooperation, and development of mutual legal assistance (Mitsilegas 2009). While this development has been particularly pronounced in the European Union, it has also marked international crime control efforts, including by the UN and individual states. The United States has, for example, been working multilaterally through FATF (the Financial Action Task Force), and has been able to make financial institutions across the globe to adopt a series of anti-money laundering measures (Jakobi 2013). What is of particular interest here is that these cross-border cooperation structures not only represent a different spatial dynamic from that of a territorial nation state, but also a different type of sovereignty, described by Slaughter (2004) as 'networked sovereignty'. Instead of being defined by a negative capacity to fend off external interference and preserve autonomy,

[4] Australia, the US, and the European Union have also, in the past two decades, progressively expanded their policing activities into the international domain thus externalizing their 'domestic' control functions and exporting their migration control agenda (Aas 2013; Ryan and Mitsilegas 2010; Weber and Pickering 2011).

this new type of sovereignty is concerned with augmenting state power by increasing its ability to participate in international cooperation. The result is increasingly interconnected state agencies and government networks, allowing states 'to compensate for their decreasing territorial power by increasing their global reach' (ibid.: 288).

AUTHORITY, CRIME, AND CRIMINAL JUSTICE

The discussion above brings forth the changing nature of contemporary order of crime governance. As Held observes, a 'new regime of government and governance is emerging which is displacing traditional conceptions of state power as an indivisible, territorially exclusive form of public power' (Held 2010: 37). The authority to police, criminalize, investigate, prosecute, punish, and shame, is not vested only in state agencies, but is being dispersed to a growing array of other actors above, below, and outside the state. For European countries, the final decision on the nature of a penalty or on the terms of imprisonment lies today with the European Court of Human Rights rather than individual states (Van Zyl Smit and Snacken 2009). Nor are agents of the state as easily awarded immunity from prosecution, due to the expansion of international criminal justice, as we shall see in the next section.

However, several historic and contemporary analyses have pointed out that internationalization of criminal justice and policing has been often marked by partiality. What is illegal, and how it is policed, often depends on the political interests of certain states, most notably the United States and Western Europe (Andreas and Nadelmann 2006; Aas 2013). This has been particularly evident in the international efforts to combat drug trafficking (Bowling 2010). In their comprehensive study on global policing Andreas and Nedelmann (2006: 10) argue that 'international crime control is one of the most important—and one of the most overlooked—dimensions of U.S. hegemony in world politics'. Historically, Western powers have, through international prohibition efforts (against slavery, piracy, drugs,), exported their own definitions of crime, not only for political and economic reasons, but also to promote their own morals to other parts of the world. '[T]he models, methods, and priorities of international crime control are substantially determined and exported by the most powerful states in the international system' (Andreas and Nadelmann 2006: 10).

Such actors, who have the ability to shape and influence the nature of global prohibition regimes, can be described as transnational 'moral entrepreneurs' (Jakobi 2013). While moral entrepreneurship can usually be encountered on the level of domestic crime policy, its dynamics are shaped, on the international level, by the unequal power relations between states in the international community. As Hurrell (2007: 20) observes, 'the language of "international order" or "global governance" is never politically neutral. Indeed a capacity to produce and project proposals, conceptions and theories of order is a central part of the practice of power'. The observation can serve as an important reminder of 'the particularity of globalist projects' (Tsing 2005: 76). Moreover, the case of FATF,[5] mentioned above, reveals the important role that non-state actors, such as NGOs and other agencies play in the emerging system of international governance

[5] The Financial Action Task Force (FATF)—an inter-governmental body for the combatting of money laundering.

(see also Lohne, forthcoming). These arrangements are part of a broader spectre of privatized authority that has been one of the hallmarks of globalization. Through the growing strength of privatized and supranational authorities, we are witnessing an evolution of 'a parallel institutional world for the handling of cross-border operations' (Sassen 2007: 41); a world which can be, 'extremely partial rather than universal' and 'not fully accountable to formal democratic political systems' (ibid.: 39). Global governance today is thus a complex 'multilayered, multidimensional and multi-actor system' (Held 2010: 31), where national actors interact, participate in, and cooperate with transnational governmental and non-governmental ones.

While criminologists may have been late-comers to these debates, classical criminological insight has much to offer to the understanding of the emerging global order of governance, where issues of security and crime are of central importance. Criminalization is a phenomenon which cannot be simply taken for granted, but rather something that needs explanation and there is much to be gained in examining the global processes of production of illegality. How are goods, substances, services, and people made illegal at the global level (Dauvergne 2009; Jakobi 2013)? How and why have certain activities come to be criminalized, and why do other forms of social and ecological harm still remain legal (White 2009, 2011)? Moreover, how can we understand the activities of various actors in this field?

Much of the popular discourse on illicit globalization, promoted particularly by politicians, law enforcement agencies, and popular culture, has focused on 'bad' actors and has, explicitly or implicitly, had a moralizing undertone rather than looking at economic and other imperatives behind these activities. However, critics have pointed out that part of the failure of the war on drugs, for example, lies in the fact that prohibition regimes in themselves are essential for maintaining the profitability of the illicit markets which they in turn try to abolish (Global Commission 2011; Gilman *et al.* 2011). Consequently, one should stop thinking of surveillance, intelligence, law enforcement, and punishment as elements of a war that is winnable. The strength of illicit actors lies in the unequal global economic development and the pervasive global inequality which underpin the growth of the illicit economy and put into question the viability of various militant law-enforcement practices and prohibition regimes. Rather than seeing illicit or deviant globalization as a 'removable cancer in an otherwise healthy global economy', Gilman *et al.* (2011: 5) argue that the 'truth of the matter is that deviant globalization is a massive permanent phenomenon that is central to the lives of hundreds of millions of people.

The economic strength of illicit entrepreneurs, and their political influence, is thus intrinsically connected to the mainstream globalization and the deep social divisions it helps to produce and maintain. Through activities such as human smuggling and trafficking, illegal trade in wildlife, drug trafficking, and trafficking in organs, illicit actors are meeting a range of unfulfilled demands of predominantly Northern consumers. Deviant supply is therefore essentially driven by deviant demand, 'generated by repressed desires for things that rich communities themselves either marginalized or forbade' (Gilman *et al.* 2011: 15). Resonant of Merton's work on anomie, but not directly drawing on it, Gilman *et al.* (2011) argue that deviant globalization represents a form of 'survival entrepreneurship' for those without easy access to legitimate market opportunities, through which the globally excluded are able 'to find a space to be innovative, a space in which the rules of the game have not already been stacked against them' (ibid.: 274). The issue brings to our attention the centrality of global development for understanding the dynamics of contemporary crime control and security challenges (Aas 2013). By creating conditions of permanent economic competition and precariousness, and by substantially weakening the capacities of states to provide public services, the neoliberal mantra has opened up a space which is being filled by other—often illicit—actors and activities.

This development is a good example of the weakening of the state and globalization´s ability to perforate state sovereignty. Sometimes criminal networks and other violent non-state actors are perceived to be so powerful that they, to use Carolyn Nordstrom's (2000) famous term, represent 'shadow sovereigns'. These actors, pose *de facto* sovereignty and, as Graham Denyer Willis (2015: 10) shows in his illuminating study of security in Sao Paolo, may 'carry an ability to kill, punish, and discipline with near impunity, in the absence of (or defying) sovereignty grounded in formal ideologies and structures of rule and legality'. The growing influence of violent non-state actors in the post-Cold war era can be seen as yet another testimony of the fragility of the Westphalian order, discussed previously. These actors include not only organized crime groups and terrorist organizations, but also national liberation and insurgent guerilla movements, as well as private military firms (Mulaj 2010). While violent non-state actors may not be in themselves intrinsically 'good' or 'bad'—some of them do, if successful, become legitimate state power holders—they are nevertheless marked by the ability to employ large-scale violence in the pursuit of their goals, a capacity which is traditionally seen to be the state prerogative. As such, these actors operate in, and contribute to, the conditions of limited statehood in the societies in which they operate. These conditions in some countries come close to state collapse, where the state lacks a functioning central government and is unable to provide basic services to its citizens. One such example, which has newly received academic attention, is Somalia, where due to the existence of large unregulated, 'stateless' areas, its coast has in recent years become the most pirate-infested shipping lane in the world (Townsley *et al.* 2016). The UN Security Council has passed several resolutions authorizing member states to enter Somali territorial waters and use 'all necessary means' to interdict and deter piracy (Menkhaus 2010: 357). Consequently, military vessels from NATO and EU countries, the US, China, Russia, Japan, and India, as well as armed private security companies have been involved in patrolling the Somali waters, and have extended their interventions also to the mainland.

The discussion shows the vast differences in the nature of state sovereignty globally. There are varieties of statehood which diverge from the ideal of statehood defined by and found in the global North, and which has so far received most attention within criminological scholarship. However, academic observers have pointed out that while in these states, sovereignty—in the classical, Weberian sense of monopolizing violence—is clearly limited or fragmented, it is by no means absent, but marked by the fact that 'state and non-state actors co-exist, conflict, and cooperate tacitly and implicitly' (Richani 2010: 32). The condition is well captured in Müller's (2012: 37) analysis of Mexico and his concept of the 'negotiated state', which is marked by the fact that state rulers, facing the large scale existence of autonomous power centres inside the territory, create a state space as a space of appropriation as well as to enhance the 'reach of the state'. Despite what is commonly believed, the negotiated state is not marked by the complete absence of the rule of law or anarchy, nor should its many violent local orders simply be seen as being outside or 'beyond the state'. Rather 'the formal-legal dimension is permanently overdetermined and subverted by informal politics' (Müller 2012: 36). Violence, which particularly characterizes many Latin American societies, does not signify an outright defeat of the state, but exists in an intricate 'political economy of violence', which crucially depends on the availability of various 'political entrepreneurs that lend tacit or implicit support to these groups for political and economic returns' (Richani 2010: 32). The condition is captured in Arias and Goldstein's (2010: 4) notion of 'violent pluralism' which denotes a condition of endemic violence in the society 'with states, social elites and subalterns employing violence in the quest to establish or contest regimes of citizenship, justice, rights, and a democratic social order'. This 'dirty togetherness' between a state and other organized sources of violence necessarily departs from a perceived ideal (Willis 2015: 11), but can nevertheless be encountered in numerous countries across the world. Moreover, as Lisa Miller shows in her recent study (2016), examining the economy of violence can be a productive starting point for understanding penal regimes in advanced democracies too. 'Security from violence is a basic human need, a legitimate state interest, and a core public good' (Miller 2015: 186) and provides and important context for the politics of punishment and state legitimacy.

What is of interest at this point, though, is that there are substantial global varieties in terms of institutional provision of security (Loader and Walker 2007). Security is an unevenly distributed good and there exists vast *security inequalities* mainly between countries in the global North and global South, but also within these countries themselves. As the most peaceful region in the world, Europe is in stark contrast to North Africa, the Middle East, and South America, which are marked by deteriorating levels of security (Institute for Economics and Peace 2015a). For example, while many countries in the global North have been experiencing a decrease in levels of violent crime, in Honduras, which now has the highest homicide rate in the world, there was a 48 per cent increase in the homicide rate between 2007 and 2012. Similarly, Mexico and several other Latin American countries have seen a dramatic rise in drug related levels of violence. Security inequalities reflect, and are co-related with, pervasive income inequalities as well as deprivations from the rule of law (ibid.). Moreover, these are not only inequalities between states, but also within them. Contemporary landscapes of security are patchy rather than based on unified territories. They include distinct zones with often radically different levels of presence and absence of violence and the rule of law, and different types of security providers. For example, the case of Somali piracy, mentioned above, reveals novel arrangements which have been put into place to securitize a space through which a substantial proportion of world oil is being transported, including EU and other nations' naval missions, construction of pirate courts and prisons, as well as massive private security and insurance arrangements (Townsley *et al.* 2016).

The discussion above reveals that the answer to one of the most basic questions of human life: 'Who provides protection and decides on issues of life and death?' is no longer simply the nation state, if it ever has been. Sovereign states are built on violence and exert violence, with varying levels of legitimacy and rule of law protection (Sarat and Culbert 2009). However, sovereignty as the right over life—both in terms of protection as well as killing—is increasingly also held by other actors. These arrangements have created a large '"disposable" population that states allow to be preyed on' (Willis 2015: 12); lives which are unprotected by states, whose deaths are not investigated by state agents and not counted in official state statistics. One such example is, as Weber and Pickering (2011) show, the lives of migrants lost at the borders of the affluent world, which are not counted and part of official state statistics. According to The Missing Migrants Project, conducted by the International Organization for Migration, 3,770 migrants lost their lives in the Mediterranean in 2015. Yet these deaths are not part of statistical and police records of the European border control agency, Frontex, nor of individual member states.

CRIMINAL JUSTICE, MEMBERSHIP, AND RIGHTS

In this patchy landscape of security arrangements a central question arises about the meaning and relevance of rights and legal protections. The existence of persons in limbo, outside of the law and its sphere of basic protections, is not only a matter of weak or undemocratic states, but has been also one of the consequences of the war on terror and the new security landscape in Western democracies (Cole 2004). There is therefore much evidence to confirm Giorgio Agamben's (1998) popular writing on homo sacer, whose life is marked by precariousness and bareness, as well as Zygmund Bauman's (2004) gloomy prediction about 'human waste' as being an inevitable byproduct of the spread of global modernity. On the other hand, although excluded from the nation state articulated systems of rights and protections, protection of 'bare lives' has in recent decades become the objective of an influential global discourse of solidarity, governance, and justice, namely, humanitarianism (Fassin 2011). Humanitarianism is, among other things, a cluster of sentiments and a set of laws and moral imperatives to intervene, which focuses on alleviating suffering and saving lives in times of crisis and emergency (Feldman and Ticktin 2010). It has produced an increasingly influential set of new actors, such as humanitarian NGOs who, as representatives of the so-called global civil society, increasingly also have the ability to shape issues of crime and punishment on the international arena (Lohne, forthcoming).

The globalizing process, therefore, not only demands new methods and frameworks of understanding, but significantly, also offers new possibilities for social justice and political action. It is now possible to put an issue on the global agenda, even though nation states are unwilling to put it on the national agenda. Transnational mobilization has thus been central in combating certain types of crimes such as corruption. Traditionally, governments perceived the problem of combating corruption as a matter of national sovereignty. Now, on the other hand, with NGOs such as Amnesty International and Transparency International, action on the global level is making an impact and becoming an important driving force of national change. The acknowledgement that 'justice must transcend the territorial limits it has operated within modernity' (Morrison 2006: 2), has driven a series of social mobilizations against environmental crime, state crime, and human rights violations. This of course is by no means a historical novelty. In the late

1700s, anti-slavery campaigns found people in Britain, and later other countries, politically engaging in issues at the far side of the world at a time when the social meaning of distance was much greater. Interestingly, the campaigners used some distinctly modern forms of political pressure and mobilization, such as political lobbying, celebrity endorsements, and consumer boycotts of sugar, thus revealing an awareness of the intertwining of global issues and local actions (Aas 2013). Today, international mobilizations have had an impact on numerous criminologically relevant domains from global anti-domestic violence campaigns and struggles for better prison conditions to anti-death penalty activism, to name just a few (Hood and Hoyle 2008).

Moreover, there is growing acknowledgment that '[s]trict adherence to the principle of national sovereignty is no longer acceptable, and institutions must be considered through which the international community can effectively intervene' (Savelsberg 2010: 3). We have thus in recent years seen pronounced tendencies towards the criminalization of mass atrocities and human rights violations, most notably represented by the establishment of the International Criminal Court, as well as growing criminological interest in these topics (see, *inter alia*, Findlay 2008; Savelsberg 2010; Hagan and Rymond-Richmond 2009; Schabas 2011; Braithwaite *et al.* 2010; Lohne, forthcoming). Here criminology enters a complex interdisciplinary terrain which demands an engagement with findings from political science, history, human rights and international criminal law, social psychology, and other social science traditions. The recent interest in the field of mass atrocities has been strongly related to the growing salience of human rights as well as the dynamic developments with the international criminal law. Through the progressive articulation of the global civil society, certain crimes and violations of rights are being established as issues to be addressed at the global level, a matter of common responsibility in a perceived shared space of humanitarian consciousness (Lohne, forthcoming).

These developments are part of a broader transformation in the nature of the contemporary world order which has been marked by 'a dramatic and sustained move towards more and more far-reaching international institutions and an exponential increase in the scope, range, and intrusiveness of international rules, norms, and institutions' (Hurrell 2007: 5). This move has, in the field of punishment, been most visible in the growing influence and emphasis placed on human rights (Van Zyl Smit and Snacken 2009; Savelsberg 2010). The jurisprudence of international courts, most notably the European Court of Human Rights, challenges national sovereignty on a diverse set of issues such as prison conditions and conditions of detention centres for immigrants, prisoners' voting rights, the right to a fair trial, anti-terror measures, etc. What is important here is that, for a long time, the power to punish has been primarily vested in the nation state as a prerequisite of its sovereignty, but we are now seeing this power curtailed and shaped by transnational and international actors; not only international courts and UN bodies, but also human rights organizations, NGOs, and various inter-governmental bodies. These actors operate on the international stage, and even though they may frequently be representing national and local interests, they contribute to the normative convergence of contemporary criminal justice which is slowly taking shape above the nation states, and at times against their interests.

CONCLUSION

Through the rise of human rights, the establishment of the International Criminal Court, transitional and environmental justice, and growing salience of humanitarian discourses, we are witnessing the emergence of new modes of criminal justice and governance which are moving beyond the Westphalian, sovereignty-based, pluralism of states and reveal the contours of a constitution of a different international society. However, it is easy to overstate the historical novelty and social potency of these changes (and globalization scholarship has not always been able to resist the temptation). For as much as the past two decades have given evidence of a gradual formation of a global polity, formed around common perceptions of justice and overriding considerations of state sovereignty, there have been also forceful counter-trends. The enormous investments in border control and surveillance are a testimony of a renewed importance of state sovereignty, if not in its material and functional forms, at least in its symbolic forms (Bartelson 2014). By building walls and fortifying their borders, states, as Wendy Brown (2010: 25) observes, theatrically project 'power and efficaciousness that they do not and cannot actually exercise'. They attempt to reinvigorate certain forms of identity and security, and produce subjects 'defended against worldliness' (Brown 2010: 40).

Therefore, far from being irrelevant, the nation state has gained a renewed importance in terms of membership, identity, and belonging. There is a growing body of scholarship about how these trends are also shaping the nature of contemporary penality and criminal justice (Aas and Bosworth 2013; Melossi 2015). Policing, today, is thus also a question of 'patrolling the boundaries of entitlement and belonging' (Weber 2013:173), and imprisonment is not simply a penal measure, but also about expelling the unwanted (Ugelvik 2013; Kaufman 2015). The objectives of borders control are thus increasingly inscribed into discourses about crime and punishment and into everyday practices of contemporary penal regimes. Such forms of 'bordered penality' (Aas 2014) both try to revitalize national identity and keep out the foreign and culturally different, as well as fend off those who wish to make claim on the resources, and protect welfare rights for citizens (Barker 2013; Aas 2014). Contemporary deportation regimes (De Genova and Peutz 2010) surpass those at the height of the colonial era. While an estimated 160,000 convicts were transported from Britain to Australia in the eighteenth and nineteenth centuries, we can read in the Frontex general report (2014: 56) that in 2013 alone 'a stable number of about 159,000 third-country nationals were effectively returned to third countries'.

These practices confirm the continued importance of nation states and state sovereignty. They also reveal the salience of the global which, although interconnected, is also deeply divided (Aas 2011). The lines of demarcation between the global North and South are, of course, far from simple. 'The north these days, contains much south' (Comaroff and Comaroff 2006: 18) and it is precisely this inversion of borders, of the internal and the external spaces, which makes greater knowledge of southern realities all the more urgent (Carrington *et al.* 2016). Contemporary societies are defined by a growing ability of the margins to define the centre. Due to the proliferation of spaces of colonial difference in the midst of the prosperous west, Martha Nussbaum's observation (in Harvey 2000: 531) that a society unable to look at itself through the lens of the other is, as a consequence, equally ignorant of itself, is today more salient than ever. Here lies also an imperative for criminological scholars to engage with global transformations. This involves not only an understanding of global interconnectedness, but also a greater awareness of global divisions, of geopolitical context, as well as critical self-reflection about the potential universality of our own knowledge production.

SELECTED FURTHER READING

There is a booming scholarly literature on globalization in several disciplines. McGrew and Held's *Globalization Theory: Approaches and Controversies* (2007) gives a good presentation of the concept of globalization as well as the debates surrounding it; while Kenway and Fahey's *Globalising the Research Imagination* (2009) offers an off-the-beaten track approach, based on a series of interviews with leading globalization scholars about what it might mean to globalize research imagination.

When it comes to criminological literature, Franko's *Globalization and Crime* (2013) provides a useful introduction to the field, as does Pakes' edited collection *Globalisation and the Challenge to Criminology* (2012). Comparative criminal justice has in recent years become a burgeoning field. Nelken's *Comparative Criminal Justice and Globalization* (2011) offers in-depth debates on the topic. There are of course extensive literatures on individual aspects of global justice, such as eco-global crimes, human rights violations, and responses to mass atrocities. For the former, see White's (2009, 2011) extensive body of work, while Savelsberg's *Crime and Human Rights: Criminology of Genocide and Atrocities* (2010) provides an accessible overview of the latter.

REFERENCES

AAS, K. F. (2011), 'Visions of Global Control: Cosmopolitan Aspirations in a World of Friction', in M. Bosworth and C. Hoyle (eds), *What is Criminology?*, Oxford: Oxford University Press.

AAS, K. F. (2013), *Globalization and Crime*, 2nd edn, London: Sage.

AAS, K. F. (2014), 'Bordered Penality: Precarious Membership and Abnormal Justice', in *Punishment & Society*, 16(5): 520–41.

AAS, K. F. and BOSWORTH, M. (2013), *The Borders of Punishment: Migration, Citizenship, and Social Exclusion*, Oxford: Oxford University Press.

AGAMBEN, G. (1998), *Homo Sacer: Sovereign Power and Bare Life*, Stanford: Stanford University Press.

ANDREAS, P. and NEDELMANN, E. (2006), *Policing the Globe: Criminalization and Crime Control in International Relations*, Oxford and New York: Oxford University Press.

ANDREAS, P. (2013), *Smuggler Nation: How illicit trade made America*, New York: Oxford University Press.

ANDREAS, P. and PRICE, R. (2002), 'From War Fighting to Crime Fighting: Transforming the American National Security State', *International Studies Review*, 3(3): 31–52.

ARIAS, E. D. and GOLDSTEIN, D. M. (2010), 'Violent pluralism: Understanding the New Democracies of Latin America', in E. D. Arias and D. M. Goldstein (eds), *Violent Democracies in Latin America (The Cultures and Practice of Violence)*, Duram: Duke University Press.

ASHWORTH, A. and ZEDNER, L. (2015), *Preventive Justice*, Oxford: Oxford University Press.

BARKER, V. (2013), 'Nordic Exceptionalism revisited: Explaining the paradox of a Janus-faced penal regime', *Theoretical Criminology*, 17(1): 5–25.

BARTELSON, J. (2014), *Sovereignty as Symbolic Form*, Abingdon: Routledge.

BAUMAN, Z. (2002), *Society under Siege*, Cambridge: Polity.

BAUMAN, Z. (2004), *Wasted Lives: Modernity and its Outcasts*, Cambridge: Polity.

BECK, U. (2002), 'The terrorist threat: world risk society revisited', *Theory, Culture & Society*, 19(4): 39–55.

BOSWORTH, M. (2014), *Inside Immigration Detention*, Oxford: Oxford University Press.

BOWLING, B. (2010), *Policing the Caribbean: Transnational Security Cooperation in Practice*, Oxford: Oxford University Press.

BOWLING, B. and SHEPTYCKI, J. (2012), *Global Policing*, London: Sage.

BRAITHWAITE, J., CHARLESWORTH H., REDDY, P., and DUNN, L. (2010), *Reconciliation and Architectures of Commitment: Sequencing peace in Bougainville*, Canberra: ANU E Press.

BROWN, W. (2010), *Walled States, Waning Sovereignty*, New York: Zone Books.

CARRINGTON, K., HOGG, R., and SOZZO, M. (2016), 'Southern Criminology', in *British Journal of Criminology*, 56(1): 1–20.

CASTELLS, M. (2000), *End of Millennium*, 2nd edn, Oxford: Blackwell.

CAVADINO, M. and DIGNAN, J. (2006), *Penal systems: a Comparative Approach*, London: Sage.

COLE, D. (2004), *Enemy Aliens: Double Standards and Constitutional Freedoms in the War on Terrorism*, New York and London: The New Press.

COMAROFF, J. L. and COMAROFF, J. (2006), 'Law and disorder in the postcolony: An introduction', in J. Comaroff and J. L. Comaroff (eds), *Law and Disorder in the Postcolony*, Chicago: University of Chicago Press.

DAUVERGNE, C. (2008), *Making People Illegal*, Cambridge: Cambridge University Press.

DEAN, M. (2013), *The Signature of Power: Sovereignty, Governmentality and Biopolitics*, London: Sage.

DEFLEM, M. (2002), *Policing World Society: Historical Foundations of International Police Cooperation*, Oxford: Oxford University Press.

DE GENOVA, N. and PEUTZ, N. M. (2010), *The Deportation Regime: Sovereignty, Space, and the Freedom of Movement*, Durham: Duke University Press.

ELLEFSEN, R., SOLLUND, R., and LARSEN, G. (eds) (2012), *Eco-global Crimes: Contemporary Problems and Future Challenges*, Burlington: Ashgate.

FASSIN, D. (2011), *Humanitarian Reason: A Moral History of the Present*, Berkeley, Los Angeles, London: University of California Press.

FELDMAN, I. and M. TICKTIN (eds) (2010), *In the Name of Humanity: The Government of Threat and Care*, Durham and London: Duke University Press.

FINDLAY, M. (2008), *Governing through Globalised Crime: Futures for International Criminal Justice*, Devon: Willan.

FOUCAULT, M. (2009), *Security, Territory, Population: Lectures at the College de France 1977-1978*, Basingstoke: Palgrave Macmillan.

FOUCAULT, M. (1980), *Power / Knowledge*, New York: Pantheon.

FRASER, N. (2008), *Scales of Justice*, Cambridge: Polity.

GARLAND, D. (2013), 'The 2012 Sutherland address: Penality and the Penal State', *Criminology*, 51(3): 475–517.

GARLAND, D. (2016), *The Welfare State: A Very Short Introduction*, Oxford: Oxford University Press.

GIDDENS, A. (1995), *A Contemporary Critique of Historical Materialism*, Cambridge, Polity Press.

GILMAN, N., GOLDHAMMER, J., and WEBER, S. (2011), *Deviant Globalization. Black Market Economy in the 21st Century*, New York, London: The Continuum International Publishing Group.

GLENNY, M. (2008), *McMafia: Crime Without Frontiers*, The Bodley Head Ltd.

GLOBAL COMMISSION ON DRUG POLICY (2011), *(War) on Drugs: Report of the Global Commission on Drug Policy* Source: http://www.globalcommissionondrugs.org/wp-content/themes/gcdp_v1/pdf/Global_Commission_Report_English.pdf, accessed 18 December 2016.

GOLDIN, I. and MARIATHASAN, M. (2014), *The Butterfly Defect: How Globalization Creates Systemic Risks, and What to Do about It*, Princeton and Oxford: Princeton University Press.

GOLDSMITH, A. J. and SHEPTYCKI, J. W. E. (2007), *Crafting Transnational Policing: Police Capacity-Building and Global Policing Reform*, Oxford. Hart.

GOTTSCHALK, M. (2006), *The Prison and the Gallows: The Politics of Mass Incarceration in America*, Cambridge: Cambridge University Press.

GRABOSKY, P. N. and STOHL, M. (2010), *Crime and Terrorism*, London: Sage.

GUNDHUS, H. I. and FRANKO, K. (2016), 'Global policing and mobility: Identity, territory, sovereignty', in B. Bradford, B. Jauregui, I. Loader, and J. Steinberg (eds), *The Sage Handbook of Global Policing*, London: Sage.

HAGAN, J. and RYMOND-RICHMOND, W. (2009), *Darfur and the Crime of Genocide*, Cambridge: Cambridge University Press.

HANSEN, T. B. and STEPPUTAT, F. (2006), 'Sovereignty Revisited', in *Annual Review of Anthropology*, 35: 295–315.

HARCOURT, B. E. (2011), *The Illusion of Free Markets: Punishment and the Myth of Natural Order*, Cambridge, MA: Harvard University Press.

HARVEY, D. (2000), 'Cosmopolitanism and the Banality of Geographical Evils', *Public Culture*, 12(2): 529–64.

HELD, D. (2010), *Cosmopolitanism: Ideals and Realities*, Cambridge: Polity.

HOBBS, D. (2013), *Lush Life: Constructing Organized Crime in the UK*, Oxford: Oxford University Press.

HOOD, R. and HOYLE, C. (2008), *The Death Penalty: A World-Wide Perspective*, Oxford: Oxford University Press.

HURRELL, A. (2007), *On Global Order: Power, Values, and the Constitution of International Society*, Oxford: Oxford University Press.

INSTITUTE FOR ECONOMICS AND PEACE (2015a), *Global Peace Index 2015: Measuring peace, its causes and its economic value*, available at: http://economicsandpeace.org/wp-content/uploads/2015/06/Global-Peace-Index-Report-2015_0.pdf, accessed 18 December 2016.

INSTITUTE FOR ECONOMICS AND PEACE (2015b), *Global Terrorism Index 2015*; available at: http://economicsandpeace.org/wp-content/uploads/2015/11/Global-Terrorism-Index-2015.pdf, accessed 19 January 2017.

JAKOBI, A. (2013), *Common Goods and Evils? The Formation of Global Crime Governance*, Oxford: Oxford University Press.

KALMO, H. and Q. SKINNER (2010), 'Introduction: a concept in fragments', in H. Kalmo and Q. Skinner (eds), *Sovereignty in Fragments: The Past, Present and Future of a Contested Concept*, Cambridge and New York: Cambridge University Press.

KAUFMAN, E. (2015), *Punish and Expel: Border Control, Nationalism, and the New Purpose of the Prison*, Oxford: Oxford University Press.

KENWAY, J. and FAHEY, J. (eds) (2009), *Globalising the Research Imagination*, Abingdon: Routledge.

KNEPPER, P. (2010), *The Invention of International Crime: A Global Issue in the Making, 1881-1914*, Basingstoke: Palgrave Macmillan.

KNEPPER, P. (2011), *International Crime in the 20th Century: The League of Nations Era, 1919-1939*, London: Palgrave MacMillan.

LACEY, N. (2008), *The Prisoners' Dilemma: Political Economy and Punishment in Contemporary Democracies*, Cambridge: Cambridge University Press.

LOADER, I. and WALKER, N. (2007), *Civilizing Security*, Cambridge: Cambridge University Press.

LOADER, I. and PERCY, S. (2012), 'Bringing the "Outside" In and the "Inside" Out: Crossing the Criminology/IR Divide', *Global Crime*, 13(4): 213–18.

LOHNE, K. (forthcoming) *Advocates of Humanity: Human Rights NGOs and International Criminal Justice*, Oxford: Oxford University Press.

MCGREW, A. and HELD, D. (2007), *Globalization Theory: Approaches and Controversies*, Cambridge: Polity.

MELOSSI, D. (2015), *Crime, Punishment and Migration*, London: Sage.

MENKHAUS, K. (2010), 'None-State Actors and the Role of Violence in Stateless Somalia', in K. Mulaj, *Violent Non-state Actors in World Politics*, London: Hurst.

MIKLAUCIC, M. and J. BREWER (eds) (2013), *Convergence: Illicit Networks and National Security in the Age of Globalization*, National Defense University Press, Washington, DC.

MILLER, L. (2015), 'What's violence got to do with it? Inequality, punishment, and state failure in US politics', *Punishment & Society*, 17(2): 184–210.

MILLER, L. (2016), *The Myth of Mob Rule: Violent Crime and Democratic Politics*, New York: Oxford University Press.

MITSILEGAS, V. (2009), *EU Criminal Law*, Oxford: Hart.

MORRISON, W. (2006), *Criminology, Civilisation and the New World Order: Rethinking Criminology in a Global Context*, London: Glasshouse Press.

MORSELI C. (2009), *Inside Criminal Networks*, New York: Springer.

MULAJ, K. (2010), *Violent Non-state Actors in World Politics*, London: Hurst.

MÜLLER, M.-M. (2012), *Public Security in the Negotiated State*, Houndsmills: Palgrave MacMillan.

NELKEN, D. (2011), *Comparative Criminal Justice and Globalization*, Farnham: Ashgate.

NORDSTROM, C. (2000), 'Shadows and sovereigns', *Theory Culture & Society*, 17(4): 35–54.

PAKES, F. (ed.) (2012), *Globalisation and the Challenge to Criminology*, London: Routledge.

PRATT, J. and ERIKSSON, A. (2013), *Contrasts in Punishment: An Explanation of Anglophone Excess and Nordic Exceptionalism*, London: Routledge.

PICARD, J. (2013), 'Can we estimate the global scale and impact of illicit trade?', in J. Pratt and A. Eriksson, *Contrasts in Punishment: An Explanation of Anglophone Excess and Nordic Exceptionalism*, London: Routledge.

RICHANI, N. (2010), *Fragmentation of Sovereignty and Violent Non-State Actors in Colombia*, London: C. Hurst & Co.

RYAN, B. and MITSILEGAS, V. (2010), *Extraterritorial Immigration Control: Legal Challenges*, Leiden: Nijhoff.

SALTER, M. (2015), *Making Things International 1: Circuits and Motion*, Minneapolis: University of Minnesota Press.

SARAT, A. and J. CULBERT (2009), *States of Violence War, Capital Punishment, and Letting Die*, New York: Cambridge University Press.

SASSEN, S. (2006), *Territory, Authority, Rights: From Medieval to Global Assemblages*, updated edn, Princeton and Oxford: Princeton University Press.

SASSEN, S. (2007), *A Sociology of Globalization*, New York and London: W. W. Norton & Company.

SAVELSBERG, J. J. (2010), *Crime and Human Rights*, London: Sage.

SCHABAS, W. A. (2011), 'Criminology, Accountability, and International justice', in M. Bosworth and C. Hoyle (eds), *What is Criminology?*, Oxford: Oxford University Press.

SHELLEY, L. (2014), *Dirty Entanglements: Corruption, Crime, and Terrorism*, New York: Cambridge University Press.

SLAUGHTER, A-M (2004), 'Sovereignty and power in a Networked World Order', *Stanford Journal of International Law*, 40(2): 283–327.

STRANDSBJERG, J. (2010), *Territory, Globalization and International Relations: The Cartographic Reality of Space*, Basingstoke: Palgrave Macmillan.

TOWNSLEY, M., LECLERC, B., and TATHAM, P. H. (2016), 'How super controllers prevent crimes: learning from modern maritime piracy', *British Journal of Criminology*, 56: 537–57.

TSING, A. L. (2005), *Friction: An Ethnography of Global Connection*, Princeton and Oxford: Princeton University Press.

UGELVIK, T. (2013), 'Seeing like a Welfare State: Immigration Control, Statecraft, and a Prison with Double Vision', in K. Franko Aas and M. Bosworth (eds), *The Borders of Punishment: Migration, Citizenship, and Social Exclusion*, Oxford: Oxford University Press.

VAN ZYL SMIT, D. and SNACKEN, S. (2009), *Principles of European Prison Law and Policy: Penology and Human Rights*, Oxford: Oxford University Press.

VARESE, F. (2011), *Mafias on the Move: How Organized Crime Conquers New Territories*, Princeton: Princeton University Press.

Wacquant, L. (2009), *Punishing the Poor: the Neoliberal Government of Social Insecurity*, Durham: Duke University Press.

Wacquant, L. (2010), 'Crafting the Neoliberal State: Workfare, Prisonfare, and Social Insecurity', *Sociological Forum*, 25(2): 197–220.

Wall, T. and Monahan, T. (2011), 'Surveillance and violence from afar: The politics of drones and liminal security-scapes', *Theoretical Criminology*, 15(3): 239–54.

Weber L. and Pickering, S. (2011), *Globalization and Borders: Death at the Global Frontier*, Basingtoke: Palgrave Macmillan.

Weber, L. (2013), *Policing Non-citizens*, Abingdon and New York: Routledge.

White, R. (ed.) (2009), *Environmental Crime: A Reader*, Cullompton: Willan.

White, R. (ed.) (2011), *Transnational Environment and Crime*, New York: Routledge.

White, R. (2012), 'The Foundations of Eco-global Criminology', in R. Ellefsen, R. Sollund, and G. Larsen (eds), *Eco-global Crimes: Contemporary Problems and Future Challenges*, Burlington: Ashgate.

Willis, G. D. (2015), *The Killing Consensus: Police, Organized Crime, and the Regulation of Life and Death in Urban Brazil*, Oakland, California: The University of California Press.

■ CHAPTER ACKNOWLEDGEMENTS

I am very grateful to Helene O. I. Gundhus, David Rodriguez-Goyes, and to the editors for their help in developing the arguments in this chapter. This work was supported by European Research Council Starting Grant (StG 2010).

16

BORDER CRIMINOLOGY AND THE CHANGING NATURE OF PENAL POWER

Mary Bosworth

INTRODUCTION

This chapter describes the new field of 'border criminology'[1] that examines the growing convergence between criminal justice and immigration control. Building on existing scholarship about criminal law, policing, courts, and punishment, border criminologists focus on how states around the world have put the criminal justice system to work in managing mass mobility. In their discussions of legal changes that criminalize immigration violations, new policing responsibilities at the border and within, and the changing numbers and treatment of foreign nationals in prison, border criminologists reveal how the criminal justice system has been systematically reoriented around matters of citizenship (Bosworth 2016b; Aliverti 2013; Stumpf 2006; Kaufman 2015; Kaufman and Bosworth 2014). At the same time, their research makes clear that familiar problems remain. The primary targets of intervention in border control and the criminal justice system are economically precarious (De Giorgi 2010), racialized, ethnic minority men (Philips and Bowling 2003). New criminal justice powers and responsibilities have not, in other words, entirely replaced older tasks and justifications, but rather intersect, inform, and are shaped by them.

This chapter starts with an overview of the global immigration context, before outlining key ideas and areas of scholarship within border criminology. It then turns to look more closely at penal power, drawing on fieldwork and policy analysis to explore the methodological and epistemological implications for criminology of examining citizenship and migration. It ends by arguing for greater engagement with the challenges and effects of mass mobility. As the impact of a decision to arrest in any street

[1] Often referred to in a plural form as 'border criminologies' (see, e.g., Canning 2016), this field is also sometimes known as 'the criminology of mobility' (Pickering, Bosworth, and Aas 2015).

in Britain may be felt in countries far away, it is time for criminologists to take into account more explicitly the global nature of criminal justice and reflect on its implications for how and what we study.

IMMIGRATION AND CRIMINAL JUSTICE: THE CONTEXT

An unprecedented number of people are on the move, worldwide. Figures released by the United Nations Refugee Agency, UNHRC, in 2015 reported that globally, one in every 122 people was either a refugee, internally displaced, or seeking asylum. There were 59.5 million men, women, and children displaced by the end of 2014, one third of whom (19.5) were refugees (UNHCR 2015). In addition to these people, who have been compelled to relocate either within their country or abroad due to conflict and persecution, a far larger sum emigrate for education, work, and family reunification. Within this second group, the International Organisation of Migration (IOM) counted 'an estimated 232 million international migrants' about half of whom 'reside in ten highly urbanized, high-income countries': Australia, Canada, the United States, France, Germany, Spain, the United Kingdom, the Russian Federation, Saudi Arabia, and the United Arab Emirates (IOM 2015: 2). Most are ethnic minorities from the global south.

While the sum of migrants and refugees has been growing for years, matters leaped into public consciousness in the summer of 2015 when significant numbers of Syrians, fleeing the conflict in their homeland, made their way to Europe in search of refuge. Driven out by civil war, these people have been met with varying degrees of hostility and confusion. Notwithstanding some important exceptions in Germany, Austria, and Sweden, European Union (EU) member states have been reluctant to offer them sanctuary. Disagreements about burden sharing and administrative law, in addition to significant financial uncertainty in the region during an extended period of recession and austerity have strained diplomatic relations, almost to breaking point.

Mass migration has altered more than international agreements. It has also shaped national and local laws and practices. Criminal justice has not been immune to these developments. Many jurisdictions have created a host of new criminal offences for immigration violations (Aliverti 2013; Stumpf 2006). The police have, likewise, acquired additional roles and responsibilities in determining the nationality of criminal suspects and enforcing immigration law within the border and beyond (Aliverti 2015; Eagly 2013; Weber 2013; Weber and Bowling 2004). Immigration officers are now present in prisons in many jurisdictions to identify foreigners and facilitate their deportation (Kaufman 2015; Kaufman and Weiss 2015; Ugelvik 2012). Adjacent to such institutions, new carceral spaces have sprung up in which former offenders are often placed to facilitate their identification and expulsion (Bosworth 2014; Ugelvik and Ugelvik 2013; Fili 2013).

Such developments are widespread. In the United States, for instance, immigration-related prosecutions currently outnumber all other federal criminal prosecutions, including those for drugs and weapons, while Immigration and Customs Enforcement is now the largest investigative arm of the US Department of Homeland Security (Chacón 2012; Eagly 2013; Light *et al.* 2014). In Europe, national and transnational police forces routinely intercept irregular migrants at the border and within national territory (Mutsaers 2014; Aas and Gundhus 2015). Across the continent, rapidly growing foreign populations represent on average 20 per cent of all prison inmates, reaching extraordinary highs in counties such as Switzerland (71.4 per cent), Luxembourg (68.8 per cent), Cyprus (58.9 per cent), Greece (57.1 per cent), and Belgium (44.2 per cent).[2] Countries everywhere have criminalized at least some aspects of immigration, making it harder for people to arrive legally and remain. They have also established networks of immigration detention centres in country and offshore, while extending their powers to deport (Flynn 2014; Wong 2015; Hasselberg 2016; Bosworth 2011).

As more foreigners end up in prison and as states vigorously pursue additional forms of confinement and deportation, the distinct justifications of punishment and administrative penalties have blurred (Aas and Bosworth 2013; Stumpf 2013). Under these circumstances, it is time to ask whether criminological explanatory concepts, terminology, and methods work. What about the secondary literature on which we draw? Are our traditional analytical strategies fit for purpose, or must new approaches be forged to understand these developments? These questions animate this chapter and much of the wider field of border criminology.

CITIZENSHIP, SOVEREIGN POWER, AND CRIMINAL JUSTICE

With a few notable exceptions, criminologists have not been particularly interested in matters of citizenship. In large part, their indifference stems from the fact that criminal justice is usually meted out within one jurisdiction bounded by the nation state (Aas 2007). Like the laws and practices criminologists examine, the traditional framework of analysis in our discipline has been territorial (although see Nelken (2010)). More critically, given that most of those subject to border control are from the global south, the lack of engagement with citizenship has been exacerbated by a related disinterest in race and ethnicity (Bowling 2013; Parmar 2016).

Yet, it would be an overstatement to claim that all accounts of criminal justice fail to examine citizenship, or that none take a comparative or transnational approach (Bowling and Sheptycki 2012). Indeed, a concern with foreigners dates to the first criminological studies produced by the Chicago School sociologists. For these scholars, migrants were distinctive in the ways in which they were bound to their earlier cultures and mores, yet anxious to integrate and succeed in their new homeland. New arrivals created separate communities within the city, some of which, these early sociologists argued, were more prone to social disorganization (Shaw and McKay 1942).

[2] See http://www.prisonstudies.org/info/worldbrief/, accessed 31 December 2016. See also Ugelvik (2015) and Bosworth, Hasselberg, and Turnbull (2016a).

Once individuals and groups integrated, they usually moved on. Some never left (Wirth 1928).

From these ethnographic origins, a more quantitative tradition in US criminology developed, focusing on the criminal activities of immigrant populations and their descendants (Tonry 1996; Bucerius and Tonry 2014). In this body of work, authors provide statistical evidence of lower crime rates among the foreign born (Mears 2011). They also examine connections in the policing of migrant and ethnic minority citizen communities (Hagan and Palloni 1999; Tonry 1996).

So, too, a large body of transnational and comparative criminology can be found. In the field of prison studies, in particular, international comparisons of prison populations (Cavadino and Dignan 2005) and penal practices (Pratt and Eriksson 2014) have generated important insights about local practices, while in the policing literature studies of transnational practices and global policing have shown significant interconnections between countries in their pursuit of security (Bowling 2010; Bowling and Sheptycki 2012; Bradford *et al.* 2016). Comparative legal scholarship (Nelken 2010; Van Zyl Smit and Snacken 2009) has likewise been a fertile and illuminating area of analysis.

Border criminology engages with and owes much to these areas of scholarship. It also diverges from them. In contrast to the predominantly quantitative US literature on migration, for example, border criminology is more usually qualitative, theoretically engaged, and interdisciplinary. While sharing a number of methodological and intellectual roots with the transnational and comparative literature, its focus on the intersections between criminal justice and migration control leads to different topics and techniques of analysis. Authors in this field explore the constitutive relationship between borders, migration control, and criminal justice. They concentrate on how and why certain activities like human smuggling (Sanchez 2014), sex work (Pickering and Ham 2014), or document fraud (Aliverti 2015), have been criminalized, while exploring fresh forms of coercive state power (Bosworth 2014; Aas 2014; Barker 2011, 2016a). Most draw on concepts from a range of disciplines including feminist theory, refugee and immigration studies, postcolonial studies, human rights, immigration and refugee law, politics and international relations.

Since the terrorist attacks on New York City and Washington, DC in September 2001, migration has been conceptualized in much government policy and legislation as a potential security threat. This approach has meant that asylum and labour migration have been recast as possible 'routes in' for foreign terrorists, firmly embedding them in discussions of and policies about national security (Bigo 2006; Bosworth and Guild 2008; HM Government 2015). In making sense of these developments, border criminologists draw on literature and ideas from the sociology of punishment and security studies (Pickering, Bosworth, and Aas 2015). Work by Foucault on governmentality (1991) and biopolitics (2004), Bauman on modernity (2001) as well as Agamben's (2004) notion of the 'state of exception' have been particularly influential (see, e.g., Aas 2007, 2013; Eriksson 2016). Elsewhere, Ahmed's account of 'the stranger' (2000), and Butler's (2004) consideration of why some people are considered 'grievable' while others are not, have been used to illuminate aspects of current policy and public attitudes (Bosworth 2014).

Finally, in recognition of the racialized nature of most border controls (Bhui 2016), border criminologists increasingly integrate issues of race and ethnicity in their analysis, although, as critics observe (Garner 2015), more needs to be done (see, *inter alia*, Bowling 2013; Sanchez 2014; Bosworth and Kellezi 2013a). Most of those subject to border controls are from the global south. Many are from former colonies of the country they seek to enter. Under these conditions, Hall's (2001) notion of colonial amnesia and Gilroy's (2002, 2006) study of Empire have been particularly productive (Kaufman 2015; Bowling 2013). More descriptively, considerable efforts have been made to document the racially disproportionate impact of legislation (Vazquez 2011; Chacón 2012) and penal practice (Mehta 2016; Kaufman 2015; Bhui 2016; Hernandez 2012).

In deploying this conceptual literature, border criminologists revisit the relationship between state sovereignty and criminal justice (Garland 1996; Simon 2007). It is not just crime that the sovereign state cannot fully control, authors in this subfield point out, but also mobility (Bosworth 2008; Aas 2007; Barker 2016b). While nations strive to limit their obligations to resources, security, and justice, citizenship offers a flexible new means of allocation. As Barker succinctly puts it, in this global, mobile world, 'membership matters most' (Barker 2013b; Aas 2014).

Under these circumstances it is unsurprising to find that foreigners no longer receive the same treatment as citizens in the criminal justice system. From policing to imprisonment, the emphasis on immigration status has affected all parts of the criminal justice system. These days, in many countries, police may hold foreigners not for criminal activity, but for immigration violations (Weber 2013; Aliverti 2015). This same logic propels the police across their territorial border, to other zones altogether, to prevent irregular entry of the foreign born—even those who seek to make humanitarian claims for protection (Aas and Gundhus 2015; Bowling 2010). In the courts, too, nationality is becoming ever more pertinent as judges and magistrates may add a deportation order to a criminal sentence (Aliverti 2016; Eagly 2013; Stumpf 2013). Though the numbers remain small in England and Wales at least, foreigners face conviction for a range of immigration offences, that by definition, citizens do not. At the most extreme end, and thus in smaller numbers still, a handful of individuals found guilty of terrorist-related offences may lose their citizenship altogether, even, in the UK, if they do not hold another (Zedner 2016).

In all these ways, practices and notions of justice and due process as well as ideas about punishment have been trumped by identity, identification, and belonging (Zedner 2010; Stumpf 2013; Eagly 2013). Over the next sections, I will map out these developments in the field of incarceration, demonstrating how national prisons have changed (Kaufman 2015) while novel forms of incarceration in immigration detention centres (Bosworth 2014) and exclusionary practices of deportation have expanded (Kanstroom 2012; Golash-Boza 2015; Barker 2016a). As I will show, such places and practices are characterized by high levels of uncertainty as well as racial disproportionality. The state is both present and absent, working with and through the private sector, NGOs, international agencies, other governments and, sometimes, different arms of itself.

MASS MIGRATION AND PENAL POWER

PRISONS

Currently there are 9,300 foreign nationals serving prison sentences in England and Wales (HMIP 2015: 3). Accounting for 11 per cent of the total incarcerated population, this sum has recently stabilized after expanding rapidly in the first decade of the twenty-first century. Until 2006, foreign offenders rarely figured in public debates about crime or punishment. Yet, that year, following extensive coverage in the British tabloid press, then Home Secretary Charles Clark lost his job when it was discovered that, over the previous decade, 1,000 foreign prisoners had not been considered for deportation, but simply released into the British community.

Despite this relatively small sum number, public and media outcry was shrill. Foreign offenders, they claimed, posed significant threats to public safety. They were difficult to locate in the wider community of migrant residents. Why were they still in Britain?

In the media coverage and subsequent political debates, familiar, racialized concerns over young men of colour merged seamlessly with narratives about terrorism and radicalization, both upheld by enduring fears about economic migration. In so doing, both were subtly altered, as groups previously not marked out as targets of criminal justice, like young Asian men, became recast as potential terror suspects or 'illegal immigrants' and thus appropriate targets of stop and search and incarceration (Parmar 2010, 2016).

Legislatively, the response to the prisons crisis was swift and decisive. The UK Borders Act 2007 mandated deportation for all offenders from outside the European Economic Area (EEA) who had been sentenced to 12 months (or whose sentences over the previous five years add up to this total) unless there were human rights protections. EEA offenders face the same outcome for sentences of (or adding up to) 24 months. For those already incarcerated, the experience of prison also began to change. Perceived as an escape threat, foreign offenders now face considerable barriers to open conditions. Destined for deportation, they may be excluded from certain prison programs as limited resources are not to be wasted on those who will not remain (Bosworth 2007; Bhui 2007; Kaufman 2015; Warr 2016). Some are gathered together in foreign national only establishments, where they are offered a distinct regime designed to prepare them for return (Bosworth, Hasselberg, and Turnbull 2016a).[3] Finally, alongside such local initiatives, the British government, like others elsewhere, has actively pursued voluntary and mandatory prisoner transfer agreements offering a variety of incentives in assisted voluntary returns schemes and sentence reductions (Home Office 2016b; Van Zyl Smit and Mulgrew 2012).

In all these developments, prisons have been fundamentally altered (Kaufman 2015). Penal establishments in England and Wales must now determine the citizenship of each new arrival. Unless prisoners arrive with a passport, such matters are not always straightforward. As a result, prison officers rely on dubious , racialized markers, including accent and appearance to generate a list for the immigration authorities, whose task is then to determine whether or not to apply a deportation order.

[3] Other countries have created similar establishments (on Norway, see Ugelvik (2012); on the USA, Kaufman and Weiss (2015)).

Several studies have documented how prison life for foreign national prisoners diverges from that of citizen prisoners. Some matters, like communication, maintaining family contact and cultural practices, are longstanding (Bhui 2007). Yet others are more recent, shaped by the new insistence on deportation. For most foreign offenders, even those without a mandatory deportation order, prison life is far more unsettled and uncertain, since they simply cannot be sure what will happen at the end of their time behind bars (Kaufman 2012; Phillips 2012; Boe 2016; Warr 2016; Hasselberg 2016).

Notwithstanding the government's desire to move from prison to plane, for an increasing number of men and women, a period of imprisonment is followed by time in an immigration detention facility. Yet, despite these clear ties to the prison, immigration detention centres have received scant criminological attention as they officially sit outside the criminal justice system (Bosworth 2014; Aas and Bosworth 2013; Ugelvik and Ugelvik 2013; Fili 2013). In the following section, I describe these administrative sites and explore their implications for criminological understanding of penal power. I also consider the methodological challenges they present.

IMMIGRATION DETENTION

Britain, like most countries, has long had the power to detain foreign nationals under immigration act powers. Whereas many nations detain those who arrive without legal documents (Guild 2006), in the UK, detention is primarily used at the end of a person's migration, as a means to expedite expulsion.[4] In this task the state is only minimally successful, with statistics revealing that only half the detained population are forced to go (Home Office 2016a).

At the time of writing, the British system houses 3,500 men and women, across nine establishments. Most originate from former British colonies or from places of current or recent conflict. In 2015, the five most common nationality groups were India, Pakistan, Bangladesh, Nigeria, and Albania (Gower 2015). Just under half the population had claimed asylum at some point (Home Office 2016a).

These ties to the Commonwealth date to the 1969 Immigration Appeals Act, which ushered in the contemporary immigration system including the first purpose built immigration detention unit at Harmondsworth in 1970 (Bosworth 2014). Though at the time heralded as a liberal response to the duties Britain owed to its former subjects (Bosworth 2014), its racialized effects on the immigration system attract today considerable critique from detainees (and some staff).'When the British went around the world', Jonas[5] exclaimed, 'they did not apply for visas or residents permits. They just went in and took what they wanted . . . This is modern slavery', he concluded, angrily. (Uganda, IRC Tinsley House, cited in Bosworth 2014: 105).

In most other respects, the contemporary immigration detention estate owes much to the new millennium, when the New Labour governments of Blair and Brown passed numerous pieces of legislation about immigration and asylum that significantly

[4] Until a successful legal challenge in 2015, certain asylum seekers in the UK could also be held under a 'fast track' scheme if their case was pre-determined as unlikely to succeed. At the time of writing this system has been suspended and its replacement is under review.

[5] Not his real name. Participants have been allocated pseudonyms.

expanded the population subject to detention and deportation. As the previous Conservative government had with prisons, so, too, Labour relied on the private sector to build and open new detention sites quickly. Each centre is run under contract for the Home Office by a range of private custodial firms (currently G4S, Mitie, Serco, and GEO) or HM Prison Service.[6]

In 2001, British detention centres were renamed 'immigration removal centres' (IRCs), to more clearly signify their intent. Notwithstanding this promise of a brief stay, however, nearly all facilities opened since that date have been built to Category B high security prison design or have been situated in former penal establishments run as IRCs under contract by HM Prison Service. These are secure institutions. They are all located behind razor wire, with considerable interior surveillance (closed circuit television) and security (drug dogs, patrols, room searches, surveillance, and so on). Detainee Custody Officers (DCOs) within them wear uniforms and carry keys. Senior staff who run them have all worked in the prison service.

The implications of these matters are hard to avoid. Detainees and staff often feel they are held or work within a prison. These are not sites of removal, such views imply, but of punishment.

Many are worried about the similarities between the two institutions. 'They shouldn't lock the door on us', Innocent exclaimed. 'We're not prisoners!' (Rwanda, IRC Colnbrook). Officers are usually more ambivalent in their assessment (Bosworth 2016a). While some believe IRCs should be run more like prisons, others are less sure. 'I don't think personally that anyone detained should have to live in wings', Alisa stated, 'because they've only broke the law of paperwork haven't they really?' (DCO, IRC Tinsley House).

Some detainees are glad of the differences between IRCs and prisons. For them, access to a mobile phone and the internet, along with regular visits, and more time out of their locked rooms, mitigate their experience of custody. Many, like Innocent, are keen to mark out their non-criminal status. Most, however, interpret their confinement with reference to the prison. Without it, detention makes little sense. From those arrested at work, to others who had been signing on at the Home Office, the lament is the same: 'This place is worse than prison', Ala complained (Kashmir, IRC Yarl's Wood).

For Ala, the problems inhere in the building and regime. 'There is nothing to do', she moaned. 'This place needs more relaxing, how the building is designed, living room, living rooms look like waiting rooms. Don't feel comfy and cosy, just cold' (Kashmir, IRC Yarl's Wood). For Giv, however, who had served a four-year custodial sentence, the distinction between the two establishments and the reason why IRCs were worse, sprang from its unclear purpose. 'Some privileges like mobile, like visits, things like that, you get more, you know. Okay, that's okay', he acknowledged. 'But . . . the mentality in the prison, you set your time up. Is routine there, regime is there, . . . Is routine there, is law working there and you have to respect the law. Either officer or prisoner have to

[6] Globally the use of the private sector varies. In Australia, for instance, all the sites of detention are contracted out to one company (currently Serco). The US, like the UK, relies on a range of companies, as well as state, local, and federal corrections. Many other countries, however, eschew the private sector altogether, with nearly all EU member states staffing their detention sites with border police instead (Bosworth and Vannier 2016).

respect that law. Is routine there. Okay, they all banged up, that's why you a prisoner because, you know, so that's something you get on with it, you know. And, but here first of all, you think is why I'm locked up—detention, why?' (Iran, IRC Colnbrook). For most people, confinement for immigration matters is hard to understand.

It is not just detainees who wonder about the purpose of detention. Officers are often confounded about the institution in which they work (Bosworth 2016a; Bosworth and Slade 2014). They, too, search around for alternative non-penal explanations of their job yet rarely settle on anything particularly consistent or persuasive. Some characterize their jobs in caring terms, suggesting they are social workers, or even a medical professional. 'I'm here to look after their welfare', Azima asserted, 'just like doctors are there to save people's lives, in a different way' (Detainee Custody Officer, IRC Harmondsworth). For Joyce, the appropriate comparison is a boarding school: 'To me, you know, there's people held here. They're learning stuff. They've come from all different backgrounds. You're kind of thrown together like you would be in a school, with people you might get on with, you might not get on with' (Detainee Custody Manager, IRC Colnbrook).

At the same time, most staff recognize the impact of the built environment and the institutional policies. In a lengthy reflection on the relationship between the two kinds of institutions, Saul begins by denying the similarities. 'I'm not a Prison Officer', he baldly asserts, 'cos the guys that we look after are not prisoners, they are detainees and there is a difference'. A few moments later in the conversation, however, he changes tack. 'Lets not beat around the bush here', he admits, 'You've got metal fencing with razor wire, you've got bars at the window, you've got locks, bolts on doors, okay, so yes, it is theoretically, a prison environment' (Detainee Custody Officer, IRC Harmondsworth). Mishal, at IRC Colnbrook next door, agrees. 'I think it is prison', she acknowledges, 'in a sense. Because everything else is exactly like prison apart from the fact that they can keep their phone and have their visits all the time' (Detainee Custody Manager, IRC Colnbrook).

Legally, of course, IRCs are not prisons. Most of those detained have not been found guilty of a criminal offence. Nobody is (still) serving a sentence, although some of those with criminal convictions may be on parole.[7] Notwithstanding their punitive effect, these are not sites of punishment in the law (Bosworth, Hasselberg, and Turnbull 2016b).

For staff, such contradictions raise ethical and practical questions. Many are uncomfortable with the lack of judicial oversight. Few support a totally open-ended period of confinement. Such concerns, it is important to note, are not necessarily driven by moral concerns or philosophical values. They are often animated by more pragmatic factors. It is difficult to work in institutions that look and feel like prisons without the rules, regulations, coercive powers, and thus legitimacy, of formal punishment (Bosworth 2013; Sparks, Bottoms, and Hay 1996). 'Although it looks like a prison', Mishal pointed out, 'it's not run like a prison. We don't have the power that prison officers have. So we have to really, really work hard with our interpersonal skills to keep the place safe and

[7] Precise statistics are difficult to obtain. According to the most recently available ones set out in the 2016 *Review into the welfare in detention of vulnerable persons*, 1,050 out of 3,532 women and men in detention in March 2015 had been referred by the police under Operation Nexus or by the Criminal Case Directorate (Shaw 2016: 34–5). While not all of the former will have been convicted of a crime, those in the latter category would have been.

calm and it just takes a few members of staff to rock that and cause a mess for the rest of us' (Detainee Custody Manager, IRC Colnbrook).

For detainees, issues are more personal and, consequently, more painful. The system of administrative law offers them far fewer protections and detainees have little agency over their treatment. Many will not have been to court and thus will have had no opportunity to communicate his or her side of the story. While a deportation order may be handed down as part of a criminal sentence, the decision to detain is an administrative one. Unless a detainee applies for bail to an immigration tribunal, the grounds for his or her confinement may never be subject to judicial oversight.[8] Instead, immigration caseworkers in offices around the country make decisions based on files and paperwork (HMIP and ICIBI 2012).

Most women and men are not detained for long; two-thirds are removed, deported, or released within 28 days. Yet, for the remaining third, the duration of confinement varies widely because, in contrast to the rest of Europe, there is no statutory upper limit to the period of detention in the UK (Bosworth and Vannier 2016; APPG 2015). A small number in each IRC will have been held for over a year. Some appear to be stuck (Turnbull 2016). In 2016, HM Inspector of Prisons (2016) found one man who had been detained for five years in IRC Harmondsworth.

All these aspects of detention differentiate it from penal confinement. Yet, IRCs remain associated with the prison by those within and outside (Leerkes and Broeders 2010). As a result, considering them through the lens of prison sociology can be illuminating. To the extent that there are some similarities with experiences in the high-security prison estate (Liebling *et al.* 2012), IRCs have wider relevance for thinking about penal power more broadly.

At the same time, however, the exercise of administrative power demands its own framework of analysis (Bosworth 2016c). It is far easier to deprive people of their liberty on the basis of citizenship, than for a criminal offence. This aspect alone has profound implications for how we might judge the purpose and nature of these sites. As I have written elsewhere, questions of legitimacy, used so effectively to critique imprisonment, have little traction or application to this method of confinement (Bosworth 2013).

IRCs defy easy explanation. In an era of austerity they are expensive. Although designed to encourage removal, they are not particularly effective in getting people to go. While many support them, particularly those who would reduce net migration to the UK, IRCs also attract considerable criticism (AAPG 2015; Shaw 2016). Their inefficiency in managerialist terms, their economic cost, and their impact on human rights, attracts ongoing critique. Nonetheless states around the world remain committed to this form of border control.

The contested and unclear nature of IRCs affects the research field. The politicized nature of confinement for immigration purposes means that the state and the private companies guard research access to them jealously. Such strictures shape the kind of evidence available. Most of what is published about detention is produced by NGOs (Phelps 2009), and government agencies (HMIP 2016), or gleaned from interviews

[8] In May 2016, the Immigration Bill 2016 passed through various amendments, introducing mandatory judicial oversight after four months of detention.

conducted with former detainees or over the phone (Griffiths 2014). A considerable amount of work is conducted surreptitiously in visit halls. Institutional ethnographies, the mainstay of much prisons research, are rare (Hall 2012; Bosworth 2014). At the time of writing I remain the only academic in the UK with permission to conduct research freely in the centres, a position I have held since 2009.

Gaining formal access is only the start of the challenge. Once inside, detention centres are particularly complex. First, there are multiple layers of governance with conflicting goals and responsibilities. Although run by private custodial companies, the state is not totally absent. IRCs house onsite immigration agents from the Home Office whose job is to pass information between detainees and offsite case workers, while monitoring the contract with the company. Since 2014 the NHS has managed healthcare in detention, by contracting it out, rather than providing it. Before then healthcare was delivered by the custodial company. IRCs, like prisons, are inspected by the Prison Inspectorate (HMIP 2016) and monitored by local Independent Monitoring Board (IMB) teams. They are also each serviced by a local support group, who offer social visits to those within.

In all these figures as well as in the person of the detainee, IRCs draw together otherwise distinct legal frameworks of refugee law, immigration law, and criminal law, and, for those detainees with children, family law as well. Making sense of this range of roles and responsibilities, not to mention the relationships between these different systems and their impact is difficult. Power flows in many directions, not all of it directed towards expulsion.

Conducting research with detainees poses distinct challenges. Most obviously, although most of those confined speak some English, few are totally fluent. Criminologists, however, are often monolingual; language instruction is not part of our postgraduate training. The sheer cultural, religious, and ethnic diversity of this population can also be confusing. Spending time in an IRC requires a quick study of geography and world religions. Once again, such matters are usually absent from the criminology curriculum, and from most publications.

The temporal uncertainty of detention further compounds matters. Most detainees are profoundly anxious and depressed (Bosworth and Kellezi 2013b). 'What we doing here?' Ayesha cried out one day. 'I'm just eating and sleeping and just thinking: "What happen next, what happen next?"' (Pakistan, IRC Yarl's Wood). Research with people in pain has to proceed carefully. Communication difficulties hamper attempts to garner trust, to soothe or comfort, as well as understanding (Bosworth and Kellezi 2016).

More practically, those who have agreed to be interviewed may be suddenly removed, released, or transferred, making interviews difficult to plan. A fieldnote from May 2011 illustrates the point: After driving 90 minutes to IRC Brook House, parking, being searched, and then walking over to the legal corridor, I note in an exasperated tone, 'my first interviewee did not show up. UKBA [the Home Office] transferred him yesterday to Tinsley House. You might have thought they would have known that earlier on, i.e. yesterday, when these arrangements were made' (Fieldnotes, IRC Brook House, 10 May 2011). Sampling is shaped by this temporal uncertainty. So too, is the nature of the testimonies. Gathered in haste, across a language divide, stories are often fragmented.

Detainees are not alone in the uncertainty they face. Long-term prisoners experience some of the same factors. They also find it hard to make plans, and are likely to feel hopeless, anxious, and depressed (Liebling 2014). However, the nature and ubiquity of the uncertainty of detention is distinct. Its duration and various outcomes are impossible to predict. Will they be deported or removed? What about release? If they are bailed or offered temporary admission, how long before the state seeks to remove them again?

Migration control reaches into the future as well as the past, erasing people's aspirations, while also, by insisting people leave the country, negating their previous experiences. Time spent in the UK, children, work-experience, tax, all of it is deemed insufficient justification to remain. 'My whole life is going to erase', Tahir notes sadly, 'Just imagine that! You know when you erase old numbers from your mobile phone? Just imagine if your whole life was erased just like that?' (Sudan, IRC Campsfield House) (cited in Bosworth 2014: 177).

Above all, the rationale for the loss of liberty is indistinct in immigration detention. Many simply do not understand why they are locked up. As Innocent observed, they are not prisoners. Why then are they held in places that look like prison?

Together these factors create environments where, even those who are held for lengthy periods tend to have their attention trained elsewhere, usually on their immigration case. Despite being places of bricks and mortar, IRCs are just staging posts. Internal matters, like regimes and relationships, so pivotal to understanding the prison, do little to illuminate these sites of confinement. Instead, like those whom they study, researchers must take a wider view, looking beyond the institution to make sense of life within.

DEPORTATION

Although nearly half of those detained are released, at least temporarily, back into Britain, deportation and removal[9] loom large for all who are confined. For nearly everyone in IRCs, the prospect of forced return is unwelcome. Many speak of it as a form of humiliation. They are embarrassed to return without gifts, having failed in their life abroad. Some fear a more terrifying outcome. In either case, few look forward to 'going home'. Instead of re-entry and reunification, with their implicit promise, however hard to achieve in practice, of the possibility of a new beginning, removal or deportation are experienced and understood as further punishment (Hasselberg 2016).

The criminal justice system plays an important role in facilitating deportation and other forms of administrative expulsion (Brotherton and Barrios 2011; Bosworth 2011; Kaufman and Weiss 2015). Sometimes, as in the UK Borders Act 2007, expulsion is triggered by a particular length of custodial sentence.[10] At other times, no conviction is necessary. In the USA, for example, state and federal police are now required to run fingerprints of suspects through the immigration database. Even if the police drop the criminal case, migrants may be held on immigration detainers pursuant to their deportation (Manuel 2015).

[9] Although different legal categories of expulsion, deportation, and removal have the same effect, banishing individuals and restricting their return within a period of time.

[10] In 2014 Australia brought in similar legislation to deport foreign offenders.

Notwithstanding the range of mechanisms available to the government, forcing people to go can be difficult (Gibney 2008). Like detention, expulsion is often contested. Those asked to leave can delay their departure for some time by refusing to go, 'losing' their passport, and even resisting on the plane. These are all desperate strategies and ones that are dangerous for the individual. Ultimately, they will be ineffective in the face of state power.

While scholars like Gibney (2008) in political science focus on the challenges in forcing out long-term residents or asylum seekers, a criminological lens directs our attention to the contradictory impact of this administrative penalty on the logic of criminal justice. Deportation is an additional consequence that cannot be meted out to citizens and, as such, undermines the expectation of equal treatment before the law. It is not necessarily subject to judicial oversight, despite its profound impact on those subject to it. In the UK, while judges and magistrates may add a deportation order onto a criminal sentence, civil servants can also decide to enforce departure.

For those forced to leave, deportation hollows out the promise of rehabilitation and reintegration that had, at least in part, justified their punishment. Waldo, who had served numerous sentences for drug related crimes, explains. 'When I went to prison', he said, 'I done numerous courses, and then obviously I've realised what I was doing wrong, and where I went wrong when I end up in jail . . . at that time I thought to myself, "look, I have to do something, innit? Because I can't keep going in and out of prison". So I started doing the course that will help me to, like, better myself for when I get released and that, so that I don't go back to certain things that I used to do, you know. But while I was about to get released, that's when they came in with this deportation order' (Ghana, IRC Brook House). Deportation also fits uneasily into ideas of deterrence or just deserts. While politicians currently assert that tough immigration laws make Britain 'hostile' to irregular migrants and foreign offenders, immigration numbers rise and fall unconnected to criminal justice policy.

CONCLUSION

As mass migration continues to shape all aspects of society, it is not surprising to find that the criminal justice system is being affected as well. These days, the impact of imprisonment stretches far beyond institutional walls, not only seeping into the community in which it is based (Beckett and Murakawa 2012), but reaching across the world (Sudbury 2005). In so doing, the prison joins with other, putatively non-penal institutions and practices like immigration detention and deportation in the service of border control and regulation of foreigners on national soil (Bosworth 2008; Bosworth and Guild 2008; Fekete and Webber 2010).

Criminologists are well placed to explore these developments, as we can capitalize on our existing ties to the criminal justice system to gain access to these more hidden sites and practices. Border criminologists can also learn from existing studies. As criminal sentences lengthen, for instance, prisoners report growing levels of hopelessness and distress (Liebling *et al.* 2012, 2014). Uncertainty is a consequence of more than just border control. Criminologists have also long documented the retreat of the state and the growing involvement of the private and voluntary sector (Garland 1996; Tomczak 2014). This scholarship is relevant to these new forms of state power as well.

These points of commonality are important to acknowledge. Yet, border criminology offers more than just 'new wine in old bottles'. In shifting the frame of analysis, to take account of the global in the local, it offers a fresh perspective that highlights the relevance of citizenship, race, and ethnicity and reinterprets the role and nature of sovereignty and power (Bosworth 2008; Barker 2016b).

In a global, interconnected yet profoundly unequal world, the nation state is both vulnerable and increasingly muscular. Deploying the logic and the practice of criminal justice for the purpose of border control allows for the expansion of state power offshore and out of sight. Such developments destabilize many of the core principles of criminal justice, while also altering the nature of migration control and even international aid and development. They also shift the expectations we have about accountability and efficacy. The state seems to have more leeway to experiment and expand in coercive actions taken against foreigners than it does with citizens (Bosworth 2017).

All these matters raise important and urgent questions about the kind of society that is being constructed at home and abroad. What does it mean for a multicultural country like Britain, with its long tradition of immigration, to prioritize exclusion for so many within? What are we to make of the ties to the colonial past? Given that, as this chapter has demonstrated, the state faces a number of barriers in its bid to expel, how are we to reconcile the symbolic role of its extensive powers with their practical effect?

It is not just that laws passed against foreigners have a habit of being applied to citizens, as David Cole (2007) once observed about terrorism laws in the United States, but also that they are entrenching practices in societies through which certain members are denied the same rights and protections of others. History is littered with examples of the perils of this logic. In drawing these issues into the discipline, border criminology seeks to reanimate moral and political debate about justice, inclusion, and exclusion. What kind of society do we live in and where is it heading? Who belongs in it, and how far will we go to secure it? These are the questions of our time, and ones that deserve greater reflection.

SELECTED FURTHER READING

For those interested in exploring immigration detention in more depth, Bosworth's *Inside Immigration Detention* (2014) and Hall's *Border Watch* (2012) offer the only two ethnographic accounts of everyday life in immigration detention centres. Other, comparative, legal accounts can be found in Wilsher's *Immigration Detention: Law, History and Politics* (2011), and Wong's, *Rights, Deportation, and Detention in the Age of Immigration Control* (2015). For those interested in policing and border control, Weber's *Policing Non-Citizens* (2013) offers a detailed account of practices in Australia, while, for a critical account of the intersections between criminal law and immigration control, see Aliverti's *Crimes of Mobility* (2013). Conceptually, the edited collection, *The Borders of Punishment* by Katja Aas and Mary Bosworth (2013) explores how putting the criminal justice system to work in managing migration changes ideas and practices of punishment, while Pickering and Ham's, *Routledge*

Handbook on Crime and International Migration (2014), offers a thorough overview of literature on border criminology. Students who wish to follow the most up-to-date research in this field should consult Border Criminologies' blog at https://www.law.ox.ac.uk/research-subject-groups/centre-criminology/centreborder-criminologies/blog.

REFERENCES

Aas, K. F. (2007), 'Analysing a world in motion: Global flows meet "criminology of the other" ', *Theoretical Criminology*, 11(2): 283–303.

Aas, K. F. (2013), 'The Ordered and the Bordered Society', in K. F. Aas and M. Bosworth (eds), *The Borders of Punishment: Migration, Citizenship and Social Exclusion*, Oxford: Oxford University Press.

Aas, K. (2014), 'Bordered Penality: Precarious Membership and abnormal justice', *Punishment & Society*, 16(5): 520–41.

Aas, K. F. and Bosworth, M. (eds) (2013), *The Borders of Punishment: Citizenship, Crime Control, and Social Exclusion*, Oxford: Oxford University Press.

Aas, K. F. and Gundhus, H. (2015), 'Policing Humanitarian Borderlands: Frontex, Human Rights and the Precariousness of Life', *British Journal of Criminology*, 55(1): 1–18.

Agamben, G. (2004), *The State of Exception*, Chicago: University of Chicago Press.

Ahmed, S. (2000), *Strange Encounters: Embodied Others in Post-Coloniality*, London: Routledge.

Aliverti, A. (2016), 'The global criminal court', in M. Bosworth, C. Hoyle, and L. Zedner (eds.), *The Changing Contours of Criminal Justice*, Oxford: Oxford University Press.

Aliverti, A. (2015), 'Enlisting the Public in the Policing of Immigration', *British Journal of Criminology*, 55(2): 215–30.

Aliverti, A. (2013), *Crimes of Mobility: Criminal Law and the Regulation of Immigration*, Abingdon: Routledge.

APPG (2015), *The Report of the Inquiry into the Use of Immigration Detention in the United Kingdom, A Joint Inquiry by the All Party Parliamentary Group on Refugees & the All Party Parliamentary Group on Migration*. London: House of Commons. Available at: https://detentioninquiry.files.wordpress.com/2015/03/immigration-detention-inquiry-report.pdf

Barker, V. (2016), 'On Bauman's Moral Duty: population registries, REVA and eviction from the Nordic realm', in A. Eriksson (ed.), *Punishing the Other*, Abingdon: Routledge.

Barker, V. (forthcoming), 'Nordic Vagabonds: The Roma and the Logic of Benevolent Violence in the Swedish Welfare State', *European Journal of Criminology*.

Barker, V. (2013), 'Democracy and deportation: Why membership matters most', in K. Aas and M. Bosworth (eds), *The Borders of Punishment: Criminal Justice, Citizenship and Social Exclusion*, Oxford: Oxford University Press.

Barker, V. (2011), 'Global Mobility and Penal Order: Criminalizing Migration, A View from Europe', *Sociology Compass*, 6(2): 113–21.

Bauman, Z. (2001), *Modernity and the Holocaust*, Cambridge: Polity.

Beckett, K. and Murakawa, N. (2012), 'Mapping the Shadow Carceral State: Toward an Institutional Capacious Approach to Punishment', *Theoretical Criminology*, 16(2): 221–44.

Bhui, H. S. (2007), 'Alien experience: Foreign national prisoners after the deportation crisis', *Probation Journal*, 54(4), 368–82.

Bhui, H. S. (2013), 'Introduction: Humanizing Migration Control and Detention', in K. F. Aas and M. Bosworth (eds.), 'The Borders of Punishment: Migration, Citizenship and Social Exclusion', Oxford: Oxford University Press.

Bhui, H. S. (2016), 'The place of 'race' in understanding immigration control and the detention of foreign nationals', *Criminology & Criminal Justice*, 18(3): 267–85.

Bigo, D. (2006), 'Security, Exception, Ban and Surveillance', in D. Lyon (ed.), *Theorizing Surveillance: The Panopticon and Beyond*, Abingdon: Routledge.

Boe, C. (2016), 'From Banlieue Youth to, Undocumented Migrant: Illegalized Foreign-Nationals in Penal Institutions and Public Space', *Criminology & Criminal Justice*, 16(3): 319–36.

Bosworth, M. (2007), 'Immigration Detention in Britain', in M. Lee (ed.), *Human Trafficking*, Collumpton: Willan.

Bosworth, M. (2008), 'Border Control and the Limits of the Sovereign State', *Social & Legal Studies*, 17(2): 199–215.

Bosworth, M. (2011), 'Deporting Foreign National Prisoners in England and Wales', *Citizenship Studies*, 15(5): 583–95.

Bosworth, M. (2013), 'Can Immigration Detention be Legitimate?', in K. Aas and M. Bosworth (eds.), *The Borders of Punishment Migration, Citizenship and Social Exclusion*, Oxford: Oxford University Press.

Bosworth, M. (2014), *Inside Immigration Detention*, Oxford: Oxford University Press.

Bosworth, M. (2016a), 'Immigration Detention, Ambivalence and the Colonial Other', in A. Eriksson (ed.), *Punishing the Other*, Abingdon: Routledge.

Bosworth, M. (2016b), 'Border Criminology: How Migration is changing criminal justice', in M. Bosworth, C. Hoyle, and L. Zedner (eds), *The Changing Contours of Criminal Justice*, Oxford: Oxford University Press.

Bosworth, M. (2016c), 'Administrative power and staff in immigration detention: Paperwork and the file', conference paper, Monash University, 2 February 2016.

Bosworth, M. (2017), 'Penal Humanitarianism? Punishment in an era of mass migration', *New Criminal Law Review*, 20(1): 39–65.

Bosworth, M. and Guild, M. (2008), 'Governing through migration control: Security and Citizenship in Britain', *The British Journal of Criminology*, 48(6): 703–19.

Bosworth, M., Hasselberg, I., and Turnbull, S. (eds) (2016a), 'Punishment, Citizenship and Identity: The Incarceration of Foreign Nationals', *Special issue of Criminology & Criminal Justice*, 16(3): 257–66.

Bosworth, M., Hasselberg, I., and Turnbull, S. (2016b), 'Imprisonment in a Global World: Rethinking Penal Power', in Y. Jewkes, B. Crewe, and J. Bennett, (eds), *Handbook on Prisons*, 2nd edn, Abingdon: Routledge.

Bosworth, M. and Kellezi, B. (2013a), 'Citizenship and Belonging in a Women's Immigration Detention Centre', in C. Philips and C. Webster (eds), *New Directions in Race, Ethnicity and Crime*. Abingdon: Routledge.

Bosworth, M. and Kellezi, B. (2013b), 'Developing a Measure of the Quality of Life in Detention', *Prison Service Journal*, 205: 10–15.

Bosworth, M. and Kellezi, B. (2016), 'Doing Research in Immigration Removal Centres: Ethics, Emotions and Impact', *Criminology and Criminal Justice*, Online First.

Bosworth, M. and Slade, G. (2014), 'In Search of Recognition: Gender and Staff-Detainee Relations in a British Immigration Detention Centre', *Punishment & Society*, 16(2): 169–86.

Bosworth, M. and Vannier, M. (2016), 'Human Rights and Immigration Detention in France and the UK', *European Journal of Migration and Law*, 18(2): 157–76.

Bowling, B. (2010), *Policing the Carribean: Transnational Security Cooperation in Practice*, Oxford: Oxford University Press.

Bowling, B. (2013), 'Epilogue: The Borders of Punishment: Towards a Criminology of Mobility', in K. F. Aas and M. Bosworth (eds), *The Borders of Punishment: Migration, Citizenship and Social Exclusion*, Oxford: Oxford University Press.

Bowling, B. and Sheptycki, J. (2012), *Global Policing*, London: Sage.

Bradford, B., Jauregui, B., Loader, I., and Steinberg, J. (2016), *The SAGE Handbook of Global Policing*, London: Sage.

Brotherton, D. and Barrios, L. (2011), *Banished to the Homeland: Dominic Deportees and Their Stories of Exile*, New York: Columbia University Press.

Bucerius, A. and Tonry, M. (eds) (2014), *The Oxford Handbook of Ethnicity, Crime and Immigration*, New York: Oxford University Press.

Butler, J. (2004), *Precarious Life: The Powers of Mourning and Violence*, London: Verso.

Canning, V. (2015), 'Unsilencing Sexual Torture: Responses to Refugees and Asylum Seekers in Denmark', *British Journal of Criminology*, 56(3): 438–55.

Cavadino, M. and Dignan, J. (2005), *Penal Systems: A Comparative Approach*, London: Sage.

Chacón, J. (2012), 'Overcriminalizing Immigration', *Journal of Criminal Law and Criminology*, 102(3): 613–52.

Cole, D. (2007), 'Against Citizenship as a Predicate for Basic Rights', *Fordham Law Review*, 75: 2541–8.

Eagly, I. (2013), 'Criminal Justice for Non-Citizens: An analysis of variation in law enforcement', *New York University Law Review*, 88: 1126–223.

Eriksson, A. (ed.) (2016), *Punishing the Other: The Social Production of Immorality Revisited*, Abingdon: Routledge.

Fekete, L. and Webber, F. (2010), 'Foreign nationals, enemy penology and the criminal justice system', *Race & Class*, 51(4): 1–25.

Fili, A. (2013), 'The Maze of Immigration Detention Greece: A Case Study of the Athens Airport Detention Facility', *Prison Service Journal*, 205: 34–38.

Flynn, M. (2014), ' How and Why Immigration Detention Crossed the Globe', Global Detention Project Working Paper Series, Geneva: Global Detention Project, available at: http://www.globaldetentionproject.org/publications/working-papers/diffusion.html, accessed 27 December 2016.

Foucault, M. (1991), 'Governmentality', in G. Burchell, C. Gordon, and P. Miller (eds), *The Foucault Effect: Studies in Governmentality*, Chicago: University of Chicago Press.

Garland, D. (1996), 'The Limits of the Sovereign State', *British Journal of Criminology*, 36(4): 445–71.

Garner, S. (2015), 'Crimmigration: When Criminology (Nearly) Met the Sociology of Race and Ethnicity', *Sociology of Race and Ethnicity*, 1(1): 198–203.

Gibney, M. (2008), 'Asylum and the Expansion of Deportation in the United Kingdom', *Government and Opposition*, 43(2): 146–67.

Gilroy, P. (2002), *There Ain't No Black in the Union Jack: The Cultural Politics of Race and Nation*, Abingdon: Routledge.

Gilroy, P. (2006), *After Empire or Postcolonial Melancholia*, New York: Columbia University Press.

Giorgi, de, A. (2010), 'Immigration control, post-Fordism, and less eligibility A materialist critique of the criminalization of immigration across Europe', *Punishment & Society*, 12(2): 147–67.

Golash-Boza, T. (2015), *Deported: Policing Immigrants, Disposable Labor and Global Capitalism*, New York: New York University Press.

Gower, M. (2015), *Immigration Detention in the UK: An Overview*, House of Commons Library Briefing Paper, Number 7294, London: House of Commons.

Griffiths, M. (2014), 'Out of time: The temporal uncertainties of refused asylum seekers and immigration detainees,' *Journal of Ethnic and Migration Studies*, 40(12): 1991–2009.

Guild E. (2006), *Briefing Paper: A Typology of Different Types of Centres for Third Country Nationals in Europe*, Brussels: European Parliament, available at: http://www.europarl.europa.eu/RegData/etudes/note/join/2006/378268/IPOL-LIBE_NT(2006)378268_EN.pdf, accessed 27 December 2016.

HAGAN, J. and PALLONI, A. (1999), 'Sociological Criminology and the Mythology of Hispanic Immigration and Crime', *Social Problems*, 46(4): 617–32.

HALL, A. (2012), *Border Watch: Cultures Of Immigration Detention And Control*, London: Pluto.

HALL, S. (2001), 'Conclusion: The Multicultural Question', in B. Hesse (ed.), *UN/Settled Multiculturalisms: Diasporas, Entanglement, Transruptions*, London: Zed.

HASSELBERG, I. (2016), *Enduring Uncertainty: Deportation, Punishment and Everyday Life*, London: Berghahn.

HERNÁNDEZ, C. C. G. (2012), 'The perverse logic of immigration detention: unravelling the rationality of imprisoning immigrants based on markers of race and class otherness', *Columbia Journal of Race and Law*, 1(3): 353–64.

HM GOVERNMENT (2015), *National Security Strategy and Strategic Defense and Security Review 2015: A Secure and Prosperous United Kingdom*, Cm 9161, London: HMSO.

HMIP (2015), *People in Prison: A Findings paper by HM Inspectorate of Prisons*, London: Her Majesty's Inspectorate of Prisons, available at: https://www.justiceinspectorates.gov.uk/hmiprisons/wp-content/uploads/sites/4/2015/11/HMIP-Immigration-detainees-findings-paper-web-2015.pdf, accessed 27 December 2016.

HMIP (2016), *Report on an unannounced inspection of Heathrow Immigration Removal Centre—Harmondsworth site (7–18 September 2015)*, London: Her Majesty's Inspectorate of Prisons, available at: https://www.justiceinspectorates.gov.uk/hmiprisons/wp-content/uploads/sites/4/2016/02/Harmondsworth-web-2015.pdf, accessed 27 December 2016.

HMIP and ICIBI (2012), *The effectiveness and impact of immigration detention casework. A Joint thematic review by HM Inspectorate of Prisons and the Independent Chief Inspector of Borders and Immigration*. London: HMIP and ICIBI. Available at: http://www.justice.gov.uk/downloads/publications/inspectorate-reports/hmipris/thematic-reports-and-research-publications/immigration-detention-casework-2012.pdf.

HOME OFFICE (2016a), *Immigration Statistics: October to December 2015*, available at: https://www.gov.uk/government/statistics/immigration-statistics-october-to-december-2015, accessed 27 December 2016.

HOME OFFICE (2016b), *The Facilitated Return Scheme*, available at: https://www.gov.uk/government/uploads/system/uploads/attachment_data/file/558202/Facilitated-returns-scheme-v8_0.pdf, accessed 9 January 2017.

IOM (2015), *World Migration Report 2015*, Geneva: IOM, available at: http://publications.iom.int/system/files/wmr2015_en.pdf, accessed 27 December 2016.

KANSTROOM, D. (2012), *Aftermath: Deportation Law and the New American Diaspora*, New York: Oxford University Press.

KAUFMAN, E. (2012), 'Finding Foreigners: Race and the Politics of Memory in British Prisons', *Population, Space and Place*, 18(6): 701–14.

KAUFMAN, E. (2013), 'Hubs and Spokes: The Transformation of the British Prison', in K. F. Aas and M. Bosworth (eds), *The Borders of Punishment: Migration, Citizenship, and Social Exclusion*, Oxford: Oxford University Press.

KAUFMAN, E. (2015), *Punish and Expel: Border Control, Nationalism, and the New Purpose of the Prison*, Oxford: Oxford University Press.

KAUFMAN, E. and BOSWORTH, M. (2013), 'Prison and National Identity: Citizenship, Punishment and the Sovereign State', in D. Scott (ed.), *Why Prison?*, Cambridge: Cambridge University Press.

KAUFMAN, E. and WEISS, S. (2015), 'The Limits of Punishment', in K. Reiter and A. Koenig (eds), *Extreme Punishment*, London: Palgrave.

LEERKES, A. and BROEDERS, D. (2010), 'A Case of Mixed Motives? Formal and Informal Functions of Administrative Immigration Detention', *British Journal of Criminology*, 50(5): 830–50.

LIEBLING, A. (2014), 'Moral and Philosophical Problems of Long-Term Imprisonment', *Studies in Christian Ethics*, 27(3): 258–73.

LIEBLING, A., ARNOLD, H., and STRAUB, C. (2012), *An Exploration of Staff-Prisoner Relationships at HMP Whitemoor: Twelve Years on*, London: National Offender Management Service.

LIGHT, M. T., MASSOGLIA, M., and KING, R. D. (2014), 'Citizenship and Punishment: The Salience of National Membership in U.S. Criminal Courts', *American Sociological Review*, 79(5): 825–47.

MANUEL, K. (2015), *Immigration Detainers: Legal Issues, Congressional Research Service*, Washington, DC: CRS, available at: https://fas.org/sgp/crs/homesec/R42690.pdf, accessed 12 May 2016.

MEARS, D. (2011), 'The Immigration-Crime Nexus: Toward an Analytic Framework for Assessing and Guiding Theory, Research, and Policy', *Sociological Perspectives*, 44(1): 1–19.

MEHTA, R. (2016), 'Borders: A View from Nowhere', *Criminology & Criminal Justice*, 16(3): 286–300.

MUTSAERS, P. (2014), 'An Ethnographic Study of the Policing of Internal Borders in the Netherlands: Synergies Between Criminology and Anthropology', *British Journal of Criminology*, 54(5): 831–48.

NELKEN, D. (2010), *Comparative Criminal Justice: Making Sense of Difference*, London: Sage.

PARMAR, A. (2016), 'The changing contours of race, ethnicity and criminal justice', in M. Bosworth, C. Hoyle, and L. Zedner, (eds), *The Changing Contours of Criminal Justice*, Oxford: Oxford University Press.

PHELPS, J. (2009), *Detained Lives*, London: LDSG.

PHILIPS, C. (2012), *The Multicultural Prison: Ethnicity, Masculinity and Social Relations Among Prisoners*, Oxford: Oxford University Press.

PHILIPS, C. and BOWLING, B. (2003), 'Racism, Ethnicity and Criminology: Developing Minority Perspectives', *British Journal of Criminology*, 43(2): 269–90.

PICKERING, S., BOSWORTH, M., and AAS, K. F., (2015), 'The Criminology of Mobility', in S. Pickering and J. Ham (eds), *The Routledge Handbook on Crime and International Migration*, Abingdon: Routledge.

PICKERING, S. and HAM, J. (2014), 'Hotpants at the Border', *British Journal of Criminology*, 54(1): 2–19.

PRATT, J. and ERIKSSON, A. (2014), *Contrasts in Punishment: An Explanation of Anglophone Excess and Nordic Exceptionalism*, Abindgon: Routledge.

SANCHEZ, G. (2014), *Human Smuggling and Border Crossings*, Abingdon: Routledge.

SHAW, C. R. and MCKAY, H. D. (1942), *Juvenile Delinquency and Urban Areas: A Study of Rates of Delinquents in Relation to Differential Characteristics of Local Communities in American Cities*, Chicago: University of Chicago Press.

SHAW, S. (2016), *Review into the welfare in detention of vulnerable persons, m 9186*, London: HMSO.

SIMON, J. (2007), *Governing Through Crime*, New York: New York University Press.

SPARKS, R., BOTTOMS, A. E., and HAY, W. (1996), *Prisons and the Problem of Order*, Oxford: Oxford University Press.

STUMPF, J. (2006), 'The Crimmigration Crisis: Immigrants, Crime, and Sovereign Power', *American University Law Review*, 56(2): 367–419.

STUMPF, J. (2013), 'The process is the punishment in crimmigration law', in K. Aas and M. Bosworth (eds), *The Borders of Punishment*, Oxford: Oxford University Press.

SUDBURY, J. (ed.) (2005), *Global Lockdown: Race, Gender and the Prison Industrial Complex*, Abingdon: Routledge.

TOMCZAK, P. (2014), 'The penal voluntary sector in England and Wales: Beyond neoliberalism', *Criminology & Criminal Justice*, 14(4): 470–86.

TONRY, M. (ed.) (1996), *Ethnicity, Crime and Immigration: Comparative and Cross-National Perspectives*, Chicago: University of Chicago Press.

TURNBULL, S. (2016), 'Stuck in the Middle: Waiting and Uncertainty in Immigration Detention', *Time & Society*, 25(1): 61–79.

UGELVIK, S. and UGELVIK, T. (2013), 'Immigration control in Ultima Thule: Detention and exclusion, Norwegian style', *European Journal of Criminology*, 10(6): 709–24.

UGELVIK, T. (2012), 'Imprisoned on the border: subjects and objects of the state in two Norwegian prisons', in S. Ugelvik and B. Hudson (eds), *Justice and Security in the 21st Century: Risks, Rights and the Rule of Law*, Abingdon: Routledge.

UGELVIK, T. (2015), 'The Incarceration of Foreigners in European Prisons', in S. Pickering and J. Ham (ed.), *The Routledge Handbook on Crime and International Migration*, Abingdon: Routledge.

UNITED NATIONS (2015), http://www.unhcr.org/558193896.html, accessed 27 December 2016.

VAN ZYL SMIT, D. and MULGREW, R. (2012), *Handbook on the International Transfer of Sentenced Persons*, New York: United Nations, available at: https://www.unodc.org/documents/organized-crime/Publications/Transfer_of_Sentenced_Persons_Ebook_E.pdf, accessed 27 October 2015.

VAN ZYL SMIT, D. and SNACKEN, S. (2009), *Principles of European Prison Law and Policy: Penology and Human Rights*, Oxford: Oxford University Press.

VAZQUEZ, Y. (2011), 'Perpetuating the Marginalization of Latinos: A Collateral Consequence of the Incorporation of Immigration Law into the Criminal Justice System', *Howard Law Journal*, 54(3): 639–74.

WARR, J. (2016), 'The Deprivation of Certitude, Legitimacy and Hope: Foreign National Prisoners and the Pains of Imprisonment', *Criminology and Criminal Justice*, 16(3): 301–18.

WEBER, L. (2013), *Policing Non-Citizens*, Abingdon: Routledge.

WEBER, L. and BOWLING, B. (2004), 'Policing Migration: A framework for investigating the regulation of global mobility', *Policing & Society*, 14(3): 195–212.

WILSHER, D. (2011), *Immigration Detention: Law, History and Politics*, Cambridge: Cambridge University Press.

WIRTH, L. (1928), *The Ghetto*, Chicago: University of Chicago Press.

WONG, T. (2015), *Rights, Deportation, and Detention in the Age of Immigration Control*, Stanford: University of Stanford Press.

ZEDNER, L. (2016), 'Citizenship deprivation, security and human rights', *European Journal of Migration and Law*, 18(2): 222–42.

ZEDNER, L. (2010), 'Security, the State, and the Citizen: The Changing Architecture of Crime Control', *New Criminal Law Review*, 13(2): 379–403.

CHAPTER ACKNOWLEDGEMENTS

I would like to thank Alison Liebling, Michal Bosworth, Sarah Turnbull, and Vanessa Barker for their useful comments on earlier drafts. The time to write this chapter and much of the research on which it draws was funded by my European Research Council Starter Grant 313356.

17

CRIMINOLOGY AND TRANSITIONAL JUSTICE

Kieran McEvoy, Ron Dudai, and Cheryl Lawther

The notion of Transitional Justice comprises the full range of processes and mechanisms associated with a society's attempt to come to terms with a legacy of large-scale past abuses, in order to ensure accountability, serve justice and achieve reconciliation. It consists of both judicial and non-judicial processes and mechanisms, including prosecution initiatives, facilitating initiatives in respect of the right to truth, delivering reparations, institutional reform and national consultations.

(United Nations 2004: 4)

INTRODUCTION

While transitional justice has only really emerged as an area of inquiry in the last 30 years, it has very quickly acquired all of the trappings of academic 'respectability' (McEvoy and Mallinder 2016). Originally viewed as a sub-specialism of political sciences which focused on the political transition from conflict or authoritarianism (O'Donnell and Schmitter 1986; Arthur 2009), it now attracts serious scholarship from lawyers, anthropologists, psychologists, sociologists, and of course criminologists. There are numerous academic books and articles, university courses, two specialist journals, book series, major research grants, and all of the other accoutrements of a vibrant area of study.

The field is also a lively one for policy and practice. Transitional justice attracts the interests of politicians, policy-makers, the UN, the World Bank, many local and international civil society actors, and other important players which cumulatively amount to what McCargo (2015) has called a 'transitional justice industry'. The arguable 'swagger' which characterizes elements of this field is underpinned by the enormous expenditure of resources involved and the popularization of some of the key elements of the transitional justice toolkit. The creation of ad hoc tribunals for the former Yugoslavia and Rwanda, the International Criminal Court (ICC), and hybrid courts (involving a combination of domestic and international law) in places like Sierra Leone and Cambodia have cost billions.[1] Almost all post conflict or post authoritarian countries have reparations programmes designed to help victims and survivors and these too have become increasingly expensive.[2] In addition, 'rule of law' programmes are now seen as central to almost all democratic reform, peace-making or economic liberalization processes—often, for example, being a precondition for loans from the Word Bank and other institutions—and thus securing huge amounts of resources from the international donor community (May 2014).[3] In addition, elements of transitional justice have become increasingly well-known in popular culture. High profile international trials of former presidents (e.g. Slobodan Milošević, Radovan Karadžić, Charles Taylor) and the work of the International Criminal Court in particular have meant that, for example, former world leaders such as Tony Blair are regularly the subject of calls in the press or social media that he should be 'tried for war crimes at the Hague'—regardless of the legal impossibility of such proceedings ever taking place.[4] Similarly, such has been the spread and popularization of processes such as truth commissions (over 40 in the last three decades) that settled democracies have increasingly adapted such mechanisms to deal with their troubled histories, drawing explicitly from the transitional justice experience (Niezen 2013).[5] Truth commissions, especially the South African one, have also filtered into popular culture, becoming a topic of films and novels.[6] In short, serious people spend a serious amount of money on transitional justice and the field has at least some purchase on the popular imagination—all contributing to a degree of self-importance in the area.

Almost a decade ago one of the authors suggested the need for a criminology of transitional justice (McEvoy 2007). In part, that call was informed by a perception that some of the more hubristic traits evident in the field were due to the dominance of lawyers in transitional justice. Identifying a number of features including the *seductive qualities of legalism*, the oversold *triumph of human rights* and a tendency towards *seeing like a state,* that paper sketched out briefly (in one subsection) how criminology could provide something of a buttress against the negative consequences of these

[1] For example, the most recent published annual running costs for the International Criminal Tribunal for Yugoslavia (established in 1993) is $180 million in 2014–15, $250 million in 2012–13, $286 million in 2010–11. See http://www.icty.org/en/about/tribunal/the-cost-of-justice, accessed 31 December 2016. By 2014, the International Criminal Tribunal for Rwanda had cost over $2 billion in its two decades of operation. See *The Mail & Guardian*, 'Rwanda Genocide Court Closes after 20 years and $2bn', 17 December 2014. The International Criminal Court has an annual budget of over $140 million and has cost well in excess of $1 billion to date. 'International Criminal Court: 12 Years, $1 Billion, 2 Convictions', *Forbes Magazine*, 12 March 2014.

[2] Recent estimates concerning the comprehensive reparations programme in Colombia have suggested that the costs will be in excess of $30 billion. See International Centre for Transitional Justice (2015), *Challenges of Implementing Reparations for Massive Violations in Colombia*, New York: ICTJ.

[3] In 2006 the World Bank estimated that it had supported 330 'rule of law' programmes in over 100 countries at a cost of $3.8 billion—see further Santos (2006).

[4] 'Outrage as War Crimes Prosecutors Say Tony Blair will not be Investigated over Chilcot's Iraq War Report—but British Soldiers could be', *Daily Telegraph*, 2 July 2016.

[5] Indeed on 2 March 2009 the *New York Times* ran an editorial asking the question, 'A Truth Commission for the Bush Era?' with regard to the actions of US forces during the War on Terror. President Obama ultimately concluded that such a commission should not be established. 'No Truth Commission on Torture, says Obama', *Irish Times*, 25 April 2009.

[6] *Red Dust*, Gillian Slovo's novel on the South African Commission, also turned into a film starring Hillary Swank, is one of many such examples.

features. In particular, because of its status as what David Downes famously described as 'rendezvous subject' between different disciplines, it was suggested that criminology could provide the prism through which to ask more philosophical questions about *what is transitional justice for* as well as *who it is intended to benefit* which would, in turn, provide some benchmarks to make practical assessments as to whether not it could be deemed to be *working*. Although as was noted above, the breadth of academic disciplines now working in transitional justice is impressive and challenging the dominance of legalism has arguably become normalized in the past 10 years, few would contest the continued power and influence of lawyers in the area. Bearing that in mind, the power of criminology as an interdisciplinary bulwark against legalism in the field remains strong. We have therefore taken this opportunity to expand on the utility of a number of familiar criminological themes to the particular contexts of transitional justice—namely the punishment of offenders, the construction of victimhood, and the broader intersection between transitional justice and social control. Before examining these in some detail however, we must address the central problem concerning how the discipline of criminology—largely developed in settled democracies—is of relevance in the context of post-conflict or post-authoritarian societies.

EXCEPTIONALISM, TRANSITIONAL JUSTICE, AND CRIMINOLOGY

The challenges of applying criminological theories to the exceptional circumstances of post-conflict or authoritarian regimes is a familiar one. With regard to conflicts themselves, Ruth Jamieson (1998) memorably described criminology as being 'largely aloof and unmoved' by the desire to better understand war, a tendency which Jock Young (2011) termed one of the 'ten ironies' of critical criminology. The authors have grown up in conflict zones (Northern Ireland and Israel) and experienced, at least in Northern Ireland, the out-workings of a peace process and a sustained engagement with transitional justice.[7] As such, we are familiar with an occasional sense amongst some criminological colleagues from settled democracies that our experiences were a little too exotic or exceptional to have much to offer to 'mainstream' criminological theory. Obviously the inclusion of this chapter is a sign that the struggles of such societies to deal with the legacies of the past is of some interest to criminologists. It also true that in the last decade or so there has been increasing serious and engaged criminological work on war, mass violence, genocide, terrorism, and of course state crime (e.g. Jamieson 2014; Walklate and McGarry 2015; Rafter 2016; Ruggiero 2006; Green and Ward 2006)—all of which speaks encouragingly to an expanding of the criminological imagination in this area. While other criminologists have a long-standing interest in

[7] While the Israeli–Palestinian conflict is of course still ongoing, some civil society groups in the region have engaged in initiatives which draw explicit inspiration from transitional justice mechanisms elsewhere (Dudai and Cohen 2010).

the intersection between human rights and criminology and the role of criminology in peace-making (e.g. Weber *et al.* 2016; McEvoy and Newburn 2003; Braithwaite *et al.* 2010), it remains the case that transitional justice remains somewhat off-piste from the majority. Two other factors may have contributed to criminology's lingering 'blind-spot' in relation to transitional justice. First, criminological knowledge tends to privilege theories, assumptions, and methods based largely on the specificities of the global North (Carrington *et al.* 2016), while transitional justice mechanisms have operated, at least initially, mainly in the global South. Second, the fact that so much recent and highly influential criminological writings have been oriented toward a critique of excessive punishment (mainly in the US context; see, e.g., Garland 2001; Simon 2007), has probably rendered some elements of transitional justice where the value of punishment remains undiminished (explored in the next section) appear out of sync with criminological thinking. These and other factors may in turn have served to limit the engagement of transitional justice scholars and practitioners with criminology, a discipline seen by many as having comparatively little interest in the global South or, until recently, in political and ethnic violence.

As noted above, the origins of transitional justice in trying to understand and assist with the transitions from authoritarian regimes in Latin America and the former Soviet bloc have heavily influenced developments in the field. One challenge raised by these transitions, almost of all of which were characterized by horrendous human rights abuses, was how to strike a balance between the quest for 'justice' and political stability. As is discussed further below, these 'exceptional' circumstances contributed to the emergence of theorizations of transitional justice as compromised justice (Teitel 2003; Mallinder 2014), inevitably partial or imperfect and conditioned by local realities such as compromised legal and criminal justice systems, underdeveloped democratic institutions, compelling social or economic problems and, in some cases at least, a nervous military which appeared willing to retake power by force if pressed too hard (Teitel 2008; Olsen *et al.* 2010). Thus mechanisms and processes evolved such as truth commissions; reparations programmes for victims of conflict; disarmament, demobilization and reintegration programmes for former combatants; lustration and vetting procedures of former state actors involved in previous human rights abuses; mechanisms designed to facilitate acknowledgement, apology, and memorialization; and of course, as discussed further below, the continued use of and refinement of the tried and tested post-conflict measure, amnesties.

The exceptionalist argument within transitional justice has been critiqued from a number of vantage points. First, some human rights activists and scholars have resisted such arguments, responding that recourse to such special pleading is often a version of old fashioned impunity dressed up in the fancy language of transitional justice and reconciliation which undermines binding international legal obligations to punish human rights abusers and thus reassert the rule of law (Orentlicher 1991; Snyder and Vinjamuri 2004; Leebaw 2008). Second, at a conceptual level, others have argued that sometimes the exceptional nature of a post-conflict or post-authoritarian context is exaggerated. The best known of such critiques is that advanced by Posner and Vermuele (2004: 764) in which they claim that transitional justice specialists have 'gone wrong' by failing to grasp that such contexts are merely on one end of the continuum of change which is faced by settled democracies and 'ordinary law' all of the time and as such they do not present '. . . a distinct set of moral and jurisprudential dilemmas'. Third, as mentioned above, the fact that settled democracies such as Canada, Australia, and elsewhere are explicitly utilizing the theory and practice of transitional justice to deal with past abuses again suggests that whatever its exceptional origins as a field, it does have relevance and resonance in more settled contexts. Finally, the fact that transitional justice mechanisms have continued to develop and be deployed in such a diverse set of geographical and political contexts has meant that at least to some degree it moved 'from the exception to the norm' (Teitel 2003).

Our own instincts on this exceptionalism debate are what we would term critical but pragmatic. On the key issue of political, cultural, and contextual variety, we are intuitively sympathetic to the view of Hardie Bick and colleagues that 'any criminology worthy of the name should contain a comparative dimension' (2005: 1). As academics who have actually been involved in quite a lot of international comparative research on transitional justice,[8] we would argue that it is possible to draw out broad themes from very diverse experiences while remaining sensitive to local context-specific variables—striking a balance between ethnocentrism and relativism (Nelken 2009). In practice this means understanding and acknowledging the very different experiences of Belfast, Bogota, Kigali, or Jerusalem to London, New York, or Sydney—while at the same time being alive to the possibilities of theoretical and indeed practical insights emerging from any and indeed all of these settings and more. Bearing in mind the very specific contexts in which some of the themes discussed have arisen, in the following section we will make the argument that transitional justice does indeed have something to contribute to criminology more broadly and vice versa.

PUNISHMENT AND RESTORATION IN TRANSITIONAL JUSTICE

In this section we wish to focus on those who have been involved in acts of violence or other human rights abuses—the 'offenders' or 'perpetrators'—in our exploration of *what is transitional justice for*. Of course, as we discuss in greater detail below with regard to victimhood, the notion that one that one can easily divide the world into 'guilty perpetrators' and 'innocent victims' sometimes does not match the messy reality of transitional contexts. For the moment however, we will concentrate our attentions

[8] The ideas developed in this chapter emerge from a number of comparative and jurisdiction specific transitional justice projects in which the authors have been engaged involving fieldwork in Argentina, Uruguay, Chile, Colombia, Tunisia, South Africa, Rwanda, Uganda, Sierra Leone, Israel, Palestine, Spain (Basque Country), Cambodia, and Northern Ireland. These projects have variously been funded by Joseph Rowntree Charitable Trust & Merck Foundation (Prisoner Release and Reintegration: A Comparative Study); Atlantic Philanthropies (Transitional Justice from Below); The Arts and Humanities Research Council (AHRC *AH/E008984/1* Beyond Legalism: Amnesties, Transition and Conflict Transformation, *AH/J013897/1* Amnesties Prosecutions and the Public Interest and *AH/N001451/1* Voice, Agency and Blame: Victimhood and Imagined Community in Northern Ireland); and the Economic and Social Research Council (*ES/J009849/1* Lawyers, Conflict and Transition and *ES/N010825/1* Apologies, Abuses and Dealing with the Past). See also Dudai (2012a, 2012b).

on wrongdoers. Broadly, the transitional justice approach to offenders is to try to punish at least some of them through retributive trials, provide some with an amnesty and/or related efforts to shift them away from violence, and engage them in broader social and communal efforts of peace-making and reconciliation. By examining such processes through a criminological lens we will argue that some of the strengths and limitations of these approaches can be seen much more clearly.

With regard to punishment of offenders in transitional contexts, certainly at the international level, it is clear that much of the focus is upon what Henman has described as 'predominantly retributive and marginally deterrent' (2004: 36). In Hegelian terms, 'the criminal has done, so it should be done to him' (Hegel 1952: 71). Judges at the international tribunals often focus on retribution and deterrence as the primary goals of sentencing, 'dismissing any significant consideration of rehabilitation of social reinsertion' (Schabas 2011: 348). Given the heinous nature of some crimes involved—including genocide, war crimes, torture, sexual violence as a strategy of subjugation—retribution being visited against those deemed most responsible is an obvious intuitive response, coupled with the desire to deter other would-be offenders from engaging in similar acts of horror (Roberts 2003; Drumbl 2007). In seeking to examine the force of the predominant retributive thinking regarding the reasons for *doing* transitional justice, a number of features come to the fore, particularly with regard to issues of legality, proportionality, and selectivity; and the expressive functions of punishment. In addition, we shall also examine briefly some of the key elements of deterrence which are, as noted above, often grouped with retribution.

For those who view retribution as perhaps the key role of punishment, law is at the very core of the punishment project. From such a perspective, crime is viewed as 'lawbreaking' and therefore the response must be 'lawful'—a reassertion of the primacy of law (Golash 2005). Many of those who argue for retribution in transitional justice, particularly human rights lawyers, argue that states are legally bound to punish perpetrators because of the 'duty to prosecute' the most serious of international crimes—namely genocide, war crimes, and crimes against humanity (Orentlicher 1991; Mills 2015). In practice, as McEvoy (with Mallinder 2013) has argued in greater detail elsewhere, there are significant divergences in law and practice about how all-encompassing the duty to prosecute is even in such extreme circumstances. For example, with regard to the crime of genocide, the duty to prosecute is often described as 'absolute' (e.g. Scharf 1996; Jackson 2007). However, in practice, the definition of genocide presents quite a high threshold to trigger the duty to prosecute. Under the Genocide Convention of 1948 genocide requires that violent actions are taken with 'intent to destroy, in whole or in part, a national, ethnical, racial or religious group'. Thus, murder campaigns directed against political groups—such as, for example, 'communists' or 'subversives' in South America's 'dirty wars'—would place such mass killings beyond the scope of the Genocide Convention. Similarly with regard to war crimes the duty to prosecute (under the Geneva Conventions of 1949 and Additional Protocol of 1977) refers to 'grave breaches' committed during *international* conflict—thus ruling out the numerous internal armed conflicts of the last seven decades. Moreover, as is discussed further below, the Geneva Conventions and the reality of state practice in post-conflict societies for hundreds of years mean that the granting of amnesties remain a key element of the transitional justice toolkit. In sum, therefore, using law and legal obligations as the key rationale for punishment in transitional justice is mitigated by the fact that there are often competing interpretations of law, its meaning, applicability, and consequences. The so-called 'human rights as trumps' perspective (Ignatieff 2003) only takes one so far.

Other difficulties for retributivists in transitional justice relate to questions of *selectivity* and *proportionality*. In contexts where thousands or indeed hundreds of thousands of individuals have been involved in serious violence or human rights abuses, prosecutions will inevitably be selective (Cryer 2005; Akhavan 2013). Much has been written about the range of political factors which led to the creation of the tribunals to deal with the crimes of Rwanda and Yugoslavia but not in other contexts (e.g. Schabas 2012). Once international, hybrid or indeed local trials are established to deal with past abuses, decisions have to be taken regarding who to prosecute and for what crimes. Often prosecutors seek to indict senior people—those deemed 'most responsible' but such a focus may in turn offer *de facto* impunity to thousands of middle and lower level individuals who were enmeshed in the most brutal elements of past violence and human rights abuses (Takemura 2007). Similarly with regard to the issue of proportionality, another central component of retributivist thinking, devising lawful punishments which match the nature of the crimes committed in many of these contexts is a very significant challenge. As Hannah Arendt has famously argued with regard to Nazi atrocities, 'For these crimes, no punishment is severe enough' (1992: 54) and any search for real proportionality with such crimes is 'inadequate and absurd' (1973: 439).

Finally it is worth exploring in a little more detail the closely linked position of deterrence as a reason for punishment in transitional justice. Needless to say, deterrence has long been a politically popular element of the philosophy of punishment (Bentham 1830; Brooks 2012). Whether it is geared towards specific or general deterrence, the basic assumption is that one of the reasons for punishing an offender today for a particular offence or offences is the knowledge that a similar punishment will feature in the decision-making of future offenders (Von Hirsch *et al.* 1999). Variations of this premise are reproduced as a key rationale for prosecutions in multiple UN documents, preambles to the establishment of the ICTY, ICTR, and indeed the Rome Statute which established the International Criminal Court.

Lawyers, judges, and policy-makers involved in international justice regularly invoke deterrence for doing what they do. However, as Schabas has remarked, many of these pronouncements are 'marked by amateurishness . . . driven more by intuition than anything else' (2011: 349). The great caution about over-stating the effectiveness of deterrence—which is such a strong feature of the criminological literature regarding determining which offenders may be deterred from committing which crimes in which circumstances in settled democracies (e.g. Tonry 2008; Kennedy 2008; Jacobs 2010)—has clearly not yet permeated into the world of international criminal justice. That confidence in deterrence within international criminal justice is in our view misplaced.

Notwithstanding the developments outlined above, the fact remains that the statistical chances of being successfully prosecuted in the post-conflict or post-transitional contexts under review remains very slight (UNSC 2004: para 26; Drumbl 2007). A combination of a lack of resources, lack of evidence, corrupt or inefficient local justice systems, a lack of political will or indeed local amnesties will often ensure that only a tiny fraction, if any, former human rights abusers will be brought to justice. In addition, the applicability of deterrence theory to such contexts is further undermined by its explicit assumption that the actors involved will make rational calculations regarding risk before engaging upon campaigns of mass violence. While that may be true of some elite leaders (Akhavan 2001; Rosenberg 2012), they will of course be reassured by the low risks of ever being prosecuted. Moreover, often those involved in directing the worst kinds of genocidal violence are inherent military and political risk-takers. For example, Ku and Nzelibe (2006) examine the deterrent effect of international tribunals by looking at what happened to those leaders who tried to achieve political ends by violence across 17 countries in Africa through 348 coups or attempted coups. 28 per cent were executed or otherwise murdered and 22 per cent were exiled or imprisoned. Despite these very daunting life prospects, many of these individuals appeared undeterred by a 50\50 chance of being killed or imprisoned by their own state. To assume that they would be deterred by the perhaps more abstract threat of international prosecution is 'highly debateable' (Ku and Nzelibe 2006: 831). For those on the ground, the relevance of deterrence theory may be even more dubious. If one is seeking to influence the behaviour of genocidal fanatics in Rwanda, abused or coerced child soldiers in Uganda or Congo, or radicalized jihaddists in Syria or Iraq—easy assumptions about the efficacy of deterrence are arguably of limited utility.

We would like now to consider two other important and interrelated elements of the transitional justice toolkit with regard to offenders—amnesties and Disarmament, Reintegration and Rehabilitation (DDR) programmes. Again our own views on these topics have been heavily influenced by criminological theory and practice—in particular those emanating from restorative justice.

At first blush, amnesties would appear to be the polar opposite of any attempt to try to render an offender accountable through punishment. An amnesty is the formal extinguishment of an individual or group of individuals criminal (and often civil) liability for past crimes or human rights abuses (Mallinder 2008). Originating in the power of the sovereign to 'show mercy' in the way of such conflicts, amnesties have been a key element of making peace for centuries and remain remarkably popular.[9] Historically, the scope of such amnesties was as broad as the state or sovereign in question wished them to be (Joinet 1985). However, with the developments in international human rights law since the end of the Second World War and in particular the importance afforded to 'the fight against impunity', the shape of amnesties has gradually changed. In the 1970s sweeping 'blanket amnesties' were often a central demand of outgoing military dictators and other authoritarian regimes as a condition of handing over political power. Perhaps inevitably, amnesties became synonymous with impunity for many activists and were often seen as a denial of the rights of victims to the versions of justice discussed above (Laplante 2008). However, such unconditional amnesties have gradually been whittled away by domestic and international legal challenges, pressure from victims and other civil society groups, and a general reluctance by key

[9] In her seminal overview of world-wide amnesties Mallinder (2012) reviewed 529 amnesty laws in 138 countries and suggested that on average there continue to be approximately a dozen amnesties introduced world-wide per year.

international institutions such as the United Nations to countenance such measures (Freeman 2009; Collins 2010).[10] It is now much more common to see amnesties or amnesty-like measures linked to or indeed conditional upon other transitional measures such as participation in truth recovery processes, disarmament and demobilization, reparations, or forms of acknowledgement to victims (Du-Bois Pedain 2011; Jeffery 2014).

It is easy to see how amnesties became synonymous with impunity and a failure of accountability. However, the increased linkage of such measures with these other transitional justice processes above mean that many commentators now argue that amnesties should instead be viewed through the lens of restorative justice rather than simply as evidence of the absence of accountability (e.g. Braithwaite 2002; McEvoy and Mallinder 2013; Jeffrey 2014). For example, the South African Truth and Reconciliation Commission (TRC) explicitly drew upon restorative justice as an explanatory rationale for its use of amnesties in exchange for truth recovery. Responding to criticism that the amnesty amounted to a denial of justice, the TRC final report argued that amnesty could be viewed as a form of justice if justice is conceived not as retribution, but restoration. The report stated '. . . that amnesty in return for public and full disclosure (as understood within the context of the Commission) suggests a restorative understanding of justice, focusing on the healing of victims and perpetrators and on communal restoration' (SATRC 1999: para 55).

In some instances, such as Sierra Leone, Northern Ireland, or more recently the 52-year conflict in Colombia, it would arguably have been impossible to have successfully concluded peace negotiations without some form of an amnesty being part of the peace accord. Combatants or prisoners imprisoned for politically motivated offences are often important constituencies of armed groups (non-state and state) and bringing such constituencies 'over the line' in reaching a peace deal is often a key challenge for those seeking to make peace (McEvoy 2001). Moreover, as transitional societies seek to deal with their violent past through the establishment of a truth recovery body such as a truth commission, it is simply not realistic to expect that those previously involved in violence or human rights abuses will come forward to tell the truth if they are likely to face prosecution as a result. Therefore the 'trade-off' of truth for non-prosecution—as was the case in South Africa, has become increasingly normalized in transitional contexts (Hayner 2011). Bearing in mind those twin realities, John Braithwaite has suggested that amnesties may be compatible with restorative justice provided that they contribute to ending a war, all stakeholders are given a voice in the amnesty negotiations, and that those who will benefit are willing to 'show public remorse for their crimes and to commit to the service of the new nation and its people and repair some of the harm they have done' (2002: 203).

[10] For example, in 1999 the Lomé Agreement was signed between the government of Sierra Leone and the Revolutionary United Front (RUF) bringing to an end a decade-long and incredibly brutal civil war. The Agreement contained a blanket amnesty to all participants in the conflict. At the very end of the negotiations, which had been facilitated by the United Nations, the UN Special Representative of the Secretary General appended a disclaimer to the Agreement stating that the amnesties provisions contained therein would not apply to crimes of genocide, crimes against humanity, war crimes, and other serious violations of international human rights law. In 2004, the Appeal Chamber of the Special Court for Sierra Leone confirmed that the amnesties provisions of the Lomé Accord were no bar to prosecutions before it for such crimes. See further Meisenberg (2004).

It is possible for amnesties to fulfil Braithwaite's criteria of a restorative amnesty. Of course amnesties were historically crafted to exclusively suit the interests of the political or military elites with little heed for the needs of victims. However, in recent years, meaningful participation by victims and affected communities has become much more common. For example, in Northern Ireland, the *de facto* amnesty which has resulted in the return of 12 of the 16 people murdered and disappeared (mostly by the IRA) during the conflict was introduced specifically at the request of the affected families (Dempster 2016). In Uganda, the mobilization which led to the Amnesty Act of 2000 again came about following a campaign by religious, cultural, and political leaders from the region worst affected by the conflict between the Ugandan government and the Lord's Resistance Army (LRA) (Khadiagala 2001). More recently, victims' voices have been a very powerful force in the design of the partial amnesty which is an element of the Colombian peace agreement which was recently agreed between the Colombian government and FARC in Havana Cuba (Joint Communiqué 93, 2016).

Braithwaite also asked the question whether an amnesty can 'contribute to ending a war' (2002: 203) in determining whether or not it can be adjudged restorative. We have interpreted this to mean not just is the amnesty part of process that brings violent conflict to an end, but also does it 'work' in terms of 'identifying paths to prevention'. It isn't enough in a transition to simply remove the threat of prosecution. Former combatants also need to be able to avail of programmes designed to facilitate their reintegration—sometimes (controversially) also referred to as 'rehabilitation'.[11] Of course offender reintegration has long been a key objective of restorative justice in settled democracies (Bazemore and Maruna 2009; Bazemore and Dooley 2015). The argument that offenders need to be helped and to take responsibility themselves for desisting from offending as part of the process of restoring relations with victims and communities affected by their previous actions is arguably all the more compelling in transitional societies.

Such work with former combatants is normally approached through the framework of disarmament, demobilization, and reintegration (DDR) programmes that entail removing and/or destroying weapons, disbanding armed groups, and returning individuals to civilian life (Patel *et al.* 2009; Kahl 2011). Huge amounts of resources are spent on these programmes. By way of illustration, in the year 2007 $1.599 billion was spent on DDR programmes across 19 countries in the world, 9 of which were amongst the lowest ranked countries in socio-economic development (Camares/Sanz 2008). In one programme which ran for seven years, the World Bank and other partners were working across seven countries in the Great Lakes region of Central Africa assisting with the demobilization of over 300,000 ex-combatants at a cost of $450,000 million (World Bank 2010).

In reviewing the literature on such programmes, the challenges with regard to DDR programmes mirror some of the debates in reintegration, desistance, and rehabilitation studies in general. For example, there is the tentative emergence of a 'what works' movement in transitional justice which is seeking to adjudge value for money and effectiveness of transitional justice measures such as DDR by reference to a range of

[11] Many ex-combatants take the view that they have been engaged in justified armed struggle and therefore as politically motivated ex-combatants are in no need of rehabilitation, a term they associate with 'ordinary' criminals (see further Shirlow and McEvoy 2008).

indicators including levels of violence and ex-combatant recidivism rates (Van der Merwe *et al.* 2009; Olsen *et al.* 2010; Backer 2010; Dancy 2010; Hamber *et al.* 2010; Thoms *et al.* 2010)—but it is very underdeveloped. Amongst the studies which detail the difficulties for demobilized ex-combatants in getting jobs, issues with family relations, mental health, drug and alcohol abuse, and in some instances involvement in 'ordinary crime', one sees a different emphasis upon structural, cultural, political, and individualized arguments between why such projects succeed or fail (e.g. Gear 2002; Humphreys and Weinstein 2007; Rolston and Artz 2014; Banholzer 2014). Elsewhere, McEvoy (with Shirlow 2009) has offered a strong critique of some of these programmes drawing explicitly from the criminological desistance literature arguing that the assumed *passivity* of the offender or ex-combatant in such programmes is a central weakness. An assumption that DDR is something that is done *to* or *for* ex-combatants fails to grasp the central role of agency amongst such ex-combatants and indeed their capacity to provide leadership in the transformation of deeply entrenched cultures of violence precisely because of their previous involvement in violence. Adjudging therefore whether an amnesty process or a DDR programme can be adjudged restorative by helping in 'ending a war' requires that the individual ex-combatant is given space to exercise individual agency and where appropriate, leadership.

Finally with regard to both amnesties and DDR programmes, there is the complex and challenging issue of offender 'remorse'. As noted above, Braithwaite has argued that for an amnesty to be considered restorative, offenders should show 'public remorse' as well as commit to the service of the new nation. Our own instincts on this issue are that acts of apology and remorse need to emerge from organizations and individuals who have been involved in past acts of violence rather than being 'forced' from them in return for concessions if they are to be viewed as genuine by victims and affected communities. Certainly in the context of the early release of prisoners in Northern Ireland, McEvoy (with Gormally 1995) argued strongly that such a process could not be conditional upon an expression of remorse from the prisoners. In fact a series of apologies have been forthcoming from both Republican and Loyalists groupings (and the state) during the Northern Ireland peace process, but these have largely emerged organically, either to coincide with anniversaries or as a result of truth recovery efforts concerning the events (Healing Through Remembering 2016).[12] As noted above, the restorative component of amnesties may be used to incentivize ex-combatant participation in such truth recovery processes. Transitional justice scholars and activists commonly argue that such truth recovery is important for preventing a repetition of crimes and contributing to the healing of victims and society (Hayner 2011; Wiebelhaus-Brahm 2010; Kovras 2014). However, it may also help ex-combatants. Participation in truth

[12] More recent experiences in the Colombian context are also instructive. In 2014, at a press conference in Havana, Cuba, while negotiations were ongoing between FARC and the government of Colombia, the guerrilla group issued a public apology for the killing of 79 civilians in the West Colombian town of Bojaya for what has become known as the 'Bojaya Massacre'. In 2015, FARC followed up this public apology with a private apology to the victims and survivors in the town itself. A number of FARC leaders and former guerrillas also took part in a ceremony in the town where FARC again formally apologized and vowed to 'compensate for the damage done, repair the victims of these acts, as well as not ever to repeat situations like this.' See 'FARC asks Forgiveness For Killing 79 In 2002 Bojaya Massacre', *Colombia Reports*, 18 December 2014; 'FARC asks Town for Forgiveness for 2002 Tragedy that Killed 80', TeleSUR, 8 September 2015.

recovery may also enable ex-combatants to 'tell their own story and allow them to gain back the control over their position and their role in the conflict, and later also their place in the community' (Parmentier *et al.* 2008: 347). Furthermore, through publicly answering for their actions, offenders are arguably subjected to thicker and more complex versions of accountability (Mallinder and McEvoy 2011). Remorse may of course form part of the process of truth recovery, or it may emerge organically after such a process. Regardless, for truth recovery to be effective, it requires ex-combatant participation.

In sum, in looking at the applicability of criminological theory and practice to better understand 'what is transitional justice for' with regard to offenders, there are significant limitations regarding the utility of either retribution or deterrence as explanatory constructs for the punishment focused variants of transitional justice. Instead, as is discussed further below, we are more persuaded about the place of punishment as one element of broader social control strategies and as an important element of censure in establishing or re-establishing a meaningful attachment to the rule of law in post-conflict or post-authoritarian societies. In addition, we believe that there are compelling arguments to view offender related work in transitional justice through the prism of restorative justice. Whether in the guise of amnesties, usually linked to truth recovery processes, or DDR programmes designed to assist ex-combatant reintegration, it is possible to design processes which privilege ex-combatant agency and responsibility in seeking to 'make good' in Maruna's terms—putting behind their violent past 'as a necessary prelude to a productive and worthy life' (Maruna 2001: 87) and trying to repair some of the damage they have done and to restore relations with victims and communities who they have previously wronged.

VICTIMS AND VICTIMHOOD IN TRANSITIONAL SOCIETIES

In this section we wish to explore question of victims and victimhood in addressing the question of what and who is transitional justice for. The importance of victims and victimhood to transitional societies has been the subject of significant scholarly and policy attention in recent years. What Walklate (2007) has called the 'imagined victim'—the innocent, vulnerable victim who is deserving of justice—has provided justification for the more abstract aims of transitional justice (e.g. securing justice, deterrence, upholding the rule of law, and seeking truth about the past etc.) as well as the creation of the range of transitional justice mechanisms discussed above (e.g. international criminal tribunals, truth commissions, and community-based or 'bottom up' programmes (Clarke 2009; Hayner 2011; McEvoy and McGregor 2008). Indeed, victims serve a key practical and symbolic role in what Barker (2001: 6) has termed the 'self-legitimation' of almost all of those who work in the field of transitional justice.

Again our views on victims and victimhood in transitional societies have been heavily influenced by criminological writings regarding the treatment of victims in more settled democracies (McEvoy and McConnachie 2012, 2013; Dudai 2012a, 2012b; Lawther 2014). While space does not permit an exhaustive examination of the criminology/victimology literature, key themes which have shaped our views have included the historical rise of the victim in Western criminology scholarship and policy-making, the politics of victimhood, and the creation of binary oppositions between victims and perpetrators (Garland 2001; Simon 2007). Accordingly, we look more closely at the extent to which transitional justice lives up to the promise that it is 'for' victims, the ways in which victims and victimhood are sometimes politically appropriated in transitional contexts, and the particular constructions of victimhood in transitional justice which bifurcates the world into 'innocent' victims and 'guilty' perpetrators—a process which not only obscures the complexity of conflict but which also helps to create and sustain dubious hierarchies of victimhood.

As is much discussed, as the field of transitional justice has evolved, it has increasingly been described as 'victim centred' (Robins 2011). Victims are often offered as the legitimizing basis for prosecutions, truth commissions, reparations, memorialization, and the plethora of other measures deployed in transitional justice contexts (see, e.g., Fletcher 2015; Hayner 2011; Waterhouse 2009). In particular with regard to retribution in transitional justice, victims are often deployed as the central symbolic justification for the enormous financial, political, legal, and psychological effort to deal with the consequences of past violence in many of these societies. More broadly, victims make real what might otherwise be rather abstract justifications for transitional justice—such as securing justice, deterrence, establishing the 'rule of law', and determining the truth about the past. All of these might appear rather ethereal without the tangible suffering personified by victims.

The impetus towards doing transitional justice in the name of victims is of course premised upon a series of assumptions concerning what victims want or should want. As occurs in settled democracies, the imagined victim can all too easily become a political tool used to justify and legitimize particular political or policy agendas. For example, while victims are often cited as the raison d'être of international criminal tribunals, Schabas (2010) has argued that at the ICTY and ICTR at least, justice has been 'in the name of victims', but with little recognition that victims are individuals with needs and a legitimate interest in the process. Such instrumentalization constitutes a classic version of what Christie (1977) described as the 'theft' of conflict, whereby victims' voices are picked out, appropriated and re-presented to suit the aims of politicians, policy-makers, lawyers, and other elite-level actors (Madlingozi 2010). Such appropriation of victims' voices may also strip victims of their agency (Weinstein 2014). Equally, truth commissions, particularly the South African Truth and Reconciliation Commission, have been criticized on the grounds of prioritizing those victims' voices which fitted with the demands of the political landscape and the project of national reconciliation. In South Africa, the voice of the 'forgiving' victim was eulogized and large sections of the TRC report were devoted to 'exemplary' accounts of seeking and granting forgiveness (Wilson 2001; Moon 2008; Hamber 2009). Victims may in some instances be victimized twice—once by the original incident and second by their political compatibility/incompatibility with the prevailing socio-legal and political mood of the transitional justice process in which they are engaged.

Inherent to the danger of the capturing and instrumentalization of victims' voices in transitional justice is the way in which victimhood is often constructed around competing notions of 'innocent' and 'guilty' victims. For Christie (1986), the 'ideal victim' is innocent, vulnerable, and engaged in responsible behaviour when victimized. In contrast, the 'wicked' perpetrator is evil, uncivilized, and deserving of punishment or reciprocal violence (Moffett 2016). On one level, an emphasis on innocence is often a natural and expected reaction to traumatic loss, competition over victimhood, and strong emotions such as fear, anger, hurt, and loss that may be associated with past suffering (Enns 2012; Ferguson *et al.* 2010). However, such dynamics are arguably more potent in transitional contexts where victimhood is used to claim legitimacy and justification for past actions and where innocence becomes a symbol around which contested notions of past violence and suffering are constructed and reproduced (Cohen 2001; McEvoy and McConnachie 2013).

By implication, to be outside this categorization of victimhood is to be aligned with notions of guilt, illegitimacy, and complicity. Victimhood hence becomes competitive and innocence and guilt mutually dependent—the positioning of the guilty perpetrator is required to satisfy and exempt the innocent victim (Lawther 2014). These dynamics are readily identifiable in Northern Ireland, Israel/Palestine, South Africa, Argentina, Spain, and a range of other transitional sites in which we have worked. To take one example, in Northern Ireland, pro-state politicians and some unionist victims groups have repeatedly claimed to be the 'real' and 'innocent' victims of the conflict and have refused to countenance the victimhood of 'the other'. Any effort to contest such starkly polarized definitions of 'innocent victims' and 'guilty combatants' is dismissed as creating a 'moral equivalence' between terrorists and their victims and somehow justifying or legitimating past Republican (and sometimes Loyalist) actions. Victimhood becomes the terrain on which the political contests of the past are fought.

As in non-transitional contexts, an attachment of innocence to the notion of 'true' victim status can in turn help create hierarchies of victimhood (Carrabine *et al.* 2004; McAlinden 2014; McEvoy and McConnachie 2012). Such a distinction between 'deserving' and 'non-deserving' victims turns on a politically calibrated notion of suffering and legitimacy (Walklate 2011). As McAlinden (2014) points out, such hierarchies cannot easily accommodate 'deviant' victims or 'vulnerable' offenders who lie in the middle ground between the polarities of accepted victim and offender status. While criminal justice and transitional justice discourses inevitably make frequent reference to 'victims' and 'perpetrators' as 'reified and distinct' categories, not least for ease of reference (as we have done here), such neat categorizations often do not match the real world. Often former combatants themselves have been tortured or lost family or community members so that in reality they may have inflicted and endured suffering at different stages in their lives (McEvoy and McConnachie 2012: 527). In such contexts, as Bouris (2007:10) has argued, we should make space for the notion of complex victimhood where 'a victim who is no longer chained to characteristics of complete innocence and purity, but remains a victim nonetheless'. Adhering to rigid hierarchies of victims misses the complex and messy reality of conflict and the personal, social, and political contexts in which victimization and involvement in conflict occurs.

Another important variable in transitional justice constructions of victimhood is the notion of blame. In designating individuals as 'deserving' or 'undeserving' victims, it also establishes a template for the allocation of blame and the absolution of those considered 'blameless'. As Tilly (2008: 11) has contended, blaming has a particularly strong resonance in post-conflict conflicts and he identifies key elements of the transitional 'tool box' such as truth commission as forums in which a line is 'drawn between worthy and unworthy citizens'. One sees clear evidence of a linkage between victimhood (our victimhood), denial (of the victimhood of the 'other') and blame of that other for all of the ills of the past in Israel/Palestine, the Balkans, and of course Northern Ireland. This version of blame allocation, and the parallel claiming of innocence is part of the age-old tradition of scape-goating (Girard 1977, 1989) whereby locating blame in the 'other' also absolves 'us' of any semblance of guilt or responsibility. Unless carefully managed, transitional justice processes such as trials, truth commissions, or even reparations programmes (as is currently being debated in Northern Ireland—see Moffett 2016) run the risk of reifying such scape-goating.

In sum, all of us who work in the field of transitional justice would say that we are doing this work in order to try to help those who have been previously harmed in conflict zones or former authoritarian regimes. In trying to navigate this complex and controversial terrain, again we have drawn significant guidance from the rich criminological literature on the politics of victimhood. Encouraging an empathetic but where necessary critical understanding of victims and victimhood—particularly when it is used to underpin politically exclusionary, racist, sectarian, or other analogous reactionary practices—is *sina qua non* for a more a grounded understanding of what transitional justice is for.

TRANSITIONAL JUSTICE AND SOCIAL CONTROL

Having examined the role of both offenders and victims in responding to the question what is transitional justice for, we would now like to shift our gaze to the communal and societal level. Again we will draw explicitly on criminological frameworks, in particular the notion of social control. As will become apparent, our thoughts on this topic have been heavily influenced by the inimitable Stan Cohen. While Cohen was among the key scholars to deconstruct and criticize social control (1985), the later phase of his work, informed by his work on the denial of human rights violations (Cohen 2001), suggested that perhaps social control wasn't an entirely bad thing (Cohen 2011). In particular, elements of social control discourses—the classification of certain acts as deviance and the deployment of control tools to stigmatize, regulate, and punish them (Innes 2003)—can sometimes be put to positive uses as a bulwark against conservative or reactionary discourses which often deny or otherwise attempt to minimize past wrongs. This is the prism through which we wish to explore the social or communal purpose of transitional justice.

Prior to a political transition, past regimes invariably contest human rights violations—such as extrajudicial killings, torture, rape, disappearances, or genocide—by either denying them outright or else trying to contest or reshape public understandings of such abuses (Cohen 2001). At a societal level, a key task of transitional justice is therefore to counter such denial, to assert that such events happened, to locate them within the broader social or political context in which they occurred, and to mark them as deviant. To explore the ways in which this is done we want to look in particular at truth recovery as a retroactive version of social control, then look at the role of celebration of 'heroes' in transitional justice and finally at the role that civil society can play in advocating for a variant of social control from below in transitional contexts.

First we should expand a little on the notion of denial. Cohen (2001) distinguished three forms of denial. The first is what he termed literal denial: 'nothing happened' (e.g. no-one was killed). The second form is interpretive denial ('what happened is really something else'), where through denial of responsibility, isolation, and other techniques, those responsible reject the interpretive framework placed on events (e.g. someone was killed but it was unauthorized, isolated, or not by a state agent). The third form is what he termed implicatory denial: that is, this did happen but 'it was justified'. Implicatory denial may include arguments that what happened was 'necessary' or should be seen in the context of higher loyalties (e.g. someone was killed but it was a justified response to subversion threatening the nation) (Cohen 2001, esp. 103–12). These overlapping versions of denial are a constant thread in transitional contexts, part of what Cohen termed 'memory wars' (Cohen 2001: 241) over how to frame, present, and re-present the past.

If we view the common thread running through transitional justice mechanisms as countering these different forms of denial, it follows that the function they serve is often that of a political, judicial, social, and cultural reclassification of how past events should be categorized. In essence, it means categorizing as deviant the actions and policies (torture, the murder of political opponents, systemic discrimination, arrests without trial etc.) which before the transition may have routinely been accepted, authorized, normalized, or unacknowledged. This has broader and deeper manifestations and meanings than punishing offenders or a public recording of the facts: it involves acknowledgment that the past regime involved deliberate suffering and not just mistakes or misplaced idealism (Cohen 1995: 39). Innes and Clarke (2009) have offered a useful variant of what they term 'retroactive social control'. In the context of cold-case reviews of homicides in ordinary policing, they argue that retroactive social control captures a process wherein 'a previously authored official "definition of the situation" is challenged and subsequently revised' (Innes and Clarke 2009: 544). In transitional justice contexts, the version of social control we are postulating refers not only to efforts to politically or socially control a society or community but to help shape how such societies think about the past, how they see their own history.

Almost all versions of transitional justice have a role to play in such social control processes. For example, an explicit part of the function of the post-Second World War trials at Nuremberg or the international tribunals after the horrors of Rwanda or the former Yugoslavia was to 'make public memory publicly'—to use law to document and place the reality of past abuses 'on the record' (Osiel 1999). Similarly, the work of truth commissions and similar bodies in transitional contexts means more than establishing 'factual' truth (countering 'literal denial' in Cohen's terms), it is also required to address interpretive and implicatory denials. The challenge is not just to uncover new details and facts but to alter how events and policies are socially understood and remembered (Wilson 2001, 2011). Truth commissions which are investigating that human rights violations such as torture took place, often also have to frame those incidents as part of a wider pattern or of a formal policy, a symptom of broader structural problems, or indicative of many more unacknowledged similar incidents (Gready 2011). They may be required to redesignate responsibility for crimes. For example, murders or other crimes which had previously been viewed as the responsibility of a paramilitary organization may in fact be reinterpreted as the responsibility of the state which was colluding with or otherwise using such proxy organizations for its own purposes (Jamieson and McEvoy 2005; McGovern 2016). Putting together the mosaic of past atrocities, framing them in terms of the broader causes, context, and consequences of those past abuses and reframing the ways in which such events were either misunderstood or deliberately misinterpreted are central elements of any transitional society in trying to take control of its own past.

Transitional justice may require not only redefining as deviant acts previously treated as normal but also reclassifying some deviants as heroes. As Brogden (2000) has argued, to maintain social control societies need to rely not only on social censure but also on: 'social celebration'—an exultation of virtues and an elevation of the 'good'. Such social celebration complements the censure of opponents, together creating a political imagery which produces saints as well as sinners (see also Ellison 2000). While the 'celebration of heroes', assigning and reassigning prestige as a means of social control, is common in all societies (Goode 1978), the politics of praise and the use of exemplary stories and positive role models can be more profound in the transitional context. Transitional regimes may struggle to instil a respect in the new regime for human rights, democracy, and the rule of law where societies and communities have little experience of such values.

For example, the eulogizing of those involved in the struggle against apartheid in South Africa has been described as key to the process of constructing a 'new nation' (Marschall 2006; Baines 2007). Similarly in the Irish context, the 100 year anniversary of the 1916 Easter Rising has seen an interesting and reflective consideration of the role that the leaders of the rising and others have played in how the Irish revolution is remembered and its place in the nation's transition to democracy (McCarthy 2012; Ferriter 2015). The ambivalence associated with these and other contexts of the involvement of such heroes in armed struggle—and the suffering and violence that accompanied that involvement—is a common theme in many post-conflict contexts.

Less familiar however is the focus in some transitional contexts on 'rescuers': individuals who acted to protect members of an opposing ethnic or national group during genocides and ethnic conflicts such as, for example, Hutus who saved Tutsis in Rwanda (Rosoux 2006). As part of their efforts 'to deal with the past', some transitional societies have commemorated and praised the actions of such rescuers as part of efforts of public education for new values in the aftermath of identity-based conflicts (Dudai 2012b). Such acts of rescue were outlawed or socially disapproved of prior to transition (Dudai 2012b: 8); their use as role models after transition, with a social and political 'celebratory imprimatur' (Brogden 1997: 29), aims to signify the change in norms. This type of social reclassification provides transitional societies with 'narratives of altruism and intervention', demonstrating 'an alternative set of motivational accounts to be encouraged' (Cohen 2001: 267) in the new post-transition social landscape. Moreover, such celebration of rescuers and of internal 'resisters' to repressive regimes (Leebaw 2013) may also serve as an implicit censure of passive bystanders who stood by and did nothing.

Finally, in considering the social and communal role of transitional justice we wish to explore the particular role of civil society in combating denial. While transitional justice can have a tendency to focus on top down, state-like processes and institutions, the role of human rights organizations, social movements, victims groups, and others has also been identified as a crucial component in transitional justice policies and practices (McEvoy 2007; Gready 2011). Civil society groups often complement the activity of formal transitional institutions such as truth commissions, and indeed their work was identified as indispensable to the success of certain mechanisms (Crocker 2010). For example, social movements and organizations assist the work of truth commissions, courts, or reparation programmes through passing information and documentation, outreach to victims, making commissions accessible to local communities, disseminating their findings, and so on (Backer 2003). In this supportive role, civil society groups fill in the granular details of broader social control efforts initiated from above.

Yet in many other transitional cases civil society groups have acted in opposition to or independent of formal interventions, filling the gap in the context of state inaction and neglect. In this sense they exercise a form of 'social control from below' (Baumgartner 1984). In this vein, the perspective of 'transitional justice from below' (McEvoy and McGregor 2008) draws attention to bottom up projects and interventions by civil society groups and challenge the state-centred policies and discourses. These efforts include, for example, the advocacy and protest of victims groups, which view the actions of post-transition regimes in addressing past abuses as unsatisfactory and continue to apply pressure for profound steps toward redress. The activities of the South African Khulumani Support Group, challenging the post-apartheid governments for their failure to provide meaningful reparation and accountability; the Madres de Plaza de Mayo in Argentina, protesting post-transition governments' failure to resolve the 'disappearances' issue; or Colombian groups which contest the official discourse of transition from civil war and claim that reconciliation rhetoric hides the lack of truth and justice (Diaz 2008; Moon 2012), all illustrate this practice.

At other times, and perhaps most intriguingly in the context of social control from below, civil society groups have acted to fill the gap in the absence of state action. A compelling illustration is the establishment of 'unofficial truth commissions' or 'truth projects' by civil society groups: these unofficial bodies, inspired by the establishment of official truth commissions elsewhere, seek to expose truths and fight denial when the state is unwilling or unable to establish an effective truth commission. They have operated in relation to diverse contexts such as Brazil or Cambodia (Bickford 2007). In the USA, a non-official truth commission was established in Greensboro, North Carolina, to examine the legacy of racism and violence in the area, triggered by the unresolved legacy of a 1979 incident in which Ku Klux Klan members killed several participants in a civil rights march (Williams 2009). Similarly, in Northern Ireland, a nationalist community concerned by the official efforts' to focus primarily on IRA and Loyalist violence and airbrush the experiences of victims of state violence established its own unofficial localized documentation initiative, challenging official post-conflict discourses and narratives (Lundy and McGovern 2008). Other modes of informal truth-seeking mechanisms include informal 'courts', especially 'women's courts' which focus on abuses against women, for example in relation to the war in Bosnia (Clark 2016). Subversive commemorations of past abuses, carried out by oppositional civil society groups in Israel (Dudai and Cohen 2010) or Serbia (Simic and Daly 2011), which are often designed to invert official commemorations, have similarly aimed to push the state into accepting responsibility and ending denial of abuses, again speaking to the role of social control from below.

To recapitulate, at the communal and social level, transitional justice mechanisms and interventions can be viewed as engaging in a version of the key social control task of reclassifying the past. This process may also involve an effort to posit an alternative progressive set of norms and values as key to underpinning a new society for the future. For criminology more generally, these backward- and forward-looking variants of social control in transitional justice may be seen as illustrative of broader efforts to move the term away from some of its primarily negative associations and connotations about the capacity of the powerful to dominate the powerless. Transitional justice processes are by definition heightened spaces of contest and resistance. As Innes and Clarke (2009: 559) have noted, contests over the past and its contemporary meaning 'can articulate and animate changes in the architecture of power relations in the present . . . altering conditions for how social control can be imagined and practiced.'

CONCLUSION

As argued above, the ways in which post-conflict or post-authoritarian societies respond to 'system criminality' (Nollkaemper 2009)—crimes against humanity, war crimes, and mass human rights violations—has until recently remained beyond the remit of conventional criminology. As a result, the empirical and theoretical insights developed by criminologists remain under-used in the transitional justice field. While that gap has started to be filled, we believe that there is much further potential criminological scholarship to be done in the field.

The push-and-pull of 'ordinary' rule of law and 'exceptional' transitional mechanisms will likely remain as a key area of enquiry animating the theory and practice of the criminology of transitional justice. Transitional societies have often seen the 'rule of law' held out as panacea for all ills. Indeed, the early days of transitional justice were characterized by the then bold claim that the ordinary categories of crime, law, and punishment should be applied to what had hitherto been seen as 'political' questions to which ordinary law enforcement does not apply (Cohen 1996). While the potential of rule of law as a remedy has certainly been 'over-sold' to such societies by Western elites (McEvoy 2007), there is no doubt that criminal justice reforms are key elements of the broader process of rebuilding transitional societies. Thus, for example, policing, an institution which is intimately concerned both with pre-transition human rights violations and post-transition re-imagining of national ideals (Loader and Mulcahy 2003), has been a key issue in transitional reforms in places such as South Africa or Northern Ireland (Lawther 2010). Other criminal justice reforms, for example decisions to abolish—and at times to retain—the death penalty in post-conflict countries (Futamura and Bernaz 2013), likewise reflect how such societies imagine themselves and the lessons they draw from the past, expressing their responses to crises through the idiom and framework of the rule of law.

At the same time, it appears that in more and more cases established democracies respond to crises of legitimacy by appealing to the forms and the idiom of the 'exceptional' transitional justice mechanisms. Canada's decision (referred to above) to establish a truth commission to address its treatment of 'First Nations' is a compelling illustration of an appreciation in the global North that ordinary rule of law mechanisms—even in the most advanced democracies—are insufficient to address a legacy of structural abuses. In what is a further interesting intersection of criminology and transitional justice, the crises of mass incarceration and policing violence in the US has led, especially in the aftermath of Ferguson and subsequent incidences, to calls to establish a truth commission there.[13] If transitional societies seem to have often had a misplaced optimism in the power of US-style rule of law, it may be that we witness now an ironic reversal in which Americans and others have an equally optimistic view of the power of South African-style truth commissions. At any case, these developments again demonstrate that as much as transitional justice scholars can no longer ignore criminological insights on punishment and restoration, those interested in addressing the crisis of criminal justice would do well to explore the insights of transitional justice scholars.

Beyond the questions already pursued in this chapter, a research agenda for a criminology of transitional justice could also involve a systematic revisiting of some of the familiar foundational questions on responding to crime and justice, while applying them to the context of mass atrocities and their legacies. What would Durkheim have made of an International Criminal Court? How would Foucault have assessed the work of truth commissions? How can transitional justice be interpreted by enthusiasts of Norbert Elias as a 'civilizing process' framework? Engaging in such analyses can not only bring to the fore the often-overlooked social, cultural, and governmental functions of transitional justice mechanisms, but also open up for refinement and reinterpretation some basic criminological tenets—a challenging two-way process which should keep those of us interested in both fields engaged for a few years to come.

[13] Noted commentator Nicholas Kristof wrote, for example, in this context: 'let's borrow a page from South Africa and impanel a Truth and Reconciliation Commission', while Todd Landman justified his call for establishing a truth commission in the United States by pointing out that the total number of deaths from gun violence over the last three decades far exceeds the total of those killed in many civil wars around the world where such commissions were established. See 'When Whites Just Don't Get It', *New York Times*, 29 November 2014; 'Why America needs a truth commission', *Open Democracy*, 13 July 2016.

SELECTED FURTHER READING

For those interested in the historical applications of transitional justice, Elster's *Transitional Justice in Historical Perspective* (2004) traces variants of transitional justice from ancient Greece to Latin America in the 1980s, Bourbon monarchy in France in the nineteenth century and the Algerian war of independence in the late 1950s and early 1960s. Teitel's *Transitional Justice* (2000), although by no means an easy read, remains a classic in the field—particularly to explore the intersection between law and politics in a political transition. For an optimistic account of the power of human rights in transition and the possibility of holding accountable those who have committed the most egregious human rights abuses, Sikkink's *The Justice Cascade* (2011) is the 'go to' source. On specific key aspects of transitional justice, Mallinder's *Amnesty, Human Rights and Political Transitions* (2008), Hayner's *Unspeakable Truths: Transitional Justice and the Challenge of Truth Commissions* (2nd edn, 2011), and De Greiff's *Handbook of Reparations* (2006) are all excellent sources for a more rounded understanding of amnesties, truth recovery, and reparations respectively. Finally, for those interested in some self-consciously critical readings of transitional justice theory and practice, three edited collections will give students and scholars a good grasp of the contours of such critiques—Roht-Arriaza and Mariecurrena's *Transitional Justice In The Twenty-First Century* (2006), McEvoy and McGregor's *Transitional Justice from Below* (2008), and Palmer, Clarke, and Granville's *Critical Perspectives on Transitional Justice* (2012).

REFERENCES

AKHAVAN, P. (2001), 'Beyond Impunity: Can International Criminal Justice Prevent Future Atrocities?', *American Journal of International Law*, 95(1): 7–31.

AKHAVAN, P. (2013), 'The Rise, and Fall, and Rise, of International Criminal Justice', *Journal of International Criminal Justice*, 113(3): 527–36.

ARENDT, H. (1973), *The Origins of Totalitarianism*, London: Deutsch.

ARENDT, H. (1992), *Hannah Arendt, Karl Jaspers Correspondence 1926-69*, San Diego: Harcourt Brace Jovanovich.

ARTHUR, P. (2009), 'How "Transitions" Reshaped Human Rights: A Conceptual History of Transitional Justice', *Human Rights Quarterly*, 31(2): 321–67.

BACKER, D. (2003), 'Civil society and transitional justice: possibilities, patterns and prospects', *Journal of Human Rights*, 2(3): 297–313.

BACKER, D. (2010), 'Watching a Bargain Unravel? A Panel Study of Victims' Attitudes about Transitional Justice in Cape Town, South Africa', *International Journal of Transitional Justice*, 4(3): 443–56.

BAINES, G. (2007), 'The Politics of Public History in Post-Apartheid South Africa', in Stolten E. (ed.), *History Making and Present Day Politics: The Meaning of Collective Memory in South Africa*, Uppsala: Nordic Africa Institute.

BANHOLZER, L. (2014), *When Do Disarmament, Demobilisation and Reintegration Programmes Succeed?*, Bonn: Deutsches Institut für Entwicklungspolitik.

BARKER, R. (2001), *Legitimating Identities: The Self-Presentations of Rulers and Subjects*, Cambridge: Cambridge University Press.

BAUMGARTNER, M. P. (1984), 'Social control from below', in D. Black, (ed.), *Toward a General Theory of Social Control*, Orlando, FL: Academic.

BAZEMORE, G. and DOOLEY, M. (2015), 'Restorative Justice and the Offender: The Challenge of Reintegration', in G. Bazemore and M. Schiff (eds), *Restorative Community Justice: Repairing Harm and Transforming Communities*, Abingdon: Routledge.

BAZEMORE, G. and MARUNA, S. (2009), 'Restorative Justice in the Reentry Context: Building New Theory and Expanding the Evidence Base', *Victims and Offenders*, 4(4): 375–84.

BENTHAM, J. (1830), *The Rationale of Punishment*, London: R. Heward.

BICKFORD, L. (2007), 'Unofficial truth projects', *Human Rights Quarterly*, 29(4): 994–1035.

BOURIS, E. (2007), *Complex Political Victims*, Bloomfield, CT: Kumarian.

BRAITHWAITE, J. (2002), Restorative *Justice and Responsive Regulation*, Oxford: Oxford University Press.

BRAITHWAITE, J., CHARLESWORTH, H., REDDY, P., and DUNN, L. (2010), *Reconciliation and Architectures of Commitment: Sequencing Peace in Bougainville*, Canberra: ANU E Press.

BROGDEN, M. (2000), 'Burning Churches and Victim Surveys: The Myth of Northern Ireland as Low-Crime Society', *Irish Journal of Sociology*, 10(1): 27–48.

BROOKS, T. (2012), *Justice and Capabilities Approach*, Aldershot: Ashgate.

CAMARES, A. and SANZ, E. (2008), *DDR 2009. Analysis of Demobilisation, Disarmament, Reintegration*

(DDR) Programmes in the World during 2008, Bellaterra: School for a Culture of Peace.

Carrabine, E., Inganski, P., Lee, M., Plummer, K., and South, N. (2004), *Criminology: A Sociological Introduction*, Abingdon: Routledge.

Carrington, K., Hogg, R., and Sozzo, M. (2016), 'Southern Criminology', *British Journal of Criminology*, 56(1): 1–20.

Christie, N. (1977), 'Conflicts as Property', *British Journal of Criminology*, 17(1): 1–15.

Christie, N. (1986), 'The Ideal Victim', in E. A. Fattah (ed.), *From Crime Policy to Victim Policy*, London: Macmillan.

Clark, J. N. (2016), 'Transitional Justice as Recognition: An Analysis of the Women's Court in Sarajevo', *International Journal of Transitional Justice*, 10(1): 67–87.

Clarke, K. M. (2009), *Fictions of Justice: The International Criminal Court and the Challenges of Legal Pluralism in Sub-Saharan Africa*, Cambridge: Cambridge University Press.

Cohen, S. (1985), *Visions of Social Control: Crime, Punishment And Classification*, Cambridge: Polity.

Cohen, S. (1995), 'State crimes of previous regimes: Knowledge, accountability, and the policing of the past', *Law and Social Inquiry*, 20(1): 7–50.

Cohen, S. (1996), 'Crime and politics: spot the difference', *The British Journal of Sociology*, 47(1): 1–21.

Cohen, S. (2001), *States of Denial*, Cambridge: Polity.

Cohen, S. (2011), 'Whose side are we on? The Undeclared Politics of Moral Panic Theory', *Crime, Media, Culture*, 7(3): 237–43.

Collins, C. (2010), *Post-transitional Justice: Human Rights Trials in Chile and El Salvador*, Pennsylvania: Pennsylvania State University Press.

Crocker, D. (2010), 'Truth Commissions, Transitional Justice and Civil Society', in R. I. Rotberg and D. Thompson (eds), *Truth v. Justice: The Morality of Truth Commissions*, Princeton: Princeton University Press.

Cryer, R. (2005), *Prosecuting International Crimes: Selectivity and the International Criminal Law Regime*, Cambridge: Cambridge University Press.

Dancy, G. (2010), 'Impact Assessment, Not Evaluation: Defining a Limited Role for Positivism in the Study of Transitional Justice', *International Journal of Transitional Justice*, 4(3): 355–76.

De Greiff, P. (2006), *Handbook of Reparations*, Oxford: Oxford University Press.

Dempster, L. (2016), 'The Republican Movement, "Disappearing" and Framing the Past in Northern Ireland', *International Journal of Transitional Justice*, 10(2): 250–71.

Diaz, C. (2008), 'Challenging Impunity from Below: The Contested Ownership of Transitional Justice in Colombia', in K. McEvoy and L. McGregor (eds), *Transitional Justice from Below: Grassroots Activism and the Struggle for Change*, Oxford: Hart.

Drumbl, M. (2007), *Atrocity, Punishment and International Law*, Cambridge: Cambridge University Press.

Du Bois-Petain, A. (2011), *Transitional Amnesty in South Africa*, Cambridge: Cambridge University Press.

Dudai, R. (2012a), 'Informers and the Transition in Northern Ireland', *British Journal of Criminology*, 52(1): 32–54.

Dudai, R. (2012b), 'Rescues for Humanity: Rescuers, Mass Atrocities and Transitional Justice', *Human Rights Quarterly*, 34(1): 1–38.

Dudai, R. and Cohen, H. (2010), 'Dealing with the Past when the Conflict Is Still Present: Civil Society Truth-Seeking Initiatives in the Israeli-Palestinian Conflict', in R. Shaw, L. Waldorf, and P. Hazzan (eds), *Localizing Transitional Justice: Interventions and Priorities after Mass Violence*, Stanford: Stanford University Press

Ellison, G. (2000), 'Reflecting all shades of opinion', *British Journal of Criminology*, 40(1): 88–111.

Elster, J. (2004), *Closing the Books: TransitionalJjustice in Historical Perspective*, Cambridge: Cambridge University Press..

Enns, D. (2012), *The Violence of Victimhood*, Pennsylvania: Penn State University Press.

Ferriter, D. (2015), *A Nation and Not a Rabble: The Irish Revolutions, 1913-23*, London: Profile Books.

Futamura, M. and Bernaz, N. (2013), *The Politics of the Death Penalty in Countries in Transition*, Abingdon: Routledge.

Ferguson, N., Burgess, N., and Hollywood, I. (2010), 'Who are the Victims? Victimhood Experiences in Post-Agreement Northern Ireland', *Political Psychology*, 31(6): 857–86.

Fletcher, L. (2015), 'Refracted Justice: The Imagined Victim and the International Criminal Court', in S. De Vos, S. Kendall, and C. Stahn (eds), *Contested Justice: The Politics and Practice of International Criminal Court Interventions*, Cambridge: Cambridge University Press.

Freeman, M. (2009), *Necessary Evils: Amnesties and the Search for Justice*, Cambridge: Cambridge University Press.

Garland, D. (2001), *The Culture of Control: Crime and Social Order in Contemporary Society*, Oxford: Oxford University Press.

Gear, S. (2002), 'Wishing Us Away: Challenges Facing Ex-Combatants in the "New" South Africa', *Violence and Transition Series*, 8, Johannesburg: Centre for the Study of Violence and Reconciliation.

Girard, R. (1977), *Violence and the Sacred*, P. Gregory (trans), Baltimore, MD: John Hopkins University Press.

Girard, R. (1989), *The Scapegoat*, Baltimore, MD: John Hopkins University Press.

Golash, D. (2005), *The Case Against Punishment: Retribution, Crime Prevention and the Law*, New York: New York University Press.

Goode, W. J. (1978), *The Celebration of Heroes: Prestige as a Control System*, Berkeley: University of California Press.

Gormally, B. and McEvoy, K. (1995), *Release and Reintegration of Politically Motivated Prisoners in Northern Ireland: A Comparative Study of South Africa, Israel/Palestine, Italy, Spain, The Republic of Ireland and Northern Ireland*, Belfast: NIACRO.

GREADY, P. (2011), *The Era of Transitional Justice. The Aftermath of the Truth and Reconciliation Commission in South Africa and Beyond*, Abingdon: Routledge.

GREEN, P. and WARD, T. (2006), *State Crime: Governments, Violence and Corruption*, London: Pluto.

HAMBER, B. (2009), *Transforming Societies After Political Violence*, Heidelberg, Germany: Springer.

HAMBER, B., SEVCENKO, L., and NAIDU, E. (2010), 'Utopian Dreams or Practical Possibilities? The Challenges of Evaluating the Impact of Memorialization in Societies in Transition', *International Journal of Transitional Justice*, 4(3): 397–420.

HARDIE-BICK, J., SHEPTYCKI, J., and WARDAK, A. (2005), 'Transnational and Comparative Criminology in a Global Perspective', in J. Sheptycki and A. Wardak (eds), *Transnational and Comparative Criminology*, London: GlassHouse.

HAYNER, P. (2011), *Unspeakable Truths: Transitional Justice and the Challenge of Truth Commissions*, Abingdon: Routledge.

HEALING THROUGH REMEMBERING (2016), *Apologies, Acknowledgement and Dealing with the Past in and About Northern Ireland*, Belfast: Healing Through Remembering, unpublished report, copy on file with authors.

HEGEL, G. (1952), *Hegel's Philosophy of Right*, translated by T. Knox, Oxford: Oxford University Press.

HENMAN, R. (2004), 'Conceptualizing Access to Justice and Victims' Rights in International Sentencing', *Social and Legal Studies*, 13(1): 27–56.

HUMPHREYS, M. and WEINSTEIN, H. (2007), 'Demobilization and Reintegration', *Journal of Conflict Resolution*, 51(4): 531–67.

IGNATIEFF, M. (2003), *Empire Lite: Nation Building in Bosnia, Kosovo and Afghanistan*, London: Vintage.

INNES, M. (2003), *Understanding Social Control*, Berkshire: Open University Press.

INNES, M. and CLARKE, A. (2009), 'Policing the past: cold case studies, forensic evidence and retroactive social control', *The British Journal of Sociology*, 60(3): 543–63.

JACKSON, M. (2007), 'The Customary International Law Duty to Prosecute Crimes Against Humanity: A New Framework', *Tulane Journal of International and Comparative Law*, 16(1): 117–56.

JACOBS, B. (2010), 'Deterrence and Deterrability', *Criminology*, 48(2): 417–41.

JAMIESON, R. (1998), 'Towards a Criminology of War in Europe', in V. Ruggiero, N. South, and I. Taylor (eds), *The New European Criminology*, London: Routledge.

JAMIESON, R. (ed.) (2014), *The Criminology of War*, Abingdon: Routledge.

JAMIESON, R. and MCEVOY, K. (2005), 'State Crime by Proxy and Juridical Othering', *British Journal of Criminology*, 45(4): 504–27.

JEFFERY, R. (2014), *Amnesties, Accountability and Human Rights*, Pennsylvania: University of Pennsylvania Press.

JOINET, L. (1985), 'Study on Amnesty Laws and Their Role in the Safeguard and Protection of Human Rights', UN Doc E/CN.4/Sub.2/1985/16.

JOINT COMMUNIQUÉ 93 (2016), Havana, Cuba, 24 August 2016, available at: https://www.mesadeconversaciones.com.co/sites/default/files/comunicado-conjunto-93-24-de-agosto-de-2016-vf-ingles-1472131587.pdf, accessed 27 December 2016.

KAHL, M. (2011), *Disarmament, Demobilisation and Reintegration: The Challenge of Socio-Economic Reintegration of Ex-Combatants After War and the Role of the International Financial Institutions*, Saarbrucken: VDM Verlag Dr. Muller.

KENNEDY, P. (2008), *Deterrence and Crime Prevention: Reconsidering the Prospect of Sanction*, Abingdon: Routledge.

KHADIAGALA, G. M. (2001), The *Role of the Acholi Religious Leaders' Peace Initiative (ARLPI) in Peace Building in Northern Uganda*, Washington: USAID.

KOVRAS, I. (2014), *Truth Recovery and Transitional Justice: Deferring Human Rights Issues*, Abingdon: Routledge.

KU, J. and NZELIBE, J. (2006), 'Do International Criminal Tribunals Deter or Exacerbate Humanitarian Atrocities?', *Washington Law Review*, 84(4): 777–833.

LAPLANTE, L. (2008), 'Outlawing Amnesty: The Return of Criminal Justice in Transitional Justice Schemes', *Virginia Journal of International Law*, 49(4): 915–82.

LAWTHER, C. (2010), '"Securing" the Past: Policing and the Contest over Truth in Northern Ireland', *British Journal of Criminology*, 50(3): 455–73.

LAWTHER, C. (2014), *Truth, Denial and Transition: Northern Ireland and the Contested Past*, Abingdon: Routledge.

LAWTHER, C. (2014), 'The Construction and Politicisation of Victimhood', in O. Lynch and J. Argomaniz (eds), *Victims of Terrorism: A Comparative and Interdisciplinary Study*, Abingdon: Routledge.

LEEBAW, B. (2008), 'The Irreconcilable Goals of Transitional Justice', *Human Rights Quarterly*, 30(1): 95–118.

LEEBAW, B. (2013), 'Lost, Forgotten, or Buried? Transitional Justice, Agency, and the Memory of Resistance', *Politica and Società*, 2(2): 237–64.

LOADER, I. and MULCAHY, A. (2003), *Policing and the Condition of England: Memory, Politics and Culture*, Oxford: Oxford University Press.

LUNDY, P. and MCGOVERN, M. (2008), 'Whose Justice? Rethinking Transitional Justice from the Bottom Up', *Journal of Law and Society*, 35(2): 265–92.

MADLINGOZI, T. (2010), 'On transitional justice entrepreneurs and the production of victims', *Journal of Human Rights Practice*, 2(2): 208–28.

MALLINDER, L. (2008), *Amnesty, Human Rights and Political Transitions: Bridging the Peace and Justice Divide*, Oxford: Hart.

MALLINDER, L. (2014), 'Amnesties in the Pursuit of Reconciliation, Peacebuilding and Restorative Justice', in D. Philpott and J. Llewellyn (eds), *Restorative Justice, Reconciliation and Peacebuilding*, Oxford: Oxford University Press.

MALLINDER, L. and MCEVOY, K. (2011), 'Rethinking Amnesties: Atrocity, Accountability and Impunity in Post Conflict Societies', *Contemporary Social Science*, 6(1): 107–28.

Marschall, S. (2006). 'Commemorating "Struggle Heroes": Constructing a Genealogy for the New South Africa', *International Journal of Heritage Studies*, 12(2): 176–93

Maruna, S. (2001), *Making Good: How Ex-Convicts Reform and Rebuild Their Lives*, Washington, DC: American Psychological Association.

McAlinden, A. M. (2014), 'Deconstructing Victim and Offender Identities in Discourses on Child Sexual Abuse: Hierarchies, Blame and the Good/ Evil Dialectic', *British Journal of Criminology*, 54(2): 180–98.

McCargo, D. (2015), 'Transitional Justice and Its Discontents', *Journal of Democracy*, 26(2): 5–20.

McCarthy, M. (2012), *Ireland's 1916 Rising: Explorations of History-Making, Commemoration & Heritage in Modern Times*, London: Ashgate.

McEvoy, K. (2001), *Paramilitary Imprisonment in Northern Ireland: Resistance, Management and Release*, Oxford: Oxford University Press.

McEvoy, K. (2007), 'Beyond Legalism: Towards a Thicker Understanding of Transitional Justice', *Journal of Law and Society*, 34(4): 411–40.

McEvoy, K. and Mallinder, L. (2013), 'Amnesties, Transition and the Governing of Mercy', in J. Simon and R. Sparks (eds), *Handbook of Punishment and Society*, London: Sage.

McEvoy, K. and Mallinder, L. (2016), 'Politics, Theory and Praxis: The "Respectibilisation" of Transitional Justice', in K. McEvoy, and L. Mallinder (eds), *Transitional Justice*, Abingdon: Routledge.

McEvoy, K. and McConnachie, K. (2012), 'Victimology in transitional justice: Victimhood, innocence and hierarchy', *European Journal of Criminology*, 9(5): 527–38.

McEvoy, K. and McConnachie, K. (2013), 'Victims and Transitional Justice: Voice, Agency and Blame', *Social and Legal Studies*, 22(4): 489–513.

McEvoy, K. and McGregor, L. (2008), *Transitional Justice from Below: Grassroots Activism and the Struggle for Change*, Oxford: Hart.

McEvoy, K. and Newburn, T. (2003), *Criminology, Conflict Resolution and Restorative Justice*, Basingstoke: Palgrave Macmillan.

McEvoy, K. and Shirlow, P. (2009), 'Re-Imagining DDR: Ex-Combatants, Leadership and Moral Agency in Conflict Transformation', *Theoretical Criminology*, 13(1): 31–59.

Mills, K. (2015), *International Responses to Mass Atrocities in Africa. Responsibility to Protect, Prosecute, and Palliate*, Pennsylvania: University of Pennsylvania Press.

Moffett, L. (2016), 'Reparations for "Guilty Victims": Navigating Complex Identities of Victim-Perpetrators in Reparation Mechanisms', *International Journal of Transitional Justice*, 10(1): 146–67.

Moon, C. (2008), *Narrating Political Reconciliation: South Africa's Truth and Reconciliation Commission*, Plymouth: Lexington Books.

Moon, C. (2012), '"Who'll Pay Reparations on My Soul?" Compensation, Social Control and Social Suffering', *Social and Legal Studies*, 21(2): 187–99.

Nelken, D. (2009), 'Comparative Criminal Justice Beyond Ethnocentrism and Relativism', *European Journal of Criminology*, 6(4): 291–311.

Niezen, R. (2013), *Truth and Indignation: Canada's Truth and Reconciliation Commission on Indian Residential Schools*, Toronto: University of Toronto Press.

Nollkaemper, A. (2009), *System Criminality in International Law*, Cambridge: Cambridge University Press.

O'Donnell, G. and Schmitter, P. (1986), *Transitions from Authoritarian Rule: Prospects for Democracy—Tentative Conclusions about Uncertain Democracies*, London: John Hopkins University Press.

Olsen, T., Payne, L., and Reiter, A. (2010), 'The Justice Balance: When Transitional Justice Improves Human Rights and Democracy', *Human Rights Quarterly*, 32(4): 980–1007.

Orentlicher, D. F. (1991), 'Settling Accounts: The Duty to Prosecute Human Rights Violations of a Prior Regime', *The Yale Law Journal*, 100(8): 2537–615.

Osiel, M. (1999), *Mass Atrocity, Collective Memory, and the Law*, New Brunswick: Transaction.

Palmer, N., Clarke, P., and D. Granville (eds) (2012), *Critical Perspectives in Transitional Justice*, Antwerp: Intersentia.

Parmentier, S., Vanspauwen, K., and Weitkamp, E. (2008), 'Dealing with the legacy of mass violence: changing lenses to restorative justice', in S. Alette and H. Roelof (eds), *Supranational Criminology: Towards a Criminology of International Crimes*, Antwerp: Intersentia.

Patel, A., De Greiff, P., and Waldorf, L. (2009), *Disarming the Past: Transitional Justice and Ex-Combatants*, New York: Social Science Research Council.

Posner, E. A. and Vermeule, A. (2004), 'Transitional Justice as Ordinary Justice', *Harvard Law Review*, 117(3): 761–825.

Rafter, N. (2016), *The Crime of All Crimes. Toward a Criminology of Genocide*, New York: New York University Press.

Roberts, P. (2003), 'Restoration and Retribution in International Criminal Justice: An Exploratory Analysis', in A. von Hirsch, J. Roberts, A. Bottoms, K. Roach, and M. Schiff (eds), *Restorative Justice and Criminal Justice: Competing or Reconcilable Paradigms?*, Oxford: Hart.

Robins, S. (2011), 'Towards victim-centred transitional justice: Understanding the needs of families of the disappeared in postconflict Nepal', *International Journal of Transitional Justice*, 5(1): 75–98.

Roht-Arriaza, N. and Mariecurrena, J. (eds) (2006), *Transitional Justice In The Twenty-First Century: Beyond Truth Versus Justice*, Cambridge: Cambridge University Press.

Rolston, B. and Artz, L. (2014), 'Re-entry problems: the post-prison challenges and experiences of former political prisoners in South Africa and Northern Ireland', *International Journal of Human Rights*, 18(7–8): 861–80.

ROSENBERG, S. (2012), 'The Relationship between the International Criminal Court and the Prevention of Mass Atrocities', Jerusalem: Genocide Prevention.

ROSOUX, V. (2006), 'The Figure of the Righteous Individual in Rwanda', *International Social Science Journal*, 58(189): 491–9.

RUGGIERO, V. (2006), *Understanding Political Violence. A Criminological Analysis*, Berkshire: Open University Press.

SCHABAS, W. (2010), 'Victor's Justice: Selecting "Situations" at the International Criminal Court', *The John Marshall Law Review*, 43(3): 535–52.

SCHABAS, W. (2011), 'Criminology, Accountability and International Justice', in M. Bosworth and C. Hoyle (eds), *What is Criminology?*, Oxford: Oxford University Press.

SCHABAS, W. (2012), *Unimaginable Atrocities*, Oxford: Oxford University Press.

SCHARF, M. (1996), 'The Letter of the Law: The Scope of the International Legal Obligation to Prosecute Human Rights Crimes', *Law and Contemporary Problems*, 59(Fall): 41–62.

SIKKINK, K. (2011), *The Justice Cascade: How Human Rights Prosecutions Are Changing World Politics*, New York: WW Norton and Co.

SHIRLOW, P. and MCEVOY, K. (2008), *Beyond the Wire: Former Prisoners and Conflict Transformation in Northern Ireland*, London: Pluto.

SIMIĆ, O. & DALY, K. (2011). 'One Pair of Shoes, One Life': Steps towards Accountability for Genocide in Srebrenica', *International Journal of Transitional Justice*, 5(3): 477–91.

SIMON, J. (2007), Governing *through Crime: How the War on Crime Transformed American Democracy and Created a Culture of Fear*, New York: Oxford University Press.

SNYDER, J. and VINJAMURI, L. (2004), 'Trials and Errors. Principle and Pragmatism in Strategies of International Justice', *International Security*, 28(3): 5–44.

SOUTH AFRICAN TRUTH AND RECONCILIATION COMMISSION (1998), *Truth and Reconciliation Commission of South Africa Report*, Cape Town: Juta.

TAKEMURA, H. (2007), 'Big Fish and Small Fish Debate—An Examination of the Prosecutorial Discretion', *International Criminal Law Review*, 7(4): 677–85.

TEITEL, R. (2000), *Transitional Justice*, Oxford: Oxford University Press.

TEITEL, R. (2003), 'Human Rights in Transition: Transitional Justice Genealogy', *Harvard Human Rights Journal*, 16: 69–94.

TEITEL, R. (2008), 'Editorial Note—Transitional Justice Globalized', *International Journal of Transitional Justice*, 2(1): 1–4.

THOMS, O., RON, J., and PARIS, R. (2010), 'State level effects of transitional justice: What do we know?', *International Journal of Transitional Justice*, 4(3): 329–54.

TILLY, C. (2008), *Credit and Blame*, Princeton: Princeton University Press.

TONRY, M. (2008), 'Learning from the Limitations of Deterrence Research', *Crime and Justice*, 37(1): 279–312.

UNITED NATIONS SECURITY COUNCIL (2004), *The Rule of Law and Transitional Justice in Conflict and Post-Conflict Societies*, UN Doc S/2004/616.

VAN DER MERWE, H., BAXTER, V., and CHAPMAN, A. (2009), *Assessing the Impact of Transitional Justice: Challenges for Empirical Research*, Washington: United States Institute of Peace Press.

VON HIRSCH, A., BOTTOMS, A., BURNEY, E., and WIKSTRÖM, P. O. (1999), *Criminal Deterrence and Sentencing Severity*, Oxford: Bloomsbury.

WALKLATE, S. (2007), *Imagining the Victim of Crime*, New York: McGraw-Hill.

WALKLATE, S. (2011), 'Reframing Criminal Victimization: Finding a Place for Vulnerability and Resilience', *Theoretical Criminology*, 15(2): 179–94.

WALKLATE, S. and MCGARRY, R. (eds) (2015), *Criminology and War: Transgressing the Borders*, Abingdon: Routledge.

WATERHOUSE, C. (2009), 'The good, the bad, and the ugly: Moral agency and the role of victims in reparations programs', *University of Pennsylvania Journal of International Law*, 31(1): 257–94.

WEBER, L., FISHWICK, E., and MARMO, M. (2016), *The Routledge International Handbook of Criminology and Human Rights*, Abingdon: Routledge.

WEINSTEIN, H. (2014), 'Victims, Transitional Justice and Social Reconstruction: Who is Setting the Agenda?', in I. Vanfraechem, A. Pemberton, and F. Mukwiza Ndahinda (eds), *Justice for Victims: Perspectives on Rights, Transitions and Reconciliation*, New York: Routledge.

WIEBELHAUS-BRAHM, E. (2010), *Truth Commissions and Transitional Societies. The Impact on Human Rights and Democracy*, London: Routledge.

WILLIAMS, J. E. (2009), 'Legitimacy and effectiveness of a grassroots Truth and Reconciliation Commission', *Law and Contemporary Problems*, 72(2): 143–150.

WILSON, R. (2001), *The Politics of Truth and Reconciliation in South Africa: Legitimizing the Post-Apartheid State*, Cambridge: Cambridge University Press.

WORLD BANK (2010), *Multi-Country Demobilization and Re-integration Program Final Report. Overview of Program Achievements*, Washington: World Bank.

YOUNG, J. (2011), *The Criminological Imagination*, Oxford: Polity.

18

RETHINKING COMPARATIVE CRIMINAL JUSTICE

David Nelken

INTRODUCTION

Since the last edition of this *Handbook* was published the literature relevant to comparing criminal justice has grown exponentially, reflecting increased knowledge of what is going on elsewhere, as well as the perceived need for more collaboration in the light of changes in crime threats and responses. There is now a marked and welcome increase in writing geared explicitly to cross-national description and explanation.[1] To a lesser extent, more attention is also beginning to be given to the theoretical and methodological challenges of cross-cultural comparison.[2] Criminologists (especially those working outside the USA) are now less likely to take American society as the default background to their work, even if assumptions based on the shape of crime and the role of criminal justice in the global North remain well entrenched.

This chapter is a considerably rewritten version of the one in the previous edition of the *Handbook*. It does not attempt the impossible task of summarizing what is known about different systems of criminal justice around the world but rather continues to focus on the underlying point of the exercise. Why do we do such research, and what approaches can we draw on? How should we go about finding similarities and differences? What are the main challenges currently facing the field? Last, but not least, which are the best methods to use in gathering our data?

[1] In the last five years, the *European Journal of Criminology*, for example, has included cross-national articles on topics such as the effects of suspended sentences; children's experiences of contact with imprisoned parents; confidence in the (criminal justice) system and attitudes to punishment; contrasts in the place and role of victims; differences in trust of the police amongst different groups of citizens—and differences in how far the police trust the populations they police.

[2] See the special issue of the *European Journal of Criminology* in 2015 (Vol. 12(4–5), and papers published in recent years in the *British Journal of Criminology, Punishment and Society, Crime, Law and Social Change*, and *Theoretical Criminology*.

APPROACHING CRIMINAL JUSTICE COMPARATIVELY

What is comparative criminal justice good for? This depends on what we are trying to achieve. We can pursue more theoretical goals, involving classification, description, explanation, and interpretation (Nelken 2010), or more practical and policy oriented purposes to do with borrowing from other places or helping them change (Frase 1990). Problematizing cultural assumptions can be both intellectually stimulating and practically relevant. British writing on the police used to take it as a universal truth that nothing could be more ill-advised than for them to risk losing touch with the public by relying too much on military, technological, or other impersonal methods of crime control. The results of this, it is claimed, could only be a spiral of alienation that would spell the end of 'policing by consent'. In Italy, however, two of the main police forces are still part of the military, and this insulation from the pressures of local people is actually what inspires public confidence.

As this suggests, the aims of learning about or from difference often overlap. On the other hand, practical goals can sometimes lead us astray. Are we trying to understand better 'the other' or ourselves? The answer must be the one in the light of the other. But we may be in such a hurry to draw policy conclusions that we foreshorten or distort our accounts of other places, producing what can be described as 'foil comparisons' (Nelken 2015a) that end up reinforcing existing assumptions and values rather than startling us into understanding ourselves anew in the light of others.[3]

What is the relationship between comparative criminal justice and criminology? Can studying criminal justice comparatively help in reducing crime? Michael Tonry, a world-leading penologist, has recently written that such work tries to teach us about 'better ways of dealing with familiar problems' (2015: 507). It can also help in 'examining conditions under which countries successfully import ideas from elsewhere' (Tonry 2015: 506). Finally and 'most important', it can 'put national policies and practices into cross-national contexts in order to know what differences they make in national patterns of crime and punishment'.(ibid.: 506) But, strikingly, he also warns the many policy-makers eager to borrow more 'effective' forms of crime control that the news is not encouraging. 'Crime rates and patterns' he argues, 'appear largely oblivious to criminal justice policies and to be shaped by deep cross-national forces. Punishment policies and practices to the contrary are products of distinctive national histories and political cultures and have little effect on crime rates and patterns' (ibid.: 511–12).

The evidence from victim surveys carried out over the last 30 years suggests that changes over time in national prison rates and cross-national differences in incarceration are not well correlated with changing rates of crime. Likewise, official sanctions are only one of the factors that affect crime rates amongst the many other more important determinants (also because so few cases of offending are normally apprehended and punished). But it is not clear how far we should take his argument. Are crime rates

[3] '... the end of our exploring. Will be to arrive where we started. And know the place for the first time' (Eliot 1943).

really 'oblivious' to criminal justice? (It can often be hard to draw a line between the two.[4]) From a theoretical point of view, deviance and control are intimately related; the response to behaviour is often constitutive of what counts as crime, and plays a crucial role in shaping how and when primary deviance becomes secondary deviation—as well as in explaining why crime 'waves' rise and fall (Ditton 1979).

The empirical reasons given for why criminal justice practices are unlikely to influence crime rates are still more puzzling. The claim that crime rates are shaped by 'deep cross-national forces', whereas criminal justice policies are the product of 'distinctive national histories and political cultures', whilst often true, could just as easily be reversed. Some crime trends, for example gun crime in USA or the roots of organized crime in Italy, are nationally idiosyncratic. Conversely, trends in responding to crime are frequently shaped by ideas, blueprints, and initiatives that arise elsewhere and spread internationally. It is more plausible to argue that both crime and criminal justice can be either shaped by local or by cross-national factors and that the task for comparative criminal justice is to trace the possible connections between them.

In any case Tonry's point is not that criminal justice and crime are unrelated, but, on the contrary, the need for policy-makers to recognize that they play a part in making the connection. 'Mass imprisonment in the USA', he tells us 'was not the inexorable product of rising or high crime rates, but the consequential result of conscious policy choices' (Tonry 2015: 507). But if, as he argues, we have only weak levers for reducing crime, what can be meant by 'better ways of dealing with problems' or the 'successful' importation of ideas? Could this refer to introducing improvements in criminal procedure or finding ways to increase public confidence? Interestingly, the extent to which systems of criminal justice are judged mainly by their success in reducing crime and recidivism is itself a cultural variable. Many Anglo-American writers assume that what is right is what 'works' (in terms of reducing crime rates); in some continental European countries such as Italy commentators are more inclined to say that which works is what is right. The secret of good comparative research is coming up with and exploring such contrasts.

In taking such research further we can distinguish three main approaches. There is first of all the sort of work that aims to validate explanatory theories of crime or social control (often described as 'behavioural science' or 'positivist' social science). The currently renewed interest in establishing and spreading 'evidence-based', trans-cultural knowledge of 'what works' in responding to crime (Sherman *et al.* 1997) is an important example of the search for universal knowledge in this field. As David Farrington recently put it '[t]he main justification for cross-national comparisons is to establish the generalisability of theories and results and the boundary conditions under which they do or do not hold. It is also important to investigate to what extent interventions to prevent or reduce offending have similar effects in different times' (Farrington 2015: 387).

[4] In some situations crime (as in so-called honour killings) can itself be seen as a form of criminal justice (Black 1983). In others, criminal justice is arguably akin to crime, for example the criminalization of indigenous resistance to colonization which silenced criticism of the mass dispossession and the theft of land (Cunneen 2011).

By contrast, authors who follow the 'interpretivist' approach are more concerned to investigate the ways the meaning of crime and criminal justice is embedded within changing historical and cultural contexts. Writers following this approach seek to uncover the local understandings of the factors and variables that positivist social scientists take as the starting or end points of their comparisons. The various meanings (or lack of meaning) of concepts such as prison, police, security, appeal, even the idea of criminal justice itself, need careful excavation. Terms like 'discretion', for example, can be treated as a variable to be compared in studying processes of decision-making or interrogated as a pointer to distinct sets of political concerns (Nelken 1994). Universalistic claims such as the assumption that all legal systems must find ways of relieving caseload pressures (if not by allowing plea-bargaining then through some other 'functional equivalent') turn out to be cultural projections rather than social scientific truisms. If the positivist approach operationalizes 'culture' (or deliberately simplified aspects of it) so as to explain variation in levels and types of crime and social control, this second approach tends to use evidence about crime and criminal justice as an 'index' of culture.

Care needs to be taken not to take for granted that any given practice or discourse of criminal justice necessarily 'resonates' with the wider culture (Nelken 2011c). In many societies there is a wide gulf between legal and general culture, as where the criminal law purports to maintain principles of impersonal equality before the law in polities where clientalistic and other particularistic practices are widespread. Specific ideals and values of criminal justice may also be the subject matter of fierce debates. It is not easy to decide which are relatively enduring features and which only contingent aspects of given cultures. What are taken to be entrenched cultural practices in the sphere of criminal justice can be overturned with remarkable rapidity. Relying on simplistic ideas of national character would make it difficult to reconcile the defiance of law in Weimar Germany as compared to the over-deference of the Fascist period.

There is, finally, a more legal literature that focuses on the rules, ideals, and 'law in action' in other jurisdictions (the approach followed by 'legal comparativists' and 'policy researchers). This approach highlights above all the role of criminal justice institutions and criminal procedure.[5] The advantage of giving attention to jurisdictionally circumscribed rules and ideals is that this connects with what legal actors say they are trying to do. Its weakness lies in assuming that social actors always know the causes and consequences of their actions, and it has difficulty in deciding how far what legal actors say they are trying to do should trump what the observer says they are doing (as seen in the famous debate over the relationship between prosecutors and police in European systems compared to the USA; see Goldstein and Marcus 1977; Langbein and Weinreb 1978).

Noting the differences between these approaches can help make sense of key debates in the field such as that over the alleged recent rise in punitiveness. Most of the running has been made by a search for explanatory factors. Originally emphasis was laid on the 'culture of control' of late modernity, that was seen as a result of cultural changes including the increasing exposure to crime of the middle classes (Garland 2001).

[5] See, e.g., the journals *Criminal Law Forum; European Journal of Crime, Criminal Law and Criminal Justice*; and *Journal of Crime, Criminal Law and Criminal Justice*. This writing normally avoids engagement with sociological theory. For an interesting exception see Wandall (2006).

The thesis came to be modified as applying mainly to the USA, and, to a lesser extent, other places affected by the growth of neoliberal ideology. Evidence was provided to show that imprisonment rates varied from high to low amongst four types of political economy: neoliberal, conservative-corporatist, social democratic, and oriental-corporatist (Cavadino and Dignan 2006). Amongst many other causal independent variables canvassed, attention has been given to institutional arrangements and political factors such as proportional representation (Lacey 2008) and the role of the media (Savelsberg 1994; Greene 2008). Not all of these contributions come from positivists, but the flavour of this style of argument is seen when Lappi-Seppälä (2008: 368) tells us that, 'among western European countries, about half of imprisonment rate variation is explained by type of democracy and degree of corporatism'.

The role of more interpretative approaches is best seen in their discussion of the possible meanings of the dependent variable of punitiveness (Hamilton 2014). The starting point is the operationalization of this key concept. Are incarceration rates the best way of getting at punitiveness? Many of the countries that have low incarceration rates, such as Sweden, use shorter prison terms but actually send relatively more people to prison than those with higher overall rates. Does this show less punitiveness than sending fewer people for longer periods? What of harshness more generally (Whitman 2003)? Is leniency the opposite of punitiveness or could it be permissiveness, indulgence, favouritism, neglect, indifference, impunity, denial, or collusion (Nelken 2005, 2006a)? Whose views matter and why?

In addition, the legal process must be seen as an important part of any explanation of criminal justice outcomes. In Italy, for example, the procedural guarantees of the adversarial system (relying on the forensic contest of the trial) introduced in the 1989 reform of criminal procedure, were simply added to the ones that belong to the inquisitorial tradition. Even quite minor cases go through a series of procedural hoops and are reviewed by a large number of judges. There are two stages of appeal (the first stage being a retrial on the facts). Uniquely, the so-called 'prescription', statute of limitations period, after which criminal proceedings become null and void, continues to run until the cassation court has given its final verdict. Imprisonment rate are low therefore because of the high rate of attrition—many cases start out but few arrive at a conclusion. Yet such attrition is not related in any simple way with differences in processes of social and economic inclusion.

The best writing about comparative criminal justice tries to draw on all these approaches so as to balance generalizing claims with sensitivity to different social meanings and legal traditions (Nelken 2010). Hamilton for example, in her recent comparative study of youth justice regimes, quotes one policy-making informant who suggests that Scotland's relatively lenient approach to young offenders is 'based upon Presbyterianism or indeed Calvinism. It's part of the egalitarian interest of Scotland: 'We're all Jock Tamson's bairns; these are our kids. These kids who are misbehaving, there's some right bad people who have to go to prison but the rest of them, they're our laddies . . . they're our folk. We can't send them to the colonies' (Hamilton 2013: 162; see also Hamilton 2016). She adds that 'The roots of this culture . . . may be related to the higher levels of poverty in certain Scottish cities such as Glasgow, its history of trade unionism or indeed democratic traditions within the Church'. On the other hand, such claims about long-standing reasons for leniency can underestimate the importance of law, such as the radical change represented by the introduction in 1970 of the Children's Hearing System based on welfare principles and representation of the community in decision-making. Before that (or so we were told as new Panel members in the training for our roles), children were processed in ways that treated them more like adults.

UNDERSTANDING SIMILARITIES AND DIFFERENCES

In practice the choice of what to compare is often a matter of convenience and ease of access. In larger collective works, for example, academics or practitioners are just asked to tell the story of what has been happening in their jurisdiction. In this sort of 'comparison by juxtaposition' it is left to the reader (or sometimes to the editor) to decide what, if anything, makes the places chosen commensurable. But similarities and differences are always relative. We need to think about why exactly places are being compared, in relation to which issues, and from what 'starting point'. If we write about 'exceptional' places (and the list of places described in this way grows ever longer) we beg the question of what we are taking to be 'normal' and why.

If we choose to write say about the Japanese way of justice (Johnson 2000, 2001) or French criminal justice (Hodgson 2005) who are our potential readers, what we can take for granted, and what do we think they need to know? Lacey and Zedner, for example, marvel at what they call the 'significant absence' of reference to 'community' in discourse about crime prevention in Germany (Zedner 1995; Lacey and Zedner 1995, 1998). But the absence is one that depends on the Anglo-American starting point (in Italy the term community tends to be applied mainly to religious groups).

The problem of building sound comparisons is sometimes posed as ensuring that we 'compare like with like'. But what this means is not obvious. If places were not at least in some respects unalike there would be no point in comparing them. But if they are too unalike there may not be much to learn from any comparison. Take again the debate about relative punitiveness. The fact that criminal justice is but one aspect of the larger field of formal and informal social controls (themselves shaped by and expressing social structure and culture) seriously complicates any claims we may want to make. US prison rates went up sevenfold after the end of slavery. Is this evidence of more or less repression? How are we to make sense of the fact that as Kazakhstan or Belorussia have become more autocratic their leaders have cut back on their prison populations?

All this gets in the way of explanations that base themselves only on official crime statistics. What of police extrajudicial killings in Brazil, Pakistan, or the Philippines[6]

[6] More than a thousand Filipinos have reportedly been murdered or disappeared as a result of President Duterte's war on drugs—in little more than a month since he took charge. See https://www.theguardian.com/commentisfree/2016/aug/09/kill-list-phillipines-duterte-mass-murder-china-united-states-rivalry-war-on-drugs, accessed 10 August 2016.

(or the USA)? Going beyond the official system (but the line is not always easy to draw) the types of 'informal' social control exerted in Saudi Arabia, Switzerland, or Japan are crucial to the reduced role of criminal justice in those places.[7] We can hardly learn anything useful from India's low prison rates without knowing much more about the forms of local social control—or protection—of offenders (Baxi 2014). When we compare the lower rate of prison use by the juvenile courts in Italy, on the one hand, and England and Wales, on the other, is the strength of the Italian family the key to explaining the difference or something that undoes the point of the comparison? And, from an interpretivist stance, what are we to make of the charge that Italian families keep their children in a 'golden prison' (Nelken 2005)?

The point of comparing is to produce unexpected, and therefore new, findings. Such findings can either result from discovering similarities where the existing academic literature would otherwise suggest differences—or differences where it would predict similarities. Examples of similarities despite differences could be the supposed global similarities in what people think of as serious crimes (Newman 1999), or the allegedly similar ranking by police forces round the world of the seriousness of various types of police misconduct (Klockars, Ivkovitch, and Haberfeld 2003). Illustrations of differences despite similarities could be differences in prison rates (despite allegedly similar levels of crime), or the different levels of independence of prosecutors in Russia and Poland despite allegedly similar legal traditions and political backgrounds (Polak and Nelken 2010).

Even where a potentially relevant common issue, trend, or hypothesis has been found, caution needs to be exercised about assuming that it is similarly salient in the places being compared. It is not just that there will of course be variation—that is after all what interests us—but rather that we may be missing the point. Is neoliberalism really the best way of understanding differences in youth justice (Bailleau and Cartuyvels 2007)? Is 'the problem' we need to resolve too much punitiveness or too much impunity? If we are too intent on explaining 'governing through crime' (Simon 2007) we are unlikely to notice the need to make sense of 'ruling through leniency' (Melossi 1994). In the Italian, as opposed to Anglo-American, literature, the main debate about prosecutors is only indirectly concerned with their relationship with the police, who are seen, rightly or wrongly, as playing a much more subservient role than in Anglo-American cultures (Montana and Nelken 2011). Against a background of sharp struggle between judges and politicians, especially during the Berlusconi years, the issue is rather whether prosecutors' independence is at threat from the politicians or whether, on the contrary, they are themselves liable to abuse their powers.

This has special bearing on the concepts that we use to examine cross-cultural variation. If, for example, we want to compare levels of prosecutorial independence we need to ask what it means locally to say that prosecutors are, or should be, independent. Of/from what and whom? The police, the judges, the heads of prosecution offices, the minister of justice, politicians in general, parliament, or even the general public? In Italy, for example, careful distinctions are made between the independence of the category of judges/prosecutors as a whole and single judge/prosecutors; as well as between external autonomy—the independence of all prosecutors from outside conditioning,

[7] Whilst Cavadino and Dignan offer Japan as the best example of a regime of low punitiveness they entitle the detailed chapter describing their system of criminal justice 'iron fist in a velvet glove'.

and internal independence—the independence of the single prosecutor from hierarchical control by his or her superior (Nelken 2013).

When it comes to comparing the values pursued by different systems, comparative scholars need to avoid the opposite dangers of ethnocentrism and relativism (Beirne 1983/1997; Leavitt 1990/1997; Nelken 2009a), either assuming that our system already has the right answers or that no one can have them. But there is also a more subtle way of projecting our own standards that is more common and more difficult to recognize. Here the problem is to assume that what is good or bad about criminal justice processes and outcomes in other systems must always be a result of what we think of as good or bad causes.

The punitiveness debate is again a good example of this. Most criminologists link higher prison rates to other matters they consider negative in their own right, such as lower welfare levels, less effort to ensure economic equality, or less public participation in political life.[8] By contrast, Jim Whitman's explanation of the relative harshness of the treatment of criminals in the USA in comparison to Continental Europe is refreshingly different. His argument is that whereas France and Germany 'levelled up' their treatment of criminals, on the basis of long-standing more respectful treatment for higher-status prisoners, in America criminals suffered from a general levelling-down process that presupposed status equality (Whitman 2003; Nelken 2006b).

Increasingly—often through the writings of insider-outsiders—we are learning more about the complex links between what an outside observer might consider positive features of a given criminal justice systems and its less positive ones. Vanessa Barker, for example, has recently explained how the inclusiveness promoted by the welfare state in Sweden (one of the countries with the lowest rates of incarceration) is linked to what she calls Nordic nationalism and its 'politics of belonging'. It can justify heavy medical interventions and psychological paternalism for those it includes, and exclude those who are not seen as belonging to the 'national home' (Barker 2013). With closer acquaintance it turns out that we may like the outcomes achieved by other systems of criminal justice, but not the means they use to get there, or vice versa.

Our understanding of the range of possible similarities and differences amongst criminal justice systems is artificially limited if we confine ourselves to commonly studied places like USA, Europe or, more generally, the economically developed world including Japan. Fortunately more countries are now being heard from.[9] But it is not easy for reports from such places to show both the relevance of the findings and values of mainstream criminology whilst also opening up new questions. The editors of a recent special issue focusing on crime and criminal justice in the post-Soviet region warn explicitly that 'conceptual frames and theories developed in western industrialized democracies, such as the rise of the "culture of control" or "governing through crime", may not be applicable to the study of criminal justice phenomena elsewhere'

[8] Of course punitiveness may have roots in other matters we disapprove of. But it could also be linked to the rise in concern for victims, or the introduction of determinate sentencing through sentencing guidelines intended to reduce arbitrariness in decision-making and create more national standardization. Prison building restarted in the Netherlands in part to keep faith with the principle of one person to a cell. More important, the 'evil causes evil' fallacy blurs the question of how matters are perceived locally.

[9] See, e.g., the papers published in *The Asian Journal of Criminology*. On China we now have the more legal approach of McConville and Pils (2013) and the more criminological approach of McConville (2011).

(Slade and Light 2015; Nelken 2015b). The individual contributions, however, pivot between drawing on existing theories of crime control in the West and showing their limits.

The problem of controlling hate crime in Russia for example, has many similarities with that faced in the West. But, insofar as the state makes use of some of the groups who engage in it, it is also subtly different (Arnold 2015). Is this conceptual category then the right one to use (cf. Garland and Chakraborti 2012)? Again, the world over, prisoners play some role in running their prisons. But Post-Soviet 'carceral collectivism' we learn, is more than a functional necessity: 'It also stems from a systematic Soviet preference for collective arrangements in all aspect of social life, which in turn reflects a particular model of mutual surveillance, or "polyopticism", in which citizens monitored one another on behalf of the state' (Slade and Light: 153). Because this part of the world is in transition the past persists in the form of legacies that are found in mental, social, and physical structures.[10] As Piacentini and Slade demonstrate, the previous overseer system was not destroyed but rather reshaped. What the authors call 'carceral collectivism' therefore continues to place limits on the modernization of the prison estate (Piacentini and Slade 2015). On the other hand the current and future trajectories of these criminal justice systems are also shaped by 'pull' factors, especially the need to comply with the recommendations of the European council and the remit of the European Court of Human Rights.

In the view of the contributors to the special issue (who include scholars coming from the countries under examination), criminal justice practices in most of the post-Soviet region fall well below acceptable standards and are in need of major reform. The challenge is not only that of finding ways to reduce the prison population, but also of transforming its existing role as an element of a capillary network of politically directed social control. In addition much needs to be done to overcome racial bias in the judiciary and end its compliant subservience to prosecutors. Last but not least, there is the problem of taming the police, not only so that they respect the accused's rights while aiming for 'crime control', but, more fundamentally, so that they are no longer used to crush political opponents or allowed to prey on the general population.

These values cannot be characterized as only relevant to Western nations. On the contrary it is not always clear where 'the Western' standards that the commentators take as examples of better practice are located. Are we speaking of the USA or of Europe? Certainly there may be almost as much of a contrast in the use of prison in the USA and Finland as between the USA and ex-Soviet Union countries. It would be interesting rather to compare these latter countries with other ex-communist countries now within the orbit of the European Union. Whilst there is nothing wrong in itself with wanting to criticize poor practices there can be some danger that this fails to engage with the subtleties of debates about criminal justice in their own cultural contexts. The term 'political malfeasance' seems far from such debates. What did Putin mean when arguing that the 'dictatorship of law has not been achieved'. How are such statements actually understood locally?

[10] In general, much of the scholarship on ex-communist countries argues that communist penal practices created a specific 'culture of control' that still makes a crucial contribution to current crime control policies (for a recent study, see Tripkovic (2016)).

BEYOND COMPARATIVE CRIMINAL JUSTICE?

We are all comparativists now—in the sense of increasingly wanting to see our own criminal justice systems in the light of others—or else being obliged to do so. But, for that very reason, writing about comparative criminal justice as if nation states were self-contained units has lost any small plausibility it might have had. Neither the sources of crime threats nor the responses to them are confined to the national level. If we are 'to acknowledge the effects that distant conflicts and developments have on national crime and security concerns and vice versa' (Aas 2007: 286) we need to think about the spread of security fears worldwide as well as the ways social exclusion operates at the global level.

A key phenomenon here is the growth of so-called crimmigration (Stumpf 2006; Bosworth, this volume) and xeno racism (racism displaced onto foreigners). Recent contributions to the debate about incarceration levels have rightly noted that the proportion of non- nationals in European prisons is vastly out of proportion to their number in the population of the country (Solivetti 2010).Whereas the pattern in the USA used to be different (Melossi 2016), there too prosecutions of illegal entry are now a driving force in mass incarceration.[11] European countries now choose to rely on Turkey (as before they did on Libya) to block the immigrants and refugees trying to reach our shores, even though (or rather precisely because) this means that they are subjected to the sort of repressive measures that they would not be able to use. At the same time (inconsistently) Turkey is also warned that it cannot join the European Union if it breaches its standards by reintroducing the death penalty for offenders after the failed military coup in 2016.

As nation states are incorporated into the global economy and informational cyberspace, state sovereignty is challenged by international courts, human rights conventions, multinational private security enterprises, cross-border policing, policy networks and flows, and technologies of global surveillance (Nelken 1997, 2011b). Singly and collectively, they try to deal with such threats as organized crime, terrorism, human trafficking, corruption, illegal dumping of waste, computer crime, money-laundering, and tax evasion. Key crime initiatives now link regional or local centres of power (Edwards and Hughes 2005) or are delegated to the private sector.[12] Studies of comparative criminal justice increasingly overlap with those concerned with international and transnational criminal law, international human rights and peace-making. Are the goals of punishment, such as retribution, deterrence, reform, and reparation, the same in international criminal law settings as in domestic courts? Should they be?

[11] A report from Justice Strategies and Grassroots Leadership quoted in *The Guardian* in July 2016 reported that illegal entry prosecutions made up half of all criminal cases in the US federal court system in 2015. Non-citizens currently make up nearly a quarter of the total federal prison population, with Mexican nationals alone accounting for 15 per cent.

[12] A recent topical example here is the allegation that torture was used in Australia's offshore detention regime by a private company to whom these tasks had been delegated: https://www.theguardian.com/australia-news/2016/aug/10/the-nauru-files-2000-leaked-reports-reveal-scale-of-abuse-of-children-in-australian-offshore-detention, accessed 1 January 2017.

Who is 'the community' that needs to be served (see, e.g., Findlay and Henman 2005)? With its new 'responsibility to protect', the citizens of the nation state are no longer the only subjects of its interventions. But what happens on the ground is far from reassuring when the objectives of protecting state security clash with the needs of vulnerable groups in precarious life situations (Aas and Gundhus 2015).

On the other hand, the decline of the nation state should not be overstated. There are important and systematic differences in criminal justice institutions and practices, as in the relationship between law and politics, the role of legal and lay actors, levels of leniency, degrees of delay, and so on. State boundaries still often coincide with language and cultural differences, national jurisdictions represent the main source of the rules of criminal law and of criminal statistics, and the imposition of a common legal code and the common training of legal officials forms part of attempts to achieve and consolidate national identity. Criminal law continues to be a powerful icon of sovereignty: the state promotes itself as guardian of internal and external security and 'borders' remain a key site where the insecurities and uncertainties brought about by (economic) globalization are supposed to be 'resolved'.

As Muncie puts it:

> the argument that criminal justice is becoming a standardised global product can be sustained only at the very highest level of generality. Economic forces are not uncontrollable, meet resistance, and have effects that are neither uniform nor consistent. Nor should we expect that policy transfer be direct, complete, exact or successful. Rather, it is mediated through national and local cultures, which are 'themselves changing at the same time'. (Muncie 2011: 100; see also Savelsberg 2011)

Even if USA think tanks played a role in exporting ideas of the penal state (Wacquant 2009a, 2009b), as Cavadino and Dignan showed, neoliberal trends have had differential effects on prison rates across the world. The same applies to the spread of blueprints about the proper organization of criminal justice. Large countries such as China or the USA (Garland 2010) succeed in holding on to the death penalty despite calls for its abolition, but so do smaller ones in Asia (Johnson and Zimring 2009). Because the models on offer are plural this allows local policy-makers room for manoeuvre (Blaustein 2016). Likewise, a state such as Greece can resist international and domestic pressure to improve its immigrant detention centres by claiming to be especially gifted at providing hospitality (Cheliotis 2013). Just as there are significant national differences in responding to socially problematic behaviours such as prostitution/sexwork (as seen in the controversial reception of the so-called Swedish Model of punishing the clients), so there are very different approaches being taken to the alleged 'global' threat of human trafficking (Nelken 2011a).

In examining interactions between the national and the transnational it can be helpful to distinguish analytically between convergence, copying, and collaboration (Nelken 2010). Convergence can come about indirectly as a result of other processes of social change (Sergi 2015). Or it can be actively pursued, for example as part of the implementation of European integration or by non-governmental organizations and intergovernmental organizations and influential think tanks who formulate internationally influential blueprints (see, e.g., Karstedt 2007; Melossi *et al.* 2011; Newburn and Sparks 2004). A wide variety of matters can spread—scripts, norms, institutions, technologies, fears, ways of seeing, problems, solutions—new forms of policing, punitiveness, or conceptual legal innovations such as 'the law of the enemy', mediation, or therapeutic justice.

Copying, by contrast, involves individual countries actively seeking similarity through borrowing or imitation—which may or may not then lead to greater overall convergence (Nelken and Feest 2001). Sometimes they may seek out 'best practices' from places with very different histories and cultures (often with notable success, as the institution of the ombudsman shows). More often, however, those who borrow look to what they take to be similar systems. Thus, as Hamilton tells us, 'the Canadian "what works" research has been influential in prisons and probation policy in New Zealand, Ireland and Scotland. For Ireland and Scotland, geographical proximity also meant that England's criminal justice policies were very influential' (Hamilton 2016: 160).

But borrowing can have unpredictable results even where similar systems are involved. Jones and Newburn studied the outcomes in England and Wales of attempts to introduce USA practices regarding private prisons: 'three strikes and you're out', sentencing reforms, and zero tolerance policing. They showed that borrowing did take place. But they concluded that this led to only limited changes in actual practices (Jones and Newburn 2006). By contrast, Nolan, in his description of the way USA-type 'problem- solving courts' were introduced into five other common law jurisdictions, reaches somewhat different conclusions about the influence of USA models of criminal justice. He stresses not only how much was successfully taken over but also the way that such borrowing inevitably brings about the spread of central aspects of USA popular culture (Nolan 2009).

Those who examine processes of collaboration seek to understand the way action needs to be coordinated even if—or especially if—those concerned do not intend to copy practices from elsewhere. Jacqueline Ross shows how hard it can be for those in the USA criminal justice system to align their working practices for given purposes with those belonging to other systems of criminal justice. She argues that the United States and European nations conceptualize, legitimate, and control undercover policing in very different ways and that this has consequences for cooperating in the battle against transnational organized crime. In comparing American and Italian ways of regulating such practices she tells us that Americans worry mainly about how to stop undercover agents from corrupting innocent targets. By contrast, the concern in Italy focuses on the way covert operations can assist state-sanctioned lawlessness (Ross 2004, 2007).

A further implication of the increasing entwinement between the national and transnational is the way an increasing number of actors (not only criminologists) help produce 'official knowledge' of crime and criminal justice. In their study of the work of Frontex (the European agency policing the Mediterranean), for example, Aas and Gundhus (2015) describe how those who patrol migrants distribute the task of recording the number of those who die in the process of emigrating—and warn of the implications of such failed record keeping. What we can call 'second-order comparison' (studying these social processes of comparison and its consequences) can also help in understanding why criminal justice responses change independently of crime rates. Returning to the debate over changes in imprisonment rates, the most famous example here is the way Finland's incarceration rates declined sharply (whilst levels of criminality remained unaffected) because its policy elite chose to bring its prisons' rates in line with (other) Scandinavian countries with which it wanted to be compared (Lappi-Seppälä 2007; Von Hofer 2003). But self understandings of differences in national practices also shape the work of those in international and transnational agencies. Aas and Gundhus tell us that 'officials from different countries in our interviews frequently invoked differences between East and West, North and South of Europe, and described themselves in terms of their national policing culture which they saw as distinct from, and superior to, other nations' (Aas and Gundhus 2015: 7).[13]

The many changes in the significance of state borders and global links have a variety of implications for the boundaries of comparative criminal justice as an academic subject. But, perhaps understandably, scholars are struggling to integrate the study of recent developments into their traditional classificatory and descriptive schemes. One introductory textbook now eclectically stretches the topics it covers to go beyond police, courts, and prisons by including discussion, for example, about privatized policing and security, criminal justice in the Middle East (including Sharia law), and cybercrime, including reference to the 'great firewall of China' (Pakes 2015: 1). Some authors relegate material about transnational and international crime and criminal justice that fits awkwardly into the normal comparative paradigm to an early chapter (Reichel 2008), to a closing one (Dammer, Fairchild, and Albanese 2005) or even to a separate book (Reichel 2007).

For other scholars it is the mainstream paradigm itself that needs to be changed. Sheptycki and Wardak, in their edited collection, suggest that we distinguish 'area studies', 'transnational crime issues', and 'transnational control responses' (Sheptycki and Wardak 2005). Larsen and Smandych, in introducing their text, tell us that 'the effects of rapid globalization have changed social, political, and legal realities in such a way that comparative and international approaches to crime and justice are inadequate to capture the full complexity of these issues on a global scale' (Larsen and Smandych 2008: xi). Pakes has proposed that the comparative approach could be seen as just a matter of methodology whereas globalization is an 'object of study' (Pakes 2010b: 18–19; but see also Pakes 2014). On the other hand, both critics of 'methodological nationalism' (Beck and Sznaider 2006) as well as those who draw our attention to the different 'scales' of security problems (Valverde 2009) would argue that we cannot easily keep separate the object of study and our approach to it.

This point links to the larger call to decentre Western criminology (Aas 2012) and to privilege gender, race, and outsider perspectives.[14] It is argued that 'criminology is a product of a particular set of narratives within Western social sciences— a set of narratives that were fashioned in relation to the experience of the [European] Diaspora and in the construction of complexly stratified societies within and around the urban conurbations of Western cities' (Cunneen 2011). A 'Criminology of the South', on the other hand, holds the promise of being able 'to elucidate the power relations embedded in the hierarchal production of criminological knowledge that privileges theories, assumptions and methods based largely on empirical specificities of the global North' (Carrington *et al.* 2016).

[13] Others have reported that international organizations create their own new legal culture whereby their members give their loyalty to each other and develop new norms (Arold 2007; Nelken 2009b). There is a clear need for more empirical research here.

[14] For an example with reference to the imprisonment of foreigners, see Matos (2016).

Of special relevance for our purpose, a post-colonial criminological perspective also enables a much wider focus for criminology: questions of sovereignty and citizenship become core concerns (Cunneen 2011). Where much mainstream research on transnational threats such as human trafficking, the war on terror, illegal immigrants, and the transnational flow of peoples, it is argued, still sees them as primarily a problem for Western states, a post-colonial perspective on human trafficking would start instead from the states that supply such victims and the factors that shape their migration projects. More generally, the risks of unreflexively exporting home grown solutions to crime to the South has been illustrated, yet again, in a recent analysis of a toolkit for evidence-based crime prevention developed for the Inter-American Development Bank in 2012 (Blaustein 2016). But this new more reflexive criminology would seem to require even more, rather then less, sensitivity to the similarities and differences in object, approaches, and values that studies in comparative criminal justice, and comparative sociology of law more generally, can help to nurture (Nelken 2016b).

DOING RESEARCH INTO COMPARATIVE CRIMINAL JUSTICE

How should we go about gathering evidence of similarities and differences? Most introductory texts about comparative criminal justice say relatively little about the actual process of carrying out cross-cultural research. We might assume that this is because there is nothing special in the methods available for researching criminal justice comparatively. It will involve, just as in research on domestic criminal justice, collecting information, reading official texts, court cases or other documents, and employing the normal instruments of questionnaires, interviews, and observation. On the other hand it would be a mistake to underestimate the pitfalls in acquiring insider knowledge of another culture. The researcher not only faces problems posed by the unreliability of statistics, lack of appropriate data, and the meaning of foreign terms, but also less obvious obstacles to understanding what can often be profound differences in other practices and world views.

These difficulties are complicated by the very cultural differences that we are seeking to uncover: apparently technical issues about 'equivalence' frequently conceal more difficult questions of legal, social, and cultural commensurability. Re-presenting the 'other' can turn out to be especially tricky where those being portrayed have their own (criminological and other) spokespeople able and willing to contest our accounts, arguing that the observer's assessments have been too critical (e.g. Balvig 1988; Killias 1989) or too generous (e.g. Downes 1988, 1990; Franke 1990; Pratt and Eriksson 2103, Ugelvik and Dullum 2012). Such debates between cultural insiders and outsiders are illuminating in their own right, but they also offer a useful corrective to the pretensions of a discipline that too often studies the powerless who cannot answer back.

In practice, however, almost all reports about other places rely directly or indirectly on what is said by members of the society concerned. How this works out in practice depends on whether the researcher chooses to cooperate with foreign experts, to go abroad to interview legal officials and others, or to draw on direct experience of living and working in the place being investigated (strategies that I have labelled 'virtually there', 'researching there', or 'living there', see Nelken 2000, 2010a. See also Heidensohn 2009).

The first of these strategies allows for a variety of different forms of international collaboration. In a comparison between the Netherlands and England and Wales, for example, scholars asked why each of their jurisdictions responded differently to the rise of covert and proactive policing (Brants and Field 2000). Such collaboration, we are told, requires a high degree of mutual trust and involves 'negotiating' mutually acceptable descriptions of legal practice in each of their home countries. The lesson they seek to drive home is that correct interpretation of even the smallest detail of criminal justice organization requires sensitivity to broader institutional and ideological contexts. Similar issues arise in the increasingly popular action-research projects involving scholars and practitioners from different countries (Edwards and Hughes 2005), such as those encouraged by EU funded COST research projects (http://www.cost.eu/).[15]

In a bid to learn more about the broader contexts many scholars advocate going in person to the research site. This gives the researcher the opportunity to become directly involved in the experience of cultural translation. On the basis of his regular visits to France, Crawford, for example, offered a sophisticated reading of the contrasting meanings of mediation in two different settings (Crawford 2000). In France, he argues, the move to introduce mediation was best seen as part of a project of 'bringing law to the people' both by making the criminal justice response more immediate in time and also by subtly transforming its referent. But it was not about involving the 'community' in the actual delivery of criminal justice. By contrast, the familiar conception of 'community' built into the mediation movement, he argued, had a meaning and appeal which is strongly tied to the Anglo-American type of political and social order. In France it had historically been the role of the state to represent the larger community, and its social institutions had it as their fundamental task to lead those who were not yet part of the polis into becoming bona fide French citizens.

'Researching there' also provides the chance for open-ended enquiry that can lead to the discovery of new questions and findings about the 'law in action'. Some things are never written down because they belong to 'craft rules of thumb', whilst other matters may be considered secrets that should not be written down (Hodgson 2000). But research visits can still involve over-reliance on local experts and practitioners. Indeed obtaining their views is usually the whole point of the exercise. At the least it is important not to draw uncritically on such insiders and to ask why we consider them as experts. What do they know—and how do they know it? And what are they able and willing to tell us?

Practitioners may be especially likely to paint an 'official' picture insofar as they are subject to the constraints of the organizations they work for. But this can vary by culture. In some places judges will eagerly bad mouth politicians. In others, professed political neutrality is fundamental. Some police officers will criticize what goes on in their

[15] See, for example, Edwards and Hughes on crime prevention in Europe (Edwards and Hughes 2005).

force, in other places enormous importance is placed on face-saving (Johnson 2003). Such differences carry implications for cross-national comparisons of levels of corruption in politics or the police.

Much the same applies to repeating what we are told by academics. When we think of experts in our own culture we will normally, without much difficulty, be able to associate them with 'standing' for given political or policy positions. But we sometimes forget this when we cite experts from abroad. In many places in Latin America or Continental Europe it is considered quite appropriate for academics to identify and to be identified as members of a faction. In France some commentators are strongly against importing ideas from the common law world, others are less antagonistic; in Italy, some academics are notoriously pro-judges, others are anti-judges. In such societies the question of social and political affiliation is one of the first questions that needs to be raised in considering the point and validity of academic criticisms of current practices and of corresponding proposals for reform (Nelken 2013).

In Anglo-American cultures, the approved practice may often be to do one's best to avoid such identification. In some cases this just makes the process of establishing affiliation more elusive. Alternatively, the extent of political consensus, or of admiration for allegedly neutral criteria based on 'results' or 'efficiency', may be such that academics are indeed less pressed to take sides, or intellectuals may simply count for less politically! (And there are fewer examples than on the continent of professors moving in and out of political life.) The point again is that without knowledge about their affiliations, and an understanding of the responsibilities attached to different roles in the culture under investigation, it can be hard to know what credit to give to the arguments of any expert about criminal justice.

Even if we can assume that our sources are not politically 'partial' (or, better still, if we try to make proper allowance for this) there still remains the problem that experts and practitioners are undoubtedly part of their own culture. This is after all why we consult them. But this also means that they do not necessarily ask or answer questions based on where the researcher is 'coming from' (and may not even have the basis for understanding such questions). In a multitude of ways both their descriptions and their criticisms will belong to their own culture. In Italy, local commentators regularly attack a principled but inefficient system on grounds of principle; in England and Wales, a system highly influenced by managerial considerations, sometimes at the expense of principle, will tend to be criticized for its remaining inefficiencies.

Amongst other advantages, longer-term involvement in another culture, actually 'being there' as an insider-outsider, makes it easier to grasp the intellectual and political affiliations of the insiders. More generally, everyday experience of another culture, in the form of 'observant participation', also allows the researcher to fill in the 'taken-for-granted' background to natives' views and actions. It makes it possible to get beyond media presentations—important as they are—to decide which events may be less newsworthy but more representative of quotidian routine.[16] In research based on short visits the vital issue of what are the 'right' questions to ask is often glossed

[16] Brilliant books can be written about killings by and of young people based on newspaper reports and cinema dramatizations of cause celebre (Nerenburg 2012). But only close inspection of the case files and appreciation of the relative insulation of the Italian juvenile court from public scrutiny can help explain how most murders dealt with there end up with sentences of no more than pre-trail probation· (Field and Nelken 2010).

over because of the implicit collusion between the researcher and those she engages with which privileges what the enquirer wants to know. The long-stay researcher, by contrast, is engaged in a process of being slowly resocialized. She will increasingly want to reformulate the questions others back home wish to address to the foreign setting. Direct experience and involvement with what is being studied can help give the researcher's accounts the credibility that comes from being part of the story.

This said, the heavy investment required by 'observant participation' or sustained ethnography may not always be feasible. Often our choice of what to compare will be limited by considerations of access, language skills or funding, whether one is able to visit the country concerned, and with what sort of time commitment. There are also the usual trade-offs amongst methodologies. It is possible to cover a large number of cases with questionnaires or interviews only by dispensing with in-depth observation. What is more, the insider-outsider cannot possibly experience everything at first hand so her findings are again in large part the result of interviews and consultation of experts and practitioners, sometimes obtained in ways that are less systematic than those followed by the other approaches. The short-termer can usefully pretend to be naïve in ways that the long-term researcher must abandon, since that is part of what it means to become an insider-outsider.

To a large degree these points about method can be applied in carrying out research at the increasingly important level of interactions between the national and the transnational. Here too we have to accept inevitable trade-offs in choosing whether to consult with, interview, or observe the many non-governmental and inter-governmental organizations that play a central role in making, implementing, and enforcing this or other regional or international standards. A valuable recent study of different national responses to human trafficking chose Thailand, Serbia, and Australia as examples of supply, transit, and demand countries (Segrave *et al.* 2009). No doubt practical considerations weighed heavily in choosing these particular countries for comparison.

In researching 'second-order comparison', however, method itself becomes the topic. How do the comparative strategies used by non-governmental and inter-governmental organizations in their collection and processing of information about what is going on in different places shape their accounts? Large scale comparisons involved in 'measuring the world' (Merry 2011) so as to rank places in terms of global social indicators of matters such as corruption, the rule of law, or human trafficking typically means relying on arms length 'virtual' comparisons, through collating reports from people on the ground, rather than the methods of 'researching there' or 'being there'. Given the loss of contextual nuance as information comes up through the hierarchy of knowledge the results can often best be described (on analogy with 'junk science' in the courtroom) as 'junk comparisons' that only make sense in terms of the knowledge and governance 'effects' of such indicators (Davis *et al.* 2012).

In studying such processes we can explore what happens at the local, national, subnational and supranational levels. How is agreement achieved amongst signatories to conventions or those subject to regulatory networks, or those involved in making and monitoring cross- national standards? Who translates supposedly transnational standards into the vernacular (Merry 2006)? Whose interests and values do they represent and how are or could they be they contested (Merry *et al.* 2015; Nelken 2015c)? Do those who monitor human rights succeed in creating a fruitful dialogue with those whose practices they are describing and evaluating (Kruckenberg 2012)? Who should have the last word?

Often an imaginary view from 'nowhere' (positivist criminology) or from 'everywhere' (as with human rights) is presupposed by which supposedly 'global' indicators are taken to be applicable to countries with very different social circumstances. This makes it hard to pin down the local starting point and salience of allegedly universal standards (Nelken 2014, 2016a).

SELECTED FURTHER READING

The best way to learn the trade of researching into comparative criminal justice is to start with mainstream studies of specific societies or systems such as, amongst many others, Barker's article 'Nordic Exceptionalism revisited: Explaining the paradox of a Janus-faced penal regime' (2013); Cavadino and Dignan's *Penal Systems: A Comparative Approach* (2006); Downes' *Contrasts in Tolerance* (1988); Green's *When Children Kill Children: Penal Populism and Political Culture* (2008); Hodgson's *French Criminal Justice* (2005); Hamilton's *Reconceptualising Penality: A Comparative Perspective on Punitiveness in Ireland, Scotland and New Zealand* (2016); Johnson's *The Japanese Way of Justice* (2001); Pratt *et al.*'s *The New Punitiveness: Current Trends, Theories, Perspectives* (2005); or Pratt and Ericksson's *Contrasts in Punishment* (2013).

Useful texts or collections of papers about comparative criminal justice/transnational criminal justice include Drake *et al.*'s *Criminal Justice, Local and Global* (2009); Karstedt and Nelken's *Crime and Globlization* (2013); Larsen and Smandych's *Global Criminology and Criminal Justice: Current Issues and Perspectives* (2008); Muncie *et al.*'s *Crime: Local and Global* (2009); Nelken's *Comparative Criminal Justice: Making Sense of Difference* (2010); Pakes' *Comparative Criminal Justice* (2015); Sheptycki and Wardak's *Transnational and Comparative Criminology* (2005); and Winterdyk *et al.*s *A Guided Reader to Research In Comparative Criminology/Criminal Justice* (2009). For a recent bibliography, see Winterdyk *et al.*'s *A Guided Reader to Research In Comparative Criminology/Criminal Justice* (2009), and, for a set of biographical essays, Winterdyk and Cao's *Lessons from International/ Comparative Criminology/Criminal Justice* (2004).

Illustrations of policy oriented cross-national perspectives on crime and criminal justice may be found in Newman's *Global Report on Crime and Justice* (1999), Tonry's *Crime and Justice vol 36: Crime, Punishment and Politics in Comparative Perspective* (2007), and Van Dijk's *The World of Crime* (2007), For discussions of blueprints, convergence, and cross-national borrowing, see Melossi *et al.*'s *Travels of the Criminal Question: Cultural Embeddedness and Diffusion* (2011); Newburn and Sparks' *Criminal Justice and Political Cultures: National and International Dimensions of Crime Control* (2004); Jones and Newburn's *Policy Transfer and Criminal Justice* (2006); and Nolan's *Legal Accents, Legal Borrowing: The International Problem-Solving Court Movement* (2009).

Serious work in this field now needs to take into account writing about globalization and crime e.g. Aas and Gundhus' 'Policing Humanitarian Borderlands: Frontex, Human Rights and the Precariousness of Life' (2015) and immigration and crime e.g. Melossi's *Crime, Punishment and Migration* (2016).

As I have tried to illustrate in this chapter, critical research on global social indicators is also increasingly relevant e.g. Merry *et al.*'s *The Quiet Power of Indicators* (2015). This may induce wariness when reading websites describing efforts to handle a host of global evils from corruption to human trafficking. In general, 'information' on governmental and official websites on criminal justice systems in specific countries should be treated more as presentational data in need of explanation rather than as a solid basis for cross-cultural comparison. Similar caution should be exercised when using the sites of inter-governmental and non-governmental organizations.

Beyond this, depending on the topic in hand, the student of comparative criminal justice will want to sample literatures that touch on a variety of disciplines and may need to make some hard methodological decisions (even if the best work often straddles divides). A lot of the running in anything to do with judges, for example, is made by political scientists. Works inspired by the comparative law or interpretative approaches to comparative criminal justice often do not communicate much with debates in the policy-oriented positivist criminological mainstream. Those, on the other hand, who want to move to the more sceptical end of the continuum (or hold a torch for diversity) could read about the difficulties of translation in Glanert's *Comparative Law—Engaging Translation* (2014), or discover the lack of reflexivity in much comparative legal scholarship critiqued by Frankenberg's *Critical Comparative Law* (2016).

■ REFERENCES

Aas, K. F. (2007, 2nd edn, 2015), *Crime and Globalisation*, London: Sage.

Aas, K. F. (2012), 'The Earth is one but the world is not': Criminological theory and its geopolitical divisions', *Theoretical Criminology*, 16(1): 5–20.

Aas, K. F. and Gundhus, O. I. (2015), 'Policing Humanitarian Borderlands: Frontex, Human Rights and the Precariousness of Life', *British Journal of Criminology*, 55(1): 1–18.

Arnold, R. (2015), 'Systematic racist violence in Russia between "hate crime" and "ethnic conflict"', *Theoretical Criminology*, 19(2): 239–56.

Arold, N. L. (2007), *The Legal Culture of the European Court of Human rights*, Amsterdam: Martinus Nijhoff.

Bailleau, F. and Cartuyvels, Y. (2007), *La justice pénale des mineurs en Europe. Entre modèle Welfare et inflexions néo-libérales*, Paris: L'Harmattan.

Balvig, F. (1988), 'The Snow White Image: The Hidden Reality of Crime in Switzerland', *Scandinavian Studies in Criminology*, 17, Oslo: Norwegian University Press, Scandinavian Research Council for Criminology.

Barker, V. (2013), 'Nordic Exceptionalism revisited: Explaining the paradox of a Janus-faced penal regime', *Theoretical Criminology*, 17(1): 5–25.

Baxi, P. (2014), *Public Secrets of Law: Rape Trials in India*, Delhi: Oxford University Press.

Beck, U. and Sznaider, N. (2006), 'Unpacking cosmopolitanism for the social science research agenda', British Journal of Sociology, 57: 1–23.

Beirne, P. (1983/1997), 'Cultural relativism and comparative criminology', reprinted in P. Beirne and D. Nelken (eds), *Issues in Comparative Criminology*, Aldershot: Dartmouth.

Black, D. (1983), 'Crime as Social Control', *American Sociological Review*, 48(1): 34–45.

Blaustein, J. (2016), 'Exporting criminological innovation abroad: Discursive representation, "evidence-based crime prevention" and the post-neoliberal development agenda in America', *Theoretical Criminology*, 20(2): 165–84.

Brants, C. and Field, S. (2000), 'Legal Culture, Political Cultures and Procedural Traditions: Towards a Comparative Interpretation of Covert and Proactive Policing in England and Wales and the Netherlands', in D. Nelken (ed.), *Contrasting Criminal Justice*, Aldershot: Dartmouth.

Carrington, K., Hogg, R., and Sozzo, M. (2016), 'Featured: Southern Criminology', *British Journal of Criminology*, 56(1): 1–20.

Cavadino, M. and Dignan, J. (2006), *Penal Systems: A Comparative Approach*, London: Sage.

Cheliotis, L. (2013), 'Behind the veil of philoxenia: The politics of immigration detention in Greece', *European Journal of Criminology*, 10(6): 725–45.

Crawford, A. (2000), 'Contrasts in Victim/Offender Mediation and Appeals to Community in Comparative Cultural Contexts: France and England and Wales', in D. Nelken (ed.), *Contrasting Criminal Justice*, Aldershot: Dartmouth.

Cunneen, C. (2011), 'Postcolonial Perspectives for Criminology', in C. Hoyle and M. Bosworth, *What is Criminology?* Oxford: Oxford University Press.

Dammer, H., Fairchild, E., and Albanese, J. (2005), *Comparative Criminal Justice*, Belmont, CA: Thomson.

Davis, K. E., Fisher, A., Kingsbury, B., and Merry, S. E. (2012), *Governance by Indicators: Global Power Through Classification and Rankings*, Oxford: Oxford University Press.

DITTON, J. (1979), *Controllogy. Beyond the new Criminology*, London, Macmillan.

DOWNES, D. (1988), *Contrasts in Tolerance*, Oxford: Clarendon.

DOWNES, D. (1990), 'Response to H. Franke', *British Journal of Criminology*, 30(1): 94–6.

DRAKE, D., MUNCIE, J., and WESTMARLAND, L. (eds) (2009), *Criminal Justice, Local and Global*, Collumpton: Willan.

EDWARDS, A. and HUGHES, G. (2005), 'Comparing the governance of safety in Europe', *Theoretical Criminology*, 9(3): 345–63.

ELIOT, T. S. (1943), *Little Gidding*: section V, London: Faber and Faber.

FIELD, S. and NELKEN, D. (2010), Reading and writing youth justice in Italy and Wales', *Punishment and Society*, 12(3): 287–308.

FARRINGTON D. P. (2015), 'Cross-national comparative research on criminal careers, risk factors, crime and punishment', *European Journal of Criminology*, 12(4): 386–99.

FINDLAY, M. and HENHAM, R. (2005), *Transforming International Criminal Justice*, London: Routledge.

FRANKE, H. (1990), 'Dutch Tolerance: Facts and Fallacies', *British Journal of Criminology*, 30(1): 81–93.

FRANKENBERG, G. (2016), *Critical Comparative Law*, Cheltenham, Edward Elgar.

FRASE, R. S. (1990), 'Comparative Criminal Justice as a Guide to American Law Reform', *California Law Review*, 79(3): 539.

GARLAND, D. (2001), *The Culture of Control*, Oxford: Oxford University Press.

GARLAND, D. (2010), *Peculiar Institution. America's Death Penalty in an Age of Abolition*, Cambridge: Harvard University Press.

GARLAND, J. and CHAKRABORTI, N. (2012), 'Divided by a common concept? Assessing the implications of different conceptualizations of hate crime in the European Union', *European Journal of Criminology*, 9(1): 38–51.

GLANERT, S. (2014), *Comparative Law—Engaging Translation*, Abingdon: Routledge.

GOLDSTEIN, A. and MARCUS, M. (1977), 'The Myth of Judicial Supervision in Three Inquisitorial Systems: France, Italy and Germany', *Yale Law Journal*, 87(2): 240.

GREEN, D. A. (2008), *When Children Kill Children: Penal Populism and Political Culture*, Oxford, Oxford University Press.

HAMILTON, C. (2013), 'Punitiveness and political culture: Notes from some small countries', *European Journal of Criminology*, 10(2): 154–67.

HAMILTON, C. (2014), 'Reconceptualizing Penality', *British Journal of Criminology*, 54(2): 321–43.

HAMILTON, C. (2016), *Reconceptualising Penality: A Comparative Perspective on Punitiveness in Ireland, Scotland and New Zealand*, Aldershot: Ashgate.

HEIDENSOHN, F. (2009), 'Contrasts and Concepts: Considering the Development of Comparative Criminology', in T. Newburn and P. Rock (eds), *The Politics of Crime Control*, Oxford: Oxford University Press.

HODGSON, J. (2000), 'Comparing Legal Cultures: The Comparativist as Participant Observer', in D. Nelken (ed.), *Contrasting Criminal Justice*, Aldershot: Dartmouth.

HODGSON, J. (2005), *French Criminal Justice*, Oxford: Hart.

JOHNSON, D. (2000), 'Prosecutor Culture in Japan and USA', in D. Nelken (ed.), *Contrasting Criminal Justice*, Aldershot: Dartmouth.

JOHNSON, D. (2001), *The Japanese Way of Justice*, Oxford: Oxford University Press.

JOHNSON, D. (2003), 'Police Integrity in Japan', in C. B. Klockars, S. K. Ivkovich, and M. R. Haberfeld (eds), *The Contours of Police Integrity*, London: Sage.

JOHNSON, D. and ZIMRING, F. (2009), *The Next Frontier: National Development, Political Change, and the Death Penalty in Asia*, Oxford: Oxford University Press.

JONES, T. and NEWBURN, T. (2006), *Policy Transfer and Criminal Justice*, Milton Keynes: Open University Press.

KARSTEDT, S. (2007), 'Creating Institutions: Linking the "Local" and the "Global" in the Travel of Crime Policies', *Police Practice and Research: An International Journal*, 8(2): 145–58.

KARSTEDT, S. and NELKEN, D. (eds) (2013), *Crime and Globlization*, Abingdon: Routledge.

KILLIAS, M. (1989), 'Book review of Balvig', *British Journal of Criminology*, 29(3): 300–5.

KLOCKARS, C. B., IVKOVIC, S. K., HABERFELD, M. R. (eds) (2003), *The Contours of Police Integrity*, New York: Sage.

KRUCKENBERG, L. J. (2012), *The UNreal World of Human Rights: An Ethnography of the UN Committee in the Elimination of Racial Discrimination*, Baden Baden: Nomos.

LACEY, N. (2008), *The Prisoners' Dilemma: Political Economy and Punishment in Contemporary Democracies*, Cambridge: Cambridge University Press.

LACEY, N. and ZEDNER, L. (1995), 'Discourses of Community in Criminal Justice', *Journal of Law and Society*, 22(1): 301–20.

LACEY, N. and ZEDNER L. (1998), 'Community in German Criminal Justice: A Significant Absence?', *Social and Legal Studies*, 7(1): 7–25.

LANGBEIN, J. and WEINREB, L. (1978), 'Continental Criminal Procedure: Myth and Reality', *Yale Law Journal*, 87(8): 1549.

LAPPI-SEPPÄLÄ, T. (2007), 'Penal Policy in Scandinavia, Crime and Justice', *Crime, Punishment, and Politics in a Comparative Perspective*, 36(1): 217–95.

LAPPI-SEPPÄLÄ, T. (2008), 'Trust, Welfare, and Political Culture: Explaining Differences in National Penal Policies', *Crime and Justice*, 37(1): 313–87.

LARSEN, N. and SMANDYCH, R. (eds) (2008), *Global Criminology and Criminal Justice: Current Issues and Perspectives*, Buffalo, NY: Broadview Press.

LEAVITT, G. C. (1990/1997), 'Relativism and Cross-Cultural Criminology: A Critical Analysis', reprinted in

P. Beirne and D. Nelken (eds), *Issues in Comparative Criminology*, Aldershot: Dartmouth.

MATOS, R. (2016), 'Trajectories and identities of foreign national women: Rethinking prison through the lens of gender and citizenship', *Criminology and Criminal Justice*, 16(3): 350–65.

MCCONVILLE, M. (2011), *Criminal Justice in China: An Empirical Inquiry*, Cheltenham: Elgar.

MCCONVILLE, M. and PILS, E. (eds) (2013), *Comparative Perspectives on Criminal Justice in China*, Cheltenham: Elgar.

MELOSSI, D. (1994), 'The "economy" of illegalities: Normal crimes, Elites and Social Control in comparative analysis', in D. Nelken (ed.), *The Futures of Criminology*, London: Sage.

MELOSSI, D. (2016), *Crime, Punishment and Migration*, London, Sage.

MELOSSI, D., SOZZO, M., and SPARKS, R. (eds) (2011), *Travels of the Criminal Question: Cultural Embeddedness and Diffusion*, Oxford: Hart.

MERRY, S. E. (2006), *Human Rights and Gender Violence: Translating International Law into Local Justice*, Chicago, University of Chicago Press.

MERRY, S. E. (2011), 'Measuring the World: Indicators, Human Rights, and Global Governance', *Current Anthropology*, 52(S3): S83–S95.

MERRY, S. E., DAVIS, K. E., and KINGSBURY, B. (eds) (2015), *The Quiet Power of Indicators*, Cambridge: Cambridge University Press.

MONTANA, R. and NELKEN, D. (2011), 'The ambivalent role of Italian Prosecutors and their resistance to "moral panics" about crime', in C. S. Smith, S. X. Zhang, and R. Barberet (eds), *Routledge Handbook of International Criminology*, London: Taylor and Francis.

MUNCIE, J. (2011), 'On globalization and exceptionalism', in D. Nelken (ed.), *Comparative Criminal Justice and Globalization*, Aldershot: Ashgate.

MUNCIE, J., TALBOT, D., and WALTERS, R. (eds) (2009), *Crime: Local and Global*, Cullompton: Willan.

NELKEN, D. (1994), 'Whom can you trust? The future of comparative criminology', in D. Nelken (ed.), *The Futures of Criminology*, London: Sage.

NELKEN, D. (1997), 'The Globalisation of Crime and Criminal Justice: Prospects and Problems', in M. Freeman (ed.), *Law at the Turn of the Century*, Oxford: Oxford University Press.

NELKEN, D. (ed.) (2000), *Contrasting Criminal Justice*, Aldershot: Dartmouth.

NELKEN, D. (2005), 'When is a Society non-punitive? A case study of Italy', in J. Pratt, D. Brown, S. Hallsworth, M. Brown, and W. Morrison, (eds), *The New Punitiveness: Current Trends, Theories, Perspectives*, Cullompton: Willan.

NELKEN, D. (2006a), 'Italy: A lesson in tolerance?', in J. Muncie and B. Goldson (eds), *Comparative Youth Justice: Critical Issues*, London: Sage.

NELKEN, D. (2006b), 'Patterns of Punishment', *Modern Law Review*, 69(2): 262–77.

NELKEN, D. (2009a), 'Comparative Criminal Justice: Beyond Ethnocentricism and Relativism', *European Journal of Criminology*, 6(4): 291–311.

NELKEN, D. (2009b), 'The Temple of Rights': Review essay of Nina-Louisa Arold's The legal culture of the European Court of Human Rights, *European Journal of Public Law*, 3(15): 447–56.

NELKEN, D. (2010), *Comparative Criminal Justice: Making Sense of Difference*, London: Sage.

NELKEN, D. (2011a), 'Human Trafficking and Legal Culture', *Israel Law Review*, 43(1): 479–513.

NELKEN, D. (ed.) (2011b), *Comparative Criminal Justice and Globalization*, Aldershot: Ashgate.

NELKEN, D. (2011c), 'Theorising the embeddedness of punishment', in D. Melossi, M. Sozzo, and R. Sparks (eds), *Travels of the Criminal Question: Cultural Embeddedness and Diffusion*, Oxford: Hart.

NELKEN, D. (2013), 'Can Prosecutors be too Independent? An Italian case- study', in T. Daems, S. Snacken, and D. van Zyl Smit (eds), *European penology?*, Oxford: Hart.

NELKEN, D. (2014), 'The changing roles of social indicators: from explanation to governance', in P. Alldridge, L. Cheliotis, and V. Mitsilegas (eds), *Globalisation, Criminal Law and Criminal Justice: Theoretical, Comparative and Transnational Perspectives*, Oxford: Hart.

NELKEN, D. (2015a), 'Foil comparisons or foiled comparisons? Learning from Italian juvenile justice', *European Journal of Criminology*, 12(5): 519–34.

NELKEN, D. (2015b), 'Post-Soviet criminal justice and comparative criminology', *Theoretical Criminology*, 19(2): 289–95.

NELKEN, D. (2015c), 'Afterword: Contesting social indicators?', in S. E. Merry, K. E. Davis, and B. Kingsbury (eds), *The Quiet Power of Indicators*, Cambridge: Cambridge University Press.

NELKEN, D. (2016a), 'From pains-taking to pains-giving comparisons', in N. Creutzfeldt, A. Kubal, and F. Pirie (eds), 'Exploring the comparative in socio-legal studies', *International journal of Law in Context* (special issue), 12(4): 1–14.

NELKEN, D. (2016b), 'Comparative legal research and legal culture: Facts, approaches and values', *Annual Review of Law and Social Science*, 12: 1–21.

NELKEN, D. and FEEST, J. (eds) (2001), *Adapting Legal Cultures*, Oxford: Hart.

NERENBURG, N. (2012), *Murder Made in Italy*, Bloomington: Indiana University Press.

NEWBURN, T. and SPARKS, R. (eds) (2004), *Criminal Justice and Political Cultures: National and International Dimensions of Crime Control*, Cullompton: Willan.

NEWMAN, G. (ed.) (1999), *Global Report on Crime and Justice*, Oxford: Oxford University Press.

NOLAN, J. (2009), *Legal Accents, Legal Borrowing: The International Problem-Solving Court Movement*, Princeton: Princeton University Press.

PAKES, F. (2010b), 'The Comparative method in Globalised Criminology', *Australian and New Zealand Journal of Criminology*, 43(1): 17–34.

PAKES, F. (ed.) (2014), *Globalisation and the Challenge to Criminology*, Abingdon: Routledge.

PAKES, F. (ed.) (2015), *Comparative Criminal Justice*, 3rd edn, Cullompton: Willan.

PIACENTINI, L. and SLADE, G. (2015), 'Architecture and attachment: Carceral collectivism and the problem of prison reform in Russia and Georgia', *Theoretical Criminology*, 19(2): 179–97.

POLAK, P. and NELKEN, D. (2010), 'Polish Prosecutors, Corruption and Legal Culture', in A. Febbrajo and W. Sadurski (eds), *East-Central Europe After Transition: Towards a New Socio-Legal Semantics*, Aldershot: Ashgate.

PRATT, J., BROWN, D., HALLSWORTH, S., BROWN, M., and MORRISON, W. (eds) (2005), *The New Punitiveness: Current Trends, Theories, Perspectives*, Cullompton: Willan.

PRATT, J. and ERIKSSON A. (2013), *Contrasts in Punishment*, Abingdon: Routledge.

REICHEL, P. (2007), *Handbook of Transnational Crime and Justice*, 4th edn, New York: Sage.

REICHEL, P. (2008), *Comparative Criminal Justice Systems*, 5th edn, Upper Saddle River, NJ: Prentice Hall.

ROSS, J. E. (2004), 'Impediments to Transnational Cooperation in Undercover Policing: A Comparative Study of the United States and Italy', *American Journal of Comparative Law*, 52(3): 569–624.

ROSS, J. E. (2007), 'The Place of Covert Policing in Democratic Societies: A Comparative Study of the United States and Germany', *American Journal of Comparative Law*, 55(3): 493.

SAVELSBERG, J. (1994), 'Knowledge, domination and criminal punishment', *American Journal of Sociology*, 99(4): 911–43.

SAVELSBERG, J. (2011), 'Globalization and States of Punishment', in D. Nelken (ed.), *Comparative Criminal Justice and Globalization*, Aldershot: Ashgate.

SEGRAVE, M., MILIVOJEVIC, S., and PICKERING, S. (2009), *Sex Trafficking: International Context and Response*, Cullompton: Willan.

SERGI, A. (2015), 'Divergent mind-sets, convergent policies: Policing models against organized crime in Italy and in England within international frameworks', *European Journal of Criminology*, 12(6): 658–80.

SHEPTYCKI, J. and WARDAK, A. (2005), *Transnational and Comparative Criminology*, London: Glasshouse.

SHERMAN, L., GOTTFREDSON, D., MACKENZIE, D., ECK, J., REUTER, P., and BUSHWAY, S. (1997), *Preventing Crime, What Works, What Doesn't, What is Promising*, Rockville: National Institute of Justice.

SIMON, J. (2007), *Governing Through Crime*, Oxford,: Oxford University Press.

SLADE, G. and LIGHT, M. (2015), 'Crime and criminal justice after communism: Why study the post-Soviet region?', *Crime and Criminal Justice in the Post-Soviet Region* (special issue), *Theoretical Criminology*, 19(2): 147–58.

SOLIVETTI, L. (2010), *Immigration, Social Integration and Crime: A Cross-National Approach*, Abingdon: Routledge.

STUMPF, J. (2006), 'The Crimmigration Crisis: Immigration, Crime and Sovereign Power', *American University Law Review*, 56(2): 367.

TONRY, M. (ed.) (2007), *Crime and Justice vol 36: Crime, Punishment and Politics in Comparative Perspective*, Chicago: University of Chicago.

TONRY, M. (2015), 'Is cross-national and comparative research on the criminal justice system useful?', *European Journal of Criminology*, 12(4): 505–16.

TRIPKOVIC, M. (2016), 'Beyond punitiveness? Governance of crime and authoritarian heritage in Serbia', *Punishment & Society*, 18(3): 369–86.

UGELVIK, T. and DULLUM, J. (ed.) (2012), *Penal Exceptionalism? Nordic Prison Policy and Practice*, Abingdon: Routledge.

VALVERDE, M. (2009), 'Jurisdiction and Scale: Legal "Technicalities" as Resources for Theory', *Social Legal Studies*, 18(2): 139–57.

VAN DIJK, J. (2007), *The World of Crime*, London: Sage.

VON HOFER, H. (2003), 'Prison populations as political Constructs: the Case of Finland, Holland and Sweden', *Journal of Scandinavian Studies in Criminology and Crime Prevention*, 4(1): 21–38.

WANDALL, R. H. (2006), 'Equality by numbers or words: a comparative study of sentencing structures in Minnesota and in Denmark', *Criminal Law Forum*, 17(1): 1–41a.

WACQUANT, L. (2009a), *Prisons of Poverty*, Minneappolis: University of Minnesota Press.

WACQUANT, L. (2009b), *Punishing the Poor: The Neoliberal Government of Social Insecurity*, Durham, NC: Duke University Press.

WHITMAN, J. (2003), *Harsh Justice*, Oxford: Oxford University Press.

WINTERDYK, J. and CAO, L. (2004), *Lessons from International/Comparative Criminology/Criminal Justice*, Toronto: De Sitter.

WINTERDYK, J., REICHEL, P., and DAMMER, H. (2009), *A Guided Reader to Research In Comparative Criminology/Criminal Justice*, Bochum: Brockmeyer Verlag.

ZEDNER, L. (1995), 'In Pursuit of the Vernacular: Comparing Law and Order Discourse in Britain and Germany', *Social and Legal Studies*, 4(4): 517–35.

19

UNDERSTANDING STATE CRIME

Penny Green and Tony Ward

INTRODUCTION

With a few honourable exceptions, criminology has ignored a simple truth about crime—that serious crime is predominantly committed by states and their officials. State crimes are generally easy to recognize: genocide (though rarely in the early stages), war crimes, torture, police violence, and 'grand corruption'—the organized plunder of national resources by a ruling elite. Other forms of state crime, however, are less recognizable: forced eviction, land grabbing, the avoidable effects of many natural disasters. The framework that we offer in this chapter seeks both to provide the conceptual tools to enhance 'recognition' and to explain state crime in a way that relates it to the disciplinary concerns of criminology while drawing on the contributions of other disciplines.

The questions asked by scholars of state crime are essentially those major political and sociological concerns that have informed critical criminology for at least four decades and relate to the exercise of governance and abuse of power by state agents; the relationship between state, capital, and crime; class, gender, and ethnic relations and conceptions of justice and the challenge to state power from below. These concerns, however, have not been addressed exclusively by scholars who would embrace the label 'critical'. For example a great deal of mainstream policing scholarship is concerned with abuses of state power and cannot avoid engaging with issues of class, even if not in the (neo-)Marxist spirit that pervades much of the overtly critical literature (see, e.g., Hinton and Newburn 2009; Punch 2010, 2012). What distinguishes critical criminology is its central concern with demystifying state-defined conceptualizations of crime as a highly selective, class-based censure of social harms. Critical criminology made clear in the 1980s that the harms of the powerful far outweighed the harms of the powerless, and that the criminal label was often employed by the state as a weapon against those sections of society which challenged it or its corporate allies. It took some time, however, before scholars committed to theorizing state criminality and even longer before empirical investigations into state deviance were to be conducted on a serious and global scale.

We are now witnessing a surge in scholarship that seeks to apprehend, interpret, and expose the orchestrated harms of states and corporations (and often the confluence of both) as crimes. This has involved the repositioning of traditional representations of the protagonists—so that conventional conceptions of the state as 'protector' against, and victim of, crime are replaced by, or combined with, the often more accurate representation of the state as perpetrator of crime. Sophisticated, challenging, and courageous methodologies now provide an increasingly powerful evidence base for state crime scholarship.

We begin this chapter by discussing the vexed question of how to define state crime. We then discuss the extent of plainly criminal state activity in today's world, before considering various approaches to the explanation of state crime and the methods by which criminologists can study it.

The notion of state crime raises some obvious definitional problems. First, what is a state? As Weber (1970) famously argued, states claim a monopoly of the legitimate use of force in their territory. Unpacking this definition, we can say that a state is an organization that both exercises, if not a monopoly, at least dominance over the use of organized force within some significant territory, and lays claim to political legitimacy. By these criteria, the 'so-called Islamic State' is indeed a state, and a criminal one.

Like the study of corporate crime, state crime scholarship imputes criminal acts and intentions to group agents (List and Pettit 2011): groups of people whose actions are coordinated to achieve shared goals, in ways which presuppose the truth of certain beliefs about the world. States are complex and internally differentiated, and while in certain contexts they may be regarded as single agents it is often more realistic to impute acts and intentions to specific state *agencies* without supposing that they are shared by the state as a whole (ibid.: 40). Group agents may be nested one within another—a particular police squad may have shared beliefs and goals but may (or may not) also act in concert with other units to achieve the goals of the force as a whole. At times, and particularly in times of crisis (e.g. the UK miners' strike: Green 1990) so many state agencies may be acting in a coordinated way that it is reasonable to treat 'the state' as a single group agent.

What, then, is state *crime?* In this chapter we adopt a definition we have advocated elsewhere (Green and Ward 2000, 2004): it is *organizational deviance*, by *state agencies* (in the sense just explained), which *violates human rights.* As Robert Agnew observes, our definition attempts to 'integrate the essentialist and constructionist perspectives' on crime (Agnew 2011: 29). The 'essentialist' element is an assumption that some acts are *objectively harmful* to human beings, and that human beings have *prima facie* moral rights not to be harmed in those ways. We can leave aside philosophical arguments about whether the existence of human rights is an objective moral reality: it suffices to say that we (and, we hope, most criminologists) have a moral commitment to certain basic rights that we think states ought to respect. We can also leave aside Agnew's view, shared by some state crime scholars (e.g. Rothe 2009), that international law provides an 'objective' definition of harmful behaviour. International human rights instruments do a reasonable job of categorizing the sorts of harm with which we are concerned (torture, deprivation of liberty, denial of essential healthcare, etc.), but understanding the basic needs or interests of human beings as creatures capable of agency is not a matter in which social scientists need to defer to the law (see Doyal and Gough 1981).

The 'constructionist' perspective on crime emphasizes that it is behaviour that is *seen* as harmful and wrong by the state and/or some significant social audience. In the nature of state crime, it is typically not 'labelled' or censured as culpable behaviour by the state itself. This labelling or censuring role is primarily played, rather, by a range of organizations that make up 'civil society': associations independent of the state with some capacity for formulating or advocating norms of conduct and disseminating information about their violation. The term 'civil society' is broad enough to cover international non-governmental organizations (NGOs) like Amnesty, local grass roots organizations, media outlets independent of the state, and religious bodies. Civil society can exist, and effectively censure and resist state crimes, even in repressive states that offer it little or no legal protection (Beyerle 2014: 16–17).[1]

Some state crime attracts formal, legal censure from bodies such as the International Criminal Court (ICC), but this is comparatively rare (23 cases at the ICC up to the time of writing), and to confine our attention to these cases would be to take a very narrow view of state crime. The selection and processing of cases by international tribunals is, however, a fertile field for criminological inquiry (see e.g. Hagan 2003; Mullins 2011).

Agnew (2011) offers his own combination of 'essentialist' and 'constructivist' perspectives which brings state crime within a comprehensive definition and classification of crimes. He proposes that criminologists should rank actions according to the degree to which they: (1) amount to blameworthy harms, that is, harms inflicted intentionally, recklessly, or negligently and without justification or excuse; (2) are condemned by significant sections of the public; and (3) are subject to state sanctions. Acts which meet *any* of these criteria to a significant degree fall within the scope of criminology, but 'core crimes', the paradigmatic subject matter of conventional criminology, rank high on all three. Agnew's approach resembles ours inasmuch as he combines a human-rights-based definition of harm with a recognition that either the state or the public may censure behaviour as harmful and blameworthy. He refers to both Kauzlarich and Kramer's (1998) and our own (Green and Ward 2004) work on state crime as examples of how criminologists might elaborate on the classification of crime that he offers. In this spirit, we would like to suggest that the most serious forms of state crime fall into a category not clearly recognized in Agnew's own work. What may be termed 'core state crimes' are identical to Agnew's 'core crimes'—murder, rape, theft, etc.—except that, while clearly harmful, blameworthy, widely condemned and in most cases illegal, they carry little risk of a state-imposed sanction, at least in the short term. These 'core' crimes should be distinguished—even if the dividing line is blurred—from, for example, 'the intersection of global warming, governmental action—or inaction—and corporate behaviour in ways that produce state-corporate crimes of global warming' (Lynch and Stretesky 2010: 71). Without questioning that this is an immensely important category of harm and of legitimate interest to criminologists, we do question whether it is helpful to equate it with genocide (ibid.: 72). Core state crimes and ambiguously criminal state harms call for different kinds of analysis. We turn to the

[1] This aspect of civil society was the subject of a research project by the authors and colleagues at the International State Crime Initiative: 'State Crime and Resistance: A Comparative Study of Civil Society' funded by Economic and Social Research Council grant no ES/I030816/1 (see Green and Ward, forthcoming).

analysis of core crimes in the next section, but for reasons of space will touch only briefly on more ambiguous cases.

THE MODERN CRIMINAL STATE

State crime is ubiquitous. In 2014 Amnesty International recorded human rights violations in 160 of the world's 196 states and territories and documented torture in 131 of them (Amnesty International 2015).

We are all familiar with the 'core' crimes committed by states, even if we haven't constructed them as such: the ongoing genocides in Sudan's Darfur region and Burma's Rakhine state; the Israeli bombing of Gaza in 2014; the US torture of Iraqi prisoners in Abu Ghraib; the brutality of Ben Ali's Tunisian police state; the terror and corruption of the Egyptian ruling elite represent some of the more egregious acts of state crime. The scale of state killing and systematic theft by ruling elites is staggering and the organized and planned criminality of governments has resulted in immeasurable pain and suffering. Yet the shroud of secrecy, official resistance, and an ideological/juridical culture which confines hegemonic understandings of criminality to the actions of the powerless results in an absence of state crime statistics, a misplaced sense of public fear, and a resistance within criminology to invoking the state as perpetrator. Even for those crimes acknowledged in international law—torture, genocide, crimes against humanity, and war crimes—governments have shown at best only a selective interest in monitoring and measuring. There is no doubt that impunity, secrecy, and a lack of political will impose enormous challenges to the accurate recording of state criminality.

The few attempts there have been to quantify the scale of state crime are inevitably challenged by these complexities. R. J. Rummel, nonetheless, has calculated that 262 million people died between 1900 and 1999 through the 'murder of any person or people by a government including, genocide, politicide and mass murder' (Rummel n.d.). While the great majority of these murders (around 85 per cent) occurred in China (under both Communist and Nationalist regimes), the USSR, the Third Reich, and the colonies of the European powers, there are numerous other regimes who contributed at least hundreds of thousands of deaths to the century's record of carnage.

There have been a number of more recent attempts to quantify the state murder of civilians in individual conflicts. One of the most notable is that conducted by the NGO, Iraq Body Count (2011). They estimated that state, militia, and insurgent killing resulted in between 99,704 and 108,856 violent deaths of civilians in Iraq between the 2003 invasion and January 2011. When the Wikileaks Iraq War Logs data on 15,114 new civilian deaths is added, the total figure of estimated civilian deaths rises to 123,960 (https://www.iraqbodycount.org/analysis/numbers/warlogs/). The Syrian Center for Policy Research (SCPR) has calculated that since the beginning of the war in 2011, 470,000 Syrians have been killed (SCPR 2016: 61) and according to the Syrian Network for Human Rights (whose estimated death toll of civilians between March 2011 and November 2015 was 180,879) 95 per cent were victims of President Bashar Al Assad's forces. In the course of Israel's 'Operation Cast Lead' 23-day bombardment of Gaza between 27 December 2008 and 18 January 2009, approximately 1,440 Palestinians were killed (over half estimated to be civilians), compared with 13 dead (including four civilians) on the Israeli side (Congressional Research Centre 2009).

Mary Kaldor identifies human rights violations and war crimes (i.e. state crimes) as 'a central methodology' of modern armed conflict where politics frames rather than determines the 'violent enterprise' (Kaldor 2006: 121–2). Instead of isolated actions of criminal soldiers or military units, crimes of war now extend to the core of modern armed conflict and are fuelled by looting, illegal trading in diamonds, minerals and timber, corruption, and transnational criminal networks (Green and Ward 2004). Moreover, as Kaldor observes, 'we have good and accurate statistics for the deaths of men in state-based uniforms, but information about the vast majority of victims is totally inadequate' (Kaldor 2013: 9).

If we combine these few attempts to quantify the scale of state crime with the vast and increasing body of work by human rights NGOs, journalists, and academics from a range of disciplines it is clear that state violence and corruption can no longer be left in criminology's hinterlands—rather, state crime should be central to any adequate definition of the scope of criminology.

According to the World Health Organization (WHO), in 2000 some 310,000 people were killed as a result of collective or war-related violence (2002: 10); this represented 20 per cent of all global violent deaths at the time. The WHO acknowledges that this figure, which excludes domestic deaths at the hands of police and security forces, is the tip of an iceberg given the secrecy and denial which envelops so much state violence. One measure of the states' capacity for violence is military expenditure. Evidence from the Stockholm International Peace Research Institute (SIPRI 2015) suggests that in 2014 world military expenditure (estimated at $1,776 billion) represented 2.3 percent of world GDP. While overall global military spending declined by 0.4 per cent between 2013–14 this was largely a function of decisions in the US, South America, and Europe. China, Russia, and Saudi Arabia all increased military expenditure substantially during the period (SIPRI 2015).

Of course, not every death in war is the result of a war crime; the very idea of a war crime presupposes that some killing in war is lawful. Ruggiero (2005) has argued for a pacifist criminology that would treat war itself as criminal. Such an approach would, however, ignore the very significant differences in the degrees to which states and insurgent forces seek to conduct their operations in a lawful manner. For example, ongoing research by Alicia de la Cour Venning[2] explores the apparent adoption of norms of international humanitarian law by Myanmar's armed ethnic Kachin Independence Army (KIA) in its long-running war with the Myanmar state. She seeks to determine how the adoption of these norms, within the context of an armed conflict, can be conceptualized as an effective strategy for challenging a criminal regime. The Myanmar state's criminality is relevant as it characterizes the context within which the KIA must make decisions. Her research has the potential to extend state crime theory by

[2] De la Cour Vening (2016) unpublished doctoral research, 'To what extent do Kachin Independence Army perceptions of international humanitarian norms conform with development of its policies and practice?' (Queen Mary University of London).

investigating the extent to which compliance with international humanitarian norms impacts effective strategies of resistance to prolonged and brutal state criminality.

EXPLAINING CORE STATE CRIME

Brannigan (2013) highlights three features of genocide and similar mass atrocities that criminology needs to explain. The first of these 'paradoxes' is that atrocities are committed for the most part by 'ordinary men' (Browning 1998), and sometimes by ordinary women (see e.g. Sharlach 1999), in the absence of psychopathology, acute provocation, or duress. The second is that although most of these actions are recognized by national and international law as grave crimes, they are or have been 'conventionalized', that is, they remain technically proscribed but are rarely punished (Carson 1979; Brannigan 2013: 32–3). It is this feature that chiefly distinguishes 'core state crimes' from 'core crimes' in Agnew's sense, which attract severe state sanctions as well as public disapproval. The third 'paradox' is that the enormous 'dark figure' of state-instigated violence eclipses that of serious 'street' crime and yet it has received far less attention from criminology.

Faced with these paradoxes, there are two ways that an attempt at criminological explanation can go. One is to suggest that atrocities are not, after all, so very different from other core crimes. In very broad and abstract terms, the same kinds of criminogenic factors are present: motivation, opportunity, and an absence of effective control. What has to be taken into account in analysing state crimes is that these factors operate on several different organizational levels as well as the level of the individual perpetrator. This approach has been developed most systematically in the 'integrated theory' which underpins much of the state crime scholarship of the last two decades, especially in the USA (Kauzlarich and Kramer 1998; Mullins and Rothe 2008). An analysis by Hoofnagle (2011) of mass murder and rape in Burundi provides a typical example of this approach. She identifies *motivational drives* such as international economic policies; *opportunities* afforded by a chaotic situation, coupled with unclear lines of command in the military; some limited *constraint* on the violence provided, albeit haphazardly, by international peace-keeping efforts; and some mechanisms of *control*, that is, would-be deterrent measures taken after the event, which were not implemented effectively. While accounts such as this encapsulate a variety of causal factors in a way that is easily assimilated to mainstream criminological theory, they are open to criticism for being essentially descriptive and offering limited insight into any deeper and less easily legible process that might underlie the surface phenomena (Lasslett 2010). The use of parallels with 'street' crime is perhaps most productive when it yields insights into the emotional and interpersonal dynamics of extreme violence, as in Rafter's (2016) recent work on genocide.

Another response to Brannigan's 'paradoxes' is to emphasize that core state crime is fundamentally different from other crimes by reason of its essentially conformist, rather than deviant, nature. In the phrase coined by Kelman and Hamilton (1989), they are 'crimes of obedience'. As Smeulers puts it:

> a crime qualifies as a crime of obedience when it is supported by the authority structure . . . This very fact turns the whole analytical framework which underlies criminological theory upside down . . . [W]e have to focus on the question why [the perpetrators] are *obedient,* why they followed the group, why they *do* live by the (deviant and immoral) rules. (Smeulers 2008: 236–7)

Talk of 'deviant rules', however, raises the question as to whether this is really a complete inversion of mainstream criminology, rather than a variant of differential association theory. After all, employees of dishonest corporations and members of mafia-like organizations might also be said to live by deviant rules.

The classic study of immoral obedience to authority is Milgram's (1974) notorious series of experiments (partially replicated by Burger 2009) in which a majority of subjects were prepared to inflict what they were told were high-voltage electric shocks on another participant (in reality an actor). What can be learnt from Milgram's seriously flawed and unethical experiments is a highly controversial question (Brannigan 2013, Russell and Gregory 2015). The artificial setting in which subjects were confronted with unexpected demands under the direct supervision of an authority figure (a white-coated 'scientist') cannot be considered a realistic model for the position of state-appointed torturers and murderers who must carry out extreme violence repeatedly over long periods, often without direct supervision.

While highly critical of Milgram's use of his findings to explain the Holocaust, Brannigan (2013) is also in the camp that sees mass atrocities in terms of conformity rather than deviance. Brannigan draws on the work of Elias (2000 [1939]) who related the monopolization of violence by European states since the middle ages to changing sensibilities regarding violence in everyday life. Although the relation between the two is not simple or direct, the concentration of legitimate violence in the hands of the state has developed hand-in-hand with the 'civilizing process' of increasing self-restraint by individuals in the exercise of violence and other bodily functions such as eating and sex. Brannigan argues that modern genocide must be understood as the actions of individuals who are 'civilized' in this sense. He disagrees with Elias' (1996) suggestion that Nazi Germany witnessed a partial regression to 'barbarism'. Germany remained, he argues, a thoroughly controlled and, in Elias' sense, a 'civilized' society; and the more recent genocide in Rwanda also occurred in the context of a tightly controlled, bureaucratic state (see Straus 2006). Brannigan sees genocidal behaviour as a form of deviance resulting from an excess, rather than a deficit of control, paralleling Durkheim's 'altruistic' and 'fatalistic' forms of suicide.[3] There is a kind of altruism in the perpetrators' sense of duty and commitment to the genocidal ideology of the state, and a kind of fatalism in the willingness to persist in genocide even in the face of inevitable defeat.

Our own analysis of state violence (Green and Ward 2008, 2009) shares Brannigan's debt to Elias but sees an important truth in Elias' view that there are 'decivilizing'

[3] In Durkheim's explanatory scheme, altruistic suicides (driven by duty and self-sacrifice), derive from deficient individuation, while fatalistic suicides, such as those of slaves, derive from an excess of regulation (Durkheim 1952: 217–21, 276 n.).

counterflows at work within the 'civilizing process'. Along with subjection to the state comes a licence to use violence creatively and autonomously in pursuit of the state's goals. De Swaan's (2001) concept of *enclaves of barbarism* captures this synthesis within an Eliasian perspective. For de Swaan, the key feature of the 'bureaucratization of barbarism' is the *comparmentalization* of the target population, the sites of torture or murder, the roles of the perpetrators, and their emotional experiences:

> wildness and brutality are let loose, or maybe even instilled, and at the same time instrumentalized, for specific purposes, within demarcated spaces at an appointed time: an archipelago of enclaves where cruelty reigns while being reined in all the while . . . [T]he regime creates and maintains compartments of destruction and barbarism, in meticulous isolation, almost invisible and well-nigh unmentionable. (de Swaan 2001: 269)

Within these 'enclaves', including the Nazi concentration camps and the sites of mass slaughter in Rwanda, what takes place is not simply routinized, efficient killing but a wide variety of acts of extreme cruelty that go well beyond dutifully carrying out orders and owe much of their social meaning to their 'excessive' character (see, e.g., African Rights 1994; Sofsky 1997).

The contradiction between 'civilized' sensibilities (in Elias' sense) and the demands of the violent state is manifested most acutely when extremely repressive policies take root in states that have experienced relatively liberal forms of democratic political rule. States of this kind have been the subject of several exemplary studies, including Schirmer's (1998) of the Guatemalan military in the 1980s, Huggins' work on Brazilian torturers and murders (Huggins *et al.* 2002), Haritos-Fatouros' (1988, 2003) and Gibson's (1990) work on torture under the Greek junta, and the work of Feitlowitz (1998), Marchak (1999), and others on Argentina.

Whilst there are many nuances and regional particularities, we can identify a number of general explanatory themes in this body of scholarship. The first is a tendency for states which engage in systematic state violence to promote a monolithic sense of cultural identity (e.g. the project of the architects of the Turkish Republic). A supposedly indivisible 'imagined community' (Anderson 1991) defines itself through exclusion of minorities whose claims to recognition and respect threaten the integrity of the monolith. When those claims take the form of active resistance against the state then clear ideological enemies are defined and the state may engage in a dehumanization process which excludes those enemies from the 'universe of obligation' (Fein 1990) within which ordinary moral rules apply. Monolithic cultures are frequently authoritarian in character and those agents of the state most likely to rise to its defence are found to be attracted to far right wing and fascist ideologies (Staub 1989).

A second theme that emerges clearly from the psychological research is that most torturers and purveyors of state terror, who are for the most part psychologically normal, require training, often of a very brutal and brutalizing nature, to counter long-held socialized norms against the use of cruelty (Haritos-Fatouros 1988; Gibson 1990). Specialized elite units, such as those to which virtually all torturers of the Greek and Brazilian regimes belonged (Gibson and Haritos-Faturos 1986; Huggins *et al.* 2002) also appear to be essential.

The literature reveals, thirdly, that even when states portray torture and terror as essential to combat perceived threats to social order, there is a recognition on the part of state agents that this violence stands outside the bounds of political legitimacy (Cohen 1981; Green and Ward 2004).

Denial, of the various kinds analysed by Cohen (2001a) is a ubiquitous response on the part of states whose wrongdoing is exposed. This is closely allied to neutralization (Sykes and Matza 1957), the difference being that neutralization occurs before or during the event rather than after it. Techniques of neutralization enable perpetrators or instigators of state crime to make radical departures from conventional moral norms appear justifiable or excusable (Cohen 2001b; Alvarez 2010). New research is revealing exactly how states and corporations mobilize significant legal, financial, and human resources, to conceal their illicit practices from public scrutiny. MacManus (2016) refers to a dialectical interplay between civil society condemnation and exposure of state-corporate crime and state-corporate practices of denial as a 'process of labelling and counter-labelling . . . conducted in the public'. In recent decades PR companies have been 'routinely employed by governments for "crisis management", i.e. to deal with any potentially damaging public reaction to perceived state deviance or crime' (MacManus 2016).

The economic, strategic, and political interests of the major powers are also important in sustaining criminal practices and their denial, as can be seen in the cases of Israel and Myanmar. According to the Congressional Research Service, Israel is the 'largest cumulative recipient of U.S. foreign assistance since World War II'. In 2015 the US administration funded Israel to the tune of $3.7 billion—$3.1 billion in direct bilateral military aid with a further $619.8 million for 'joint' US–Israel missile defence programs. US support directly enables Israel's well documented crimes in the occupied West Bank and Gaza (extrajudicial killings, ethnic cleansing, forced evictions, illegal settlements, apartheid against civilian Palestinians (Sharp 2015)).

In Myanmar, where the state is in the process of a genocidal campaign to annihilate its ethnic minority Rohingya population (Green *et al.* 2015), the regional powers, China and India, have ignored the plight of the Rohingya as they seek to exploit Myanmar's natural resources with, for example, the Shwe gas pipeline and the Kaladan Multimodal Transit Transport Project—projects which will benefit Myanmar's rulers but not the inhabitants of the country's second poorest state (Green *et al.* 2015).

CORRUPTION, COLLUSION, AND AMBIGUITY

Apart from illegitimate state violence, the other major form of state crime is that which involves the illegitimate use of state agencies' powers over the allocation of resources. Much of corruption falls under the heading of core state crime: theft and fraud which is unambiguously illegal and generally condemned by the public. But there is also much about corruption that is legally and morally ambiguous—and its ambiguity does not necessarily make it less serious.

In Papua New Guinea, for example, the corruption of greatest concern to local civil society activists[4] is not so much the blatant scams and embezzlement for which the country is notorious (Sharman 2012) as forms of state-corporate collusion in the (sometimes ambiguously) illegal acquisition of land rights (Ward 2016).

[4] We draw here on Kristian Lasslett's contributions to the research mentioned in n. 1 above.

One of the most important insights to emerge from the economic study of corruption is the tendency of states to gravitate towards either a high or low equilibrium, that is, a stable level of corruption (Andvig and Feldstad 2000). Levels of corruption appear to be driven by either virtuous or vicious circles. In the virtuous circle, because corruption is rare, offering a bribe is risky and accepting one carries heavy 'moral costs' (guilt and the risk of detection). In the vicious circle, because corruption is common, offering a bribe stands a good chance of success with a low risk of adverse consequences, and the costs of accepting a bribe are likely to be low. As in the case of violence, behaviour that is deviant according to one set of standards may amount to conformity to the expectations of those who can apply the most effective pressure to the individual actor. In a metaphor used by Hong Kong police officers, you can get on the bus (participate in corruption) or run alongside the bus (abstain from corruption but not interfere with it), but if you stand in front of the bus you are liable to be run over (Kutnjak Ivkovic 2005).

Corruption is important both as a major form of crime in its own right and as a factor in understanding some forms of state violence. For example, the vulnerability of certain populations to natural disasters (the 1999 Marmara earthquake, Hurricane Katrina in 2005, the Haitian earthquake, and the Pakistan floods of 2010) is directly attributable to corrupt decision-making processes and the resulting deaths can be considered a form of indirect state violence. Many states collude with criminal organizations to carry out violence as well as illicit business and numerous violent regimes rely on corrupt networks to sustain their power (see e.g. Heyman 1999; Green and Ward 2004).

At its most extreme, this contradiction between the formal rules of government and the real exercise of power manifests itself in a 'shadow state' (Reno 1995), where the legally constituted system is little more than a façade erected to secure international respectability and aid. In Weberian terms such states can be classed as 'neo-patrimonial' (Médard 2001)—patrimonialism (personal and economic ties between rulers and subordinates) is the real basis of the rulers' power, and of such domestic legitimacy as they may possess, but the formal structure of authority presents itself as a rational–legal one. Bayart *et al.* (1999) have discussed some extreme examples of the 'criminalization of the state in Africa', where relatively small states such as the Comoros Islands and Equatorial Guinea were largely financed by smuggling. Another extreme form of corruption is 'kleptocracy' where the theft of public resources by a ruling elite appears to be the ruling principle of the state. Examples include Liberia under (and before) Charles Taylor and Zaire under Mobutu (Schatzberg 1988).

STATE CRIME AND THE ETHNOGRAPHIC TRADITION

Given the strong Marxist antecedents informing the study of state violence and corruption, it is unsurprising that research in the field has been impelled by three main drivers: (1) the political and economic context in which these crimes take place; (2) the primacy of victims' perceptions; and (3) an intimate examination of perpetrator agency. Combined with an implicit distrust of state-produced and packaged knowledge researchers are thus led to rely far more on the direct testimony of victims and perpetrators and detailed examinations of political economy.

Criminology has a narrowly drawn but important tradition of ethnographic research dating back to the Chicago School of the 1920s and Robert Park's injunction to young scholars to 'go out and get your hands dirty in real research' (Park 1966: 71). A revival of criminological ethnography in the late 1990s saw the method again confined to the marginalized and familiar constituents of criminology's oeuvre (see in particular Ferrell and Hamm 1998)—and also to deviance within the police (e.g. Westley 1970; Holdaway 1982; Choongh 1997; Westmarland 2011).

Where ethnography first begins to address other state crime issues, however, is unsurprisingly within the domain, not of criminology, but of anthropology, the original home of ethnography (see, e.g., Sluka 1999; Keenan 2009, 2013; Jensen and Jefferson 2009). Mehmet Kurt for example, in studying notions of violence, state, religion, and belonging in Turkey's Kurdish Hizbullah employed his former status as an imam to secure access and trust from his participants. Kurt examines in intimate detail the manner in which Islamic civil society has taken root in a region where ethnic identity has been the primary organizing tool against a repressive and violent state. Despite the rise of Islamic radicalization in Kurdish South East Turkey, almost all scholarly work has focused on mainstream Islamic civil society organizations (Jenkins 2008). This body of work concludes that Turkish Islamist groups have found a 'peaceful' way to compromise with the secular regime and the ruling Peace and Development Party's (AKP) political administration (Turam 2007). Kurt's research suggests this is a misleading picture of Islamism in Turkey and that Kurdish Islamist CSOs, such as Özgür-Der and Ay-Der, which have flourished in the region since at least 2005, are not only becoming increasingly radicalized, but that many hundreds of their members are joining the IS and Al Nusra Front in the jihadist war in Syria (Kurt 2015).

Through ethnographic field work and extensive interviews with members, leaders, and supporters of Hizbullah we are not only given an insight into the workings of a rather clandestine form of 'civil society' but an explanation of why Hizbullah has proved so attractive to young Kurds and why so many of them have crossed the border into Syria to fight with Islamic State. Kurt's work captures both an Islamist response to state criminality and a source of the growth of a new kind of criminal state, Islamic State (Kurt, forthcoming).

NEW DATA, NEW METHODS

The dangers and difficulties involved in researching state crime continue to foster particular forms of creative resourcefulness with regard to methodology and access. Those working on state crime are, perhaps, predisposed to seek non-traditional and alternative data sources given the guarded nature of the subject. Accepting that the state does not provide neatly packaged statistical documentation on state deviance, and given the critical framework within which these scholars work, data is necessarily sought elsewhere.

One of the most innovative methods of securing research access was conceived by the Harvard Humanitarian Initiative and its local partners in the Democratic Republic of Congo, the Centre d'Assistance Medico-Psychosociale (CAMPS). In order to interview Mai Mai militia combatants active in the southern Kivu province and heavily involved in the perpetration of sexual and other violence, lead researcher Michael van Rooyen negotiated with a commanding colonel living in the forest outside the town of southern Kivu town of Kamituga. As Kamituga was under the control of the Congolese National Military, researchers negotiated a 48-hour amnesty for the combatants who were then required to disarm at the entrance to the town before entering for interviews (HHI 2009: 13).

A further example, drawn from one of the authors' own work, relates to negotiating access in an environment of absolute denial. In researching the genocidal processes faced by the Muslim ethnic Rohingya in Myanmar, Green and her colleagues met a wall of silence when seeking to locate Rohingya detention camps to the west of Rakhine state's capital Sittwe. The Myanmar state denies the very existence of the Rohingya identity (use of the term Rohingya is forbidden in the country), and because of the complete segregation which operates in southern Rakhine state, locating camps in the region of Mrauk U proved extremely difficult. However, with the aid of a GPS, bone rattling bicycles, a UNOCHA[5] map, and the air of naïve tourists it was (after several hours cycling across dry paddy fields and peasant tracks) possible to locate a Rohingya village and nearby camp and to conduct interviews and observations before being pursued by Myanmar security forces (see Green *et al.* 2015).

While fieldwork remains the central core of data gathering there are rich sources to be plumbed beyond the academy: eyewitness accounts from reputable journalists and quality print and broadcasting media (see especially the reports and films of Egypt's Mosireen Collective, Robert Fisk, Al Jazeera's Phil Rees, and John Pilger); civil society organizations, former state agents, legal firms, and NGOs can provide a wealth of valuable and reliable data. Social media, camera phones, and web technologies have encouraged the phenomenon of 'citizen journalism' and thereby provided a means through which civil society can reach large global audiences without recourse to traditional forms of media. Increasing numbers of human rights and advocacy groups have joined forces with citizen journalists (especially during the Arab uprisings of 2011), encouraging them to document abuses in order to frustrate censorship and expose state repression, violence, and corruption. During the Libyan uprising of February 2011 Google set up an account so that anyone in the country with a phone could call one of a range of numbers and leave a voice message about what was happening on the streets. The message was then automatically translated into a tweet in order to evade the communication blackout that Gaddafi's regime had imposed (Al Jazeera 2011). While not an immediately obvious research tool Google nonetheless provided a mechanism which allowed real time data to flow into the international public domain.

Other researchers are analysing social media content in order to source data on events which they would otherwise be unable to study (see Saeb Kasm's work on Egypt's Mosireen Video Collective, forthcoming). For scholars of state crime these developments hold exciting promise but they must also be approached with rigorous regard to issues

[5] United Nations Office for the Coordination of Humanitarian Affairs.

of data verification. Determining the provenance of human rights abuse claims through text, images, and footage and ascertaining the veracity and authenticity of sources is thus opening new methodological challenges to scholars drawing on new media data.

As we saw in the section on 'mapping', reliable quantitative data on state violence are hard to come by, and scholars often have to resort to 'meta-guesstimates' arrived at by averaging out the widely varying estimates available. Some more sophisticated demographic techniques for estimating death rates are discussed by Bijleveld (2008). Hagan and Rymond-Richmond used data from the Darfur Atrocities Documentation Project, the US State Department's survey into genocidal processes in Sudan[6] to advance their claim that genocide had taken place in Darfur; that a criminology of genocide was required; and that such a criminology could be used to advocate against genocide (Hagan and Rymond-Richmond 2008).

A newer methodology which has a particular value for the state crime scholar exploring state terror, ethnic cleansing, war crimes, and genocide is that of satellite earth observation imagery, already pioneered in archaeology for the protection and management of cultural heritage. Researchers may hire satellite capacity in order to monitor troop or militia movements; village destruction; population displacement; and the destruction of farm and pastureland. The costs remain high but the Satellite Sentinel Project which was launched by human rights organization Not on Our Watch to monitor troop movements in Southern Sudan in 2011 has demonstrated the potential of satellite data for researching criminal state practices (http://satsentinel.org/; McGreal 2010).

Investigating crimes of powerful state agents can be difficult, harrowing, and sometimes dangerous (Schirmer 1998; Nordstrom 2004; Green 2003). One of the reasons why so few researchers venture into empirically investigating crimes committed by generals, politicians, and state officials is the assumption that access to the powerful and their criminogenic processes will be denied. Access to powerful perpetrators may, however (with persistence, creativity and tenacity), be less difficult to secure than imagined, as the work of many of the authors cited above demonstrates. Whyte's (2012) empirical research on the criminal restructuring of the Iraqi economy following the 2003 US-led invasion is a case in point. Attendance at Iraq reconstruction conferences provided a rare opportunity to observe, analyse, and participate in the political/corporate dealings of the occupation. Uninvited, Whyte (2012) secured valuable data relating to the political and corporate underpinnings of Iraqi reconstruction by boldly assuming rights of access to Iraqi Restructuring meetings that he did not formally possess. Adopting the confidence of 'white men in suits' was enough, as it turned out, to open the door.

State crime researchers tend, however, to side with those for whom change brings freedom from state abuses. In so doing state crime researchers are adopting Scheper-Hughes' notion of 'ethical orientation' in which the personal accountability of the researcher is answerable to the 'other' (Scheper-Hughes 1992: 24). This ethical orientation speaks to a commitment to justice and moral alignment with the victims of state violence and corruption, in the pursuit of truth and change.

[6] 1,136 eyewitnesses in refugee camps in Chad were interviewed by the research team, 'a sample large enough to be a statistically significant representation of the estimated 200,000 Darfuri refugees in Chad', Genocide Watch, available at: http://www.genocidewatch.org/provinggenocidedarfur.html, accessed 2 January 2017.

CONCLUSION

State crime scholarship is an expanding field and one that is no longer confined to a few marginalized critical voices. It remains the case that most work on genocide, corruption, torture, and other state crimes is not carried out by people who define themselves as criminologists; but criminology can provide both a meeting place for ideas deriving from other disciplines and make a distinctive contribution through its focus on rules, transgression, and processes of censure.

It is over 150 years since Proal (1898: 2) began his pioneering study by quoting Seneca's observation that '[t]he desire to rule and the exercise of authority teach fraud and violence'. If crime can be defined, as Gottfredson and Hirschi argued, as 'acts of force or fraud undertaken in pursuit of self-interest' (1990: 15) then criminology's recognition of Seneca's ancient insight is long overdue. Work such as Agnew's 'unified' approach—not to mention the inclusion of this chapter in the *Oxford Handbook*—suggests that mainstream criminology is beginning to take notice of the obvious importance of state crime, even if it does not yet occupy a place within the discipline commensurate with its scale and destructiveness.

SELECTED FURTHER READING

An indispensable starting point for the study of state crime is Cohen's *States of Denial: Knowing About Atrocities and Suffering* (2001). Chambliss, Kramer, and Michalowski, individually and collectively, have made many important contributions, including their co-edited, *State Crime in the Global Age* (2010). Among the best empirical studies of state functionaries as criminal actors is Huggins, Haritos-Fatouros, and Zimbardo's *Violence Workers: Police Torturers and Murderers Reconstruct Brazilian Atrocities* (2002). Brannigan develops an approach to genocide of particular interest to criminologists in *Beyond the Banality of Evil: Criminology and Genocide* (2013). Lasslett's *State Crime on the Margins of Empire* (2015) is a powerful example of exciting new developments in the field. For the latest in cutting-edge research see the journal of the International State Crime Initiative (ISCI), *State Crime*, and ISCI's website: http://statecrime.org.

The approach we have set out in this chapter draws on our monograph *State Crime: Governments, Violence and Corruption* (2004).

REFERENCES

African Rights (1994), *Rwanda: Death, Despair and Defiance*, London: African Rights.

Agnew, R. (2011), *Toward a Unified Criminology*, New York: New York University Press.

Al Jazeera (2011), 'How Did Egypt become so Corrupt?', *Inside Story* aired 7 February 2011, available at: http://www.aljazeera.com/palestinepapers/2011/01/201112214310263628.html, accessed 13 January 2017.

Alvarez, A. (2010), *Genocidal Crimes*, London: Routledge.

Amnesty International (2015), *Amnesty International Report 2014: The State of the World's Human Rights*, available at: http://thereport.amnesty.org/facts-and-figures. https://www.amnesty.org/en/latest/news/2015/02/annual-report-201415-facts-and-figures/, accessed 28 December 2016.

Anderson, B. (1991), *Imagined Communities: Reflections on the Origin and Spread of Nationalism*, London: Verso.

Andvig, J. C. and Feldstad, O-H. (2000), *Research on Corruption: A Policy Oriented Survey*, Oslo: Chr.

Michelsen Institute and Norwegian Institute for International Affairs.

Bayart, J-F., Ellis, S., and Hibou, B. (1999), *The Criminalization of the State in Africa*, Oxford: James Currey.

Beyerle, S. (2014), *Curtailing Corruption: People Power for Accountability & Justice*, Boulder: Lynne Rienner.

Bijleveld, C. (2008), 'Missing Pieces. Some Thoughts on the Methodology of the Empirical Study of International Crimes and other Gross Human Rights Violations', in A. Smeulers and R. Haveman (eds), *Supranational Criminology: Towards a Criminology of International Crimes*, Antwerp: Intersentia.

Brannigan, A. (2013), *Beyond the Banality of Evil: Criminology and Genocide*, Oxford: Oxford University Press.

Browning, C. (1998), *Ordinary Men: Reserve Police Batallion 101 and the Final Solution in Poland*, New York: Harper Perennial.

Burger, J. M. (2009), 'Replicating Milgram: Would People Still Obey Today?', *American Psychologist*, 64(1): 1–11.

Carson, W. G. (1979), 'The Conventionalisation of Early Factory Crime', *International Journal for the Sociology of Law*, 7(1): 37–60.

Chambliss, W., Michalowski, R., and Kramer, R. (eds) (2010), *State Crime in the Global Age*, Cullompton: Willan.

Choongh, S. (1997), *Policing as Social Discipline*, Oxford: Clarendon Press.

Cohen, S. (1981), 'Footprints on the Sand: A Further Report on Criminology and the Sociology of Deviance in Britain', in M. Fitzgerald, G. McLennan, and J. Pawson (eds), *Crime and Society: Readings in History and Theory*, London: Routledge & Kegan Paul.

Cohen, S. (2001a), *States of Denial: Knowing About Atrocities and Suffering*, Cambridge: Blackwell.

Cohen, S. (2001b), 'Memory Wars and Peace Commissions', *Index on Censorship*, 30(1): 38–48.

Congressional Research Service (2009), *Israel and Hamas: Conflict in Gaza (2008-2009)*, available at: https://www.fas.org/sgp/crs/mideast/R40101.pdf, accessed 28 December 2016.

De Swaan, A. (2001), 'Dyscivilization, Mass Extermination and the State', *Theory, Culture & Society*, 18(2–3): 265–76.

Doyal, K., and Gough, I. (1981), *A Theory of Human Need*, Basingstoke: Macmillan.

Durkheim, E. (1952), *Suicide*, trans. J. A. Spaulding and G. Simpson, London: Routledge & Kegan Paul.

Elias, N. (1996), *The Germans*, Cambridge: Polity.

Elias, N. (2000), *The Civilizing Process*, Oxford: Blackwell.

Fein, H. (1990), 'Genocide: A Sociological Perspective', *Current Sociology*, 38(1): 1–111.

Feitlowitz, M. (1998), *A Lexicon of Terror: Argentina and the Legacies of Terror*, Oxford: Oxford University Press.

Ferrell, J. and Hamm, M. (1998), *Ethnography at the Edge: Crime, Deviance and Field Research*, Boston: Northeastern University Press.

Festinger, L. (1962), *A Theory of Cognitive Dissonance*, Stanford: Stanford University Press.

Gibson, J. T. (1990), 'Factors contributing to the Creation of a Torturer', in P. Suedfeld (ed.), *Psychology and Torture*, New York: Hemisphere.

Gibson, J. T. and Hartos-Fatouros, M. (1986), 'The Education of a Torturer', Copenhagen: Denmark Torture Rehabilitation Centre, RCT, 16 November: 50–8.

Gottfredson, M. R. and Hirschi, T. (1990), *A General Theory of Crime*, Stanford: Stanford University Press.

Green, P. (1990), *The Enemy Without: Policing and Class Consciousness in the Miners' Strike*, Milton Keynes: Open University Press.

Green, P. (2003), 'Researching the Turkish State', in S. Tombs and D. Whyte, *Unmasking the Crimes of the Powerful*, New York: Peter Lang.

Green, P. and Ward, T. (2000), 'State Crime, Human Rights and the Limits of Criminology', *Social Justice* 27(1), 101–15.

Green, P. and Ward, T. (2004), *State Crime: Governments, Violence and Corruption*, London: Pluto.

Green, P. and Ward, T. (2008), 'Torture and the Paradox of State Violence', in B. Clucas, G. Johnstone, and T. Ward (eds), *Torture: Moral Absolutes and Ambiguities*, Baden-Baden: Nomos.

Green, P. and Ward, T. (2009), 'Violence and the State', in R. Coleman, J. Sim, S. Tombs, and D. Whyte (eds), *State, Power, Crime*, London: Sage.

Green, P. and Ward, T. (2012), 'State Crime: A Dialectical View', in M. Maguire, R. Morgan, and R. Reiner (eds), *The Oxford Handbook of Criminology*, Oxford: Oxford University Press.

Green, P. and Ward, T. (forthcoming), *Civil Resistance to State Crime*, London: Routledge.

Green, P., MacManus, T., and de la Cour Venning, A. (2015), *Countdown to Annihilation: Genocide in Myanmar*, London: International State Crime Initiative.

Hagan, J. (2003), *Justice in the Balkans: Prosecuting War Crimes in the Hague Tribunal*, Chicago: University of Chicago Press.

Hagan, J. and Rymond-Richmond, W. (2008), *Darfur and the Crime of Genocide*, Cambridge Studies in Law and Society, New York: Cambridge University Press.

Haritos-Fatouros, M. (1988), 'The Official Torturer: a learning model for obedience to an authority of violence', *Torture (RCT)*, 26: 69–97.

Haritos-Fatouros, M. (2003), *The Psychological Origins of Institutionalized Torture*, London: Routledge.

Harvard Humanitarian Initiative (HHI) (2009), *Characterizing Sexual Violence in the Democratic Republic of the Congo: Profiles of Violence, Community Responses, and Implications for the Protection of Women*, August 2009, Final Report for the Open Society Institute, Cambridge, MA: Harvard Humanitarian Initiative and Open Society Institute, available at: http://www.hhi.harvard.edu/images/resources/reports/final report for the open society institute—1.pdf, accessed 28 December 2016.

HEYMAN, J. M. (ed.) (1999), *States and Illegal Practices*, Oxford: Berg.

HINTON, M. S. and NEWBURN, T. (2009), *Policing Developing Democracies*, Abingdon: Routledge.

HOLDAWAY, S. (1982), *Inside the British Police*, Oxford: Blackwell.

HOME OFFICE (2011), *Research and Development Statistics 2011*, available at: http://rds.homeoffice.gov.uk/rds/pubsintro1.html.

HOOFNAGLE, K. (2011), 'Burundi: A History of Conflict and State Crime', in D. L. Rothe and C. W. Mullins (eds), *State Crime: Current Perspectives*, New Brunswick: Rutgers University Press.

HUGGINS, M. K., HARITOS-FATOUROS, M., and ZIMBARDO, P. G. (2002), *Violence Workers: Police Torturers and Murderers Reconstruct Brazilian Atrocities*, Berkeley: University of California Press.

INTERNATIONAL STATE CRIME INITIATIVE (ISCI), http://www.statecrime.org, accessed 28 December 2016.

IRAQ BODY COUNT (2011), https://www.iraqbodycount.org/database/, accessed 28 December 2016.

JENKINS, G. (2008), *Political Islam in Turkey Running West Heading East*, New York: Palgrave Macmillan.

JENSEN, S. and JEFFERSON, A. (2009), *State Violence and Human Rights: State Officials in the South*, London: Routledge.

KASM, S. (forthcoming), 'Reframing Narratives in Egypt's Contested Revolution: The Power of Digital and Cultural Resistance'.

KALDOR, M. (2006), *New and Old Wars*, 2nd edn, Cambridge: Polity.

KALDOR, M. (2013), 'In Defence of New Wars', *Stability*, 2(1): 1–16.

KAUZLARICH, D. and KRAMER, R. C. (1998), *Crimes of the American Nuclear State: At Home and Abroad*, Boston: Northeastern University Press.

KEENAN, J. (2013), *The Dying Sahara: US Imperialism and Terror in Africa*, London: Pluto.

KEENAN, J. (2009), *The Dark Sahara: America's War on Terror in Africa*, London: Pluto.

KELMAN, H. C. and Hamilton, V. L. (1989), *Crimes of Obedience*, New Haven: Yale University Press.

KURT, M. (2015), 'Din, Şiddet ve Aidiyet Türkiye'de Hizbullah' (Hizbullah in Turkey: Religion, Violence and Belonging), İstanbul: İletişim Yayınları.

KURT, M. (forthcoming), *Hizbullah in Turkey: Religion, Violence and Belonging*, London: Pluto.

KUTNJAK IVKOVIC, S. (2005), *Fallen Blue Knights: Controlling Police Corruption*, New York: Oxford University Press.

LASSLETT, K. (2010), 'Scientific Method and the Crimes of the Powerful', *Critical Criminology*, 18(3): 211–28.

LIST, C. and PETTIT, P. (2011), *Group Agency: The Possibility, Design and Status of Corporate Agents*, Oxford: Oxford University Press.

LYNCH, M. J. AND STRETESKY, P. B. (2010), 'Global Warming, Global Crime: A Green Criminological Perspective', in R. White (ed.), *Global Environmental Harm: Criminological Perspectives*, Cullompton: Willan.

MACMANUS, T. (2016), 'The denial industry: public relations, "crisis management" and corporate crime', *The International Journal of Human Rights*, 20(6): 785–97.

MCGREAL, C. (2010), 'George Clooney and Google launch satellite plan to avert Sudan violence', *The Guardian*, 29 December.

MARCHAK, P. (1999), *God's Assassins: State Terrorism in Argentina in the 1970s*, Montreal: McGill-Queen's University Press.

MÉDARD, J-F. (2001), 'Corruption in the Neo-patrimonial States of Sub-Saharan Africa', in M. Johnston and A. J. Heidenheimer (eds), *Political Corruption: Contexts and Consequences*, New Brunswick: Transaction.

MILGRAM, S. (1974), *Obedience to Authority*, New York: Harper & Row.

MULLINS, C. W. (2011), 'The Current Status and Role of the International Criminal Court', in D. L. Rothe and C. W. Mullins (eds), *State Crime: Current Perspectives*, New Brunswick: Rutgers University Press.

MULLINS, C. W. and ROTHE, D. (2008) *Blood, Power and Bedlam: Violations of International Criminal Law in Postcolonial Africa*, New York: Peter Lang.

NORDSTROM, C. (2004), *Shadows of War: Violence, Power, and International Profiteering in the Twenty-First-Century*, Berkeley, Los Angeles, London: University of California Press.

PARK, R. E. (1966), 'Unpublished Statement made by Robert E. Park and Recorded by Howard Becker while a Graduate Student at Chicago in the Twenties', in J. C. McKinney (ed.), *Constructive Typology and Social Theory*, New York: Appleton-Century-Crofts.

PROAL, L. (1898), *Political Crime*, London: T. Fisher Unwin.

PUNCH, M. (2010), *Shoot to Kill: Police Accountability, Firearms and Fatal Force*, Bristol: Policy.

PUNCH, M. (2012), *State Violence, Collusion and the Troubles*, London: Pluto.

RAFTER, N. (2016), *The Crime of All Crimes: Toward a Criminology of Genocide*, New York: New York University Press.

RENO, W. (1995), *Corruption and State Politics in Sierra Leone*, Cambridge: Cambridge University Press.

ROTHE, D. L. (2009), *State Criminality: The Crime of All Crimes*, Lanham, MD: Lexington.

RUGGIERO, V. (2005), 'Criminalizing War: Criminology as Ceasefire', *Social & Legal Studies*, 14(2): 239–57.

RUMMEL, R. J. (n.d.), '20th Century Democide', available at: http://www.hawaii.edu/powerkills/20TH.HTM and http://www.hawaii.edu/powerkills/DBG.CHAP2.HTM, accessed 28 December 2016.

RUSSELL, N. and GREGORY, R. (2015), 'The Milgram-Holocaust Linkage: Challenging the Present Consensus', *State Crime*, 4(2): 128–53.

SCPR (2016), *Forced Dispersion: A Demographic Report on Human Status in Syria*, available at: http://scpr-syria.org/publications/forced-dispersion-syrian-human-status-the-demographic-report-2016/, accessed 17 January 2017.

SCHATZBERG, M. G. (1988), *The Dialectics of Oppression in Zaire*, Bloomington: Indiana University Press.

Scheper-Hughes, N. (1992), *Death without Weeping*, Berkeley: University of California press.

Schirmer, J. (1998), *The Guatemalan Military Project*, Philadelphia: University of Pennsylvania Press.

Sharlach, L. (1999), 'Gender and Genocide in Rwanda: Women as Agents and Objects of Genocide', *Journal of Genocide Research*, 1(3): 387–99.

Sharman, J. (2012), *Chasing Kleptocrats' Loot: Narrowing the Effectiveness Gap*, Oslo: Christian Michelsen Institute.

Sharp, J. (2015), 'U.S. Foreign Aid to Israel', The Congressional Research Service's Report, 10 June 2015.

Sluka, J. (ed.) (1999), *Death Squad: The Anthropology of State Terror*, Philadelphia: University of Pennsylvania Press.

Smeulers, A. (2008), 'Perpetrators of International Crimes: Towards a Typology', in A. Smeulers and R. Haveman (eds), *Supranational Criminology: Towards a Criminology of International Crimes*, Antwerp: Intersentia.

Sofsky, W. (1997), *The Order of Terror: The Concentration Camp*, Princeton: Princeton University Press.

Staub, E. (1989), *The Roots of Evil: The Origins of Genocide and Other Group Violence*, Cambridge: Cambridge University Press.

Stockholm International Peace Research Institute (2015), *Recent Trends in Military Expenditure*. Stockholm: SIPRI, available at: http://www.sipri.org/research/armaments/milex/recent-trends, accessed 28 December 2016.

Straus, S. (2006), *The Order of Genocide: Race, Power and War in Rwanda*, Ithaca: Cornell University Press.

Sykes, G. and Matza, D. (1957), 'Techniques of Neutralization: a Theory of Delinquency', *American Sociological Review*, 22(6): 664–70.

Syrians For Human Rights (2015), 'Death Toll', available at: http://sn4hr.org/blog/category/victims/death-toll/, accessed 28 December 2016.

Syrian Network For Human Rights (2016), Syria: *Confronting Fragmentation!*, available at: http://www.sy.undp.org/content/syria/en/home/library/poverty/confronting-fragmentation/, accessed 10 February 2017.

Turam, B. (2007), *Between Islam and the State: The Politics of Engagement*, Stanford: Stanford University Press.

Ward, T. (2016) 'Civil Society Perspectives on Corruption and Human Rights: The Case of Papua New Guinea', in L. Weber, E. Fishwick, and M. Marmo (eds), *The Routledge International Handbook of Criminology and Human Rights*, London: Routledge.

Weber, M. (1970), 'Politics as a Vocation', in H. Girth and C. Wright Mills (eds), *From Max Weber: Essays in Sociology*, London: Routledge & Kegan Paul.

Westley, W. A. (1970), *Violence and the Police*, Cambridge, MA: MIT Press.

Westmarland, L. (2011), 'Blowing the Whistle on Police Violence: Gender, Ethnography and Ethics', *British Journal of Criminology*, 41(3): 523–35.

Whyte, D. (2012), 'Between Crime and *Doxa*: Researching the Worlds of State-Corporate Elites', *State Crime*, 1(1): 88–108.

World Health Organization (2002), *World Report on Violence and Health*, available at: http://www.who.int/violence_injury_prevention/violence/world_report/en/, accessed 28 December 2016.

20

MAKING AND MANAGING TERRORISM AND COUNTER-TERRORISM: THE VIEW FROM CRIMINOLOGY

Martin Innes and Michael Levi

INTRODUCTION

On Friday 13 November 2015 two acts of politically motivated violence with geopolitical consequences captured public attention. In the morning, a story broke into the news cycle that Mohammed Emwazi, who had gained international notoriety as 'Jihadi John'—responsible for beheading a number of hostages on behalf of the so-called Islamic State—had been killed in a targeted assassination. Four military drones fired missiles into a location on the basis of intelligence collected from a blend of human and electronic intercept sources to end his life.

That same evening, three cells of armed men used guns, grenades, and suicide vests to kill 130 people in Paris. The response to this lasted for several weeks, resonating across Europe, as police and security agencies sought to establish who was involved in planning, supporting, and executing the attacks. This was one of a series of terrorist acts that have taken place across a growing number of global cities.

Taken together, these two events and the responses to them encapsulate a number of the key themes and issues involved in understanding the contemporary configuration of terrorism and counter-terrorism. They capture the complex ways in which the attack methodologies of terrorist groups are evolving and adapting. Those performing such acts include highly organized individuals and networks displaying a clear long-term ideological motivation, as well as more spontaneous and less highly organized lone-actors and small groups (though retrospective analysis, sometimes shows longer-term planning and connectivity). The two cases also capture the ways counter-terrorism responses increasingly blend military and criminal justice interventions. Most importantly however, the events of 13 November clearly illuminate how acts of terrorism and counter-terrorism interweave in what Smelser (2007) labelled 'a rhetorical battle of symbols'.

In this chapter, absent space for a more comprehensive review, our intention is to set out ideas and concepts derived from criminology that provide insights into how and why terrorist ideologies and acts occur, as well as why responses to these are organized in the ways that they are. The chapter is organized around six principal sections. It starts by mapping out the potential domain of criminological knowledge in a space replete with alternative 'ways of knowing', before considering the role played by labels and particular definitions of the situation. This is followed by a review of key findings about how and why people join and support terrorist campaigns and engage more directly in violence, as well as desist from such activities. The next section switches focus to engage with what is known about the functions and organization of counter-terrorism. The conclusion seeks to connect these two elements to understand the symbiotic relations that exist between acts of terrorism and the counter-measures arrayed against them.

KNOWING TERRORISM

As terrorism's status as a social and political problem has grown in recent years, it has been constructed through multiple 'ways of knowing'. It is important to understand where *academic* discourses and ideas sit within the plethora of influential 'problem formulations' in public circulation. In the years since 2001, there has been a vast increase in funding directed towards counter-terrorism activity of various kinds across Europe and the North America. In addition to profits generated for what President Eisenhower called 'the military industrial complex', which now includes private military and cybersecurity companies, this has been manifestly exploited by a variety of moral entrepreneurs and claims-makers who, despite a relatively weak evidence base, have confidently offered risk mitigation solutions and policy prescriptions. Set against such a backdrop, it is necessary to clarify what the particular value of a criminologically inflected account of terrorism and counter-terrorism is.

The rapidly growing literature on terrorism encompasses journalistic accounts, biographies, and political treatises. Functioning as a 'first cut of history', several journalists have provided richly descriptive documentaries of and insights into key geopolitical events and conflicts that have, in many ways, surpassed in insights more formal academic treatises (e.g. Wright 2006; Burke 2014). At the other end of the spectrum, there have been a series of explicitly and implicitly politically motivated accounts, emanating from the offices of government officials, think-tanks and assorted non-governmental organizations, where the agenda is to provoke or justify a particular course of action. Layered on top of these has been a series of (auto)biographical accounts from individuals in contact with violent extremist groups (Husain 2007; Nawaz 2012). The latter use their apparent authenticity often to segue into offering thoughts on policy development opportunities.

In academia, terrorism has been studied from a multitude of disciplinary vantage points, especially international relations, politics, and psychology, accenting different epistemological and disciplinary background knowledge and predilections (Weston and Innes 2010). Within this polyphony of voices, criminology is a minor chord (by contrast with, e.g., the study of serial killings *not* conventionally defined as 'terrorism'), and is a relative newcomer. Nevertheless, a criminologically inflected voice offers something special to how we understand the dynamics of terrorism and counter-terrorism. This is predicated upon criminology's disposition to study the processes of 'making laws, breaking laws and reacting to the breaking of laws' (Sutherland and Cressey 1955). As will be demonstrated, these are all critical issues in the study of terrorism and our reactions to it.

A 'Criminology of terrorism and counter-terrorism' should aspire—we contend—to provide a normatively agnostic position that is led by empirical evidence in its formulation of 'middle range' theories. It is precisely this approach that we seek to model in this chapter, in recognition that this has not often happened to date. 'Administrative criminology' accounts have tended towards 'abstracted empiricism', and have not highlighted enough the ways that state institutions have dictated the boundaries between categorizations. At the other extreme, some studies have been so keen to demonstrate their 'critical' credentials and speak truth to power, that they neglect the fact that there is a complex social problem in play that instigates relatively indiscriminate violence, harm, and destruction by persons other than the state, whose target appears to be to terrify the general population and the state, and to inspire others to act locally and impact globally. It is our intent to navigate a path between these two extremities.

Moreover, criminologists are conceptually especially well resourced to engage with how criminal justice agencies have been appropriated to play an increasingly important role in Western state responses. Criminology has a long established tradition of interrogating official classifications of deviant and transgressive behaviour to show how official definitions shape patterns of response. Finally, there are clear resonances between terrorists' vocabularies of motive and what has been learned by criminologists over the past hundred years about how certain individuals and groups come to acquire their violent motivations, and how they act these out.

DEFINING TERRORISM

The signature attribute of terrorism is the use of communicative violence. The perpetrators of terrorist attacks are usually described as non-state actors struggling against a more powerful adversary, with the former invoking extreme violence in an effort to 'terrorize, polarize and mobilize' a public audience. Although terrorist violence is rarely large enough to pose a fundamental (as contrasted with symbolic) existential threat to the more powerful entity, the latter still need to perform responses that aim to inhibit the potential for the impacts of terror, group polarization, and mass mobilization to occur. Understood in this way, many terrorist incidents are coherent with Innes' (2014) logic of signal crimes—events that alter how people, groups, and institutions, think, feel, and act in relation to their security.

It is evident that the series of terrorist killings from 11 September 2001 onwards in cities across Western Europe have had profound effects upon the institutional and interactional ordering of social life. This ranges from the revision and enhanced investment in the counter-terrorist apparatus (Omand 2012), to the politics of terrorist risk management (Suskind 2006), and patterns of surveillance and social sorting (Lyon 2006; Gandy 2006; Marx 2016). As part of these recalibrations, the ontologies of a number of everyday objects have been redefined. Neyland (2009) notes that several hitherto mundane and ordinary items have been cast as potential terrorist weapons. The most obvious is the list of articles prohibited from hand luggage on board aeroplanes: liquids, gels, and creams can only be carried in small quantities lest they carry the chemical components of a bomb. Such developments gesture to how, although terrorist violence and campaigns only rarely accomplish their aims, they nonetheless have transformative effects.

Many of those participating in what Black (2004) identified as a form of 'self help' against more powerful opponents refute and resist the idea that what they are doing is 'terrorism'. Cromer (2001) fruitfully applied Sykes and Matza's (1957) 'techniques of neutralisation' to describe how groups attempt to resist being defined as terrorists. Depending upon their aims and orientations, those engaging in ideologically inspired violence: deny responsibility; deny injury; deny the victim; condemn the condemners; and appeal to higher loyalties. Similar techniques appear where nation states implement communicative violence against their own citizens in pursuit of their own political objectives, causing destruction, fear, and panic. As authors such as Cohen (2001) have forcefully argued, a comprehensive and coherent definition of terrorism needs to encompass acts sponsored or sanctioned by nation states, as well as lesser entities: though this would lead us to reject non-state actors as a *necessary* component of the definition of terrorism (see, more generally, Karstedt 2014). Critics might argue that terrorism serves the interests of the military industrial complex by generating profits, surveillance, and extra powers. The latter consequences are undeniable, but the deaths and maimings are real, even if Western media and governments count them unevenly to focus on victims from the global North, and some Islamic groups conversely focus on their own injured to inflame co-religionists globally to inspire 'lone wolf' or 'small pack' attacks.

Sykes and Matza's approach was closely aligned with labelling theory in criminology. From this vantage point, the institutions of law and the processes of criminal justice they embody, create and sustain particular orders of reality that define certain acts and actors as 'extremism' requiring interventions, whilst other ostensibly similar events are treated differently. Such power and ideological considerations are directly relevant to the study of terrorism, reflecting how scholars have wrestled with delineating a politically agnostic definition of terrorism—one that works independently of and outside the machinations of political power. Over a quarter of a century ago, Schmid and Jongman (1988) could list over 100 different definitions of terrorism, and two decades later there were many more in circulation (Smelser 2007). As a consequence, recent surveys of the field have introduced 'meta-distinctions' to identify where proposed conceptualizations gravitate around similar constructs. English (2009) distinguishes 'analytic' approaches from more avowedly practical ones. Crelinsten (2009) suggests competing definitions can be grouped together under four broad headings: (1) 'Tactical' definitions that are common in international legal conventions and accent the 'how' of terrorism; (2) 'Perpetrator'-based approaches that pivot around 'who' the individuals and groups involved are'; (3) 'Motive' oriented accounts that focus upon 'why' terrorist actors do what they do; or (4) a 'behavioural' approach that is most concerned with 'what' is done.

As English (2009) identifies, terrorist type activities are frequently embedded within the conduct of wars and other conflicts (Hoffman 2006; Kilcullan 2009), alongside ongoing criminality such as the trafficking of minerals and diamonds, and other commodities that are illicit (people smuggling/trafficking) or *per se* criminal (counterfeits, drugs) (Shelley 2014). The way we categorize such acts can influence whether they are deemed to require a 'military' or 'criminal justice' response.

Though definitions of terrorism remain contested, there does appear to be something approaching a consensus that there are at least three necessary conditions for so labelling an act:

- Political violence—a key consideration for defining an act as terrorist and thus distinguishing it from some other forms of violence is that it is conducted in pursuit of a political objective;
- Communicative violence—almost all definitions acknowledge that terrorist acts are marked by a desire to communicate an intimidatory message beyond the immediate victims;
- Asymmetry of power—terrorist violence tends to arise when a relatively powerless group identifies a need to mobilize a response to a more powerful adversary. Whilst others contest this, on the grounds that it makes an unwarranted distinction between the acts of states and citizens (and perhaps fails to take account of state actor support for rebellions that use terror tactics), an asymmetrical power dynamic certainly is present.

These issues about how to define terrorism have become more prominent recently because of how the social problem of terrorism has been evolving and adapting. This is the focus of the next section.

CHANGING TERRORISM

The rapid rise in the study of terrorism reflects the evolving risks and threats for the interests of the global North that have been presenting on the world stage. These have, for example, been manifest in: the initial emergence of Al-Qaeda as a network of networks (Sageman 2004) and its eclipse by Islamic State (Burke 2014); a so far, more limited, resurgence of extreme far-right political violence conducted by individuals such as Anders Breivik, reminding us of the dangers of looking only at the risks from Islamist violence; changes in the preferred attack methodologies from complex plots against transport infrastructure, towards less sophisticated but no less brutal violence (Nesser 2014); an increasingly fuzzy boundary (though almost never a complete merger) between some 'organized crime' and terrorist actors, as the latter engage with the networks of the former to source weaponry and funding (Callimachi 2016); a similar blurring with issues of global migration, as conflicts around the world trigger large-scale population movements (and large income flows for people smuggling groups, some of them affiliated with terror networks); and the adoption of social media technologies to amplify the impacts of assaults across social space and time, as well as to facilitate the meeting of minds and bodies.

Thus terrorism has a simultaneous local and international reach (Wilkinson 2001). It is, according to Hobbs' conceptualization (1988), a 'glocal' issue. Militaristic counter-terrorism actions are being undertaken in several middle-eastern countries to confront the state building programme of Daesh, whilst simultaneously, domestic policing and criminal justice-led responses have seen significant increases in investment and effort across many nation states. Similar shifts can be observed transnationally also.

The emergence of what Sageman (2004) labelled 'leaderless jihad' has meant the ideas, sentiments, and communications these groups propagate serve to inspire other 'lone actors', often with mental health issues, to autonomously engage in violence (Corner *et al.* 2015). As in Nice and many conflict zones in the global South, their acts often achieve a capacity for 'shock and awe' owing to brutality and apparent unpredictability.

In light of these ongoing changes, there is an understandable demand for a scaling of risks. By the end of July 2016, an estimated 850 people had travelled from the UK to Syria, a significant proportion of whom were not previously 'on the radar' of the police or security service, and a further 900 have been prevented from doing so. The UK Counter-Terrorism Network claim they have been taking down around 1,000 websites a week linked to jihadist propaganda, but these are rapidly replaced. The Commissioner of the Metropolitan Police stated that in the year to the end of October 2015, six viable mass casualty plots were disrupted, where a few years ago they were dealing with one maybe two per annum. Between 2010–15, over 140 individuals were convicted in the UK courts of terrorism related offences, and in 2014 there were 327 arrests, up 32 per cent on the previous year. The Director General of the UK Security Service stated in the latter months of 2015 that in excess of 3,000 individuals were subject to active monitoring. This is almost double the number in 2006. By the end of July 2016, there had been an increase from 30 to 46 in the number of designated 'Prevent' areas in Britain—hotspots where people are judged to be 'at risk' of radicalization. In our judgement, these rises are not merely a reflection of increased surveillance capacities.

DOING TERRORISM

Research shows that there are multiple pathways to radicalization, to which a diverse range of people are more or less susceptible. This echoes older studies such as Lofland (1966), who conceptualized several 'involvement sequences' by which people were indoctrinated into an established cult or religious group. Recognition of this has been important in depathologizing both the people who are radicalized and the social-psychological processes via which this happens. Both Horgan (2005) and Atran (2010) trenchantly argue for the 'ordinariness' of the majority of people who engage in, or socially support terrorist violence. This is consistent with information about the petty crime records of Belgian and French terrorists. Both accounts also accent how the acquisition of extremist narratives and grievances is predicated upon well documented techniques of influence and persuasion.

Sageman (2004) focuses on the role played by social networks in initial contacts with extremist groups and subsequent involvement with members. Likewise, Atran's (2010) more qualitative approach enriches our understanding of how social bonds can be harnessed to recruit and radicalize. Others however, place markedly more emphasis on theology (Lincoln 2006), the social structuring consequences of Islamic identity politics (Kepel 2004), and the working of social psychological influence and persuasion (Horgan 2005) in explaining why some individuals are radicalized. Wiktorowicz (2006) identifies how personal crises often provide a 'cognitive opening' in terms of making people more susceptible to extremist influences. Based upon his work examining the group Al-Muhajiroun, he unpacks the techniques operationalized when people are effectively more 'radicalizable'. Developing the concept of 'culturing', Wiktorowicz shows how a blend of theological, social psychological, and social devices are deployed to induce people to commit to the new group, by insulating them from any counter-influences. This perspective has been adopted in thinking about the role played by online information and digital technologies. Indeed, an enduring feature of 'the new terrorism' is the empathy of Muslims (including converts) throughout the world towards their co-religionists, and the propensity of some to be enraged by social media coverage of these perceived injustices to the point of self-radicalization.

There is a growing consensus evident in the academic literature that people tend to be radicalized when they are exposed to a combination of several necessary and sufficient conditions. Richardson (2006: 14) argues that terrorism is grounded in subjective perceptions melding with:

> . . . a lethal cocktail containing a disaffected individual, an enabling community and a legitimizing ideology . . . terrorist behaviour can be understood in terms of both long-term political motivations, which differ across different types of groups, and more immediate short-term motives, which very different types of terrorists share.

She identifies the presence of 'a conducive surround' of active and/or passive public support as a component of long-term terrorist campaigns. If this explains the inception of a terrorist campaign, then it is a desire for 'revenge, renown, and reaction' that influences individual actors to participate in it. Richardson does not develop the implications of this point (and it is similarly neglected by many others), but what this points to is the importance of deconstructing the label of 'terrorist' and what it means to be involved in 'doing' terrorism. Many terrorist campaigns involve a division of labour. Only a minority of individuals engage directly in the most serious kinds of violence, with greater numbers performing other functions such as financing, recruiting, and testing out members, developing and disseminating propaganda, procuring weapons, and so forth (Nesser 2014). Others may just supply social support (Sluka 1989).

Reflecting this insight, the more compelling and persuasive accounts of radicalization delineate multiple pathways via which people come to join terrorist groups and networks, with multiple interacting forces in play in moving them through this process. One early account to propose a multi-factorial approach was the 'situational model of violent radicalisation' (SMOVR) that accented the co-occurrence of 'push factors' that repel young people away from non-extremist individuals and ideas, and 'pull factors' ('attractors') that encourage people towards violent extremism (Innes *et al.* 2007). It is a social-psychological process akin to the 'differential association' construct familiar to generations of criminologists (Sutherland and Cressey 1955). Importantly, the SMOVR model also differentiated between 'deeper' and 'shallower' forms of radicalization—while supporting a group's ideas and values, not all radicalized individuals are willing to commit violence.

To become a terrorist requires more than just the acquisition of motivation. The motivated terrorist also needs tradecraft to execute a successful attack in order to not arouse the suspicions of others, avoid detection by the authorities, and perform the violence. Small cells in particular require some form of social interactional competency. These are all elements of the 'tradecraft' of terrorism (Hoffman 2006) that are not suited to the participation of a wild and errant individual—although such persons can function as 'lone actors'. Indeed, there are claims that many terrorist organizations such as Al-Qaeda are quite careful to avoid recruiting such dysfunctional individuals. Daesh are reputed to be less bothered and indeed show converts how to attribute their violence to 'Islamic State' (Callimachi 2016), potentially misdirecting us to an exaggerated view of its tentacles.

Collins (2008) identifies an important axiom—that contrary to popular expectations, 'competent' violence is difficult to accomplish. Most violence is chaotic and messy, rather than calculating and clinical. This is particularly so at close-quarters, where a basic 'confrontational tension' functions to render violence difficult. He contends that this is why many terrorist groups adopt 'confrontation minimizing' tactics. The use of remote-controlled bombs and Improvised Explosive Devices (IEDs) is one example of this, but more contentiously, so is suicide bombing. According to Collins, the tactic of suicide bombing enables the bomber to outwardly maintain the aura of normal appearances until the moment of detonation, thereby avoiding direct interpersonal confrontation with potential victims. In effect, it keeps them 'depersonalized', cognitively easing the ability to envision their obliteration (we would add that this concealment also makes it harder to identify and stop them).

The process of converting human beings into 'human bombs' to combine dying with killing is one that appears to exert a 'gravitational pull' for a number of scholars. Unlike those who commit 'ordinary' suicide, 90 per cent of whom are depressed or have diagnosable mental conditions, suicide attackers do not typically display such traits. Most bombers are young unmarried men, although not all are—globally around 15 per cent were female at the time of one study (Pape 2006; see also Brunner 2016), though in the global South, there has been a marked increase in the number of women and child suicide bombers. Suicide bombers tend to be comparatively well educated and from a higher social background when related to the communities to which they belong (Gambetta 2005; Pape 2006). In this sense, their actions align well with Durkheim's (1952/1897) construct of 'the altruistic suicide'.

Whilst suicide bombing is oftentimes an effective tactic, judged in terms of its capacity to secure public and political attention, and to elicit fear and fascination, it remains a relatively rare method even today. There are a panoply of other terrorist methods including kidnap, extortion, assassination, and hijacking that in aggregate have been more commonly deployed than suicide bombing. In respect of these methods, a frequently overlooked issue is how terrorist groups learn from each other in terms of 'what works', 'what doesn't', and 'what's promising' (to them). There is an international trade in 'terrorist tradecraft'. For example, there is evidence of contacts between the Basque separatist group ETA and Provisional IRA, and that the latter were also involved in training FARC groups in Colombia in the use of firearms and explosives. On the other hand, the many conflicting Islamist groups are unlikely to share much interpersonally.

There has been a growing interest in patterns of individual and group desistance. Foremost amongst these has been Cronin's (2009) cross-national review of how terrorism ends, due to consistent ongoing pressure upon individuals and their relationships with each other, and a continual risk of implosion amongst groups, emanating from mistakes, burnout, and collapse. Sometimes these stresses are nudged along by intelligent, carefully targeted pressure from the police or military. Cronin argues that criminal justice agencies and/or military interventions, especially when they cohere with other trends, can promote desistance from terrorism, though this is hard to separate out and quantify.

Gary LaFree and colleagues (2009) aimed to test precisely what impacts flow from criminal justice interventions. Informed by data on six key counter-terrorist interventions conducted in Northern Ireland between 1969 and 1992, they constructed two alternative hypotheses. The first was a 'deterrence model' founded on the belief that assertive policing would deter individuals and groups from future violence. The second was that such interventions would actually induce a 'backlash' and more violence. The analysis found that only one of the military surges appeared to have deterred violence, whereas three out of the six interventions appeared to have promoted 'backlash effects'. All the interventions tested were assertive, intrusive, and coercive. As Wilkinson (2001: 102) contends, since 1969 the conflict in Northern Ireland exemplified counter-terrorism grounded in 'the use of military in aid of the civil power'. Whilst distinct from the full militarization of counter-terrorism seen elsewhere, it represents a departure from the view that criminal justice should always be the default option for liberal democratic polities (English 2015). The interventions tested by LaFree and colleagues perhaps lacked some of the more 'soft power' dimensions that much research identifies as an important component of effective counter-terrorism. This leads us to a more detailed analysis of counter-terrorism responses.

COUNTERING TERRORISM

The growth in multi-disciplinary terrorism studies has paid far more attention towards understanding how and why terrorist violence is performed, than towards the dynamics of counter-terrorist policy and practice (English 2015). There are several reasons for this. One is difficulties with securing access to reliable and insightful materials, given agency sensitivities about secrecy and protection of 'tradecraft'. However, some counter-terrorism (CT) studies are illuminating. One such is Foley's (2014) comparative analysis of the CT regimens in France and the UK, which poses: 'why is it that the CT policy and practice responses in these two countries are so markedly different, given that the profile of risks and threats they face are broadly similar?' He traces how before the mid-2000s, the approach in the UK was relatively tolerant of extremist groups with possible connections to violence, certainly when compared with the more 'muscular' French policies and interventions that implemented mass arrests and large-scale initiatives. This is explicable by 'deep' institutional and cultural norms, which frame how the problem of terrorism is configured and understood, and what kinds of counter-measures are deemed appropriate.

However, these 'deep structures' are not immutable, and can shift in the aftermath of high-profile mass casualty terrorist attacks, as has begun to happen between European countries during 2016. As Innes (2014) contends, the series of attacks in Western cities have induced profound 'institutional effects' upon the social organization of counter-terrorism. Since 2001, a 'legislative reflex' has come to the fore where, following terrorist atrocities, politicians need to be seen to be 'doing something', frequently in the form of bringing forward new legislation. In the UK this has included: the Anti-terrorism, Crime and Security Act 2001, which allowed for detention without trial (later overturned by the courts); the Prevention of Terrorism Act 2005, introducing the 'control order' (also overturned); the Terrorism Act 2006, which extended the detention of suspects without charge from 14 to 28 days; the Terrorism Order 2006, enabling the Treasury to freeze the assets of suspects; the Counter-Terrorism Act 2008, under which police were permitted to continue questioning suspects after charge; the Terrorist Asset-Freezing Act 2010; and the Counter-Terrorism and Security Act 2015. New laws have become a routinized societal response to terrorist attacks, as they have to other transnational social bads, such as anti-money laundering measures to deal with grand corruption and 'organized crime' (Levi 2007).

Accompanying these legislative initiatives, many countries have reconfigured the counter-terrorism apparatus. Conceptual discussions of counter-terrorism in the academic literature typically distinguish between 'intelligence-led', 'military', and 'criminal justice' oriented modes (Steven and Gunaratna 2004), and between 'offensive' and 'defensive' postures (Crelinstein 2009). However, the contemporary scene is marked by the ways that offensive and defensive are being blended into *both* more proactive and reactive measures (English 2015).

Internationally, it has been argued that the mobility of contemporary terrorist groups and actors require far more effective intelligence-sharing mechanisms between states to respond to the spectrum of risks and threats (Jacobson 2006). This extends to multilateral intelligence clearing houses to move data without comprising the source or agency methods (Ganor 2005; Steven and Gunaratna 2004). However, national intelligence and even police agencies are often reluctant to pool into such 'fusion centres'.

An even more profound movement may be in the routinized connectivity between 'high' and 'low' policing (Brodeur 2010), integrating principles, processes, and practices originating in the community policing tradition into the delivery of local counter-terrorism interventions (Pickering *et al.* 2008; Innes *et al.* 2011). Thacher (2005) described the emergence of joint-terrorism task forces (JTTFs) as an improvised solution to the problem of getting US local law enforcement agencies to implement proactive and intrusive counter-terrorism methods, preferring 'community protection' strategies grounded in target-hardening and emergency response. They feared that the kinds of surveillance required would lead minority communities to question the agencies' overall legitimacy and crime control mission. Instigating JTTFs was a way of trying to circumvent such resistance and to join up the infamously complex policing and intelligence landscape of North America.

Some commentators, such as Deflem (2010), have questioned whether such contemporary configurations are sustainable, and maintain that local domestic policing should stay away from counter-terrorism work, leaving the latter to specialized central agencies (see also Manning 2010). Faced with such critiques, it is worth positing a counterfactual scenario, about what a viable response *without* community policing style tactics would look like. In this respect there are important lessons from history. There is compelling evidence from multiple studies that the intelligence-led 'hard policing' style pursued in the 1970s and 1980s in particular, exacerbated the Northern Irish conflict, increasing rather than reducing levels of social support for organisations like the Provisional IRA and INLA (Sluka 1989; English 2015).

This is not the only counterfactual possibility to integrating local policing that could be imagined. An alternative would be more covert technologies to guide and prioritize coercive interventions against nominated suspects (Lyon 2006; Marx 2016). Surveillance technologies have triggered considerable critique and consternation, most interestingly from Molotch (2012) who argues that many of the socio-technological assemblages have made us feel profoundly *in*secure rather than more secure.

However, these are not mere counterfactuals. Counter-terrorism changes over the past decade and a half have adopted all three of these approaches (i.e. the co-optation of community policing strategies; the blending of military and criminal justice responses; and increasingly sophisticated surveillance technologies). This holistic approach is reflected also in how policy framings have evolved and been developed.

In 2004, the UK government introduced the cross-governmental CONTEST strategy to provide a comprehensive and coordinated response to international terrorism, organized around four key pillars of activity: Prepare; Prevent; Protect; and Pursue (HM Government 2009, 2016). It is a highly influential framework that has shaped European policy and has also been imported into the UK's national strategies for serious organized crime (HM Government 2013) and cybersecurity (Levi *et al.* 2015). Of the four strands, Protect and Pursue most closely focus upon the kinds of activity traditionally associated with counter-terrorism. Except for arrests and prosecutions (stated to be the preferred option), they tend to be less publicly visible, and are typically led by the Security Service domestically and the Secret Intelligence Service overseas. In contrast, Prepare and Prevent are more innovative and public facing. The four strands can be differentiated and defined as follows (HM Government 2016):

- Pursue—the investigation and disruption of terrorist attacks;
- Prevent—work to stop people becoming terrorists or supporting terrorism;

- Protect—improving our protective security to stop a terrorist attack; and
- Prepare—working to minimize the impact of an attack and to recover as quickly as possible.

Of all the dimensions of CONTEST, Prevent has been most public-facing and politically charged. However, the surveillance and disruption components of Pursue have also generated controversy.

The many policy commentaries and critiques, and the smaller number of genuinely empirical studies of CONTEST have stressed how the prevailing posture is precautionary, preventive, and pre-emptive (Walker and Mckay 2015; Mythen *et al.* 2013). Ashworth and Zedner (2014), for instance, cast this as an inflection of a more general contemporary preventative 'pre-crime' policy orientation; while Heath-Kelly (2013) suggests that the Prevent strategy, in particular, represents a manifestation of the prevalent risk of governance discourse. Innes (2006) notes that some of the tribulations experienced by Prevent stem from a profound uncertainty about precisely what problem(s) it is trying to solve.

The task of preventing 'violent extremism' has proven to be the most visible and contentious aspect of CONTEST. There have been repeated allegations that Prevent institutionalizes a governmental programme to 'spy' upon communities (Kundani 2009), casting Muslims as a *de facto* 'suspect community' (Pantazis and Pemberton 2009). Innes *et al.* (2011) reported that despite its 'toxic brand' in some quarters, Muslim community attitudes and perceptions were more subtle. Data showed that people from Muslim faith backgrounds exhibit higher levels of trust and confidence in the police than did the general population. Young Muslim men had marginally more negative perceptions and attitudes than other young men, but nearly 4 out of 10 of them expressed positive views of policing. It is uncertain that this is still the case, with some evidence of increasing scepticism and disengagement from Prevent processes and structures by Muslim groups and organizations (O'Toole *et al.* 2016).

Prevent has been subject to three systemic revisions. In 2008 reform was triggered because CONTEST had not shifted enough to prevention from 'Pursue'. The change of government led to revisions in 2011 to instantiate a much clearer distinction between counter-terrorism, and integration and cohesion work. In 2015, the Conservative administration explicitly widened Prevent's focus, from violent extremism to all forms of extremism—albeit this was never adequately defined (HM Government 2015). These tensions remain in the 2016 review of the CONTEST strategy (HM Government 2016).

Given the levels of political contestation that swirl around contemporary counter-terrorism policy frames, it is important that efforts to provide independent and rigorous assessments of these allow researchers to step outside the categories that policy-makers and practitioners use. It is necessary to devise a conceptually agnostic analytic apparatus through which key approaches can be independently described and thought about. However, studying attempts to prevent and inhibit violent and non-violent extremism 'in depth' and 'at scale' is extremely difficult, and there are relatively few robust empirical studies upon which to develop such a framework.

One possible alternative is to derive the conceptual base for such a framework from the literature on general crime prevention. Ekblom and Hirschfield's (2014) meta-synthesis of key tested and validated crime prevention mechanisms, which distils these down into 11 'principles of intervention', can help, even though only some work with CT.[1] With this in mind we can distinguish interventions designed to:

- Defend and Discover—these are measures designed to identify the prevalence and distribution of risks and threats, and then apply broad-based responses to these in order to protect specific people, places, events, and objects that are adjudged to have an escalated risk of being targeted. Often, this is because they are perceived as possessing some sort of symbolic value to the perpetrators. Visible examples of this are the physical target hardening measures that have been placed around many public landmarks in European cities.
- Deter and Divert—deterrence and diversion are integral to most crime prevention strategies. In relation to preventing violent extremism, they cover a range of activities focused upon individuals deemed vulnerable to radicalization, designed to steer them away from exposure to any such risks.
- Disrupt and Degrade—for those who cannot be deterred or diverted in terms of their interests, the next modality seeks to interfere with their capacity and capability to act. Disruptions tend to be more immediate and have a shorter time horizon, whereas 'degrading' a group or network adopts a slightly longer-term perspective. Counter-terrorism efforts to degrade the operational capacity of violent extremist groups and networks increasingly encompass a range of offline and online activities. This includes economic measures, as discussed in more detail below, but also legal powers whereby groups are officially proscribed.
- Detect and Detain—the most targeted, most intensive forms of domestic counter-terrorism interventions involve the application of criminal sanctions, or attempts to impose these. These focus upon securing 'detections' for specific offences and the physical detention of those committing these offences.

Figure 20.1 connects these modes to convey how they collectively constitute an overarching strategic response to terrorism. Relative to each other, they are increasingly targeted towards fewer and fewer people, but with the intensity of the intrusion and focus being progressively sharpened.

Limitations on space prohibit a full and detailed treatment of all of these components. Instead, we will focus upon: the use of financial interventions to degrade terrorist groups and networks; disruption; and detection and detaining suspects, as exemplars to illuminate how empirical CT research is generating new insights into the ways terrorist risks and threats are being managed.

DEGRADING FINANCIAL CAPABILITY

Interdictions directed towards what is increasingly termed 'threat finance' (Levi 2010), involve trying to cut off licit and illicit sources of finance by: threatening criminal and regulatory penalties, and private civil lawsuits against financial intermediaries (e.g. banks, lawyers); as well as against those individuals, organizations, and governments

[1] The 11 are: defeat; disable; deter; direct/deflect; deter known and unknown offenders; discourage; demotivate; deceive; disconcert; detect; detain.

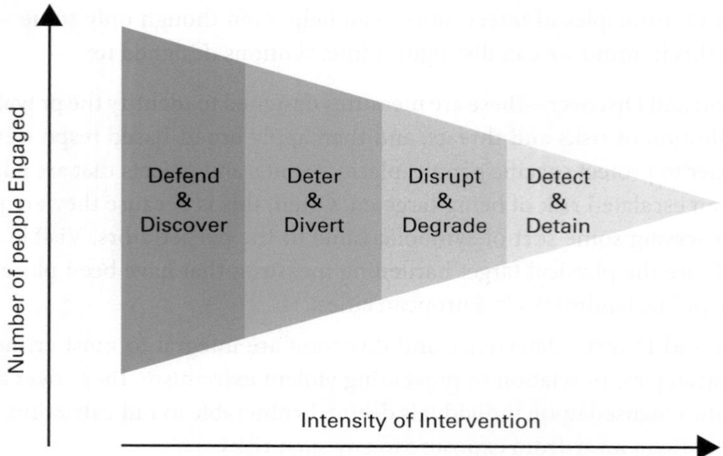

Figure 20.1 High level schematic of the counter-terrorism process

who wish to directly give money or facilities to terrorists. Anti-money laundering regulations were first operationalized in 1986 as part of the 'War on Drugs'. In the aftermath of 9/11, governments have adapted these instruments to respond to 'Islamist terrorism' and 'rogue States' (Eckert and Biersteker 2010; Biersteker *et al.* 2016).

There are strong advocates for cutting off the financial lifeblood to degrade the efficacy of terrorist operations (Gurule 2015; Zarate 2013) and equally passionate (but far fewer) opponents of the social costs (intended and unintended) of such measures, given the alleged 'problem inflation' induced (Hayes 2012; Mueller and Stewart 2011; Walker 2014; Wesseling 2014). For example, Daesh's income has been successfully reduced (leading to claims of victory for counter-terrorist finance): but a more subtle analysis would suggest that this has been achieved largely by the military attacks on trucks travelling to and from the oil well-heads—a visible area of vulnerability.

There is also ambiguity over what the category of 'terrorist finance' includes. Operationally, little money is required to mount a successful terrorist operation: '9/11' cost less than $500,000 to organize; the London and Madrid bombings less than £10,000; and these are among the more expensive compared with hiring a truck to kill Nice pedestrians, or slitting the throat of a Catholic priest in rural France. As one Norwegian study of 40 terrorist attacks (Oftedal 2015: 3) summarized, European terrorists' financial activities are remarkably ordinary. Jihadis who have plotted attacks in Western Europe most commonly relied on funding from the cell members' own salaries and savings. The vast majority of the cells studied were entirely self-financed, with only a quarter receiving economic support from international terrorist organizations such as Al-Qaeda. Moreover, three quarters of the plots were estimated to have cost under $10,000. To degrade this sort of funding would be almost impossible unless key suspects or nodes were already under surveillance.

Though the pattern of financial support varies—and Daesh is an outlier in its financial capacities arising from control over large swathes of territory and the ability to extort from business (FATF 2015a; 2015b)—those interested in promoting violent extremism can obtain funds via multiple channels:

- Licit sources (including 'rogue states' as well as wealthy sympathizers, or smaller donations gathered through registered or informal charities);
- Contraband (e.g. smuggled alcohol, fuel, tobacco);
- Illicit 'market offences' (e.g. drugs, extortion/tribute for permitting smuggling, export of prohibited goods like oil from sanctioned territories);
- Acquisitive property crimes (fraud, robbery, and theft).

The latter three categories are covered by criminal law and proceeds of crime controls. For the most part, terrorists prefer to source their income from licit sources, bringing less risk of victim/law enforcement action against them before they have achieved their objectives. Some money is moved via charities (where the licensing regime in the UK is stronger than elsewhere) and via Money Service Businesses (like Western Union and MoneyGram) and by informal value transfers (Passas 2003, 2006).

A key policy movement in operationalizing these financial control instruments has been the 'responsibilization' of the banks. They have been required to try to spot funds destined to aid terrorism and weapons of mass destruction. The expectation of the authorities is that the prospect of being identified: (1) puts potential donors on notice that they may lose their liberty and their assets for assisting terrorism; (2) deters them from participation; or (3) leads to their apprehension and prosecution *pour décourager les autres*. One unintended side effect of such policies has been that banks have become risk averse. They have closed the accounts of many Money Service Businesses and smaller banks in developing countries, with detrimental effects to business enterprises and remittance flows there, risking the intensification of support for terrorism locally (Artingstall *et al.* 2016; CGD 2015).

One specific intervention designed to degrade the operating capacity of terrorist organizations is to freeze their assets. The United States can impose legal sanctions on 'Specially Designated Global Terrorists' and 'Foreign Terrorist Organisations' (FTOs). As of 1 June 2015, 59 organizations and under 1,000 individuals were so designated. The US Treasury has blocked about $22 million in assets relating to 7 of these 59 designated FTOs (GAO 2015; US Treasury 2016). These sums look quite trivial compared with the amounts allegedly accruing to terrorist groups, especially to Daesh (FATF 2015a, b), much of which is generated locally and does not require international transfer.

Certainly, there is a need for closer liaison between countries, and public and private sectors if the system is to work more efficiently. In practice then, controlling 'threat finance' is a modest element in the risk policing and prevention of terrorism, rather than being its core. It is perhaps unsurprising, therefore, that terrorist finance cases are not clogging up the courts or prisons—the number prosecuted in England and Wales in 2001–14 was 17 (UK Government 2015). However, these (and asset freezing) are not the only yields. *After the event*, the pursuit of financial records enables linkages to be made; and controls may have a chilling effect on donations by the wealthy, whose funds may be used to support terrorist group activities. But what such a situation does point to is the constraints that apply to the capacities and capabilities of government, police, private sector, and civil society actions to impact upon terrorist activities. As such, it is important to differentiate between the status of the 'law in books' and 'in action'. Terrorist capability may have been degraded somewhat by public and private sector efforts around the globe. But 'the threat analysis' may mislead us into an exclusive focus on the bigger organizational entities and into missing right-wing, non-Islamist terror threats. Determining what levels of terrorism would have been without the controls is extremely contentious, but for example, it is plausible that in the absence of financial sanctions, Iran would not have reduced its nuclear capabilities and that the Irish peace settlement would have happened later.

DISRUPTIONS

Disruptions can be divided into two principal types (Innes and Sheptycki, 2004). Criminal disruptions involve prosecuting suspects for offences other than those that they were originally being investigated for. The logic is that by engaging the criminal justice process against them, it will interfere with their ability to operate. This is distinct from 'extra-legal' disruption, where the intent is to impact upon illegal or troublesome activities without recourse to criminal law.

In their study of Prevent policing in the UK, Innes *et al.* (2011) documented that disruption has been playing an increasingly significant role in the local delivery of counter-terrorism. Confronted by increasing numbers of 'subjects of interest', disrupting their activities provides a way of managing the potential risk they pose, where there are insufficient police or intelligence resources to mount full criminal investigations against all individuals who might warrant this. Innes *et al.*'s study provides several case studies of how disruption works in practice, including the following:

> Another Mosque in (xxxx) rang up one of my sergeants and said we've got three guys coming here, and they were doing the proper radicalization thing. They were trying to draw kids in, they were trying to have little meetings, they were being quite radical. We'd appreciate your support if you could come and help us, and speak to these three individuals because we don't want them here but we're a little bit concerned. So [Name]'s gone down, confronted the three individuals. The Mosque don't want you here, what are you about? Do you want to talk to me about it? They didn't. They went. We know where they went. (Innes *et al.* 2011: 28)

The concept of disruption has been featuring increasingly prominently in discussions of counter-terrorism, as the 'demand' for counter-terrorism interventions is outstripping the available capacity to 'supply' them. Disrupting plots and conspiracies, rather than prosecuting, does something about troublesome situations which are worrying but perhaps not an immediate priority. But the recourse to a language of disruption signals something else as well. That is, a recognition of the limitations of what can be achieved through criminal justice interventions oriented towards opponents who are profoundly and deeply inspired by ideological motivations rather than 'rational choice' as commonly understood.

DETECT AND DETAIN

There is a near absence of independent primary research on the processes and systems of police counter-terrorism investigations (reflecting a more general lack of research evidence on major crime investigations more generally). The paucity of research reflects practitioner concerns that enabling research would decrease their efficacy by providing insights into policing methodologies that can be exploited by terrorist groups. Trial and media transcripts provide snatched glimpses of this facet of counter-terrorism policing from which insightful inferences can be drawn. Considerable emphasis is placed upon the use of covert methods, including intercepts and human intelligence sources, with much information initially being developed by the Security Service before being passed over to the police to perform the investigative function and construct a case for prosecution. Significant effort is invested in protecting these sources via 'parallel sourcing' of information wherever possible, to avoid them having to be disclosed to the defence and wider public.

In one of the few pieces of work conducted in this area, the Royal United Services Institute's analysis of arrest statistics for 2014 on behalf of Sky News reported that of 289 terrorism-related arrests, 102 were charged with a terror offence. At 35 per cent, this is lower than the charge rate of 58 per cent for all criminal offences. This is supplemented by data that 315 people were arrested in the year to November 2015, including 50 women, a figure which is reportedly double that for the previous year. These figures were used by Sky's reporters to draw negative inferences about the quality and precision of police counter-terrorism investigations.[2] However, it appears that they failed to appreciate some important differences between police general crime and counter-terrorism-based investigative work. Most importantly, CT investigations routinely arrest to disrupt a potential harm from occurring (as discussed earlier), whereas many general crime arrests are post-crime. Indeed, many offences are identified only after arrest.

Fundamentally then, the 'Pursue' strand of investigative activity is part of a risk management system. Decisions and judgements are taken by actors working within the counter-terrorism apparatus about which suspects and cases to take forward to try to secure a conviction, versus which should be tackled by other interventions. Serious questions can be asked about the performance of this risk-based diagnostic approach; nearly all suspects in attacks in Western countries over the past decade and a half have retrospectively been found to have been 'known' to the police or intelligence services. As Nesser (2014) documents at the European level, this includes individuals who have been convicted and imprisoned for activities associated with terrorism, who have subsequently engaged in more serious violence.

Of the 35 per cent of people arrested and prosecuted by the police under counter-terrorism legislation and convicted by the courts in the UK, several sources outline important information about the management of these individuals (Anderson 2015; Home Office 2015; Dean 2014). There remain difficult and complex decisions about how to manage such people. For example, should they be dispersed throughout the prison system, thereby limiting the contact between already radicalized individuals, but risking their influence upon other prisoners unless placed in solitary confinement for years? Alternatively, should they be located in a single specialist unit, to limit their contacts with 'ordinary' prisoners, but acknowledging that this will make it harder to

[2] http://news.sky.com/story/1603052/police-terror-tactics-radicalising-muslims, accessed 10 December 2015.

'deradicalize' any of those so categorized because they are in constant contact with like-minded people? Looking across Europe, it is intriguing to see variations in national responses. The UK has until very recently tended to the former approach, whilst the French have adopted the latter.

That such differences exist illustrates not just cultural differences, but disagreement about the current state-of-the-art in respect of countering terrorism. It would be wrong to assert that there is a clear-cut solution, or established suites of interventions that we can turn to or can be recommended. There is no correlation between the confidence of 'expert' consultants and NGOs and the evidence for effectiveness. The state of our knowledge is simply not that advanced. Accordingly, our aims and aspirations need to be more modest. In a situation where the risks of mass-casualty terrorist attacks look like they will be part of social organization of the political order for the foreseeable future, we can understand some of the causes and consequences that flow from these forms of violence, whilst recognizing that this does not yield total attack-prevention capacities.

CONCLUSIONS: INTERACTING TERRORISM AND COUNTER-TERRORISM

Terrorism is a particular, and in many ways, peculiar kind of violence. It is typically, as Donald Black (2004) famously described it, 'social control from below', involving a less powerful group engaging a more powerful one over some politically inflected grievance. The violence invoked is designed to send a message that will travel beyond the actual physical harm, to impact upon the perceptions of a wider public audience (Altheide 2006). This is why the attacks are often so profoundly violent, either in terms of the scale of destruction caused, or its focused intensity. Translated into the preferred terminology of the social sciences, it is as much 'expressive' as it is 'instrumental'.

Until relatively recently, research on terrorist violence was dominated by ideas and perspectives emanating from the disciplines of international relations, political science, and psychology. More recently however, increasing numbers of criminologists have sought to engage with these issues. Whilst it would be misleading to imply that there is a coherent 'criminological voice' in terms of understanding terrorism, this 'disciplinary insurgency' has disrupted the field of terrorism studies. These developments reflect criminology's long tradition of studying different forms of violence, situated across an array of settings. There is also a considerable track record of studying how individuals join, participate in, and disengage from groups engaging in criminal and antisocial activities. Furthermore, much of the criminological canon has been concerned with mapping social reactions to crime. And there is a growing consensus within the academic community, if not the political one, that the most effective and sustainable responses to terrorism occur when it is treated as a crime, through criminal justice mechanisms which offer greater legitimacy.

A key thrust for this chapter has been to assert that rather than seeing acts of terrorism and counter-terrorism as discrete, it is more insightful to connect them and subject them to analysis that positions them as interacting and recursively adapting events and actions. Terrorists and those organized to interdict and prevent their acts are continually seeking to innovate in ways that give them a temporary advantage over their adversaries. There is a sequence of point and counter-point, as one side seeks to do something that their opponent was not expecting.

Attending to these interactional dynamics where terrorist and counter-terrorist strategies and tactics mutually adapt, provides a greater sense of the complexities involved in analysing the causes and consequences of terrorist incidents and campaigns. There is certainly evidence to suggest that when counter-terrorist responses are publicly perceived as overly aggressive and over-reactions, they amplify social support for their adversaries (English 2015; Sluka 1989). The more effective responses are more discriminating in using targeted criminal justice interventions against suspects, as opposed to collective interventions that target whole groups of people indiscriminately (English 2015).

Reviewing the literature on counter-terrorism, a key observation is its relative neglect compared to the rapid growth in studies seeking to explain terrorism itself. Second, more practically, much of it is predicated upon anticipatory logics of prediction, pre-emption, and prevention. Given the strong tradition in criminological scholarship of studying criminal justice agencies and the work of social control, this is an area where a concerted effort might be especially productive and insightful in terms of contributing to knowledge.

An additionally fecund area of engagement might be in understanding more precisely the connections between 'crimes' and 'terrorism'. A number of commentators have posited that terrorism should be treated as ontologically similar to particular types of crime—particularly organized crime. Based upon our reading of the extant literature, such an approach seems to be both conceptually and empirically problematic. Some species of terrorism are quite closely aligned with the social organization of organized crime, but others are not. On occasion (e.g. post the Irish Peace Agreement), terrorism has transitioned into organized crime, and vice versa. There are forms of terrorism effectively conducted by individual actors, devoid of any material support from others; whereas other types of terrorism are nurtured and supported by a vast array of illicit activities; and others still that are undergirded by entirely legal behaviours. Some individuals who support or engage in terrorist violence transition from criminal career pathways into violent extremism, but others do not.

Finally, criminology overall has shown a capacity to blend an engagement with real world problems with an independent and slightly sceptical viewpoint on the more assertive claims emanating from state agencies tasked to respond to them. In an intellectual and policy moment where the perceived risks of terrorism are being presented as highly accentuated, the value of this should not be under-estimated. Clear-sighted, independent analysis is required if we are to understand how and why such risks emerge, and what the reactions and responses to them should be and should not be.

SELECTED FURTHER READING

The literature on terrorism and counter-terrorism, including both academic and informed comment, has been proliferating at a considerable rate in recent years. There are now a number of texts giving a general overview of the field. The best of these are Richardson's *What Terrorists Want: Understanding the Terrorist Threat* (2006), Wilkinson's *Terrorism Versus Democracy: The Liberal State Response* (2001), and Hoffman's *Inside Terrorism* (2006). A more explicitly sociological perspective is provided by Smelser's *The Faces of Terrorism: Social and Psychological Dimensions* (2007). Nesser's *Islamist Terrorism in Europe* (2014) provides a useful documentary record of the plots and attacks that have occurred in Europe over the past decade. The most incisive contributions on counter-terrorism are Foley's comparative study, *Countering Terrorism in Britain and France: Institutions, Norms and the Shadow of the Past* (2014) and the collection of essays in the volume edited by English, *Illusions of Terrorism and Counter-Terrorism* (2015). For those coming to the subject of terrorism from a criminological background, the collection of chapters in LaFree and Freilich's *Handbook of the Criminology of Terrorism* (2016) are particularly interesting. Grabosky and Stohl's short book, *Crime and Terrorism* (2010), also provides a clearly written overview of the key issues.

REFERENCES

ALTHEIDE, D. (2006), *Terrorism and the Politics of Fear*, Lanham, MD: Rowman & Littlefield.

ANDERSON, D. (2015), 'The Terrorism Acts in 2014: Report of the Independent Reviewer on the Operation of the Terrorism Act 2000 and Part 1 of the Terrorism Act 2006', cited 15 September 2015, available at: https://terrorismlegislationreviewer.independent.gov.uk/wp-content/uploads/2015/09/Terrorism-Acts-Report-2015-Print-version.pdf, accessed 28 December 2016.

ARTINGSTALL, D., DOVE, N., HOWELL, J., and LEVI, M. (2016), *Drivers and Impacts of Derisking*, London: Financial Conduct Authority.

ATRAN, S. (2010), *Talking to the Enemy: Violent Extremism, Sacred Values and What it Means to be Human*, London, Allen Lane.

ASHWORTH, A. and ZEDNER, L. (2014), *Preventive Justice*, Oxford: Oxford University Press.

BIERSTEKER, T., ECKERT, S., and TOURINHO, M. (2016), *Targeted Sanctions: The Impacts and Effectiveness of United Nations Action*, London: Routledge.

BLACK, D. (2004), 'The geometry of terrorism', *Sociological Theory*, 22(1): 14–25.

BRODEUR, J-P. (2010), *The Policing Web*, New York: Oxford University Press.

BRUNNER, C. (2016), 'Female suicide bombing', in J. Steans and D. Belfrage (eds), *Handbook on Gender in World Politics*, Cheltenham: Edward Elgar.

BURKE, J. (2014), *The New Threat From Islamic Militancy*, London: Vintage.

CGD (2015), *Unintended Consequences of Anti–Money Laundering Policies for Poor Countries*, available at: http://www.cgdev.org/sites/default/files/CGD-WG-Report-Unintended-Consequences-AML-Policies-2015.pdf, accessed 28 December 2016.

CALLIMACHI, R. (2016), 'How a Secretive Branch of ISIS Built a Global Network of Killers', *New York Times*, August 3.

COHEN, S. (2001), *States of Denial: Knowing About Atrocities and Suffering*, Cambridge: Polity.

COLLINS, R. (2008), *Violence: A Micro-Sociological Perspective*, Princeton: Princeton University Press.

CORNER, E., GILL, P., and MASON, O. (2015), 'Mental health disorders and the terrorist: A research note probing selection effects and disorder prevalence', *Studies in Conflict and Terrorism*, 39(6): 560–68.

CRELINSTEN, R. (2009), *Counter-Terrorism*, Cambridge: Polity.

CROMER, G. (2001), 'Terrorist tales', in G. Cromer (ed.), *Narratives of Violence*, Aldershot: Ashgate.

CRONIN, A. (2009), *How Terrorism Ends: Understanding the Decline and Demise of Terrorist Campaigns*, Princeton: Princeton University Press.

DEAN, C. (2014), 'The healthy identity intervention: The UK's development of a psychologically informed intervention to address extremist offending', in A. Silke (ed.), *Prisons, Terrorism and Extremism: Critical Issues in Management, Radicalisation and Reform*, London: Routledge.

DEFLEM, M. (2010), *The Policing of Terrorism: Organizational and Global Perspectives*, New York: Routledge.

DURKHEIM, E. (1952/1897), *Suicide: A Study in Sociology*, London: Routledge & Kegan Paul.

ECKERT, S. and BIERSTEKER, T. (2010), '(Mis)Measuring success in countering the financing of terrorism', in P. Andreas and K. M. Greenhill (eds), *Sex, Drugs, and Body Counts: The Politics of Numbers in Global Crime and Conflict*, Ithaca, NY: Cornell University Press.

EKBLOM, P. and HIRSCHFIELD, A. (2014), 'Developing an alternative formulation of SCP principles—the Ds (11 and counting)', *Crime Science*, 3/2.

ENGLISH, R. (2009), *Terrorism: How to Respond*, Oxford: Oxford University Press.

ENGLISH, R. (2015), 'Introduction: the enduring illusions of terrorism and counter-terrorism', in R. English (ed.), *Illusions of Terrorism and Counter-Terrorism*, Oxford: Oxford University Press.

FATF (2015a), *Emerging Terrorist Financing Risks*, Paris: OECD.

FATF (2015b), *Financing of the Terrorist Organisation Islamic State in Iraq and the Levant*, Paris: OECD.

FOLEY, F. (2014), *Countering Terrorism in Britain and France: Institutions, Norms and the Shadow of the Past*, Cambridge: Cambridge University Press.

GAO (2015), *Combating Terrorism; Foreign Terrorist Organization Designation Process and U.S. Agency Enforcement Actions*, Washington, DC: US Government Accountability Office.

GANOR, B. (2005), *The Counter-Terrorism Puzzle: A Guide for Decision-Makers*, Edison, NJ.: Transaction.

GAMBETTA, D. (2005), 'Can we make sense of suicide missions?', in D. Gambetta (ed.), *Making Sense of Suicide Missions*, Oxford: Oxford University Press.

GANDY, O. (2006), 'Data mining, surveillance and discrimination in the post 9-11 environment', in K. Haggerty and R. Ericson (eds), *The New Politics of Surveillance and Visibility*, Toronto: University of Toronto Press.

GRABOSKY, P. and STOHL, M. (2010), *Crime and Terrorism*, Thousand Oaks: Sage.

GURULE, J. (2015), 'Holding Banks Liable Under The Anti-Terrorism Act For Providing Financial Services To Terrorists: An Ineffective Legal Remedy In Need Of Reform', *Journal of Legislation*, 41:(2), Article 2, available at: http://scholarship.law.nd.edu/jleg/vol41/iss2/2, accessed 28 December 2016.

HAYES, B. (2012), *Counter-terrorism, Policy Laundering and the FATF (Financial Action Task Force): Legalizing Surveillance, Regulating Civil Society*, Amsterdam: Transnational Institute/Statewatch.

HEATH-KELLY, C. (2013), 'Counter-Terrorism and the Counterfactual: Producing the "Radicalisation" Discourse and the UK PREVENT Strategy', *The British Journal of Politics and International Relations*, 15(3): 394–415.

HM GOVERNMENT (2009), *Pursue, Prevent, Protect, Prepare: The United Kingdom's Strategy for Countering International Terrorism*, London: Crown Stationery Office.

HM GOVERNMENT (2013), *Serious and Organised Crime Strategy*, London: Crown Stationery Office.

HM GOVERNMENT (2015), *Counter Extremism Strategy*, London: Crown Stationery Office.

HM GOVERNMENT (2016), *CONTEST The United Kingdom's Strategy for Countering Terrorism—Annual Report 2015*, London: Crown Stationery Office.

HOFFMAN, B. (2006), *Inside Terrorism*, 2nd edn, New York: Columbia University Press.

HOME OFFICE (2015), 'Operation of police powers under the Terrorism Act 2000 and subsequent legislation: Arrests, outcomes, and stop and search, Great Britain, quarterly update to September 2015', London: Office for Security and Counter-Terrorism.

HORGAN, J. (2005), *The Psychology of Terrorism*, London: Routledge.

HUSAIN, E. (2007), *The Islamist*, London: Penguin.

INNES, M. (2006), 'Policing uncertainty: countering terror through community intelligence and democratic policing', *Annals of the American Academy of Political and Social Science*, 605(1): 222–41.

INNES, M. (2014) *Signal Crimes; Social Reactions to Crime, Disorder and Control*, Oxford: Oxford University Press.

INNES, M. and SHEPTYCKI, J. (2004), 'From detection to disruption: some consequences of intelligence-led crime control in the United Kingdom', *International Criminal Justice Review*, 14: 1-14.

INNES, M., ABBOTT, L., LOWE, T., and ROBERTS, C. (2007), *Hearts and Minds and Eyes and Ears: Reducing Radicalisation Risks Through Reassurance-Oriented Policing*, London: ACPO.

INNES, M., ROBERTS, C., INNES, H., LOWE, T., and LAKHANI, S. (2011), *Assessing the Effects of Prevent Policing*, London: ACPO.

JACOBSON, M. (2006), *The West at War: US and European Counterterrorism Efforts, Post-September 11*, Washington: Washington Institute for Near-East Policy.

KARSTEDT, S. (2014), 'State Crime. The European Experience,' in S. Body-Gendrot, M. Hough, K. Kerezsi, and R. Lévy (eds), *The Routledge Handbook of European Criminology*, London: Routledge.

KEPEL, G. (2004), *The War for Muslim Minds: Islam and the West*, Cambridge, MA: The Belknap Press of Harvard University Press.

KILCULLAN, D. (2009), *The Accidental Guerrilla: Fighting Small Wars in the Midst of a Big One*, New York: Oxford University Press.

KUNDANI, A. (2009), *Spooked! How Not to Prevent Violent Extremism*, London: Institute of Race Relations.

LAFREE, G., MORRIS, N., and DUGAN, L. (2010), 'Cross-national patterns of terrorism: Comparing trajectories for total, attributed and fatal attacks 1970-2006', *British Journal of* Criminology, 50(4): 622–49.

LAFREE, G., and FREILICH, J. (2016), *The Handbook of the Criminology of Terrorism*, New York: Wiley.

LEVI, M. (2007), 'Pecunia non olet? The control of money-laundering revisited', in F. Bovenkerk and M. Levi (eds), *The Organised Crime Community*, New York: Springer.

LEVI, M. (2010), 'Combating the financing of terrorism: A history and assessment of the control of "threat finance"', *British Journal of Criminology Special Issue Terrorism: Criminological Perspectives*, 50(4): 650–69.

LEVI, M., DOIG, A., GUNDUR. R., WALL, D., and WILLIAMS, M. (2015), *The Implications of Economic Cybercrime for Policing*, London: City of London Corporation, available at: http://www.cityoflondon.gov.uk/business/economic-research-and-information/research-publications/Pages/

The-implications-of-economic-crime-for-policing.aspx, accessed 28 December 2016.

LINCOLN, B. (2006), *Holy Terrors: Thinking About Religion After September 11*, Chicago: University of Chicago Press.

LOFLAND, J. (1966), *Doomsday Cult: A Study of Conversion, Prosletysation and Maintenance of Faith*, New York: Prentice-Hall.

LYON, D. (2006), '9/11, synopticon, and scopophilia: watching and being watched', in K. Haggerty and R. Ericson (eds), *The New Politics of Surveillance and Visibility*, Toronto: University of Toronto Press.

MANNING, P. (2010), *Democratic Policing in a Changing World*, Boulder: Paradigm.

Marx, G. (2016), *Windows into the Soul: Surveillance and Society in an Age of High Technology*, Chicago: University of Chicago Press.

MOLOTCH, H. (2012), *Against Security: How We Go Wrong at Airports, Subways and Other Sites of Ambiguous Danger*. Princeton: Princeton University Press.

MUELLER, J. and STEWART, M. (2011), *Terror, Security and Money*, Oxford: Oxford University Press.

MYTHEN, G., WALKLATE, S., and KHAN, F. (2013), 'Why Should We Have to Prove We Are Alright? Counter-Terrorism, Risk and Partial Securities', *Sociology*, 5(3): 1–16.

O'TOOLE, T., MEER, N., NILSSON DEHANAS, D., JONES, S., and MODOOD, T. (2016), 'Governing through Prevent? Regulation and contested practice in Muslim-state engagement', *Sociology*, 50(1): 160–77.

NAWAZ, M. (2012), *Radical: My Journey Out of Islamist Extremism*, London: WH Allen.

NESSER, P. (2014), *Islamist Terrorism in Europe*, London: Hurst.

NEYLAND, D. (2009), 'Mundane terror and the threat of everyday objects', in K. Aas, H. Gundus, and H. Lovell (eds), *Technologies of Insecurity: The Surveillance of Everyday Life*, Abingdon: Routledge-Cavendish.

OFTEDAL, E. (2015), 'The financing of jihadi terrorist cells in Europe', Oslo: Norwegian Defence Research Establishment (FFI).

OMAND, D. (2012), *Securing the State*, London: C. Hurst & Co.

PANTAZIS, C. and PEMBERTON, S. (2009), 'From the "Old" to the "New" Suspect Community Examining the Impacts of Recent UK Counter-Terrorist Legislation', *British Journal of Criminology*, 49(5): 646–66.

PAPE, R. (2006), *Dying To Win: The Strategic Logic of Suicide Terrorism*, Random House: New York.

PASSAS, N. (2003), 'Informal value transfer systems, terrorism and money laundering', Report to the National Institute of Justice, Boston: Northeastern University.

PASSAS, N. (2006), 'Fighting terror with error: the counter-productive regulation of informal value transfers', *Crime, Law and Social Change*, 45(4–5): 315–36.

PICKERING, S., MCCULLOCH, J., and WRIGHT-NEVILLE, D. P. (2008), *Counter-terrorism Policing: Community, Cohesion and Security*, New York: Springer.

RICHARDSON, L. (2006), *What Terrorists Want: Understanding the Terrorist Threat*, London: John Murray.

SAGEMAN, M. (2004), *Understanding Terror Networks*, Philadelphia: University of Pennsylvania Press.

SCHMID, A. and JONGMAN, A. (1988), *Political Terrorism: A Research Guide to Concepts, Theories, Data Bases and Literature*, Amsterdam: North Holland.

SHELLEY, L. (2014), *Dirty entanglements: Corruption, Crime, and Terrorism*, Cambridge: Cambridge University Press.

SLUKA, J. (1989), *Hearts and Minds, Water and Fish: Support for the IRA and INLA in a Northern Ireland Ghetto*, Connecticut: JAI Press.

SMELSER, N. (2007), *The Faces of Terrorism: Social and Psychological Dimensions*, Princeton: Princeton University Press.

STEVEN, G. and GUNARATNA, R. (2004), *Counter-terrorism: A Reference Handbook*, Santa Barbara: ABC Clio.

SUSKIND, R. (2006), *The One Percent Doctrine: Deep Inside America's Pursuit of Its Enemies Since 9/11*, London: Simon and Schuster.

SUTHERLAND, D. and CRESSEY, D. (1955), *Principles of Criminology*, 5th edn, Washington, DC: Lippincott.

SYKES, G. and MATZA, D. (1957), 'Techniques of neutralization: A theory of delinquency', *American Sociological Review*, 22(6): 664–70.

THACHER, D. (2005), 'The local role in Homeland Security', *Law and Society Review*, 39(5): 635–76.

UK GOVERNMENT (2015), *UK National Risk Assessment of Money Laundering and Terrorist Financing*, London: HM Treasury and Home Office.

US TREASURY (2016), TERRORIST ASSETS REPORT, Calendar Year 2015 Twenty-fourth Annual Report to the Congress on Assets in the United States Relating to Terrorist Countries and International Terrorism Program Designees, available at: https://www.treasury.gov/resource-center/sanctions/Programs/Documents/tar2015.pdf, accessed 17 January 2017.

WALKER, C. (2014), 'Terrorism Financing and the Policing of Charities: Who pays the price?', in C. King and C. Walker (eds), *Dirty Assets: Emerging Issues in the Regulation of Criminal and Terrorist Assets*, Ashgate: Farnham.

WALKER, C., and MCKAY, S. (2015), 'Community Surveillance and Terrorism', in J. Pearse (ed.), *Investigating Terrorism: Current Political, Legal and Psychological Issues*, Chichester: Wiley-Blackwell.

WESSELING, M. (2014), *Evaluation of EU Measures to Combat Terrorism Financing*, Brussels: European Parliament.

WESTON, N. and INNES, M. (2010), 'Terrorism', in F. Brookman, M. Maguire, H. Pierpoint, and T. Bennett (eds), *Handbook on Crime*, Cullompton: Willan.

WIKTOROWICZ, Q. (2006), *Radical Islam Rising: Muslim Extremism in the West*, Maryland: Rowman and Littlefield.

WILKINSON, P. (2001), *Terrorism Versus Democracy: The Liberal State Response*, Abingdon: Frank Cass.

WRIGHT, L. (2006), *The Looming Tower: Al Qaeda and the Road to 9/11*, London: Allen Lane.

ZARATE, J. (2013), *Treasury's War*, New York: Public Affairs.

21

RELIGION, CRIME, AND VIOLENCE

Simon Cottee

INTRODUCTION

The relationship between religion, crime, and violence is one of the most contentious and urgent public issues of our time. Yet it has attracted little sustained attention in criminology, much less a criminological manifesto or school devoted to its study. This chapter aims to fill in some of the gaps by focusing on the more controversial aspects of the intersections between religion, crime, and violence. Drawing on a range of sources from both inside and outside criminology, it explores the following questions: Why is the relationship between religion and violence the object of such fierce controversy? Does religion have a 'true face', as both its detractors and defenders claim? Is religion a force for good in the world, or is it a force for ill? How, historically, has criminology understood religion and its relationship to crime and control? Is religion really about religion, or is it about politics? If religious belief does figure causally in religious violence, how should its role be understood? These are difficult questions, and in order to make them more tractable this chapter concentrates on one of the most potent and widely debated forms of religious violence in the world today: Islamist-inspired violence. Islam, it is necessary to clarify at the outset, does not have a monopoly over the use of violence in the name of God; indeed all monotheistic religions, including Christianity, have violent pasts that extend into the present (Juergensmeyer 2001). But of all the violent religious actors in the world today, radical Islamism is undoubtedly one of the most prevalent. It is also one of the most vigorously disputed and misunderstood, and thus represents an important case study for analysis.

The chapter is divided into five parts. The first part introduces some key questions at the centre of debates over religion and violence by focusing on a recent and widely disseminated article on the links between the so-called Islamic State or ISIS and its theological beliefs. The article in question—Graeme Wood's 'What ISIS Really Wants', published in *The Atlantic* in March 2015—contended that ISIS is 'very Islamic', and that what the group does is intimately and inextricably connected to its foundational religious beliefs. Wood's article is intensely controversial, and the nature of this controversy is explored throughout the chapter. The second part contextualizes the question of religious violence against the background of the global religious revival. The third part focuses on criminology and its treatment of religion, and how that treatment reflects a pro-religious bias. The fourth part concentrates on the treatment of religious violence in terrorism studies, using this to help sketch out some methodological suggestions for the criminological study of religious violence. The fifth and final part of the chapter looks at the broader climate of 'the new religious intolerance' (Nussbaum 2012) in which current debates over religion, crime, and violence now take place.

RELIGION, VIOLENCE, AND CONTROVERSY

In March 2015 *The Atlantic* published an article by Graeme Wood, a contributing editor at the magazine and Fellow at the Council on Foreign Relations. The subject of the article could not have been more topical: 'What ISIS Really Wants'.

In June the previous year, ISIS (the Islamic State of Iraq and al-Sham), also known as Islamic State, ISIL (the Islamic State of Iraq and the Levant), or 'Daesh' (Hamid and McCants 2014), had seized Mosul, Iraq's second largest city, and in the following months captured large swathes of territory in Syria and Iraq, including, notably, Fallujah, Ramadi, and Palmyra (Stern and Berger 2015; Wood 2014; Chulov 2014; Chulov 2015). It had also, by that point, recruited more foreign fighters to its ranks than any other jihadist mobilization in recent history (Hegghammer 2013),[1] eclipsing its chief competitor Al Qaeda (Watts 2015; Wood 2015; Lister 2016) as the world's preeminent jihadist group (Watts 2015; Wood 2015; Lister 2016).

Wood's article was 10,500 words long, and its tone was sober and scholarly. Despite this, it went viral (Wright 2015). According to the web analytics company Chartbeat (Edmonds 2015), it was the best read digital article of 2015, receiving a total of 100 million minutes of engaged reading time. In the months following its online publication it attracted approximately 10,000 views a day. On the night of the November 2015 Paris attacks it received an extraordinary 1.9 million views.

The article, in part, served a polemical purpose and was an attempt to refute the view, prevalent in Washington political circles in mid-2014, that ISIS was just a bunch of thugs and psychopaths who posed no serious strategic threat to the Middle East or the wider world.[2] But it was also a serious attempt to explain the nature of the group, its origins, aims, and broader ideological vision.

'There is a temptation', Wood (2015) argued, citing Peter Bergen's (2002) classic study of Al Qaeda *Holy War, Inc.* to think 'that jihadists are modern secular people,

[1] In December 2015, the Soufan Group (2015) reported that between 27,000 and 31,000 people had travelled to Syria and Iraq to join ISIS and other violent extremist groups from at least 86 countries. Around 5,000 are thought to have come from Western Europe, including just over 750 from Britain.

[2] In January 2014 President Barack Obama dismissed ISIS as a 'JV [junior varsity] team' of Al Qaeda. 'The analogy we use around here sometimes, and I think is accurate, is if a jayvee team puts on Lakers uniforms that doesn't make them Kobe Bryant', he told the *New Yorker*'s David Remnick (2014).

with modern political concerns, wearing medieval religious disguise—and make it fit the Islamic State'. This would be a mistake, he insisted. Indeed, 'much of what the group does looks nonsensical except in light of a sincere, carefully considered commitment to returning civilization to a seventh-century legal environment, and ultimately to bringing about the apocalypse'. Drawing on official ISIS statements and interviews with prominent ISIS supporters, Wood summarized the core of his argument in this way:

> The reality is that the Islamic State is Islamic. *Very* Islamic. Yes, it has attracted psychopaths and adventure seekers, drawn largely from the disaffected populations of the Middle East and Europe. But the religion preached by its most ardent followers derives from coherent and even learned interpretations of Islam. (Wood 2014, emphasis in original)

'Muslims can reject the Islamic State; nearly all do', he added. But: 'pretending that it isn't actually a religious, millenarian group, with theology that must be understood to be combatted, has already led the United States to underestimate it and back foolish schemes to counter it.' He was particularly critical of what he described as 'a well-intentioned but dishonest campaign to deny the Islamic State's medieval religious [and specifically Islamic] nature'. 'Many mainstream Muslim organizations', he wrote, 'have gone so far as to say the Islamic State is, in fact, *un-Islamic* (emphases in original)', a view shared by President Obama, who has denounced ISIS as 'not Islamic' (Blake 2014; Killough 2014),[3] and French President François Hollande, who contemptuously refers to the group as 'Daesh' (Mark 2015).[4] According to Wood, this is flatly 'preposterous', given how closely and assiduously the leaders of the Islamic State follow, however selectively, 'the Prophetic methodology' of early Islam. It is also reflective, he suggested, of a deeper 'Western bias': namely, that 'if religious ideology doesn't matter much in Washington or Berlin, surely it must be equally irrelevant in Raqqa or Mosul'.

Wood's article attracted great interest and fierce controversy. It is not difficult to understand why. ISIS has become notorious for its brutality and violence. Since its dramatic rise to prominence in the summer of 2014, the group has slaughtered thousands of defenceless Iraqi soldiers and Shiite civilians, gunning them into trenches (McCoy 2014; Arango 2014a). It has raped and enslaved hundreds of women (Naili 2014; McDuffee 2014; Human Rights Watch 2014; Callimachi 2015; Callimachi 2016). It has brutalized children by forcing them to watch scenes of horrific cruelty (Bloom 2015; Horgan and Bloom 2015; Bloom, Horgan, and Winter 2016). It has presided over public crucifixions in its current stronghold of Raqqa, Syria (Abdelaziz 2014). It has coerced boys as young as 14 to carry out suicide missions (Arango 2014b). It has launched a campaign of murderous aggression against gay men (Cowburn 2016). It

[3] US Secretary of State John Kerry went even further, condemning ISIS as 'apostates' (Kaplan 2016), a highly charged term of contempt for those who have left the fold of Islam (Cragun and Hammer 2011: 154; Cottee 2015a: 9). 'Daesh', he declared, 'is in fact nothing more than a mixture of killers, of kidnappers, of criminals, of thugs, of adventurers, of smugglers and thieves'. 'And', he continued, 'they are above all apostates, people who have hijacked a great religion and lie about its real meaning and lie about its purpose and deceive people in order to fight for their purposes.' (Quoted in Taylor 2016.) Given that takfirism, the practice of one Muslim declaring another to be an apostate (Hafez 2010), is so controversial within Islam (in many Muslim majority countries the penalty for apostasy is death (Cottee 2015b)), Kerry's invocation of the term was unwise (Al-Awsat 2014), especially since ISIS itself is a takfirist group (Wood 2015).

[4] The term 'Daesh' is based on an Arabic acronym al-Dawla al-Islamiya fil Iraq wa'al Sham, which translates as Islamic State of Iraq and Sham (Syria), but is similar to 'Dahes' or 'one who sows discord' (Martinson 2015).

has stolen and destroyed ancient and irreplaceable artefacts (Jeffries 2015). And it has created a vast library of snuff movies that degrades not only the victims whose deaths they depict, but also the viewers who watch them (Cottee 2014a; Cottee 2016a). To say that all this inhumanity is rooted in, or somehow connected to, Islam challenges one of the prevailing mantras of polite modern political discourse: namely that Islam is 'a religion of peace'.[5]

The contention, at the heart of Wood's article, that ISIS is fundamentally Islamic was strongly challenged by Juan Cole (2015a), who accused Wood of engaging in 'essentialism' for failing to recognize that ISIS, far from having an 'Islamic essence', is in fact a 'destructive Muslim cult', radically at odds with the ideals of Islam as understood and practiced by most Muslims. Indeed, he asserted, 'the refusal to see ISIL in these terms is just a form of Orientalism, a way of othering the Middle East and marking its culture as inherently threatening'. Cole (2015b) argued that there is 'a center of gravity to any religion such that observers can tell when something is deviant', concluding, 'Why pretend that we can't judge when modern Muslim movements depart so far from the modern mainstream as to be a cult?'

Mehdi Hasan (2015) was similarly emphatic, discounting religion 'as a useful analytical prism through which to view the rise of ISIS'. By way of substantiation, he summarized the views of terrorism expert Marc Sageman, who he paraphrased as saying that ISIS 'are using religion to advance a political vision, rather than using politics to advance a religious vision'. He also emphasized the decidedly secular enthusiasms of western jihadists, referring to a 2008 classified MI5 briefing note on radicalization, in which it is reported that many are 'religious novices' with 'a high propensity for "drug-taking, drinking alcohol and visiting prostitutes"'. It is particularly instructive, he observed, that Mohammed Ahmed and Yusuf Sarwar, two British Muslim men who were convicted on terrorism charges in 2014 after travelling to fight in Syria, purchased copies of *Islam for Dummies* and *The Koran for Dummies* from Amazon prior to their departure. 'It cannot be said often enough', Hasan said:

> It isn't the most pious or devout of Muslims who embrace terrorism, or join groups such as ISIS. Nor has a raft of studies and surveys uncovered any evidence of a 'conveyor belt' that turns people of firm faith into purveyors of violence. Religion plays little, if any, role in the radicalisation process . . . To claim that ISIS is Islamic is egregiously inaccurate and empirically unsustainable, not to mention insulting to the 1.6 billion non-violent adherents of Islam across the planet.

The controversy surrounding Wood's article on ISIS reflected a larger controversy, first sparked by the 9/11 attacks, over the nature or 'faces' of Islam and, more broadly, the relationship between religion and violence. Is there something inherently violent about extreme or fundamentalist versions of religion (let alone Islam), or is the violence carried out in the name of religion at root politically motivated and thus primarily secular

[5] Even President George W. Bush (2001)—widely reviled across the Muslim world and beyond for launching wars in Afghanistan and Iraq—was adamant, as he put it in a speech just after the 9/11 attacks, that 'Islam is peace'. 'These acts of violence against innocents', he said of the attacks, 'violate the fundamental tenets of the Islamic faith. And it's important for my fellow Americans to understand that.' Following the Pakistani Taliban's attack on a school in Pakistan in December 2014, the British Prime Minister David Cameron was similarly forthright in his view that it had 'nothing to do with one of the world's great religions—Islam, which is a religion of peace. This is a perversion.'

in character? What causal role, if any, do religious doctrines and beliefs play in terrorism? Is religion a force for good in the world or a source of evil? ISIS, because of the vigour and fastidiousness with which it has sought to justify its actions as divinely mandated, has brought these wider questions to the fore.

THE GLOBAL RELIGIOUS REVIVAL AND THE AMBIVALENCE OF THE SACRED

Before considering the deeper questions about religion and violence raised by Wood's article, it is important to briefly describe the broader context out of which these questions have emerged. This is the context of the global religious revival. 'Half a century ago', Michael Cook (2014: 443) writes, 'it was widely thought that in the modern world religion was doomed to fade away.' This presumption, or the 'secularization' thesis, is the historical 'process by which religious institutions, actions and consciousness lose their social significance' (Wilson 1966: 14; see also Berger 1967: 107).[6] It was a presumption widely shared among a wide spectrum of nineteenth-century thinkers, ranging from Auguste Comte, Herbert Spenser, Emile Durkheim, Max Weber, Sigmund Freud, Karl Marx, Friedrich Engels, and Ferdinand Tönnies (see Bruce 1992: 170–94; Aldridge 2000; Turner 1992: 102), who all confidently supposed that the development of capitalism would profoundly and inexorably undermine the social and cultural bases of traditional religion. C. Wright Mills (1959: 32–33) narrates the thesis like this:

> Once the world was filled with the sacred—in thought, practice, and institutional form. After the Reformation and the Renaissance, the forces of modernization swept across the globe and secularization, a corollary historical process, loosened the dominance of the sacred. In due course, the sacred shall disappear altogether except, possibly, in the private realm.

This thesis held sway until the latter decades of the twentieth-century (Norris and Inglehart 2011: 3; Beck 2010: 20), at which point it came under sustained attack. Religion, critics of secularization theory contend, remains a vital aspect of social life across the globe, evidenced, variously, in the enduring popularity of churchgoing in the United States, the emergence of New Age spirituality in Western Europe, the rise of Islamist movements in the Muslim world, and the growth of Pentecostalism and Charismatic Catholicism in Latin American and Africa. These developments prompted Peter L. Berger (1999: 2), one of the leading exponents of the secularization thesis in the 1960s, to renounce his earlier claims: 'The world today, with some exceptions', he acknowledged, 'is as furiously religious as it ever was, and in some places more so than ever.' 'This means', Berger concluded, 'that a whole body of literature by

[6] Secularization must be distinguished from secularism—the conviction that religion should be a strictly private matter into which the state should not intrude nor vice versa. On the various dimensions of secularization, see Dobbelaere (1981).

historians and social scientists loosely labeled "secularization theory" is essentially mistaken.' Rodney Stark and Roger Finke (2000: 79) were no less categorical: 'After nearly three centuries of utterly failed prophesies and misrepresentations of both present and past, it seems time to carry the secularization doctrine to the graveyard of failed theories, and there to whisper "requiescat in pace".' Thus many contemporary social theorists are now apt to speak of a 'postsecular' age, in which 'the vigorous continuation of religion in a continually secularizing environment must be reckoned with' (Habermas 2005: 26). Olivier Roy (2010), for example, has argued that secularization, far from eradicating religion, has in fact paved the way for its revival, transforming it into a 'decultured', or culturally diluted, set of beliefs, practices, and identities. About the 'return of the religious', Roy writes, 'It does not mean that religious observance has increased, but that it has become more visible, especially with the appearance of "fundamentalist" forms of religious expression, in which the believer refuses to restrict his faith to the private realm but insists on its being recognized as an integral dimension of his public self, believing that religion should govern every aspect of his personal behavior.' According to Roy (2005: 3), what is distinctive about new forms of religious expression, whether charismatic Christianity (in all its manifestations), orthodox Judaism, 'sects', such as the Jehovah's Witnesses or Muslim fundamentalism, is that they are *individualistic* (membership is a choice, not necessarily a cultural inheritance), *institutionally weak* (mistrustful of churches and representative authorities), and *anti-intellectual* (unconcerned with theological niceties).

The confidence with which nineteenth-century social theorists supposed that religion would diminish in the modern world was not entirely misplaced: after all, as Cook (2014: 443) points out, in Western Europe, 'it continues to hold up rather well' (see also Berger 1999: 9–11). There may be even be a case for suggesting that it has held up elsewhere, too, including, notably, the United States (Bruce 2002). Yet today, as Cook also makes clear, 'as a generalization about humanity at large, the conjecture is false'. Indeed, he argues, 'the massive Islamic revival is in itself enough to refute it'. Cook (2014: 444) suggests that there are three dimensions to this revival: private religiosity, the expansion of Islam into conventional politics, and jihadism. The first of these is the most widespread: 'an increase in religiosity whereby large numbers of people "get religion", for the most part without any involvement in political activism or militancy.'[7] The second refers to the proliferation of Islamist political parties, whose aspiration is to replace existing political arrangements with an intrinsically Islamic political order. The third is the rise of jihadist groups, whose goals are to defend or recapture territory by means of violence (Pape 2003, 2005), or, as in the case of ISIS, to violently annex and occupy new territory in an effort to create a revolutionary political entity that transcends the bounds of the conventional nation state—namely, the 'caliphate' (Cottee 2016b; Stern and Berger 2015).

It is against this background, and particularly the dramatic upsurge in religious violence across the globe in the past twenty years (Juergensmeyer 2001; Juergensmeyer, Griego, and Soboslai 2015; Selengut 2008), that current controversies over the nature and role of religion in contemporary social and political life must be understood. It

[7] For a contrasting view, see Fish (2011: 24–6, 45): 'Muslims are not dramatically more religious than non-Muslims and are only slightly more religious—if even that—than Christians'.

certainly helps explain the sensitivities and militancy of the so-called 'new atheist' critics of religion, for whom the question 'is there really something rotten at the heart of religion?' warrants an unequivocal 'yes' (Harris 2004; Dawkins 2006). Among the most articulate and ardent of the 'new atheists' is the late Christopher Hitchens, whose polemic *God is Not Great* sought to show that religion not only impedes progress, but, in the words of its subtitle, 'poisons everything' (Hitchens 2007). In a chapter titled 'Religion Kills', Hitchens cites case after case of what he takes to be 'religiously inspired' acts of cruelty, asserting that in many zones of conflict throughout the world 'religion has been an enormous multiplier of tribal suspicion and hatred' (Hitchens 2007: 18, 36). Even when religious believers perform good deeds Hitchens insists that they are acting not out of fidelity to their religious beliefs, but instead to a secular commitment to humanism (2007: 27).

Hitchens' position is acutely problematic from a sociological point of view. First, instead of trying to intellectually make sense of the meaning and centrality of religion in social life and throughout history, Hitchens' chief concern is to morally condemn it. This is not a sound basis on which to say anything insightful about religion and its appeal to millions of people who hold religious beliefs, engage in religious practices, or self-define in religious terms.

Second, the idea that religion is essentially and irredeemably malevolent is so preposterously one-sided and reductive that it cannot be taken fully seriously (Hall 2013: 365–6). Religion and religious identity, to be sure, have often been the source of violence in the world, but it is not the *only* source: for a great many evils have been perpetrated in the name of secular dogmas, too. (Think, e.g., of Nazi Germany and the Holocaust (Goldhagen 1996; Browning 1992), or of the tens of millions who died under Soviet Communism (Conquest 1990, 1999).) At the same time, it is an incontestable empirical fact that countless numbers of people have been inspired by their religious beliefs to do good and to stop or ameliorate all manner of injustices (Appleby 2000). Hitchens (2007: 27) is obliged to recognize this, but he refuses to credit religion as the animating motive in these cases, arguing that any good a believer does is 'a compliment to humanism, not to religion'. Of Martin Luther King, a committed Christian who used the language of the Old Testament and who frequently invoked the theme of the 'promised land' to inspire the Civil Rights movement, and who preached non-violence in the struggle against racism, Hitchens says that he was not a 'real' Christian: 'When Dr. King took a stand . . . he did so as a profound humanist and nobody could ever use his name to justify oppression or cruelty . . . his legacy has very little to do with his professed theology . . . In no real as opposed to nominal sense, then, was he a Christian' (Hitchens 2007: 180, 176).[8] The circularity in this position is obvious. Because he starts with the assumption or conviction that religion is inherently evil Hitchens must rhetorically redefine the good done in the name of religion as not properly religious. He also adopts the same circular logic in his discussion of the atrocities carried out in the name of secular creeds: these, he contends, were, for all intents and purposes, faith-based initiatives, because they were mandated by infallible leaders whose authority was sacred in character.[9]

[8] On the intimate relationship between King's religious beliefs and his social activism, see Branch (1989).

[9] This is not unlike the circular logic of early radical criminologists who sought to argue that because 'true' socialism was a perfect model of society and politics, 'actually existing' socialist societies which had yet to

Third, Hitchens has a tendency to reify religion, characterizing it as a thing in itself, independent of those who practice it and make sense of it. This is sociologically untenable, because it neglects to acknowledge the multiple and complex ways in which people reflexively recreate religion in and through their everyday routine activities or 'praxis'. This is a particularly important point to stress, given how so much contemporary public discourse on religion, and particularly Islam, reproduces Hitchens' fundamental methodological error. Consider, for example, Republican presidential candidate Donald Trump's claim that Islam is antithetical to the West, especially America: 'Islam hates us', he told CNN host Anderson Cooper, although he did not specify the nature or degree of this apparent hatred, still less contrive to substantiate this claim (Schleifer 2016). Or consider President Barack Obama's converse assertion that 'Islam is a religion that preaches peace.' [10] Obama's view is clearly the more politically responsible, but both exhibit the same reifying impulse, constructing Islam as a thing that somehow possesses its own agency and whose essential moral character is fixed outside of time and space. But, from a sociological perspective, Islam doesn't *do* anything, and like all religions its meaning is created and recreated by those who practice it. As Will McCants (2016) nicely expresses it, taking both Trump and Obama to task, 'Islam neither hates nor preaches—its followers do. Islam is what people make of it, and they have made it many different things.' According to McCants, 'Muslims abstain and Muslims drink . . . Muslims defend and Muslims demolish . . . Muslims kill and Muslims tolerate . . . Muslims war and Muslims ally'. And so on. McCants' point is that Islam encompasses an extraordinarily diverse and contradictory range of actions and practices. There is not one Islam, but a plurality of Islams, and what Islam means is determined not by 'ancient, immutable scripture' but by Muslims and their ever-evolving approaches to their faith. 'Rather than talk about what Islam does and what Islam believes', McCants argues, 'politicians should talk about what its followers do and what its followers believe.'

This makes good sociological sense, and applies not just to Islam but to all religions. Religion, from this perspective, is a moral, cultural, and intellectual resource on which people draw and which they use for a variety of private and public purposes. It provides the guiding scripts and rituals for a whole range of social activities (Van Gennep 1960). But it is equally important to recognize that just as religion enables, it also constrains in significant ways, limiting the scope of that which is permissible and hence possible.[11] Moderate Muslims, for example, have sought to question the ruling, accepted across the major schools of Islamic law (Peters and De Vries 1976–7; Friedmann 2003), that the penalty for apostasy is death (Akyo 2011: 274–5). Their hermeneutic efforts have centred on reinterpreting Chapter 2: verse 256 of the Quran (2004: 29)—'There is no compulsion in religion'—as a doctrine of religious tolerance, instead of a judgement denying the feasibility of coercion in matters of faith

usher in this model were not 'really' socialist, and that any pathologies they displayed had their roots in the pathologies of the capitalist societies they had replaced (Downes 1979).

[10] See http://www.realclearpolitics.com/video/2014/09/28/obama_islam_is_a_religion_that_preaches_peace.html, last accessed 2 April 2016.

[11] This is a characteristic it shares with all social practices: see Giddens (1984).

(Friedmann 2003: 94).[12] Given that the Quran is emphatic that unrepentant apostates should forever burn in hell,[13] it is an interpretive stretch to suggest that it is a document of religious freedom.[14] But a case can be made for it. By contrast, it is far more difficult to find in the Quran, still less the hadith (the collected sayings of the Prophet Muhammad), a warrant for same-sex marriage. And it is precisely for this reason that Muslim-majority countries, in which lesbian, gay, bisexual, and transgender rights are systematically withheld,[15] are unlikely to legalize same-sex marriage. (Conversely, it is unlikely that the United States Congress would pass a law mandating the stoning to death of women for marital infidelity, given the interpretive difficulties of finding a justification for this in the US Constitution.) Like all religions, Islam is malleable, but not indefinitely so. This is Cook (2014: xii):

> I have sometimes been tempted to think of a religious heritage as a set of circuits that the politically inclined may or may not choose to switch on or as a menu from which they may or may not choose to make a selection; that is to say, an ancient religion, like a menu, provides its modern adherents with a set of options that do not determine their choices but do constrain them.

In a footnote to this, Cook (2014: xii) adds, by way of qualification, that 'even this may exaggerate the degree of freedom of choice. Often one should perhaps think rather of a menu dispensed by a waiter anxious to sell the house specials'. 'I have no great sympathy', Cook elaborates, 'with the idea that religious traditions are putty in the hands of exegetes—as if a heritage could successfully be interpreted to mean whatever one wanted and all interpretations were equally plausible to one's fellow believers.'

This raises a difficult question. Are some religions more malleable for progressive political purposes than others? Or, conversely, are some religions more malleable for anti-democratic or inhumane purposes? A further question is whether there is something *intrinsically* problematic about religion itself,[16] in that it necessarily embodies an exclusivist outlook that divides the world into believers and non-believers, into an 'us' and 'them' (Juergensmeyer, Griego, and Soboslai 2015: 66; Juergensmeyer 2001: 7)[17] and invokes transcendental values that inhibit compromise (Hoffman 1995: 272–4).

[12] The entirety of 2: 256 reads: 'There is no compulsion in religion: *true guidance has become distinct from error*, so whoever rejects false gods and believes in God has grasped the firmest hand-hold, one that will never break (emphases added).' Some classical Islamic scholars have taken this to mean that because the truth of Islam is so self-evident no one is in need of being coerced into it; rather, they need only to open their eyes and heart to it (Friedmann 2003: 105).

[13] 'If any of you revoke your faith and die as disbelievers, your deeds will come to nothing in this world and the Hereafter, and you will be inhabitants of the Fire, there to remain' (The Quran 2004, 2: 217: 24). An apostate or disbeliever is someone who renounces their faith (Cottee 2015a: ch. 2).

[14] At the time at which the Quran was composed the idea of religious freedom, as it is now conventionally understood in the democratic societies of the West, simply did not exist.

[15] Same-sex sexual activity is illegal in more than 30 Islamic countries (Cviklová 2012).

[16] See, classically, Girard (1972), who argues that scapegoating—the killing of a 'surrogate victim' standing in for wider evils—is a primordial religious act intended to preserve the sacred from pollution.

[17] 'The seed of religiously motivated violence', writes Beck (2010: 54), 'lies in the universalism of the equality of believers which withholds from non-believers what it promises to believers: dignity for fellow human beings and equality in a world of strangers.'

RELIGION, CRIME, AND CRIMINOLOGY

Criminology is necessarily interested in the boundaries between 'them' and 'us', between 'good' and 'evil', how these distinctions are policed, and with what consequences. The discipline is also naturally interested in violence and injustice and how these are legitimated by means of discourses that make judgements about categories of persons based on their ethnicity, class, or gender. Yet it remains largely silent on the question of religion and the 'them' and 'us' master narratives that underpin it and legitimize the many violent acts and injustices carried out in its name. This silence has not gone unnoticed among criminologists. Discussing the neglect of religion in the criminological mainstream, Francis T. Cullen (2012: 151) reports that a raid of his bookshelf revealed that out of the 16 titles he selected, including notable classics (Akers 1998; Gottfredson and Hirschi 1990; Sampson and Laub 1993; Lilly, Cullen, and Ball 2007), not a single reference to religion was to be found in their indices. A scan of the entire back-catalogue of the *British Journal of Criminology*, one of the key institutional sites of academic international criminology, reveals a similar absence. Between July 1960, the month in which the first volume of the *British Journal of Criminology* was published and January 2014, which saw the publication of the first issue of its 54th volume, the crime-religion theme is addressed in just three articles: Junger and Polder (1993), Mahabir (2012), and Hamm (2009).

Jeffery T. Ulmer (2012: 163) echoes Cullen's lament about the neglect of religion in criminology. 'Sociologists since Durkheim', he writes, 'have recognized that religion is a core element of culture and that it therefore is a powerful potential motivator of and control on behavior'. Criminology, however, 'has yet to locate religion centrally in the field'. This failing is all the more notable, he observes, given that the study of religion is currently enjoying 'a renewed vitality in sociology and new thinking in psychology'.

Yet it would be misleading to suggest that the neglect of religion in criminology is wholesale. On the contrary, there is a sizeable criminological literature on religion as a *crime-reducing* facet of social control. Indeed, Byron R. Johnson and Sung Joon Jang (2012), in a comprehensive review, identify 270 published studies on this theme. These studies invariably construct religion not as a cause of crime, but as an important bulwark against it. Johnson and Jang (2012: 120–1) write:

> We find religion to be a robust variable that tends to be associated with the lowered likelihood of crime or delinquency. Also, the vast majority of studies document the importance of religious influences in protecting youth from harmful outcomes as well as promoting beneficial and prosocial outcomes.

This recalls the cultural conservatism of William Bennett, John Dilulio, and James Walters' 1996 study *Body Count*, according to which the root cause of 'predatory street crime' is 'moral poverty' (Bennett *et al.* 1996: 56). Far from being a product of economic deprivation or structural inequalities, crime is a function of bad secular parenting. Like Johnson and Jang, *Body Count* asserts that 'religion is the best and most reliable means we have to reinforce the good' (Bennett *et al.* 1996: 208).

It is beyond the remit of this chapter to assess the validity of Johnson and Jang's contention that religion has 'prosocial effects' as a restraining force against criminal impulses, although it is obviously highly contentious (Cragun 2013: 92–6). But it is necessary to register the one-sidedness of Johnson and Jang's discussion and their failure to address, much less explore, the possibility that in addition to the 'prosocial effects' of religion, religious involvement may also have 'antisocial effects'. In an age in which religious violence and sectarian religious disputes are among the dominant forms conflict worldwide (Juergensmeyer 2001; Stern 2003; Selengut 2008), the side-stepping of this issue is untenable.

Cullen (2012) and Ulmer (2012), who, as we have seen, both regret the neglect of religion in criminology, do not seem overly troubled by such a one-sided account. In fact, they endorse it. For his part, Cullen suggests that 'a criminology of religion' should focus on the ways in which religion, and specifically a belief in a 'loving God', can help not only to restrain baser impulses but also to cultivate positive emotional predispositions:

> Religion is not strictly about a retributive God who seeks to evoke guilt when His commandments are violated and who threatens Hellfire for transgressions. Religion also is about God's love and about the invitation to spread the good word and to be good. Exploring the impact of faith in a loving God thus appears worthy of further exploration. (Cullen 2012: 155)

This is quite extraordinary. Cullen is a professional criminologist, not a theologian, yet here he is stipulating what religion is and what it is not. 'Religion also is about God's love', he claims. This makes the same fundamental methodological error as those who insist that religion is 'really' about God's hate. But, as we have seen, religion is not a fixed entity independent of those who practice it. It is neither about love nor hate. Rather, it is about what believers, within certain bounds, take it to be. Historically, they have taken it to be many things, both loving and hateful.

No less extraordinary is Ulmer's (2012, emphasis in original) claim that religion

> is a source of definitions and moral messages that discourage interpersonal violence, stealing, dishonesty, illicit substance use, etc. Religion thus likely involves differential association processes entailing exposure to and internalization of *definitions*—values, attitudes, and beliefs that reject crime and delinquency.

This is less a neutral description of religion than a stark affirmation of it as a social good. It is also vulnerable to the rejoinder that, as well as being a source of 'prosocial' definitions, religion can also offer a multitude of commands, prohibitions, and prejudices that legitimize as morally right or necessary a number of inhumane practices and acts (Hitchens 2007; Jones 2008: 44–5, 143). As Albert Bandura (1990: 164) remarks, 'Over the years, much reprehensible and destructive conduct has been perpetrated by ordinary, decent people in the name of religious principles, righteous ideologies, and nationalistic imperatives. Throughout history, countless people have suffered at the hands of self-righteous crusaders bent on stamping out what they consider evil.' Charles Selengut (2008: 2) is more succinct: 'Religion can tell us that it is ultimately right to love our neighbors, but it can also instruct us that it is our sacred duty to kill them.'

Ronald L. Akers (2010: 1), though sensitive to the inhumane purposes to which religion can be put, reinforces Johnson and Jang's view that religion, by and large, is a force for good in the world, serving as a restraining moral counter-weight against base and lawless human impulses:

> While religious extremism (as is true for extremism of any type) can provide motivation and support for deviant actions, crime and violence, and religious groups and beliefs can develop in direct opposition to the established and prevailing society and culture, the expectation is that religion generally provides institutional support for conformity to conventional culture. That is, religious beliefs, worship, doctrines, commitment, and activities work against violating the laws and norms of good and civil behavior in society. Certain Christian doctrines, for instance, teach respect and obedience to both government and religious authorities, and if one truly believes such doctrines as 'do unto others as you would have them do unto you,' and 'love your neighbor as yourself,' it is difficult to bring oneself to cheat, defraud, or do violence against others.[18]

It is instructive to note that when Akers (2010: 4) concedes that there have been cases in which religion has had 'an antisocial impact', he describes these as 'extreme', suggesting that religion's 'pro-social, anti-criminal impact on society' is the norm. It is also revealing that in the course of making this point Akers refers to the 'misuse and distortion of religion to justify criminal acts'. This carries the assumption that religion can only justify criminal acts if it is *misapplied* in some way, and that religion is at heart fundamentally pacific. Not only is this a normatively biased reading; it is also unsociological, attributing to religion a 'true' face or essence against which it is possible to measure distortions or deviations.

Why have criminologists tended to ignore religion as a possible cause of crime or as an animating emotion in the subjectivity of the offender? There are at least two central reasons for this.

First, criminology, from its historical beginnings, framed the criminal offender as an essentially secular subject (Cottee 2014b). It was the Italian positivist school, spearheaded by Cesare Lombroso, which laid the foundations for this framing, rejecting outright theological notions of evil and sin as incompatible with its revolutionary scientific ethos (Sparks 1999; Vold *et al.* 2002: 1–17; Beirne 1993).The offender, as Lombroso saw him (this was well before feminist criminology blazed its trail), was genetically abnormal, not fallen, still less possessed of the devil. Correspondingly, he was in need of clinical treatment (Radzinowicz 1966: 53–6), not clerical intervention, still less redemption and forgiveness. Although contemporary criminology has uniformly discarded Lombroso's work and self-reflexively adopted a variety of post-Enlightenment discourses (Nelken 1994), the foundational Lombrosian construction of the offender as a primarily secular subject lives on in its master paradigms as a 'domain assumption' (Gouldner 1970). The brutalized inadequate; the detached egoist; the frustrated social climber; the resentful rejector; the virtuous victim, 'more sinned against than sinning'; the quasi-insurgent; the self-maximizing consumer; the bored thrill seeker: these images of the offender, despite being crude caricatures, capture something important about the broader theoretical narratives to which they belong, and hint at what few professional criminologists would like to admit: that criminology is as much a morality-play as a science, where the offender, conjured into existence by

[18] Akers clearly underestimates the vast scope for denial and cognitive dissonance in human affairs (Cohen 2001), and how the 'the breastplate of righteousness' can mask a multitude of sins (Humphreys 1975).

his criminological creator, strikes a moral pose and invites a judgement (Cottee 2013). Yet it is a field in which the religious believer is conspicuous by his/her absence, and where notions of evil, sin, damnation, sacrifice, salvation, and the soul do not find any footing alongside the more worldly states of deprivation, alienation, strain, stigma, inequality, and injustice.

Second, there is a pro-religious bias in criminology. This has two dimensions: the first is the conviction that religious belief or a community of believers serve as a safeguard against crime and antisocial—and presumably *secular*—tendencies or corruptions. The second is more subtle and harder to capture: a generalized sense that religion is a valuable source of identity, belonging, and meaning, and that linking it to criminality is somehow disrespectful or even demonizing toward religious believers, especially those from minority communities. Few criminologists would confess to harbouring any such sense, but a theory or study which blames religion, still less a specific religion, for crime or injustices is unlikely to catch on in criminological circles. This, as Cullen (2012: 153) helpfully suggests, is connected to a broader scepticism among criminologists toward explanations that link culture and specifically 'bad morals' to crime, 'unless the culture itself is explained by structural disadvantage'—or politics more broadly.

If criminology is to fully engage with religion, it must overcome its historical secularism and recognize the salience of religion in social and political life. It must also adopt a more neutral stance toward the relationship between religion, crime, and control, instead of simply valorizing religion as a mechanism for peace and 'pro-social' behaviour. Moreover, in keeping with its critical traditions, criminology must acknowledge the role of mainline or allegiant religions in legitimizing the social control of deviants, apostates, heretics and, crucially and notoriously, women (Eltahawy 2015).

RELIGION, VIOLENCE, AND POLITICS

Like criminology, terrorism studies is a 'rendezvous subject' (Downes 1988), where scholars from a variety of disciplines pass through and meet to discuss common points of interest. But unlike criminology, terrorism studies has a tradition of vigorous and illuminating debate over the meaning and nature of religious violence. Some six years before the 9/11 attacks, Bruce Hoffman, a leading terrorism studies scholar, argued that 'holy terror' is not like 'secular terror' (1995: 272–3). For the religious terrorist, unlike his/her secular twin, 'violence first and foremost is a sacramental act or divine duty executed in direct response to some theological demand or imperative'. The religious terrorist, furthermore, is 'unconstrained by the political, moral or practical constraints that seem to affect other [non-religious] terrorists'. And their mission is not to sway an audience, but to engage in acts of sacrificial violence for the greater glory of a divine god or being: 'Where the secular terrorist sees violence primarily as a means to an end, the religious terrorist tends to view violence as an end in itself' (1995: 273).

Hoffman's position acquired a particular salience in the wake of the 9/11 attacks. Were the perpetrators and their sponsors rational political actors or where they religious fanatics whose purposes did not extend beyond what they felt was a religious duty to punish and avenge the 'great Satan' of the United States of America? In his seminal study on suicide bombing, *Dying to Win: The Strategic Logic of Suicide Terrorism*, Robert Pape (2005: 23) took up the former position, arguing that 'the bottom line is that suicide terrorism is mainly a response to foreign occupation.' From a dataset of 315 suicide attacks from 1980 to 2003, Pape concluded that strategic logic, rather than ideology or religion, explains 95 percent of all suicide attacks around the world. They are 'organized, coherent campaigns' to compel a modern democracy to withdraw military forces from a group's domestic territory. 'Suicide terrorism', he wrote, 'is mainly a strategy to compel democracies to make concessions that will enable a community to achieve self-determination' (2005: 92). Referring to Al Qaeda, he acknowledged that religion matters for the group, 'but mainly in the context of national resistance to foreign occupation' (2005: 104).

From Pape's perspective, suicide bombing, far from being a sacramental—and hence a primarily expressive—act, is a political tactic adopted for its expediency. It is horrifying and cheap and, above all, lethal.[19] And, crucially, it is intended for a wider audience—the political elites and citizenry of the occupier. As can be seen, this is a thoroughly and unapologetically secular thesis (Friedman 2016; Cottee 2016b): suicide bombing is an overwhelmingly *political* phenomenon. It is about territory, not religion: 'Religion is rarely the root cause, although it is often used as a tool by terrorist organizations in recruiting and in other efforts in service of the broader strategic objective.' (Pape 2005: 2)

Pape's study provoked vigorous controversy, chiefly because it was taken to suggest that the blame for suicide bombing lies not with religion, but foreign occupations. More specifically, it was read as a scathing indictment of the 2003 American-led war in Iraq: far from inoculating Iraq from the threat of Al Qaeda and jihadism (Otterman 2003; Milbank and Pincus 2004), the war served as a rallying cry for a new generation of international jihadists and Iraq became the focal point of their activities. In addition to this, Pape's thesis fell right across the fault-line in a wider argument over the nature, meaning, and origins of jihadist militancy. This argument reached fever pitch just after the 9/11 attacks: was Al Qaeda an insurgency against western, and especially American, imperial aggression and overreach or was it simply a murderous religious cult?[20] The rise of ISIS has reignited this debate.

Assaf Moghadam (2008/09: 55) is especially critical of Pape's (2005: 115) characterization of Al Qaeda as 'a coalition of nationalist groups seeking to achieve local change in their home countries, not a truly transnational movement seeking to spread Islam or any other ideology to non-Islamic populations'. Religion, he insists, *contra* Pape, plays a central role in Al Qaeda's ideology and mission. By way of illustration, he quotes from a 2001 statement in which Bin Laden declared, 'This war is fundamentally religious . . . Under no circumstances should we forget this enmity between us

[19] 'The main reason that suicide terrorism is growing', he writes, 'is that terrorists have learned that it works' (2005: 61).

[20] For an overview of the key lines of controversy, see Cottee and Cushman (2008: 1–36).

and the infidels. For the enmity is based on creed' (Moghadam 2008/09: 55). Bruce Hoffman (2006: 82) concurs with Moghadam's overall assessment: 'the religious motive [for Al Qaeda] is overriding'.

Although Pape's study is primarily about suicide bombing and jihadist violence, it also raises deeper questions about the role of religion or ideology in social and political life. This, too, explains why it proved so controversial. According to James W. Jones (2008: 19), Pape's claims 'that religion is primarily a marker of cultural difference and a rhetorical device used by political leaders seem like a rather superficial understanding of the role of religion in human life'.

What would a more solid understanding of that role look like? At a minimum, it would need to take seriously the following three possibilities. First, it must acknowledge that religious belief is not merely an *ex post facto* rationalization for social action, but can serve as a motive in itself, *prompting* action. This type of social action would fall under the category of what Max Weber (1978: 25) calls 'value-rationality', where persons, 'regardless of possible costs to themselves, act to put into practice their convictions of what seems to them to be required by duty, honor, the pursuit of beauty, a religious call'.[21] These actions serve not as means to an end, but are ends in themselves, valued for their own sake. They are intrinsically meaningful for the person who undertakes them, and there is often a ritualistic and symbolic aspect to their performance that does not make obvious rational sense to external observers.

It is instructive to note that it is precisely this aspect of suicide bombing—its performative and ritualistic dimension—that Pape's critics take him to task for failing to address. Mark Juergensmeyer (2001: 124), for example, has argued, referring to the 9/11 attacks and other 'dramatic displays of power', that 'these creations of terror' are done not to achieve a strategic goal but to make a symbolic statement'. They are the climactic expression of a 'sacred drama' in which the perpetrators see themselves as heroic figures in a cosmic battle against evil. Suicide bombing, in short, is 'performance violence'. A similar theme runs through Ann Marie Oliver and Paul F. Steinberg's (2005: 72–3) haunting ethnography of Palestinian suicide bombing. 'You will never understand anything about the lure of martyrdom', they write, 'until you realize that someone who has decided to take that path as his own sees himself not only as an avenging Ninja, but also as something of a movie star, maybe even a sex symbol—a romantic figure at the very least, larger than life.' They also make the following observation about the ghosts in Hamas martyrdom videos: 'These guys knew they're going to die. Life in the meantime has become unbearable. They just want to get it over with. At the same time, we get the feeling that life has never seemed better to them—so intense, so exuberant, so full of meaning. Perhaps that's why they keep on smiling' (2005: 118). As Juergensmeyer (2001: 190) suggests, for those engaged in a holy struggle 'there may be something exhilarating, perhaps even rewarding, about the struggle itself'.

Second, a fully serious engagement with religion would need to address its role in legitimizing or concealing self-interest and political power (Fox 2000: 11–17). What looks like religiously inspired violence may in fact be secularly inspired violence under a religious cloak. As Charles Selengut (2008: 9) observes, individuals or groups may

[21] Scott Atran (2006: 138) describes these convictions as 'sacred values'. Selengut's preferred terminology (2008: 194) is 'sacred visions'.

'utilize religious sentiment in order to gain political or economic advantage, to punish a historical rival, or to maintain power over a subordinate group'. This can be seen in the current conflict in Syria, where ISIS has selectively used Islamic scripture to justify its sectarian killing and state-building project.

Juergensmeyer (2001: xi) has similarly argued that religion is 'crucial' for acts of religious violence, in that 'it gives moral justifications for killing and provides images of cosmic war that allow activists to believe that they are waging spiritual scenarios'. 'This does not mean that religion causes violence', he adds, 'nor does it mean that religious violence cannot, in some cases, be justified by other means. But it does mean that religion often provides the mores and symbols that make possible bloodshed—even catastrophic acts of terrorism.' In other words, religion, as well as prompting acts of violence and destruction, can also serve as a legitimizing device for these acts, enabling their occurrence by giving them legitimacy. In this sense, religious beliefs and doctrines, selectively mined and interpreted, provide, *contra* Ulmer (2012), 'a source of definitions and moral messages' that neutralize (Sykes and Matza 1957) and hence *encourage* 'interpersonal violence, stealing, dishonesty' etc.

Third, any serious attempt to address the role of religion in violence must acknowledge the enormous methodological difficulties of assigning political or religious motives to actors whose actions could plausibly be understood as manifesting either. As Stephen Holmes (2005: 132–3) observes, the problem 'is not so much that individuals with secretly secular purposes may feign religious goals to burnish their reputations for purity', but rather that 'one and the same decision could have been taken for either religious or secular reasons'. This makes it difficult 'to tell which motive played the dominant role'. By way of example, Holmes says that an Islamic husband, living in Germany, 'may lock his wife inside the house because he wants to be pious and thinks that female sequestration is what piety demands; but he may also do it to exercise arbitrary power and thereby compensate psychologically for feelings of impotence and passivity that afflict the rest of his miserable life'. According to one account, Islamic beliefs govern his behaviour, whereas according to the other, Islamic beliefs merely provide an acceptable pretext. 'So how', Holmes asks, 'can we decide which account is more persuasive in any particular case?' Or, as Oliver McTernan (2003: x) inquires, referring directly to the 9/11 attackers:

> Who can claim to understand fully the minds and motives of those young, educated and talented men, all of whom spent the last months of their lives meticulously planning the destruction of themselves and thousands of others? Who can claim with certainty that it was grievance, real or imagined, and not their profoundly held religious beliefs that motivated their use of commercial aircraft to commit mass murder on the working communities of New York and Washington?

There is no easy answer to this question. What can be certain, however, is that a polemical interest in assigning either a religious or a political motive to violence will do little to advance our interpretive efforts. Holmes, for his part, after a searching and balanced exploration of the available empirical evidence, concludes that a possible mix of personal frustration, political protest, and religious conviction may have driven Mohammad Atta, the lead hijacker of the 9/11 attacks. The broader significance of Holmes' analysis lies in his methodological approach, which is empirically driven and resistant to any bias either for or against religion.

CONCLUSION: THE NEW RELIGIOUS INTOLERANCE

'Anyone who lives in the early twenty-first century and follows the news', Michael Cook (2014: xi) writes, 'will have noticed that ancient religions play a significant part in modern politics'. They will also have noticed how insistently religion has become enmeshed in modern political violence. According to US State Department statistics, religion has been associated with more instances of public violence in the last 30 years than at any time in the last two hundred years (Juergensmeyer, Griego, and Soboslai 2015: 30). Indeed, as Charles Selengut (2008: 2) puts it, 'religious violence is among the most pressing and dangerous issues facing the world community'. It is also one of the most controversial, as the current debate over ISIS with which this chapter began clearly shows.

Martha Nussbaum (2012) has written of a 'new religious intolerance' in western democracies. For example, in Britain, in recent years, there has been an upsurge in religiously motivated hate crime, mainly targeted at Muslims. According to official statistics (Corcoran, Lader, and Smith 2015: 1), between 2012–13 and 2014–15, there were an estimated 222,000 hate crimes each year for the five monitored strands.[22] Of these, 38,000 were linked to victims' religion.[23] In the majority of cases, the religion in question was Islam (2015: 20). Other official sources suggest that hate-crimes against Muslims are on the increase. In September 2015 the London Metropolitan Police reported a 70.7 per cent increase in 'Islamophobic' offences between July 2014 and July 2015.[24] Given the mounting evidence of significant non-reporting of anti-Muslim hate crimes by victims, official statistics may provide an incomplete picture of the scale of anti-Muslim bigotry and hate crime.[25]

There is a substantial body of research documenting anti-Muslim hate, and the wider culture of suspicion and contempt in which it is rooted. This centres on the much-contested concept of Islamophobia (Halliday 1999), which has been defined by Neil Chakraborti and Irene Zempi (2012: 271) as 'a fear or hatred of Islam that translates into ideological and material forms of cultural racism against obvious markers of "Muslimness"'.[26]

Broadly speaking, there are two key themes running through this research: first, that Islamophobia, however defined, is widespread and growing across western

[22] The five monitored strands are: race, religion, sexual orientation, disability, and gender-identity.

[23] According to police statistics, offences linked to victims' religion increased by 43 per cent in 2014–15 (Corcoran, Lader, and Smith 2015: 5).

[24] A total of 816 offences were recorded in this period, up from 478 for the previous year: http://news.met.police.uk/news/met-s-response-to-rise-in-islamophobic-hate-crime-in-london-128144, accessed 9 April 2016. An Islamophobic offence is defined as 'any offence which is perceived to be Islamophobic by the victim or any other person, that is intended to impact upon those known or perceived to be Muslim': (http://www.met.police.uk/crimefigures/textonly_month.htm#c41, last accessed 9 April 2016).

[25] See especially, EU-MIDIS Data in Focus Report 2: Muslims, available at: http://fra.europa.eu/en/publication/2010/eu-midis-data-focus-report-2-muslims, last accessed 9 April 2016; and Githens-Mazer and Lambert (2010: 12).

[26] For a more expansive definition, see the Runnymede Trust (1997) report.

democratic countries; and second, that Islamophobia serves to fuel and legitimize abuses against Muslims, ranging from everyday acts of symbolic degradation to murderous violence. A connected theme is how Islamophobic discourse licenses repressive social control measures against Muslims (Githens-Mazer and Lambert 2010; Kundnani 2009). The picture that emerges is that Muslims are victims and that their communities are indeed 'under siege' (Zempi 2014: 115). Referring to the criminological literature on British Muslims, Julian Hargreaves (2015: 21) writes, 'Muslims are frequently depicted as a population blighted by personal crime victimization distinct in nature and extent from that faced by other minority groups in the United Kingdom'.

This broader context of bigotry and suspicion toward Muslims has made it difficult to speak openly and critically about Islam and its connection to crime and violence, especially for scholars whose progressive politics dissuades them form probing the dark side of what they see as an 'already embattled minority' (Buruma 2006: 33; Daveed Gartenstein-Ross 2012). It has also made it difficult to speak about hate crime *within* Muslim communities, and how differences in terms of gender, sexuality, ethnicity, and belief, including non-belief, may serve as the focal point for conflict and abuses among Muslims (Cottee 2015a; Butt 2009).

Criminology is of course no stranger to controversy, and Jock Young and his fellow 'left realists' did not hesitate to intervene in highly politicized debates over the black crime rate in the 1980s, imploring 'left idealists' to take street crime seriously (Cottee 2002). Yet there is no comparable willingness among criminologists to wade into the current controversies over religion, violence, and Islam.

Despite Cullen's (2012: 158) efforts, the idea of a 'criminology of religion' still remains undeveloped. 'Ever since its emergence in the industrialized, urbanized world of the mid-nineteenth century, criminology', David Garland and Richard Sparks (2000: 189) reflect, 'has been, or has sought to be, a contemporary, timely, worldly subject'. Yet its retreat from religion, or willingness to engage with it only as a 'pro-social' control variable or else as a badge of victimhood, would suggest a more imaginatively cramped and unworldly outlook. This is an invitation for a more open criminological engagement with one of the most important issues of our time.

SELECTED FURTHER READING

On the relationship between religious violence and the emotions, the following two texts are particularly illuminating: Juergensmeyer's *Terror in the Mind of God* (2001) and Stern's *Terror in the Name of God* (2003). On radical Islamic activism, Wiktorowicz's *Radical Islam Rising* (2005) is superb, fusing rich ethnographic research with social movement theory to provide a compelling account of Islamist radicalization in the West. On ISIS, see, notably, Stern and Berger's *ISIS: The State of Terror* (2015), and Atwan's *Islamic State: The Digital Caliphate* (2015). For a balanced account of the role of religion in international politics, see Appleby's *The Ambivalence of the Sacred* (2000). On the culture of religious violence, see Oliver and Steinberg's *The Road to Martyrs' Square: A Journey into the World of the Suicide Bomber* (2005). For a brilliantly lucid and insightful analysis of Islamic ethics, see Cook's *Forbidding Wrong in Islam: An Introduction* (2003).

REFERENCES

ABDELAZIZ, S. (2014), 'Death and desecration in Syria: Jihadist group "crucifies" bodies to send message', cnn.com, 2 May 2014, available at: http://edition.cnn.com/2014/05/01/world/meast/syria-bodies-crucifixions/, accessed 27 March 2016.

AKERS, R. L. (1998), *Social Learning and Social Structure*, Boston, MA: Northeastern University Press.

AKERS, R. L. (2010), 'Religion and Crime', *The Criminologist*, 35(6): 1–6.

AKYO, M. (2011), *Islam without Extremes: A Muslim Case for Liberty*, New York: W.W. Norton & Company.

AL-AWSAT, A. (2014), 'Egypt's Al-Azhar stops short of declaring ISIS apostates', aawsat.com, 13 December, available at: http://english.aawsat.com/2014/12/article55339431/egypts-al-azhar-stops-short-of-declaring-isis-apostates, accessed 27 March 2016.

ALDRIDGE, A. (2000), *Religion in the Contemporary World*, Cambridge: Polity.

APPLEBY, R. S. (2000), *The Ambivalence of the Sacred*, Rowman & Littlefield.

ARANGO, T. (2014a), 'Escaping Death in Northern Iraq', *The New York Times*, 3 September, available at: http://www.nytimes.com/2014/09/04/world/middleeast/surviving-isis-massacre-iraq-video.html, accessed 27 March 2016.

ARANGO, T. (2014b), 'A Boy in ISIS. A Suicide Vest. A Hope to Live', *The New York Times*, 26 December, available at: http://www.nytimes.com/2014/12/27/world/middleeast/syria-isis-recruits-teenagers-as-suicide-bombers.html, accessed 2 January 2016.

ATRAN, S. (2006), 'The Moral Logic and Growth of Suicide Terrorism', *The Washington Quarterly*, 29(2): 127–47.

ATWAN, A. (2015), *Islamic State: The Digital Caliphate*. London: Saqi.

BANDURA, A. (1990), 'Mechanisms of Moral Disengagement', in W. Reich (ed.), *Origins of Terrorism: Psychologies, Ideologies, Theologies, States of Mind*, Washington: The Woodrow Wilson Centre Press.

BECK, U. (2010), *A God of One's Own*, Cambridge: Polity.

BEIRNE, P. (1993), *Inventing Criminology*, Albany: SUNY.

BENNETT, W., DILULIO, J., Jr., and WALTERS, J. (1996), *Body Count*, New York: Simon and Schuster.

BERGEN, P. (2002), *Holy War, Inc: Inside The Secret World Of Osama Bin Laden*, New York: Touchstone.

BERGER, P. L. (1967), *The Sacred Canopy: Elements of a Sociological Theory of Religion*, New York: Doubleday.

BERGER, P. L. (ed.) (1999), *The Desecularization of the World: Resurgent Religion and World Politics*, Washington, DC: William B Eerdmans.

BLAKE, A. (2014), 'Obama says the Islamic State "is not Islamic". Americans disagree', *The Washington Post*, 11 September, available at: https://www.washingtonpost.com/news/the-fix/wp/2014/09/11/obama-says-the-islamic-state-is-not-islamic-americans-are-inclined-to-disagree/, accessed 27 March 2016.

BLOOM, M. (2015), 'Cubs of the Caliphate: The Children of ISIS', *Foreign Affairs*, 21 July, available at: https://www.foreignaffairs.com/articles/2015-07-21/cubs-caliphate, accessed 27 March 2016.

BLOOM, M., HORGAN, J., and WINTER, C. (2016), 'Depictions of Children and Youth in the Islamic State's Martyrdom Propaganda', *CTC Sentinel*, 18 February, available at: https://www.ctc.usma.edu/posts/depictions-of-children-and-youth-in-the-islamic-states-martyrdom-propaganda-2015-2016, accessed 27 March 2016.

BRANCH, T. (1989), *Parting the Waters: America in the King Years 1954-63*, New York: Simon & Schuster.

BROWNING, C. (1992), *Ordinary Men: Reserve Police Battalion 101 and the Final Solution in Poland*, New York: HarperCollins.

BRUCE, S. (ed.) (1992), *Religion and Modernization*, Oxford: Oxford University Press.

BRUCE, S. (2002), *God is Dead: Secularization in the West*, Oxford: Blackwell.

BURUMA, I. (2006), *Murder in Amsterdam: Liberal Europe, Islam, and the Limits of Tolerance*, New York: Penguin.

BUSH, G. W. (2001), '"Islam is Peace" Says President', georgewbush-whitehouse.archives.gov/, 17 September, available at: http://georgewbush-whitehouse.archives.gov/news/releases/2001/09/20010917-11.html, accessed 28 March 2016.

BUTT, R (2009), 'Muslims in Britain have zero tolerance of homosexuality, says poll', *The Guardian*, 7 May, available at: http://www.theguardian.com/uk/2009/may/07/muslims-britain-france-germany-homosexuality, accessed 9 April 2016.

CALLIMACHI, R. (2015), 'ISIS Enshrines a Theology of Rape', *The New York Times*, 13 August, available at: http://www.nytimes.com/2015/08/14/world/middleeast/isis-enshrines-a-theology-of-rape.html, accessed 27 March 2016.

CALLIMACHI, R. (2016), 'To Maintain Supply of Sex Slaves, ISIS Pushes Birth Control', *The New York Times*, 12 March, available at: http://www.nytimes.com/2016/03/13/world/middleeast/to-maintain-supply-of-sex-slaves-isis-pushes-birth-control.html, accessed 27 March 2016.

CHAKRABORTI, N. and ZEMPI, I. (2012), 'The Veil under Attack: Gendered Dimensions of Islamophobic Victimisation, *International Review of Victimology*, 18(3): 269–84.

CHULOV, M. (2014), 'ISIS insurgents seize control of Iraqi city of Mosul', *The Guardian*, 10 June, available at: http://www.theguardian.com/world/2014/jun/10/iraq-sunni-insurgents-islamic-militants-seize-control-mosul, accessed 27 March 2016.

CHULOV, M. (2015), 'First Ramadi, then Palmyra: Isis shows it can storm bastions of Syria and Iraq', *The Guardian*, 22 May, available at: http://www.theguardian.com/world/2015/may/21/

isis-palmyra-ramadi-advances-say-more-about-state-weakness-than-jihadi-strength, accessed 27 March 2016.

COHEN, S. (2001), *States of Denial: Knowing about Atrocities and Suffering*, Cambridge: Polity.

COLE, J. (2015a), 'How "Islamic" Is the Islamic State?', *The Nation*, 24 February, available at: http://www.thenation.com/article/how-islamic-islamic-state/, accessed 28 March 2016.

COLE, J. (2015b), 'Today's Top 7 Myths about Daesh/ISIL', juancole.com, 17 February available at: http://www.juancole.com/2015/02/todays-about-daesh.html, accessed 28 March 2016.

CONQUEST, R. (1990), *The Great Terror: A Reassessment*, New York: Oxford University Press.

CONQUEST, R. (1999), *Reflections on a Ravaged Century*, London: John Murray.

COOK, M. (2003), *Forbidding Wrong in Islam: An Introduction*, Cambridge: Cambridge University Press.

COOK, M. (2014), *Ancient Religions, Modern Politics: The Islamic Case in Comparative Perspective*, Princeton: Princeton University Press.

CORCORAN, H., LADER, D., and SMITH, K. (2015), *Hate Crime, England and Wales, 2014/15, Statistical Bulletin 05/15*, 13 October, available at: https://www.gov.uk/government/uploads/system/uploads/attachment_data/file/467366/hosb0515.pdf, accessed 9 April 2016.

COTTEE, S. (2002), 'Folk devils and moral panics: 'Left idealism' reconsidered', *Theoretical Criminology*, 6(4): 387–410.

COTTEE, S. (2013), 'Judging Offenders: The Moral Implications of Criminological Theories', in M. Cowburn *et al.* (eds), *Values in Criminology and Community Justice*, Bristol: Policy.

COTTEE, S. (2014a), 'The Pornography of Jihadism', *The Atlantic*, 12 September, available at: http://www.theatlantic.com/international/archive/2014/09/isis-jihadist-propaganda-videos-porn/380117/, accessed 27 March 2016.

COTTEE, S. (2014b), 'We Need To Talk About Mohammad: Criminology, Theistic Violence and the Murder of Theo Van Gogh', *British Journal of Criminology*, 54(6): 981–1001.

COTTEE, S. (2015a), *The Apostates: When Muslims Leave Islam*, London: Hurst.

COTTEE, S. (2015b), 'Flights From Islam', *The Pacific Standard*, 14 August, available at: http://www.psmag.com/books-and-culture/ex-muslims-face-an-uphill-battle, accessed 27 March 2016.

COTTEE, S. (2016a), 'Translating ISIL's atrocity porn', *The National Post*, 25 January, available at: http://news.nationalpost.com/full-comment/simon-cottee-translating-isils-atrocity-porn, accessed 27 March 2016.

COTTEE, S. (2016b), 'Is There Any "Logic" to Suicide Terrorism?', *The Atlantic*, 29 March, available at: http://www.theatlantic.com/international/archive/2016/03/suicide-terrorism-theories-logic/475821/, accessed 30 March 2016.

COTTEE, S. and CUSHMAN, T. (eds) (2008), *Christopher Hitchens and His Critics: Terror, Iraq, and the Left*, New York: New York University Press.

COWBURN, A. (2016), 'ISIS has killed at least 25 men in Syria suspected of being gay, group claims', *The Independent*, 5 January, available at: http://www.independent.co.uk/news/world/middle-east/isis-has-killed-at-least-25-men-in-syria-suspected-of-being-gay-group-claims-a6797636.html, accessed 27 March 2016.

CRAGUN, R. T. (2013), *What You Don't Know About Religion (But Should)*, Durham, NC: Pitchstone.

CRAGUN, R. T. and HAMMER, J. H. (2011), '"One Person's Apostate is Another Person's Convert": What Terminology Tells Us about Pro-Religious Hegemony in the Sociology of Religion', *Humanity & Society* 35(1–2): 149–75.

CULLEN, F. T. (2012), 'Toward a Criminology of Religion', in R. Rosenfeld, K. Quinet, and C. Garcia (eds), Papers From the American Society of Criminology 2010 Conference: 151–61, available at: http://www.baylorisr.org/wp-content/uploads/Jang-and-Johnson_Religion-and-Crime1.pdf, accessed 4 April 2016.

CVIKLOVÁ, L. (2012), 'Advancement of human rights standards for LGBT people through the perspective of international human rights law', *Journal of Comparative Research in Anthropology and Sociology*, 3(2): 45–60.

DAWKINS, R. (2006), *The God Delusion*, London: Random House.

DOBBELAERE, K. (1981), 'Secularization: A Multi-Dimensional Concept', *Current Sociology*, 29(2): 1–216.

DOWNES, D. (1979), 'Praxis Makes Perfect', in D. Downes and P. Rock (eds), *Deviant Interpretations: Problems in Criminological Theory*, London: Martin Robertson.

DOWNES, D. (1988), 'The Sociology of Crime and Social Control in Britain, 1960-87', in P. Rock (ed.), *A History of British Criminology*, Oxford: Oxford University Press.

EDMONDS, R. (2015), 'The Best-read Digital Story of 2015? It's The Atlantic's "What ISIS Really Wants" ', pointer.org, 31 December, available at: http://www.poynter.org/2015/the-best-read-digital-story-of-2015-its-the-atlantics-what-isis-really-wants/390382/, accessed 26 March 2016.

ELTAHAWY, M. (2015), *Headscarves and Hymens: Why the Middle East Needs a Sexual Revolution*, New York: Farrar, Straus and Giroux.

FISH, M. S. (2011), *Are Muslims Distinctive?: A Look at the Evidence*, New York: Oxford University Press.

FOX, J. (2000), 'The Ethnic-Religious Nexus: The Impact of Religion on Ethnic Conflict', *Civil Wars*, 3(3): 1–22.

FRIEDMAN, U. (2016), 'The "Strategic Logic" of Suicide Bombing', *The Atlantic*, 23 March, available at: http://www.theatlantic.com/international/archive/2016/03/brussels-attacks-terrorism-isis/474858/, accessed 6 April 2016.

FRIEDMANN, Y. (2003), *Tolerance and Coercion in Islam: Interfaith Relations in the Muslim Tradition*, New York: Cambridge University Press.

GARLAND, D. and SPARKS, R. (2000), 'Criminology, social theory and the challenge of our times', *British Journal of Criminology*, 40(2): 189–204.

Gartenstein-Ross, D. (2012), 'A Blind Spot', defenddemocracy.org, 2 November, available at: http://www.defenddemocracy.org/media-hit/a-blind-spot/, accessed 11 May 2016.

Giddens, A. (1984), *The Constitution of Society: Outline of the Theory of Structuration*, Cambridge: Polity.

Girard, R. (1972), *Violence and the Sacred*, P. Gregory, (trans.), Baltimore: Johns Hopkins University Press.

Githens-Mazer, J. and Lambert, R. (2010), *Islamophobia and Anti-Muslim Hate Crime: A London Case Study*, Exeter: European Muslim Research Centre, available at: https://lemosandcrane.co.uk/resources/Islamophobia_and_Anti-Muslim_Hate_Crime.pdf, accessed 9 April 2016.

Goldhagen, D. (1996), *Hitler's Willing Executioners: Ordinary Germans and the Final Solution*, New York: Knopf.

Gottfredson, M. and Hirschi, T. (1990), *A General Theory of Crime*, Stanford: Stanford University Press.

Gouldner, A. (1970), *The Coming Crisis of Western Sociology*, New York: Harper.

Habermas, J. (2005), 'Equal Treatment of Cultures and the Limits of Postmodern Liberalism', *Journal of Political Philosophy*, 13(1): 1–28.

Hafez, M, (2010), 'Tactics, *Takfir*, and Anti-Muslim Violence', in A. Moghadam and B. Fishman (eds), *Self-Inflicted Wounds: Debates and Divisions within al-Qa'ida and its Periphery*, Washington: Harmony Project, West Point.

Hall, J. R. (2013), 'Religion and violence from a sociological perspective', in M. Juergensmeyer, M. Kitt, and M. Jerryson (eds), *The Oxford Handbook of Religion and Violence*, Oxford: Oxford University Press.

Halliday, F. (1999), '"Islamophobia' reconsidered', *Ethnic and Racial Studies*, 22(5): 892–902.

Hamid, S. and McCants, W. (2014), 'John Kerry won't call the Islamic State by its name anymore. Why that's not a good idea', *The Washington Post*, 29 December, available at: https://www.washingtonpost.com/posteverything/wp/2014/12/29/john-kerry-is-calling-the-islamic-state-by-the-wrong-name-and-its-helping-the-islamic-state/, accessed 27 March 2016.

Hamm, M. (2009), 'Prison Islam in the Age of Sacred Terror', *British Journal of Criminology*, 49(5): 667–85.

Hargreaves, J. (2015), 'Half a Story? Missing Perspectives in the Criminological Accounts of British Muslim Communities, Crime and the Criminal Justice System', *British Journal of Criminology*, 55(1), 19–38.

Harris, S. (2004), *The End of Faith: Religion, Terror and the Future of Reason*, London: Free Press.

Hasan, M. (2015), 'How Islamic is Islamic State?', *New Statesman*, 10 March, available at: http://www.newstatesman.com/world-affairs/2015/03/mehdi-hasan-how-islamic-islamic-state, accessed 27 March 2016.

Hegghammer, T. (2013), 'Syria's Foreign Fighters', *Foreign Policy*, 9 December, available at: http://foreignpolicy.com/2013/12/09/syrias-foreign-fighters/, accessed 27 March 2016.

Hitchens, C. (2007), *God is Not Great: How Religion Poisons Everything*, New York: Twelve.

Hoffman, B. (1995), 'Holy Terror', *Studies in Conflict & Terrorism*, 18(4): 271–84.

Hoffman, B. (2006), *Inside Terrorism*, New York: Columbia University Press.

Holmes, S. (2005), 'Al-Qaeda, September 11, 2001', in D. Gambetta (ed.), *Making Sense of Suicide Missions*, New York: Oxford University Press.

Horgan, J. and Bloom, M. (2015), 'This Is How the Islamic State Manufactures Child Militants', *Vice*, 8 July, available at: https://news.vice.com/article/this-is-how-the-islamic-state-manufactures-child-militants, accessed 27 March 2016.

Human Rights Watch (2014), 'Iraq: Forced Marriage, Conversion for Yezidis', hrw.org, 11 October, available at: https://www.hrw.org/news/2014/10/11/iraq-forced-marriage-conversion-yezidis, accessed 27 March 2016.

Humphreys, L. (1975), *Tearoom Trade: Impersonal Sex in Public Places*, Chicago: Aldine.

Jeffries, S. (2015), 'Isis's destruction of Palmyra', *The Guardian*, 2 September, available at: http://www.theguardian.com/world/2015/sep/02/isis-destruction-of-palmyra-syria-heart-been-ripped-out-of-the-city, accessed 27 March 2016.

Johnson, B. R. and Jang, S. J. (2012), 'Crime and Religion: Assessing the Role of the Faith Factor', Papers from the American Society of Criminology 2010 Conference: 117–49, available at: http://www.baylorisr.org/wp-content/uploads/Jang-and-Johnson_Religion-and-Crime1.pdf, accessed 4 April 2016.

Jones, J. (2008), *Blood That Cries Out From the Earth: The Psychology of Religious Terrorism*, New York: Oxford University Press.

Juergensmeyer, M. (2001), *Terror in the Mind of God*, Berkeley, CA: University of California Press.

Juergensmeyer, M., Griego, D., and Soboslai, J. (2015), *God in the Tumult of the Global Square: Religion in Global Civil Society*, Berkeley, CA: University of California Press.

Junger, M. and Polder, W. (1993), 'Religiosity, Religious Climate and Delinquency Among Ethnic Groups in the Netherlands', *British Journal of Criminology*, 33(3): 416–35.

Kaplan, M. (2016), 'ISIS Not Islamic? John Kerry Calls Terror Group "Apostates"', *International Business Times*, 3 February, available at: http://www.ibtimes.com/isis-not-islamic-john-kerry-calls-terror-group-apostates-2291791, accessed 27 March 2016.

Killough, A. (2014), 'Strong reaction to Obama statement: "ISIL is not Islamic"', CNN, 11 September, available at: http://edition.cnn.com/2014/09/10/politics/obama-isil-not-islamic/, accessed 27 March 2016.

Kundnani, A. (2009), *Spooked! How Not To Prevent Violent Extremism*, London: Institute of Race Relations, available at: http://www.irr.org.uk/publications/issues/spooked-how-not-to-prevent-violent-extremism/, accessed 6 January 2017.

LILLY, J., CULLEN, F., and BALL, R. (2007), *Criminological Theory: Context and Consequences*, 4th edn, Thousand Oaks, CA: Sage.

LISTER, C. (2016), 'Jihadi Rivalry: The Islamic State Challenges al-Qaida', Brookings Doha Center Analysis Paper Number 16, January, available at: http://www.brookings.edu/~/media/research/files/papers/2016/01/27-the-islamic-state-challenges-alqaida-lister/en-jihadi-rivalry.pdf, accessed 27 March 2016.

MAHABIR, C. (2012), 'Allah's Outlaws: The Jamaat al Muslimeen of Trinidad and Tobago', *British Journal of Criminology*, 53(1): 59–73.

MARK, M. (2015), 'ISIS, ISIL, Daesh Or Islamic State? After Paris Terror Attacks, French And U.S. Officials Debate Name Of Militant Group', *The International Business Times*, 14 November, available at: http://www.ibtimes.com/isis-isil-daesh-or-islamic-state-after-paris-terror-attacks-french-us-officials-2185029, accessed 27 March 2016.

MCCANTS, W. (2016), 'Barack Obama and Donald Trump are both wrong about Islam: For better and worse, the faith is what people make of it', *New York Daily News*, 13 March, available at: http://www.nydailynews.com/opinion/mccants-obama-trump-wrong-islam-article-1.2561804, accessed 2 April 2016.

MCCOY, T. (2014), 'ISIS, beheadings and the success of horrifying violence', *The Washington Post*, 13 June, available at: https://www.washingtonpost.com/news/morning-mix/wp/2014/06/13/isis-beheadings-and-the-success-of-horrifying-violence/, accessed 27 March 2016.

MCDUFFEE, A. (2014), 'ISIS Is Now Bragging About Enslaving Women and Children', *The Atlantic*, 13 October, available at: http://www.theatlantic.com/international/archive/2014/10/isis-confirms-and-justifies-enslaving-yazidis-in-new-magazine-article/381394/, accessed 27 March 2016.

MCTERNAN, O. (2003), *Violence in God's Name: Religion in an Age of Conflict*, London: Darton, Longman and Todd.

MARTINSON, J. (2015), 'BBC to review use of "Islamic State" after MPs protest against term', *The Guardian*, 29 June, available at: http://www.theguardian.com/media/2015/jun/29/bbc-to-review-use-of-islamic-state-after-mps-protest-against-term, accessed 27 March 2016.

MILBANK, D. and PINCUS, W. (2004), 'As Rationales for War Erode, Issue of Blame Looms Large', *The Washington Post*, 10 July, available at: http://www.washingtonpost.com/wp-dyn/articles/A39833-2004Jul9.html, accessed 6 April 2016.

MOGHADAM, A. (2008/09), 'Motives for Martyrdom: Al-Qaida, Salafi Jihad, and the Spread of Suicide Attacks', *International Security*, 33(3): 46–78.

NAILI, H. (2014), 'Iraq Women's Shelter Responds to Growing Crisis', Women's eNews, 19 June, available at: http://womensenews.org/2014/06/iraq-womens-shelter-responds-growing-crisis/#.U7J7p0JdXih, accessed 27 March 2016.

NELKEN, D. (ed.) (1994), *The Futures of Criminology*, London: Sage.

NORRIS, P. and INGLEHART, R. (2011), *Sacred and Secular: Religion and Politics Worldwide*, 2nd edn, Cambridge: Cambridge University Press.

NUSSBAUM, M. C. (2012), *The New Religious Intolerance*, Cambridge, MA: Harvard University Press.

OLIVER, A. M. and STEINBERG, P. F. (2005), *The Road to Martyrs' Square: A Journey into the World of the Suicide Bomber*, New York: Oxford University Press

OTTERMAN, S. (2003), 'Iraq: America's Rationale for War', 21 April, Council on Foreign Relations, available at: http://www.cfr.org/iraq/iraq-americas-rationale-war/p7693#p11, accessed 6 April 2016.

PAPE, R. (2003), 'The Strategic Logic of Suicide Terrorism', *American Political Science Review*, 97(3), available at: http://www.columbia.edu/itc/journalism/stille/Politics%20Fall%202007/readings%20weeks%206-7/Strategic%20Logic%20of%20Suicide%20Missions.pdf, accessed 30 March 2016.

PAPE, R. (2005), *Dying to Win: The Strategic Logic of Suicide Terrorism*, New York: Random House.

PETERS, R. and DE VRIES, G. (1976–7), 'Apostasy in Islam', *Die Welt des Islams*, 17.

RADZINOWICZ, L. (1966), *Ideology and Crime*, London: Heinemann.

REMNICK, D. (2014), 'Going the Distance: On and off the road with Barack Obama', *The New Yorker*, 27 January, available at: http://www.newyorker.com/magazine/2014/01/27/going-the-distance-david-remnick, accessed 27 March 2016; http://www.nybooks.com/articles/2015/09/24/slavery-isis-rules/, accessed 7 April 2016.

ROY, O. (2005), 'La Crise de l'État Laïque et les Nouvelles Formes de Religiosité', *Esprit*, 312(2) (February): 27–44, available at: http://www.diplomatie.gouv.fr/en/IMG/pdf/0101Roy_gb.pdf, accessed 30 March 2016.

ROY, O. (2010), *Holy Ignorance: When Religion and Culture Part Ways*, R. Schwartz (trans.), London: Hurst.

SAMPSON, R. and LAUB, J. (1993), *Crime in the Making*, Cambridge, MA: Harvard University Press.

SELENGUT, C. (2008), *Sacred Fury*, Maryland: Rowman and Littlefield.

SCHLEIFER, T. (2016), 'Donald Trump: "I think Islam hates us." ', CNN, 10 March, available at http://edition.cnn.com/2016/03/09/politics/donald-trump-islam-hates-us/, accessed 2 April 2016.

SPARKS, R. (1999), 'Review of Adventures in Criminology', *British Journal of Criminology*, 39(3): 452–5.

STARK. R. and FINKE, R. (2000), *Acts of Faith: Explaining the Human Side of Religion*, Berkeley, CA: University of California Press.

STERN, J. (2003), *Terror in the Name of God*, New York: HarperCollins.

STERN, J. and BERGER, J. M. (2015), *ISIS: The State of Terror*, New York: Harper Collins.

SYKES, G. and MATZA, D. (1957), 'Techniques of Neutralization: A Theory of Delinquency', *American Sociological Review*, 22(6), 664–70.

THE QURAN (2004) (trans.) M. A. S. Abdel Haleem, New York: Oxford University Press.

THE RUNNYMEDE TRUST, (1997), *Islamophobia: A Challenge for Us All*, London: The Runnymede Trust.

THE SOUFAN GROUP (2015), 'Foreign Fighters: An Updated Assessment of the Flow of Foreign Fighters into Syria and Iraq', 2 December, available at: http://soufangroup.com/wp-content/uploads/2015/12/TSG_ForeignFightersUpdate3.pdf, accessed 26 March 2016.

TURNER, B. (1992), *Max Weber: From History to Modernity*, Routledge: London.

ULMER, J. T. (2012), 'Religion as a Unique Cultural Influence on Crime and Delinquency', Papers from the American Society of Criminology 2010 Conference: 163–71, available at: http://www.baylorisr.org/wp-content/uploads/Jang-and-Johnson_Religion-and-Crime1.pdf, accessed 4 April 2016.

VAN GENNEP, A. (1960), *The Rites of Passage*, M. Vizedom and G. Caffee (trans.), Chicago: The University of Chicago Press.

VOLD, G. B., BERNARD, T. J., and SNIPES, J. B. (2002), *Theoretical Criminology*, 5th edn, Oxford: Oxford University Press.

WATTS, C. (2015), 'ISIS and al Qaeda Race to the Bottom', *Foreign Affairs*, 23 November, available at: https://www.foreignaffairs.com/articles/2015-11-23/isis-and-al-qaeda-race-bottom, accessed 27 March 2016.

WEBER, M. (1978), *Economy and Society*, G. Roth and C. Wittich (eds), Berkeley: University of California Press.

WIKTOROWICZ, Q. (2005), *Radical Islam Rising*, London: Rowman and Littlefield.

WILSON, B. (1966), *Religion in Secular Society*, London: Penguin.

WOOD, G. (2014), 'What ISIS's Leader Really Wants', *New Republic*, 1 September, available at: https://newrepublic.com/article/119259/isis-history-islamic-states-new-caliphate-syria-and-iraq, accessed 27 March 2016.

WOOD, G. (2015), 'What ISIS Really Wants', *The Atlantic*, March, available at: http://www.theatlantic.com/magazine/archive/2015/03/what-isis-really-wants/384980/, accessed 27 March 2016.

WRIGHT, R. (2015), 'The Clash of Civilizations That Isn't', *The New Yorker*, 25 February, available at: http://www.newyorker.com/news/news-desk/clash-civilizations-isnt, accessed 29 March 2016.

WRIGHT MILLS, C. (1959), *The Sociological Imagination*, Oxford: Oxford University Press.

ZEMPI, I. (2014), 'Responding to the Needs of Victims of Islamophobia', in N. Chakraborti and J. Garland (eds), *Responding to Hate Crime*, Bristol: Policy.

22

CHARACTER, CIRCUMSTANCES, AND THE CAUSES OF CRIME: TOWARDS AN ANALYTICAL CRIMINOLOGY

Per-Olof H. Wikström

If they are true to their calling, all criminologists have to be interested in morality.

(Anthony Bottoms (2002))

INTRODUCTION

This chapter will discuss and advocate the advantages of analysing and explaining crime as moral actions (i.e. actions guided by what is the right or wrong thing to do) within an analytical criminology framework. That people's acts of crime have something to do with their 'character' (their personal morals and ability to exercise self-control) and something to do with the 'circumstances' they experience in their daily lives (the moral contexts of the opportunities and frictions they encounter) seems a reasonable proposition. After all, crimes are breaches of rules of conduct about what is right or wrong to do (or not do) in particular circumstances.

Arguably, the causes of crime are situational. People express their character in actions in response to the circumstances of the settings in which they take part and, therefore, the explanation of why acts of crime happen ultimately depends on understanding the role of the interaction between 'character' and 'circumstances' in crime causation. Specifically, it may be argued that *people commit acts of crime because they find them acceptable in the circumstances (and there is no relevant and strong enough deterrent) or that they fail to act in accordance with their own personal morals (i.e. fail to exercise self-control) in circumstances when externally pressured to act otherwise.*

Arguing that the causes of crime are situational does not mean that cultural and structural and development factors and processes are unimportant in the analysis of crime causation. Quite the contrary, but they are best analysed as 'causes of the causes'. Such factors and processes do not directly explain what moves people to commit particular acts of crime, but help explain (1) why particular interactions between kinds of people ('characters') and kinds of places ('circumstances') occur creating the criminogenic situations in which acts of crime may happen, (2) why people develop certain and different crime propensities (based on their personal morals and ability to exercise self-control), and why environments develop specific and different criminogenic inducements (depending on the moral contexts of the opportunities and frictions they provide). Specifically it may be argued that *differences in people's crime involvement depend on processes of social and self selection that place some people in criminogenic settings more often than others, and processes of emergence that make some people more crime prone than others (personal emergence) and some settings more criminogenic than others (social emergence).*

Analysing acts of crime as moral actions does not (necessarily) entail a 'moralistic' approach to the study of crime and its causes. Assuming that people's actions are guided by their personal morals and ability to exercise self-control and the moral contexts in which they take part does not imply any assumptions, for example, that all existing laws and prevailing moral norms (necessarily) represent some higher universal moral order. The question of why we have certain laws and common moral norms is a separate question from that of whether people's actions are essentially guided by their personal morals and the moral contexts in which they take part. For example, one reason why people may find it acceptable to violate a particular law may be that they disagree with or even find the particular law immoral. Some laws are more contested on moral grounds than others.

This chapter is organized in three sections. The first provides background by outlining some common problems of current criminological theorizing and research, such as the lack of a shared definition of crime, the poor integration of knowledge about the role of people and places in crime causation, the frequent confusion of causes and correlates, and the lack of an adequate action theory, and proposes a more analytical criminology as the remedy. The second section introduces and outlines Situational Action Theory (SAT), a general, dynamic and mechanism-based theory about crime and its causes. SAT advocates that the explanation of acts of crime should centre around three basic kinds of mechanisms: the perception-choice process (the action mechanism linking people and places to explain why crime happens); processes of selection (linking macro and micro features to explain how particular people and place interactions occur); and processes of emergence (addressing development and change to explain how people and environments become as they are). The final section briefly discusses the main implications for policy and prevention.

CENTRAL PROBLEMS IN CRIMINOLOGICAL THEORIZING AND RESEARCH

> Criminology risks being a field of study in which many ideas are developed and all are chosen—in which all theories have equal claim to legitimacy and in which only the most highly specialized scholars can separate the theoretical wheat from the chaff.
>
> (Frank Cullen *et al.* (2008))

> Criminology lacks an accepted and general theoretical structure for guiding integrative inquiry into the causes of crime.
>
> (Per-Olof H. Wikström and Robert J. Sampson (2006))

Criminology is a multifaceted discipline. It is the study of crime and its causes, and scholars from all kinds of academic backgrounds (e.g. biologists, psychologists, and sociologists) engage in criminological study. This is one of the most exciting features of criminology—its potential for multidisciplinary inquiry—but also the feature that creates most of its problems—its lack of multidisciplinarity. Criminological knowledge and key insights are largely fragmented and poorly integrated (e.g. Bernard 1990; Liska *et al.* 1989; Tittle 1995). The advancement of criminological theory and research are particularly hampered by the lack of a clear and shared definition of crime, poor integration of knowledge about the role of people and places (environments) in crime causation, the frequent confusion of causes and correlates, and the lack of an adequate action theory. Arguably, what is needed to take the discipline forward is a theoretical framework for the integrative study of crime and its causes that can better organize current knowledge and more effectively guide future research.

THE IMPORTANCE OF CLEARLY DEFINING WHAT A THEORY OF CRIME CAUSATION SHOULD EXPLAIN

Many criminological theories and empirical research studies fail to clearly define what it is they propose to explain, if they define it at all. This is a crucial omission because an explanation has to be an explanation of something (we can have effects without specifying their causes, but not causes without specifying their effects). Without clearly defining what it is we try to explain (what crime is) it is difficult to assess the relevance and importance of current knowledge and develop an in-depth understanding of what causes crime. Of those theories and studies which do define crime, the definitions may vary significantly (compare, e.g., Gottfredson and Hirschi 1990: 15; Felson 2006: 35) and it has been observed that there are 'questions whether the dependent variable is the same in different theories' (Akers 1989: 25).

There are many different kinds of actions that constitute acts of crime (e.g. rape, insider trading, shoplifting, assault, and tax evasion). What is crime in one jurisdiction (e.g. country) may not be crime in another (e.g. acts of homosexuality) and what is crime in the same jurisdiction may change over time (e.g. parents physically punishing their children). These kinds of observations have made some scholars despair about the possibility of developing a general theory of crime causation (e.g. Wilson and Herrnstein 1985: 21) and others to suggest that explanations of crime should be crime-specific (e.g. Cornish and Clarke 2008: 26). Objections to the possibility of a general theory are clearly stronger if the focus is on explaining the performances of the many different kinds of actions that constitute crime but less problematic if the focus is on explaining the rule-breaking that is common to all crimes.

There is little question that the concept of crime has to do with morality. Morality is about what we 'ought to do and not to do' (Hare 1999: 9). The law is a set of formalized moral rules aimed at influencing behaviour. A moral rule is a rule of conduct that prescribes what is the right or wrong thing to do (or not do) in particular circumstances. A crime is breaking a rule of conduct stated in law. To explain crime is thus to explain *why* people breach rules of conduct stated in law. In principle, there is no difference between rules of conduct stated in law and rules of conduct more generally; 'The legal norm /. . . / is merely one of the rules of conduct, of the same nature as all other rules of conduct' (Ehrlich [1936] 2008). A theory of crime causation may therefore be regarded as a special case of a more general theory of the grounds for human action.

THE IMPORTANCE OF INTEGRATING KNOWLEDGE ABOUT THE ROLE OF PEOPLE AND PLACES (ENVIRONMENTS) IN CRIME CAUSATION

Some people are more involved in acts of crime than others, and some places (environments) have more crime than others. These are two key stable criminological findings. Crime is typically strongly concentrated in the population, that is, few commit a lot of the crimes (e.g. Piquero, Farrington, and Blumstein 2007: 17–19; Wikström 1990; Wolfgang, Figlio, and Sellin 1972). Many kinds of acts of crime are also strongly concentrated in certain places (and times), often referred to as crime hot spots (e.g. Sherman, Gartin, and Buerger 1989; Weisburd, Groff, and Yang 2012; Wikström 1991). Figure 22.1, with data from the PADS+longitudinal study in Peterborough (for details

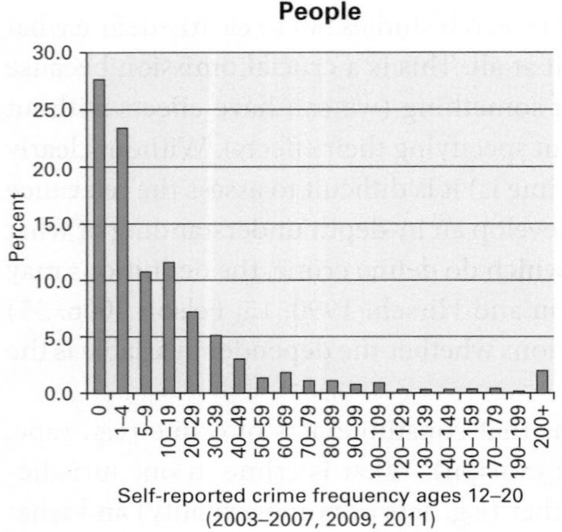

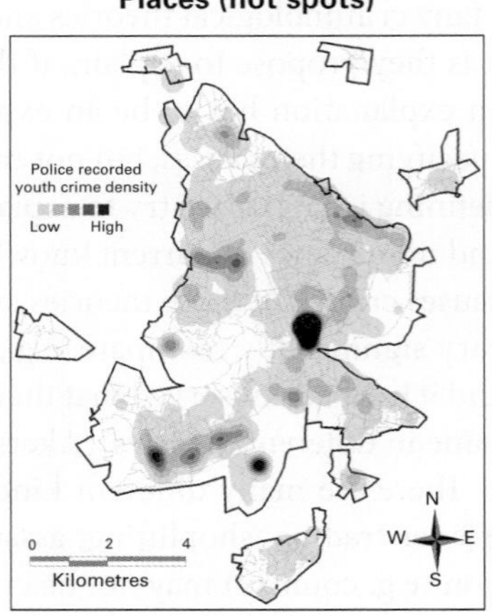

Figure 22.1 The distribution of self-reported crime in the population and the concentration of police recorded crime in space. Young people in Peterborough.

Source: BREAKING RULES: THE SOCIAL AND SITUATIONAL DYNAMICS OF YOUNG PEOPLE'S URBAN CRIME by Per-Olof Wikström, Dietrich Oberwittler, Kyle Treiber, and Beth Hardie (2013): Fig. 5.3 (p. 225). By permission of Oxford University Press, USA (www.oup.com).

of the study, see Wikström, Oberwittler, Treiber, and Hardie (2012: 44-106)), illustrates the highly skewed distribution of self-reported crime in the population (e.g. 5 per cent are responsible for 55 per cent of the crimes) and the strong spatial concentration of acts of police recorded crimes among young offenders (so called, crime hot spots). The question is why do people and places vary in their crimes?

People are different. They have different characteristics and experiences. It would be surprising if personal differences would have no bearing on people's propensities to engage in acts of crime or particular acts of crime (e.g. Lahey and Waldman 2003:79). The key question is rather which of people's many different characteristics and experiences are relevant for their crime propensity? Research demonstrates hundreds of personal characteristics and experiences (e.g. Ellis *et al.* 2009; Farrington 1992: 256) that are correlated with crime involvement (from single genetic polymorphisms to features of neighbourhoods), most of which are likely to have no causal relevance (a topic I shall return to and develop below). Given that acts of crime are moral actions, a strong but reasonable assumption is that people's 'character'—their personal morals (value-based rules of conduct) and ability to exercise self-control (to act in accordance with their own personal morals)—is a crucial factor as regards their crime propensity.

Places (environments) are different. They provide different opportunities and create different frictions. They also provide different moral contexts (moral norms and their enforcement) of the opportunities and frictions they present. For example, some places create a high amount of frictions in a moral context that tends to encourage (or, at least, not discourage) the use of violence as a response to provocations, while other places have low levels of frictions and a moral context that strongly discourage the use of violence. It would be surprising if such differences would not influence the criminogeneity of places and thus have a significant influence on the actions of people exposed to the particular place, with relevance for how much and what kinds of acts of crime will occur at the place. 'Collective efficacy' (Sampson *et al.* 1997) and 'code of the streets' (Anderson 1999) are examples of concepts that capture the importance of places' moral context in the explanation of why crime happens.

People act, but they do not act in a social vacuum. It is therefore vital to understand the role of the person–environment interaction for human action (e.g. Lewin 1936; Magnusson 1988). For example, *different* people may react differently in the same circumstance (e.g. being called a loser by a stranger in a pub) and the *same* person may react differently in different circumstances (being called a loser by his mother at home or by a stranger in a pub). It is a reasonable assumption that some people may be more crime prone than others, and that some places may be more criminogenic than others, and, crucially, that the combination of a crime prone person and a criminogenic setting is particularly conducive to acts of crime happening.

Criminological theory and research typically focus on understanding the role of differences between people (personal characteristics and experiences) *or* differences between places (environmental features) in crime causation. In fact, it is, broadly speaking, possible to talk about person-oriented and place-oriented approaches in the study of crime and its causes. While each of these research traditions undoubtedly harbour important insights and knowledge about crime and its causes the roles of people and places are rarely analysed and studied within a unified framework. In fact, there is often tension, and even conflict, between those advocating people-oriented and place-oriented approaches, sometimes to the effect that they ignore or strongly downplay the importance of the other (e.g. Wilcox *et al.* 2003).

The problem of how to jointly account for personal and environmental factors in the explanation of crime has been with us for a long time, and continues to be a central problem for criminological theory (e.g. Reiss 1986). The person-oriented and place-oriented traditions clearly need better integration. Arguably, one cannot be adequately understood without the other. For example, people may commit more crime because they are more crime prone and/or more exposed to criminogenic places and places may have more crimes because they are more criminogenic and/or have more crime prone people among their visitors. The lack of integration of insights from and joined up study of the two traditions may be regarded as one of the major obstacles for the advancement of knowledge about crime and its causes. True integrative and situational approaches are rare (Birkbeck and LaFree 1993). Most 'situational' explanations of crime confuse the 'immediate environment' and 'situation' and are essentially environmental rather than situational explanations (Wikström and Treiber 2015). We need dynamic theory to account for, and dynamic methodology to test, the role of the people-and-place interaction in crime causation.

THE IMPORTANCE OF NOT CONFUSING CORRELATION AND CAUSATION

When analysing and studying the causes of crime it is obviously important to think about what constitutes a cause and what can be a cause of acts of crime. People do not commit acts of crimes because they are male, 17 years old, Lithuanian, or black. Attributes like sex, age, ethnicity, and race cannot be causes of crime, or of anything else for that matter (Holland 1986: Bunge 2001: 70). Neither are people moved to steal a car, beat up a stranger, engage in insider trading, pollute a river, or blow up a tube train, because they, for example, live in council housing, have a poor educational record, had a mother who smoked in their infancy, or a slow resting heart rate. While factors like these (often referred to as risk factors) may be more or less (generally less) good predictors of people's crime involvement, they are not causes of their acts of crime. At best they are markers or symptoms (factors correlated with true causes or their effects). However, some may be somewhat implicated in analyses of the 'causes of the causes' (see further below).

Much empirical research in criminology is done within a risk factor approach. Risk factors are predictors (correlates that precede the outcome). It is well-known that predictors are not the same as causes. In fact, David Farrington has stressed that 'a major problem with the risk factor paradigm is to determine which risk factors are causes and which are merely markers or correlated with causes' (2000: 7). Despite this warning, risk factors are often treated in the public debate and among some academics as if they always have causal efficacy (which they typically lack) and recommendations are sometimes made that the best way to achieve effective prevention is to reduce the risk factors (which obviously will not work for the many risk factors that lack causal efficacy). When addressing the causes of crime, it is imperative to clearly differentiate between predictors and causes (causes are always predictors, but predictors are not necessarily causes). Strong prediction is helpful when the task is to identify 'at risk groups of people' or 'at risk places', but, again, it is crucial not to confuse risk factors and causes, because the factors that predict 'at risk' for crime may not be the factors that cause crime. The classic example of the importance of differentiating between predictors and causes in the philosophical literature on causation is the barometer. The barometer is a very good predictor, but clearly not a cause of, the weather (e.g. Woodward 2003: 16).

Arguably, the causes of crime are situational. People do what they do because of who they are and the settings in which they take part. Causes may be defined as 'triggers of processes that produce an effect' (generally on the problem of causation, see, e.g., Bunge 2004; Psillos 2002; Salmon 1998). Crimes are actions that break rules of conduct stated in law and hence causes of crime are triggers of processes that result in an action breaking a rule of conduct (stated in law). When we analyse human action, triggers are typically the result of the intersection and interaction of people (propensities) and places (environmental inducements), against the backdrop of motivations (temptations or provocations), that set in motion a (mental) process that results in an action. When analysing human action this process is active and guiding. Depending on the nature of the situation, the relevant mental processes may be more or less deterministic, ranging from fully habitual (automated) to fully deliberative ('free will' exercised within the constraints of perceived action alternatives).

Causes may be differentiated from 'causes of the causes'. 'The background is frequently cited, what people do being traced back to their childhood, to a strict or slack education, often to poverty, to abuse, to bad parenting. Matters of that sort cannot be ignored, but their bearing is indirect. The background at most predisposes' (Schick 1997: 15). Causes of the causes refers to processes further back in a causal chain such as psychosocial processes which help form and shape a person's crime propensities or socio-ecological processes that mould places' criminogeneity.

It is crucial in the analysis of crime causation to clearly differentiate the role of causes and 'causes of the causes'. When we analyse and study the causes of crime we focus on the situational factors and processes that move people to action. When we analyse and study the 'causes of the causes' we are concerned with the contemporaneous selection processes that create the circumstances (people–place interactions) that may move people to crime and the historical processes of emergence responsible for people's development of different crime propensities (person emergence) and that places and the broader environment develop different criminogenic influences (social emergence). Many of the insights about the 'causes of the causes' will draw upon knowledge from non-criminological research, such as studies into processes of segregation and how these may influence the creation of criminogenic interactions between people and places, or research into human development and its relevance to people's development of crime propensities.

THE IMPORTANCE OF HAVING AN ADEQUATE ACTION THEORY

At the heart of a proper explanation of why crime happens is an adequate action theory. An action theory is a theory that specifies what moves people to action.[1] Action theories generally presume that people have agency—powers to make things happen intentionally—and are primarily concerned with explicating the role of the process of

[1] For a detailed discussion of the role of action theory in the explanation of crime, see Wikström (2006).

choice in human action. An adequate action theory helps us link people (propensities), places (inducements), and action choices. It also provide a foundation for assessing what cultural, structural, and historical factors and processes (as causes of the causes) are relevant and important in the explanation of human actions such as acts of crime. Understanding on what grounds people see action alternatives and make action choices is crucial for the explanation of why people follow or break rules of conduct (stated in law).

A central problem in criminological theorizing is that most criminological theories lack a developed and explicit theory of action (Wikström 2004). Without such a theory it is difficult to effectively explain how proposed personal characteristics and experiences (e.g. weak social bonds) or environmental features (e.g. weak collective efficacy) are supposed to transform into acts of crime. When criminological theories do have some conception of the grounds for action they typically allude to some version of rational choice theory; actors are seen as self-interested (egoistic) and rational (utilitarian) (e.g. Agnew 2014). However, rarely is the role of rational choice in the theory explicated in any detail (e.g. Hirschi 1986: 109–11). For example, Marcus Felson states that Routine Activity Theory 'implied a decisional offender, but did not make the decision process explicit' (2008: 73).

Rational choice theory,[2] arguably, has limits when it comes to the explanation of human action, such as acts of crime. The process of choice is typically treated as deliberative (weighing pros and cons) and future and outcome-oriented, thereby, ignoring the importance of more automated (habitual) choice-processes that commonly guide human action. Rational choice theory also typically assumes that people's actions are driven by self-interest, although this is not a necessary assumption of a rational choice perspective as pointed out by Elster (2007: 193). However, human action is not only about optimizing personal advantage but may also be driven by prosocial motives and commitments. Without denying that people make rational choices (when they deliberate) and that self-interest, at times, play a role in crime causation, it is questionable whether rational choice theory provides a good foundation for criminological theory (for a discussion, see, e.g., Wikström and Treiber 2015).

TOWARDS AN ANALYTICAL CRIMINOLOGY

An analytical criminology focuses on answering *why* and *how* questions and aims to explicate the key basic causal processes involved in crime causation. Specifically, it seeks to identify the key situational, developmental, and social processes (mechanisms) involved in crime causation. It aspires to move beyond mapping out correlations and making predictions to establishing causation and, crucially, providing explanation.

Analytical criminology takes a realist approach (e.g. M. Bunge 2006) to the study of crime and its causes. Two important assumptions of realism are that:

1. the world exists independent of our theorizing about it (e.g. in science we do not invent causes, we discover them), and

[2] On rational choice theory generally as applied in the social sciences, see Wittek, Snijders, and Nee (2013). See McCarthy (2002) on the use (and lack of use) of [rational] choice theory within criminology.

2. many important explanatory processes are unobservable, or partly unobservable (i.e. scientific knowledge is not only what is observable).

From a realist perspective simply establishing causation (i.e. demonstrating that manipulating X will change Y in predicted ways) is not enough to provide a scientific explanation; one also has to demonstrate through what process the alleged cause/s make/s the effect happen. A proper theory of crime causation provides explanation by suggesting plausible causal processes (mechanisms) that link the putative cause/s and the effect and thus tells us *how* the outcome is produced, and thereby answers the question of *why* people engage in acts of crime (see, e.g. Wikström 2011).

Analytical criminology advocates theory-driven empirical research, arguing that empirical study without guiding theory (at worst) risks just being the charting of (mostly causally irrelevant) correlations, but also that theorizing without supporting empirical research (at its worst) risks just being (inadequate) guesswork. It stresses the importance of developing integrative theory with clear, empirically testable implications.

Empirical research can establish correlations, allow us to make predictions, and sometimes demonstrate causal dependency through manipulation (experimentation). However, only theory can provide explanation by answering why questions (why does X cause Y) and thereby specify how the studied outcome is produced by the putative cause (e.g. Bunge 1999: 51). An adequate scientific explanation may be defined as a theory (hypothesis) that:

1. is consistent with relevant (statistical) correlates and predictions,
2. is, as far as possible, supported by manipulations (experiments) which demonstrate relevant changes in hypothesized causal relationships, and, crucially,
3. provides explanation by suggesting plausible causal processes (mechanisms) that link putative causes to the effect and thereby tells us how the outcome is produced.

DYNAMIC THEORY: SITUATIONAL ACTION THEORY (SAT)

> Human beings must be treated as agents acting according to rules.
>
> (Rom Harré and Paul Secord (1972))

Why do people drive while drunk? Why do they bully their workmates? Why do they download music without paying? Why do they vandalize others' fences? Why do they take office stationery home for private use? Why do they starve their animals? Why do they avoid paying taxes? Why do they drive a lorry into a crowd of people? Why do they racially abuse other people? Why do they park in spaces reserved for disabled people? Why do they engage in insider trading? Why do they beat up their partners? Why do they burgle others' houses? Why do they claim benefits to which they know they are not entitled? Why do they sexually molest young children? Why do they detonate bombs in tube stations? Why do they take things from shops without paying? Why do they embezzle others' savings? Why do they headbutt strangers? Why do they knowingly pollute rivers with toxic chemicals?

Can all these actions be explained in the same way? The bold suggested answer is 'yes'. They all represent acts that break rules of conduct; if we can explain why people follow and break rules of conduct (identify the basic factors and processes involved) we will have an explanation that is applicable to all these different acts. If we can accomplish this we can also explain why people with different attributes and from different backgrounds are differently involved in different acts of crime, and why people's crime involvement may change over time. *Situational Action Theory* (SAT)—a general, dynamic, and mechanism-based theory—proposes to do just that (e.g. Wikström 2004, 2005, 2006, 2010; Wikström, Oberwittler, Treiber, and Hardie 2012: 3–43).

SAT was developed to address common shortcomings in criminological theorizing (as previously discussed) and provide an integrative analytical framework for the study of crime and its causes which has clear testable implications (e.g. Wikström, Oberwittler, Treiber, and Hardie 2012). It analyses crime as moral actions (i.e. actions guided by rules about what is the right or wrong thing to do in particular circumstances). Explaining crime as moral action has many advantages. It makes a general theory possible because the definition covers the essence of what crime is and what all crimes (at all places in all times) have in common, that is, rule-breaking. It helps delimit what personal and environmental factors and processes may be causally relevant by emphasizing the primary importance of factors and processes that directly, or indirectly, affect whether people follow or break rules of conduct.

BASIC ASSUMPTIONS—ANALYSING CRIME AS RULE-GUIDED ACTIONS

The basic assumptions of Situational Action Theory are that:

1. People are essentially rule-guided creatures[3] and society (social order) is based on (more or less) shared rules of conduct (moral norms). To be rule-guided means to express one's desires (wants), and respond to frictions, within the context of rule-guided choice.
2. People are the source of their actions; they perceive, choose, and execute their actions, but
3. the causes of their actions are situational; people's particular perception of action alternatives, process of choice, and execution of action are triggered and guided by the relevant input from the person–environment interaction.

Analysing human action as rule-guided choices in response to motivators (temptations, provocations) avoids the risk of developing an overly deterministic view of human behaviour (or an 'oversocialized conception of man', as Wrong [1961] puts it). Guidance means guidance. People may decide to follow or ignore particular

[3] For a review of evidence from cognitive neuroscience about how we use rules to select actions, see Bunge 2004. On the importance of rule-guidance for human behaviour, see also Bunge and Wallis 2008; Lyons, Young, and Keil 2007; and Wellmans and Miller 2008.

rule-guidance. Rule-guidance may be more or less automated, allowing for elements of predictability ('automaticity') and deliberation ('free will') in action choices. Rules of conduct (internal, external) may in some circumstances be in conflict, making the rule-guidance less straightforward and action choices more difficult, promoting stronger deliberation. People may be unaware of or misunderstand particular moral norms (and even laws) with obvious implications for their action choices.

THE SITUATIONAL MECHANISM—THE PERCEPTION-CHOICE PROCESS

The *situational mechanism* that links people and their immediate environments to their actions is the perception-choice process (see Wikström 2006: 76–84). This is the basic causal process that explains human action. The perception-choice process is initiated and guided by relevant aspects of the interaction between a person and the immediate environment (the part of the environment that person at that particular moment can experience with his or her senses). The perception-choice process is crucial for the action outcome because *perception* (the selective information we get from our senses) links the person to the environment and *choice* (the formation of the intention to act in one way or another) links the person to his or her actions. What action takes place depends on what kind of person he or she is and what kind of setting he or she is taking part in. An act of crime will happen if a person sees crime as an acceptable action alternative in the circumstances (and there is no relevant and strong enough deterrence) or fails to act in accordance with his or her own personal morals (i.e. fails to exercise self-control) in a circumstance when externally pressurized to act otherwise. The key steps of the action process as applied to acts of crime are summarized in Figure 22.2.

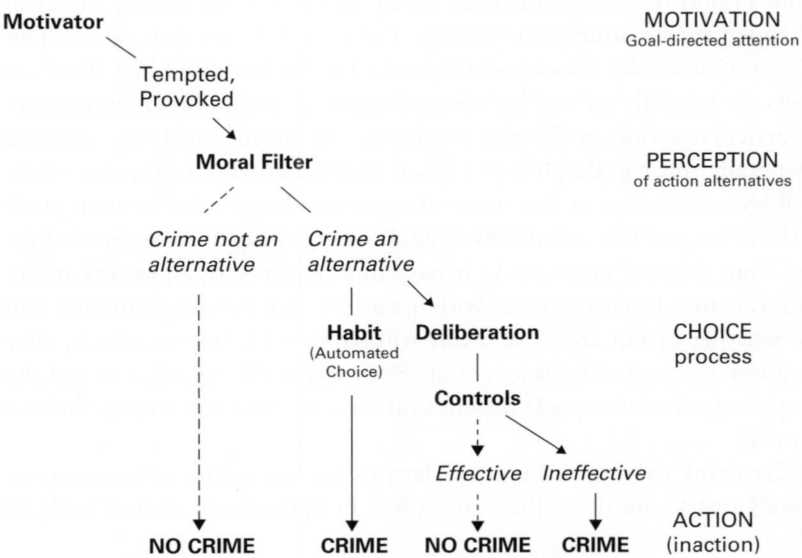

Figure 22.2 Overview of the key steps in the perception-choice process

Motivation and rule-guidance drive the action process. *Motivation* (goal-directed attention), which initiates the action process, is an outcome of the interaction between a person's preferences, commitments, or sensitivities *and* the opportunities or frictions presented by the setting (immediate environment) in which he or she is taking part. If a person has the opportunity to satisfy a desire (want, need) or fulfil a commitment, a temptation is formed. If a person encounters a friction (an unwanted external interference) that causes anger or annoyance, this may create provocation. People vary in their preferences and commitments and therefore what kinds of opportunities may create temptation will vary. People also vary in their sensitivities and therefore what kinds of frictions may create provocation will vary.

Motivation is a necessary but not sufficient situational factor in the explanation of action. The moral filter governs what action alternatives (if any) a person perceives. The *moral filter* is the moral-rule induced selective perception of viable action alternatives in relation to a particular motivator (temptation or provocation). People bring their personal morals (value-based rules of conduct) to particular moral contexts (settings' perceived shared rules of conduct), and the interaction between these personal morals and moral contexts create the moral filter that distils what actions (if any) are seen as action alternatives in response to a motivator, and, crucially, whether any of the alternatives involve an act of crime. If crime is not an alternative there will be no crime. Importantly, the process of choice plays no part in this first stage of the action process; perception of action alternatives precedes the process of choice because choice requires alternatives even if there is only one salient alternative that is automatically chosen (as is the case in habitual action processes).

However, if a person sees an act of crime as an action alternative in response to a motivator the process of choice will be crucial for the outcome. The process of choice may be primarily either automated—expressing a habit—or rational deliberative—weighing the pros and cons of different alternatives (on dual thought processes see, e.g. Evans and Frankish 2009; Kahneman 2003). In the case of habits, an act of crime will happen (or be attempted) because the actor will see only one salient alternative (even if he or she is aware in the back of his or her mind that there are others). Habits are typically created by repeated exposure to similar circumstances in which a particular action in the past produced a recurrent satisfying outcome (on habits generally see, e.g. Bargh 1997; Wood and Quinn 2005). In cases where the actor deliberates, whether or not an act of crime will happen (or be attempted) depends on the efficacy of the *controls* involved. If seeing an act of crime as an alternative results from external pressures to behave in a certain way, a person's ability of self-control (i.e. to act in accordance with his or her own personal morals[4]) will be crucial to whether or not an act of crime will happen. In cases in which, after some deliberation, the person finds an act of crime acceptable, whether or not the crime will happen (or be attempted) depends on the relevance and strength of any deterrent present.

Let's consider drink driving through the lens of this suggested action process. A person attends a party. She drove there so she has the opportunity to drive home in

[4] The conception of self-control in SAT is different from that presented in Gottfredson and Hirschi's *General Theory of Crime* (1990). For a discussion of this difference, see Wikström and Treiber (2007).

her own car. During the evening she gets drunk (well over the legal limit, and she is aware of this). According to SAT there are four ideal typical ways in which the action process may play out. *Case one*. The actor believes it is totally unacceptable to drive while drunk. She believes the other party goers hold the same view. Knowing that she is drunk she only considers taking the bus or a cab home but not driving herself. In this case there will be no crime of drink driving because she doesn't see driving herself as an option. It is not on her radar. *Case two*. The actor has gone to a lot of parties before and successfully driven home while over the legal limit so she doesn't see this as a big problem. In fact, this is the only option she considers, so she drives home. She will commit an act of drink driving crime out of habit. She does as she normally does in such circumstances without giving it much thought. *Case three*. The actor thinks it is really not acceptable to drive home when drunk but other partygoers try to talk her in to doing so (saying things like 'It's no big deal', 'I have done it many times without a problem'). She deliberates over the alternatives. Whether or not she will drive home depends on her ability to act in accordance with her own personal morals (that drink driving is wrong) and withstand the 'peer pressure' (that it is OK). It is a question of her ability to exercise self-control. *Case four*. In the final case the actor may think that it is no big deal to drive home when she is a bit drunk but other partygoers insist it is wrong and that she should take a cab. They may even threaten to call the police if she decides to drive. Whether or not she will drive home drunk depends on how relevant and serious she perceives the views and threats from other partygoers. Will they disapprove of her if she drives home in her car, and does she care? Will they really call the police? The extent to which she will be deterred by the others' reactions will determine whether or not she will drive home drunk. If this is a group of people whose opinion she strongly cares about this may be enough to prevent her driving drunk. Or if not, her action may be prevented if she takes the threat of calling the police seriously.

THE CAUSES OF THE CAUSES: SELECTION PROCESSES

In the conclusion of her seminal work 'Social Sources of Delinquency', Ruth Kornhauser argues for the need 'to search for the root causes of delinquency in social structure and situation' (1978: 253). However, the role of situations conducive to acts of crime, and their dependency on social structure (and culture), have not figured much in subsequent criminology.[5]

Situational analysis explains why crime happens by detailing the interactions and action mechanisms involved in crime causation. However, it does not tell us much about how criminogenic situations (interactions) come about, and the role of structural

[5] With the exception of Routine Activity Theory (Cohen and Felson 1979), which suggests that criminogenic convergences (seen as convergences of likely offenders and suitable targets in the absence of capable guardians) is an outcome of people's routine activities (e.g. recurrent spatial and temporal patterns in family, work, and leisure activities) because 'illegal activities must feed upon other activities' (ibid.: 590). However, RAT is rather undeveloped; it really does not explain how the proposed convergences cause acts of crime (other than at times alluding to rational choices) and does not give much detail about *how* routine activities create criminogenic convergences other than referring to the dependence of illegal activities on legal activities (for a discussion of RAT and SAT, see Wikström and Treiber 2015).

and cultural factors in this. To link macro properties of society (e.g. patterns of segregation) with micro events (e.g. criminogenic situations) we need to understand the mechanisms by which the former affects the latter.

Situational Action Theory proposes that understanding what connects 'structure' and 'culture' to criminogenic situations requires an understanding of *processes of selection*, how processes of social and self-selection place certain kinds of people ('characters') in certain kinds of places ('circumstances') and thereby creates particular kinds of interactions, some of which may be criminogenic. For example, processes that introduce people who sees violence as an acceptable response to frictions to settings with high levels of frictions. Selection processes explain why criminogenic interactions arise (where and when and at what rate) but also why some people (and categories of people) are more exposed to criminogenic settings than others. As drivers of differential exposure, they help us understand and raise important questions about the role of factors such as inequality, integration, and segregation (as causes of the causes) in crime causation.

Social selection refers to the social forces (dependent on general systems of formal and informal rules and the differential distribution of personal and institutional resources in a particular jurisdiction) that enable (encourage or compel) or restrict (discourage or bar) particular kinds of people from taking part in particular kinds of time- and place-based activities. The content of the cultural ('rules-based') and structural ('resource-based') social forces driving social selection will vary between jurisdictions (countries, regions, cities) and hence the outcome of such processes (the production of particular kinds of people and kinds of place interactions) will also vary; some will produce more criminogenic interactions than others (i.e. interactions between crime prone people and criminogenic settings).

However, people are not purely at the mercy of forces of social selection; their exposure to particular kinds of settings also depends on self-selection. *Self-selection* refers to the agency and preference-based choices people can make to attend particular time and place-based activities within the constraints of the forces of social selection (e.g. people do not always have the resources, or are allowed, to take part in some activities they prefer). People vary in their agency (their power to influence what settings they take part in) depending on their age[6] and their access to human capital (e.g. skills), financial capital (e.g. money) and social capital (i.e. resourceful relationships). People also vary in their activity preferences, largely as a result of their previous life-history.

The dynamic of social and self-selection processes is crucial for understanding people's exposure, and differential exposure, to criminogenic settings. People will differ in how they actively and successfully manage their own life within the constraints of forces of social selection. A good illustration of this with criminological relevance is the discussion by Anthony Bottoms (2013) about the role of self-selection (although he doesn't use this concept) in the process of desistance; when persistent offenders aim to quit a 'life of crime', some actively, and more and less successfully, try to avoid taking part in settings that may get them into further difficulties.

[6] People start life with little or no agency but develop their capacity to influence what settings they take part in throughout their lives, but especially during childhood and adolescence (albeit at different rates).

THE CAUSES OF THE CAUSES: PROCESSES OF EMERGENCE

While situational analysis helps identify which are the important personal and environmental factors involved in crime causation, and analysis of contemporaneous selection processes helps explain how criminogenic situations (interactions) are created, what still remains to be addressed is the question of why people come to have certain crime propensities and why places come to have certain criminogenic features (and why some jurisdictions produce more crime prone people and criminogenic settings than others). According to Situational Action Theory this is essentially a question of understanding (historical) processes of emergence (i.e. the process of how something becomes as it is).

SAT asserts that the development of and changes in people's crime propensities largely depend on psychosocial processes of *personal emergence*, particularly processes of moral education and cognitive nurturing which are relevant to people's crime propensities (their law-relevant personal morals and abilities to exercise self-control; see further Wikström and Treiber 2017). These processes form and change how people see their action alternatives and make choices when confronted with specific motivators in particular circumstances, including whether they see and choose to commit acts of crime. This is consistent with Urie Bronfenbrenner's definition of individual development as 'a lasting change in the way a person perceives and deals with his environment' (1979: 3).

Moral education refers to the learning and evaluation process by which people actively come to adopt and change value-based rules of conduct about what it is right or wrong to do in particular circumstances. The key proposed mechanisms through which this happens are instruction, observation, and trial and error. People are told rules of conduct and when they apply, they observe others' adherence to rules of conduct and the consequences of any breaches, and they try out and test what happens when they follow or break particular rules of conduct. However, people are not simply passive recipients of moral experiences, but actively evaluate (and re-evaluate) those experiences in the context of their previously acquired personal morals and cognitive capabilities. Social institutions like the family and education system play a particularly important role in moral education, especially in the formative years.

Cognitive nurturing refers to the experiential processes (limited by a person's neurological constitution and baseline capacities) which positively influence neurocognitive capacities and their expression. A person's cognitive capacities (executive functions[7]) are important for his or her ability to exercise self-control, but may also be relevant for his or her ability to acquire, understand, and apply rules of conduct (particularly if he or she has cognitive deficiencies). Again, the workings of family and educational institutions, especially in the formative years, are of prime importance for this process (perhaps even more so than for moral education).

SAT suggests that places' criminogeneity largely depends on socioecological processes of *social emergence*, processes of population and activity differentiation of

[7] Executive capabilities are higher order cognitive functions implicated in attention, inhibition, and the activation, evaluation, organization, and integration of (internally and externally derived) action relevant information (Morgan and Lilienfeld 2000). Specifically on the Neuroscientific Basis of Situational Action Theory, see Treiber (2011).

relevance to the occurrence of (time and) place-based motivators and law-relevant moral norms and their enforcement. The moral norms of a setting and their level of enforcement depend on the activities that take place within them and, related to that, the kind and mix of people present. Some activities are more likely than others to encourage the breaking of particular rules of conduct, and some people are more likely than others to hold views that support the breaking of particular rules of conduct. The extent to which a place is criminogenic depends thus on its people and activity mix. The emergence of particular patterns of people and place interactions (with consequences for the production of criminogenic interactions) is a result of historical processes of population and activity spatial and temporal differentiation (e.g. dependent on market forces and planning and technological advances, for example in transport).

TOWARDS A COMPREHENSIVE ANALYSIS OF CRIME CAUSATION

Situational analysis is arguably the core of the study of crime and its causes (Wikström and Treiber 2015). However, to give a comprehensive account of the question of crime causation, situational analyses need to be complemented with analyses and, particularly, empirical investigations of how contemporaneous processes of social and self-selection and past processes of social and person emergence are implicated (as the 'causes of the causes') in the creation of the situations that cause acts of crime (Table 22.1). We need to know much more about how processes of social and self-selection interact in creating criminogenic situations, and their dependency on broader cultural (rule-based) and structural (resource-based) conditions. We also need to know much more about how processes of personal emergence (through moral education and cognitive nurturing) influence the development and change of people's crime propensities, and how processes of social emergence (through people and activity differentiation) help create criminogenic places (settings).These are the main challenges criminology has to meet to advance knowledge about crime and its causes and to provide a more solid foundation for the creation of effective crime policy and prevention.

IMPLICATIONS FOR CRIME PREVENTION POLICY

> . . . current prevention theory and practice reflects a vigorous but undisciplined marketplace of competing ideas, often without sound foundations in either theory or research . . .
>
> (Peter Greenwood (2006))

The fragmentation and poor integration of knowledge that characterizes the study of crime and its causes are unsurprisingly reflected in crime prevention policies and interventions. Not only are there many different and conflicting ideas about why people commit crime, but also about the best policies and interventions to tackle the problem of crime. There is also no shared definition of crime prevention. The dominance of risk-focused prevention in crime prevention policy has not helped counter its fragmentation. Arguably, there is a need for policy and prevention to move away from a risk-factor approach (targeting predictors that often lack causal efficacy) towards an approach that tackles the key causal processes that lead to crime.

Situational Action Theory proposes that there are three basic kinds of processes involved in crime causation (Table 22.1) and suggests that focusing on developing policies and interventions that address these processes may help organize crime prevention efforts and increase their efficacy.

The following basic arguments can be made based on a SAT-founded analytical approach to crime prevention (for a detailed discussion of these arguments and their foundations, see Wikström and Treiber 2016):

1. Effective crime prevention results from policies and measures that successfully target causes or causal processes involved in crime causation.
2. Effective crime prevention requires interventions to successfully change the input into people's perception-choice process by changing (a) people's crime propensities, by changing their law-relevant personal morals and ability to exercise self-control, or (b) environments' criminogenic inducements, by changing the moral context of motivators or (c) that change people's exposure to criminogenic environments.
3. Changing people's crime propensities is a question of promoting people's perception of crime (or particular kinds of crimes) as unacceptable behaviour and strengthening their ability to withstand external incitements to break the law through relevant moral education and cognitive nurturing.
4. Changing places' (environments') criminogenic inducements is a question of making them less encouraging (or more deterring) of acts of crime through interventions that change the moral context of their motivators (i.e. change or counter moral norms that encourage acts of crime as a response to opportunities and frictions).

Table 22.1 Situational Action Theory: Key basic suggested causal mechanisms and their role in crime causation

Main mechanisms	Role in crime causation
Causes *Perception-choice*	*Action mechanism. Links the interaction between people and their environment to their actions* (explains why crime happens)
Causes of the causes *Selection* (social and self-selection)	*Places particular people in particular settings and thereby creates particular kinds of interactions to which people's actions are a reaction* (explains why criminogenic situations appear and why certain groups of people have a higher exposure to criminogenic settings than others)
Emergence (person and social emergence)	*Psychosocial processes that create specific personal propensities (person emergence) and socioecological processes that create particular place-based environmental inducements (social emergence)* (explains why people come to vary in their crime propensities and why places come to vary in their criminogeneity)

5. Changing people's exposure to criminogenic settings is a question of influencing processes of social and self-selection with the aim of reducing the prevalence of criminogenic interactions. This may involve anything from broad policies targeting selection processes arising from inequality and segregation which affect the criminogenic convergence of people and activities, to more specific interventions aimed at altering or counteracting people's personal preferences which encourage them to take part in criminogenic settings.

A comprehensive crime prevention policy involves long- and short-term measures that focus on altering or counteracting key criminogenic processes and their consequences. Effectively influencing processes of selection and emergence is not an easy task, but if successful it may have a major impact on crime. In fact, it is plausible that major societal changes in levels of crime—such as the heavily discussed 'crime drop'—are consequences of significant changes in relevant processes of social and personal emergence and/or processes of social and self-selection impacting on people's crime propensities and criminogenic exposure.

The major challenge for crime prevention policy is thus to develop and effectively implement policies that successfully influence people's crime propensities and criminogenic exposure by altering or counteracting relevant psychosocial and socio-ecological processes of emergence and relevant processes of social and self-selection selection. A better understanding of how processes of emergence and selection help create criminogenic situations may also help politicians and policy-makers better foresee any consequences of their policy decisions. Many social and economic policies (not just those particularly concerned with the problem of crime) may have short- and long-term effects on levels of crime as an unintended consequence of their impact on crime relevant processes of emergence and selection.

CONCLUSION

In this chapter I have advocated the advantages of analysing and explaining crime as moral actions within an analytical criminology framework. I have reviewed some common key problems of criminological theorizing and research I believe such an approach may help to overcome. I have presented Situational Action Theory as an example of a general, dynamic, and mechanism-based theory that adopts an analytical criminology approach and briefly also discussed its general implications for crime prevention policy. I have particular suggested that to advance knowledge about crime and its causes we need to better understand and research how the generation of criminogenic situations are dependent on processes of selection and emergence and their changes.

Arguably, thinking about crime and crime prevention in terms of moral actions and the basic causal process that generates such actions also have other advantages. It draws attention to that how we view crime, and particular kinds of crime, and how we view those committing crime, and particular acts of crime, has to do with morality (views on what we ought and not ought to do). It further draws the attention to that crime policy and prevention has to do with morality—since the aim is to influence people to behave in preferred ways—and therefore involve moral considerations. It may encourage us to think about why we have the laws we have, why some laws have been abolished and others appeared, and to what extent they are grounded in human nature and the requirements for a functioning social order.

SELECTED FURTHER READING

For readers interested in the empirical foundation and tests of the core assumptions of Situational Action Theory (SAT), the best single source is Wikström *et al.*'s *Breaking Rules: The Social and Situational Dynamics of Young People's Urban Crime* (2012).

For those interested in an application of SAT to the role of social disadvantage in crime causation, a good source is Wikström and Treiber's paper *Social Disadvantage and Crime: A Criminological Puzzle*, which was published open access in the *American Behavioral Scientist* in 2016.

A comprehensive introduction to the problem of causation can be found in Psillos' *Causation and Explanation* (2002). Bunge's paper *How Does it Work? The Search for Explanatory Mechanisms* (2004) gives a brilliant case for the importance of mechanistic explanation.

REFERENCES

AGNEW, R. (2014), 'Social concern and crime: Moving beyond the assumption of simple self-interest', *Criminology*, 52(1): 1–32.

AKERS, R. L. (1989), 'A Social Behaviorist's Perspective on Integration of Theories on Crime and Deviance', in S. F. Messner, M. D. Krohn, and A. E. Liska (eds), *Theoretical Integration in the Study of Deviance and Crime: Problems and prospects*, Albany: State University of New York Press.

ANDERSON E. (1999), *Code of the Street: Decency, Violence, and the Moral Life of the Inner City*, New York: W. W. Norton and Company.

BARGH, J. (1997), 'The automaticity of everyday life', in J. Bargh and R. Wyer (eds), *The Automaticity of Everyday Life. Advances in Social Cognition, Volume 10*, Mahwah, NJ: Lawrence Erlbaum.

BERNARD, T. J. (1990), 'Twenty years of testing theories: What have we learned and why?', *Journal of Research in Crime and Delinquency*, 27(4): 325–47.

BIRKBECK, C. and LAFREE, G. (1993), 'The situational analysis of crime and deviance', *Annual Review of Sociology*, 19: 113–37.

BOTTOMS, A. E. (2002), 'Morality, Crime, Compliance and Public Policy', in A. E. Bottoms and M. Tonry (eds), *Ideology, Crime and Criminal Justice: A Symposium in Honour of Sir Leon Radzinowicz*, Cullompton: Willan.

BOTTOMS, A. E. (2013), 'Learning from Odysseus: Self-Applied Situational Crime Prevention as an Aid to Compliance', in P. Ugwudike and P. Raynor (eds), *What Works in Offender Compliance*, New York: Palgrave Macmillan.

BRONFENBRENNER, U. (1979), *The Ecology of Human Development*, Cambridge, MA: Harvard University Press.

BUNGE, M. (1999), *The Sociology-Philosophy Connection*, New Brunswick: Transaction.

BUNGE, M. (2001), 'Scientific Realism', in M. Mahner (ed.), *Selected Essays by Mario Bunge*, Amherst, NY: Prometheus.

BUNGE, M. (2004), 'How Does it Work? The Search for Explanatory Mechanisms', *Philosophy of the Social Sciences*, 34(2):182–210.

BUNGE, M. (2006), *Chasing reality: Strife over realism*, Toronto: University of Toronto Press.

BUNGE, S. A. (2004), 'How we use rules to select actions: A review of evidence from cognitive neuroscience', *Cognitive, Affective and Behavioral Neuroscience*, 4(4): 564–79.

BUNGE, S. A. and WALLIS, D. (2008), *Neuroscience of Rule-Guided Behavior*, Oxford: Oxford University Press.

CORNISH, D. and CLARKE, R. (2008), 'The rational choice perspective', in R. Wortley and L. Mazerolle (eds), *Environmental Criminology and Crime Analysis*, Abingdon: Routledge.

CULLEN, F. T., WRIGHT, J. P., and BLEVINS, K. R. (2008), *Taking Stock: The Status of Criminological Theory, Advances in Criminological Theory*, vol. 15, New Brunswick: Transaction.

Ehrlich, E. ([1936] 2008), *Fundamental Principles of the Sociology of Law*, New Brunswick: Transaction.

Ellis, L., Beaver, K., and Wright, J. (2009), *Handbook of Crime Correlates*, San Diego: Academic.

Elster, J. (2007), *Explaining Social Behavior: More Nuts and Bolts For the Social Sciences*, Cambridge: Cambridge University Press.

Evans, J. and Frankish, K. (2009), *In Two Minds: Dual Processes and Beyond*, Oxford: Oxford University Press.

Farrington, D. P. (1992), 'Explaining the beginning, progress and ending of antisocial behavior from birth to adulthood', in J. McCord (ed.), *Facts, Frameworks, and Forecasts, Advances in Criminological Theory, vol. 13*, New Brunswick: Transaction.

Felson, M. (2006), *Crime and Nature*, Thousand Oaks: Sage.

Felson, M. (2008), 'Routine activity approach', in R. Wortley and L. Mazerolle (eds), *Environmental Criminology and Crime Analysis*, Abingdon: Routledge.

Gottfredson, M. and Hirschi, T. (1990), *A General Theory of Crime*, Stanford: Stanford University Press.

Greenwood, P. W. (2006), *Changing Lives: Delinquency Prevention as Crime-Control Policy*, Chicago: University of Chicago Press.

Hare, R. M. (1999), *Objective Prescriptions and Other Essays*, Oxford: Clarendon.

Harré, R. and Secord P. (1972), *The Explanation of Social Behaviour*, Oxford: Blackwell.

Hirschi, T. (1986), 'On the Compatibility of Rational Choice and Control Theories of Crime', in D. B. Cornish and R. V. Clarke (eds), *The Reasoning Criminal*, New York: Springer.

Holland, P. W. (1986), 'Statistics and Causal Inference', *Journal of The American Statistical Association*, 81(396): 945–60.

Kahneman, D. (2003), 'A perspective on judgement and choice: Mapping bounded rationality', *American Psychologist*, 58(9): 697–720.

Kornhauser, R. R. (1978), *Social Sources of Delinquency*, Chicago: University of Chicago Press.

Lahey, B. B. and Waldman, I. E. (2003), 'A Developmental Propensity Model and the Origins of Conduct Problems during Childhood and Adolescence', in B. B. Lahey, T. E. Moffitt, and A. Caspi (eds), *Causes of Conduct Disorder and Juvenile Delinquency*, New York: The Guilford Press.

Lewin, K. (1936), *Principles of Topological Psychology*, New York: McGraw-Hill.

Liska, A. E., Krohn, M. D., and Messner, S. F. (1989), 'Strategies and requisites for theoretical integration in the study of crime and deviance', in S. F. Messner, M. D. Krohn, and A. E. Liska (eds), *Theoretical Integration in the Study of Deviance and Crime: Problems and Prospects*, Albany: State University of New York Press.

Lyons, D., Young, A., and Keil, F. (2007), 'The hidden structure of over-imitation, *Proceedings of the National Academy of Sciences*, 104(50): 19751.

Magnusson, D. (1988), *Individual Development from an Interactional Perspective*, Hillsdale, NJ: Earlbaum.

Morgan, A. B. and Lilienfeld, S. O. (2000), 'A meta-analytic review of the relation between antisocial behavior and neuropsychological measures of executive function', *Clinic Psychological Review*, 20(1): 113–36.

Piquero, A., Farrington, D., and Blumstein, A. (2007), *Key Issues in Criminal Career Research: New Analyses of the Cambridge Study in Delinquent Development*, Cambridge: Cambridge University Press.

Psillos, S. (2002), *Causation and Explanation*, Montreal: McGill-Queen's University Press.

Reiss, A. J. (1986), 'Why Are Communities Important in Understanding Crime?', in A. J. Reiss and M. Tonry (eds), *Communities and Crime, Volume 8 of Crime and Justice: A Review of Research*, Chicago: University of Chicago Press.

Salmon, W. C. (1998), *Causality and Explanation*, Oxford: Oxford University Press.

Sampson, R. J., Raudenbush, S. W., and Earls, F. (1997), Neighborhoods and Violent Crime: A Multilevel Study of Collective Efficacy', *Science*, 277(5328): 918–24.

Schick, F. (1997), *Making Choices. A Recasting of Decision Theory*, Cambridge: Cambridge University Press.

Sherman, L. W., Gartin, P. R., and Buerger, M. E. (1989), 'Hot Spots of Predatory Crime: Routine Activities and the Criminology of Place', *Criminology*, 27(1): 27–55.

Tittle, C. R. (1995), *Control Balance: Toward a General Theory of Deviance*, Boulder, CO: Westview.

Treiber, K. (2011), 'The Neuroscientific Basis of Situational Action Theory', in K. Beaver and A. Walsh (eds), *The Ashgate Research Companion to Biosocial Theories of Crime*, Surrey: Ashgate.

Weisburd, D., Groff, E., and Yang, S. M. (2012), *The Criminology of Place. Street Segments and our Understanding of the Problem of Crime*, New York: Oxford University Press.

Wellmans, H. and Miller, J. (2008), 'Including deontic reasoning as fundamental to theory of mind', *Human Development*, 51(2): 105–35.

Wikström, P.-O. (1990), 'Age and crime in a Stockholm cohort', *Journal of Quantitative Criminology*, 6(1): 61–84.

Wikström, P.-O. (1991), *Urban Crime, Criminals and Victims*, New York: Springer.

Wikström, P.-O. (2004), 'Crime as alternative: Towards a cross-level situational action theory of crime causation', in J. McCord (ed.), *Beyond Empiricism: Institutions and Intentions in the Study of Crime*, New Brunswick: Transaction.

Wikström, P.-O. (2005), 'The social origins of pathways in crime: Towards a developmental ecological action theory of crime involvement and its changes', in D. Farrington (ed.), *Integrated Developmental and Life-course Theories of Offending. Advances in Criminological Theory, vol. 14*, New Brunswick: Transaction.

Wikström, P.-O. (2006), 'Individuals, settings, and acts of crime: Situational mechanisms and the explanation of crime', in P.-O. H. Wikström and R. J. Sampson (eds), *The Explanation of Crime: Context, Mechanisms and Development* (pp. 61–107), Cambridge: Cambridge Univerity Press.

Wikström, P.-O. (2010), 'Explaining crime as moral actions', in S. Hitlin and S. Vaisey (eds), *Handbook of the Sociology of Morality* (pp. 211–39). New York: Springer Verlag.

Wikström, P.-O. (2011), 'Does everything matter? Addressing problems of causation and explanation in the study of crime', in J. M. McGloin, C. J. Silverman, and L. W. Kennedy (eds), *When Crime Appears: The Role of Emergence*, New York: Routledge.

Wikström, P.-O. and Sampson, R. (2003), 'Social mechanisms of community influences on crime and pathways in criminality', in B. Lahey, T. Moffitt, and A. Caspi (eds), *The Causes of Conduct Disorder and Serious Juvenile Delinquency*, New York: Guilford Press.

Wikström, P.-O. and Sampson, R. (2006), 'Introduction: Toward a Unified Approach to Crime and Its Explanation', in P.-O. Wikström and R. J. Sampson, *The Explanation of Crime: Context, Mechanisms and Development*, Cambridge: Cambridge University Press.

Wikström, P.-O. and Treiber, K. (2007), 'The Role of Self-Control in Crime Causation. Beyond Gottfredson and Hirschi's General Theory of Crime', *European Journal of Criminology*, 4(2): 237–64.

Wikström, P.-O. and Treiber, K. (2015), 'Situational theories: The importance of interactions and action mechanisms in the explanation of crime', in A. R. Piquero (ed.), *Handbook of Criminological Theory*, Hoboken, NJ: Wiley-Blackwell.

Wikström, P.-O. and Treiber K. (2016), 'Beyond Risk Factors: An Analytical Approcah to Crime Prevention', in B. Teasdale and M. Bradley (eds), *Preventing Crime and Violence (Advances in Prevention Science)*, New York: Springer.

Wikström, P.-O. and Treiber K. (2016), 'Social Disadvantage and Crime. A Criminological Puzzle', *American Behavioral Scientist*, 60(10): 1232–59.

Wikström, P.-O. and Treiber, K. (2017), 'The Dynamics of Change: Criminogenic Interactions and Life Course Patterns in Crime', in D. P. Farrington, L. Kazemian, and A. R. Piquero (eds), *The Oxford Handbook on Developmental and Life-Course Criminology*, Oxford: Oxford University Press.

Wikström, P.-O., Oberwittler, D., Treiber, K., and Hardie, B. (2012), *Breaking Rules: The Social and Situational Dynamics of Young People's Urban Crime*, Oxford: Oxford University Press.

Wilcox, P., Land K. C., and Hunt, S. A. (2003), *Criminal circumstance. A dynamic multicontextual criminal opportunity theory*, New York: Aldine de Gruyter.

Wilson, J. Q. and Herrnstein, R. J. (1985), *Crime and Human Nature*, New York: Touchstone.

Wittek, R., Snijders, T., and Nee, V. (2013), 'Introduction: Rational choice social research', in R. Wittek, T. Snijders, and V. Nee (eds), *The Handbook of Rational Choice Social Research*, Stanford: Stanford University Press.

Wolfgang, M., Figlio, R., and Sellin, T. (1972), 'Delinquency in a Birth Cohort', Chicago: University of Chicago Press.

Wood, W. and Quinn, J. (2005), 'Habits and the structure of motivation in everyday life', in J. Forgas, K. Williams, and S. Laham (eds), *Social Motivation: Conscious and Unconscious Processes*, Cambridge: Cambridge University Press.

Woodward, J. (2003), *Making Things Happen. A Theory of Causal Explanation*, Oxford: Oxford University Press.

Wrong, D. H. (1961), 'The Oversocialized Conception of Man in Modern Sociology', *American Sociological Review*, 26(2): 183–93.

23

CRIME AND THE CITY: URBAN ENCOUNTERS, CIVILITY, AND TOLERANCE

Jon Bannister and John Flint

INTRODUCTION

There is an inherent paradox at the heart of contemporary debates about urban crime, violence, and antisocial behaviour. On the one hand, there is a transnational reduction in the levels of recorded crime in many Western nations at national and individual city levels and authors, such as Pinker (2011), have argued that global levels of violence and conflict are historically low and continue to decline. On the other hand, fear of crime and perceptions of antisocial behaviour among populations remain persistently high. Indeed there appears to be a broader and more pervasive sense of insecurity centred on encounters with difference within urban populations: differences relating to physical and economic well-being and life opportunities. Arguably this has been exacerbated by tensions relating to terrorism, ethno-religious conflict, cultural clashes of civilizations and large scale migrations across and within national territorial boundaries (Young 2007). As the planet becomes increasingly urbanized, these dynamics play out in urban spaces that provide the landscapes and arenas for encounters between populations and where processes of both cohesion and division are manifested.

This chapter begins by identifying the importance of cities and concepts of the urban to understandings of civility. It continues by exploring debates about the extent to which urban civility and tolerance are declining. The chapter then turns to definitions of civility and theories of how urban behaviour is influenced by changing urban economic and social conditions and how these are being transformed in the contemporary urban age. Drawing heavily on the work of Wyly (2015) we consider the extent to which urban processes may be conceptualized as a form of social Darwinism in which new forms of competition reconfigure social tensions and exclusion or, alternatively, whether urbanity is primarily characterized (or might be enhanced) by cooperation and cohesion. The chapter discusses key debates about propinquity as a mechanism for enhancing civility and tolerance and the various techniques of urban governance that are deployed to shape urban encounters and manage hyper-diversity. We conclude that new global forms of urban connectivity are reframing the urban contexts of civility and tolerance and their relationships with (perceptions of) crime and antisocial behaviour in the cities of the twenty-first century.

THE JANUS-FACED CITY: URBAN ENCOUNTERS AND (IN)CIVILITY

Cities have always been conceptualized as producers of civilization and as arenas in which civility may be enacted. According to David Hume, civil populations 'flock[ed] into cities' as sites where they could 'communicate knowledge [and] show their wit or their breeding' (Hume 1985: 271). Mumford (1996 [1937]) argued that in cities: 'Men . . . are withdrawn from barbarous fixity and force to a certain mildness of manners, and to humanity and justice . . . good behaviour is yet called urbanitas because it is rather found in cities than elsewhere'. In these terms, the city may be understood as a place of encounter and assembly (Lefebvre 1970), and through these mechanisms as a driver of public sociability (Sennett 1996). By equal measure, cities have also been viewed as fostering incivility and antipathy. Engels (1934: 24), in his account of the *Condition of the Working Class in England in 1844*, states: 'The very turmoil of the streets has something repulsive . . .The brutal indifference, the unfeeling isolation of each in his private interest becomes the more repellent and offensive, the more . . . individuals are crowded together, within a limited space'. Cities, therefore, have always been recognized as Janus-faced: they inculcate the highest standards of urban refinement and achievements of citizenship, whilst simultaneously possessing qualities that threaten chaos and the breakdown of social order. As de Tocqueville writes of Manchester in 1835: 'Here . . . humanity attains its most complete development and its most brutish; here civilisation works its miracles and civilised man is turned back almost into a savage' (quoted in Hall 1998: 310). Contemporary variations of these themes continue. For commentators such as Glaeser (2011: 26) cities are our greatest invention, enhancing wealth, intelligence, health, and well-being, while for others the contemporary neoliberal city is increasingly characterized by segregation and the intensifying exclusion of particular social groups (Wacquant 2008).

There are strong linkages between the physical and social environments of the city and both the perceptions and realities of civility, crime, and antisocial behaviour. The physical environment, its architecture, conduits, public and private spaces can shape interactions between individuals and groups, influencing opportunities for disorder and its control (Felson 2008; Clarke 1980; Brantingham and Brantingham 1984). Similarly, the social environment, manifest in terms of the levels of trust and cooperation within and between groups of urban residents, conceptualized as social capital (Putnam 2001) or 'collective efficacy' (Sampson *et al.* 1997), is posited to hold a direct relationship with rates of antisocial behaviour, crime, and violence. Many forms of antisocial behaviour or crime occur in the public spaces of neighbourhoods and have a strong determinant on residents' perceptions of their neighbourhoods and neighbours. The most common forms of complaints about antisocial behaviour in neighbourhoods are those relating to noise and phenomena such as littering, vandalism, public consumption of alcohol, and groups congregating. The fact that in the United States these behaviours are termed 'incivilities' indicates how they are seen to undermine public sociability, cohesion, and cooperation in urban areas.

DECLINING URBAN CIVILITY?

Forces operating at an international scale impact on civility in cities. Green and Germen Janmaat (2012) argue that, despite variations, globalization and its inherent crises have reduced social cohesion in many nations. Recognition of declining civility, of the reality or perceived threat of intergroup conflict, has found form in community cohesion and antisocial behaviour policies across Europe and beyond. In the UK, the New Labour governments of 1997 to 2010 prioritized tackling antisocial behaviour and promoted a Respect Agenda on the basis that the 'values necessary to support respect are becoming less widely held—and that this change has led to an increase in disrespectful behaviour' (Respect Task Force 2006: 5; see Powell and Flint 2009). This paradigm was retained in the notion of a 'Broken Britain' developed by Conservative thinkers (Social Justice Policy Group 2006). Commentators, such as Browne (2008), cite survey evidence indicating a widespread perception amongst the British population that there has been a decrease in civility, morals, and respect for authority, and an increase in antisocial behaviour. This narrative is countered by Griffith *et al.* (2011) who challenge the objective evidence for any decline in civility, arguing that Britain is largely a well-mannered and courteous society, which has experienced a long-term decline in casual violence, racism, and antisocial behaviour. Indeed, Williams and McConnell (2011) argue that urban public space can be predominately characterized as a site of everyday moments of co-existence, cooperation, and exchange. Similarly, and in the United States, Lee (2006) describes how urban interactions between different racial groups are characterized by civility, routine, and 'business as usual' as the norm, whilst Bloom *et al.* (2015) provide strong evidence to counter the myths of chronic antisocial behaviour, incivility, and racial tensions in public housing. For Lee (2006) this prosaic routine can intermittently be ruptured by 'explosive tension', with recent examples being the rioting across urban France in 2005 and in urban England in 2011. Such outbreaks of urban violence and criminality in turn generate new forms of moral panic about declining morality, civility, and social cohesion. In turn, elites and governing authorities undertake 'civilizing offensives' in an endeavour to renew civic values and forms of responsibility perceived to have eroded amongst targeted populations such as youths, the working class, or ethnic minorities (see Powell and Flint 2011). Yet, and irrespective of the impact of 'civilizing offensives' on actual behaviours, a pervasive sense of urban insecurity persists.

The multi-various and interlocking forces that shape the city have resulted in its accommodation of vast differences. Multiple identities drawn on cultural, material, religious, and ethnic lines find co-presence in residential, public, and commercial spaces (Bannister and Kearns 2013). The propinquity of difference, however, does not serve to engender encounters nor a sense of well-being when encounters do take place. Valentine *et al.* (2015), for example, have identified triggers to negative emotions and prejudice within the realities of everyday proximity. Demographically and ethnically mixed neighbourhoods can be characterized by a lack of engagement or overt hostility between groups (Amin 2012; Byrne *et al.* 2006; Gijsberts *et al.* 2011). Such existence without depth or meaning to relationships (Byrne *et al.* 2006) results in what Amin (2012) terms a civility of indifference. The 'parallel lives' lived by residents in polarized or segregated urban communities serves to negate the permeability of neighbourhoods and the potential of social interaction (Valins 2003). These insights are suggestive of an increased social and spatial separation of urban populations, whereby the propinquity of difference leads people to withdraw, to 'hibernate' (Putnam 2000). The realities or perception of a declining urban civility, of an antipathy towards difference, demands that we consider the meaning of civility and tolerance and their role in an emergent planetary urbanism.

CIVILITY, TOLERANCE, AND PLANETARY URBANISM

Civility enables us to negotiate encounters with difference. The 'formal' expression of civility elides, in Boyd's (2006: 864) view, with 'the manners, politeness, courtesies, or other formalities of face-to-face interactions in everyday life'. Though superficial and lacking in intensity, these interactions and actions enable surety to replace risk, in that they act as 'an instrument of social control' (Boyd 2006: 869). The 'formal' expression of civility, however, rests on an appreciation of the legitimate presence of others and is therefore based on a 'substantive' civility, which 'denotes a sense of standing or membership in the political community with its attendant rights and responsibility' (Boyd 2006: 864) and 'presupposes an active and affirmative moral relationship between persons. Being civil is a way of generating moral respect and democratic equality . . . civility is a moral obligation borne out of an appreciation of human equality' (ibid.: 875).

For Boyd (2006) the notion of civility was uniquely associated with the modern socio-economic order of the emerging market economy from the eighteenth century. Crucially, the commercial society and the city, as its epitome, facilitated forms of social cooperation through trade, socializing, and residential proximity that did not necessitate a resolution of the fundamental moral, religious, cultural, and philosophical disputes that had characterized Western Europe, and its bloody ethno-religious conflicts, in earlier centuries. The ubiquity of these tensions, however, is highlighted by the re-emergence of what has been termed 'the fundamentalist city' (AlSayyad and Massoumi 2011), in which, often exclusionary, socio-spatial, ultra-religious practices reshape global urban spaces. Such religious urbanism engages in a struggle with key tenets of modernity, including individualism, tolerance of diversity, and the permeability of the city. Equally, although such tenets are manifested in liberal regimes such as Britain and the United States, equality has never been conceptualized as a necessary condition of social cohesion (Green and Germen Janmaat 2012).

The growth in urban populations and their diversity, which resulted in the 'constant and intense' propinquity of difference in modern urbanism, made civility a requirement for the city to function (Boyd 2006). Elias (2000) described how, in what he termed the civilizing process, the growing organizational complexity of commercial urban societies was the catalyst for a process of psychologization whereby 'more people are forced more often to pay more attention to more other people' (Goudsblom 1989, quoted in Mennell 1990: 209). This increasing complexity through the growing differentiation and integration of social functions results in a reflexive requirement to behave with greater consideration of the feelings and interests of more people, for more of the time and thereby mutually expected self-restraint has risen (Wouters 1986; Elias 2000). This socialization process remains directly linked to the economic order: 'The hyperspecialisation of the urban economy means that we are entirely dependent for the satisfaction of even our most basic needs on a multitude of individuals who are necessarily strangers to us' (Boyd 2006: 871). Griffith *et al.* (2011: 26) similarly argue that civility increases in modern society, as 'we have to be so polite because we are so different'. This self-restraint extends to the notion of tolerance: of not interfering with conduct, practices, or beliefs that we disapprove of (Furedi 2011). In these terms, tolerance functions as a mechanism to enable social harmony, to make possible socio-economic advance, in diverse and multicultural urban societies (Browne 2008; Waltzer 1997; Bannister and Kearns 2013). The social constraint of individuals was also linked to the pacification of social spaces, including those that evolved into cities (Elias 2000).

But, if civility and tolerance were products of previous economic orders, manifest in the daily encounters of industrial and post-industrial cities, are these being transformed in our own era? If civility and tolerance are a mechanism through which our connectivity to others is performed, are these being reconfigured in light of what Wyly (2015) terms new forms of planetary connectivity? Wyly (2015) engages with Teilhard de Chardin's (1964) notion of the noosphere as a planetary super stage of consciousness in which humanity would move toward unheard-of and unimaginable degrees of organized complexity and of reflective consciousness to become ultra-reflexive. This resonates with Elias' (2000) notion of civilizing processes, such that as structures of societies become more complex, manners, culture, and personality also change. Crucially, Elias (2000) argued that such processes occur firstly among elite groups then gradually more widely (Mennell 1990: 207). Contemporary elites are emerging through reconfigured networks of diverse, dynamic global cities constituted through planetary communication circuits resulting in a new type of 'cognitive-cultural capitalism' (Wyly 2015; Moulier-Boutang 2012). Such cognitive cultural capitalism is defined by increasingly diverse pathways from cultural identity and creativity to the valorization of success through competition, increasingly mediated by socially networked information technologies, driven by those corporations who own and develop the technology and platforms for these circuits, such as Apple, Google, and Facebook (Wyly 2015). The new elites become conceptualized as 'cosmopolitan patriots' (Appiah 1997), who in response to global crisis and insecurity offer an alternative to a fortress mentality bounded by space and sovereignty (Wyly 2015). Florida (2003), with reference to globally circulating technology, talent, and tolerance, has described a 'new industrial revolution inside people's heads' (quoted in Wyly 2015), in which the primacy of creativity and knowledge over other forms of identity and legitimacy require forms of tolerance in the same way that the enactment of forms of civility among diverse populations was necessary for the industrial city to function. Thus, Wyly argues, Webber's (1964) idea of a non-place urban realm of community without propinquity takes new planetary and transnational forms (Wyly 2015).

How we fundamentally understand urban connectivity shapes the conceptualization of the role of civility and tolerance in cities. For writers such as Mumford (1937) the urban phenomena was characterized by social cooperation and the formation of 'cities where men by mutual society and company together do grow to alliances, commonalities and corporations.' Similarly, Dewey (1920) believed that the environment changed through an evolution that was a collective social process based on cooperation and communication. Dewey argued that human beings could control and manage human affairs. This idea—that the future could be predicated and influenced; that urban problems were not intractable but that cities could be made—was at the very heart of the birth of modern town planning and governance in nations such as France, Britain, and the United States, where its proponents sought to impose order on the chaos of urban experience.

But an alternative understanding is that competition is the fundamental component of urban experience and that (perceptions of) antisocial behaviour, incivilities, and crime are one manifestation of such competition made visible. The physical propinquity of diversity does not, of itself, deliver social harmony. Rather, it serves to dissolve social connections: 'Warm attachments, born of ancient, local contiguity and personal intercourse vanished in the fierce contest for wealth among thousands who had never seen each other's faces before' (Toynbee 1884, quoted in Hunt 2004: 16; see also Engels 1934 and Zorbaugh 1924, for similar accounts of nineteenth-century Manchester and twentieth-century Chicago respectively). The urban existence is, in this reading, essentially a form of social Darwinist competition, involving the survival of the fittest (Glass 1964). Wyly (2015) observed that this Darwinist competition became disguised in the urban ecology, and its naturalized narratives, that developed through the Chicago School. Further, he suggests that the contemporary urban era represents a new human ecology of social Darwinist competition that is manifested in the transformations of urban space (see also Zukin 1991). For Thrift (2005), elements of antagonism as well as solidarity are inherent to urban existence, while Flint (2009a) argues that the non-antagonistic city is an ill-conceived fantasy, despite attempts to integrate class, cultural, and ethno-religious differences into a global, cosmopolitan smooth space absent of friction or conflict (Diken 2004).

Such attempts deny the extent to which confinement, insulation, and exclusion can be characterized as enduring responses to urban difference, finding form in: the Jewish ghettos of medieval European cities; the workhouse, prison, and lunatic asylum of the nineteenth century (Foucault 1977); the periphery public housing estates of the twentieth century (including the French banliues that epitomize ethno-religious tensions and urban disorder); the sanitization of commercial and formerly public spaces in city centres (Davis 1990; Sorkin 2008); and, the global growth of gated communities and common interest developments of the late twentieth and early twenty-first centuries.

Elite groups have sought to physically insulate themselves from difference in the contemporary city (Atkinson and Flint 2004). In part, this represents a continuum of the segregation of classes that Engels (1934) and others described in the industrial city of the nineteenth century. A recent and controversial example of this phenomenon has been the use of 'poor doors' through which a socio-spatial segregation of different income groups is achieved by the use of separate entrances for different tenure groups in new 'mixed' residential developments. Effectively, separate entrances serve to minimize the physical proximity of, and consequently the potential for urban encounters between, social classes (Osborne 2014).

THE GOVERNANCE OF URBAN INSECURITIES

So, whilst planetary urbanism has ushered in a new era of hitherto unimaginable connectivity, its in-place manifestation as a constant and intense propinquity of difference has delivered friction and competition over harmony and cooperation. Friction and competition, perhaps as it has always done, has served to provoke a societal preference for confinement, insulation, and exclusion. It is these processes that have served to shape the urban landscape in which markedly intensive governance of urban interactions occurred from the 1990s.

The governance of public housing has been central to processes of urban segregation. Public housing authorities have been ambiguous in their governance of diversity, both strongly promoting mixed communities (of income, ethnicity, and age) to reduce social marginalization, whilst also using forms of geographical segregation, such as enacting age restrictions to separate younger and older populations, to reduce social conflict. However, there is also a prominent history of more hidden forms of segregation and exclusion that have sought to reduce social tension and antisocial behaviour by denying access to marginalized groups in the first place. This includes, for example, the very restrictive allocation eligibility criteria used by the New York Housing Authority to insulate its developments from the most vulnerable or problematic households and the increasing use in the UK of probationary tenancies and the denial of access to individuals with a history of antisocial behaviour. The examination of contemporary housing and urban systems provides clear evidence to support Wyly's (2015) arguments about social Darwinism. Working class, ethnic minority, and younger populations have become increasingly displaced from central urban areas through: what has been termed domicide (Shao 2013) and state violence, both symbolic and real (Allen 2008; Slater 2012); rising property prices, demolition, relocation, and urban renewal programmes (Goetz 2013); significant reductions in housing-related welfare support to individuals (such as the imposition of 'the bedroom tax' in the UK to address the alleged over-occupation of some social housing properties); and, through reduced subsidies to social housing agencies. In the Netherlands, the so-called 'Rotterdam Law' now enables municipalities to forbid households from weaker socio-economic positions from moving to specific neighbourhoods (Uitermark *et al.* 2015). Governance regimes are not limited to national polities. Municipalities in Western Europe and the United States have sought to deny specific groups, particularly immigrants, access to housing or other welfare support (Gilbert 2009), for example the recent banning of male refugees from swimming pools in Borhheim, Germany in the context of controversies of sexual harassment (Guardian 2016). In addition, private companies play an increasingly prominent role in the social and physical governance of diversity, illustrated by the controversy over G4S allegedly using the colour of doors to demarcate the residences of asylum seekers in England (Mason *et al.* 2016).

The governance of urban interactions, as of any policy context, is an inherently political process (Davies and Nutley 2001) involving ideology, vested interests, institutional norms, and path dependencies (Weiss 2001). In these terms, it is necessary to consider the weighting ascribed to different policy drivers (or forms of knowledge) and their relation to specific stages of the policy-making process. To this end, Tenbensel (2008) recommends deployment of a typology of knowledge based on the Aristotelian 'intellectual virtues' of episteme, techne, and phronesis. Episteme accords with the conception of knowledge as rational, positive, and value free. The scientific community is typically responsible for generating this form of knowledge. Techne, or practical knowledge, relates to the understanding of what works in particular situations; it represents the knowledge formed by practitioners and others engaged in policy implementation. Finally, phronesis like techne involves experiential knowledge, but pertains more closely to ultimate ends rather than means. Phronetic knowledge centres on what matters to individuals and groups in society. In this sense, it is political and rests on the underlying values interests of the citizenry as they are engaged in the policy-making process.

Examining the governance of urban interactions, it is striking the extent to which phronetic knowledge is demanded by the polity and the centrality of the role that the polity accords that knowledge in the policy-making process. For example, exploring the evidential underpinnings of antisocial behaviour policies in the UK (1997–2010), Bannister and O'Sullivan (2014) find public perceptions of antisocial behaviour rather than its objective measurement to hold prominence in problem definition and by inference in the assessment of problem resolution. In his account of the lessons learnt whilst in charge of Tony Blair's Delivery Unit, Barber (2007: 370) suggests that New Labour policy-makers were keenly aware of the requirement for policies to attend to phronetic knowledge, stating: 'the numbers are important but not enough: citizens have to see and feel the difference'. Thus, and as Tonry (2010: 388) suggests, New Labour's policies were largely 'expressive', intended to acknowledge public anxieties and in so doing prevent a deterioration of morale and allay anxieties pertaining to the quality of urban life.

Not only do public preferences drive the direction of policies in this area, they also inform their character. If (perceptions of) antisocial behaviour can be understood as arising from the absence or breakdown of community relations, government could in principle formulate its policy response in a number of alternative ways in terms of the nature of the role assigned to itself or its nominated agencies for the purpose of bringing about improved intergroup relations. First, government could attempt to fully insert itself between groups, acting as a 'mediator' and addressing community tensions on a bilateral basis but with no direct attempt to bring the groups together. Second, government could act as a 'facilitator' in the search for forms of mutual engagement that would enhance intergroup civility. Third, government could act to create space (both physical and socio-political) for groups to constructively explore and address problems for themselves, essentially creating the space for this to happen while playing the role of 'supervisor'. The final and least active alternative would see government adopting the role of 'observer', expecting groups to work things out for themselves (see Bannister and O'Sullivan 2013). Reflecting on the substance of antisocial behaviour policy in the UK, Clarke *et al.* (2011) find that it has centred on the protection of victim groups, even if this has been attained through targeting perpetrators. Government agencies are firmly positioned between aggrieved groups and (perceived) perpetrators, adopting the role of 'mediator'. Though there have been occasions where policy-makers have proposed active roles for aggrieved groups in the management of antisocial behaviour, they have gained limited foothold as these groups 'prefer' mediated arrangements to be maintained (Home Office 2011; Scottish Government 2009). In overview, the character of antisocial behaviour policies have tended to support the public desire not to engage with others in an endeavour to lessen intergroup friction.

In turn, the nature of policies aimed at targeting (perceptions of) antisocial behaviour, can be characterized as supporting the dominant privilege (or competitive edge) of one group over another, in terms of their access to, control and use of urban resources. Thus, a series of new legal measures, including Antisocial Behaviour Orders and Dispersal Orders in the UK and the use of exclusion notices by public housing authorities in the US, sought to limit the presence of certain individuals or groups in public space and prohibited forms of behaviour in specific urban localities. There were also governmental projects to inculcate required levels of civility and tolerance among populations. These included good neighbour agreements signed by residents (replicating the detailed covenants and behavioural requirements in common interest developments and gated communities) and tenant reward schemes. In direct response to increasing migration and ethno-religious diversity, information packs sought to codify required standards of 'British' behaviour and etiquette, including queuing, attending appointments, spitting, and congregating in public space (see Flint 2009b for a full account).

In these terms, the governance of urban insecurities can be seen as an endeavour by the state as 'mediator' to lessen the frictions, or intolerance, arising from the propinquity of difference. Its strategy is to demand, in line with an idealized and dominant set of values (informed by the public), that those identified as 'others' show us respect, or risk exclusion. Khan (2007) refers to this as 'evaluative' respect. However, these strategies can only hold ameliorative effect on our sense of urban insecurity if the behaviour, actions, and qualities of the 'other' are demonstrably the same as our own. For Sennett (2012: 8) this desire to 'neutralize difference, to domesticate it, arises from anxiety about difference', but he cautions that to follow this path will only serve to weaken our motivation to engage with difference. In sum, and viewed in light of the forces shaping planetary urbanism that deliver an ever-increasing in-place manifestation of difference, can these policies be viewed (however necessary they are deemed to be) anything other than a sticking-plaster solution? Further, is this not evidenced by the persistence of urban insecurities?

What then of the current prospect of the governance of urban insecurities? A clear conditioning factor is that of austerity. The global financial crisis of 2008 has served to usher in an era in which a significant reduction in public expenditure has been sought. In the UK, and under the Coalition government, the 'austerity agenda' clearly underpinned all public service thinking between 2010 and 2015, though resource pressures pre-date—and will presumably outlive—austerity. Garside and Ford (2015), drawing on data from Her Majesty's Treasury report, identified an 18 per cent (£4 billion) reduction in criminal justice expenditure in England and Wales between 2010 and 2015. In terms of police service funding, a reduction in excess of 20 per cent was achieved (in part) by an 11 per cent reduction in the number of police officers. Here, it is important to note that the dramatic reduction in police numbers might well have been enforced by austerity, but it was certainly enabled by evidence of falling crime. Nevertheless, and in clear consequence, the governance of urban insecurities will require to be achieved with more limited means.

The UK Coalition government approach to public policy in general and to criminal justice in particular was to adopt state re-treatment and increased marketization as a driver for reform (Garside and Ford 2015). There are, however, evident continuities with what has gone before. There has been renewed emphasis on community engagement, community problem-solving, and community mobilization (Hodgkinson and Tilley 2011), with the intention that the community is enabled 'to make decisions and take the lead in making change happen, with agencies available to assist' (Home Office 2011: 11). The precise way in which this might manifest in practical application, however, is uncertain. Or rather, it is evident that strategies aimed at tackling urban insecurities will aim to capture the public's voice whilst the state will retain the role of 'mediator', or via its agents the role of 'facilitator'. The reform of police–public relations in England and Wales under the Police Reform and Social Responsibility Act (2011) presents a clear example of the intention to centre public demands in local police service delivery. Here, the public's voice has been captured through the direct election of Police and Crime Commissioners, though the extent to which this serves to capture the 'democratic' voice of the citizenry and will ensure sensitivity local area needs has been questioned (Joyce 2011; Independent Police Commission 2013).

PUBLIC PERCEPTIONS OF CRIME, ANTISOCIAL BEHAVIOUR, AND INCIVILITIES

Given the extent to which the governance of urban insecurities is built upon the capture of public perceptions, it remains an essential task to consider how and where perceptions of crime, antisocial behaviour, and incivilities take form. Here, and surely, it is in the qualities of urban interaction (as broadly conceived) that we must find the answer.

To live in the presence of difference, indeed the effective functioning of cities, demands that the vast majority of our encounters with difference are ephemeral. However, there are also spaces in which our encounters, of practical necessity, hold the potential to be enduring. Commercial, residential, and recreational spaces all demand that we coexist in cooperative fashion or that we act to exert influence over these spaces, to compete for their resource.

Bannister and Kearns (2013) posit that the perception of incivilities (as they find form in public survey or political action), of urban insecurities in general, captures value judgement and risk assessment, both conditioned by the qualities of urban living that inform urban interactions. Building upon the conception of civility outlined earlier, value judgements depend on whether we perceive those with whom we interact to be 'deserving' or 'undeserving' of our consideration, whilst risk assessments depend on the calculation of the consequences or impact of that interaction for our self and for others. The social and spatial fragmentation and segregation that characterize the city require that we deploy 'stereotype' and 'metaphor' as crude proxy when making these calculations. A lack of familiarity with certain social groups, underpinned by limited or fleeting direct engagement, leads us to 'stereotype' the *threat* posed by any encounter with members of that group based on the actual behaviour or the (media) portrayal of individuals comprising that group. In the United States, Sampson (2009) has found evidence of the stereotyping of certain groups in relation to disorder, whilst Emerson *et al.* (2001) found that Whites actually avoid living in neighbourhoods with 'non-token' Black populations (above 15 per cent Black) because they equate such groups with crime and low educational attainment. On the other hand, the very presence of certain social groups serves to act as a 'metaphor' for the relative powerlessness of the observer, and by extension of the community and the state, to exercise control through the imposition of their own values in that space, a malaise held to enable the undesired presence of other to flourish and inhibit their confrontation (Sampson 2009; Sampson and Raudenbush 2004).

This reading holds parallels with wider narratives of 'social disparagement', of the 'othering' of those regarded as threatening to our general welfare and detrimental to social solidarity, and serves to generate negative views of individuals on the basis of their membership of certain population groups rather than on the basis of their actual behaviour or personal worth (Young 2007; Sveinsson 2009). Sennett (2012: 3), goes as far as to characterize the United States as a tribal society comprising 'people adverse to getting along with those who differ' and which 'couples solidarity with others like yourself to aggression to those who differ'. In this vein, Bottoms (2006) draws on Barbelet (1998) to differentiate the 'resentment' we feel towards those thought to behave (or simply to be) counter to our view of established rights (the threat imposed by others) and, the 'vengefulness' we feel towards those perceived as dispossessing our right to levy our own values on the use of public space.

There is a vital contextual dimension to these assessments: the importance we place on urban interactions varies across the city (see, *inter alia*, Madanipour 2003; Watson 2006). In other words, there are locations in which our capacity to avoid contact with others is constrained, as a consequence of our employment, travel, and living arrangements. Here, our assessments are informed by two key questions: *what is at stake*? And, *what are we used to*? The former encompasses the consideration of the threat (both risk assessment and value judgement), whilst the latter encompasses our familiarity with others. Collectively, these questions probe the extent to which the presence of the 'other' (and their behaviours) seem 'in' or 'out-of-place', consistent or not with what we would expect and/or want to happen. The less familiarity we have with the 'other' the greater the likelihood that we fall back on our use of stereotype and metaphor; the greater the threat that they pose, the more likely that their presence will provoke intolerance and anxiety.

There are two outcomes to this interplay, which hold clear resonance with the strategies designed to govern urban interactions. First, that 'resentment' and 'vengefulness' can only (seemingly) be satiated through removal of the 'other', or that their behaviours be modified in line with our own values. Second, that the demand to enforce this expulsion, in the perceived absence of our own capacity to do so, be placed upon *formal* agents of control. However, strategies that endeavour to *impose* a mode of social interaction, which treat difference as illegitimate, clearly run the risk of perpetuating a cycle of intolerance of maintaining seemingly disproportionate levels of urban insecurity.

ENGENDERING CIVILITY AND PROMOTING TOLERANCE: MEANINGFUL INTERACTION

In light of our sense of urban insecurity being founded on the deployment of stereotype and metaphor, we echo Tonry and Bildsten's (2009: 595) plea that we 'need to find ways to bring . . . fractured populations together rather than to split them . . . to strengthen the relations between majority and minority populations rather than to weaken them'. Further, and given the assessment of threat is bound to the urban experience as competition for resource, it prompts consideration of whether and under what terms the urban experience can instead be one of communication and social cooperation (Mumford 1937; Dewey 1920). Thus, if civility and the tolerance of difference are founded on the existence of a shared language of social interaction, then how might we develop such a language? Through greater interaction with those whom we share the city, threats can lose their generic or random nature (Carvahlo and Lewis 2006) and become particular to specific events, places, and individuals. Holding a greater capacity to contextualize the presence of difference (and associated behaviours) decreases our reliance upon stereotype and metaphor as interpretive tools, ameliorating our perception of threat (risk). In these terms, the perception of a threat holds, at least to an extent, a relational quality as opposed to the presence of difference (exclusively) embodying a threat.

Relatedly, engagement can stimulate mutual respect, not only demanding but also offering respect, 'treating with respect the need perceived in another when acting together' (Sennett 2003: 53). Indeed, greater identification with those whom we share urban arenas can serve to provoke cooperation (Tyler and Fagan 2008). If this reading holds true, it opens the potential that other benefits might also be accrued. In an era of austerity, communication and engagement offer the prospect of significant resource savings for those agencies charged with managing urban interactions and addressing urban insecurities. The demands placed on agencies of social control might not only be more precise, but also more limited in nature.

What then are the qualities required of engagement to stimulate these benefits? By engagement we are referring to meaningful and purposeful social interaction and collective activity with others. As we have seen, co-presence alone does not engender interaction of this nature, nor do the fleeting contacts that necessarily characterize the majority of urban encounters. Allport (1954: 281), through what has become known as the 'contact' hypothesis, argued that prejudice: 'may be reduced by equal status contact between majority and minority groups in the pursuit of common goals. The effect is greatly enhanced if this contact is sanctioned by institutional supports (i.e. by law, custom or local atmosphere), and provided it is of a sort that leads to the perception of common interests and common humanity between members of the two groups'. Crucially, however, for this effect to take hold it is necessary that there is an equality of status between the groups involved and that the purpose of cooperative endeavour is directed toward the achievement of common goals. Where there is a lack of (perceived) equality, contact is likely to aggravate rather than lessen intergroup prejudice (Brewer and Gaertner 2001). In these terms, equality of status can be understood as being founded on a 'substantive' conception of civility (Boyd 2006) with its attendant citizenship rights and responsibilities. Here, the role of the state is fundamental, both in its recognition and promotion of the legitimacy of difference in the urban realm and through its capacity to provide the means and spaces for intergroup contact. Providing that the situational requirements of contact can be met, there is a substantial body of research in support of the contact hypothesis and its use to promote intergroup tolerance (Pettigrew and Tropp 2005; Hewstone 2009).

Despite the compelling evidence that meaningful social interactrion can stimulate tolerance and promote cooperative endeavour, this prospect requires to be set against the forces shaping the experience of contemporary urbanity and its governance. Urban populations are increasingly diverse, segregated, and isolated possessing (seemingly) neither the capacity nor the desire to engage in meaningful social interaction. Moreover, government would require adopting the role of 'facilitator' or to a lesser extent 'supervisor', rather than 'mediator'. This, as we have seen, is something that governments have been reluctant to do in the governance of urban insecurities and might be less inclined to do so under the constraints of austerity. In these terms there seems little likelihood of meaningful social interaction arising organically or through government sponsorship. In other words, there appears to be a shortfall in the conditions or 'built-in equipment' required to enable 'strangers to dwell in peace together' (Jacobs 1961: 83).

Set against these challenges, recent years have witnessed a dramatic shift in the way in which people can learn about one another and in the way in which they communicate. The Internet enables fingertip access to a vast array of materials, whilst urban populations now possess a digital voice through the advent of social media platforms. In the UK, eight in ten adults aged 16 or over go online, whilst six in ten use a smart phone (Ofcom 2014). The widespread access to smart phones, for example, enables citizens to document their surroundings through videos, recordings, and text and to communicate these instantly. People are sharing an ever-increasing proportion of their lives on these 'digital commons' (Omand *et al.* 2012). Of those online in the UK, two-thirds have a presence on a social networking site, typically Facebook (Ofcom 2014). Extending beyond personal interaction, social media has an increasing presence in political/social mobilization and public debate. Twitter, for example, played a key role in enabling and shaping political discourse as well as in mobilizing protestors in the Arab Spring (Howard *et al.* 2011).

Given the extent to which social media platforms have become a key means of communication prompts consideration of whether this form of (non-physical) interaction can serve to stimulate civility and tolerance and in so doing confront (perceptions of) urban insecurities. However, the emergent literatures tend to pay greater attention to the Internet and social media as a resource to perpetrate crime and engender social disharmony. The Office for National Statistics (2015), for example, calculated that there were 2.5 million cybercrimes in England and Wales in 2014, whereas social media platforms were accused of fuelling the London riots of 2011 (Halliday 2012) and have been central to global controversies over Charlie Hebdo, the burning of the Koran, and disruption of remembrance services. Social media is becoming intertwined with a new phenomenon within conceptualizations of incivility and intolerance, namely 'offensiveness'. That said, the extent to which offensiveness should be recognized as a form of incivility and subject to governmental regulation is disputed (Waiton 2013). There is evidence that mass-mediated interaction can promote beneficial changes to public perception. Shiappa *et al.* (2005), for example, found that 'parasocial' or mass-mediated contact held the capacity to change public beliefs about gay men and transvestites, lowering pre-existing levels of prejudice. It is also clear however that the public, reflecting physical practices of confinement, insulation, and exclusion, tend to engage in intragroup rather than intergroup contact. Morozov (2012), for example, and reflecting on the changing use of the Internet and social media, believes that the dominance of these media by corporations such as Apple, Google, and Facebook is serving to narrow exploration and intergroup contact. Thus whilst Facebook serves to remove anonymity and promote social interaction, such interaction is founded on intragroup communication.

To date, the uptake of social media in the governance of urban insecurities has been both experimental and haphazard. Few approaches are grounded in formal strategies with clearly articulated objectives or protocols for deployment and data handling, yet a greater number of applications are emergent (Denef *et al.* 2012). In this context, the Norwegian police use a one-way twitter feed to communicate with citizens, whilst in the Netherlands, public security practitioners use a multi-media platform (CrowdSense 2015) in an endeavour to mitigate the risks associated with large-scale social gatherings. There is also clear resonance with the nature of approach typically adopted by the state in the governance of physical interactions, inserting itself as 'mediator' and protecting victim groups through targeting perpetrators. For example, the media has been used to advance new mechanisms of using public shaming as a mechanism of deterrence, including publicizing individuals subject to Antisocial Behaviour Orders in the UK or lists of individuals banned from US public housing. These techniques have also increasingly been used by commercial transport companies to shame fare dodgers (Powell and Flint 2009: Croll 1999). Recently, Los Angeles has considered naming and effectively 'drought shaming' residents who use a disproportionate amount of water (Walters 2015). In Scotland, the Offensive Behaviour at Football and Threatening Communications (Scotland) Act 2012 includes a specific focus on prohibiting sectarian, homophobic, or racist content in internet communications. In overview, whilst the advent of and engagement with new communication technologies holds the potential to reframe urban encounters, supporting interactions that are not bounded in space, the direction of travel for typical users bears relation to traditional physical and socially bounded modes of interaction. New communication technologies are also creating new social problems, holding influence on how uncivil or antisocial behaviour are conceived. Non-physical interaction via communication technologies can also manifest in physical realities. Governing authorities are moving to insert themselves in this arena, though the direction of travel here also bears relation to traditional modes of the governance of urban insecurities.

CONCLUSION

Cities are vital to the conceptualization and manifestations of civility, tolerance, and perceptions of antisocial behaviour and crime. However, the encounters with difference that characterize the propinquity of urban experience need to be situated within a wider contemporary planetary urbanism fundamentally transforming social connectivity and conflict. There is evidence that new forms of social Darwinism are driving urban insecurities in which urban encounters with diversity are defined by the perceived incivility of other groups or where the sites for such encounters are systemically reduced by displacement, segregation, and the exclusion of 'others' through physical, legal, political, and cultural mechanisms. New technologies of connectivity within the hyper-diversity of planetary urbanism do not, inherently, necessitate an acceleration of Darwinist competition or conflict. They could, alternatively, generate new forms of cooperation and tolerance as envisaged by Dewey (1920) and captured in the concept of a global noosphere of hyper-connectivity. However, this would require a return to Boyd's (2006) emphasis on a substantive reading of civility characterized by inclusive citizenship and forms of urban encounter underpinned by greater levels of equality between groups. The contemporary governance of urban diversity and civility is complex and ambiguous; in which some governmental projects to foster propinquity between groups are countered by state ambivalence towards, or indeed proactive facilitation of, urban forces driving intolerance and conflict.

What is evident is that governmental projects to avoid the complexity and challenges of managing hyper-diversity through reducing the visibility or prominence of such diversity in urban arenas are insufficient. It is equally fanciful for the state to hope that other actors will autonomously resolve conflicts and generate the civil city. At present we appear trapped in a cycle in which the primacy of phronesis as a driver of governmental action, at national and city scales, results in the cumulative fears of urban populations and elites about diversity being mirrored back and forth and thereby intensified. Governments respond to the alleged fears of the citizenry and, in turn the discourses and policies of government heighten the fears of urban residents. In such a scenario, the relatively strong evidence for recent declines in the levels of urban crime in many cities, and the longer-term historical fall in urban inter-personal violence and forms of intolerance, will not translate into popular public perceptions of safer cities. Without achieving such a new understanding, the calculations of risk involved in urban encounters with difference will continue to be founded on (often unwarranted) fears, inculcating acts of avoidance and separation, rather than generating the meaningful interactions the civil city requires.

SELECTED FURTHER READING

Boyd's 'The Value of Civility?' (2006) provides an excellent discussion of the conceptualization of urban civility, and the other papers in this issue of the journal are also on urban (in)civility. Wyly's 'Gentrification on the planetary urban frontier: The evolution of Turner's noosphere' (2015) provides a full discussion of many of the concepts used in this chapter. Bannister and Kearns' 'The function and foundations of urban tolerance: encountering and engaging with difference in the city' (2013) provides a conceptualization of how urban tolerance may be understood and how it is manifested in cities. Sennett's *Together: The Rituals, Pleasure and Politics of Cooperation* (2012) explores the tendency for society to become ever more complicated while people tend socially to avoid people unlike themselves. It interrogates how this situation has arisen and what might be done about it. Flint's 'Cultures, Ghettos and Camps: Sites of Exception and Antagonism in the City' (2009) examines an increasing racial and religious segregation and the potential of urban policy to facilitate civility between diverse populations.

REFERENCES

ALLEN, C. (2008), *Housing Market Renewal and Social Class*, London: Routledge.

ALLPORT, G. W. (1954), *The Nature of Prejudice*, Cambridge, MA: Addison-Wesley.

AMIN, A. (2012), *Land of Strangers*. Cambridge: Polity.

APPIAH, K. W. (1997), 'Cosmopolitan Patriots', *Critical Inquiry*, 23(3): 617–39.

ALSAYYAD, N. and MASSOUMI, M. (eds) (2011), *The Fundamentalist City? Religiosity and the Remaking of Urban Space*, London: Routledge.

ATKINSON, R. and FLINT, J. (2004), 'Fortress UK? Gated communities, the spatial revolt of the elites and time-space trajectories of segregation', *Housing Studies*, 19(6): 875–92.

BANNISTER, J. and KEARNS, A. (2013), 'The function and foundations of urban tolerance: encountering and engaging with difference in the city', *Urban Studies*, 50(13): 2700–17.

BANNISTER, J. and O'SULLIVAN, A. (2013), 'Civility, community cohesion and antisocial behaviour: Policy and social harmony', *Journal of Social Policy*, 42(1): 91–110.

BANNISTER, J. and O'SULLIVAN, A. (2014), 'Evidence, antisocial behaviour and the policy cycle', *Evidence and Policy*, 10(1): 77–92.

BARBELET, J. M. (1998), *Emotion, Social Theory and Social Structure: A Macrosociological Approach*, Cambridge: Cambridge University Press.

BARBER, M. (2007), *Instruction to Deliver*, London: Politico's.

BLOOM, N. D., UMBACH, F., and VALE, L. J. (eds) (2015), *Public Housing Myths: Perception, Reality and Social Policy*, Ithaca and London: Cornell University Press.

BOTTOMS, A. (2006), 'Incivilities, offence, and social order in residential communities', in A. Von Hirsch and A. P. Simester (eds), *Incivilities: Regulating Offensive Behaviour*, Oxford: Hart.

BOYD, R. (2006), 'The Value of Civility?', *Urban Studies*, 43(5/6): 879–902.

BRANTINGHAM, P. J. and BRANTINGHAM, P. L. (1984), *Patterns in Crime*, New York: Macmillan.

BREWER, M. and GAERTNER, S. L. (2001), 'Toward Reduction of Prejudice: Intergroup Contact and Social Categorization', in R. Brown and S. L. Gaertner (eds),

Blackwell Handbook of Social Psychology: Intergroup Processes, Oxford: Blackwell.

Browne, A. (2008) *Has There Been a Decline in Values in British Society?*, York: Joseph Rowntree Foundation.

Byrne, J., Hansson, U., and Bell, J. (2006), *Shared Living: Mixed Residential Communities in Northern Ireland*, Belfast: Institute for Conflict Research.

Carvahlo, I. and Lewis, D. A. (2006), 'Beyond community: reactions to crime and disorder among inner-city residents', *Criminology*, 41(3): 779–812.

Clarke, A., Williams, K., Wydall S., Gray, P., Liddle, M., and Smith, A. (2011), *Describing and Assessing interventions to address anti-social behaviour*, Research Report 51, London: Home Office.

Croll, A. (1999), 'Street Disorder, surveillance and shame: regulating behaviour in the public spaces of the late Victorian Town', *Social History*, 23(4): 250–67.

Clarke, R. V. (1980), '"Situational" crime prevention: Theory and practice', *British Journal of Criminology*, 20(2): 136–47.

CrowdSense.co (2015), CrowdSense. Available at: http://crowdsense.co/, accessed 15 January 2016.

Davies, H. T. O. and Nutley, S. M. (2001), 'Evidence-based policy and practice: moving from rhetoric to reality', Paper presented at the Third International, Inter-disciplinary Evidence-Based Policies and Indicator Systems Conference, 86–95.

Davis, M. (1990), *City of Quartz: Excavating the Future in Los Angeles*, London: Verso.

Denef, S., Kaptein, N., Bayerl, P. S., and Ramirez, L. (2012), 'Best Practice in Police Social Media Adaptation, COMPOSITE Project', available at: http://www.composite-project.eu/tl_files/fM_k0005/download/COMPOSITE-social-media-best-practice.pdf, accessed 15 January 2016.

Dewey, J. (1920), *Reconstruction in Philosophy*, New York: Henry Holt.

Diken, B. (2004), 'From refugee camps to gated communities: biopolitics and the end of the city', *Citizenship Studies*, 8(1): 83–106.

Elias, N. (2000), *The Civilizing Process*, Oxford: Blackwell.

Emerson, M. O., Yancey, G., and Chai, K. J. (2001), 'Does race matter in residential segregation? Exploring the preferences of White Americans', *American Sociological Review*, 66: 922–35.

Engels, F. (1934), *The Condition of the Working Class in England*, London: Allen and Unwin.

Felson, M. (2008), 'Routine Activities Approach', in R. Whortley and L. Mazerolle (eds), *Environmental Criminology and Crime Analysis*, Portland: Willan.

Flint, J. (2009a), 'Cultures, Ghettos and Camps: Sites of Exception and Antagonism in the City', *Housing Studies*, 24(4): 417–32.

Flint, J. (2009b), 'Migrant Information Packs and the Colonisation of Civility in the UK', *Space and Polity*, 13(2): 127–40.

Florida, R. (2003), 'Cities and the Creative Class', *City and Community*, 2(1): 3–19.

Foucault, M. (1977), *Discipline and Punish: The Birth of the Prison*, London: Penguin.

Furedi, F. (2011), *On Tolerance: A Defence of Moral Independence*, London: Continuum.

Garside, R. and Ford, M. (2015), *UK Justice Policy Review, vol. 4*, London: Centre for Crime and Justice Studies.

Gijsberts, M., Van Der Meer, T., and Dagevos, J. (2011), '"Hunkering down" in multi-ethnic neighbourhoods? The effects of ethnic diversity on dimensions of social cohesion', *European Sociological Review*, doi:10.1093/esr/jcr/022.

Gilbert, L. (2009), 'Immigration as local politics: Re-Bordering Immigration and Multiculturalism through Deterrence and Incapacitation', *International Journal of Urban and Regional Research*, 33(1): 26–42.

Glaeser, E. (2011), *Triumph of the City: How Our Greatest Invention Makes Us Richer, Smarter, Greener, Healthier and Happier*, New York: Penguin.

Glass, R. (1964), 'Introduction', in ***Centre for Urban Studies, London: Aspects of Change***, London: MacGibbon and Kee.

Goetz, E. (2013), *New Deal Ruins: Race, Economic Justice and Public Housing Policy*, New York: Cornell University Press.

Goudsblom, J. (1989), 'Styles and Civilisation', *De Gids*, 152: 720–2.

Green, A. and Germen Janmaat, J. (2012), *Regimes of Social Cohesion: Societies and the Crisis of Globalization*, Basingstoke: Palgrave.

Griffith, P., Norman, W., O'Sullivan, C., and Ali, R. (2011), *Charm Offensive: Cultivating Civility in 21st Century Britain*, London: Young Foundation.

The Guardian (2016), 'German town bans male refugees from swimming pool', *The Guardian*, 15 January 2016, available at: http://www.theguardian.com/uk-news/2016/jan/20/asylum-seekers-north-east-claim-identifiable-red-doors-houses, accessed 22 January 2016.

Hall, P. (1998), *Cities in Civilisation*, London: Weidenfeld and Nicolson.

Halliday, J. (2012), 'UK riots "made worse" by rolling news, BBM, Twitter and Facebook', *The Guardian*, 28 March 2012, available at: http://www.theguardian.com/media/2012/mar/28/uk-riots-twitter-facebook, accessed 15 January 2016.

Hewstone, M. (2009), 'Living Apart, Living Together? The Role of Intergroup Contact in Social Integration', *Proceedings of the British Academy*, 162: 243–300.

Hodgkinson, S. and Tilley, N. (2011), 'Tackling anti-social behaviour: Lessons from New Labour for the Coalition Government', *Criminology and Criminal Justice*, 11(4): 283–305.

Home Office (2011), *More Effective Responses to Anti-Social Behaviour*, London: Home Office.

Howard, P. N., Duffy, A., Freelon, D., Hussain, M., Mari, W., and Mazaid, M. (2011), 'Opening closed regimes: What was the role of social media during the Arab Spring?', Project on Information Technology & Political Islam, Social Science Research Network, available at: http://ssrn.com/abstract=2595096, accessed 15 January 2016.

HUME, D. (1985), Essays: Moral, Political and Literary', E. Millar (ed.), Indianpolis, IA: Liberty Fund.

HUNT, T. (2004), *Building Jerusalem: The Rise and Fall of the Victorian City*, London: Weidenfeld and Nicolson.

INDEPENDENT POLICE COMMISSION (2013), *Policing for a Better Britain. Report of the Independent Police Commission, The Lord Stevens of Kirkwhelpington QPM*, Essex: Anton Group.

JACOBS, J. (1961), *The Death and Life of Great American Cities*, New York: Random House.

JOYCE, P. (2011), 'Police reform: from police authorities to police and crime commissioners', *Safer Communities*, 10(4): 5–13.

KHAN, O. (2007), 'Rights, respect and criminal justice policy', *Safer Society*, 34: 2–5.

LEE, J. (2006), 'Constructing Race and Civility in Urban America', *Urban Studies*, 43(5/6): 903–18.

LEFEBVRE, H. (2003 [1970]), *The Urban Revolution*, Minneapolis: University of Minnesota Press.

MADANIPOUR, A. (2003), *Public and Private Spaces of the City*, London: Routledge.

MASON, R., PIDD, H., and KNOMAMI, N. (2016), 'Asylum seekers in north-east claim they are identifiable by red doors', *The Guardian*, 20 January 2016, available at: http://www.theguardian.com/uk-news/2016/jan/20/asylum-seekers-north-east-claim-identifiable-red-doors-houses, accessed 22 January 2016.

MENNELL, S. (1990), 'Decivilizing processes: theoretical significance and some lines of research', *International Sociology*, 5(2): 205–23.

MOROZOV, E. (2012), 'The death of the cyberflaneur', *The New York Times*, 4 February 2012, available at: http://www.nytimes.com/2012/02/05/opinion/sunday/the-death-of-the-cyberflaneur.html?pagewanted=all&_r=1, accessed 15 January 2016.

MOULIER-BOUTANG, Y. (2012), *Cognitive Capitalism*, Cambridge: Polity.

MUMFORD, L. (1996 [1937]), 'What is a City?', in R. T LeGates and F. Stout (eds), *The City Reader*, 4th edn, London: Routledge.

OFCOM (2014), *Adults' Media Use and Attitudes Report 2014*, 29 April 2014, available at: http://stakeholders.ofcom.org.uk/market-data-research/other/research-publications/adults/adults-media-lit-14/, accessed 18 January 2016.

OMAND, D., BARTLETT, J., and MILLER, C. (2012), 'A balance between security and privacy online must be struck . . .', DEMOS, available at: http://www.demos.co.uk/publications/intelligence, accessed 15 January 2016.

ONS (2015), 'Improving Crime Statistics in England and Wales', Office for National Statistics, 15 October 2015, available at: http://www.ons.gov.uk/ons/rel/crime-stats/crime-statistics/year-ending-june-2015/sty-fraud.html, accessed 18 January 2016.

OSBORNE, H. (2014), 'Poor-doors: The segregation of London's inner-city flat dwellers', *The Guardian*, 25 July 2014.

PETTIGREW, T. F. and TROPP, L. R. (2005), 'Allport's Intergroup Contact Hypothesis: Its History and Influence', in J. F. Dovidio, P. Glick, and L. A. Rudman (eds), *On the Nature of Prejudice: fifty years after Allport*, Oxford: Blackwell.

PINKER, S. (2011), *The Better Angels of Our Nature: The Decline of Violence and Its Causes*, London: Allen Lane.

POWELL, R. and FLINT, J. (2011), 'The English City Riots of 2011, "Broken Britain" and the Retreat into the Present', *Sociological Research Online*, 17(3).

POWELL, R. and FLINT, J. (2009), '(In)formalization and the Civilizing Process: Applying the Work of Norbert Elias to Housing-Based Anti-social Behaviour Interventions in the UK', *Housing, Theory and Society*, 26(3): 159–78.

PUTNAM, R. (2000), *Bowling Alone: The Collapse and revival of American Community*, New York: Simon and Schuster.

SAMPSON, R. (2009), 'Disparity and diversity in the contemporary city: social (dis)order revisited', *British Journal of Sociology*, 60(1): 1–31.

SAMPSON, R. J. and RAUDENBUSH, S. W. (2004), 'Seeing disorder: Neighbourhood stigma and the social construction of "broken windows" ', *Social Psychology Quarterly*, 67(4): 319–42.

SAMPSON, R. J., RAUDENBUSH, S., and EARLS, F. (1997), 'Neighborhoods and Violent Crime: A Multilevel Study of Violent Crime', *Science*, 277: 918–24.

SCOTTISH GOVERNMENT (2009), *Promoting Positive Outcomes: Working Together to Prevent Antisocial Behaviour in Scotland, vol. 1*, Edinburgh: Scottish Government.

SENNETT, R. (1996), *The Uses of Disorder: Personal Identity and City Life*, London: Faber and Faber.

SENNETT, R. (2003), ***Respect: the formation of character in an age of inequality***, London: Allen Lane.

SENNETT, R. (2012), *Together: The Rituals, Pleasure and Politics of Cooperation*, New Haven: Yale University Press.

SHAO, Q. (2013), *Shanghai Gone: Domicide and Defence in a Chinese Megacity*, Lanham, MD: Rowman and Littlefield.

SHIAPPA, E., GREGG, P. B., and HEWES, D. E. (2005), 'The parasocial contact hypothesis', *Communication Monographs*, 72(1): 92–115.

SLATER, T. (2012), 'From 'criminality' to marginality: Rioting against a broken state', *Human Geography*, 4(3): 106–15.

SOCIAL POLICY JUSTICE GROUP (2006), *Breakdown Britain*, London: Social Policy Justice Group.

SORKIN, M. (ed.) (2008), *Indefensible Space: The Architecture of the National Insecurity State*, New York and London: Routledge.

SVEINSSON, K. P. (ed.) (2009), *Who Cares About the White Working Class?*, London: Runnymede Trust.

TEILHARD DE CHARDIN, P. (1964), *The Future of Man*, New York, Doubleday.

TENBENSEL, T (2008), 'The role of evidence in policy: how the mix matters', Paper presented at the International Research Society for Public Management, Queensland University of Technology, Brisbane, Australia, 26–28 March 2008.

Thrift, N. (2005), 'But malice aforethought: cities and the natural history of hatred', *Transactions of the Institute of British Geographers*, 30(2): 133–50.

Tonry, M. (2010), 'The costly consequences of populist posturing: ASBOs, victims, "rebalancing" and diminution in support for civil liberties', *Punishment & Society*, 12(4): 387–413.

Tonry, M. and Bildsten, H. (2009), 'Antisocial behaviour', in M. Tonry (ed.), *Crime and Public Policy*, Oxford: Oxford University Press.

Toynbee, A. (1884), *Toynbee's Industrial Revolution*. Newton Abbott.

Tyler, T. R. and Fagan, J. (2008), 'Legitimacy and cooperation: Why do people help the police fight crime in their communities', *Ohio State Journal of Criminal Law*, 6: 231–75.

Uitermark, J., Hoschtenbach, C., and Van Gent, W. (2015), 'The statistical politics of exceptional territories', Paper presented at Sheffield Hallam University, 3 December 2015.

Valentine, G. *et al.* (2015, forthcoming), 'Tolerance: popular understandings of diversity and peaceful coexistence in Europe'.

Valins, O. (2003), 'Stubborn identities and the construction of socio-spatial boundaries: ultra-orthodox Jews living in contemporary Britain', *Transactions of the Institute of British Geographers*, 25: 158–78.

Wacquant, L. (2008), *Urban Outcasts: A Comparative Sociology of Advanced Marginality*, Cambridge: Polity.

Waiton, S. (2013), 'The New Sectarians', in J. Flint and J. Kelly (eds), *Bigotry, Football and Scotland*, Edinburgh: Edinburgh University Press.

Walters, J. (2015), 'Los Angeles considers officially "drought shaming" water wasters', *The Guardian*, 1 November 2015, available at: http://www.theguardian.com/us-news/2015/nov/01/los-angeles-california-drought-shaming, accessed 22 January 2016.

Waltzer, M. (1997), *On Toleration*, New Haven, CT and London: Yale University Press.

Watson, S. (2006), *City Publics: The (Dis)enchantments of Urban Encounters*, London: Routledge.

Webber, M. M. (1964), 'The Urban Place and the Nonplace Urban Realm', in M. M. Webber, J. W. Dyckman, D. L. Foley, A. Z Gutternberg, W. L. C. Wheaton, and C. Bauer Wurster (eds), *Explorations into Urban Structure*. Philadelphia, PA: University of Pennsylvania Press.

Weiss, C. H. (2001), 'What kind of evidence in evidence-based policy?', Paper presented to third international, inter-disciplinary evidence-based policies and indicator systems conference, July, University of Durham.

Williams, P. and McConnell, F. (2011), 'Critical geographies of peace', *Antipode*, 43L 927–31.

Wouters, C. (1986), 'Formalization and informalization: changing tension balances in civilizing processes', *Theory Culture and Society*, 3(2): 1–18.

Wyly, E. (2015), 'Gentrification on the planetary urban frontier: The evolution of Turner's noosphere', *Urban Studies*, 52(14): 2515–50.

Young, J. (2007), *The Vertigo of Late Modernity*, London: Sage.

Zorbaugh, H. W. (1924), *The Gold Coast and the Slum: A Sociological Study of Chicago's Near North Side*, Chicago: Chicago University Press.

Zukin, S. (1991), *Landscapes of Power: From Detroit to Disneyworld*, Berkeley, CA: University of California Press.

24

PRISON ARCHITECTURE AND DESIGN: PERSPECTIVES FROM CRIMINOLOGY AND CARCERAL GEOGRAPHY

Yvonne Jewkes and Dominique Moran

INTRODUCTION: WHY ARCHITECTURE AND DESIGN MATTER TO OUR UNDERSTANDING OF IMPRISONMENT

This is the sixth edition of the *Oxford Handbook*, yet it is the first to include a chapter on prison design. Indeed, aside from the many historical accounts of the early evolution of prison architecture (among others, Brodie *et al.* 1999, 2002; Evans 1982; Fairweather and McConville 2000; Grant and Jewkes 2015; Jewkes and Johnston 2007; Johnston 2000; Spens 1994), the topic has received only fleeting or tangential mention in post-war criminological scholarship. One exception to this neglect by the academy came in 1961, when a special issue of the *British Journal of Criminology* (Volume 1, Issue 4) was devoted to 'prison architecture'. Compiled at the time of the 'largest [prison] building programme to be undertaken in this country for a century' ('Editorial', 1961: 305), at a cost of £12 million (approximately £250 million today), the idea that new prison buildings must reflect both the most up-to-date scholarship and the most progressive penal philosophies in currency is deeply embedded in these early *British Journal of Criminology* articles, written by the Chairman of the Prison Commission, A. W. Petersen, sociologist, John Madge, architect and professor of architecture, Norman Johnston, and architectural theorist, Leslie Fairweather. We feel that theirs is an aspiration worth reviving and, with this in mind, we will pay close attention to the arguments put forward by these 'founding fathers' as this chapter unfolds.

When approaching the task of writing our contribution for this new edition of the *Handbook*, we have a few (perhaps obvious) questions at the forefront of our minds.

Why is this topic important? Why now? Why us? And—after such a long absence from the mainstream of criminological discourse and debate—how might we convince you, the reader, that prison architecture and design have meaning and relevance to scholars in criminology and related disciplines beyond the relatively small handful of people who study custodial buildings and carceral spaces? In communicating why we think the architecture and design of prisons is pivotal to 'prison studies', this chapter is divided into three sections, each of which takes a different approach to the question of why the topic of prison architecture and design matters. First, it will examine the extent to which penal philosophy and evolving penological ideas have been reflected in prison design through history. As Wener (2012) suggests, prison environments represent both an 'overt' agenda that seeks to provide adequate, measurable, and reasonably consistent living and working conditions for those individuals sentenced to imprisonment; and a 'covert' agenda that reflects what or who prisoners 'are' in the minds of those who commission prisons and in the wider society. This first section of the chapter explores what this 'covert' agenda has been through the ages of punishment.

In the second section we turn our attention to the recent policy context. This is a rare moment in the penal history of England and Wales as, at the time of writing, it has been announced that new, modern prisons for both adult men and women will be designed and built, in addition to HMP Berwyn, a 2,106 bed facility, which will open in Wrexham, North Wales in 2017. The announcement follows the closure of several old nineteenth-century jails, including Shrewsbury, Gloucester, and Reading, with more closures to come. Not since the middle of the nineteenth century, when 54 prisons were constructed on the same panoptic template as Pentonville, followed by a slightly less ambitious building programme in the 1960s in response to the problems of overcrowding, has such a wide-scale prison-building programme been contemplated. The current government plans thus represent a once-in-a-generation opportunity, not only to build facilities that are fit-for-purpose, but to re-assess what prisons are for and how their design might assist with the philosophies that underpin them.

Developing these ideas, the third and final section of the chapter discusses *society*'s relationship with the prison. We have argued elsewhere that prisons function simultaneously as technologies of control *and* systems of cultural symbolism (Jewkes *et al.* 2016). This section explains this idea further in relation to the ongoing prison modernization programme. In a sense, this will bring us full circle, as we discuss why the public appear to want prisons to *feel* like nineteenth-century places of severe and unremitting punishment, while *looking* like the kinds of buildings that populate twenty-first-century business parks and modern industrial sites. Finally, we suggest that a novel approach to prison design in England and Wales (one that follows the Scandinavian model, for example) might open up new spaces for discussion concerning how (and how much) we choose to punish. In other words, far from being about creating 'softer' or 'prettier' prisons, a focus on designing humanizing prison spaces that are focused on supporting rehabilitation and desistance could be a vital component in achieving radical justice reform, including decarceration.

This volume is self-evidently aimed primarily at students and scholars of criminology, but throughout the chapter we will make reference to the influence of other disciplines on criminological understandings of prison architecture and design, including architectural research, environmental psychology, and critical organization studies. Of particular importance in our discussion is carceral geography, a new and vibrant field of geographical research into practices of incarceration, which has in recent years made a significant contribution to criminological understandings of the prison. Its work is largely centred around three main themes: the nature and experience of carceral spaces, the geographies of carceral systems, and the relationship between the carceral and an increasingly punitive state (Moran 2013). Although the first geographical studies of spaces of confinement were disparate works in diverse contexts and with different aims and theoretical framings, research in this field now reflects a growing dialogue with the work of Foucault (1979) on the development of the prison, surveillance, and the regulation of space and docility of bodies, and of Agamben (1998, 2005) on the notion of exception, where sovereign power suspends the law, producing a zone of abandonment.

Innovative analyses of incarceration from a carceral geography perspective include explorations of bed-space (Mitchelson 2014); space and safety (Morin 2013); spaces of flirtation (Dardel 2013); visiting spaces (Moran 2013); and personal space and the personalization of cells (Sibley and van Hoven 2009). Meanwhile, scholars from criminology now routinely refer to the 'affective' dimensions of carceral space (Earle and Phillips 2012), the 'emotional geography' of prisons (Crewe *et al.* 2013), the 'penal palimpsest' (Fiddler 2007), prisons as 'non-places' for 'non-people' (Jewkes *et al.* 2016), and so on. In this chapter we are informed by carceral geographies of architecture (e.g. Moran *et al.*, forthcoming), in which a long-standing representationalist focus on the symbolism of buildings as sites of meaning and 'texts' to be read (Cosgrove 1998; Pratt 2002), has been displaced by consideration of the 'dynamic encounters' (Jacobs and Merriman 2011) between buildings, their constituent elements and spaces, those involved in their planning and design, and those who encounter them in a range of different ways. In paying attention to both the architectural symbolism of incarceration (the ways in which prison buildings are manifestations of punitive philosophies) and the ways in which they may reflexively shape such philosophies through real, virtual, or vicarious 'encounters', we seek to position prison architecture and design as a key site of negotiation of evolving penal philosophies. This, then, answers the question, 'why us?' as we are currently conducting the first major comparative international research study of prison architecture and design[1] and are bringing to the project our cross-disciplinary expertise in criminology and carceral geography respectively. As the authors in the *British Journal of Criminology* special issue understood, such interdisciplinary modes of inquiry are crucial to expanding our knowledge base and perceptions of the lived experience of imprisonment.

[1] ESRC Standard Grant ES/K011081/1,'Fear-suffused environments' or potential to rehabilitate? Prison architecture, design and technology and the lived experience of carceral spaces' (with Research Associate Jen Turner and doctoral candidate Ellie Slee).

A BRIEF HISTORY OF THE EVOLUTION OF PENAL PHILOSOPHIES AND PRISON ARCHITECTURE

As previously noted, relatively little has been written about prison design within criminology. Yet in the aforementioned special edition of *British Journal of Criminology* on prison architecture, several of the points made by Petersen, Madge, Fairweather, and Johnston appear depressingly familiar because they remain unresolved over half-a-century later. To take just a few examples; all the *British Journal of Criminology* contributors emphasize the importance of enabling as many prisoners as possible to serve their sentences within a reasonable distance of their home; an argument still being made by contemporary desistance theorists (Farrall and Calverley 2006; McNeill and Schinkel 2016; Schinkel 2014) and commentators on the 'collateral damage' inflicted on prisoners' families when a parent is incarcerated (Condry *et al.* 2016; Scharff Smith 2014). The question of why the use of small institutions should be 'economically prohibitive' (Madge 1961: 364) is another concern that has become even more salient since the 1960s, when the maximum number of prisoners envisaged for any given establishment was 450 (Petersen 1961). The proposition from both Johnston and Fairweather that small prisons are more operationally effective and more likely to result in rehabilitated prisoners is given added weight by recent research that finds that smaller prisons are better than larger facilities at housing prisoners in safe and secure conditions, providing them with meaningful work, education, and training, encouraging purposeful activity, and fostering healthy relationships between prisoners and prison staff (Liebling with Arnold 2004; Johnsen *et al.* 2011).

The fallacy of creating standardized prison designs, with only minor differences applied (e.g. to strength of construction materials) depending on the level of security required is an issue raised by Fairweather and Johnston, anticipating current concerns about 'value engineering' and 'future proofing' prison designs, which will be explored below. Relatedly, the need (identified by Fairweather) to build custodial facilities that meet known demand, rather than future projections, speaks to actuarial assessments of risk at the heart of the 'new penology' (Feeley and Simon 1992) and is a perennial concern to criminologists who write about the tendency of the media to exaggerate potential threats in times of particular sensitivity to risk (Jewkes 2015). The 'moral panic' had not yet been named in 1961, but scaremongering news reports inflected political debates about how the prison estate should respond to the abolition of the death penalty in the early 1960s, just as, arguably, they continue to do today, with possible terrorist attacks uppermost on media and political agendas.

These four examples from the first volume of the *British Journal of Criminology* in 1961 (and there are many others) underline that the history of imprisonment is characterized by continuity and consistency. The question of why the field of criminology has not been able to exert more influence on challenging a form of punishment that, by almost any measure applied, emphatically does not work, is not a issue that can be dealt with here (but see Garland 1990). Suffice to say that every major prison expansion programme of the last two hundred years has been a knee-jerk response to predictable problems—rising prisoner numbers, chronic overcrowding, and buildings that become dangerously outdated. As Fairweather (1961) notes, we do not appear to learn from our mistakes.

'HISTORY REPEATS ITSELF'

The suggestion that prisons represent a 'covert' agenda that reflects predominant attitudes towards offenders (Wener 2012) has underpinned the design of penal institutions since the late eighteenth century, when the celebrated prison reformer and 'architects' mentor' John Howard was instrumental in forcing those legislating and managing the prison system to re-think their philosophy of criminal justice and its fulfilment in prison architecture. Following outbreaks of serious, contagious illnesses in many gaolhouses, it was recognized that the squalid and chaotic prisons of the day were not suitable environments for the containment of large numbers of people in very close confines (see Jewkes and Johnston 2007, for an overview). Howard's reformist experience and his understanding of architecture made him the ideal candidate for an advisory role and in 1793, three years after his death, his principles for the construction of an 'ideal county gaol' were realized in the construction of Shrewsbury prison. The interior of Shrewsbury consisted of highly organized buildings that embodied the philosophy of reformation rather than retribution, with prison cells that were, for their day, comfortable and airy, including some that even commanded 'a beautiful view of the country' (Owen 1808: 433, cited in Jewkes and Johnston 2007). In many respects, then, Shrewsbury prison was ahead of its time—a very early exemplar of the 'healthy prison'[2]—and John Howard's mission to improve prison conditions underpinned radical changes in penal design globally; particularly in relation to ventilation, hygiene, segregation (to prevent contagion of criminality as well as disease), and religious servitude.

However, it must be remembered that Howard's prominence was largely because reform was urgently needed and, for all his good work, this was not an era of unmitigated enlightenment. Prison hulks and transportation were still being used and the site of the first national 'penitentiary' (so named because prisoners were to undergo a process of expiation and penance, and the emphasis was on hard but unproductive labour) was selected in 1799, the year of the Penitentiary Act, and established in 1816. The site chosen for the new Millbank penitentiary was boggy marshland on the banks of the river Thames, the unsuitability of which contributed to the enormous financial cost of the build (Johnston 2015). At Millbank, a period of strict and severe seclusion was followed by a second, more moderate phase of confinement, whereby some association was permitted—by which time the initial period of solitary confinement had already caused many prisoners to go insane. Indeed, the regime was so brutal that over 30 prisoners died in the first few years of its operation, leading to critical newspaper reports and political intervention, which testify to the lack of legitimacy of the prison in this early period (ibid.).

[2] A concept adopted by the World Health Organisation and developed as part of their inspection criteria by Her Majesty's Inspectorate of Prisons, http://www.justiceinspectorates.gov.uk/hmiprisons/about-our-inspections/inspection-criteria/, accessed 5 January 2017.

By 1842, when a 'new model prison' was deemed necessary to break the 'chain of [convicts'] former habits' prior to transporting them to the colonies (Sir John Graham, cited in Johnston 2015: 109), the 'separate system' of total solitude had been established. The model prison was Pentonville and prisoners there were kept apart at all times and monitored from a central observation point, in line with Bentham's panoptic vision, conceived in 1791. In the six years following Pentonville's construction, 54 further prisons were built to the same radial template, with the exception of the anomalous Wormwood Scrubs, constructed between 1875 and 1891 to a 'telegraph-pole' design, which Shrewsbury prison replicated when it was substantially altered at around the same time to reflect a move away from reform to a new emphasis on deterrence (see further below). While there was nothing especially novel about the use of solitary confinement in prisons, Pentonville represented the first time that the design of the prison became unified with the enforcement of the regime; a grim harmonization that finds its modern form in many of the self-contained, supermax-style segregation units found in high-security facilities, where seclusion through architecture overcomes the need for physical punishment, but results in many prisoners experiencing extreme mental anguish. Even as the last bricks were being laid, social commentators of the day were expressing their views that the new prison would be 'unnecessarily cruel' and that 'madness will seize those whom death has spared' (*The Times*, 20 May 1841; cited in Johnston 2015: 109). Moreover, observers of the new prison, standing on a six-acre site and encompassed by 25-foot-high walls, can have been left in little doubt about the uncompromising nature of criminal justice:

> To the inhabitants of Islington who daily look upon the high walls of Pentonville with its grim blackened cell houses, it is a visible sign of the most severe sanctions the law can impose—the deprivation of liberty and the possibility of death itself, for Pentonville is a 'hanging prison'. First and foremost the prison punishes, and there can be little doubt about this, for the physical apparatus of a maximum security prison is suggestive of little else beyond the curtailment of freedom. The architectural quality of the prison is not only functional but dramatic, part of the same body of symbolism which clothes the Judge of Assize in scarlet. (Morris and Morris 1963: 20)

Located in the very heart of the urban neighbourhood from which it drew its clientele, Pentonville heralded the collapse of the ideal of reformation and the emergence of new objectives—deterrence and repression. Its design also gave full expression to the Victorian obsession with discipline, certainty, and systematic uniformity and, despite its foreboding appearance, it was one of the most advanced prisons of its time (indeed, one of the most cutting-edge buildings of its era). Nearly two hundred years later, many of these late nineteenth-century jails are finally earmarked for closure,[3] having been described by then Prime Minister David Cameron, as 'ageing, ineffective, creaking, leaking and coming apart at the seams' (http://www.politics.co.uk). Nonetheless, we might speculate that the architect of Pentonville, Joshua Jebb, would be surprised that his prison remained in operation 175 years after it was built and that his influence

[3] Thirteen older prisons have been decommissioned so far with a further raft of closures expected imminently. Although no official announcement has yet been made regarding the closure of Pentonville, its demise is widely anticipated, not least because of the potential value of the site. It is worth noting, though that some of the smaller Victorian prisons are or were high-performing in relation to prisoner well-being.

is still to be seen in the radial wings, galleried landings, cellular compartments, and other design features of prisons constructed in the twenty-first century.

As the quote from Morris and Morris (1963) illustrates, just as John Howard's design principles based on the need for air and ventilation were abandoned in favour of cellular accommodation that was cramped and enclosed, the exteriors of prisons were becoming more expansive and formidable. For example, when Shrewsbury was redeveloped, the exterior was transformed into a façade of 'massive, strong and impressive character' (Anon 1894: 14, cited in Jewkes and Johnston 2007). These design strategies had parallel aims: the ostentatious, austere, and dramatic external façades were intended to deter people in the community from offending; while the dark and claustrophobic interior spaces, sparse conditions, and harsh regimes were aimed at deterring prisoners from future reoffending (Pratt 2002; Hancock and Jewkes 2012).

By the twentieth century, and especially in the immediate post-war period, when the prison population spiked and expansionism of the estate was once again on the political agenda, several prisons were, of necessity, opened in more rural locations. Converted from disused army camps, airfields, military hospitals, lunatic asylums, and country houses, some prisoners are to this day still housed in former Nissan huts and other accommodation that was only ever intended to be a temporary solution to an immediate crisis. This was the period when penal philosophies began to embrace a more therapeutic discourse—a process that had reached its apogee at the time that the special issue of the *British Journal of Criminology* was published in 1961. By then, the bleak surroundings of the crumbling Victorian prison had become viewed as an obstacle to progressive penal thinking (Pratt 2002) and the form and fabric of prison buildings was regarded as secondary to the therapeutic mission pursued within. 'Open' prisons, had also been established (the first started operating in the 1930s), allowing a relatively unrestricted degree of movement, including within the surrounding land, which was commonly used for farming and horticulture. Not only did the new open establishments bring flexibility to a system previously concerned only with uniformity, but they facilitated links between prisons and the communities in which they were located for the first time in over a century (Dunbar and Fairweather 2000; Jewkes and Johnston 2007).

NEW ERA, OLD IDEAS

The 1961 special issue of the *British Journal of Criminology* on 'prison architecture' was a response to the publication of the White Paper on Penal Practice in a Changing Society (HMSO 1959). This landmark policy document outlined proposals to build 40 new prisons to ease the overcrowding that blighted prisons in the post-war years (the first of which was HMP Blundeston in Suffolk, opened in 1963). The contributors to the *British Journal of Criminology* were invited to 'express their views' ('Editorial', 1961: 305) and the narrative thread running through their articles is familiar to contemporary prison scholars, that is, that the new prison-building programme was a chance to put right the mistakes of the past and build new prisons with a vision that went far beyond a straightforward solution to housing the inexorably rising prison population. In his contribution, Fairweather condemns the prison estate as 'an embarrassing legacy of extremely permanent buildings expressing an outdated and outworn penal philosophy' (1961: 340). The new building programme thus represented a once-in-a-generation opportunity in an age of architectural experimentation, new modern methods, and materials of construction (including pre-fabrication), and an as yet unwavering belief in prisons as places of human(e) experimentation. At this time, the predominant 'treatment model' resulted in criminal justice being influenced by a new raft of professional experts, including social workers, psychologists, health professionals, and academics. The new emphasis on treatment and therapy also permeated discussions about what the new prisons should look like: Prison Commissioner Peterson proclaims, 'Changes in treatment may bring with them changes in architecture, and research into treatment methods is developing rapidly' (1961: 375).

Fairweather, however, expresses cynicism regarding what kinds of prison buildings would be realized, which might strike a chord with the views of sceptics anticipating the current government's plans for prison reform. Under the subtitle 'History repeats itself', Fairweather comments that it is 'hardly surprising . . . but bitterly disappointing, that the first new prison of major importance to be built in this century—at Everthorpe Hall, Yorkshire, in 1958—should be a very close imitation of the type of prison erected during the previous century' (1961: 340). It was, he states, 'completely out of date before it even left the drawing board' and 'so far out of sympathy with current penal thought that it will very seriously hamper the use and development of more effective treatment methods' (Fairweather 1961: 340). Of course, with the benefit of hindsight, we know that the rehabilitative, treatment model had another decade in it, before it came to be seen as a further expression of the state's repressive disciplinary tendencies, involving excessive intervention, denying offenders their due rights, and inappropriately using indeterminate sentencing whereby prisoners would be treated for as long as it took to make them 'better'. It was finally sunk by a doctrine that, in the 1970s, had a swift and profound impact on policy and practice—'nothing works' (Martinson 1974; see Jewkes 2012; Cullen and Gendreau 2001 for overviews).

But even as 1950s austerity was giving way to 1960s optimism, Fairweather was calling for a re-think of the 'whole problem of prison design' to avoid building another Everthorpe which, he says, 'stands as a depressing reminder of the consequences of architectural stagnation' (1961: 340). Concurring with this view, President of the Prison Reform Trust, Lord Douglas Hurd denounced the prison designs of the post-war period as 'shoddy, expensive and just a little inhuman' (Hurd 2000: xiii-xiv). As Home Secretary (1985–89) Hurd said he was never asked to adjudicate on matters of prison design, nor was the subject raised in official reports or by pressure groups. This absence of public and policy discussion about prison design continued until very recently, when the opening of HMP Oakwood in 2012 reignited heated debate that recalls Fairweather's excoriation of Everthorpe and raises questions about the prison's perceived legitimacy. Following a series of well-documented problems that appear to have out-lived their dismissal by various interested parties as 'teething troubles',[4] there is now tacit acceptance on the part of key stakeholders, including government

[4] Although the much-publicized problems besetting its operator, G4S (at the 2012 Olympics and concerning Medway Secure Training Centre, to name but two), may have contributed to intense press coverage, it is nevertheless the case that HMP Oakwood has been the subject of an unusually high number of newspaper articles. For a perspective on different political responses to Oakwood, see: http://tinyurl.com/h5gev55; http://tinyurl.com/zwlp8dx; http://tinyurl.com/hd33vz8, accessed 5 January 2017.

ministers and their advisers, that a more ambitious and innovative approach to prison design might help to achieve their desired outcomes of reform and rehabilitation. The next section of this chapter will explore this policy context.

POLICY CONTEXT IN THE TWENTY-FIRST CENTURY: A FOCUS ON SIZE AND SECURITY

In recent years prisons in England and Wales have witnessed multiple ascending trends: more severe sentencing policies resulting in rising prisoner numbers and leading to further overcrowding; the growing prominence of security concerns within and outside the penal estate; the radicalization of prisoners to fundamentalist faiths; an influx of 'legal highs', mobile phones, and other contraband; an unprecedented number of murders; and a dramatic rise in self-harm and suicide after periods of relative stability and/or decline. These pressing problems have all had an impact on the detail of prison design; for example, internal fixtures and fittings must be designed without ligature points to prevent suicide attempts, in-cell phones are being introduced in some prisons in a bid to reduce the number of illicit devices, and perimeter walls are usually double-skinned so that contraband thrown over the wall lands in the gap in between.

Amid the negative, 'upward' outcomes, one of the few measurable indices of performance to travel in the other direction has been escapes from prison, which have fallen by 75 per cent since 2009 (Hansard 2015). In part this decline can be explained by a hardening of penal architecture and design, which has accompanied, and arguably given material form to, the intensifying 'depth', 'weight', and 'tightness' of imprisonment that are achieved administratively (Crewe 2009). Prison walls are higher, prison space is sequestered through zoning, prisoner movement is severely restricted, CCTV cameras and other (e.g. biometric) technologies proliferate, and fewer prisoners are housed in open conditions. This systemic and structural emphasis on surveillance, security, containment, and control in pursuit of compliance is characteristic of the 'new penology' first identified by Feeley and Simon (1992), which has replaced the earlier therapeutic discourses that shaped the thoughts of the *British Journal of Criminology* contributors on prison architecture. And, at the turn of the current century, with the emergence of a dominant concern for managing aggregates of 'dangerous' groups as economically and as efficiently as possible (as opposed to focusing on individual clinical diagnosis and treatment, for example), the rationale for building bigger and cheaper prisons rapidly overtook discussions about imaginative prison design, humane treatment, and attention to rehabilitation.

Of course, an important driver of these developments has been private investment which has, since the mid-1990s, had an undeniable impact on the design of prisons; partly because there is an expectation that the private sector will bring to the prison system quality improvement, cost reduction, and innovation; but not least because private companies are subject to significant financial penalties for failure to meet government-set performance targets on the kinds of incidents highlighted above. Introduced by a Conservative administration in 1992, the Private Finance Initiative (PFI) enabled 'Public-Private Partnerships' (PPPs) to fund public infrastructure projects with private capital and two years later the 1994 Criminal Justice and Public Order Act allowed for the private *provision* as well as operation and maintenance of prisons.[5] Following a tendering process in which the public sector was barred from participating, Group 4 (now G4S) was awarded a contract to manage HMP Wolds, a newly built remand prison that opened near Hull in April 1992. What started as an 'experiment', however, soon became routine policy and in 1997 the incoming New Labour government adopted PFI, with HMP Altcourse in Liverpool and HMP Parc, at Bridgend, being the first PFI builds under Labour in England and Wales respectively. There are currently 14 private prisons that are contractually managed by three companies: G4S, Sodexo, and Serco.

Assessments of privatization are mixed (see Metzger 2003; Crewe, Liebling, and Hulley 2011). There can be little argument that private prisons are leading the way in innovation, for example regarding prisoners' access to personal technology, but many critics have lingering concerns that short-term innovation simply improves long-term efficiency by drastically reducing staffing costs. One of the most controversial outcomes of private sector involvement in the prison estate is the size of new correctional facilities. In 2009, the then Labour government announced that it was shelving its plans to build so-called 'Titan' prisons and, a year later, the new Conservative Secretary of State for Justice, Kenneth Clarke promised a 'rehabilitation revolution', which led to some hope that money would be diverted instead into smaller prisons and community-based alternatives. But now the Titan has returned in all but name, and reform groups predict that shortly half of all prisoners will be warehoused in 'super-prisons' (PRT 2014). Advised by the right-wing think tank Policy Exchange, successive ministers have been persuaded that not only do very large establishments on multi-prison sites offer much-needed economies of scale, they have the added benefit of providing jobs and financial growth in parts of the country that suffered during the economic downturn. Aside from the moral questions implicit in the idea of taking England and Wales down the same path of 'profit from punishment' as many US states, this political stance ignores the wealth of evidence to the contrary. For example, Genter *et al.* (2013) found that not only did prisons *not* improve job prospects for inhabitants of host communities, but that the privatization of prisons in the US has actually impeded local economic growth. In the UK there has been a great deal of opposition to super-sized prisons, on the grounds that 'effectiveness' and 'efficiencies' are incompatible goals (Owers 2008; Liebling 2008); and that 'effectiveness' must be measured in terms of the quality of life offered (Liebling with Arnold 2004), as well as performance measures that prioritize prison security, offender risk management, and local economic growth.

The other, less well-known, characteristic of the most recently built prisons in England and Wales, which also raises concerns that prisoners' quality of life and

[5] In a nutshell, under this initiative an integrated supply team is appointed to design, construct, manage, and finance a development and then to operate it for a period of time. A special purpose vehicle (SPV), of which the integrated supply team is a part, finances the project and leases it to the government for an agreed period (usually 25 years) after which the development reverts to government ownership.

well-being fall a long way behind the drivers of 'effectiveness' and 'efficiency', is that the sites and buildings are 'future-proofed'. This means that, although they are Category C prisons—officially 'medium-security' facilities, holding those prisoners who are unlikely to try to escape—the prisons are constructed with all the security paraphernalia of (at least) a Category B institution, intended to house prisoners for whom the potential for escape should be made very difficult. The rationale is that, if at some point in the future, it needs to be used to accommodate high-security prisoners, it can do so without the need for expensive retro-fitting of enhanced situational security measures. Consequently, Category C prisoners, who would normally anticipate living in somewhat 'open' conditions (relatively speaking), as they are prepared for the minimum-security conditions of a Category D facility and/or release into the community, are accommodated within high fences and walls with locked gates every few metres inhibiting their movement.

HMP Berwyn (due to open in Wrexham, North Wales, in 2017) has been designed to the same template as HMP Oakwood in Wolverhampton (opened in 2012). Both have an over-securitized design for the category of prisoner they hold and both have 2,106 beds, making them among the largest prisons in Europe. Many criminologists view these prison warehouses as a retrograde step that runs counter to all the knowledge and evidence that has found that smaller institutions nurture the humanistic values (e.g. respect, trust, and empathy) that are central to forging positive prisoner–staff relationships and successful outcomes (Drake 2012; Liebling with Arnold 2004; PRT 2014; HMCIP 2009; Jewkes and Moran 2014; Johnsen *et al.* 2011; Madoc-Jones *et al.*, forthcoming). Writing at a time when a prison holding in excess of 400 prisoners was considered 'very large' (Liebling 2008), Leslie Fairweather could not have anticipated just how vast prisons would become when he wrote in 1961:

> The internal arrangement of a building can influence the degree and quality of personal relationships within it to a remarkable degree. These relationships will not develop healthily in huge impersonal blocks of cells where the individual is dwarfed by the overpowering size of the structure. They can only be attempted in buildings which respect the quality of the individual by being attractive, as normal in appearance as possible, and suitable in scale. (Fairweather 1961: 340)

'VALUE-ENGINEERING' AND THE ROLE OF THE ARCHITECT

Fairweather would also not have been able to predict that the architects of these new super-size prisons have little creative input into the designs. The rise of the computer-aided, simulation-based software known as Building Information Modelling (BIM) has replaced the old-fashioned drawing board and introduced further standardization of the penal estate, with arguably negative consequences both for the ways in which architects think about buildings representationally and creatively, and also in terms of the lived experience of those who occupy them. Reflecting on one of the current buzzwords in prison planning, 'value-engineering', one of the architects who worked on the plans for Oakwood lamented:

> I'm sorry, but with the Ministry of Justice it's just a cost-cutting exercise. And that's all it is. It's just reducing costs again and again and again . . . [I]t's really sad but we've got to a stage where we're actually stripping back our designs (cited in Moran *et al.*, forthcoming).

The restriction of space for architectural creativity and the managerialist, regulatory, and risk-averse context of prison procurement mean that even the most benign and well-intended design decisions can get vetoed at an early stage. For example, the planting of trees around prison sites is widely acknowledged (not least by architects) to 'soften' the environment and have 'therapeutic' benefits for prisoners, but proposals for landscaping in prison grounds are frequently thwarted by security minded officials who argue that trees interrupt sight-lines and gardens are expensive to keep tidy and can be used to hide contraband. Moreover, the emphasis on value-engineering means that, on the whole, prison buildings are constructed from 'hard' materials such as bricks and pre-fabricated concrete panels, while materials more commonly seen in 'signature buildings' such as arts centres, airport buildings, office blocks, and specialist healthcare environments (wood, steel, huge glass panels, etc.) are rejected on grounds of cost.

In other parts of Europe, however, there are prisons that can justifiably be described as signature buildings. Underpinned by a utopian vision, prison designers in Norway,[6] Iceland, and Denmark have focused on the rehabilitative function of imprisonment, and have experimented with progressive and highly stylized forms of penal architecture. Internal prison spaces exhibit soft furnishings, colour zoning, maximum exploitation of natural light, displays of art and sculpture, and views of nature through vista windows without bars, while outdoor space and encompassing landscape are utilized to maximum effect. For example, in designing a new prison in Greenland (its first 'closed' prison, in fact), the Danish architects Schmidt Hammer Lassen aim to design the 'world's most scenic prison'. Set within a stunning, rugged landscape, the prison will exploit the 'contrast between the rough and the beautiful':

> The whole idea behind the project is to add qualities to the complex that will enhance rehabilitation and diminish physical and psychological violence . . . The thought process behind this is that access to nature—watching the clouds, birds, daylight, weather, and so on, can aid in rehabilitation. (http://www.archdaily.com/375056/ny-anstalt-correctional-facility-winning-proposal-schmidt-hammer-lassen-architects/)

Carceral geographers regard such designs as generic expressions of 'affect' that evoke certain kinds of creative inhabitation (Kraftl and Adey 2008). Characterized by openness, flexibility, and 'humane' treatment, they may promote personal and intellectual growth, and even a lightness and vividness of being (Hancock and Jewkes 2012). This link between affect and creative, experiential inhabitation echoes parallel developments in organization studies and criminological research into architecture as 'technologies of (dis)enchantment' (Hancock and Jewkes 2012; Jewkes 2013). In simple terms, it has been suggested that the purposeful incorporation into a building of an

[6] Although Halden prison in southern Norway is commonly held up as an exemplar of humane prison design, and one that is 'effective' at meeting its 'quality-of-life' objectives, it is not regarded by the Norwegian prison authorities as being 'efficient' (partly because it occupies a large site that requires staff to spend much of their time escorting prisoners around the scattered buildings). As Norway plans its own prison modernization/expansion strategy (under a recently elected Conservative-led government), future 'closed' custodial facilities will be BIM-designed, standardized, modular units with relatively restricted movement—in other words, inexpensive to construct and operate. They will, however, remain small in size in comparison to prisons in the UK and will contain elements and amenities that are still considered 'controversial' in England and Wales.

aesthetic code designed to blunt or depress the senses ('an-aesthetics') produces a non-cognitive reaction that enhances feelings of disenchantment, estrangement, and banality on the part of all those who interact with it (Dale and Burrell 2003; Jewkes 2013); and possibly even limits the subjective growth of those confined, contributing to the pains of imprisonment (Hancock and Jewkes 2012).

The bland, unassuming, and uniform exterior style that has been favoured in recent prison construction projects, with its vast expanses of brick, few, small windows, limited landscaping, visible surveillance, and no unnecessary decoration, are arguably a manifestation of how architecture, design, and technology contribute to the generation of an anaesthetized subjectivity, one perfectly suited to control from above and between (Dale and Burrell 2003). While we would hesitate to claim that a prison in England and Wales could not, or will never be, a 'signature' building in the manner of Nuuk Prison in Greenland, or Halden Prison in Norway, the research we have conducted with architects, contractors, engineers, and other buildings professionals, and with representatives of the MoJ, strongly suggests that within the dynamic encounters between these different parties, discussion of the logics and philosophies of imprisonment has barely featured at all. Regulations, schedules, structures, and technologies that exist to standardize delivery, speed up build times, and drive down build costs, all marginalize opportunities for design innovation; or even for discussion of what it is that the prison is intended to achieve beyond simply incapacitating offenders for a period of time.

LOOKING TO THE FUTURE: THE 'BIGGEST SHAKE-UP OF PRISONS SINCE THE VICTORIAN ERA'

Having said all of the above, there is, as this volume goes to press, a new chapter unfolding in the evolution of prison design in England and Wales. In a speech delivered at the Prisoner Learning Alliance (PLA) in July 2015, then Secretary of State for Justice, Michael Gove, announced that nine new prisons would be built by 2020 and stated that his aim for these new facilities was 'to design out the dark corners which too often facilitate violence and drug-taking . . . [and] build a prison estate which allows prisoners to be rehabilitated' (http://www.gov.uk). In February 2016 the Prime Minister of the time, David Cameron, pledged to support his minister in the 'biggest shake-up of prisons since the Victorian era', and announced that in addition to the new facilities, a further six existing establishments would become 'reform prisons' with governors given greater autonomy over the financial and operational management of their prisons. Conceiving of the new establishments as places of care, as well as punishment, both Gove and Cameron acknowledged the extent to which the buildings and spatial design of prisons are conducive to rehabilitating offenders and helping them 'find meaning in their lives' (http://www.

politics.co.uk). The other side of the modernization plan, said Cameron, involves relinquishing the parts of the estate that are no longer fit-for-purpose. Such prisons, he commented, were barely fit for human habitation when they were built, and are 'much, much worse today' (ibid.).

Of course, the UK now has a new Prime Minister (Theresa May) and Secretary of State for Justice (Liz Truss), but the early signs are that their predecessors' prison reform plans remain broadly on course. Looking forward, then, there is a possibility that the prison estate will look very different by 2020, as the proposed modernization programme brings the opportunity not only to radically reform the prison landscape, but in doing so, to nurture a different philosophy of punishment in the minds of politicians, policy-makers, and the public at large. One aspect of this might be to look at examples of good practice in prison design in other parts of the world, especially those with lower rates of recidivism and lower numbers of suicides, self-harm, and violent assaults than those that blight our own penal system. Once again, those who are sceptical about the political will to embrace truly reformist ideas might point to Petersen's article in the special issue of the *British Journal of Criminology*, which notes that the Prison Commission had taken account of 'recent work in foreign countries . . . [including] several Scandinavian establishments' (1961: 374). Their influence is difficult to determine in the facilities that were built.

One of the most significant factors in not following the lead of our Scandinavian neighbours in applying to the design of new prisons architectural and aesthetic principles that encourage personal and intellectual creativity, is the perception—fuelled by the popular press—that there is no public appetite for it, and therefore no votes in it. Politicians habitually employ 'public opinion' and 'public interest' to justify Draconian policies and, while prison designers in Norway, Iceland, and Denmark have experimented with progressive and highly stylized forms of architecture, and internal prison spaces that explore more open, flexible, and normalized spatial planning, with comfortable furnishings, attractive colour schemes, and a maximum exploitation of natural light, even tentative discussions about how to humanize prison environments in England and Wales have met with concerns from politicians and civil servants about whether they would pass the '*Daily Mail* test'.[7]

Given the very particular brand of punitive populism that frames media reporting of anything relating to prison conditions, one might expect new prisons to look as stark and foreboding as their Victorian predecessors, but contemporary prison architecture is the material embodiment of prevailing expectations that prisons should be as inoffensive in outward appearance as possible, while being sufficiently punitive within to punish offenders and deter them from offending in future. The prototypical prison may be a constant reminder to society of the perils of transgression and a reassurance of the severe deprivations within, but it also generates disproportionate fears about diminished public safety, low 'civic pride', and a belief that the disrepute of the

[7] An example related to us during our research illustrates the point: a discussion among prison planners about bars on cell windows concluded that horizontal bars (which permit a better view of the outside vista) would be acceptable in women's facilities and those holding children and young people, but that in adult male prisons, vertical bars were important signifiers of 'punishment'. The idea that windows could be installed *without* bars, as is common in other parts of the UK and Europe, has not yet penetrated planning discussions in England and Wales.

prison will cause property values to plummet.[8] For all these reasons, the 'Victorian' archetype has been submerged by a desire to disguise penal institutions so that they resemble countless other 'chillingly-blank', 'barn-like buildings' (Hatherley 2010: 11). Supermarkets, schools, DIY outlets, Amazon warehouses, Premier Inns, prisons, and countless commercial, civic, and institutional buildings all wear the same camouflage, forming a heterogeneous mass to merge seamlessly into the 'archi-texture' of the city (Davis 1990: 256; Jewkes *et al.* 2016).

Interestingly, both Northern Ireland and the Republic of Ireland are proposing a more progressive design agenda for future prison planning, while Scotland has three new prisons established since 2012—HMP Low Moss, HMP Shotts, and HMP Grampian—all of which are relatively striking in appearance (they are much closer to what might be described as 'signature buildings') and are viewed as a 'nod to Scandinavia' (Armstrong 2014). Of course, the idea of a new prison simply being a bold design statement or architectural vanity project would be as unpalatable as the deliberate designing-in of bleakness or ugliness as a punitive aesthetic (Jewkes 2013). But in the Scottish examples, their progressive, 'community-facing' designs signal an explicit commitment to the principles of desistance. Moving away from a traditional 'deficits-based' approach of identifying what's wrong with offenders and trying to fix it, towards an 'assets-based' model of identifying offenders' strengths and building on them (rhetoric which was echoed in David Cameron's speech in February 2016), HMP Grampian and the others have been characterized as statements of Scottish separatism—the ambition of a Nationalist government seeking to 'do punishment differently, and specifically, differently from England' (Armstrong 2014: np).[9]

The characteristics of contemporary prison architecture described so far represent the overt agendas of penal design, reflecting a punitive turn from which, we might cautiously suggest, the prison services of the UK and Ireland appear to be in various stages of retreat. But what of the covert agendas that speak to underlying societal perceptions of offenders? The most recently built prisons in England and Wales may share a (relatively) inoffensive vernacular with retail warehouses or low-budget, chain hotels, but arguably they are no less scripted in their visual appearance than their turreted and curlicued Victorian cousins (Jewkes *et al.* 2016). And like their grandiose predecessors, the contemporary prison's visual reach of control and anaesthetization extends far beyond the prisoner, or even the staff and visitors who populate and move through carceral spaces, to the myriad of users and things that come into its contact in numerous, complex, planned, embodied, multi-sensory, spontaneous, and unexpected ways, and are resonant of the power structures that exist both within and outwith the building (Jacobs and Merriman 2011). The new architecture of incarceration thus provides a common (and 'common-sense') visual vocabulary for current political, economic,

[8] The name as well as the appearance of a prison can be contentious. While welcoming the selection of a former Firestone industrial site in North Wales because of the jobs it might provide, the people of Wrexham nonetheless did not want their new prison to be named after, and thus closely associated with, the town; hence HMP Berwyn.

[9] Whether or not they are succeeding in this aim is debatable; like all new prisons they have experienced some teething troubles and it is perhaps too early to say whether their design is positively affecting their operation and outcomes (although we plan to publish further on this in the future).

social, cultural, and spatial understandings of incarceration (Schept 2014), just as it did when Jebb designed the magnificent but maleficent Pentonville Prison.

So, if Pentonville stands as a statement of sovereign power and retribution, while Everthorpe is a manifestation of political timidity and architectural stagnation, and Grampian is a radical experiment (in its building, if not yet in its culture) with a separatist intent, what do the unremarkable carceral buildings of the current age in England and Wales say? What are the aesthetic principles being mobilized—as technologies of control and as systems of cultural symbolism? We suggest that contemporary carceral aesthetics in England and Wales have a mimetic quality, sequestering offenders, sanitizing the pains of imprisonment, and eliciting ignorance and apathy in the spectator (Jewkes *et al.* 2016). The 'humming, fortress-like invincibility' (Schept 2014: 200) of an edifice like that of Pentonville or Wormwood Scrubs elicits 'layers of questions' about 'the physical and symbolic place of incarceration . . . and about the role of the state and capital in structuring the future of communities' (ibid.). It is a potent, challenging force. In contrast, the bland and indistinct presence of Oakwood or Berwyn serves to conceal the implications of its power. It barely raises any questions at all, except this; do we turn a blind eye to the plight of the confined and to the historical structures of power that support the carceral complex when we diminish the visibility of the buildings that contain them? The affective dimensions of spectatorship in relation to the prisons built in the nineteenth century are frequently rousing, sensate experiences, but the buildings that administer contemporary criminal justice are 'neither forbidding nor overly welcoming . . . [but are] simply there, like everything else in the neighbourhood'. (Davis 1990: 168). It is arguable, then, that an anaesthetizing aesthetic extends beyond the affective power to deaden the senses of those who inhabit prison buildings and permeates the wider, collective conscience as well (Jewkes *et al.* 2016).

CONCLUDING THOUGHTS

This chapter has attempted to show how viewing the concepts and theories that have dominated the study of prisons over the last half-century through the lens of architecture and design generates a nuanced and sensate understanding of imprisonment. We have made reference to the negative effects of architecture and design which, as eloquently described in numerous prisoner biographies and testimonies (among others, Boyle 1977, 1984; Hassine 2010; Wayne 1994; McWatters 2013), give material context to the 'pains of imprisonment' (Sykes 1958). Two-hundred-year-old discourses of legitimacy and non-legitimacy (Sparks and Bottoms 1995) have resurfaced in criticism of modern prison warehouses that do little to rehabilitate the offender and arguably do even less to engage the public with questions about the purpose of imprisonment and the harms that prisons do. Their high-security architecture (to hold medium-security prisoners) might be regarded as a barometer for understanding the methods and parameters of state power, as security in prisons has run parallel to its rise in prominence in an increasingly risk-attuned and retributive society (Drake 2012). Changes in penal architecture and design have reflected evolving penological ideas, from Howard's philosophies about reform and 'healthy' prisons, to a Victorian emphasis on order, discipline, deterrence, and repression, through a faith in individually tailored treatment and rehabilitation, to the challenge of an administrative focus known as the 'new penology' (Feeley and Simon 1992). As the aesthetics of carceral spaces have reformed and rationalized the delivery of punishment, resulting in 'deeper', 'heavier', and 'tighter' experiences of incarceration (Crewe 2009), a resurgence of the doctrine of less eligibility has led to public acquiescence and apathy about the conditions that prisoners are held in.

Nonetheless, a growing recognition that our bloated penal system is unsustainable,[10] and is failing in numerous respects, has precipitated a change in government rhetoric. The notions of 'reform' and 'healthy' prisons are once again in common currency, in ways that would be recognizable to John Howard. Moreover, for those who believe that advocating a more progressive prison design agenda—be it based on principles of normalization, humanization, human rights, therapy, well-being, or any number of other concerns—is actually about creating 'softer' or 'prettier' prisons, and/or that it is doing nothing to challenge the institution of the prison itself, we argue that a focus on designing prison spaces that support rehabilitation and desistance could be a vital component in achieving radical justice reform, including decarceration. Put simply, prisons that are designed to be hard, ugly, and either sensorially depriving or sensorially overloading (which prisons often are simultaneously; Wener 2012), support a view of the prisoner as deserving of such disenchanting environments. However, when a prison communicates positive attributes (e.g. hope, trust, empathy, respect), the design challenges the cultural stereotype of what a prison is—and through this—who prisoners are, and it becomes considerably harder to hold the view that prisoners 'deserve' to be held in brutal conditions. Taking this a step further if, through design, the idea of housing people in a 'prison' is not significantly different from housing people in a well-designed hospital or student hall of residence, it may not be a huge conceptual leap to connect the prison to notions of justice that can be achieved while 'prisoners' remain in the community (Jewkes and Lulham 2016).

As we contemplate the closure of more iconic Victorian prisons and the opening of 10 new prisons (including Berwyn) by 2020, it is tempting to return to the parallels between the discussions published in the *British Journal of Criminology* more than half-a-century ago and current debates about what England and Wales' new prisons should look like, what they should be trying to achieve, and how their design might assist these aims. Although carceral spaces, and the forms of inhabitation they encourage, have subtly altered over the decades, prison architecture has not evolved very much since the Pentonville model, with wings radiating from a central hall and cellular confinement remaining the norm. In 1961, Leslie Fairweather wrote of Everthorpe that, like its Victorian predecessors, it consists of 'long, noisy, open halls with banks of cells rising on each side' which are, he says, 'abhorrently familiar features of our prison system [that] need no further description' (1961: 340). This description might just as

[10] That is, unsustainable in both human and financial terms, arguments which are also germane in the USA where several states have experienced recent decreases in their prison populations.

easily have been written about any of the prison houseblocks constructed in the last five years.

If prisons continue to be designed as they have been over the last 150 years, 'modern' prisons will continue to inherit 'Victorian' problems, as Fairweather predicted in 1961, and as has been documented by the Prisons Inspectorate numerous times since. For example, within a year of re-opening in 1983, the 'new' Holloway Prison was criticized by HMIP for engendering a form of torture that could result in acute mental illness (Home Office 1985), recalling criticism in the 1840s of the numbers of prisoners who became insane under the separate system (Jewkes and Johnston 2007). A decade later, in December 1995, Chief Inspector David Ramsbotham walked out of an inspection of Holloway in disgust.[11] More recently, HMP Doncaster (built in 1994) has come under heavy criticism for its high rates of violent assaults, incidents of self-harm, and deaths in custody; all of which may be a partial consequence of poor environmental conditions, including cells 'in a terrible state, with filth, graffiti, and inadequate furniture' (HMIP 2016: 5), stinking, unscreened toilets, broken windows, exposed wiring, dirty bedding, and areas that were littered and contained vermin (ibid.: 17). Meanwhile, reports that HMP Oakwood is expanding its capacity by 500, by converting single occupancy cells to double rooms, does little to alleviate the impression that the system is once again in crisis.

Given the wealth of evidence that has been accumulated since the last major wave of prison expansion, it is hoped that ministers will take notice of the opinions of experts with 'open, fertile and creative minds' (Madge 1961: 371) and accept that our recent history of building 'huge impersonal blocks of cells where the individual is dwarfed by the overpowering size of the structure' (Fairweather 1961:) has negative effects; and on staff, as well as prisoners.[12] Just as in 1961, when Madge warned of the futility of preserving established practice (given all the evidence that prison does not 'work') and appealed for a 'more adequate prison architecture' in a time of experimentation, the planners, architects, and designers currently working on the template for the nine new facilities indisputably have a 'decisive influence on their success or failure' for at least a generation to come (1961: 371).

As long ago as 1931, Robert Davison, Director of Research for the Architectural Record, published a caustic article castigating both US prison commissioners and penologists for being 'surprisingly insensitive to the enormous importance of the building in the treatment of the prisoner' (1931: 39). Recognizing that the design of prisons seemed to be a blind spot for the criminal justice system, he advocated that it was the job of the architect—even though they could 'scarcely be expected to be a penal expert'—to indicate the 'necessity for a prolonged and careful study of this problem', and for 'thorough research in [prison] building'[13] (Davison 1931: 39). Although the

[11] The 'inadequate and antiquated' Holloway is one of the prisons that will close to make way for '21st century solutions to criminality', according to Michael Gove in his speech in 2015 (http://www.gov.uk, accessed 5 January 2017).

[12] In addition to the growing body of academic scholarship that finds that smaller prisons are more successful on a range of outcomes, Her Majesty's Inspectorate of Prisons has also reported that large prisons are not as effective as small ones (Madoc-Jones *et al.*, forthcoming).

[13] That a group of architects working on early designs for the new prisons arrived at a meeting with us recently, armed with an impressive stack of criminology and carceral geography books, suggests that Davison's advice is being taken seriously!

UK Government has eschewed proposals to hold an architectural design competition (for reasons of expediency), as is common in many European countries, the inclusion of 'designing-architects' in the planning process gives us some grounds for optimism. It is hoped, then, that the designers of the new prisons mobilize aesthetic and spatial values and practices to signify and support a different model of criminal justice than the one that has singularly failed to achieve any of the aims of imprisonment, other than (usually) temporary incapacitation. A new approach to prison architecture and design is at least 55 years overdue. Let us finally learn from the mistakes of the past.

SELECTED FURTHER READING

Although primarily focused on prisons in North America, Wener's *The Environmental Psychology of Prisons and Jails: Creating Humane Spaces in Secure Settings* (2012) discusses principles of architecture and environment that have universal application, and is an erudite yet accessible compilation of 30 years of research by one of the world's leading scholars of penal design and its effects. Spens' *Architecture of Incarceration* (1994) remains a pictorially beautiful and informative collection, which includes an essay by Leslie Fairweather. The collection edited by Fairweather and McConville, *Prison Architecture: Policy, Design and Experience* (2000), contains contributions from some of the leading experts in prison design from the worlds of architecture, the Prison Service, the Inspectorate, and academia. For more recent analyses, the authors of this chapter have written several contributions. Among them, Jewkes has written 'The Aesthetics and Anaesthetics of Prison Architecture' (2013) and 'Penal aesthetics and the art of prison architecture'. Moran has written 'Prison Buildings and the Design of Carceral Space' (2015). Collaboratively, they have written an overview of the topic: Moran *et al.*, 'Prison design and carceral space' (2016); and a discussion of the subject from the perspective of visual criminology, Jewkes *et al.*, 'The visual retreat of the prison: non-places for non-people' (2016). The special issue of the *British Journal of Criminology* (1961: 1(4)) devoted to 'prison architecture' is a fascinating snapshot of expert thinking about prison design at the time of the last major expansion programme, and is a pertinent reminder of the perils of not learning from past mistakes.

REFERENCES

AGAMBEN, G. (1998), *Homo Sacer: Sovereign Power and Bare Life*, Stanford: Stanford University Press.

AGAMBEN, G. (2005), *State of Exception*, Chicago: University of Chicago Press.

ARMSTRONG, S. (2014), 'Scotland's newest prison is another nod to Scandinavia', *The Conversation*, available at: https://theconversation.com/scotlands-newest-prison-is-another-nod-to-scandinavia-24145, accessed 4 January 2017.

BOYLE, J. (1977), *A Sense of Freedom*, London: Pan.

BOYLE, J. (1984), *The Pain of Confinement*, Edinburgh: Canongate.

BRODIE, A., CROOM, J., and DAVIES, J. O. (1999), *Behind Bars: The Hidden Architecture of England's Prisons*, English Heritage: Swindon.

BRODIE, A., CROOM, J., and DAVIES, J. O. (2002), *English Prisons: An Architectural History*, English Heritage: Swindon.

CONDRY, R., KOTOVA, A., and MINSON, S. (2016), 'Social Injustice and Collateral Damage: The Families and Children of Prisoners', in Y. Jewkes, J. Bennett, and B. Crewe (eds), *Handbook on Prisons*, 2nd edn, Abingdon: Routledge.

COSGROVE, D. E. (1998), *Social Formation and Symbolic Landscape*, Madison, WI: University of Wisconsin Press.

CREWE, B. (2009), *The Prisoner Society: Power, Adaption, and Social Life in an English Prison*, Oxford: Oxford University Press.

CREWE, B., LIEBLING, A., and HULLEY, S. (2011), 'Staff culture, use of authority and prisoner quality of life in public and private sector prisons', *Australian & New Zealand Journal of Criminology*, 44(1): 94–115.

CREWE, B., WARR, J., BENNETT, P., and SMITH, A. (2013), 'The emotional geography of prison life', *Theoretical Criminology*, 18(1): 56–74.

CULLEN, F. T. and GENDREAU, P. (2001), 'From nothing works to what works: Changing professional ideology in the 21st century', *The Prison Journal*, 81(3): 313–38.

DALE, K. and BURRELL, G. (2003) 'An-Aesthetics and Architecture', in A. Carr and P. Hancock (eds), *Art and Aesthetics at Work*, Basingstoke: Palgrave.

DARDEL, J. (2013), 'Resisting "Bare Life": Prisoners' Agency in the New Prison Culture Era in Colombia', in D. Moran, N. Gill, and D. Conlon (eds), *Carceral Spaces: Mobility and Agency in Imprisonment and Migrant Detention*, Farnham: Ashgate.

DAVIS, M. (1990), *City of Quartz*, London: Pimlico.

DAVISON, R. L. (1931), 'Prison architecture', *Annals of the American Academy of Political and Social Science*, 157: 33–9.

DRAKE, D. (2012), *Prisons, Punishment and the Pursuit of Security*, London: Palgrave.

DUNBAR, I. and FAIRWEATHER, L. (2000), 'English prison design', in L. Fairweather and S. McConville (eds), *Prison Architecture: Policy, Design and Experience*, Oxford: Architectural Press.

EARLE, R. and PHILLIPS, C. (2012), 'Digesting men? Ethnicity, gender and food: Perspectives from a "prison ethnography" ', *Theoretical Criminology*, 16(2): 141–56.

'EDITORIAL' (1961), *British Journal of Criminology*, special issue on 'Prison Architecture', 1(4): 305–6.

EVANS, R. (1982), *The Fabrication of Virtue: English Prison Architecture, 1750-1840*, Cambridge: Cambridge University Press.

FAIRWEATHER, L. (1961), 'Prison Architecture in England', *British Journal of Criminology*, special issue on 'Prison Architecture', 1(4): 339–61.

FAIRWEATHER, L. and MCCONVILLE, S. (eds) (2000), *Prison Architecture: Policy, Design, and Experience*, Oxford: Elsevier.

FARRALL, S. and CALVERLEY, A. (2006), *Understanding Desistance from Crime*, Maidenhead: Open University Press.

FEELEY, M. M. and SIMON, J. (1992), 'The New Penology: Notes on the Emerging Strategy of Corrections and its Implications', *Criminology*, 30(4): 449–74.

FIDDLER, M. (2007), 'Projecting the prison: The depiction of the uncanny in The Shawshank Redemption', *Crime, Media, Culture: An International Journal*, 3(2): 192–206.

FOUCAULT, M. (1979), *Discipline and Punish: The Birth of the Prison*, New York: Vintage.

GARLAND, D. (1990), *Punishment and Modern Society*, Chicago: University of Chicago.

GENTER, S., HOOKS, G., and MOSHER, C. (2013), 'Prisons, jobs and privatization: The impact of prisons on employment growth in rural US counties, 1997–2004', *Social Science Research*, 42(3): 596–610.

GRANT, E. and JEWKES, Y. (2015), 'Designs on punishment: evolving models of spatial confinement in Australia and the USA', *The Prison Journal*, 95(2): 223–43.

HANCOCK, P. and JEWKES, Y. (2012), 'Penal aesthetics and the pains of imprisonment', *Punishment & Society*, 13(5): 611–29.

HANSARD (2015), 'Prison escapes: written question - 9484', available at: http://www.parliament.uk/business/publications/written-questions-answers-statements, accessed 4 January 2017.

HASSINE, V. (2010), *Life Without Parole: Living and Dying in Prison Today*, New York: Oxford University Press.

HATHERLEY, O. (2010), *A Guide to the New Ruins of Great Britain*, London: Verso.

HOME OFFICE (1985), *HM Prison Holloway: Report by Chief Inspector of Prisons*, London: Home Office.

HMIP (2016), 'Report on an unannounced inspection of HMP', Doncaster, 5-16 October 2015, London: Her Majesty's Chief Inspector of Prisons.

HMSO (1959), *Penal Practice in a Changing Society*, Cmnd 645, London: HMSO.

HURD, D. (2000), *Memoirs*, London: Little Brown.

Independent (2016), 'Prison overcrowding: HMP Oakwood to convert single cells into doubles to make room for 500 extra inmates', available at: http://ind.pn/1ouKCf1, accessed 4 January 2017.

JACOBS J. M. and MERRIMAN P. (2011), 'Practising architectures', *Social & Cultural Geography*, 12(3): 211–22.

JEWKES, Y. (2012), 'Prisons', in M. Tonry (ed.), *The Oxford Handbook of Crime and Criminal Justice*, Oxford: Oxford University Press.

JEWKES, Y. (2013), 'The Aesthetics and Anaesthetics of Prison Architecture', in J. Simon, N. Temple, and R. Tobe (eds), *Architecture and Justice*, Farnham: Ashgate.

JEWKES, Y. (2015), *Media and Crime*, revised 3rd edn, London: Sage.

JEWKES, Y. and JOHNSTON, H. (2007), 'The evolution of prison architecture', in Y. Jewkes (ed.), *Handbook on Prisons*, Cullompton: Willan.

JEWKES, Y. and LULHAM, R. (2016), 'Provoking criminal justice reform: a presentation in the Empathy "Things" Workshop', 50th Anniversary Design Research Society Conference—'Future focused thinking', June 27–30, Brighton, UK.

JEWKES, Y. and MORAN, D. (2014), 'Bad design breeds violence in sterile megaprisons', *The Conversation*, available at: https://theconversation.com/bad-design-breeds-violence-in-sterile-megaprisons-22424, accessed 4 January 2017.

JEWKES, Y., SLEE, E., and MORAN, D. (2016), 'The visual retreat of the prison: non-places for non-people', in M. Brown and E. Carrabine (eds), *The Routledge Handbook of Visual Criminology*, Abingdon: Routledge.

JOHNSEN, B., GRANHEIM, P. K., and HELGESEN, J. (2011), 'Exceptional prison conditions and the quality of prison life: prison size and prison culture in Norwegian closed prisons', *European Journal of Criminology*, 8(6): 515–29.

JOHNSTON, H. (2015), *Crime in England, 1815-1880: Experiencing the Criminal Justice System*, Abingdon: Routledge.

JOHNSTON, N. (2000), *Forms of Constraint: A History of Prison Architecture*, Chicago: University of Illinois Press.

KRAFTL, P. and ADEY, P. (2008), 'Architecture/affect/inhabitation: geographies of being-in buildings', *Annals of the Association of American Geographers*, 98(1): 213–31.

LIEBLING, A. with ARNOLD, H. (2004), *Prisons and Their Moral Performance: A Study of Values, Quality, and Prison Life*, Oxford: Oxford University Press.

METZGER, G. (2003), 'Privatization as Delegation', *Columbia Law Review*, 103(6): 1367–502.

MCNEILL, F. and SCHINKEL, M. (2016), 'Prisons and desistance', in Y. Jewkes, J. Bennett, and B. Crewe (eds), *Handbook on Prisons*, 2nd edn, Abingdon: Routledge.

MCWATTERS, M. (2013), 'Poetic testimonies of incarceration: towards a vision of prison as manifold space', in D. Moran, N. Gill, and D. Conlon (eds), *Carceral Spaces: Mobility and Agency in Imprisonment and Migrant Detention*, Farnham: Ashgate.

MADGE, J. (1961), 'Trends in prison design', *British Journal of Criminology*, special issue on 'Prison Architecture', 1(4): 362–71.

MADOC-JONES, I., WILLIAMS, E., HUGHES, C., and TURLEY, J. (2016), 'Prisons: "Does size still matter?', *Prison Service Journal*, 277(Sept): 4–10, available at: https://www.crimeandjustice.org.uk/sites/crimeandjustice.org.uk/files/PSJ%20227%20September%202016.pdf, accessed 17 January 2017.

MARTINSON, R. (1974), 'What Works? Questions and Answers About Prison Reform', *Public Interest*, 35(Spring): 22–54.

MITCHELSON, M. L. (2014), 'The production of bedspace: prison privatization and abstract space', *Geographica Helvetica*, 69(5): 325–33.

MORAN, D. (2013), 'Carceral geography and the spatialities of prison visiting: visitation, recidivism, and hyperincarceration', *Environment and Planning D: Society and Space*, 31(1): 174–90.

MORAN, D. (2015), *Carceral Geography: Spaces and Practices of Incarceration*, Farnham: Ashgate.

MORAN, D., TURNER, J., and JEWKES, Y. (2016), 'Becoming big things: Building events and the architectural geographies of incarceration in England and Wales', *Transactions of the Institute of British Geographers*, 41(4): 416–28.

MORIN, K. M. (2013), '"Security here is not safe": violence, punishment, and space in the contemporary US penitentiary', *Environment and Planning D: Society and Space*, 31(3): 381–99.

MORRIS, P. and MORRIS, T. (1963), *Pentonville: A Sociological Study of an English Prison*, London: Routledge.

OWERS, A (2008), 'Evidence to Justice Committee', *Towards effective sentencing*, 22 July, HC 184-ii, 2007–08, Q375-77.

PETERSEN, A. W. (1961), 'The prison building programme' and 'The prison building programme: a postscript', *British Journal of Criminology*, special issue on 'Prison Architecture', 1(4): 307–16 and 372–75.

PRATT, J. (2002), *Punishment and Civilization*, London: Sage.

PRISON REFORM TRUST (2014), *Titan Prisons: A Gigantic Mistake*, London: PRT.

SCHARFF SMITH, P. (2014), *When the Innocent are Punished: The Children of Imprisoned Parents*, London: Palgrave.

SCHEPT, J. (2014), '(Un)seeing like a prison: counter-visual ethnography of the carceral estate', *Theoretical Criminology*, 18(2): 198–223.

SCHINKEL, M. (2014), *Being Imprisoned: Punishment, Adaptation and Desistance*, London: Palgrave.

SIBLEY, D. and VAN HOVEN, B. (2009), 'The contamination of personal space: boundary construction in a prison environment', *Area* 41(2): 198–206.

SPARKS, R. and BOTTOMS, A. E. (1995), 'Legitimacy and Order in Prisons', *British Journal of Sociology*, 46(1): 45–62.

SPENS, I. (1994), *Architecture of Incarceration*, London: Academy.

SYKES, G. (1958), *The Society of Captives: A Study of a Maximum Security Prison*, Princeton: Princeton University Press.

WAYNE, P. (1994), 'Prison design in the twentieth century', in I. Spens (ed.), *Architecture of Incarceration*, London: Academy Editions.

WENER, R. E. (2012), *The Environmental Psychology of Prisons and Jails: Creating Humane Spaces in Secure Settings*, Cambridge: Cambridge University Press.

PART III

DYNAMICS OF CRIME AND VIOLENCE

25

INTERPERSONAL VIOLENCE ON THE BRITISH ISLES, 1200–2016

Manuel Eisner

INTRODUCTION

In this chapter I review interpersonal violence across the British Isles during the past 800 years, roughly covering the period between 1200 and the present. The focus will be on the big patterns, the long-term trends, and their theoretical explanations. After an introduction to the theoretical framework I discuss the sources that historians use to understand and analyse interpersonal violence. I then provide an overview of the current knowledge of the long-term trend in homicide rates. This is followed by an analysis of trends in infanticide as a distinct category of lethal interpersonal violence. A next section examines interpersonal violence in four historical periods, namely the High and Late Middle Ages (1200–1500), the early modern period (1500–1800), the Industrial Age (1800–1950), and the post-Second World War period. For each period I will briefly review the literature that examines characteristics of homicide in their historical context, focusing on the social and cultural mechanisms that influenced change in the manifestations of violence. The chapter concludes with a review of the broader implications of the historical evidence.

THEORETICAL PERSPECTIVES ON THE LONG-TERM TREND

Much historical research is shaped by hermeneutic thinking: based on a careful reading of historical sources, it aims to reconstruct the world of beliefs, meanings, motivations, and institutions within which individuals' actions unfolded in a historical context. Yet social and cultural historians increasingly recognize that especially work on crime, violence, and punishment needs to be informed by social science theory: analyses of medieval violence require assumptions about the motivations that drove criminal behaviour in the past; theories about stigma and prejudice are involved when historians examine the social groups accused of witchcraft in the seventeenth century; work on the rise of a professional police or correctional service invariably becomes part of wider debates about the role of the state in modern societies.

Two general themes are particularly relevant to criminologists. The first revolves around the role of human nature in historical explanations of violence (e.g. Wood 2011). Traditionally, historians conceptualize violence mainly as meaningful action shaped by cultural forces, respectively a mode of communication learned by individuals. They emphasize that the perception of what constitutes violence is variable over time and space, that humans must learn rituals such as dueling or knife-fighting from others, that cultural paradigms shape the perpetration of violence, and that social norms can promote or control aggressive behaviour (Schwerhoff 2002; Skoda 2013). Other historians, in contrast, read violence through a more behaviourist lens. It entails the idea that murder, rape, and robbery have similar roots in all cultures (Roth 2011; Hanlon 2007; Daly and Wilson 1997). In this perspective universal hard-wired psychological mechanisms, possibly shaped during the evolution of the human species, are the deep motivational drivers for violence and cooperation in all societies, at all times (Eisner 2009). Scholars who adopt this view tend to emphasize the similarities of age and sex distributions of perpetrators across history, highlight the universal role of jealousy, anger, revenge, and power as motivators for violence, and search for the general social control mechanisms that influence the potential for violent behaviour.

Consequently, researchers who examine historical change through a behaviourist perspective assume that universal psychological and social mechanisms influence whether levels of violence in a society increase or fall. For example, they expect that a loss of legitimacy and lack of good governance are universally associated with increasing interpersonal violence.

A second debate revolves around the question of whether a 'civilizing process'—a growing concentration of the legitimate use of force in the hands of the state, the expansion of methodical self-control, and the rising abhorrence of judicial torture, maltreatment of children, cruelty against animals, and bullying in schools—permeates the historical manifestations of violence (Spierenburg 2008; Muchembled 2008; Eisner 2003; Pinker 2011). The idea has recently been popularized by Steven Pinker's best-seller *Better Angels of our Nature* (Pinker 2011), which develops the notion that all forms of violence—interpersonal violence, civil war, and international war—have followed a long-term declining trajectory, possibly over thousands of years. For historians of crime the most influential theoretical anchor remains the Theory of the Civilizing Process, developed by the sociologist Norbert Elias in the 1930s (Elias 1978). His theoretical framework explains the increasing self-restraint and culture of shame that characterizes the civilizing process as a result of two processes: the increasing centralization of power and the legitimate use of force in the hands of the state and the expanding interconnectedness between individuals in evermore complex societies.

The first process was shaped, according to Elias, by the increasing control that the emerging central powers exerted over knightly warriors from the early to the high Middle Ages. As a result, the qualities required for political success shifted from fighting skills to the ability to forge alliances, and to engage in sophisticated diplomacy, taste, and civility. Over time, the state expanded its monopoly of power over wider groups and larger spaces. Within these emerging nation states, violent disruptions of daily life became rarer, open displays of cruelty became increasingly loathed, and the intensity of emotions was dampened.

Elias' second argument, namely that increasing interdependency within and between societies favours self-control and peaceful behaviour, borrows heavily from enlightenment philosophers. In *The Wealth of Nations*, for example, Adam Smith argued that the rise of commerce and functional interdependence introduces 'order and good government, and with them, the liberty and security of individuals' (Smith 1776, III.iii, 8). The argument developed by Elias does not assume that chains of interdependence result in empathy or compassion for another person. Rather, they have the effect that individuals increasingly learn to emotionally neutralize interactions among strangers, and to rely on culturally shared rules that allow for long-term reciprocal interactions.

Also, increasing interdependence and openness of societies means that actors can harm others by non-violent means, for example by selecting alternative partners for the exchange of goods, services, and information. These structures, Elias argues, reward disciplined and good mannered behaviour, while a lack of low self-control and reliability have damaging effects on the maintenance of complex networks.

SOURCES

A large variety of sources inform historical research on interpersonal violence. Text documents dominate, but researchers also use visual material such as prints, signs of violent trauma in archeological records of skeletons, or physical objects such as weapons. Textual sources can be subdivided into four groups: the first comprises archival records of cases processed by representatives of the state: police, court, and prison records, forensic and other medical notes, and criminal statistics. Interpreted with an understanding of the limits of the underlying source, they can give insight into historical patterns of violent behaviour. Hanawalt (1979), for example, has examined about 20,000 fourteenth-century criminal court cases to draw a rich picture of crime and conflict in late medieval England. A second group is normative and didactic material—laws and parliamentary debates, expert reports, moral treatises, or advice literature. Such sources have been used, for example, to understand the criminalization of marital violence between the seventeenth and the nineteenth century (Foyster 2005) or to analyse the legal discourse around the insanity defence (Walker 1968). Pamphlets, broadsheets, newspapers, and magazines are a third major type of sources that help to understand beliefs around violence. A study by Martin (2007), for example, shows how an emerging popular understanding of the motives and circumstances of female murderers documented in sixteenth and seventeenth-century broadside stories may have contributed to their increasingly frequent acquittal. Finally, much can be learned through autobiographies, correspondences, private notebooks, or—for the recent past—oral histories. For example, Morgan and Rushton (2003) analysed a notebook by an eighteenth century magistrate in North-East England to highlight the importance of negotiating peace over the conviction of the culprit at the level of local courts.

QUANTIFICATION AND THE LIMITS OF JUDICIAL RECORDS

Thanks to the extraordinary richness of British historical judicial archives historians of crime have often found it useful to analyse source material using quantitative methods. Most historians agree that using quantitative methods to summarize information in often-formulaic large-N documents (e.g. coroners' records, police files, indictments, newspaper crime reports) is a meaningful complement to more traditional hermeneutic work. There is less agreement about whether historical records can also be used to estimate actual levels of violence in the past. The one candidate for such an approach is homicide, the only violent crime likely to leave traces in judicial records from the thirteenth century onwards (Roth 2001; Eisner 2014).

To make comparisons historians of crime generally calculate homicide rates, which are the number of homicide cases in a year divided by the population of the respective geographic area and expressed as 'per 100,000 of the population', The calculation of homicide rates is fraught with limitations. Throughout the Middle Ages and the early modern period law enforcement was at best patchy, meaning that many homicides may have remained undiscovered (such as infanticide and gerontocides), that perpetrators often remained unknown, that known suspects fled and were never brought to justice, or that cases were dealt with informally and outside the judicial system. For example, only around 30 per cent of the cases recorded by medieval coroners were brought to court and only around 10 per cent resulted in a conviction (Hanawalt 1976). But problems are not limited to pre-modern sources. Archer (2008), for example, shows that homicide records in late nineteenth-century North-West England were likely incomplete, and that infants, immigrants, and female victims may have been underrepresented.

Also, in comparisons over the centuries a number of factors affect the likelihood that an assault results in a death. Eisner (2014) has proposed grouping these factors into changing 'technologies of healing' such as wound treatment and changing 'technologies of killing' such as better and more effective weapons. For example, before the advent of wound antiseptics and emergency wards many victims died of wounds that would not be lethal today (Eisner 2014). Finally, the population figures used to calculate historical homicide rates are often crude and possibly biased estimates, and over longer periods of time change in the age structure of the population needs to be taken into consideration.

THE BIG PICTURE: HOMICIDE FROM 1200–2015

Research on historical homicide trends began in the early 1970s when social historians first examined large numbers of judicial records, using social science methodologies such as systematic coding of information and statistical data analyses. This pioneering work includes Given's (1977) extensive statistical analysis of homicides in thirteenth-century eyre court records, Hanawalt's (1979) massive study of the gaol delivery commissions in the fourteenth century, the examinations of late sixteenth and early seventeenth-century assize court records by Samaha (1974) and Cockburn (1977), and Beattie's (1974) analysis of higher court records between 1660 and 1800. Since then new research has shed light on historical levels of homicide in other counties of England, as well as various regions in Wales, Ireland, and Scotland (Cockburn 1991; Sharpe 1983; Summerson 1992; Jobson 2006; Howard 2008; Garnham 1997).

As a result, an increasingly detailed statistical picture is beginning to emerge. It not only allows us to outline long-term trends, but also to trace situational patterns, describe offender and victim profiles, and map out regional differences over long periods. In conjunction, the data are becoming increasingly useful in testing and refining theoretical frameworks such as Elias' Theory of the Civilizing Process (Elias 1978).

With this goal in mind, Eisner (2001; 2003; 2014) began in the late 1990s with the development of a database that aims to document all estimates of homicide rates generated by historians of crime across Europe. It currently comprises over 900 local estimates across Europe for the period before 1800, and national series on homicide rates for 25 countries, mostly from the 1850s onwards. Figure 25.1 shows all estimates currently available for the British Isles over the past 800 years. Before the onset of national statistics each dotted line represents a series relating to a local unit such as a county (e.g. Essex, Cheshire) or the city of London. The solid lines starting in the early nineteenth century represent the national homicide

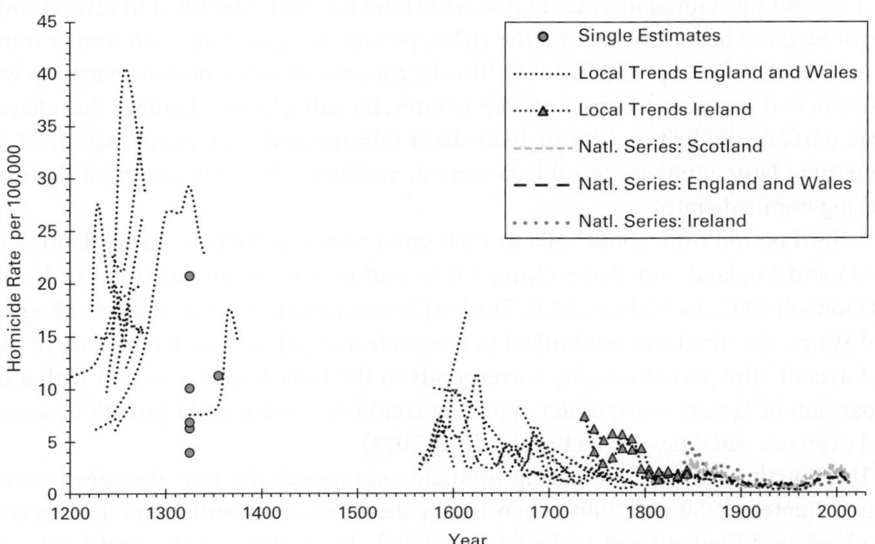

Figure 25.1 Trend in homicide rates on the British Isles, 1200–2016

Sources: History of Homicide Database, see Eisner (2014).

rates based on the mortality statistics or police statistics of Scotland, Ireland, and England and Wales.

The data suggest two main 'big picture' conclusions: first, they document a long-term declining trend in homicide rates in England over the past 800 years. It takes average homicide levels from about 20–25 per 100,000 in the thirteenth century to an all time low of about 0.3–0.5 per 100,000 in the decades between about 1930 and 1950. This trend had first been discovered by Ted Robert Gurr in the early 1980s when he combined findings from the first generation of quantitative studies of historical court records into a single graph (Gurr 1981). Since then new data from additional counties or based on different sources have confirmed the basic pattern with astonishing regularity (e.g. Sharpe and Dickinson 2016b; Sharpe and Dickinson 2016a). Although it remains important to recognize the limitations of the data on which these estimates are based, most historians of crime hence agree that it mirrors a real change in actual behaviour (Sharpe and Dickinson 2016b; Stone 1983; Emsley 2005b). Also, the gap in estimates between about 1350 and 1550 makes it impossible to determine the onset of the decline. What we do know, however, is that the long-term trend initially discovered in England is part of much wider decline in every area of Europe where pertinent data are available (Eisner 2014).

Second, the data point to at least four periods of mounting homicide—and possibly interpersonal violence more generally: for the Middle Ages the records suggest a possible increase in homicide towards the end of the thirteenth century. Certainly, there is a contemporary sense of a loss of law and order in those decades. The Statute of Winchester (1285), in particular, complained that 'from day to day robberies, homicides and arsons are more often committed than they used to be' (Summerson 1992). It may have been linked to declining real wages due to a growing population pressure, but limitations in the data make any firmer conclusions impossible (Clark 2007; Hanawalt 1979).

A second substantial increase in homicide rates has been identified in several counties of England between 1590 and the 1620s, possibly in synchrony with similar trends in other areas of Europe (Roth 2001). The decades saw severe economic hardship with drops in real wages and a series of crop failures, including severe famines that affected large parts of the British Isles in 1622–1624 (Sharpe and Dickinson 2016b). At the same time large numbers of soldiers were demobilized, possibly contributing to the soaring homicide rates.

A third period from about 1800 to 1850 saw a homicide increase in Scotland (King 2011) and England and Wales (King 2013), and possibly a similar trend in Ireland (O'Donnell 2005; McMahon 2013). Emsley (2005a) has shown that, at least in England and Wales, the trend was not limited to homicide, but part of a wider increase in theft and assault. The period roughly corresponds to the Industrial Revolution with a fast expansion of factory work under appalling conditions and a rapid growth of squalid and overcrowded cities across Britain (King 2013).

The fourth period of increasing homicide comprises the four decades between approximately 1960 and 2000 when homicide followed a similar trend in Ireland, Scotland, and England and Wales (Eisner 2008). The pattern on the British Isles followed a trend that occurred similarly across much of Europe, Northern America, and Australia (Lappi-Seppälä and Lehti 2014).

CHANGE AND STABILITY IN STRUCTURAL CHARACTERISTICS

Historians of crime agree that tracing homicide levels over time may be useful, but that such figures remain largely meaningless without an understanding of what these events were, who was involved, and where and when they happened. Scholars interested in broader generalizations have therefore used criminal justice records to draw statistical profiles of changing homicide characteristics across time. The kind of information that can be retrieved varies between sources, but generally it is possible to distinguish three types of information, namely:

- characteristics of the perpetrator and the victim such as sex, age, and social background,
- characteristics of the crime itself, such as the type of wound, the weapon used, the time and location of the crime, and the presence of third parties,
- information about the events following the crime including, for example, confiscation of goods, arrest, and conviction.

For criminologists, such information is particularly valuable when it allows for comparison across studies and hence an assessment of different theories of crime and explanations of crime trends. We illustrate this potential using the example of the sex of perpetrators of homicides, excluding infanticide.

Throughout the Middle Ages and the early modern period the overwhelming majority of violent perpetrators were male. But why? Some historians of crime have argued that the main mechanisms were culturally rooted notions of masculinity that emphasized physical prowess and honour (Shoemaker 2001). This resembles the sociological emancipation-crime hypothesis, developed by criminologist Freda Alder 40 years ago (1975). It maintains that women become more criminal as their participation in public life and the workforce increases over time, and as expectations about femininity progressively embody qualities such as assertiveness and autonomy. It leads us to expect a higher proportion of female perpetrators of violence as levels of gender equality went up.

Interestingly, research reveals a more complex historical reality that defies simple explanations. Sex ratios for murder and robbery, in particular, have been barely affected by change in women's legal status, cultural roles, or access to education over the past eight centuries. In thirteenth-century England (Given 1977) women committed 8.6 per cent of all homicides (excluding infanticides). The corresponding early twenty-first-century figure was 9.1 per cent (ONS 2013), and a scattering of data for the centuries in between shows very limited variation (Eisner 2014).

But why has the proportion of female killers changed so little although they spend less time in domestic roles, are more visible in public space, their legal rights have improved, and gender roles have become much less polarized? One answer comes from evolutionary psychologists such as Archer (2004) and Daly and Wilson (1988). They argue that we should not expect much cross-cultural variation in gender ratios for serious violence, because the predominance of male murderers reflects universal mechanisms that have shaped sex differences in violent propensities during the course of human evolution (Eisner 2011; Eisner 2014).

However, the evidence is not unequivocal. Recent historical work shows notable historical variation in female violent offending for some types of violence, but not in a way that can easily be explained by the emancipation-crime framework. Thus, a cluster of studies suggests an astonishingly high female involvement in assault during the second half of the eighteenth century: in Boldon, a rural parish on the way from Sunderland to Newcastle, 31 per cent of all accusations of assault between 1750 and 1764 concerned women (Morgan and Rushton 2003). In the City of London women accounted for 29 per cent of the defendants in assault cases at the Guildhall Justice room between 1784 and 1794 (Gray 2007). In Portsmouth, a large harbour city and a major military base, 31 per cent of violent assailants recorded by the authorities between 1653 and 1781 were female (Warner *et al.* 2005: 293). And in the Scottish lowlands almost 35 per cent of those indicted for violent crimes at the Scottish Justiciary Court between 1750 and 1815 were women (Kilday 2007; also see Ewan 2010).

These are remarkably high figures, also in comparison to contemporary statistics. In 2010, for example, merely 18 per cent of suspects for 'violence against the person' were female, a rate that is only slightly higher than late Victorian rates of around 14 per cent for common assault (Zedner 1991; ONS 2013).

The reasons are unclear. Nothing suggests that late eighteenth-century femininity ideals even remotely supported swearing, fighting, or participation in public protests. Leaving the possibility of a statistical fluke aside scholars have proposed a series of hypotheses that are only partly satisfactory. Warner *et al.* (2005) highlight the importance of autonomous female honour in Portsmouth where women were often running the households while their husbands were abroad and where the flourishing prostitution may have engendered violent conflict. Similarly, Zedner (1991) noted that women were highly visible in the eighteenth-century cities, actively participating in markets and trades with ample opportunities for conflicts leading to assault. This might explain why women involved in assault cases in Surrey tended to be in respectable positions, often married to men of substance, tradesmen, artisans, or yeomen (Beattie 1975: 101). And for Scotland Kilday (2007) speculates that women's growing public presence may have led them to become more independent, but she equally considers the possibility that the judicial records reflect a tendency by the Scottish authorities to punish wayward women more severely than their male counterparts.

INFANTICIDE

One category of lethal interpersonal violence that requires separate consideration is infanticide. The phenomenon has become extremely rare in contemporary society and is usually associated with severe mental illness of the mother (Spinelli 2004). For much of European history, however, it was far more widespread. Depending on the period and region, infanticide could represent up to about 40 per cent of total indictments for homicide, and some scholars believe that a much larger number may have remained hidden from the authorities. Public attitudes were torn between sympathy, abject horror, and pragmatism (Kilday 2013). In complex ways, its history is intimately intertwined with the history of Christian images of the caring mother, attitudes towards premarital sex, the conditions of lower-class women, and increasing control by the emerging nation state over its population.

Across Europe, infanticide increasingly drew the attention of the criminal justice system in the late sixteenth century (Kilday 2013). In England the political discourse culminated in the 1624 Act to Prevent the Destroying and Murthering of Bastard Children, which made the concealment of a birth and death of a newborn by an unmarried woman punishable by death (Wrightson 1975; Gowing 1997). It remained a capital crime until the Infanticide Act of 1922, but the last woman taken to the gallows for 'murder of a bastard' was 24-year old Mary Smith in 1834 (Goc 2013: 21ff).

The 1624 act marks a movement away from a more ambiguous attitude in the Middle Ages when infanticide tended to be considered a sin rather than a crime (Kellum 1974; Damme 1978). Thus ecclesiastical courts dealt with most documented cases in medieval England, while the records of secular courts are almost entirely silent on the issue (Hanawalt 1976; Dean 2001). Also, the criminalization of infanticide in the early seventeenth century was part of a broader movement to regulate moral behaviour. Contemporaries associated infanticide with 'lewd and unnaturall women' who committed the most 'horrid' and 'unnatural' 'barbarity', and the 1624 legislation coincided with efforts to criminalize moral transgressions such as bastardy, adultery, incest, and fornication (Wrightson 1975).

Throughout the sixteenth to nineteenth centuries there was little change in the socio-demographic profile of defendants: they were overwhelmingly single mothers in their mid-twenties, often domestic servants of low education. In Scotland, for example, 93 per cent of those accused between 1700 and 1820 were employed in the domestic service, probably documenting the tension between the rigid expectations of chastity and childlessness and the likelihood of extra-marital sexual relationships, whether consensual or coercive (Kilday 2013: 38). The number of those brought to court tended to decline in England, Wales, and Scotland during the eighteenth century, and there was probably an even greater decline in the number of convictions (Kilday 2013; Francus 1997). At the same time, the language softened and a more humanitarian and compassionate approach to infanticide can be found in the public and expert discourse.

Between the 1800s and the 1860s police data suggest a massive increase in recorded infanticides in England, Wales, and Scotland (Kilday 2013: 122). In the mid-nineteenth century the panic over murderous mothers led Thomas Wakley, member of parliament and coroner, to declare that 'child murder was going on to a frightful, to an enormous, a perfectly in-credible extent', claiming a huge number of unrecorded infanticides each year in London (Higginbotham 1989: 319). Especially, members of the medical profession turned their attention to the presumed epidemic of infanticide (Higginbotham 1989: 337; Goc 2013). It was primarily a discourse of social reform and moral betterment, whose origins reach back into the eighteenth century. It revolved around protecting vulnerable children, helping mothers, protecting the sanctity of the bourgeois home, and changing the social conditions that led to infanticide (Higginbotham 1989).

It also resonated the growth of psychiatry which began developing an understanding of post-natal depression, under the label of *puerperal insanity*, and its effects on mothers (Marland 2004).

E. Farrell (2013) has recently examined the history of infanticide in post-Famine Ireland. In line with trends in England and Wales she documents a decline in recorded infanticides during the second half of the nineteenth century. She shows that women who killed their infants were treated surprisingly leniently. Although the crime was punishable with the death penalty, only 29 out of the 2,726 cases identified by Farrell for Ireland in the nineteenth century resulted in a death penalty. None was effectively executed.

In the last decades of the nineteenth century the frequency of infanticide started to decline rapidly across Europe, becoming an extremely rare event in contemporary society (Chesnais 1981; Kilday 2013). Various factors likely played a role, including the gradual disappearance of birth at home combined with the normality of medical care for pregnant women, and the wider availability of contraception, first of condoms, then the contraceptive pill.

HOMICIDE TRENDS AND PATTERNS IN FOUR HISTORICAL PERIODS

Any closer analysis of the role of violence across history requires an understanding of how violence was embedded into the daily routines, behaviour expectations, and authority patterns of various social groups in any particular historical period, as well as a grasp of the broader cultural and legal framework within which interpersonal conflicts were interpreted and addressed. In this section we provide a selective overview of some core issues in four historical periods, namely the Middle Ages (1200–1500), the early modern period (1500–1800), the Industrial Age (1800–1950), and the post-Second World War period.

THE MIDDLE AGES: 1200–1500

Several types of documents provide information about homicide in medieval England. But by far the most informative source are the coroner's rolls, records of the inquests held in the presence of a jury by an appointed official who had the duty to investigate all cases of violent death.

Studies like Hammer's (1978) analysis of homicide in medieval Oxford or Hanawalt's (1976) comparative examination of murder cases in Northamptonshire, London, and Oxford provide a rich picture of medieval homicide. They show a society where violence was a common part of daily life. Hanawalt's (1976) study of the surviving coroner's records in early fourteenth-century London and Northamptonshire still provides a unique insight into the structure of murder cases in the fourteenth century. Much looks surprisingly familiar to criminologists: In the countryside, homicide followed the seasonal activity with higher levels during the spring and summer period; especially in the cities the weekends were the days when most murders occurred, and like in modern societies homicide followed a distribution over the time of the day with a peak in the evening or night hours. Most of it happened in public space, usually between men, often in the context of taverns and other places of sociability. The killings were almost never planned but often arose out of trivial altercations that escalated and went wrong. Clearly, men expected that they needed to fight in public space. The lethal wounds recorded by the coroners were almost always inflicted with dedicated fighting instruments—knives, swords, staffs, axes, or bow and arrow. In contrast, killings committed with bare hands or objects accidentally available to the assailant accounted for less than 4 per cent of cases. Conviction was rare. Offenders often absconded and were subsequently outlawed. And among those who were brought to trial only a minority of around 20 per cent were convicted by the jury (Hanawalt 1976).

Medieval records are somewhat ambiguous about the social class background of perpetrators. In the Oxford coroners' records, a third of perpetrators were members of the university, roughly in line with their share in the general population (Hammer 1978). In line with work on other university towns in Europe this suggests that medieval students were a rather rowdy crowd, prone to rioting and fighting whenever the occasion arose (Dean 2001). However, members of the upper classes rarely appear in the court records, a pattern that may reflect a tendency to settle violent elite conflicts outside the legal system. In fact, the ruling elites of England certainly experienced very substantial violence until the end of the Middle Ages: Between 1350 and 1500, 19 per cent of the secular peers summoned to parliament died a violent death—executions for treason, involvement in feuds and civil wars, and accidents by sea and on land (Rosenthal 1973). The trend was increasing over these 150 years, and among those born between 1401 and 1450 a full 36 per cent died from violence.

The decline of the blood-feud in Scotland and Wales

The thousands of criminal cases carefully recorded by clerks on the rolls of the thirteenth-century itinerant judges are a telling manifestation of the transition to a centralized and bureaucratic justice in England that had been propelled forward by the reforms introduced by Henry II at the Assize of Clarendon in 1166. In Scotland, Wales, and Ireland, however, systems of private justice through feud and reconciliation coexisted with state intervention through indictment and criminal law for several more centuries (Wormald 1980; Davies 1969; Brown 1986; McLeod 2004).

In Scotland, the payment of compensation to the kin of the man who had been killed, followed by a recognition that full and satisfactory compensation had been received, remained a core mechanism to conduct and settle conflicts among members of the nobility until the early seventeenth century. As Wormald (1980) shows, it persisted thanks to a complex judicial system in which decentralized baronial and a more centralized royal justice coexisted, and where private kin-based justice remained an often successful mechanism for maintaining social order. Between 1573 and 1625 at least 50 feuds were being carried on in any year, only to disappear astonishingly quickly during the century after James IV's accession to the English throne in 1603 (Brown 1986). Their decline was a complex story. Efforts to render state justice more efficient and control the power of the nobility, the wider availability of trained lawyers, and the growing sense that reconciliation between members of kin was inadequate as a way of dealing with homicide played a role (Brown 1986). Behind much of the dynamic stood the influence of the Calvinist church, which considered the practice of feuding with its emphasis on obligations to kin and lord as a sign of moral corruption that needed to be substituted with the allegiance to God (Wormald 1980: 93).

THE EARLY MODERN PERIOD (C 1550–1800)

Except for the increase during the first decades of the seventeenth century, the history of homicide rates between 1550 and 1800 is broadly one of sustained long-term decline, at least in England and Wales. In the Palatinate of Cheshire, homicide rates as measured by cases tried at the Court of Great Sessions rose to about 8–12 per 100,000 in the 1620s, falling to 2 per 100,000 in the 1690s and slightly under 1 per 100,000 in the second half of the eighteenth century (Sharpe and Dickinson 2016b; Sharpe and Dickinson 2016a). A similar trend can be found in Kent, where the number of cases in the assize records peaked at around 6 per 100,000 in the 1590s, falling to 3.6 in the 1690s, and 2 by the end of the eighteenth century (Cockburn 1991).

Recent work suggests notable differences between regions of the British Isles. In Scotland, an analysis of all homicide cases brought to the High Court of Justiciary during the eighteenth century suggests an astonishingly low homicide rate of about 0.35 per 100,000, a rate that, if true, would qualify as amongst the lowest rates ever observed in any human society. The finding probably needs further scrutiny, but Knox and Thomas (2015) point to the fact that Scotland was a 'tightly policed society with ruling groups exercising enormous authority over subordinate constituencies through their control of the kirk, the courts and the economy'. In Ireland, in contrast, records for Armagh and Fermanagh in Ulster suggest much higher homicide rates of 3–8 per 100,000 in the first half of the eighteenth century, but falling quickly as the century progressed (McMahon 2013).

A number of structural changes co-occurred with the drop in homicide rates from the sixteenth to the late eighteenth century: For example, there is now good evidence on weapon use since the Middle Ages suggesting that the proportion of cases committed with fighting instruments such as knives, swords, or staffs fell, while relatively more crimes were committed with bare hands or non-specific objects—bottles, farming tools, or stones (Eisner 2014). Both in Kent and in Cheshire the decline in homicide rates parallels the disappearance of rapiers, knives, or staffs as murder instruments. Probably this means that as public space became more pacified during the eighteenth century people became less inclined to carry arms in anticipation of a fight. Among the lower classes violent male-on-male conflicts were increasingly channeled into more formalized fights, usually on open fields, that were fought with bare fists and could sometimes result in the death of one opponent (Sharpe and Dickinson 2016a).

Also, the decline was accompanied by a withdrawal of the respectable classes from interpersonal violence. Exactly when this happened is not clear. During the Tudor period peers and gentry appear to have continued to be involved in violence, although the manifestations began to change: the medieval proclivity to robber barons and the taste for private warfare gradually gave way to more ritualized duels and litigation in the courts (Sharpe 2001). In seventeenth-century Cheshire, gentlemen and yeomen—the two highest social classes distinguished in the source material—still accounted for 35 per cent of all male prime homicide suspects, while labourers accounted for only 21 per cent (Sharpe and Dickinson 2016b: 11). Several cases involving gentlemen killing other gentlemen with rapiers were probably duels. By the second half of the eighteenth century, the picture had changed completely. The Cheshire gentry had almost completely retreated from homicidal violence, with only 10 per cent of the defendants being described as gentlemen and yeomen, while labourers now accounted for 40 per cent of the accused (Sharpe and Dickinson 2016a).

A great gauge to track change in beliefs and attitudes towards male honour among the British male elites is the duel—the arranged combat between two individuals with matched weapons. The judicial duel as an approach to truth-finding had disappeared in the high Middle Ages. The duel as a way of settling matters of honour, in contrast, was invented in Italy in the mid-sixteenth century and arrived on the British Isles via France in the 1570s. Its popularity initially peaks in the first decades of the seventeenth century, experiencing a revival after the Restoration (1688) and probably another wave of popularity in the last decades of the eighteenth century (Shoemaker 2002; Kelly 1995; Peltonen 2003).

Several historians have examined the vanishing of the duel from the seventeenth to the nineteenth centuries (Andrew 1980; Banks 2010; Shoemaker 2002). Various mechanisms were probably involved: they include the broader withdrawal of elites from public violence, the changing ways in which reputations were established, the spread of reformed norms of masculine conduct, and the growing role of print culture in conducting disputes (Shoemaker 2002). In other words: the decline of the duel was inversely associated with the rise of the urban gentleman, whose status depended on money and conduct rather than a coat of arms and a sword. In London, wearing a sword went out of fashion in the 1720s and 30s, and the growing opposition to dueling meant that fights needed to be arranged in places removed from public view, thereby undermining their function as public male formidability displays (Shoemaker 2002).

The final demise of the duel in the nineteenth century was partly a triumph of the rule of law, but it was probably much more a sign of the deeper underlying transformation of elite masculinity. Its key ingredient was the notion of civility: men were no longer to be ruled by the tyranny of passion but were expected to master themselves and subjugate their will to reason (Pollock 2007). It culminated in the ideal of a man of dignity, focused on forethought, reasonableness, prudence, and command over himself (Wiener 2004).

Insults

Historians have used a variety of sources to track the interplay between change in the social bases for reputation and aggressive behaviour. One trail of evidence that has attracted substantial academic interest are insults. Their importance in the close-knit societies of the medieval and early modern world is revealed by legal terminology: in Scotland, as in German judicial language, insults were classed as 'verbal injuries', often requiring compensation in excess of that for physical assaults (Ewan 2010). This reflects the idea that being honourable was not merely a desirable personal quality. Rather, it was a moral gold standard that determined good standing in business exchanges and on the marriage market, creditworthiness, and social inclusion. Insult and slander were hence massive threats, often resulting in defamation cases in church or consistory courts between the sixteenth and the eighteenth centuries (e.g. Hurl-Eamon 2005; Sharpe 1980; Hollander 2006).

Insults appear to have been quite similar across Europe, and they were highly gender-specific: typical insults against women were 'whore', 'witch', and 'bitch', although 'cheat' and 'thief' were not uncommon. Insults against men were somewhat more varied and included 'rogue', 'thief', 'knave', 'cuckold', 'rascal', 'dog', 'bastard', or 'villain'—usually fortified by colourful adjectives like 'stinking', 'rotten', or 'damned' (see, e.g., Shoemaker 2000: 114; Leneman 2000; Hollander 2006; Sharpe 1980).

Shoemaker (2000) has examined the career of public insults as a mechanism of community regulation in early modern London. He shows a surge in defamation cases at the consistory court in the late sixteenth and early seventeenth centuries, followed by shrinking numbers from around 1640 to 1800. Their gradual disappearance as a behaviour that merits being taken to court probably means that insults gradually lost their harm-doing power. Witnesses seem to have become increasingly sceptical about whether defamatory words would necessarily damage reputations, articulating a more individualistic norm that people should mind their own business (Shoemaker 2000: 111). At the same time, Shoemaker also observes a growing refinement of public conversation in eighteenth and nineteenth-century London, where higher standards of politeness possibly meant fewer opportunities for friction. Also, as relationships became more fleeting, people could be more selective about whom they interacted with. The spoken word lost some of its power to destroy social standing, while business contacts, church activities, family and kin, and print culture became the main reference for public reputation and respectability.

THE INDUSTRIAL AGE (1800–1950)

In Scotland as well as in England and Wales national reports begin to present murder and manslaughter statistics in the first decades of the nineteenth century, while Irish mortality statistics start in 1841 (King 2013; O'Donnell 2004). From then onwards, the Judicial Statistics provide insight into national trends as well as regional differences and some offender and offence characteristics. Until about 1950 the data suggest two main trend periods: quite a marked increase from around 1800 until the 1850s, and then a gradual decline continuing until the 1950s (O'Donnell 2005; Eisner 2008). The declining trend is not only documented for homicide. Rather, the Judicial Statistics of all three nations suggest a similar drop in serious and common assault, robbery, and crime levels more generally (Finnane 1997; Gatrell 1980; Emsley 2005b).

New research using these data shows important differences across Great Britain (King 2011; King 2013). In the 1830s and 1840s homicide rates varied dramatically between regions. In England, a band of high homicide rates stretched across the fast urbanizing north-west industrial counties, while the rural counties of the East of England, Wales, and the south west had the lowest rates (King 2013). In Scotland, the incidence of lethal violence was even more spatially polarized. In the industrial areas around Glasgow and Edinburgh homicide rates were five or six times higher than on the periphery (King 2013).

These regional differences became much smaller during the second half of the nineteenth century as homicide rates dropped over-proportionally in those urbanized and industrialized areas that had seen violence peak in the first half of the century. Perhaps, the convergence is a sign of declining deprivation during the decades when urban infrastructure improved, living standards increased, and levels of absolute poverty declined. Possibly, also, the convergence is related to change in levels of social conflict and political strife. Thus, early nineteenth century working-class political protest such as the Chartist movement was mostly concentrated in the industrial cities. As protest subsided and a more consensual society developed in the mid-Victorian years, crime rates dropped particularly in these cities (King 2013).

But why did crime and violence fall overall in the midst of rapid urbanization and industrialization? No simple answers exist. Some credit should probably be apportioned to broader structural change such as rising incomes, better education, and improving welfare provision (Wiener 2004: 289). But most specialists of the period agree that conscious efforts and strategies—a Victorian 'civilising offensive'—played an important role (Wiener 2004; Wood 2004; Emsley 2005b). Its core was a cultural model of the conduct of life, reinforced through social institutions, that emphasized self-control as an ideal of personality; domesticity and familialism as guidelines for private life; and respectability as the yardstick for public appearance (Eisner 2008).

For one, Victorian moral entrepreneurs took various initiatives at societal moral regulation that targeted a wide spectrum of behaviours believed to be associated with violence. The British temperance movement identified alcohol as the source of vice, promoting sobriety as a core element of a respectable identity (Yeomans 2011: 43), leading to the 1872 licensing act, which introduced fixed closing hours and penalties for varying degrees of drunkenness. Alcohol consumption in England and Wales declined considerably from the 1880s until the 1950s, and so did violence (Eisner 2014).

Also, in the 1830s reformers began to work towards an ambitious society-wide reform of leisure time activities—recognizing the concentration of violence and many other types of 'vice' in places of unregulated leisure-time activities of young working-class men. The movement became known under the ideal of 'rational recreation' (Bailey 1978). It meant that leisure activities should be respectable, controlled, ordered, and morally improving, while vulgar and unregulated activities were to be suppressed. For example, prize fighting in open space, which often resulted in the death of participants, gradually became transformed into boxing as a regulated and respectably indoor activity. Modern association football with its emphasis on team spirit and civilized, rule-bound physicality replaced the older game of large crowds battling to drag a pig bladder to one corner of a village, a game that often ended with rowdy, violent behaviour (Emsley 2005b). The judiciary played an important role in molding these new practices of urban leisure, using criminal law to clear the streets of traditional activities, creating a legal framework for recreational land use, and regulating indoor commercial entertainment in public houses, music halls, or the emerging cinemas (Vorspan 2000).

But efforts to control violence were not limited to the public sphere. Wiener (2004) has tracked the growing sensitization of the Victorian public to domestic violence. Especially towards the end of the nineteenth century the ideal of a more companionate relationship based on affection rather than domination increased the authorities' willingness to prosecute and punish in cases of wife-beating (Bailey and Giese 2013). The husband's right to chastise his wife was repealed in 1891. It did away with a long-held view which distinguished between legitimate physical and psychological chastisement and correction within a patriarchal arrangement and 'marital cruelty', which was disproportionate and unjustified violence that could, if supported in court, lead to support for the separation from the husband (Bailey and Giese 2013).

POST-SECOND WORLD WAR: 1950–2016

Over the past 70 years the frequency of lethal interpersonal violence has followed a wave-like pattern across the British Isles: between 1950 and 1959 homicide rates were at the lowest levels ever recorded, with rates of 0.2 per 100,000 in Ireland (1954), 0.4 in Scotland (1951), and 0.6 in England and Wales (1957). Then they began to trend upwards for about four decades, peaking around 2000 at levels of 1.5 in Ireland (2001), 2.7 in Scotland (1993), and 2.1 in England and Wales (2001). Since then, homicide has consistently fallen and is currently at levels less than half of the peak seen 20 years ago.

The homicide trends broadly mirror trends in violence and crime in general, although for most crimes other than homicide the upper turning point was in the mid 1990s. Rates of police recorded robbery and assault, for example, increased by about 9 per cent every year in England and Wales between 1950 and the late 1980s, and both types of crime have fallen since the mid 1990s (Field 1990). Similarly, the Crime Survey of England and Wales—the most comprehensive instrument for assessing crime trends since the early 1980s—and hospital admission data suggest a peak of interpersonal violence in around 1993, followed by a more or less continuous decline over more than 20 years (Shepherd *et al.* 1993; Sivarajasingam *et al.* 2010) (also see Maguire, this volume).

Some demographic groups experienced a much stronger increase than others. In Ireland, homicide victimization grew most for men in the age bracket of between 20 and 40 years (O'Donnell 2005). Over the same period, there was a fall in the proportion of family homicides and an increase in stranger homicides. Trends in England and Wales point in the same direction. Here, too, the strongest upturn occurred for young male victims, and it affected the poorest areas over-proportionally (Shaw *et al.* 2005; Eisner 2008). Oral testimonies provided by three generations of people in London's working-class East End corroborate this interpretation. While some violence among young working class men was widespread in the 1950s, it was socially accepted as part of a 'rough' masculine identity (Hood and Joyce 1998). By the 1990s, however, residents perceived a widespread decay of social and moral order linked to, amongst others, heroin addiction and street robbery, and a much more antagonistic relationship between police and local youth, both black and white.

The reasons for the late twentieth-century upswing in street robbery, gang-fights, and homicide between disadvantaged young men in public space remain controversial. Some have pointed to economic and structural factors such as 'increased consumption, a growing emphasis on the material and an upswing in alcohol consumption' (O'Donnell 2009). In particular, economic growth and consumerism may have created new opportunities for violence, especially the expansion of night-time economies in the city centres, the use of recreational drugs and alcohol among young people, and the growth of black markets as a side effect of widespread property crime (Farrell *et al.* 2011). Its effects may have been exacerbated by the technological and economic transformations in the period, which eroded the 'traditional' working class cultures that provided a sense of identity (Fukuyama 1999) (also see Hobbs and Fraser, this volume).

Others have attempted to explain the increase as the result of a 'decivilizing process' associated with relaxation of controls and 'loosening of morals' that began in the 1960s and 70s (e.g. Mennell 1990). Eisner (2008) and Pinker (2011) have interpreted the surge as a result of a cultural turn towards permissive, hedonistic, and risk-seeking youth subcultures that undermined the ethos of respectability and self-control rooted in Enlightenment civil society. Thus, each of the working-class subcultures emerging since the 1950s like the Teddy boys, the mods, the rockers, and the skinheads were variously associated in the public discourse with delinquency and violence. The punk subculture of the late 1970s, for example, powerfully combined messages of 'anarchy', 'revolution', subversive art, and anti-establishment anger into a counterculture that endorsed provocation, rudeness, fun, rebellion, and violence (Simonelli 2002). The spread of illegal drugs, often in the wake of new subcultures, may have played a role. In England and Wales, the rise and fall of property crime between 1980 and 2010 closely tracks the timing of heroin/crack epidemics—and at least in the United States the crack epidemic has been linked to trends in violent crime as well (Morgan 2014; Blumstein 2000).

There is also little consensus about the reasons for the decline in interpersonal violence since the mid-1990s, which was entirely unexpected by criminological experts. Recent overviews distinguish a dozen or so explanations (G. Farrell 2013). They include, amongst others, a reduction in lead poisoning; fewer unwanted children due to more liberal abortion laws, the decline of the crack-cocaine market, better policing, higher imprisonment, strong economies, more comprehensive surveillance, and demographic change.

Attempts to explain the decline over the past two decades as a result of cultural change point to a lower society-wide tolerance for many manifestations of violence, including violence against women and children, sexual minorities, racism, bullying, violence against animals, violence in institutions, and violence against disabled persons. Since the 1960s, for example, there has been an enormous change in the perception of sexual violence and intimate partner violence that has addressed deeply ingrained stereotypes, mobilized stakeholders, changed legislation, and led to better and more comprehensive prevention and intervention measures (McMahon and Baker 2011; Barner and Carney 2011). Attitudes towards child abuse and corporal punishment have also changed dramatically in the Western world (Straus 2010). Wherever survey data are available they show a declining support for corporal punishment. The exact causes are unknown. Candidates include demographic change towards smaller families and higher levels of education, a general expansion of human rights including the Convention on the Rights of Children, the transition to a post-industrial society that values autonomy more highly, and the gradual delegitimation of corporal punishment through psychological and criminological research.

CONCLUSION

Much progress has been made, over the past four decades, in our understanding of the history of interpersonal violence across the British Isles. This review focused on the 'big picture' long-term changes in levels, geographic patterns, and structural characteristics of homicide, the violent crime that was most likely to leave traces in historical records. It showed evidence for a long-term decline in levels of homicide over many centuries. This broad trend was linked to long-term structural change, including the withdrawal of elites from interpersonal violence and the pacification of interactions in public space, which is documented, amongst others, in the declining tendency to carry weapons in daily life. The trend in homicide probably mirrors a wider decline in interpersonal violence, but the extent to which this is the case remains disputed. In particular, as the overview of the history of infanticide showed, different types of interpersonal violence follow their own trajectories. Also, the extent to which various kinds of aggression such as slander and insult are either dealt with informally or taken to court varies over time, showing changing sensitivities to specific aggressions and varying expectations about the role of the justice system.

We don't currently understand well what social, economic, and cultural mechanisms are responsible for the long-term ups and downs in levels of interpersonal violence. The notion of a civilizing process that manifested itself in a growing sensitization to violence and the development of increased controls over aggressive behaviour remains the best-known framework. It can be observed, for example, in the growing monopolization of judicial powers during the Middle Ages, the changing notions of masculinity and honour during the early modern age, or in the Victorian efforts to establish a paradigm of 'rational recreation'. Using the example of the sex distribution of violent offenders over the past 800 years I showed how criminological theories can potentially be tested with historical material. However, limited work has been done to put specific hypotheses to more stringent tests, for example by collecting historical indicators that represent theoretically relevant aspects of the civilizing process such as various kinds of social control (but see, e.g., Eisner 2014).

Understanding such mechanisms is not of merely academic interest. Rather, better models of why interpersonal violence sometimes falls over decades or even centuries can help to inform current and future policies aimed at reducing violence across the world.

■ SELECTED FURTHER READING

Sharpe's *A Fiery & Furious People: A History of Violence in England* (2016) is a fascinating overview of the long-term history of interpersonal violence in England from the Middle Ages to the present. Anybody interested in the big picture should read Pinker's extraordinary *The Better Angels of our Nature* (2011), a beautifully written interpretation of the role of violence across human history. Dean's *Crime in Medieval Europe* (2001) is still the best one-volume overview of crime and responses to crime in Europe during the Middle Ages. Given's 'Society and Homicide in Thirteenth-Century England' (1977) remains an extraordinary analysis of statistical patterns of homicide more than seven centuries ago. Walker's *Crime, Gender and Social Order in Early Modern England* (2003) is the most sophisticated analysis of the relationship between gender, crime, and justice in early modern England. Kilday's *A History of Infanticide in Britain* (2013) is a comprehensive overview of the long-term change in infanticide from 1600. Emsley's *Hard Men* (2005) provides a compelling analysis of major changes in behaviour patterns and attitudes towards violence from 1750 until the present, while Wiener's *Men of Blood* (2004) provides a compelling analysis of domestic violence in Victorian England.

REFERENCES

ANDREW, D. T. (1980), 'The code of honour and its critics: the opposition to duelling in England, 1700–1850', *Social History*, 5(3): 409–34.

ARCHER, J. (2004), 'Sex differences in aggression in real-world settings: A meta-analytic review', *Review of General Psychology*, 8(4): 291–322.

ARCHER, J. E. (2008), 'Mysterious and Suspicious Deaths: Missing Homicides in North-West England (1850-1900)', *Crime, Histoire et Sociétés—Crime, History and Societies*, 12(1): 45–63.

BAILEY, J. and GIESE, L. (2013), 'Marital cruelty: reconsidering lay attitudes in England, c. 1580 to 1850', *The History of the Family*, 18(3): 289–305.

BAILEY, P. (1978), *Leisure and Class in Victorian England: Rational Recreation and the Contest for Control, 1830–1885*, London: Routledge.

BANKS, S. (2010), *A Polite Exchange of Bullets: The Duel and the English Gentleman, 1750–1850*, Woodbridge: Boydell & Brewer.

BARNER, J. R. and CARNEY, M. M. (2011), 'Interventions for intimate partner violence: A historical review', *Journal of Family Violence*, 26(3): 235–44.

BEATTIE, J. M. (1974), 'The pattern of crime in England 1660–1800', *Past and Present*, 62(1): 47–95.

BEATTIE, J. M. (1975), 'The criminality of women in 18th century England', *Journal of Social History*, 8(4): 235-44.

BLUMSTEIN, A. (2000), 'Disaggregating the violence trends', in A. Blumstein and J. Wallman (eds), *The Crime Drop in America*, Cambridge: Cambridge University Press.

BROWN, K. M. (1986), *Bloodfeud in Scotland 1573-1625: Violence, Justice and Politics in an Early Modern Society*, Edinburgh: John Donald Publishers.

CHESNAIS, J.-C. (1981), *Histoire de la Violence en Occident de 1800 à Nos Jours*, Paris: Robert Laffont.

CLARK, G. (2007), 'The long march of history: Farm wages, population, and economic growth, England 1209–1869', *The Economic History Review*, 60(1): 97–135.

COCKBURN, J. S. (1977), 'The nature and incidence of crime in England 1559–1625; A preliminary survey', in J. S. Cockburn (ed.), *Crime in England 1550–1800*, London: Methuen.

COCKBURN, J. S. (1991), 'Patterns of violence in English society: Homicide in Kent, 1560-1985', *Past and Present*, 130: 70–106.

DALY, M. and WILSON, M. (1988), *Homicide*, New York: Aldine Gruyter.

DALY, M. and WILSON, M. (1997), 'Crime and conflict: Homicide in evolutionary psychological perspective', *Crime and Justice—A Review of Research*, 22: 51–100.

DAMME, C. (1978), 'Infanticide: the worth of an infant under law', *Medical History*, 22(1): 1–24.

DAVIES, R. (1969), 'The survival of the bloodfeud in medieval Wales', *History*, 54(182): 338–57.

DEAN, T. (2001), *Crime in Medieval Europe; 1200-1550*, London: Pearson.

EISNER, M. (2001), 'Modernization, self-control and lethal violence—The long-term dynamics of European homicide rates in theoretical perspective', *British Journal of Criminology*, 41(4): 618–38.

EISNER, M. (2003), 'Long-term historical trends in violent crime', *Crime and Justice; A Review of Research*, 30: 83–142.

EISNER, M. (2008), 'Modernity strikes back? A historical perspective on the latest increase in interpersonal violence (1960-1990)', *International Journal of Conflict and Violence*, 2(2): 289–316.

EISNER, M. (2009), 'The uses of violence: An examination of some cross-cutting issues', *International Journal of Conflict and Violence*, 3(1): 40–59.

EISNER, M. (2011), 'Human evolution, history and violence: An introduction', *British Journal of Criminology*, 51(3): 473–8.

EISNER, M. (2014), 'From swords to words: Does macro-level change in self-control predict long-term variation in levels of homicide?', *Crime and Justice—A Review of Research*, 43(1): 65–134.

ELIAS, N. (1978), *The Civilizing Process (Vols. I and II)*, Oxford: Oxford University Press.

EMSLEY, C. (2005a), *Crime and Society in England*, 1750–1900, Harlow: Pearson.

EMSLEY, C. (2005b), *Hard Men—Violence in England since 1750*, London: Hambledon and London.

EWAN, E. (2010), 'Disorderly damsels? Women and interpersonal violence in Pre-Reformation Scotland', *The Scottish Historical Review*, 89(228): 153–71.

FARRELL, E. (2013), *'A Most Diabolical Deed': Infanticide and Irish Society, 1850–1900*, Oxford: Oxford University Press.

FARRELL, G. (2013), 'Five tests for a theory of the crime drop', *Crime Science*, 2(1): 1–8.

FARRELL, G., TSELONI, A., MAILLEY, J., and TILLEY, N. (2011), 'The crime drop and the security hypothesis', *Journal of Research in Crime and Delinquency*, 48(2): 147–75.

FIELD, S. (1990), *Trends in Crime and their Interpretation: A Study of Recorded Crime in Post War England and Wales*, London: HM Stationery Office.

FINNANE, M. (1997), 'A decline in violence in Ireland? Crime, policing and social relations, 1860-1914' , *Crime, Histoire, et Sociétés—Crime, History and Societies*, 1(1): 51–70.

FOYSTER, E. (2005), *Marital Violence: an English Family History, 1660–1857*, Cambridge: Cambridge University Press.

FRANCUS, M. (1997), 'Monstrous mothers, monstrous societies: infanticide and the rule of law in Restoration and eighteenth-century England', *Eighteenth-Century Life*, 21(2): 133–56.

FUKUYAMA, F. (1999), *The Great Disruption: Human Nature and the Reconstitution of Social Order*, New York: Free Press.

GARNHAM, N. (1997), 'How violent was eighteenth-century Ireland?', *Irish Historical Studies*, 30(119): 377–92.

GATRELL, V. A. C. (1980), 'The decline of theft and violence in Victorian and Edwardian England', in V. A. C. Gatrell, B. Lenman, and G. Parker (eds), *Crime and the Law; The Social History of Crime in Western Europe since 1500*, London: Europa Publications.

GIVEN, J. B. (1977), *Society and Homicide in Thirteenth-Century England*, Stanford: Stanford University Press.

GOC, N. (2013), *Women, Infanticide and the Press, 1822–1922: News Narratives in England and Australia*, Farnham: Ashgate.

GOWING, L. (1997), 'Secret births and infanticide in seventeenth-century England', *Past and Present*, 156: 87–115.

GRAY, D. D. (2007), 'The regulation of violence in the metropolis; the prosecution of assault in the summary courts, c. 1780–1820', *The London Journal*, 32(1): 75–87.

GURR, T. R. (1981), 'Historical trends in violent crime: A critical review of the evidence', *Crime and Justice—An Annual Review of Research*, 3: 295–350.

HAMMER, C. I., JR. (1978), 'Patterns of homicide in a medieval university town: Fourteenth-century Oxford', *Past and Present*, 78: 3–23.

HANAWALT, B. A. (1976), 'Violent death in fourteenth- and early fifteenth century England', *Comparative Studies in Society and History*, 18(3): 297–320.

HANAWALT, B. A. (1979), *Crime and Conflict in English Communities, 1300–1348*, Cambridge: Cambridge University Press.

HANLON, G. (2007), *Human Nature in Rural Tuscany: an Early Modern History*, New York: Palgrave.

HIGGINBOTHAM, A. R. (1989), '"Sin of the Age": Infanticide and illegitimacy in Victorian London', *Victorian Studies*, 32(3): 319–37.

HOLLANDER, M. (2006), *Sex in Two Cities: the Formation and Regulation of Sexual Relationships in Edinburgh and York, 1560–1625*, PhD thesis, University of York, available at: http://etheses.whiterose.ac.uk/11027/.

HOOD, R. and JOYCE, K. (1998), 'Three generations: Oral testimonies on crime and social change in London's East End', *British Journal of Criminology*, 39(1): 136–60.

HOWARD, S. (2008), *Law and Disorder in Early Modern Wales; Crime and Authority in the Denbighsire Courts, c. 1660–1730*, Cardiff: University of Wales Press.

HURL-EAMON, J. (2005), *Gender and Petty Violence in London, 1680–1720*, Columbus: Ohio State University Press.

JOBSON, A. L. (2006), *The Oxfordshire Eyre Roll of 1261*, PhD thesis, University of London.

KELLUM, B. A. (1974), 'Infanticide in England in the later middle ages', *History of Childhood Quarterly*, 1(3): 367–88.

KELLY, J. (1995), *'That Damn'd Thing Called Honour': Duelling in Ireland, 1570–1860*, Cork: Cork University Press.

KILDAY, A.-M. (2007), *Women and Violent Crime in Enlightenment Scotland*, Woodbridge: Boydell & Brewer.

KILDAY, A.-M. (2013), *A History of Infanticide in Britain, c. 1600 to the Present*, Houndmills: Palgrave Macmillan.

KING, P. (2011), 'Urbanization, rising homicide rates and the geography of lethal violence in Scotland, 1800–1860', *History*, 96(323): 231–59.

KING, P. (2013), 'Exploring and explaining the geography of homicide: patterns of lethal violence in Britain and Europe 1805–1900', *European Review of History: Revue europeenne d'histoire*, 20(6): 967–87.

KNOX, W. W. J. and THOMAS, L. (2015), 'Homicide in eighteenth-century Scotland: Numbers and theories', *The Scottish Historical Review*, 94(1): 48–73.

LAPPI-SEPPÄLÄ, T. and LEHTI, M. (2014), 'Cross-comparative perspectives on global homicide trends', *Crime and Justice—A Review of Research*, 43: 135–230.

LENEMAN, L. (2000), 'Defamation in Scotland, 1750–1800', *Continuity and Change*, 15(2): 209–34.

MARLAND, H. (2004), *Dangerous Motherhood: Insanity and Childbirth in Victorian Britain*, Basingstoke: Macmillan.

MARTIN, R. (2007), *Women, Murder, and Equity in Early Modern England*, London: Routledge.

MCLEOD, N. (2004), 'The blood-feud in medieval Ireland', in P. O'Neill (ed.), *Between Intrusions: Britain and Ireland between the Romans and the Normans*, Papers from the 2003 Melbourne Conference (2003), Sydney: Celtic Studies Foundation.

MCMAHON, R. (2013), *Homicide in Pre-famine and Famine Ireland*, Oxford: Oxford University Press.

MCMAHON, S. and BAKER, K. (2011), *Changing Perceptions of Sexual Violence over Time*, Harrisburgh: National Resource Center on Domestic Violence. (http://vawnet.org/material/

changing-perceptions-sexual-violence-over-time, accessed 20 January 2017).

MENNELL, S. (1990), 'Decivilising processes: theoretical significance and some lines of research', *International Sociology*, 5(2): 205–23.

MORGAN, G. and RUSHTON, P. (2003), 'The magistrate, the community and the maintenance of an orderly society in eighteenth-century England', *Historical Research*, 76(119): 54–77.

MORGAN, N. (2014), *The Heroin Epidemic of the 1980s and 1990s and Its Effect on Crime Trends–Then and Now (Home Office Research Report 79)*, London: Home Office.

MUCHEMBLED, R. (2008), *Une histoire de la violence*, Paris: Editions du Seuil.

O'DONNELL, I. (2004), 'Lethal violence in Ireland, 1841 to 2003; Famine, celibacy, and parental pacification', *British Journal of Criminology*, 45(5): 671–95.

O'DONNELL, I. (2005), 'Violence and social change in the Republic of Ireland', *International Journal of the Sociology of Law*, 33(2): 101–17.

O'DONNELL, I. (2009), 'The Fall and Rise of Homicide in Ireland', in S. Body-Gendrot and P. Spierenburg (eds), *Violence in Europe: Historical and Contemporary Perspectives*, New York: Springer.

ONS (2013) 'Crime in England and Wales, Year Ending June 2013', London: Office for National Statistics.

PELTONEN, M. (2003), *The Duel in Early Modern England: Civility, Politeness and Honour*, Cambridge: Cambridge University Press.

PINKER, S. (2011), *The Better Angels of our Nature; Why Violence has Declined*, London: Viking.

POLLOCK, L. A. (2007), 'Honor, gender, and reconciliation in elite culture, 1570–1700', *The Journal of British Studies*, 46(1): 3–29.

ROSENTHAL, J. T. (1973), 'Mediaeval longevity: and the secular peerage, 1350–1500', *Population Studies*, 27(2): 287–93.

ROTH, R. (2001), 'Homicide in early modern England, 1549–1800: the need for a quantitative synthesis', *Crime, Histoire et Société—Crime, History and Society*, 5(2): 33–68.

ROTH, R. (2011), 'Biology and the deep history of homicide', *British Journal of Criminology*, 51(3): 535–55.

SAMAHA, J. (1974), *Law and Order in Historical Perspective; The Case of Elisabethan Essex*, New York: Academic Press.

SCHWERHOFF, G. (2002), 'Criminalized violence and the civilizing process—A reappraisal', *Crime, Histoire et Sociétés—Crime, History and Societies*, 6(2): 103–26.

SHARPE, J. and DICKINSON, J. (2016a), 'Homicide in eighteenth-century Cheshire', *Social History*, 41(2): 192–209.

SHARPE, J. and DICKINSON, J. (2016b), 'Revisiting the "violence we have lost": Homicide in seventeenth-century Cheshire', *The English Historical Review*, 131(549): 293–323.

SHARPE, J. A. (1980), *Defamation and Sexual Slander in Early Modern England: the Church Courts at York*, York: Borthwick Institute of Historical Research.

SHARPE, J. A. (1983), *Crime in Seventeenth-Century England; A County Study*, Cambridge: Cambridge University Press.

SHARPE, J. A. (2001), 'Crime', in A. F. Kinney and T. W. Copeland (eds), *Tudor England: An Encyclopedia*, New York: Garland.

SHARPE, J. (2016). *A Fiery & Furious People: A History of Violence in England*, London: Random House.

SHAW, M., TUNSTALL, H., and DORLING, D. (2005), 'Increasing inequalities in risk of murder in Britain: trends in the demographic and spatial distribution of murder, 1981–2000', *Health and Place*, 11(1): 45–54.

SHEPHERD, J. P., HUGHES, A., and LEVERS, B. (1993), 'Trends in urban violence: a comparison of accident department and police records', *Journal of the Royal Society of Medicine*, 86(2): 87–8.

SHOEMAKER, R. B. (2000), 'The decline of public insult in London, 1660-1800', *Past and Present*, 169: 97–131.

SHOEMAKER, R. B. (2001), 'Male honour and the decline of public violence in eighteenth-century London', *Social History*, 26(2): 190–208.

SHOEMAKER, R. B. (2002), 'The taming of the duel: Masculinity, honour and ritual violence in London, 1660-1800', *The Historical Journal*, 45(3): 525–45.

SIMONELLI, D. (2002), 'Anarchy, pop and violence: Punk rock subculture and the rhetoric of class, 1976-78', *Contemporary British History*, 16(2): 121–44.

SIVARAJASINGAM, V., WELLS, J., MOORE, S., PAGE, N., and SHEPHERD, J. (2010), *Violence in England and Wales in 2010: an Accident and Emergency Perspective*, Cardiff: Violence and Society Research Group.

SKODA, H. (2013), *Medieval Violence: Physical Brutality in Northern France, 1270–1330*, Oxford: Oxford University Press.

SMITH, A. (1776), *An inquiry into the Wealth of Nations*, London: Strahan and Cadell.

SPIERENBURG, P. (2008), *A History of Murder; Personal Violence in Europe from the Middle Ages to the Present*, Cambridge: Polity.

SPINELLI, M. G. (2004), 'Maternal infanticide associated with mental illness: prevention and the promise of saved lives', *American Journal of Psychiatry*, 161(9): 1548–57.

STONE, L. (1983), 'Interpersonal violence in English society, 1300–1980', *Past and Present*, 101: 22–33.

STRAUS, M. A. (2010), 'Prevalence, societal causes, and trends in corporal punishment by parents in world perspective', *Law and Contemporary Problems*, 73(2): 1–30.

SUMMERSON, H. (1992), 'The enforcement of the Statute of Winchester, 1285–1327', *The Journal of Legal History*, 13(3): 232–50.

VORSPAN, R. (2000), 'Rational recreation and the law: The transformation of popular urban leisure in Victorian England', *McGill Law Journal*, 45: 891–973.

WALKER, G. (2003), *Crime, Gender and Social Order in Early Modern England*, Cambridge: Cambridge University Press.

WALKER, N. (1968), *Crime and Insanity in England. Vol 1. The Historical Perspective*, Edinburgh: Edinburgh University Press.

WARNER, J., GRAHAM, K., and ADLAF, E. (2005), 'Women behaving badly: Gender and aggression in a military town, 1653–1781', *Sex Roles*, 52(5): 289–98.

WIENER, M. J. (2004), *Men of Blood; Violence, Manliness and Criminal Justice in Victorian England*, Cambridge: Cambridge University Press.

WOOD, J. C. (2004), *Violence and Crime in Nineteenth Century England: The Shadow of our Refinement*, London: Routledge.

WOOD, J. C. (2011), 'A change of perspective: Integrating evolutionary psychology into the historiography of violence', *British Journal of Criminology*, 51(3): 479–98.

WORMALD, J. (1980), 'Bloodfeud, kindred and government in early modern Scotland', *Past and Present*, 87(1): 54–97.

WRIGHTSON, K. (1975), 'Infanticide in earlier seventeenth-century England', *Local Population Studies*, 15: 10–22.

YEOMANS, H. (2011), 'What did the British temperance movement accomplish? Attitudes to alcohol, the law and moral regulation', *Sociology*, 45(1): 38–53.

ZEDNER, L. (1991), 'Women, crime, and penal responses: A historical account', *Crime and Justice—A Review of Research*, 14: 307–62.

26

URBAN CRIMINAL COLLABORATIONS

Alistair Fraser and Dick Hobbs

INTRODUCTION

Metaphors of communal transgression, for instance the gang, mob, firm, outfit or organization carry implicit essences of consolidated, concentrated, undiluted deviant intent. When presented as collectivities, criminals compound the threats posed by the actions of individual deviants, and the resultant categories become easily objectified by law enforcement agencies, and valorized by the mass media. However, not all collaborative criminal activity is presented in terms of collectivities, for instance fraud and white collar crime are generally exempt from these emotive terms (Levi 1981). It is overwhelmingly social groups emanating from the urban working class who are regarded as suitable for plural as opposed to individual consideration. As will be discussed in this chapter, while criminological categorizations such as these emerged from academic efforts to conceptualise live social problems, they represent at best loose approximations of a complex social reality, at worst a wilful blindness toward forms of crime perpetrated by more powerful groups. The categories developed or adopted by criminologists have nonetheless had a major impact upon the way in which we understand crime, and the footprint of a criminological category tends to have a long life, perhaps, as we will discuss in this chapter, outliving the phenomena that inspired its creation.

The chapter will focus first on categorizations of urban criminal collaboration involving young people, specifically efforts to define street-based, urban youth under the concepts of 'gangs' and subcultures. As will be seen, though there is a clear trajectory of scholarship on youthful collaboration, which has become central to the criminological canon, the groups these terms attempt to depict constantly evade definition. In the context of large-scale shifts in society, particularly the wrench from industrialism to post-industrialism, we argue that it is increasingly difficult to press the breadth and diversity of urban groups through narrow categorizations. The chapter will then connect these considerations of haphazard youthful subcultural experimentations to adult collaborations via a consideration of changes in the urban political economy, and discuss the shifting efforts of criminologists to categorize these groups through a range of terms ranging from neighbourhood crime groups to professional crime. Some of these affiliations operate within confederations that have been labelled as organized crime, a concept that presents a somewhat ambiguous threat to the contemporary political and economic order. In tracing these categorizations, however, it must be noted that adult collaborations have not received the same level of criminological attention as their youthful counterparts. Contemporary criminological scholars have proved somewhat reluctant to engage with mature urban transgressive settings. The criminological orthodoxy, particularly in the UK, seldom features adult confederations unless they feature as a law enforcement driven social problem such as organized crime. Consequently we draw in this section from across disciplinary boundaries under headings that, while lacking the chronological parameters of the criminology of youth, make explicit our central argument concerning the need to embrace concepts and theoretical frameworks that have tended to be ignored. In the conclusion, we summarize this argument through reference to the notion of epochs, which construct broad brush typifications of criminal actions, and discuss the limitations of epochalist categorization in relation to the chaos of contemporary social and economic life.

In tracing these efforts to categorize the complexities of urban criminal collaborations, a central theme of the chapter will be on the social, cultural, and structural processes underpinning both criminal and academic labour. Both urban criminal collaborations and urban criminological collaborations respond to forces and pressures beyond their everyday control, in particular the changing character of the political economy. Our emphasis is on the influence of the political economy upon successive generations of criminal collaborations—their origins, *modus operandi*, and the principles around which they are organized—but also the changing parameters of the criminological field, the demand for funding, and the entrepreneurial efforts of scholars to respond to perceived social problems. As we will discuss, the changing character of the political economy has ensured that many of the traditional theoretical props and categories upon which criminologists have framed their work are not fit for purpose. In some cases this has resulted in a blurring of categories which renders them as little more than convenient indicators of the division of academic labour. The rigidity of these categories ignores the flexibility of criminal actors, who should be considered by addressing both the sweeping social changes that have reshaped urban life, and the methodological sensibilities that these changes require in order to conduct innovative research into criminal lives.

YOUTHFUL URBAN COLLABORATIONS

Much of the collective criminological product is concerned with youth, and as will become apparent from these studies, scholarship on youthful collaborations have a traceable chronology. As Reiss and Farrington (1991) indicate, approximately half of all offences involve co-offending, and male co-offenders tend to have longer criminal careers than solitary criminals. Co-offenders also tend to share not only gender, but also age and neighbourhood, as well as living close to the site of offences. While these similarities between offenders decline with age, youthful co-offenders share in territorial and gender specific activities and this tendency for delinquency to manifest itself as a male territorially based group activity (Shaw and McKay 1942) has become central to criminological curricula. However, the social history of categorizations such as 'gang' do not always match with the social history of the street culture they seek to depict. This section will explore a range of ways in which these activities have been studied and labelled over time by criminologists, incorporating discussion of a number of these classic contributions.

THE CHICAGO SCHOOL GANG

Although social groups, particularly men, banding together for criminal or political purposes have a longer genealogy (Pearson 1983), it was not until the end of the nineteenth century, in the United States, that the categorization of 'gang' for these forms of criminal collaborations developed momentum. Initially used to describe frontier outlaws and prisoners, it was only in the wake of urbanization that usage became attached to street-based groups of young people. As Sanchez-Jankowski argues:

> The social science academy's research on gangs has its own history, and the focus of this research has in turn been influenced largely by what society has considered the major social problems of the period. (Sanchez-Jankowski 1991: 1)

Research focusing specifically on youthful collaborations under the label of 'gangs' began in earnest in the early twentieth century, in the work of Asbury in New York (1927) and Thrasher in Chicago (1927/1963). Asbury's book was a journalistic account of the conflicts between differing criminal groups in the Bowery and Five Points areas of Manhattan, and documents in detail their violent struggles for supremacy.[1] Thrasher's book, by contrast, grew out of the urban sociology of the Chicago School of Sociology, which sought to distinguish generic patterns of social interaction within a developing urban milieu (Deegan 2001: 11–25).

Thrasher developed an explanation of youth gangs that was rooted in a combination of social, cultural, and urban processes, arguing that gangs emerge in neighbourhoods with high densities of population, with limited space and resource, in which large numbers of children and young people congregate in public space (Thrasher 1963: 23). As children form into peer-groups, so they are forced to defend this space from other groups (Thrasher 1963: 117), becoming 'integrated through conflict' (Thrasher 1963: 193).

> The gang is an interstitial group originally formed spontaneously . . . It is characterized by the following types of behaviour: meeting face to face, milling, movement through space as a unit, conflict, and planning. The result of this collective behaviour is the development of tradition, unreflective internal structure, esprit de corps, solidarity, morale, group awareness, and attachment to a local territory. (Thrasher 1963: 57)

[1] The book was made famous 75 years later when it formed the basis for a feature film, directed by Martin Scorsese, *Gangs of New York* (2002).

Notably Thrasher documented a range of different groups that exhibited 'gang-like' features, including sports clubs, fraternity houses, and various adult associations as well as organized criminal groups and political parties. While these groups may carry out criminal acts, for Thrasher this was not their *raison d'être* (Thrasher 1963: 51). Following in the Chicago tradition, scholars sought to situate youthful gang associations within the context of broader socio-cultural forces. For instance, in Shaw's classic study (1930/1966), youths flow in and out of gang activities, while Whyte's classic study (1943) revealed the often banal routine that patterned gang life, and the importance of situating gang identification within the broader fabric of social relations in the community.

What these early studies of gangs have in common is an effort to seek out general explanations of youthful, urban collaborations using a form of categorization that was apt for reformist spirit of the time: 'the gang'. While not entirely neutral, it did not carry with it the criminal implications that has become a familiar aspect of contemporary US gang research. In this sense these early studies are rooted in sociological perspectives on deviance, which emphasize the social and cultural causes of crime. The term 'gang' was used as a relatively neutral descriptor of a type of social group, rather than as a specific, definable or universalized phenomenon. Nonetheless, it must be recognized that these studies were premised on a view of social life that paid little attention to the role of gender, ethnicity, or social class in structuring social life in communities. Much of this early research was premised on studies of working-class, male, mostly white, street-based youth, whose involvement in crime was relatively disorganized: African-American gangs, for example, made up only 7 per cent of Thrasher's sample (Thrasher 1927: 139–40). In this sense the early body of US scholarship was structured by the broader ethnocentrism and gender-bias that characterized the broader field of criminology at that time (Chesney-Lind and Hagedorn 1999).

The exception to this general trend was the overlap between youth gang research and the subcultural theories of the 1960s, which opened the door to an analysis of political economy in the field. Cohen (1955) incorporated an analysis of class-relations into the study of gang formation. For Cohen, the middle-class 'measuring rod' of the school created oppositional subcultures, in which the values of the school were turned on their head in a process of 'reaction-formation'. For Cloward and Ohlin (1960), youth groups and adult criminality had to be understood as an ecological whole, with the evolution of a youthful street-gang into a more organized criminal enterprise contingent on the illegitimate opportunity structures that existed in the community. Cohen, along with Cloward and Ohlin were heavily influenced by the aspirational assumptions of North American society, and a perception that youth gangs and subcultures were reactions to these aspirations being blocked (Merton 1938).

POST-WAR SUBCULTURAL STUDIES

Downes (1966) considered these subcultural theories in a UK context, and echoing earlier findings from Scott (Scott 1956), found that 'American-style' gangs were absent. Downes argued that Cohen's theory of 'status frustration' did not apply easily to his observations on the streets of the Stepney and Poplar boroughs of London. For Downes the middle-class values of Cohen's theory had not been internalized by young men in the community and instead they had relatively low aspirations. Downes stressed the process of dissociation through which all aspects of middle-class life, and in particular the primary engine of aspirational culture, education, is rejected. Further, as structural inequalities within working-class communities were cross-generational, working-class youths took over traditional practices from the parent culture, and as a consequence, rather than a theory of gang formation, this was closer to a theory of class reproduction. Other studies from this period followed a similar pattern. As Parker argued similarly in his study of 'Roundhouse', '[t]he Boys are not a gang, they do not possess such rigid defining criteria; they are a network, a loose-knit social group' (Parker 1974: 64. See also Wilmott 1966. Gill 1977). The key to these British studies was not youthful resistance or rebellion, but adaption to the material conditions that young people shared with their parent culture.[2]

The loose-knit confederacy of, 'Anarchists, CND, Young Communists and International Socialists' (Cohen 1974: 27) that constituted the National Deviancy Conference (NDC) (see Cohen 1971: ch. 1), was a self-conscious effort to break away from what was perceived to be the positivist dogma of the period, and studies of youth were prominent in their agenda. Heavily influenced by the Chicago School and interactionism, prominent studies focused on processes of labelling (Young 1971) and moral panic (S. Cohen 1972).[3] Elements of resistance lay at the core of much of the work that emerged from the Centre for Contemporary Cultural Studies (CCCS), or 'Birmingham School', who focused on the symbolic meanings and stylistic responses of youth to the tensions and contradictions within the 'parent' working-class culture as traditional industries fell into decline (Hebdige 1979; Clarke 1975; Jefferson 1975). Through music, fashion, and aesthetics, Cohen argued, 'the latent function of subculture is ... to express and resolve albeit "magically", the contradictions of the parent culture' (P. Cohen 1972: 23). Willis, in his famous study of working-class 'lads' in Hammertown, was less concerned with such 'magical' resolutions,[4] and focused instead on social reproduction, detailing the ways in which strategies of resistance the 'lads' at school prepared them for the manual shop-floor culture they were soon to enter (Willis 1977. See also Corrigan 1979).

The overlapping concerns of the NDC and the CCCS trained attention on the ways in which forms of exclusion and labelling were institutionalized in the bureaucracies of the state, while also placing attention on the ways in which these modes of exclusion were internalized by young people growing up, resulting in cultural reproduction. Hall and colleagues' collective CCCS work (1978) proceeded to deconstruct the complex ideological and social apparatus that underpinned the emergence of a new moral panic over 'mugging' in 1970s Britain. Demonstrating that the phenomenon was thoroughly

[2] The one notable exception from this period is James Patrick's *A Glasgow Gang Observed* (1973)—now infamous for the authors' use of covert participant observation explains the persistence of gang phenomenon in Glasgow as related to the 'interconnecting and cumulative forms of inequality' that were embedded in the city's fabric, producing 'feelings of frustration, rage and powerlessness' (1973: 170). Further he argues that 'available evidence ... points to the conclusion that there is no English equivalent of the Glasgow gang' (Patrick 1973: 164–5).

[3] The utopianism of a 'fully social' (Taylor *et al.* 1973: 268–82) theory of deviance became honed towards neo-Marxism (Taylor *et al.* 1975), and was rejected by formal Marxists for whom the relationship between the industrial working class and the (criminal) lumpenproletariat was set in stone (Hirst 1975: 203–44).

[4] See Stan Cohen's devastating critique of such 'magical thinking' (Cohen 1980).

racialized, targeting young men of African-Caribbean origin, the authors bring the politics of race and racism centre-stage in the analyses of youth and crime (Jefferson 2008).

In a climate of post-war counterculture and the expansion of higher education in the UK, the categorization of youthful collaborations as 'subcultures' represented a significant break with previous generations of criminological classification. Due in part to the study of crime being carried out from within sociology departments, the role of culture and political economy were brought to the fore. As in the early gang research in the United States, however, theories of youthful subcultures were largely rooted in the social patterning of industrialism, particularly in a perspective of stability between youth and parent cultures. While critical theories of race and class were brought to the fore, much of the work remained focused on male, working-class subcultural groups, and the role of young women and gendered relations was left unexamined (McRobbie and Garber 1976; McRobbie 1980). In the context of the shift to post-industrialism, some of these predictable continuities have fragmented with corresponding impacts on youthful street cultures (Hobbs 2013). While the concept of 'subculture' has fallen away amid a post-industrial context of 'neo-tribes' and 'post-subcultures' (Bennett 1999, 2011), the categorization of 'gangs' has emerged once more. As will be seen, however, this may reflect more of the changing parameters of academic labour in the UK than definable changes in urban youth themselves.

THE CRIMINOLOGIST'S 'GANG'

In recent years, in both the United States and—increasingly—the United Kingdom, the criminological categorization of 'gang' has emerged with renewed vigour. Increasingly, however, researchers are disinterested with either social improvement as in the Chicago School, or social inequality as in the Birmingham School, but more narrowly on ways of constructing categories of definition that are predicated on efforts at social control. Rather than responding to complexity with categorizations that capture fluidity and change, marketization and migration, researchers have tended to reach back to the 'gang' label. Mirroring developments in the United States, 'the gang' has become a convenient scapegoat for a host of deep-seated social anxieties in the United Kingdom.[5] It is not uncoincidental that recent academic interest in gangs in the UK occurred in the aftermath of Prime Minister Cameron's declaration of 'all-out war on gangs and gang culture'.[6] Academic labour occurs in the same climate of marketized entrepreneurialism and political economy as the street-based criminal collaborations they seek to depict.

In some parts of the world, it is clear that violent youthful groups pose a clear threat—as paramilitary groups, militias, or as adjuncts of the State (Hazen and Rodgers 2014) that demonstrate significant change over time. In others, it is evident that street-based, urban collaborations of youth have become institutionalized in communities where the state is absent, either due to a weak state or active retrenchement in policy-making (Wacquant 2008), forming community structures that incorporate both adults

[5] Gangs have been connected recently with 'violent women' (Batchelor 2009; T. Young 2011), knife crime, ethnicity (Aldridge *et al.* 2007), asylum and violent extremism (Alexander 2008).

[6] BBC (2011) 'Riots: David Cameron's statement in full', available at: http://www.bbc.co.uk/news/uk-politics-14492789, accessed 16 January 2017.

and young people, engaged in both organized and disorganized forms of crime, individually and collectively, in ways that defy easy categorization. These groups tend to react responsively to the social and economic environment in which they develop, particularly the forms of inequality in their community. Gangs have in some cases formed in prisons (Skarbek 2014), with the experience of prison reinforcing community-based collaborations in the 'free world' (Moore 1978). Other groups have adopted entrepreneurship as a central ethos (Padilla 1992), with some members graduating to international drug trafficking (Dowdney 2007).

In the United States, gang research has grown into a vast academic industry, as federal and state governments attempt to control the violence affecting communities across the country (Coughlin and Venkatesh 2003; Sanchez-Jankowski 2003). As Klein argues, summarizing the ascendancy of criminal justice orientations to criminological orthodoxy: 'Whatever may have been the history of the term gang and whatever may have been the desire—in many ways legitimate—to avoid stigmatizing youth groups with a pejorative term, it is time to characterize the street gang specifically for its involvement, attitudinal and/or behavioural, in delinquency and crime' (Klein 1995: 23). In this context, there have been few efforts to devise new categorizations for global complexity and the changing parameters of gang meanings (Moore 1998; Vigil 2003; Venkatesh 2008; Hagedorn 2015). Katz and Jackson-Jacobs depict this paradox as akin to the activity of a criminal gang seeking a monopoly in a territorial area.[7] In a chapter titled 'The Criminologist's Gang', they characterize the debate over definition of a gang as being 'essentially an argument over the correct description of a ghost' (Katz and Jackson-Jacobs 2004: 106).

In recent years, particularly in the aftermath of England's 'summer of violent disorder' in 2011 (Treadwell *et al.* 2013; Smithson *et al.* 2013), a comparable debate has emerged in the UK. On one side, scholars have drawn on the conceptual vocabularies of subcultural theory to argue that local identity and group conflict represent an enduring feature of life in working-class communities across the UK, and as such that territorial 'gangs' are nothing new (Alexander 2000; Hallsworth and Young 2008; Hallsworth 2013; Wilson 2016). From this perspective, categorization of this behaviour as 'gang-related' represents a cynical example of academic entrepreneurialism (Hallsworth 2011) that follows a trend for punitive social policy toward 'gang-related' activity (Cottrell-Boyce 2013). This strand of debate focuses attention on the role of academic, political, and media audiences in constructing 'the gang' as a contemporary 'folk devil' which cloaks racialized stereotypes (Alexander 2008; Williams 2015).

On the other side, researchers have argued that the subcultural theories of the 1970s are no longer relevant, and that the social and structural shifts brought on by the post-industrial era have resulted in the emergence of new street-based groups for whom the term 'gang' is a meaningful descriptor (Pitts 2008; Pitts 2011; Densley 2013). From this perspective, identifiable groups of street-based youth—with group names, organizational capacity and criminal entrepreneurialism—have emerged in urban centres in

[7] The shift from Chicago School approaches is epitomized most clearly in the work of the Eurogang network (Klein *et al.* 2001), a group of European and American gang researchers who have developed a set of common definitional criteria for the purposes of cross-national research, comprising 'any durable, street-oriented youth group whose involvement in illegal activity is part of its group identity' (van Gemert 2005: 148).

recent years, as an evolution from the street-based subcultural groups of previous eras. This view has found notable support in recent policing and policy changes in the UK, with flagship gang policies introduced, and 'anti-gang' units introduced across a range of police forces in England (HM Government 2011; Smithson *et al.* 2013). While both sides agree that the shift to post-industrialism has had significant and divisive implications for urban youth, there is intense debate as to whether the 'gang' label is a useful descriptor for this heavily politicized issue (Squires *et al* 2008).[8]

In the context of these debates, it is notable that the empirical basis for knowledge of gangs in the UK remains relatively undeveloped. Although there has been a recent upswing in gang research, findings vary significantly according to methodological approach, epistemological underpinning, and geographical context of the study. For example, survey-based methods tend to find relatively high levels of gang membership, though varying by cohort and questions (Bennett and Holloway 2004: 311; Sharp *et al.* 2006; Smith and Bradshaw 2005). Contrastingly, qualitative and ethnographic research often finds that gang identification to be relatively fluid and contingent (Aldridge *et al.* 2007: 17; see also Young *et al.* 2007).

Much work still needs to be done before an empirical basis for a distinctive case for a UK 'gang' is to be made. Critical developments in sociological and criminological theory—challenging researchers to analyse the complex intersections of race, class, and gender in contemporary street collectives, as well as reflexively engaging with feminist critiques of the 'malestream'—have scarcely touched contemporary gang scholarship (Young 2009, 2011; Batchelor 2009, 2011). Similarly, critical scholarship of the racialized impact of knife and gun crime (Solomos 1993:125), and more recently gang policies (Williams and Clarke 2015), as well as the impact of gang labelling practices of the police (Ralphs *et al.* 2009; Fraser and Atkinson 2013) have yet to fully register. There is, moreover, growing evidence of significant differences in the nature and meaning of 'gangs' in the different UK cities, making it inherently problematic to talk of 'gang in the UK' as a unified whole (Medina *et al.* 2013; Fraser 2015).

What is clear from these debates is that there have been significant changes to urban life in recent years, and traditional conceptualizations and categorizations may need substantial revision and reconstruction. Most contemporary youths do not belong to gangs (Sharp *et al.* 2006),[9] and often share space with peers who exhibit normative traits, a phenomena once described by academics as distinctly subcultural (Wilson 2016). Amongst these traits are dissociation from middle-class norms, and the adoption of key characteristics of a parent culture that is at least one generation removed from the high employment and relative prosperity enjoyed by the post-Second World War industrial working class (Armstrong *et al.* 2016: ch. 2). Yet criminology has tended to shy away from regarding contemporaneous youth from a historically nuanced perspective (Fraser 2015), that embraces both the chaos of the post-industrial city (Hobbs 2013; Winlow and Hall 2006), and the economic plight of youth in relation to the

[8] Alternative descriptions such as 'on road' (Hallsworth and Young 2008), 'street culture' (Bourgois 1995; Ilan 2015) or 'street capital' (Sandberg 2008) have sought to present a more complex picture.

[9] In their study of the policing of the London borough that hosted the 2012 Olympics, Armstrong *et al.* explain that while some gangs existed in the borough, most youths could not be described as gang 'members' or even 'associates'. Indeed, most violent crime was committed by this non-gang majority (Armstrong *et al.* 2016).

parent culture (MacDonald 1997, 1998). To do so would be to refigure and revise subcultural analysis, but instead the concept has been associated with an epoch now deemed redundant, and reduced to a few verses in a criminological karaoke primed by chronocenterism, 'the belief that one's own times are paramount, that other periods pale in comparison' (Fowles 1974: 249; Rock 2005).

The key variable that binds both the subcultural and gang eras is class, and more specifically the territories that cumulatively constitute the working-class city. As we saw earlier, street collaborations of the industrial era were categorized in the USA as gangs, whose formation was attributed to blocked aspiration. However, with notable and significant exceptions, in the UK where working-class aspiration was minimal, youthful collaborations were typified as, '[l]oose collectivities or crowds within which there was occasionally some more structured grouping, based on territorial loyalty' (Cohen 1972: 128). In industrial society this emphasis on territoriality was reinforced by the parent culture's long-term affiliation to neighbourhoods in close proximity to centres of employment, and to related institutions and agencies of informal order and social control: in particular the hegemony of a single class social structure built upon the firm foundations of unionized manual labour, the extended family, and the ecology of the working-class street (Cohen 1972). The family and the street provide the two central props in understanding the way in which the youth collaborations discussed above can mutate into adult crime collaborations.

ADULT URBAN COLLABORATIONS

While it has long been one of the few indisputable empirically established 'facts' of the criminological enterprise that most youths 'mature out' of delinquency (Hirschi and Gottfredson 1983), the confidence with which criminologists have wielded concepts such as subcultures and gangs in order to categorize deviant youth has not been apparent in scholarly approaches to adult urban criminal collaborations; a category of transgression that has been poorly served by criminological scholarship. As we discussed above, within territorially based youth collaborations conflict is crucial in forming identities, creating reputations, and moulding communal distinctiveness in the face of opposition. These groups occupy spaces or interstices between sections of the city that are frequently situated within 'delinquency areas' typified by working-class territorial imperatives defined by the experiences of low income, poor housing, and poor health (Shaw and McKay 1942). This is the locale where adult criminal careers were nurtured amongst youth formulated associations (Yablonsky 1962: 147–8).

NEIGHBOURHOOD CRIME GROUPS

The morphing from territorially based youth collaborations into adult acquisitive crime with the neighbourhood providing new recruits via the local delinquent subculture, has been documented by a wide range of writers, commenting on disparate urban milieus (Chin 1990: 120–45, 1996; Boyle 1977; Capeci and Mustain 1992; Thrasher 1927: 281–92; Cummines 2015). However, here we will discuss the phenomena with particular reference to the importance highlighted above by Thrasher of bringing to bear local, historical, and contextual analysis to attempt to understand the complexity of urban criminal collaborations.

Working-class communities of the industrial era were not homogeneous, but were made up of, 'a social patchwork of intensively localist culture and sentiment' (Robson 1997: 7), where adjacent territories were regarded with deep mistrust (Davies 2008, 2013). Neighbourhood-based groups abounded, and territorial imperatives featuring individual, local, and family reputations were forged in youthful combat that was ideal preparation for the world of acquisitive adult crime (McDonald 2001). Often bound by family affiliation (Lambrianou 1992: 29), these territorially based groups proved especially potent units when exploiting local entrepreneurial opportunities, before locating vulnerable targets in adjacent territories (Whyte 1943: 10; Boyle 1977) with variations of extortion and territorial domination providing the most common entry level activities (Hobbs 2013).[10]

Informal networks of violent entrepreneurs evolved from loose-knit youth groups into enduring adult criminal affiliations of professional criminals (McIntosh 1971, 1975), providing 'a sphere of *continuity* in the life of the area' (Robson 1997: 9). For instance analysis of the London-based criminal careers of the Sabini,[11] Kray,[12] and Richardson[13] families show how iconic adult crime collaborations emerged from youthful territorial violence, and into extortion before morphing into more entrepreneurial pursuits while retaining their culturally embedded violent potential. All three groups retained and nurtured their traditional bases, and refused to be constricted by the parochial restraints of the working-class neighbourhood. While retaining their neighbourhood roots, what marks out all three of these groups of extortioners turned entrepreneurs was their ability to reach beyond the locale that nurtured them (Hobbs 2013: 58–88). Throughout the industrial era these predators tended to be defined as professional criminals.

PROFESSIONAL CRIME

The concept of professional crime has long been associated with urban alcoves where regimentation of the poor was most ineffective (Tobias 1974; Salgado 1977; Stedman Jones 1971). However, while historians have documented the world of professional criminals (Klockars 1975: ch. l; Hay 1975; Munsche 1981; McMullan, 1982, 1984), it was left once more to the sociologists of the Chicago School to devise an analytic template for their practice and culture.

Sutherland (1937) challenged the then dominant Chicagoan explanation of crime being the result of social disorganization, and located a cohesive group that shared

[10] Extortion is not only a highly effective vehicle for consolidating control over territory (Falcone 1993: 116), it also assures market dominance (Gambetta 1988: 140).

[11] See Shore (2012, 2015).

[12] See Pearson (1973, 2001).

[13] See Richardson (1992), Robson (1997).

technical skill, consensus via a shared ideology, differential association, status, and organization. While Sutherland established the foundation for an important body of subsequent sociological work (see also Maurer 1955; Einstadter 1969; Shover 1973), some scholars highlighted professional criminal activity that required no collaboration and little skill (Lemert 1958), while others stressed the importance of non-specialist adaptable 'hustlers' (Holzman 1983; Polsky 1964, 1971; Roebuck and Johnson 1962; Williams and Milton 2016), who engage in a wide range of criminal endeavours, while displaying a distinct lack of any shared consensus with other hustlers.[14] This calls to question the notion of a cohesive behaviour system, and while commitment to making a living from crime (Letkemann 1973) provides a useful criterion for identifying these 'full-time miscreants' (Mack 1964), Mack's emphasis upon subcultures is a useful reminder of the commonality of urban working-class origins within adult as well as youthful criminal collaborations. Indeed, in the UK we can see a distinct urban working-class subculture of robbery emerging from working-class neighbourhoods that had been bypassed by the disciplining functions of industrial society (R. Smith 2005; T. Smith 2005; Hobbs 1995: 47; Mason 1994: 126–33). The violent potential and instrumental physicality of industrial cultures were ideally suited to armed robbery, whose rationale was often explicitly hedonistic (McVicar 1979: 158; Reynolds 2000: 116).[15]

THE UNDERWORLD

The world of the professional criminal has been commonly located within an urban underworld,[16] an iconic, essentially transgressive cultural space, 'a passive screen on to which the righteous project their own inhibited lusts and rapacities' (Benney 1936: 194–5). Inextricably associated with, 'That dangerous class which is found occupying a position between pauper and convict' (Archer 1865), and with its origins in urban working-class neighbourhoods, the underworld was essentially a transgressive annexe of proletarian industrial culture populated by those who were unable or unwilling to engage with the industrial project, yet with 'too little moral restraint to starve' (Archer 1865), and dominated by an occupational group defined by their level of commitment to illegal economic activities (see Becker 1960).[17] Further, by providing physical boundaries for the underworld within specific working-class urban alcoves crime is stabilized and concentrated (Rock 1973: 30), reducing our perception of the criminal population to those resident within those boundaries.

The decline of industrial society has impacted massively upon the working-class neighbourhoods from which both youthful and adult urban criminal collaborations have emerged (Hobbs 1995, 1997). The activities once associated exclusively with

[14] See Irwin (1970) and Irwin and Cressey (1962), which stress that the most crucial aspect in determining an inmate's adaptation to prison is the culture that is imported from the working-class urban milieu, which in turn also informs the identity of the professional criminal (Cohen and Taylor 1972; McVicar 1982; Fraser 1994; Mason 1994; Foreman 1996; Cummines 2015).

[15] See Hobbs (2013) and Matthews (2002).

[16] For an historical overview of the concept, see Shore (2015).

[17] Mack and Kerner (1975) include 'background operators' and 'service providers' such as accountants, lawyers, and corrupt police officers amongst this population.

professional crime are no longer the sole prerogative of an 'underworld' (cf. Haller 1990: 228–9). The mid 1970's rise of the drug trade marked a shift towards entrepreneurial relationships that mimicked the legitimate political economy, and the notion of a self-contained criminal underworld became increasingly redundant. Similarly, post-industrialism destroyed traditional communities and assured the fragmentation of working-class populations and the disintegration of extended family networks. Both mainstream and criminal economies along with their accompanying cultures have been redefined by this post-industrial shift which in turn has fostered clusters of decentred, unpredictable, and fractious trading economies (Hobbs 2013).

Working-class neighbourhoods have been erased, eroded, and colonized by bourgeois incomers, and their populations dispersed and relocated to locales often lacking the pragmatic economic logic that bound working-class communities of the industrial era. Neighbourhood crime firms and armed robbery teams were very much part of this process of fragmentation and relocation, and fragments of the working-class city's old underworld became attached to entrepreneurial opportunities that were no longer linked to neighbourhood-based affiliations. Criminal labour mimicked its legitimate counterpart and became negotiated within networks of small flexible firms characterized by short-term contractual commitments (Lash and Urry 1987), determined by market demand (Castells 1996: 272), and manifested themselves, '. . . as fluid sets of mobile marauders in the urban landscape alert to institutional weakness in both legitimate and illegitimate spheres' (Block 1983: 245).

Crimes previously central to the concept of a professional criminal underworld, for example armed robbery, whose practitioners were embedded in urban working-class neighbourhoods (Hobbs 2013), have become essentially amateur excursions utilizing base levels of competence (Matthews 2002; Smith 2005). Meanwhile, extortion evolved to accommodate demands for muscle in the night-time economy (Hobbs *et al.* 2003), as professional criminals followed the post-industrial route into entrepreneurship. With the demand for recreational drugs driving criminal activity and coinciding precisely with deindustrialization and the fragmentation of traditional communities, trading relationships, albeit within post-industrial urban settings, now provide the basis for contemporaneous criminal collaborations.

The gangsters and robbers of the old underworld, and the youths that fed their ranks emerged from working-class neighbourhoods that were products of industrial society. Deindustrialism marked the end of this culture and, in response to the hedonism and rampant entrepreneurship promoted by post-industrialism, contemporary street-based working-class collaborations of youths and adults are now mediated through market engagements that transcend traditional transgressive categories, making it difficult for family-based units to establish the kind of parochial dominance they once enjoyed. Yet kinship along with neighbourhood roots are far from redundant in post-industrial crime collaborations, and should be regarded as a highly instrumental trust variables, assuring loyalty by appealing to something other than self-interest (Gambetta 1988; Reuter 1985). 'If a group all speaks the same language, has the same village roots, possesses the same myth and culture norms, then it can function as a unit with greater trust and understanding . . .' (Lupsha 1986: 34; see Reuter 1983: 115).

However, criminal collaborations must constantly evolve, and the level and extent to which a criminal enterprise is embedded in the so called 'upperworld'—the sphere of legitimate transactions—is a major factor in its effectiveness. 'The more embedded a criminal market is in the upperworld, the easier it is for financial sources to be found' (Antonopoulos *et al.* 2015: 14). In the post-industrial era carefully nuanced market engagements with the upperworld enabled professional criminals to access new arenas that exceed circumscribed terrain (Lashmar and Hobbs, forthcoming), and these arenas are entrepreneurially orientated; supportive of networks that constitute an ideal environment for a range of both legal and illegal opportunities. Operating in accord with local conditions, '... flexible, adaptive networks that readily expand and contract to deal with the uncertainties of the criminal enterprise' (Potter 1994: 12) emerged from the 'inherited basic architecture' (Castells 1996: 146) of the working-class city.

The entrepreneurial habitas of post-industrial society has created collectivities that are linked via networks of illegal trading to strategically relevant pragmatic partnerships (Taylor 1999: 171–3), and urban street collaborations, however they are branded by commentators, are vital components to the dynamics of this unlicensed form of capitalism whose indistinct parameters are defined by the chaos and fragmentation of deindustrialization and the subsequent pragmatics of the working-class city.

ORGANIZED CRIME

> the study of organised crime—part science, part gossip, part theology (Lacey 1991: 367).

In spite of some resistance from British politicians and police, who prefered to emphasize 'professional', as opposed to 'organized' criminality to describe serious criminal collaborations in the UK (Home Affairs Committee 1994: 16–17), international pressures led to the adoption in the 1990s of 'organized crime', essentially a transnational phenomena that was attributed to foreigners (Woodiwiss 1988: 11–15; Nadelmann 1993: 470; Sheptycki 2003: 127). Specialist police budgets rapidly benefitted as the UK adopted a form of alien conspiracy theory (Cressey 1969, 1972),[18] and the essentially racist assumptions embedded in transnational organized crime narratives (Raine and Cilluffo 1994), were reproduced in early1990s UK police rhetoric (NCIS 1993a, 1993b). However, unlike studies of youth and the professional criminal collaborations and cultures into which they morphed, when the British version of organized crime was launched (Woodiwiss and Hobbs 2009), the indigenous urban origins of British criminal collaborations were ignored, and as a consequence, organized crime was confirmed in British political discourse as the product of globalization and the practice of foreigners (See Hobbs 2013, ch. 2).[19]

By ignoring the importance of urban social ecology in favour of a concentration upon transnational networks of deviant foreigners, organized crime has been rendered problematic as an analytic category. While the contemporary working-class street is now a profoundly multicultural entity 'vernacular cosmopolitanism' (Diouf 2000) this does not denote transnationalism. The important point is that contemporary working-class urban street collaborations increasingly share domains of interest with apparently

[18] For critiques of alien conspiracy theory, see Block (1983); Morris and Hawkins (1970); Smith (1975); Hawkins (1969).

[19] Subsequently the concept expanded to embrace threats as diverse as the Taliban, Somali Pirates, and 'delinquent youth gangs' (Cabinet Office Strategy Unit 2009). See also Home Office (2004).

legal actors operating within a post-industrial entrepreneurial habitas, and both unlicensed capitalism and the community of practice within which it resides are central to the way that we now live (Hobbs 2013).

The quest for order that seeks to capture and package criminal collaborations in convenient theoretical and distinctly non-empirical categories has also been extended to adult collaborations, and with the demise of the industrial era underworld, the notion of organized crime has proved to be a particularly potent phantom that has rapidly colonized law enforcement agencies and their allies in the academic community (Van Duyne 1996). Whatever transgressional sobriquet is applied to them, contemporary urban criminal collaborations both youth and adult alike, are integral to the assemblage that constitute the 'community of practice' that has replaced the self-contained proletarian underworld of industrial society. This community of practice is not exclusively reliant upon the cultures of the urban working class, for the fragmentation of entrenched communities produced disordered mutations of traditional culture which are enlivened by post-industrial entrepreneurial engagement mixed with cosmopolitan influences and their accompanying irregular trading networks, constituting, 'a far less exclusive zone than traditional underworld narratives would suggest' (Hobbs 2013: 230). Within this disparate collection of marketized scavengers the notion of extra-legal governance (see Varese 2010) is not apparent and, 'there is no imminent tendency towards the consolidation of large scale modern illegal bureaucracies' (Paoli and Fijnaut 2004: 610). However, the trope of the street remains vital in contextualizing a community of practice responding to interpretations of global markets operationalized via local identities and sensibilities (Hobbs 2013).

CONCLUSION: PROBLEMATIZING CRIMINOLOGICAL CATEGORIZATION

> a great deal of social scientists tend to describe the present as the *dawn of a new epoch* in human history, in one way or another marking a profound break with hitherto existing social structures of modern societies. (Osrecki, 2015: 131)

The tendency of much academic discourse to adopt a particularly rigid model of criminological epochs such as subcultures, gangs, professional crime, and organized crime fails to reflect the messy realities of urban life. While some of these products of the academy have their origins in the corridors of government, cumulatively these convenient collaborative categories, should not be taken as literal epochalist models (see Savage 2009), for while 'sociological epochalisms can be regarded as a legitimate strategy of raising public awareness for sociological debates' (Osrecki 2015), they are essentially genres of reasoning that lack historical consciousness, and do not constitute clear-cut unambiguous categories. For instance, both industrialism and post-industrialism constitute social processes that overlap, and the neighbourhoods from which urban working-class collaborations have emerged are subjected to the these processes, which in turn can both conflict and compliment. Consequently, the epochs of subcultures, gangs, professional crime and organized crime should be regarded as academic genres with contested boundaries.

Although the changing categories used to define such groups reflect the shifting contours of criminology, these shifts take place within a broader social and political context in which policing and political priorities have contributed considerably to shaping the field. In this chapter we have endeavoured to examine the changing nature of urban working-class criminal collaborations, in particular the impact of shifts from industrialism to post-industrialism, and the implications of this change for life in former working-class communities. Formulated by academics and often supported by institutions of welfare and law enforcement, categories of transgression may not be acknowledged by proponents of transgression. The messy realities, shifting identities, and fluid economies of the post-industrial city produce forms of transgression that tend to fall outside of political or administratively convenient categories. Working-class lives are rather more chaotic and less conveniently ordered (Winlow and Hall 2006) than is suggested by either the literal transplantation of gang or organized crime urban narratives from the USA. For instance the definitions of Thrasher (1963 [1927]), or Landesco (1968) were created in the maelstrom of industrial era Chicago, and their relevance to contemporary post-industrial urban populations are limited. However, this has not prevented politicians and law enforcement agencies from utilizing potent media enhanced narratives relating to gangs and organized crime in order to generate electoral clout, or budgetry leverage.

Importantly, the rapidly changing urban milieu has rendered these rigid criminological categorizations problematic. Their persistence in curricula and textbooks can be largely attributed to the emergence of criminology as a self-contained discipline whose self-imposed parameters are generated by an increasingly narrow set of market led criminological concerns (Hobbs 2012). However, gentrification, rehousing, and a proletarian residue constantly enhanced by a shifting, churning cosmopolitan population, has created a chaotic contemporary urban reality that can no longer rely upon the predictability that emanated from settled working-class neighbourhoods imbued with the certainties and hierarchies of industrial society. The post-industrial drift of working-class communities away from their traditional urban heartlands have bloated the periphery with new towns and extended suburbs. Criminal collaborations are integral to this proletarian diaspora, and they will continue to mutate.

SELECTED FURTHER READING

For a starting point on the 'gang' categorization, Thrasher's *The Gang* (1927) stands the test of time. On gangs in a global context, see Hagedorn (2008), Dowdney's *Neither War Nor Peace: International Comparisons of Children and Armed Youth in Organised Armed Violence* (2007), and Brotherton's *Youth Street Gangs: A Critical Appraisal* (2015). For discussion of contemporary debate in UK gang research, see Goldson's *Youth in Crisis? 'Gangs', Territoriality and Violence* (2011). Classical approaches to youth, crime, and subcultures in the UK come in the form of Downes' *Delinquent Solution* (1966), Taylor, Walton, and Young's *The New Criminology* (1973), Cohen's *Folk Devils and Moral Panics* (1972), Pearson's *Hooligan: A History of Respectable Fears* (1983), Hall *et al.*'s *Policing the Crisis* (1976) and *Resistance through Ritual* (1978). Critical questioning of these points can be found in recent special issues of the *British Journal of Criminology* (49/1) and *Crime Media Culture* (4/1). Finally, Fraser's ethnography of gangs in Glasgow, *Urban Legends: Gang Identity in the Post-Industrial City* (2015), brings our understanding of urban youth collaborations into the post-industrial era.

On adult criminal collaborations, Sutherland's *The Professional Thief* (1937), Klockars' *The Professional Fence* (1974), Hobbs' *Bad Business* (1995), and Taylor's *In the Underworld* (1983), along with Levi's classic study of 'Long Fraud', *The Phantom Capitalists* (1981) all provide classic accounts of professional crime. Chinn's study of Chinatown, *Chinatown Gangs* (1996) and Shore's study of the move from the neighbourhood into violent entrepreneurship, 'Criminality and Englishness in the Aftermath: The Racecourse wars of the 1920s' (2012), along with Pearson's classic account of the Kray twins, *The Profession of Violence* (1972) provide valuable studies of neighbourhood crime groups. On organized crime, Alan Block's superb history of organized crime in New York, *East Side-West Side: Organizing Crime in New York* (1983), Gambetta's study of Sicily *The Sicilian Mafia* (1993), Reuter's down to earth account of how organized crime actually operates, *Disorganised Crime: Illegal Markets and the Mafia* (1984), and Hobbs' (2013) study of how youth and adult criminal collaborations come together in post-industrial society all provide a foundation for further study.

REFERENCES

Aldridge, J., Medina, J., and Ralphs, R. (2007), 'Youth Gangs in an English City: Social Exclusion, Drugs and Violence', Full Research Report ESRC End of Award Report, RES-000-23-0615, Swindon: ESRC.

Aldridge, J., Ralphs, R., and Medina, J. (2011), 'Collateral Damage: territory and policing in an English gang city', in B. Goldson (ed.), *Youth in Crisis? 'Gangs', Territoriality and Violence*; Abingdon: Routledge.

Alexander, C. (2000), *The Asian Gang: Ethnicity, identity, masculinity*, Oxford: Berg.

Alexander, C. (2008), *(Re)thinking Gangs*, London: Runnymede Trust.

Antonopoulos, G. A., Hall, A., Levi, M., and Rusev, A. (2015), 'Understanding criminal finances: policy and methodological framework', in *Financing of Organised Crime*, Center for the Study of Democracy, University of Trento, Teesside University.

Archer, T. (1865), *The Pauper, The Thief and the Convict: Sketches of Some of their Homes, Haunts and Habits*, London: Groombridge and Sons.

Armstrong, G., Giulianotti, R., and Hobbs, D. (2016), *Policing the 2012 London Olympics: Legacy and Social Exclusion*, London: Routledge.

Asbury, H. (1927), *The Gangs of New York: An Informal History of the Underworld*, Garden City, NY: Garden City Publishing Company.

Batchelor, S. (2009), 'Girls, gangs and violence: assessing the evidence', *Probation Journal*, 56(4): 399–414.

Batchelor, S. (2011), 'Beyond dichotomy: towards an explanation of young women's involvement in violent street gangs', in B. Goldson (ed.), *Youth in Crisis? 'Gangs', Territoriality and Violence*, London: Routledge.

Becker, H. (1960), 'Notes on the Concept of Commitment', *American Journal of Sociology*, LXVI: 32–40.

Bennett, A. (1999), 'Subcultures or Neo-Tribes? Rethinking the Relationship between Youth, Style and Musical Taste', *Sociology*, 33(3): 599–617.

Bennett, A. (2011), 'The post-subcultural turn: some reflections 10 years on', *Journal of Youth Studies*, 14(5): 493–506.

Bennett, T. and Holloway, K. (2004), 'Gang Membership, Drugs and Crime in the UK', *British Journal of Criminology*, 44(3): 305–23.

Benney, M. (1936), *Low Company*, Facsimile edn, Sussex (1981): Caliban Books.

Block, A. (1983), *East Side-West Side: Organizing Crime in New York, 1930-1950*, Newark, NJ: Transaction.

Bourgois, P. (1995), *In Search of Respect: Selling Crack in El Barrio*, Cambridge University Press: Cambridge.

Boyle, J. (1977), *A Sense of Freedom*, London: Pan.

Brotherton, D. (2015), *Youth Street Gangs: A Critical Appraisal*, London: Routledge.

Cabinet Office Strategy Unit (2009), *Extending our Reach: A Comprehensive Approach to Tackling Serious Organised Crime*, Norwich: The Stationery Office.

Capeci, J. and Mustain. G. (1992), *Gotti: Rise and Fall*, New York: Onyx.

Castells, M. (1996), *The Rise of the Network Society*, Oxford: Blackwell.

Chesney-Lind, M. and Hagedorn, J. (1999), *Female Gangs in America: Essays on Girls, Gangs and Gender*, Chicago: Lake View Press.

Chin, K. (1990), *Chinese Subculture and Criminality*, Westport, CT: Greenwood.

Chin, K. (1996), *Chinatown Gangs*, New York: Oxford University Press.

Clarke, J. (1975), 'The Skinheads and the Magical Recovery of Community', in S. Hall and T. Jefferson (eds), *Resistance through Rituals*, Birmingham: Centre for Contemporary Cultural Studies.

Cloward, R. and Ohlin, L. (1960), *Delinquency and Opportunity*, New York: Free Press.

Cohen, A. (1955), *Delinquent Boys: The Culture of the Gang*, Glencoe: Free Press.

Cohen, P. (1972), 'Subcultural Conflict and Working-Class Community', *Working Papers in Cultural Studies*, 2 (Spring): 5–52.

Cohen, S. (1972), *Folk Devils and Moral Panics: The Construction of the Mods and Rockers*, London: MacGibbon and Kee.

Cohen, S. (1974), 'Criminology and the Sociology of Deviance in Britain', in P. Rock and M. McIntosh (eds), *Deviance and Social Control*, Tavistock: London.

Cohen, S. (1980), Symbols of Trouble: Introduction to the New Edition, *Folk Devils and Moral Panics*, 2nd edn, London: MacGibbon and Kee.

Corrigan, P. (1979), *Schooling the Smash Street Kids*, London: MacMillan.

Cottrell-Boyce, J. (2013), 'Ending Gang and Youth Violence: A Critique', *Youth Justice*, 13(3): 193–206.

Coughlin, B. C. and Venkatesh, S. (2003), 'The Urban Street Gang after 1970', *Annual Review of Sociology*, 29: 41–64.

Cressey, D. (1969), *Theft of the Nation: The Structure and Operations of Organized Crime in America*, New York: Harper and Row.

Cressey, D. (1972), *Criminal Organisation*, London: Heinemann

Cummines, B. (2015), *I Am Not a Gangster*, London: Ebury.

Davies, A. (2013), *City of Gangs: Glasgow and the Rise of the British Gangster*, London: Hodder & Stoughton.

Deegan, M. J. (2001), *The Chicago School of Ethnography*, in M. Atkinson, S. Delamont, A. Coffey, J. Lofland, and L. Lofland (eds), *The Sage Handbook of Ethnography*, London: Sage.

Densley, J. (2013), *How Gangs Work: An Ethnography of Youth Violence*, London: Palgrave.

Diouf, M. (2000), 'The Senegalese Murid trade diaspora and the making of a vernacular cosmopolitanism', *Public Culture*, 12(3): 679–702.

Dowdney, L. (2007), *Neither War Nor Peace: International Comparisons of Children and armed Youth in Organised Armed Violence*, UN: COAV.

Downes, D. (1966), *The Delinquent Solution: A Study in Subcultural Theory*, London: Routledge & Kegan Paul.

Einstadter, W. J. (1969), 'The Social Organisation of Armed Robbery', *Social Problems*, 17(1): 64–83.

Falcone, G. (1993), *Men of Honour*, London: Warner.

Fowles, J. (1974), 'On Chronocentrism', *Futures*, 6(1): 65–8.

Fraser, A. (2015), *Urban Legends: Gang Identity in the Post-Industrial City*, Oxford: Oxford University Press.

Fraser, A. and Atkinson, C. (2014), 'Making Up Gangs: Looping, Labelling and the New Politics of Intelligence-Led Policing', *Youth Justice*, 14(2): 154–70.

Fraser, F. (1994), *Mad Frank*, London: Little Brown.

Gambetta, D. (1988), 'Fragments of an Economic Theory of the Mafia', *Archives Européennes de Sociologie*, 29(1): 127–45.

Gambetta, D. (1993), *The Sicilian Mafia: The Business Of Private Protection*, Cambridge, MA, London: Harvard University Press.

Gill, O. (1977), *Luke Street: Housing Policy, Conflict and the Creation of the Delinquent Area*, London: Macmillan.

Goldson, B. (ed.) (2011), *Youth in Crisis? 'Gangs', Territoriality and Violence*, London: Routledge.

Hagedorn, J. (2015), *The In$ane Chicago Way: The Daring Plan by Chicago Gangs to Create a Spanish Mafia*, Chicago: University of Chicago Press.

Hagedorn, J. (2008), *A World of Gangs: Armed Young Men and Gangsta Culture*, University of Minnesota Press: Minnesota.

Hall, S. M. and Jefferson, T. (1976), *Resistance Through Rituals: Youth Subcultures in Post-War Britain*, London: Hutchinson.

Hall, S. M., Critcher, C., Jefferson, T., Clarke, J., and Roberts, B. (1978), *Policing the Crisis: Mugging, The State and Law and Order*, London: MacMillan.

Haller, M. (1990), 'Illegal Enterprise: A Theoretical and Historical Interpretation', *Criminology*, 28(2): 207–35.

Hallsworth, S. (2011), 'Gangland Britain? Realities, fantasies and industry', in B. Goldson (ed.), *Youth in Crisis? 'Gangs', Territoriality and Violence*, London: Routledge.

Hallsworth, S. (2013), *The Gang and Beyond: Interpreting Violent Street Worlds*, Basingstoke: Palgrave.

Hallsworth, S. and Young, T. (2008), 'Gang Talk and Gang Talkers: A Critique', *Crime, Media, Culture*, 4(2): 175–95.

Hawkins, G. (1969), 'God and the Mafia', *The Public Interest*, 14–Winter: 24–51.

Hay, D. (1975), 'Property, Authority and the Criminal Law', in D. Hay *et al.*, *Albions Fatal Tree*, London: Allen Lane.

Hazen, J. and Rodgers, D. (2014), *Global Gangs: Street Violence Across the World*, Minneapolis, MN: University of Minnesota Press.

Hebdige, D. (1979), *Subculture: the meaning of style*, London: Methuen.

Hirschi, T. and Gottfredson, M. (1983), 'Age and the Explanation of Crime', *The American Journal of Sociology*, 89(3): 552–84.

Hirst, P. (1975), *Marx and Engels on Law, Crime and Morality*, in I. Taylor, P. Walton, and J. Young (eds), *Critical Criminology*, London: Routledge & Kegan Paul.

HM Government (2011), *Ending Gang and Youth Violence*, London: Home Office.

Hobbs, D. (1995), *Bad Business: Professional Criminals in Modern Britain*, Oxford: Oxford University Press.

Hobbs, D. (1997), 'Criminal Collaboration: Youth Gangs, Subcultures, Professional Criminals and Organized Crime', in M. Maguire, R. Morgan, and R. Reiner (eds), *The Oxford Handbook of Criminology*, Oxford: Oxford University Press.

Hobbs, D. (2012), 'It was never about the money: market society, organised crime and UK criminology', in S. Hall and S. Winlow (eds), *New Directions in Criminological Theory*, London: Routledge.

Hobbs, D. (2013), *Lush Life: Constructing Organized Crime in the UK*, Oxford: Oxford University Press.

Hobbs, D., Hadfield, P., Lister, S., and Winlow, S. (2003), *Bouncers: Violence, Governance and the Night-time Economy*, Oxford: Oxford University Press.

Holzman, H. R. (1982), 'The Serious Habitual Property Offender as Moonlighter: An Empirical Study of Labour Force participation among robbers and burglars', *Journal of Criminal Law and Criminology*, 73(4): 1774–92.

Home Affairs Committee (1994), *Organised Crime: Minutes and Memoranda*, London: Home Office.

Home Office (2004), 'One Step Ahead: A 21st Century Strategy to Defeat Organised Crime', London: Home Office, available at: https://www.gov.uk/government/uploads/system/uploads/attachment.../6167.pdf , accessed 16 January 2017.

Ilan, J. (2015), *Understanding Street Culture: Poverty, Crime, Youth and Cool*, Basingstoke: Palgrave Macmillan.

Jefferson, T. (1975), 'Cultural Responses of the Teds: The defence of space and status', in S. Hall and T. Jefferson (eds), *Resistance Through Rituals*, Birmingham: Centre for Contemporary Cultural Studies.

Jefferson, T. (2008), 'Policing the crisis revisited: The state, masculinity, fear of crime and racism', *Crime Media Culture*, 4(1): 113–21.

Junger-Tas, J., Marshall, I. H., Enzmann, D., Killias, M., Steketee, M., and Gruszczynska, B. (2012), *The Many Faces of Youth Crime: Contrasting Theoretical Perspectives on Juvenile Delinquency Across Countries and Cultures*, New York: Springer.

Katz, J. and Jackson-Jacobs, C. (2004), 'The Criminologists' Gang', in C. Summer (ed.), *The Blackwell Companion to Criminology*, Oxford: Blackwell.

Klein, M. (1995), *The American Street Gang: Its Nature, Prevalence, and Control*, New York: Oxford University Press.

Klein, M. with Kerner, H.-J., Maxson, C. L., and Weitekamp, E. G. M. (eds) (2001), *The Eurogang Paradox*, Kluwer Academic Press: London.

Klockars, C. (1975), *The Professional Fence*, London: Tavistock.

Lacey, R. (1991), *Little Man*, New York: Little Brown.

Lambrianou, T. (1992), *Inside the Firm*, London: Pan.

Lash, S. and Urry, J. (1987), *The End of Organised Capitalism*, Cambridge: Polity.

Lashmar, P. and Hobbs, D. (forthcoming), *Hatton Garden: Heist*, **History and Organised Crime**.

Lemert, E. (1958), 'The Behaviour of the Systematic Check Forger', *Social Problems*, 6(2): 141–9.

Letkemann, P. (1973), *Crime as Work*, New Jersey: Prentice Hall.

Levi, M. (1981), *The Phantom Capitalists*, Aldershot: Gower.

Lupsha, P. (1986), 'Organised Crime in the United States', in R. Kelly (ed.), *Organised Crime: A Global Perspective*, Totowa, NJ: Rowman and Littlefield.

MacDonald, R. (1997), 'Informal working, survival strategies and the idea of an underclass', in R. Brown (ed.), *The Changing Shape of Work*, Basingstoke: Macmillan.

MacDonald, R. (1998), 'Youth, transitions and social exclusion: some issues for youth research in the UK', *Journal of Youth Studies*, 1(2):163–76.

Mack, J. (1964), 'Full-time Miscreants, Delinquent Neighbourhoods and Criminal Networks', *British Journal of Sociology*, 15: 38–53.

Mack, J. and Kerner, H. (1975), *The Crime Industry*, Lexington: Saxon House, Levington Books.

Mason, E. (1994), *Inside Story*, London: Pan.

Matthews, R. (2002), *Armed Robbery*, Devon: Willan.

Maurer, D. W. (1955), *The Whizz Mob*, New Haven: College and University Press.

McDonald, B. (2001), *Elephant Boys*, Edinburgh: Mainstream.

McIntosh, M. (1971), 'Changes in the Organisation of Thieving', in S. Cohen (ed.), *Images of Deviance*, Harmondsworth: Penguin.

McIntosh, M. (1975), *The Organisation of Crime*, London: Macmillan.

McMullan, J. (1982), 'Criminal Organisation in Sixteenth and Seventeenth Century London', *Social Problems*, 29(3), 311–23.

McMullan, J. (1984), *The Canting Crew: London's Criminal Underworld, 1550-1700*, New Brunswick, NJ: Rutgers University Press.

McRobbie, A. (1980), 'Settling Accounts with Subcultures: A Feminist Critique', *Screen Education*, 39(Spring): 37–49.

McRobbie, A. and Garber, J. (1976), 'Girls and subcultures: an exploration', in S. Hall and T. Jefferson (eds), *Resistance through Rituals*, London: Hutchison.

McVicar, J. (1979), *McVicar By Himself*, London: Arrow.

Medina, J., Aldridge, J., and Ralphs, R. (2013), 'Gang Transformation, Changes or Demise: Evidence from an English city', in C. L. Maxson, A. Egley Jr, J. Miller, and M. W. Klein (eds), *The Modern Gang Reader*, Los Angeles: Oxford University Press.

Merton, R. (1938), 'Social structure and anomie', *American Sociological Review*, 3(5): 672–82.

Moore, J. (1978), *Homeboys: Gangs, Drugs, and Prison in the Barrios of Los Angeles*, Philadelphia: Temple University Press.

Moore, J. (1998), 'Understanding Youth Street Gangs: Economic Restructuring and the Urban Underclass', in M. W. Watts (ed.), *Cross-Cultural Perspectives on Youth and Violence*, Stanford: JAI Press Inc.

Morris, N. and Hawkins, G. (1970), *The Honest Politician's Guide to Crime Control*, Chicago: University of Chicago Press.

MUNSCHE, P. (1981), *Gentlemen and Poachers*, Cambridge: Cambridge University Press.

NADELMANN, E. (1993), *Cops Across Borders: The Internationalization of U.S. Criminal Law Enforcement*, University Park: Penn State Press.

NCIS (1993a), *An Outline Assessment of the Threat and Impact by Organised/Enterprise Crime Upon United Kingdom Interests*, London: NCIS.

NCIS (1993b), *Organised Crime Conference: A Threat Assessment*, London: NCIS.

OSRECKI, F. (2015), 'Constructing Epochs: The Argumentative Structures of Sociological Epochalisms', *Cultural Sociology*, 9(2): 131–46.

PADILLA, F. (1992), *The Gang As an American Enterprise*, New Brunswick, NJ: Rutgers University Press.

PAOLI, L. and FIJNAUT, C. (2004), 'Comparative Synthesis of Part 2', in L. Paoli and C. Fijnaut (eds), *Organised Crime in Europe*, Netherlands: Springer.

PARKER, H., (1974), *View From the Boys: A Sociology of Down-Town Adolescents*, Newton Abbot: David and Charles Holding.

PATRICK, J. (1973), *A Glasgow Gang Observed*, London: Eyre-Methuen.

PEARSON, J. (1972) *The Profession of Violence: The Rise and Fall of the Kray Twins*, London: Weidenfeld and Nicolson.

PEARSON, G. (1983), *Hooligan: a History of Respectable Fears*, London: Macmillan.

PEARSON, J. (1973), *The Profession of Violence*, London: Granada.

PEARSON, J. (2001), *The Cult of Violence*, London: Orion.

PITTS, J. (2008), *Reluctant Gangsters: The Changing Face of Youth Crime*, Devon: Willan.

PITTS, J. (2011), 'Mercenary territory: are youth gangs really a problem?', in B. Goldson (ed.), *Youth in Crisis? 'Gangs', Territoriality and Violence*, London: Routledge.

POLSKY, N. (1964), '"The Hustler", *Social Problems*, 12(1) Summer: 3–15.

POLSKY, N. (1971), *Hustlers, Beats and Others*, Harmondsworth: Pelican (1st edn. 1967).

POTTER, G. W. (1994), *Criminal Organisations*, Illinois: Waveland.

RAINE, L. and CILLUFFO, F. (eds) (1994), *Global Organized Crime: The New Empire of Evil*, Washington, DC: Center for Strategic and International Studies.

RALPHS, R., MEDINA, J., and ALDRIDGE, J. (2009), 'Who needs enemies with friends like these? The importance of place for young people living in known gang areas', *Journal of Youth Studies*, 12(5): 483–500.

REISS, A. J. and FARRINGTON, D. P. (1991), 'Advancing knowledge about co-offending: Results from prospective longitudinal survey of London males', *Journal of Criminal Law and Criminology*, 82(2): 360–95.

REUTER, P. (1984), *Disorganised Crime: Illegal Markets and the Mafia*, Cambridge, MA: MIT Press.

REUTER, P. (1985), *The Organisation of illegal Markets: An Economic Analysis*, Washington, DC: US Department Of Justice.

REYNOLDS, B. (2000), *The Autobiography of a Thief*, London: Virgin.

RICHARDSON, C. (1992), *My Manor*, London: Pan.

ROBSON, G. (1997), *Class, Criminality and Embodied Consciousness: Charlie Richardson and a South East London Habitus*, London: Goldsmiths College.

ROCK, P. (1973), *Deviant Behaviour*, London: Hutchinson.

ROCK, P. (2005), 'Chronocentrism and British Criminology', *British Journal of Sociology*, 6(3): 473–791.

ROEBUCK, J. and JOHNSON, R. (1962), 'The Jack of All Trades Offender', *Crime and Delinquency*, 8(2): 172–81.

SALGADO, G. (1977), *The Elizabethan Underworld*, London: Dent.

SANCHEZ-JANKOWSKI, M. (1991), *Islands in the Street: Gangs and American Urban Society*, Berkeley, CA: University of Berkeley Press.

SANCHEZ-JANKOWSKI, M. (2003), 'Gangs and Social Change', *Theoretical Criminology*, 7(2): 191–216.

SANDBERG, S. (2008), 'Street capital: ethnicity and violence on the streets of Oslo', *Theoretical Criminology*, 12(2): 153–71.

SAVAGE, S. (2009), 'Against Epochalism: An Analysis of Conceptions of Change in British Sociology', *Cultural Sociology*, 3(2): 217–38.

SCOTT, P. (1956), 'Gangs and Delinquent Groups in London', *British Journal of Delinquency*, 7(1): 4–26.

SHARP, C., ALDRIDGE, J., and MEDINA, J. (2006), *Delinquent Youth Groups and Offending Behaviour: Findings from the 2004 Offending, Crime and Justice Survey*, Home Office: London.

SHAW, C. and MCKAY, H. D. (1942), *Juvenile Delinquency and Urban Areas*, Chicago: University of Chicago Press.

SHAW, C. (1966), *The Jackroller: A Delinquent Boy's Own Story*; Chicago and London: University of Chicago Press.

SHEPTYCKI, J. (2003), 'Against transnational organised crime', in M. E. Beare (ed.), *Critical Reflections on Transnational Organised Crime, Money Laundering and Corruption*, Toronto: University of Toronto Press.

SHORE, H. (2012), 'Criminality and Englishness in the Aftermath: The Racecourse wars of the 1920s', *Twentieth Century British History*, 22(4): 474–97.

SHORE, H. (2015), *London's Criminal Underworlds, c. 1720—c. 1930: A Social and Cultural History*, London: Palgrave.

SHOVER, N. (1973), 'The Social Organisation of Burglary', *Social Problems*, 20(4): 499–514.

SKARBEK, D. (2014), *The Social Order of the Underworld: How Prison Gangs Govern the American Penal System*, New York: Oxford University Press.

SMITH, D. (1975), *The Mafia Mystique*, New York: Basic Books.

SMITH, R. (2005), *A Few Kind Words and a Loaded Gun*, London: Penguin.

SMITH, T. (2005), *The Art of Armed Robbery*, London: Blake.

Smith, D. J. and Bradshaw, P. (2005), 'Gang Membership and Teenage Offending', *Edinburgh Study of Youth Transitions and Crime*; Publication Number 8.

Smithson, H., Ralphs, R., and Williams, P. (2013), 'Used and Abused: The Problematic Usage of Gang Terminology in the United Kingdom and its Implications for Ethnic Minority Youth', *British Journal of Criminology*, 53(1): 113–28.

Solomos, J. (1993), *Race and Racism in Britain*, London: Macmillan.

Squires, P. (2011), 'Young people and "weaponisation" ', in B. Goldson (ed.), *Youth in Crisis? 'Gangs', Territoriality and Violence*, London: Routledge.

Squires, P., Silverstri., A. with Grimshaw, R. and Solomon, E. (2008), *Street Weapons Commission: Knives and Street Violence*, London: Centre for Crime and Justice Studies.

Stedman-Jones, G. (1971), *Outcast London*, Oxford: Oxford University Press.

Sutherland, E. (1937), *The Professional Thief*, Chicago: University of Chicago Press.

Taylor, I. (1999), *Crime in Context*, Cambridge: Polity.

Taylor, I. and Taylor, L. (eds) (1973), *Politics and Deviance: Papers from the National Deviance Conference*, Middlesex: Pelican.

Taylor, I., Walton, P., and Young, J. (1973), *The New Criminology: For a Social Theory of Deviance*, London: Routledge & Kegan Paul.

Thrasher, F. (1963), *The Gang: A Study of 1,313 Gangs in Chicago*, 2nd edn, Chicago, Ill: University of Chicago Press.

Tobias, J. (1974), *Prince of Fences: The Life and Crimes of Ikey Solomons*, London: Valentine Mitchell.

Treadwell, J., Briggs,. D., Winlow, S., and Hall, S. (2013), 'Shopocalypse Now: Consumer Culture and the English Riots of 2011', *British Journal of Criminology*, 53(1): 1–17.

Varese, F. (2010), 'What is Organised Crime?', Introduction in F. Varese (ed.), *Organised Crime*, London: Routledge.

Van Duyne, P. C. (1996), 'The phantom and threat of organized crime', *Crime, Law and Social Change*, 24(4): 341–77.

van Gemert, F. (2005), 'Youth groups and gangs in Amsterdam: A Pretest of the Eurogang Expert Survey', in S. Decker and F. Weerman (eds), *European Street Gangs and Troublesome Youth Groups*, Oxford: AltaMira Press.

Venkatesh, S. (2008), *Gang Leader for a Day: A Rogue Sociologist Crosses the Line*; London: Allen Lane.

Vigil, J. (2003), 'Urban Violence and Street Gangs', *Annual Review of Anthropology*, 32: 225–42.

Wacquant, L. J. D. (2008), *Urban Outcasts: A Comparative Sociology of Advanced Marginality*, London: Polity.

Whyte, W. F. (1993) [1943], *Street Corner Society: The Social Structure of an Italian Slum*, 4th edn, Chicago and London: University of Chicago Press.

Williams, P. (2015), 'Criminalising the other: challenging the race-crime nexus', *Race & Class*, 56(3): 18–35.

Williams, P. and Clarke, B. (2015), *Dangerous Associations: Joint Enterprise, Gangs and Racism*, London: Centre for Crime and Justice Studies.

Willis, P. (1977), *Learning to Labour: How Working Class Kids Get Working Class Jobs*, Hampshire: Gower.

Wilmott, P. (1966), *Adolescent Boys of East London*, Harmondsworth: Penguin.

Wilson, A. (2016), 'The Same Old Song?: The Contemporary Relevance of Subcultures', in D. Hobbs (ed.), *Mischief, Morality and Mobs: Essays in Honour of Geoffrey Pearson*, London: Routledge.

Winlow, S. and Hall, S. (2006), *Violent Night: Urban Leisure and Contemporary Culture*, Oxford: Berg.

Woodiwiss, M. (1988), *Crime, Crusades and Corruption: Prohibitions in the United States, 1900-1987*, London: Pinter.

Woodiwiss, M. and Hobbs, D. (2009), 'Organized Evil and the Atlantic Alliance: Moral Panics and the Rhetoric of Organized Crime Policing in America and Britain', *British Journal of Criminology*, 49(1): 106–28.

Yablonsky, L. (1962), *The Violent Gang*, New York: Macmillan.

Young, J. (1971), *The Drugtakers: The Social Meaning of Drug Use*, London: Paladin.

Young, J. (2004), 'Voodoo criminology and the numbers game', in J. Ferrell, W. Morrison, and M. Presdee (eds), *Cultural Criminology Unleashed*, London: Glasshouse.

Young, T. (2009), 'Girls and Gangs: "Shemale" Gangsters in the UK?', *Youth Justice*, 9(3): 224–38.

Young, T. (2011), 'In search of the "shemale" gangster', in B. Goldson (ed.), *Youth in Crisis? 'Gangs', Territoriality and Violence*, London: Routledge.

Young, T., FitzGerald, M., Hallsworth, S., and Joseph, I. (2007), 'Groups, gangs and weapons', London: Youth Justice Board; available at: http://www.yjb.gov.uk/publications/Resources/Downloads/gangs%20Guns%20and%20Weapons%20Summary.pdf, accessed 1 August 2013.

27

DEVELOPMENTAL AND LIFE-COURSE CRIMINOLOGY: INNOVATIONS, IMPACTS, AND APPLICATIONS

Lesley McAra and Susan McVie

> An academic discipline is in substantial measure an institutionally bounded community, a tradition, a set of practices, a market-place, a network for communication and an organised way of seeing the world
>
> (Rock 1994: 125)

> If there is one thing I have stood for in my career, it is that we should never, never withdraw from the policy making arena. We must give answers; we must be about doing good where doing harm so often now prevails
>
> (Cullen 2011: 23)

INTRODUCTION

The term 'developmental and life-course criminology' (DLC[1]) is used to describe the field of study which explores age-based changes in individual offending behaviour. It is distinct from other related fields of enquiry by its conceptual focus on crime and antisocial behaviour *across the life-span* of the *individual* (i.e. *within* individual change) and is characterized by a methodological approach which involves longitudinal exploration of key developmental stages and transitions over the life-course. DLC's roots lie firmly in a scientific–empirical approach to the study of crime. It is predicated on

[1] We use the combined term 'developmental and life-course criminology' in this chapter because the two elements are commonly connected or used interchangeably in the literature; however, we acknowledge that some scholars make a distinction between 'developmental' and 'life-course' criminology on conceptual, methodological, and theoretical grounds. See Sampson and Laub (2005, 2016) for further details.

the notion that knowledge is progressive and universalizable. Core assumptions of the paradigm are that human behaviour is measurable and quantifiable, and that there are law-like regularities in social encounters and individual responses that enable predictions to be made. It is in these ways that DLC is, at heart, a 'modernist creation' (Garland 1997).

In the previous edition of the *Handbook*, we offered a critical review of theory and method in DLC and its impacts on programmes for offender management (McAra and McVie 2012a). On undertaking this recommission some five years later, we have found ourselves reflecting on the questions raised by recent innovations in DLC for the discipline of criminology more generally, namely:

- How do paradigms (in Rock's terms 'organised way of seeing the world') emerge and endure, with specific reference to the social, political, and economic (market-led) organization of knowledge production?
- What are the lessons that can be drawn from DLC with regard to the ways in which particular theories are constructed and gain approval within criminology?
- How do methodological developments, linked particularly to technological advances, make certain types of knowledge possible (and what are the consequences of this)?
- What are the circumstances under which criminological knowledge is taken up and deployed by policy-makers and practitioners?

In offering an explication of these interrelated questions, we aim to conduct an appreciative review of DLC scholarship and highlight what we believe to be its (sometimes unrecognized) radical potential in terms of innovation and impact. For these reasons, we would claim, the DLC paradigm speaks to those in criminology who, in Cullen's terms are 'about doing good where doing harm so often now prevails'.

We begin by reviewing the contexts in which developmental and life-course criminology emerged and has endured. We then turn to a critical review of theoretical and methodological innovation and advancement within the paradigm. This is followed by an exploration of policy solutions offered by the DLC paradigm and its more recent policy impacts. The chapter concludes with some final reflections on the questions posed above.

THE EMERGENCE AND DURABILITY OF THE DEVELOPMENTAL AND LIFE-COURSE PARADIGM

Developmental and life-course criminology emerged in the early to mid-twentieth century, drawing inspiration from the statistical movement led, *inter alia*, by Quetelet in the mid-nineteenth century and the expert knowledge-base of social work and psychiatry which had evolved from the late nineteenth century onwards.

The *scientific* ambition of the embryonic developmental perspective had much in common with early sociological theories and variants of biological and physiological positivism. However, a key difference was its primary unit of analysis. Rather than focusing solely on the body (as per biological and physiological positivism) or social 'facts' (as per early sociological criminology), the developmental approach initially adopted what may be termed a 'bio-psycho-social' approach to the study of the individual.

Sheldon and Eleanor Glueck were amongst the earliest and most influential protagonists of the developmental approach. During the 1930s they instigated a longitudinal research project following a cohort of 1,000 boys in Boston. The core objects of this study were the body, the mind, and the social milieu of the individual youth. They concluded that delinquency in childhood was a strong predictor of adult criminality; and that family relationships were key, with weak discipline, sundered emotional ties and social deprivation all featuring in the lives of the youngsters at greatest risk of long-term criminal careers. Other contributing factors were low IQ, mental disturbance, and body shape, with mesomorphic tendencies being linked to delinquent propensity (Glueck and Glueck 1950; Sampson and Laub 1993).

The developmental perspective expanded over the course of the twentieth century, gaining particular purchase within US criminology from the 1970s onwards. Of key salience was a study by Wolfgang *et al.* (1972), *Delinquency in a Birth Cohort,* which highlighted the fact that a small group of young offenders was responsible for a disproportionately high number of offences. This was a major source of inspiration for the subsequent focus on 'criminal careers' research in the US, taken forward by the Panel on Research on Criminal Careers led by a group of leading scholars and funded by the National Institute of Justice in 1983 (see Blumstein *et al.* 1986a, 1986b). One of the outcomes of this Panel was a proliferation of longitudinal studies, including a collective group known as the *Causes and Correlates* studies which were launched in the late 1980s, comprising the Pittsburgh Youth Survey (see Loeber *et al.* 2003), the Rochester Youth Development Study (see Thornberry *et al.* 2003), and the Denver Youth Survey (see Huizinga *et al.* 2003).

The last two decades of the twentieth century were an especially productive time for developmental criminologists, and some of the most innovatory contributions to theory and method stem from this period (as we shall discuss later). However, it was also a time when the field faced particularly harsh criticism from the emergent radical and later post-modern and cultural criminology perspectives, which eschewed the precepts of scientific criminological inquiry as failing to engage sufficiently with the 'human meaning' of crime (see Young 1988, 2004). Adherents to such critical perspectives have dismissed quantitative approaches to criminology generally, and developmental approaches in particular, for oversimplifying individual experiences, failing to take account of structural contexts and cultural difference, and being insufficiently driven by or contributing too little to theory (see Case and Haines 2009; Cullen 2011). Even some of the most influential life-course theorists are critical of the paradigm's overall failure to incorporate macro-level social change (Sampson 2015; Sampson and Laub 2016). Given such harsh criticism then, why has the paradigm endured, and what has made it so resilient in spite of its critics?

DURABILITY OF THE PARADIGM

A large part of DLC's durability can be attributed to its inter-disciplinary origins and its methodological approach. Many of those who became interested in criminological research in the 1970s migrated from other fields with special expertise in quantitative research, including psychology, psychiatry, education, medicine, and public health. In addition, the vast increase in computational power, rapid advances in statistical modelling, and an explosion in available crime data, including administrative data (see Maguire and McVie, this volume), have greatly enhanced the methodological capabilities of scholars to develop and test complex causal hypotheses.

Arguably, however, its longevity has also been due to: (1) the willingness of researchers within the paradigm to engage with policy; and (2) the fact that the interventions and solutions proffered by such entrepreneurial activity continue to 'make sense' to policy-makers as one element of the complex and contradictory policy framework which has come to characterize youth justice (especially) in the first two decades of the twenty-first century (McAra, forthcoming; see also McAra this volume). We offer some comments on each in turn.

Policy entrepreneurs

Since the 1990s, developmental scholars on both sides of the Atlantic have been highly active in attempting to engage with policy-makers and practitioners about the policy implications of their research, with varying degrees of success. This is exemplified, in particular, by the number of longitudinal studies in both North America and continental Europe which have developed interventions and tested their efficacy as part of their research. These include: the *Montreal multi-modal intervention programme* developed by Tremblay *et al.* (1995) which focused primarily on family support; the *Seattle Social Development Project* developed by Hawkins *et al.* (1991) which focused on parenting, teacher training, and skills development for young people and led to the development of the highly influential *Communities that Care programme*, now implemented in over 500 communities worldwide (see Hawkins *et al.* 2014); and the *Zurich Project on the Social Development of Children* (z-proso), in which two prevention programmes (family-based parenting skills programme and a school-based social skills programme in schools) were embedded into the longitudinal study, to test their long-term effectiveness under real world conditions (see Eisner *et al.* 2012). Within the UK, David Farrington too has been heavily involved in government sponsored working groups, as well as a range of international and UK-based campaigning and expert research groups such as the Campbell Collaboration (a network which aims to improve the evidence base for government decision-making through systematic research reviews, see http://www.campbellcollaboration.org/about_us/index.php). As co-directors of the Edinburgh Study of Youth Transitions and Crime, the authors of this chapter have actively engaged with government and practitioners, using a range of strategies ranging from sustained, purposive, and targeted knowledge-exchange activities to engaging with justice leaders and local communities using art and drama to explore the impact of crime and justice issues on individual well-being (see McAra, forthcoming).

Key narratives 'make sense'

The second factor contributing to the longevity of the DLC paradigm, we contend, is the way in which some, but not all, of the solutions stemming from this research have had 'uptake' from governments. There is strong evidence that governments seek out research to support a view already taken, rather than critically engaging with a wider field of knowledge, some of which may contradict or confound political perception (Mears 2007; McAra, forthcoming). Thus, opportunities for research to impact on policy most often occur where research findings have some commonality with dominant political narratives. Significantly, these narratives (the bedrock of penal politics) are shaped, in turn, by the vagaries of their wider social, economic, and cultural contexts (Lacey 2008; see also Morgan and Smith, and Garland, this volume), and this leads to (often) short-term enthusiasms for particular modes of intervention.

Within UK jurisdictions there have been two recent phases in which the developmental paradigm has come to play a key role in legitimizing and sustaining emergent policy portfolios (see also McAra, this volume). Firstly, a range of individual 'risk factors' identified from developmental research (in particular the Cambridge Study in Delinquent Development, Farrington 2007) was drawn on to underpin a shift towards preventative and more actuarial strategies in youth justice within England, Wales, and Scotland from around 1997 to 2010. And secondly, research evidence on the detrimental impact of labelling by juvenile justice agencies on young people (influenced by findings from the Edinburgh Study of Youth Transitions and Crime, McAra and McVie 2005, 2007, 2010) provided support for a new diversionary approach to youth justice in Scotland that was rolled out nationally from 2011 onwards.

In terms of the first phase, a number of commentators have argued that core dimensions of the crime policy narratives which came to predominance over the millennium and first decade of the twenty-first century, (particularly populist punitivism but more especially, for the purpose of this chapter, actuarialism) were tied to the conditions of late modernity (Young 2011; Wacquant 2006). Just as the emergence of theory is closely linked to its temporal and spatial context, so too did such policy responses at this time reflect the uncertainties and anxieties produced by the risk society (in Bauman's phrase 'ambient fear' (1998: 22)), the loss of nation-state sovereignty, and the growth of what Sparks (2006) has termed structurally redundant populations in the context of macro socio-economic transformations. Arguably, however, these broader changes also opened up a conceptual 'space' in which narratives of certainty (predictability) were found to be politically comforting as a lexicon which talked of (individual) resilience rather than fundamental transformation of extant structures (see Armstrong and McAra 2006). The DLC perspective offered policy-makers a concrete set of 'solutions' that were apparently based on robust empirical evidence, subject to concrete measurements and, above all, made it appear as if the government was having an impact.

More recently, policy contexts within the UK have undergone a further shift, marked in particular by the global economic crash in 2008 and the context of austerity. Currently, policy solutions aimed at reducing the scale and intensity of intervention are most likely to gain traction as are solutions which focus on process management as much as, if not more than, offender outcomes (see Bateman 2012). This wider systemic approach makes sense to politicians, in a context of fiscal uncertainty: an approach in which there is an imprimatur of control (led by targets and efforts to support better systemic linkage across criminal justice institutions), and opportunities for cost-cutting by reducing the number of people who are sucked into the criminal justice system (McAra and McVie 2014). The DLC paradigm, we would argue, has proved agile in responding to such shifting markets for research and flexible in offering policy-makers a requisite evidence-base on which to underpin radical systemic change.

We will return to the nature and efficacy of these solutions later in this chapter.

THREATS TO THE PARADIGM

Whilst the DLC paradigm has endured, it has for some years become something of a niche paradigm (particularly in a UK context). Longitudinal studies, the staple of DLC research, are very expensive and are many years in the making. Research funders can be reluctant to sponsor them (not least because funder themselves are subject to the whims of fast moving political agendas), and, as a consequence, very few longitudinal studies received sustained, long-term investment. Answering some of the major theoretical challenges currently facing the paradigm will require new complex and accelerated designs (with multiple cohorts); however, in a context where there have been major cuts to research funding (especially in the UK), such studies are unlikely to find favour. Younger scholars not immediately part of an existing research team are heavily reliant on open access to datasets but, within the UK at least, researchers have not always made rapid efforts to deposit their data in national archives. As a consequence, the DLC paradigm's future becomes more dependent on capacity building within extant programmes (with the potential for conceptual stasis as narrow conceptual framings are recursively produced).

Established DLC scholarship has also showed signs of increasing introspection. A recent review of five top international criminology journals found that nine of the top ten most cited scholars were involved in research on developmental and life-course criminology and criminal careers (Cohn and Iratzoqui 2015). Indeed, many DLC scholars adopt a scientific approach to publication (i.e. multiple co-authors and numerous short incremental papers) and publish in a much wider range of outlets (including non-social science journals) than is typical within criminology. However, the DLC paradigm has been dominated for many years by a relatively small and close-knit group of scholars who are very proactive in critiquing each other's theory and methods, thus rendering the citation process highly self-referential. Moreover, the establishment of a new Journal of *Developmental and Life Course Criminology* (launched in March 2015) poses a danger of the DLC specialism becoming a conversation with itself. In this context, Cullen's call (made during his Sutherland Address to the American Society of Criminology in 2011) for DLC scholars to reach out and embrace mainstream criminology has particular resonance.

There are, however, some indications of change. Indeed we are witnessing the gradual emergence of a new generation of DLC scholars working across a range of more specialized topics, such as: football-related violence (Leal *et al.* 2016), sexual offending, and the sex industry (Blokland and Lussier 2015; Mancini *et al.* 2014), serious and organized crime (Francis *et al.* 2013; Otu and Elechi 2015), and victims of human trafficking (Reid 2012). DLC has also been applied to study the criminal careers of places rather than people (Yang *et al.* 2014). Furthermore, the paradigm is becoming increasingly international in reach with important studies in: Sweden (e.g. Estrada *et al.* 2015), the Netherlands (e.g. Blokland *et al.* 2005), Australia (e.g. McGrath 2015); Canada (e.g. Lussier *et al.* 2015); Nigeria (e.g. Otu and Elechi 2015); and Japan (e.g. Farrington *et al.* 2015).

As well will go on to discuss, such conceptual and empirical expansion is essential if DLC is to avoid intellectual stasis.

THEORETICAL INNOVATION

Although there is some evidence that aetiological research has been in decline within the UK (see editors' introduction), DLC scholarship has, arguably, bucked this trend. Indeed, internationally it has become one of the most prolific fields in terms of theory building, with almost every large-scale longitudinal study constructing its own theory to account for its findings. We begin this section by deconstructing a number of the leading theoretical positions that have evolved within DLC over recent decades, with a particular focus on modes of theory construction, and the ways in which particular accounts have come to predominance within the paradigm. This is followed by a review of more recent debates within DLC on age, period, and cohort effects and their implications for future theory building.

THEORY BUILDING

Examples of the leading theoretical positions that have evolved within DLC are set out in Table 27.1. For reasons of space, our review of DLC theory is necessarily selective and we have focused on examples which demonstrate variant approaches to theory building.[2] As we will argue, our review shows why DLC cannot and should not distance itself from mainstream criminology, given the extent to which contemporary DLC theorizing is for the most part a bricolage of constructs borrowed from different criminological traditions and paradigms. As Table 27.1 illustrates, there is no settled conception of offender aetiology across the DLC paradigm, with differences being particularly marked around whether or not scholars have embraced taxonomic, integration, or 'core construct 'approaches to conceptual development. We discuss each of these in turn.

Taxonomy

For some, taxonomy lies at the heart of theory development, with the longitudinal method naturally lending itself to the analysis of different pathways of offending over time. Within DLC, scholars have focused on describing different offender 'types'

[2] We have omitted Situational Action Theory as it is discussed in detail in Wikström, this volume. For more detailed reviews of DLC theories see Farrington and Ttofi (2015) and Piquero (2015).

Table 27.1 Examples of the leading theoretical positions that have evolved within DLC

Leading author(s)	Summary	Generation of theory	Personhood	Social relations	Evidence-base
Moffitt	**Dual Taxonomy Theory** *Life course persistent*—neuropsychological deficit exacerbated by family-adversity risk factors in childhood, continues through life but behaviour differentiated by age and stage *Adolescent limited*—reaction to exogenous risk factors combined with maturational development and rebellion against controls, mimics LCP	Taxonomic: Explaining continuity and change	Bio-psycho-social Autonomy compromised by endogenic features (neurocognitive deficits in LCP and maturational development in AL) Behaviour reactive to immediate environment (in both LPC and AL)	Primacy of the individual within immediate family and peer context	Dunedin Multi-Disciplinary Health and Development Study1037 boys and girls born between 1 April 1972 and 31 March 1973
Loeber	**Developmental Pathways Theory** *Authority conflict pathway*—commences early childhood as stubborn behaviour, second stage defiance and disobedience; third stage authority avoidance (truancy or running away) *Covert pathway*—first stage minor behaviour (e.g. lying, shoplifting), second stage property damage, final stage more serious property crimes (breaking and entering) *Overt pathway*—aggression (e.g. annoying others, bullying), physical fighting, and violence (e.g. rape, strong-arming)	Taxonomic: Explaining continuity and change and types of offending	State-dependence Early behaviour shapes pathway compromising autonomy (uni-directional)	Primacy of the individual	Pittsburg Youth Study, began 1987–88, three cohorts of boys (1,512) who were in the first, fourth, and seventh grades in Pittsburg public school system, random selection
Thornberry Thornberry and Krohn	**Interactional theory** Weakened bonds (especially those linked to parental attachment, commitment to school, and conventional beliefs) interacting with structural variables including social class and residential area Causal influences vary over life course, and bi-directional (weak bonds can be the result of offending and vice versa) Later development of theory:	Synthetic: Social control Social learning Initially general theory of delinquency Later development—taxomonic explaining continuity and change	Psycho-social Soft-determinism, choice within constraints Delinquency occurs where social bonds weak and behaviours learnt and reinforced by immediate peer interactions	Social structures (class, neighbourhood, poverty) shape familial and peer environment (and hence can determine strength of bonds) Functionalist	Rochester Youth Development Study 1,000 students from seventh and eighth grade selected from Rochester, New York Public Schools during 1987–88

	Precocious—very early onset (pre-school) and long-term career Linked to individual traits (including neuropsychological deficits), ineffective parenting, and structural adversities, cumulative disadvantage (family, peers, school, and beliefs) over the life course *Early onset*—commence between 6 and 12, parental and social structural deficits, continuity until encounter improved social environment *Later onset*—commence during adolescence and mostly stops at end of adolescence (autonomy wars linked to maturation and environmental risk factors) *Late bloomers*—commence late adolescence/early adulthood, loss of childhood protective buffers and more exposed to life stressor and deviant peer influence				Sample selected to over-represent youth at high risk for serious delinquency and drug use (initial sample 73 per cent male)
Farrington	**Integrated Cognitive Antisocial Potential (ICAP)** Antisocial potential and modes of cognitive reasoning combine to produce between individual variation and within individual change over time *Long term AP*—motivation linked to lack of legitimate means to achieve key goals (material gain, status, excitement, sexual satisfaction), exacerbated by poor attachment and exposure to delinquent role models, significant life events, and impulsivity. *Short-term AP*—motivation boredom, anger, alcohol (frustration with male peers), coupled with criminal opportunities and suitable victims. Short-term AP has consequences for long-term AP if impacts of behaviour reinforce or punish Translation from AP to actual behaviour dependent on cognitive processes assessing opportunities, victims, risks, and rewards	Synthetic: Strain Social control Labelling Rational choice General theory Single developmental pathway explaining continuity and change	Bio-psycho-social Soft-determinism, choice within constraints Autonomy decreases as consequence of exogenous factors (labelling) and pressures (strain) to achieve structural goals	Functionalist	Cambridge Study in Delinquent Development Sample of 411 males, selected from boys aged 8–9 in 1961–62 who were on the registers of six state primary schools located within a one-mile radius of a research office that had been established in the east end of London

Table 27.1 Continued

Leading author(s)	Summary	Generation of theory	Personhood	Social relations	Evidence-base
Catalano and Hawkins	**Social development model** Offending driven by hedonistic desire to seek satisfaction and realize self-interests and dependent on balance between antisocial and prosocial bonding	Synthetic: social control, social learning differential association General theory	Psycho-social Soft determinism, choice within constraints	Functionalist—determining opportunity structures encountered by young people	Seattle Social Development Project Cohort of 808 boys and girls drawn from fifth grade students in 1985, regular follow-ups with both students and parents
LeBlanc	**Integrative Multi-Layered Control Theory** Mechanisms of control—bonding to society (family, school peers, marriage, work) Psychological development over time (egocentric to allocentric) Modelling (pro or antisocial constraints) Environmental factors (social class, neighbourhood) influence bonding, whilst biological capacity (e.g. difficult temperament) influences psychological development Three types of offending: *Persistent* (weak bonds, antisocial modelling, low constraints, high frequency and high serious but often ends in mid 30s) *Common* (adolescence, opportunistic, more minor) *Transitory* (adolescent and sometimes late onset, but rapid increase and then declining in persistent and seriousness, includes some serious crimes)	Synthetic: Social control Social learning Bio-psycho development Taxonomic Explaining continuity and change in serious and frequency of offending	Bio-psycho-social Soft determinism, choice within constraints	Social structures (class, neighbourhood, poverty) shape familial and peer environment (and hence can determine strength of bonds) Functionalist	The Montreal Two-Sample Two-Generation Longitudinal Study of Men (1972 onwards) A representative sample of 1,611 boys and a sample of 470 boys adjudicated at the Montreal Juvenile Court during their adolescence

Sampson and Laub	**Age-graded informal social control** Social bonds build social capital Teenage offending linked to attachments to delinquent peers Adulthood transitions provide turning points (marriage, employment)	Core construct: Social control	Autonomy constrained by exogenous factors	Social structures (class, neighbourhood, poverty) shape familial and peer environment (and hence can determine strength of bonds) Functionalist	Follow-up of Glueck and Glueck's Boston Study (1,000 boys born during the Great Depression in the United States; 500 officially defined as delinquent and a matched group of 500 from US public schools)
McAra and McVie	**Negotiated Order** Focuses on role of formal and informal (peer-related) regulatory practices in shaping offender and non-offender identities To retain sense of ego-continuity young people need to negotiate a pathway through this tutelary complex actively engaging with ascribed identities, absorbing, or fighting back	Core construct: Labelling	Soft-determinism, choice within constraints The looking glass self	Structural factors (economic, political) shape cultural practices of the tutelary complex	Edinburgh Study of Youth Transitions and Crime Cohort: 4,300 Population of young people starting secondary school in Edinburgh in 1998 (aged around 12) Males and Females

according to age of onset, duration of offending, and the prevalence and frequency of rule breaking behaviours, with theoretical development predicated on the explanation of differences between groups. Taxonomic approaches have generally held that one overarching theory is insufficient to understand the complexity of offending behaviour within the population under scrutiny. Terrie Moffitt's dual taxonomy model of offending is perhaps the best-known of these accounts within and beyond the DLC paradigm.

Using data from the Dunedin Multidisciplinary Health and Development Study, Moffitt (1993, 2003) identified a small group of 'life-course persistent' (LCP) offenders and a much larger group of 'adolescence limited' (AL) offenders. She hypothesized that LCP offending began during early childhood and manifested itself in a range of problematic behaviours (such as temper tantrums and periods of hyperactivity) as well as difficulties in other aspects of life, such as educational failure and dysfunctional social relationships. It continued to exhibit itself throughout the life-course, although the specific forms of antisocial behaviour and difficulties changed to reflect the age and stage of the individual. She proposed that antisocial behaviour was a highly stable trait amongst LCP offenders, not necessarily because early offending locked them into a cycle of later offending, but because the causal factors that underpinned their antisocial behaviour tended to be present throughout their lives. These include neuropsychological deficits, exacerbated by risk factors in the child's early social environment, typically related to familial and neighbourhood disadvantage.

In contrast to LCP, AL offending was described as a temporary phase, starting in early adolescence (around the age of puberty), rapidly escalating and then de-escalating. According to Moffitt, AL offending was a relatively normal reaction to various exogenous (often peer influenced) risk factors during the teenage years, combined with maturational development and associated rebellion against controls which mimicked the actions of the LCP offenders (Caspi and Moffitt 1995).

Moffitt's identification of different offending typologies has inspired many other scholars to empirically test this approach (for a review see Piquero and Moffitt 2005), to the extent that it has been referred to as the 'Moffittization of Criminology' (DeLisi 2013: 911). In particular, others have attempted to replicate her taxonomies, although it is notable that most have found more than two groups of offenders (this is discussed further later in the chapter). Moffitt's taxonomy, however, has been criticized for lacking an underlying construct to sufficiently explain patterns of antisocial behaviour (Farrington 2006). Indeed, Skardhamar concludes that it is unclear how to unpick the meaning, mechanisms, and causes of the different 'types' from her typology and that, based on her theoretical argument, it would actually be 'more reasonable to assume gradual differences rather than discrete types' (2009: 874).

Theoretical integration

Other approaches to theory building within the DLC paradigm include theoretical integration and synthesis. As can be seen from the Table 27.1, many theorists have borrowed from a range of perspectives to build their explanatory framings. David Farrington's Integrated Cognitive Antisocial Potential (ICAP) theory (2006, 2015), for example, draws on strain, social control, labelling, and rational choice theories in explaining continuity and change in offending over the life-course based on the construct of antisocial potential. Meanwhile, Thornberry's Interactional Theory of

Delinquency (Thornberry *et al.* 2003) attempts to show the bi-directional and intricate causal patterning that occurs at the intersection of weakened social bonds (social control theory) and situational contexts in which delinquent behaviour becomes reinforced (social learning theory), whilst also acknowledging the role of structural level dynamics on these phenomena (including social class and poverty).

Critical commentators have in the past condemned efforts at theoretical integration, claiming that the underlying constructs of theories such as social control and strain differ in such fundamental ways as to make synthesis impossible (see, for example, Hirschi 1989, Kornhauser 1978). However, in an important rebuttal, Bernard and Snipes (1996) argue that it is possible to create a single theory which incorporates three dimensions: the structural conditions associated with high crime rates; the processes explaining why individuals who experience these structural conditions are more likely to engage in crime; and the individual characteristics that make it more or less likely that an individual will engage in crime regardless of structural conditions. Although Bernard and Snipes question the practical (as opposed to theoretical) desirability of integration (given the complexities of the requisite analysis), they acknowledge that multi-level frameworks may be useful. Indeed, methodological advances in the time since these debates were first aired, have rendered multi-level analysis far more feasible than hitherto.

Core construct approaches

A third approach to theory building, identified in Table 27.1, might be termed 'core construct': with theory deriving from one dominant factor or central set of ideas. Examples are, most notably, Sampson and Laub's age-graded social control theory, but also McAra and McVie's (2012b) theory of negotiated order (with roots in symbolic interactionism and labelling).

Using data collected by the Gluecks in their Boston Study and following their male cohort beyond age 70, Sampson and Laub (1993, 2003) proposed that social bonds were key to explaining involvement in offending because they enabled people to build social capital which, in turn, reduced the likelihood of criminal offending. They argued that strong social bonds were dependent on positive attachments or emotional ties, usually developed through relationships (e.g. family and peers in the early years and partners in adulthood) and through institutional belonging (e.g. employment and, for their cohort, the military). People who socialize and bond well with conventional others grow their social capital: a store of positive relationships emanating from social networks and built on norms of reciprocity and trust, upon which the individual can draw for support. However, age-graded theory also emphasizes the role of human agency (i.e. individual choice or free will) in determining the direction of an individual's behaviour.

For Sampson and Laub, it is essential to examine the interplay of offending across the entire life-course, rather than focus on specific periods of development, although they acknowledge that behaviour needs to be understood in an 'age-graded' way. They consider factors occurring in childhood as important for influencing behaviour in adolescence, but less so in adulthood because that is more likely to be affected by later, age-appropriate life events and transitions. A key claim is that offending during the peak teenage years is caused by a general weakening of social bonds (due to lower discipline and supervision) and greater attachment to delinquent peers. However, as people move into adulthood they experience a series of social and institutional transitions or 'turning points' (including marriage and employment) that can change a person's life trajectory in pro-social directions. Essentially, they contend that all offenders eventually desist, and many of them simply need a 'nudge' in the right direction (Sampson and Laub 2016).

As with Moffitt, Sampson and Laub's theory has been highly influential in informing debate within DLC. However, a number of recent studies have tested elements of the theory to determine whether it applies to contemporary society and different social groups. Studies on the effect of marriage as a turning point suggest it may not have the same significance in modern society as it did at the time of Gluecks' study. For example, Skardhamar *et al.* (2014) found that marriage was not necessarily a 'turning point' in promoting desistance, as that process had usually started several years before marriage. Testing the effect of gender, Doherty and Ensminger (2013) found strong evidence of a marriage effect for men, but less of an effect for women. Craig (2015) examined racial differences and found that marriage led to changes in levels of offending among whites and Hispanics but not blacks. Research on the effect of employment as a turning point has also reported equivocal results. Skardhamar and Savolainen (2014), for example, showed that most offenders had desisted prior to the employment transition and that very few (only around 2 per cent) offenders became employed during an active phase of the criminal career and experienced substantial reductions in criminal offending thereafter. These recent studies suggest that there may be gaps in the original theory that need to be addressed. Nevertheless, there continues to be significant support for the proposition that social bonds act as a 'change catalyst' in transforming the direction and meaning of individual offending (see Cid and Marti 2012).

VALORIZING THEORY

As the above discussion demonstrates, DLC contains a multitude of perspectives derived from different methods of theory building. Wolfgang *et al.* (1972: 4) once warned that criminological research had failed to generate a coherent analytical framework for the study of offending, with the potential danger of producing 'a million modest little studies that produce a million conflicting results'. This opens up to question the value judgements we bring to bear as scholars when determining what constitutes a 'good' theory; and the appropriateness of the data and methods we utilize in the construction of concepts.

The review of theory building indicates that parsimony may be one of the key characteristics of 'good theory' for DLC scholars. This may account for the reach and impact of Moffit's dual taxonomy theory discussed above, and the influence of Sampson and Laub's borrowings from social control theory: the predominance of both accounts being evidenced by heavy citations and an expansion in the number of studies testing out their key constructs. Whilst explanatory frameworks which have emerged from the integrationist method of theory building have tended to be more complex in orientation (in terms of the multiplicity of constructs utilized and of the pathways analysis in which such constructs are sequenced), the overall dynamic of integration or synthesis is one which is again aimed at gaining the most parsimonious account (see Bernard and Snipes 1996). As noted above, the further development of theory within the DLC paradigm is crucially dependent on technological advances to enable more sophisticated modes of data analysis. Statistical advances however, will almost certainly introduce greater complexity into explanatory framings, with software development enabling analysis of multi-scale and multi-dimensional modelling. Value judgements which have led to the dominance of particular theories may as a consequence be challenged by emergent methodological possibilities (a point to which we return later in this chapter).

As the above review of theory building also demonstrates, one of the most established approaches within DLC for determining the value of theory is the replicability (or indeed falsifiability) of its constructs across other studies. Whilst this is in keeping with DLC's scientific epistemological standpoint, as a method of valorization, it presents some challenges. Tests of replicability can only take place where studies utilize the same measures. Whilst the causes and correlates studies in the US bear close affinity to each other, and most studies openly publish their research instruments, major differences are still evident across longitudinal research programmes worldwide in terms of access to official records (as e.g. health, criminal conviction, or educational records), and in terms of the measures used. Moreover a (questionable) assumption underpinning DLC theories as they have evolved over time, is that measures are mostly transferrable from jurisdiction to jurisdiction and across different cultural and structural contexts: whereas 'sense-making' of constructs may be closely bound up with spatial and temporal locale. These points suggest that there will be 'selection effects' in terms of which theories come to predominate within the paradigm (meaning that some potentially strong explanatory frameworks do not get picked up, primarily because they are based on constructs that other studies do not measure), and limitations on the capacity for cross-national comparison and deployment of theory (with a requirement that studies consider more reflexively whether or not the vagaries of their locale have implications for replicability).

As Weisburd and Piquero (2008: 485) remind us:

> Most tests of theory are limited . . . Theories are seldom measured completely or with fully defensible measures . . . accordingly the problem of low variance may be less with criminologists' theories, than with capacities to measure and access them.

FUTURE DIRECTIONS FOR THEORY: AGE, PERIOD, AND COHORT EFFECTS

As the DLC paradigm has matured and more extensive longitudinal data has become available (covering the life-span of individuals), scholars are now beginning to take more seriously the need to explore broader historical and contextual factors (beyond families and neighbourhoods) which shape individual experience and behaviour (see Sampson 2015). Arguably, this highlights the need for more substantive discussions within DLC around 'age', 'cohort', and 'period' effects.

The DLC theories reviewed above, have generally focused on age effects (that is the effect of changing age on offending). Indeed, it is a universally accepted fact within the paradigm, that there is an 'age-crime curve'. This is found in aggregate crime data when plotted against age and typically takes the form of an 'asymmetrical bell shape', representing a sharp rise in offending during the teenage years, which peaks in the late teens or early twenties and then declines, steeply at first and then steadily, into adulthood (Farrington 1986; Loeber and Farrington 2014). The precise shape of the curve and the age at which the peaks emerge, however, varies depending on a range of factors, including the type of data used (convictions data tend to show a later peak than self-report survey data), gender (peaks occur earlier and are shallower for females than males), type of crime (curves for violence typically peak later than those for property crime), era (the shape and peak of the curve has varied over time) and jurisdiction (peculiarities in justice systems, including recording practices and working cultures can impact on the shape of the age-crime curve) (see Loeber and Farrington 2014).

In terms of theory building, variations in the shape, scale, and nature of the age-crime curve over time and space raise questions about the influence of structural contexts and their transformations over time (as recommended by Sampson and Laub 2016) and the nature and operation of formal institutional arrangements for dealing with crime and their impacts over time (as asserted by McAra and McVie 2012b). This highlights a need for both 'diachronic' analysis (in other words, analysis of structural and institutional changes that occur within single jurisdictions over time) and 'synchronic' analysis (i.e. comparative analysis of such changes across jurisdictions at specific time-points). Fundamental to such analysis is the need to disentangle the age effects described above, from *period effects* (i.e. societal change that impacts equally across people of all ages) and *cohort effects* (i.e. societal change that impacts only on people born at a specific time point).

The most active work in relation to age, period, and cohort effects is being conducted by criminologists investigating the so-called 'crime drop' of the 1990s (see Maguire and McVie, this volume), very few of whom are currently core to DLC scholarship. Rather than focusing on individual-level explanations of the age-crime curve (which, as noted above, has been the common preserve of the DLC paradigm historically), emphasis is now being placed on macro-level analysis, examining whether the aggregate fall in crime (across the USA, UK, and other parts of Europe) reflects a reduction in offending for people of all age groups or whether it reflects a disproportionate fall in crime amongst people of some age groups or born during particular periods compared with others (Kim *et al.* 2016; Matthews and Minton, forthcoming).

The evidence so far is indicative of a significant cohort effect that influenced a decline in offending behaviour within recent generations. Farrell *et al.* (2015), for example, examined age-crime curves in US arrest data for violence and property crime before (1980), during (1994), and after (2010) the crime drop. They found that, while the overall shape of the age-crime curve remained familiar, there was a large decline in the peak of the curve following the crime drop. In other words, arrest rates for both violence and property crime had reduced significantly amongst those at the peak age of arrest, that is, during adolescence and early adulthood. There were also modest declines in arrest rates up to age 40 for both crime types; however, the arrest rates for those aged over 40 increased after the crime drop. Drawing on earlier work (Farrell *et al.* 2011) which had examined the impact of improving situational crime prevention, especially security technologies, on falling rates of crime, Farrell *et al.* (2015) concluded that the decline in arrest rates for those aged 40 and under was a cohort effect caused by a reduction in opportunities for crime during the 1990s and 2000s (due to increased securitization) that made adolescents and early adults far less likely to begin or to continue offending. Whereas, the increased rate of offending amongst the over 40s was the result of a legacy of plentiful crime opportunities that had increased the onset and continuation of criminality in the 1970s and 1980s.

Using similar US data, Kim *et al.* (2015) also concluded that the changing age-crime distribution was likely to be due to a cohort effect, because the fall in arrest rates was concentrated in more recent birth cohorts. Although, they also noted a significant age-period interaction effect for those aged 16 to 20 years during the very early years of the crime drop, suggesting that arrest rates fell particularly sharply for this group. Like Farrell *et al.* (2015), they concluded that the decline in arrest rates did not reflect a universal drop in crime across different age groups, but was disproportionately influenced by declining crime amongst younger people.

The gap in offending rates between males and females also declined during the latter part of the twentieth century (see Lauritsen *et al.* 2009), which raises further questions about the changing nature of the age-crime curve. Estrada *et al.* (2015) tested this in the context of the crime drop using Swedish register data across a number of birth cohorts (born in 1965, 1975, and 1985) and found that the narrowing of the gender gap was almost entirely attributable to a change amongst those aged under 22. Moreover, the narrowing gap was a product of both decreasing convictions for men and increasing convictions for women, which suggests opposing patterns of change. Using data on parental income, Estrada and his colleagues were also able to identify that, for violent offending, the gender gap had declined across all income groups, but declined most amongst the wealthiest and least amongst the poorest for both men and women; whereas, for theft, the decline in the gender gap was greatest amongst the higher income groups. Overall, they concluded that any increases in conviction had occurred predominantly amongst those in the lowest income groups, especially women; whereas, men in the highest income groups had witnessed a decline in convictions for both violence and theft. What does this mean for the age-crime curve? Again, it suggests a cohort effect, but one that was both gendered and socio-economically driven.

Recent work in Scotland has confirmed some of these findings. Using continuous data from the Scottish Offenders Index to examine the age-specific rate of all convicted offences per 10,000 population from age 16 to 60 over a 30-year period, Matthews and Minton found that the conviction rate for both men and women up to their mid-twenties had declined over time; while those from their late twenties to mid-forties had seen increased rates of conviction (Matthews 2014; Matthews and Minton, forthcoming). The relative magnitude of the changes varied by sex, with conviction rates declining more for young men than young women, and increasing more for older women than older men. In other words, the shape of the age-crime curves had become much flatter and similar for men and women over time, although the overall conviction rate was still higher for men. Notably, however, Matthews and Minton found three very distinct periods of change. Between 1989 and 2000, there was a marked decline in rates of conviction for young men under the age of 25, but no change for older men or for women; from 2001 to 2006, there was no change in the conviction rates for young men or women, but increased conviction rates for those from their mid-20s to early 40s; while from 2007 to 2011, there was a rapid decline in conviction for men and, especially, women under the age of 20, but stable conviction rates for those aged 30 and above.

These studies reveal two important challenges for the DLC paradigm. Firstly, they suggest that the crime drop was predominantly influenced by a reduction in offending amongst young people, particularly young men. Therefore, whatever societal forces caused crime to decline across the Western world they did not impact equally by age or gender. Secondly, the crime drop (at least in Scotland) was not a linear process and different social, economic, or political mechanisms may have led to different phases of change; indeed, Matthews and Minton (forthcoming) observe a marked similarity between trends identified in the conviction patterns and key eras of change in Scottish justice policy (see McAra and McVie 2015).

The research reviewed above is critical for the evolution of developmental and life-course theories because it demonstrates the importance not only of individual-level change, but of wider macro-level societal, economic, and political changes that impact on the life-course in complex and dynamic ways. Indeed we would argue that any credible DLC theory must explicitly account for age, period, and cohort effects. However, almost all of the crime-drop research referred to above, uses administrative data on arrests or convictions as a measure of 'crime' rather than self-reported data. Self-reported offending careers do not overlap cleanly with criminal conviction careers (McAra and McVie 2010, forthcoming), largely because administrative data (including criminal convictions data) are themselves culturally constructed and, consequently, are as much a signifier of institutional practices as they are of individual behaviour.

In taking forward theory building within DLC, therefore, critical attention needs to be paid to: gathering the requisite data (which will involve accelerated cohort designs, linkage of self-report and convictions data, and enable more detailed exploration of gender differences); the cross-comparative contexts of knowledge production; and the methods of analysis needed to capture multi-level temporal and spatial dynamics. By introducing greater complexity into extant methodological and explanatory frameworks, evolving scholarship requires more open conversation about the ways in theories are valorized and validated. The next section turns to a more detailed discussion of challenges of methodological innovation in this field.

METHODOLOGICAL INNOVATION IN DEVELOPMENTAL AND LIFE-COURSE CRIMINOLOGY

Probably more than any other sub-discipline within criminology, DLC has contributed significantly to the application and expansion of advanced quantitative methodologies. Methodological innovation has been facilitated by increased linkage of administrative data to individual level longitudinal self-report data (see Stewart *et al.* 2015; Farrington 2015), and the development of novel statistical methodologies (see McGee and Mazerolle 2016). These advances have enabled DLC scholars to examine patterns of criminal offending across the full life-course (Laub and Sampson 2003), explore the existence of groups of offenders and their offending trajectories (Nagin and Land 1993;

D'Unger *et al.* 1998), identify possible correlates or explanations of different offender trajectories (Blokland *et al.* 2005) and improve the potential for predicting future offending using trajectories and covariates (Sampson and Laub 2003).

As we have argued previously, methodological issues around statistical analyses tend not to inspire widespread debate amongst criminologists within the wider discipline, which is largely a consequence of both deliberate disengagement from positivist approaches and a lack of quantitative training, especially within the UK (see McAra and McVie 2012a). Amongst developmental criminologists, however, there exists a positive culture of debate and critique about the nature and validity of variant methodological approaches, including the impact of such methods on theory building. In exploring how technological advances make certain types of knowledge possible, we concentrate here on critical debates and innovations in the use of two key types of modelling: finite mixture and random effects models. These methods of analysing patterns and trends in longitudinal data are increasingly at the heart of DLC research and, as McGee and Mazerolle (2016: 2) note, 'understanding the dynamic processes of offending over time not only provides challenges for methodological innovation but it creates unique windows of opportunity whereby innovation and advances can occur'.

FINITE MIXTURE MODELS

Early efforts to explore population differences in offending involved relatively crude or arbitrary methods of grouping individuals (see Wolfgang *et al.* 1972; Blumstein *et al.* 1985). The development of finite mixture or group-based models, however, enabled radically different types of individuals to be distinguished using statistical algorithms (see Nagin and Land 1993). This method is well suited to longitudinal data as it identifies an optimal number of developmental trajectories within a population based on measures of offending recorded at different ages. Discrete groups of offenders are estimated which are internally homogenous (individuals are similar to each other within the group) but externally heterogeneous (the groups as a whole differ from each other). A key advantage of the method is that it can accommodate missing data in estimation, which allows individuals with incomplete data to be included in the analysis (an important consideration for longitudinal studies where attrition and non-response can be problematic issues).

In an early test of Moffitt's taxonomic theory, Nagin and Land (1993) applied group-based modelling techniques to study trajectories of criminal propensity. They identified four latent classes grouped on the basis of their patterns of conviction (including one class of individuals who were never convicted). In line with Moffitt's theory, these included a long-term, high-rate trajectory that matched the life-course persistent offender group and a late-onset, short-term trajectory that matched the adolescence limited group. In addition, however, they identified a low-rate chronic class of offenders that did not conform to Moffitt's taxonomy. This class was distinguishable from all the others in terms of their disproportionately low IQ, although it was quite different from the high-rate chronic class on a host of dimensions. Nagin and Land (1993: 355) concluded that the 'low-rate chronics appear to be comparatively docile individuals who, because of their low intelligence, either blunder into or are easily led into crime'.

Since Nagin and Land's early study, group-based modelling has become one of the most popular methodologies used within DLC. However, the question of how many offender groups exist in the population remains controversial. Piquero (2008) identified 80 studies that used trajectory models to study offending and found that most reported between three and five distinct groups. More recently, Jennings and Reingle (2012) identified 105 studies that used finite mixture models to study trajectories in violence, aggression, and delinquency, and found the number of groups ranged from two to seven. Most studies reported three or, more commonly, four groups, which included groups that were similar to Moffitt's Life-course Persistent and Adolescence Limited offenders. The number of groups that are found in crime data does, however, seem to be contingent on a number of exogenous factors, including: the data used to measure offending (such as self-report, arrest, or convictions data), the nature of the cohort under study, the context of the community from which the sample was drawn, the developmental phase of the life-course studied, and the length of the observation period (see D'Unger *et al.* 1998; Eggleston *et al.* 2004; Jennings and Reingle 2012).

Finite mixture models have been subject to 'unusually robust criticism' (Sweeten 2014, 1991). A common reproach is that, while the use of such models may have been stimulated by theory, the application of the technique amongst DLC scholars has tended to be largely atheoretical and exploratory (Sampson *et al.* 2004; Osgood 2005; Jennings and Reingle 2012). Greenberg (2016: 28) has noted that using group-based methods for exploratory purposes is 'unobjectionable', especially where no theory currently exists. However, there have been strong calls from DLC scholars for finite mixture modelling to go beyond mere description and test theoretical predictions about how many groups are present (see Brame *et al.* 2012).

Another contentious issue which affects the finite mixture modelling approach is that absolute 'groups' of offenders may not exist in reality within the population (see Sweeten 2014). Using data from the Glueck's classic study, Sampson and Laub (2003) tested the retrospective selection of groups based on the finite mixture model against a prospective theory-based approach that predicted a number of groups based on childhood risk factors. They found quite different patterns in the age-crime curve for each approach, and failed to find a life-course persistent group using the group-based model. Sampson and Laub concluded that group-based trajectory models were seductive in terms of giving the appearance of distinct and predictable groups when these did not necessarily exist. Using a more elaborate simulation test, Skardhamar (2010) also found that group-based modelling techniques were unreliable and could distinguish groups within data where no groups actually existed. In his seminal textbook on group-based models, Nagin (2005) made it clear that it was a heuristic device and that the groups identified should not be interpreted as reflecting real underlying discrete groups in the population. He noted later, however, that the technique was 'vulnerable to misappropriation by those pre-disposed to believe in the idea of certain types of offenders' (Nagin and Piquero 2010: 111).

RANDOM EFFECTS MODELS

An alternative approach adopted by some scholars is the random effects or growth-curve model (also variously known as multi-level models, hierarchical linear models, or mixed effects models; see Erosheva *et al.* 2014). This method is equivalent in many respects to the latent class approach, in the sense that it seeks to identify patterns in the data over time. Rather than placing individuals into groups, however, the approach estimates *individual* growth-curves (or trajectories). A regression model is then used to estimate the relationships between individual characteristics and differences between growth-curves. Restrictions placed on the data ensure that the growth-curves are 'smoothed', which means that the curves are artificially adjusted to look smoother than they may actually be and sharp changes or chaotic patterns can sometimes be obscured. As a result, such models are efficient for plotting long-term, gradual change, but less good for reflecting short-term or erratic change in behaviour. When growth-curves are interpreted, it is generally assumed that all the within-individual change is being measured; however, Osgood (2005) estimates that growth-curves typically account for less than half of all within-individual variance (in other words, some aspects of change are not being reflected). He argues that this is not necessarily a shortcoming of the method, but it is important for analysts to interpret the results of such models carefully and accurately: 'growth-curves are useful summaries of the more consistent aspects of patterns of change, but they are only a partial picture, not some deeper reality' (Osgood 2005: 205).

In a comparison of the two types of model, Kreuter and Muthen (2008) found that the random effects growth-curve model did not fit the data as well as the finite mixture model alternative. However, Osgood (2005) has argued that growth-curve models are preferable over the grouping approach for three reasons. Firstly, comparisons of trajectory typologies show that the number and distribution of the typologies vary depending on the underlying measures used. Second, there is a danger that despite the warnings of scholars such as Nagin, researchers will treat and interpret them as 'real' groups. And third, policy-makers presented with offender groups may be more punitive towards those in the 'high chronic' groups without justification.

Random effects models have also been used to counter concerns about the potential 'over-extraction' of groups from the finite mixture model approach. Greenberg (2016), for example, argues that finite mixture modelling finds groups because it is designed to do so; however, researchers rarely test whether the shape of the distribution of criminal career trajectories across individuals is discrete (i.e. has different groups) or continuous. This is of theoretical importance because whether the distribution of criminal careers is discrete or continuous 'may bear on our theoretical understanding of the processes that generate or inhibit criminal conduct' (Greenberg 2016: 13). Using multi-level modelling and individual time series techniques, Greenberg analysed arrest data for 3,432 males released by the California Youth Authority and found little clear evidence of sharply discrete arrest trajectories. Finite mixture modelling identified too many arrest groups, and these did not cluster into statistically or substantively meaningful classes. He recommends using similar techniques for other studies, and warns that reanalysis is likely to identify fewer groups than previously found.

Taken together the methodological innovations outlined above open up major new fields of enquiry, and have the potential to offer a more nuanced understanding of life-course transitions and events. However, DLC needs to ensure that the complexities of new statistical techniques do not result in a situation where method rather than theory becomes king. As other criminologists before us have warned, just because something is possible analytically does not necessarily result in sense-making at a conceptual level (Walker 1987). Indeed DLC needs to guard itself against trajectory fetishism and the reification of what are ultimately heuristic devices. It also needs to communicate clearly with non-DLC specialists, including policy-makers and practitioners, the possibilities and limitations of innovation in method. It is to this conversation between DLC and policy that we now move.

INNOVATIVE CONTRIBUTIONS TO POLICY AND PRACTICE

As noted earlier, one of the reasons for the enduring appeal of DLC has been its value to policy-makers and practitioners working in the fields of juvenile and adult criminal justice. In keeping with the theoretical and methodological debates just described, there is controversy within the field over the application of findings to policy. Differences of opinion exist over: the groups and/or population on whom intervention should be targeted; the particular stages in the life-course and/or criminal career at which intervention may be most effective; and the nature and scope of the interventions. There are also major differences regarding the appropriate 'level' at which services should be provided, such as between: *universal targeting*—developing services and support for a whole population without differentiating between those who may be more or less risky; *selective targeting*—focusing services on those groups who may not yet be involved in offending/antisocial behaviour, but whose background and family context suggest that they are at risk; and *indicative targeting*—providing support for those who are beginning to demonstrate problematic behaviours (see Hawkins *et al.* 2010 for an overview). Other distinctions have been drawn between primary (universal support targeting whole communities), secondary (providing support and services for families and schools where individual children have been identified as being at risk of offending), and tertiary (aimed at preventing reoffending provided by youth justice specialists) levels of prevention (see Sutton *et al.* 2004).

Building on our earlier commentary on the circumstances in which evidence from the DLC paradigm has been taken up by policy, this section gives some detailed examples of the broad range of programmes that have been developed on the basis of longitudinal research, and explores the policy contexts in which two of the most recent innovations have been deployed.

INFLUENCE OF DLC ON PROGRAMMES

Table 27.2 highlights some of the leading examples of programmes. For reasons of space this is necessarily selective and our choices represent variant levels of intervention including family, school, youth, community, and systems.

Table 27.2 Examples of interventions predicated on DLC research

Identified problem	Focus of intervention	Examples of Programmes
Early involvement in problem behaviour (hyperactivity and impulsivity, conduct disorders) Poor parental supervision and discipline Family conflict and history of problem behaviour Parental involvement in/attitudes condoning problem behaviour Low family income Poor housing	**Family** Pre-natal services Family support using home visitors Parenting information and support	Oregon Study (child-rearing—Patterson 1982) Universal Parent Management (Mason *et al.* 2003) 'Triple P' Programme (positive parenting, Sanders *et al.* 2000) Functional Family Therapy (Sexton and Alexander 2003) The Incredible Years Programme (Webster-Stratton 1984) Elmira Study (intensive home-visiting—Olds *et al.* 1986) Montreal Study—Multi-modal intervention (Tremblay *et al.* 1995) Multi-dimensional Treatment Foster Care (Chamberlin 2003)
Low achievement beginning in primary school Aggressive behaviour including bullying Lack of commitment to school including truancy School disorganization	**School and pre-school** Pre-school education Family literacy and reading schemes Reasoning and social skills education School organizational changes (whole school ethos, teacher training, and support) Preventing/tackling truancy and exclusion Further education for disaffected young people	High/Scope Perry Pre-School Project (Schweinhart and Weikart 1980) Child-Parent Centre (CPC) Programme (Reynolds *et al.* 2001) Seattle Social Development Project—multiple component programme (Hawkins *et al.* 1991) Promoting Alternative Thinking Strategies (Greenberg *et al.* 1995)
Friends involved in problem behaviour Alienation and lack of social commitment	**Youth** After-school clubs Mentoring Youth employment with education Youth work programmes	Multi-systemic Therapy (multiple component programme—Henggeler *et al.* 1992) Children at Risk (Harrell *et al.* 1999) Participate and Learn Skills (constructive leisure pursuits—Jones and Offord 1989) Job Corps (enhancing employability—Schochet *et al.* 2008)
Disadvantaged neighbourhoods Community disorganization and neglect High turnover/low neighbourhood attachment	**Community** Community mobilization Peer-led community programmes	Communities that Care (Harachi *et al.* 2003) CREATE (Homel *et al.* 2015)
Criminogenic impact of system contact	**System** Alternatives to police charges (expansion of structured activities and leisure opportunities for young people in the community) Alternatives to prosecution Alternatives to imprisonment	Diversionary paradigm for offender management (McAra and McVie 2014)

Source: Adapted from Anderson *et al.* 2008, Hawkins *et al.* 2010, McAra and McVie 2014.

Risk factor led interventions

The vast majority of interventions set out in table 27.2 are based on evidence from the risk-factor prevention paradigm. Farrington has claimed that these modes of intervention have gained policy traction precisely because they are 'based on empirical research rather than theories' (2007: 7). Importantly, scholars embracing this perspective have been highly active in designing interventions, embedding them within their own programmes of research, persuading others (including schools, local authorities, or even national governments) to implement the interventions and then evaluating outcomes. Examples here include: the Elmira Study developed by David Olds and colleagues in New York (1989), which involved intensive home visits by nurses both pre- and post-natal, and aimed to improve pregnancy outcomes, ensure that mothers gave better care to their children, and support the personal development of mothers (see Hawkins *et al.* 2010); parent management training programmes such as the Triple P programme (initially developed in Australia) and the Incredible Years programme (Farrington and Welsh 2003); the Perry High/Scope Pre-School project (implemented in Ypsilanti, Michigan USA) based on a daily pre-school programme, plus home visits on a weekly basis over two years, with the overall aim of providing intellectual enrichment, improved reasoning skills, and increased attainment levels at school (Schweinhart *et al.* 1993, 2005); the Seattle Social Development Project, which combined parent management techniques, teacher training and skills training for the youngsters involved (Hawkins *et al.* 1999); and the Multi-systemic Therapy programme which targets serious young offenders and offers tailored interventions, matched to the needs of the young person, aimed at improving home-school and community links, and enhancing cognitive skills (Littell 2005).

The efficacy of such programmes has been established in a variety of ways. Some have been validated utilizing randomized control trials or quasi-experimental methods, as for example the Elmira Study in which 400 mothers recruited to the Study were randomly assigned to intervention and control groups, with follow-ups after 2 and then 15 years revealing that the young people from the families in the intervention group had significantly fewer arrests (see Olds *et al.* 1998); and the Perry High/Scope Pre-School project, with follow-ups at ages 19 and 40 revealing better educational outcomes, greater employability, and lower levels of arrests amongst the intervention group in comparison with the controls (see Schweinhart *et al.* 1993, 2005). Still others have been validated using meta-analysis, as for example the meta-analysis of 10 evaluations of parenting management programmes conducted by Farrington and Welsh (2003) which found that such programmes reduced antisocial behaviour and delinquency by 20 per cent.

Importantly the overwhelming majority of these programmes have been evaluated in a US/Canadian context, and, as with theory building discussed earlier, there is a questionable assumption within the broader literature that such programmes can be readily transported from jurisdiction to jurisdiction without the need to consider differences in the cultural, social, and legal contexts within which such measures are to be implemented (Muncie 2002; Muncie and Goldson 2006). Critics have also argued that risk-factor derived programmes often fail to take account of potential selection effects caused by the gate-keeping practices of agencies at earlier stages of the youth justice process, and the broader (and possibly cumulative) impact of systemic contact on individual offenders as they move from stage to stage (see, e.g., McAra and McVie 2007; Case and Haines 2009).

Contextual and systemic focused interventions

Criticism of the risk factor paradigm has inspired a recent shift within DLC scholarship towards greater emphasis on generalised developmental crime prevention initiatives that can be rolled out at the population level across neighbourhoods, regions, or countries. Following theoretical advances within the paradigm, these large-scale interventions typically take much greater account of the wider contextual influences on offending behaviour. Here, we draw attention to two recent programmes that have taken such an approach and which have had impact on policy within their specific jurisdictions: the CREATE programme in Australia which focuses on community-wide intervention; and the Whole Systems Approach in Scotland which involved changing the entire systemic approach to dealing with young people who offend.

CREATE-ing a community-based approach in Australia

The Pathways to Prevention Project operated from 2002 to 2011 in a highly disadvantaged multicultural community within Brisbane, Australia (see Freiberg *et al.* 2005). It incorporated two core elements: pre-school intervention focused on communication and social skills; and parental training and support aimed at improving child development within families. Described as a 'universal "early intervention", developmental prevention project' (Freiberg *et al.* 2005: 144), it was strongly underpinned by life-course principles and aimed to intervene in the lives of disadvantaged children at a key 'turning point' in childhood—the transition to school. Four key lessons were learned from the Pathways Project: (1) much intervention work within communities was effective despite rarely being evaluated; (2) building trust within communities, and with difficult families, through strong interpersonal relationships was critical to effective practice; (3) evidence-based programmes were rarely used by practitioners; and (4) governance arrangements that divided schools, community agencies, and families undermined project success (Branch *et al.* 2012). Building on this learning, a new national place-based programme was developed across 52 disadvantaged areas within Australia. The model was named CREATE—the acronym encapsulating the main principles underpinning the model: Collaborative, Relationships-driven, Early in the pathway, Accountable, Training-focused, and Evidence-driven (see Homel *et al.* 2015).

The aim of CREATE was to build capacity to undertake population-level community-based prevention. Although the explicit focus is still on disadvantaged communities, its proponents note that it could equally be used in non-disadvantaged areas or form the basis for prevention targeted at whole populations (see Homel *et al.* 2015). CREATE is based on the concepts of 'equifinality' (i.e. young people may reach the same end, such as offending, through different pathways) and 'multifinality' (i.e. young people may begin on the same pathway but achieve different outcomes). These concepts inform the preventative approach, which is multi-systemic and involves collaboration across a wide range of partners. Importantly, the language of the scheme is framed around 'positive development' and 'child and youth well-being' rather than crime reduction, and its overarching goal is framed in terms of 'Better lives for children in disadvantaged communities' (Homel *et al.* 2015: 373). CREATE marks a significant shift in terms of developmental crime prevention because it promotes the strengthening of social bonds between both people and organizations in order to build capacity within communities for mutually supportive and integrated practices across families, schools, and local agencies that operate as a whole to benefit children (see Branch *et al.* 2012). This holistic community-based approach is at odds with many prevention strategies that are dominated by justice institutions and high-level government policies, where communities and families are often absent from the decision-making processes. CREATE is at an early stage and is subject to comprehensive evaluation, so the impact of this programme cannot yet be determined. However, the model has strong backing from the Australian government and has created 'widespread enthusiasm amongst policy people, practitioners and social entrepreneurs for collaborative approaches that achieve collective impact' (Homel *et al.* 2015: 370).

A whole systems approach to juvenile justice in Scotland

In Scotland, evidence from the Edinburgh Study of Youth Transitions and Crime has been used to develop a diversionary paradigm for juvenile justice (within the context of the tribunal-based children's hearing system; McAra and McVie 2015). Reform began with the publication of *Getting it Right for Every Child (GIRFEC): Proposals for Action* (Scottish Executive 2005), a policy document setting out a vision for children's services that ran counter to the then prevailing punitive rhetoric on youth crime. GIRFEC placed primary emphasis on individual well-being, improving outcomes for vulnerable children, and early targeted intervention. A further strategy document, *Preventing Offending by Young People: A Framework for Action* (Scottish Government 2008), set out guidelines for what national and local agencies should do to prevent, divert, manage, and change the behaviour of young people who offend or are at risk of offending. Juvenile justice underwent wholesale transformation in 2011 when the Scottish government rolled out of a new 'Whole System Approach' (WSA) for young people who engage in offending (see Burman and McVie 2016). The WSA represents a reinvigorated welfare-based system which is delivered through multi-agency partnership and a renewed commitment to education and skills. It involves 'early and effective intervention' by referring young people into suitable community-based services, rather than the children's hearing system, at the earliest signs of offending; diversion from prosecution of those aged under 18; and non-custodial disposals for those aged under 21 (Murray *et al.* 2015). The first five years of implementation were accompanied by major reductions in offence referrals to the Scottish juvenile justice system, which fell by 83 per cent; there was also a 75 per cent reduction in the rate of conviction amongst 16 and 17 year olds; custodial sentences for young people aged under 21 fell by 60 per cent; and the number of recorded crimes and offences committed by children and young people (8 to 17 year olds) decreased by 32 per cent. (NB it should be noted that these reductions form part of a slightly longer term trend and therefore caution is required in attributing causal impact directly to the WSA; nonetheless the rate of reduction has increased exponentially since 2011, see McAra this volume.) Within Scotland legislation now has decriminalized the majority of youth offending and enshrined elements of the GIRFEC model in law. These transformations have made Scottish juvenile justice 'a positive and inclusive process based on a broader vision of Scotland as a compassionate nation' (McAra and McVie 2014: 272).

The long term impacts of CREATE and the Whole Systems Approach have yet to be fully evaluated but early signs look promising. However, returning to the issues raised in the first part of the chapter, a key challenge for DLC scholars will be to persuade policy-makers and practitioners to keep faith with the possibility of such approaches in the context of the shorter-term pressures of the political cycle, and the need for implementation integrity in the context of multi-layered and multi-level interventions.

CONCLUSION

In this chapter, we have reflected on recent innovations, impacts, and applications in Developmental and Life Course Criminology. We have found a field of enquiry that is burgeoning, pushing at the methodological boundaries of social-scientific enquiry, and actively attempting to inform and influence policy-making. By way of conclusion, we return to the questions posed at the start of the chapter and would offer the following reflections.

DLC's endurance within the wider discipline of criminology, despite hostile criticism from those with other epistemological and ontological leanings, has been largely due to its social, economic, and political acumen. Socially it comprises an inner core of scholars, who work closely with each other in terms of publication, theory testing, and analytical development; and an emergent generation of scholars applying DLC to more specialist areas of study and with a more international outlook. Economically, DCL has taken advantage of markets both in terms of research funding and policy-oriented knowledge production (stepping into the fray at a time when there was a retreat from engagement with policy within critical criminological circles); and politically it has been adaptive to the vagaries of the environments of late modernity, experimenting with smarter ways of engaging with policy and practice.

These modes of endurance come with some costs, however. We have expressed concerns about DLCs self-referential dynamic and its potential for conceptual stasis due to funding models and data availability, and because of the ways in which theories have been constructed and gained esteem within the paradigm. Indeed, DLC contains a multiplicity of competing theories, predicated on several predominant modes of theory building, which are valorized to the extent that they are both parsimonious in terms of underlying constructs, and replicable across other contexts and studies. As we have argued, this drive for replicability favours theories derived from sets of studies using the same measures (reinforcing again the self-referential dynamic highlighted above), and takes little cognizance of the transferability of constructs and measures across different cultural and jurisdictional contexts. Whilst technological advances have opened up new possibilities for knowledge production, statistical developments have given greater weight to types of modelling which naturally favour taxonomical approaches to theory building. Care must be taken that these developments do not skew conceptual advances such that methodological possibility outruns theoretical imagination. Finally DLC scholarship has highlighted the fragile and contingent nature of policy engagement. The uptake and sustainability of interventions designed on the basis of DLC research has been less to do with the strength of the evidence base and more to do with cycles of government and the wider contexts of penal politics: core dynamics that are not under the control of scholars themselves.

In undertaking this review of DLC, we have at various points made mention of its radical potential. We believe that major theoretical advances both within the DLC paradigm and criminology as a whole, can be made by taking a more holistic approach to theory development and application: an approach which recognizes that conceptual development requires greater understanding of the complex and shifting structural and institutional contexts which form the backdrop to individual lives; and one which ensures that policy interventions address the dynamic interplay between individuals, communities, and systems of justice. Taken as a whole, studies within this paradigm have demonstrated that young people who are persistently and seriously involved in offending are amongst the most vulnerable and victimized groups in societies cross-nationally. By embracing Cullen's exhortation never to withdraw from the policy-making arena, we believe that DLC has the capacity to 'do good'. DLC scholarship reminds us of the need for reflexivity in the ways in which we deploy theory and method across the discipline and the value judgements we make regarding the efficacy of concepts. In sum, important lessons can be learnt from DLC, and we urge our colleagues across the wider discipline to engage.

SELECTED FURTHER READING

Seminal texts in the field of developmental criminology are the two volumes of essays titled *Criminal Careers and Career Criminals Volumes I and II*, edited by Blumstein, Cohen, Roth, and Visher (1986a and 1986b), which laid the groundwork for this paradigm. For a critical evaluation of the study of the age–crime relationship and the developmental perspective, Gottfredson and Hirschi's *A General Theory of Crime* (1990) is an excellent starting point. For key theoretical and methodological debates, Sampson and Laub's *Crime in the Making* (1993) and their follow-up text *Shared Beginnings, Divergent Lives* (Laub and Sampson 2003), and Piquero, Farrington, and Blumstein's *Key Issues in Criminal Career Research* (2007) offer a broad review of the issues and consideration of analytical techniques. The policy perspective is well captured in the collection of essays edited by Smith (2010) in *A New Response to Youth Crime*. Summaries of theories can be found in Bruinsma and Weisburd's *Encyclopedia of Criminology and Criminal Justice* (2014) and an overview of contemporary thinking can be found in Gibson and Krohn's *Handbook of Life-Course Criminology* (2013)

Key journals in the field are: *The Journal of Developmental and Life-Course Criminology; The Journal of Criminal Justice; The Journal of Research in Crime and Delinquency*; and *The Journal of Quantitative Criminology*.

REFERENCES

ARMSTRONG, S. and McARA, L. (2006), 'Audience, borders, architecture: the contours of control', in S. Armstrong and L. McAra (eds), *Perspectives on Punishment: The Contours of Control*, Oxford: Oxford University Press.

BATEMAN, T. (2012), 'Who pulled the plug? Towards an explanation of the fall in child imprisonment', *Youth Justice*, 12(1): 36–52.

BERNARD, T. J. and SNIPES, J. B. (1996), 'Theoretical Integration in Criminology', *Crime and Justice: A Review of Research, vol. 20*, 301–48.

BLOKLAND, A. J. and LUSSIER, P. (2015), *Sex offenders: A criminal career approach*, New York: Wiley-Blackwell.

BLOKLAND, A. J., NAGIN, D., and NIEUWBEERTA, P. (2005), 'Life span offending trajectories of a Dutch conviction cohort', *Criminology*, 43(4): 919–54.

BLUMSTEIN, A., FARRINGTON, D. P., and MOITRA, S. (1985), 'Delinquency careers: innocents, desisters and persisters', in Tonry and Morris (eds), *Crime and Justice: A Review of Research, vol. 6*, Chicago: University of Chicago Press.

BLUMSTEIN, A., COHEN, J., ROTH, J. A., and VISHER, C.A. (eds) (1986a), *Criminal Careers and 'Career Criminals'*, vol. I, Washington, DC: National Academy Press.

BLUMSTEIN, A., COHEN, J., ROTH, J.A., and VISHER, C.A. (eds) (1986b), *Criminal Careers and 'Career Criminals'*, vol. II. Washington, DC: National Academy Press.

BRAME, R., PATERNOSTER, R., and PIQUERO, A. R. (2012), 'Thoughts on the analysis of group-based developmental trajectories in criminology', *Justice Quarterly*, 29(4): 469–90.

BRANCH, S., HOMEL, R., and FREIBERG, K. (2012), 'Making the developmental system work better for children: lessons learned implementing an innovative programme', *Child and Family Social Work*, 18(3): 294–304.

BURMAN, M. and McVIE, S. (2016, forthcoming) 'Getting it Right for Every Child? Juvenile Justice in Scotland', in S. H. Decker and N. Marteache (eds), *International Handbook of Juvenile Justice*, 2nd edn, Cham: Springer International Publishing.

CASE, S. and HAINES, K. (2009), *Understanding Youth Offending: Risk Factor Research, Policy and Practice*, Cullompton: Willan.

CASPI, A. and MOFFITT, T. E. (1995), 'The continuity of maladaptive behaviour: from description to understanding in the study of antisocial behaviour', in D. Cicchetti and D. Cohen (eds), *Developmental Psychopathology*, vol. 2, New York: Wiley.

CID, J. and MARTI, J. (2012), 'Turning points and returning points: Understanding the role of family ties in the process of desistance', *European Journal of Criminology*, 9(6): 603–20.

COHN, E. G. and IRATZOQUI, A. (2015), 'The most cited scholars in five international criminology journals, 2006–10', *British Journal of Criminology*, 56(3): 602–23.

CRAIG, J. M. (2015), 'The effects of marriage and parenthood on offending levels over time among juvenile offenders across race and ethnicity', *Journal of Crime and Justice*, 38:2: 163–82.

CULLEN, F. T. (2011), 'Beyond adolescence-limited criminology: Choosing our future—the American Society of Criminology 2010 Sutherland address', *Criminology*, 49(2): 287–330.

DELISI, B. (2013), 'The Moffittization of Criminology', *International Journal of Offender Therapy and Comparative Criminology*, 57(8): 911–12.

DOHERTY, E. E. and ENSMINGER, M. E. (2013), 'Marriage and offending among a cohort of disadvantaged African Americans', *Journal of Research in Crime and Delinquency*, 50(1): 104–31.

D'UNGER, A.V., LAND, K. C., McCALL, P. L., and NAGIN, D. S. (1998), 'How many latent classes of delinquent/criminal careers? Results from mixed Poisson regression analyses', *American Journal of Sociology*, 103(6): 1593–630.

EGGLESTON, E. P., LAUB, J. H., and SAMPSON, R. J. (2004), 'Methodological sensitivities to latent class analysis of long-term criminal trajectories', *Journal of Quantitative Criminology*, 20(1): 1–26.

EISNER, M., NAGIN, D., RIBEAY, D., and MALTI, T. (2012), 'Effects of a universal parenting programme for highlight adherent parents: a propensity score matching approach', *Prevention Science*, 13(3): 252–66.

EROSHEVA, E. A., MATSUEDA, R. L., and TELESCA, D. (2014), 'Breaking bad: Two decades of life-course data analysis in criminology, developmental psychology and beyond', *Annual Review of Statistics and Its Application*, 1: 301–32.

ESTRADA, F., BACKMAN, O., and NILSSON, A. (2015), 'The darker side of equality? The declining gender gap in crime: historical trends and an enhanced analysis of staggered birth cohorts', *British Journal of Criminology*, 56(6): 1272–90.

FARRELL, G., TILLEY, N., TSELONI, A., and MAILLEY, J. (2011), 'The crime drop and the security hypothesis', *Journal of Research in Crime and Delinquency*, 48(2): 147–75.

FARRELL, G., LAYCOCK, G., and TILLEY, N. (2015), 'Debuts and legacies: The crime drop and the role of adolescence-limited and persistent offending', *Crime Science*, 4: 16, doi:10.1186/s40163-015-0028-3.

FARRINGTON, D. P. (1986), 'Age and crime', in *Crime and Justice: A Review of Research, vol. 7*, 189–250.

FARRINGTON, D. P. (2006), 'Building Developmental and Life-Course Theories of Offending', in F. T. Cullen, J. P. Wright, and K. R. Blevins (eds), *Taking Stock: The Status of Criminological Theory*, New Brunswick, NJ: Transaction.

FARRINGTON, D. P. (2007), 'Childhood risk factors and risk-focused prevention', in M. Maguire, R. Morgan, and R. Reiner (eds), *The Oxford Handbook of Criminology*, 4th edn, Oxford: Oxford University Press.

FARRINGTON, D. P. (2015), 'Prospective longitudinal research on the development of offending', *Australian and New Zealand Journal of Criminology*, 48(3): 314–35.

FARRINGTON, D. P., HARADA, Y., SHINKAI, H., and MORIYA, T. (2015), 'Longitudinal and criminal career research in Japan', *Asian Criminology*, 10: 255–76.

FRANCIS, B., HUMPHREYS, L., KIRBY, S., and SOOTHILL, K. (2013), *Understanding criminal careers in organised crime. Crime research and analysis no. 74*, London: Home Office.

FREIBERG, K., HOMEL, R., BATCHELOR, S., CARR, A., HAY, I., ELIAS, G., and TEAGUE, R. (2005), 'Creating pathways to participation: A community based developmental prevention project in Australia', *Children and Society*, 19(2): 144–57.

GARLAND, D. (1997), 'Governmentality and the problem of crime: Faoucault, criminology, sociology', *Theoretical Criminology*, 1(2): 173–214.

GLUECK, S. and GLUECK, E. (1950), *Unravelling Juvenile Delinquency*, New York: The Commonwealth Fund.

GOTTFREDSON, M. and HIRSCHI, T. (1990), *A General Theory of Crime*, Stanford: Stanford University Press.

GREENBERG, D. F. (2016), 'Criminal careers: Discrete or continuous?', *Journal of Developmental and Life Course Criminology*, 2(1): 5–44.

HAWKINS, J. D., CATALANO, R. F., and KUKLINSKI, M. R. (2014), 'Communities that care', in G. Bruinsma and D. Weisburd (eds), *Encyclopedia of Criminology and Criminal Justice*, New York: Springer.

HAWKINS, J. D., VON CLEVE, E., and CATALANO, R. F. (1991), 'Reducing early childhood aggression: Results of a primary prevention programme', *Journal of the American Academy of Child and Adolescent Psychiatry*, 30(2): 208–17.

HAWKINS, J. D., WELSH, B., and UTTING, D. (2010), 'Preventing Youth Crime: Evidence and Opportunities', in D. Smith (ed.), *A New Response to Youth Crime*, Cullompton: Willan.

HIRSCHI, T. (1989), 'Exploring alternatives to integrated theory', in S. F. Messner, M. D. Krohn, and A. E. Liska (eds), *Theoretical Integration in the Study of Deviance and Crime*, Albany, NY: State University of New York Press.

HOMEL, R., FREIBERG, K., and BRANCH, S. (2015), 'CREATE-ing capacity to take developmental crime prevention to scale: A community-based approach within a national framework', *Australian and New Zealand Journal of Criminology*, 48(3): 367–85.

HUIZINGA, D., SCHUMANN, K., EHRET, B., and ELLIOT, A. (2003), 'The effects of juvenile justice processing on subsequent delinquent and criminal behaviour: a cross-national study', Washington, DC: final report to the National Institute of Justice.

JENNINGS, W. G. and REINGLE, J. M. (2012), 'On the number and shape of developmental/life-course violence, aggression, and delinquency trajectories: A state-of-the-art review', *Journal of Criminal Justice*, 40(6): 472–89.

KIM, J., BUSHWAY, S., and TSAO, H-S. (2015), 'Identifying Classes of Explanations for Crime Drop: Period and Cohort Effects for New York State', *Journal of Quantitative Criminology*, 32(3): 357–75.

KORNHAUSER, R. R. (1978), 'Social Sources of Delinquency: An Appraisal of Analytic Models', Chicago: University of Chicago Press.

KREUTER, F. and MUTHEN, B. (2008), 'Anayzing criminal trajectory profiles: Bridging multilevel and group-based approaches using growth mixture modelling', *Journal of Quantitative Criminology*, 24(1): 1–31.

LAUB, J. H. and SAMPSON, R. J. (2003), *Shared Beginnings, Divergent Lives. Delinquent Boys to Age 70*, Cambridge, MA: Harvard University Press.

LAURITSEN, J. L., HEIMER, K., and LYNCH, J. P. (2009), 'Trends in the gender gap in violent offending: new evidence from the national crime victimization survey', *Criminology*, 47(2): 361–99.

LEAL, W., GERZ, M., and PIQUERO, A. R. (2016), 'Are NFL arrestees violent specialists or high frequency offenders or both?', *Deviant Behavior*, 37(4): 456–70.

LOEBER, R. and FARRINGTON, D. P. (2014), 'Age-crime curve', in G. Bruinsma and D. Weisburd (eds), *Encyclopedia of Criminology and Criminal Justice*. New York: Springer.

LOEBER, R., FARRINGTON, D. P., STOUTHAMER-LOEBER, M., MOFFITT, T. E., CASPI, A., WHITE, H. R., WEI, E. H., and BEYERS, J. M. (2003), 'The development of male offending: Key findings from fourteen years of the Pittsburgh Youth Study', in T. P. Thornberry and M. D. Krohn (eds), *Taking Stock of Delinquency: An Overview of findings from Contemporary Longitudinal Studies*, New York: Kluwer/Plenum.

LUSSIER, P., MCCUISH, E., and CORRADO, R. R. (2015), 'The Adolescence–Adulthood Transition and Desistance from Crime: Examining the Underlying Structure of Desistance', *Journal of Developmental and Life Course Criminology*, 1(2): 87–117.

MAGUIRE, M. and MCVIE, S. (2017), 'Crime Data and Criminal Statistics: A Critical Reflection', in A. Liebling, S. Maruna, and L. McAra (eds), *The Oxford Handbook of Criminology*, 6th edn, Oxford: Oxford University Press.

MANCINI, C., RECKDENWALD, A., BEAUREGARD, E., and LEVENSOND, J. S. (2014), 'Sex industry exposure over the life course on the onset and frequency of sex offending', *Journal of Criminal Justice*, 42(6): 507–16.

MATTHEWS, B. (2014), 'Where have all the young offenders gone?', AQMeN Research Briefing 4, November 2014.

MATTHEWS, B. and MINTON, J. (forthcoming), 'The age-crime curve and the crime drop in Scotland', submitted to the *European Journal of Criminology*.

MCARA, L. (2010), 'Models of Youth Justice', in D. J. Smith (ed.), *A New Response to Youth Crime*, Cullompton: Willan.

MCARA, L. (2017), 'Youth Justice', in A. Liebling, S. Maruna, and L. McAra (eds), *The Oxford Handbook of Criminology*, 6th edn, Oxford: Oxford University Press.

MCARA, L. and MCVIE, S. (2005), 'The Usual Suspects? Street-life, Young Offenders and the Police', *Criminal Justice*, 5(1): 5–36.

MCARA, L. and MCVIE, S. (2007), 'Youth Justice? The Impact of Agency Contact on Desistance from Offending', *European Journal of Criminology*, 4(3): 315–45.

MCARA, L. and MCVIE, S. (2010), 'Youth Crime and Justice: Key Messages from the Edinburgh Study of Youth Transitions and Crime', *Criminology and Criminal Justice*, 10(2): 211–30.

McAra, L. and McVie, S. (2012a), 'Critical debates in developmental and life-course criminology', in M. Maguire, R. Morgan, and R. Reiner (eds), *The Oxford Handbook of Criminology*, 5th edn, Oxford: Oxford University Press.

McAra, L. and McVie, S. (2012b), 'Negotiated order: Towards a theory of pathways into and out of offending', *Criminology and Criminal Justice*, 12(4): 347–76.

McAra, L. and McVie, S. (2014), 'The Scottish Juvenile Justice System: Policy and Practice', in J. Winterdyk, (ed.), *Juvenile Justice: International Perspectives, Models and Trends*, Boca Raton, Fl: CRC Press.

McAra, L. and McVie, S. (2015), 'The Case for Diversion and Minimum Necessary Intervention', in B. Goldson and J. Muncie (eds), *Youth Crime and Justice*, 2nd edn, London: Sage.

McGee, T. R. and Mazarolle, P. (2016), 'Special issue on methodological innovations in developmental and life-course criminology research: Editorial introduction', *Journal of Developmental and Life Course Criminology*, 2(1): 1–4.

McGrath, A. (2015), 'Exploring Patterns of Offending by Juvenile Offenders in Australia: What Is the Evidence for a Specialist Violent Offender?', *Journal of Developmental and Life Course Criminology*, 1(3): 304–24.

Mears, D. P. (2007), 'Towards rational and evidence-based crime policy', *Journal of Criminal Justice*, 35(6): 667–82.

Moffitt, T. E. (1993), '"Life-course persistent" and "adolescent-limited" anti-social behaviour: A developmental taxonomy', *Psychological Review*, 100(4): 674–701.

Moffitt, T. E. (2003), 'Life-course-persistent and adolescence-limited antisocial behaviour: A 10-year research review and a research agenda', in B. B. Lahey, T. E. Moffitt, and A. Caspi (eds), *Causes of Conduct Disorder and Juvenile Delinquency*, New York: The Guilford Press.

Muncie, J. (2002), 'Policy transfers and what works: Some reflections on comparative youth justice', *Youth Justice*, 1(3): 27–35.

Muncie, J. (2010), 'Book Review: S Case and K Haines, Understanding Youth Offending: Risk Factor Research, Policy and Practice, Willan Publishing, Cullompton, 2009', *Youth Justice: An International Journal*, 10(3): 302–4.

Murray, K., McGuinness, P., Burman, M., and McVie, S. (2015), 'Evaluation of the Whole System Approach to Young People Who Offend in Scotland', Glasgow: SCCJR Report No. 07/2015, available at: http://www.sccjr.ac.uk/wp-content/uploads/2015/06/Evaluation-of-the-WSA-approach.pdf, accessed 6 January 2017.

Nagin, D. S. (2005), *Group-Based Modelling of Development*, Cambridge, MA: Harvard University Press.

Nagin, D. S. and Land, K. C. (1993), 'Age, criminal careers and population heterogeneity: specification and estimation of a non-parametric, mixed poisson model', *Criminology*, 31(3): 327–62.

Nagin, D. S. and Piquero, A. S. (2010), 'Using the group-based trajectory model to study crime over the life course', *Journal of Criminal Justice Education*, 21(2): 105–16.

Osgood, D. W. (2005), 'Making sense of crime and the life-course', *The Annals of the American Academy of Political and Social Science*, 602: 196–211.

Otu, S. E. and Elechi, O. O. (2015), 'Pathways and Trajectories to Life-Course Persistent Armed Robbery Offending Behavior in Contemporary Nigeria: Examining the Predictors and the Risks Factors', *International Journal of Criminal Justice Sciences*, 10(1): 10–31.

Piquero, A. R. (2008), 'Taking stock of developmental trajectories of criminal activity over the life course', in A. M. Liberman (ed.), *The Long View of Crime A Synthesis of Longitudinal research* New York: Springer.

Piquero, A. R., Farrington, D. P., and Blumstein, A. (2007), *Key Issues in Criminal Career Research: New Analyses of the Cambridge Study in Delinquent Development*, Cambridge: Cambridge University Press.

Piquero, A. R. and Moffitt, T. E. (2005), 'Explaining the facts of crime: How the developmental taxonomy replies to Farrington's invitation', in D. P. Farrington (ed.), *Integrated Developmental and Life-Course Theories of Offending: Advances in Criminological Theory*, New Brunswick, NJ: Transaction.

Reid, J. A. (2012), 'Exploratory review of route-specific, gendered, and age-graded dynamics of exploitation: Applying life course theory to victimization in sex trafficking in North America', *Aggression and Violent Behavior*, 17(3): 257–71.

Rock, P. (1994), *History of Criminology*, Aldershot: Dartmouth.

Sampson, R. J. (2015), 'Crime and the life course in a changing world: Insights from Chicago and implications for global criminology', *Asian Criminology*, 10(4): 277–86.

Sampson, R. J. and Laub, J. H. (eds) (1993), *Crime in the Making: Pathways and Turning Points Through Life*, Cambridge, MA: Harvard University Press.

Sampson, R. J. and Laub, J. H. (2003), 'Life-course desisters? Trajectories of crime among delinquent boys followed to age 70', *Criminology*, 41(3): 301–39.

Sampson, R. J. and Laub, J. H. (2005), 'A General Age-Graded Theory of Crime: Lessons Learned and the Future of Life-Course Criminology', in D. P. Farrington (ed.), *Integrated Developmental & Life-Course Theories of Offending*, New Brunswick, NJ: Transaction.

Sampson, R. J. and Laub, J. H (2016), 'Turning points and the future of life-course criminology: Reflections on the 1986 Criminal Careers Report', *Journal of Research in Crime and Delinquency*, 53(3): 321–35.

Sampson, R. J., Laub, J. H., and Eggleston, E. P. (2004), 'On the robustness and validity of groups', *Journal of Quantitative Criminology*, 20(1): 37–42.

Scottish Executive (2005), 'Getting it Right for Every Child: Proposals for Action', Edinburgh: The Scottish Government.

SCOTTISH GOVERNMENT (2008), 'Preventing Offending by Young People: A Framework for Action', Edinburgh: The Scottish Government, available at: http://www.gov.scot/Resource/Doc/228013/0061713.pdf , accessed 18 January 2017.

SKARDHAMAR, T. (2010), 'Distinguishing facts and artifacts in group-based modelling', *Criminology*, 48(1): 295–320.

SKARDHAMAR, T. and SAVOLAINEN, J. (2014), 'Changes in criminal offending around the time of job entry: a study of employment and desistance', *Criminology*, 52(2): 263–91.

SKARDHAMAR, T., MONSBAKKEN, C. W., and LYNGSTAD, T. H. (2014), 'Crime and the transition to marriage', *British Journal of Criminology*, 54(3): 411–27.

SPARKS, R. (2006), 'Ordinary anxieties and states of emergency: statecraft and spectatorship in the new politics of insecurity', in S. Armstrong and L. McAra (eds), *Perspectives on Punishment: The Contours of Control*, Oxford: Oxford University Press.

STEWART, A., DENNISON, S., ALLARD, T., THOMPSON, C., BROIDY, L., and CHRZANOWSKI, A. (2015), 'Administrative data linkage as a tool for developmental and life-courese criminology: The Queensland Linkage Project', *Australian and New Zealand Journal of Criminology*, 48(3): 409–28.

SUTTON, C., UTTING, D., and FARRINGTON, D. P. (2004), *Support from the Start: Working with Young Children and their Families to Reduce the Risks of Crime and Antisocial Behaviour*, London: Department for Education and Skills (Research Brief 524).

SWEETEN, G. (2014), 'Group-based trajectory models', in G. Bruinsma and D. Weisburd (eds), *Encyclopedia of Criminology and Criminal Justice*, New York: Springer.

THORNBERRY, T. P., LIZOTTE, A. J., KROHN, M. D., SMITH, C. A., and PORTER, P. K. (2003), 'Causes and consequences of delinquency: Findings from the Rochester Youth Development Study', in T. P. Thornberry and M. D. Krohn (eds), *Taking Stock of Delinquency: An Overview of Findings from Contemporary Longitudinal Studies*, New York: Kluwer Academic/Plenum.

TREMBLAY, R. E., PAGANI-KURTZ, L., MÂSSE, L. C., VITARO, F., and PIHL, R. O. (1995), 'A bimodal preventive intervention for disruptive kindergarten boys: its impact through mid-adolescence', *Journal of Consulting and Clinical Psychology*, 63(4): 560–8.

WACQUANT, L. D. (2006), 'Penalization, Depoliticization, Racialization: On the Over-Incarceration of Immigrants', in S. Armstrong and L. McAra (eds), *Perspectives on Punishment: The Contours of Control*, Oxford: Oxford University Press.

WALKER, N. (1987), *Crime and Criminology: A Critical Introduction*, New York: Oxford University Press.

WIKSTRÖM, P.-O. (2017), 'Character, Circumstances and the Causes of Crime Towards an Analytical Criminology', in A. Liebling, S. Maruna, and L. McAra (eds), *The Oxford Handbook of Criminology*, 6th edn, Oxford, Oxford University Press.

WOLFGANG, M. E., FIGLIO, R. M., and SELLIN, T. (1972), *Delinquency in a Birth Cohort*, Chicago: University of Chicago Press.

YOUNG, J. (1988), 'Radical Criminology in Britain: the emergence of a competing paragdim, *The British Journal of Criminology*, 28(2): 159–83.

YOUNG, J. (2004), 'Voodoo criminology and the numbers game', in J. Ferrell, K. Hayward, W. Morrison, and M. Presdee, (eds), *Cultural Criminology Unleashed*, London: GlassHouse.

YOUNG, J. (2011), *The Criminological Imagination*, Cambridge: Polity.

YANG, S-M., WEISBURD, D., and GROFF, E. R. (2014), 'Criminal careers of places', in G. Bruinsma and D. Weisburd (eds), *Enclyclopedia of Criminology and Criminal Justice*, New York: Springer.

28

MENTAL HEALTH, MENTAL DISABILITIES, AND CRIME

Jill Peay

INTRODUCTION

The relationship between mental disability and crime is complex. The familiar question of whether an individual charged with a criminal offence was 'mad' or 'bad' or a bit of both has long been superseded by more nuanced questions. What is meant by crime? Who can be held responsible for it? How can culpability be assessed for the purposes of punishment in those with a mental disability? Is treatment (and if so of what nature) more appropriate than punishment? And are those with a mental disability more likely to be at risk from the criminal activities of others, or to present as perpetrators of behaviour that harms others, possibly in the most serious of ways?

Many of these questions are intractable. But the process through which the criminal justice system deals with those with mental disabilities has been subject to extensive review. The Bradley Report (2009) was an end-to-end examination of the system; it made significant recommendations, many of which have been adopted. The Criminal Justice Joint Inspection (2009) report was similarly critical of the system; and the Law Commission (2013, 2016a, and 2016b) has looked at the legal framework for insanity, automatism, and unfitness to plead, albeit their recommendations remain merely recommendations. The period of legislative turmoil which did take place concerned amendments to the Mental Health Act 1983 (MHA 1983)[1] which affected offenders with mental disability in more marginal ways than those proposed by the Law Commission. Beyond these policy and legal developments there have been important economic changes. The effects of the recession (Peay 2011a) and the subsequent policies of austerity are hard to assess empirically. But the latter have had a notable effect on police resources, and in a context where some forces have reported up to 40 per cent of their time being spent dealing with incidents triggered by mental health issues it is evident that mental disability should loom large in policy thinking.[2] Finally, it is arguable

[1] See Mental Health Act 2007, and for commentary Peay (2011b).

[2] http://www.theguardian.com/uk-news/2016/jan/27/mental-health-crisis-huge-increasing-share-police-time-40, accessed 6 January 2017.

that the public tone has changed to a more benign and understanding one towards those with mental disability, but certainly the context for any analysis is complex.

This chapter is divided into six sections with a primary focus on England and Wales. The first examines the problematic concept of 'the mentally disordered offender'. Do such individuals constitute an isolated category meriting special provision, or do the issues raised by this 'group' have wider implications for the study of criminology? Are they a minority presence or an awkward presence within the criminal justice system (Peay 2016a)? The second section considers generally issues of mental health and crime. Is there a relationship between the two: does mental disorder cause crime or does involvement in the criminal justice system bring out mental health issues in vulnerable people? Are those with mental disabilities more likely to be victims of offending than perpetrators of it? The third examines the fundamental justification for separate provision, namely treatment. It takes a critical look at evidence for the treatability of the mental disability-offending spectrum, and then focuses on a key problematic group—offenders suffering from personality disorder—who straddle the continuum. There is also a brief examination of the 'dangerous and severe personality disorder' (DSPD) initiative. The fourth section tackles some hidden agendas—bifurcation, detention for protective purposes, due process in discharge, and release mechanisms. The fifth reviews developments in policy and tries to provide an understanding of the problematic context of the conflicting themes. The themes relate to the way in which therapeutic and risk-oriented objectives have become progressively blurred; the ongoing conflict between legalism and welfarism; and the growing role for human rights developments. And the final section formulates some conclusions.

One area where the shifts have been perceptible concerns the relationship between mental disability and risk, a theme which permeates this chapter. Perceiving those with mental disability as a separate category, a perception underpinned by our discriminatory mental health legislation, can play into an unfounded attribution of enhanced risk. Indeed, the reforms to the MHA 1983, which culminated in the Mental Health Act 2007, and which arose in part out of the then government's focus on risk, had the effect of taking mental health law towards penal law and away from health law (see Fennell 2001 and Richardson 1999). This can only have contributed to a perception that those with mental health issues are more a risk to us than they are to themselves or from us, even assuming that such groupings make any sense. Yet the statistical picture suggests that this perception is misplaced (see Appleby *et al.* 2015), with vulnerability lying primarily with those with disorders, not from them. Notably, the seemingly relentless focus on homicides has shifted with the rescinding of the requirement for mandatory independent inquiries on any occasion where those who had been in contact with mental health services in the previous 12 months went on to kill (Crichton 2011; Peay 1996). And there has been a seeming shift in our perceptions with respect to those from whom we are at risk. The frenzied, irrational, or psychopathic stranger may have been replaced by terrorist ideologues, albeit that the mental health status of such terrorists never seems far from popular discourse. For both lawyers and clinicians the teasing out, in the context of the most extreme, repugnant, and incomprehensible violence, of what is disordered and what is ordered, has been laid bare in extraordinary detail by the Anders Behring Breivik case (Seierstad 2015: Syse 2014: Melle 2013).

Perhaps a kindlier and more understanding era for people with mental health difficulties has been ushered in. Maybe the government's 'What's the story?' assault on media misrepresentations has borne fruit after all.[3] These trends are hard to establish empirically, but anecdotally they are reflected in the responses of mental health law students. With each incoming crop of students I have asked them what two words come into their minds when I say the phrase 'mentally disordered offender'. Ten years ago the concepts were heavily dominated by violence, risk, and incapacitation. Most recently, students have used words like vulnerable, needy, treatment, and victim. And their responses are reflected in the new title to this chapter. Gone is the reference to the term 'mentally disordered offender' and instead there is a focus on mental disabilities.

DEFINITION, INCIDENCE, AND IMPLICATIONS

Offenders with mental disabilities are categorically awkward; being neither exclusively ill nor uncomplicatedly bad, such people 'totter between two not always compatible discourses of state intervention' (Webb and Harris 1999: 2). Are they offenders who have mental disorders, or people with mental disorders who have offended? Or both? The category itself also conjures up images of the 'unloving, unloved and unlovable' (Bean 2008: 172). Such individuals can be hard to define, challenging to deal with, and unattractive to services. It is perhaps not surprising that they have been relegated and isolated, both in theory and practice. But is it right that they be treated separately, in the way that criminology chapters have been historically devoted to issues of gender, race, or youth? It is the premise of this chapter that how we deal conceptually, practically, and in principle with those deemed 'mentally disordered offenders' is central to the scope of criminology; treating this as an isolated topic fails to reflect how mental disability infuses discussion of the criminal justice system.

Indeed, to argue for the existence of a discrete group of 'mentally disordered offenders' would presuppose a category of 'mentally ordered offenders'. This falsely comforting notion echoes Gilman's (1988) observation that setting the sick apart sustains the fantasy that the rest of us are whole. The criminal law broadly adopts such an approach, presuming rationality where there is no proof of its complete absence. Yet, such a clear-cut division is problematic. Even the notionally reasonable 'man on the Clapham omnibus' can experience moments of madness. In turn, scientific advances in our understanding of the structure, functioning, and chemistry of the brain have generated a more medical approach to some limited forms of offending and the neurological syndromes which may underlie them (Eastman and Campbell 2006). In the area of so-called normal offending, defences are rightly advanced or mitigation constructed which draw on elements of 'diminished responsibility', 'unthinking' behaviour, or

[3] http://www.mediawise.org.uk/wp-content/uploads/2011/03/Whats-the-story-reporting-mental-health-and-suicide.pdf, accessed 6 January 2017.

uncontrolled responses to extreme social stress. Concepts of limited rationality will be familiar to criminologists; the difficulties which stem from offences committed whilst people are under the influence of drink or drugs, or who fail to understand the consequence of their actions, due to immaturity or limited cognitive skills, or who process new information poorly can all intersect with issues of legal/criminal responsibility. Yet few of these individuals would wish for the special treatment that may follow a finding of 'defect of reason' integral to a finding of 'not guilty by reason of insanity'. A finding which absolves such individuals from the punishment which follows a formal finding of guilt but which potentially propels them into a system of compulsory treatment and the associated stigma which surrounds those deemed mad. As Porter (2004) observed, it might be preferable to be criminalized and maintain one's free will than to be psychiatrized and lose it.

People with mental disabilities who have offended find themselves confined in hospitals, prisons, therapeutic regimes within prisons, and, most notably, within the remand population. Underuse of the provisions within the MHA 1983, which permit the diversion of alleged disordered offenders into hospital rather than custodial remand, partially accounts for this enhanced prevalence. But the interactive stress of being charged with an offence if one is already vulnerable should not be underestimated. Offenders with mental disabilities exist in one shape or form across the entire criminal justice system; indeed, the presence of mental disability 'can affect the normal processes of the criminal justice system at several points' (Hale 2010: 145); detention, interrogation, diversion, prosecution, conviction, disposal, treatment, and release can all be affected by an individual's mental state (Criminal Justice Joint Inspection 2009).

One explanation for this infusion into the criminal justice process relates to the definition of 'mental disorder' in section 1 of the MHA 1983, namely, 'any disorder or disability of the mind'. This definition is one of acute terminological inexactitude: it acts like a concertina, expanding or contracting depending on the context in which it is applied in order to accommodate different client groups with little or no coherence. It is the gateway to hospital, to services, and to safeguards. As was pointed out to the Joint Scrutiny Committee on the 2004 Draft Mental Health Bill, the definition was potentially broad enough to include those who smoked cigarettes and would encompass all individuals with personality disorder.[4] Whether the implications of this had been fully thought through in respect of all of the points at which it would apply to those involved in the criminal justice process is a moot point; but it was clearly intended to include those with personality disorder, and hence those with DSPD, within the ambit of compulsory treatment. Thus, people with mental disabilities are unlikely to constitute a minority group. They will contribute to the totality of offending, interact with all stages of the criminal justice system, and make up a significant proportion of custodial populations.

The statistics support this. The UK prison population, like that of other jurisdictions, displays high levels of disorder both before and during custody (Stewart 2008; Fazel and Danesh 2002; Singleton *et al.* 1998) with the Singleton *et al.* study estimating levels of functional psychotic disorder at 7 per cent for sentenced men and 10 per cent

[4] See http://www.publications.parliament.uk/pa/jt200405/jtselect/jtment/79/7906.htm#a20, accessed 6 January 2017.

for men on remand. Indeed, only one in ten of the prison population does not experience some form of diagnosable disorder (albeit not all of those who are diagnosable would qualify for compulsory admission under the MHA 1983, since many have drug and alcohol dependence or experience learning disability without it being associated with abnormally aggressive or seriously irresponsible conduct[5]). Notably, the Singleton *et al.* (1998) study found levels of the more serious mental illnesses which significantly exceed those in the general population (Meltzer *et al.* 1995; Johns *et al.* 2004), even given a growing recognition that psychosis occurs on a continuum rather than being an all or nothing phenomenon. The figures for psychotic disorders were shocking because they were worse even than those found 20 years earlier by Gunn *et al.* (1978) in their survey of the south-east prison population. Moreover, the presence of mental disability generally will contribute to the high levels of suicide and self-harm amongst prisoners; figures for the latest year available show levels of self-inflicted deaths at 100, and incidents of self-harm at 32,313, persisting and, sadly, increasing despite numerous measures to combat them (Ministry of Justice 2016). Indeed, they are clearly indicative of an inappropriate environment in which to detain vulnerable individuals.

Yet at the start of the criminal justice process are these high levels of disorder present? The Bradley Review (2009: 38) estimated that the 'number of mentally disordered suspects passing through police stations varies between 2% and 20%'. Given that the definition of mental disorder is so all embracing, it is perhaps not surprising that the variation in its identification in individual suspects is significant. Undoubtedly there is a crystallization effect through the criminal justice process; a process which facilitates greater disclosure or diagnosis of disability, and which in part selectively filters into the system those with disability. Levels of disability identified at the police station have been historically low (Robertson *et al.* 1995; Littlechild 2001), which is worrying since there is a requirement for an appropriate adult to be present when questioning such individuals (Home Office 2014: Code C, paras 3.15–3.19). Indeed, the Code requires officers to be over-inclusive, stating (para 1G) 'When the custody officer has any doubt about the mental state or capacity of a detainee, that detainee should be treated as mentally vulnerable and an appropriate adult called.' Dehaghani (2016: 411), based on her observational study of booking-in procedures at a large custody suite, asserts that 'almost all suspects booked in could have been considered vulnerable in some manner'. The problem, she argues, is not the identification of vulnerability *per se*, but an interpretation by officers that the appropriate adult is not required in the specific circumstances. Since personality disorder falls within the new definition of mental disorder under the MHA 1983, appropriate adults should routinely be present at interrogations. Does not the police definition of, for example, an accused with antisocial personality disorder, require them to adhere to these special protections for those with 'mental disorder'?

Personality disorder is perhaps a telling example of where the mismatch between different agencies' expectations for, and definitions of, 'the mentally disordered' impedes the full protection to which that 'group' is entitled in law. It is worth illustrating some of those dilemmas here. Personality disorder (a clinical concept), psychopathy (a trait measurable by the Hare Psychopathy Checklist: Hare 1991) and DSPD (dangerous

[5] Section 1(3) and section 1(2A)(b) MHA 1983.

and severe personality disorder—a political/policy concept) are all terms used when exploring the association between disorders of personality and criminality. And can all be used by the various professions and agencies involved in the criminal justice system. The diagnosis of personality disorder has a long and problematic history, which has continued into the 2013 version of the Diagnostic and Statistical Manual (DSM-5) used by the American Psychiatric Association.[6] Here, the 10 distinct types of personality disorder from the previous versions of the manual have been retained, but DSM-5 changes from a multi-axial system of diagnosis to one that removes the arbitrary boundaries between personality disorders and other mental disorders. This acknowledges the fundamental similarities across disorders, recognizing that personality disorders are 'associated with ways of thinking and feeling about oneself and others that significantly and adversely affect how an individual functions in many aspects of life'. But DSM-5 also controversially includes a new alternative hybrid model, based on traits and their severity together with how an individual experiences himself or others. This appears as a separate section of the manual. This hybrid model contrasts with the categories of personality disorder approach embodied in the main manual: it is likely to facilitate further research in the area.

Of the 10 personality disorder categories listed in the manual, it is inevitable that there will be some association between personality and criminality since the concepts are by definition, in varying formats, linked. For example, both 'antisocial personality disorder' and 'borderline personality disorder'—the latter entails strong impulses to engage in reckless and irresponsible behaviour—are much more likely to be associated with criminal behaviour than, for example 'obsessive-compulsive personality disorder', which has as a feature an excessive interest in lists, timetables, and rules. Thus, in much the same way as will be discussed for the category of 'schizophrenia', 'personality disorder' can be protective rather than criminogenic when its particular form is associated with a reluctance to socialize and a withdrawn lifestyle.

On this side of the Atlantic the 2016 version of ICD 10 (the World Health Organization's International Statistical Classification of Diseases)[7] is preferred. And in the UK the approach is different again. Here, the NHS guidance and many psychiatrists think of personality disorder as falling into three clusters: A, B, and C (crudely: the mad, bad, and sad). It is cluster B, people who show patterns of behavior that are 'dramatic, erratic and threatening or disturbing',[8] who are thought to have an enhanced risk of offending and thus be more likely to engage with the criminal justice system. Ironically, the cluster approach is not so dissimilar to DSM-5.

Whilst the therapeutic, conceptual, and legal difficulties with personality disorder are manifold (Peay 2011c), and will be returned to later, it is worth stressing here that rarely do those individuals find themselves subject to civil commitment under the MHA 1983. Although those with 'personality disorder' may be extremely time consuming of GPs' energies, it is almost exclusively their involvement with the criminal justice system which brings them to the attention of mental health services (James *et al.* 2002).

[6] http://www.dsm5.org/Pages/Default.aspx, accessed 6 January 2017.

[7] http://apps.who.int/classifications/icd10/browse/2016/en: Chapter V, accessed 9 January 2017.

[8] http://www.nhs.uk/Conditions/Personality-disorder/Pages/Symptoms.aspx, accessed 9 January 2017.

Finally, it is worth noting that the lack of a detailed definition as to what constitutes mental disability poses not only challenges for services but also opportunities. One such is a recent development in the controversial use of police stations as a 'place of safety' under section 136 of the MHA 1983. Following a number of critical reports (Scott 2015; HMIC 2013; Docking *et al.* 2007) concerning the over-use by the police of their powers, change is in-hand (see Policing and Crime Act 2017). Revisions to the statutory power (MHA 2007) to remove an individual from a public place to a 'place of safety' when the person appears to be suffering from mental disorder and in immediate need of care and control have occurred and policy edicts (Department of Health and Home Office 2014) indicate further movement on the issue. For example, the police station is no longer to be used as a place of safety for those under 18 and the police are strongly encouraged to instead take people with mental disabilities to hospital or to designated place of safety suites. The substantial reversal of the numbers, now favouring hospital over police stations, is encouraging.[9] Indeed, as part of a revival in the use of diversion (Dyer 2013; Scott *et al.* 2013) after the Bradley Review (2009) some police forces are trialing mental health first responders in police cars—in effect a triage car—which helps divert those with mental disabilities from criminalization and towards hospital. Moreover, the broader Liaison and Diversion Service for England aims to serve 50 per cent of the population by 2015–16.[10]

On the other hand, at a time when mental health services are themselves extremely stretched it is hard to see how offenders with disabilities are likely to secure priority in services unless they pose an evident risk. And in a context where the lack of definitional focus permits a politicized approach to people with disabilities caught up in the criminal justice system, such individuals remain vulnerable to an inconsistent response and an arguably overly punitive response.

MENTAL DISABILITY AND CRIME

Does mental disorder cause crime, does involvement in crime and the criminal justice system cause mental disorder, and are those with mental disabilities more likely to be the perpetrators of crime or victims of it? Indeed, are crime and mental disability not related at all, but simply share common precursors? These straightforward questions are immensely complex to unpack (Peay 2011b; Bean 2008). Equally, they may not be

[9] http://www.hscic.gov.uk/searchcatalogue?productid=19118&q=title%3a%22Inpatients+formally+detained+in+hospitals+under+the+Mental+Health+Act%22+&sort=Most+recent&size=10&page=1#top, accessed 6 January 2017.

Compare with police detentions 2014–15 http://www.theguardian.com/society/2015/jun/08/police-detain-fewer-people-mental-illness, accessed 6 January 2017.

In 2005–6 the bulk of uses of section 136 were at police stations not hospitals, by 2014–15 whilst the overall numbers had increased (with 19,403 at hospitals alone) hospital detentions now significantly outnumber police detentions (for 2014–15: 4,537).

[10] https://www.england.nhs.uk/commissioning/health-just/liaison-and-diversion/ld-faqs/#cb, accessed 6 January 2017.

the best questions since the critical issue may concern why and in what ways particular symptoms or impairments could contribute to what are complex and multi-factorial causes of crime?

Whilst those with mental disabilities are over-represented in the statistics of imprisonment, that is not a basis for concluding that mental disorder causes crime, since the processes of selection and progressive disclosure of disability will account for a proportion of the disproportionality. The scope for selective inclusion of more visible offenders is obvious; combining notions of inept offending with the range of views held by the relevant 'gatekeepers' as to the needs of this problematic group will undoubtedly contribute to a highly skewed criminal justice 'output'. Earlier in the process it is difficult to disentangle the impact of various policies and diversion schemes; on the one hand they serve to filter offenders away from the formal process, while on the other hand the identification of mental disability can have a net-widening effect, whereby people with mental disability become caught up in the criminal justice system and criminalized where other individuals may be treated differently. The intersection of public order offences and mental disability is apposite.

It is, however, important to re-emphasize that surveys of the incidence of mental disability at the earliest stages will be an under-representation as the police, the CPS, and the courts are likely to identify only those with the most obvious symptomatology, while surveys of custodial populations are likely to be over-inclusive since they will count those whose disorders have been exacerbated, or brought about, by the process of prosecution and punishment. Indeed, a number of those in custody would not be sufficiently disordered to bring them within the ambit of the 1983 Act's requirements for compulsory admission. Similarly, any tendency to remand into custody to obtain psychiatric reports will contribute to this concentration effect. A tension between the desire to obtain treatment for the 'deserving' offender with a mental disability, and protective concerns where that desire may be frustrated, plays itself out amongst a shifting population.

The contribution that mental disorder makes to the totality of offending overall is difficult to quantify. Like juveniles, their offences are frequently highly visible, petty, and repeated; moreover, such offences are not dissimilar to those committed by the 'mentally ordered' (Amos *et al.* 2013). That is not to deny that for some people with mental disabilities their offences are violent; and in some cases homicidal. Yet, the best epidemiological evidence (Swanson *et al.* 1990), which comes from the United States, indicates that those individuals with major mental disorders account for only a modest proportion of the violence committed; in the US the figure is put at around 3 per cent (Monahan *et al.* 2001). Drugs and alcohol issues are much more prevalent precursors to violent crime. Other studies, for example in Sweden, have found not dissimilar low rates for the association between major mental illness and violence (Fazel and Grann 2006). Notably, even studies which report a stronger association between violent reoffending and diagnosed psychiatric disorders (see, e.g., Chang *et al.* 2015) identify drug and alcohol-use disorders as markedly most common. Indeed, the dramatically increased 'disorder' effect for violent reoffending in women (double that for men) is, of course, confined to the more limited incidence of female reoffending. In essence, what studies show is that most people with mental disabilities are not violent, and most violence is not committed by people with mental disabilities.

The majority of those who have offended with mental disabilities are to be found not on psychiatric wards but in local facilities supported by health, housing, and social services, or in prison. Properly resourcing these facilities could have a major preventive impact. It is paradoxical, therefore, as Burney and Pearson (1995: 309) observe, that 'a court appearance may be the only way that their needs will become apparent'. Yet, that very involvement with the criminal justice system may constitute the reason why community services are more problematic to access for these individuals.

Two other issues are important. First, the focus should be not on the relationship between offending and 'disorders' as diagnoses, but between particular symptoms and offending. Schizophrenia is a good example. The bald diagnosis itself is of little help in identifying those who might offend, but even if one descends to sub-classifications, for example, paranoid schizophrenia under the recognized International Classification of Diseases[11] the picture remains complex. One might presuppose false beliefs that someone is threatening you or hearing voices telling you to attack another (threat-control-override) might make you more likely to commit an assault, but the evidence is conflicted. In some cases there is a relationship, but in others the outcome may depend more on the nature of the threat, the gender of the person concerned, and/or whether negative symptomatology (more common in chronic stages of the condition) is dominant (Stompe *at al.* 2004; Swanson *et al.* 2006). Thus, in some cases, in some people, mental disability can make it less likely that a crime will be committed because of the social withdrawal and passivity associated with the particular stage of the condition. Acknowledging the importance of the role that symptoms play in the life of any potential individual has led researchers to conduct small-scale detailed studies involving individuals immediately after the alleged offending (Peterson *et al.* 2014; Junginger *et al.* 2006). These researchers have equally considered another question; namely, even if you have a mental disability is your offending necessarily linked to it? Both of these studies found only relatively small percentages of offending by those with mental disability related directly to their offending (between 8–17 per cent). In turn, this has supported Skeem and colleagues' (2011) argument that a more sophisticated approach is required to unpack the precursors of offending in those with mental disability. For some, the disability does appear to have a criminalizing effect; for others, it is more a question of a shared etiology between offending and mental disability. For the shared etiology group, mental disability plays little or no part and offending can be attributed to other common criminogenic factors. Finally, in some cases it is the response to disability—one of stigma, discrimination, and heightened fears—which is thought to lead to recidivism. Thus, Skeem and her colleagues call for a multi-disciplinary conceptual framework if recidivism is to be reduced in those with mental disability. Such a framework is equally important when thinking about the causes of crime in those with mental disabilities.

Once one starts to be alert to 'mental health' the variety of places and ways in which it manifests itself are legion. Thus, of young offenders in the 13–18 age group, 31 per cent were identified as having a mental health need (Harrington and Bailey 2005). The extensive criminal victimization of people with mental health

[11] ICD—10- CM Diagnosis Code F20.0, 2016; see http://www.icd10data.com/ICD10CM/Codes/F01-F99/F20-F29/F20-/F20.0, accessed 6 January 2017.

problems has been, until recently, an under-researched area.[12] Cape (2016), as part of his consideration of the abolition of police bail, has noted the stress of being on long-term police bail and its negative consequences for the mental health of formerly healthy individuals. Bean (2008) has questioned why it is that we understand that victims of crime can suffer from post-traumatic stress disorder, but we rarely consider how those witnessing the violence they themselves perpetrate can equally suffer traumatically afterwards? Such trauma can be guilt induced or, as is more often in, for example, the case of military veterans, attributable to the sights seen and the acts done. The relationship between cannabis use, still formally a criminal offence, and the development of psychosis, remains controversial. Vulnerable individuals and young people are particularly at psychiatric risk from some forms of cannabis use.[13]

The intricacies of the relationship between the mind, and the experiences people have, are beyond this chapter's remit; it is simply worth observing two matters. First, the links between mental disability and crime, whether violent or not, are extraordinarily complex. And hence the interventions that might successfully follow are not self-evident. Secondly, being able to benefit from psychological therapy does not necessarily imply that an individual is suffering from a mental disability that requires compulsory psychiatric intervention.[14] But some are: and considering where and in what ways treatment for offenders might be appropriate forms the next section.

OFFENDING BEHAVIOUR AND TREATMENT

Identifying the right place to deal with people who have offended who also have mental disabilities is both hard and easy. Easy because with the levels of disability amongst the offending population, and with our very narrow mental condition defences (Law Commission 2013), most of those with such disabilities will inevitably be dealt with in the penal system rather than the health system. There simply are not enough beds, enough resources or enough enthusiasm within the health system to take all those who might benefit from a health disposal. Prisons have to cope through a combination of the mental health in-reach services, the principle of equivalence (namely, that primary care services should be as good in prison as in the community), and, as a last resort, the possibility of transfer to hospital for individuals who meet the necessary criteria under the MHA 1983 (Department of Health *et al.* 2001). For some individuals, for whom compulsory treatment is deemed necessary at the point of sentence/disposal, hospital is the only viable option since it is only under section in hospital that treatment can be

[12] See the Report by Victim Support and the Institute of Psychiatry at King's College, 'At risk, yet dismissed', https://www.mind.org.uk/media/187663/At-risk-yet-dismissed-report_FINAL_EMBARGOED.pdf, accessed 9 January 2017.

[13] http://www.rcpsych.ac.uk/healthadvice/problemsdisorders/cannabis.aspx, accessed 6 January 2017.

[14] See, for example, those who have experienced female genital mutilation.

given compulsorily for mental illness, victimization by other prisoners avoided, and violent or self-harming behaviour adequately monitored and controlled.[15]

On the other hand, the question of identification is hard since, if the penal system is the default option, it is an option that is peculiarly ill-suited to offering effective therapeutic interventions. As the Home Office recognized as long ago as 1990, 'For most offenders, imprisonment has to be justified in terms of public protection, denunciation and retribution. Otherwise it can be an expensive way of making bad people worse' (para. 2.7). Custodial environments are noisy, stressful, overcrowded, frightening to many, and ill-equipped to manage genuine rehabilitative change, whilst community orders have become progressively punitive in their impact under the agendas of successive governments.[16]

It is never, of course, clear when dealing with offenders with disability quite what is meant by treatment, or what treatment is attempting to alter—the 'underlying disorder', the offending behaviour, or the link, if any, between the two? Or are these efforts really devoted largely to alleviating the distress and emotional problems individuals suffer, either those pre-existing or post-dating the offending? If it is the likelihood of criminal behaviour *per se*, the justification for treatment will not be confined to a 'mentally disordered' subgroup. These quandaries have not deterred the development of a number of rehabilitative programmes in prison.

The 'What Works' initiative (Home Office 2001) has had a significant impact on the philosophy of imprisonment, with the focus being largely on treating offending, rather than mental disorder *per se*. Cognitive behavioural programmes for sex offenders, offence-focused problem-solving (e.g. the 'Think First' programme), substance-abuse treatment programmes, controlling and managing anger (CALM), and cognitive self-change programmes for violent offenders, capture the flavour of these initiatives.

However, the extent to which treatment endeavours can be both sustained and effective remains questionable. Achieving effectiveness will be jeopardized by three enduring factors: prison overcrowding, the use of short sentences (both of which can disrupt programme completion), and the need to obtain genuine engagement in the programmes by prisoners. Such consent has come to be recognized as critical to the success of treatment endeavours with some offenders (Zlodre *et al.* 2015). Involuntary treatments can have no effect at all, or indeed, be detrimental (Martin *et al.* 2012). Finally, if sentencers believe that imprisonment will secure access to beneficial treatment programmes for persistent offenders, 'ordered' offenders may find themselves at as great a risk as disordered offenders of therapeutic sentencing, further accelerating the problem of overwhelming demand.

Emphasis is also shifting onto the importance of resettlement and providing through-care from prisons into the community. Yet, as Grant (1999) observed, this 'through-care' has had a worryingly narrow focus on crime reduction where multi-agency working has had as its objective pragmatic restraint rather than treatment *per*

[15] The UK was found to have violated Art. 2 of the ECHR—the right to life—following the killing of one mentally disordered man by another; both had been on remand and held in the same cell in Chelmsford Prison: *Paul and Audrey Edwards v The UK* (2002) Application No. 46477/99.

[16] See, most recently, Schedule 16 to the Crime and Courts Act 2013 which has required courts, unless it would be unjust to do so, to include a punitive element in all non-custodial orders.

se. He argues that it is no easy task to support the health needs of less serious offenders while managing the risk they pose and the fear they engender. The shift from broadly-based rehabilitation to offence-specific crime reduction initiatives has also had an impact on Grendon Prison.[17] Genders and Player (1995, 2010) admirably detail the way in which Grendon's therapeutic endeavours and security considerations are difficult to reconcile. Yet Grendon's record of success in *controlling* problematic prisoners is notable. Perhaps, as Genders and Player (1995) point out, the knowledge by all concerned that the rest of the prison system provides a very different form of containment may have a positive effect on prisoner behaviour.

Grendon notably takes prisoners on the personality disorder end of the spectrum of disability, rather than those with mental illness *per se*. Somewhat curiously it was not one of the designated prisons for taking offenders under the DSPD programme. But this might be because its 'voluntary' ethos was at odds with some of the more explicitly coercive objectives of the DSPD programme. A generous interpretation of the history of the DSPD initiative would suggest that it was prompted as much by a concern for the unmet needs of these diverse and un-enticing individuals as it did from a concern about their risk to others (Home Office 1999; Department of Health/Home Office 2000). As the Home Office observed, they have

> high rates of depression, anxiety, illiteracy, poor relationships and loss of family ties, homelessness and unemployment. They have high rates of suicide and high rates of death by violent means. They have high rates of substance misuse. Their behaviour is often violent. Their behaviour is of immense distress to themselves and they are frequently in the position where they are asking for help and yet finding it very difficult to access suitable help. (1999: 34)

There is, thus, considerable conflict in the objectives that policy is attempting to pursue with respect to personality disordered offenders (O'Loughlin 2014). Psychiatrists find themselves in a dilemma, being understandably wary of having to 'treat' 'personality disordered' offenders, where successful interventions are yet to be reliably established, whilst clinicians are painfully aware of the needs of such individuals and their levels of distress. Moreover, 'treatment' is arguably offered by the medical profession as a response to illness—something atypical and unwelcome for an individual. Personality disorder has rather been characterized as something integral to an individual—normal for them—and hence conventional 'treatment' approaches sit oddly when considering interventions with such individuals. Psychologists have entered this morass, but even their enthusiasm may wane if the treatment is primarily containment and control; paradoxically professionals are criticized both for a failure to offer treatment to those they regard as untreatable, and for releasing those they deem successfully treated.

Over the last 15 years, the DSPD programme has become a prime focus for service development and legislative provision with the more inclusionary definition of mental disorder adopted under the amended MHA 1983. Originally, DSPD individuals were thought to number some 2,400 men and facilities were developed in both prisons and high security hospitals, albeit the maximum number in the programmes fell significantly short of this figure. In the event the hospital-based programmes proved

[17] Grendon is a secure psychiatric facility within HM Prison Service which accepts prisoners on longer-term sentences who have volunteered to enter its therapeutic community approach.

resource-costly, with the result that the focus shifted to the prison-based programmes; indeed, the Broadmoor facility was closed[18] (O'Loughlin 2014; McRae 2015). To what extent this reveals an emphasis on containment rather than treatment, or else the tacit recognition that treatment may not be successful, is unclear. *Breaking the Cycle* (Ministry of Justice 2010: 37) envisaged an expansion of the programme, and this is now represented by the Offender Personality Disorder Pathway (OPDP), which expands the nature of the offenders included and extends the pathway into community settings. The ambitious nature of this programme should not be underestimated: some 8,007 men in custody and 7,795 men on community orders or on licence are estimated likely to pass the harm-screening test and satisfy at least one of the other five screening criteria; for women the respective figures are 655 and 2,749.[19]

On the basis of the DSPD programme, policy-makers would be well-advised to be extremely cautious. For that programme, research was initiated, but legislation proceeded without any positive findings. DSPD was not an evidence-based initiative; indeed, it had quickly transformed into a pilot. In any event, how could it have been evidence-led? There was no agreed clinical diagnosis and offenders were admitted who fell outside the specific programme criteria, there was no agreed treatment, no means of confidently assessing when the predicted risk may have been reduced, and no obvious link between the alleged underlying condition and the behaviour. In this context could outcomes be agreed upon and evaluated? The 'pilot' programme had initially recruited volunteers and had controversial results (Tyrer *et al.* 2010); yet, the legislation enacted provided the basis for compulsory transfer and treatment within the hospital system. Testing the latter by the former seemed ill-advised.

At this stage in a national evaluation of OPDP, which only commenced in August 2014, it is perhaps unedifying to describe those engaging in it as falling foul of the Pollyanna principle—namely, a subconscious bias towards the positive. But all of the problems of consent for the hospital-based offenders, and of coercion—explicit or implied—amongst the penal group, may dumbfound its enthusiasts if these problems are not properly addressed.

Thus, treatment issues embody a number of difficulties. First, given the diversity of need, 'treatment' may mean many different things—ranging from the administration of anti-psychotic medication to the acquisition of social survival skills. There may be a mismatch between health and criminal justice personnel in respect of the objectives of treatment. Secondly, if the relationship between the disorder and the offending behaviour is not primarily causal, there is less justification for excusing from punishment, and offenders should remain entitled to protection of their rights as offenders while not being denied access to voluntary treatment. However, if punishment is merited, assessing the degree of culpability in offenders with mental disabilities is more challenging than for those without disabilities, and considering the punitive–therapeutic balance more critical. Thirdly, it is important to recognize that if the individual is found not to be legally responsible for the offending, on grounds of mental disability, then there can be no punishment, only a health-based disposal. Fourthly, where an individual

[18] Albeit all three High Secure Hospitals and a number of medium secure units are now involved in OPDP.

[19] https://www.gov.uk/government/uploads/system/uploads/attachment_data/file/418307/OPD_seminar_pres_Mar_2015.pdf, accessed 6 January 2017.

is treatable and there is some causal connection between the disorder and his or her offending behaviour, there may be less (or no) justification for continued detention after treatment. Fifthly, successful treatment for a disability may have no bearing on future criminality; offenders with mental disabilities should be accorded proportionality in the length of confinement as would offenders without disabilities; release should not be determined on the basis of unreliable predictions of future offending. And finally, the choice between jurisprudential logic, which may sanction punishment for the 'culpable' disabled offender, and decades of a humanitarian response endorsing a common-sense preference for treatment rather than punishment, should perhaps focus rather on facilitating genuinely capacitous engagement with treatment in both contexts. Explicit coercion should only be used for those who do not have the capacity to consent. The need is urgent to enhance the custodial-therapeutic environment to facilitate whatever rehabilitation may be possible on a non-coerced basis. Clearly, if the numerical bulk of disorder-related offending is associated with alcohol and drug use, and/or disorders of personality, then a psychiatric hospital is probably not the best venue for 'treatment'.

PROTECTIVE SENTENCING: PROCEDURAL SAFEGUARDS VERSUS TREATMENT

Reform in the area of the trial of those with mental disorder has been devoted primarily to increasing the court's sentencing options and not to addressing issues of culpability, albeit the Law Commission (2016a, 2016b) has substantial proposals for the reform of the law of unfitness to plead and has considered insanity and automatism (Law Commission 2013). If implemented the proposals on unfitness will have a significant impact on the fairness of trials for people with disabilities, and will address a number of areas where our current law on unfitness is in conflict with our human rights obligations under the European Convention on Human Rights (ECHR) (Peay 2016a).

The bulk of individuals sentenced with mental disability gain little mitigating effect from their disabilities. The Sentencing Guidelines Council did identify 'mental illness or disability' as one of the four factors that may 'significantly lower culpability' when the seriousness of an offence is assessed (Sentencing Guidelines Council 2004: para. 1.25). Moreover, recent offence-specific guidelines, see, for example, the Definitive Guideline on Theft Offences, have specified that a medical condition can make a community order with a mental health treatment requirement a proper alternative to a moderate custodial sentence.[20] In general though, the presence of mental disorder can still lead to disproportionately long sentences where paternalistic assumptions about the 'mental disorder' element, and protective-predictive ones about the offending element, leave prisoner-patients with more than their 'just' deserts. This may arise from

[20] See p. 6 of https://www.sentencingcouncil.org.uk/wp-content/uploads/SC-Theft-Offences-Definitive-Guideline-content_FINAL-web_.pdf, accessed 6 January 2017.

either a shift in the community/custody threshold, or from the use of longer determinate sentences or more frequent use of indeterminate sentences by courts when sentencing those with mental disabilities. Notably, those serving indefinite sentences have higher rates of self-harm than those on life sentences.[21]

It is also worth reiterating that, like all offenders, the vast majority of those with mental disorder are not dangerous. However, some are. Arguments favouring limited special measures have their attractions, if only to deal with that small but worrying group; but their *quid pro quo* is that the preventive rationale should be tempered by procedural safeguards. Similarly, arguments for bifurcation are inherently appealing, where diversion into humanitarian care protects offenders from damaging penal sentences. Yet the implications of these two propositions under our existing arrangements are that the route into confinement—prison or hospital—will affect both the route out, and whether and what treatment will be given.

Concepts of dangerousness and its alleged association with mental disorder pepper the academic literature and the rhetoric of sentencing. Academics and policy-makers have been fiercely divided both on predictive grounds—will it work?—and on questions of rights. The argument embodies the distinction between statistical and legal-clinical decision-making, crudely put, the difference between risk factors associated with groups of people who have common characteristics (much of the risk-prediction literature is of this nature), and the determination of whether any one individual within that group will be amongst those where risk is realized (Buchanan and Zonana 2009). These kinds of difficult decisions are faced regularly by courts, Mental Health Tribunals (MHTs), discretionary lifer panels, the Parole Board, clinicians, and the executive (see, e.g., Boyd-Caine 2010). The findings of research concerning such decision-making bodies are consistent: despite actuarial evidence that would support the release of patients and prisoners, attributions of risk are central, overvalued, and very difficult to refute (Trebilcock and Weaver 2012).

Should offenders be entitled to a proportional measure of punishment? Walker (1996: 7) argues that there may be no such 'right' where individuals have forfeited the presumption of being harmless because they have *previously* attempted or caused harm to others. But how is precautionary sentencing to be limited? And are mentally disordered offenders at greater risk of imposition of such a sentence? These and other issues concerning the use of preventive justice have been extensively reviewed by Ashworth and Zedner (2014), but their analysis of the issues around public health law and issues of liberty as they affect those with mental disabilities is particularly telling.

Dworkin (1977) described the restraint and treatment of the 'dangerously insane' as an insult to their rights to dignity and liberty—an infringement that could be justified not where crime reduction might result, but only where the danger posed was 'vivid'. Bottoms and Brownsword (1983: 21) unpacked this concept into its elements of seriousness, temporality (that is frequency and immediacy), and certainty. Certainty was pivotal to precautionary sentencing, but even a high probability of future offending should become relevant only if the behaviour anticipated involved causing or attempting 'very serious violence'. Thus, the right to a proportional measure of punishment

[21] http://gu.com/p/4mh65/sbl, accessed 6 January 2017.

would yield a '*prima facie* right to release for the prisoner at the end of his normal term', and this would apply—in the absence of 'vivid danger'—equally to the alleged 'dangerous offender'. But at this point theory and practice diverge.

The passage of the Criminal Justice Act 2003 with its smorgasbord of objectives (crime reduction, risk management, reparation, deterrence, rehabilitation, and deserved punishment) places those with mental disabilities in triple, if not quadruple, jeopardy. Treatment for their underlying disorders, attempts to reduce independently their potential for crime through measures to change their thinking strategies, and a deterrence philosophy which may impact even less successfully on some offenders with mental disabilities, are all likely to contribute to a greater than proportionate use of incapacitation for those where offending occurs in the context of mental disability.

Under the Criminal Justice Act 2003 community sentences with a mental health treatment requirement have been little used.[22] The 2015 figures show that such orders, whether attached to community orders or suspended sentence orders, continue to make up less than 1 per cent of the orders made by the courts.[23] Whilst this is, in part, attributable to the problem of finding a willing practitioner and a consenting patient it does indicate an abject failure to address the level of need in the less serious offending population. At the other end of the spectrum, the introduction of life sentences under section 225(1)(b), where the court is of the opinion that there is 'significant risk to members of the public of serious harm occasioned by the commission . . . of further specified offences', has drawn more mentally disordered offenders into the net of indeterminacy. Notably, section 225 does not prevent the courts from making a hospital order with restrictions, where an individual satisfies the necessary conditions under the 1983 Act; indeed, only the mandatory life sentence following a conviction for murder has the capacity to trump a potential therapeutic disposal. However, in general, protective confinement is self-justifying and difficult to resist. Finally, it is of concern that the Court of Appeal, in the case of *Vowles*,[24] has recently opined that even in cases where an individual's offending is accounted for by his or her disorder, so that culpability may be of the most tenuous, a mixed punitive-therapeutic order under section 45A of the MHA 1983 is to be preferred to the therapeutic disposal under section 37/41 of the same Act (Peay 2016b). The former order allows for Parole Board release, which can entail subsequent recall in the light of the individual's risk increasing. Conditional discharge following a section 37/41 order requires, for recall, deterioration in the individual's mental health and is deemed by the court to be less flexible. Indeed, the Court of Appeal in *Vowles* even went so far as to discourage the costly use (costly to court resources) of interim hospital orders,[25] designed to ensure that only those offender-patients suited to hospital should be sent there under the MHA 1983.

[22] See Table 5 and accompanying text, https://www.gov.uk/government/uploads/system/uploads/attachment_data/file/426676/Supporting_CO_Treatment_Reqs.pdf, accessed 6 January 2017.

[23] https://www.gov.uk/government/statistics/offender-management-statistics-quarterly-july-to-september-2015, accessed 6 January 2017.

[24] [2015] EWCA Crim 45.

[25] Section 38 MHA 1983.

POLICY DEVELOPMENT IN ENGLAND AND WALES: WHY WE ARE WHERE WE ARE

Policy development in mental health and crime has been chequered. Therapeutic and risk-oriented objectives have become progressively blurred (Rutherford 2010); a conflict between legalism and welfarism is evident; and there has been a growing role for human rights developments. At face value the dominant policy is humane and therapeutic: Home Office Circular 66/90, which formally encouraged from 1990 onwards the placement of mentally disordered offenders, wherever possible, into the care of health and personal social services, received considerable support from both the recommendations of the Bradley Review (2009) and the Ministry of Justice (2010). However, these 'rehabilitative revolutions' are invariably accompanied by riders which stress the need properly to protect the public; such a nuanced approach is captured in *Breaking the Cycle:*

> We will work with the Department of Health to divert more of the less serious offenders with mental illness and drug dependency into treatment rather than prison, as long as the safety of the public is not compromised. (Ministry of Justice 2010: 2)

Perceptions and attributions of risk have had a great influence on policy development (Ashworth and Zedner 2014; Seddon 2008). Those who have offended who have a mental disability are most 'at risk' of being perceived as posing an unquantifiable danger, and thus, peculiarly apt for the ubiquitous focus on risk management. As risk is transposed into danger, dangerous individuals are singled out for special attention, and the responsibility for preventing and managing risk is transferred to those professionals dealing with or caring for them (Douglas 1992).

Evidence of this duality in policy can be seen in the development of the DSPD programme (Home Office 1999) and its wider successor, the OPDP (O'Loughlin 2014; McRae 2015). Even if these programmes were started with beneficent aims, acknowledging the neediness and vulnerability of some personality disordered offenders, their impact has been to delay release from confinement and extend control out into the community. Moreover, the introduction in 2001 of IPPs (indeterminate sentences for public protection—now abolished—Annison 2015) and the Multi-Agency Public Protection Arrangements (MAPPA), both of which drew in those with mental disabilities, had clearly protective ambitions.

MAPPA is worth considering in some detail since it encapsulates some of the difficulties of clinical professionals working alongside criminal justice personnel. The annual reports for MAPPA (Ministry of Justice 2015) detail the scheme, but in essence they are designed to ensure the identification of serious sexual and violent offenders in the community, the sharing of information among those agencies involved in the assessment of the risk, and the management of that risk as individuals move from conditions of security into the community. MAPPA embrace both registered sex offenders, violent and other sex offenders, either sentenced or disposed of as mentally disordered offenders, and some other offenders whom it is thought may cause serious harm to the public. On 31 March 2015, there were 68,214 MAPPA eligible individuals: 72 per cent were registered sex offenders[26] and 26 per cent were categorized as violent offenders (which included those on hospital orders and some sex offenders not eligible for notification requirements). The overwhelming majority in these categories were subject only to ordinary agency management (Ministry of Justice 2015). However, 1,573 individuals were 'actively managed' as they fell into the two highest risk levels.[27] Over the course of the year 2014–15, 6,506 individuals were MAPPA eligible for management at this level and 10.5 per cent were returned to custody for a breach of licence.[28] Psychiatrists are involved with these two risk categories and, since the passage of the Criminal Justice Act 2003, the various agencies, including Health Trusts, have a duty placed on them to cooperate with the responsible authority in each of the 42 MAPPA areas. Yet a psychiatrist's primary responsibility is to the health of their patients; and psychiatrists, like other health professionals, have a duty of confidentiality towards those patients, a duty that does not sit easily with the concepts of information sharing embraced by MAPPA. The tensions are evident, and as Taylor and Yakeley observe (2013: 12) in respect of information sharing 'a blurring of professional boundaries may occur at MAPPA meetings, where less experienced health representatives may be unprepared for the—often subtle—pressures placed upon them to disclose information about patients known to them'. Notably, this Royal College of Psychiatrists' Faculty Report stresses the advantages of obtaining patient consent to disclosure as a way of overcoming some of these confidentiality issues. Where it cannot be obtained disclosure is only justifiable, in the public interest, to prevent a serious and imminent threat to life of the individual or a third party or to prevent or detect serious crime.

The policy context clearly embodies both positive and negative messages. On the one hand, calls for diverting those with mental disabilities from the damaging effects of the criminal justice system are longstanding (Bradley 2009).[29] Notions of early intervention are also consistent with a philosophy that 'treatment works'; people can be changed, diverted, or protected from inappropriate or damaging experiences. Yet on the negative side, there appears to be a persistent distrust of therapeutic disposals for some offenders with mental disability.

Much of the confusion arises because of the tensions inherent across the continuum both of ordered–disordered behaviour and that of law-abiding–law-breaking behaviour. Notions of care and treatment are seen as appropriate for the seriously disordered, provided this does not arise in conjunction with offending of a worrying nature. Similarly, notions of protection and custodial punishment have been traditionally reserved for serious offenders, again assuming an absence of obvious disorder. Yet these tensions are confounded where it is argued that disorder and offending exist

[26] Registered sex offenders subject to notification requirements for life are now eligible for review of this requirement following a declaration of incompatibility by the Supreme Court under section 4 of the Human Rights Act 1998: see *R (on the application of F and Angus Aubrey Thompson) v Secretary of State for the Home Department* [2010] UKSC 17.

[27] See Table 1, which relates only to offenders managed on 31 March 2015. This figure notably includes all 255 in the 'other dangerous offenders' category, at: https://www.gov.uk/government/uploads/system/uploads/attachment_data/file/471408/mappa-annual-report-2014-15.pdf, accessed 6 January 2017.

[28] See ibid., Table 7a.

[29] See also the thoughtful report from Criminal Justice Joint Inspection, available at, https://www.justiceinspectorates.gov.uk/cjji/wp-content/uploads/sites/2/2014/04/MDO_Joint_Report_12_2009.pdf, accessed 6 January 2017.

side-by-side in one individual, or, more confusingly still, interact. Of course, part of the difficulty arises from the perception of those with mental disabilities who have offended as being in thrall to their disorders. The notorious Inquiries after Homicide fell into this trap (Peay 1996), notorious because they made an independent Inquiry mandatory wherever a homicide was perpetrated by an individual who had been in contact with mental health services in the previous year, regardless of the links between disability and the death. In turn, mental health practitioners became the focus for blame. As Szmukler (2000:7) observes:

> Inquiries . . . adopt a model of responsibility that is grossly oversimplified and distorted by retrospective analysis. The offender patient is seen as lacking agency, behaving as an automaton, like an aeroplane out of control. The patient is no longer a person with feelings, hopes, intentions or with the capacity for choice.

The resulting amplification of discriminatory practices for such individuals has led in part to calls for capacity-based legislation to apply to both mentally ordered and mentally disordered offenders (Szmukler *et al.* 2010).

The MHA 1983 is the key statutory provision dealing with those with mental disabilities; Part III deals with those involved with the criminal justice system. The Act continues uneasily to embrace both legalism and welfarism. Its emphasis on treating people for who they are has also sat uncomfortably alongside a criminal justice approach which has traditionally emphasized what people have done as the basis for a proportionate intervention. It is therefore notable that the Criminal Justice Act 2003 has the reform and rehabilitation of offenders as one of its five purposes of sentencing (section 142(1)), albeit that offenders disposed of under the MHA 1983 are explicitly exempted from all five purposes (see section 142(2)(d)). An awkward fusion is evident between mental health and criminal justice objectives, with both sets of professionals now being expected to engage in the potentially competing tasks of reformation and risk management. Arguably, this fusion of objectives favours risk management even in those cases where individuals are sufficiently disordered to be detainable under the MHA 1983 (see Peay 2016b).

Finally, the impact of the Human Rights Act 1998 is relevant. The ECHR has had a powerful influence on the relationship between the executive and the continuing detention of those with psychiatric disorders; an influence which has generally permeated discretionary decision-making (Peay 2016a). Yet, the ECHR is not a document that naturally lends itself to the protection of those with mental disorders because it explicitly permits the detention of those of 'unsound mind'. Nonetheless, the first declaration of incompatibility under the Human Rights Act occurred in a case concerning an offender-patient detained in a psychiatric hospital.[30] Perhaps this is mere coincidence. But perhaps it reflects the presence of conflicting tensions permeating the practices of all who work in this field, whether they are based in the police station or at the Court of Appeal (Eastman and Peay 1999).

In short, policy development has been much influenced by a subjective approach to the framing of mental disability and crime: achieving an approach grounded in objective facts has proved elusive. Again, this is unsurprising where disability has been so

[30] *R (on the application of H) v Mental Health Review Tribunal* [2001] 3 WLR 512.

broadly defined and objectivity itself is inherently vulnerable to a subjective filtering of fears and fancies.

CONCLUSION

If the basic premise of this chapter is accepted—namely, that individuals with disabilities who have offended are not, and should not be, treated as an isolated category—the conclusions that follow are of broader significance.

First, effort should be devoted to developing a pluralistic model of the criminal justice system. Piecemeal tinkering may provide solutions for the problems posed by specific offenders; it is insufficient as a basis for addressing problems across the ordered–disordered offending continuum. Equally, the temptation to solve problems by addressing only the back end of the process (namely, sentencing and disposal issues) distracts attention from the urgent need for the prior issues of culpability to be resolved on a fairer basis than is currently achieved.

Secondly, the impossibility of identifying such individuals consistently makes a 'diversion and transfer' solution unrealistic. Resource allocation needs to be across the board and not only in respect of a limited number of beds for potentially difficult offender-patients. Moreover, as Watson and Grounds (1993) observed, greater liaison combined with overcoming the boundaries between different parts of the criminal justice and health agencies will be insufficient all the time there is a discrepancy in expectations between agencies of who satisfies the category of 'mentally disordered offender'.

Thirdly, treatment in prison, and in community settings, needs to be properly resourced. The problem here is the use of overt compulsion. Thus, the circumstances in which treatment will be offered, to whom, and what the consequences will be where it is deemed unwelcome, unsuccessful, or inappropriate needs more careful reflection. A pluralistic model would require the same limitations on intervention for all offenders, assuming they have the capacity to consent to treatment or undergo punishment. While adoption of a proportionality-based approach would constitute a sounder foundation for greater fairness between offenders, the risk-based/treatment approach looks set to dominate the field. In turn, the problematic aspects of multi-agency working need clarifying so that all are familiar with the limited circumstances in which confidential 'health' information can be shared in the absence of consent.

Lastly, the justifications are many for singling out subsections of 'disabled offenders' for special treatment. But if one lesson emerges from an understanding of the relationship between mental health and crime it is that people are not their diagnoses. A much more sophisticated and holistic understanding is required. Special treatment can all too readily become special control; and to be seduced by the notion that risk can be managed through the containment of identifiable individuals is to allow discriminatory treatment for that group, while failing to tackle the roots of the problem.

SELECTED FURTHER READING

For those wanting a clear and short introduction to the relevant sections of the MHA 1983 relating to remand and sentence, see the Ministry of Justice's guidance, available at: https://www.justice.gov.uk/downloads/offenders/mentally-disordered-offenders/guidance-for-the-courts-mha.pdf (2008).

For a more whimsical introduction to clinical criminology, see Prins' *Offenders, Deviants or Patients? An Introduction to Clinical Criminology* (2016). The fifth edition of this book draws together Herschel Prins' unique experiences as a probation officer, psychiatric social worker, academic, and member of the Parole Board.

On the problematic relationship between mental disorder and crime, see Peay's *Mental Health and Crime* (2011b), ch. 4 and Bean's *Madness and Crime* (2008), Part 4 for fuller accounts than space permits here.

REFERENCES

Amos, T., Gordon, H., Gunn, J., Peay, J., and Walker, J. (2013), 'The majority of crime: theft, motoring and criminal damage (including arson)', in J. Gunn and P. Taylor (eds), *Forensic Psychiatry: Clinical Legal and Ethical Issues*, 2nd edn, London: Hodder Arnold Education.

Annison, H. (2015), *Dangerous Politics: Risk, Political Vulnerability and Penal Policy*, Oxford: Clarendon Press.

Appleby, L., Kapur, N., Shaw, J., Windfuhr, K., Hunt, I., Flynn, S., While, D., Roscoe, A., Rodway, C., Ibrahim, S., and Tham, S. (2015), *The National Confidential Inquiry into Suicide and Homicide by People with Mental Illness Annual Report 2015: England, Northern Ireland, Scotland and Wales*, July 2015, Manchester: University of Manchester.

Ashworth, A. and Zedner, L. (2014), *Preventive Justice*, Oxford: Oxford University Press.

Bean, P. (2008), *Madness and Crime*, Cullompton: Willan.

Bottoms, A. and Brownsword, R. (1983), 'Dangerousness and Rights', in J. W. Hinton (ed.), *Dangerousness: Problems of Assessment and Prediction*, London: Allen and Unwin.

Boyd-Caine, T. (2010), *Protecting the Public? Executive Discretion in the Release of Mentally Disordered Offenders*, Cullompton: Willan.

Bradley, Lord Keith (2009), *Lord Bradley's review of people with mental health problems or learning disabilities in the criminal justice system*, London: Department of Health, COI 2009.

Buchanan A. and Zonana H. (2009), 'Mental disorder as the cause of a crime', *International Journal of Law and Psychiatry*, 32(3): 142–6.

Burney, E. and Pearson, G. (1995), 'Mentally Disordered Offenders: Finding a Focus for Diversion', *The Howard Journal*, 34(4): 291–313.

Cape, E. (2016), *What if police bail were abolished?*, London: The Howard League for Penal Reform, available at: http://howardleague.org/publications/what-if-police-bail-was-abolished/, accessed 9 January 2017.

Chang, Z., Larsson H., Lichtenstein, P., and Fazel, S. (2015), 'Psychiatric disorders and violent reoffending: a national cohort study of convicted prisoners in Sweden', *The Lancet Psychiatry*, 2(10): 891–900.

Crichton, J. (2011), 'A review of published independent inquiries in England into psychiatric patient homicide 1995-2010', *Journal of Forensic Psychiatry and Psychology*, 22(6): 761–89.

Criminal Justice Joint Inspection (2009), *A joint inspection on work prior to sentence with offenders with mental disorders*, HMI Probation, HMI Court Administration, HMI Constabulary, and HM Crown Prosecution Service Inspectorate, available at: http://www.ohrn.nhs.uk/resource/policy/jointinspectionMDO.pdf, accessed 9 January 2017.

Dehaghani, R. (2016), 'He's just not that vulnerable: Exploring the implementation of the appropriate adult safeguard in police custody', *The Howard Journal of Crime and Justice*, 55(4): 396–413.

Department Of Health, Hm Prison Service, and National Assembly For Wales (2001), *Changing the Outlook: A Strategy for Developing and Modernising Mental Health Services in Prisons*, London: Department of Health.

Department of Health and Home Office (2000), *Reforming the Mental Health Act: Part II High Risk Patients*, Cm 5016-II, London: The Stationery Office.

Department of Health and Home Office (2014), *Review of the Operation of Sections 135 and 136 of the Mental Health Act 1983, Review Report and Recommendations*, available at: https://www.gov.uk/government/uploads/system/uploads/attachment_data/file/389202/S135_and_S136_of_the_Mental_Health_Act_-_full_outcome.pdf, accessed 6 January 2017.

Docking, M., Grace, K., and Bucke, T. (2007), 'Police Custody as a "Place of Safety": examining the use of section 136 of the Mental Health Act 1983',

Independent Police Complaints Commission, Research and Statistics Series: Paper 11.

DOUGLAS, M. (1992), *Risk and Blame: Essays in Cultural Theory*, London: Routledge.

DWORKIN, R. (1977), *Taking Rights Seriously*, London: Duckworth.

DYER, W. (2013), 'Criminal Justice Diversion and Liaison Services: A Path to Success?', *Social Policy and Society*, 12(1): 31–45.

EASTMAN, N. and CAMPBELL, C. (2006), 'Neuroscience and legal determination of criminal responsibility', *Nature Reviews Neuroscience*, 7(4): 311–18.

EASTMAN, N. and PEAY, J. (eds) (1999), *Law Without Enforcement: Integrating Mental Health and Justice*, Oxford: Hart.

FAZEL, S. and DANESH, J. (2002), 'Serious mental disorder in 23,000 prisoners. A systematic review of 62 surveys', *Lancet*, 359: 545–50.

FAZEL, S. and GRANN, M. (2006) 'The Population Impact of Severe Mental Illness on Violent Crime', *American Journal of Psychiatry*, 163(8): 1397–403.

FENNELL, P. (2001), 'Reforming the Mental Health Act 1983: "Joined Up Compulsion" ', *Journal of Mental Health Law*, 5–20.

GENDERS, E. and PLAYER, E. (1995), *Grendon: A Study of a Therapeutic Prison*, Oxford: Clarendon Press.

GENDERS, E. and PLAYER, E. (2010), 'Grendon: Ten Years On', *Howard Journal*, 49(5): 431–50.

GILMAN, S. (1988), *Disease and Representation. From Madness to AIDS*, Ithaca, NY: Cornell University Press.

GRANT, D. (1999), 'Multi-agency risk management of mentally disordered sex offenders: a probation case study', in D. Webb and R. Harris (eds), *Managing People Nobody Owns*, London: Routledge.

GUNN, J., DELL, S., and WAY, C. (1978), *Psychiatric Aspects of Imprisonment*, London: Academic Press.

HALE, B. (2010), *Mental Health Law*, 5th edn, London: Sweet & Maxwell.

HARE, R. (1991), *The Hare Psychopathy Checklist—Revised*, Toronto: Multi-Health Systems.

HARRINGTON, R. and BAILEY, S. (2005), *Mental Health Needs and Effectiveness of Provision for Young Offenders in Custody and in the Community*, Youth Justice Board for England and Wales.

HMIC (2013), *A Criminal Use of Police Cells? The use of police custody as a place of safety for people with mental health needs*, London: HMIC.

HOME OFFICE (1991), *Custody, Care and Justice*, London: HMSO.

HOME OFFICE (1999), *Managing Dangerous People with Severe Personality Disorder. Proposals for Policy Development*, London: Home Office.

HOME OFFICE (2001), *What Works: Second Report of the Joint Prison/Probation Service Accreditation Panel*, London: Home Office.

HOME OFFICE (2014), *Revised Code of Practice for the Detention, Treatment and Questioning of Persons by Police Officers Police and Criminal Evidence Act 1984 (PACE)—Code C*, London: The Stationery Office.

JAMES, D., FARNHAM, F., MOOREY, H., LLOYD, H., BLIZARD, R., and BARNES, T. (2002), *Outcome of Psychiatric Admission Through the Courts*, London: Home Office, RDS Occasional Paper No. 79.

JOHNS, L., CANNON, M., SINGLETON, N., MURRAY, R., FARRELL, M., BRUGHA, T., BEBBINGTON, P., JENKINS, R., and MELTZER, H. (2004), 'Prevalence and correlates of self-reported psychotic symptoms in the British population', *The British Journal of Psychiatry*, 185(4): 298–305.

JUNGINGER, J., CLAYPOOLE, K., LAYGO, R., and CRISTIANI, A. (2006), 'Effects of serious mental illness and substance use on criminal offence', *Psychiatric Services*, 57(6): 879–82

LAW COMMISSION (2013), 'Criminal Liability: Insanity and Automatism. A Discussion Paper', available at: http://www.lawcom.gov.uk/wp-, content/uploads/2015/06/insanity_discussion.pdf, accessed 6 January 2017.

LAW COMMISSION (2016a), 'Unfitness to Plead Report, Volume 1: Report', available at: http://www.lawcom.gov.uk/wp-content/uploads/2016/01/lc364_unfitness_vol-1.pdf, accessed 6 January 2017.

LAW COMMISSION (2016b) 'Unfitness to Plead Report, Volume 2: Draft Legislation', available at: http://www.lawcom.gov.uk/wp-content/uploads/2016/01/lc364_unfitness_vol-2.pdf, accessed 6 January 2017.

LITTLECHILD, B. (ed.) (2001), *Appropriate Adults and Appropriate Adult Schemes: Service User, Provider and Police Perspectives*, Birmingham: Venture Press.

O'LOUGHLIN, A. (2014), 'The Offender Personality Disorder Pathway: Expansion in the Face of Failure?', *Howard Journal*, 53(2): 173–92.

MARTIN, M., DORKEN, S., WAMBOLDT, A., and WOOTTEN, S. (2012), 'Stopping the revolving door: A meta-analysis on the effectiveness of interventions for criminally involved individuals with major mental disorders', *Law and Human Behavior*, 36(1): 1–12.

MCRAE, L. (2015), 'The Offender Disorder Pathway: Risking Rehabilitation?, *Medical Law Review*, 23(3).

MELLE, I. (2013) 'The Breivik case and what psychiatrists can learn from it', *World Psychiatry*, 12(1): 16–21.

MELTZER, H., GILL, B., PETTICREW, M., and HINDS, K. (1995), *OPCS Surveys of Psychiatric Morbidity in Great Britain, Report 1: The Prevalence of Psychiatric Morbidity among Adults Living in Private Households*, London: The Stationery Office.

MINISTRY OF JUSTICE (2008), 'Mental Health Act 2007: guidance for the courts on remand and sentencing powers for mentally disordered offenders', available at: https://www.justice.gov.uk/downloads/offenders/mentally-disordered-offenders/guidance-for-the-courts-mha.pdf, accessed 9 February 2017.

MINISTRY OF JUSTICE (2010), *Breaking the Cycle: Effective Punishment, Rehabilitation and Sentencing of Offenders*, Cm 7972, London: The Stationery Office.

MINISTRY OF JUSTICE (2015), 'Multi-Agency Public Protection Annual Reports 2014/15', Ministry of Justice, Statistics Bulletin.

MINISTRY OF JUSTICE (2016), *Safety in Custody Statistics, England and Wales. Deaths in Prison Custody to March 2016, Assaults and Self-harm to December 2015*, Ministry of Justice Statistics Bulletin, London: The Stationery Office.

MONAHAN, J., STEADMAN, H., SILVER, E., APPELBAUM, P., ROBBINS, P., MULVEY, E., ROTH, L., GRISSO, T., and BANKS, S. (2001), *Rethinking Risk Assessment: The MacArthur Study of Mental Disorder and Violence*, New York: Oxford University Press.

PEAY, J. (ed.) (1996), *Inquiries after Homicide*, London: Duckworth.

PEAY, J. (2011a), 'Recession, Crime and Mental Health', Papers from the British Criminology Conference, 11, 3–19, available at: http://www.britsoccrim.org/volume11/pbcc_2011_wholevolume.pdf , accessed 9 January 2017.

PEAY, J. (2011b), *Mental Health and Crime*, Routledge: Abingdon.

PEAY, J. (2011c), 'Personality Disorder and the Law: Some Awkward Questions', *Philosophy, Psychiatry and Psychology*, 18(3): 231–44.

PEAY, J. (2016a), 'An awkward fit: defendants with mental disabilities in a system of criminal justice', in M. Bosworth, C. Hoyle, and L. Zedner (eds), *Changing Contours of Criminal Justice: Research, Politics and Policy*, Oxford: Oxford University Press.

PEAY, J. (2016b), 'Responsibility, culpability and the sentencing of mentally disordered offenders: objectives in conflict', *Criminal Law Review*, 3: 152–64.

PETERSON, J., SKEEM, J., KENNEALY, P., BRAY, B., and ZVONKOVIC, A. (2014), 'How often and How Consistently do Symptoms Directly Precede Criminal Behavior Among Offenders With Mental illness?', *Law and Human Behavior*, 38(5), 439–49.

PORTER, R. (2004), 'Is mental illness inevitably stigmatizing?', in A. Crisp (ed.), *Every Family in the Land. Understanding Prejudice and Discrimination Against People with Mental Illness*, London: Royal Society of Medicine.

PRINS, H. (2016), *Offenders, Deviants or Patients? An introduction to clinical criminology*, 5th edn, Hove: Routledge.

RICHARDSON, G. (1999), *Review of the Mental Health Act 1983*, Report of the Expert Committee, London: Department of Health.

ROBERTSON, G., PEARSON, R., and GIBB, R. (1995), *The Mentally Disordered and the Police*, Research Findings No. 21, London: Home Office, Research and Statistics Department.

RUTHERFORD, M. (2010), *Blurring the Boundaries: The Convergence of Mental Health and Criminal Justice Policy, Legislation, Systems and Practice*, London: Sainsbury Centre for Mental Health.

SCOTT, D., MCGILLOWAY, S., DEMPSTER, M., BROWNE, F., and DONNELLY, M. (2013), 'Effectiveness of criminal justice liaison and diversion services for offenders with mental disorders: A review', *Psychiatric Services*, 64(9): 843–49.

SCOTT, K. (2015), 'S136 of the Mental Health Act 1983 and human rights violations: police procedure and the practice of using custody as a "place of safety" for vulnerable individuals', *Criminal Law Review*, 2: 130–41.

SEDDON, T. (2008), 'Dangerous Liaisons: Personality disorder and the politics of risk', *Punishment and Society*, 10(3): 301–17.

SENTENCING GUIDELINES COUNCIL (2004), *Overarching Principles: Seriousness*, Final Guideline, London: Sentencing Council.

SINGLETON, N., MELTZER, H., and GATWARD, R. (1998), *Psychiatric Morbidity Among Prisoners in England and Wales*, Office for National Statistics, London: The Stationery Office.

SKEEM, J., MANCHAK, S., and PETERSON, J. (2011), 'Correctional policy for offenders with mental illness: Creating a new paradigm for recidivism', *Law and Human Behavior*, 35(2): 110–26.

STEWART, D. (2008), *The Problems and Needs of Newly Sentenced Prisoners: Results from a National Survey*, London: Ministry of Justice.

STOMPE, T., ORTWEIN-SWOBODA, G., and SCHANDA H. (2004), 'Schizophrenia, delusional symptoms and violence: The threat/control-override concept reexamined', *Schizophrenia Bulletin*, 30(1): 31–44.

SEIERSTAD, A. (2015), *One of Us*, New York: Macmillan Farrar, Straus, and Giroux.

SWANSON, J., HOLZER, C., GANJU, V., and JONJO, R. (1990), 'Violence and psychiatric disorder in the community: evidence from the Epidemiologic Catchment Area surveys', *Hospital and Community Psychiatry*, 41(7): 761–70.

SWANSON. J., SCHWARTZ, M., VAN DOREN, R., ELBOGEN, E., WAGNER, R., ROSENHECK, R., STROUP, S., MCEVOY, J., and LIEBERMAN, J. (2006), A national study of violent behaviour in persons with schizophrenia', *Archives of General Psychiatry*, 63: 490–9.

SYSE, A. (2014), 'Breivik—the Norwegian Terrorist case', *Behavioural Sciences and the Law*, 32(3): 389–407.

SZMUKLER, G. (2000), 'Homicide Inquiries: What sense do they make?', *Psychiatric Bulletin*, 24: 6–10.

SZMUKLER, G., DAW, R., and DAWSON, J. (2010), 'A model law fusing incapacity and mental health legislation', *Journal of Mental Health Law*, 11: 11–22.

TAYLOR, R. and YAKELEY, J. (2013), *Working with MAPPA: guidance for psychiatrists in England and Wales*, Faculty Report FR/FP/01, London: Royal College of Psychiatrists.

TREBILCOCK, J. and WEAVER, T. (2012), 'Everybody Knows That the Prisoner is Going Nowhere: Parole Board Members' Views about Dangerous and Severe Personality Disorder in England and Wales', *International Journal of Criminology and Sociology*, 1: 141–50.

TYRER, P., DUGGAN, C., COOPER, S., CRAWFORD, M., SIEVEWRIGHT, H., RUTTER, D., MADEN, A., BYFORD, S., and BARRETT, B. (2010), 'The successes and failures of the DSPD experiment: the assessment and management of severe personality disorder', *Medicine, Science and the Law*, 50(2): 95–99.

WALKER, N. (ed.) (1996), *Dangerous People*, London: Blackstone Press.

WATSON, W. and GROUNDS, A. (eds) (1993), *Mentally Disordered Offenders in an Era of Community Care*, Cambridge: Cambridge University Press.

WEBB, D. and HARRIS, R. (eds) (1999), *Managing People Nobody Owns*, London: Routledge.

ZLODRE, J., YIEND, J., BURNS, T., and FAZEL, S. (2015), 'Coercion, Competence and Consent in Offenders with Personality Disorder', *Psychology, Crime and Law*, 22(4): 315–30.

29

DOMESTIC VIOLENCE

David Gadd

INTRODUCTION

As anyone who followed the trial of Oscar Pistorious will know, discerning clear boundaries around the study of domestic violence is not always easy. What looked to many in the domestic violence sector to be a clear case of femicide—an unarmed woman murdered while cowering in her bathroom to protect herself after an argument with her husband—was successfully presented to a Johannesburg court as a tragic case of culpable homicide. Paraolympian Pistorious claimed he believed he was heroically protecting Reeva Steenkamp from an intruder as he shot four times through their bathroom door on Valentine's day, 14 February 2013. Pistorious' defence succeeded in convincing the court that his disability contributed both to his perception of life-threatening danger and the necessity of an armed response. Legally then, in September 2014, this was neither 'domestic violence'—despite the evidence revealing Steenkamp had messaged Pistorious saying she was 'scared' of him when he 'snapped' at her—nor murder despite Pistorious' awareness that someone was being hit by the bullets he was firing at close range (BBC 2015). On the other hand, the notion that any man would leave his bed to protect his partner from an intruder without first checking whether she was still in it tested credibility to a limit raised in this case by an implicitly racist discourse about the threat of crime posed by poor blacks to wealthy whites in South Africa. That such a highly televised trial could disregard the accumulated knowledge of the millions of women who suffer domestic violence every year seemed like a terrible indictment of gender relations in the twenty-first century. And so it was. The One Billion Rising campaign that launched, coincidentally, the same day, highlighted that 'One in three women in the world will be beaten or raped in their lifetime' and called upon men and women the world over to 'express their outrage'. Only after he had been released from prison on licence, and following campaigning from The African National Congress Women's League, was Pistorious' conviction for culpable homicide overturned and replaced with a conviction for murder in November 2015. This conviction was secured, not on the grounds that Pistorious knew he was killing Steenkamp, but on the basis that he must have known he was killing someone (Supreme Court of Appeal 2015: 18).

In this chapter I will outline the key definitional and aetiological issues surrounding the perpetration of domestic violence. My position is that, without an understanding of the complexity behind what offenders do, the kind of exceptionalism evoked by the Pistorious case proliferates, producing public debate in which domestic violence is acknowledged as a threat to every woman, but perpetrators are recognized almost nowhere. There is thus a substantial void between what gets counted as domestic violence within the criminal justice system and what social scientists say about the problem. While the law is drawn to issues of proof and culpability with regard to discrete incidents, social scientists usually conceptualize domestic violence as a pattern of physically, sexually, and/or emotionally abusive behaviours that a victim, or some other person supporting a victim, has come to regard as a perpetrator's ongoing efforts to control or intimidate their current or former partner. These different manifestations of domestic violence pose particular challenges of measurement, conceptualization, and explanation, not only because of the stigma associated with being a 'perpetrator' or a 'victim' frames what people are willing to disclose, but also because both parties usually have their own versions of the same events. A push might be the beginnings of a campaign of intimidation or a thoughtless and regrettable overreaction in the heat of a crisis. Sex without explicit consent might be rape, evidence of recklessness towards the other person's feelings, or just how it has always happened in a relationship that is close enough to be confident of how the other person feels during intimacy. One person's attempt to talk a conflict through can be another's argument, 'nagging', harassment, or 'verbal aggression'. In sum, definitional, methodological, and aetiological issues abound in cases of domestic abuse and are not resolved by shifting to data addressed at an aggregate level. Questions about what happened and, more taxingly, why, are further obscured when we survey whole populations of would-be victims and offenders. Nevertheless, how we resolve these difficult questions really matters, for it often determines the 'solutions' to domestic violence that are viable, as the chapter shows.

The chapter begins with international estimates of the prevalence of domestic violence, many of which confine themselves to assessments of the percentage of women worldwide who have ever been physically or sexually assaulted by a partner. This has been important both in terms of securing meaningful comparisons across countries and in terms of generating the political impetus for action to combat violence against women. But it also reproduces a definition of domestic violence that is narrowly conceived in terms of countable incidents of assault perpetrated primarily by heterosexual adult men against their wives and girlfriends. Such an approach is not without problems as the chapter's section on historical representations of domestic violence illustrates. This reveals how nineteenth-century British attitudes towards 'wife-beaters' yielded, first to a medical-psychiatric discourse that blamed drunk and disrespectful women for provoking men with quick tempers, and then to twentieth-century feminism that exposed the fallacies of paternalistic protectionism and the inequities of married life. Where some psychiatric commentators blamed women for provoking men's violence and proposed the restoration of marital relations as a solution, feminist research confronted the sexism behind such victim-blaming and exposed how the heteronormative assumptions of the state compounded women's experiences of male violence. 'Domestic abuse', 'intimate partner violence', 'coercive control', and 'gender-based violence' are perhaps the among pervasively used terms now used to convey the range of behaviours women can experience from abusive men. Many of these terms have been adopted within government policy, revealing the degree of impact which feminist research has achieved. However, as the third section of the chapter shows, more inclusive definitions of domestic violence have also paved the way for several important critiques of explanations grounded in gender inequality. The first critique, most frequently championed by psychologists undertaking research using the Conflict Tactics Scale (CTS), points to the use of controlling tactics by both men and women in intimate relationships. Research on male victims, women arrested for violence towards partners, as well as on the personalities of perpetrators in treatment, suggests that matters are more complicated than notions of 'gender symmetry' can capture. The second critique has been engendered by those alive to the 'intersectional' dynamics that compound patterns of oppression, including violence. The privileges and prejudices associated with gender often converge with the discriminations associated with ethnicity, class, sexuality, and age complicating patterns of vulnerability to both victimization and criminalization among populations effected by domestic violence (Crenshaw 2012). This, as the chapter concludes, makes it imperative that we tackle the multiple disadvantages that make it harder for some people to leave abusive relationships and/or seek protection from the law. It also begs the question of how best to address the population of perpetrators, given diversity in their motives, backgrounds, and behaviours and that some are victimized too.

A GLOBAL PROBLEM

There were few reliable attempts to capture the pervasiveness of the problem of domestic violence across the world before the turn of the twenty-first century. The advent of methodologically sophisticated international comparative research on this topic has presented opportunities to highlight the commonality of many women's experiences but also to reconsider why the risk of victimization is unevenly distributed. The World Health Organization (WHO) estimates that '35% of women worldwide have experienced either physical and/or sexual intimate partner violence or non-partner sexual violence' (García-Moreno *et al.* 2013: 2). These figures are derived from a meta-analysis of published studies and databases that have sought to measure national prevalence rates among women aged 15 and over. Narrowing the frame to 'physical and/or sexual intimate partner violence among all ever-partnered women' through the exclusion of non-partner assaults, 'female genital mutilation, honour killings and the trafficking of women', the WHO's best estimate of rates of intimate partner violence directed against women across the world is 30 per cent (ibid.: 16). While the exclusion of non-partnered women will have inflated the headline figure,[1] the definition of violence operationalized by the WHO is much more prescriptive than that used in most national victim surveys. Those who recounted 'being slapped ... pushed or shoved, ... hit with a fist or something else ... kicked, dragged or beaten up, being choked or burnt on purpose, and/or being threatened with, or actually, having a gun, knife or other weapon used on [them]' were included in the WHO's count. Because of the absence of international consensus on what is considered abusive as opposed to 'unkind' behaviour (ibid.: 10), those exposed only to emotional abuse and controlling behaviours—such as being stalked, checked up on, being verbally abused or put down, or having one's access to friends or family restricted—were excluded from the count. Given this, One Billion Rising's 'one in three' figure is a conservative estimate of the number of women in the world today who have ever suffered any of the physical, sexual, or psychological aspects of domestic violence.

This risk of being a victim of domestic violence, however, is not evenly spread across the world's regions. In African, Eastern Mediterranean, and South-East Asian regions around 37 per cent of ever-partnered women report having experienced physical and/or sexual intimate partner violence at some point in their lives (García-Moreno *et al.* 2013). In the Americas around 30 per cent of women report lifetime exposure, while in Europe (23 per cent) and the Western Pacific (25 per cent) rates are a little lower. Part, but not all, of this variation is accounted for in terms of socio-economic factors. Poorer regions generally have higher rates of intimate partner violence than prosperous regions. Regions where there have been recent wars and conflicts have higher rates of domestic violence than those where peace has prevailed. Those living away from urban centres are at greater risk than those in the cities. Hence, in the provincial regions of many poor countries like Bangladesh (62 per cent), Ethiopia (71 per cent), and Peru (61 per cent) the majority of women report having been physically or sexually assaulted by a partner (García-Moreno *et al.* 2005). South African studies also report very high rates of domestic assault and sexual violence in some provinces (Vetten 2014). Conversely, rates of domestic violence are thought to be lowest in Japan, where 15 per cent of ever-partnered women have experienced physical or sexual violence from a partner (García-Moreno *et al.* 2005).

Meaningful comparative studies of domestic violence rates between countries are, nevertheless, hard to generate. This is because definitions of domestic violence have varied from place to place, as have the techniques used (questionnaire or computer assisted interviewing) in national surveys, the timeframes asked about (last year, last two-to-five years, lifetime), as well as the age ranges of the samples captured (Gadd *et al.* 2014; Walby and Myhill 2002). The European Union Agency for Fundamental Rights' (2014) EU-wide survey sought, not entirely successfully, to overcome these challenges. Over 42,000 women aged 15 and over from across the 28 (then) member states of the European Union were interviewed face-to-face about their experiences of physical, sexual, and psychological violence. 22 per cent of women in

[1] Never-partnered women, by definition, cannot previously have been victims of intimate partner violence. Hence, the percentage of ever-partnered women who are victims is, by definition, always greater than the proportion of the female population as a whole—ever and never partnered—who have been victims.

Europe reported having ever experienced physical or sexual violence from a partner in their lifetime. In Finland, Denmark, and Latvia lifetime prevalence rates ranged from 30–32 per cent, while in Austria, Croatia, Poland, Slovenia, and Spain around 13 per cent of women reported having experienced physical or sexual violence from a partner. The comparable figures for the UK, Sweden, France, and Germany were 29 per cent, 28 per cent, 26 per cent, and 22 per cent respectively. In sum, Western European countries generally regarded as better in terms of gender equality were found to have higher rates of intimate partner violence than some Eastern European countries with poorer records for gender equality, causing the study's authors to question the extent to which levels of consciousness about domestic violence, or the willingness to discuss it face-to-face, shaped the results. Indeed, in countries like the US, Australia, and the UK, where campaigns against domestic violence are long-standing, victim surveys suggests that rates of domestic abuse have fallen in recent years (Catalano 2012; Trewin 2005).

In the UK, both the lifetime prevalence and the annual incidence of domestic violence have been measured via the Scottish and British Crime Surveys (BCS) since the 1980s. Computer assisted self-completion technologies have been used in England and Wales since 1996 as such methods are better able to overcome the reluctance to disclose that face-to-face methods can engender (Mirrlees-Black 1999). The 2014–15 sweep of the Crime Survey for England and Wales (CSEW, successor to the BCS) reports a lifetime prevalence rate for (physical and non-physical forms of) domestic violence of 27.1 per cent for women (comparable to that reported in the EU-Wide survey) and 13.2 per cent for men (ONS 2016). The annual incidence rates—which are based on the proportion of people who have been victimized in the 12 months prior to completing the survey—are inevitably lower at 6.5 per cent of women and 2.8 per cent of men 2014–15. These compare favourably with the incidence rates for women (9.3 per cent) and men (6.5 per cent) reported for the year 2006–7, implying a decline in rates of domestic violence in England and Wales (ONS 2014), comparable to the decline in domestic abuse suggested in Scottish Crime Survey reports (MacQueen 2014: 10). It may, however, be premature to assume that this decline is a trend because the full extent of repeat victimization suffered by some women was not fully captured in previous surveys of Britons (Walby *et al.* 2014a). What is more certain is that the experiences of men counted as victims in these surveys are rarely equivalent to those of women counted as victims. Female victims are much more likely to report experiences of life threatening forms of violence, sexual assaults, and stalking than male victims (Roe 2009; ONS 2016). They are also more likely to report sustaining physical injuries and mental and emotional problems in the aftermath of violence (ONS 2016: 25). The CSEW indicates that the violence women experience is four times more likely to be accompanied by threats than the violence men experience (ibid.: 5), leading some to suggest, as explained later in the chapter, that men rarely suffer partner assaults in the context of acutely controlling relationships. Divergent rates of reporting to the police—10 per cent for men and 26 per cent for women who disclosed any partner abuse in the CESW 2014–15 in the previous year—must be interpreted in the light of differential experiences of victimization too (ibid.: 39).

HISTORICAL REPRESENTATIONS OF DOMESTIC VIOLENCE

PATERNALISTIC PROTECTIONISM

While it is rarely remarked upon in the criminological literature, the consensus among many crime historians is that tolerance of violence against female partners in England declined during the nineteenth century. Hammerton (1992) explains that it was not uncommon in the mid-nineteenth century for effigies of known wife-beaters to be paraded through the streets. Such 'rough music rituals' were not an early expression of pro-feminist sensibilities—'nagging' wives, adulterers, women said to have made false accusations of rape, drunken women, and homosexuals were also singled out for rough music too (Hammerton 1992: 14). Rather, the shaming—and occasional lynching—of wife-beaters symbolized the 'patriarchal gallantry' of men who wished to distinguish themselves from those deemed to be taking advantage of vulnerable women at a time when the protections offered by the church, custom, and law were dwindling (ibid.: 13). As attitudes to wife-beaters hardened, the courts came to see it as their job, more than the public's, to protect vulnerable women from 'brutal' 'ruffians' 'with no higher sense of what is due to womanhood' (ibid.: 60). In England, the passing of the 1853 Act for the Better Prevention of Aggravated Assault Upon Women and Children enabled magistrates to impose court orders, fine, or imprison men who assaulted their wives, and was followed, three years later, by a campaign to enable women to divorce 'wife-beating' husbands (Stark 2007: 143).

The application of such laws, however, was tinged with class and gendered expectations. As Wiener (2006: 159) explains, new ideals of domesticity meant that 'husbands' should not only 'support' and protect' but also be 'there for their wives (and children)'. Consequently, women found their domestic lives exposed to 'stricter scrutiny' as a 'wife's behaviour and character became more crucial than ever to the happiness and viability of the home' (ibid.). As Crone's (2006: 1082) account of the history of Punch and Judy shows reveals, the breakdown of supposedly 'companionate' marriages became painful for the middle classes to admit, except through satire. New expectations of domesticity thus opened up a space for those mostly middle-class men who could afford a legal defence to justify wife assault on the basis that their spouses fell short of the 'indisputable attributes of a good wife': 'industry', 'sobriety' and . . . chastity' (Weiner 2004: 159). Meanwhile, the pressures on working-class women intensified as feminists of the time pointed out (Cobbe 1878 cited in Euler 2000). Financial dependence upon male breadwinners meant that poor working-class women had few legal protections from domestic violence. The few who went to court had little option but to withdraw from legal proceedings or risk becoming destitute, losing their homes, and/or access to children (Clark 2000). Middle-class women, perceiving domestic violence to be a problem of the 'dangerous classes', often concealed their bruises (Hunt 1992), but some, nevertheless, pursued separations as a solution. Victorian divorce courts, as Foyster (2002) has shown, were willing to listen to middle-class women who could prove they had been intimidated into silence by abusive and ungentlemanly men and sympathetic to women who claimed to be 'affected by "hysterics", "fits", "freaks"...

"want of appetite and spirits", crying and "deep melancholy" as a consequence of their husbands' treatment (ibid.: 409). But it was not without risk: 'the suspicion that women could sham illness to manipulate others gave further opportunity for scrutinising the honesty and morality of the women making accusations of cruelty' (ibid.: 413).

MARRIAGE MENDING AND THE SCIENCE OF MADNESS

Indeed, the risks associated with disclosing both victimization and hysterical affects appear to have intensified for women in Britain at the very end of the nineteenth century as the judiciary became more concerned to 'reconcile wives with their violent husbands' (Hughes 2010: 2). Men who assaulted women said to have 'provoking tongues' or problems with alcoholism were more readily excused (ibid:. 22). In early twentieth-century Scotland, men who killed their wives were convicted for 'culpable homicide' and sentenced only to short prison terms instead of murder when their rage was said to be attributable to 'drunkeness' (ibid.: 26). Those who perpetrated lesser assaults could be spared criminal sanctions altogether as 'marriage mending' became the preferred discourse of the state, in part due to colonialist fears about the depletion of the British 'race' (ibid.: 31). In response the courts sought to rehabilitate 'wife-beaters without criminalizing them' (ibid.). Meanwhile, the professionalizing discourses adopted by psychoanalysis and psychiatry before and after the Second World War also addressed themselves to the possibility of resolving family dysfunctions through the treatment of hysterical women. The small body of Anglo-American practice-based literature that addressed assaults on wives in this period reveals how an oversimplified refashioning of Freudian concepts was used to justify interventions that sought to treat the masochism of women who purportedly invited victimization. Schultz (1960), a probation officer, reported on the case of an African-American man—called Jim—who had stabbed his second wife four times and killed her. Jim was the child of illiterate parents, who had little time to be affectionate to their children because, like many Southern blacks at that time, they worked exhaustingly long hours share-cropping for very low pay. Both Jim's first and second wives had been unfaithful and the second had also been violent towards Jim. The day Jim killed his second wife she had refused to kiss him and berated him for failing to pick her up from the shops, pointing out that she had called upon her 'paramour' to do so. Schultz concluded that Jim's wife had precipitated her own death by failing to recognize how Jim's 'domineering, rejecting mother' had taught him to deny his own 'emotional needs' (ibid.: 107–8).

Likewise, psychiatrists Snell *et al.* (1964: 109), perplexed as to why women who had endured many years of violence from husbands suddenly turned to the courts, focused on one case where a teenage son 'for the first time stepped in between his arguing parents and physically restrained the father'. Rather than interpret the son's behaviour as a positive attempt to protect his mother, the psychiatrists persuaded her it was time her husband's 'rival' moved out. The son, they speculated, had inadvertently disrupted a 'marital equilibrium' through which the husband's aggressive behavior' met 'the masochistic needs of the wife . . . even though she protests it' (ibid.: 110). Astoundingly, a woman who had been assaulted after refusing a husband who made 'very aggressive sexual demands when drunk' was then given therapy to address her own 'aggressiveness, masculinity, frigidity, and masochism' in order to alleviate her abusive husband's 'passivity, indecisiveness and sexual inadequacy' (ibid.: 111).

Such perspectives persisted through the 1970s when the psychiatrist Gayford (1979) published a paper on one hundred 'battered women' supported by Chiswick Women's Aid. Many had previously been diagnosed with psychiatric disturbances, over a third having previously attempted suicide. Many of the women at Chiswick had suffered abuse and incest in their childhoods—a quarter having been raped by a man other than their husband—making return to their parents homes unviable despite the concerns the majority had about the threat domestic violence posed to their own children. The husbands and boyfriends who abused them were often no less troubled. A third had histories of imprisonment. Half had problems with alcohol and just under half were regular gamblers. Two thirds were excessively jealous, and yet around half were thought to have been unfaithful. In short, this was a sample of repeatedly abused, desperate, and vulnerable women with few other options but to go into the first ever refuge or remain with men who were terrifying them and their children. And yet Gayford appraised their plight by repeating the well-worn misogynistic trope of castigating women for failing to know their places:

> The neat, efficient woman of superior intelligence to her marital partner can be provocative if her husband develops a dependency on her which she withdraws at a critical time. At the other end of the spectrum, the inadequate woman who cannot organize her domestic life is provocative. Pair each of these with a man of low frustration tolerance who has found that crises appear to be solved by outbursts of aggression and violence, add an element of suspicion of the wife's fidelity. Dissolve his inhibitions in alcohol and a battered wife can be predicted. (ibid.: 24)

Only when critical attention fell on the men so 'provoked' was there any glimmer of insight. Faulk's (1974) questionnaire-based assessment of 23 men remanded in custody for grievous assaults, murder, and attempted murder—revealed a diversity of motives among wife assaulters. Some men who saw themselves as generally pacifying their partners had suddenly 'exploded' following some 'precipitating act' by the victim; others were 'dependent and suspicious' men who had become controlling and then increasingly violent because of their own undue jealousies. Some were generally 'violent and intimidating' men who tried to solve all their problems by 'bullying' people, while others were dominating husbands 'who would brook no insubordination from their wives'. But the biggest group were a previously 'stable and affectionate group' of men who had not become abusive until a 'time of mental disturbance' (Faulk 1974: 181–2). In fact, over two thirds of the sample had suffered psychiatric disorders such as depression, delusional jealousy, paranoid illness, or dementia. A third of their victims had previously told the police that they had reason to feel unsafe.

FEMINISM AND CRIMINOLOGY

The vast body of feminist scholarship that reshaped thinking about sexism and gender from the 1970s onwards challenged the view that women were somehow to blame for the violence they experienced at the hands of men. It asked also why women's experiences were typically devalued as anecdote while men's interpretations of female victims' provocations were treated as science. Griffin (1971) underlined the 'price' many women pay for the male chivalry that promises them a very constricted form of protection in return for the acceptance of a range of rape-condoning myths. Brownmiller (1975) noted the pervasiveness of the sexual and physical violence experienced by women of all social groups across the world and history—including as a weapon of war and colonization—conceptualizing rape as part of a strategy of patriarchal domination that protected men's interests in maintaining sexual inequality. Dworkin (1974, 1981) exposed the cultural hatred of women beneath apparently banal expressions of sexism and related this to the systematic subjugation of the female body in what was then only an emerging global pornography industry trading in the consumption of women's bodies.

Criminology was a latecomer to this feminist scholarship, and a needy one at that, given its blindness to issues of gender generally and its inattention to domestic violence specifically (Smart 1990: 27). The radical sociologies of deviance that upstaged the more therapeutic and medical orthodoxies said very little about domestic violence, and were, for the most part, oblivious to the gendered nature of much crime and criminalization. Dobash and Dobash's (1979) *Violence Against Wives* was among the first feminist texts on domestic violence that spoke directly to this criminological chasm. Also drawing some of their sample from Chiswick, Dobash and Dobash noted how women at this time became conscious of their common experiences of domestic violence as they began talking about other matters: feelings of 'loneliness and isolation', for example, or how 'to seek help for problems, ranging from poor housing to alcoholism' (ibid.: 1). Asked to describe the first, worst, and last 'incidents' of violence they had suffered, the Dobashes' participants explained that it had no exact beginning or end, because violent episodes tended to permeate relationships in which conflicts about jealousies, housework, and money are continuously laden with threat.

> Violent events . . . usually take place after a build-up and take on an identity of their own which is intense and memorable . . . because of the meanings they have for each partner. Such events not only dominate the daily lives of both abuser and abused but also form a crucial part in the formation of subsequent violent events and in the continuing development of the couple's overall relationship. (Dobash and Dobash 1984: 269)

Dobash and Dobash (1979: ix) argued for a 'comprehensive explanation and understanding' of the brutal and systematic abuse of 'wives' their interviews had exposed. They argued that this explanation should incorporate: the patriarchal structures and ideology that shape expectations of women and men in relationships; the sources of conflict that lead up to and become articulated in violent episodes; and the effects of the violence, not only in terms of the physical and psychological harms caused, but also in terms of the management or avoidance of further conflict by the victim and the pressures, often imposed by the abuser, to continue the relationship as if nothing had happened. The Dobashes discovered that many abused women attempted to reason and argue with men who threatened them. Some screamed or cried in order to resist a beating. Others had pushed abusers away or hit back, because they were both angry and wanted to protect themselves. But continued exposure to violence was not inevitable. In some cases, the support of friends, neighbours, and relatives had led to the 'eventual termination' of the abuse 'either through escape from the abuser or cessation of his violent behaviour' (1984: 269).

Subsequent feminist scholarship nevertheless problematized the distinction Dobash and Dobash (1979: 11) made between 'violent relationships' entailing 'the systematic, frequent and brutal use of physical force' and 'most marriages', which they characterized as prone to minor but 'regrettable' 'physical incidents' of assault, locating the latter within a spectrum of oppressive behaviours women endure at the hands of men. In her book, *Intimate Intrusions*, Stanko (1985: 1) highlighted how women 'are continually on their guard to the possibility of men's violence' and how despite its widespread nature, women exposed to 'rape, incest, wife battering, or sexual harassment' have also to contend with a criminal justice system that construes such abuses as 'indiscretions' typically perpetrated against women of questionable respectability (ibid.: 4). Similarly, Kelly's (1988) *Surviving Sexual Violence* conceived of a 'continuum of abuse'—including sexual harassment, pressurised sex, exposure to pornography, domestic violence, incest, and rape—which women have to learn how to cope with and resist, despite the pervasive acceptance of myths about how they incite violence or even enjoy being abused. Kelly conceived of domestic violence as both an expression of men's power and evidence of women's resistance to it, the threat of force also evoked when patriarchal authority is lacking. Theoretically, this made distinguishing 'battered wives' from other women beside the point. It also begged a question as to how distinguishable male 'batterers' were from other 'normal' men. As Kelly (1987: 59) surmised:

> The fact that some women only experience violence at the more common, everyday end of the continuum is a difference in degree not in kind. The use of the term 'victim' in order to separate one group of women from other women's lives and experiences must be questioned. The same logic applies to the definition of 'offenders'.

Now much more widely understood as a feature of everyday sexism, the political importance of acknowledging that many partner assaults against women are part of a continuum of abuse should not be understated (Walby *et al.* 2014b). Recognition of the connections between the many abuses women suffer led ultimately to the: advent of national crime surveys, as described earlier, that sought to measure domestic violence; political acknowledgment of the extent of this crime and the harm it inflicts; estimates of the economic costs imposed by domestic violence and the necessity of resourcing interventions to support victims and tackle perpetrators; and the development of international policy at the levels of the UN and European Union requiring national governments to tackle gender-based violence of all kinds.

CONTEMPORARY DEBATES AND PERSPECTIVES

COERCIVE CONTROL AND THE PSYCHOLOGY OF MALE PERPETRATORS

Advances in the measurement of victimization have, however, also opened up debates with regard to the relative merits of explanations grounded in psychology, gender, and other inequalities, to which this chapter now turns. Taking leave from the notion that women experience a continuum of abuse, O' Leary (1993: 25), for example, suggests there is much to be gained from contemplating a continuum of violence perpetration:

> At the more moderate end of the continuum of physical aggression against a wife ... impulsiveness, and 'dependence' (readiness to defend oneself, suspicion of others, and a tendency to take offense easily... are ... predictive of physical aggression against a ... dating partner .. In large community studies ... the association of personality styles or traits and the use of physical aggression against a partner is small but statistically significant. In men who engage in severe acts of physical aggression and coercive tactics against a partner, the likelihood of finding that an individual has a significantly elevated score on a scale that assesses personality disorders is very high.

In other words, the differences between men who are not normally violent and those who are moderately so are subtle though measurable and more akin to nuances of personality styles than traits. This is partly because shades of sexism, suspiciousness, and sensitivity to criticism from a partner are relatively common among men. The differences between men who are not normally violent and those who are frequently and severely physically abusive are stark and easily exposed through psychometric testing.

Psychological research has suggested that there are different types of psychopathology among the clinically-known batterer population. Holtzworth-Munroe and Stuart (1994) distinguish between 'family-only batterers' (with relatively low levels of psychopathology and fairly liberal attitudes towards women) and two other types with conservative attitudes towards women: 'borderline batterers' (who also score highly on measures of low mood, jealousy, insecurity, and fear of rejection) and men who are 'generally violent' in many contexts (who score highly on measures of antisocial personality disorder, evidenced in terms of criminal records and histories of alcoholism or substance misuse). Others, like Dutton (1998), distinguish between 'instrumental' batterers (who use violence in many walks of life to get what they want) and 'impulsive' batterers (who go through cycles of being violent to their partners, giving the impression that the abuse is somehow out of character). Through psychometric testing, Dutton has shown that this latter group are more likely to have 'fearful attachment styles', evidenced by 'an unstable sense of self and an inability to tolerate aloneness', together with high scores on measures of borderline personality organization (BPO) (ibid.: 86).

> [T]hese men depend on their relationship with female partners to prevent their fragile selfhood from disintegrating and to dissipate the pervasive anxiety they feel ... The intimate relationship of the high-BPO scorer is asked to do the impossible, and when it fails, or appears in his eyes to fail, extreme anger results because his very sense of self is threatened and because his use of projection as a defense tell him that it is *her* fault that it is failing. He views her, at that phase of the relationship, as 'all bad'. If that impasse resolves, he then tends to view her as 'all good' and himself as bad ... (1998: 86–7, emphasis in original)

Compared to men who are not violent, Dutton *et al.* (1998: 145) find evidence that 'impulsive' batterers are more likely to report 'feeling rejected' or a 'a lack of warmth' from their fathers, being 'physically' and verbally abused by their fathers, and 'feeling rejected' by their mothers. This suggests that the causes of domestic violence are not only to be found in men's expectations of power, but also in their insecurities. These insecurities are often co-located both in the conflicts with their partners and in upbringings with fathers who were emotionally distant, belittling, or abusive.

SEXUAL 'SYMMETRY' AND WOMEN'S VIOLENCE

The work of psychologists has nevertheless proved contentious among many feminist criminologists because of its tendency to dismiss the role of gender in the aetiology of domestic violence as without scientific foundation (DeKeseredy and Dragiewicz 2014). This either/or—gender/personality—way of thinking about causation derives in part from the studies of Straus and his colleagues' using the Conflict Tactics Scale (CTS). The CTS is a self-report questionnaire that asks participants both what they have done to their partner and what their partner has done to them on occasions over the last 12 months when they have tended to 'disagree, get annoyed with the other person, or just have spats or fights because they are in a bad mood or tired or for some other reason' (Straus 1993: 82). Replicated in over two hundred studies across the world, findings produced using the CTS are fairly consistent (Straus 2010). Men and women report roughly equivalent usage of conflict tactics. Adjustments to the questions to include sexual violence—which women experience much more than men—have not changed the overall conclusion in part because sexual violence when measured as an 'incident' or 'tactic' is not as commonplace as either verbal abuse and minor acts of physical aggression. Consequently, Straus queries the relevance of gender to the aetiology of domestic violence. Those persuaded by his argument have called for gender-focused content to be removed from programmes that provide preventative domestic abuse education for children and from treatment interventions for perpetrators (Dixon *et al.* 2012; Dutton 2010). They have also called for the development of victim services that serve men and women equally.

Such proposals are nevertheless almost impossible to square with the demand for victim services the world over, very little of which comes from male victims, despite campaigns in some Western countries to encourage abused men to seek support. Indeed, the most likely explanation for the 'sexual symmetry' produced in studies using the CTS is a methodological one. First, as both Dobash and Dobash (1979) and Straus (1993: 79) have argued, some of the worst domestic violence happens when women who live with a batterer slap or throw 'something at a partner for doing something outrageous . . . [This] reinforces *his* moral justification for slapping her . . . as he sees it'. In sum, minor acts of aggression between men and women in heterosexual relationships become part of the moral justification some men offer for battering women. At the same time, there may be few victims who have not also been perpetrators at some point, if a perpetrator is defined rather loosely as anyone who has once acted in an abusive way, however mild, whether or not it was in retaliation or self-defence (Dobash *et al.* 1992). Second, the samples captured by the CTS are more self-selecting than those used in crime surveys. Sampling frames used in CTS studies have relied heavily on students who are younger and better educated than the general population. Completion rates of these self-report studies tend to be low with little effort made to ensure matched replacements of participants who drop out, potentially skewing the sample away from those who have the more 'shameful' experiences—whether as perpetrators or victims—to admit. Moreover, community-based surveys, especially when undertaken with adults in educational settings, tend to be over representative of educated, childless, middle-class populations and hence under-representative of those populations from which the most violent and criminally involved men tend to derive (Kimmel 2002). Such shortcomings led Johnson (2006) to conclude that the CTS primarily measures one form of domestic violence, namely 'common couple' or 'situational' violence, that is often reciprocal, rarely about power and control, and often to do with some form of specific crisis or period of separation. By contrast the refuge population mostly comprises women who have been exposed to 'intimate terrorism', what Stark (2007) calls 'coercive control', a cumulative form of subjugation that uses violence alongside a range of tactics that 'entrap' women in relationships with men by making them constantly fearful. Third, there is some evidence to suggest that both men and boys work with more constricted understandings of what constitutes violence than women when it comes to self-report surveys (Hearn 1998). Miller's (2008) *Getting Played*, for example, exposes instances where women recount experiences of gang rape orchestrated by their boyfriends, while the young men involved defined their behaviour as a consensual form of group sex called 'running trains'.

The general picture to be extracted from national victimization surveys the world over is that men who have experienced domestic abuse encounter it less repeatedly and severely than women (Tjaden and Thoennes 2000; Povey *et al.* 2008; Black *et al.* 2011). These surveys also reveal that the violence men experience from women less frequently takes life-threatening forms. Men generally suffer far fewer physical and psychological consequences from domestic violence perpetrated by women. Men less frequently require medical treatment following domestic assaults and, unlike female victims, are rarely financially disadvantaged, suggesting they are less likely to be trapped in abusive relationships. Qualitative studies of male victims and female perpetrators generally confirm the point that very little female-to-male violence can be described as 'coercive control' or 'battery' (Stark 2007; Hester 2009). Moreover, some men identified as victims in survey research regard themselves more as perpetrators who have been hit back, while some of those who perceive themselves as victims are mostly aggrieved at the loss of relationships in which no or little physical violence occurred (Gadd *et al.* 2003). Some male victims tell heroic stories of self-sacrificing restraint in which they endured relationships with unkind, unfeeling, or 'crazy' women to protect their children or out of a sense of chivalric duty to protect a vulnerable female (Alger 2016). Such stories often reveal complex imbalances of power—borne out of disabilities, income levels, or citizenship status—amidst what might look like 'common couple' violence, while the restraints victimized men use to pacify women deemed 'hysterical'—such as pinning them down—are easily reinterpreted as intimidating behaviours that evoke the fear of physical or sexual assault (Gadd *et al.* 2003). While there is no doubt that some men are victimized by women who are abusive, dangerous, or use their children against them, social researchers have struggled to find any substantial population of male victims fearful enough to merit substantial investment in refuge provision either from within those identified as victims in national population surveys (ibid.) or among those known to health professionals (Hester *et al.* 2015). Indeed, Hester *et al.* (2015) suggest it may thus be better to map men's experiences of victimization onto a wider terrain of 'negative behaviours', some of which are violent and some of which they have also perpetrated themselves, either in retaliation or in ways that pre-empted abuse directed against them. Studies of women arrested for violence against a partner reveal a population that has been victimized more often than they have perpetrated abuse and whose experiences of sexual assault are comparable to women in the refuge population (Stuart *et al.* 2006). Asked why they had abused their partners, women in Stuart and colleagues' (2006) study said they had done so for self-defence, to show anger, to express feelings that could not be put into words, to retaliate for emotional hurts, to feel more powerful, and because they had been provoked. Echoing the accounts of some male victims, a number of commentators distinguish between women who use violence as the primary perpetrators, those who use it defensively to protect themselves, and those who adopt a 'never again' mentality who strike first, having been abused by previous partners (Hamlett 1998). This latter group of women—who are sometimes cast erroneously as sufferers of 'Battered Woman Syndrome' (Walker 1984)—are often perceived by criminal justice professionals as behaving in ways that are 'mutually combative'. Yet studies of women in treatment programmes for violence suggest such offenders scare themselves more than others through their actions. Substance abuse, mental health problems, and historic experiences of child sexual abuse are part of the explanation for sudden outbursts of aggression geared towards protecting themselves or their children from threats that may be real or imagined (Swan and Snow 2006). In jurisdictions where pro-arrest policies focus on laws broken in the most immediate incident, an increasing number of women have found themselves unexpectedly arrested for domestic violence offences (Miller and Meloy 2006). Consequently, women who have endured abusive relationships without previous recourse to law can find themselves rapidly propelled into the criminal justice system for reacting in kind to violence they have long tolerated as victims (Swan and Snow 2006). In such instances, criminal justice responses can suddenly turn reluctant victims into known perpetrators, compounding experiences of abuse with injustice.

RISK AND INTERSECTIONALITY

That such unjust criminal justice outcomes would fall more heavily upon multiply oppressed women was first anticipated by Crenshaw (1993). Describing her own experiences of working for disadvantaged groups in Los Angeles, Crenshaw noted the perverse outcomes that follow when gender, race, and class intersect in the lives of battered women. While feminism had exposed how any woman, whatever her education or class status, could be a victim of domestic violence—leading some to suggest all women were equally at risk—Crenshaw pointed out that violence afflicted the poorest women and ethnic minority women the most. Black women generally have fewest protections, black rights organizations unwilling, at that time, to recognize domestic violence as a social problem affecting them. Historic experiences of police racism made many African-American women reluctant to call the police when their husbands abused them, lest this culminate in police violence directed towards the men. More reliant on finding their own solutions, African-American women were more likely to be declined places in a refuge if they admitted using violence to protect themselves. Similarly, police clampdowns could make matters worse still for immigrant women who feared deportation if they got into trouble and who struggled, if they could not speak English, to access refuge provision, making them increasingly dependent on their husbands, as is still the case today (Erez *et al.* 2009; Mason and Pulvirenti 2013). Meanwhile, the sons of battered women, Crenshaw noted, were at increased risk of imprisonment for taking it upon themselves to intervene in domestic assaults perpetrated against their mothers.

Survey research across the world continues to illustrate, though not necessarily explain, the importance of these intersections, including differences by ethnicity in terms of the risks of victimization (Black *et al*, 2010; García-Moreno *et al.* 2013; European Union Agency for Fundamental Rights 2014; ONS 2014). Younger people are at much greater risk of domestic violence than older people. Separated, separating, and pregnant women are at heightened risk of victimization relative to married, divorced, or non-pregnant women. Women with long-term illnesses and disabilities are at greater risk than those without, as are lone parent women. Similarly, women living in deprived areas are at enhanced risk, while women with higher levels of education are typically at lower risk of assault form a partner than women with no or low levels of education. Problematic drink and drug use are more common among both victims and perpetrators of domestic violence. Some of these risks factors routinely feature in government policy as rationales for providing additional support to the most vulnerable women and children. In some jurisdictions they also feature—sometimes erroneously and sometimes as a substitute for appraising perpetrators' proclivities—in practitioners' assessments of the future risks posed to abused women and their children (Robinson and Howarth 2012).

Conversely, criminological theory has attended to intersectionality by reappraising the identities of perpetrators, the structured action approach to masculinities positing that some groups of men—young, poor, minority ethnic—have fewer resources to accomplish their masculinity than others and hence use violence against women to compensate for this (Messerschmidt 1999). Structured action theory has tended, however, to overstate the social acceptability of domestic violence among men, few of whom would regard domestic abusers as the most accomplishedly masculine men (Gadd 2000). In Britain and Sweden, for example, being able to provide for and protect a partner, offer rational advice, and maintain romance and respect, are common themes in perpetrators' accounts of themselves (Gadd 2002; Gottzèn 2016). Within these contexts, going into treatment is sometimes cited by perpetrators as a way in which they will sort out shameful problems that have caused them, uncharacteristically, to 'lose control'. By way of contrast, the exceptionally high rates of violence against women to be found in South Africa cannot be disentangled from a culture, engendered by the brutality of apartheid, that encouraged men to use violence to retain control as families were broken by forced removals and police brutality, and while myths about HIV were propagated at the highest levels of the political establishment (Squire 2016). Consequently, many of the disproportionately poor, black men from the provinces who go into perpetrator programmes in South Africa commence intervention work by asking their psychotherapists how they can possibly understand where they are 'coming from' (Boonzaier and Gordon 2015: 15).

In Western Europe discussions about ethnicity and domestic violence have tended to focus more latterly on the issue of 'honour-based' or 'honour-related violence'. Such crimes are often assumed to be exclusive to Muslim populations, though they are also found in some contemporary European Christian cultures too. Honour-based violence is usually perpetrated against women who have brought shame on the family or the community through their behaviour. Dishonourable behaviour can include marrying a person of their choice against their family's wishes, divorcing an abusive partner, being raped, or entering into same-sex relationships (Idriss 2011). Violence perpetrated in the name of honour is often sanctioned by the wider community and can also be perpetrated against men who fail to redress the transgressions of their wives. The study of such crimes is complicated both by migration that has increased cultural diversity among groups of the same faith, and Islamophobia which has propagated stereotypes of Muslim men and women. Gill (2011) argues that there is actually no honour—Islamic or otherwise—in violence towards women, just gender-based social control geared towards maintaining particular forms of political and cultural authority. By way of contrast, far less attention is paid to the disproportionately high rates of domestic violence suffered by sex workers or women caught up in sex trafficking, much of which is perpetrated by men regarded as 'boyfriends' with whom the victims are in exploitative relationships (Broad 2015; Pickering and Ham 2013). Both sex industries are ones that exploit across gender and ethnic lines, with economically disadvantaged minority ethnic and 'first nation' indigenous women over-represented in these trades in many Western countries. Those who trade drugs for sex and vice versa debar themselves from legal protections and hence become prone to taking greater risks as their desperation intensifies and they become reliant on the protection of men who can present a credible threat of violence (Shannon *et al.* 2008; see also Phoenix, this volume).

The greatest challenges in terms of explaining domestic violence, however, come from studies that address questions of sexuality and age. While most feminist theory has assumed that domestic violence is perpetrated primarily by men against women, studies of lesbian, gay, bisexual, transgender (LGBT) populations reveal that domestic violence is by no means exclusive to heterosexual couples. Community-based studies of 'out' LGBT populations have tended to uncover prevalence rates similar to studies that have administered the CTS to heterosexual couples (Renzetti 1992; Roch *et al.* 2010; Donovan and Hester 2011). This has led some to suggest that domestic violence among sexual minorities is typically 'common couple' and rarely coercively controlling (Johnson 2006). The few national studies that use random sampling, however, present a more complex picture. The US National Violence Against Women Survey suggests that rates of domestic violence are lower in lesbian relationships than in straight relationships, but that men who live with male partners are potentially at greater risk (Tjaden *et al.* 1999). Likewise, the findings of the US National Intimate Partner and Sexual Violence Survey suggest that the risk of being a victim of domestic violence for gay and bisexual men is twice that for heterosexual men, while rates of domestic abuse among lesbian and heterosexual women are similar (Walters *et al.* 2013). Such figures comprise participants with only one experience of domestic violence, but there is ample evidence that LGBT people in the US also experience violence that is severe, physical, sexual, and psychological. Such findings may, of course, reflect the lesser degree of legal protection afforded to sexual minorities, reluctance to come out to the authorities through fear of homophobia, the heterosexist focus of much domestic violence provision, and the presumption among some gay and lesbian people that domestic violence is a heterosexual problem (Hester 2010). But there are also dangers of over-generalization here, some commentators pointing to subsections of the gay male population who actively pursue risky forms of intimacy via social media and/or shared drug use. Such behaviours can be conceived as subcultural reactions against heteronormative forms of social control that render same-sex intimacy inherently dangerous, generating the demand for virtual spaces where risk can be actively negotiated (Frederick and Peronne 2014). Moreover, some commentators note similar recent changes in dating patterns among young heterosexuals, alongside the risks of exploitation young women engaged in online flirtation must navigate (Lee and Crofts 2015). One might retort that if domestic violence is a feature of a continuum of power relations within intimacy then we should not be surprised to see such power relations reproduced when intimacy is navigated online. Concomitantly, warning young people who are resistant to conventions about such risks may well make the dangers more enticing to some, in much the same way that public health campaigns can generate what are known as counterproductive 'boomerang effects', with those prone to risk-taking tempted by behaviour marked anew as dangerous (Gadd *et al.* 2015).

Preoccupation with the effects of exposure to violence between adults on children has led to the neglect of the evidence suggesting that the peak age for victimization and offending lie in early adulthood or mid-to-late teens. UK studies show that around a quarter of young people admit to perpetrating an act of domestic abuse against a partner by their mid-teens and around two fifths of mid-teens who have dated have at least one experience of victimization (Barter *et al.* 2009; Fox *et al.* 2014). Tellingly, most children, like most adults, regard hitting a partner to be wrong and want perpetrators to be 'challenged' (Gadd *et al.* 2015). At the same time most young people can think of exceptions when violence might be acceptable, and many young men can empathize with those who act in controlling ways towards a partner because they feel insecure and understand how a 'fight' between a couple can become physical given the imperative to 'hit back' (ibid.; Lombard 2015). These nuances of meaning—together with popular stereotypes about what perpetrators look like—'mad' older men under stress, younger men in gangs or addicted to drugs, or ethnic minority men with religious or cultural values that are disrespectful to women—are critical parts of the explanation as to how domestic violence continues despite widespread and historically enduring antipathy towards 'wife-beaters'. Interviews with young men who had been criminalized for physically assaulting partners lend support for the view that such men tend also to lack positive experiences of trusting relationships, abusive and neglectful childhoods commonplace in their life histories (Gadd *et al.* 2015). Within this context, it becomes easier to see how the sexist attitudes that justify domestic violence fester among young men whose hope that their intimate relationships will help redress feelings of anger, low self-worth, or anxiety deriving from troubled childhoods prove false, especially when they find themselves unexpectedly behaving in ways reminiscent of fathers and stepfathers who were abusive or demeaning towards them, their siblings, or their mothers.

What happens as such men grow up has been little studied by criminologists, though it is evident from both victimization surveys and treatment evaluations that many reduce their use of abusive behaviours or even stop completely by middle age

(Bowen 2011; Kelly and Westmarland 2015). Acceptance of the criminological wisdom that settling down with a partner helps men desist is part of the reason for the absence of research in this area (Gadd and Farrell 2004). Some perpetrators are only likely to stop using violence when they can accept the need to end a relationship or live alone, and many women are endangered when told that their husband needs to stay with them in order to redress his violence (ibid.). What we do know, however, is that engaging with the perspectives of those affected by violence makes a difference to men who have become reliant upon it and that this requires the provision of support programmes for victims to empower them enough to insist that violence is no longer acceptable (Dobash *et al.* 2000; Kelly and Westmarland 2015). Interventions that engage men as fathers and support their children so that they feel safe enough to ask them directly about previous violence can also help secure change among former perpetrators (Alderson *et al.* 2012). What is less well understood is how change is secured outside of treatment contexts and what it looks like, for there is a huge difference between a relationship in which someone who has been a victim of domestic violence continues to pacify a partner to avoid enraging them and the conscious decision of the person who has been violent to ensure they never react in that way again (Walker *et al.* 2015). Morran's (2013) recent follow up of 11 ex-perpetrators who completed celebrated UK perpetrator programmes reveals that while treatment helps some men become reflexive about masculinity and sexism they once relied upon to justify violence, the desire for control and the feelings of vulnerability that underpinned it often persist.

CONCLUSION

This chapter has endeavoured to take stock of the key features of the domestic violence literature produced over the last 70 years. It has revealed the inextricable connections between definitional, methodological, and aetiological issues. Wife-beaters have long been condemned by those invested in paternalistic values. Feminist research has encouraged the world to move beyond stereotypes of victims, but this has proved difficult in part because the struggle to get recognition for victims of domestic violence has rested upon the ability to demonstrate the scale of a problem with common dimensions patterned by gender. While sexism justifies some men's violence not all sexists are abusive and domestic violence perpetrators vary in their psychological profiles. Consequently, whether or not the parties involved come to think of themselves as victims, perpetrators, or mutual combatants can depend very much on how others respond to them and/or their own psychological preparedness to listen.

Given this, two things are probably necessary to take the criminology of domestic violence forward. First, the debate about *whether* or not gender is relevant needs to be superseded by a debate about how *gender* is relevant, both in articulating the dynamics of psychopathology and in compounding the other socially structured forms of discrimination—racism, classism, homophobia, disabilism—that give rise to violence.

Second, criminologists must conceptualize domestic violence as both an expression of power and potentially symptomatic of the absence of the authority or competence perpetrators would like to have. In its illegitimacy domestic violence exposes the desire for control and recognition perpetrators often feel they are lacking. This is why it often happens in moments of conflict or crisis, why many of those who repeatedly inflict it have troubled pasts and presents, and why the subtleties of cultural misogyny, sexism, patriarchy, and masculinities provide critical but, on their own, insufficient explanations for most of its instances. Expressing outrage at the persistence of men's violence towards women has become a critical part of the process of raising consciousness and demanding legal reform. But now is perhaps the time for criminologists to reflect more fully on just what the law can and cannot achieve in this regard. Only a minority of perpetrators are brought to justice and when they are the focus is invariably on culpability with regard to one or two discrete incidents—the incorporation of 'coercive control' into official definitions of domestic violence notwithstanding. In the recounting of high profile cases, as in the Pistorious case, defence lawyers persuade that mistakes were made, that the intent was not malevolent, and that love motivated more than hate or power. Hence, few perpetrators probably see themselves as 'wife-beaters'. Moreover, because some perpetrators are also victims, and some victims are also perpetrators, law enforcement focused on discrete incidents always risks pursuing the wrong women or wrong men, reproducing the injustices the intersections of multiple inequalities generate. If there is a unifying theme to be extracted from the historical record, victims' voices, and the campaigning of feminists, it is that people need the material and legal resources to leave abusive relationships without risking poverty, estrangement from their children, or stigma. The absence of this explains, in part, why domestic violence continues to be patterned by gender, why young adults are more prone to it than older adults, and why marginalized groups can find it harder to escape from it. Finding a common academic voice to redress the role of complex inequalities in the aetiology of domestic violence should be a priority for criminologists. The time has probably also come to develop a more differentiated approach to those who perpetrate domestic violence, to recognize that attitudes, motives, and backgrounds vary among those who have been perpetrators, that many of those who have been violent are not violent most of the time, and to establish what viable change looks like for those involved in intimate partner violence. Redressing the blindspots of law and challenging sexism remain crucial parts of this project, but there is also a need to explain why some people, especially some men, rely on violence and its threat to establish authority much more than others and to explore what needs to happen during their life courses to enable them to relinquish such dependence.

SELECTED FURTHER READING

Hydén, Gadd, and Wade's (2016) *Response-Based Approaches to the Study of Interpersonal Violence* showcases international perspectives informed by the insight that whether domestic violence continues depends upon the interplay of a complex range of responses.

Westmarland's *Violence against Women* (2015) provides a comprehensive overview of the criminological literature on violence against women.

REFERENCES

ALDERSON, S., WESTMARLAND, N., and KELLY, L. (2012), 'The Need for Accountability to, and Support for, Children of Men on Domestic Violence Perpetrator Programmes', *Child Abuse Review*, 22(3): 182–93.

ALGER, S. (2016), *Inverting Assumptions*, unpublished PhD: University of Manchester.

BBC (2015), 'Oscar Pistorius trial: 10 key moments', posted 3 December 2015, available at: http://www.bbc.co.uk/news/world-africa-29018522, accessed 26 April 2016.

BARTER, C., MCCARRY, M., BERRIDGE, D., and Evans, K. (2009), *Partner Exploitation and Violence in Teenage Intimate Relationships*, London: NSPCC.

BLACK, M. C., BASILE, K. C., BREIDING, M. J., SMITH, S. G., WALTERS, M. L., MERRICK, M. T., CHEN, J., and STEVENS, M. R. (2011), 'The National Intimate Partner and Sexual Violence Survey: 2010 Summary Report', Atlanta, GA: National Center for Injury Prevention and Control.

BOONZAIER, F. and GORDON, S. (2015), 'Responding to Men's Violence Against Women Partners in Post-Apartheid South Africa', *British Journal of Criminology*, 1–19.

BOWEN, E. (2011), *The Rehabilitation of Partner-Violent Men*, Chichester: Wiley.

BROAD, R. (2015), 'A vile and violent thing', *British Journal of Criminology*, 55(6): 1058–75.

BROWNMILLER, S. (1975), *Against Our Will*, New York: Simon and Schuster.

CATALANO, S. (2012), *Intimate Partner Violence, 1993–2010, NCJ 239203*, Washington, DC: US Department of Justice.

CLARK, A. (2000), 'Domesticity and the problem of wifebeating in nineteenth century Britain', in S. D'Cruze (eds), *Everyday Violence in Britain*, Harlow: Longman.

COBBE, F. P. (1878), 'Wife torture in England', *The Contemporary Review*, 32: 55–87.

CRENSHAW, K. (1993), 'Mapping the margins: Intersectionality, identity politics and violence against women of colour', *Stanford Law Review*, 43(6): 1241–99.

CRENSHAW, K. (2012), 'From Private Violence to Mass Incarceration: Thinking Intersectionally About Women, Race, and Social Control', *UCLA Law Review*, 59(6): 1418–72.

CRONE, R. (2006), 'Mr and Mrs Punch in Nineteenth-Century England', *The Historical Journal*, 49(4): 1055–82.

DEKESEREDY, W. S. and DRAGIEWICZ, M. (2014), 'Woman abuse in Canada', *Violence Against Women*, 20(2): 228–44.

DIXON, L., ARCHER, J., and GRAHAM-KEVAN, N. (2012), 'Perpetrator programmes for partner violence', *Legal and Criminological Psychology*, 17(2): 196–215.

DOBASH, R. P. and DOBASH, R. (1979), *Violence Against Wives*, New York: Free Press.

DOBASH, R. E. and DOBASH, R. P. (1984), 'The Nature and Antecedents of Violent Events', *British Journal of Criminology*, 24(3): 269–88.

DOBASH, R. P., DOBASH, R. E., WILSON, M., and DALY, M. (1992), 'The Myth of Sexual Symmetry in Marital Violence', *Social Problems*, 39(1): 71–91.

DOBASH, R. E., DOBASH, R. P., LEWIS, R., and CAVANAGH, K. (2000), *Changing Violent Men*, London: Sage.

DONOVAN, C. and HESTER, M. (2011), 'Seeking help from the enemy', *Child and Family Law Quarterly*, 23(1): 26–40.

DUTTON, D.G. (1998), *The Abusive Personality*, London: Guildford Press.

DUTTON, D. G. (2010), 'The gender paradigm and the architecture of antiscience', *Partner Abuse*, 1(1): 5–25.

DWORKIN, A. (1974), *Woman Hating*, New York: Penguin.

DWORKIN, A. (1981), *Pornography*, London: Women's Press.

EREZ, E., ADELMAN, M., and GREGORY, C. (2009), 'Intersections of Immigration and Domestic Violence', *Feminist Criminology*, 4(1): 32–56.

EULER, C. (2000), 'The irons of their fetters have eaten into their souls'—nineteenth-century feminist strategies to get our bodies onto the political agenda', in S. D'Cruze (eds), *Everyday violence in Britain*, Harlow: Longman.

EUROPEAN UNION AGENCY FOR FUNDAMENTAL RIGHTS (2014), *Violence Against Women: An EU-Wide Survey*, Luxembourg: Publications Office of the European Union.

FAULK, M. (1974), 'Men who assault their wives', *Medicine, Science and the Law*, 4(3): 180–3.

FOX, C. L., CORR, M-L., GADD, D., and BUTLER, I. (2014), 'Young teenagers' experiences of domestic abuse', *Journal of Youth Studies*, 17(5): 510–26.

FOYSTER, E. (2002), 'Creating a veil of silence? Politeness and marital violence in the English household', *Transactions of the Royal Historical Society*, 12: 395–415.

FREDERICK, B. and PERRONE, D. (2014), '"Party N Play" on the Internet', *Deviant Behavior*, 35(11): 859–84.

GADD, D. (2000), 'Masculinities, violence, and defended psychosocial subjects', *Theoretical Criminology*, 4(4): 429–49.

GADD, D. (2002), 'Masculinities and violence against female partners', *Social and Legal Studies*, 11(1): 61–80.

GADD, D. and FARRALL, S. (2004), 'Criminal careers, desistance and subjectivity', *Theoretical Criminology*, 8(2): 123–56.

GADD, D., FARRALL, S., DALLIMORE, D., and LOMBARD, N. (2003), 'Equal victims or the usual suspects?', *International Review of Victimology*, 10(1): 95–116.

GADD, D., FOX, C., and HALE, R. (2014), 'Preliminary steps towards a more preventative approach to eliminating violence against women in Europe', *European Journal of Criminology*, 11(4): 464–80.

GADD, D., FOX, C., CORR, M-L., BUTLER, I., and ALGER, S. (2015), *Young Men and Domestic Abuse*, London: Routedge.

García-Moreno, C., Jansen, H., Ellsberg, M., Heise, L., and Watts, C. (2005), *WHO Multi-Country Study on Women's Health and Domestic Violence Against Women*, Geneva: WHO.

García-Moreno, C., Pallitto, C., Devries, K., Stöckl, H., and Watts, C. (2013), *Global and Regional Estimates of Violence Against Women*, Geneva: WHO.

Gayford, J. (1979), 'The Aetiology of Repeated Serious Physical Assaults by Husbands on Wives (Wife Battering)', *Medicine, Science and the Law*, 19(1): 19–24.

Gill, A. (2011), 'Reconfiguring "honour"-based violence as a form of gendered violence', in M. Idriss and T. Abbas (eds), *Honour, Violence, Women and Islam*, London: Routledge.

Gottzèn, L. (2016), 'Displaying shame: men's violence toward women in a culture of gender equality', in M. Hydén, D. Gadd, and A. Wade (eds), *Response-Based Approaches to the Study of Interpersonal Violence*, London: Palgrave.

Griffin, S. (1971), 'Rape: The All-American Crime', *Ramparts*, 10(3): 26–35.

Hamlett, N. (1998), *Women Who abuse in Intimate Relationships*, Minneapolis: Domestic Abuse Project.

Hammerton, A. J. (1992), *Cruelty and Companionship*, London: Routledge.

Holtzworth-Munroe, A. and Stuart, G. (1994), 'Typologies of Male Batterers', *Psychological Bulletin*, 16(3): 476–97.

Hearn, J. (1998), *The Violences of Men*, London: Sage.

Hester, M. (2009), *Who Does What to Whom?*, Bristol: University of Bristol in association with the Northern Rock Foundation.

Hester, M. (2010), 'Gender and Sexuality', in C. Itzin, A. Taket, and S. Barter-Godfrey (eds), *Domestic and Sexual Violence and Abuse: Tackling the Health and Mental Health Effects*, London: Taylor & Francis.

Hester, M., Ferrari, G., Jones, S. K., Williamson, E., Bacchus. L., and Peters, T. J. (2015), 'Occurrence and impact of negative behaviour, including domestic violence and abuse, in men attending UK primary care health clinics: a cross-sectional survey', *British Medical Journal Open*, 5(5): 1–10.

Hughes, A. (2010), 'The "Non-Criminal" Class: Wife-Beating in Scotland (c. 1800-1949), *Crime, History and Societies*, 14(2): 31–54.

Hunt, M. (1992), 'Wife Beating, Domesticity and Women's Independence in Eighteenth Century London', *Gender and History*, 4(1): 10–33.

Hydén, M., Gadd, D., and Wade, A. (eds) (2016), *Response-Based Approaches to the Study of Interpersonal Violence*, London: Palgrave.

Idriss, M. (2011), 'Honour, violence, women and Islam' in M. Idriss and T. Abbas (eds), *Honour, Violence, Women and Islam*, London: Routledge.

Johnson, M. (2006), *A Typology of Domestic Violence*, Boston: New University Press.

Kelly, L. (1987), 'The Continuum of Sexual Violence', in J. Hanmer and M. Maynard (eds), *Women, Violence and Social Control*, Basingstoke: Prometheus.

Kelly, L. (1988), *Surviving sexual violence*, Oxford: Polity.

Kelly, L. and Westmarland, N. (2015), *Domestic Violence Perpetrator Programmes: Steps Towards Change. Project Mirabal Final Report*, London and Durham: London Metropolitan University and Durham University.

Kimmel, M. (2002), '"Gender symmetry" in domestic violence', *Violence Against Women*, 8(11): 1332–63.

Lee, M. and Crofts, T. (2015), 'Gender, Pressure, Coercion and Pleasure', *British Journal of Criminology*, 55(3): 454–73.

Lombard, N. (2015), *Young People's Understandings of Men's Violence Against Women*, Surrey: Ashgate.

ONS (2014), 'Chapter 4—Intimate Personal Violence and Partner Abuse', in *Crime Statistics, Focus on Violent Crime and Sexual Offences*, 2012/13, London: Office for National Statistics.

ONS (2016) 'Chapter 4—Intimate Personal Violence and Partner Abuse', in *Crime Statistics, Focus on Violent Crime and Sexual Offences*, 2014/15, London: Office for National Statistics.

O' Leary, D. K. (1993), 'Through a Psychological Lens', in R. Gelles and R. D. Loske (eds), *Current Controversies in Family Violence*, Newbury Park: Sage.

Povey, D., Coleman, K., Kaiza, P., Hoare, J., and Jansson, K. (2008), 'Homicides, firearm offences and intimate violence 2006/2007' (Supplementary Volume 2 to Crime in England and Wales 2006/07), London: Home Office.

MacQueen, S. (2014), *2012/13 Scottish Crime and Justice Survey: Partner Abuse*, SCJR, Edinburgh: Scottish Government.

Mason, G. and Pulvirenti, M. (2013), 'Former Refugees and Community Resilience', *British Journal of Criminology*, 53(3): 401–18.

Messerschmidt, J. (1999), *Nine Lives*, Boulder: Westview.

Miller, J. (2008), *Getting Played*, New York: NYU Press.

Miller, S. and Meloy, M. (2006), 'Women's Use of Force', *Violence Against Women*, 12(1): 89–115.

Mirrlees-Black, C. (1999), *Domestic Violence: Findings from a New British Crime Survey Self-completion Questionnaire*, HORS 191, London: Home Office.

Morran, D. (2013), 'Desisting from domestic abuse', *Howard Journal of Criminal Justice*, 52(3): 306–20.

Pickering, S. and Ham, J. (2013), 'Hot Pants at the Border', *British Journal of Criminology*, 54(1): 2–19.

Renzetti, C. (1992), *Violent Betrayal*, Thousand Oaks: Sage.

Robinson, A., and Howarth, E. (2012), 'Judging Risk: Key Determinants in British Domestic Violence Cases', *Journal of Interpersonal Violence*, 27(8): 1489–518.

Roch, A., Ritchie, G., and Morton, J. (2010), *Out of Sight, Out of Mind*, Edinburgh: Scottish Transgender Alliance.

Roe, S. (2009), 'Intimate violence: 2007/08 British Crime Survey', in D. Povey (ed.), *Homicides, firearm offences and intimate violence 2007/08*, 3rd edn, Home Office Statistical Bulletin 02/09, London: Home Office.

SCHULTZ, L. (1960), 'The Wife Assaulter', *Journal of Social Therapy*, 6: 103–11.

SHANNON, K., KERR, T., ALLINOTT, S., CHETTIAR, J., SHOVELLER, J., and TYNDALL, M. (2008), 'Social and structural violence and power relations in mitigating HIV risk of drug-using women in survival sex work', *Social Science Medicine*, 66(4): 911–21.

SMART, C. (1990), 'Feminist Approaches to Criminology or Postmodern Woman Meets Atavistic Man', in L. Gelsthorpe and A. Morris (eds), *Feminist Perspectives in Criminology*, Buckingham: Open University Press.

SNELL, J. R., ROSENWALD, R., and ROBEY, A. (1964), 'The Wifebeater's Wife', *Archives of General Psychiatry*, 11: 107–13.

SQUIRE, C. (2016), 'Narratives as Responses to Physical Interpersonal Violence', in M. Hydén, D. Gadd, and A. Wade (eds), *Response-Based Approaches to the Study of Interpersonal Violence*, London: Palgrave.

STANKO E. (1985), *Intimate Intrusions*, London: Routledge.

STARK, E. (2007), *Coercive Control: How Men Entrap Women in Personal Life*, New York: Oxford University Press.

STRAUS, M. (1993), 'Physical Assaults by Wives', in R. Gelles and D. Loske, (eds), *Current Controversies in Family Violence*, Newbury Park: Sage.

STRAUS, M. (2010), 'Thirty Years of Denying the Evidence on Gender', *Partner Abuse*, 1(3): 332–62.

STUART, G., MOORE, T., GORDON, K., HELLMUTH, J., RAMSEY, S., and KAHLER C. (2006), 'Reasons for intimate partner violence perpetration among arrested women', *Violence Against Women*, 12(7): 609–21.

SUPREME COURT OF APPEAL (2015), The Supreme Court of Appeal Of South Africa Judgment, Reportable Case No: 96/2015, In The Matter Between: Director Of Public Prosecutions, Gauteng Appellant and Oscar Leonard Carl Pistorius, available at: http://cdn.24.co.za/files/Cms/General/d/1801/db3888fd1bc-24611805612316c9e413b.pdf, accessed 26 April 2016.

SWAN S. and SNOW, D. (2006), 'The development of a theory of women's use of violence in intimate relationships', *Violence Against Women*, 12(11): 1026–45.

TJADEN, P., THOENNES, N., and ALLISON, C. (1999), 'Comparing violence over the life span in samples of same-sex and opposite-sex cohabitants', *Violence and Victims*, 14(4): 413–25.

TJADEN, P, and THOENNES, N. (2000), *Full Report of the Prevalence, Incidence, and Consequences of Violence Against Women*, Washington: National Institute of Justice.

TREWIN, D. (2005), 'Personal safety survey Australia', Melbourne: Australia Bureau of Statistics.

VETTEN, L. (2014), 'Domestic violence in South Africa', *Policy Brief 71*, Pretoria: Institute for Security Studies.

WALBY, S. and MYHILL, A. (2002), 'New Survey Methodologies in Researching Violence Against Women', *British Journal of Criminology*, 41(3): 502–22.

WALBY, S., TOWERS, J., and FRANCIS, B. (2014a), *The Decline in the Rate of Domestic Violence has Stopped*, Lancaster: Lancaster University.

WALBY, S., TOWERS, J., and FRANCIS, B. (2014b), 'Mainstreaming domestic and gender-based violence into sociology and the criminology of violence', *The Sociological Review*, 62(2): 187–214.

WALKER, L. (1984), *The Battered Woman Syndrome*, New York: Springer.

WALKER, K., BOWEN, E., BROWN, S., and SLEATH, E. (2015), 'Desistance from Intimate Partner Violence', *Journal of Interpersonal Violence*, 30(15): 2726–50.

WALTERS, M., CHEN J., and BREIDING, M. J. (2013), *The National Intimate Partner and Sexual Violence Survey (NISVS): 2010 Findings on Victimization by Sexual Orientation*, Atlanta: National Center for Injury Prevention and Control.

WESTMARLAND, N. (2015), *Violence against Women*, London: Routledge.

WIENER, M. (2006), *Men of Blood*, Cambridge: Cambridge University Press.

30

PROSTITUTION AND SEX WORK

Jo Phoenix

INTRODUCTION

The aims of this chapter are threefold: to explore the characteristics and contexts of prostitution as they have evolved into the twenty-first century; to examine the ways in which such phenomena have been conceptualized within criminology; and to review the shifting modes of regulation that have shaped responses to sex work over time, with a specific focus on UK developments. As the chapter will demonstrate, there is now such a rich body of academic literature on prostitution that it is possible to speak of a sub-field of 'sex-work studies'. However, prostitution remains a subject of intense debate and there is little or no consensus amongst academics, politicians, policy-makers, or campaigners regarding definitional, explanatory, or regulatory questions. Indeed as a field, sex work research is beset with epistemological, methodological, and political schisms and consequently risks losing sight of some basic questions including: how is prostitution shaped by the social, economic, and cultural contexts in which it is situated; how can we account for the 'passage' of individuals who become involved in prostitution over time (to borrow from Young 1987); and how can scholars utilise the answers to these questions better to illuminate political and policy debates?

The chapter begins with a review of the changing empirical realities of prostitution and sex work. It then explores in more detail the ways in which women's involvement in prostitution has been conceptualized within criminology. This is followed by a review of current regulatory frameworks and the ways in which these have been influenced by both emergent criminological knowledge and context.

EMPIRICAL REALITIES—CHANGE AND CONTINUITY

In comparison with the nineteenth and twentieth centuries, the twenty-first century has witnessed significant changes to the ways in which sex can be bought, sold, and financially exploited, as broader social, political, and economic forces alter and multiply sex 'markets', old and new.

As a social institution, prostitution is more than an exchange of sex for money. It comprises heterogeneous relationships between sex workers, their clients, the local neighbourhoods, and regulatory agencies such as the police, social workers, or health-care professionals. It takes many different shapes and forms: from street-based sex work to indoor work which, in itself, is variable in terms of how it is organized, the business model upon which it is fashioned, and the ways in which it is regulated. The internet and smart phones have provided the technology for an assumed massive expansion, diversification, and reorganization of prostitution and new and different commercial sexual experiences and products (take cybersex for instance), as well as novel ways to organize the sale and purchase of sex (see punternet.org as an example) (Weitzer 2007, 2009).

Globalization and the spread of neoliberal economic policies have given rise to what is (now) more commonly referred to as a globally organized 'sex industry', rather than prostitution. Not only are national and international companies and corporations structuring these new 'markets' (Brents and Sanders 2010), the sex industry has become as intertwined with licit, global economic 'markets' (such as sex tourism) as it is with older illicit 'markets' (such as drugs markets). Globalization and mass migration have also altered routes into prostitution and the conditions experienced by those involved have become more tied to the global flows of capital and human beings and, consequently, more precarious (O'Connell Davidson 2015). Along with this expansion and diversification in the way that prostitution is structured and organized, locally and globally, women's experiences of prostitution also vary enormously, as between different sectors of the sex industry and different parts of the world in which such activities are pursued (Chin and Finckenauer 2012; Kempadoo *et al.* 2015).

Amidst all this diversity, there nevertheless remain a few unchanging themes. In particular, there remain endemic levels of exploitation and violence in the industry just as there remain links with organized crime (Campbell 2000; Turnbull *et al.* 2001; Church 2003; Hester and Westmarland 2004; Galatowicz *et al.* 2005). Small-scale empirical research confirms that for women, entrance into prostitution tends to be shaped by everyday political and economic structures that: maintain women's economic dependency on men and families; shape their relative poverty to men; limit their access to full-time secure employment; place on women the burden of childcare and domestic responsibilities; ensure that welfare security is mediated by and through women's relationships in families and with men; and maintain welfare benefits at near destitution level. In this context, sex remains—as ever—a key economic resource in women's attempts to provide for themselves and any dependents they may have. These processes and structures become more pronounced for women who struggle with multiple disadvantage and compound social-welfare and health needs (Phoenix 1999). As in earlier centuries, where activities associated with prostitution were criminalized, the burden of regulation today falls disproportionately on the women in prostitution rather than the men (Edwards 1987).

Given this backdrop of both change and continuity, how then has criminology engaged with questions relating to prostitution?

THEORIZING PROSTITUTION

This section charts the evolution of criminological theory from early positivism to more recent debates within feminist criminology and offers a critique of the core precepts which underscore attempts to analyse and explain women's involvement in prostitution.

POSITIVISM, AETIOLOGY, AND SUBCULTURES

For the better part of the last 150 years, the prostitution-related question that captured the imagination of criminologists was: why do women do it? This aetiological question was generated by two sets of assumptions. Firstly, prostitution was somehow disconnected from mainstream social institutions and activities and thus women's involvement in it required explanation. Secondly, being involved in prostitution meant *selling* sex which, for women, was deemed pathological, and a deviant, or abnormal social activity (in contrast to the purchase of sex by men which was considered to be normal).

Two of the most well-known positivistic explanations for women's involvement in prostitution were put forward by Lombroso and Ferrero (1898) and Sheldon and Eleanor Glueck (1934). Briefly, Lombroso's and Ferrero's (1898) explanation of prostitution was an application of Lombroso's earlier positive method of social science and his theory of atavism as the cause of criminality. Lombroso and Ferrero started with the observation that there appeared to be fewer atavistic women than men and certainly fewer criminal women than men. They argued that this was because the reproductive and maternal functions of women produced a retardation of evolution. However, once they collected detailed physiognomic data from women involved in prostitution, they noted that such women exhibited more atavistic qualities and certainly more criminal characteristics than 'normal' women. They concluded, therefore, that prostitution must be the form that women's criminality takes.

In a similar fashion, the Gluecks also conceptualized prostitution as a form of women's criminality. In their study, they included women who committed crime as well as women in prostitution, with over half their sample engaged in some form of sex work. They argued that involvement in either was a result of the individual's supposed pathological nature. However, rather than prostitutes possessing a physiological pathology (such as atavism) the Gluecks argued that prostitutes were women who were 'burdened with feeblemindedness psychopathic personality and marked instability [who] find it difficult to survive by legitimate means' (Gluecks 1934: 300). Put simply, these women's psychological pathologies were what caused their involvement in prostitution.

Whilst early positivistic accounts were reductive, later positivistic explanations took rather subtler forms. For instance, in her exposition of sex work in England, Wilkinson (1955) conceptualized prostitution as a deviant subculture (in keeping, it should be noted, with dominant explanations for youth delinquency at the time). The question that arises from such a conceptualization remains an aetiological one, namely: what causes women to become 'prostitutes'—that is a member of a deviant subculture? Wilkinson's specific claim was that such women experienced a process of extrusion. First, at some point in their lives the various social institutions within which they were located 'failed' them. Second, these women became dislocated from 'normal society', which created a 'drifting and disorganised state' (see generally the Chicago School and social ecological explanations for criminality (Shaw and McKay 1942; Burgess and Akers 1966; Sutherland *et al.* 1992)). Third, whilst drifting 'women may hear of friends, or may even work with women who are prostitutes and eventually accept the suggestion of some friend that they should go out with her' (Wilkinson 1955: 108). For Wilkinson, there is no one cause of women's involvement in prostitution: just a series of contributory factors. She states:

> There is a danger in this over-simplification of factors which are no more than phases of a dialectical process, and the analysis of these factors is submitted in the belief that any factor alone is insignificant and none can be isolated with the comment: 'This is the cause'. The cause is past experience, plus present situation, plus personal interpretation of them both. (Wilkinson 1955: 243).

Fast forward to the end of the twentieth and beginning of the twenty-first centuries and such explanations continue to have currency in the shape of 'pathways' models. Dodsworth's (2012) 'routes into sexual exploitation' uses much the same logic as Wilkinson: 'a complex pattern emerged . . . in which various 'push' and/or 'pull' factors, interconnected and overlapped with incidents of going missing. The meaning participants gave to these experiences . . . appeared to precipitate them along different pathways . . .' (Dodsworth 2012: 2). And many other pathways studies start with the usual description of demographics: women in prostitution tend to come from abusive families, have been excluded from school, have grown up in Local Authority Care, may have experience of drug and alcohol issues, mental health issues, have housing difficulties, are unemployed, underemployed, or in precarious labour (Chesney-Lind 1989; Galvin *et al.* 2003; Cusick 2006; Coy 2008; Coy 2009; Pearce 2009; Dodsworth 2012; Chesney-Lind and Shelden 2013). Hoigard and Finstad (1992) made more explicit reference to the impact of subcultures in their ethnography of prostitution in Sweden, and made the case (again in a manner akin to Wilkinson) that women's involvement in criminal subcultural milieus creates the conditions for many to enter sex work. Similarly O'Neill (2001) notes that involvement in prostitution is caused by a variety of factors—not least of which being women's poverty, particularly in capitalist, male dominated societies. Indeed, many ethnographies and qualitative studies of prostitution demonstrate that sex workers themselves also author such explanations (McKeganey and Barnard 1996; Melrose *et al.* 1999; Matthews and O'Neill 2003; Kinnell 2008).

The problems of biological and psychological positivism are well-known and dealt with extensively elsewhere (Phoenix 1999). However, subcultural and pathways explanations are also not without problems. In common with most subcultural explanations for criminality, there is a tendency within this body of work to overstate the differences between the criminal and/or prostitution subculture and the mainstream culture and the institutions 'out of which' women and girls have fallen. In doing so, this mode of theorizing merely reproduces the binary of normal/abnormal which inheres in earlier positivist accounts. Moreover, at the empirical level, research from England investigating the impact of street-based prostitution on communities has demonstrated—contrary to what is often assumed within subcultural or pathways explanations—that residents consider the women who work in the community to be part of, rather than different to, their community (Scoular *et al.* 2007; O'Neill, Campbell, *et al.* 2008). Additionally, explanations that focus on specifying risk factors, routes, or pathways to deviance or criminality, no matter how complex, tend to confuse correlation with causation (Sampson and Laub 1995) (see also O'Mahony (2009) for a critique of risk factors in relation to complex social behaviour, such as youth offending). Finally, no matter how careful the academic is to specify that such pathways or routes into prostitution are rational choices taken by women and would be taken by other women too, there is nevertheless the underpinning assumption that it is *these* individuals whose sexual or economic lives warrant an explanation—and indeed a 'special' explanation. Perhaps all that can be said for subcultural and pathways studies, is that they offer little more than well nuanced demographic descriptions of women *already* involved in prostitution.

ANTI-POSITIVISM AND SHIFTING OBJECTS OF EXPLANATIONS

By the end of the twentieth century, new more politically radical and academically critical questions were being asked about sex, sexualities, and regulation—questions that had a profound impact on the way that prostitution was conceptualized. Critical sexuality studies made the case that 'sexuality' varies according to social and historical context (McIntosh 1968; Gagnon and Simon 1973; Plummer 1981; Weeks 1981; Weeks 2000). Feminist scholarship challenged ideologies of gender as they shaped biologistic assumptions about male and female sex and sexuality and drew connections between these ideologies and the maintenance of social structural inequalities (Brownmiller 1976; McIntosh 1978; Smart and Smart 1978; Daly 1979; Eisenstein 1979; Shulman 1980; Dworkin 1981; Barry 1984; see also Burman and Gelsthorpe, this volume). Foucault's ground-breaking *History of Sexuality, vol. 1* made the case that the notion of 'sexuality' is an historical construct, rather than a biological category with an essential and unvarying empirical reality (Foucault 1979). Together, this body of work challenged one of the dominant assumptions underpinning positivistic explanations of women and prostitution: that prostitution served as a necessary safety valve given the biological necessity of men's sexual drive and the absolute need for men to sate their sexual desires. Deconstructing such essentialist logic raised other important questions: if prostitution was not about sex *per se*, then what was 'it'? If ideologies and practices of sex and sexuality were socially constructed in societies marked by fundamental gender-based inequalities, then what did this say about prostitution, women's involvement in sex work, and the ways in which it was regulated and policed?

In addressing the above questions, new binaries emerged that have constituted both the theorizing of prostitution as well as its politics. Prostitution was seen to be *either* a form of labour in a materially unequal society (McIntosh 1978) *or* an expression of male violence in a patriarchal society (Millett 1975). Indeed, a new space was opened which allowed for a more sociological exploration of the shape and form of prostitution. Subsequently, the period of 1980s and 1990s bore witness to an explosion of theoretically informed (mostly feminist and criminological) empirical studies focusing on the meanings of prostitution for the women involved. The debate provoked by these innovative investigations focused on: the possible relationships between women's economic circumstances and their involvement in prostitution, and the relationship between men's violence and women's involvement in prostitution. Were both men's violence against women and prostitution social institutions resulting from patriarchy (Høigård and Finstad 1992; Barry 1996; O'Neill *et al.* 1997)? Or, could women's experiences in prostitution be better explained by reference to class and labour-based inequalities (Davidson 1998; Agustín 2001; Agustín 2007)? Or both (Phoenix 1999)?

Prostitution as victimization

Prostitution as victimization is a theoretical model that is shaped by the precepts of radical feminism and offers an understanding of how a patriarchal social structure determines both the shape and form that prostitution takes and the experiences of women within it. To remind readers, as a sociological concept, 'patriarchy' refers to an unequal social structure that supports, sustains, and reproduces male domination of females. Feminist scholarship in the 1980s focused on specifying the contours of a patriarchal state and identifying how specific social and ideological practices maintained patriarchy. Fundamental to this perspective were the following claims: that gender-based ideologies of femininities and masculinities differentiate between men and women in an hierarchical and normative fashion; that women do not have control of their reproductive capacities because such control is mediated by powerful social institutions and ideologies (such as the family, religious ideologies, and a variety of medical practices); that women have less access to economic resources, largely because they are located in the private sphere of the family and have the burden of caring responsibilities; and, ultimately, that male sexual violence is socially structured.[1]

There are several basic propositions which comprise the prostitution-as-victimization approach. The first is that prostitution is a social institution shaped and determined by gender-based inequalities. Second, within patriarchal societies prostitution is not a deviant or pathological social institution, but rather a mainstream one that serves particular functions—the details of which will be highlighted below. Third, critical to the functioning of patriarchal societies is the privileging of men's sexual agency and the denigration of women's which finds expression in the commodification of women's sexuality and their bodies. Fourth, whilst sexual violence is a manifest example of both patriarchal social structures and the privileging of men's sexuality,

[1] For a comprehensive discussion of feminist interpretations of the concept of patriarchy which were relevant in shaping the prostitution as victimization explanation, see Beechey, V. (1979), 'On Patriarchy', available at: http://www.palgrave-journals.com/fr/journal/v3/n1/full/fr197921a.html, accessed 7 January 2017.

one function prostitution performs is an ideological one, normalizing sexual violence and the commodification of women's sexualities and bodies. The most clear expressions of this perspective were put forward by writers such as: Kate Millett (1975, 2000) who argued that prostitution speaks to the heart of women's social and political conditions in patriarchal societies—prostitution, in the form of a cash exchange, is women's subjection made public (without the mystification of marriage and love), it is also a declaration of the totality of women's value (a commodifiable vagina); Kathleen Barry (1984, 1996) who describes the processes, practices, laws, and institutional regulations which ensure women's sexual victimization (including prostitution) and keep women in a state of sexual 'slavery'; and, Shelia Jeffreys (1999, 2008) who has charted how women's sexual victimization within prostitution has become normalized, and latterly how the institutionalization of such sexual victimization has been shaped, influenced, and given dynamic force through global capitalism.

In each case, the arguments are functionalist in logic in that they chart the role that the social institution of prostitution plays in relation to patriarchal sexuality and sexual violence. More recently still, such logic has been inverted as the notion of violence has given way to the notion of harm—that is to say that gender-based inequalities are seen as producing prostitution and the commodification of women's bodies which, in turn, are seen as producing particular types of gender-based harms. With that, a new generation of feminist scholars are charting the various globalizing and social processes that create the sorts of harms that continue to characterize many individual women's experiences of prostitution (see various chapters in Coy (2013), especially Coy's opening chapter).

Prostitution as work

Conceptualizing prostitution as work has its roots within a broader socialist-feminist perspective. Like radical feminism, it is a form of critical inquiry that seeks to excavate the conditions determining women's oppression in order to craft a politics of liberation. However, unlike radical feminism, social (or materialist) feminist analyses located the sources of oppression in the ways in which patriarchy and capitalism combined. The basic premises of this perspective are as follows. Prostitution is a social institution shaped and determined by both gender-based and class-based inequalities. Within patriarchal-capitalist societies, women's economic survival is mediated by and through their relationships with men (in marriage, in families) because of their exclusion from the public sphere (of politics, of employment, and so on). Ideologies of gender that separate women into 'good women' and 'bad women' help to mystify the economic nature of all sexual relationships.

The most clearly articulated example of this perspective was first put forward in the now classic *Working Women: Prostitution Now* by McLeod (1982). She made the case that women involved in prostitution are not different from other women in capitalist societies. Like all women, they are engaged in a struggle against their disadvantaged social position. Prostitution is simply the social institution that confirms that women's most saleable commodity in a capitalist economy is sex. Yet, as sex workers, any chance of being able to control their labour is mitigated by male violence, male economic domination, 'whore stigma', and hypocritical laws that punish women but not men, for their involvement in prostitution.

By the late 1990s, there was an expanding literature drawing on McLeod's (1982) theorization and charting, not just the meanings of prostitution for the women involved, but also the social organization of prostitution, and the historically and socially specific contours of power that are expressed within, and made manifest at, the local, national, and global levels (see for instance Kempadoo and Doezema (1998)). Underpinning many of these studies was a shared concern to understand the nature of prostitution as a form of 'labour' within and across (late) (modern) capitalist societies.

More recently though, other scholars began exploring the socio-cultural context of sex work (Sanders *et al.* 2009). Starting with the basic premise of the prostitution-as-work perspective, prostitution was also conceptualized as just one part of a broader sex industry which encompasses everything from street-based prostitution to lap dancing, from pornography to adult only stores, from sex toys to strip clubs. There has been a proliferation of small-scale studies that describe the 'everyday lives, businesses and relationships' that comprise the sex industry (see for instance Hardy *et al.* (2010) and Sanders and Hardy (2013)). Often theorizing the 'sex industry' as a new (or expanding) market, industry, or economy in consumer capitalism, these micro analyses have also sought to understand social, economic, and cultural changes that make the markets possible as well as to analyse the various ways in which this market is similar (or not) to other 'markets' within capitalism. So, for instance, Bernstein (2007), after examining sexual markets in San Francisco, Stockholm, and Amsterdam, makes the case that in the late twentieth century, 'the sex industry' as a market began to change in both social and spatial terms. Socially, it moved from street-based sex work, with its embeddedness in communities, to individual, technologically mediated encounters. Spatially, the market moved from outdoors to indoors. Indeed Bernstein (2007:102) argues that late twentieth-century 'sex markets' could be characterized and described as a 'new post-industrial paradigm of commercial sex' which itself was made possible by a broader change in the socio-cultural signification and meanings of sex—whereas once it was framed within a relational ethic, it is now framed by and within *recreational* ethics.

Focusing more on the economics of the new sex markets, Brents and Hausbeck demonstrate how the brothel industry in Nevada uses very similar marketing and business strategies to late twentieth-century leisure and tourist industries. From this they argue that the sex industry is best examined and understood as a 'mainstream' business industry and as part of the rise in late capitalist global forms of consumption (Brents and Hausbeck 2007; Brents *et al.* 2010). In a similar fashion, Brents and Sanders (2010) make the case that as the sex industry expands the distance between it and licit economies is closing. At the same time however 'social ambivalence' (i.e. the normative evaluation of the sex industry as transgressive and/or deviant) facilitates its further expansion and also shapes its regulation. To these micro studies can be added an incredibly diverse set of largely ethnographic and descriptive studies of many different forms of sexual services including male prostitution, sex tourism, male stripping, transgendered sex work, that highlight, *inter alia*, a bewildering set of occupational cultures, strategies, and tactics, drug use, organizational and individual business practices—including health, safety, and risk (see ch. 3 in Sanders *et al.* 2009).

Understanding prostitution as just one part of a wider sex market (that in turn forms just one part of a global economic system no longer founded upon production, but upon consumption) did create a space for a noteworthy growth in studies—even if those studies remain, largely, descriptive. Mirroring the sociology of deviance, the commitment has been to 'humanize' or indeed normalize 'the deviant', or in this case, the supposedly deviant market. These more recent studies (of sex work as part of the sex industry) are distinguished from earlier approaches (such as Macleod's) which drew (often explicitly) on Marxian notions of 'labour' and particularly the exploitative and alienating nature of waged labour. Instead, contemporary approaches are underpinned by an implicit acceptance of a free market economics—best exemplified in their efforts to map the sex industry in relation to the 'mainstream' economic system.

Critique

The two theoretical positions of prostitution as 'victimization' or as 'work', were never really as distinct as some have assumed. Women themselves often see their involvement in prostitution as both work *and* a form of gendered victimization (Phoenix 1999). Research also shows that consent, control, choice, and agency are often exercised in subtle ways and individuals' capacity to make choices is shaped by both their wider social position (as working class women, BME women, young women, and so on) and the form of prostitution in which they are located.[2] Indeed the empirical realities of prostitution are far more complex than theoretical models, such as those just described, could ever hope to capture.

As much as contemporary theories have critiqued the orthodoxies of earlier more positivistic accounts, they too have a tendency towards reductionism. They reduce the complexities of involvement in prostitution to prostituting, that is the act of selling or swapping sex, as much as they reduce the diversity of prostitution to (mostly) street-based and other exploitative forms of prostitution. They reduce the totality of individuals' social lives to their lives in prostitution in that women's experiences in prostitution (alone) require explanation. And, as this section has demonstrated, in challenging the positivistic binaries of normal/abnormal (criminal) women, these newer perspectives have invoked two further sets of binaries (work/violence; consent/coercion). As a consequence much of the debate has become mired in the structure/agency, voluntarism/determinism tropes that characterized criminological theorizing for a century or more. What seems to be missing from many of these perspectives is the recognition that we all make choices, but not in conditions of our own choosing and that critical to the criminology of prostitution is the need for further theorizing with regard to the historical and social specificity of those conditions, how they shape both prostitution and the choices women make, and ultimately their consequences for governance and regulation. Fundamentally, the concept of prostitution may limit the field of study in important ways; indeed it may be more methodologically, theoretically, and epistemologically meaningful to speak of prostitutions rather than prostitution.

[2] For example women working in the legal brothels of Victoria, Australia, or Nevada have fundamentally different meanings attached to their involvement than, say, homeless girls exchanging sex for money in order to make sure they have accommodation for the night.

REGULATING PROSTITUTION

From this review of theory, the chapter now turns to a more detailed exploration of the ways in which prostitution and sex work has been regulated.

Over the course of the late twentieth and early twenty-first centuries, the UK (and much of Western Europe) has witnessed an apparent reversal in the declared trajectory of regulation. Once, formal regulation explicitly targeted 'fallen women' and the threat they caused to young men's health, young women's morals, and family inheritances (see Walkowitz 1982). Now, the main stated targets are predatory and powerful males, 'sexual abusers', 'pimps', 'traffickers', and 'organized criminal gangs' because of the threats of abuse and exploitation that they pose to 'society', 'the vulnerable', and 'the victimized'. Arguably this apparent reversal is a result of the intricate interconnections between knowledge production, official constructions of 'the problems' of prostitution, assumptions about the shifting shape and forms of prostitution, together with transformations in the configuration of policing and the process of policy reform itself. Yet, it will also be demonstrated that the apparent reversal has also created a bifurcated system of regulating prostitution: one which still focuses on women as the subjects of intervention, despite its stated aims.

NUISANCE AND THE TARGETING OF PUBLIC WOMEN

Legal definitions of prostitution tend to focus on the individual (i.e. prostitutes) and define, tautologically, prostitution as those sexual acts undertaken by prostitutes. For instance, in England and Wales, section 51(2) of the Sexual Offences Act 2003 defines 'prostitutes' as being:

> . . . a person (A) who, on at least one occasion and whether or not compelled to do so, offers or provides sexual services to another person in return for payment or a promise of payment to A or a third person; and 'prostitution' is to be interpreted accordingly.

The legal approach favoured in the UK and most of Western Europe can be characterized as negative regulationism or partial criminalization.[3] Prostitution-related behaviours that are seen as harmful or injurious to individuals are criminalized, whilst the actual act of selling and (for the most part) buying of sex is not (see Phoenix 2009). For example, in England and Wales it is currently illegal: for a prostitute to loiter or solicit in a public place for the purposes of prostitution; for anyone to keep a brothel or cause, incite, or control prostitution for financial gain; for anyone to pay for sexual services from a child and/or from a prostitute 'subject to force'; for anyone to sexually exploit a child through prostitution and/or involvement in pornography; for anyone to groom children online for the purposes of sexual exploitation; or for anyone to traffic

[3] This is to be distinguished from decriminalization and legalization. See Phoenix (2009) for a discussion of the differences between partial criminalization, decriminalization, abolition, and legalization.

individuals, that is arrange or facilitate the travel into, around, or out of the UK for the purposes of sexual exploitation.[4]

This approach was adopted in England and Wales following the Report of the Committee on Homosexual Offences and Prostitution (1957) which subsequently formed the basis of the Street Offences Act 1959. The Wolfenden Report, as it came to be known, drew a sharp line of distinction between matters of private sexual morality and the role of criminal law in 'preserving public order and decency' and protecting individuals from the 'injurious' or 'offensive' behaviours of others. Prostitution, it claimed, was a private matter of sexual morality except where it caused a public nuisance, such as the visibility of street prostitution. The Report further recommended that the policing of prostitution ought to focus on those whose presence causes affront: sex workers.

Post-Wolfenden, police attention was generally focused on controlling visible street-based sex work via the arrest of street working women, whilst the objective of government was to manage the problems associated with prostitution rather than attempt to abolish it. Towards the end of the twentieth century, the standard disposal for convictions of soliciting and loitering became a fine. The irony of this was notable, particularly given that empirical research confirmed that many women involved in street-based prostitution were precisely those who could least afford to pay fines. Thus in targeting this population of sex workers, Wolfenden inaugurated a system of regulation whose effect was to catch one of the most marginalized groups of sex workers in a cycle of revolving doors between prostitution and arrest, prosecution and punishment (for a full account of the legal regulation and policing of prostitution post-Wolfenden, see Phoenix (1999) especially chapter 2).

PUBLIC HEALTH AND THE RISE OF MULTI-AGENCY WELFARE PROVISION

Approaches to regulation underwent radical transformation in the last two decades of the twentieth century.

Throughout the 1980s and 1990s and in response to concerns about an HIV/AIDS pandemic, fears grew about the impact of prostitution on the sexual health of the general populace. Within popular discourse, prostitution had long since been identified as a bridge between the undeserving and diseased few, and the healthy, moral many.[5] The tone of the public discussion about prostitution and the spread of HIV/AIDS was comparatively harsh, with various calls being made to restrict sex workers' freedom of movement and to segregate them. Despite this, however, the focus of public health and medical research was not on risky people (prostitutes) but on risky behaviours and lifestyles (promiscuity, intravenous drug use, anal sex) in an endeavour to understand the epidemiology of HIV/AIDS. Largely as a result of this burgeoning literature, a plethora of new services started to develop with the aim of minimizing the potential

[4] The Crown Prosecution Service for England and Wales provides a comprehensive list of the laws pertaining to prostitution and exploitation of prostitution, available at: http://www.cps.gov.uk/legal/p_to_r/prostitution_and_exploitation_of_prostitution/, accessed 7 January 2017.

[5] Please also see the Contagious Diseases Acts 1984, 1866, and 1869 and the Defence of the Realm Act 1914 (section 40D) in England and Wales (see Walkowitz 1982).

health risks *to* sex workers who engaged in many of the risky behaviours associated with HIV/AIDS.

This 'public health' approach to prostitution was new in the UK (see Kinnell 2008). The services created were shaped by a non-judgemental approach. The aim of intervention was not to try to reduce or abolish prostitution or compel or convince women to leave. Rather it was to minimize the risks and harms that sex workers encountered. Throughout the 1990s, the Department of Health put considerable financial resources into developing these services via genito-urinary clinics and sexual health outreach projects. Most local sexual health and drugs projects were pragmatic in orientation and adopted a multi-agency approach in which everything from general and sexual health concerns (most often, the sexual health outreach services provided free condoms to sex workers), drugs and alcohol abuse and misuse, housing and homelessness, and domestic violence were addressed. Involvement by sex workers with the agencies was purely voluntary. That same pragmatism also marked the relationships that many of these services developed with the local police constabularies. These projects began to identify violence from clients as being a key threat to the health of sex workers and also sought to liaise with local police about the arrest and prosecution of violent clients and local men who were exploiting and abusing the women: see for instance the Ugly Mugs scheme which was pioneered at the SAFE project in Birmingham in the 1990s.

There were three effects of the rise in concerns about sex workers being a threat to public health. Firstly, as sexual health outreach projects matured and as their relationships with local police constabularies strengthened, there was a noticeable decline in the numbers of women being arrested and convicted for loitering and soliciting for the purposes of prostitution. So for instance in 1989, there were over 15,739 women cautioned or convicted for soliciting. By 2002, this number had fallen to 4,102. Whilst this might have been attributable to street-based sex workers moving indoors, the change did occur prior to the widespread adoption of the internet and smart-phone technology (which has been credited with providing the means by which women can avoid street-based sex work). Secondly, by the turn of the millennium, the UK Network of Sex Workers Projects was established (see http:uknswp.org) working for and on behalf of sex workers, providing practical help and advice for sex workers, and acting as a powerful lobbying voice at the local, regional, and national governmental levels. Thirdly, in order to fulfil their funding requirements, many of these organizations kept detailed records about the lives and experiences of the women they worked with. In practice this meant that by the end of the twentieth century there was an alternative (to the police) source of information and knowledge about prostitution and most importantly about the problems of prostitution from the perspective of those working within it (see Kinnell 2008).

VICTIMIZATION, NEW CATEGORIES OF WOMEN TO POLICE, AND THE CREATION OF NEW FORMS OF PROSTITUTION-RELATED PROBLEMS

During the first decade of the twenty-first century, there was an exponential expansion in government-led initiatives relating to prostitution. Six new guidance documents were issued by the Department of Health, the Home Office, the Ministry of

Justice, and/or The Department of Child and Family Services aimed at 'tackling' prostitution, childhood sexual exploitation, trafficking, and street prostitution. That first decade also saw the introduction of six major pieces of legislation amending earlier statutes and introducing new police powers in terms of prostitution, together with the first major proactive, national policing operation into human trafficking (Operation Pentameter in 2006). Sentencing for prostitution-related offences also changed. The practice of fining women for loitering or soliciting for the purposes of prostitution was replaced with the full range of sentences for summary offences (up to and including imprisonment) and a new sentencing framework of 'enforcement plus support' was adopted. Recommended tariffs for other prostitution-related offences were significantly increased.

The political rhetoric justifying these changes to the formal regulation of prostitution was simple: prostitution is not a victimless crime. Its main victims are vulnerable women and girls. Its main offenders are predatory men who profit from trading in that vulnerability and violent men for whom sex workers are 'easy targets'.[6] Yet, despite this rhetoric actual policing remained largely focused on the women, who became the sources of information in the policing of predatory men. For example, whilst Operation Pentameter did result in several arrests and was hailed as a tremendous success, especially by the Crown Prosecution Service, records showed that it failed to find any victims of trafficking (Davies 2009). Indeed, many analyses of these policy changes have concluded that the rhetoric of vulnerability and victimhood was little more than window-dressing and that the changes to policy, in effect, created new categories of women to target with criminal justice interventions (see Phoenix 2009 for a detailed analysis of these changes as they apply to different categories of sex workers, including children and male sex workers).

CRITICAL REFLECTIONS ON KNOWLEDGE, POLITICS, AND IMPACTS OF REGULATION

The recent history of regulation points to a troubling relationship between criminological knowledge and politics, such that the rapid expansion of descriptive research on prostitution in the late twentieth century helped to create the very subject positions that justified the changes to regulation, changes which have had very limited impact on the lived experiences of women involved in prostitution and sex work.

Many of the changes described above occurred in the heyday of Tony Blair's New Labour government, and were part of its manifesto promises to modernize law and create 'evidence-based policy'. It is possible to opine that there was an unintended coalescence of new information about women's experiences in prostitution and a government desire to modernize. But, such an argument relies on a view of government law and policy-making as a linear process of enlightenment (with better, more 'truthful' information comes better, more 'authentic' policy and law) and fails to recognize

[6] It is important to note that Scotland and England and Wales were not alone in Europe in changing the trajectory of policy and in creating new frameworks for regulating prostitution. So, for instance, Sweden and many of the Nordic countries began the process of criminalizing the purchase of sex, rather than its sale, in 1999 (see Skilbrei and Holmstrom 2013).

the gaps that exist between the intentions of policy-makers, the rhetoric justifying policy changes, and the actual practices of regulation, policing, and governance.

A different argument might suggest that the twenty-first century has merely brought a change in discourse, rather than a change in the practice of regulation, *per se*, and that this is part and parcel of broader shifts in the neoliberal governance of troubling populations (see O'Neill and Scoular (2007) for a good example of this, see also Carline and Scoular (2015)). The justification for making this argument is the recognition that little has actually changed. Women are still the targets of regulation. Interventions are often experienced as punishment and sex workers remain under-protected in terms of the crimes committed against them. Arguably, the studies of late 1990s and early 2000s, had their part to play. They challenged the notion that prostitution was victimless and/or a matter of private morality by describing women's experiences of poverty, of alcohol, and drug issues, of the risks and realities of violence and exploitation (from clients, from boyfriends, and from managers in indoor locations) and more than anything else, the deleterious effects of law enforcement practices that targeted women in prostitution more so than those who commit crimes against them. In creating a victim persona for women involved in prostitution, and in highlighting the ways in which legal protections were routinely denied, such research played a key role in constructing the problem to which government responded.

Twenty-first-century shifts in prostitution laws and policies have provided fertile ground for research and have given new energy to the polarized political stances often taken by academics researching prostitution policy reform. Most of this new research has attempted to deconstruct the discourses that provided the rationale for transformations in regulation and highlight the complexity of the empirical realities faced by many individuals in prostitution. It has shown that it is not so easy to distinguish the willing, voluntary sex worker from the coerced prostituted woman and that in reality these subject positions blur. Scholars have questioned the taken-for-granted 'victimization and vulnerability' discourses that bring so many sex workers under official surveillance and makes them over-vulnerable to subsequent prosecution and criminalization (Scoular 2015). They have demonstrated how these 'victimization and vulnerability' discourses work in a range of contexts to sustain (or, occasionally, destabilize) the operation of material, gendered, cultural, or state-based inequalities. (For more details on how discourses on human trafficking help to underpin increasingly repressive immigration regimes, see Turner and Kelly 2009; O'Connell Davidson 2011; Anderson 2013.) Such studies have also highlighted how the rhetoric of exploited and/or prostituted women may engender and sustain austere welfare policies which women and girls experience as punishment rather than protection (Phoenix 2009). And, in tracing out how, for instance, 'trafficked women' are discursively distinguished from 'migrant sex workers'; how young sex workers become defined as victims of childhood sexual exploitation; or how exploited or prostitute women are distinguished from 'consensual' sex workers (Phoenix 2002; Chapkis 2005; Agustín 2006; Sanders *et al.* 2009; Phoenix and Oerton 2013), the binary division of women into agents who choose their destinies and victims who are targeted—by either punitive welfare agencies or predatory and exploitative males—persists (see also Della Guista and Munro (2008)). These modes of differentiation are given life as those responsible for enacting policies and regulating prostitution then inscribe the subject positions created by the differentiations on to actual women in prostitution.

So, the irony: in the process of studying prostitution, the shape and form of prostitution itself also changes. To borrow from Cohen's (2002) notion of a control wave, the more that agencies and organizations use trafficking laws and policies in order to do something with, for, or to, a specific individual that comes within their ambit, the more the problem of trafficking is created and once created, the greater the imperative to do something about it.

CONCLUSION

This chapter has provided an overview of the ways in which prostitution and sex work have been theorized within criminology and the complex relationships that have evolved between criminological knowledge and regulatory practices. In doing so it highlights a number of theoretical, methodological, and political challenges for criminologists working within the field.

At the theoretical level a key challenge is how to represent the sheer complexity and heterogeneity of what is being studied. More pertinently, is it possible or even desirable to study *prostitution*? Or, ought we reconceptualize 'prostitution' and draw lines of demarcation between particular forms that criminal or deviant commercial sexual exchanges take, then study one or other form in its own historical and social specificity (such as, for instance, street-based sex work, escort work)? At the methodological level, a key challenge is how to address the conundrum that much of what is known about prostitution has come from relatively small-scale qualitative research on individual experience, yet most of the theorizing about the changing nature of prostitution focuses on macro-level transformations, such as globalization and the feminization of migration. Few studies, if any, have asked what the necessary or sufficient conditions are for the changes which have been observed, nor have they traced with any degree of detail the mechanisms that might help to account for the ways in which street-based sex work, for example, has all but vanished from many of the UK's cities.

More fundamentally this chapter has demonstrated the political challenges inherent in the application of prostitution research to questions of public policy. The political utility and effect of knowledge produced about prostitution is constantly changing and the chapter has demonstrated how criminological knowledge and its uptake by policy can, in turn, shape the form which prostitution takes. As prostitution research enters the field of formal politics and researchers start lobbying for (or against) specific types of reform, new configurations of knowledge are constructed. Thus, whereas once feminist understandings of prostitution as violence helped to (successfully) challenge the way that the most vulnerable women in prostitution (street-based sex workers) were under-protected and over-policed, now the same understandings underpin what many see as being illiberal forms of regulation that seek to distinguish between the 'deserving' victims and the 'undeserving'. In the same way, calls for scholars to engage in lobbying for the decriminalization of prostitution (see specifically Shaver (2005) and Weizter (2011)), fail to recognize that decriminalization will not in itself stop the governance and regulation of prostitution, it will merely mark a shift in the regulatory context from the criminal justice to the economic sphere.

Selling sex places women at risk of violence, of exploitation, of poverty, and of criminalization. The history of prostitution shows that such women have often become the victims of regulatory practices that reinforce rather than ameliorate the wider social and economic opportunity structures that in turn shape the contours of prostitution itself. In engaging with the theoretical, methodological, and political challenges outlined above, scholars will be better placed to develop new, alternative visions of the future, visions which transcend the binary categories besetting earlier attempts at theorizing prostitution and sex work, and thus lay the groundwork for a politics of liberation.

SELECTED FURTHER READING

The literature on prostitution is now so voluminous that there are textbooks provided to help students navigate their way through the empirical studies. The best of these is Sanders *et al*.'s *Prostitution: Sex work, Policy and Politics* (2009). Three early empirical studies that set the tone for many of the contemporary debates about the politics of prostitution are Davidson's *Prostitution, Power and Freedom* (1998), O'Neill's *Prostitution and Feminism: Towards a Politics of Feeling* (2001), and Phoenix's *Making Sense of Prostitution* (1999). For a scholarly deconstruction of discourses of prostitution see Scoular's *The Subject of Prostitution: Sex Work, Law and Social Theory* (2015). In relation to human trafficking Agustín's 'Sex workers and violence against women: utopic visions or battle of the sexes?' (2001) and 'The disappearing of a migration category: migrants who sell sex' (2006) provides some of the accessible critiques of both international policy and organizations working with women. Two extremely good websites are: http://beyond-the-gaze.com/ and http://www.uknswp.org/. For male sex work, see Browne and Minichiello's 'The social meanings behind male sex work: Implications for sexual interactions' (1995); Hubbard and Sanders' 'Making space for sex work: female street prostitution and the production of urban space' (2003); Scott, *et al*.'s 'Understanding the new context of the male sex work industry' (2005), Friedman's 'Male Sex Work from Ancient Times to the Near Present' (2014), Minichiello and Scott's *Male Sex Work and Society* (2014).

REFERENCES

Agustín, L. M. (2001), 'Sex workers and violence against women: utopic visions or battle of the sexes?', *Development*, 44(3): 107–10.

Agustín, L. M. (2006), 'The disappearing of a migration category: migrants who sell sex', *Journal of Ethnic and Migration Studies*, 32(1): 29–47.

Agustín, L. M. (2007), *Sex at the Margins: Migration, Labour Markets and the Rescue Industry*, London: Zed.

Anderson, B. L. (2013), *Us and them?: The Dangerous Politics of Immigration Control*, Oxford: Oxford University Press.

Barry, K. (1984), *Female Sexual Slavery*, New York: New York University Press.

Barry, K. L. (1996), *The prostitution of sexuality*, New York: New York University Press.

Bernstein, E. (2007), *Temporarily Yours: Intimacy, Authenticity, and the Commerce of Sex*, Chicago: University of Chicago Press.

Brents, B. G. and Hausbeck, K. (2007), 'Marketing sex: US legal brothels and late capitalist consumption', *Sexualities*, 10(4): 425–39.

Brents, B. G. and Sanders, T. (2010), 'Mainstreaming the sex industry: economic inclusion and social ambivalence', *Journal of Law and Society*, 37(1): 40–60.

Browne, J. and Minichiello, V. (1995), 'The social meanings behind male sex work: Implications for sexual interactions', *British Journal of Sociology*, 46(4): 598–622.

Brownmiller, S. (1976), *Against our Will: Men, Women and Rape*, Harmondsworth: Penguin.

Burgess, R. L. and Akers, R. L. (1966), 'A differential association-reinforcement theory of criminal behavior', *Social Problems*, 14(2): 128–47.

Campbell, C. (2000), 'Selling sex in the time of AIDS: the psycho-social context of condom use by sex workers on a Southern African mine', *Social Science & Medicine*, 50(4): 479–94.

Carline, A. and Scoular, J. (2015), 'Saving fallen women now? Critical perspectives on engagement and support orders and their policy of forced welfarism', *Social Policy and Society*, 14(01): 103–12.

Chapkis, W. (2005), 'Soft glove, punishing fist: The Trafficking Victims Protection Act of 2000', in E. Bernstein and L. Schaffner (eds), *Regulating Sex: The Politics of Intimacy and Identity*, New York: Routledge.

Chesney-Lind, M. (1989), 'Girls' crime and woman's place: Toward a feminist model of female delinquency', *Crime & Delinquency*, 35(1): 5–29.

Chesney-Lind, M. and Shelden, R. G. (2013), *Girls, Delinquency, and Juvenile Justice*, New York: John Wiley & Sons.

Chin, K.-l. and Finckenauer, J. O. (2012), *Selling Sex Overseas: Chinese Women and the Realities of Prostitution and Global Sex Trafficking*, New York: New York University Press.

Church, S. L. (2003), *The Social Organisation of Sex Work: Implications for Female Prostitutes' Health and Safety*, Glasgow: University of Glasgow.

Cohen, S. (2002), *Folk Devils and Moral Panics: The Creation of the Mods and Rockers*, London: Routledge.

Coy, M. (2008), 'Young women, local authority care and selling sex: findings from research', *British Journal of Social Work*, 38(7): 1408–24.

Coy, M. (2009), 'This body which is not mine: The notion of the habit body, prostitution and (dis) embodiment', *Feminist Theory*, 10(1): 61–75.

Coy, M. (2013), *Prostitution, Harm and Gender Inequality: Theory, Research and Policy*, London: Ashgate.

Cusick, L. (2006), 'Widening the harm reduction agenda: From drug use to sex work', *International Journal of Drug Policy*, 17(1): 3–11.

Daly, M. (1979), *Gyn/ecology: The metaethics of Radical Feminism*, London: The Women's Press.

Davidson, J. O. C. (1998), *Prostitution, Power and Freedom*, Cambridge: Polity.

Davies, N. (2009), Inquiry fails to find a single trafficker who forced anyone into prostitution, *The Guardian*, available at: https://www.theguardian.com/uk/2009/oct/20/government-trafficking-enquiry-fails, accessed 13 January 2017.

Della Giusta, M. M. and Munro, V. E. (2008), *Demanding Sex: Critical Reflections on the Regulation of Prostitution*, London: Ashgate.

Dodsworth, J. (2012), 'Pathways through sex work: Childhood experiences and adult identities', *British journal of social work*, 42(3): 519–36.

Dworkin, A. (1981), *Pornography: Men possessing Women*, London: Women's Press.

Edwards, S. (1987), 'Prostitutes: Victims of law, social policy and organised crime', in P. Carlen and A. Worrall (eds), *Gender, Crime and Justice*, Buckingham: Open University Press.

Edwards, S. (1997), 'The legal regulation of prostitution', in G. Scambler and S. Scambler (eds), *Rethinking Prostitution: Purchasing Sex in the 1990s*, London: Routledge.

Eisenstein, Z. R. (1979), *Capitalist Patriarchy and the Case for Socialist Feminism*, New York/London: Monthly Review Press.

Foucault, M. (1979), *Discipline and Punish: The Birth of the Prison*, London: Penguin.

Foucault, M. (1979), *The History of Sexuality*, London: Allen Lane.

Friedman, M. (2014), 'Male Sex Work from Ancient Times to the Near Present', in V. Minichiello and J. Scott (eds), *Male Sex Work and Society*, New York: Harrington Park Press.

Gagnon, J. H. and Simon, W. (1973), *Sexual Conduct: The Social Origins of Human Sexuality*, Chicago: Aldine.

Galatowicz, L., Pitcher, J., and Woolley, A. (2005), *Report of the Community-Led Research Project Focusing on Drug and Alcohol Use of Women Sex Workers and Access to Services*, Coventry: Terrence Higgins Trust.

Galvin, C., *et al.* (2003), *It's Someone Taking a Part of you: A Study of Young Women and Sexual Exploitation*, London: Jessica Kingsley.

Glueck, S. and. Glueck, E. (1934), *500 Delinquent Women*, New York: Alfred Knopf.

Hardy, K., *et al.* (2010), *New Sociologies of Sex Work*, Ashgate.

Hester, M. and Westmarland, N. (2004), *Tackling Street Prostitution: Towards a Holistic Approach*, London: Home Office Research, Development and Statistics Directorate.

Høigård, C. and Finstad, L. (1992), *Backstreets: Prostitution, Money, and Love*, London: Polity,

Home Office (1957), *Report of the Committee on Homosexual Offences and Prostitution*, London: Home Office.

Hubbard, P. and Sanders, T. (2003), 'Making space for sex work: female street prostitution and the production of urban space', *International Journal of Urban and Regional Research*, 27(1): 75–89.

Jeffreys, S. (1999), 'Globalizing sexual exploitation: Sex tourism and the traffic in women', *Leisure studies*, 18(3): 179–96.

Jeffreys, S. (2008), *The Idea of Prostitution*, Melbourne: Spinifex Press.

Kempadoo, K. and Doezema, J. (1998), *Global Sex Workers: Rights, Resistance, and Redefinition*, London: Routledge

Kempadoo, K., Sanghera, J., and Pattanaik, B. (2015), *Trafficking and Prostitution Reconsidered: New Perspectives on Migration, Sex work, and Human rights*, London: Routledge.

Kinnell, H. (2008), *Violence and Sex Work in Britain*, London: Routledge.

Lombroso, C. and Ferrero, W. (1898), *The Female Offender*, New York: D. Appleton and Company.

Matthews, R. A. and O'Neill, M. (2003), *Prostitution*, London: Ashgate.

May, T., Harocopos, A., and Turnbull, P. (2001), *Selling Sex in the City An Evaluation of a Targeted Arrest Referral Scheme for Sex Workers in Kings Cross*, Social Science Research Paper No. 14 London: Criminal Policy Research Unit, South Bank University.

McIntosh, M. (1968), 'The homosexual role', *Social Problems*, 16(2): 182–92.

McIntosh, M. (1978), 'Who Needs Prostitutes? The Ideology of Male Sexual Needs', in C. Smart and B. Swart (eds), *Women, Sexuality and Social Control*, London: Routledge & Kegan Paul.

McKeganey, N. P. and Barnard, M. (1996), *Sex Work on the Streets: Prostitutes and their Clients*, Buckingham: Open University Press.

McLeod, E. (1982), *Working women: Prostitution now*, London: Croom Helm.

Melrose, M. *et al.* (1999), *One Way Street? Retrospectives on Childhood Prostitution*, London: The Children's Society.

Millett, K. (1975), *The Prostitution Papers: A Candid Dialogue*, St. Albans: Paladin.

Millett, K. (2000), *Sexual Politics*, Champaign: University of Illinois Press.

Minichiello, V. and Scott, J. (2014), *Male Sex Work and Society*, New York: Columbia University Press.

O'Connell Davidson, J. (1998), *Prostitution, Power and Freedom*, Michigan: University of Michigan Press.

O'Connell Davidson, J. (2011), 'Moving children? Child trafficking, child migration, and child rights', *Critical Social Policy*, 31(3): 454–77.

O'Connell Davidson, J. (2015), *Modern Slavery: The Margins of Freedom*, London: Palgrave Macmillan.

O'Mahony, P. (2009), 'The risk factors prevention paradigm and the causes of youth crime: A deceptively useful analysis?', *Youth Justice*, 9(2): 99–114.

O'Neill, M. (2001), *Prostitution and Feminism: Towards a Politics of Feeling*, Chichester: John Wiley & Sons.

O'Neill, M., *et al.* (1997), 'Prostitute women now', in G. Scambler and A. Scambler (eds.), *Rethinking Prostitution: Purchasing Sex in the 1990s*, London: Routledge.

O'Neill, M., *et al.* (2008), 'Living with the Other: Street sex work, contingent communities and degrees of tolerance', *Crime, Media, Culture*, 4(1): 73–93.

Pearce, J. J. (2009), *Young People and Sexual Exploitation: 'It's Not Hidden, You Just Aren't Looking'*, London: Routledge.

Phoenix, J. (1999), *Making Sense of Prostitution*, London: Macmillan.

Phoenix, J. (2002), 'In the name of protection: Youth prostitution policy reforms in England and Wales', *Critical Social Policy*, 22(2): 353–75.

Phoenix, J. (2009), *Regulating Sex for Sale: Prostitution, Policy Reform and the UK*, Bristol: Policy.

Phoenix, J. and Oerton, S. (2005), *Illicit Illegal*, Cullompton: Willan.

Plummer, K. (1981), 'Building a sociology of homosexuality', *The making of the modern homosexual*, New York: Barnes & Noble, Inc, 17–29.

Sampson, R. J. and Laub, J. H. (1995), *Crime in The Making: Pathways and Turning Points Through Life*, Cambridge, MA: Harvard University Press.

Sanders, T. and Hardy, K. (2013), 'Sex work: the ultimate precarious labour?', *Criminal Justice Matters*, 93(1): 16–17.

Sanders, T., O'Neill, M., and Pitcher, J. (2009), *Prostitution: Sex work, Policy and Politics*, London: Sage.

Scott, J., Minichiello V., Mariño, R., Harvey, G. P., Jamieson, M., and Browne, J. (2005), 'Understanding the new context of the male sex work industry', *Journal of Interpersonal Violence*, 20(3): 320–42.

Scoular, J. (2015), *The Subject of Prostitution: Sex Work, Law and Social Theory*, Abingdon: Routledge.

Scoular, J. and O'Neill, M. (2007), 'Regulating Prostitution Social Inclusion, Responsibilization and the Politics of Prostitution Reform', *British Journal of Criminology*, 47(5): 764–78.

Scoular, J., *et al.* (2007), 'What's anti-social about sex work? The changing representation of prostitution's incivility', *Safer Communities*, 6(1): 11–17.

Shaver, F. M. (2005), 'Sex work research methodological and ethical challenges', *Journal of Interpersonal Violence*, 20(3): 296–319.

Shaw, C. R. and McKay, H. D. (1942), *Juvenile Delinquency and Urban Areas*, Chicago: University of Chicago Press.

Shulman, A. K. (1980), 'Sex and Power: Sexual Bases of Radical Feminism', *Signs*, 5(4): 590.

Smart, C. and Smart, B. (1978), *Women, Sexuality and Social Control*, London: Routledge & Kegan Paul.

Sutherland, E. H., Cressey, D. R., and Luckenbill, D. G. (1992), *Principles of Criminology*, Lanham: Rowman & Littlefield.

Turner, J. and L. Kelly (2009), 'Trade Secrets: Intersections between Diasporas and Crime Groups in the Constitution of the Human Trafficking Chain', *The British Journal of Criminology*, 49(2): 184.

Walkowitz, J. (1982), *Prostitution and Victorian Society*, Cambridge University Press: Cambridge.

Weeks, J. (1981), *Sex, Politics, and Society: The Regulation of Sexuality Since 1800*, London, New York: Longman.

Weeks, J. (2000), *Making Sexual History*, Cambridge: Polity.

Weitzer, R. (2007), 'Prostitution: facts and fictions', *Contexts*, 6(4): 28–33.

WEITZER, R. (2009), *Sex for Sale: Prostitution, Pornography, and the Sex Industry*, Abingdon: Routledge.

WEITZER, R. (2011), 'Sex trafficking and the sex industry: The need for evidence-based theory and legislation', *The Journal of Criminal Law and Criminology*, 101(4): 1337–69.

WILKINSON, R. (1955), *Women of the Streets: A Sociological Study of the Common Prostitute*, London: British Social and Biology Council.

YOUNG, J. (1987), 'The tasks facing a realist criminology', *Contemporary Crises*, 11(4): 337–56.

31

DRUGS: CONSUMPTION, ADDICTION, AND TREATMENT

Toby Seddon

INTRODUCTION

It probably seems obvious why this *Handbook* should cover drugs. After all, every standard criminology textbook does. But is this really so obvious? Why should the intoxicants that we label as 'drugs' be worthy of criminological attention but not others? Why not the substance ranked by some experts as the most harmful of all (alcohol) (see Nutt *et al.* 2010), or the one that kills the most people every year (tobacco) or, for that matter, the one that is the most popular globally amongst consumers (coffee)? Some might say the answer is simple: substances labelled as 'drugs' are the only ones that are prohibited, meaning that suppliers and users are subject to criminal sanctions. But this is a circular answer and, of course, a Western-centric one, as there are several countries in Africa and the Middle East where alcohol is currently prohibited. I will argue in this chapter that understanding the nature of today's global drug problem requires a broadening of our gaze to make full sense of this most perplexing phenomenon.

The drug problem is undoubtedly one of the thorniest and most difficult challenges facing the world in the twenty-first century. Whilst it may have been possible to claim otherwise in the twentieth century, it is now without question a fully *global* phenomenon, with almost no corner of the planet unaffected. The global drug trade is estimated to be worth US$ 320 billion (UNODC 2005) which makes drugs amongst the most traded commodities, matching the size of markets in many very mainstream licit goods, such as, animal and vegetable oils or tea and coffee.[1] Officials estimate there are roughly 246 million current drug users across the world, including 12 million drug injectors (UNODC 2015). In many producer and transit countries, involvement in the drug supply chain is bound up with serious problems of poverty and insecurity. The most obvious example of this is probably Afghanistan, whose position as a major

[1] The measurement challenges here are formidable and the figure for the global drug trade has been questioned (e.g. Thoumi 2005; Reuter and Greenfield 2001).

source country in the world heroin economy has been a central factor in the sad story of political instability, violence, and corruption that has unfolded there over the last 40 years (McCoy 1972; Chouvy 2006). More recently, several countries in West Africa which have become transit points in the cocaine trade, connecting South American producers with European consumer markets, have seen violence and organized crime destabilize places that were already facing significant development challenges (UNODC 2008; Collodi 2014). The region has also seen public health risks like HIV and Hepatitis C rapidly worsen as domestic drug problems have taken hold in the wake of the arrival of cocaine, heroin, and drug money (WACD 2014). Globally, outside sub-Saharan Africa, drug injecting accounts for approximately a third of all new cases of HIV infection (UNODC 2012: 15). At the consumer end of the drug supply chain, typically in more developed economies, drugs have been experienced for many decades as an entrenched social problem, fuelling crime, poverty, and ill-health (Seddon 2006).

Given this seemingly intractable and global web of problems, it is perhaps of little surprise that politicians and leaders around the world have tended to adopt fairly entrenched policy positions on drugs, revolving around strong moral condemnation coupled with expressed aims of eliminating the drug trade through prohibition (see Stevens, this volume, for a discussion of the legal and policy responses that have been developed to deal with drugs). Summarizing this strand quite neatly, the then British Prime Minister David Cameron declared in 2014, in response to a report which failed to find links between 'tough' law enforcement and lower levels of drug consumption:

> I don't believe in decriminalising drugs that are illegal today. I'm a parent with three children; I don't want to send out a message that somehow taking these drugs is OK or safe.

This chapter will examine three inter-connected areas which underpin the drug problem and are key to understanding precisely what this phenomenon actually is: the human attraction to mind-altering substances (*consumption*); understandings of why some people experience problems associated with habitual consumption (*addiction*); and how we have sought to help those experiencing these problems (*treatment*). In all three areas, the aim is to set out a critical and historically informed perspective, designed to equip readers to be able to question and challenge conventional ideas and debates about drugs. Many common assumptions about drugs, the things we take for granted or see as self-evident, turn out to be less straightforward than they appear at first sight. For the purposes of this chapter, the term 'drug' will be used to refer to those substances controlled under the Misuse of Drugs Act 1971, the most familiar of which are cannabis, cocaine (including crack), heroin, ecstasy, amphetamine, and LSD (for a critical account of the drug concept, see Seddon (2016)).

CONSUMPTION

The human desire for intoxication has a history which is long and wide. Rituals and practices that involve the consumption of mind-altering substances can be found across the globe, and historians have traced these all the way back to the ancient civilizations of Mesopotamia, Sumeria, and Egypt some 6,000 years ago (Berridge 2013: 9). Even further back, into the very distant past before the invention of the written word—human history in 'deep time' (Shyrock and Smail, 2011)—signs of intoxicant use can be found amongst the evidence that archaeologists and palaeo-scientists have unearthed (Smail 2009). Based on this historical longevity and cultural ubiquity, Siegel (1989) famously argued that the desire for intoxication is the fourth fundamental driver of human behaviour, after hunger, thirst and sexual desire.

This sense of the universality of human psychoactive desire might suggest that the story of our engagement with mind-altering substances is equally universal and unvarying. In fact, the opposite is the case. One of the consistent features of the history of intoxicant use in society is how practices and preferences are culturally and geographically bound. The examples here are endless but include: wine drinking in ancient Greece and Rome and later the European side of the Mediterranean; coca leaf chewing in the Andean region of South America; hashish smoking in Asia and the Middle East; and beer drinking in Northern Europe. This tells us something very important: practices of intoxication are bound up with and deeply embedded within the way of life of a society and so are rich with insights for the keen cultural observer. These different cultural histories of intoxication are shaped by multiple factors: geography, climate, religion, politics, and trade. In an important sense, these psychoactive histories provide a window through which we can see much more general and wide-ranging histories of human existence. The converse is also true: if we only understand trajectories of preferences and practices of intoxication as very particular stories in a narrow sense, without seeing them as part of a bigger picture, then our vista is myopic.

For example, heroin is usually regarded as the most harmful of all the illicit drugs, highly damaging to individuals and communities. What, though, is the particular story of Britain's encounter with this drug? Morphine, the principal active alkaloid in opium, had been isolated for the first time in 1827. In 1874, a new ester of morphine, diamorphine, was created in a laboratory in a West London hospital. It was given the name heroin by the German company Bayer & Co and marketed for the first time in 1898 as a 'sedative for coughs', advertised alongside Bayer's other new 'wonder drug', aspirin (see Sneader 1998).

For a short period, heroin was a commercial success as a medicine, with lucrative markets in the United States and across Europe. Fairly quickly, however, concerns about its addictive potential began to accumulate and by the end of the First World War it had been banned in Britain by the Dangerous Drugs Act 1920 (Seddon 2007). Yet this ban was not in response to a new heroin problem of any significance. In fact, for the next three decades the number of heroin users in Britain remained not only extremely small but also largely concentrated amongst the professional classes, particularly doctors and others who had special access to diamorphine. There was no particular connection with crime or other social problems. In fact, as late as the 1970s, Home Office research found that a majority of heroin users had no criminal history and even amongst the minority with convictions, many were for drug possession offences only (Mott 1975). In other words, one aspect of what might be seen as a defining characteristic of heroin use—that it is inextricably connected with crime—turns out not to be so after all.

In the early 1960s, there was an upsurge in heroin use in Britain, as part of the emergence of a new drug subculture (Spear 1969). The new heroin users were younger than their predecessors. Whereas in 1959, 89 per cent of heroin users had been aged 35 or over, by 1964 this had dropped to 60 per cent (Ministry of Health, 1965: 5). A study by Bewley (1965) of addicts admitted as patients to a London hospital found that nearly half were aged 25 or under. As well as being younger, the new users were also more diverse, with more coming from working-class backgrounds, but also many living 'bohemian' lifestyles as students or musicians. However, this new heroin 'scene' was largely London-based and was very small in terms of absolute numbers (Pearson 2001) and certainly nothing like the epidemics which had affected some cities in the US in the previous couple of decades (Chein *et al.* 1964). During the 1970s, the London scene grew older and largely stabilized in size and Britain could still be accurately described as having a 'slumbering, almost non-existent encounter' with heroin (Pearson 2001: 55). However, a profound shift was around the corner.

In 1979, reports began to circulate of cheap brown heroin becoming available in a number of places outside London which had no previous history of the drug, notably in northern England and Scotland. The scale of the increase was significant: numbers on the index of new addicts notified to the Home Office rose from just over 1,000 in 1980 to nearly 6,000 by 1985 (Home Office 1990). To set those numbers in context, 20 years earlier in 1965, the number of new addicts was a mere 259, itself a sharp rise from 1960 when it had been just 24 (Spear 1969). The new heroin users were young, mostly unemployed and lived in the most deprived neighbourhoods in cities like Liverpool, Manchester, and Glasgow (Pearson 1987a; Parker *et al.* 1988). By the early 1980s, commentators were describing this as a heroin 'epidemic' and linking it to the austere economic policies of the Thatcher government (Peck and Plant 1986; Pearson 1987b). The new users were also highly involved in crime, especially car theft and burglary, making significant contributions to the worsening of local crime problems (Parker and Newcombe 1987; Hammersley *et al.* 1989). This constellation of issues—deprivation, unemployment, crime—has come to be seen as an inherent feature of localized heroin problems, even though it was certainly not the case in Britain prior to 1980. A further important aspect of the 1980s epidemic is that it only became possible because of the arrival of cheap heroin from Iran and Pakistan, a development driven by political developments in that region.

What does this brief account of the British experience with heroin have to tell us? Firstly, it shows that some of the features that we may view as intrinsic features of heroin, are in fact rooted in specific times and places, that is, they are historically and culturally contingent (e.g. the links between heroin and crime). Secondly, it shows us that heroin is a substance of modernity—still less than 150 years old—which owes its existence to the emergence in nineteenth-century Europe of industrial chemical production methods, a development which in turn laid the foundations for the global pharmaceutical industry. Bayer, for example, is now a global multinational company which had revenue of $46 billion in 2015. Thirdly, it demonstrates that heroin's origins were therapeutic, a fact that is not unusual for many of today's illegal drugs (e.g. cocaine was widely used in dentistry up until the early twentieth century (Enever 2010)). Fourthly, it shows us that there are often important connections between local drug problems and global developments (in this case, political events in the Golden Crescent region which opened up new sources of heroin supply).

DRUG-TAKING AS DEVIANCE

If we broaden our perspective to look at other drugs used in Britain over the last half-century, some trends are clear. As already noted, the 1960s witnessed the emergence of a new youth drug subculture. This had several strands: cannabis as part of an underground youth culture; amphetamines within mod culture; and LSD within 'hippie' culture. Criminological understandings of these new drug scenes were heavily influenced by the 'new deviancy theories' that were being developed at the time in North America. Perhaps the most influential contribution was Howard Becker's series of essays from the late 1950s and early 1960s (Becker 1963). Key to this approach was a commitment to 'appreciating' deviance from the perspective of the 'deviants'. Rather than seeing criminality as dysfunctional or pathological, the new deviancy theorists set out to understand the world as seen by the rule-breakers themselves. Looked at in this way, drug-taking appeared quite different. Becker argued that motivation to experiment with drugs is generally not caused by pre-existing personality traits or psychological 'weaknesses'; rather, it is a learned experience (people 'learn how to get high'). Further, for some social groups, drug use is a meaningful activity that may be understood as beneficial, providing 'solutions' to problems they were experiencing.

Other work in this vein includes a classic essay by Harold Finestone (1957), entitled 'Cats, Kicks and Color', which explored drug use by young African American men in Chicago. In a British context, Jock Young's (1971) book, *The Drugtakers*, presented a study of cannabis smoking by students in West London in the late 1960s. Both shared Becker's emphasis on the need to understand drug consumption very precisely within its specific context. They showed how the meanings, practices, and effects of consuming a particular substance are not fixed or universal.

It is worth remembering that drug consumption in Britain was still a minority pursuit in the 1960s and 1970s. The vast majority of young people had no contact with drugs. The Wooton Report in 1968 estimated that 300,000 people had tried cannabis which was by far the most commonly used substance at the time (Advisory Committee on Drug Dependence 1968: para. 36). There was, in other words, a relatively small drug subculture, associated with young people, music, and fashion, and based primarily around cannabis. It emerged most strongly from the mid-1960s and came to be associated with the 'counter-culture' of the time. Famously, a full-page advert appeared in *The Times* newspaper on 24 July 1967 from leading counter-cultural figures, calling for the legalization of cannabis. Amongst the 64 signatories were all four Beatles, radical psychiatrist R. D. Laing, pop artist Richard Hamilton, political activitist Tariq Ali and, somewhat incongruously from a twenty-first century vantage point, journalist David Dimbleby!

NORMALIZATION OF DRUG USE

In the 1980s, things began to change. As already noted, the British heroin epidemic emerged during the first half of the decade, and was firmly connected with the parallel economic recession and rise in youth unemployment. Additionally, a new youth-culture phenomenon started to develop in the late 1980s, as a series of dance and clubbing cultures rapidly spread, with the consumption of ecstasy (MDMA) and other stimulants central to the experience (Measham *et al.* 2001). Throughout the 1990s, this trend of drug-taking becoming increasingly part of mainstream youth culture continued to develop. As experimentation with drugs became more commonplace, the usefulness of 'deviancy' perspectives started to be questioned by criminologists. Put simply, if young people taking drugs was no longer exceptional, what sense did it make to understand it as deviant?

The strongest challenge to the deviancy framework came from a group of researchers led by Howard Parker and based at the University of Manchester. They carried out a longitudinal study of young people in the North West of England. The baseline data involved a survey of nearly 800 14 year olds undertaken in 1991, with the cohort then followed up at intervals (Parker *et al.* 1998; Aldridge *et al.* 2011; Williams 2012). Based on their emerging findings from the early phases, they argued that by the mid-1990s, drug-taking in England had undergone a process of *normalization*, moving 'from the margins *towards* the centre of youth culture' (Parker *et al.* 1998). Indicators of normalization include increased availability, higher rates of drug-trying and sustained drug use, greater peer tolerance of 'sensible' drug-taking, and a wider societal or cultural tolerance of drugs. Significantly, as part of this 'mainstreaming' of drugs, the demographics of recreational drug-taking also shifted, towards a more balanced profile in terms of gender and class (Aldridge *et al.* 2011; Measham *et al.* 2011).

The normalization thesis has not been without its critics. Shiner and Newburn (1997, 1999) have argued that it exaggerates the degree of change that has taken place and that drug use remains a minority pursuit within youth culture and one that is viewed negatively by the majority. Nevertheless, despite these criticisms, the prevailing view today, some 20 years since the idea was first articulated, is that young people's experience of drugs in many Western developed countries has been transformed in the last couple of decades. Studies from around Europe (Zobel and Gotz 2011), in the US (Hunt *et al.* 2010), and elsewhere have repeatedly substantiated Parker's findings. Further, the idea of a move 'from the margins to the mainstream' appears to capture the essence of this transformation, even if there is disagreement about the precise scale of the change. The language of 'deviance' simply no longer fits the way that it once did. In a broader sense, too, in societies shaped by consumer capitalism, recreational consumption—whether of drugs, alcohol, or anything else—is *required* to keep the economic wheels turning.

NEW PSYCHOACTIVE SUBSTANCES (NPS)

Changes in patterns of consumption continue to appear, usually unheralded and unforeseen. In the last few years, there has been a global proliferation of new psychoactive substances (NPS), often called 'legal highs' (see Shapiro 2016). This rather loose term describes a range of stimulants, synthetic cannabinoids, and hallucinogens which are typically not (yet) controlled by legislation. The pace at which new substances have emerged has left policy-makers floundering and searching for new legal and policy solutions (Seddon 2014). In the UK, for example, a 'blanket ban' has been introduced via the Psychoactive Substances Act 2016, whilst in other places different approaches have been taken, including in New Zealand an innovative selective approval and licensing system. From the perspective of understanding trends in consumption, the lesson from the 'legal highs' phenomenon is very simple: human beings continue to seek out psychoactive experiences with whatever substances are available at any given time and place. Two further lessons can be drawn. The first concerns the role of technological developments. Just as the development of laboratory chemistry in the nineteenth century led to the synthesis of heroin, so the emergence of the internet has shaped the new markets in NPS, as online fora such as *Silk Road* have rapidly opened up the availability of new substances (see Martin 2014). The second lesson, which has been much less remarked on, also has earlier parallels. One of the drivers for the rapid proliferation of NPS has been the supply of cheap chemicals from China. This, in turn, has been driven by the vast capacity of the Chinese chemical and pharmaceutical industries, as China has overtaken Europe and the US as the global sectoral leader.

From the vantage point of the present, the NPS phenomenon and the moving of (some) drug markets online appear to be fundamental game-changers in terms of consumption practices. And they may well turn out to be. Yet our critical historical perspective also tells us that continuity (the human desire for intoxication) and change (the variations in consumption preferences) are the twin characteristics of the long story of human engagement with psychoactive substances and perhaps NPS will prove to be less exceptional than we might think.

ADDICTION

One of the recurring features of experiences with drugs is that they lead some individuals into severe difficulties, usually involving heavy and habitual consumption that gets 'out of control'. Members of the British public are familiar with media accounts and shared stories of the suffering experienced by heroin or crack addicts and, in turn, of the troubles they themselves cause to their families, friends, and neighbours. These drug-related difficulties are typically discussed in terms of the concept of *addiction*. But what exactly is addiction? What causes it? Why do some people become addicts but not others?

In a classic article, Harry Levine (1978) traces what he terms the 'discovery of addiction' back to a point around 200 years ago. He argues:

> The essentials of the modern . . . understanding of [addiction] first emerged . . . at the end of the 18th and the beginning of the 19th century. Around that time a new paradigm was created . . . This new paradigm or model defined addiction as a central problem in drug use and diagnosed it as a disease, or disease-like. (1978: 143)

Prior to this point, according to Levine, we lived in a 'world without addiction' in which the 'vocabulary of compulsion' was simply not used when talking about, for example, habitual drunkenness, which was conceived largely in terms of choice and (sometimes) sin. It was only at the start of the nineteenth century that terms like 'irresistible', 'overpowering', and 'overwhelming' began to be used to describe this new notion of addiction. A pioneer of the concept was American physician, Dr Benjamin

Rush, who wrote an essay in 1805 on 'The Effects of Ardent Spirits Upon Man'. A year earlier in 1804, Thomas Trotter's 'Essay on Drunkenness' had covered similar ground. The Rush/Trotter conception contained all the elements core to a contemporary idea of addiction: a condition centred around compulsion or loss of control; characterized as a disease; and with total abstinence as the only proper cure.

From a twenty-first century perspective, it is striking that Levine's account shows that Western cultures have not always had this idea of addiction and that 'excessive' or compulsive consumption of psychoactive substances used to be understood quite differently. His analysis also reveals that the modern addiction concept was first worked out for alcohol. It was only later in the nineteenth century that it began to be applied to opium and opiates. Over the last 100 years, there has been a progressive widening-out of the ambit of the concept, so that today it covers habits from shopping and using the internet, through to 'traditional' addictions like heavy drinking or heroin use. Still, across that continuum, the same core ideas hold, around compulsion and loss of control. Debate does however continue about whether this condition is best understood as a disease or not.

As the historian Virginia Berridge (1979) has shown, the disease model was always something of a hybrid, bringing together the idea of addiction as a medical condition with the older notion of it being a moral failing:

> Addiction was disease *and* vice; it was 'moral bankruptcy', 'disease of the will', 'a form of moral insanity' . . . This continuing moral component ensured a disease theory which was individually oriented, where the addict was responsible, through volition, for his own condition. Addiction was 'medicalised', but failure to achieve a cure was a failure of self control, not medical science. (Berridge 1979: 77)

This is an important point, as it helps explain an otherwise puzzling feature of contemporary attitudes to addiction. If we understand addiction as some sort of medical condition or disease, why are addicts so often stigmatized, despised, or feared? Why would we condemn a person for having a disease? The answer lies partly in this hybridity, rooted in the historical development of the concept during the nineteenth century: addicts are viewed as ill but, at the same time, partly responsible for their condition through making 'bad' choices.

CONCEPTS AND CAUSES OF ADDICTION

Debate about the nature of addiction can be understood as revolving around the two poles brought together in this hybrid model: at one end, compulsion generated by a medical condition; at the other, a bad habit caused by immoral choices. At the former end, we can place contributions such as E.M. Jellinek's (1960) classic book *The Disease Concept of Alcoholism* or what is known as the NIDA brain disease paradigm (see Courtwright 2010) which remains a highly influential perspective especially in North America. At the other end, there is a range of interesting work which emphasizes the choice-making involved in addiction, from psychologist Stanton Peele's (1985) *The Meaning of Addiction* to Nobel prize-winning economist Gary Becker's 'rational theory of addiction' (Becker and Murphy 1988). A particularly interesting contribution at this end of the continuum is John Booth Davies' (1992) iconoclastic book *The Myth of Addiction* in which he argues that what we call addiction is no more or less than a set of accounts drug users give to justify what is actually voluntaristic and reasoned behaviour.

So debate continues about what addiction actually is. Closely connected is the question of what causes it. How you answer this largely depends on what you understand addiction to be. For a person like Nora Volkow, director of NIDA (National Institute on Drug Abuse), this is simple: it is a brain disease with an underlying neurobiological basis (Goldstein and Volkow 2002). For Stanton Peele, on the other hand, addiction is a way of coping with yourself and your world, that is, it is caused by an interaction between an individual and their social environment (Peele and Brodsky 1992). Simplifying somewhat, the debate about causation could be characterized as a specific version of the old argument about 'nature v nurture' which has dogged the social and human sciences for centuries.

Perhaps reflecting this rather unsatisfactory state of knowledge about the addiction concept and its aetiology, there have been periodic attempts to create alternative and less elusive concepts. In the 1960s, the notion of drug dependence rose to prominence, initially after recommendation in 1964 by an expert committee of the World Health Organization (WHO). In essence, it signified a shift away from emphasizing physical effects (e.g. withdrawal symptoms) towards more psychological understandings of compulsive consumption. Through the 1970s, it was probably the dominant concept in research and policy circles. For example, in Britain, the new treatment centres set up in 1968 were called Drug Dependency Units (DDUs) and were based in the large London teaching hospitals, led primarily by psychiatrists. Interestingly, and reversing what happened with addiction, in the 1970s the idea of dependence was then borrowed from the drugs field and applied to alcohol, starting with a famous paper by Edwards and Gross (1976).

In the 1980s, another new concept was developed, the notion of 'problem' use (see Seddon 2011). Like addiction, this had been previously worked out for alcohol in the 1960s and was first applied to drugs in 1982 in a report by the Advisory Council on the Misuse of Drugs (ACMD 1982). As a concept, problem use pulled back from arguments about causation and instead focused on the harmful behaviours and consequences of compulsive and 'out of control' drug-taking. In Britain and Europe, and to some extent elsewhere, the problem drug user has largely replaced the addict as the target of policy and the object of research.

So what to make of this rather confusing picture about addiction? The following conclusions are certainly justified:

- Some individuals get into difficulties with their consumption of psychoactive substances, which can appear compulsive and 'out of control'.
- Societies have labelled these difficulties in different ways over the last 200 years. Before 1800 they were usually understood simply as 'moral transgressions' or 'bad habits'.
- Social and medical scientists are unsure precisely why these difficulties occur for some people and not others, but causes are likely to be a combination of, and interaction between, particular substances, individual characteristics, and social environment.

WHO BECOMES ADDICTED?

A further important question is whether there are patterns in who experiences these drug-related difficulties. In other words, is addiction an equal opportunities condition or are some types of people more susceptible to it? Viewed in historical perspective, we might conclude there are no fixed patterns. After all, a typical heroin addict in early 1950s Britain would have been a middle-class professional, often a doctor, and not the unemployed youth from a poor neighbourhood that we saw in the 1980s. We should be wary then of claims about universal relationships between, for example, addiction and unemployment or addiction and crime. In other words, these relationships and patterns are always context-specific, linked to particular times and places, rather than inevitable or automatic connections.

As was noted in the previous section, in recent decades, 'recreational' drug-taking has become much more widespread as part of a process of normalization and to a great extent now cuts across class, gender, and race boundaries. It is worth emphasizing, too, that most use does not become dependent or problematic. But who are the people who *do* become addicted? If we look at profiles of people who end up in drug treatment in England (Public Health England 2015), we see that they are:

- Predominantly male (70 per cent)
- Mainly white (89 per cent)
- Distributed across the age range (from 18–70) but mainly people in their 20s, 30s, and 40s
- Around one fifth with current housing problems (19 per cent) and over three-quarters unemployed (77 per cent).

Treatment populations, of course, may not be representative of all who experience serious drug-related difficulties. Analysis by Alex Stevens sheds some further light on this question. He argues, firstly, that when looking at a broad range of indicators and data, it is clear that drug use is most likely to become dependent or addictive for people living in situations of socio-economic deprivation (Stevens 2011: 13–32). Secondly, he suggests that this leads to an unequal distribution of drug-related harms. For example, in one study, the age-adjusted mortality rate for drug users seeking treatment was six times that of the general population (Stevens 2011: 26). He argues that we should therefore understand addictive or problematic drug use as one of the 'afflictions of inequality' that Wilkinson and Pickett (2009) describe in their important work on unequal societies (see also Wilkinson 1996). Through a cross-national comparative study they found that within richer, developed countries, levels of socio-economic inequality are associated with a series of social ills, from violence and ill-health to premature death. In other words, once a country reaches a certain level of wealth, it is inequality that drives rates of social problems rather than levels of aggregate wealth. Drug addiction appears to be one more of these inequality-driven afflictions.

Arguably, this focus on deprivation also provides a better way of understanding one of the recurring preoccupations of criminologists in the drug field: the relationship between drug addiction and crime. The starting point in the drugs-crime debate is a simple observation: at every stage of the criminal justice system one finds a disproportionate number of people who use drugs or have drug-related problems, compared to the general population. The standard explanation for this has been the 'drugs-cause-crime' model: addicts are compelled to steal to fund their drug habit. There is considerable empirical support for this model, as, for example, summarized in a widely cited meta-analysis of 30 studies from around the world (Bennett *et al.* 2008). Yet, other studies have suggested alternative causal explanations. Starting from the observation that first involvement in crime tends to happen at an earlier age than first drug experimentation, some researchers have suggested that the causal link actually runs in the opposite direction. Auld *et al.* (1986) argued that as a means of economic survival, people experiencing socio-economic difficulties often get involved in the semi-criminal informal economy where they encounter drugs. It is, in other words, the need for marginalized groups to engage in economic activity that brings drugs and crime together. An insightful essay by Pearson (1987b), building on this argument, shows how active involvement in the 'hustler' lifestyle of the drug-using offender—the daily challenge of generating enough cash to buy drugs—can be a way to make life more bearable for young people whose prospects in the legitimate economy might be decidedly bleak. This points to a third position: that drugs-crime connections vary over time and that they can only be understood in their specific social, cultural, and economic context (Seddon 2006). In this sense, attempts to find 'universal' causal accounts of the drug-crime link are doomed to fail.

TREATMENT

In the late 1980s, consultant psychiatrist Dr John Marks became (in)famous for prescribing smokeable heroin to heroin addicts in Merseyside in northwest England (Marks *et al.* 1991). To some, Marks' approach was in the best tradition of radical and humane medical practice; to others, it was a reckless undermining of the fundamental goal of drug policy, namely to reduce drug-taking to a minimum. As Marks (1990) himself observed, drug policy is built on a series of paradoxes and this idea of treating addiction by providing a supply of a (substitute) drug has been one of the puzzles at the heart of policy and practice debates for at least a century.

Before examining those debates about maintenance and substitution treatment, there is, however, a deeper paradox underlying the drug treatment endeavour that is important to understand. In a nutshell, many of the substances we consider as 'illicit drugs'—which lead to addiction that then requires treatment—were themselves once used therapeutically or as medicines. Opium, for instance, has been used for millennia for its therapeutic benefits. As historian Virginia Berridge (1999) showed in her classic book *Opium and the People*, in nineteenth-century Britain, opium was part and parcel of everyday life, used to cure or alleviate all manner of ills, from diarrhoea to toothache, even being one of the ingredients of infant 'soothing syrups'. Similarly, morphine and later diamorphine (heroin) were synthesized by pharmaceutical companies for pain relief, and were both widely used to that end. Morphine remains one of the most common medicines for treating severe pain; less well-known is that diamorphine is also *still* used in medical practice in Britain, particularly in palliative care with cancer patients (Gossop *et al.* 2005). A similar story can be told about cocaine or amphetamines and their origins as medicines. Nor is this just a historical matter. Medical marijuana dispensaries are proliferating in a number of countries, including several European states, Israel, Canada, and the US. There has also been renewed interest in recent years in the potential for using hallucinogens like LSD, psilocybin, and MDMA for the treatment of mental health problems, including depression, anxiety, and Post-Traumatic Stress Disorder (Tupper *et al.* 2015). So these demonized psychoactive substances, consumers of which may require treatment, can themselves be used therapeutically and medicinally. Indeed, in many cases, they were often first developed for that very purpose.

MAINTENANCE TREATMENT AND TREATMENT EFFECTIVENESS

In one sense, it is partly this underlying paradox that inflames debates about maintenance treatment. But how did the idea of maintenance become established? The rise of drug treatment was, of course, the corollary of the emergence of the disease model of addiction in the nineteenth century. Treatment in the 1880s and 1890s was extremely varied in methods and practice—from Turkish baths to beef soup!—often involving institutional cures which typically combined custody, exercise, and healthy diet. A range of patent medicines were used, both within treatment institutions but also as bottled cures for home use, although many of these actually contained alcohol, cocaine, or codeine (White 1998). Moving into the twentieth century, the 1912 Opium Convention agreed at The Hague stipulated that use of morphine, cocaine, and opium should be restricted to 'legitimate medical purposes', although there was considerable debate as to what that might encompass.

In 1924, the British Home Office established a committee to resolve this question. The Committee's 1926 report—known as the Rolleston Report after its chair—became a drug-policy landmark as it established the legitimacy of medical control of heroin and morphine addiction by prescribing 'patients' their drug of addiction in order to enable them to lead a useful life. This approach became known as the 'British System' which set the parameters for treatment in Britain up until the 1950s (see Berridge 1980). In the 1960s, partly influenced by an important study by American researchers (Dole and Nyswander 1965), and driven also by anxieties about the growing numbers of heroin users, there was a shift towards use of methadone (a long-acting synthetic opioid) in maintenance treatment rather than heroin. The switch to methadone quickly became entrenched, to such an extent that by the 1980s John Marks' experiment in Merseyside with heroin prescribing was perceived as deeply controversial.

In the 1980s, alongside the heroin epidemic described earlier, the other challenge for treatment services was the emergence of HIV as a public health threat, particularly in relation to injecting drug use. Accessible methadone prescribing services were seen as important for attracting users into treatment where they could be monitored and given HIV prevention advice. The philosophy of *harm reduction*—built around low-threshold prescribing plus new initiatives like syringe exchange schemes—became dominant (Newcombe 1987), until at least the mid-1990s. Harm reduction refers to an approach which focuses on reducing the adverse effects of drug-taking, rather than on preventing drug use itself. Arguably, methadone maintenance has continued to be the principal treatment modality ever since and a perceived weakness with the British treatment system has been a lack of adaptability to other drug problems, such as the rise of crack-cocaine in the 1990s (Gossop *et al.* 1994; Hunter *et al.* 1995).

One important moment in the British treatment field is now often forgotten. This was a review of treatment effectiveness commissioned in the mid-1990s by the Department of Health and somewhat curiously chaired by a physicist and priest, the Reverend Dr John Polkinghorne. Rather to the surprise at the time of many in the field, Polkinghorne's review concluded that, in broad terms, 'treatment works' (Department of Health 1996). More significantly, it recommended the establishment of a scientific study to investigate treatment effectiveness more rigorously. This became the National Treatment Outcome Research Study (NTORS) which was later followed by the Drug Treatment Outcome Research Study (DTORS). Both NTORS and DTORS came to establish the evidence base on which significant investment in treatment was justified, particularly from 2000 onwards. Key findings from NTORS were that treatment led to reductions in heroin use, non-prescribed methadone use, injecting risk behaviour and criminality, as well as improvements in psychological health and functioning, with these changes still detectable at five-year follow-up (Gossop *et al.* 2003). Outcomes for alcohol and crack-cocaine were less positive. The follow-up study, DTORS, produced broadly similar findings, measured at one-year follow-up, with treatment leading to reductions in drug use, offending, and risk behaviours, as well as improvements in social functioning and psychological health (Jones *et al.* 2009). The study suggested that most of these gains occurred in the early months of treatment engagement and were then sustained at that level, rather than further extended, after that.

It may have been relatively uncontroversial to claim during this period that treatment 'worked', however, a long-standing problem has concerned differential patterns of accessing treatment. Put bluntly, British treatment populations have tended to be dominated by white, male heroin users. The male to female ratio in treatment has remained at around 3:1 for many years (Neale 2004). This may be partly because men are more likely to experience drug problems but it has also been argued that women are much less likely to access treatment services even when they require help. A series of studies have indicated that there are several barriers which have tended to make it harder for women drug users to access support from treatment and other services, including persistent negative stereotyping and associated stigmatization, lack of adequate childcare, and a failure to provide services that meet women's specific needs (Weissman *et al.* 1995; Becker and Duffy 2002). Some have argued that there is a need to rethink fundamentally how we conceptualize women's drug use and their support needs (Ettorre 2004).

The 'whiteness' of treatment populations has led to a similar set of debates. Akhtar and South (2000) argue that there is a 'hidden history' of heroin use within some minority ethnic communities in Britain, implying a significant group of users who are largely not in contact with treatment services (see also Pearson and Patel 1998). As one of the respondents in a study by Awiah *et al.* (1990) put it, mainstream community drug services could feel like 'the last place I would go', the perception being that they are run by and for white people. This lack of what has been termed 'cultural competence' in the treatment sector does not appear to have been addressed in any serious or sustained way during the period of investment and expansion post-2000. An evidence review published in 2010 (UKDPC 2010) found much the same picture as Awiah and colleagues had some 20 years earlier. The injustice of the failure to tackle this issue properly is further compounded by evidence from research which shows that when it comes to the enforcement of drug laws, it is exactly this group who bear the brunt of police attention (Eastwood *et al.* 2013). At a broader level, racial injustice is one of the long-running seams that we find in the archaeology of how we have constructed and responded to the drug problem over the last century or so (see Seddon 2016).

THE RECOVERY MODEL

Since around 2008, first slowly but gradually building momentum, there has been a growing disquiet about the philosophy and practice of maintenance-based treatment which has coalesced under the sign of *recovery* as a new paradigm for helping people with drug problems. This disquiet is not new, of course. As Hall (2000: 1274) rightly notes, ever since the release of the Rolleston Report in 1926 policy-makers and politicians have been 'deeply ambivalent about the morality and legitimacy of maintenance prescribing for opiate addiction'. In this sense, the emergence of the recovery model—defined in broad terms as an approach which is curative, rather than one that is focused on long-term stability and problem management (UKDPC 2008)—is merely a resurfacing of anxieties about maintenance that have always been there. Even Rolleston had expressed what Hall (2000) describes as a 'grudging' support for maintenance, recognizing its troubling and somewhat paradoxical character.

One of the interesting aspects about the recovery agenda is how rapidly it has become the new paradigm for treatment (see Wardle 2012). This is partly because it represents a reworking of old questions and concerns, rather than an entirely novel direction. There was also perhaps an unusual alignment of interests, particularly in the period from 2008, with at least four different agendas coming together and pointing in the same direction:

- Cutting spending on expensive clinical and pharmacological interventions, in favour of cheaper community/voluntary provision, as part of public-sector austerity.
- Progressive concerns that an over-reliance on methadone prescribing had condemned some people to narrow and impoverished lifestyles absent of hope and optimism.
- More conservative concerns that the maintenance approach was part of a broader dependency culture in which some sectors of the population were 'taking' from society and not contributing.
- A political desire by the incoming Conservative-led coalition government in 2010 to reverse key aspects of New Labour social policy.

In some respects the recovery agenda is an adjustment to an issue that has already become outdated, as heroin use has been in decline over the last few years (Morgan 2014: 49–65). The new challenge for treatment is going to be how to deal with the new types of drug-related problems experienced by people using the wide range of new psychoactive substances which have become available, notably highly potent synthetic cannabinoids, new stimulants, and hallucinogens, as well as the re-emergence of old favourites like MDMA. Treatment research and practice faces a very steep learning curve to get to grips with this new world. The rise of recovery may turn out to be a blind alley and an unhelpful distraction from the real challenge ahead in terms of how we help people who get into difficulties with their use of psychoactive substances. Of course, it should be remembered too that most people who take drugs experience few or no problems.

CONCLUSION

At the start of this chapter, the question was posed as to why criminologists should be interested in drugs at all. In his foundational criminology text, first published in 1924, Edwin Sutherland defined the subject as the scientific study of law-making (criminalization), law-breaking (criminality), and responses to law-breaking (criminal justice). Applied to drugs, these three elements point us to the fundamental issues and guide us towards what the intellectual agenda for the field ought to be. First, the very concept of a drug is the product of the *criminalization* of a sub-set of psychoactive substances at the beginning of the twentieth century (Seddon 2016). A critical future agenda for research and policy has to include a serious re-examination of this and a willingness to consider radical alternatives. Second, the endless debate about why people take drugs is in one sense a specific version of the general question of the causes of *criminality*. But if we accept Siegel's claim that the human desire for intoxication is timeless and universal, we perhaps need to ask ourselves some more searching questions about precisely what we are trying to explain about drug-taking. Third, following these first two elements, the question of what *criminal justice* should mean then becomes difficult and troubling. Can the enforcement of drug laws ever be compatible with justice?

Perhaps then our grasp today of the drugs question is not so different from how Stan Cohen described criminology back in 1981, as a field of study struggling to meet the intellectual and political challenges of the times. Cohen famously ended his essay with a quotation from the English astronomer and physicist Sir Arthur Eddington, warning of the dangers of excessive scientific navel-gazing. Yet Eddington's words have a rather different resonance for the study of drugs and drug use, which, as we have seen in this chapter, has often been so lacking in critical self-reflection that it has failed to see what has been staring us in the face for a very long time:

> We have found a strange footprint on the shores of the unknown. We have devised profound theories, one after another, to account for its origins. At last, we have succeeded in reconstructing the creation that made the footprint. And Lo!, it is our own. (Eddington quoted in Cohen 1981: 243)

SELECTED FURTHER READING

For those interested in exploring the historical aspects in more depth, Berridge's *Demons* (2013) is an excellent single-volume synthesis of her lifetime's work in this area. For a longer and more global history, Courtwright's masterwork *Forces of Habit* (2001) is hard to beat, whilst Kohn's *Dope Girls* (1992) adds an all too rare focus on gender to the historical picture and tells a compelling story. On more contemporary ground, Stevens' *Drugs, Crime and Public Health* (2011) is an extremely readable and insightful analysis of the failings of drug policy and the need to understand the drug problem in a broader social and political context. MacCoun and Reuter's classic *Drug War Heresies* (2001) is probably still the best book on the policy issues. On some of the more recent changes to global drug markets, Martin's short book *Drugs on the Dark Net* (2014) is an invaluable guide. Lastly, the United Nations Office on Drugs and Crime publishes an annual *World Drug Report* which brings together important global data on the latest trends in markets and prevalence and is an invaluable source of information for all students of drugs.

REFERENCES

Advisory Committee on Drug Dependence (1968), *Cannabis*, London: Home Office, ('The Wootton Report').

Advisory Council on the Misuse of Drugs (ACMD) (1982), *Treatment and Rehabilitation*, London: HMSO.

Akhtar, S. and South, N. (2000), '"Hidden from Heroin's History": Heroin use and dealing within an English Asian community—a case study', in M. Hough and M. Natarajan (eds), *Illegal Drug Markets: From Research to Prevention Policy*, Crime Prevention Studies, Vol 11, Monsey, New York: Criminal Justice Press.

Aldridge, J., Measham, F. and Williams, L. (2011), *Illegal Leisure Revisited: Changing Patterns of Alcohol and Drug Use in Adolescents and Young Adults*, Hove: Routledge.

Auld, J., Dorn, N. and South, N. (1986), 'Irregular work, irregular pleasures: heroin in the 1980s', in R. Matthews and J. Young (eds), *Confronting Crime*, London: Sage.

Awiah, J., Butt, S., and Dorn, N. (1990), '"The Last Place I Would Go": Black people and drug services in Britain', *Druglink*, Sept/Oct 14–15.

Becker, G. and Murphy, G. (1988), 'A Theory of Rational Addiction', *Journal of Political Economy*, 96(4): 675–700.

Becker, H. (1963), *Outsiders: Studies in the Sociology of Deviance*, New York: Free Press.

Becker, J. and Duffy, C. (2002), *Women Drug Users and Drugs Service Provision*, DPAS Paper 17, London: Home Office.

Bennett, T., Holloway, K., and Farrington, D. (2008), 'The Statistical Association between Drug Misuse and Crime: A Meta-analysis', *Aggression and Violent Behavior*, 13(2): 107–18.

Berridge, V. (1979), 'Morality and Medical Science: Concepts of Narcotic Addiction in Britain, 1820-1926', *Annals of Science*, 36(1): 67–85.

Berridge, V. (1980), 'The making of the Rolleston report, 1908-1926', *Journal of Drug Issues*, 10(1): 7–28.

Berridge, V. (1999), *Opium and the People*, Revised edn, London: Free Association.

Berridge, V. (2013), *Demons: Our Changing Attitudes to Alcohol, Tobacco, & Drugs*, Oxford: Oxford University Press.

Bewley, T. (1965), 'Heroin and Cocaine Addiction', *The Lancet*, 285(7389): 808–10.

Chein, I., Ferard, D., Lee, R., and Rosenfeld, F. (1964), *The Road to H: Narcotics, Delinquency and Social Policy*, London: Tavistock.

Chouvy, P.-A. (2006), 'Afghanistan's Opium Production in Perspective', *China and Eurasia Forum Quarterly*, 4(1): 21–4.

Cohen, S. (1981), 'Footprints on the sand: a further report on criminology and the sociology of deviance in Britain', in M. Fitzgerald, G. McLennan, and J. Pawson (eds), *Crime and Society: Readings in History and Theory*, London: Routledge.

Collodi, J. (2014), *External Stresses in West Africa: Cross-Border Violence and Cocaine trafficking*, IDS Policy Briefing Issue 60, Brighton: Institute of Development Studies.

Courtwright, D. (2001), *Forces of Habit: Drugs and the Making of the Modern World*, Cambrige, MA: Harvard University Press.

Courtwright, D. (2010), 'The NIDA Brain Disease Paradigm: History, resistance and spinoffs', *BioSocieties*, 5(1): 137–47.

Davies, J. B. (1992), *The Myth of Addiction: An Application of the Psychological Theory of Attribution to Illicit Drug Use*, Reading: Harwood.

Department of Health (1996), *Report of an Independent Review of Drug Treatment Services in England (Task Force Report)*, London: HMSO ('The Polkinghorne Review').

Dole, M. and Nyswander, V. (1965), 'A Medical Treatment for Diacetylmorphine (Heroin) Addiction. A Clinical Trial with Methadone Hydrocholoride', *Journal of the American Medical Association*, 193(8): 646–50.

Eastwood, N., Shiner, M., and Bear, D. (2013), *The Numbers in Black and White: Ethnic Disparities in the Policing and Prosecution of Drug Offences in England and Wales*, London: Release.

Edwards, G. and Gross, M. (1976), 'Alcohol dependence: provisional description of a clinical syndrome', *British Medical Journal*, 1(6017): 1058–61.

Enever, G. (2010), 'The history of dental anaesthesia', in I. Shaw, C. Kumar, and C. Dodds (eds), *Oxford Textbook of Anaesthesia for Oral and Maxillofacial Surgery*, Oxford: Oxford University Press.

Ettorre, E. (2004), 'Revisioning women and drug use: gender sensitivity, embodiment and reducing harm', *International Journal of Drug Policy*, 15(5–6): 327–35.

Finestone, H. (1957), 'Cats, kicks, and color', *Social Problems*, 5(1): 3–13.

Goldstein, R. and Volkow, N. (2002), 'Drug Addiction and Its Underlying Neurobiological Basis: Neuroimaging Evidence for the Involvement of the Frontal Cortex', *American Journal of Psychiatry*, 159(10): 1642–52.

Gossop, M., Griffiths, P., Powis, B., and Strang, J. (1994), 'Cocaine: patterns of use, route of administration, and severity of dependence', *British Journal of Psychiatry*, 164(5): 660–4.

Gossop, M., Marsden, J., Stewart, D., and Kidd, T. (2003), 'The National Treatment Outcome Research Study (NTORS): 4-5 year follow-up results', *Addiction*, 98(3): 291–303.

Gossop, M., Keaney, F., Sharma, P., and Jackson, M. (2005), 'The unique role of diamorphine in British medical practice: a survey of general practitioners and hospital doctors', *European Addiction Research*, 11(2): 76–82.

Hall, W. (2000), 'Rolleston revisited', *Addiction*, 95(8): 1273–4.

Hammersley, R., Forsyth, A., Morrison, V., and Davies, J. (1989), 'The relationship between crime and opioid use', *British Journal of Addiction*, 84(9): 1029–44.

Home Office (1990), *Statistics of the Misuse of Drugs: Addicts Notified to the Home Office, United Kingdom 1989*, Home Office Statistical Bulletin 7/ 90, London: Home Office.

Hunt, G., Moloney, M., and Evans, K. (2010), *Youth, Drugs and Nightlife*, New York: Routledge.

Hunter, G., Donoghoe, M., and Stimson, G. (1995), 'Crack use and injection on the increase among injecting drug users in London', *Addiction*, 90(10): 1397–400.

Jellinek, E. (1960), *The Disease Concept of Alcoholism*, New Haven, CT: Hillhouse.

Jones, A., Donmall, M., Millar, T., Moody, A., Weston, S., Anderson, T., Gittins, M., Abeywardana, V., and D'Souza, J. (2009), *The Drug Treatment Outcomes Research Study (DTORS): Final outcomes report*, Research Report 24, London: Home Office.

Kohn, M. (1992), *Dope Girls: The Birth of the British Drug Underground*, London: Granta.

Levine, H. (1978), 'The Discovery of Addiction: Changing Conceptions of Habitual Drunkenness in America', *Journal of Studies on Alcohol*, 39(1): 143–74.

MacCoun, R. and Reuter, P. (2001), *Drug War Heresies: Learning from other Vices, Times, and Places*, Cambridge: Cambridge University Press.

McCoy, A. (1972), *The Politics of Heroin in Southeast Asia*, London: HarperCollins.

Marks, J. (1990), 'The Paradox of Prohibition', in J. Hando and J. Carless (eds), *Controlled Availability: Wisdom or Disaster?*, NDARC Monograph No 10. Sydney: National Drug and Alcohol Research Centre, University of New South Wales.

Marks, J., Palombella, A., and Newcombe, R. (1991), 'The smoking option', *Druglink*, May/June 10–11.

Martin, J. (2014), *Drugs on the Dark Net: How Cryptomarkets are Transforming the Global Trade in Illicit Drugs*, Basingstoke: Palgrave Pivot.

Measham, F., Aldridge, J., and Parker, H. (2001), *Dancing on Drugs: Risk, Health and Hedonism in the British Club Scene*, London: Free Association.

Measham, F., Williams, L., and Aldridge, J. (2011), 'Marriage, Mortgage, Motherhood: What longitudinal studies can tell us about gender, drug "careers" and the normalisation of adult "recreational" drug use', *International Journal of Drug Policy*, 22(6): 420–7.

Ministry of Health (1965), *Drug Addiction. Second Report of the Interdepartmental Committee*, London: HMSO ('The Second Brain Report').

Morgan, N. (2014), *The Heroin Epidemic of the 1980s and 1990s and its Effect on Crime Trends—Then and Now: Technical Report*, London: Home Office.

Mott, J. (1975), 'The criminal histories of male non-medical opiate users in the United Kingdom', *Bulletin on Narcotics*, 27(4): 41–8.

Neale, J. (2004), 'Gender and Illicit Drug Use', *British Journal of Social Work*, 34(6): 851–70.

Newcombe, R. (1987), 'High time for harm reduction', *Druglink*, 2(1): 10–11.

Nutt, D., King, L., and Phillips, L. (2010), 'Drug harms in the UK: A multicriteria decision analysis', *The Lancet*, 376(9752): 1558–65.

Parker, H. and Newcombe, R. (1987), 'Heroin use and acquisitive crime in an English community', *British Journal of Sociology*, 38(3): 331–50.

Parker, H., Bakx, K., and Newcomber, R. (1988), *Living with Heroin: The Impact of a Drugs 'Epidemic' on an English Community*, Milton Keynes: Open University Press.

Parker, H., Aldridge, J., and Measham, F. (1998), *Illegal Leisure: The Normalization of Adolescent Recreational Drug Use*, London: Routledge.

Pearson, G. (1987a), *The New Heroin Users*, Oxford: Basil Blackwell.

Pearson, G. (1987b), 'Social deprivation, unemployment and patterns of heroin use', in N. Dorn and N. South (eds), *A Land Fit for Heroin?*, London: Macmillan.

Pearson, G. (2001), 'Drugs and Poverty', in S. Chen and E. Skidelsky (eds), *High Time for Reform: Drug Policy for the 21st Century*, London: Social Market Foundation.

PEARSON, G. and PATEL, K. (1998), 'Drugs, Deprivation and Ethnicity: Outreach among Asian Drug Users in a Northern English City', *Journal of Drug Issues*, 28(1): 199–224.

PECK, D. and PLANT, M. (1986), 'Unemployment and illegal drug use: concordant evidence from a prospective study and national trends', *British Medical Journal*, 293(6552): 929–32.

PEELE, S. (1985), *The Meaning of Addiction*, San Francisco: Jossey-Bass.

PEELE, S. and BRODSKY, A. (1992), *The Truth About Addiction and Recovery*, New York: Simon & Schuster.

PUBLIC HEALTH ENGLAND (PHE) (2015), *Adult Substance Misuse Statistics from the National Drug Treatment Monitoring System (NDTMS). 1 April 2014—31 March 2015*, London: Public Health England.

REUTER, P. and GREENFIELD, V. (2001), 'Measuring Global Drug Markets: How good are the numbers and why should we care about them?', *World Economics*, 2(4): 159–73.

SEDDON, T. (2006), 'Drugs, Crime and Social Exclusion: Social context and social theory in British drugs-crime research', *British Journal of Criminology*, 46(4): 680–703.

SEDDON, T. (2007), 'The regulation of heroin: Drug policy and social change in early twentieth-century Britain', *International Journal of the Sociology of Law*, 35(3): 143–56.

SEDDON, T. (2011), 'What is a problem drug user?', *Addiction Research and Theory*, 19(4): 334–43.

SEDDON, T. (2014), 'Drug policy and global regulatory capitalism: The case of new psychoactive substances (NPS)', *International Journal of Drug Policy*, 25(5): 1019–24.

SEDDON, T. (2016), 'Inventing Drugs: A genealogy of a regulatory construct', *Journal of Law and Society*, 43(3): 393–415.

SHAPIRO, H. (2016), *NPS Come of Age: A UK overview*, London: DrugWise.

SHINER, M. and NEWBURN, T. (1997), 'Definitely, maybe not? The normalisation of recreational drug use among young people', *Sociology*, 31: 511–29.

SHINER, M. and NEWBURN, T. (1999), 'Taking Tea with Noel: The Place and Meaning of Drug Use in Everyday Life', in: N. South (ed.), *Drugs: Cultures, Controls and Everyday Life*, London: Sage.

SHYROCK, A. and SMAIL, D. (eds) (2011), *Deep History: The Architecture of Past and Present*, Los Angeles: University of California Press.

SIEGEL, R. (1989), *Intoxication: Life in the Pursuit of Artificial Paradise*, New York: E. P. Dutton.

SMAIL, D. (2009), *On Deep History and the Brain*, Oakland, CA: University of California Press.

SNEADER, W. (1998), 'The discovery of heroin', *The Lancet*, 352(9141): 1697–9.

SPEAR, H. B. (1969), 'The Growth of Heroin Addiction in the United Kingdom', *British Journal of Addiction*, 64(2): 245–55.

STEVENS, A. (2011), *Drugs, Crime and Public Health: The Political Economy of Drug Policy*, Abingdon: Routledge.

THOUMI, F. (2005), 'The Numbers Game: Let's all guess the size of the illegal drugs industry!', *Journal of Drug Issues*, 35(1): 185–200.

TUPPER, K., WOOD, E., YENSEN, R., and JOHNSON, M. (2015), 'Psychedelic Medicine: A re-emerging therapeutic paradigm', *Canadian Medical Association Journal*, 187(14): 1054–59.

UK DRUG POLICY COMMISSION (UKDPC) (2008), *The UK Drug Policy Commission Recovery Consensus Group: A Vision of Recovery*, London: UKDPC.

UK DRUG POLICY COMMISSION (UKDPC) (2010), *The Impact of Drugs on Different Minority Groups: Ethnicity and Drug Treatment. Evidence Review*, London: UKDPC.

UNITED NATIONS OFFICE ON DRUGS AND CRIME (UNODC) (2005), *World Drug Report 2005*, New York: United Nations.

UNITED NATIONS OFFICE ON DRUGS AND CRIME (UNODC) (2008), *Drug Trafficking as a Security Threat in West Africa*, New York: United Nations.

UNITED NATIONS OFFICE ON DRUGS AND CRIME (UNODC) (2012), *World Drug Report 2012*, New York: United Nations.

UNITED NATIONS OFFICE ON DRUGS AND CRIME (UNODC) (2015), *World Drug Report 2015*, New York: United Nations.

WARDLE, I. (2012), 'Five years of recovery: December 2005 to December 2010—From challenge to orthodoxy', *Drugs: Education, Prevention and Policy*, 19(4): 294–8.

WEISSMAN, G., MELCHIOR, L., HUBA, G., SMERECK, G., NEEDLE, R., MCCARTHY, S., JONES, A., GENSER, S., COTTLER, L., BOOTH, R., and ALTICE, F. (1995), 'Women living with drug abuse and HIV disease: Drug abuse treatment access and secondary prevention issues', *Journal of Psychoactive Drugs*, 27(4): 401–11.

WEST AFRICA COMMISSION ON DRUGS (WACD) (2014), *Not Just in Transit: Drugs, the State and Society in West Africa*, An Independent Report of the West Africa Commission on Drugs, Accra, Ghana: WACD.

WHITE, W. (1998), *Slaying the Dragon—The History of Addiction Treatment and Recovery in America*, Bloomington: Lighthouse Training Institute.

WILKINSON, R. (1996), *Unhealthy Societies: The Afflictions of Inequality*, London: Routledge.

WILKINSON, R. and PICKETT, K. (2009), *The Spirit Level: Why More Equal Societies Almost Always Do Better*, London: Allen Lane.

WILLIAMS, L. (2012), *Changing Lives, Changing Drug Journeys: Drug taking decisions from adolescence to adulthood*, Abingdon: Routledge.

YOUNG, J. (1971), *The Drugtakers: The Social Meaning of Drug Use*, London: MacGibbon & Kee.

ZOBEL, F. and GOTZ, W. (2011), 'Drug use in Europe: specific national characteristics or shared models?', in G. Hunt, M. Milhet, and H. Bergeron (eds), *Drugs and Culture: Knowledge, Consumption and Policy*, Farnham: Ashgate.

32

WHITE-COLLAR AND CORPORATE CRIME

Michael Levi and Nicholas Lord

INTRODUCTION

This chapter has one main objective: to present a succinct overview of key debates and ideas associated with theory, research, and practice in the area of white-collar and corporate crimes. First, we think about white-collar and corporate crimes in the twenty-first century, contextualizing these phenomena and reinforcing their criminological significance, despite their analysis remaining at the margins of mainstream discourse. Second, we revisit ongoing conceptual debates, identifying central analytical features of white-collar and corporate crimes before going on to argue in favour of shifting attention towards understanding how white-collar crimes are organized and the conditions that shape this over time. Third, we look at ways of explaining these behaviours, ranging from consideration of individual propensities and rationality, through organizational context and culture, to wider social conditions. Fourth, we analyse current policing and regulation strategies. We conclude with a discussion of key themes in white-collar crime research and scholarship.

WHITE-COLLAR AND CORPORATE CRIMES IN THE TWENTY-FIRST CENTURY: A BRIEF HISTORY OF THE PRESENT

We begin writing this chapter in the shadow of several corporate scandals where otherwise non-criminal, legitimate business organizations and their employees have been implicated in a diverse array of criminal and illicit activities. Volkswagen and its corporate associates committed globally massive deliberate falsification of toxic diesel emission levels to enhance corporate sales targets and profits, while Mitsubishi also falsified data in Japan for similar motives: this would normally be analysed as white-collar crime, but it is also properly labelled as 'organized crime'. In addition, car industry political lobbyists successfully (and legally) sustained inappropriate lab-based testing to make European emissions and fuel consumption look much better than they really were. In the political sphere, the Brazilian President, Dilma Rousseff, was impeached in 2016 and replaced by others also accused of corruption, voted out of power by many Brazilian parliamentarians awaiting trial for far more serious corruption and other offences than hers. In 2015, the Romanian Prime Minister was forced to resign following anti-corruption protests. The South African President Jacob Zuma has been embroiled in a range of corruption allegations relating to personal enrichment and the purchase of inappropriate aircraft for the air force, and in July 2016 was ordered by the Constitutional Court to repay $ 400,000 of personal benefit in refurbishment of his home. FIFA continues its well-merited reputation for corruption, and was until 2015 safe from criminal justice interventions. Its case is an exemplar of how, once the veil of secrecy is penetrated by arrests and/or whistle-blowers, a mass of revelations can follow. Motivated more by national prestige than money, systemic state-sponsored Russian athletics doping scandals led to the suspension of track and field and some other Russians from the 2016 Rio Olympics, and all athletes from the Rio Paralympics. This is merely a selection of recent high-profile cases.

Tombs and Whyte note that, in addition to the dramatic cases that make headline news (such as the above), corporations are responsible for wide-ranging and cumulatively substantial 'routine, everyday harm' (Tombs and Whyte 2015: 37). They document this with respect to four key areas: corporate theft and fraud (particularly in the retail financial services sector); crimes against consumers (e.g. food unsafety); crimes against workers (workplace safety crimes); and crimes against the environment (e.g. air pollution) (ibid.: 37–50). In addition, there is a range of 'middle-class crimes' in which tax and other frauds are committed by people who regard themselves as respectable and are so regarded by others (Karstedt 2016).

Dominant representations and constructions of the crime phenomenon often reflect common-sense conceptions of criminality associated with the 'street' or 'serious and organized' criminal who is characterized by an inherent propensity to offending and presented as an external threat to moral society. Yet 'crimes' and misconduct by those in elite political and economic positions can de-legitimate the system politically (Levi 2012) and harm firms, groups, and individuals both within and outside their socio-economic class. Shifting analytical focus away from 'crimes on the streets' and 'organized crime' towards 'crimes in the suites' disturbs popular stereotypes about the composition of 'threats to society' and attempts to represent criminality as a single type of person driven by risk appetites and social pathology. Accounting for such a diverse range of criminal actors, acts, and responses to them—criminal, civil, and regulatory—poses a fascinating set of research questions, including the conditions under which at least *some* forms of white-collar crime become or fail to become social problems that 'require' the intervention of *criminal justice* rather than *regulation* (Katz 1980; Levi 2009a).

WHAT IS WHITE-COLLAR AND CORPORATE CRIME?

White-collar crime is a term best viewed as a sensitizing rather than a definitive concept (Blumer 1969), and though no definition is satisfactory, the label retains its appeal. A brief analysis of associated behaviours highlights the centrality of supposedly legitimate actors in the context of otherwise legitimate business, institutional, and market environments in undertaking inherently harmful and exploitative behaviours. For instance, Edward A. Ross' 'criminaloid' characterized the inherent business duplicity of legitimate actors alongside a pretence of respectability and piousness, driven by the same motivations as others (Ross 1907: 47–50). In a more Marxist European than populist American tradition, Bonger (1916) argued that lower and upper-class offending alike are explicable as a product of opportunities of the 'capitalist economic production regime'. The integration of these key themes led Edwin Sutherland to 'approximately' define white-collar crime as 'a crime committed by a person of respectability and high social status in the course of his occupation' (Sutherland 1949: 9). Sutherland's empirical focus was on the violations of the 70 largest US corporations at that time and of elite executives within these, though much of his actual research incorporated a diverse array of offences such as workplace theft, fraud by mechanics, and deception by shoe sales persons. As Slapper and Tombs (1999: 4–5) summarize, Sutherland's concept demonstrated (1) that the common image of typical crimes and typical criminality (i.e. the preoccupation with volume crimes) was inaccurate, (2) that a reductionist criminology explaining criminality in terms of lower-class pathology (i.e. such as general theories foregrounding strain or social/individual pathology) was inadequate, (3) that the scope of criminology needed to include a wider range of criminal behaviours and the process of criminalization (i.e. the offences of elite actors and their integration with political processes), and (4) that one must explain both the predatory crimes by the wealthy against the poor and the abuses of power by the wealthy (i.e. recognize in whose interests laws are created). However, Sutherland's definition is clouded in various ambiguities (see Nelken 2012) and 'has itself become an imprisoning framework that confuses the offender with the offense and inadequately attends to the structural aspects of white-collar crimes' (Pontell and Geis 2007: xiv).

A key issue is that 'in using social status as a defining element of crime . . . it cannot then be used as an explanatory variable because it is not allowed to vary independently of the crime' (Benson and Simpson 2009: 7). Aligned with analyses foregrounding how the deficiencies inherent in Sutherland's definition 'rendered white collar crime an impotent construct for theory building in sociology' (Braithwaite 1985: 3), Shapiro (1990) argued that we ought to 'collar the crime, not the criminal'. This and a general focus on deception (Edelhertz 1970) brings into scope many 'blue-collar' occupational crimes that would otherwise fall outside Sutherland's construct, watering down the elite component and broadening the public policy challenges (Geis 2016: 35; Pontell 2016: 39), which we suggest should be broadened further still by including Mafia-type 'organized crime' involvement in major bankruptcy and VAT frauds, counterfeiting, alcohol and tobacco tax evasion/smuggling, and public corruption activities. But offender-based and offence-based approaches can be compatible, as we can analyse how elite occupational positions and high social esteem provide access to opportunities to commit particular white-collar offences; to possess the knowledge, techniques, networks, locations, and skills needed to carry them out; and to disarm or even deter the *potential* suspicions of auditors, media, police, and regulators.

Sutherland included as 'crime' acts sanctioned through criminal, civil, and administrative proceedings because there were more feasible alternatives to prosecution for such misconduct, a situation that exists today, except for some jurisdictions that operate a 'legality principle' which obliges prosecution whenever there is sufficient evidence to justify it (admittedly, a term of art that is seldom reviewable by outsiders in practice). Some lawyers argued that it was too loose a criterion (Tappan 1947), though we note that all crime-survey and victim-survey data make precisely the same assumption. Some corporations and individuals may admit to regulatory offences to reduce hassle and time, whereas they would strongly defend and sometimes succeed against criminal charges because of their imputation of dishonesty and the collateral consequences of conviction for their right to bid for government contracts. However, as Aubert (1952: 266) put it:

> For purposes of theoretical analysis it is of prime importance to develop and apply concepts which preserve and emphasize the ambiguous nature of the white-collar crimes and not to 'solve' the problem by classifying them as either 'crimes' or 'not crimes.' Their controversial nature is exactly what makes them so interesting from a sociological point of view and what gives us a clue to important norm conflicts, clashing group interests, and maybe incipient social change. One main benefit to be derived from the study of white-collar crimes springs from the opportunity which the ambivalence in the citizen, in the businessman, and among lawyers, judges, and even criminologists offers as a barometer of structural conflicts and change-potential in the larger social system of which they and the white-collar crimes are parts.

Criminology, as a discipline, may be broad enough also to include arguably harmful but not criminal behaviours (e.g. tax avoidance). Those from a more critical position may argue that we need to transcend state definitions, but foregrounding a classification system based on 'informed morality' opens up the problem of who chooses the harm criteria and what is the role of intention in criminal liability. Lobbying and political finance can influence criminalization in law and in practice. However, while debates over how widely to define 'white-collar crime' are important for scholars and activists, they may be irrelevant to those with the task of responding to 'it' who require definitive offences and frameworks within which to pursue such white-collar offenders. Hence, the importance of the details in contested legislation in the UK such as the Fraud Act 2006 and the Bribery Act 2010, and the Financial Institutions Reform, Recovery and Enforcement Act 1989 and much other civil and criminal legislation in the US. At times, there can be a political preference for criminalization, although (or to the ultra-cynical, even because) regulatory enforcement might arguably be more efficient and effective (Beaton-Wells and Fisse 2011; Engdahl and Larsson 2015).

The definitions of 'white-collar crime' that we construct have theoretical, empirical, and policy implications (see Pontell 2016). How we define and conceptualize our research focus shapes how white-collar crime is represented, measured, explained, prevented, regulated, and sanctioned. Various conceptualizations have been advanced over the years, which have significant differences of nuance: 'corporate crime' (Clinard and Yeager 1980; Braithwaite 1985; Slapper and Tombs 1999) and 'occupational crime' (Clinard and Yeager 1980; Green 1997); 'organizational deviance' (Ermann and Lundman 1978); 'organizational crime' (Schrager and Short 1978); 'crimes of the powerful' (Pearce 1976); 'crimes of the middle classes' (Weisburd, Wheeler, and Waring 1991); 'crimes of deception' (Gottfredson and Hirschi 1990); 'crimes of the suites' (Timmer and Eitzen 1989); 'crimes of specialized access' (Felson and Eckert 2015); and 'middle-class crime' (Karstedt 2016). There are common analytical features across these definitions, such as the focus on unlawful acts and omissions in the course of an occupation and/or in an organizational setting (public or private), the foregrounding of a violation or abuse of trust characterized by some form of deception or dishonesty, and the misuse of otherwise legitimate business or institutional procedures and practices to conceal behaviours.

Occupational crimes are offences committed by individuals, or small groups of individuals, for themselves in the course of their occupations, often against their employers (Clinard and Quinney 1973; Clinard and Yeager 1980: 18). In contrast, corporate/organizational crimes are those committed by corporate officials acting for the corporation and by the corporation itself (Clinard and Quinney 1973; Clinard and Yeager 1980: 16–18). But individuals can act for personal gain *and* for the gain of the business (i.e. 'by the firm, for the firm' (Hartung 1950)). Sutherland (1983: 227), and Wang and Holtfreter (2012) stress levels of corporate recidivism.

Focusing on the organization or corporation as an offender can create problems for criminal law frameworks that are geared towards individual guilt and intent: a corporation or organization, as a hollow entity, cannot have intent or guilt. Organizations are constellations of individuals who carry our behaviours on their behalf, although it may be ambiguous whether these behaviours have clear criminal intent, are acts of negligence or involve an omission of duty, creating obstacles to investigation and prosecution for 'crime'. Different jurisdictions approach this issue in different ways, the US making corporate criminal responsibility easier via the rule that junior employees can be deemed to act for the corporation; the UK and some other jurisdictions via absolute or vicarious liability for health and safety offences, for example. The OECD and Financial Action Task Force have pressurized countries into enhancing corporate liability for transnational bribery and all forms of money-laundering.

WHITE-COLLAR AND CORPORATE CRIME AS 'ORGANIZED' CRIME

Sutherland (1983: 229–30) recognized white-collar crimes as 'organized crime', not in the contemporary sense where organized crime discourse is associated with illegitimate, external criminal gangs and criminal enterprise, but in the need to understand the formal and informal 'organization' of the white-collar crime activities. Thus, 'offenders' may organize their behaviours collaboratively, through structures such as 'gentlemen's agreements' (usually male), trade associations, cartels, and so on, with the aim of influencing legislation or restricting law enforcement as well as fixing prices etc. In less regulated economies, businesses may seek to manipulate or restrain trade in their favour, for example, a corporation would more likely reward their advertising agencies that increase sales, irrespective of the honesty of their methods. For Sutherland (1983: 230) one of the few significant points of difference between the white-collar criminal and the 'professional thief' is their self- and public perception.

With this in mind, we can usefully consider how contemporary white-collar and corporate crimes are organized. By analysing 'organization', we can identify those relations and practices that are necessary and those that are contingent to the accomplishing of criminal enterprise (see Lord and Levi 2016). This implies understanding (1) how and why motivated offenders recognise and exploit such financial crime opportunities, (2) how they generate and manage the finances for and from the bribes, (3) the types of skill sets, knowledge, and expertise that they need (or need to recruit) to organize the bribes, and (4) the conditions that facilitate this organization. By thinking in terms of 'how would-be offenders confront problems of gaining finance, gaining access to crime opportunities, and retaining their freedom and crime proceeds' (Levi 2009b: 225), we can begin to understand how social/criminal networks are established and maintained for criminal enterprise within legitimate business structures, networks, and situations. If we begin to organize our thinking to consider bribery in terms of the 'skill sets, contacts, start-up capital, and running costs that they require' (Levi 2009b: 231), we can recognize necessity in terms of the convergence in space and time of a specific situation (e.g. a vulnerability in the procurement chain converging at a time and location), a target (e.g. the perceived simplicity of bribery through hospitalities), and the absence of capable guardians (e.g. inadequate anti-corruption regulation and oversight). Offenders need to have skills and confidence as well as motivation.

EXPLAINING WHITE-COLLAR AND CORPORATE CRIMES

There are a number of different foci in the explanation of these crimes, just as there are for other forms of crime but with the additional issue that many white-collar and corporate crimes are policed by non-police agencies, all with their varied approaches to regulation and use of the criminal law. We should analyse (1) the immediate actions of individuals (and their nature) in the contexts of offending environments, (2) how and why opportunities are 'made the most of' by individuals, and (3) how these issues relate to the wider economic and structural landscape.

INDIVIDUAL DIFFERENCES AND WHITE-COLLAR CRIME

The Lombrosian methodology for distinguishing 'criminals' from 'the rest of us' excluded *white-collar* criminals because they were not in an imprisoned dataset.

Gottfredson and Hirschi's (1990) general theory of crime did include fraud, but its focus was not on elite managers (few of whom are convicted) but on the much larger number of high-frequency deceivers (like credit card and welfare fraudsters) who have high impulsivity and such like ill discipline common among other 'mainstream' delinquents. It might be fruitful to examine the links between impulsivity, the various cultures of masculinity and high-risk economically harmful decisions taken by financial speculators, as well as by senior banking executives in search of those short-term performance-related bonuses that will make them into the wolves of Wall Street or avoid becoming the failures on the wrong side of the Art of the Deal: however, little such research has been done, and senior bankers are less accessible than market traders to cortisol/testosterone measurement (Levi 1994; Benson 2013; Coates 2013; Piquero and Piquero 2016). Some self-report studies have challenged the unusualness of low-end white-collar crime. Karstedt and Farrall (2006, 2007) surveyed a random sample of over 4,000 25–65 year-olds in England and Wales, the former East Germany and the former West Germany. 61 per cent self-reported that they committed at least one out of a list of offences against business, government, or against employers at work: common practices were paying cash in hand to avoid taxation, keeping money when given too much change, wrongly using and swapping identity cards for own gain and cheating in second-hand sales.

A focus on differences between individuals in the propensity to commit crime may lead us to neglect situational influences on criminality, including the sheer length of time taken for some white-collar and corporate offences to unfold. Thus, Levi (2008) examined bankruptcy (and other) frauds in terms of a threefold typology:

1. pre-planned frauds, in which the business scheme is set up from the start as a way of defrauding victims (businesses, public sector and/or individuals)
2. intermediate frauds, in which people started out obeying the law but consciously turned to fraud later and
3. slippery-slope frauds, in which deceptions spiralled, often in the context of trying—however absurdly and over-optimistically—to rescue an essentially insolvent business or set of businesses, escalating losses to creditors.

One aspect upon which Sutherland and his followers focused was on the learned attitudes to the situational morality of business conduct—later described as 'techniques of neutralization' by sociologists and 'cognitive dissonance' by psychologists. In both academic and forensic professional circles, a popular concept is the 'fraud triangle', which has received a great deal of research attention, and which outlines necessary conditions in the commission of fraud. Albrecht *et al.* (1982: 34) follow Cressey (1953) in his classic study of embezzlement in arguing that people became embezzlers if and only if all three conditions of the fraud triangle are evident: 'There must be (1) a non-sharable problem, (2) an opportunity for trust violation, and (3) a set of rationalizations that define the behaviour as appropriate in a given situation'. In one recent study, Switzerland and Austria's 'elite' white-collar offenders with high professional standing and respectability were interviewed (Schuchter and Levi 2015). They consider that though perceived pressure from peers outside and inside the firm is salient to most frauds, the common core is only motivation. Schuchter and Levi (2015) concluded that the frequently cited 'rationalization' is too simplistic: rather, among those interviewed, a fraud-inhibiting inner voice before the crime and a guilty conscience after it were present. Whether this is true more generally remains to be determined.

PERSONALITY DIFFERENCES VERSUS LEARNING TO COMMIT FRAUD

It is not clear whether there is any personality difference between 'fraudsters' and others (as argued by Babiak and Hare (2007), who see fraudsters as an identifiable subset of psychopaths),[1] or whether fraud results more from differential socialization into particular (sub)cultures (see Shover and Hochstetler 2006; Benson and Simpson 2015). The latter 'fraud is normal' (at least in particular occupational settings) view over-predicts the actual incidence of fraud among those with opportunities to commit it, whereas the 'fraudsters are psychopaths' view under-estimates the prevalence of deception in the general population by focusing on high-frequency career fraudsters. Both models have difficulty in accounting for change in general levels of fraud between societies, over time and—for individuals—over the life course. The foci on personality attributes and on differential association may not be mutually exclusive: indeed it seems unlikely that fraud is fully explicable in either framework alone. Psychiatrists long held that there was a category of 'creative psychopaths' who were successful liars, though why they became such was unexplained. Some psychobiologists consider that such persons can be identified from questionnaires and brain scans, and Babiak and Hare (2007) suggest that 'snakes in suits' most commonly suffer from narcissistic personality disorder: showing an excessive need for admiration, a sense of superiority and entitlement, and a lack of empathy. So individual differences in propensity to commit white-collar crime is moulded both by heredity and environment, within a context of different situational opportunities (Duffield and Grabosky 2001).

Like most of the embezzlers studied by Nettler (1974)—critiquing Cressey (1953)—pre-planned bankruptcy fraudsters knew what they were doing and that what they were doing was against the criminal law. By and large, they did not seem unduly troubled morally by this, having quite cynical views about the morality of ordinary business and being unchallenged by those around them (Levi 2008). Notwithstanding, the most serious (but not the most commonly committed) frauds are committed not by vanishing swindlers using false personal names and/or intentionally short-term corporate names, but by senior executives using their own names, manipulating—with the knowing, wilfully blind, or unwitting assistance of their professional advisers (or 'enablers' in the parlance of the police)—the exchange values of largely phony financial instruments while hoping to enjoy long executive careers with multiple corporate partners.

Wheeler (1992) argues that elites engage in crime not because of greed or financial gain but because of the fear of losing their possessions and standing. Therefore, fear of falling may be more important than the fear of failing to explaining involvement in intermediate or slippery-slope white-collar crime. The sense of entitlement, combined with confidence in impunity, can account for the clear abuse of corporate facilities

[1] It may be impossible to tell when accounts by offenders (and non-offenders) of their motivations (a) are genuinely believed by the fraudsters, and (b) represent their 'true' motivations at the time they contemplated and committed their offences (Levi 2008).

(jets, hotels, and restaurants) for private benefit by senior executives. What the effects of prosecutions for the latter offences may be on general deterrence remain unknown (Paternoster 2016).

CRIMINAL CAREERS AND WHITE-COLLAR CRIMES

Once someone has decided to offend, what specific avenues of white-collar criminality are selected as part of rational choice can vary according to the self-confidence, technical, and social skills and contact set possessed, as well as the situation in which each individual is placed: as Cressey (1955) noted, all accountants can embezzle, and the same applies to other professionals with the capacity to defraud or to launder money (Middleton and Levi 2015). How available 'crime networks' are to the willing white-collar offender affects 'crime capacitation': an issue often neglected in context-free individualized explanations of involvement in crime. Age also impacts choice of what type of white-collar crime to commit. Those currently over-50s might be over-challenged by cyber-enabled crimes, and they might not know or trust younger co-offenders. This is a general proposition about the relationship between age and risk-taking/innovation, but current millennials or digital natives might not be similarly anxious about technology when they reach their 50s.

KPMG (2016) examined 'company fraud' cases which its forensic departments investigated over recent years, whether or not prosecuted: unstated, the willingness of clients to pay to hire KPMG means that such frauds are more likely to be serious in impact and involve senior personnel. Most fraudsters are between the ages of 36 and 55 (69 per cent of fraudsters investigated); predominantly male (79 per cent compared with 85 per cent in 2007); 65 per cent are employed by the company (38 per cent for over six years); hold an executive or director level position (35 per cent); described as autocratic (18 per cent) and are three times more likely to be regarded as friendly as not; likely to have colluded with others (62 per cent of frauds, down from 70 per cent in the 2013 survey); and motivated by personal gain (60 per cent), greed (36 per cent) and the sense of 'because I can' (27 per cent). Why greed is different from personal gain—rather than just an expression of moral condemnation—is not considered. The Association of Certified Fraud Accountants conducts biennial surveys of its worldwide members, though with a poor response rate which—as with most such surveys—makes it hard to know what to infer from it about *typical* behaviour: the most recent gives many interesting details about perpetrators, victims, and contexts, and shows that the more senior the insider offender, the greater the losses (ACFE 2016). None of these datasets include frauds against individuals perpetrated from outside otherwise legitimate businesses.

In the criminal careers literature, late onset and non-violent offenders have been neglected: longitudinal studies tend to start at age 8–10 and end before major white-collar crime opportunities present themselves. Convicted white-collar offenders in the US, UK, and the Netherlands are typically male, white, and about 10 years older than non–white-collar offenders, and are from the middle class of society; have previous arrests and convictions (though not at the same rate as non–white-collar offenders); and have committed both white-collar and non–white-collar types of crimes (Onna *et al.* 2014; Piquero and Piquero 2016; Soothill *et al.* 2012). Some Dutch fraud offenders are early onset, high frequency offenders, whereas others are late onset, low frequency offenders (Onna *et al.* 2014); a construct also supported by the Organised Crime Monitor data from the Netherlands, showing a substantial proportion apparently turning to major fraud and organized crime business-enabled offences in middle age (van Koppen *et al.* 2010a, 2010b).

Soothill *et al.* (2012: 782) in the last of a series of thoughtful follow-up studies of middle-class offenders over 35 years, concluded that 'middle-class offenders who are more prolific tend to be generalists (including committing white-collar crime) rather than specialists in a particular type of crime', but a quarter of low-rate white-collar offenders were reconvicted of white-collar offences. However, what such studies have not yet told us is how the type of offences change over time, as perhaps it becomes harder for those convicted to gain specialized access that would enable them to commit particular offences (or to go straight).

White-collar offenders had *longer* criminal careers (Piquero and Weisburd 2009). Some of the offenders continued into their 70s, as did some British offenders (Levi 2008). Piquero and Benson (2004) argue that this is best understood as *punctuated situationally dependent offending*, in which some traditional offending similar to other offenders occurs in late adolescence, and then white-collar crime develops later in life when most people have given up crime altogether. The opportunity to offend—whether that ends up being labelled as white-collar crime, organized crime, or not crime at all—may become available to the individual only after he or she has obtained a certain occupational position; and the motivation may be activated only if the individual experiences some crisis in his or her personal or occupational life. On the other hand, many frauds do not require any established organizational role—indeed in the case of many cyber-enabled and cyber-dependent frauds, they may be in a different continent!—and one lesson from all this research is that it is absurd to expect a coherent pattern of criminality and criminal careers from such a variegated set of criminal activities. Finally, Sutherland (1983: 227) and Wang and Holtfreter (2012) stress levels of *corporate* recidivism, which is a different focus from that on individuals in the analyses above.

THE IMPORTANCE OF THE ORGANIZATIONAL CONTEXT, STRUCTURE, CULTURE, AND OPPORTUNITY

We might explain individual offending behaviour in relation to (1) the rational choices that those with opportunities make in pursuit of personal (or organizational) gain as the lure of offending, together with a lack of restraint and oversight, and perhaps changing circumstances, becomes more tempting (see Shover and Hochstetler 2006), (2) how such individuals might rationalize or 'neutralize' their offending behaviour (e.g. 'everyone is at it', 'I was protecting the business'), or (3) the lack of attachments that such individuals have to society (e.g. perceiving there to be no direct victims as is the case of most 'conventional' crimes). However, individual level explanations do not sufficiently account for the influence of organizational cultures or wider political-economic/cultural structures and can 'underestimate the pressures within society and organizational structures which impel those individuals to commit illegal acts' (Schrager and Short 1978: 410). Thus, contextualized theories of rational choice, and the dynamics between choice, organization, opportunity, and context (Benson *et al.* 2016) are most promising in explaining white-collar and corporate crimes. Such theories 'build from a rational actor framework that shows how offending decisions are affected by instrumental and normative considerations. Such theories can take into account micro-, meso-, and macro-level influences and have important policy implications' (Simpson 2013: 325; see also Vaughan 2007).

We can analyse these different levels through the lens of the organization and organizational cultures. The organization provides the means, setting, rationale, and opportunity for corporate deviance (Punch 1996, 2011). Some organizations may exhibit pathological characteristics (e.g. a diffusion of responsibility, an absence of clear operating procedures, low internal compliance, or destructive social dynamics), but such associations and internal linkages are difficult to test empirically. Except where a trail of emails and internal phone recordings make them manifest—as in recent banking rate fixing scandals—it can be difficult to prove beyond reasonable doubt that senior staff had active knowledge of misconduct. Such difficulties in attributing liability are quite unlike those in areas of crime for gain where we have merely to link the actor to the act.

The attitudes of senior managers have long been recognized as important (Clinard and Yeager 1980) as the 'tone from the top' shapes how behaviours are (re)defined as acceptable or not. But rather than having a cohesive and singular 'corporate culture', there may also be subcultures in organizational and institutional settings that can be in tension, with the key being to understand how and why the priorities of certain cultures, groups, or departments are considered more important than others. For instance, the professional ethics of lawyers or accountants may give way to commercial pressures to advise how far companies can get away with certain activities, as they try to hit their own personal commercial targets set by the firm. The organizational mindset is further reinforced through processes of organizational selection and socialization while 'walls of secrecy and silence' may also emerge as colleagues, through cognitive dissonance, concerted ignorance, or an absence of interest or fear of disclosing the truth, do not blow the whistle on deviance within the workplace (van de Bunt 2010).

Organizations, occupations, and industries vary in the pressures and opportunities for crime and deviance. For example, recent cases involving businesses using 'defeat devices' to falsify emissions data in the auto industry, bribing doctors to prescribe their medical products, or adulterating food products with cheaper—sometimes toxic—alternatives, raise questions about how pervasive criminal behaviour is in certain industries, which are sometimes hard to prove or to falsify. Some would argue that business is criminogenic (Clarke 1990; Punch 1996; Slapper and Tombs 1999) and that to 'understand the social embeddedness of deviant and criminal business behaviour it is essential to grasp that the business organization is the weapon, the means, the setting, the rationalization, the offender, *and* the victim' (Punch 1996: 214). Managers, in response to internal and external business pressures, engage in a wide spectrum of deviant behaviours at certain times and under certain conditions to cope with the problems they encounter in the corporate working environment (Punch 1996: 214).

However, there is a danger of sociological or organizational determinism. *Pace* Clarke (2012), opportunity alone does not 'make the thief' but if the cultural conditions are conducive, then offending is more likely. Practices, processes, and collective decisions to benefit the corporation become more than simply the sum of individual actions (Fisse and Braithwaite 1993; Punch 1996). In such settings, the morality, voice, and internal restraints of 'good' individuals may be suspended and become lost in the 'groupthink' of the organization, a context reinforced by the potential for the depersonalization of one's actions and the cognitive dissonance of colleagues. Rationality becomes bounded with amoral calculations for the benefit of the business taking priority (Kagan and Scholz 1984). Thus, the structure, culture, and personality/identity of business are key variables that help us explain why some companies and managers turn to deviant solutions/practices (Punch 1996). The same logic can be applied to Russian and other drug cheating in the Olympics and World Championships.

Fligstein and Roehrkasse (2016) try to integrate these different levels, noting that the financial crisis of 2007 to 2009 was marked by widespread fraud in the mortgage securitization industry, shown by large regulatory settlements in which many of the largest banks paid multibillion-dollar penalties. They found that theories emphasizing the impact of deregulation or technical opacity identify only necessary, not sufficient, conditions. Their argument focuses instead on changes in competitive conditions and firms' positions within and across markets. As the supply of mortgages began to decline around 2003, mortgage originators lowered credit standards and engaged in predatory lending to shore up corporate unit profits (and, in our view, their personal bonuses). In turn, mortgage-backed securities issuers and underwriters who were part of giant banks and building societies committed securities fraud to conceal this misconduct and to enhance the value of other financial products.

We must also consider the wider cultural and political-economic context for white-collar and corporate offending. For instance, the geo-historical context has seen the emergence of an enterprise culture that promotes individualism, together with free-market principles and deregulation. This has produced social inequality and a high-risk culture accompanied by legal and political support (e.g. the creation of limited liability companies to reduce risk of failure). For Slapper and Tombs (1999: 141), the 'structural necessities of contemporary capitalism' require the prioritization of profit leading to amoral calculations on the part of corporations and shapes the extent to which such crime is seen as more or less acceptable. While this may be persuasive to many readers, such a perspective over-predicts criminality as economic markets are relatively stable, as ethical and morally responsible corporate policies can be profitable, and as notable legal and regulatory improvements (under consumer and worker pressure) have been made to govern business criminality. Furthermore, the detection of serious violations can threaten profitability—though such threats may be beyond the short time-horizons of staff enjoying performance bonuses—while we also see frauds in several non-business contexts (e.g. charity organizations, state institutions) where we might expect the organizational cultures to be different.

POLICING, PROSECUTING, AND REGULATING

We have established that white-collar and corporate crimes are varied in their victim/offender relationships, size, longevity, and skills required, as are the offenders and explanations of their behaviour. There is further diversity regarding policing strategies and who is responsible for these. Note the use of 'policing' rather than 'the police' here, because although 'plural policing' (Jones, this volume) has been increasingly used to describe the way formal social control operates in the sphere of 'ordinary' crimes and public order, the number and diversity of modes of policing for white-collar and corporate crimes is arguably much greater. Indeed, the history of business regulation is shot through with specialist bodies that have been set up apart from the police (in rough historical order) to handle direct and indirect taxes, workplace health and safety, food and drink adulteration, pollution, financial services regulation, etc. For these bodies, criminal prosecution is overwhelmingly the road not taken, and though studies of the police in many countries have highlighted the role of discretion, criminal prosecution is much more routinized for theft, robbery, and street violence than it is for their equivalents in crimes by or even against the corporation.

Myriad state authorities are involved in the investigation and prosecution of white-collar and corporate crimes. In the UK, these include government and non-government licensed regulatory authorities (including the Financial Conduct Authority (FCA), Prudential Regulation Authority (PRA), HM Revenue and Customs (HMRC), Health and Safety Executive (HSE), Environment Agency (EA), the Solicitors Regulation Authority and other regulators of the professions, and the Department for Business, Energy and Industrial Strategy (BEIS) Companies Investigation Branch); law enforcement authorities—including the Serious Fraud Office (SFO), National Crime Agency (NCA) and economic and specialist crime units within police forces, for example, primarily the City of London Police (CoLP) Economic Crime Directorate (Doig and Levi 2013); and international agencies (including the European Fraud Office (OLAF), Europol, and Interpol. A similar variation exists within the US. The FBI (including its IC3 internet fraud reporting process), the New York Department of Financial Services, the Manhattan District Attorney's Office, and the Department of Justice (DoJ) are the principal criminal investigation and prosecution bodies. However, the Securities and Exchange Commission (SEC), the US Secret Service (for counterfeiting and payment card fraud), and the Federal Trade Commission also have oversight of fraud, and there is a plethora of regulators with enforcement powers. In Federal systems (including Australia, Germany, and the US), there are usually State as well as Federal criminal investigation bodies. Civil Law systems tend to have more unified systems in which white-collar crimes are dealt with in the same ways as others: but they may be decentralized and under pressure to deal with large numbers of cases, generating delays and short cuts. There is no space in this chapter for a review of regulatory processes, but they tend to be based around particular issues like health and safety at work or pollution.

This diversity of responsibility presents difficulties in establishing what an 'adequate enforcement' framework should look like (see Lord and Levi 2015). For instance, competing ideologies have shaped arguments over the most appropriate model of policing white-collar and corporate crimes, containing both symbolic and instrumental elements, where there is often a significant problem in measuring levels of misconduct and assessing the effects of enforcement decisions, often cross-border. The 1980s and 1990s saw debates around the purported role of criminal prosecution as being a tool of last resort or a fundamental part of the enforcement response (Reiss 1984), and often characterized by the contrast between the 'compliance' (Clarke 1990; Hawkins

2002) and 'deterrence' (Pearce and Tombs 1998; Slapper and Tombs 1999) approaches. Croall (2003) analysed the primary strategies, arguments, and assumptions of these binary positions. She suggests that 'regulation' seeks to secure and maintain standards by encouraging compliant behaviour through persuasion and cooperation (assuming potential offenders are willing to comply), with self-regulation and private remedies being the preferred outcomes; while 'crime control' seeks to punish and prosecute offenders, foregrounding deterrence (assuming potential offenders are amoral calculators) and moral condemnation through public justice. Attempts to persuade are argued to be more effective due to the inherent complexity of the offences (i.e. difficult to detect, evidential obstacles) and associated delay and financial costs of prosecution, but alternatively less effective as low prosecution rates undermine deterrence and the close relations between regulator and regulatee can risk regulatory capture (which may be deliberate on the part of business and the career prospects of regulators). The discourse associated with the two models also varies, with the regulated activities being viewed respectively as technical violations (i.e. *mala prohibita*) and inherently 'bad' like 'real crimes' (i.e. *mala in se*). 'Occupational crimes' involving specific individual accused and where the organization is a victim are more likely to be subject to criminal law, while 'organizational crimes' where individual responsibility is harder to establish and where the business has benefited, are more likely subject to regulatory control.

There is much overlap between the models in practice, and not just as a reflection of the 'punish or persuade' pyramid of enforcement espoused by Ayres and Braithwaite (1992) in the context of the regulation of 'repeat players'. 'The lines between regulatory and criminal procedures are becoming more tangled and blurred' and in the area of corporate crime, the 'enforcement of criminal law . . . increasingly uses classic regulatory techniques of negotiation and settlement' (Wells 2011: 15, 13), although increased political will, proactive inspectorial strategies, and increased resources can enable prosecution (Slapper and Tombs 1999: 186; see also Almond 2013; Pearce and Tombs 1998; Tombs and Whyte 2007). Current 'policing' of variegated white-collar and corporate crimes incorporates features of both 'Old Governance' (i.e. state-centric, centralized, bureaucratic expertise, mandatory rules) and 'New Governance (i.e. state orchestration, decentralized, dispersed expertise, soft law) (Abbott and Snidal 2009) in 'regulatory capitalism' (Braithwaite 2008). Additionally, policing incorporates a range of state and non-state actors, such as inter-governmental and non-governmental organizations (see Braithwaite and Drahos 2000; Djelic and Sahlin-Andersson 2006; Abbott and Snidal 2013), who interact with both public and private actors in pursuing harmonized, transnational legal and normative standards. Models of 'responsive regulation' remain at the forefront of attempts to control and change the undesired behaviours (see Grabosky 2013; Mascini 2013; Parker 2013) but critique emanates from the political left who use low prosecution rates to expose the neoliberal hypocrisy of capitalist societies' crime control ideologies (Tombs and Whyte 2013, 2015). Furthermore, there is a lack of credibility in graduated sanctions models when prosecutions are so rare (Lord 2014a; Lord and Levi 2015). Anti-money laundering measures have featured heavily in the fight against Grand Corruption and other crimes, alongside an array of prosecutions, Deferred Prosecution Agreements against large banks and accounting firms, and civil and regulatory sanctions, but the effects of these on underlying crimes are largely unanalysed (Levi *et al.*, forthcoming; Halliday *et al.* 2014).

Due to the diversity of the crimes, it is difficult to conceptualize the policing response to specific white-collar offences. Distinctions in response have been made between 'crimes against social regulation' (i.e. offences causing physical, human harms) and 'crimes against economic regulation' (i.e. offences of a financial nature, often against the state and economic system) (Slapper and Tombs 1999: 196), though this focuses away from many blue-collar and white-collar crimes. This is most clear in the fines levied against business for such offences. For example, at the time of writing, the highest British fine levied for the death of an employee was £700,000 against Baldwins Crane Hire by Preston Crown Court/Health and Safety Executive (HSE) in December 2015. (Since the coming into force of the Corporate Manslaughter and Homicide Act 2007 there have been 11 prosecutions, almost all for smaller firms in which it is easier to show a connection between the harm and the demonstrable acts of senior people.) In contrast, Barclays Bank was fined £284 million in 2015 by the Financial Conduct Authority (FCA) for Forex failings; the FCA imposed a total of £905,219,078 in fines in 2015 alone against 39 firms. Comparators with the treatment of 'ordinary' property crimes are too problematic because few such thefts are anywhere near as large as the median economic crimes, but also because the range of regulatory and self-regulatory sanctions is simply unavailable for them, making it policing by the police or nothing, though restorative and community penalties are possible.

PROSECUTING WHITE-COLLAR AND CORPORATE CRIMES

Readers may wonder why there is such a difference between the ways we treat white-collar and 'ordinary' crimes for gain: this may be understood as a mix of ideology, the 'revolving door' between business and regulation; and the difficulties of proving cases against respectable firms. But there are differences between the policing and prosecution of social security fraud and of fraud scams against consumers and investors, on the one hand, and the pursuit of health and safety violators and serious tax evaders, on the other. In the former cases, provided that the crimes are detected and investigated to a criminal standard, prosecution tends to be routine (though in more recent years, 'change of circumstances' social security fraudsters may be dealt with by suspension of/deduction from benefits instead); in the latter, non-criminal justice mechanisms for control are typically explored, with prosecution or indeed law only as a last resort (Hawkins 2002; Levi 2010a; Tombs and Whyte 2015).

Some prosecutors in the US have been using techniques developed against organized crime, for example, in insider dealing and telemarketing cases where they get one network member to give evidence against others, even extending to insiders wearing wires to tape conversations if the conspiracy is still going on. This has not been the case elsewhere, except where Mafia-type crime groups are involved in public sector corruption contracts, VAT frauds, or counterfeit products.

Early 2016 saw the UK's first concluded criminal prosecution and sentencing of a company, Sweett Group PLC, for 'failing to prevent bribery' by its employees in a foreign jurisdiction,[2] and the later case involving Rolls Royce which had engaged in systematic bribery between 1989 and 2013 in a range of countries (*SFO v Rolls Royce*, 17 January 2017, https://www.judiciary.gov.uk/judgments/serious-fraud-office-v-rolls-royce/).

[2] https://www.sfo.gov.uk/cases/sweett-group/, accessed 8 January 2017.

The boundaries of corporate obligations to prevent corruption and/or money laundering are a contested area. The inability of the SFO to prosecute reflects the impact of the antiquated system of corporate criminal liability in England and Wales in shaping the normal enforcement response to corporate bribery of accommodation and non-prosecution, despite willingness to prosecute (see Lord 2014a, 2014b): note that the after the SFO dropped the case, US authorities continued their parallel Forex investigation, operating on a different set of corporate criminal liability principles. If prosecutions fail, this may imperil the prosecuting body if they are seen as 'ideological' or incompetent; if they always succeed in court, prosecutors may be accused of being too timid.

SENTENCING WHITE-COLLAR AND CORPORATE CRIMINALS

Sentencing tends to follow the routines of just deserts, general and specific deterrence, and incapacitation that are observed in other offence types, but with some special twists based around sentencers' perceptions of harm and dangerousness, and the relative absence of criminal records among most of those convicted which enables them to plead that their offences were 'out of character'. Because of the symbolic component of white-collar crime's association with elites, there is also the general issue of perceived fairness of treatment in relation to offenders with less grace from which to fall. (Restorative justice campaigners might use white-collar crime sanctioning as a role model for how to handle other types of crime.) In most cases, there is not the tabloid hysteria that greets 'lenient sentencing' for many other offences, and few fraudsters unconnected with 'organized crime' are seen as *generally* dangerous. On the other hand, there has been an increasing level of publicity about the prevalence and seriousness of fraud (especially but not only cybercrime), and so it is little surprise that sentencing has been rising for both elite and 'middle-class' criminals (though we would add 'blue-collar', like most payment card as well as social security fraudsters) (Levi 2010b, 2016; Stadler *et al.* 2013). These individual sentencing models cannot, however, be read across to the sentencing of corporations, where we must also factor in the economic consequences of conviction and of scandal independent of prosecution (Fisse and Braithwaite 1984; Levi 2002). Imprisonment is usually an option only for those cases in which there is clear evidence that owners personally instructed or implemented reckless or intentional business decisions, for example, where corporate manslaughter charges can be connected to individuals like the West Virginia mine owner Donald Blankenship, jailed for a year in 2016 for misdemeanour after workers died due to his refusal to undertake expensive safety measures. Otherwise, corporate fines may reflect guidelines influenced by judicial perceptions of intent, harm, and future likelihood of offending, some aspects of which may be mentioned in court as mitigation or by the prosecutor (except in the UK, where it is rare for prosecutors to advocate at the sentencing hearing). In the growing number of Deferred Prosecution Agreement and/or Monitorship cases which bypass criminal trial, there appears to be awareness by the regulators and prosecutors of the general level of sanctions.

In the top 10 global banks (two of which were British), poor disclosure to clients was a factor in the $25 billion of fines paid by US banks in a 2012 settlement for abusive foreclosure practices. The second most expensive issue for the banks was failures in how they sold residential mortgage securities, which resulted in a penalties total of

$27.7 billion. The banks paid $20.2 billion in fines in relation to securitization failures; and 'rate setting' fines came to $14.6 billion, partly stemming from banks' manipulation of foreign exchange and interest rates (*Financial Times*, 27 March 2016). These data reflect relatively aggressive US regulation, but exclude most of the £30 billion paid to victims of 'mis-selling' of personal protection insurance, and the large fines imposed on other banks outside the Top Ten. But they in turn raise issues of what constitutes 'credible deterrence' in the financial services sector, as well as the relationship between large headline figures for fines and the proportionality to profits *from that activity*, profits *as a whole*, and wealth. There is no doubt that enforcement has had a big impact on the rising costs of compliance departments. Time (and transparency) may tell whether it has a similar effect on corporate behaviour.

Below is a selection of sentences in spectacular and mostly well-publicized (see Levi 2006, 2010b) US white-collar crime cases in this century that shows what, by the standards of the rest of the world, are long sentences; where sentences are lower, this usually reflects plea and charge bargaining and/or substantial assistance to prosecutors:

- For a Ponzi scheme (in which investors are paid from incoming funds from new investors but there is little genuine investment) defrauding investors of around $17.3 billion, Bernie Madoff received a sentence of 150 years (and his brother received 10 years for assisting him).
- For a Ponzi scheme defrauding investors of around $7 billion, American Allen Stanford received 110 years (after a not-guilty plea) in 2012, and separately was stripped of his English knighthood.
- Russell Wasendorf Sr., ex-CEO of Peregrine, who defrauded clients of $215 million over 20 years, was given a 50-year sentence.
- Minor Vargas Calvo, owner of Provident Capital Indemnity (PCI) Ltd., ran a criminal reinsurance company that fraudulently guaranteed almost half a billion dollars of life settlement investments worldwide, and was sentenced to 60 years.
- In the Galleon insider-dealing case, Raj Rajaratnam, CEO of Galleon, was sentenced to 11 years (plus $156 million in financial penalties) and Rajat Gupta, former director of McKinsey and of Goldman Sachs, was given a two-year sentence (plus a $5 million fine and one year of supervised release).
- Bernard J. Ebbers, the WorldCom Chief executive who masterminded an $11 billion accounting fraud, got 25 years.
- In Enron, Jeffrey Skilling initially received 24 years' imprisonment, reduced substantially in 2013 in a deal that led to his dropping his appeal and repaying $40 million in his seized assets to creditors (but not reinstating the more than 5,000 jobs and $1 billion in employee retirement funds lost when Enron collapsed).
- In Enron, Andy Fastow got a reduced sentence of six years after pleading guilty and giving evidence against Skilling and Kenneth Lay (who died before serving his sentence).

Critical criminologists may seek to explain this as symbolic gestures to mollify the retributive instincts of the masses, but though there is an element of truth in this, it is difficult to conclude that this is a sufficient explanation, either at the *verstehen* level of how judges feel and think about their decisions (Wheeler *et al.* 1988) or at a more analytical level (judges can only sentence the people put before them). Moreover, looking comparatively (Levi 2010b), it would not explain the national variations in sentencing, a subject that has been little examined.

CONCLUSION

White-collar crimes (as defined in US Federal statutes) are a broad category, ranging from credit card and insurance frauds that most people could commit, to insider trading and price-fixing that require significant positions of trust and socio-economic status. White-collar criminals are a heterogeneous group in terms of their backgrounds, their involvement with 'mainstream' offenders, their consciousness of transgressing social as well as legal norms, and the levels of social disapproval their offences elicit. Weisburd and Waring (2001) usefully distinguish between occasional 'crime as an aberration' offenders, intermittent 'opportunity seekers' and chronic 'stereotypical criminals'; and Piquero and Weisburd (2009) note that a focus on the propensity to commit crime is valuable only for the last category. The general invisibility and non-prosecution of frauds make comparisons between offenders and non-offenders perilous, but it is clear that some offenders are exceptionally low in empathy, conscience, and 'shameability'. We now have a reasonable understanding of both motivational and situational pathways into (though not out of) fraud, but we do not yet have a full explanation of *why* some people commit white-collar crimes and others, similarly placed, do not.

We agree with Haines (2016) that control measures are best understood when framed not only around the methods of control (punishment or persuasion) but also around the degree to which they explicitly attempt to reshape who can and should influence business behaviour and the institutional conditions under which business activity occurs. But the amount and composition of effort to achieve controls is shaped not merely by economic interests but by culture, political traditions, and the history of legal powers. The US historically has been the most aggressive prosecutorial nation across the board; China is taking increasing action on corruption (at least when not connected to current elites) and counterfeit dairy products, but there is less action on other white-collar crimes; and other countries have varied sanctioning records. But we still know only a modest amount about the effectiveness of controls in different contexts, and there remain fundamental tensions between symbolic efforts at parity in the treatment of offending and offenders 'across the board' and narrower efficiency and effectiveness measures in looking for the optimal impact on behaviour for any given level of control expenditure. Thus despite the opportunities for regulation as well as criminal and other sanctions, the moral philosophy of punishment and the science of control remain far apart in white-collar crime, as they are in other arenas of crime control.

SELECTED FURTHER READING

First, read the original research of Edwin Sutherland's *White-collar Crime: the Uncut Version*, (1983). This monograph presents Sutherland's analysis of the 'criminal' activities of the 70 largest corporations in the US at the time of writing. Second, read Sutherland's 'Is "White-Collar Crime" Crime?' (1945). This original article from Sutherland provides excellent insight into the origins of the concepts of white-collar crime and the central analytical dilemma over the 'crime, or not crime' debate. As you read the article, bear in mind the geographical and historical context (i.e. 1940s USA) in which it was written. Follow this by reading Tappan's 'Who is the criminal?' (1947). This is Tappan's response to Sutherland. It provides a more formal legal perspective on the nature of crime, the criminal, and criminality. Third, the following texts provide analysis from established white-collar crime scholars on key issues in white-collar and corporate crime scholarship: Van Slyke, Benson, and Cullen's *The Oxford Handbook of White-Collar Crime* (2016); Benson's and Simpson's (2015) *Understanding White-Collar Crime: An Opportunity Perspective* (2015); Simpson and Weisburd's *The Criminology of White-Collar Crime* (2009); Pontell and Geis' *International Handbook of White-Collar and Corporate Crime* (2007).

REFERENCES

ACFE (2016). *Report to the nations on occupational fraud and abuse: 2016 global fraud study*, Austin, TX: ACFE, http://www.acfe.com/rttn2016/docs/2016-report-to-the-nations.pdf, accessed 8 January 2017.

Abbott, K. and Snidal, D. (2006), *The Governance Triangle: Regulatory Standards Institutions and the Shadow of the State*, Working Paper, Global Governance Project, Oxford University.

Abbott, K. and Snidal, D. (2009), 'Strengthening International Regulation Through Transnational New Governance: Overcoming the Orchestration Deficit', *Vanderbilt Journal of Transnational Law*, 42: 501–78.

Abbott, K. and Snidal, D. (2013), 'Taking responsive regulation transnational: strategies for international organizations', *Regulation and Governance*, 7(1): 95–113.

Albrecht, W. S., Romney, M. B., Cherrington, D. J., Payne, R., and Roe, A. V. (1982), *How to Detect and Prevent Business Fraud*, Englewood Cliffs: Prentice Hall.

Almond, P. (2013), *Corporate Manslaughter and Regulatory Reform, Crime Prevention and Security Management*, Basingstoke: Palgrave Macmillan.

Aubert, V. (1952), 'White-Collar Crime and Social Structure', *American Journal of Sociology*, 58(3): 263–71.

Ayres, I. and Braithwaite, J. (1992), *Responsive Regulation: Transcending the Deregulation Debate*, New York: Oxford University Press.

Beaton-Wells, C. and Fisse, B. (2011), *Australian Cartel Regulation: Law, Policy and Practice in an International Context*, Cambridge: Cambridge University Press.

Benson, M. L. (2013), *Crime and the Life Course: An Introduction*, 2nd edn, New York: Routledge.

Benson, M. L. and Simpson S. S. (2009), *White-Collar Crime: An Opportunity Perspective*, Abingdon, Oxfordshire: Routledge.

Benson, M. L. and Simpson S. S. (2015), *White-Collar Crime: An Opportunity Perspective*. 2nd edn, Abingdon, Oxfordshire: Routledge.

Benson, M., Van Slyke, S. R., and Cullen, F. T. (2016), 'Core Themes in the Study of White-Collar Crime', in S. R. Van Slyke, M. L. Benson, and F. T. Cullen (eds), *The Oxford Handbook of White-Collar Crime*, Oxford: Oxford University Press.

Bonger, W. A. (1916), *Criminality and Economic Conditions*, Boston: Little, Brown.

Braithwaite, J. (1985), 'White-Collar Crime', *Annual Review of Sociology*, 11: 1–25.

Braithwaite, J. (2008), *Regulatory Capitalism: How It Works, Ideas for Making It Work Better*, Cheltenham: Edward Elgar.

Braithwaite, J. and Drahos, P. (2000), *Global Business Regulation*, Cambridge: Cambridge University Press.

Babiak, P. and Hare, R. (2007), *Snakes in Suits: When Psychopaths Go to Work*, New York: Harper Collins.

Beaton-Wells, C. and Fisse, B. (2011), *Australian Cartel Regulation: Law, Policy and Practice in an International Context*, Port Melbourne: Cambridge University Press.

Blumer, H. (1969), *Symbolic Interactionism: Perspective and Method*, Berkeley: University of California Press.

Clarke, M. (1990), *Business Crime. Its Nature and Control*, Oxford: Polity.

Clarke, R. V. (2012), 'Opportunity makes the thief. Really? And so what?', *Crime Science*, 1(3): 1–9.

Clinard, M. B. and Quinney, R. (1973), *Criminal Behavior Systems: A Typology*, revised edn, New York: Holt, Rinehart & Winston.

CLINARD, M. B. and YEAGER, P. C. (1980), *Corporate Crime,* New York: Free Press.

COATES, J. (2013), *The Hour Between Dog and Wolf,* London: Fourth Estate.

CRESSEY, D. (1953), *Other People's Money,* New York: Free Press.

CROALL, H. (2003), 'Combating financial crime: Regulatory versus crime control approaches', *Journal of Financial Crime,* 11(1): 45–55.

DJELIC, M-L. and SAHLIN-ANDERSSON, K. (2006), *Transnational Governance: Institutional Dynamics of Regulation,* Cambridge: Cambridge University Press.

DOIG, A. and LEVI, M. (2013), 'A Case of Arrested Development? Delivering the UK National Fraud Strategy within Competing Policing Policy Priorities', *Public Money and Management,* March, 33(1): 1–8.

DUFFIELD, G. and GRABOSKY, P. (2001), *The Psychology of Fraud,* Trends and Issues 199, Canberra: Australian Institute of Criminology, available at: http://www.aic.gov.au/media_library/publications/tandi_pdf/tandi199.pdf, accessed 10 January 2017.

EDELHERTZ, H. (1970), *The Nature, Impact and Prosecution of White-Collar Crime,* Washington, DC: US Department of Justice.

ENGDAHL, O. and LARSSON, B. (2015), 'Duties to Distrust: The Decentring of Economic and White-Collar Crime Policing in Sweden', *British Journal of Criminology,* 56(3): 515–36.

ERMANN, M. D. and LUNDMAN, R. J. (1978), 'Corporate and Governmental Deviance: Origins, Patterns, and Reactions', in M. D. Ermann and R. J. Lundman (eds), *Corporate and Governmental Deviance: Problems of Organizational Behavior in Contemporary Society,* New York: Oxford University Press.

FELSON, M. and ECKERT, M. (2015), *Crime and Everyday Life,* 5th edn, London: Sage.

FISSE, B. and BRAITHWAITE, J. (1984), *The Impact of Publicity on Corporate Offenders,* Albany: Suny.

FISSE, B. and BRAITHWAITE, J. (1993), *Corporations, Crime, and Accountability.* Cambridge: Cambridge University Press.

FLIGSTEIN, N. and ROEHRKASSE, A. F. (2016), 'The Causes of Fraud in the Financial Crisis of 2007 to 2009: Evidence from the Mortgage-Backed Securities Industry', *American Sociological Review,* 81(4): 617–43.

GEIS, G. (2016), 'The Roots and Variant Definitions of the Concept of "White-Collar Crime" ', in S. R. Van Slyke, M. L. Benson, and F. T. Cullen (eds), *The Oxford Handbook of White-Collar Crime,* Oxford: Oxford University Press.

GOTTFREDSON, M. and HIRSCHI, T. (1990), *A General Theory of Crime,* Stanford: Stanford University Press.

GRABOSKY, P. (2013), 'Beyond Responsive Regulation: The expanding role of non-state actors in the regulatory process', *Regulation and Governance,* 7(1): 114–23.

GREEN, G. S. (1997), *Occupational Crime,* 2nd edn, Chicago: Nelson-Hall.

HALLIDAY, T., LEVI, M., and REUTER, P. (2014), *Global Surveillance of Dirty Money: Assessing Assessments of Regimes To Control Money-Laundering and Combat the Financing of Terrorism,* Chicago: American Bar Foundation, available at: http://www.lexglobal.org/files/Report_Global%20Surveillance%20of%20Dirty%20Money%201.30.2014.pdf, accessed 8 January 2017.

HAINES, F. (2016), 'Taming Business? Understanding Effectiveness in the Control of Corporate and White-collar Crime', in R. Matthews (ed.), *What is to Be Done About Crime and Punishment?,* London: Palgrave Macmillan.

HARTUNG, F. E. (1950), 'White-Collar Offenses in the Wholesale Meat Industry in Detroit', *American Journal of Sociology,* 56(July): 25–34.

HAWKINS, K. (2002), *Law as Last Resort: Prosecution Decision-Making in a Regulatory Agency,* Oxford: Oxford University Press.

KAGAN, R. and SCHOLZ, J. (1984), 'The "Criminology of the Corporation" and Regulatory Enforcement Strategies', in K. Hawkins and J. M. Thomas (eds), *Enforcing Regulation,* Boston, MA: Kluwer-Nijhoff.

KATZ, J. (1980), 'The social movement against white-collar crime', *Criminology Review Yearbook,* 2: 161–84.

KPMG (2016), *Global Profiles of the Fraudster,* London: KPMG International.

KARSTEDT, S. (2016), 'Middle-Class Crime: Moral Economies Between Crime in the Streets and Crime in the Suites', in S. van Slyke, M. Benson, and F. Cullen (eds), *The Oxford Handbook of White-Collar Crime,* New York: Oxford University Press, doi: 10.1093/oxfordhb/9780199925513.013.9.

KARSTEDT, S. and FARRALL, S. (2006), 'The moral economy of everyday crime markets, consumers and citizens', *British Journal of Criminology,* 46(6): 1011–36.

KARSTEDT, S. and FARRALL, S. (2007), *Law-abiding majority?: the everyday crimes of the middle classes,* London: Centre for Crime and Justice Studies, King's College London.

LEVI, M. (1994), Masculinities and white-collar crime', in T. Newburn and B. Stanko (eds), *Just Boys Doing Business,* London: Routledge.

LEVI, M. (2002), 'Suite justice or sweet charity? Some explorations of shaming and incapacitating business fraudsters', *Punishment and Society,* 4(2): 147–63.

LEVI, M. (2006), 'The Media Construction of Financial White-Collar Crimes', *British Journal of Criminology,* Special Issue on Markets, Risk and Crime, 46(6): 1037–57.

LEVI, M. (2008), *The Phantom Capitalists: the Organisation and Control of Long-Firm Fraud,* 2nd edn, Aldershot: Ashgate.

LEVI, M. (2009a), 'Suite Revenge? The Shaping of Folk Devils and Moral Panics about White-Collar Crimes', *British Journal of Criminology,* 49(1): 48–67.

LEVI, M. (2009b), 'Financial crimes', in M. Tonry (ed.), *The Oxford Handbook of Crime and Public Policy,* Oxford Handbooks in Criminology and Criminal Justice, New York: Oxford University Press.

LEVI, M. (2010a), 'Serious tax fraud and non-compliance: A review of evidence on the differential impact of criminal and non-criminal proceedings', *Criminology and Public Policy,* 9(3): 493–513.

LEVI, M. (2010b), 'Hitting the suite spot: sentencing frauds', *Journal of Financial Crime*, 17(1): 116–32.

LEVI, M. (2012), 'How well do anti-money laundering controls work in developing countries?', in P. Reuter (ed.), *Draining Development? Controlling Illicit Flows from Developing Countries*, Washington, DC: World Bank Press.

LEVI, M. (2016) 'Sentencing Respectable Offenders', in S. van Slyke, M. Benson, and F. Cullen (eds), *The Oxford Handbook of White-Collar Crime*, New York: Oxford University Press.

LEVI, M., REUTER, P., and HALLIDAY, T. (forthcoming), 'Can the AML/CTF System Be Evaluated Without Better Data?', *Crime, Law and Social Change*.

LORD, N. (2014a), *Regulating Corporate Bribery in International Business*, Farnham: Ashgate.

LORD, N. (2014b), 'Responding to transnational corporate bribery using international frameworks for enforcement', *Criminology and Criminal Justice*, 14(1): 100–20.

LORD, N. and LEVI, M. (2015), 'Determining the adequate enforcement of white-collar and corporate crimes in Europe', in J. van Erp, W. Huisman, G. Vande Walle (eds), *The Routledge Handbook of White-Collar and Corporate Crime in Europe*, London: Routledge.

LORD, N. and LEVI, M. (2016), 'Organising the Finances For and the Finances From Transnational Corporate Bribery', *European Journal of Criminology*, doi: 10.1177/1477370816661740.

MASCINI, P. (2013), 'Why was the enforcement pyramid so influential? And what price was paid?', *Regulation and Governance*, 7(1): 48–60.

MIDDLETON, D. and LEVI, M. (2015), 'Let Sleeping Lawyers Lie: Organised Crime, Lawyers and the Regulation of Legal Services', *British Journal of Criminology*, 55(4): 647–68, doi: 10.1093/bjc/azv001.

NELKEN, D. (2012), 'White-Collar and Corporate Crime', in M. Maguire, R. Morgan, and R. Reiner (eds), *The Oxford Handbook of Criminology*, 5th edn, Oxford: Oxford University Press.

NETTLER, G. (1974), 'Embezzlement without problems', *British Journal of Criminology*, 14(1): 70–7.

VAN ONNA, J. H., VAN DER GEEST, V. R., HUISMAN, W., and DENKERS, A. J. (2014), 'Criminal Trajectories of White-collar Offenders', *Journal of Research in Crime and Delinquency*, 51(6): 759–84.

PARKER, C. (2013), 'Twenty years of responsive regulation: An appreciation and appraisal', *Regulation and Governance*, 7(1): 2–13.

PATERNOSTER, R. (2016), 'Deterring Corporate Crime', *Criminology and Public Policy*, 15(2): 383–6.

PEARCE, F. (1976), *Crimes of the Powerful*, London: Pluto.

PEARCE, F. and TOMBS, S. (1998), *Toxic Capitalism: Corporate Crime and the Chemical Industry*, Aldershot: Ashgate.

PIQUERO, N. L. and BENSON, M. (2004), 'White-Collar Crime and Criminal Careers: Specifying a Trajectory of Punctuated Situational Offending', *Journal of Contemporary Criminal Justice*, 20(2): 148–65.

PIQUERO, N. L. and WEISBURD, D. (2009), 'Developmental Trajectories of White-Collar Crime', in: S. Simpson and D. Weisburd (eds), *The Criminology of White-Collar Crime*, New York: Springer.

PIQUERO, N. L. and PIQUERO, A. R. (2016), 'White-Collar Criminal Participation and the Life Course', in S. R. Van Slyke, M. L. Benson, and F. T. Cullen (eds), *The Oxford Handbook of White-Collar Crime*, Oxford: Oxford University Press.

PONTELL, H. (2016), 'Theoretical, Empirical, and Policy Implications of Alternative Definitions of "White-Collar Crime": "Trivializing the Lunatic Crime Rate" ', in S. R. Van Slyke, M. L. Benson, and F. T. Cullen (eds), *The Oxford Handbook of White-Collar Crime*, Oxford: Oxford University Press.

PONTELL, H. and GEIS, G. (2007), 'Preface', in H. Pontell and G. Geis (eds), *International Handbook of White-Collar and Corporate Crime*, New York: Springer.

PUNCH, M. (1996), *Dirty Business: Exploring Corporate Misconduct*, Sage: London.

PUNCH, M. (2011), 'The organizational component in corporate crime', in J. Gobert and A-M. Pascal (eds), *European Developments in Corporate Criminal Liability*, London: Routledge.

REISS, A. (1984), 'Consequences of Compliance and Deterrence Models of Law Enforcement for the Exercise of Police Discretion', *Law and Contemporary Problems*, 47(4): 83–122.

ROSS, E. A. (1907), 'The criminaloid', *The Atlantic Monthly*, 99: 44–50 (January).

SCHRAGER, L. S. and SHORT, J. F. (1978), 'Towards a sociology of organisational crime', *Social Problems*, 25: 407–19.

SCHUCHTER, A. and LEVI, M. (2015), 'Beyond the Fraud Triangle: Swiss and Austrian elite fraudsters', *Accounting Forum*, 39(3): 176–87, doi:10.1016/j.accfor.2014.12.001.

SHAPIRO, S. P. (1990), 'Collaring the Crime Not the Criminal: Liberating the Concept of White-Collar Crime', *American Sociological Review*, 55(1): 346–69.

SHOVER, N. and HOCHSTETLER, A. (2006), *Choosing White-Collar Crime*, Cambridge: Cambridge University Press.

SIMPSON, S. (2013), 'White-collar crime: A review of recent developments and promising directions for future research', *Annual Review of Sociology*, 39(July): 309–31.

SLAPPER, G. and TOMBS, S. (1999), *Corporate Crime*, London: Longman.

SOOTHILL, K., HUMPHREYS, L., and FRANCIS, B. (2012), 'Middle-Class Offenders: A 35-Year Follow-Up', *British Journal of Criminology*, 52(4): 765–85.

STADLER, W., BENSON, M., and CULLEN, F. T. (2013), 'Revisiting the Special Sensitivity Hypothesis: The Prison Experience of White-Collar Offenders', *Justice Quarterly*, 30(6): 1090–114.

SUTHERLAND, E. H. (1949), *White Collar Crime*, New York: Holt, Rinehart, and Winston.

SUTHERLAND, E. H. (1983), *White-collar Crime: the Uncut Version*, New Haven, CT: Yale University Press.

TAPPAN, P. W. (1947), 'Who is the Criminal?', *American Sociological Review*, 12(1): 96–102.

Timmer, D. A. and Eitzen, D. S. (1989), *Crime in the Streets and Crime in the Suites: Perspectives on Crime and Criminal Justice*, Boston: Allyn and Bacon.

Tombs, S. and Whyte, D. (2007), *Safety Crimes*, Cullompton: Willan.

Tombs, S. and Whyte, D. (2013), 'Transcending the deregulation debate? Regulation, risk, and the enforcement of health and safety law in the UK', *Regulation and Governance*, 7(1): 61–79.

Tombs, S. and Whyte, D. (2015), *The Corporate Criminal: Why Corporations Must Be Abolished*, Abingdon: Routledge.

Van de Bunt, H. (2010), 'Walls of secrecy and silence', *Criminology and Public Policy*, 9(3): 435–53.

Van Koppen, M. V., De Poot, C. J., Kleemans, E. R., and Nieuwbeerta, P. (2010a), 'Criminal trajectories in organized crime', *British Journal of Criminology*, 50(1): 102–23.

van Koppen, M. V., De Poot, C. J., and Blokland, A. A. (2010b), 'Comparing criminal careers of organized crime offenders and general offenders', *European Journal of Criminology*, 7(5): 356–74.

Vaughan, D. (2007) 'Beyond Macro- and Micro-Levels of Analysis, Organizations, and the Cultural Fix', in H. Pontell and G. Geis (eds), *International Handbook of White-Collar and Corporate Crime*, New York: Springer.

Wang, X. and Holtfreter, K. (2012), 'The effects of corporation- and industry-level strain and opportunity on corporate crime, *Journal of Research in Crime and Delinquency*, 49(2): 151–85.

Weisburd, D., Wheeler, S., and Waring, E. (1991), *Crimes of the Middle Classes: White Collar Offenders in the Federal Courts*, Princeton: Yale University Press.

Weisburd, D. and Waring, E. with Chayet, E. (2001), *White-Collar Crime and Criminal Career*, Cambridge: Cambridge University Press.

Wells, C. (2011), 'Containing corporate crime. Civil or criminal controls?', in J. Gobert and A-M. Pascal (eds), *European Developments in Corporate Criminal Liability*, London: Routledge.

Wheeler, S. (1992), 'The Problem of White Collar Crime Motivation', in K. Schlegel and D. Weisburd (eds), *White Collar Crime Reconsidered*, Boston: Northeastern University Press.

Wheeler, S., Mann, K., and Sarat, A. (1988), *Sitting in Judgment: The Sentencing of White-Collar Criminals*, New Haven, CT: Yale University Press.

33

DESISTANCE FROM CRIME AND IMPLICATIONS FOR OFFENDER REHABILITATION

Joanna Shapland and Anthony Bottoms

INTRODUCTION

Most people who are convicted of crimes—even persistent offenders—eventually desist; and to a significant extent they do this on their own initiative. Although this statement is backed by a considerable amount of empirical evidence, until recently its full significance has not been grasped either by criminologists or, in most countries, by those responsible for developing criminal policy. Indeed, this is the first time that a chapter specifically on 'desistance' has been included in the *Handbook*. Previously the topic has been discussed in the *Handbook*'s chapter on criminal careers, but the explosion of desistance research in the last 15 years now demands separate treatment. In what follows, we shall try to summarize this research, together with various theoretical perspectives on desistance, so as to provide an accurate account of what has become an exciting, fast-moving, and still developing field of study.

The chapter first addresses a number of key issues in desistance research, such as how 'desistance' should be defined, and the importance of various kinds of 'age-crime curve'. Attention then turns to how desistance can be researched, and to summaries of the main research and theorization. For convenience, these research summaries are divided into sections covering the more individually-focused and the more socially-focused research, although of course these categories overlap. But not all offenders' paths to desistance are the same, so disparities in desistance in terms of gender and culture are briefly considered. The chapter concludes with a look at what the criminal justice system is doing, and might be doing, to promote desistance rather than to impair it.

KEY ISSUES IN THE STUDY OF DESISTANCE

DEFINING DESISTANCE

There is no agreed definition of 'desistance'. There is a common understanding that it means stopping committing crime, but beyond that definition becomes difficult. For example, to be classed as a 'desister', does a person have to have entirely stopped offending of all kinds, or just to be appreciably slowing up in the rate of commission of offences? If complete stopping is the criterion, for how long should the desister have stopped—a month, a year, or 10 years? These questions are particularly important when considering desistance by persistent offenders, because we now know that most such offenders desist gradually rather than suddenly.

Indeed, uncertainty is intrinsic to the idea of desistance itself. One can look back at someone's life and say, yes, after that point no more offences were committed (or at least the person was not caught committing offences). But it is not possible to consider a living person and say that they will never commit another offence. Even the person himself or herself may not be sure: there might be no intention to commit another offence, but given particular circumstances they might feel they could be tempted. This is why Piquero and colleagues (2007) have said that it is not possible to classify a person as having desisted until they die.

Accordingly, no definition of desistance can be perfect. But a useful heuristic definition is that recently offered by Kirkwood and McNeill (2015), who see desistance as 'the process of moving from offending to successful social integration (and with it compliance with law and social norms)'. This adds 'social integration' to the basic requirement of 'stopping offending', but in doing so it captures the sense of social recognition that most would-be desisters aspire to, and most correctional agencies work towards.

CRIME-FREE GAPS AND THE AGE-CRIME CURVE

When scientific criminology burgeoned in the middle of the twentieth century, the focus was on the pathways into crime in adolescence, and how to prevent children becoming attracted to crime. Perhaps because most criminologists study crime, rather than conformity or compliance, until recently much less attention has been paid to desistance, but now this has begun to change. In the early history of British criminology, there was however an interesting forerunner to modern desistance studies: the psychiatrist Donald West (1963) identified a group of male habitual offenders who had a significant period (minimum four years) during which they were not convicted. On the best evidence from police, relatives, and the men themselves, these were genuine 'crime free gaps'—although there was a subsequent return to offending. Of particular interest was that, during these 'crime free gaps', the men were usually in some kind of supportive environment—a point to which we shall return.

Another important precursor to modern desistance studies has been the so-called 'age-crime curve'. The age-crime curve is one of the few criminological constants, which has been found in very similar shapes in different countries for a hundred years or more. As normally drawn, an age-crime curve is cross-sectional; that is, it shows official convictions and cautions (or, in some countries, arrests) for people of different ages during a given short time span, usually a year. Figure 33.1 shows a cross-sectional bar chart of this kind for England and Wales. The shape of the curve for males is a very skewed distribution, with steeply increasing proportions of offenders from 10 (the age of criminal responsibility) to around age 19, and then a sharp descent in the twenties, after which it slows gradually, but never quite reaches zero. The curve for women has a much smaller peak (fewer women are convicted) and a more gradual descent from mid-adolescence. In other words, for both genders, after around the age of 20 people are increasingly unlikely to be convicted, and convictions after 30 are rare.

Of course, plotting a cross-section of the proportions of the population who are convicted at different ages does not tell us whether individuals who frequently commit crimes follow the same temporal path in their own criminality. A key strand in the development of research on desistance has therefore been the emergence of what is called 'life-course criminology'.

LIFE-COURSE CRIMINOLOGY

Longitudinal studies following children from birth through school and into adolescence have a long history in both Britain and the United States in the fields of health, child development, and parenting studies; and, from the mid-twentieth century, criminological scholars followed their example.

Life-course criminology researchers have been able to define some key features of criminal careers: these include the age of onset of criminal activity, whether people persist in offending, and the length of criminal careers (Carlsson and Sarnecki 2016). From early longitudinal studies of boys, it quickly became clear that those who went on to commit many criminal offences tended to have an early age of onset. Those who began criminal activity later often dropped out again after a short time—a group which Moffitt (1993) has termed 'adolescence-limited offenders'. A significant part of the 'hump' of the cross-sectional age-crime curve (Figure 33.1) is due to this adolescence-limited group, which makes it the more interesting to look at the temporal patterns of crime among more persistent offenders.

A major element in attracting interest towards desistance from crime came from the work of John Laub and Robert Sampson, who were able to plot criminal careers over time by re-examining and extending the classic early research by Sheldon and Eleanor Glueck (1950), who had studied a sample of male adolescent persistent offenders. Sampson and Laub's (1993) first work re-examined the Gluecks' longitudinal data to age 32, using more modern statistical methods. Later, they followed the same sample into their sixties through criminal record searches (Laub and Sampson 2003), and through this work they found, remarkably, that the aggregate temporal pattern of individual pathways of criminality closely resembled in shape the traditional cross-sectional age-crime curve (Figure 33.2). There were some variations for different offenders, with some persistent offenders not starting to desist until their thirties or forties, but the general shape remained. The marked pattern of desistance—including early desistance—that Figure 33.2 displays also raised the possibility of developing

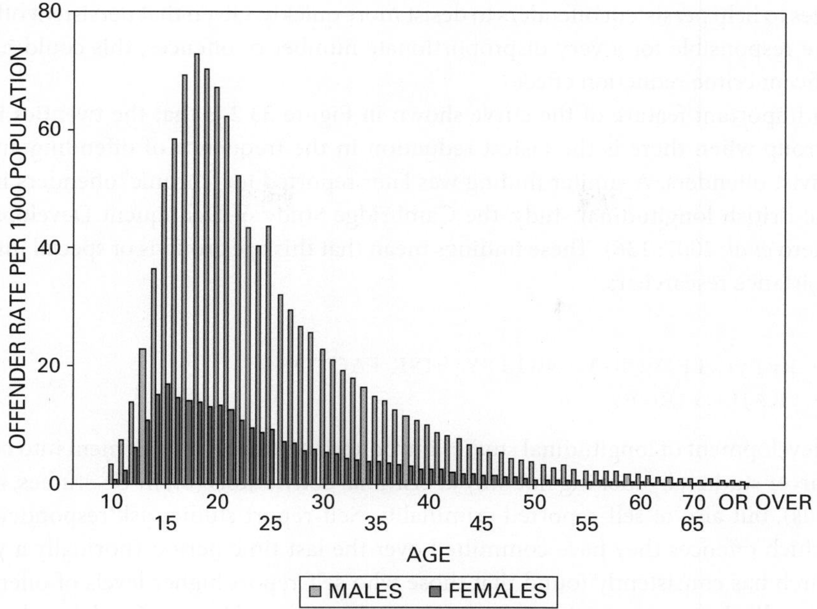

Figure 33.1 Recorded offender rates per 1,000 relevant population by age and gender, England and Wales, 2000

Source: Bottoms *et al.* (2004: 370)

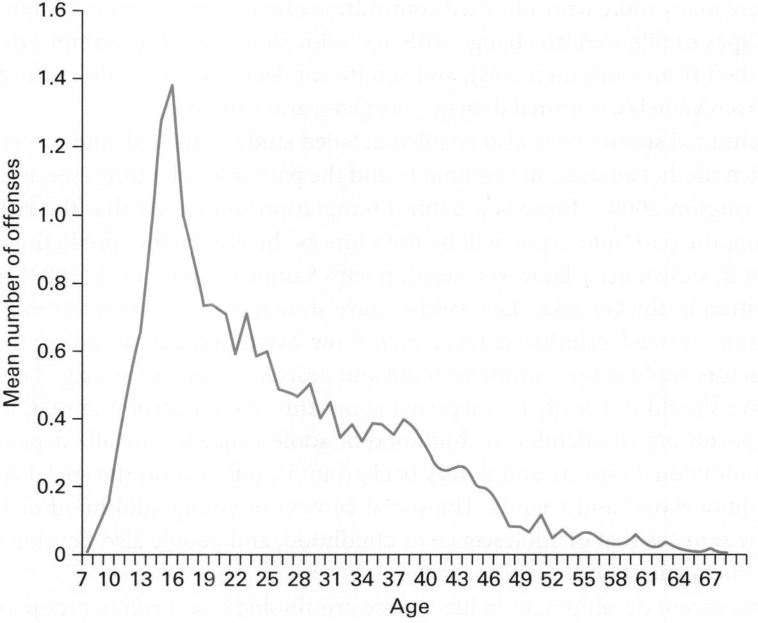

Figure 33.2 Longitudinal age-crime curve in a US persistent offender sample: mean number of offences, ages 7–70

Source: Laub and Sampson (2003: 86). Copyright © 2003 by the President and Fellows of Harvard College.

policies to help persistent offenders to desist more quickly. Given that persistent offenders are responsible for a very disproportionate number of offences, this could have a significant crime reduction effect.

An important feature of the curve shown in Figure 33.2 is that the twenties is the age group when there is the fastest reduction in the frequency of offending among recidivist offenders. A similar finding was later reported for 'chronic' offenders in the classic British longitudinal study, the Cambridge Study of Delinquent Development (Piquero *et al.* 2007: 136). These findings mean that this age group is of special interest to desistance researchers.

SELF-REPORTED CRIMINALITY, RISK FACTORS, AND TRAJECTORIES

The development of longitudinal studies introduced another major element into criminal career studies, by looking not only at criminal convictions (or, in US studies, arrest records), but also at self-reported criminality. Self-report studies ask respondents to say which offences they have committed over the last time period (normally a year). Research has consistently found that those who self-report higher levels of offending are more likely to come to the notice of the authorities and be convicted, but the ratio of self-reported offending to official offending varies considerably with age. In adolescence, some offending (self-reported) is relatively common—in the Cambridge Study, 78 per cent of 402 London boys aged 10–14 admitted offending, as did 76 per cent of those aged 15–18 (Farrington *et al.* 2006: 33). However, the ratio of self-reported to officially convicted offenders was quite high (7.4 and 4.1 respectively: p. 35)—so there were many more who admitted committing offences than were ever convicted for them. Types of offence also change with age, with shop theft, for example, decreasing (whilst theft from work increases), and significant decreases after adolescence in theft of and from vehicles, criminal damage, burglary, and drug use.

Longitudinal studies have also enabled detailed study of the risk and protective factors which predict adolescent criminality and the path into offending (see, e.g., Loeber and Farrington 2000). There is a natural temptation to assume that the risk factors predicting the path into crime will be the same as the risk factors predicting the path out (that is, desistance). However, starting with Sampson and Laub's (1993) initial re-examination of the Gluecks' data, studies have shown that it is incorrect to make this assumption. Instead, criminal careers often show 'asymmetrical causation'; that is, different factors apply at the commencement and desistance stages (see, e.g., Loeber *et al.* 2016). We should not really be surprised about this. As Wikström\ *et al.* (2012) have shown, becoming an offender in childhood or adolescence is crucially dependent not only on individual aspects and family backgrounds, but also on the social context of the neighbourhood and friends. The social context of young adulthood or older life is not the same as that of adolescence or childhood, and people also develop different aspirations in adulthood.

A more recent development in life-course criminology has been to group longitudinal patterns of criminality into clusters, or 'trajectories', and to examine which factors define each pattern. Two studies have carried out such analyses over a whole lifetime (into the sixties). Laub and Sampson (2003: 104) found that their US sample was best described statistically by six groups, varying in the persistence, frequency, and age-range of their criminality. They found, interestingly, that the offending levels of even their highest-rate 'chronic' group declined with age. Blokland and colleagues (2005) examined a much larger national sample of offenders convicted in The Netherlands, aged between 12 (the age of criminal responsibility) and 20 at the time of their first conviction in 1977. Encouragingly, they reported rather similar results to those of Laub and Sampson: the data was best described using four groups, again varying in frequency and persistence (namely: sporadic offenders with very few convictions apart from the first; low-rate desisters; moderate-rate desisters; and a small number (1.6 per cent) of high-rate persisters). This last group—which was not found in Laub and Sampson's study—did not comprise serious offenders; instead, they regularly committed minor property offences even in their sixties.

One difficulty with trajectory analysis is how to classify those individuals whose pattern of offending may fall between the main groups. This is a key reason why different studies have, statistically, created different numbers of groups which best fit the data. Another issue is whether it is the prevalence, frequency, or seriousness of offending which is the major target for the analysis; it is highly likely that there are slightly different age-crime curves for each of these, though few analyses have looked at all three (Loeber *et al.* 2016).

We noted above that desistance rarely involves a sudden cessation of all offending; diminution of the frequency (and often of the seriousness) of offending is more the norm. The reasons for this are not hard to understand. Even leaving aside drug and alcohol addiction, if one has been offending regularly, and most of one's friends are also offending, then committing a crime may have become the default response in certain situations, such as when money is short. One might have decided to try to stop, but if the rent is due and there is no cash in the house . . .

We need now to look at how desistance can be researched, before turning to what might be driving processes of desistance.

RESEARCHING DESISTANCE

Since desistance means stopping offending, the population to research clearly needs to be an offending population. One cannot 'desist' from having committed only one offence in one's life, particularly if that means one self-reported offence. Most of the male population in most Western countries say they have committed at least one criminal act in adolescence, although few say they have committed many offences. Given the rapid drop-off between the proportion of the population committing *any* offence, and those who commit many, using a general population sample to research desistance is likely to be costly—although, of course, longitudinal studies such as the Cambridge Study have contributed important insights to our understanding of desistance (Farrington *et al.* 2006).

For these reasons, most studies of desistance have started with populations which are already known to be offending. So, for example, the follow-up by Laub and Sampson (2003) of the Gluecks' (1950) original sample studied boys who were residents in correctional schools in Massachusetts in the 1930s, and so had originally been persistently delinquent. The large Dutch study by Blokland *et al.* (2005) started with a representative sample of 4 per cent of those convicted of a serious offence in the Netherlands in 1977.

As with many topics in criminology, desistance research has included both quantitative and qualitative studies. Both kinds of study have yielded important insights, and in this chapter we draw freely on each of them.

Another important contrast in desistance research has been that between prospective and retrospective studies. Since desistance from persistent offending is often gradual, there are some obvious advantages in studying it prospectively, and many researchers have done so. However, there has also been some very valuable retrospective research into desistance, notably Maruna's (2001) matched study of desisters and persisters in Liverpool, and the retrospective interviews conducted by Laub and Sampson (2003) with 52 of the Gluecks' men when they were in their sixties. There is some evidence, to be discussed later, that the early and the later stages of desistance involve different processes, and retrospective studies have provided some of our best accounts of the final stages of desistance.

Farrall and colleagues (2014) have proposed some desiderata for researching desistance. Amongst other things, they argue that studies should preferably be longitudinal, prospective, with a long-term follow-up (and good re-contact rates), collecting both quantitative and qualitative data, and collecting data from multiple sources. While other kinds of study can be valuable, it is hard to disagree with these recommendations for mainstream desistance research.

UNDERSTANDING THE PROCESS OF DESISTANCE: INDIVIDUAL DIMENSIONS

Why and how do people desist? As we shall see, a variety of reasons and mechanisms have been suggested in the literature, and these can broadly be characterized as predominantly individual and predominantly social—although of course there is always an overlap between the individual and the social. We shall adopt this distinction in what follows, and we begin with the individual dimension.

WHY DESIST?

A first question, which is not always addressed in desistance research, is: 'why should someone who has been offending persistently even think about desisting?'

This is a valid question, because offending can bring some significant benefits. Committing crimes can supply some people with much of their income, while for others it provides extra money to lead the lifestyle they wish to have (e.g. entertainment at weekends, or meeting the cost of drugs or alcohol). Less materially, it can be genuinely exciting to commit crimes, and/or to try to outwit the police, perhaps especially in late adolescence. But obviously, crime can bring problems and disadvantages as well. There is the constant potential of being caught, prosecuted, convicted, and—particularly as offenders become older and have longer criminal records—imprisoned for increasing periods. Imprisonment also brings the possibility of impaired contact (or indeed loss of contact) with partners and children. There are also potential threats from criminal associates, and the general perils of living off the informal economy, rather than having formal employment (Verhage and Shapland 2013). Yet the process of desisting, as we shall see, often involves a drop in income and/or significant difficulty in changing one's lifestyle. So why embark on it?

Broadly speaking, researchers have suggested two main types of reason. One is instrumental, and has been particularly proposed by Paternoster and Bushway (2009). They suggested that one element propelling offenders towards desistance is fear of what they might become if they continue to offend. These authors see everyone as having a 'working self', which embodies his or her present identity, including their preferences and social networks; but they suggest that everyone also envisages possible futures, including what they want or hope to become (the 'desired self') and anxiety over what they fear they might become (the 'feared self'). According to Paternoster and Bushway (2009), people continue with their working self until the cost of remaining committed to it becomes larger than the perceived benefits, at which point there is a 'crystallization of discontent'. This dissonance then provides an initial motivation to change, by moving away from the working self and towards the desired self. Other researchers (including ourselves) have doubted whether this simple cognitive cost-benefit analysis gives a sufficient account of the start of desistance, but most desistance scholars would agree that the concepts of the feared self and the desired self have merit in helping to explain the impetus to start to change, and the process of maintaining momentum if and when things later become difficult (see, e.g., Bottoms and Shapland 2016; Maruna 2001). Those who have been convicted often fear, for example, spending much of their life in prison, becoming isolated through losing their partners and friends, or becoming a dependent addict.

In some contrast to this instrumentalist account, others have emphasized normative factors as reasons to turn away from crime. There are two versions of this view, which are not necessarily in conflict. The first is that those who have been offending sometimes come into contact with new people and/or fresh social contexts (e.g. a romantic partner, a really interesting job, or a religious community) where they encounter fresh and attractive social norms. Gradually, these new norms and interests become increasingly central to the person's life. Indeed, it can even sometimes be the case that, in these fresh normative contexts, people can make 'a commitment to go straight without even realising it'—a process that has been called 'desistance by default' (Laub and Sampson 2003: 278–9).

The alternative normative account is particularly applicable to those in their early twenties. On the basis of our own research with this age group, we have argued that at around age 20, many persistent offenders, like others of their age group, reassess their lives and think about what kind of adult they want to be. The answer, overwhelmingly often, is that their desired future would be one in which they are living a 'normal life'—that is, they would not be offending, and would be respected by those around them, including their family and relations. The Sheffield Desistance Study studied prospectively, from approximately age 20, a sample of 113 mostly persistent male convicted offenders (Bottoms and Shapland 2011, 2016). Participants were interviewed up to four times, at intervals of about a year. Asked in the first interview, 'What kind of person would you like to become?' (with more than one response allowed), the main answers were: 'going straight/being drug and alcohol free'; living a normal/regular life; be successful; be a good person—be responsible; and be a family man (Shapland and Bottoms 2011). These are very conventional goals. We also asked respondents how important they thought it was that people in general should keep the law—and 79 per cent said it was 'very' or 'fairly' important. We asked them how serious they thought a range of criminal offences were, and to rate them. The most serious offences were mugging/robbery/bag snatch, murder, rape, and child abuse, but burglary and theft of cars were also rated as very serious. In fact, the severity order was identical to that used by the Home Office of England and Wales at the time. So although these young men were persistent offenders, they still held many mainstream values, which they were able to draw upon as they tried to move towards their 'desired selves'.

MATURATION AND AGE

It is not accidental that men in the Sheffield sample were considering their futures at around age 20, because this is a normal feature of maturation at around this age (see, e.g., Tanner (2006) on 'recentering' in the transition to adulthood). Given that the early twenties is the fastest period of deceleration of offending among those offending persistently, this raises the issue of potential links between desistance and the physical and psychological processes of maturation. Accordingly, there has been much criminological interest in the recent physiological evidence that—contrary to the previously received view—in normal humans the pre-frontal cortex in the brain, and therefore the capacity for full impulse control, does not complete its development until the mid-twenties (Johnson *et al.* 2009). This is clearly of potential relevance to the decline in offending levels in the early twenties.

Issues of psychological maturity are being particularly researched in the ongoing Pathways to Desistance study, which is being carried out in two US metropolitan areas, and is following over 1,300 serious adolescent offenders into young adulthood (Mulvey and Schubert 2016). A finding of particular interest concerns the 'temperance scores' (which measure ability to control impulses) of five trajectories of the sample from age 14 to age 25. The two trajectories labelled 'desister' and 'persister' both had identical temperance scores at age 14, but by age 25 their scores were widely separated, which suggests that 'maturity (especially self-regulation) is an important developmental feature that accompanies the cessation of serious crime' (Mulvey and Schubert 2016: 135). This finding also falsifies Gottfredson and Hirschi's (1990) earlier suggestion that the rank ordering of individuals' ability to exercise self-control remains unchanged from an early age. Given these findings, maturity of judgement is a factor that future research into desistance needs to add to the long list of other elements requiring attention.

But not all desistance happens in the twenties. From the trajectory analyses of Laub and Sampson (2003) in the US and Blokland *et al.* (2005) in the Netherlands, we know that some men only start to desist considerably after the peak of the age-crime curve, in their thirties and forties. Such men are likely to have a longer experience of the criminal justice system, and a longer time for offending behavioural patterns to have become habitual; hence it might be more difficult for them to desist. Indeed, F.-Dufour and Brassard (2014) found in their sample of mid-thirties male desisters from (primarily) property offending, that prior to desisting they were both entrenched in criminal activities and held pro-criminal views—although this was a very small sample. Yet they still desisted. There is a real need for further research on older desisters, to pinpoint whether, for example, the death of a relative, increasingly bad health or later marriage may be important in providing the stimulus for the decision to move away from offending—as Laub and Sampson (2003) suggest for some of their sample.

AGENCY AND IDENTITY

But although physiological and psychological maturation is important, we need also to remember that humans are reflexive creatures, who can shape their futures by their own decisions and actions. This key input of the would-be desister in the path towards desistance is usually called 'agency'. It includes decisions to start desisting, actions towards that end, and elements of how the desisters regard themselves—that is, their identity and their view of the future. The idea of agency tended to be only sketchily present in early theories of desistance (e.g. Laub and Sampson 2003), but more recently the cognitive component of desistance has become more emphasized. Partly this increased emphasis may be because desistance is primarily the study of adults changing their lives, and so how would-be desisters are thinking is both accessible (as far as it is to themselves) and appropriate. Partly it is based on empirical findings that it is very difficult to predict exactly who will desist from any combination of external factors impinging on that individual, however sophisticated the analysis (Laub and Sampson 2003). Partly it stems from empirical results of longitudinal studies, which indicate that offenders saying they intend to desist at one point in time (when they are still offending) does predict subsequent reductions in offending (e.g. Le Bel *et al.* 2008; Bottoms and Shapland 2011).

Giordano's (2016) theory of cognitive transformation was developed from her study of a sample of girls from a correctional institution in the US, together with an equivalent sample of boys. Originally interviewed in 1982, they were re-interviewed at about the age of 30 and then again at around 39 years in 2010. Though her original perspective concentrated on the external social circumstances of the women and men, and on how 'hooks for change' could arise (discussed later), the qualitative interviews showed that 'individual-level cognitive changes were integral to desistance processes, and this was not just an artifact of our reliance on a narrative approach (i.e., the idea that respondents themselves would inevitably cast themselves as the stars of their own stories)' (Giordano 2016: 13). Using an approach derived from the sociological theory of symbolic interactionism, Giordano stresses that 'cognitive shifts and the individual's related agentic moves are implicated in desistance, particularly when this requires significant changes in life direction' (ibid.). These cognitive shifts include being open to change; differential receptivity to particular catalysts (such as a new partner or job: 'hooks for change'); realizing that these external changes have happened and are important to use; and beginning to fashion a 'replacement self' that can supplant the old one, which has to be left behind.

Bushway and Paternoster (2013) have suggested that this identity change comes first, but both Giordano (2016) and Bottoms and Shapland (2016) would argue that identity development and change are ongoing, occurring simultaneously with changing one's ideas about how to lead one's life, and attempts to change one's behaviour. All of these are simultaneously also engaging with the external situation surrounding the desister, so that we are likely always to be left with the question posed by LeBel *et al.* (2008) concerning 'The "chicken and egg" of subjective and social factors in desistance from crime'. Cognitive, identity and social elements are all implicated in successful desistance, which as we have seen often takes place over a period of time.

Carlsson (2016), echoing Shover (1996), suggests that as individuals age into adulthood, they become more interested in conventional lifestyles and their rewards, whilst offending changes from having the excitement it possessed in adolescence to having more of a negative stigma. Not only do potentially desisting offenders become more open to grabbing the 'hooks for change' that external circumstances present, but they may, agentically, tend to manoeuvre themselves into a position to encounter that 'hook'. A reverse process of a similar kind has been identified by Bottoms and Shapland (2016), whereby would-be desisters manoeuvre themselves away from influences that would tempt them to continue offending—for example, by avoiding bars where they know that violence is likely to erupt, or by staying away from certain areas where they would encounter former friends who might tempt them to return to crime. Bottoms and Shapland described this kind of future planning as 'diachronic self-control'.

Although there is as yet little detailed research on the unfolding of desistance processes over time, there is tentative evidence that there are some significant differences between early and late desistance. It seems that in the early stages of desistance, as individuals wish to change and realize they can change, they may be 'preoccupied with "becoming normal", and their goals are more likely to revolve around finding conventional roles in work and family life' (Healy 2013: 561). By contrast, in the later stages of desistance, people may move on to a 'deeper' set of concerns, including the creation of a different self-identity, and the development of a more 'other-centred' (empathetic) set of concerns (Porporino 2010: 73).

The work of Shadd Maruna (2001) has particularly emphasized the changes in identity that may occur during the desistance process, and he argues that to desist from crime, ex-offenders need eventually to develop a coherent, prosocial identity for themselves. His data came from the Liverpool Desistance Study, which researched two groups who were carefully matched on their previous history—but members of one group had now desisted, while the others were still offending. Maruna analysed the life histories of both groups, and showed that in the later stages of desistance, ex-offenders may often seek strongly to distinguish their past and present selves, and to 'knife off' who they were before as separate, more immature people. This sometimes involved (perhaps particularly among ex-drug users) developing a 'redemption script' which 'allows the [desisting] person to rewrite a shameful past into a necessary prelude to a productive and worthy life' (Maruna 2001: 87). The Liverpool Study has also been influential in encouraging other scholars to undertake narrative research into how people understand themselves and their circumstances as they face the continuing challenges of sustaining a new way of life.

Before leaving the topic of agency, we should note that there remain difficult theoretical questions about how this concept should best be understood. These questions have been addressed recently by a number of desistance researchers (e.g. Healy 2013; Carlsson 2016; Weaver 2016: ch. 3), but the issues are too complex to summarize here. Linked to this issue is our own suggestion that 'mainstream desistance theory has not [yet] seriously grappled with "the ethics of everyday life"' (Bottoms and Shapland 2016: 117), notwithstanding the obvious ethical struggles that are inevitably involved in desistance from persistent offending.

SOCIAL CONTEXTS AND THEIR INFLUENCE ON DESISTANCE

We turn now to the social elements in the journey to desistance, and we begin with a topic that has been the subject of much recent discussion, namely whether key life events can provide a 'turning point' or stimulus for individuals on the road to desistance.

'TURNING POINTS' AND INFORMAL SOCIAL CONTROL

The idea of a 'turning point' in relation to desistance was originally raised in Sampson and Laub's (1993) statistical analysis of the life course of offending in the Gluecks' sample. They found that offending often decreased (desistance occurred) after the men married, obtained a job, or went into the armed forces. Laub and Sampson (2003: 40) caution that these events were not turning points for all: 'some transitions lead to no change in a life trajectory . . . some transitions merely accentuate pre-existing characteristics rather than promoting change'. In considering the evidence from this study, it is also necessary to bear in mind that the Gluecks' sample were in late adolescence or their early twenties at the time of the Second World War, when social conditions were very different. Applying the idea of turning points to today, one needs to be aware that the social meaning of marriage, the nature and likelihood of military service, and even having a full-time job, are different for today's young people.

How might a turning point affect someone who is offending? In relation to marriage, Laub and Sampson (2003) and others have indicated that what matters is not the institution or occasion itself, but rather a response to an enduring attachment to a partner who has prosocial views. Changing one's life following marriage may result from a real attraction to the partner and her/his way of life; and/or the thought of losing the partner if one is sent to prison; and/or lifestyle changes which mean that the person spends more time with the partner/family and less with former delinquent friends (on which see Warr 2002). Obtaining a 'steady job' can similarly be seen as a transition that draws the person into a more prosocial lifestyle, which would be put at risk by continuing offending, and creates changes in time patterns and lifestyles. These changes can therefore be characterized as desistance arising from fresh *social bonds* which create new styles of *informal social control*. The prosocial and social control aspects of turning points echo the 'hooks for change' in Giordano's theory, but Laub and Sampson (2003: 278) place less emphasis than Giordano on cognitive transformation, and indeed they argue that 'the image of "desistance by default" [see earlier discussion] best fits the desistance process we found in our data'.

Recently, some scholars have argued that turning points do not always precede desistance; instead, behavioural change towards desistance may create the possibility of the turning point event occurring. Skardhamer and colleagues (Skardhamer and Savolainen 2016; Skardhamer *et al.* 2016) show that although the literature indicates strong marriage effects on desistance, the causality of these has not really been tested. Does marriage cause desistance, or does reducing offending promote partner attachment (on both sides, possibly) which leads to marriage? Their data from Norway allowed them to plot the time course of offending—and they showed that offending started to decline several years before marriage, with marriage itself sometimes creating a 'rebound' effect (more offending). However, one could argue that marriage today (unlike for Laub and Sampson's sample) can be the culmination of several years of cohabitation or having a strong relationship, so it is the relationship which is important. It is clear that more research is needed on the timelines between relationships, marriage, and offending to be sure which aspects are the more important and when; but the importance of a strong social bond to a prosocial person seems now to be well established (see also Horney *et al.* 2012). Similar issues arise in relation to employment, particularly given that a 'job for life' is becoming rarer in today's economies. Thus, as social circumstances and mores change, exactly what are key turning points is becoming less clear—and far harder to measure.

OBSTACLES TO DESISTANCE: LEARNING TO LIVE A NON-CRIMINAL LIFE

On the basis of the Sheffield study, we have suggested that one key element to desistance is that the person trying to desist has to learn how to live a desisting life in the community (Bottoms and Shapland 2016). This means not only that they have to break away from elements in their lifestyles that are pulling them back towards reoffending, but also that they need to find new ways to earn money, solve accommodation and debt issues, find people to be around and different things to do. There are some real challenges, particularly for persistent offenders, in solving these issues, and we have called them 'obstacles to desistance'.

In the Sheffield Desistance Study, the final level of offending, after following the men for about four years, was best predicted by a combination of the lifetime official criminality of the offender and their actual or perceived social circumstances (relating to substance abuse, employment, delinquent friends, and the total of obstacles to desistance that they perceived). This prediction brings together the sheer weight of previous criminality (the length of time and amount of offending, particularly those leading to official convictions) with the current circumstances of potential desisters—*as they perceive them*. Those who perceived more obstacles to stopping offending were less likely to desist.

Many studies have documented particular obstacles to desistance. For example, while only about half of persistent offenders have a significant drug or alcohol abuse habit, the evidence suggests that this group find it particularly difficult to desist. Another major obstacle is money, given that persistent property offenders who desist often experience a reduction in income. The main legitimate source of money is employment, but persistent offenders are likely to have had difficult school histories, with exclusion and lack of qualifications being common, so their ability to find skilled employment is low. Although some are able to take courses in custodial establishments to remedy the lack of qualifications, their lack of a documented work history will also not serve them well. Calverley (2013) has shown how some families and indeed ethnic groups may be able to make a difference for those trying to desist, by offering a chance for work with relatives or in the community, but others do not have these social supports. Given this, and the technological revolution that has eliminated many unskilled manual jobs, Farrall *et al.* (2010) have argued that societal and political changes over the last half century or so are making the obstacle-strewn path to desistance harder.

Sometimes, people find the obstacles so great that they stop offending, but in a socially isolated way—for example, by staying at home all the time, partly because they cannot find work, and partly to avoid the temptations they fear they would encounter if they went out to meet old friends. Evidence about cases of this kind led Kirkwood and McNeill (2015) to define desistance as 'the process of moving from offending to successful social integration'. They wanted to emphasize that, from a social policy perspective, governments should be looking beyond the mere cessation of offending and towards the goal of integrating ex-offenders into society in a full sense.

FRESH PERSPECTIVES ON THE SOCIAL ASPECTS OF DESISTANCE

Recently, two fresh studies have enhanced theoretical understanding of the social dimensions of desistance. The first study is by Cid and Marti (2015), based on research in Spain in which a small sample of men was interviewed in prison and after release. Cid and Marti found that a significant mechanism favouring desistance was the provision by the men's families of strong social support, which mitigated the strains of both imprisonment and the post-release experience. The authors provide good reasons for differentiating the mechanism of 'social support in conditions of strain' from Laub and Sampson's concept of informal social control; in particular, Laub and Sampson's concept implies entry into and commitment to a new social role, but social support can be offered and received in other circumstances. Interestingly, this suggested mechanism of support would seem to fit well with the data in West's (1963) pioneering study of crime-free gaps, discussed earlier.

The second fresh study was conducted by Beth Weaver (2016) in Scotland. This is a very innovative narrative study which was focused on a male friendship group who once committed offences together, but gradually moved away from crime while also turning to new concerns and evolving different relationships with one another.

Theoretically, the study places centre stage Donati's (2011) 'relational sociology', which attempts to transcend the standard sociological distinction between 'agency' and 'structure' and to focus on social relations as the key to understanding social change. Within this framework, Weaver's analysis revealed that, for this group, desistance was:

> variously enabled or constrained by the interaction of the social relations of friendship, intimate relations, families of formation, faith communities and employment as reflexively mediated through the lens of a given individual's personal priorities, values, aspirations and relational concerns. ... Ultimately, desistance emerged for these men as a means to realizing and maintaining their individual and relational concerns with which continued offending became (sometimes incrementally) incompatible ... Desistance, in this sense, occurs in the context of shifting engagements with, commitments to, and reflexivity about different facets of civil society. (2016: 241)

Weaver has thus raised some important fresh issues for desistance scholars, and it will take time for the refreshing challenges that she poses to be fully worked through.

GENDER AND CULTURE

Desistance processes may obviously play out differently for those in different social circumstances. The relevant issues have been researched to a limited extent in relation to both gender and culture.

GENDER

Not surprisingly, most desistance research has focused on men, given that men form the great majority of more persistent offenders. We might reasonably expect that processes of desistance will be different for women, given the presence of gender-specific elements around family responsibilities, employment and income, housing, victimization, and indeed patterns of offending. However, Rodermond *et al.* (2016), in their systematic review of female desistance, found that the same kinds of life changes are important in shaping desistance for women as for men: marriage, finding a stable partner, having children, employment, having prosocial supportive friendships, coming off drugs and being able to be economically independent. They stress, though, that for women there are complex interactions between these factors, such that those trying to desist need to have a wide range of assistance related to housing, financial support, relationships, employment, and drug use (see also Sharpe 2015 on the stigmas associated with young motherhood and offending). Accordingly, several studies reported that having more than one kind of social capital and support (e.g. from friends as well as a partner) is important. Caring for children can also be a catalyst for change, as women come to realize that their lifestyle is not good for their children. In response, women, like men, may need to move away from their previous social world or deliberately avoid certain social situations (as we saw above with men, in relation to diachronic self-control).

Though similar elements pertain to desistance in both men and women, there are subtle nuances which create differences. So, young men are more likely to affiliate to delinquent peers, and need then subsequently to get away from them. While romantic partnerships are important for both women and men, 'given the known base rates of crime according to gender, it is important to highlight that men, on average, are more likely to marry up (that is, in the direction of a prosocial . . . partner)' (Giordano 2016: 24). Again, women's narratives of change focus to a greater extent on family relationships, yet Andrea Leverentz (2014) found in her ethnographic study of women desisters in the US that this focus could in itself create some confusion and conflict. For example, some family relationships were complicated by long histories of abuse and neglect, and these were sometimes highlighted by social workers as potential 'triggers' for relapse that the women should avoid. Yet, reports Leverentz (2014: 113) 'it was also important for their sense of self for the women to be the good mothers, daughters and sisters that they had failed to be in the past, even when this came into conflict with their desistance understandings and attempts'.

CULTURES

When we turn to consider differences in desistance between those from different cultures, we are currently very limited in terms of the research available. The most relevant British research is the qualitative study by Adam Calverley (2013), who found significant differences in the experiences and strategies reported by desisting offenders of Indian, Bangladeshi, and Black and dual-heritage ethnic origin. For example, the families of origin of Bangladeshi-origin offenders 'played a critical part in prompting, encouraging and maintaining the [desistance] process' and in adopting an attitude of forgiveness which gave the offenders 'hope that a possible life without crime was indeed possible' (ibid.: 186). Additionally, and in contrast to the other two ethnic groups studied, religion (Islam) 'featured prominently in directing and shaping the decision and motivations of Bangladeshis to desist'; it also provided them with 'places of desistance where their new pro-social identity as "good" Muslims was acknowledged' (ibid.: 187). By contrast, for Black and dual heritage offenders 'the experience [of desistance] was generally a much lonelier journey' because 'they lacked social capital'. 'Isolated from strong networks of family and community support', they faced threats to their desistance from 'the "code of the street" . . . and criminally active peers'. They responded to their situation by 'investing in themselves', for example by '"pumping iron" in the gym and attending courses or participating in voluntary work in order to improve their CV' (ibid.: 187–8).

Cid and Marti (2016) also observed cultural contrasts in their Spanish study. Their sample included a group of immigrant prisoners, who lacked the family support which—as previously noted—was key for the Spanish prisoners who were able to desist. This study highlights the very strong role of the family in Spanish culture, which creates an expectation that relatives will support prisoners in prison and after release.

These fascinating examples not only illustrate the importance of social capital and cultural context for any given individual's possible road to desistance, they also highlight the markedly different ways in which desistance processes can play out in different cultural contexts.

THE CRIMINAL JUSTICE SYSTEM AND DESISTANCE

The fact that most offenders desist is a potential spur to the criminal justice system. Could the system, through rehabilitational or other efforts, speed up the rate of desistance? If so, it could make a remarkable difference to amounts of victimization, because a few persistent offenders are responsible for a considerable amount of crime. It is this realization that has driven recent efforts in a number of countries to experiment with new ways of trying to rehabilitate offenders, which derive from desistance theory. As McNeill (2012: 13) has put it 'Most people stop offending sometime, with or without interventions, and sometimes even in spite of them . . . [T]he practical challenge is to help them to do so more swiftly and certainly'.

Readers might think it remarkable that the effects of the criminal justice system on desistance have been largely absent from our narrative so far. The reason for this is that most would-be desisters try to fashion their own way of staying out of trouble, often with relatively little direct input from criminal justice personnel. But obviously, two of the key aims of criminal justice systems are to deter reoffending and to attempt to rehabilitate offenders, so it is reasonable to ask how these aims link with the research previously described.

As regards deterrence, a large-scale statistical study by Macleod and colleagues (2012) found that there were no differential effects on criminal careers as between custodial and non-custodial sentences; moreover, on release from prison the expected duration of the residual criminal career was the same as after a non-custodial sentence (hence, prison had no incapacitative effect). What *did* have an effect, however, was simply getting convicted, leading the authors to state that, from the point of view of the criminal justice system at least, 'the most important influence on desistance is getting convicted' (ibid.: 209). This is an interesting conclusion, which fits well with the evidence from qualitative desistance studies about the 'feared self'.

Turning to rehabilitation and the criminal justice system, some efforts to rehabilitate offenders have tended to proceed from a 'top-down' perspective—that is, to 'do' things to offenders that it is thought will provide beneficial treatment. Many of these are valuable, as the literature on recidivism and offender management shows; and clearly, learning to lead a non-offending life in the community will often be helped by improved employability, literacy, and social skills. The key element that desistance theory has added, however, is the realization that many offenders are already trying to desist in their own way, so the criminal justice system should develop programmes of 'assisted desistance'; that is, doing things *with* not *to* the offender (Porporino 2010). This implies that such assistance should focus, in supervision, on future-oriented goals, rather than mainly on the (past) offence, and—bearing in mind the evidence about asymmetric causation—to build on offenders' strengths and capabilities rather than focusing mostly on deficits.

PROBATION SUPERVISION

A number of studies of desistance have found that those attempting to desist have not, at that time, ascribed their success to their supervision by probation staff (Farrall 2002;

Shapland *et al.* 2012b)—though some have indicated how much their probation supervisors have tried (Healy 2016). Would-be desisters have often commented that probation practice has tended to focus upon their general social situation, welfare issues and their ways of thinking, rather than helping them to overcome practical obstacles which they saw as preventing them from desisting. Farrall *et al.* (2014), however, re-interviewing former probationers who had desisted, found that they remembered what their supervisors had said and encouraged them to do into the future, and that this had been influential in maintaining them on the path to desistance when things had become difficult. Supervision, as traditionally practised, may thus have a long-term effect despite its apparently limited success in the early stages of desistance.

Probation supervision can include a wide variety of elements. Research shows that probation staff and those on probation generally tend to have similar views about what makes good quality probation—but it has consistently been found that probation staff tend to emphasize relational and welfare aspects, whilst those on probation find there is not enough emphasis on coping with practical difficulties (Shapland *et al.* 2012a). Given that desistance is not only about cognitive change but also about finding a new lifestyle, providing help on key aspects of that lifestyle, such as accommodation, substance abuse, coping with debt, accessing employment or benefits, and avoiding temptations is obviously important. Here probation staff may need not just to 'signpost' their supervisees to appropriate agencies, but help them to make appointments and overcome any bureaucratic obstacles, as well as thinking carefully with them about daily routines.

RE-ENTRY AND OVERCOMING PRACTICAL OBSTACLES

A key point at which practical obstacles become apparent is on release from prison. There has been significant investment in some countries into re-entry programmes following release, targeted around accommodation, employment, and mentoring. Lero Jonson and Cullen (2016) have reviewed the major initiatives in the USA since the turn of the millennium. They show that the results have been mixed: implementation of programmes has often been difficult, despite strong political backing for the movement, and though the overall effect has been to reduce recidivism, not all programmes have done so (and there have been few rigorous evaluations). Characteristics which seem to make programmes more effective are where there is continuity of care between prison and community; where treatment is given consistently; and where high risk individuals are targeted.

However, we may have given up too soon on simple employment programmes. Re-analysis of a 1970s programme which provided jobs to those leaving prison and drug treatment found that those given jobs had a significantly lower subsequent rate of arrest (by 46 per cent) than a randomly assigned control group (Uggen and Blahnik 2016). However, though having considerable effects on arrest for criminal offences, the programme had no effect on drug relapse. This illustrates the problematic dilemmas for funders and policy-makers that re-entry programmes can create: is it better to reduce crime, but also possibly slightly increase (illegal) drug use, some of it funded by the job programme?

Of course, one of the key practical obstacles to desistance is the fact of having a criminal record itself, and its potential effects on employment and housing. Healy (2016), comparing the 'Tiger' years in Ireland with the subsequent economic downturn, has shown that in economic hard times, even those offenders trying to desist are likely to fail because employers will look elsewhere in the pool of unemployed labour. Uggen and Blahnik (2016) describe how even one minor arrest in the US makes it less likely that employers will call back applicants for interview for a job, with particularly high effects for African-Americans. US state bans on those with convictions being able to access public assistance for housing etc. have tended to *increase* criminality.

In the US, there have been some attempts to mitigate those effects by 'sealing' criminal records after a crime-free period. So, for example, many US states keep the criminal records of young offenders private and allow for them to be sealed or expunged after a period of time. Most states also do this for adult offenders, though policies vary considerably in their detail. In England and Wales, legislation with a similar purpose has been in place since 1974 (the Rehabilitation of Offenders Act), and this was extended in its scope in 2014. Maruna (2011) has pointed out, however, that though sending someone to prison is replete with symbolic rituals emphasizing criminality, and those 'sticky labels' (Uggen and Blahnik 2016) continue to mark out those released afterwards, societies have not managed to produce symbolic labels or ceremonies celebrating desistance or reintegration into society.

Restorative justice, often run in parallel with criminal justice, brings those affected by the offence (offender, victim, etc.) together with a neutral facilitator. It has been suggested that restorative justice conferencing may provide a platform upon which intending desisters can set out, in front of their supporters and victims, that they do take responsibility for the offence, that they wish to change their lives, and that they are sorry for the harm the offence has caused (to the victim and supporters) (Shapland *et al.* 2011). The outcome agreement arising from the restorative justice conference, which is agreed by all those present, who are all involved in putting it together, then is effectively like an individualized rehabilitation plan for that offender—but one which is supported by and working in tune with what the offender wants. In other words, it could be seen as a desistance plan. Some forms of restorative justice, if and when the plan is successfully completed, may then have a celebration that the offender has been reintegrated. Drug courts often work in the same way. In relation to maintaining desistance, as Maruna (2011) suggests, should we then think about introducing such celebratory rituals by criminal justice for offenders who do desist—and maybe also make it an occasion to seal the records of the past?

CONCLUSION

We have seen that, though not everyone desists from crime, most offenders, even most persistent offenders, do desist. However, having a longer criminal career makes it harder to desist and may make that journey longer, though starting offending early does not necessarily make desistance less likely. The time course of desistance varies considerably between individuals—there is desistance from childhood or adolescent conduct disorders (Loeber *et al.* 2016), and some do not desist until after age 40, but most start desisting in their twenties or thirties.

Sudden desistance, because some major event has occurred, is not unknown, but for most people, desistance is a process, which frequently involves obstacles, and sometimes relapses. There is still debate in the literature as to whether people first take a decision to desist and then, gradually, become able to implement it, or whether life changes ('hooks for change' or 'turning points') occur and the person is then able to build on these. Whichever occurs for an individual, the agentic choice of that individual, psychological maturation and social circumstances (as well as social-structural features such as opportunities for employment) all seem to be important.

The potential for the criminal justice system to hasten desistance, and so to reduce reoffending and crime rates generally is tantalizing—but that potential has not yet been realized. Probation supervision seems only rarely to be perceived by probationers as helping their own efforts to desist at the time—but there is encouraging evidence that it may have a lagged effect, and so help to maintain desistance. Certainly, desistance research suggests that rehabilitative efforts of the 'top-down' variety would be better reshaped to generate a process of working *with* offenders to enhance their desisting goals. The fear of being repeatedly convicted does seem to provide an impetus for offenders to think about changing their lives, but there remain many obstacles to overcome if these desisting impulses are be converted into successfully leading a non-offending life in the community. Indeed, in some countries political decisions about how society treats ex-offenders (e.g. preventing access to housing assistance; not allowing the sealing of criminal records) have actually increased the practical obstacles to desistance.

There remain many gaps in the research literature on desistance, but the explosion of research and theorization in the last 15 years or so means that we now know much more than we did about processes that ex-offenders have been quietly accomplishing for years. In criminal policy terms, however, desistance remains a relatively new strategic policy goal which still requires considerable work. It is therefore perhaps helpful to end this chapter as we began it, by referring to Kirkwood and McNeill's (2015) definition of desistance as 'the process of moving from offending to successful social integration (and with it compliance with law and social norms)'. In other words, to encourage desistance is to encourage recognition and good citizenship, and this is in the interests of all citizens, whether or not they have ever been convicted.

SELECTED FURTHER READING

Research on desistance is notable for the major longitudinal studies that have been carried out in various parts of the world. Reviews of the findings from many of these can be found in Shapland, Farrall, and Bottoms' *Global Perspectives on Desistance* (2016). Two of the major theorists from the US, who followed a group of persistent male delinquents until they were in their sixties and beyond, are Laub and Sampson whose *Shared Beginnings, Divergent Lives* (2003), explores how differently their lives turned out. Maruna describes how desisters (and persisters) themselves see their desistance journey and their own identity in *Making Good: How Ex-Convicts Reform and Rebuild their Lives* (2001). In a rather different cultural context, Healy's *Dynamics of Desistance: Charting Pathways Through Change* (2010) explores the difficult journeys towards desistance of male offenders in Ireland. A key question for desistance researchers is whether the desistance process is the same for men and for women. Women's desistance is explored by Giordano, Cernkovich, and Rudolph in their article, 'Gender, crime and desistance: toward a theory of cognitive transformation' (2002), and updated by Giordano in her chapter in *Global Perspectives on Desistance*. Women's desistance in the context of women's lives is the centre of Leverentz's *The Ex-Prisoner's Dilemma: How Women Negotiate Competing Narratives of Reentry and Desistance* (2014). Reflections on the potential role of the criminal justice system in promoting desistance, or putting barriers in the way of offenders desisting, can be found in McNeill's 'A desistance paradigm for offender management' (2006) and in Uggen and Blahnik's chapter in *Global Perspectives on Desistance*.

REFERENCES

Blokland, A. A. J., Nagin, D., and Nieuwbeerta, P. (2005), 'Life span offending trajectories of a Dutch conviction cohort', *Criminology*, 43(4): 919–54.

Bottoms, A. E. and Shapland, J. (2011), 'Steps towards desistance among male young adult recidivists', in S. Farrall, M. Hough, S. Maruna, and R. Sparks (eds), *Escape Routes: Contemporary Perspectives on Life after Punishment*, London: Routledge.

Bottoms, A. E. and Shapland, J. (2016), 'Learning to desist in early adulthood: the Sheffield Desistance Study', in J. Shapland, S. Farrall, and A. E. Bottoms (eds), *Global Perspectives on Desistance: Reviewing What We Know, Looking to the Future*, London: Routledge.

Bottoms, A. E., Shapland, J., Costello, A., Holmes, D., and Muir, G. (2004), 'Towards desistance: theoretical underpinnings for an empirical study', *Howard Journal of Criminal Justice*, 43(4): 368–89.

Bushway, S. and Paternoster, R. (2013), 'Desistance from crime: a review and ideas for moving forward', in C. Gibson and M. Krohn (eds), *Handbook of Life-Course Criminology*, New York: Springer.

Calverley, A. (2013), *Cultures of Desistance: Rehabilitation, Reintegration and Ethnic Minorities*, London: Routledge.

Carlsson, C. (2016), 'Human agency, criminal careers, and desistance', in J. Shapland, S. Farrall, and A. E. Bottoms (eds), *Global Perspectives on Desistance: Reviewing What We Know, Looking to the Future*, London: Routledge.

Carlsson, C. and Sarnecki, J. (2016), *An Introduction to Life-Course Criminology*, London: Sage.

Cid, J. and Marti, J. (2015), 'Imprisonment, social support and desistance: a theoretical approach to pathways of desistance and persistence for imprisoned men', *International Journal of Offender Therapy and Comparative Criminology*, online first, doi.org/10.1177/0306624X15623988.

Cid, J. and Marti, J. (2016), 'Structural context and pathways to desistance: research in Spain', in J. Shapland, S. Farrall, and A. E. Bottoms (eds), *Global Perspectives on Desistance: Reviewing What We Know, Looking to the Future*, London: Routledge.

Donati, P. (2011), *Relational Sociology: A New Paradigm for the Social Sciences*, London: Routledge.

Farrall, S. (2002), *Rethinking What Works with Offenders: Probation, Social Context and Desistance from Crime*, Cullompton: Willan.

Farrall, S., Bottoms, A., and Shapland, J. (2010), 'Social structures and desistance from crime', *European Journal of Criminology*, 7(6): 546–70.

Farrall, S., Hunter, B., Sharpe, G., and Calverley, A. (2014), *Criminal Careers in Transition: the Social Context of Desistance from Crime*, Oxford: Oxford University Press.

Farrington, D. P., Coid, J. W., Harnett, L. M., Jolliffe, D., Soteriou, N., Turner, R. E., and West, D. J. (2006), *Criminal Careers up to Age 50 and Life Success up to Age 48: New Findings from the Cambridge Study in Delinquent Development*, 2nd edn, Home Office Research Study 299, London: Home Office.

F.-Dufour, I. and Brassard, R. (2014), 'The convert, the remorseful and the rescued: three different processes of desistance from crime', *Australian and New Zealand Journal of Criminology*, 47(3): 313–35.

Giordano, P. (2016), 'Mechanisms underlying the desistance process: reflections on "A theory of cognitive transformation"', in J. Shapland, S. Farrall, and A. E. Bottoms (eds), *Global Perspectives on Desistance: Reviewing What We Know, Looking to the Future*, London: Routledge.

Giordano, P., Cernkovich, S., and Rudolph, J. (2002), 'Gender, crime and desistance: toward a theory of cognitive transformation', *American Journal of Sociology*, 107(4): 990–1064.

Glueck, S. and Glueck, E. (1950), *Unraveling Juvenile Delinquency*, New York: Commonwealth Fund.

Gottfredson, M. R. and Hirschi, T. (1990), *A General Theory of Crime*, Stanford: Stanford University Press.

Healy, D. (2010), *Dynamics of Desistance: Charting Pathways Through Change*, Cullompton: Willan.

Healy, D. (2013), 'Changing fate?: agency and the desistance process', *Theoretical Criminology*, 17(4): 557–74.

Healy, D. (2016), '"I've always tried but I hadn't got the willpower": understanding pathways to desistance in the Republic of Ireland', in J. Shapland, S. Farrall, and A. E. Bottoms (eds), *Global Perspectives on Desistance: Reviewing What We Know, Looking to the Future*, London: Routledge.

Horney, J., Tolan, P., and Weisburd, D. (2012), 'Contextual influences', in R. Loeber and D. P. Farrington (eds), *From Juvenile Delinquency to Adult Crime: Criminal Careers, Justice Policy and Prevention*, New York: Oxford University Press.

JOHNSON, S. B., BLUM, R. W., and GIEDD, J. N. (2009), 'Adolescent maturity and the brain: the promise and pitfalls of neuroscience research in adolescent health policy', *Journal of Adolescent Health*, 45: 216–21.

KIRKWOOD, S. and MCNEILL, F. (2015), 'Integration and reintegration: comparing pathways to citizenship through asylum and criminal justice', *Criminology & Criminal Justice*, 15(5): 511–26.

LAUB, J. H. and SAMPSON, R. J. (2003), *Shared Beginnings, Divergent Lives: Delinquent Boys to Age 70*, Cambridge, MA: Harvard University Press.

LE BEL, T., BURNETT, R., MARUNA, S., and BUSHWAY, S. (2008), 'The "chicken and egg" of subjective and social factors in desistance from crime', *European Journal of Criminology*, 5(2): 131–59.

LERO JONSON, C. and CULLEN, F. (2016), 'Prisoner reentry programs', *Crime and Justice*, 44(1): 517–75.

LEVERENTZ, A. M. (2014), *The Ex-Prisoner's Dilemma: How Women Negotiate Competing Narratives of Reentry and Desistance*, New Brunswick, NJ.: Rutgers University Press.

LOEBER, R. and FARRINGTON, D. P. (2000), 'Young children who commit crime: epidemiology, developmental origins, risk factors, early interventions, and policy implications', *Development and Psychopathology*, 12(4): 737–62.

LOEBER, R., STOUTHAMER-LOEBER, M., and AHONEN, L. (2016), 'Key behavioural aspects of desistance from conduct problems and delinquency', in J. Shapland, A. E. Bottoms, and S. Farrall (eds), *Global perspectives on Desistance*, London: Routledge.

MACLEOD, J. F., GROVE, P. G., and FARRINGTON, D. P. (2012), *Explaining Criminal Careers: Implications for Justice Policy*, Oxford: Oxford University Press.

MARUNA, S. (2001), *Making Good: How Ex-Convicts Reform and Rebuild their Lives*, Washington, DC: American Psychological Association.

MARUNA, S. (2011), 'Re-entry as a rite of passage', *Punishment and Society*, 13(1): 3–28.

MCNEILL, F. (2006), 'A desistance paradigm for offender management', *Criminology and Criminal Justice*, 6(1): 39–62.

MCNEILL, F. (2012), 'Four forms of "offender" rehabilitation: towards an interdisciplinary perspective', *Legal and Criminological Psychology*, 17(1): 18–36.

MOFFITT, T. E. (1993), 'Adolescence-limited and life-course-persistent antisocial behavior: a developmental taxonomy', *Psychological Review*, 100: 674–701.

MULVEY, E. and SCHUBERT, C. (2016), 'Issues to consider in future work on desistance from adolescence to early adulthood: observations from the Pathways to Desistance study', in J. Shapland, S. Farrall. and A. E. Bottoms (eds), *Global Perspectives on Desistance: Reviewing What We Know, Looking to the Future*, London: Routledge.

PATERNOSTER, R. and BUSHWAY, S. (2009), 'Desistance and the feared self: toward an identity theory of criminal desistance', *Journal of Criminal Law and Criminology*, 99(4): 1103–56.

PIQUERO, A. R., FARRINGTON, D. P., and BLUMSTEIN, A. (2007), *Key Issues in Criminal Career Research: New Analyses of the Cambridge Study in Delinquent Development*, Cambridge: Cambridge University Press.

PORPORINO, F. J. (2010) 'Bringing sense and sensitivity to corrections: from programmes to "fix" offenders to services to support desistance', in J. Brayford, F. Cowe, and J. Deering (eds), *What Else Works?: Creative Work with Offenders*, Cullompton: Willan.

RODERMOND, E., KRUTTSCHNITT, C., SLOTBOOM, A-M., and BIJLEVELD, C. (2016), 'Female desistance: a review of the literature', *European Journal of Criminology*, 13(1): 3–28.

SAMPSON, R. and LAUB, J. (1993), *Crime in the Making*, Cambridge, MA: Harvard University Press.

SHAPLAND, J. and BOTTOMS, A. E. (2011), 'Reflections on social values, offending and desistance among young adult recidivists', *Punishment and Society*, 13: 256–82.

SHAPLAND, J., BOTTOMS, A., FARRALL, S., MCNEILL, F., PRIEDE, C., and ROBINSON, G. (2012a), 'The Quality of Probation Supervision—A Literature Review', Centre for Criminological Research Occasional Paper no. 3, Sheffield: University of Sheffield, available at: http://www.shef.ac.uk/polopoly_fs/1.159010!/file/QualityofProbationSupervision.pdf, accessed 3 February 2016.

SHAPLAND, J., BOTTOMS, A. E., and MUIR, G. (2012b), 'Perceptions of the criminal justice system among young adult would-be desisters', in F. Losel and A. E. Bottoms (eds), *Young Adult Offenders: Lost in Transition?*, London: Routledge.

SHAPLAND, J., FARRALL, S., and BOTTOMS, A. E. (2016), *Global Perspectives on Desistance: Reviewing What We Know, Looking to the Future*, London: Routledge.

SHAPLAND, J., ROBINSON, G., and SORSBY, A. (2011), *Restorative Justice in Practice*, London: Routledge.

SHARPE, G. (2015), 'Precarious identities: "young" motherhood, stigma and desistance', *Criminology and Criminal Justice*, 15(4): 407–22.

SHOVER, N. (1996), *Great Pretenders: Pursuits and Careers of Persistent Thieves*, Colorado: Westview Press.

SKARDHAMER, T. and SAVOLAINEN, J. (2016), 'Timing of change: are life course transitions causes or consequences of desistance?', in J. Shapland, S. Farrall, and A. E. Bottoms (eds), *Global Perspectives on Desistance: Reviewing What We Know, Looking to the Future*, London: Routledge.

SKARDHAMER, T., SAVOLAINEN, J., AASE, K., and LYNGSTAD, T. (2016), 'Does marriage reduce crime?', *Crime and Justice: A Review of Research*, 44: 385–446.

TANNER, J. L. (2006), 'Recentering during emerging adulthood', in J. J. Arnett and J. L. Tanner (eds), *Emerging Adults in America: Coming of Age in the 21st Century*, Washington, DC: American Psychological Association.

UGGEN, C. and BLAHNIK, L. (2016), 'The increasing stickiness of public labels', J. Shapland, S. Farrall, and A. E. Bottoms (eds), *Global Perspectives on Desistance: Reviewing What We Know, Looking to the Future*, London: Routledge.

VERHAGE, A. and SHAPLAND, J. (2013), 'Getting by or getting rich, or simply looking for a better life? The informal economy in times of economic crisis', in P. Saitta, J. Shapland, and A. Verhage (eds), *Getting by or Getting Rich? The Formal, Informal and Criminal Economies in a Globalised World*, The Hague: Eleven.

Warr, M. (2002), *Companions in Crime*, Cambridge: Cambridge University Press.

Weaver, B. (2016), *Offending and Desistance: The Importance of Social Relations*, London: Routledge.

West, D. J. (1963), *The Habitual Prisoner*, London: Macmillan.

Wikström, P-O., Oberwittler, D., Treiber, K., and Hardie, B. (2012), *Breaking Rules: The Social and Situational Dynamics of Young People's Urban Crime*, Oxford: Oxford University Press.

PART IV

RESPONSES TO CRIME

34

POLICING AND THE POLICE

Trevor Jones, Tim Newburn, and Robert Reiner

INTRODUCTION

This chapter reviews some of the key themes in scholarly work on policing, now one of the major sub-fields within criminology. We begin with definitions of 'policing', before outlining the emergence of policing as an area of academic research. The chapter then moves on to consider the nature of police discretion, the factors that shape police decision-making and the implications for the accountability and governance of policing agents and organizations. The next section reviews contrasting styles or models of policing that have come to prominence over recent years. Finally, we explore two overarching developments within contemporary policing, pluralization and internationalization. The focus is primarily upon policing in the United Kingdom though many of the themes are similar across all western democracies.

DEFINING 'POLICE' AND 'POLICING'

For decades, academic studies of policing focused exclusively upon the *police*; the specialist state agency tasked with crime control, order maintenance, and emergency response. However, from the 1990s onwards, policing activities undertaken by a wide range of individuals and institutions—within, beyond, below, and above the nation state (Loader 2000)—came under increasing academic scrutiny and it is now commonplace to distinguish the concept of *policing* from *the police*. We take policing to be a subset of social control that involves:

> organized forms of order-maintenance, peace-keeping, rule or law enforcement, crime investigation and prevention and other forms of investigation and information-brokering—which may involve a conscious exercise of coercive power—undertaken by individuals or organizations, where such activities are viewed by them and/or others as a central or key defining part of their purpose. (Jones and Newburn 1998: 18–19)

A diverse range of policing organizations has always existed, and in recent years proliferated, which has led to the debates about 'pluralization' discussed later in the chapter. However, within this more complex landscape it is only the state agency with special legal powers and an omnibus mandate that is understood by the label *the* police.

Policing originated in collective processes of social control, but it was the emergence of social inequality, hierarchy, and more centralized state systems that led to the development of specialist police agencies (Robinson and Scaglion 1987: 109; Williams 2014). Communal policing forms were converted gradually to state-dominated ones, which operated as agents of class control rather than sources of impartial protection. The complex and contradictory function of contemporary police, as simultaneously embodying the quest for general and stratified order—'parking tickets' as well as 'class repression' (Marenin 1983)—is inscribed in their origins.

The police are required to perform a miscellany of tasks, from traffic control to counter-terrorism. The defining feature of police work, however, is not a particular social function, whether that be crime control, social service, order maintenance, or political repression. Rather, it is that all demands on the police involve 'something that ought not to be happening and about which someone had better do something **now**!' (Bittner 1974: 30, emphasis in original). In other words, policing tasks arise in emergency situations, often where there is an element of social conflict (Brodeur 2007). The police deploy a variety of tactics to keep the peace without formal resort to their legal powers, but underpinning their approach is their potential power to wield legal sanctions, ultimately the use of legitimate force (Bittner 1970, 1974: 35; Brodeur 2010).

THE DEVELOPMENT OF POLICE RESEARCH

Academic research on the police emerged in the early 1960s on both sides of the Atlantic (Newburn and Reiner 2012). Concerns about police violations of civil rights were the key driver of early US police research. Socio-legal researchers analysed how the police role, organization, and occupational culture respectively shaped malpractices (Sklansky 2008: ch. 2). In the late 1960s as 'law and order' displaced 'civil rights' as the key domestic political issue in the USA, policy-oriented work on police effectiveness became increasingly prominent.

Police research in Britain developed at a time when the post-war consensus about British police efficiency and integrity was being increasingly questioned (Reiner 2010). Banton's (1964) pioneering empirical study found the police role was primarily 'peacekeeping' rather than law enforcement. Much of the emergent work in the 1970s focused on the backstage life of the police—contrasting its disciplined, rule-bound image with the more complex, divided and occasionally deviant reality.

The politicization of 'law and order' in the later 1970s stimulated two new strands of research. Within universities, a body of critical, Marxist-influenced work developed (e.g. Hall *et al.* 1978; Hain 1979, 1980; Brogden 1982; Scraton 1985; Grimshaw and Jefferson 1987). At the same time, a more policy-oriented form of police research emerged, much of it conducted or funded by government (e.g. Clarke and Hough 1984). Since that period, policing research has continued to expand with both critical and more policy-oriented strands continuing to be visible. More recently, a body of 'evidence-based policing' has begun to emerge. Stimulated both by governmental interests and funding, and by growing academic interest in experimental and quasi-experimental methods, such work has as its central focus 'making decisions about "what works" in policing: which practices and strategies accomplish police missions most cost-effectively' (Sherman 2013: 1). Alongside such work—though rarely in a dialogue with it—sits the more critical scholarship which since the 1990s has come to be more influenced by Foucault and Bourdieu than by Marx (though that may well change as the continuing economic crisis post-2008 draws attention back to political economy). It has focused on subjects such as the use of police surveillance powers and, more particularly, on questions of equality and discrimination in the modern globalized world (e.g. Brodeur 2010; Fassin 2013; Mutsaers 2014).

POLICE DISCRETION: ITS NATURE, OPERATION, AND CONTROL

The police organization is often seen as a rule-bound bureaucracy, potentially implying the mechanistic enforcement of the law (Allen 1976). In practice, there is a very wide degree of discretion in frontline police decision-making. Breaches of the law outstrip police capacity to process them, so choices about priorities are inevitable. Discretion is also logically necessary as legal rules require interpretation in unpredictable situations and, indeed, a police force has the 'special property . . . that within it discretion increases as one moves down the hierarchy' (Wilson 1968: 7). For many years, it has been argued that police discretion is hard to regulate partly because the dispersed character of routine police work gives it 'low visibility' (Goldstein 1960). However, the rapid spread of digital recording technologies has increasingly enabled some individuals and organizations subjected to police control and surveillance to themselves record and monitor the activities of the controllers (Wilson and Serisier 2010). For example, recent high profile scandals relating to unlawful police violence against black people in the USA have arisen due to the availability of video evidence from bystanders that discredited the accounts of the officers involved (Rosenfeld 2015). Concerns about police use of force have led, in some areas, to the introduction of body-worn cameras with the aim of both improving police conduct and enhancing police legitimacy (Ariel *et al.* 2015). Such technologies may somewhat level the playing field between police and those they suspect of crime or disorder.

In the late 1970s a structuralist critique argued that although a degree of discretion was inescapable, English and Welsh law took an unnecessarily permissive stance to police powers by formulating elastic and vague rules (McBarnet 1978, 1979). This paved the way for more detailed studies of the interaction between legal rules and police practice (Dixon 1997; Cape and Young 2008).

POLICE DISCRETION IN PRACTICE: UNEQUAL POLICING

A central finding of police research across many national contexts is that relatively powerless groups are both over-policed *and* under-protected. Most police resources are devoted to uniformed patrol of public space, but privacy has a class dimension (Stinchcombe 1963). The lower the social class of a person, the more their lives take place in public space, and the more 'available' they are to come to police attention (Quinton *et al.* 2000; Waddington *et al.* 2004). Adversarial policing falls disproportionately on young men in the lowest socio-economic groups, but a range of marginalized sub-groups have also found themselves coming into conflict with the police. Whilst recent research has explored the relationship between policing and sexualities (Jones 2015), the predominant focus over the past 20 years or so has concerned ethnicity and gender.

Numerous studies have shown that police powers are disproportionately deployed against black people (Bowling and Phillips 2002, 2007; Weber and Bowling 2013; Phillips and Bowling, this volume). This results from a complex interaction between police discrimination and social pressures that generate disproportionate offending by young black men (Reiner 1993, 2010: 159–75). Ethnic minorities are victimized disproportionately by crime of all kinds (Ministry of Justice 2015), and often perceive the police response as inadequate (Bowling 1999; Foster *et al.* 2005; Ministry of Justice 2015). In addition, ethnic minorities remain under-represented *within* the police service, and research has demonstrated unequal treatment of black and minority ethnic officers and staff within the police organization (Holdaway 2009). The police service in England and Wales has come under increasing official pressure to improve its relationship with ethnic minority populations.

With regard to gender, women are significantly less likely than men to find themselves on the end of adversarial police powers, although this does not mean that forms of gender discrimination do not operate (Newburn and Reiner 2012). There is much clearer evidence of discrimination against women in their treatment by the police as victims. Calls to domestic disturbances have always been a significant part of the police workload, but officers were often reluctant to use formal powers even where evidence of assault is present. 'Domestics' are seen as messy, unproductive, and not 'real' police work in traditional cop culture. This issue has become highly charged in the last three decades around the world, and police forces have attempted to improve their response to domestic assaults, with debatable results (Hoyle 1998). There has also been much concern about insensitive treatment of rape victims, an issue dramatically highlighted 35 years ago by Roger Graef's TV documentary on the Thames Valley Police, which filmed the interrogation of a rape victim (BBC 1, 18 January 1982). Despite considerable improvements since then, the treatment of rape victims by police remains problematic (Horvath and Brown 2010; Hohl and Stanko 2015). The recruitment of women officers has increased over time (by 2015 they accounted for about 28 per cent of police officers) as has their presence in senior ranks (several women chief constables have been appointed in the last 20 years). However, the persistence of gender discrimination within the service has been widely documented (Heidensohn 1992, 2008; Brown and Heidensohn 2000; Silvestri 2003, 2007).

FACTORS SHAPING POLICE DISCRETION

One straightforward explanation of the patterns outlined above has it that police work attracts people with distinctively conservative and authoritarian personalities. However, there is little evidence to support this (Waddington 1999a). The most common explanation of police working practices found in the research literature points to the informal culture of the rank and file as a primary factor. Occupational police cultures can be defined as beliefs, norms, working practices, and informal rules that help police officers to make sense of their world (Reiner 2010). Early studies of policing—based on observation of the work of uniformed patrol officers—proposed a relatively stable set of dimensions that appeared to characterize 'cop culture'. In Skolnick's (1966) classic formulation, the tensions associated with policing in liberal societies foster a common set of cultural responses (see also Reiner 2015). The police in liberal democracies are faced with a basic dilemma. They are under pressure to achieve results in the form of law enforcement, but the rule of law restricts the methods they can use. They are also visible embodiments of social authority, exposing them to danger and creating tensions in all their social relationships. The development of a set of informal rules, rites, and recipes is a collective 'coping mechanism' for dealing with such pressures: a subculture that is transmitted by storytelling, a toolkit of examples for dealing with police work (Shearing and Ericson 1991).

Skolnick identified three main aspects of cop culture: suspiciousness, internal solidarity coupled with social isolation, and conservatism. Suspiciousness arises from the pressure to achieve results by catching offenders, and the concern with danger: people and places are constantly scrutinized for signs of crime or risk. Suspiciousness also makes the police prone to operate with prejudiced stereotypes of potential 'villains' and 'troublemakers'. Internal solidarity and social isolation are mutually reinforcing. Solidarity is knitted from the intense experience of confronting shared dangers, and the need to be able to rely on colleagues in tight spots. Isolation results from organizational aspects of the work such as the shift system, and people's wariness in interacting with authority figures.

Many reforms in the last 30 years, have aimed to moderate, if not eliminate, these characteristic traits of traditional rank-and-file police culture (Henry and Smith 2007; Rowe 2007; Cockcroft 2012) and/or constrain discretion and thus potential discrimination via 'rule-tightening' (Chan 1997). There does appear to be some progress in controlling the overt display of prejudice (Foster *et al.* 2005). However, ethnographic and other research suggests that key aspects of traditional police culture remain resilient in the face of these reforms (Loftus 2008, 2009, 2010; O'Neill *et al.* 2007; O'Neill and McCarthy 2014). Studies of police culture have been criticized for presenting a monolithic picture, overlooking differences between and within forces (Chan 1997), though such variations have actually been a staple part of police studies for a long time (see Reiner 2010: ch. 4).

The major analyses of police culture do not support the notion of a freestanding phenomenon into which successive generations of police are socialized as passive cultural dopes. The culture is generated and sustained by the problems and tensions of the police role, structured by legal and social pressures. In the absence of fundamental transformations in the mandate and pressures the police have to deal with their culture is unlikely to alter dramatically. However, culture does not determine practice, but is enacted in concrete situations where other factors are important (Waddington *et al.* 2017). For example, officers who are racially prejudiced may nonetheless be restrained from acting in overtly discriminatory ways by clear and effectively sanctioned rules (Smith *et al.* 1983; Waddington 1999b).

THE CONTROL OF POLICE DISCRETION

The formal control of police discretion in Britain is limited by the common law doctrine of constabulary independence. As stated by Lord Denning, this holds that a 'constable . . . is not the servant of anyone, save of the law itself. No Minister of the Crown can tell him that he must, or must not, keep observation on this place or that; or that he must, or must not, prosecute this man or that one. Nor can any police authority tell him so. The responsibility for law enforcement lies on him' (*R v Metropolitan Police Commissioner, ex p. Blackburn* [1968] 2 QB 136). Though its constitutional status has been much contested (Lustgarten 1986) the 'principle' affords British police officers a considerable measure of legitimate discretion. In considering how such discretion is governed we may distinguish between the processes by which individual officers are held to account, and the means by which broader force policy and action is overseen and subjected to outside direction and control.

Individual accountability

There are two principal channels for holding individual officers to account for alleged wrongdoing: the courts and the complaints process.

Legal accountability

Two aspects of legal accountability will be discussed here. The first concerns civil litigation about particular incidents, and the second relates to the legal regulation of police powers. The use of civil law as a remedy for police misconduct has increased in recent decades in England and Wales, as well as in other jurisdictions (Smith 2003). This can take a number of forms, including actions against the police for abuse of their powers (e.g. assault, false imprisonment, negligence), as well as for breaches of other legal codes relating to anti-discrimination, or health and safety. Individual police officers themselves can take legal action against their own forces for alleged breaches of employment laws, discrimination, or other forms of unreasonable behaviour. Although civil actions attempt to gain redress primarily via retrospective provision of financial compensation to claimants, writers have also underlined their potential deterrent value in relation to police deviance (Ransley *et al.* 2007).

Turning to the second aspect of legal accountability, the main statutory powers of the police are codified in the Police and Criminal Evidence Act 1984 (PACE), although they have been expanded since. PACE attempted for the first time to develop what the 1981 Royal Commission on Criminal Procedure (RCCP) that preceded it described as a 'fundamental balance' between a comprehensive set of police powers and safeguards for suspects. The safeguards—which provide for legal advice in the police station, set limits on detention, and govern how interviews with suspects are to be conducted among other things—are set out partly in the Act itself, partly in Codes of Practice accompanying it.

In the decade following PACE there was extensive research evaluating the impact of PACE on police practice (for summaries see Dixon 1997; Brown 1997; Reiner 2010: ch. 7). Some studies suggested that suspects systematically fail to receive their rights (McConville *et al.* 1991; Choongh 1997). Most commentators found, however, that the new procedures achieved some improvements in the treatment of suspects, although since the mid-1990s there has been a clear trend to extending powers without balancing safeguards (Cape and Young 2008).

When the government was forced to establish the Royal Commission on Criminal Justice in 1991 in the wake of the successful appeals by the Birmingham Six and Guildford Four, it was hoped by civil libertarians that the protection of suspects would be boosted further. In the event its recommendations on police powers and safeguards (Royal Commission 1993) amounted only to detailed footnotes to PACE, and they were implemented in an unbalanced way. Most new powers recommended by the 1993 Royal Commission Report were incorporated into the Criminal Justice and Public Order Act 1994,which extended stop and search powers (section 60) and gave new powers to control trespassers and raves. Most fundamentally, it introduced the right for the prosecution to comment adversely on a suspect's exercise of the right to silence in police interviews, with a corresponding change in the caution given beforehand. This resulted in a decline in the proportion of suspects exercising their right of silence in relation to some or all questions (Bucke *et al.* 2000).

Since that time, expansion of police powers has accelerated. New powers to intercept communications, conduct covert operations, stop-and-search, and arrest, and new public order offences have been created. The clear trend is for enhanced powers and reduced safeguards, reflecting the law-and-order politics that have prevailed since the early 1990s (see Newburn and Reiner 2012 for a summary). The one significant exception in recent years has resulted from government intervention in relation to police powers to stop and search. In the aftermath of the 2011 English riots, where it once again became clear that stop and search was a highly divisive issue, the then Home Secretary, Theresa May, announced a review of police use of this power. Undertaken by HMIC the outcome was significant pressure on police forces to limit the use of the power in order to demonstrate greater effectiveness in its deployment (HMIC 2013). In the year 2014–15 a 40 per cent drop in the use of stop and search powers was recorded (ONS 2015). The stop and search example notwithstanding, it remains the case that the broader trend, not least in relation to issues such as surveillance and communications interception (such as are contained in the Investigatory Powers Bill) is firmly in the direction of the growth of police power.

The complaints process

Prior to the early 2000s, there was widespread concern about the relative lack of independence of the police complaints process in England and Wales from the police organization. Ultimately, police officers investigated serious complaints against other officers, although there was an independent element in the supervision of such investigations by the Police Complaints Authority (PCA) (Newburn and Reiner 2012). The

Police Reform Act 2002 established the Independent Police Complaints Commission (IPCC), staffed entirely by non-police officers and with a greater remit and more powers than the old PCA (Smith 2009a, 2009b). Experience in other countries suggests independent investigation of complaints is not a panacea for regulating police misconduct (Goldsmith and Lewis 2000). No matter who does the investigating, complaints against the police are hard to sustain, because of the low visibility of most encounters. The fact that the majority of IPCC staff have been ex-police officers also raised concerns. Indeed, as Smith (2013: 95) observed, it seemed 'inconceivable that the presence of a large body of investigators with a police background and vast experience of criminal investigations and years of exposure to police occupational culture has not impacted significantly on IPCC working practice generally. Such concerns prompted the Chair of the IPCC to seek to recruit and train significant numbers of non-police investigators (Savage 2013).

In recent years concern that the IPCC may have an insufficiently prominent and robust role in the oversight of policing has been stimulated by a number of *causes célèbres*—including the ongoing Hillsborough scandal, Operation Yewtree (investigations into historic child abuse), and Operation Elveden (into police corruption). Referring to the high number of successful appeals against decisions made by internal police force complaints departments, the House of Commons Home Affairs Committee (HAC) (2013) said that the 'root of the problem is that the front line of the police complaints system is not working'. To counter the continuing serious problems affecting the system of complaints the HAC recommended further enhancement of a non-police element in investigations, a greater role for Her Majesty's Inspectorate of Constabulary (HMIC), a change of the culture which was alleged to treat police officers differently from members of the public, and an overhaul of the IPCC's communications systems in order to avoid the problems of misinformation so signally illustrated during the 2011 riots (Riots, Communities and Victims Panel 2012). Finally, noting the changing nature of the landscape, and the dangers highlighted by cases such as that involving the death of Jimmy Mubenga[1] (Fekete 2011), the HAC recommended that the IPCC's jurisdiction should be extended to cover private sector companies in their delivery of policing services and that resources should be made available to enable them to undertake such work.

Policy accountability

Until recently the formal structure of police governance in England and Wales was set out in the Police Act 1964 and the Police and Magistrates' Court Act 1994, consolidated as the Police Act 1996. These enshrined the so-called 'tripartite' system of accountability for the 41 provincial forces in England and Wales, comprising local police authorities, the Home Secretary, and chief constables. In London, the Metropolitan Police had the Home Secretary as their police authority until 1999, when the Greater London Authority Act created a police authority for the Met. The City of London force is accountable to the Common Council of the City of London (the Aldermen and Mayor), as well as the Home Secretary.

[1] Jimmy Mubenga died whilst being restrained by three G4S security guards after boarding a flight from Heathrow airport for his deportation to Angola. The guards were subsequently tried but acquitted for manslaughter.

The Tripartite structure divided responsibility for the framing and monitoring of police policy between chief constables, the Home Office, and local police authorities. The local dimension of this structure became progressively weaker during the last decades of the twentieth century. Local police authorities had limited legal powers, and most adopted a passive role in policy-making (Jones 2008). At the same time, the Home Office was increasingly proactive in promoting central government priorities (Reiner 2010). The development of national level policing institutions during the late 1990s also contributed to centralization of control. These included the National Crime Agency (NCA), consolidating a number of other national bodies. In addition, the senior officers' professional association—the Association of Chief Police Officers (ACPO)—emerged as a significant policy-making and lobbying body at the national level (Savage *et al.* 2000). ACPO was replaced by the National Police Chiefs Council (NPCC) in 2015.

One of the most significant centralizing influences on police governance has been the rigorous 'performance model' promoted by successive governments from the 1990s onwards. The establishment of national policing objectives with allied key performance indicators in the 1990s developed into an increasingly centralized performance management framework. The trend accelerated after the Police Reform Act 2002. This required the Home Secretary to issue an annual National Policing Plan and with a plethora of associated performance objectives and targets. A Home Office 'Police Standards Unit' was established to improve the performance of all basic command units across the country. In the early 2000s, the then Labour government planned a major amalgamation programme (HMIC 2005), abandoned because of fierce opposition (McLaughlin 2007). This centralization trend was increasingly challenged during the late 2000s, with growing cross-party consensus about the need to invigorate local input into shaping policing. In the 2010 General Election all the main party manifestos offered proposals for this.

The Coalition government that took office in May 2010 set out explicitly to reverse the centralization of police governance in England and Wales.[2] It scrapped a significant proportion of the performance indicator regime to which forces had been increasingly subjected and in 2011 passed the Police Reform and Social Responsibility Act to establish Police and Crime Commissioners (PCCs). PCCs were to be elected in each provincial force area for a four-year term, replacing Police Authorities as the local 'democratic' body within the statutory framework of police governance (Jones *et al.* 2012). Police authorities were by this point widely viewed to be an impotent mechanism of accountability (see, e.g., Flanagan 2008). Supporters of PCCs claimed the reform would reconnect the public with the police by ensuring that responsibility for local policing was 'moved out of Whitehall' and returned 'to Chief Constables, their staff and the communities they serve' (Home Office 2010: 2). The direct election of PCCs, it was argued, would ensure they gained a strong local democratic mandate to hold the police to account on behalf of local communities (see Herbert 2011).

[2] The system of police governance in Scotland, already distinct from that in England and Wales, has followed the opposite trajectory with the abolition of eight regional forces and their replacement by a single national police force for Scotland in April 2013 (see Fyfe 2014), a point to which we return later.

The responsibilities of PCCs include securing the maintenance of the local police force, ensuring that it is efficient and effective, as well as holding the chief constable to account for the exercise of her or his duties. Each PCC must publish a Police and Crime Plan setting out the strategic policing objectives for the force area. They are also required to work cooperatively with community safety partners and foster joined-up responses to local problems of crime and disorder. They have responsibility for commissioning community safety services as well as services for victims of crime. Crucially, the PCC appoints the chief constable and, under specific circumstances, may suspend him or her, as well as calling upon them to resign or retire. Each PCC is nominally answerable to a Police and Crime Panel comprising local councillors. This panel has a duty to 'scrutinize' and 'support' the activities of the PCC, although the powers of these panels are very limited (Lister 2014; Newburn 2012).

The first elections of PCCs took place in November 2012, with the second round of elections in May 2016. The concerns of some critics prior to the first elections appeared to have been partly borne out, with a turnout averaging 15 per cent (the lowest in British electoral history) and record numbers of deliberately spoiled ballot papers bringing into question the democratic mandate of the PCCs (Lister and Rowe 2014). There were a number of difficulties during the first term of the PCCs, including disputes with chief constables, concerns about appointments of deputies and assistants, and some other local problems. However, despite difficulties and variation across England and Wales, overall it seems fair to say that the worst fears of the critics of the reforms were not realized during the first term. Indeed, many erstwhile critics of the original reforms began to argue that PCCs could be a positive form of local police governance (Loader and Muir 2016). Whatever the arguments for and against the institution, the outcome of the 2015 General Election confirmed that PCCs will be part of the police governance landscape for the foreseeable future. The second round of PCC elections in 2016 saw an improved overall turnout of 26 per cent, partly because the elections took place on the same day as local elections in England and National Assembly elections in Wales. However, these figures remain worryingly low for supporters of the PCC idea, which has yet to catch the imagination of the voting public. The view of the House of Commons Home Affairs Committee (HAC) two years after the reforms had been introduced—that for many the concept of PCCs had to be considered still to be 'on probation' (HAC 2014)—remains apposite today.

By contrast with England and Wales, Northern Ireland has long had a single police force, the Royal Ulster Constabulary (previously the Royal Irish Constabulary) which had been in existence since the 1920s being replaced by the Police Service for Northern Ireland (PSNI) in 2001. The PSNI was created in the aftermath of the publication of the report on the Independent Commission on Policing for Northern Ireland (the Patten Commission) (Independent Commission 1999), with responsibility for policing devolved to the Northern Ireland Assembly. Governance of policing is overseen by the Northern Ireland Policing Board which, similar to local police authorities in England and Wales prior to the introduction of PCCs, has the responsibility for securing 'and effective and efficient local police service', and appointing and potentially dismissing chief officers. There is, in addition, an independent Police Ombudsman, responsible for investigation of complaints against the police.

In a further centralizing move in 2012 the Police and Fire Reform (Scotland) Act created a new single force, Police Scotland, to replace the eight previously existing forces. From 2013, when the new force became operational, it was divided into three regions, aligned with the boundaries of the old forces, and was subject to a new form of governance in the shape of the Scottish Police Authority (SPA) comprising appointed rather than elected members. The SPA's functions include the maintenance of the Police Service of Scotland, promoting and supporting improvement, and holding the chief constable to account, though a recent review (Flanagan 2016) has suggested these are in need of fairly urgent clarification.

Developments in both Northern Ireland and Scotland appear more in line with changes in a number of European countries in recent years—not least the Netherlands and the Scandinavian countries which have seen significant reductions in force numbers—than they do with recent reforms in England and Wales. The organization of policing, and its governance, vary quite markedly in Northern Ireland, Scotland and England and Wales reflecting, at least in part, the different political realities that exist in each country (Fyfe 2014).

MODELS OF POLICING

The original mandate of Peel's Metropolitan Police placed greatest emphasis on the prevention of crime primarily via visible patrol (Emsley 2009). During the course of the nineteenth century a detective function was added and these two strategies—preventive patrol and criminal investigation—have continued to form the core of policing over the past century or more. Nevertheless, recent decades have witnessed some important developments in policing, many prompted by the pressures under which all criminal justice agencies were placed by governments increasingly concerned to secure 'value for money' and 'economy, efficiency, and effectiveness' in public services (Savage 2007). They were also partly a reaction against the 'nothing works' penal pessimism of the 1970s, the rise in recorded crime rates after the mid-1950s (largely reversed since the mid-1990s), and the apparently precipitous decline in public confidence in policing from roughly the same time.

From the 1970s research in Britain and the USA had begun seriously to question the efficacy of patrol (Clarke and Hough 1984). The Kansas City experimental study of preventive car patrol found little impact on reported crime, fear of crime, or confidence in the police (Kelling *et al.* 1974). Subsequent large-scale research on foot patrol in Newark in the USA found some evidence of impact on fear of crime, and ratings of the police, though not on crime levels (Pate and Skogan 1985). The Newark study played a significant role in maintaining faith in routine visible patrol as a cornerstone of contemporary policing. The study was a strong influence on Wilson and Kelling's much-cited (1982) 'Broken Windows' article, which argued that police action against minor incivilities was an important factor in preventing the development of more serious crime (for a thorough critique, see Harcourt 2001).

In recent years policing has seen the regular appearance of what are alleged to be new 'models' of police work, each claiming to refashion policing in ways that represent a significant departure from traditional methods and predicated on varying diagnoses of the failure of traditional patrol and investigation methods. Many of these have been little more than fancy labels and promotional devices rather than genuine developments in policing styles and tactics. However, a number of developments in policing are worthy of more detailed discussion and analysis. Weisburd and Eck (2004), focusing primarily on American developments, draw attention to three—community policing, problem-oriented policing, and hotspots policing—to which two others might be added: one also seemingly originating in the US, zero tolerance policing; the second a British variant on problem-oriented policing, called 'intelligence-led policing'. What links all these innovations is the diagnosis that policing hitherto has been too reactive and should become more proactive (Tilley 2003). Many commentators, practitioners, and academics have suggested that these innovations played a large part in the recorded crime reduction since the 1990s.

COMMUNITY POLICING

Community policing approaches propose greater citizen involvement in the identification of the problems that should form priorities for police attention as well as in the responses to those problems (Trojanowicz and Bucqueroux 1990). Community policing emerged from the growing acceptance that at best the police could often only offer a very partial solution to the difficulties they confronted (Morgan and Newburn 1997). In both the USA and the UK community policing supporters recognized that police–community relations had deteriorated significantly, particularly with some minority ethnic communities (Skogan and Hartnett 1997). Community policing initiatives proliferated in the 1980s, though the available evidence suggests many were of very limited impact. Nevertheless, in the UK in the aftermath of the urban riots of the early 1980s, and Lord Scarman's plea for greater police–community consultation, ideas associated with community policing became the accepted policing orthodoxy, at least amongst senior officers (Reiner 1991). Indeed, continuing senior police scepticism about aggressive police patrol tactics was a very significant stumbling block when politicians began extolling the virtues of 'zero tolerance policing' in the mid- to late 1990s (Jones and Newburn 2007). So well established has community policing become in the USA that it has been described as the 'national mantra of the American police' (Greene 2000: 301).

The major difficulties with community policing are contained in the term itself. It is sufficiently broad to allow for almost any policing activity to be included under its rubric (Bayley 1994). Moreover, with its connotations of inclusiveness, consensus, communication, and consultation, an idea such as community policing, however difficult to pin down, is as almost impossibly seductive as cherry pie (Brogden 1999; Herbert 2006). Nevertheless, there have been numerous attempts both to define and to evaluate community policing. Skogan (2009: 43) describes it as 'an organizational strategy which supplements traditional crime fighting with problem-solving and prevention-oriented programmes that emphasize new roles for the public'. It is clear that the intention behind community policing is that it should be geared to locally identified priorities and that it should adopt locally appropriate tactics and styles. Consequently, it is a model of policing which will encompass a wide array of approaches. Such variety is partly what makes it difficult to define and contributes to difficulties in evaluation. To the extent that reliable evidence is available, it suggests that such approaches may increase satisfaction with police, aspects of police legitimacy, and citizen perceptions of disorder. There is, as yet, relatively little evidence that community-oriented policing reduces fear of crime or officially recorded crime levels (Gill *et al.* 2014).

PROBLEM-ORIENTED POLICING

At the heart of many community policing initiatives is the idea of police as 'problem-solvers' (Eck and Spelman 1987). Often considered a variant of community policing, 'problem-oriented policing' (POP) is an explicit attempt to make police work more analytical in the identification of the 'problems' to be addressed, and constructive in the solutions applied to the problems identified (Goldstein 1990). The underlying assumption is that much policing treats incidents brought to its attention as if they were discrete—having no connection or pattern. By contrast, POP looks for connections and patterns, with the aim of finding lasting solutions to ongoing problems (Moore 1992). As a consequence a number of 'tools' have come to be associated with this approach, notably the problem analysis triangle (the PAT, consisting of the offender, the victim, and the location) and the SARA process in which four sequenced stages—scanning, analysis, response, and assessment—form the basis for problem-solving (Tilley 2008).

A focus on problem-solving has given rise to a number of linked policing strategies concentrating on such patterning as repeat or prolific offenders (Everson and Pease 2001), repeat victimization (Farrell and Pease 2001), and hotspots (Sherman 1990) among others. Indeed, there is a growing literature particularly around 'hotspots policing' (Braga and Weisburd 2010; Braga *et al.* 2012). There have been a number of experimental studies in which focused and increased police patrols in areas where there are particular problems have had a measurable impact on levels of crime and disorder (Sherman and Weisburd 1995; Braga *et al.* 1999; Weisburd *et al.* 2010). However, as with community policing, there has also been considerable cultural resistance within the police to POP (Read and Tilley 2000; Scott 2000). There remains a very strong enforcement orientation in policing and an attachment to the excitement and glamour of the flashing blue lights of emergency response. The more sedate world of data collection and analysis holds fewer attractions. It is also something that few police departments are well equipped to deal with. Although the police are increasingly concerned with information brokerage and knowledge production (Ericson and Haggerty 1997), they tend still to be short on those skills that would make for successful problem-solving (Bullock and Tilley 2003), meaning that much policing practice falls well short of the ideals espoused by Goldstein (Eck 2006).

Arguably, it is precisely the identification of such limitations that lay behind the emergence of a further variation—so-called 'intelligence-led policing' (ILP) (see Maguire 2008; James 2013, 2016). This approach departs somewhat from problem-oriented and community policing in its tendency to privilege crime fighting and enforcement over other policing functions. Its underlying assumption is that these functions can be performed more efficiently and effectively through greater stimulation and use of intelligence. The link with POP lies in its emphasis upon the search for patterns in offending and victimization. One of the latest variants on such approaches, particularly consequent on contemporary developments in relation to 'big data', is what is increasingly referred to as 'predictive policing', an approach that seeks 'to identify likely targets for police intervention and prevent crime or solve past crimes by making statistical predictions'(Perry *et al.* 2013).

Where POP, community policing, and related models might be argued to have arisen out of public concerns, primarily about police community relations, police legitimacy and, to a lesser extent, police efficiency, the final model discussed here arose in the early 1990s as a reaction that there was little the police could do to stem the rising tide of crime. 'Zero-tolerance policing' is primarily associated with New York City and, more particularly, with the so-called 'New York miracle' which saw dramatic declines in all index crimes beyond those experienced in all other major American cities in the same period (Newburn and Jones 2007). More regularly referred to as 'quality of life policing', and much influenced by Wilson and Kelling's (1982) 'Broken Windows' thesis, the tactics adopted included aggressive enforcement operations against 'low level' crime problems such as graffiti, fare evasion, and public drunkenness, and the utilization of computer-aided police management systems, often referred to as COMPSTAT (Weisburd *et al.* 2003). Assessments of quality of life policing have been mixed (Katz *et al.* 2001; Golub *et al.* 2003). There has been a contentious debate about the relative contribution of policing practices and other factors to falling crime rates (see contributions to Welsh *et al.* 2015; Reiner 2016: 165–85). Concerns were also raised about the impact of aggressive enforcement-oriented policing approaches upon police–community relations and upon the incidence of police brutality (Greene 2000; McArdle and Erzen 2001). A recent influential study, however, argued that the operational strategy adopted by the Police Department—including the use of 'hotspots' approaches, a focus on the destruction of open air drugs markets, the use of aggressive enforcement and COMPSTAT—was one important factor in New York City's extraordinary crime decline toward the end of the century (Zimring 2012). Although some of the exceptional recorded crime decline in New York may have been produced by statistical data rigging by the police, perversely stimulated by COMPSTAT (Eterno and Silverman 2012), there is statistical evidence that the adoption of COMPSTAT by other US police forces was associated with a 5–15 per cent decline of crime (Roeder *et al.* 2015: 10). Whilst there is recent evidence that serious crimes not recorded effectively by either police or crime survey statistics—notably domestic violence and cybercrime—have increased not fallen (Walby *et al.* 2016; ONS 2016: s. 11), innovative policing models have contributed to the decline in the conventional crime figures. Nonetheless, the substantial decline in traditionally recorded crime is largely attributable to other factors than policing, and much remains to be explored (Reiner 2016: 165–85).

PLURALIZATION

The last three decades have seen significant challenges to the state-centric focus of much policing research by the growing recognition that liberal democracies in the twenty-first century are policed by a diverse array of organizations and individuals (Rowland and Coupe 2014; Crawford 2008; Walker 2008; Jones and Newburn 2006a). This 'pluralized' policing landscape includes a vibrant commercial security sector (Wakefield 2003), new forms of public sector policing auxiliaries such as local authority patrol forces and municipal wardens (Crawford 2008; Jones *et al.* 2009), the creation of new patrolling ranks—such as 'Police Community Support Officers' (PCSOs)—within public police organizations (O'Neill 2017), and the appearance of informal community self-policing forms such as vigilantism (Johnston 1996; Sharp and Wilson 2002). There has also been a growing emphasis on the active promotion of partnerships between these different policing bodies (Button 2007).[3]

Such has been the pace and extent of change in this area that two leading commentators have argued that 'future generations will look back on our era as a time when one system of policing ended and another took its place' (Bayley and Shearing 1996: 585). They argue that the period since the mid-1960s has seen the 'end of a monopoly' by the public police (though see Jones and Newburn 2002 and Reiner 2010 for a critique) and the emergence of what they call a 'multilateralized' system of security provision (Bayley and Shearing 2001). Through this term they seek to draw attention to the increasing complexity of policing, in terms not just of its provision, but also of its authorization or governance (Shearing 2006). Shearing and colleagues have thus argued for the use of the term 'governance of security' in preference to the state-centric term 'policing' (Johnston and Shearing 2002; Wood and Dupont 2006).

We here focus upon the growth of commercial security as the key development that has sparked discussions of pluralization.

PRIVATE SECURITY

In recent decades an increasingly complex division of labour has emerged in which private security personnel far outstrip police in numerical terms (Jones and Newburn 1998, 2006b). The proliferation of private security has involved the spread of new technologies, such as closed-circuit television (CCTV) (Lyon 2001), and the growing incursion of the private sector into forms of work, or areas of activity, hitherto associated with public policing such as the enforcement of parking and traffic regulations, the transport and guarding of prisoners, and most importantly—certainly for the way we view policing—the patrolling of public streets. Though some of these are relatively recent developments, a degree of caution has to be exercised when discussing the degree to which this is a departure from previous arrangements (Zedner 2006). In fact, there is good evidence to suggest that by the late 1950s/early 1960s the numbers employed in the private security industry already exceeded the number of police officers (Jones and Newburn 2002). Despite this, it is arguably only in the last two decades that the police service's dominant position in the public mind as the 'thin blue line' protecting the public from crime and lawlessness has come under sustained challenge.

The private security sector includes staffed services; security equipment; and investigation. Accurate estimates of the size of the private security sector are hard to find

[3] In addition, there has been increasing scholarly attention paid to the activities of a range of governmental regulatory and investigatory agencies undertaking important 'policing' tasks, although these activities are far from new (e.g. Hutter 1988; Brannigan and Pavlich 2007).

(Jones and Newburn 2006b). Research using industry data suggests the turnover in the sector had reached close to £2 billion by 2003 (Crawford *et al.* 2005) and other work (Keynote Report 2004) estimates that the figure may be closer to £5 billion. More recent reports suggest that whilst industry turnover has continued to increase, there has been significant market concentration with a reduction in the number of firms active in the market (Keynote Report 2014). The main industry association active in the sector estimates that by 2015 was worth over £6 billion to the UK economy and employed 356,000 people (British Security Industry Association 2015). The most visible manifestation of the growth of private security is the provision of staffed security services including guarding and asset protection services, body-guarding (or 'close protection'), the escort of cash-in-transit, door supervision for public houses and nightclubs, debt collection, and alarm monitoring/response services (Jones and Lister 2015). Market growth has been maintained in recent years, partly explained by a continued trend away from in-house security provision and towards contracting-in guarding services (White and Gill 2013; Keynote Report 2014). The most significant growth area in recent times has been in the proliferation of security hardware and, in particular, the expansion of the use of CCTV (McCahill and Norris 2002; Norris *et al.* 2004; though for a corrective to some dramatic claims about the numbers of cameras see Tarleton 2009). Many companies now also offer highly sophisticated integrated security systems including various forms of tracking and recognition technology. Satellite tracking has emerged relatively recently within the British criminal justice landscape, and provides the potential of continuous electronic monitoring of the position of GPS-tagged individuals wherever they are. There have been a number of local initiatives in which the policing applications of such technology are being explored (Nellis 2005; Hudson and Jones 2016).

Explanations for the expansion of private security vary. Some have argued that such growth results from increasing financial constraints on the police who, as a consequence, are unable to meet the demands placed upon them (Spitzer and Scull 1977). Despite generally increasing expenditure on public policing in recent decades, it is clear that a 'demand gap' exists (Morgan and Newburn 1997). Despite recent downward trends in crime, public perceptions of safety and security have not entirely followed suit and demands for increased policing provision continue to be regularly heard. Another factor is undoubtedly the growing privatization of urban space, notably the growth of 'mass private property' (Shearing and Stenning 1981; though see Jones and Newburn 1999) and the gradual emergence of gated residential communities—though these remain less in the UK than in the USA and Canada (Blakely and Snyder 1997; Atkinson and Flint 2004).

A third factor is the direct privatization of public functions by government. Although the private security sector was a very substantial—if generally undiscussed—presence much earlier, it was not until the 1980s that privatization emerged as a formal element of government policy and began to have an effect on the police. Initially this approach focused on general attempts to encourage efficiency and cost savings by applying private-sector management methods to the public sector, and imposing market disciplines on them (Rawlings 1991). Up until the second decade of the 2000s, privatization—directly or by contracting out— was only a minor factor in the changing face of policing in contemporary Britain. Nevertheless, some functions have been transferred entirely to the private sector, a number of which have been both symbolically significant and, for critics of privatization, the first practical step onto a slippery slope. For example, since the 1991 Criminal Justice Act came into force in England and Wales, the security arrangements for prisoners in transit have been the responsibility of private contractors, and magistrates' courts have been able to contract-in security officers to maintain order. Subsequent reforms have enabled the contracting out of the construction and management of custody centres, reception duties, and post-charge administration—including the taking of fingerprints, photographs, DNA samples, and PNC checks. Since 2010, police forces in England and Wales have faced unprecedented pressure on budgets due to the austerity policies followed by the Coalition government and its Conservative successor. In the face of significant cuts, a desire to protect 'frontline' policing increased the pressure to consider further contracting (Neyroud 2010). Police managers have become increasingly required 'to do more with less' and find ways of maintaining 'frontline' policing services whilst implementing major expenditure cuts.[4] This new context has shifted dramatically the perceptions of police managers of 'out-sourcing' functions to the private sector (Crawford 2013). In 2012 Lincolnshire Police signed a contract with the major private security company G4S, worth £200 million over 10 years, to outsource 18 police functions, including custody services, enquiry officers, force control room, the crime management bureau, and firearms licensing (White 2014). This agreement was closely followed by an announcement that two forces (West Midlands and Surrey) were collaborating in the preparation of multi-million pound contracts to outsource to private contractors a wide range of police functions and tasks. In the event, both forces abandoned these proposals following controversy over the failure of G4S to deliver on its security contract for the 2012 Olympics (Home Affairs Committee 2012). Nevertheless, given continued pressure on police budgets and a political context favourable to such experimentation as evidenced in both the health and education sectors, further developments in this direction seem inevitable.

Fundamental changes in the nature of crime threats faced by policing agencies during the late twentieth and early twenty-first centuries have played an important part in reshaping the balance between public and private policing, and no doubt contributed to the expansion of the latter. In particular, it has been long-established that public constabularies have played only a limited part in the response to fraud and serious financial crime (Levi 2008; Levi and Lord, this volume). The majority of policing activity relating to UK public sector fraud is undertaken by departmental investigators rather than the police, and most frauds against business are reported to the police via corporate actors (Levi 2010). Williams (2005) charted the rapid emergence of a 'forensic accounting and corporate investigation (FACI) industry' and argued that these forms are characterized by a clear division of labour that challenges notions of the blurring of the public–private divide in the governance of crime. More broadly, the rapid acceleration and spread of digital technologies has provided for a broad range of 'cybercrimes' including frauds, but also a range of other criminal acts including the

[4] Following the HMIC, 'frontline policing' here involves 'those who are in everyday contact with the public and who directly intervene to keep people safe & enforce the law' (HMIC 2011: 18).

sale and distribution of child pornography, the distribution of illegal drugs, organization of terrorist activities, and the spread of damaging 'hate speech' (Williams 2015). Cybercrime poses daunting challenges to the public police, both in terms of the practical difficulties in gathering evidence about the extent and nature of the problem, and in terms of their own resources and expertise. Scholars and practitioners in this area have for some time argued that effective regulatory responses require the development of partnerships that incorporate a range of public and private actors, including the police (Wall and Williams 2014; Levi *et al.* 2017). The inclusion of cybercrime and online fraud figures for the first time in the 2015 Crime Survey for England and Wales saw a doubling of the estimated crime rate to 11.6 million offences due to the inclusion of an estimated 7.6 million offences of online fraud and cybercrime (ONS 2016; Levi *et al.* 2017; Maguire and McVie, this volume). As Wall and Williams have argued, 'cybercrime is now the typical high-volume property crime in the UK, impacting upon more of the public than traditional acquisitive crimes such as burglary and car theft' (2013: 409).

INTERNATIONALIZATION

Much criminological literature on pluralization focuses on the policing activities undertaken within particular national boundaries, but an important aspect of growing complexity has related to developments 'above' the level of the nation state (Loader 2000). There has been an expansion of scholarly work on what is now generally referred to as 'transnational policing' (Sheptycki 2000a)—activities undertaken by policing bodies that draw their authority from polities that lie beyond individual nation states. Bowling and Sheptycki (2012) have undertaken a detailed analysis of the ways in which transnational policing has increasingly impacted on developments at the local level. They suggest that a new 'global policing architecture' has emerged, largely in response to the construction of global security threats by powerful actors, though it is clearly important not to over-state the dominance of 'neoliberal' transnational policing forms or underestimate the ability of local actors to resist and rework policing forms on the ground (Blaustein 2015).

EUROPEAN DEVELOPMENTS

Early European initiatives in transnational policing activity date back to the late nineteenth century (Deflem 2002). The International Criminal Police Commission was established in Vienna in 1923, succeeded after the Second World War by the International Criminal Police Office or Interpol (Walker 2000). Interpol expanded significantly and has participating bureaux in nearly two hundred countries. Despite this, and its widening functional remit (Cameron-Waller 2008; Ling 2010), Interpol is no longer the primary site of transnational policing activity. In particular European countries began making other arrangements because of Interpol's perceived shortcomings in relation to anti-terrorist policing, as well as concerns about the security of its communications network (House of Commons 1990). Very significant expansions in the area of European transnational police cooperation have taken place in the last three decades. Two key factors have been significant in stimulating such activity, notably the growing international reach of US law-enforcement activities (Nadelmann 1993) and, at least until recently, the expanding power of the European Union (Anderson *et al.* 1995). The internationalization of policing was given particular impetus by America's 'War on Drugs' and its use of the military as well as its Drug Enforcement Agency and the FBI in its interdiction efforts (Nadelmann 1993), though non-state actors have also played an important role (Sheptycki 2000b). As part of this effort a series of Mutual Legal Assistance Treaties were signed providing a legal basis for cross-border police activity, particularly covert activity (Manning 2000).

According to Bigo (2000) the 1970s were the watershed in the process of Europeanization of crime and policing issues. The establishment of TREVI in 1976 was followed by the initial Schengen Agreement in 1985, comprising five member states, and a more extensive Implementation Agreement in 1990 which established the computerized Schengen Information System and police cooperation in activities such as 'hot pursuit' (Walker 2000).

Following the signing of the Maastricht Treaty in 1992 Europol has been established as the Europe-wide police intelligence agency that would receive and supply information to the police forces of member states, though it did not become fully operational until 1999 (Walker 2003). There has been significant expansion of European policing activity since that point, not least as the repercussions of the attacks in the United States on 11 September 2001 were felt across the Atlantic (Andreas and Nadelmann 2006). The European security agenda which is driving such developments is now focused primarily on transnational organized crime (Dorn and Levi 2007) and the threat of international terrorism. In particular, the scale of the terrorist threat—exemplified by the mass casualty attacks on Paris in 2015 and Brussels in 2016—seems to have overcome many remaining national concerns about the growing power of Europol and related EU institutional arrangements. Moreover, the post-9/11 security agenda has vastly increased EU cooperation with the USA in relation to the exchange of intelligence and personal data and significantly enhanced US involvement in EU border policing and security planning (Den Boer and Monar 2002).

In the last five years Europol's mandate has been extended to allow it to investigate murder, kidnapping, hostage-taking, racism, corruption, unlawful drug-trafficking, people-smuggling, and motor vehicle crime (Lavranos 2003). European Union sharing of information and intelligence with the USA has occurred primarily through Europol, but also through the establishment of Eurojust—the EU inter-governmental institution responsible for judicial cooperation around crime (Dubois 2002). The European arrest warrant came into force in 15 member states in January 2004 enabling the transnational transfer of accused persons (Walker 2003). It is important, however, not to exaggerate the nature and reach of such policing initiatives (Andreas and Nadelmann 2006). Although current European developments fall some way short of the emergence of a transnational FBI, domestic reforms suggest that this is the direction in which European policing is heading even though they may take a couple of decades or more to reach that stage.

The international dimension of policing surfaced briefly in the debate prior to the Brexit Referendum in the UK in June 2016. The Director of Europol, Rob Wainwright claimed that a vote for Brexit would seriously compromise the UK security agencies' ability to counter terrorism and other cross-border crime (*Guardian* 22 June 2016). The referendum result has led to much speculation about what in practice Brexit would mean in terms of international police cooperation. It is clear that the UK's participation in the EU has resulted in increased cooperation in matters such as extradition and the exchange of police information. Peers (2016) has argued that the advent of Brexit will likely lead to a reduction in the overall levels of information exchange, although it is likely that (as with other non-EU countries) the UK could renegotiate some limited participation in the relevant EU laws. Similarly, non-EU countries such as Norway can participate in EU-wide policing agencies as associates, although this means a more limited involvement than is open to full EU member states.

All this comes at a time when the need for closer police cooperation is arguably more vital than ever. The challenge of combatting transnational crime has not diminished and in recent years the major refugee crisis that has emerged worldwide has further exacerbated the already daunting problems facing international policing. A combination of wars, ecological disasters, and global economic instability has led to mass population movement, and a major migration and refugee crisis in Europe, as well as in other parts of the world. One consequence of this has been a shift of policing resources to enforcement of border control, both at physical crossing points and in terms of everyday investigation and enforcement relating to illegal immigration (see Bosworth, this volume). Loftus (2013, 2015a, 2015b) has demonstrated how contemporary border policing provides an exemplar of the pluralization discussed early, in that it involves a range of different state agencies, private actors, and commercial bodies. It also raises a number of key issues for policing, such as the risks posed by vigorous enforcement to the human rights of migrants, the involvement of organized criminal networks in people smuggling operations, and the challenge of accountability within these complex networks of agencies engaged in border control.

CONCLUSION: FUTURES OF POLICING

The nineteenth-century architects of the British police constructed a distinctive image—that of a totemic national symbol of unity and order—partly to counter the widespread social and political opposition to the establishment of a specialized police institution (Reiner 2010; Emsley 2008, 2009; Rawlings 2008). This image looks increasingly anomalous in a world transformed by fundamental social, political, and cultural shifts. In particular, the raft of changes associated with neoliberalism have reconfigured the economic and social framework, globalizing production and consumption and increasing economic inequality, both within and between countries. Within the UK, levels of inequality have increased over recent years, exacerbated by government austerity policies. This has further confirmed the social and economic exclusion of a substantial and growing 'underclass' (Taylor 1999; Young 1999; Reiner 2007). Certainly with the continued dominance of free-market economic policies there is little prospect of the incorporation of such groups into the general social order. At the same time, a combination of economic instability, violent conflict, and environmental disasters in various parts of the world have led to unprecedented levels of migration, and a humanitarian crisis of historic proportions. Whilst the sustained 'crime drop' (see Maguire and McVie, this volume) perhaps took a good deal of the sting out of political debates on crime and punishment, public fears and insecurities have increasingly focused upon economic uncertainty on the one hand, and the threat of mass casualty terror attacks in Europe on the other. Both of these have become increasingly bound up in the public imagination with wider concerns about mass immigration, a fact that populist politicians on the right have been quick to exploit.

In this context, the British conception of the police as a body with an omnibus mandate, symbolizing order and harmony, becomes increasingly anachronistic but also more vital to many as the sole remaining national symbol (Loader and Mulcahy 2003). The increasingly global nature of many crime and security issues facing the British police will continue to drive them towards the international pattern of specialist national units for cybercrime, serious and organized crime, terrorism, public order, large-scale fraud, and other national or international problems. At the same time, the June 2016 vote for 'Brexit' has raised serious questions about the extent and nature of future UK participation in European-wide police cooperation. On the other hand, local police providing services to particular communities will remain, although the role that public policing plays within this has been much truncated by the impact of the austerity policies of the past six years. It seems likely that the major shifts towards out-sourcing in such forces as Lincolnshire will become the norm across England and Wales in future years. The distinctions between 'service'-style police organizations in stable suburban areas, and 'watchman' bodies with the rump duties of the present police, keeping the lid on underclass crime in symbolic locations, will almost certainly become more marked.

For the better-off, provision of security will be increasingly privatized, either in residential areas or in the 'mass private property' sector where more and more middle-class leisure and work takes place (Shearing and Stenning 1983; South 1988; Johnston 1992, 2000; Jones and Newburn 1998; Button 2007). The rapid development of new digital technologies, robotics, satellite-tracking, other forms of electronic surveillance drones, and ever more sophisticated crime prevention technologies, have huge implications for the future shape of policing. In particular, it is likely that specialized 'human' forms of policing will play a reduced role in the wider range of impersonal or automated control processes built into the environment, technological control, and surveillance devices, and the self-policing activities of ordinary citizens. Indeed, such developments play a substantial part in the shifting pattern of crime and the reduction of conventionally measured offences. *The* police will thus be supplemented and in some cases supplanted by a pluralized assortment of bodies with policing functions, and a more diffuse array of policing processes. Whether this constitutes a fundamental qualitative transformation to a completely new mode of policing can be debated (Bayley and Shearing 1996; Jones and Newburn 2002; Johnston and Shearing 2002; Reiner 2010: pt I). But there is little doubt that the profound changes in social structure, culture, crime, and order in an age of increasing global interdependence and insecurity will have momentous implications for the policing that seeks to regulate them.

The time of writing (mid-2016) is especially problematic for crystal-ball gazing. The fundamental social and political-economic transformations associated with neoliberal hegemony have become ever more evident, problematic, and challenged from different angles, as shown in the UK's EU referendum, and in the 2016 US Presidential campaign. To return to the starting point, the police, the repository of state-authorized legitimate force, constitute a social litmus paper on which the deepest troubles and conflicts are registered most vividly. Whatever the outcomes, the current increasingly fractious political, economic, and cultural tensions will impact on all the policing issues discussed above.

SELECTED FURTHER READING

The most comprehensive coverage of policing issues is to be found in the fourth edition of Reiner's, *The Politics of the Police* (2010), in Newburn's *Handbook of Policing* (2008), and its accompanying reader, *Policing: Key Readings* (2005). More particular overviews of developments in UK policing include: Ellison and Brogden's *Policing in the Age of Austerity* (2013); Donnelly and Scott's *Policing Scotland* (2010); Donnelly's *The Scottish Police Officer* (2013); Mulcahy's *Policing Northern Ireland* (2005); and Rae and Masefield's *Policing in Northern Ireland: Delivering the new beginning?* (2014).

REFERENCES

ALLEN, R. J. (1976), 'The police and substantive rulemaking: reconciling principle and expediency', *University of Pennsylvania Law Review*, 125(1): 62–118.

ANDERSON, M., DEN BOER, M., CULLEN, P., WILLMORE, W., RAAB, C., and WALKER, N. (1995), *Policing the European Union*, Oxford: Oxford University Press.

ANDREAS, P. AND NADELMANN, E. (2006), *Policing the Globe*, New York: Oxford University Press.

ARIEL, B., FARRAR, W. A., and SUTHERLAND, A. (2015), 'The effect of police body-worn cameras on use of force and citizens' complaints against the police: A randomized controlled trial', *Journal of Quantitative Criminology*, 31, 509, doi: 10.1007/s10940-014-9236-3.

ATKINSON, R. AND FLINT, J. (2004), 'Fortress UK? Gated communities, the spatial revolt of the elites and time–space trajectories of segregation', *Housing Studies*, 19(6): 875–92.

BANTON, M. (1964), *The Policeman in the Community*, London: Tavistock.

BAYLEY, D. (1994), *Police For The Future*, New York: Oxford University Press.

BAYLEY, D. and SHEARING, C. (1996), 'The Future of Policing', *Law and Society Review*, 30(3): 586–606.

BAYLEY, D. and SHEARING, C. (2001), *The Worldwide Restructuring of the Police*, Washington, DC: National Institute of Justice.

BIGO, D. (2000), 'Liaison Officers in Europe: New Officers in the European Security Field', in J. W. E. Sheptycki, *Issues in Transnational Policing*, London: Routledge.

BITTNER, E. (1974), 'Florence Nightingale in Pursuit of Willie Sutton: A Theory of the Police', in H. Jacob (ed.), *The Potential for Reform of Criminal Justice*, Beverly Hills, CA: Sage.

BITTNER, E. (1970), *The Functions of the Police in Modern Society*, Chevy Chase, Md.: National Institute of Mental Health.

BLAKELY, E. J. and SNYDER, M. G. (1997), *Fortress America: Gated Communities in the United States*, Washington, DC: Brookings Institution.

BLAUSTEIN, J. (2015), *Speaking Truths to Power: Policy Ethnography and Police Reform in Bosnia and Herzegovina*, Oxford: Oxford University Press.

BOWLING, B. and SHEPTYCKI, J. (2012), *Global Policing*, London: Sage.

BOWLING, B. (1999), *Violent Racism*, Oxford: Oxford University Press.

BOWLING, B. and PHILLIPS, C. (2002), *Racism, Crime and Justice*, Harlow: Longman.

BOWLING, B. and PHILLIPS, C. (2007), 'Disproportionate and discriminatory: Reviewing the evidence on police stop and search', *Modern Law Review*, 70(6): 936–61.

BRAGA, A. A. and WEISBURD, D. (2010), *Policing Problem Places: Crime Hotspots and Effective Prevention*, Oxford: Oxford University Press.

BRAGA, A. A., WEISBURD, D., WARING, E. J., MAZEROLLE, L., SPELMAN, W., and GAJEWSKI, F. (1999), 'Problem-oriented policing in violent crime/places: A randomized controlled experiment', *Criminology*, 37(3): 541–80.

BRANNIGAN, A. and PAVLICH, G. (2007) (eds), *Governance and Regulation in Social Life: Essays in Honour of W. G. Carson*, New York: Routledge-Cavendish.

BRITISH SECURITY INDUSTRY ASSOCIATION (2015), *Securing the Nation's Future: British Security Industry Association Manifesto: General Election 2015*, London: BSIA.

BRODEUR, J. -P. (2007), 'High and low policing in post-9/11 times', *Policing*, 1(1): 25–37.

BRODEUR, J. -P. (2010), *The Policing Web*, Oxford: Oxford University Press.

BROGDEN, M. (1982), *The Police: Autonomy and Consent*, London: Academic Press.

BROGDEN, M. (1999), 'Community Policing As Cherry Pie', in R. Mawby (ed.), *Policing Across the World*, London: UCL Press.

BROWN, D. (1997), *PACE Ten Years On: A Review of the Research*, Home Office Research Study 155, London: HMSO.

BROWN, J. and HEIDENSOHN, F. (2000), *Gender and Policing: Comparative Perspectives*, London: Macmillan.

BUCKE, T., STREET, R., and BROWN, D. (2000), *The Right of Silence: The Impact of the CJPO 1994*, Home Office Research Study 199, London: HMSO.

BULLOCK, K. and TILLEY, N. (eds) (2003), *Crime Reduction and Problem-Oriented Policing*, Cullompton: Willan.

BUTTON, M. (2007), *Security Officers and Policing*, Aldershot: Avebury.

CAMERON-WALLER, S. (2008), 'Interpol: a global service provider', in S. D. Brown, *Combating International Crime: The Longer Arm of the Law*, London: Routledge Cavendish.

CAPE, E. and YOUNG, R. (eds) (2008), *Regulating Policing: The Police and Criminal Evidence Act 1984—Past, Present and Future*, Oxford: Hart.

CHAN, J. (1997), *Changing Police Culture*, Cambridge: Cambridge University Press.

CHOONGH, S. (1997), *Policing as Social Discipline*, Oxford: Oxford University Press.

CLARKE, R. and HOUGH, M. (eds) (1984), *Crime and Police Effectiveness*, London: Home Office Research Unit.

COCKCROFT, T. (2012), *Police Culture: Themes and Concepts*, London: Routledge.

CRAWFORD, A. (2008), 'The Pattern of Policing in the UK: Policing Beyond the Police', in T. Newburn, *Handbook of Policing*, 2nd edn, Cullompton: Willan.

CRAWFORD, A. (2013), 'The police, policing and the future of the "extended police family" ', in J. Brown (ed.), *The Future of Policing*, London: Routledge.

CRAWFORD, A., LISTER, S., BLACKBURN, S., and BURNETT, J. (2005), *Plural Policing: The Mixed Economy of Visible Patrols in England and Wales*, Bristol: Policy.

DEFLEM, M. (2002), *Policing World Society: Historical Foundations of International Police Co-operation*, Oxford: Clarendon Press.

DEN BOER, M. and MONAR, J. (2002), '11 September and the Challenge of Global Terrorism to the EU as a Security Actor', *Journal of Common Market Studies*, 40(1): 11–28.

DIXON, D. (1997), *Law in Policing*, Oxford: Oxford University Press.

DORN, N. and LEVI, M. (2007), 'European Private Security, Corporate Investigation and Military Services: Collective Security, Market Regulation and Structuring the Public Sphere', *Policing and Society*, 17(3): 213–38.

DUBOIS, D. (2002), 'The attacks of 11 September: EU-US cooperation against terrorism in the field of justice and home affairs', *European Foreign Affairs Review*, 7(3): 317–35.

ECK, J. (2006), 'Science, values and problem-oriented policing: why problem-oriented policing?', in D. Weisburd and A. A. Braga (eds), *Police Innovation: Contrasting Perspectives*, Cambridge: Cambridge University Press.

ECK, J. and SPELMAN, W. (1987), 'Who ya gonna call? The police as problem-busters', *Crime and Delinquency*, 33(1): 31–52.

EMSLEY, C. (2008), 'The Birth and Development of the Police', in T. Newburn (ed.), *Handbook of Policing*, Cullompton: Willan.

EMSLEY, C. (2009), *The Great British Bobby*, London: Quercus.

ERICSON, R. and HAGGERTY, K. (1997), *Policing Risk Society*, Oxford: Oxford University Press.

ETERNO, J. and SILVERMAN, E. (2012), *The Crime Numbers Game: Management by Manipulation*, Boca Raton, FL: CRC.

FARRELL, G. and PEASE, K. (eds) (2001), *Repeat Victimization: Crime Prevention Studies Series 12*, Monsey, NY: Criminal Justice Press.

FASSIN, D. (2013), *Enforcing Order*, Cambridge: Polity.

FEKETE, L. (2011), 'Accelerated removals: the human costs of EU deportation policies', *Race & Class*, 52(4): 89–97.

FLANAGAN, A. (2016), *Review of Governance in Policing*, Edinburgh: SPA.

FLANAGAN, R. (2008), *The Review of Policing: Final Report*, London: HMSO.

FOSTER, J., NEWBURN, T., and SOUHAMI, A. (2005), *Assessing the Impact of the Stephen Lawrence Enquiry*, London: Home Office.

FYFE, N. (2014), 'A Different and Divergent Trajectory? Reforming the structure, governance and narrative of policing in Scotland', in J. Brown (ed.), *The Future of Policing*, London: Routledge.

GILL, C., WEISBURD, D., TELEP, C.W., VITTER, Z., and BENNETT, T. (2014), 'Community-oriented policing to reduce crime, disorder and fear and increase satisfaction and legitimacy among citizens: a systematic review', *Journal of Experimental Criminology*, 10(4): 399–428.

Goldsmith, A. and Lewis, C. (2000), *Civilian Oversight of Policing*, Oxford: Hart.

Goldstein, H. (1990), *Problem-Oriented Policing*, New York: McGraw Hill.

Goldstein, J. (1960), 'Police Discretion Not To Invoke the Criminal Process: Low Visibility Decisions in the Administration of Justice', *Yale Law Journal*, 69(4): 543–94.

Golub, A., Johnson, B. D., and Taylor, A. (2003), 'Quality of life policing: Do offenders get the message?', *Policing*, 26(4): 690–707.

Greene, J. (2000), 'Community Policing in America', in J. Horney (ed.), *Criminal Justice 2000 Vol. 3: Policies, Processes and Decisions of the Criminal Justice System*, Washington, DC: National Institute of Justice.

Grimshaw, R. and Jefferson, T. (1987), *Interpreting Policework*, London: Unwin.

Hain, P. (ed.) (1979), *Policing the Police*, London: Calder.

Hall, S., Critcher, C., Jefferson, T., Clarke, J., and Roberts, B. (1978), *Policing the Crisis*, London: Macmillan.

Harcourt, B. (2001), *Illusion of Order: The False Promise of Broken Windows Policing*, Cambridge, MA: Harvard University Press.

Heidensohn, F. (1992), *Women in Control? The Role of Women in Law Enforcement*, Oxford: Oxford University Press.

Heidensohn, F. (2008), 'Gender and Policing', in T. Newburn (ed.), *Handbook of Policing*, Cullompton: Willan.

Henry, A. and Smith, D. J. (eds) (2007), *Transformations of Policing*, Aldershot: Ashgate.

Herbert, N. (2011), 'A new era in policing', speech to the Institute for Government, 21 November, available at: http://www.homeoffice.gov.uk/media-centre/speeches/a-new-era-for-policing?version=1, accessed 8 January 2017.

Herbert, S. (2006) *Citizens, Cops and Power: Recognizing the Limits of Community*, Chicago: Chicago University Press.

HMIC (2005), *Closing the Gap*, London: Her Majesty's Inspectorate of Constabulary.

HMIC (2013), *Stop and Search Powers: Are the police using them effectively and fairly?*, London: Her Majesty's Inspectorate of Constabulary.

Hohl, K. and Stanko, E. A. (2015), 'Complaints of rape and the criminal justice system: Fresh evidence on the attrition problem in England and Wales', *European Journal of Criminology*, 12(3): 324–41.

Holdaway, S. (2009), *Black Police Associations*, Oxford: Oxford University Press.

Home Affairs Committee (2012), *Olympics security*, Seventh Report of Session 2012–13, Volume I, London: HMSO.

Home Affairs Committee (2013), *Independent Police Complaints Commission*, London: HMSO.

Home Affairs Committee (2014), *Police and Crime Commissioners*, London: HMSO.

Home Office (2010), *Policing in the 21st Century: Reconnecting police and the People*, London: Home Office.

Horvath, M. and Brown, J. (2010) (eds), *Rape: Challenging Contemporary Thinking*, London: Routledge.

House of Commons (1990), *Practical Police Cooperation in the European Community*, Home Affairs Committee (7th Report), Session 1989–90, London: HMSO.

Hoyle, C. (1998), *Negotiating Domestic Violence: Police, Criminal Justice and Victims*, Oxford: Oxford University Press.

Hudson, K. and Jones, T. (2016), 'Satellite tracking of offenders and integrated offender management: A Local Case Study', *Howard Journal of Crime and Justice*, 55(1–2): 188–206.

Hutter, B. (1988), *The Reasonable Arm of the Law? Law Enforcement Procedures of Environmental Health Officers*, Oxford: Oxford University Press.

Independent Commission on Policing for Northern Ireland (1999), *Final Report*, Belfast: HMSO.

James, A. (2013), *Examining intelligence-led policing: developments in research, policy and practice*, Basingstoke: Macmillan.

James, A. (2014), 'Forward to the past: reinventing intelligence-led policing in Britain', *Police Practice and Research*, 15(1): 75–88.

Johnston, L. (1992), *The Rebirth of Private Policing*, London: Routledge.

Johnston, L. (2000), *Policing Britain*, London: Longman.

Johnston, L. and Shearing, C. (2002), *Governing Security*, London: Routledge.

Jones, M. (2015), 'The complexities of researching sexuality in Policing Contexts', in M. Brunger, S. Tong, and D. Martin (eds), *Introduction to Policing Research: Taking Lessons from Practice*, Abingdon: Routledge.

Jones, T. (2008), 'The Accountability of Policing', in T. Newburn (ed.), *Handbook of Policing*, 2nd edn, Cullompton: Willan.

Jones, T. and Lister, S. (2015), 'The Policing of Public Space: Recent developments in plural policing in England & Wales', *European Journal of Policing Studies*, 2(3): 245–66.

Jones, T. and Newburn, T. (1998), *Private Security and Public Policing*, Oxford: Oxford University Press.

Jones, T. and Newburn, T. (1999), 'Urban Change and Policing: Mass Private Property Reconsidered', *European Journal of Criminal Policy and Research*, 7(2): 225–44.

Jones, T. and Newburn, T. (2002), 'The Transformation of Policing? Understanding Current Trends in Policing Systems', *British Journal of Criminology*, 42(1): 129–46.

Jones, T. and Newburn, T. (2006a) *Plural Policing*, London: Routledge.

Jones, T. and Newburn, T. (2006b), 'Understanding plural policing', in T. Jones and T. Newburn (eds), *Plural Policing: A Comparative Perspective*, London: Routledge.

JONES, T. and NEWBURN, T. (2007), *Policy Transfer and Criminal Justice*, Buckingham: Open University Press.

JONES, T. , NEWBURN, T., and SMITH, D. (2012), 'Democracy and police and crime commissioners', in T. Newburn, and J. Peay (eds), *Policing: Politics, culture and control*, Oxford: Hart.

JONES, T., VAN STEDEN, R., and BOUTELLIER, H. (2009), 'Pluralisation of policing in England & Wales and the Netherlands: exploring similarity and difference', *Policing and Society*, 19(3): 282–99.

KATZ, C. M., WEBB, V. J. and SCHAEFER, D. R. (2001), 'An Assessment of the Impact of Quality of Life Policing on Crime and Disorder', *Justice Quarterly*, 18(4): 825–76.

KELLING, G. and WILSON, J. Q. (1982), 'Broken Windows: The Police and Neighborhood Safety', *The Atlantic Monthly*, 249(3): 29–38.

KELLING, G. *et al.* (1974), *The Kansas City Preventive Patrol Experiment*, Washington, DC: Police Foundation.

KEYNOTE REPORT (2004), *The Security Industry: Industry Report*, September 2004 (see also https://www.keynote.co.uk).

KEYNOTE REPORT (2014), *Private Security Activities*, available at: https://www.keynote.co.uk//market-digest/security-defence/private-security-activities, accessed 7 August 2016.

LAVRANOS, N. (2003), 'Europol and the fight against terrorism', *European Foreign Affairs Review*, 8(2): 259–75.

LEVI, M. (2008) 'Policing fraud and organized crime', in T. Newburn (ed), *Handbook of Policing*, 2nd edn, Cullompton: Willan.

LEVI, M. (2010), 'Public and private policing of financial crimes: the struggle for coordination', *Journal of Criminal Justice and Security*, 12(4): 343–54.

LEVI, M., DOIG, A., GUNDUR, R., WALL, D., and WILLIAMS, M. (2017), 'Cyberfraud and the implications for effective risk-based responses: Themes from UK research', *Crime, Law and Social Change*, doi: 10.1007/s10611-016-9648-0.

LING, C. W. (2010), 'Mapping Interpol's Evolution: Functional Expansion and the Move to Legalization', *Policing*, 4(1): 28–37.

LISTER, S. (2014), 'Scrutinising the role of the Police and Crime Panel in the new era of police governance in England and Wales', *Safer Communities*, 14(1): 22–31.

LISTER, S. and ROWE, M. (2015), 'Electing Police and Crime Commissioners in England and Wales: prospecting for the democratization of policing', *Policing and Society*, 25(4): 358–77.

LOADER, I. (2000), 'Plural policing and democratic governance', *Social and Legal Studies*, 9(3): 323–45.

LOADER, I. and MUIR, R. (2016), *Embracing Police and Crime Commissioners: Lessons from the Past, Directions for the Future*, London: Police Foundation.

LOADER, I. and MULCAHY, A. (2003), *Policing and the Condition of England*, Oxford: Oxford University Press.

LOFTUS, B. (2008), 'Dominant Culture Interrupted: Recognition, Resentment and the Politics of Change in an English Police Force', *British Journal of Criminology*, 48(6): 778–97.

LOFTUS, B. (2009), *Police Culture in a Changing World*, Oxford: Oxford University Press.

LOFTUS, B. (2010), 'Police Occupational Culture: Classic Themes, Altered Times', *Policing and Society*, 20(1): 1–22.

LOFTUS, B. (2015a), 'Policing assemblages and the vulnerable border', *European Journal of Policing Studies*, 3(2): 238–54.

LOFTUS, B. (2015b), 'Border regimes and the sociology of policing', *Policing and Society*, 25(1): 115–25.

LUSTGARTEN, L. (1986), *The Governance of the Police*, London: Sweet & Maxwell.

LYON, D. (2001), *Surveillance Society*, Maidenhead: Open University Press.

MCARDLE, A. and ERZEN, T. (eds) (2001), *Zero Tolerance: Quality of Life and the New Police Brutality in New York City*, New York: NYU Press.

MCBARNET, D. (1978), 'The Police and the State', in G. Littlejohn, B. Smart, J. Wakeford, and N. Yuval-Davis (eds), *Power and the State*, London: Croom Helm.

MCBARNET, D. (1979), 'Arrest: The Legal Context of Policing', in S. Holdaway (ed.), *The British Police*, London: Edward Arnold.

MCCAHILL, M. and NORRIS, C. (2002), 'CCTV in Britain', Urban Eye Working Paper No.3, available at: http://www.urbaneye.net/results/ue_wp3.pdf, accessed 8 January 2017.

MCCONVILLE, M., SANDERS, A., and LENG, R. (1991), *The Case for the Prosecution: Police Suspects and the Construction of Criminality*, London: Routledge.

MCLAUGHLIN, E. (2007), *The New Policing*, London: Sage.

MAGUIRE, M. (2008), 'Criminal Investigation and Crime Control', in T. Newburn (ed.), *Handbook of Policing*, Cullompton: Willan.

MANNING, P. K. (2000), 'Policing new social spaces', in J. Sheptycki, (ed.), *Issues in Transnational Policing*, London: Routledge.

MARENIN, O. (1983), 'Parking Tickets and Class Repression: The Concept of Policing in Critical Theories of Criminal Justice', *Contemporary Crises*, 6(2): 241–66.

MINISTRY of JUSTICE (2015), *Statistics on Race and the Criminal Justice System 2014*, London: Ministry of Justice.

MOORE, M. (1992), 'Problem-Solving and Community Policing', in M. Tonry and N. Morris (eds), *Modern Policing*, Chicago: Chicago University Press.

MORGAN, R. and NEWBURN, T. (1997), *The Future of Policing*, Oxford: Oxford University Press.

MUTSAERS, P. (2014), 'An ethnographic study of the policing of internal borders in the Netherlands', *British Journal of Criminology*, 54(5): 831–48.

NADELMANN, E. (1993), *Cops Across Borders: The internationalization of U.S. criminal law enforcement*, Pennsylvania: Pennsylvania State University Press.

NELLIS, M. (2005), 'Out of this World: The Advent of Satellite Tracking of Offenders in England & Wales', *Howard Journal of Criminal Justice*, 44(2): 125–50.

NEWBURN, T. (2012), 'Police and crime commissioners: The Americanization of policing or a very British reform?', *International Journal of Law, Crime and Justice*, 40(1): 31–46.

NEWBURN, T. and JONES, T. (2007), 'Symbolising crime control: reflections on zero tolerance', *Theoretical Criminology*, 11(2): 221–43.

NEWBURN, T. and REINER, R. (2012), 'Policing and the Police', in M. Maguire, R. Reiner, and R. Morgan (eds), *The Oxford Handbook of Criminology*, 5th edn, Oxford: Oxford University Press.

NEYROUD, P. (2010), 'Protecting the frontline: a recessionary dilemma, *Policing*, 44(1): 1–3.

NORRIS, C., MCCAHILL, M., and WOOD, D. (2004), 'The growth of CCTV: a global perspective on the international diffusion of video surveillance in publicly accessible space', *Surveillance and Society*, 2(2/3): 111–35.

ONS (2015), *Police powers and procedures England and Wales year ending 31 March 2015*, London: Office for National Statistics.

ONS (2016), *Crime in England and Wales, Year ending December 2015*, London: Office for National Statistics.

O'NEILL, M. (2017), 'Police Community Support Officers in England: A dramaturgical analysis', *Policing and Society*, 27(1): 21–39.

O'NEILL, M., MARKS, M., and SINGH, A-M. (eds) (2007), *Police Occupational Cultures*, Oxford: JAI.

O'NEILL, M. and MCCARTHY (2014), '(Re)Negotiating Police Culture through Partnership Working: Trust, Compromise and the "new" Pragmatism', *Criminology and Criminal Justice*, 14(2): 143–59.

PATE, A. M. and SKOGAN, W. G. (1985), *Coordinated community policing: The Newark experience. Technical report*, Washington, DC: Police Foundation.

PEERS, S. (2016), *How would Brexit impact the UK's involvement in EU policing and criminal law?*, EU Referendum Brief 5, available at: http://eulawanalysis.blogspot.co.uk/2016/06/eu-referendum-brief-5-how-would-brexit.html, accessed on 6 August 2016.

PERRY, W. L., MCINNES, B., PRICE, C. C., SMITH, S. C. and HOLLYWOOD, J. S. (2013), *Predictive Policing: The Role of Crime Forecasting in Law Enforcement Operations*, Santa Monica, CA: Rand.

QUINTON, P., BLAND, N., and MILLER, J. (2000), 'Police Stops, Decision-Making and Practice', *Police Research Paper 130*, London: Home Office.

RANSLEY, J., ANDERSON, J., and PRENZLER, T. (2007), 'Civil litigation against police in Australia: Exploring its extent, nature and implications for accountability', *Australian and New Zealand Journal of Criminology*, 40(2): 143–60.

READ, T. and TILLEY, N. (2000), *Not Rocket Science: Problem-solving and Crime Reduction*, Crime Reduction Series Paper No. 6, London: Home Office.

REINER, R. (1991), *Chief Constables*, Oxford: Oxford University Press.

REINER, R. (1993), 'Race, Crime and Justice: Models of Interpretation', in L. Gelsthorpe and W. McWilliams (eds), *Minority Ethnic Groups and the Criminal Justice System*, Cambridge: Institute of Criminology.

REINER, R. (2007), *Law and Order: An Honest Citizen's Guide to Crime and Control*, Cambridge: Polity.

REINER, R. (2010), *The Politics of the Police*, 4th edn, Oxford: Oxford University Press.

REINER, R. (2015), 'Three seminal founders of the study of policing: Michael Banton, Jerome Skolnick and Egon Bittner', *Policing and Society*, 25(3): 308–27.

REINER, R. (2016), *Crime*, Cambridge: Polity.

RIOTS, COMMUNITIES AND VICTIMS PANEL (2012), *After the Riots: Final Report*, London: Riots, Communities and Victims Panel.

ROBINSON, C. D. and SCAGLION, R. (1987), 'The Origin and Evolution of the Police Function in Society', *Law and Society Review*, 21(1): 109–53.

ROEDER, O., EISEN, L-B., and BOWLING, J. (2015), *What Caused the Crime Decline?*, New York: Brennan Center.

ROSENFELD, R. (2015), 'Ferguson and police use of deadly force', *Missouri Law Review*, 80: 1077–97.

ROWE, M. (ed.) (2007), *Policing Beyond Macpherson*, Cullompton: Willan.

ROWLAND, R. and COUPE, T. (2014), 'Patrol officers and public reassurance: A comparative evaluation of police officers, PCSOs, ACSOs and private security guards', *Policing and Society*, 24(3): 265–84.

ROYAL COMMISSION ON CRIMINAL JUSTICE (1993), *Report*, Cm. 2263, London: HMSO.

SAVAGE, S. (2007), *Police Reform*, Oxford: Oxford University Press.

SAVAGE, S. (2013), 'Thinking Independence', *British Journal of Criminology*, 53(1): 94–112.

SAVAGE, S., CHARMAN, S., and COPE, S. (2000), 'The policy-making context: who shapes policing policy?', in F. Leishman, B. Loveday, and S. Savage (eds), *Core Issues in Policing*, 2nd edn, Harlow: Longman.

SCOTT, M. (2000), *Problem-oriented Policing: Reflections on the First 20 Years*, Washington, DC: Department of Justice.

SCRATON, P. (1985), *The State of the Police*, London: Pluto.

SHEARING, C. (2006), 'Reflections on the Refusal to Acknowledge Private Governments', in J. Wood and B. Dupont (eds), *Democracy, Society and the Governance of Security*, Cambridge: Cambridge University Press.

SHEARING, C. and ERICSON, R. (1991), 'Culture As Figurative Action', *British Journal of Sociology*, 42(4): 481–506.

SHEARING, C. and STENNING, P. (1981), 'Modern Private Security: Its Growth and Implication', in M. Tonry and N. Morris (eds), *Crime and Justice, Volume 3*, Chicago: Chicago University Press.

SHEARING, C. and STENNING, P. (1983), 'Private Security: Implications for Social Control', *Social Problems*, 30(5): 493–506.

SHEPTYCKI, J. (ed.) (2000a), *Issues in Transnational Policing*, London: Routledge.

SHEPTYCKI, J. (2000b), 'Policing the virtual launderette: money laundering and global governance', in J. Sheptycki (ed.), *Issues in Transnational Policing*, London: Routledge.

SHERMAN, L. W. (2013), 'The rise of evidence-based policing: Targeting, testing, and tracking', *Crime and Justice*, 42(1): 377–451.

SHERMAN, L. W. and WEISBURD, D. (1995), 'General deterrent effects of police patrol in crime "hot spots": A randomized, controlled trial', *Justice Quarterly*, 12(4): 625–48.

SILVESTRI (2003), *Women in Charge: Policing, Gender and Leadership*, Cullompton: Willan.

SILVESTRI (2007) '"Doing" police leadership: enter the "new smart macho"', *Policing & Society*, 17(1): 38–58.

SKLANSKY, D. (2008), *Democracy and the Police*, Stanford: Stanford University Press.

SKOGAN, W. (2009), 'An overview of community policing: Origins, concepts and implementation', in T. Williamson (ed.), *The Handbook of Knowledge-Based Policing*, Chichester: Wiley.

SKOGAN, W. and HARTNETT, S. (1997), *Community Policing, Chicago Style*, New York: Oxford University Press.

SKOLNICK, J. (1966), *Justice Without Trial*, New York: Wiley.

SMITH, D., GRAY, J., and SMALL, S. (1983), *Police and People in London*, London: Policy Studies Institute.

SMITH, G. (2009a), 'Actions for damages against the police and the attitudes of claimants'. *Policing and Society*, 13(4): 413–22

SMITH, G. (2009b), 'Why Don't More People Complain Against the Police?', *European Journal of Criminology*, 6(3): 249–66.

SMITH, G. (2013), 'Oversight of the police and residual complaints dilemmas: independence, effectiveness and accountability deficits in the United Kingdom', *Police Practice and Research*, 14(2): 92–103.

SOUTH, N. (1988), *Policing For Profit*, London: Sage.

SPITZER, S. and SCULL, A. (1977), 'Social Control in Historical Perspective', in D. Greenberg (ed.), *Corrections and Punishment*, Beverly Hills, CA: Sage.

STINCHCOMBE, A. (1963), 'Institutions of Privacy in the Determination of Police Administrative Practice', *American Journal of Sociology*, 69(2): 150–60.

TARLETON, A. (2009), 'Factcheck: How many CCTV cameras?', *Significance*, 6(4): 191–2.

TAYLOR, I. (1999), *Crime in Context*, Cambridge: Polity.

TILLEY, N. (2003), 'Community Policing, Problem-Oriented Policing and Intelligence-Led Policing', in T. Newburn (ed.), *Handbook of Policing*, Cullompton: Willan.

TROJANOWICZ, R. and BUCQUEROUX, B. (1990), *Community Policing*, Cincinnati, Ohio: Anderson.

WADDINGTON, P. A. J. (1999a), *Policing Citizens*, London: UCL Press.

WADDINGTON, P. A. J. (1999b), 'Police (Canteen) Sub-culture: An Appreciation', *British Journal of Criminology*, 39(2): 287–309.

WADDINGTON, P. A. J., STENSON, K., and DON, D. (2004), 'In Proportion: Race and Police Stop and Search', *British Journal of Criminology*, 44(6): 889–914.

WADDINGTON, P. A. J., WILLIAMS, K., WRIGHT, P., and NEWBURN, T. (2017), *How People Judge Policing*, Oxford: Oxford University Press.

WAKEFIELD, A. (2003) *Selling Security: The Private Policing of Public Space*, Cullompton: Willan.

WALBY, S., TOWERS, J., and FRANCIS, B. (2016), 'Is Violent Crime Increasing or Decreasing? A New Methodology to Measure Repeat Attacks Making Visible the Significance of Gender and Domestic Relations', *British Journal of Criminology*, 56(6): 1203–34.

WALL, D. and WILLIAMS, M. (2013), 'Policing cybercrime: networked and social media technologies and the challenges for policing', *Policing and Society*, 23(4): 409–12.

WALKER, N. (2000), *Policing in a Changing Constitutional Order*, London: Sweet & Maxwell.

WALKER, N. (2008), 'The Pattern of Transnational Policing', in T. Newburn (ed.), *Handbook of Policing*, 2nd edn, Cullompton: Willan.

WEBER, L. and BOWLING, B. (2013), *Stop and Search: Police Power in a Global Context*, London: Routledge.

WEISBURD, D., MASTROFSKI, S. D., MCNALLY, A-M., GREENSPAN, R., and WILLIS, J. J. (2003), 'Reforming to preserve: COMPSTAT and strategic problem-solving in American Policing, *Criminology and Public Policy*, 2(3): 421–56.

WEISBURD, D. and ECK, J. E. (2004), 'What can the police do to reduce crime, disorder and fear?', *The Annals*, 593 (May): 42–65.

WEISBURD, D., TELEP, C., HINKLE, J., and ECK, J. (2010), 'Is problem-oriented policing effective in reducing crime and disorder?', *Criminology and Public Policy*, 9(1): 139–72.

WELSH, B. C., BRAGA, A. A., BRUINSMA, G. J. N. (eds) (2015), 'Re-imagining broken windows: from theory to policy', special issue of *The Journal of Research in Crime and Delinquency*, 52(4): 447–629.

WHITE, A. (2014), 'Post-Crisis Policing and Public-Private Partnerships: The Case of Lincolnshire Police and G4S', *British Journal of Criminology*, 54(6): 1002–22.

WHITE, A. (2014), *The Politics of Private Security: Regulation, Reform and Re-Legitimation*, Basingstoke: Palgrave Macmillan.

WHITE, A. and GILL, M. (2013), 'The Transformation of Policing: From Ratios to Rationalities', *British Journal of Criminology*, 53(1): 74–93.

WILLIAMS, C. A. (2014), *Police Control Systems in Britain, 1775-1975: From Parish constable to National Computer*, Manchester: Manchester University Press.

WILLIAMS, J. (2005), 'Governability Matters: The Private Policing of Economic Crime and the Challenge of Democractic Governance', *Policing and Society*, 15(2): 187–211.

WILLIAMS, M. (2015), 'Guardians upon high: an application of routine activities theory to online identity theft in Europe at the country and individual level, *British Journal of Criminology*, 56(1): 21–48.

WILSON, J. Q. (1968), *Varieties of Police Behaviour*, Cambridge, MA: Harvard University Press.

WILSON, D. and SERISIER, T. (2010), 'Video Activism and the Ambiguities of Counter-Surveillance', *Surveillance & Society*, 8(2): 166–80.

WOOD, J. and DUPONT, B. (eds) (2006), *Democracy, Society and the Governance of Security*, Cambridge: Cambridge University Press.

YOUNG, J. (1999), *The Exclusive Society*, London: Sage.

ZEDNER, L. (2006), 'Policing Before the Police', *British Journal of Criminology*, 46(1): 78–96.

ZIMRING, F. (2012), *The City That Became Safe: New York's Lessons For Urban Crime and its Control*, New York: Oxford University Press.

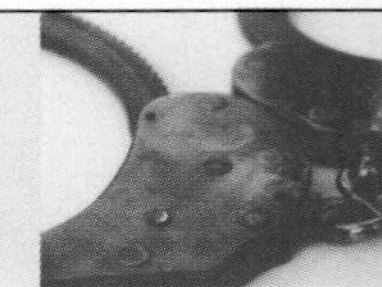

35

CRIME PREVENTION AND COMMUNITY SAFETY

Adam Crawford and Karen Evans

INTRODUCTION

Crime prevention and community safety as a field of scholarly interest and practical advances has expanded over recent years into a sub-discipline in its own right. It has its own theories, intellectual perspectives, policy debates, and moral entrepreneurs, as well as a host of practitioner and student texts, 'handbooks' (e.g. Tilley 2005; Farrington and Welsh 2012), journals, practitioner toolkits, guides, and websites resources.[1] It is not the purpose of this chapter to provide an overview of this rich tapestry, nor to offer some definitive compendium of 'what works' in crime prevention practice (see Sherman *et al.* 2002), but rather to assess the nature and shape of developments and shifts over time and to reflect upon the journey travelled thus far and possible future directions. The chapter draws as its focus developments in the UK, and where appropriate situates these in a broader international context.

We begin by tracing the historic emergence of the modern 'preventive turn' and its institutionalization. The following sections trace significant developments in crime prevention policy and practices from the 1980s to the current day. Our consideration of each substantive theme suggests three broad periods that structure the voyage taken. The first period, the 1980s to 1990s, marks the moment at which prevention gained national significance and the focus of concern was opened up to social and political considerations, providing considerable innovation and development. The second period from the mid-1990s to the late 2000s represents the point during which prevention was incorporated as a key strategy of governance. During these first two phases the parameters of crime prevention opened up to incorporate community safety, anti-social behaviour, and perceptions of insecurity fostered through inter-organizational partnerships. We then go on to argue that crime prevention has entered a third period represented as the austerity decade within which an intensification of social problems and an ideological shift away from the public provision of services has necessitated a

[1] See for instance: http://thecrimepreventionwebsite.com/ and https://www.police.uk/crime-prevention-advice/, accessed 9 January 2017.

further change in policy direction. This has seen a degree of retrenchment, refocusing, redrawing of boundaries, and reframing of inter-agency relations. Since we are currently embroiled in this particular moment our concluding remarks will be more tentative but point to the direction which we believe that practice and policy may follow into the future and on the significant part which crime prevention policy to date has played in sustaining this particular shift. In so doing, we consider the extent to which the 'preventive turn' has lived up to earlier expectations and review progress in particular fields of: situational crime prevention; community safety; social/developmental crime prevention; and the partnership approach. In relation to each, we review the journey taken and the emergent issues to which they give rise. We conclude with some thoughts on emerging fault-lines and possible future directions.

THE PREVENTIVE TURN

The history of modern crime prevention now stretches back for over 200 years and its founding principles are still those which, to a large extent, govern our preventive behaviours as individuals and as institutional actors today. It has become commonplace to understand the problem of crime as it was set out by the classical liberal philosophers in the eighteenth century. Their understanding of society rested on a view of humanity where *homo prudens*, or the rational man, prevailed. Society was characterized as driven by a multitude of rational actors who would make decisions on utilitarian principles, aiming to maximize any pleasure that might be gained by any particular life-choice and to minimize any pain which might also result (Garland 2000). The prevention of crime therefore took on two key, related elements. First, it was important to ensure that crime did not pay and that the consequences of committing crime far outweighed the advantages which accrued to the law-breaker. This necessitated the building of a state infrastructure of policing, courts, and prisons which would ensure that breaking the law did not go undetected and that convicted law-breakers would face a certain punishment. Secondly, each citizen was expected to adopt behaviours which would ensure that they would protect themselves from the pains associated with becoming a victim of crime—this involved a rational calculation on behalf of the individual as to how to best counter the threat of criminality. The state and the individual thereby worked together in a symbiotic and mutually beneficial relationship to create the conditions through which crime became both more risky and difficult to commit and the safety of society was thereby ensured. This relationship was further cemented with the creation of uniformed and state-funded police forces which became a blueprint for tackling crime in other countries across the globe (Zedner 2006).

It is only in the last 40 years or so that the philosophy and practices of crime prevention have come under any real scrutiny. Without any critical attention to the concept, crime prevention was absorbed into the work of the police. Under their direction it became a highly specialized and technical activity which was nevertheless considered as marginal to the real 'task' of policing; the detection, arrest, and prosecution of the criminal. As Weatheritt observed of the police: 'the crime prevention job remains an activity performed on the sidelines while the main action takes place elsewhere' (1986: 49). It is unsurprising that in these circumstances the subject ossified with research in the field limited to the development of more effective technological fixes. A growing consumer industry developed to supply crime prevention hardware to individual consumers and the state's role was limited to policies that encouraged individuals to adopt self-protection strategies. Little attention was paid to the social environment in which crime took place and crime prevention remained 'situational', focused on the protection of property via what became known as 'target hardening'—the (re)design and manipulation of the physical environment to reduce the opportunities in which crime might be committed.

Rising crime rates in the 1960s and 1970s forced a change in orientation towards crime and its prevention. A new-found pessimism upset and replaced the erstwhile 'rehabilitative ideal', most starkly evoked in Martinson's (1974) infamous phrase 'nothing works'. As faith in the traditional criminal justice establishment began to ebb and wane, practitioners and policy-makers looked elsewhere (Home Office 1977: 9–10). At this point the prevention of crime became a concern of the political classes which came under increasing pressure to intervene to reverse the upward trend. It was no longer sufficient to rely on the old, police-led methods. Instead, existing and aspiring politicians sought to present a social narrative through which they could explain the rise in crime and persuade the voting populace that they could put in place the social and political policies which could start to make a difference. Research into crime and its prevention took on a new significance as a consequence, adding social crime prevention policies concerned with measures aimed at tackling the root causes of crime to the crime prevention mix (Graham and Bennett 1995). The incorporation of crime prevention as a tool in the political repertoire has transformed the subject in many ways.

In reflecting on the 'path taken' and in assessing the impact and implications of the 'preventive turn' in crime control heralded by many scholars (O'Malley 1992; Crawford 1997, 1998; Gilling 1997; Hughes 1998, 2007a; Tilley 2009; Evans 2011), it is useful to consider the 'futures past' (Koselleck 2004): more precisely, the past possibilities and prospects, past conceptions, and expectations of the future. Over two decades ago, David Garland boldly stated that the 'preventive turn' in crime control policy (in the UK in particular) was intimately tied to a 'new mode of governing crime' which he characterized as 'a *responsibilisation strategy*' (1996: 452). He described it thus:

> This involves the central government seeking to act upon crime not in a direct fashion through state agencies (police, courts, prisons, social work, etc.) but instead by acting indirectly, seeking to activate action on the part of non-state agencies and organisations. This is the essence of the new crime prevention approach . . . Its key phrases are terms such as 'partnership', 'inter-agency cooperation', 'the multi-agency approach', 'activating communities', creating 'active citizens', 'help for self-help'.

Garland was no doubt correct in aligning the renewed focus on 'prevention' with the ambitions of a major restructuring of responsibilities for crime control and, as such, a re-articulation of relations between the state, market, and civil society. If prevention had become the new goal, the means to achieve it was to be through partnerships bringing diverse actors and agencies together in a common approach to pool expertise, information, capabilities, and resources. As Garland (2001: 126) subsequently elaborated, 'preventive partnerships' were to conjoin the goals of crime prevention with a de-differentiated and pluralist approach that sought to mobilize and harness non-state organizations, thus challenging a core assumption of penal modernism that crime control is 'a specialist task best concentrated within differentiated state institutions'. This was the essential message set out in the inter-departmental circular on 'crime prevention' 8/1984 emerging out of the inter-departmental working group on crime reduction established by Margaret Thatcher which declared that:

> since some of the factors affecting crime lie outside the control or direct influence of the police, crime prevention cannot be left to them alone. Every individual citizen and all those agencies whose policies and practices can influence the extent of crime should make their contribution. Preventing crime is a task for the whole community. (Home Office 1984)

The flurry of government-initiated activities that followed over the ensuing years—including the Five Towns Initiative and the Safer Cities Projects—led Bottoms (1990: 5) to conclude that: 'The 1980s, we can safely assert, has put crime prevention firmly on the map'. The influential Morgan Report (1991)—albeit at the time dismissed as ideologically inconvenient by the then Conservative government—advocated a 'partnership approach' to community safety. A *joint* statutory duty upon the police and local authorities to establish local partnership arrangements was later introduced by the new Labour government as a key element in its flagship Crime and Disorder Act 1998. By the turn of the millennium, the infrastructure to deliver on Garland's vision, of a 'de-differentiated' response that is not compartmentalized but affords a generalized, non-specialist activity built into the routines and consciousness of all citizens and organizations, had arrived.

This new approach recognized that the levers and causes of crime lie far from the traditional reach of the criminal justice system. It acknowledged that there is no single agency solution to crime, which is multi-faceted in both its causes and effects. Furthermore, it recognized the need for social responses to crime which reflect the nature of the phenomenon itself and its multiple aetiology; allowing for an holistic approach to crime, community safety, and associated issues which were to be 'problem-focused' rather than 'bureaucracy-premised'; and afforded the potential coordination and pooling of expertise, information, and resources. As we will describe, the local community safety partnerships which were to be spawned challenged many bureaucratic assumptions about professional expertise, specialization, and disciplinary boundaries.

SITUATIONAL CRIME PREVENTION

The prevailing view of crime prevention in the Britain—in England and Wales in particular—since the 1980s has been that it has been dominated by situational approaches at the expense of more socially oriented ones (King 1989; Hope 2009). Linked to theories of routine activities (Cohen and Felson 1979), rational choice

(Clarke and Cornish 1985), and opportunities (Felson and Clarke 1998), situational crime prevention (SCP) offers a variety of practical and pragmatic approaches to problem-solving (Clarke 1995) focused on the 'management, design or manipulation of the immediate physical environment' so as to reduce the opportunities for specific crimes (Hough *et al.* 1980: 1). As such, they challenged the conventional dispositional bias of much criminology which sought to explain the criminality of behaviour rather than the situational context (and opportunities) that surround or inform the act and fostered a remarkable growth in scholarly activity concerned with opportunity-reduction and SCP. Under Gloria Laycock's leadership, the Crime Prevention Unit in the Home Office and subsequently the Police Research Group published some 150 research reports, testing and developing diverse aspects of situational and environmental crime prevention (see Clarke 2012: 5).

What Garland (1996) referred to as 'the criminologies of everyday life' offered positive and up-beat—albeit often small-scale and targeted—forms of preventive adaptations in a response to the wider 'crisis of penal modernism'. It was also deemed to constitute a powerful vehicle for putting a Thatcherite ideological vision into practice (King 1989). There were close echoes here with O'Malley's (1992: 265) forceful portrayal of SCP as reflecting a neoliberal understanding of human behaviour, in which 'not only is the knowledge of the criminal disarticulated from a critique of society, but in turn, both may be disarticulated from the reaction to the offender'. For O'Malley (1992: 263), the triumph of situational, over social, crime prevention, in Anglophone countries signified 'the displacement of socialised risk management with privatised prudentialism'. Furthermore, for him this needed to be understood as being connected to, and an extension of, the neoliberal political programmes with which it was aligned in those jurisdictions—most notably in the UK but also in Australia (O'Malley 2001).

In the UK, SCP projects began as locally based and designed to solve very specific problems. In the 1970s and 1980s the government's focus was on 'high-crime' neighbourhoods and SCP was considered as an ideal fit. Then as political focus turned to economic decline and the impacts of deindustrialization, situational approaches were introduced as key aspects of government-led regeneration strategies. At this point, SCP presented a problem-solving adaptation to crime that defied wider concerns with structural or social issues. By the mid-1990s, however, situational measures which were more wide-reaching in their targets and impact began to be adopted. This reached its zenith in the wide-ranging Crime Reduction Programme, launched in 1999 (Maguire 2004).[2] The most noticeable such development was the growth of CCTV surveillance systems which, although originally developed to protect individual commercial premises began to appear on city streets, surveilling public areas and utilized as a primary form of monitoring and prevention for many different types of crime as well as antisocial behaviour. While their effectiveness as a crime reduction tool was questioned and research in this area produced mixed results (Painter and Tilley 1999; Gill and Spriggs

[2] Initially intended to run for 10 years, the programme was unique in British history in its scale and scope, the extent of the funding, and its commitment to evaluation. With a particular focus on reductions in vehicle crime and burglary, the aim was to use research-based knowledge and accumulate new knowledge about the effectiveness of a wide range of interventions for dissemination. To this end, some 10 per cent of the initial £250 million budget was to be allocated to evaluation. In the event, however, the programme only ran from 1999 to 2002 and few projects were fully implemented (Maguire 2004).

2005), they were heralded as an important reassurance tool, serving as constant, silent watchers, more effective than the traditional 'bobbies on the beat'. In 2013, it was estimated by the British Security Industry Authority (BSIA) that there were up to 5.9 million closed-circuit television cameras in Britain, including some 750,000 in 'sensitive locations' such as schools, hospitals, and care homes (Barrett 2013). The survey's maximum estimate works out at one for every 11 people in the UK, although the BSIA calculated the most likely figure as 4.9 million cameras in total, or one for every 14 people.

Over the decades situational approaches have moved on from an initial concern with target-hardening and 'bars, bolts and barriers' (Pease 2002: 952) to encompass protective and total surveillance systems. Technological advances have meant that it is now possible that every phone call, text and post on social media can be recorded, monitored, and scrutinized by national authorities. A lingering objection to SCP has long been that it can be highly intrusive and threatens civil liberties (Crawford 1998: 100; Tilley 2009: 134). Ironically, in the UK there appears to be a relative lack of popular concern regarding the use of such invasive surveillance measures, perhaps betraying the extent to which adaptive, preventive practice has been normalized and absorbed into the fabric of everyday life. Ironically, whilst the British were keen to defend their interests against the spectre of the intrusive surveillance state in the nineteenth century in contrast to their French rivals, today the situation appears to have reversed as legal restrictions and public sentiments are more sensitive to the intrusions of surveillance cameras in France! A marked fall in the costs of technology has seen technological solutions increasingly adopted by private citizens, installing CCTV in their homes, adding motion-sensor and infrared lighting equipment around private spaces, and even adding monitoring devices to cars, sometimes initiated by insurance companies. In these ways, risk-management has been dispersed and individuals have to some extent taken responsibility for their own crime protection, which is considered an example of common-sense and risk-averse behaviour which should be adopted by all (O'Malley 1992).

Undoubtedly, situational approaches occupy a prominent place in UK policy, as outlined in *The Government's Approach to Crime Prevention* (Home Affairs Committee, 2010).[3] More broadly, the role of 'architecture' in influencing the flow of events and shaping human interactions—including criminal behaviour—has been increasingly recognized (Thaler and Sunstein 2008), and now constitutes another pervasive development in prevention. Stimulated by 'defensible space' theory (Newman 1972), an array of design practices clustered under the heading of 'crime prevention through environmental design' (CPTED) (Jeffrey 1971; Schneider and Kitchen 2007) seek to embed control features through the creation of a physical and social fabric that fosters informal policing and removes opportunities for deviancy. This includes 'designing out' crime and disorder features of the physical environment and capitalizing upon civilian or 'natural' surveillance. As elsewhere in the field of security and crime prevention, the commercial sector has often been at the forefront of innovations.

[3] Interestingly, rather than celebrating its wide-scale implementation and reception, the doyen of SCP, Ron Clarke (2012: 6) has lamented the lack of take up, notably in the US: 'To date, however, situational prevention has made relatively little impression on American criminology, perhaps because American criminology is focused even more strongly on dispositional theory than the criminology of other countries'.

In assessing these trends, Mike Davis presented a powerful, dystopian vision of the future in which crime prevention aligns with and drives an 'obsession with physical security systems' and the 'architectural policing of social boundaries'. This, he contends, will increasingly come to constitute a 'master narrative in the emerging built environment movement' (1990: 223). In what Davis (1998) calls the 'fortress city', prevention through exclusion is a dominant factor in dividing urban areas and social groups; here, security becomes a positional good. Similar concerns about visible and symbolic representations of 'preventive exclusion' are to be found elsewhere among critical urban scholars and criminologists (von Hirsch and Shearing 2000)—most notably in discussions about 'gated communities' (see Blandy 2011). Yet often insufficient attention is accorded to the less visible and 'softer' forms of exclusion and social control at play in urban environments. Contrary to Davis' 'militarization' thesis, Flusty argues that 'interdictory space' has adapted to become more socially agreeable. He highlights two components through which forms of surveillance and control—crime prevention through environmental design—have become rendered 'publicly acceptable'. These, he refers to as including, first, a 'process of naturalisation', whereby 'control becomes so deeply embedded in our daily lives that we simply fail to notice it', and secondly, a dynamic of 'quaintification', by which forms of control that are too harsh to fade into the background 'are symbolically rehabilitated as both unthreatening and even laudatory' (Flusty 2001: 660). At a more mundane level, alley-gating and the use of grills and bars are also good examples of these features. Flusty concludes that the 'banality of interdiction' is becoming a defining feature of urban spaces. A dominant characteristic of this banality has been the embedding of forms of security, crime prevention, and policing into the design, layout, and physical structure of the urban environment.

Under conditions of austerity the individualization of risk-management and protective practices leaves the state to use its much-reduced capacity differently. In this economic environment, the state has been less inclined to fund large-scale capital-intensive projects which rebuild and reshape the physical environment but has endorsed the principle of 'regulated self-regulation' such as the use of signage which reminds people of the consequences of rule-breaking. The state has taken on the indirect role of enabler, promoting the ideology of 'self-help' with the private sector filling the vacuum left by the withdrawal of public funding. Increasingly, private sector organizations have become the specialists in preventative work, developing solutions to the problem of crime which can be sold to the private consumer, public authorities, and law enforcement bodies alike. However, situational approaches cannot simply be characterized as a top-down governmental perspective (Shapland 2000), as its more widespread adoption has seen its principles and practices embedded in the everyday life of the private citizen, its measures commercialized, and individualized risk management considered once again as a normal assumption for the prudent actor.

THE 'CRIME DROP' AND THE SECURITIZATION HYPOTHESIS

For some commentators, SCP measures have been a key driving force behind the historic 'crime drop'—notably declining property crime—since the early to mid-1990s both in the UK and other countries (Farrell *et al.* 2011, 2014; van Dijk *et al.* 2012). This 'security-hypothesis' contends that crime fell because of a reduction in crime opportunities caused by improvements in the level and quality of security. This includes, most prominently, improved vehicle security, particularly electronic immobilizers and central deadlocking systems, and enhanced household security via burglar alarms and security design standards (given the erstwhile volume of car theft and burglary). There are also suggestions that falling property crime may have reduced violence as an indirect effect of the same processes (Farrell *et al.* 2016). The explanatory link is made via criminal career research, which finds that most criminal careers are dominated by property crime and that property crimes are often the debut crimes that begin a criminal career. Consequently, if security improvements have reduced the volume of property crimes, it is suggested that this may have caused the less prevalent violent crimes also to decline on the basis that much violence would likely be linked with acquisitive crime in some way. At a macro-level these research findings suggest limited displacement effects—which for long had been the Achilles heel of situational approaches. To this end, they appear to reinforce the findings of others (Guerette and Bowers 2009).

Nevertheless, there have been some significant critiques of the 'security hypothesis'. The most prominent is the displacement to new forms of online, electronic, and cyber-enabled crime (ONS 2016). 'Cyber-crime' is rarely taken into consideration largely given difficulties in recording and assessing the volume of crime across time. Yet, the British Retail Consortium (2015) estimates that online credit card fraud accounts for 69 per cent of all retail card fraud. For similar reasons, the focus has been almost exclusively on victimization to households and individuals, largely ignoring patterns of crime in the commercial sector (Hopkins 2016). Whilst reductions in traditional crimes (i.e. shoplifting) in the commercial sector have been reported over recent years (Williams 2016), the real level of online crime remains uncertain. Consequently, the 'crime drop' may be as much a product of the established methods of counting crimes (through victimization surveys and police recorded crime) as it is a reflection of a fundamental reduction in the level of criminality. If traditional volume crime—burglary, shoplifting, theft, and vehicle theft—are being displaced by other forms of online crime and fraud, then this raises significant implications for opportunity theories—notably routine activities and rational choice theories—as explanations of spatial and temporal patterns. It also raises questions about the efficacy of online forms of crime prevention, bearing in mind the fears of some working in the sector that: 'Cyber threats will continue to multiply. The advent of the digital world, and the inherent interconnectivity of people, devices and organisations, opens up a whole new playing field of vulnerabilities' (Ernst & Young 2014). Nonetheless, even if displacement is occurring on a massive scale then this is reflective, at least to a certain degree, of substantial changes in opportunity structures with significant implications for crime prevention and the prevailing policy choices regarding the 'placement' of crime (Barr and Pease 1990). Regardless, the 'crime drop' debate exposes the fact that it is citizens, businesses, and other private organizations who are the prime drivers of change—be it a 'crime drop' or 'crime migration'—rather than the criminal justice system or government *per se*. It is harder to attribute these complex shifts in patterns of crime to a 'top-down' or state-centred *responsibilization strategy* rather than dynamics at play within the market and civil society.

COMMUNITY SAFETY

As noted earlier, Home Office interdepartmental circular 8/1984 announced a major philosophical shift in crime prevention practice. It took crime prevention out of its police-led silo and declared that 'preventing crime is a task for the whole community'. The vehicle to deliver this new message was the Safer Cities Programme which together ran from the mid-1980s to the mid-1990s. By providing limited short-term funding and a coordinator these local projects sought to draw together emergent partnerships and ignite crime prevention activities across the private and public sectors. The intention was to incorporate a wide range of organizations and interests including representatives of businesses, the voluntary sector, and public sector to consider local crime problems and preventive measures. The Morgan Committee, established in 1990 to review developments since circular 8/84, advanced a series of key recommendations (Morgan 1991). The two most important were conceptual and institutional. Conceptually, it suggested that the term 'community safety' be preferred to 'crime prevention'. The latter was seen to be too narrow and too closely associated with police-related responsibilities. Community safety, by contrast, was perceived to be open to wider interpretation which could encourage 'greater participation from all sections of the community in the fight against crime' (Morgan 1991: 13). Community safety was also seen as an umbrella term under which situational and social approaches could be combined rather than juxtaposed. Institutionally, the Morgan Report recommended that local authorities should be given 'statutory responsibility' for the prevention of crime, working *with* the police, for the development and promotion of community safety.

From its inception and subsequent legitimation in the Morgan Report, the concept of community safety has been associated with neighbourhood-based solutions, partnership working, and participatory frameworks. More than this, however, community safety was imagined as offering a proactive approach to local problems which placed crime and criminality into their wider social context and which required the development and implementation of systems-based, holistic solutions. Perhaps the most notable aspect of the community safety approach was that, in its emphasis on community capacity and the search for collective solutions, it recognized and affirmed the significance of lay knowledge and expertise and of the presence of systems of local social order which could only be 'known' and understood by residents, community organizations, and professionals situated on the ground and dealing with neighbourhood problems on a day-to-day basis. Consequently, the community safety approach necessitated a combination of lay and professional expertise and interventions, networked horizontally, to deliver local solutions to local problems. It took crime prevention out of the narrow confines of formal policing and opened it up to include a far wider layer of social control mechanisms, both formal and informal, working at the neighbourhood level.

While circular 8/84 emphasized local partnerships, under a series of Conservative administrations, in reality policy was informed by an apparent agenda of 'responsibilization'. Collective solutions were eschewed in favour of utilizing citizens in a more personal capacity as 'the eyes and ears of the police' as members of Neighbourhood and Street Watch schemes. These measures tended to be ad hoc, piecemeal, poorly coordinated at a national level, and in practice quite unlike the holistic, centrally coordinated solutions proffered by Morgan. Where community safety projects were established under national Conservative governments they were often relatively small in scale and supported by Labour-leaning local authority areas and national charities such as Crime Concern and NACRO. They were funded through pots of local, national, and European monies accessed through competitive process and made available to areas struggling economically and socially and characterized as high crime locales. European funding in particular required evidence that local residents and community organizations were involved in the design and implementation of strategies to improve their neighbourhoods and also that ongoing beneficial impacts on the local community were clearly demonstrated. Consequently, community safety solutions in this period were neighbourhood-based and involved the setting up of collaborative frameworks which included an area's residents, community organizations, and other stakeholders such as private businesses, schools, and youth services (Crawford and Evans 2012). In many senses, community safety work in this period offered an oppositional framework which reflected an ongoing commitment to public services and welfare provision and which also recognized the presence of social and public harms which were structural rather than individually based but which had long been denied at a national level (Hughes *et al.* 2002).

A fundamental change to this uneasy co-existence of competing perspectives came into being in 1997, with the election of a Labour-led government which appeared readily to embrace the concept of community safety, enshrined it in legislation in the Crime and Disorder Act 1998, and set about building a national institutional framework within which community safety professionals would be linked, learn their craft, and disseminate their practice. In an apparent convergence of national and local policies, local authorities were given a 'statutory responsibility' to work closely with the police to prevent crime, share information, and develop joint strategies alongside a wide range of other agencies from the public, private, voluntary, and community sectors. A network of Crime and Disorder Reduction Partnerships—renamed 'community safety partnerships' in 2010—based in local authority areas across England and Wales were set up to deliver the strategy. The 1998 Act also imposed a duty on local authorities to consider the crime and disorder implications of any policy changes and to do all that they reasonably could to prevent crime and disorder in the regions under their care (Gilling 2007).

Alongside the crime prevention elements of the Act, the Labour government also turned its attention to what it termed 'disorder' and activity which might be perceived as troublesome or as a nuisance but which fell far short of criminality. Their emphasis on tackling antisocial behaviour and 'youth disorder' led to the design and implementation of a new set of control mechanisms, from orders applied by the court to foster the curbing of individual behaviour deemed problematic, to the intermittent imposition of youth curfews in particular streets (Crawford 2009). While the actions which these orders and curfews were designed to control were not criminal, in themselves, the breaking of such orders could culminate in a criminal record. The architects of these control orders were most obviously influenced by Kelling and Wilson's (1982) 'Broken

Windows' thesis. This postulated that minor misdemeanours, gone unchecked, were likely to lead to further and more serious breaches of order in the future and that they should be tackled to reassure communities that any behaviour which might upset or distress residents would not be tolerated. The new framework was designed to counter what had been considered a breakdown of community and a 'crisis of the social' by the application of coercive interventions which would force a change in behaviour and ultimately attitudes. It was informed by New Labour's commitment to communitarian ideals—fostering an intolerance to poor behaviour would, it was argued, open up the space for the law-abiding and the active citizen to build strong communities which could collectively condemn and confront the troublesome and look towards a more prosocial future. Alongside the establishment of new mechanisms and institutional frameworks designed to establish orderly and law-abiding communities, successive Labour governments expressed a particular concern over 'problem youth', developing a new multi-disciplinary infrastructure of local Youth Offending Teams and Youth Justice Board to work with young people on the ground and to design and implement strategies at a national level (see Lewis *et al.* 2016).

Labour's moral authoritarian approach (Hughes 2007a) further developed over the ensuing 13 years in which they remained in office notably under the antisocial behaviour and respect agendas. During this period the steer from government became more pronounced with 'success' in prevention of crime and maintenance of order measured by the setting of managerialist performance targets. This reached its highpoint in 2009 with the introduction of the (short-lived) Single Confidence Target which tied the performance of community safety partnerships (police and local authorities, in particular) to increases in public perceptions of safety and confidence as measured by the annual Crime Survey for England and Wales (Rix *et al.* 2009).[4] In part, the close monitoring of organizations involved in the new government structures was a consequence of an initial reluctance on behalf of local authorities to implement the antisocial behaviour and control agenda proposed in the new legislation, demonstrating that the seeming convergence of local and national priorities might have been less solidly in place than the architects of the 1998 Act imagined (Phillips 2002). On the ground the different agencies required to find common purpose and approaches to community safety work found a clash of cultures put obstacles in the way to information-sharing and to the building and sustaining of trust (Crawford and Cunningham 2015). Central government responded with further legislation strengthening control orders and by more actively monitoring the outputs and outcomes of community safety partnerships, co-opting more agencies into the community safety agenda and incentivizing success through the control of access to funding—rewarding those partnerships and projects which hit their targets with further government grant income.

The institutionalization of community safety structures has been accompanied by a continuing fall in crime rates in the UK. Whether the two were linked remains a moot point, especially as the fall in recorded crime has been noted as a more general trend internationally (Young 1999). The coincidence of these trends in the UK, however, has allowed a consensus to develop across the political spectrum with a shared 'dominant discourse' which emphasizes focused work with 'at risk' individuals, increasing

[4] The Single Confidence Target was abandoned in 2010, when the Coalition government came to power.

regulation of problematic behaviours, the reduction of state involvement in the prevention of crime, and a more prominent role for the private sector and citizen. While the institutional frameworks within which community safety work takes place are still nominally present, the localism of the community safety approach is now taken forward through elected Police and Crime Commissioners (PCCs), charged with working closely with community safety partnerships to develop policing strategies and prevention policies. In effect, therefore, the principle of community safety from below has been replaced by more top-down managerial interventions which, while using the language popularized by community safety interventions, are far removed from its incipient ideals.

SOCIAL/DEVELOPMENTAL CRIME PREVENTION

Despite the long-standing association with SCP in the UK, the last two decades have also witnessed the growing importance of social crime prevention measures that seek to affect and target social processes and collective relationships (Crawford and Traynor 2012). They address the dispositions of individuals to offend and seek to tackle the root causes of crime. Thus, social crime prevention incorporates interventions aimed at both reducing individual motivations to offend via their social influences and institutions of socialization; and altering social relationships and/or the social environment, through a collective focus on communities, neighbourhoods, or social networks. Elsewhere in the literature, the former is often referred to as 'developmental' (Tremblay and Craig 1995) or 'risk-focused' prevention (Farrington 2007) and the latter frequently assumes the moniker of 'community crime prevention' or 'community safety'. The conceptual boundaries between developmental and community crime prevention, however, are porous. Whilst developmental approaches have largely focused on individual level risk factors, including those expressed in the interactions that individuals have with others—be they in families, kinship relationships, peer groups, and school settings—community level factors have also been drawn into these analyses. Some community-based interventions, such as the 'Communities That Care' programmes (Crow *et al.* 2004), have adopted a risk-focused approach that largely conceptualizes communities as aggregates of individual risk profiles. Furthermore, other community approaches assume a developmental logic that underpins both the factors that render certain communities high crime areas and those that foster the crime preventive capacities of certain communities. Also influenced heavily by Wilson and Kelling's (1982) 'Broken Windows' thesis, the assumption evident here is that low-level behavioural problems are harbingers of more serious criminality (either at an individual or community level) if not pre-empted, prevented, or—in contemporary policy parlance—'nipped in the bud'.

Developmental approaches of various kinds have grown in importance. They entail intervention early in personal pathways that may result in criminal behaviours and other social problems to prevent the development of criminal potential in individuals. Developmental crime prevention is based on the idea that offending is determined by behavioural and attitudinal patterns learned and produced throughout the course of an individual's life. It proceeds from the basis that risk factors exist at different ages and that life events affect the course of development. Consequently, developmental prevention concerns the manipulation of multiple risk and protective factors at crucial transition points across a lifetime. Hence, it focuses largely on childhood development and the opportunities present at critical junctures during the life-course, to prevent the onset of offending in the early years (see McAra and McVie 2012a). These developmental stages offer opportunities to target prevention resources at those most at risk of offending, where long-term benefits might accrue. Within this developmental frame, the most prevalent form of social crime prevention has come to constitute what van Dijk and de Waard (2009: 138–9) term 'secondary offender-oriented crime prevention', namely early intervention programmes targeted at children and young people (and their parents) identified as 'at risk' of offending (Farrington 2007; Farrington and Welsh 2007). Risk assessment and classification and actuarial profiling have become increasingly influential aspects of contemporary criminal (notably youth) justice systems, sometime after Feeley and Simon (1992) highlighted their emergence. They have become aligned to forms of early intervention and up-stream preventive solutions to crime problems.

Whilst often eschewing the language of 'prevention'—preferring the term 'crime reduction' given its measurable outcome-orientation (Gilling 2007)—New Labour pursued an active and aggressive antisocial behaviour agenda, which foregrounded and deployed the emerging discourse of 'pre-emption' and 'early intervention' (Allen 2011). The very term 'antisocial behaviour' is itself a form of what Zedner (2007: 262) aptly terms 'pre-crime', in that it 'shifts the temporal perspective to anticipate and forestall that which has not yet occurred and may never do so. The shift is not only temporal but also sectoral; spreading out from the state to embrace pre-emptive endeavours only remotely related to crime'. This highlights various forms of behaviour or activities which come to be seen as 'troublesome' and hence 'criminalizable' not in and of themselves (i.e. because they are directly harmful to others *per se*) but because of the way in which they are conceived—from a developmental and temporal perspective—as in some way precursors to criminal behaviour. This includes behaviour that is not-yet-criminal but which is deemed to be an indicator of likely or potential future criminal conduct. This same developmental logic is present in the *Prevent* counter-terrorism focus on 'radicalization' as a precursor to possible violent extremism.

FAMILY-FOCUSED PREVENTION

In this vein, in 2006 Tony Blair announced targeting families and screening for risk of future criminality to prevent problems developing when children grow older. He justified this by articulating a classic precautionary approach: 'If we are not prepared to predict and intervene far more early, children are going to grow up in families that we know perfectly well are completely dysfunctional'. Despite Blair's apparent certainty and confidence in the predictive capacity of developmental criminology's risk-focused prevention in relation to juvenile criminality, a government scientific report a few years earlier had arrived at a very different conclusion:

> [A]ny notion that better screening can enable policy makers to identify young children destined to join the 5 per cent of offenders responsible for 50-60 per cent of crime is fanciful. Even if there were no ethical objections to putting 'potential delinquent' labels round the necks of young children, there would continue to be statistical barriers . . . [Research] shows substantial flows *out of* as well as *in to* the pool of children who develop chronic conduct problems. As such [there are] dangers of assuming that antisocial five-year olds are the criminals or drug abusers of tomorrow. (Utting 2004: 99, emphasis in original)

Consequently, many practitioners prefer universal programmes to targeted ones, despite their obvious resource implications.

One of New Labour's most ambitious early intervention programmes was the Sure Start initiative, which aimed to support young children and their families by integrating early education, childcare, healthcare, and family support services in disadvantaged areas. Sure Start was influenced, *inter alia*, by the research evidence that emerged from the High/Scope Perry Pre-School Programme in the US (Berrueta-Clement *et al.* 1984). The Sure Start initiative sought to break the intergenerational transmission of poverty, school failure, social exclusion, and delinquency. However, the national evaluation of Sure Start produced equivocal and rather unimpressive findings with regard to the impact of Children's Centres in the UK (Belsky *et al.* 2007). The Sure Start initiative highlights the porous boundaries between social crime prevention and social policy more generally. Unlike the US Perry Pre-school project, which was conceptualized—at least by government and officials in the late 1980s and 1990s—in large part as a crime prevention programme (see Sherman *et al.* 2002), Sure Start was conceived in terms of wider social, educational, and developmental benefits. However, since 2010 and in the face of widespread funding cuts, Sure Start has been pared back to target 'the neediest families' through early intervention (HM Government 2010: 19).

A similar approach to early intervention with 'at risk' families also informed the Troubled Families programme. With its roots firmly in the approaches born of the antisocial behaviour and respect agendas, the programme was officially launched in the aftermath of the 2011 'riots'. Only implemented in England, the programme was designed to 'turn around' the 120,000 most 'troubled families' in England by May 2015, with £448 million funding from 2012–15. 'Troubled families' were officially defined as those families that met three of the four following criteria: (1) are involved in youth crime or antisocial behaviour; (2) have children who are regularly truanting or not in school; (3) have an adult on out-of-work benefits; or (4) cause high costs to the taxpayer in responding to their problems (Department for Communities and Local Government 2012: 3). The families were to be considered 'turned around' if educational attendance went above 85 per cent, youth crime reduced by 33 per cent and antisocial behaviour reduced by 60 per cent across the family, or a family member moved off out-of-work benefits and into continuous employment for three or six months, depending on the initial benefits. Despite local authority cuts over the ensuing years, a government press release in March 2015 claimed: 'More than 105,000 troubled families turned around saving taxpayers an estimated £1.2 billion' (Department for Communities and Local Government 2015), suggesting a success rate of 98.9 per cent. As a result of this apparent success, the second phase of the Troubled Families programme was launched in 2015.

The delayed publication of the independent evaluation of the programme left much scepticism about government claims. In large part, this was because the only information relating to the effectiveness of the programme had been collected from local authorities receiving funding for delivering the programme and under pressure to demonstrate compliance with the set timetable. Crossley (2015: 7) concluded that: 'Few of the claims made, regarding the need for the programme or for its success, stand up to any form of scrutiny'. In October 2016, the long-awaited report from the National Institute of Economic and Social Research was published, drawing on official data from 56 local authorities covering the first 18 months of the programme. It concluded that across a wide range of outcomes covering the key objectives—including unemployment, truancy, and criminality—the Troubled Families programme had no 'significant or systematic impact' (Day *et al.* 2016: 49). The vast majority of impact estimates were statistically insignificant, with a very small number of positive or negative results. These results are also consistent with, and complemented by, the findings of impact analysis of administrative data (Bewley *et al.* 2016), survey data (Purdon and Bryson 2016), process evaluation (White and Day 2016), and qualitative research with families (Blades *et al.* 2016). In a reversal of accepted wisdom, the Troubled Families programme appears to have represented an example of *policy-based evidence* rather than *evidence-based policy*.

More generally, however, early intervention schemes also raise crucial normative concerns. Gatti (1998: 120) notes that the right of children and young people not to be classified as future delinquents, whether they go on to become delinquents or not, represents 'one of the greatest ethical problems raised by early prevention programmes'. This stigmatizing potential was also evident in the Troubled Families initiative. Early intervention risks not only labelling young people as possible offenders of the future and hence drawing them into the 'net' of criminalization, but also subjecting those 'at risk' to greater surveillance and monitoring which provide opportunities for self-fulfilling feedback loops (Lewis *et al.* 2016). As a result, the risk-based prediction becomes directly or indirectly part of the cause itself on the basis of positive feedback between belief and behaviour. The Edinburgh Study (McAra and McVie 2007) provides ample evidence of the cyclical processes through which official contact with young people at risk can foster more and more serious police contact such that 'discipline . . . begets further and greater discipline' (McAra and McVie 2012b: 368).

'PREVENTIVE PARTNERSHIPS': ASSESSING PROGRESS

With advantages of a further two decades of hindsight, the aspired dawning of a new (local) governance of crime has proved to be something of a 'false dawn'. Whilst the discourse of partnerships is now accepted wisdom and institutional frameworks exist (some rooted in statute) in parts of the crime control field to coordinate collective responses and pursue collaborative delivery, nevertheless, progress has been hesitant, uneven and constrained. Moreover, the fear is that some of the early developments may be in the process of being reversed or undermined. The talk of 'partnerships' still belies the reality of single agency particularistic responses, whereby state organizations preserve their control over segments of the criminal justice 'turf' like fiefdoms. Delivering a 'joined-up', 'networked' approach to crime prevention has proved more complex and the obstacles much more stubborn than were often assumed (Crawford 2001). To assess with greater specificity the progress made, it is instructive to disaggregate certain distinct dimensions that Garland conflates in his 'responsibilization' thesis, namely:

- The degree to which the forces driving prevention and its promotion are primarily located within governmental edicts, laws, and policy initiatives;
- The extent to which the state—via public sector organizations—has combined to realize a less differentiated and segmented but more coordinated, holistic, and problem-oriented approach to prevention through partnerships;
- The vitality and impact of 'preventive partnerships' in fostering a preventive logic;
- The nature of the relations between the state, market, and civil society that have been initiated by and through 'preventive partnerships'; and
- The extent to which responsibilities for crime prevention and control have, in fact, been redistributed.

First, there clearly has been—in Garland's terms—'a whole new infrastructure' assembled in the name of prevention, added to which diverse new laws have been promulgated, policy initiatives launched, and funding streams instigated. Increasingly, new criminal laws and hybrid 'civil orders' have been fashioned to prevent or reduce the risk of anticipated future harm (Crawford 2009). These diverse measures constitute forms of 'preventive justice' (Ashworth and Zedner 2014), in ways that often challenge existing criminal legal principles. Notions of prevention and the architecture of preventive partnerships have reached into areas of crime control policy often perceived to be the preserve of regalian state forms of coercive penality. This has been particularly notable with regard to the UK's counter-terrorism *Prevent* strategy, which explicitly recognizes 'analogies' with 'other forms of crime prevention' (HM Government 2011: 8, para 3.29).[5] Interestingly, much of the controversy that surrounded the introduction of *Prevent* related to accusations of covert spying, intrusive surveillance, and disproportionate restrictions on free speech. These were precisely the same kinds of indictments levelled at early forms of nineteenth-century prevention—associated notably with post-Napoleonic French policing's use of *agent provocateurs*, spies, and covert surveillance—which did much to thwart the adoption of preventive approaches

[5] The *Prevent* strategy defines prevention as: 'reducing or eliminating the risk of individuals becoming involved in terrorism. *Prevent* involves the identification and referral of those susceptible to violent extremism into appropriate interventions. These interventions aim to divert the susceptible from embarking down the path to radicalisation.' (HM Government 2011: 108)

in Britain (Emsley 1991). This would seem to confirm the wide-ranging reception and embrace of the preventive turn.

However, the responsibilization thesis accepts, too readily, the idea that across the nineteenth and twentieth centuries the sovereign state came to play a dominant, monopolistic role, albeit perversely it seeks to highlight, in more contemporary times, the increasingly mythical status of state sovereignty. Historical research shows the enduring role that the security industry and prevention played from the nineteenth century onwards (Churchill 2016). While Garland (2001: 126) recognizes the 'basic sociological truth: that the most important processes producing order and conformity are mainstream social processes, located within the institutions of civil society', he accords too central a role to governments and state policy-makers. In so doing, he fails to connect sufficiently with wider developments and shifts in informal control, prevention, and regulation outside the narrow field of crime. The responsibilization thesis largely downplays the crucial role that institutions—in civil society and the marketplace—have played and continue to play as agents of social control and prevention in the regulation of both deviant and conformist behaviour. Importantly, Braithwaite (2003) reminds us that there is a very different history of policing and prevention to be derived from the business regulatory field as distinct from the 'police-prisons' arena. One of the principal historical lessons drawn from the diverse body of regulatory agencies established in the nineteenth century is the manner in which they prioritized non-punitive modes of enforcement, preferring strategies rooted in persuasion through market-based disciplines and mentalities with a more explicit preventive orientation. As one of us wrote some time ago:

> The story of the contemporary genesis and growth of crime prevention is often written as if it was something imposed by governments upon the citizenry through programmes of 'responsibilisation'—emanating outwards from the centre—and evidenced by key policy initiatives. Yet, much of the credit should properly be attributed to small-scale, local and pragmatic developments within civil society and the business sector. In reality, both criminology and government policy were relative late-comers to a preventive way of thinking. (Crawford 2007: 900-1)

As scholars of private security noted some time ago, the strategies of commercial security tend to differ significantly from those of the traditional police in that they are more instrumental than moral, offering proactive prevention rather than reactive prosecution as an approach to problem-solving (Shearing and Stenning 1981). The private security sector has tended to be more concerned with loss prevention and risk reduction rather than with law enforcement or the detection and conviction of criminals. Security guards are more likely to prioritize the plugging of security breaches in the future, the exclusion of likely offenders, and ensuring that security is not compromised. Shearing (2001) juxtaposes a past-regarding, reactive, morally toned, and punitive mentality of 'justice' against a risk-based, instrumental, and future-oriented mentality of 'security'—the latter with its roots in the private sector and marketplace and the former with its origins firmly in the state apparatuses. Whilst this birfurcation may be becoming less entrenched (Crawford 2011; White and Gill 2013), as commercially oriented strategies that combine dynamics of inclusion and exclusion now increasingly structure public ordering of city centres and street corners, and private security guards and managers appeal to the public good and have recourse to public powers, nevertheless, the locus of a preventive logic has firm origins and driving forces in the commercial sectors.

Research has also highlighted the role of the insurance industry as 'agents of prevention' and its part in helping to spread actuarial logics and technologies of prediction as well as fostering networks with state agencies that have been instrumental in the ascendancy of crime prevention (Ericson *et al.* 2003). It was only following the advent of mass consumerism and the associated growth in interest in securing property combined with the steep rise in crime risks (from the 1960s) that insurance companies sought to narrow their risk pools and foster a preventive mentality on the part of insurers. This goes some way to explaining the relatively late development of prevention in relation to crime risks as contrasted, for example, with the field of fire prevention (O'Malley and Hutchinson 2007). Whilst the insurance industry may have been relatively slow to recognize and use its potential power to influence behaviour with regard to crime risks (Litton 1982), its subsequent sway in stimulating a 'preventive mentality' is undoubted. In the ensuing years, the insurance industry has played a significant part in fostering preventive thinking and action simultaneously through networks with the police and government agencies and via diverse forms of insurance cover which have served to promote the spread and use of certain situational measures, notably forms of target-hardening.

It would be wrong, however, to suggest that crime prevention inevitably preoccupies businesses. Many businesses prefer not to acknowledge—especially publicly—their crime-related risks. It was only after the Home Office published a Car Theft Index (Houghton 1992) and the Home Secretary invited manufacturers to discuss its implications, that manufacturers actively took notice and subsequently incorporated anti-theft designs into cars. Much crime or fraud is tolerated simply because it costs less than the efforts required to prevent it. The cost of crime may be accepted as an overhead expense which is part of the business calculation. Not all crime prevention initiatives are seen by business managers as inevitably desirable, particularly if they might involve adverse publicity. Prevention unless embedded in an unobtrusive manner can literally get in the way of business. The tension between crime prevention and business goals alerts us to the fact that ultimately crime prevention will often be weighed against other (economic) goals.

Secondly, the community safety partnerships spawned by the Crime and Disorder Act have always been predominantly about public sector relations, with limited (and, sometime, no viable) private or voluntary sector involvement. Engagement with the private sector has often been patchy and the role of the voluntary sector frequently marginalized. From the outset (in the 1980s) the private sector was largely seen as a source of sponsorship and additional resources—to be untapped (as reflected in the establishment of Crime Concern in 1988)—a perception that was invariably shunned by many business leaders who felt that they were already paying for state provision of policing and criminal justice through taxes. The growth of the private security industry over the last three decades or so and the growing involvement of the private sector in crime control and policing has largely been overseen by a parallel, segmented, and very different regulatory architecture (White 2010). In many senses, the developments in the public and private sectors have passed like ships in the night, often evidencing mutual distrust and disinterest (Crawford *et al.* 2005). Where successful preventive partnerships have been forged—such as within Youth Offending Teams, Safeguarding Boards and community safety partnerships—they have almost exclusively revolved around public sector organizations as the key partners, often supported by dedicated funding streams.

Such has been the political disappointment with community safety partnerships—despite the steady decline of aggregate crime rates since the mid-1990s—that in late 2004, the then Labour government announced a major review of their activities, governance, and accountability, acknowledging that: 'a significant number of partnerships struggle to maintain a full contribution from key agencies and even successful ones are not sufficiently visible, nor we think accountable, to the public as they should be' (Home Office 2004: 123). The question then is why have their high hopes been so severely curtailed? And what has happened to derail such aspirations? One response might be that the initial claims of a rupture with the past were exaggerated. Another is that the obstacles—structural, organizational, and cultural—that stand in the way of realizing a genuine partnership approach are more substantial, entrenched, and engrained than otherwise acknowledged. Furthermore, the absence of genuinely critical debate about the processes involved in delivering multi-agency partnerships may serve to impede practice. The development of good practice conversely requires the recognition and exploration of the many unspoken problems that both practitioners face and are implied by practice.

The main barriers to successful partnerships include a reluctance of some agencies to participate (especially health, education, and social services); the dominance of a policing agenda; unwillingness to share information; conflicting interests, priorities and cultural assumptions on the part of different agencies; local political differences; lack of inter-organisational trust; desire to protect budgets; lack of capacity and expertise; and over-reliance on informal contacts and networks which lapsed if key individuals moved on. The involvement of the private sector has often been patchy and the role of the voluntary sector frequently marginalized. In practice, partnerships experience considerable problems in reaching agreements or protocols about what data they could legitimately share and on what basis. As a result, concerns over confidentiality often hinder partnership working and problematize inter-organizational trust relations.

Consequently, the optimism that accompanied the wave of community safety partnerships and other inter-organizational collaborations in diverse areas of crime prevention and control some two decades ago, has dissipated. The community safety partnership have themselves become a shell of what they portended to be; focused largely on delivering their core statutory responsibilities. Moreover, the central focus on crime reduction potentially constrained the preventive reach of the partnership approach from the outset. Elsewhere preventive partnerships are most robust where they have a legal foundation and formal structure—such as safeguarding, youth offending, multi-agency public protection panels, and local criminal justice boards. Outside of those that derive from statutory responsibilities, local partnerships tend to be more informal and uneven in nature (Crawford and L'Hoiry 2015). But even in relation to statutory responsibilities like safeguarding children—where multi-agency Local Safeguarding Children Boards have statutory responsibilities to safeguard and promote the welfare of children and young people (HM Government 2015)—working across divergent occupational cultures and organizational boundaries remains challenging.[6]

FUTURE PROSPECTS

We have entered into a period dominated by the language of 'austerity' and the refrain that the state can no longer provide services of a range and extent which were previously enjoyed. Few areas of state provision have escaped from significant reorganizations and cuts to funding as subsequent governments attempt to rebalance budgets and shrink national debt. This has left 'thinner' state services which have had to pare back delivery to their statutory responsibilities which must be provided by law. Formerly, the police and other security services have been largely protected from the withdrawal of state funding, however, under austerity politics this preferred status can no longer be expected to prevail, with spending on police services down year on year together with the subsequent loss of both back office and frontline staff (Association of Police and Crime Commissioners (APCC) 2015). This has resulted in unprecedented reductions in budgets and staff numbers. Frontline police officer and PCSO numbers in England and Wales, for example, fell by nearly 16 per cent—over 25,000 officers—between 2010 and 2016 (Hargreaves *et al.* 2016).[7] At the same time, the police have faced severe criticism from government ministers demanding that police forces respond to a reduction in funds by improving their efficiency, effectiveness, and integrity. Long-running sagas of police malpractice and misconduct, such as the Hillsborough tragedy and the independent review of the Police Federation (Travis 2013), have severely weakened police authority and legitimacy in the eyes of government and public. The police have responded, in turn, by questioning the viability of government proposals to transform policing functions and raising concerns as to whether current funding levels are sustainable or will result in increasing crime and security threats. This open spat between police and government raises questions about the future trajectory of policing under austerity conditions and their place within wider partnership arrangements.

Many preventive partnerships have been brought into being facilitated and sustained by the incentives of accessing resources and new funding streams. Hence, the recent period of austerity in public sector funding, presents critical challenges for the future of preventive partnerships. On the one hand, austerity has added a powerful dynamic to radically rethink the nature of public services, problem-solving, and the

[6] For example, the independent report into child sexual exploitation (CSE) in Rotherham (Jay 2014) concluded that whilst Rotherham saw the development of good inter-agency policies and procedures applicable to CSE, the weakness in their approach was that members of the Safeguarding Board rarely checked whether these were being implemented or whether they were working. Nearly three decades on from the *Inquiry into Child Abuse in Cleveland 1987* chaired by Elizabeth Butler-Sloss (1988), it appears that many of the same problems of partnership working persist.

[7] Overall police workforce numbers (including civilian staff), have declined over the same period by nearly 18 per cent, from 244,497 to 200,922, over 43,500 officers and staff.

relationship between different (public, private, and voluntary) providers. It might provide an incentive to shift to greater emphasis on prevention, in the ultimate quest for cost savings. It might prompt more fundamental questions about purpose, expertise, responsiveness, and effective service delivery. It might encourage collaborative advantages through partnerships as a means of finding longer-term cost efficiencies. Such prompting might also see investments in 'up-stream' preventive solutions to crime problems and away from reactive fire-fighting. This would require initial investment in terms of financial and human capital which, in the current context, may not be available. Moreover, as decades of policing research has demonstrated, such far-reaching thinking would necessitate significantly bold shifts in police organizational culture and working practices. The extent to which either, or a combination of both, these scenarios prevail; only time will tell. However, the manner in which police and other public sector leaders respond to austerity will undoubtedly shape the next phase in the development and institutionalization of preventive partnerships.

How the public and voluntary sectors respond to austerity is also uncertain. A number of possible scenarios might be envisaged in the face of sustained fiscal pressures. First, relevant organizations might retreat into their 'silos'; retracting from inter-organizational collaborations, redrawing their boundaries to focus on core objectives, and seeking to off-load responsibilities to others, wherever possible. Short-term cost savings may arise at the expense of partnership commitments, particularly where key individuals or posts are lost to early retirements or workforce reorganizations. There are signs that recent government reforms have narrowed the police mandate to a focus on crime-fighting—as signalled in the 2010 White Paper declaration that the 'key priority for the police is to cut crime' (Home Office 2010: para. 1.22).[8] This may see the police retract from wider community safer commitments and engagement with local partnerships. A report from the HMIC entitled *Policing in Austerity: Rising to the Challenge* suggested that, collaborations between police forces, let alone partnership relations were 'deeply disappointing' (HMIC 2013: 18). Despite falling crime rates, demands on the police service remain high and the changing crime mix means that costs of crime for the police have not fallen proportionally (College of Policing 2015). In particular, complex crimes, such as large volumes of historic CSE cases have added to police workloads. Under these conditions, preventative work may simply be abandoned in favour of reducing crime by meeting arrest and detection targets. Consequently, prevention may be reduced to the old tried and trusted theories of deterrence pared back to the rational choice models of criminality developed within classical criminology. Insights which have been more critical of this approach and suggest more nuanced, complex, and sociologically oriented aetiologies of crime may well be abandoned and a narrower understanding of the problem of crime may re-assert itself in the perspective of the police and in the mindset of individual officers.

There is some evidence that the police and other public services are finding themselves under continuing pressure to focus on the most vulnerable in society, targeting services which are designed to ensure the safeguarding of vulnerable children and adults over the rest of the population (APCC 2015: 23–4). With resources committed to

[8] After more than a decade in which the police role became more pervasive, as their mission widened to include non-crime activities such as antisocial behaviour.

these populations and dealing with issues which are complex and time-consuming the more routine policing and crime prevention functions which have become expected by the general public in previous periods may simply be considered as a luxury which can no longer be afforded. Some chief constables have already suggested that their officers can no longer attend to routine calls for help and that these should be logged through websites which will automatically generate crime reference numbers which can be used for insurance purposes. At the same time, primary crime prevention has taken a significant blow and vital crime reduction initiatives are 'increasingly at risk' (APCC 2015: 22). These changes may have significant and long-term consequences for the relationship between police and public, with implications for local relationships of trust that have built up over years. They may also fragment the complex, yet vital, partnership relations that have been build up over many years that support more holistic problem-solving approaches to local crime problems.

In addition to austerity there are other (somewhat tentative and volatile) developments that may influence the shape and fortunes of crime prevention going forward. The first is the growing involvement of the private sector in public service delivery. As argued earlier, commercial businesses have more often been innovators in preventive logics and technologies. For good or for ill, we may see greater cross-fertilization of ideas and practices through greater public–private partnership, the growth of Business Improvement Districts, and private management of city-centres (Crawford 2011), as well as the wholesale privatization of public services (as seen in the fields of prisons and probation). The arrival of novel horizontal or transversal linkages between private sector providers (such as G4S for instance) in different domains of crime control and criminal justice raises new fundamental issues concerning conflicts of interests. More profoundly, it evokes questions about whether crime control and policing (broadly conceived) should be viewed as a single, integrated 'system' or as a series of intricate partnership relations in which 'independent interdependence' prevails.

Additionally, the recent introduction of PCCs into the governance architecture adds a potentially interesting new dynamic. Championed as 'the most radical change in policing for half a century' (Home Office 2010: 10), the introduction of PCCs was intended to constitute 'a massive transfer of power from the government to the people', according to the then Home Secretary, Theresa May (2011). Importantly, PCCs' remit extends beyond the police to encompass responsibilities for crime and community safety. In addition to the Police budget, other funding streams, including Community Safety Partnership funding, Victims Fund, and Home Office special grants, as well as new forms of income generation such as the levy on night-time economy service users have been streamlined into a single PCC funding pot. Significant here is the level of discretion elected PCCs will have over these considerable resources; to set objectives, fix budgets, and commission services (within but also beyond existing public service providers). Much debate has focused on the responsibility that PCCs have over the police, but their function is more extensive including a duty to cooperate with community safety and criminal justice partners.[9] Consequently, there are evident possibilities (and

[9] Explicit in the role is the overarching statutory requirement to work in partnership across a range of agencies at local and national levels 'to ensure there is a unified approach to preventing and reducing crime' (sections 10 and 88 and Schedule 11 of the Police Reform and Social Responsibility Act 2011).

some might suggest a distinct likelihood) that over time PCCs will become increasingly promiscuous in pushing the boundaries of their role more extensively into the domains of crime prevention and criminal justice.[10] As it becomes clearer to PCCs that policing and crime are subject to the socio-economic and political forces that originate far from the reach of the police organisation, they will likely be drawn into policy realms and social issues beyond the narrowly defined orbit of the police and policing. In theory, at least, the PCCs might herald a revisiting of the initial policing mission 'that the principal object to be obtained is the prevention of crime' (as in the Metropolitan Police's first instruction book published in 1829).

There are, however, real dangers that the introduction of PCCs with a capacious role will reduce and subsume community safety and crime prevention to police-related policy concerns, rather than seeing policing as an element or subset of community safety (Crawford 2016). To do so, would be to retreat back to the myth of public monopoly over policing and police monopoly over crime. Just as Wiles and Pease (2000) argued that the Crime and Disorder Act of 1998 inappropriately subsumed community safety under a focus on crime reduction rather than a 'pan-hazard approach' to diverse harms, recent reforms—including the Police Reform and Social Responsibility Act 2011—may come to construct community safety through a narrow police (or at best 'policing') lens. As we have sought to show, much of the recent history of crime prevention and community safety through a partnership approach has been wrapped up with attempts to break free from the narrow constraints of a police focus endemic in much work.

CONCLUSION

Undoubtedly, future directions in crime prevention will be shaped by technological advances and innovations, as yet unknown. The history of crime prevention reminds us that much prevention serves as an attempt to 'retrofit' solutions to novel criminal opportunities that are created by new technologies. As Pease noted some time ago (2001: 27): 'if the cycle of innovation-harvest-retrofit has been for all practical purposes universal . . . it means that in terms of an arms race, we wait to lose a lot of battles before we update our armoury'. As such, there is often an historic lag to preventive efforts; as they respond to problems once these become perceived as 'problematic'. However, prevention also embodies a palpable future-orientation. Crime prevention seeks to shape the future by intervening into the present. The difficulty for crime prevention, however, is that futures prevented remain unknown and hard to measure or account for.

Nonetheless, prevention fits well with the prevailing concern for 'governing the future'; to avert potential harms, through foresight, anticipation and pre-emption

[10] The Anti-Social Behaviour, Crime and Policing Act 2014, for example, extended the responsibilities of PCCs to include commissioning victims' services.

(Zedner 2009). Yet this raises vexed issues concerning the knowledge and evidence upon which causal assumptions and developmental trajectories are premised and how knowledge generated is subsequently utilized. In the 'Petabyte Age' of 'Big Data' analytics, the criminological quest for causation—that situational prevention challenged three decades ago—may now be undermined further (Chan and Bennett-Moses 2016). The *volume*, *variety*, and *velocity* of new forms of data enable interventions in the present that shape the future in diverse (and as yet unimaginable) ways that eschew the search for causality (Mayer-Schönberger and Cukier 2013), with evident implications for security. Real-time data enable the generation of knowledge and its application in compressed time-horizons and prompts a perspective of emergent causality. It elicits a reflexive approach to knowledge creation and application as both relational and as a state of being, with feedback loops and changes through iterative processes (Chandler 2015). Such Big Data provides possible insights into shifting patterns and changing contexts, potentially enabling real-time reflexive awareness and management of risks and problems as they arise. It presages forms of 'algorithmic justice' where the preventive designs are built into the algorithms that determine how information is used. As Amazon and Google seek to predict your taste, so too the algorithms of future services, providers, and utilities may seek to prevent 'bad risks' (Harcourt 2015). Nevertheless, what remains constant is the fact that crime prevention strategies—whether initiated or conducted by citizens, civil society organizations, groups, businesses, state institutions, or computerized objects—are always and inevitably informed by assumptions about human behaviour and political choices with distinct ethical and social implications. A clearer grasp of these directions of travel should enable a greater capacity to shape future trajectories.

SELECTED FURTHER READING

The literature on crime prevention and community safety is vast and covers many different aspects of this wide-ranging field. Hughes' (2007b) *The Politics of Crime and Community* and Tilley's (2009) *Crime Prevention* remain useful in outlining the theory of situational and social crime prevention techniques while situating these within a broader political and theoretical backdrop. For readers wishing to engage with some of the original texts Wilson's *Thinking About Crime* (1975) and Newman's *Defensible Space* (1972) represent classic expositions of ideas associated with 'preventive governance', which remain influential decades on. More recently, Thaler and Sunstein's *Nudge* (2008) demonstrates how far the situational approach to behavioural change has been adopted and adapted within wider policy agendas such as health, housing, schooling, and economic decision-making. For critical reflections on the trajectory of crime prevention policy, readers might turn to Burney's *Making People Behave* (2009) and Squires and Stephen's *Rougher Justice* (2005), which reveal the dangers inherent in the adoption of punitive, top-down approaches and 'pre-crime' policies. Ashworth and Zedner's *Preventive Justice* (2014) gives a valuable background to and analysis of the 'architecture of security' and of the coercive measures that many states now take in the name of 'prevention'.

REFERENCES

ALLEN, G. (2011), *Early Intervention: The Next Steps*, London: Cabinet Office.

Association of Police and Crime Commissioners (2015), *Prospects for 2015 to 2020: Continuity with Change – The Police and Commissioners' Perspective*, available at: http://www.nottinghamshire.gov.uk/DMS/Document.ashx?czJKcaeAi5tUFL1DTL2UE4zNRBcoShgo=kU89EnoKRbG233, accessed 11 January 2017.

ASHWORTH, A. and ZEDNER, L. (2014), *Preventive Justice*, Oxford: Oxford University Press.

BARR, R. and PEASE, K. (1990), 'Crime Placement, Displacement and Deflection', *Crime and Justice*, 12: 277–318.

BARRETT, D. (2013), 'One surveillance camera for every 11 people in Britain, says CCTV survey', *The Telegraph*, 10 July.

BELSKY, J., BARNES, J., and MELHUISH, E. C. (eds) (2007), *The National Evaluation of Sure Start: Does Area-Based Early Intervention Work?*, Bristol: Policy.

BEWLEY, H., GEORGE, A., RIENZO, C., and PORTES, J. (2016), *National Evaluation of the Troubled Families Programme: National Impact Study Report, Findings from the Analysis of National Administrative Data and Local Data on Programme Participation*, London: Department for Communities and Local Government.

BERRUETA-CLEMENT, J. R., SCHWEINHART, L. J., BARNETT, W. S., EPSTEIN, A. S., and WEIKART, D. P. (1984), *Changed Lives*, Ypsilanti, Michigan: High/Scope.

BLADES, R., ERSKINE, C., and DAY, L. (2016), *National Evaluation of the Troubled Families Programme. Families' Experiences and Outcomes*, London: Department for Communities and Local Government.

BLANDY, S. (2011), 'Gating as Governance: The Boundaries Spectrum in Social and Situational Crime Prevention', in A. Crawford (ed.), *International and Comparative Criminal Justice and Urban Governance*, Cambridge: Cambridge University Press.

BOTTOMS, A. E. (1990), 'Crime Prevention Facing the 1990s', *Policing and Society*, 1(1): 3–22.

BRAITHWAITE, J. (2003), 'What's Wrong with the Sociology of Punishment?', *Theoretical Criminology*, 7(1): 5–28.

BRITISH RETAIL CONSORTIUM (2015), *Retail Crime Survey 2014*, London: BRC.

BURNEY, E. (2009), *Making People Behave*, 2nd edn, Cullompton: Willan.

BUTLER-SLOSS, E. (1988), *Report of the Inquiry into Child Abuse in Cleveland 1987*, London: HMSO.

CHAN, J. and BENNETT-MOSES, L. (2016), 'Is Big Data Challenging Criminology?', *Theoretical Criminology*, 20(1): 21–39.

CHANDLER, D. (2015), 'A World without Causation: Big Data and the Coming of Age of Posthumanism', *Millennium*, advanced access, 43(3): 833–51.

CHURCHILL, D. (2016), 'Security and Visions of the Criminal: Technology, Professional Criminality and Social Change in Victorian and Edwardian Britain', *British Journal of Criminology*, 56(5): 857–76.

CLARKE, R. V. (1995), 'Situational Crime Prevention', *Crime and Justice*, 19: 91–150.

CLARKE, R. V. (2012), 'Opportunity makes the thief. Really? And so what?', *Crime Science*, 1(3): 1–9.

CLARKE, R. V. and CORNISH, D. B. (1985), 'Modelling Offenders' Decisions', *Crime and Justice*, 6: 147–85.

COHEN, L. E. and FELSON, M. (1979), 'Social Change and Crime Rate Trends: A Routine Activity Approach', *American Sociological Review*, 44(4): 588–608.

COLLEGE OF POLICING (2015), *Estimating Demand on the Police Service*, available at: http://www.college.police.uk/Documents/Demand_Report_21_1_15.pdf, accessed 9 January 2017.

CRAWFORD, A. (1997), *The Local Governance of Crime*, Oxford: Clarendon Press.

CRAWFORD, A. (1998), *Crime Prevention and Community Safety*, Harlow: Longman.

CRAWFORD, A. (2001), 'Joined-Up but Fragmented', in R. Matthews and J. Pitts (eds), *Crime, Disorder and Community Safety: A New Agenda?*, London: Routledge.

CRAWFORD, A. (2007), 'Crime Prevention and Community Safety', in M. Maguire, R. Morgan, and R. Reiner (eds), *The Oxford Handbook of Criminology*, 4th edn, Oxford: Oxford University Press.

CRAWFORD, A. (2009), 'Governing through Anti-Social Behaviour: Regulatory Challenges to Criminal Justice', *British Journal of Criminology*, 49(6): 810–31.

CRAWFORD, A. (2011), 'From the Shopping Mall to the Street Corner: Dynamics of Exclusion in the Governance of Public Space', in A. Crawford (ed.), *International and Comparative Criminal Justice and Urban Governance*, Cambridge: Cambridge University Press.

CRAWFORD, A. (2016), 'The Implications of the English and Welsh Experiment in Democratic Governance of Policing through Police and Crime Commissioners', in T. Delpeuch and J. E. Ross (eds), *Comparing the Democratic Governance of Police Intelligence*, Cheltenham: Edward Elgar.

CRAWFORD, A. and CUNNINGHAM, M. (2015), 'Working in Partnership: The challenges of working across organisational boundaries, cultures and practices', in J. Fleming (ed.), *Police Leadership—Rising to the Top*, Oxford: Oxford University Press.

CRAWFORD, A. and EVANS, K. (2012), 'Crime Prevention and Community Safety', in M. Maguire, R. Morgan, and R. Reiner (eds), *The Oxford Handbook of Criminology*, 5th edn, Oxford: Oxford University Press.

CRAWFORD, A. and L'HOIRY, X. (2015), *Partnerships in the Delivery of Policing and Safeguarding Children*, Leeds: CCJS Press, available at: http://www.law.leeds.ac.uk/assets/files/research/N8PRP/Safeguarding-Report-Final-for-web.pdf, accessed 9 January 2017.

CRAWFORD, A., LISTER, S., BLACKBURN, S., and BURNETT, J. (2005), *Plural Policing*, Bristol: Policy Press.

CRAWFORD, A. and TRAYNOR, P. (2012), 'La Prévention de la Délinquance chez les Anglais: From community-based strategies to early interventions with young people', in E. Baillergeau and P. Hebberecht (eds), *Social Crime Prevention in Late Modern Europe*, Brussels: VUB.

Crossley, S. (2015), *The Troubled Families Programme: The Perfect Social Policy?*, Briefing 13, London: Centre for Crime and Justice Studies.

Crow, I., France, A., Hacking, S., and Hart, M. (2004), *Does Communities that Care work? An Evaluation of a Community-Based Risk Prevention Programme in Three Neighbourhoods*, York: Joseph Rowntree Foundation.

Davis, M. (1990), *City of Quartz: Excavating the Future in Los Angeles*, London: Verso.

Davis, M. (1998), *Ecology of Fear: Los Angeles and the Imagination of Disaster*, New York: Metropolitan Books.

Day, L., Bryson, C., White, C., Purdon, S., Bewley, H., Kirchner Sala, L., and Portes, J. (2016), *National Evaluation of the Troubled Families Programme: Final Synthesis Report*, London: Department for Communities and Local Government.

Department for Communities and Local Government (2012), *The Troubled Families programme: Financial Framework for the Troubled Families Programme's Payment-by-results Scheme for Local Authorities*, London: Department for Communities and Local Government, 28 March.

Department for Communities and Local Government (2015), 'More than 105,000 troubled families turned around saving taxpayers an estimated £1.2 billion' press release, 10 March, available at: https://www.gov.uk/government/news/more-than-105000-troubled-families-turned-around-saving-taxpayers-an-estimated-12-billion, accessed 9 January 2017.

Emsley, C. (1991), *The English Police: A Political and Social History*, London: Routledge.

Ericson, R., Doyle, A., and Barry, D. (2003), *Insurance as Governance*, Toronto: University of Toronto Press.

Ernst & Young (2014), *Get Ahead of Cybercrime: EY's Global Information Security Survey 2014*, available at: http://www.ey.com/Publication/vwLUAssets/EY-global-information-security-survey-2014/$FILE/EY-global-information-security-survey-2014.pdf, accessed 9 January 2017.

Evans, K. (2011), *Crime Prevention: A Critical Introduction*, London: Sage.

Farrell, G., Tseloni, A., Mailley, J., and Tilley, N. (2011), 'The Crime Drop and the Security Hypothesis', *Journal of Research in Crime and Delinquency*, 48(2): 147–75.

Farrell, G., Tilley, N., and Tseloni, A. (2014), 'Why the Crime Drop?', *Crime and Justice*, 421–90.

Farrell, G., Tseloni, A., and Tilley, N. (2016), 'Signature dish: Triangulation from data signatures to examine the role of security in falling crime', *Methodological Innovations*, 9: 1–11.

Farrington, D. P. (2007), 'Childhood Risk Factors and Risk-Focused Prevention', in M. Maguire, R. Morgan, and R. Reiner, (eds), *The Oxford Handbook of Criminology*, 4th edn, Oxford: Oxford University Press.

Farrington, D. P. and Welsh, B. C. (2007), *Saving Children from a Life of Crime: Early Risk Factors and Effective Intervention*, Oxford: Oxford University Press.

Farrington, D. P. and Welsh, B. C. (2012) (eds), *The Oxford Handbook of Crime Prevention*, Oxford: Oxford University Press.

Feeley, M. and Simon, J. (1992), 'The New Penology', *Criminology*, 30(4): 449–74.

Felson, M. and Clarke R. V. (1998), *Opportunity Makes the Thief*, Police Research Series, Paper 98, London: Home Office.

Flusty, S. (2001), 'The Banality of Interdiction: Surveillance, Control and the Displacement of Diversity', *International Journal of Urban and Regional Research*, 25(3): 658–64.

Garland, D. (1996), 'The Limits of the Sovereign State', *British Journal of Criminology*, 36(4): 445–71.

Garland, D. (2000), 'Ideas, Institutions and Situational Crime Prevention', in A. Von Hirsch, D. Garland, and A. Wakefield (eds), *Ethical and Social Perspectives on Situational Crime Prevention*, Oxford: Hart Publishing.

Garland, D. (2001), *The Culture of Control*, Oxford: Oxford University Press.

Gatti, U. (1998), 'Ethical issues raised when early intervention is used to prevent crime', *European Journal on Criminal Policy and Research*, 6(1): 113–32.

Gill, M. and Spriggs, A. (2005), *Assessing the Impact of CCTV*, Home Office Research Study 292, London: Home Office.

Gilling, D. (1997), *Crime Prevention: Theory, Policy, Politics*, London: UCL press.

Gilling, D. (2007), *Crime Reduction and Community Safety*, Cullompton: Willan.

Graham, J. and Bennett, T. (1995), *Crime Prevention Strategies in Europe and North America*, Helsinki: HEUNI.

Guerette, R. T. and Bowers K. (2009), 'Assessing the Extent of Crime Displacement and Diffusion of Benefits: A Review of Situational Crime Prevention Evaluations', *Criminology*, 47(4): 1331–68.

Harcourt, B. E. (2015), *Exposed: Desire and Disobedience in the Digital Age*, Cambridge, MA: Harvard University Press.

Hargreaves, J., Cooper, J., Woods, E., and McKee, C. (2016), *Police Workforce, England and Wales, 31 March 2016*, Statistical Bulletin 05/16, London: Home Office.

HMIC (2013), *Policing in Austerity: Rising to the Challenge*, London: Her Majesty's Inspectorate of Constabulary.

HM Government (2010), *The Coalition: Our Programme for Government*, London: Cabinet Office.

HM Government (2011), *Prevent Strategy*, Cm 8092, London: The Stationery Office.

HM Government (2015), *Working Together to Safeguard Children: A Guide to Inter-Agency Working to Safeguard and Promote the Welfare of Children*, London: HM Government.

Home Affairs Committee (2010), *The Government's Approach to Crime Prevention*, HC 242-I, London: The Stationery Office.

HOME OFFICE (1977), *Review of Criminal Justice Policy 1976*, London: Home Office.

HOME OFFICE (1984), *Crime Prevention*, Circular 8/1984, London: Home Office.

HOME OFFICE (2004), *Building Communities, Beating Crime*, London: Home Office.

HOME OFFICE (2010), *Policing in the 21st Century: Reconnecting the Police and the People*, London: The Stationery Office.

HOPE, T. (2009), 'The political evolution of situational crime prevention in England and Wales', in A. Crawford (ed.), *Crime Prevention Policies in Comparative Perspective*, Cullompton: Willan.

HOPKINS, M. (2016), 'The crime drop and the changing face of commercial victimisation', *Criminology and Criminal Justice*, 16(4): 410–30.

HOUGH, J. M., CLARKE, R. V. G., and MAYHEW, P. M. (1980), 'Introduction', in R. V. G. Clarke and P. M. Mayhew (eds), *Designing out Crime*, London: HMSO.

HOUGHTON, G. (1992), *Car Theft in England and Wales: The Home Office Car Theft Index*, London: Home Office.

HUGHES, G. (1998), *Understanding Crime Prevention*, Buckingham: Open University Press.

HUGHES, G. (2007a), *Crime and Community*, London: Palgrave.

HUGHES, G. (2007b), *The Politics of Crime and Community*, Basingstoke: Palgrave.

HUGHES, G., MCLAUGHLIN, E., and MUNCIE, J. (2002) (eds), *Crime Prevention and Community Safety: New Directions*, London: Sage.

JAY, A. (2014), *Independent Inquiry into Child Sexual Exploitation in Rotherham 1997-2013*, Rotherham Council.

JEFFREY, C. R. (1971), *Crime Prevention Through Environmental Design*, Beverly Hills, CA: Sage.

KING, M. (1989), 'Social Crime Prevention à la Thatcher', *Howard Journal*, 28(4): 291–312.

KOSELLECK, R. (2004), *Futures Past: On the Semantics of Historical Time*, Studies in Contemporary German Social Thought (trans. Keith Tribe), Cambridge, MA: MIT.

LEWIS, S., CRAWFORD, A., and TRAYNOR, P. (2016), 'Nipping Crime in the Bud? The Use of Anti-Social Behaviour Interventions with Young People in England and Wales', *British Journal of Criminology*, advanced access.

LITTON, R. A. (1982), 'Crime Prevention and Insurance', *Howard Journal*, 21(1): 6–22.

MAGUIRE, M. (2004), 'The Crime Reduction Programme in England and Wales', *Criminal Justice*, 4(3): 213–37.

MARTINSON, R. (1974), 'What Works?—Questions and Answers about Prison Reform', *The Public Interest*, 35(1): 22–54.

MAY, T. (2011), 'The deal: one year on', Speech, 9 May, available at: http://www.homeoffice.gov.uk/media-centre/speeches/one-year-on, accessed 9 January 2017.

MAYER-SCHÖNBERGER, V. and CUKIER, K. (2013), *Big Data: A Revolution that will Transform How We Live, Work and Think*, London: John Murray.

MCARA, L. and MCVIE, S. (2007), 'Youth Justice? The Impact of System Contact on Patterns of Desistance from Offending', *European Journal of Criminology*, 4(3): 315–45.

MCARA, L. and MCVIE, S. (2012a), 'Critical Debates in Developmental and Life-Course Criminology', in M. Maguire, R. Morgan, and R. Reiner (eds), *The Oxford Handbook of Criminology*, 5th edn, Oxford: Oxford University Press.

MCARA, L. and MCVIE, S. (2012b), 'Negotiated Order: The Groundwork for a Theory of Offending Pathways', *Criminology and Criminal Justice*, 12(4): 347–75.

MORGAN, J. (1991), *Safer Communities: The Local Delivery of Crime Prevention Through the Partnership Approach*, London: Home Office.

NEWMAN, O. (1972), *Defensible Space: People and Design in the Violent City*, London: Architectural Press.

ONS (2016), *Crime in England and Wales: year ending Mar 2016*, London: Office for National Statistics, available at: http://www.ons.gov.uk/peoplepopulationandcommunity/crimeandjustice/bulletins/crimeinenglandandwales/yearendingmar2016, accessed 9 January 2017.

O'MALLEY, P. (1992), 'Risk, Power and Crime Prevention', *Economy and Society*, 21(3): 252–75.

O'MALLEY, P. (2001), 'Risk Crime and Prudentialism Revisited', in K. Stenson and R. Sullivan (eds), *Crime, Risk and Justice*, Cullompton: Willan.

O'MALLEY, P. and HUTCHINSON, S. (2007), 'Reinventing Prevention: Why did Crime Prevention Develop so Late?', *British Journal of Criminology*, 47(3): 373–89.

PAINTER, K. and TILLEY, N. (1999), 'Seeing and Being Seen to Prevent Crime', *Crime Prevention Studies*, 10: 1–13.

PEASE, K. (2001), *Cracking Crime Through Design*, London: Design Council.

PEASE, K. (2002), 'Crime Reduction', in M. Maguire, R. Morgan, and R. Reiner (eds), *The Oxford Handbook of Criminology*, Oxford: Oxford University Press.

PHILLIPS, C. (2002), 'From Voluntary to Statutory Status', in G. Hughes, E. McLaughlin, and J. Muncie (eds), *Crime Prevention and Community Safety: New Directions*, London: Sage.

PURDON, S. and BRYSON, C. (2016), *National Evaluation of the Troubled Families Programme. Technical report: Impact Evaluation Using Survey Data*, London: Department for Communities and Local Government.

RIX, A., JOSHUA, F., MAGUIRE, M., and MORTON, S. (2009), *Improving Public Confidence in the Police: A Review of the Evidence*, Research Report 28, London: Home Office.

SCHNEIDER, R. H. and KITCHEN, T. (2007), *Crime Prevention and the Built Environment*, London: Routledge.

SHAPLAND, J. (2000), 'Situational Prevention: Social Values and Social Viewpoints', in A. Von Hirsch, D. Garland, and A. Wakefield (eds), *Ethical and Social Perspectives on Situational Crime Prevention*, Oxford: Hart.

SHEARING, C. (2001), 'Punishment and the changing face of governance', *Punishment and Society*, 3(2): 203–20.

SHEARING, C. and STENNING, P. (1981), 'Modern Private Security: Its Growth and Implications', *Crime and Justice*, 3: 193–245.

SHERMAN, L., FARRINGTON, D. P., WELSH, B. C., and MACKENZIE, D. L. (2002) (eds), *Evidence-Based Crime Prevention*, London: Routledge.

SQUIRES, P. and STEPHEN, D. (2005), *Rougher Justice: Young People and Anti-social Behaviour*, Cullompton: Willan.

THALER, R. H. and SUNSTEIN, C. R. (2008), *Nudge: Improving Decisions about Health, Wealth, and Happiness*, New Haven, CT: Yale University Press.

TILLEY, N. (2005) (ed.), *Handbook of Crime Prevention and Community Safety*, Cullompton: Willan.

TILLEY, N. (2009), *Crime Prevention*, Cullompton: Willan.

TRAVIS, A. (2013), 'Police Federation's legitimacy queried in tough post-plebgate review', *The Guardian*, 30 October, available at: https://www.theguardian.com/uk-news/2013/oct/30/police-federation-plebgate-review, accessed 9 January 2017.

TREMBLAY, R. and CRAIG, W. (1995), 'Developmental Crime Prevention', *Crime and Justice*, 19: 151–237.

UTTING, D. (2004), 'Overview and Conclusion', in C. Sutton, D. Utting, and D. Farrington (eds), *Support from the Start: Working with Young Children and their Families to Reduce the Risks of Crime and Anti-Social Behaviour*, London: Department for Education and Skills.

VAN DIJK, J. and DE WAARD, J. (2009), 'Forty years of crime prevention in the Dutch polder', in A. Crawford (ed.), *Crime Prevention Policies in Comparative Perspective*, Cullompton: Willan.

VAN DIJK J., TSELONI, A., and FARRELL, G. (2012) (eds), *The International Crime Drop*, London: Palgrave Macmillan.

VON HIRSCH, A. and SHEARING, C. (2000), 'Exclusion from Public Space', in A. Von Hirsch, D. Garland, and A. Wakefield (eds), *Ethical and Social Perspectives on Situational Crime Prevention*, Oxford: Hart.

WEATHERITT, M. (1986), *Innovations in Policing*, London: Croom Helm.

WHITE, A. (2010), *The Politics of Private Security*, London: Palgrave Macmillan.

WHITE, A. and GILL, M. (2013), 'The Transformation of Policing: From Ratios to Rationalities', *British Journal of Criminology*, 53(1): 74–93.

WHITE, C. and DAY, L. (2016), *National Evaluation of the Troubled Families Programme. Final Report on the Process Evaluation*, London: Department for Communities and Local Government.

WILES, P. and PEASE, K. (2000), 'Crime Prevention and Community Safety: Tweedledum and Tweedledee?', in S. Ballintyne, K. Pease, and V. McLaren (eds), *Secure Foundations: Key Issues in Crime Prevention, Crime Reduction and Community Safety*, London: IPPR.

WILLIAMS, L. (2016) (eds), *Crime Against Businesses: Findings From the 2015 Commercial Victimisation Survey*, Statistical Bulletin 03/16, London: Home Office.

WILSON, J. Q. (1975), *Thinking About Crime*, New York: Vintage.

WILSON, J. Q. and KELLING, G. (1982), 'Broken Windows: The Police and Neighbourhood Safety', *The Atlantic Monthly*, 249(3): 29–38.

YOUNG, J. (1999), *The Exclusive Society*, London: Sage.

ZEDNER, L. (2006), 'Policing before and After the Police', *British Journal of Criminology*, 46: 78–96.

ZEDNER, L. (2007), 'Pre-Crime and Post-Criminology', *Theoretical Criminology*, 11(2): 261–81.

ZEDNER, L. (2009), 'Fixing the Future? The pre-emptive turn in criminal justice', in B. McSherry, A. Norrie, and S. Bronitt (eds), *Regulating Deviance: The Redirection of Criminalisation and the Futures of Criminal Law*, Oxford: Hart Publishing, pp. 35–58.

36

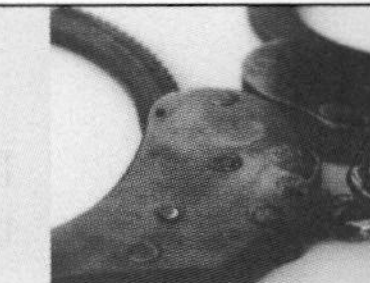

PRINCIPLES, PRAGMATISM, AND PROHIBITION: EXPLAINING CONTINUITY AND CHANGE IN BRITISH DRUG POLICY

Alex Stevens

INTRODUCTION

The assumption that drugs involve criminality is central to our concept of what a drug is (Seddon 2016). We have other names for substances that have similar effects but are not illegal to possess, like alcohol, tobacco, and medicines. The category of 'drugs' has come to include only those substances which are legally prohibited. How did this come to be? Why is it a crime to possess cannabis, but not vodka? How can we explain the development and contents of British drug policies? And what effects do these policies have? These are the questions that this chapter seeks to answer.

One way to go about answering such questions would be to assume that drug policy is a product of a rational, evidence-based process. It would involve the creation of objective information about the nature and scale of the harms and benefits of drug use. It would then test measures to reduce harms and enhance benefits. Only those measures which proved to be effective and humane would be implemented. But drug policy—like most other public policies—is not made this way (Cairney 2011; Hill 2009). For example, the potential benefits of drug use are very rarely considered in drug policy discussions, although there have been many estimates of the harms (e.g. Godfrey *et al.* 2002; MacDonald *et al.* 2005; Nutt *et al.* 2010). Some policies which have proven to be effective in reducing harms in the UK and elsewhere have been ended or never officially started. Examples include the provision of heroin-assisted treatment and safe drug consumption rooms for people who inject drugs (Potier *et al.* 2014; Strang *et al.* 2015). Other policies which have never been properly evaluated—like major investment in the policing of drug users, in border control and in long-term imprisonment of drug law offenders—continue in the absence of evidence that they reduce harms (Babor *et al.* 2010).

This chapter will argue, in contrast, that drug policy results from the complex interplay of history, long-standing disagreements over the right principles to live by, and the process of argument between social groups who have won the power to influence drug policy. This includes professions inside the 'medico-penal' framework that took control of British drug policy in the early twentieth century and retains its influence to this day (Berridge 2013). Drug policy therefore reflects and reproduces inequalities between social groups. It involves the imposition of power by some groups of people over others. So it also involves argument. Paying attention to these inequalities and arguments allows us to examine the 'political economy of drug policy' (Stevens 2011).

This chapter first gives a chronological history of the arguments that have shaped British drug policy, largely based on the works of Virginia Berridge, James Mills, and Susanne MacGregor. It then uses three stories to show how British drug policy continues to be created through these processes of contestation. These stories involve the 'absorption' of recovery, the absurdity of the Psychoactive Substances Act 2016, and the 'silent silencing' of heroin-related deaths.

The chapter is theoretically informed by the emphasis of critical theorists on policy as a form of communication that reflects and reproduces social asymmetries in power (Habermas 2002; Thompson 1990). It uses Habermas' (1986: 241) idea that we can explain the outcome of legal and—by extension—policy processes 'in terms of interest and power constellations'. Methodologically, it takes the approach of within-case process tracing (Collier 2011). The UK is treated as a case within which it is possible to link events, actions, and arguments to create an understanding of how continuity and change in policy has been produced. Data for this analysis have been gathered from secondary sources, policy documents, media reports, ministerial speeches, and other forms of discourse, as well as through participant observation of the British drug policy process over the last 20 years.

For the purposes of this chapter, drug policy includes the laws, decisions, funding programmes, and instructions by which the state affects discourses and practices on illicit drugs. Discourses include the way people think, talk, and write. Practices include the actions that are done by, to, and for consumers, producers, and sellers of these substances. Policy is one of the ways in which governments exercise power, but—following Steven Lukes (1974)—we should remember that power is not merely the ability of governments to control decisions. Power is created and shared by social actors (within and outside the state) who have won the ability to shape how knowledge is produced and used in achieving their desired goals. The goals that these groups desire to achieve are various and often conflicting. They may include, for example, the capture of wealth, the promotion of behaviours that they think of as morally good, and the reproduction of their own privileged social positions.

A SHORT HISTORY OF BRITISH DRUG POLICY ARGUMENTS

The use of some psychoactive substances became prevalent before others. Alcohol and even tobacco became popular before the birth of the modern British state. By the time the state had developed the will and capacity to ban people's consumption practices, the use of these substances was already deeply embedded in commercial and everyday life. There was opposition to their use, particularly among those influenced by the puritan strand of Protestantism. State control of intoxication, which was initiated in 1552 by the licensing of ale-houses, accompanied the spread of both Protestantism and capitalism (Nicholls 2011). But even at the height of London's 'gin craze' of the early eighteenth century, alcohol was not banned, but rather taxed and regulated (Warner 2002). The use of some psychoactive substances has long been common across social classes. Such substances are viewed as 'domestic', compared to those 'foreign' substances (like cocaine and cannabis) that were brought to the UK in the twentieth century (Harris 2005). The history of British drug policy can be seen as a history of arguments over how to define and deal with such 'foreign' substances.

In the nineteenth century, when opium poppies were grown in the Cambridgeshire fens and their products were widely available to the British public, opium could also be seen as a domestic substance (Berridge 1999). But in the 1850s and 60s, concern grew over the number of deaths among children who were given opium-based products by their parents, sometimes as pacifiers while they were at work. Doctors and chemists were able to use these concerns to win control of these effective painkillers. The 1868 Pharmacy Act gave exclusive rights to sell opium products to registered pharmacists. It was opposed by other retailers who were profiting from such sales. There have been disagreements about who gets to control drugs ever since. As we will see, these arguments often use the deaths of children and young people.

The next major developments in international—if not British—drug policy resulted from geopolitical rather than professional disagreements. As an imperial power, Britain itself profited from sales of opium and cannabis that were produced in its colonies. It had fought two wars (in 1839–42 and 1856–60) to force China to accept the import of opium produced in Bengal. By the early twentieth century, however, the moral and commercial interests of other powers (primarily the USA) led them to call for international control of opium at the International Opium Commission of 1909, and Britain could no longer resist (Musto 1999). By the time of the Hague Convention of 1912, British civil servants were arguing that cocaine (in which Britain had no significant commercial interest) should be included in the international system of prohibition (Mills 2014). However, these international agreements had little impact on drug policy within the UK. Domestic legislation was only developed after the Home Office gained control of drug policy during the First World War (Berridge 2013). The first British law to ban possession of opium and cocaine was introduced in 1916 by regulation 40B of the 1914 Defence of the Realm Act. This followed concern over the sale of cocaine to soldiers on their way to fight in the trenches. After the war, the Hague convention was incorporated into the Treaty of Versailles, and thence into British law. Moral concern arose over the supposed corruption of young white women by Chinese sellers of opium (Kohn 2001). Possession of heroin and cocaine were included as offences in the 1920 Dangerous Drugs Act. It did not become a crime to possess cannabis until 1928, after another international convention (in Geneva in 1924/5) had included this plant in the international drug control system. Britain again opposed such international law, in part because taxes were still being gathered from the sale of Indian cannabis, but also because there was very little use of cannabis in the UK at the time (Mills 2003).

The opiate medicine diacetylmorphine had been marketed under its brand name, heroin, by the Bayer pharmaceutical company since 1898. Concern over an increasing number of 'addicts' and overdose deaths grew in the 1920s. A committee of inquiry, chaired by Sir Humphrey Rolleston, was convened to consider how best to respond. It heard evidence from doctors who worked in and outside prisons. Those who worked in prison tended to argue for punitive control of heroin users, including abrupt abstinence. Doctors outside prison tended to see a more genteel class of heroin user. They favoured a less harsh, maintenance approach. Rolleston's report agreed with them that heroin use should be treated as a disease, not a crime. This led to the development of the 'British system' of prescribing heroin to people who could not stop using it (Berridge 1999). But heroin 'addiction' was not treated as a purely medical issue. In the decades that followed, Berridge (2013) observes the continued development of the 'medico-penal framework', with medical professionals, the Home Office, and the police negotiating the development of drug policy, largely between themselves.

There was little change until the late 1950s, when fears grew of the use of cannabis by visiting African American jazz musicians and African-Caribbean immigrants in blues clubs (Yates 2002). So began an era of 'moral panics'. The previously 'subterranean' values (Matza 1961) of hedonism, excitement, and instant consumption broke through the puritanical surface of industrial capitalism, with its emphasis on hard work and the deferral of gratification. Criminologists of the time, including Jock Young (1971), observed a 'deviancy amplification spiral' in action. New behaviours (such as the use of cannabis and LSD) challenged existing moral values, leading to press coverage, leading in turn to both perceived and real increases of the new behaviour, accompanied by increasing demands that 'something must be done'. Something was legislation. Parliament passed Dangerous Drugs Acts in 1964 and 1965, the Drugs (Prevention of Misuse) Act in 1964, the Dangerous Drugs (Supply to Addicts) Regulations in 1968, and the Misuse of Drugs Act in 1971. These laws and their enforcement were opposed by new organizations, such as Release and the Soma Research Association, which developed out of the 'alternative society' of the 1960s and were concerned with the human rights of drug users (Abrams 2008; Mold 2006).

The laws of the early 1960s followed a new international treaty which is still in force: the UN Single Convention on Narcotic Drugs of 1961. They brought amphetamines, LSD, and the cultivation of cannabis under the criminal law. The principal effect of the 1968 Regulations was to restrict permission to prescribe heroin to doctors who were specifically licensed by the Home Office. This restriction was a response to concerns over excessive prescription by a small number of private doctors, as expressed by another committee, chaired by Lord Brain. Yet another committee, chaired by Baroness Wootton, was commissioned to examine the rising use of cannabis. It concluded that cannabis was less harmful than other illicit drugs, and therefore should be subject to lighter punishments (the law of the time had the same sentences for cannabis as for heroin and cocaine). But while the Home Office had acted quickly to implement the Brain committee's recommendations for more restrictive regulation, the Wootton report of 1969 was immediately rejected by the then Home Secretary, James Callaghan. He argued that it would give the impression that the government did not take cannabis offences seriously (Oakley 2012). Callaghan's more liberally minded cabinet colleagues eventually overruled him. He introduced the bill that became the Misuse of Drugs Act (MDA) in 1971. This set up the current legal system of classificatory control. It was intended to calibrate the punishments for drug offences to the drug's capacity to cause a 'social problem'. Cannabis was placed in class B. Heroin, cocaine, and LSD were placed in class A. The MDA also set up the Advisory Council on the Misuse of Drugs (ACMD) as an independent body to advise ministers on drug classification and the reduction of drug-related harms.[1]

In the late 1960s and 70s, treatment of people who were dependent on heroin was moved from independent physicians into specialist drug dependency units (DDUs). Doctors in the DDUs increasingly used the opiate substitute methadone, rather than heroin itself, to stave off their patients' cravings. This did not prevent a substantial increase in the following years in the numbers of 'registered addicts'. There were a few hundred in the mid-1960s, largely supplied by doctors in London. By the end of 1970s, there were a few thousand, supplied by a burgeoning illegal market.

The 1980s saw the triple epidemics of social inequality, heroin, and HIV. The growth of the economy, wages, and the welfare state had reduced inequality after the Second World War. This reversed sharply after 1978. The incomes of the richest grew much faster than those of the poorest. In the following decade, heroin markets spread rapidly from London to the areas of Scotland, South Wales, and the north of England where rapid deindustrialization produced mass unemployment. As the illegal markets expanded, and other sources of meaningful occupation disappeared, a generation of 'new heroin users' took up the drug (Pearson 1987). Non-medical heroin use had previously been associated with bourgeois dissolution and the bohemian, 'beatnik' lifestyle. As many young members of the working class started injecting heroin, and the HIV virus reached the UK, the figure of the 'junkie' came more firmly to be associated with the threats of crime and disease. In 1986, it was estimated that up to 85 per cent of people who were injecting drugs in Edinburgh were HIV positive (Robertson *et al.* 1986); a dramatic figure which again led to calls for action.

In 1988, the ACMD advised the government that the threat from HIV was greater than that from drug use itself. So the priority should be to reduce the harms of drug use rather than to end it. It was thought at the time that HIV might spill out from injecting drug users into the general population through sexual transmission. Faced with an apparent public health emergency, the government accepted the ACMD's advice. It provided new funding for harm reduction services, such as syringe exchange programmes and methadone maintenance treatment, including by organizations other than the DDUs (MacGregor 1998). This was a successful policy. The HIV epidemic was mitigated. Rates of infection among people who inject drugs have been consistently lower in the UK than in countries, such as Russia and the USA, which have been more reluctant to implement harm reduction measures.

[1] At the time of writing (summer 2016), I am a member of the ACMD. However, the views presented in this chapter should not be taken to represent those of the ACMD as a whole.

Paradoxically, this success in preventing HIV transmission made it harder for drug treatment professionals to attract funds to treat the still-growing numbers of heroin users. A new reason to fund treatment was found in the connection between drugs and crime. The rise in the use of crack that occurred in the 1990s helped in creating the link. This crystallized form of cocaine had acquired a discursive linkage with violent crime by black people in the USA (Reinarman and Levine 1997). The use of 'heroin and/or crack' came to be taken as the defining feature of the criminal 'high harm causing user' in the UK (PMSU 2003). There is a very strong correlation between illicit drug use and other crimes. People who commit crimes are more likely to use illicit drugs, and vice versa (Bennett and Holloway 2007). Politically, claims were made (e.g. by Tony Blair in 1994) that half of all acquisitive crime was caused by drug users. Academically, it was claimed that drugs accounted for half of all murders in New York City at the height of the crack epidemic (Goldstein *et al.* 1989). As I have shown elsewhere (Stevens 2011), both claims are highly questionable. But they were rarely questioned. They proved very useful in persuading the New Labour government of 1997 to invest in drug treatment as a crime reduction measure.

In addition to this new funding, the government also created new laws to direct drug using offenders into treatment. The Crime and Disorder Act of 1998 created the drug treatment and testing order (DTTO), which was superseded (in England and Wales) by the drug rehabilitation requirement (DRR) in the Criminal Justice Act of 2003. Both the DTTO and the DRR enable courts to place conditions on offenders who consent to treatment that they must attend it for a certain amount of time and submit to drug testing. In England and Wales, the Drugs Act of 2005 was used to expand the Drug Interventions Programme. Under the slogan of 'Tough Choices', some police services used new powers to test arrestees for drugs and to require those who tested positive to attend a treatment assessment (Seddon *et al.* 2012). Expansion of treatment services and of the use of these new powers increased the numbers of people in treatment, largely methadone maintenance. As such services have good evidence that they reduce crime and drug-related death, this probably had two beneficial effects. One was to contribute to the reduction in acquisitive crime that has occurred since the mid-1990s (Morgan 2014). The other was to limit the growth in drug-related deaths. It has been estimated that treatment services in England were preventing about 880 deaths per year by the late 2000s (Pierce *et al.* 2015).

Cannabis use also rose in the 1990s, to the point where academic arguments broke out over whether the activity had become 'normalized' (Parker *et al.* 1998; Shiner and Newburn 1999). Concerns were still being expressed that the harms imposed by criminalization were disproportionate to the harms of cannabis itself. These concerns were clearly expressed in a report by a group of experts brought together by the Police Foundation, chaired by Dame Runciman (Independent Inquiry into the Misuse of Drugs Act 1971, 2000). As Home Secretary, David Blunkett moved cannabis from class B to class C of the MDA in 2004. This led to much debate in the media and between experts (Monaghan 2010). The government consulted repeatedly with the ACMD, which repeatedly advised that cannabis should stay in class C. But cannabis was moved back up to class B in 2009. This was a victory for the arguments of those informed by puritan moralism, including the then prime minister, Gordon Brown. In 2007, he claimed the drug was 'lethal' and that tighter classification was needed to 'send out a message' to young people.[2]

THE MEDICO-PENAL CONSTELLATION IN BRITISH DRUG POLICY

Some general themes arise from this brief historical review. The first is the enduring conflict between differing moral principles. This can be seen in the expressed desires of successive politicians to use drug policy to send messages about appropriate behaviour, rather than to follow evidence on levels of harmfulness. The inherently moral argument over whether people should be free to intoxicate themselves has never been decisively resolved. But when these moralities conflict, as they did at the Rolleston committee in the 1920s, in the debate over cannabis that followed the Wootton Report in the 1960s, and in the response to HIV/AIDS in the 1980s, a pragmatic response can emerge. Such pragmatic 'fudging' of the moral issues enables British drug policy to adapt to changing patterns of drug use and the different contexts within which it takes place (MacGregor 1998).

So the second theme to emerge from this account is the possibility of pragmatic use of the available evidence. This tends to occur at times where dramatic increases are perceived to be occurring in drug use or related harms. A third theme is the relatively closed processes that are adopted for the resolution of such debates. While there have often been lively discussions in the media, drug policy decisions in the UK are not taken by voting in referenda, as they sometimes are in the USA and Switzerland. Rather, the government tends to deal with publicly expressed concerns by referring them to expert committees which then take evidence and conduct debate, largely behind closed doors. Their findings are turned into concrete policy proposals by civil servants, who are also able to shape ministerial initiatives to conform to existing practices. Members of the public—including drug users themselves—rarely get a direct voice in these discussions.

A fourth theme is the persistent, productive tensions between the imperatives of public health and of law and order within such processes. For many years now, the dominant forces in drug policy discussions have been—on the one hand—public health professionals and parts of the medical establishment and—on the other—Home Office civil servants and the police. Of course, there is much scope for overlap between these groups and their priorities. Public health policies have often involved coercive measures. Some people who are in methadone maintenance treatment experience it as a form of social control (Harris and McElrath 2012).

[2] Gordon Brown later told the Leveson Inquiry into press standards that his decision to put cannabis back to class B was not because of pressure from the media, but because he personally held 'strong views' on the subject; views that are consistent with his Presbyterian protestant background.

So the people and organizations at the centre of British drug policy-making can be thought of as a medico-penal constellation;[3] a set of actors who are linked by overlapping beliefs as well as by their professional positions and interests. It is the members of this constellation who create British drug policy. People outside these groups who are motivated by other concerns—such as moral attachments to sobriety or individual freedom—have had less direct influence. As Habermas (1986: 241) has noted, when there is a clash between value preferences, it is those that are held by the most powerful constellations that tend to prevail. In the field of drug policy, this has included those agencies which implement the state's monopoly of physical force and coercion over its own citizens, which includes the Home Office, prisons, and the police. But it also includes those who deploy what Joe Sim (1990)—following Michel Foucault—has referred to as 'medical power'. This is the form of power that has been gained by state-accredited medical experts to decide who is and who is not 'normal', to define and correct the bodies and behaviours of those who are considered deviant through processes of assessment and classification. This form of power can be used on individual patients, but it can also be applied to groups within society; groups which experts can create as targets for policy through epidemiological methods of measurement and categorization. As Sim notes, the exercise of such biomedical discipline is highly compatible with more directly coercive practices of social control. More recently, Roger Matthews has argued that, rather than 'governing through crime' in accordance with the ideas of Jonathan Simon (2007), the focus of Western governments has shifted to 'governing through health and lifestyle'. This includes 'moral crusades' against consumption practices that are seen as unhealthy (Matthews 2014: 149). In the field of British drug policy, both forms of governance have been applied to those people who have been identified by criminological and medical experts as deviating from acceptable norms in both their offending and their health behaviours.

As Sim (1990) also notes, the deployment of these forms of power creates resistance. Members of other, contesting constellations have been able to put pressure on actors within the medico-penal constellation, especially during the opening of 'policy windows' (Kingdon 1984). These are conjunctions of events and political circumstances that create opportunities to change policy discourses and practices. Of course, elected politicians have the final say, but they are rarely the source of innovation in British drug policy. Rather, they have tended either to block or approve proposals that have come from or through the medico-penal constellation.

[3] 'Constellation' is a term that has recently been imported into the study of drug policy by Giulia Zampini (2016). It is used in social network analysis to describe a group of people who share social proximity and connections, without necessarily sharing all the same interests or beliefs. The term 'constellation' is preferred to 'framework' as it implies a connected group of policy actors within a broader policy network. It is used instead of the word 'coalition' (which is more common in policy studies; Sabatier and Jenkins-Smith 1993) because the latter implies both homogeneity between the beliefs of its members and deliberate coordination of their actions. I suggest that the members of the medico-penal constellation may not share core beliefs about the moral principles of drug policy, may indeed have conflicting beliefs about appropriate policies to pursue, and do not operate through central coordination of their actions.

CONTESTATION IN ACTION IN CONTEMPORARY BRITISH DRUG POLICY

These themes emerge from an analysis of recurring patterns in the drug policy arguments of the nineteenth and twentieth centuries. They can also help us understand the content of contemporary policy. In this section, I will tell three stories about the recent development of British drug policy. They will illustrate how it is made, and why it is as it is. The main players in these stories will be the organizations that are involved in the medico-penal constellation. On the side of this constellation that is most concerned with public health are public health officials, as well as the doctors, psychiatrists, pharmacists, and other professionals that they work with and fund. It also includes many of the members of the ACMD. This committee involves some police and probation representatives. It also contains some social scientists—like me—who favour individual freedom as well as public health. But most of its members are drawn from the medical and pharmacological professions. On the other side of this constellation, where the priority lies with law enforcement for social control, we can place civil servants in the drug and alcohol sections of the Home Office and their counterparts in Wales, Scotland, and Northern Ireland, as well as most representatives of prisons and the police. Another significant actor, in recent years, has been the right-of-centre think tank, the Centre for Social Justice (CSJ). This has pushed puritan policies from outside the medico-penal constellation, and has used its influence within the Conservative party to do so. Organizations that prioritize individual freedom and the human rights of drug users, such as Release and Transform, have developed relationships with the Liberal Democrats. They have produced proposals to legalize cannabis that are interesting, but not yet influential (e.g. Rolles *et al.* 2016).

THE 'ABSORPTION' OF RECOVERY

As the threat of HIV receded at the end of the twentieth century, long-running arguments between those who favour harm reduction and abstinence re-emerged. The former group tends to have a moral preference for the state not to punish or coerce people. They focus on the evidence that heroin dependence is a 'chronic, relapsing condition' and that harm reduction services save lives. Those who prefer abstinence tend to focus on a moral distaste for drug use and the evidence that most drug users who enter treatment want to become 'drug-free' (McKeganey *et al.* 2004). These debates came to focus on the symbolic term 'recovery'. This was imported from the USA, where it had been defined as involving the achievement of sobriety. It also has a profoundly moralistic tone. The effect of social inequality in providing the conditions for higher rates of drug use and dependence is replaced, in the right-wing discourse of recovery, with an emphasis on the individual's responsibility to choose to stop taking drugs; to become self-reliant rather than dependent. Opponents of harm reduction argued that drug services were not being ambitious enough for their patients. They claimed that thousands of these people were being 'parked' on methadone. These people should instead be encouraged to recover.

In Scotland, such arguments were taken up directly into drug policy in the country's 2008 drug strategy document, *The Road to Recover*. The response in England was rather more ambivalent. Many people in the field of drug treatment saw the emphasis on recovery as a direct attack on the harm reduction services that they perceived as successful. But they could also see, as the 2010 general election approached and the prospect of a Conservative government loomed, that they could not simply ignore or rebut calls for recovery (as was done in Australia; Lancaster *et al.* 2015). Prospective ministers, like Chris Grayling and Iain Duncan Smith, were echoing the CSJ's call for resources to be switched from methadone maintenance to abstinence-based rehabilitation. So, as would be expected by the criminologist Thomas Mathiesen, this challenge to the prevailing way of doing things was 'absorbed'. Mathiesen (2004: 15) writes that challenges which cannot be ignored tend to be 'integrated in the prevailing order in such a way that dominant interests continue to be served'.

This was done partly by redefining what 'recovery' means. For example, the UK Drug Policy Commission (a self-appointed body made up largely of senior people from the liberal wing of the medico-penal constellation) created a 'consensus group' to report on recovery (UKDPC 2008). Instead of being about sobriety, they stated that recovery is about 'control' over drug use. The difference is crucial, as it allows people who are currently prescribed methadone or other opiate substitutes into the category of the recovering drug user. It enables such treatment to be relabelled as 'recovery-oriented', as was duly done. The English drug strategy of 2008 did not make extensive use of the term recovery, but it did put a focus on improving the quality of drug treatment to enable more people to leave it free of drugs. Wales—like Scotland—is covered by the MDA but has its own health system. Its 2008 strategy placed much less emphasis on recovery and continued to prioritize harm reduction, as could be seen in its title: *Working Together to Reduce Harm* (Lloyd 2009).

When the Conservative Party entered government in 2010 it did not have a Parliamentary majority. Its coalition partners, the Liberal Democrats, did not support the Conservative vision of recovery, as it conflicts with their more liberal position on drug policy. The new drug strategy of 2010 announced on its cover that it was about 'supporting people to live a drug-free life'. However, the contents were nowhere near as radical as pre-election speeches by Grayling and Duncan Smith had suggested. For example, it still mentioned the need to provide heroin on prescription for some drug users. This would support suggestions that people within the civil service had been able to reduce the impact of ministerial change on policy.

The clearest official reflection of the wishes of the CSJ was published in a 2012 policy document. This was covered with the logos of eight government departments which have some role in drug policy. It was entitled *Putting Full Recovery First* (Inter-Ministerial Group on Drugs 2012). This 'recovery roadmap' claimed that the 'greatest challenge' to the success of drug treatment was the 'attitudes and practices' of treatment professionals. It promised a new era of 'payment by results', in which 'payment will be for full recovery only'. Full recovery was defined not as control over use, but as abstinence from all illicit and substitute drugs. It stated that the government would 'maximise access to abstinence-based' treatment. This would be done partly by reducing the amount of time that people would be prescribed methadone, and partly by involving 'strategic recovery champions' in the management of the drug treatment system. These would be people who have succeeded in recovering from drug addiction themselves and so could lead other drug users along the steps to sobriety.

This was an extraordinary challenge to previous practices. The established practice has been that public health professionals work with local partners to distribute funding to drug treatment services, most of whom provide opiate substitution to patients for as long as they need it. However, the aim of putting 'full recovery first' was never fully implemented. There was a pilot of the payment-by-results approach. This was unsuccessful. It produced worse outcomes than the existing model of paying for service provision (Mason *et al.* 2015). Ministers twice asked expert committees to consider putting time limits on opiate substitution treatment. On both occasions, the experts found that this would be an ineffective and even dangerous practice, due to the proven benefits of such treatments and the elevated death rates among people who leave it (ACMD 2014; Recovery Orientated Drug Treatment Expert Group 2012). Control of drug treatment in England was not given to 'recovery champions'. It was devolved to local Directors of Public Health as part of the 2013 restructuring of the National Health Service, in line with Conservative attempts to increase the use of market mechanisms and competition at the local level in the delivery of public services. Instead of growing, residential rehabilitation shrank as commissioners focused tightening funds on less expensive services (Recovery Partnership 2016).

However, the challenge of recovery was not just ignored, but absorbed. The proportion of people leaving treatment 'drug-free' became part of the English public health outcomes framework. The funding formula for local areas was changed to reward those which produced a higher proportion. Commissioners of drug treatment services increasingly used the language of payment-by-results, even if the majority of the funding continued to be payment-for-service. Continuing attempts to improve the quality of drug treatment were placed under the banner of recovery. Treatment professionals encouraged their patients to move from maintenance prescriptions to reducing towards abstinence. As one drug worker in London told researcher Fay Dennis (2016), 'we're always looking for reduction [in opiate substitution dosage]'. Another told her that harm reduction now sounded 'old-fashioned'. But many drug users have reported that the quality of service suffered. Specifically, they have reported that treatment providers—who are under pressure to produce 'drug-free' completions—have been pushing people to leave opiate substitution treatment before they are ready. As noted above, this is a dangerous practice.

THE ABSURDITY OF THE PSYCHOACTIVE SUBSTANCES ACT

The late 2000s saw a new development in the UK illicit drug market, with the arrival of substances that were known as 'legal highs' or 'novel psychoactive substances' (NPS). Since the 1960s, there had been a slow trickle of new substances into the repertoire of recreational drug use. MDMA (3,4 methylenedioxy-methamphetamine, or Ecstasy) became popular as part of the Balearic rave scene of the late 1980s. Other relatively new substances included ketamine and GHB/GBL (gamma hydroxybutyric acid and its prodrug,[4] gamma butyrolactone). MDMA had already been banned under class

[4] A prodrug is a substance that, when ingested, is turned into another active substance in the body.

A of the Misuse of Drugs Act in 1977. Ketamine was placed in class C in 2006. So was GHB/GBL in 2009. Ketamine was moved to class B in 2014.

The flow of new substances on to the market has accelerated in recent years, although their use remains concentrated among disadvantaged groups in the population (such as prisoners, the homeless and vulnerable young people). In 2008, less than 20 new substances were notified to the European Union Early Warning System. In 2014, this number was over 100 (EMCDDA 2015). Most of these have been either synthetic substances which have effects similar to (but sometimes stronger than) cannabis, or synthetic cathinone stimulants. The first synthetic cathinone to get a significant share of the UK market was mephedrone. Its effects were described by users as being similar to cocaine and MDMA. It rose in popularity during a period of low purity of both these substances. Media reports began to appear about deaths of young people who had taken mephedrone, although some turned out to be incorrect after toxicological autopsies.[5] Many of them called for the substance to be banned. Following the advice of the ACMD, in a controversial process involving arguments within the council,[6] mephedrone was placed in class B of the MDA in 2010.

The banning of mephedrone did not stop the appearance or use of NPS. Ministers asked the ACMD to advise on several new substances. A new legal measure, the temporary class drug order (TCDO), was introduced in 2011 in order to speed up the process of control. The Home Office has described this as a game of 'cat and mouse'. It presented the problem as being caused by ingenious, foreign chemists who respond to each new ban by developing new substances that are not covered by the law. This metaphor discursively excludes the idea that it is prohibition itself which causes new substances to emerge; that the demand for NPS results from the lack of legal access to cannabis, MDMA, and cocaine. The metaphor used by opponents of prohibition to illustrate this idea was the game of 'whack-a-mole'. If you crack down on one substance, this suggests, another is bound to pop up. Each of these metaphors suggests a different response. If the game is 'cat and mouse', then we need to build a better mouse trap. A method must be found to kill all the mice at once. But if we are playing 'whack-a-mole', the metaphorical suggestion is that we should stop playing this futile game and develop a more sensible approach.

The 'cat-and-mouse' metaphor fitted better with the discourses and practices of members of the medico-penal constellation, so the search was on for a better mouse trap. As usual, this task was delegated to an expert committee. Given that the junior Home Office minister who did this, Norman Baker, was a Liberal Democrat member of the coalition government, one might have expected him to prefer a liberal recommendation from the committee. But most of its members did not share his liberal approach. In its report, this 'New Psychoactive Substances Expert Panel' (2014) recommended that the government follow the example of Ireland's Criminal Justice (Psychoactive

[5] For example, in March 2010, there were many press reports on the deaths of Louis Wainwright, 18, and Nicholas Smith, 19. These reports attributed their deaths to mephedrone. However, when the inquest took place, it found that there had been no trace of mephedrone in these young men's bodies. They had recently used both alcohol and methadone.

[6] There was disagreement within the ACMD on whether mephedrone should be banned. One member of the committee, Eric Carlin, resigned over his concerns that the decision was based on media and political pressure, and that it would disproportionately criminalize young people.

Substances) Act of 2010. This introduced a blanket ban on the trade in all psychoactive substances except for those that were specifically exempted from the ban, including alcohol, tobacco, medicines, food, and substances which were already banned under other legislation.

The government quickly accepted this recommendation, despite the fact that there had been no formal evaluation of the effects of the Irish law. It did not acknowledge that such a ban breaks a fundamental legal principle that 'what is not forbidden is allowed'. Indeed, it reversed this principle. A blanket ban with exemptions implies that 'what is not specifically allowed is forbidden'. This is a major extension of the reach of the state into the lives of its citizens. The UK government compounded these problems in the Psychoactive Substances Bill, which it introduced in 2015, by using a problematic definition of the substances of which it proposed to prohibit the production, importation, or supply (Stevens *et al.* 2015). This definition included any substance which '(a) is capable of producing a psychoactive effect in a person who consumes it, and (b) is not an exempted substance'. A substance is considered to be psychoactive if 'by stimulating or depressing the person's central nervous system, it affects the person's mental functioning or emotional state'.

During the passage of the bill through Parliament, the ACMD repeatedly explained to the Home Secretary that this definition was scientifically flawed and would make it very difficult to enforce the law. There is, the ACMD stated, no way of telling whether a substance is psychoactive without doing thorough tests on human beings. As such tests would be lengthy, costly, and unethical, this would create the absurd situation where it is impossible for courts to distinguish between substances that the law does and does not cover.

The new law was enacted in 2016 despite these problems and absurdities. This provides a very interesting example of how evidence—or even logical coherence—is not necessary as a basis for drug policy when a proposed policy chimes with dominant moralities and discourses within the medico-penal constellation. It also shows again that this constellation is not homogeneous. Several people who are within it, including some of those who were on the NPS expert panel, have criticized the Psychoactive Substances Act. When arguments break out within this constellation, the balance of power lies on the side of coercive social control. The political power of ministers in the Home Office enables them to select which proposals will make it into law and official policy. In justifying their support for this Act, they made repeated references to the urgent need to prevent deaths. In doing so, I will argue in the next section, they engaged in the 'silent silencing' of a much larger category of drug-related deaths; those related to heroin.

THE 'SILENT SILENCING' OF HEROIN RELATED DEATHS

'Silent silencing' is another concept taken from the work of Mathiesen (2004). It refers to the processes, including 'absorption', through which challenges to the prevailing order are rendered powerless, but without there being open, public conflict. Two of the other components of silent silencing that Mathiesen identifies are 'legalization' and 'masking'. The first involves the translation of social problems into a question of law, and so excluding the possibility that social changes other than new legislation may be necessary. The second involves disguising a problem under the name of another, which may be presented as amenable to solving by legislation. Both these techniques of silencing are visible in ministerial speeches that have referred to the problem of drug-related death. For example, during the second Commons reading of the Psychoactive Substances Bill, the minister responsible for it, Mike Penning, made the following statement:

> Let us see whether we can save lives, bearing in mind the 129 we lost last year. That figure is growing dramatically year on year . . . people have said to me, 'Why don't you wait for the evidence to come through?' and I am not willing to do that because too many people have died in the interim period.

Here, he draws a clear link between the problem of drug-related deaths and the urgent need for new legislation. This speech can be compared to official statistics on drug-related deaths, as shown in Figure 36.1 and 36.2. Figure 36.1 shows that there has indeed been a dramatic increase in the numbers of such deaths that have been recorded in recent years.[7] They climbed by 29 per cent from 2012 to 2014. The numbers suggest there is indeed a pressing problem with drug deaths that may require government action to solve. But which drugs would we need to focus on in order significantly to reduce these deaths? Figure 36.2 shows the number of deaths in England and Wales in which specific substances were mentioned on the death certificate in 2014. It should be noted that many of these deaths involved more than one substance. 30 per cent of them also involved the recent or long-term use of alcohol (ONS 2015). The number of death certificates that mentioned NPS was 67, a rise of 15 per cent since 2012. But we should remember that most of these substances had already been controlled under the MDA. This left 18 deaths that were linked to substances that would be newly controlled by the Psychoactive Substances Act (referred to as 'legal highs' in figure 36.2). This compares to 952 deaths in which heroin was implicated; a number that had risen by 64 per cent since 2012. So both in absolute numbers and in percentage terms, deaths from heroin could be seen as far more 'dramatic' than deaths from uncontrolled NPS. Yet the government has proposed no legal or policy changes for heroin. Instead, the government has chosen to present the problem of deaths in relation to NPS.

How can we explain this focus on NPS instead of heroin deaths? One way of doing so may be to look at press reports of such deaths, in order to see what messages and metaphors the government is receiving through the media. I carried out a search of national newspapers, using the Nexis® database, for articles published in 2014 that reported deaths related either to NPS (using the search terms 'NPS' or 'legal high') or to opiates (using the search terms 'heroin' or 'methadone'). The deaths of 15 individuals were reported as related to NPS.[8] This represents one for every eight of the deaths that Mike Penning reported in his speech. There were also 15 deaths reported from opiates, but this only represents one for every 90 people whose deaths were recorded as being related to heroin or methadone. Most people who died from heroin or methadone were over 40 (PHE 2016), but the average age of the people whose deaths were

[7] There are often long delays in the recording of deaths, so many of these deaths will have occurred in previous years to those in which they are recorded.

[8] The search was for articles reporting deaths from these substances. In some cases—for both NPS and heroin—the eventual inquest found that the death was not related to the initially reported substance.

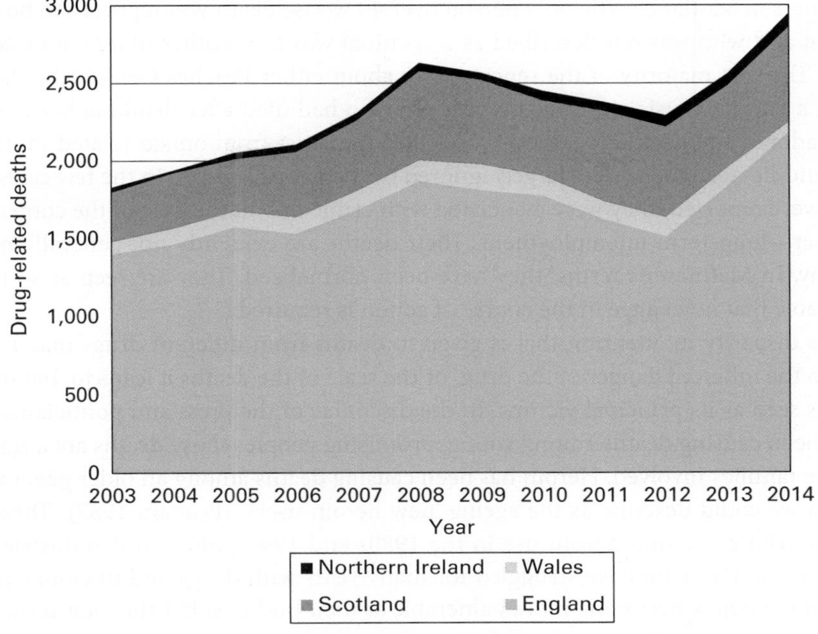

Figure 36.1 Number of drug-related deaths recorded in the UK, 2003–14
Source: ONS 2015.

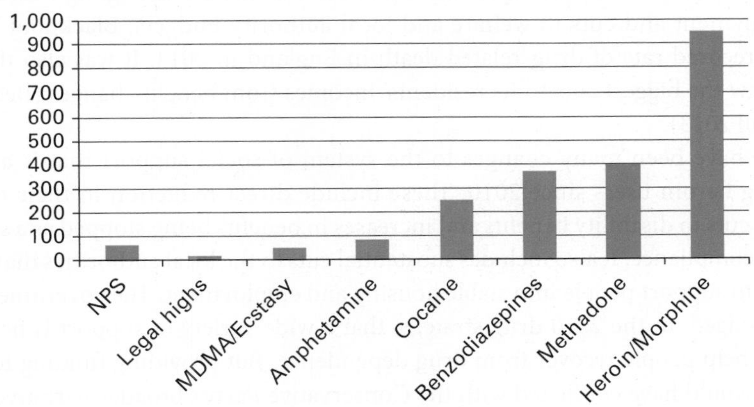

Figure 36.2 Numbers of death certificates in England and Wales that mentioned selected substances, 2014
Source: ONS 2015.

reported was 25 for both NPS and opiates. Reading these press reports, an interesting pattern emerged in the presentation of who these people were. Reports about people whose deaths were related to NPS frequently used terms like 'bright', 'student', or 'gifted'; terms that suggest a promising, middle-class life that has been tragically cut short. In contrast, the terms that were used in the reports of people who had died from opiates included 'junkie' and 'killer' (three of the deaths took place among convicted prisoners in Scotland). The only person over 40 whose death was reported to be from heroin and who was not described as a criminal was the brother of a famous comedian. The vast majority of the reports were about either Peaches Geldof (the daughter of a famous musician) or a two year old who had died after drinking her parents' methadone. The deaths of people who suffer the most from opiate-related mortality (i.e. middle-aged men) were largely ignored by the national press. In the few cases that they were reported, they were associated with crime or—in the case of the comedian's brother—long-term unemployment. Their deaths are evidently not generally newsworthy. In Mathiesen's terms, they have been normalized. They are seen as so unremarkable that no change in the course of action is required.[9]

The disparity in attention that is given to deaths from different drugs may not be due to the inherent danger of the drug, or the scale of the deaths it leads to, but due to *who* is seen as its principal victims. In the discourse of the press and politicians, NPS have been causing deaths among young, promising people whose deaths are a tragedy for the families involved. Heroin has been causing deaths among an older generation, whom we could describe as the ageing 'new heroin users' (Pearson 1987). These are people who came into heroin use in the 1980s and 1990s, often in deindustrialized areas of the UK, who have struggled for many years with drugs and unemployment, and who are now becoming more vulnerable as their bodies suffer the long-term consequences of street heroin use and inequality, often in combination with prolonged alcohol and tobacco use. The regional distribution of the deaths also suggests this pattern. Rates of death are much higher in Scotland and the north of England than in the home counties. They are especially high in towns that are struggling with ongoing unemployment and cuts to welfare and local authority budgets. Blackpool had the highest recored rate of drug-related death in England in 2014. It was also the town which saw the biggest cuts to its residents' incomes from benefit changes (Beatty and Fothergill 2013).

There have been many changes to the system of social support that is available to ageing heroin users since 2010. These include direct reduction in their incomes through cuts to disability benefits and increases in benefits being stopped as a sanction for non-compliance. It also includes substantial cuts to the local authorities that deliver services to support people into stable housing and employment. The government itself acknowledged, in the 2010 drug strategy, that a wide variety of support is needed in order to help people recover from drug dependence. But providing funding for these services would have conflicted with the Conservative Party's broader narrative on the need for cuts to both spending and taxes. Combining this withdrawal of support with pressure to leave treatment early would be expected to lead to an increase in deaths among heroin users. And this is what has occurred. Other changes, such as variations in the availability of street heroin, may also be part of the explanation of increasing deaths. What is important to note here is that the government has been silent on the potential effects of its policies on the risk of death for heroin users. It has preferred to highlight instead the much smaller rise in deaths associated with NPS as the reason for urgent, legislative action.

[9] This is a different meaning of the term 'normalization' than that used by Parker *et al.* (1998) to describe the spread in use and acceptance of cannabis among young people.

Again, this is not a homogeneous discourse within the medico-penal constellation or across the countries of the UK. Public Health England has taken steps—such as issuing guidelines and enabling the wider provision of naloxone[10]—to try and reverse the increase in heroin deaths. This response has been rather slower in England than in other parts of the UK, which have been quicker to expand access to naloxone. Wales is the only of the four UK countries to have maintained a strong emphasis on harm reduction in its strategy. It is also the only one of them to have seen significant reductions in drug-related deaths in recent years. None of these countries, however, have yet introduced some of the evidence-based harm reduction services that have emerged internationally since the 1980s. The establishment of safe drug consumption rooms has consistently been opposed by the Home Office, despite research suggesting that this would save lives by preventing overdose fatalities (Hunt and Lloyd 2008). On the basis of the evidence, funding for heroin-assisted treatment would be expanded to cover all dependent heroin users who have not been able to benefit from other opiate substitutes, as has happened in Switzerland. Instead, the three clinics that provided this service in England were closed in 2015. These services do not conform to the idea that people should use only the permitted range of psychoactive substances. They combine individual freedom with care for public health, and so do not have strong support from inside the medico-penal constellation that tends only to push for public health measures when they can also be presented as furthering social control.[11]

CONCLUSION

Drug policy is the product of discursive contestation between influential groups whose beliefs and interests overlap in the intersection of public health and social control; groups I have described as making up the medico-penal constellation. The intrusion of recovery into British policy is an example of influence from the competing constellation that favours a more puritan approach. There have also been occasional intrusions from the constellation that favours individual freedom. These include the 2004 move of cannabis to class C. Despite the 2009 reclassification back to class B, the number of police actions against cannabis users in England and Wales—including arrests and cannabis warnings[12]—has more than halved since 2008, following the removal of central targets for 'sanction detections' and cuts to the number of police officers. Neither TCDOs nor the Psychoactive Substances Act make it a crime to possess the substances

[10] Naloxone is a medicine that saves lives by quickly reversing the effect of a heroin overdose (McDonald and Strang 2016).

[11] Interestingly, the government's 2016 strategy for 'modernizing crime prevention' did include references to heroin-assisted treatment, but on the basis of its effects in crime reduction, rather than health protection.

[12] Cannabis warnings are an on-street written notice that the police in England and Wales can give to adults who are found in possession of small amounts of cannabis. It was introduced simultaneously with the 2004 reclassification of cannabis. A similar system of 'recorded police warnings' was announced for Scotland in 2015.

that they cover (except if the substance is possessed in prison; such possession was criminalized by the Act). These developments can be seen as pragmatic absorptions of the idea that it is disproportionate to criminalize simple possession. But the law still has the effect of making criminals of many of these substances' users. The dominant mode of supply of psychoactive substances is passing between friends and acquaintances who use them. Both TCDOS and the Psychoactive Substances Act criminalize supply (even without payment). This compounds the inconsistencies in legal response to different substances. If I buy you a shot of vodka, neither of us is breaking the law (as long as we are both adults). If I hand you a joint of cannabis, both of us are committing an offence. If I give you a bag of a brand new psychoactive substance, or pass you a balloon of nitrous oxide for you to inhale, only I would be classed as a criminal (unless you are in prison).

The process of contestation within and between the constellations that circle around drug policy produces policies that maintain the influence of the professions and social groups that have long dominated British drug policy (i.e. doctors, public health professionals, Home Office civil servants, and the police), while absorbing challenges that originate outside this medico-penal constellation. This constellation is inhabited by people from the most powerful social groups. Its members have been skilled in creating policies that have 'fudged' fundamental differences in principle and have been relatively successful in meeting some practical challenges. Some of the worst harms associated with illicit drug use, such as HIV infection and acquisitive crime, have been contained by the mixture of harm reduction and treatment expansion. These are consequences that were seen as risking the health and well-being of people outside the social groups who have suffered most from dependent drug use (i.e. disadvantaged members of the working class). There has been less emphasis, and less success, in reducing the harms that are concentrated on people who do take up problematic drug use, such as the recent rise in deaths by overdose. In recent years, the government has been able to silently silence these harms. On the basis of a reduction in youthful cannabis use since the early 2000s, the Home Office and senior politicians claimed that British drug policy is 'working'. They used this trend to justify the continuing criminalization of people for drug possession—which still leads to thousands of people getting criminal records every year—even though the Home Office's own research has told it that a country's drug use trends are not directly affected by the level of punishment of users (Home Office 2014).

These patterns and processes suggest some answers to the questions posed at the start of this chapter. The reason that some psychoactive substances are illegal to possess, while others are widely available and promoted, has something to do with the harms that these substances may cause. But it is also because some social groups have been able, through processes of contestation around and within the state, to reinforce their power and wealth and to promote their moral beliefs by placing controls on substances that are used by a minority of the population; a minority that can be presented as threatening 'others' in the shapes of foreign drug suppliers and unemployed heroin users, or as vulnerable young victims who must be protected from their own desires. The effect has been to produce a drug policy which seems incoherent and absurd in parts. This is not the product of a process of purely rational, deliberative communication. And it does not happen without reference to reason or evidence. It results from strategic contestation between social groups. Members of these groups have moral principles and rational abilities which they deploy in the arguments which create drug policy.

Of course, this chapter can only take us part of the way to a full explanation of the contents of British drug policy. The answers I have just given lead us on to a set of other, more sociological questions about why certain groups take certain positions, and why they have the power to win the acquiescence of others. Here, I have argued that it is essential to consider such social inequality if one wishes to understand both the history and the current, prohibitionist contents of British drug policy, which is the product of arguments and agreements between these social groups.

SELECTED FURTHER READING

I provide fuller examination of both the political economy of drug policy and the drug-crime link in my book, *Drugs, Crime and Public Health* (2011). Essential histories of the use and control of opiates and cannabis in the UK are provided by Berridge's *Opium and the People* and *Demons* (1999, 2013), and by Mills' *Cannabis Britannica* and *Cannabis Nation* (2003, 2013). Another interesting perspective on the development of our thinking on drugs and drug policy is provided by Seddon's *History of Drugs* (2010). Readers are also encouraged to seek out the various articles and chapters by Mold, Duke, Monaghan, and MacGregor, as well as Shiner's *Drug Use and Social Change* (2009) for information on how British drug policy has developed since the 1960s. For more on patterns of youthful drug use, see publications by Judith Aldridge, Fiona Measham, and their colleagues, including *Illegal Leisure Revisited* (2011). Those interested in the analysis and effects of different policies to reduce drug-related harms should read MacCoun and Reuter's *Drug War Heresies* (2001) and Babor *et al.*'s, *Drug Policy and the Public Good* (2010). A different view on harm reduction and recovery is given by McKeganey's *Controversies in Drugs Policy and Practice* (2010). Recent statistics on the drug situation in the UK are published annually in the reports of the UK National Focal Point on Drugs to the European Monitoring Centre for Drugs and Drug Addiction. Reports of the ACMD on various drug policy issues are available from its website.

REFERENCES

Abrams, S. (2008), 'Soma, the Wootton Report and cannabis law reform in Britain during the 1960s and 1970s', in S. Snitzman, B. Olsson, and R. Room (eds), *A Cannabis Reader: global Issues and Local Experiences*, European Monitoring Centre for Drugs and Drug Addiction.

ACMD (2014), *Time Limiting Opioid Substitution Therapy*, London: Home Office.

Aldridge, J., Measham, F., and Williams, L. (2011), *Illegal Leisure Revisited*, Abingdon: Routledge.

Babor, T., Caulkins, J., Edwards, G., Fischer, B., Foxcroft, D., Humphreys, K., Strang, J. (2010), *Drug Policy and the Public Good*, Oxford: Oxford University Press.

Beatty, C. and Fothergill, S. (2013), *Hitting the Poorest Places Hardest: The Local and Regional Impact of Welfare Reform*, Sheffield: Sheffield Hallam University Centre for Regional Economic and Social Research.

Bennett, T. and Holloway, K. (2007), *Drug-Crime Connections*, Cambridge: Cambridge University Press.

Berridge, V. (1999), *Opium and the People*, revised edn, London: Free Association Books.

Berridge, V. (2013), *Demons: Our Changing Attitudes to Alcohol, Tobacco, and Drugs*, Oxford: Oxford University Press.

Bruggmann, P. and Grebely, J. (2015), 'Prevention, treatment and care of hepatitis C virus infection among people who inject drugs', *The International Journal on Drug Policy*, 26(1): 1, 22–6, doi:10.1016/j.drugpo.2014.08.014.

Cairney, P. (2011), *Understanding Public Policy: Theories and Issues*, Basingstoke: Palgrave Macmillan.

Collier, D. (2011), 'Understanding Process Tracing', *PS: Political Science and Politics*, 44(4), 823–30, doi:10.1017/S1049096511001429.

Dennis, F. (2016), 'More-than-harm-reduction: engaging with alternative ontologies of "movement" ', paper presented at *10th Annual Conference of the International Society for the Study of Drug Policy*, Sydney.

EMCDDA (2015), *New psychoactive substances in Europe*, Lisbon: European Monitoring Centre for Drugs and Drug Addiction.

Godfrey, C., Eaton, G., McDougall, C., and Culyer, A. (2002), *The Economic and Social Costs of Class A Drug Use in England and Wales, 2000. Home Office Research Study 249*, London: Home Office.

Goldstein, P., Brownstein, H., Ryan, P., and Bellucci, P. (1989), 'Crack and Homicide in New York: A Conceptually Based Event Analysis', *Contemporary Drug Problems*, 16(4): 651–87.

Habermas, J. (1986), *Law and morality: The Tanner Lectures on Human Values*, Boston, MA, doi:10.1007/BF00172028.

Habermas, J. (2002), 'Social Action, Purposive Activity and Communication (1981)', in M. Cooke (ed.), *On the Pragmatics of Communication*, Cambridge: Polity.

Harris, J. and McElrath, K. (2012), 'Methadone as Social Control: Institutionalized Stigma and the Prospect of Recovery', *Qualitative Health Research*, 22(6): 810–24, doi:10.1177/1049732311432718.

Harris, P. (2005), *Drug Induced: Addiction and Treatment in Perspective*, Lyme Regis: Russell House.

Hill, M. (2009), *The Public Policy Process*, 5th edn, Harlow: Pearson.

Home Office (2014), *Drugs: International Comparisons*, London: Home Office.

Hunt, N. and Lloyd, C. (2008), 'Drug consumption rooms: between evidence and opinion, in A. Stevens (ed.), *Crossing Frontiers: International Developments in the Treatment of Drug Dependence*, Brighton: Pavilion.

Independent Inquiry into the Misuse of Drugs Act 1971 (2000), *Drugs and the Law*, London: Police Foundation.

Inter-Ministerial Group on Drugs (2012), *Putting Full Recovery First*, London: HM Government.

Kingdon, J. (1984), *Agendas, Alternatives, and Public Policies*, Boston: Little, Brown.

Kohn, M. (2001), *Dope Girls: The Birth of the British Drug Underground*, London: Granta Books.

Lancaster, K., Duke, K., and Ritter, A. (2015), 'Producing the "problem of drugs": A cross national-comparison of "recovery" discourse in two Australian and British reports', *International Journal of Drug Policy*, 26(7), 617–25, doi:10.1016/j.drugpo.2015.04.006.

Lloyd, C. (2009), How we got to where we are now', in J. Barlow (ed.), *Substance Misuse: The Implications of Research, Policy and Practice*, London: Jessica Kingsley.

Lukes, S. (1974), *Power: a Radical View*, London: Macmillan.

MacCoun, R. J. and Reuter, P. (2001), *Drug War Heresies: Learning from Other Vices, Times, & Places*, Cambridge: Cambridge University Press.

MacDonald, Z., Tinsley, L., Collingwood, J., Jamieson, P., and Pudney, S. (2005), *Measuring the Harm From Illegal Drugs Using the Drug Harm Index, Home Office Online Report 24/05*, London: Home Office.

MacGregor, S. (1998), 'Pragmatism or Principle? Continuity and Change in the British Approach to Treatment and Control', in R. Coomber (ed.), *The Control of Drugs and Drug Users*, London: CRC.

Mason, T., Sutton, M., Whittaker, W., McSweeney, T., Millar, T., Donmall, M., Jones, A., and Pierce, M. (2015), 'The impact of paying treatment providers for outcomes: difference-in-differences analysis of the "payment by results for drugs recovery" pilot', *Addiction*, 110(7): 1120–8, doi:10.1111/add.12920.

Mathiesen, T. (2004), *Silently Silenced: Essays on the Creation of Acquiescence in Modern Society*, Winchester: Waterside.

Matthews, R. (2014), *Realist Criminology*, Basingstoke: Palgvrave Macmillan.

Matza, D. (1961), Subterranean Traditions of Youth, *The Annals of the American Academy of Political and Social Science*, 338(1), 102–18.

McDonald, R. and Strang, J. (2016), 'Are take-home naloxone programmes effective? Systematic review utilizing application of the Bradford Hill criteria', *Addiction*, 111(7): 1177–87, doi:10.1111/add.13326.

McKeganey, N. (2010), *Controversies in Drugs Policy and Practice*, Basingstoke: Palgrave.

McKeganey, N., Morris, Z., Neale, J., and Robertson, M. (2004), 'What are drug users looking for when they contact drug services: abstinence or harm reduction?', *Drugs: Education, Prevention, and Policy*, 11(5): 423–35, doi:10.1080/09687630410001723229.

Mills, J. H. (2003), *Cannabis Britannica: Empire, Trade and Prohibition, 1800-1928*, Oxford: Oxford University Press.

Mills, J. H. (2013), *Cannabis Nation: Control and Consumption in Britain, 1928-2008*, Oxford: Oxford University Press.

Mills, J. H. (2014), 'Cocaine and the British Empire: The Drug and the Diplomats at the Hague Opium Conference, 1911–12', *The Journal of Imperial and Commonwealth History*, 42(3): 400–19.

Mold, A. (2006), ' "The welfare branch of the alternative society?" The work of drug voluntary organization release, 1967-1978', *Twentieth Century British History*, 17(1): 50–73.

Monaghan, M. (2010), 'The Complexity of Evidence: Reflections on Research Utilisation in a Heavily Politicised Policy Area', *Social Policy and Society*, 9(01): 1–12.

Morgan, N. (2014), *The Heroin Epidemic of the 1980s and 1990s and its Effect on Crime Trends—Then and Now. Research Report 79*, London: Home Office.

Musto, D. (1999), *The American Disease: The Origins of Narcotics Control*, New York: Oxford University Press.

Nicholls, J. (2011), *The Politics of Alcohol: A History of the Drink Question in England*, Manchester: Manchester University Press.

Nutt, D. J., King, L. A., and Phillips, L. D. (2010), 'Drug harms in the UK: a multicriteria decision analysis', *The Lancet*, 376(9752): 1558–65.

Oakley, A. (2012), 'The strange case of the two Wootton Reports: what can we learn about the evidence–policy relationship?', *Evidence & Policy: A Journal of Research, Debate and Practice*, 8(3): 267–83, doi:10.1332/174426412x654022.

ONS (2015), *Statistical Bulletin Deaths Related to Drug Poisoning in England and Wales, 2014 Registrations*, London: Office for National Statistics.

Parker, H., Aldridge, J., and Measham, F. (1998), *Illegal Leisure. The Normalization of Adolescent Recreational Drug Use*, London: Routledge.

Pearson, G. (1987), *The New Heroin Users*, Oxford: Basil Blackwell.

PHE (2015), *Shooting Up: Infections Among People who Inject Drugs in the UK, 2014. An Update, November 2015*, London: Public Health England.

PHE (2016), *Trends in Drug Misuse Deaths in England, 1999 to 2014*, London: Public Health England.

Pierce, M., Bird, S. M., Hickman, M., Marsden, J., Dunn, G., Jones, A., and Millar, T. (2015), 'Impact of treatment for opioid dependence on fatal drug-related poisoning: A national cohort study in England', *Addiction*, 111(2): 298–308, doi:10.1111/add.13193.

PMSU (2003), *Strategy Unit Drugs Report. Phase 1 Report: Understanding the Issues*, London: Prime Minister's Strategy Unit.

Potier, C., Laprévote, V., Dubois-Arber, F., Cottencin, O., and Rolland, B. (2014), 'Supervised injection services: What has been demonstrated? A systematic literature review', *Drug and Alcohol Dependence*, 145: 48–68, doi:10.1016/j.drugalcdep.2014.10.012.

Recovery Orientated Drug Treatment Expert Group (2012), *Medications in Recovery: Re-orienting Drug Dependence Treatment*, London: National Treatment Agency for Substance Misuse.

Recovery Partnership (2016), *State of the Sector 2015*, London: Adfam.

Reinarman, C. and Levine, H. (1997), *Crack in America: Demon Drugs and Social Justice*, Berkeley: University of California Press.

Robertson, A. J. R., Bucknall, A. B. V., Welsby, P. D., Roberts, J. J. K., Inglis, J. M., and Brettle, R. P. (1986), 'Epidemic Of Aids Related Virus (HTLV-III / LAV) Infection Among Intravenous Drug Abusers Stable', *British Medical Journal*, 292(6519): 12–13.

Rolles, S., Barton, M., Eastwood, N., Lloyd, T., Measham, F., Nutt, D., and Sumnall, H. (2016), *A Framework for a Regulated Market for Cannabis in the UK: Recommendations from an Expert Panel*, London: Liberal Democrats.

Sabatier, P. A. and Jenkins-Smith, H. C. (1993), 'The advocacy coalition framework: Assessment, revisions, and implications for scholars and practitioners', in P. Sabatier and H. Jenkins-Smith (eds), *Policy Change and Learning: An Advocacy Coalition Approach*, Boulder, CO: Westview.

Seddon, T. (2010), *A History of Drugs: Drugs and Freedom in the Liberal Age*, London: Routledge.

Seddon, T. (2016), 'Inventing Drugs: A Genealogy of a Regulatory Concept', *Journal of Law and Society*, 43(3): 393–415.

Seddon, T., Williams, L., and Ralphs, R. (2012), *Tough Choices: Risk, Security and the Criminalization of Drug Policy*, Oxford: Oxford University Press.

Shiner, M. (2009), *Drug Use and Social Change*, London: Palgrave Macmillan.

Shiner, M., and Newburn, T. (1999), 'Taking tea with Noel: The place and meaning of drug use in everyday life', in N. South (ed.), *Drugs: Cultures, Controls and Everyday Life*, 1st edn, London: Sage.

Sim, J. (1990), *Medical Power in Prisons: The Prison Medical Service in England 1774-1989*, Buckingham: Open University Press.

Simon, J. (2007), *Governing through Crime: How the War on Crime Transformed American Democracy and Created a Culture of Fear*, Oxford: Oxford University Press.

Stevens, A. (2011), *Drugs, Crime and Public Health: The Political Economy of Drug Policy*, Abingdon: Routledge.

Stevens, A., Fortson, R., Measham, F., and Sumnall, H. (2015), 'Legally flawed, scientifically problematic, potentially harmful: The UK Psychoactive Substance Bill', *International Journal of Drug Policy*, 26(12): 1167–70.

Strang, J., Groshkova, T., Uchtenhagen, A., van den Brink, W., Haasen, C., Schechter, M. T., Metrebian, N. (2015), 'Heroin on trial: systematic review and meta-analysis of randomised trials of diamorphine-prescribing as treatment for refractory heroin addiction', *The British Journal of Psychiatry: The Journal of Mental Science*, 207(1): 5–14, doi:10.1192/bjp.bp.114.149195.

The New Psychoactive Substances Expert Panel (2014), *New Psychoactive Substances Review*. London: Home Office.

Thompson, J. B. (1990), *Ideology and Modern Culture: Critical Social Theory in the Era of Mass Communication*, Cambridge: Polity.

UKDPC (2008), *The UK Drug Policy Commission Recovery Consensus Group: A Vision of Recovery*, London: UK Drug Policy Commission.

Warner, J. (2002), *Craze: Gin and Debauchery in an Age of Reason*, London: Profile Books.

Yates, R. (2002), 'A brief history of British drug policy, 1950-2001', *Drugs: Education Prevention and Policy*, 9(2): 113–24.

Young, J. (1971), *The Drugtakers: The Social Meaning of Drug Use*, London: Paladin.

Zampini, G. (2016), *Morality Play: a Comparative Study of the use of Evidence in Drug and Prostitution Policy in Australia and the UK*, PhD Thesis, Canterbury: University of Kent.

37

SENTENCING

Andrew Ashworth and Julian V. Roberts

INTRODUCTION

Sentencing represents the apex of the criminal process and is the most public stage of the criminal justice system. Controversial sentences attract widespread media coverage, intense public interest, and much public and political criticism. Selective news coverage, populist journalism, and the complexities of sentencing explain why surveys in all western nations find that most people believe sentencing to be too lenient[1] (see also Hough and Roberts, this volume). While it is true that when researchers provide sufficient information about sentencing decisions, the 'punitiveness gap' between the public and the courts diminishes, it is the polls that attract headlines and pressure politicians to introduce tougher sentencing.

Sentencing in the United Kingdom has changed greatly in recent years, notably through the introduction of sentencing guidelines in England and Wales, and more recently, Scotland. However, there are still doubts about the fairness and consistency of sentencing practice, not least in the use of imprisonment. Among the key issues to be examined in this chapter are the tendency towards net-widening, the effects of race and gender, the impact of pleading guilty, the use of indeterminate sentences, the rise of mandatory sentences, and the role of the victim in the sentencing process. The chapter begins by outlining the methods by which cases come before the courts for sentencing. Reviewing jurisdictions across the UK, but with a particular focus on England and Wales, we summarize the sentences available to courts and examine current sentencing patterns, before turning to a more detailed exploration of sentencing guidelines, and of the key issues identified above. The chapter broadly addresses two critical questions: What is sentencing (namely who exerts the power to punish)? Does sentencing in the UK measure up to appropriate standards of fairness and consistency?

CASELOAD AND COURT STRUCTURES

Courts pass sentence for only a small proportion of the crimes committed, largely because only a small minority of all crimes are reported to the police, recorded, detected,

[1] Three-quarters of respondents to the Crime Survey of England and Wales expressed the view that sentences were too lenient (see Hough *et al.* 2013, Table 3.6).

and prosecuted to conviction (see also Maguire and McVie, this volume). Recent statistics illustrate the phenomenon. In the year ending March 2015, approximately 6.8 million crimes were reported to the Crime Survey England and Wales (CSEW, see Office for National Statistics 2015). A total of 3,811,258 crimes were recorded by the police and a charge or summons was brought in 16 per cent of these cases (Home Office 2015). However, since a large proportion of crimes are not reported to the CSEW, it is likely that only approximately 3 per cent of all offences in any given year result in court sentences (Home Office 1999). This is not to suggest that sentencing is unimportant, for it may have a social or symbolic importance considerably in excess of the small proportion of crimes resulting in a sentence. But these statistics do suggest the need for caution in assessing the crime-preventive effects of sentencing.

The selection of cases for sentence is not merely a quantitative filtering process. There are also filters of a qualitative kind, some formal, some informal. Regulatory and other agencies (e.g. HM Revenue and Customs), have various means of enforcing compliance without resort to prosecution, such as warning notices or the 'compounding' of evaded tax and duty. Within England and Wales, for example, even though the orientation of the police and the Crown Prosecution Service (CPS) is more towards prosecutions in court, they deploy a range of out-of-court disposals. When an offence is reported to the police, the choice among alternative courses (e.g. no further action; informal warning; Penalty Notice for Disorder; cannabis warning; fixed penalty notice; or passing the case to the Crown Prosecution Service with a view to prosecution) has relatively low visibility. If the case is passed to the CPS, the Code for Crown Prosecutors[2] requires them to assess whether the evidence raises a reasonable prospect of conviction and whether a prosecution would be in the public interest. If both of these tests are fulfilled, the CPS must decide whether to prosecute or to choose an alternative course, such as offering a conditional caution (specifying certain conditions, compliance with which will lead to the dropping of the charge) or returning the case to the police to impose a simple caution.

At the stage of plea, the system offers strong incentives to plead guilty and in England and Wales, negotiation is a familiar part of justice in magistrates' courts and in the Crown Court (see Ashworth and Redmayne 2010: ch. 10). In summary, therefore, the offences for which the courts have to pass sentence are both quantitatively and qualitatively different from what might be described as the social reality of crime.

CRIMINAL COURTS IN ENGLAND AND WALES

Most jurisdictions operate two or three levels of trial court. In England and Wales there are two levels: the Crown Court deals with the more serious cases and the magistrates' courts with the less serious. The Crown Court sits as a trial court with judge and jury. Two-thirds of Crown Court cases involve a guilty plea, and these are dealt with by judge alone—juries play no part in sentencing in this jurisdiction.

In almost all other common law jurisdictions sentencing is conducted by professional judges; England and Wales is almost unique in using lay adjudicators (members

[2] See https://www.cps.gov.uk/publications/docs/code_2013_accessible_english.pdf, accessed 1 September 2016.

of the public who have been appointed magistrates). The lay magistracy has existed for over six centuries in this jurisdiction.

There are approximately 21,500[3] lay magistrates in England and Wales, and they usually sit in benches of three, assisted by a legally trained adviser (Courts and Tribunals Judiciary 2015). Some magistrates' courts, particularly in large cities, have the additional resource of a professional District Judge. The maximum sentence in a magistrates' court is six months' imprisonment or a total of 12 months' imprisonment if there are two or more convictions. In 2014, fully 93 per cent of all offenders sentenced were disposed of in the magistrates' courts (Ministry of Justice 2015). For many offences a magistrates' court has the power to commit an offender to the Crown Court for sentence if it believes that its own sentencing powers are inadequate.

There is the possibility of appeal against sentence, from magistrates' court to Crown Court, or from Crown Court to the Court of Appeal. The Court of Appeal, Criminal Division hears all appeals in criminal matters from the Crown Court. During 2013, a total of 6,851 applications for leave to appeal were received, a 10 per cent reduction on 2012. Of the 6,851 applications for leave to appeal 73 per cent were sentence appeals (Ministry of Justice 2014: Table 5.7). Of the 1,535 appeals involving sentence heard in that year 1,008 or 67 per cent were successful (Ministry of Justice 2014: Table 5.8).

CRIMINAL COURTS IN SCOTLAND AND IN NORTHERN IRELAND

In Northern Ireland, the criminal courts structure is similar to that in England and Wales, starting with the magistrates' courts, then the Crown Court, with appeals going to the Northern Ireland Court of Appeal. However, the Scottish criminal justice system is different, with four main 'levels' of criminal court: the Justice of the Peace Court has lay justices and deals only with summary (less serious) cases; the Sheriff Court may sit as a summary court, with the sheriff adjudicating, or it may sit in solemn procedure (for more serious cases) with a sheriff and a jury of 15; the High Court of Justiciary deals with the most serious cases (such as murder or rape), held in front of a judge and a jury.[4] Appeals are heard in the High Court (sitting as an appeal court) and the Sheriff Appeal Court. In all criminal trials in Scotland there are three possible verdicts: *guilty, not guilty*, or *not proven*. In legal terms, the implications of a not proven verdict are the same as a not guilty verdict in that the accused is acquitted. For jury trials, a simple majority (eight out of fifteen jurors) is enough to convict.

The choice of whether to prosecute a case under solemn or summary procedure is made by the Crown Office and Procurator Fiscal Service (COPFS), which then affects the sentences available to the court on conviction (see below). The vast majority of criminal cases are dealt with under summary procedure: 94 per cent of criminal court disposals in 2014–15 were in the summary courts (COPFS 2015).

[3] The number has been declining steadily in recent years as a result of court closures and other government reforms; as recently as a decade ago there were almost 30,000 magistrates.

[4] Criminal procedure in Scotland is mainly regulated by the Criminal Procedure (Scotland) Act 1995, where the distinction is made between solemn and summary procedure. For a comprehensive overview of the Scottish court system, including the new Sheriff Appeal court which was created on 22 September 2015 to hear appeals arising out of summary criminal proceedings from both the Sheriff and Justice of the Peace courts, see Judiciary of Scotland (2015).

MAXIMUM PENALTIES

In most countries the legislature sets the maximum sentence for each offence. This is the position in all UK jurisdictions, except that there remain a few common law offences which have no fixed maximum penalty (e.g. in England and Wales, manslaughter and conspiracy to outrage public decency have no fixed maximum penalty, whilst in Scotland the maximum sentence for common law crimes is life imprisonment or an unlimited fine). Parliament has set the maxima at different times, in different social circumstances, and without any overall plan, often based on the seven times table originating in the era of transportation to Australia in earlier centuries (Radzinowicz and Hood 1990: ch. 15). The legislature continues to assign and revise maximum penalties on a piecemeal basis.[5] As we shall see below, a small number of offences carry a mandatory sentence or a mandatory minimum sentence.

KEY STATUTORY PROVISIONS

Sentencers are guided by key statutory provisions which identify the purposes and principles of sentencing, and which provide directions regarding the use of specific sanctions. In England and Wales, the objectives of sentencing are listed in section 142(1) of the Criminal Justice Act 2003. Consistent with statutes in other common law countries such as New Zealand, Canada, and Australia, the stated objectives include punishment, deterrence, crime prevention, rehabilitation of offenders, protection of the public, and achieving reparation. A common critique of this multi-purpose, smorgasbord approach to objectives is that they inevitably conflict with one another: a punitive sentence may well undermine rehabilitation, while a robust deterrent sentence is at odds with the retributive principle of proportionality.

Imprisonment is the most severe sanction and Parliament has directed courts to impose custody only when no lesser sentence would be sufficient. Section 152(2) of the Criminal Justice Act 2003 states that: 'A court must not pass a custodial sentence unless it is of the opinion that the offence, or the combination of the offence and one or more offences associated with it, was so serious that neither a fine alone nor a community sentence can be justified for the offence'. A related provision (section 153(2) states that 'the custodial sentence must be the shortest term . . . that in the opinion of the court is commensurate with the seriousness of the offence, or the combination of the offence and one or more offences associated with it.' Taken together these two sections reflect two more general sentencing principles, namely *Restraint* and *Proportionality*. Restraint (or parsimony) requires the sentencing court to impose the least onerous sanction which would be appropriate. Proportionality is relevant because in deciding whether custody must be imposed (and if so, for how long) a court is guided by the principle that the severity of sentencing outcomes should be proportionate to the seriousness of the offence,[6] rather than other considerations (such as prior record, level of dangerousness). The concepts of restraint and proportionality guide sentencing in other common law jurisdictions such as Australia, New Zealand, and Canada.

[5] For example, in England, the Criminal Justice Act 2003 raised the maxima for many summary offences and the maximum for causing death by dangerous driving was increased from 10 to 14 years.

[6] This principle is derived from the just deserts sentencing philosophy (von Hirsch 1976).

THE RANGE OF AVAILABLE SENTENCES

Within England and Wales, the available sentences may be represented in terms of three tiers. At the lowest level are the so-called 'first tier' sentences. These include the *absolute discharge*, usually reserved for a small number of cases of very low culpability; the *conditional discharge*, where the condition is that the offender does not reoffend within a specified time (one, two, or three years), and breach of which condition means that the offender will be sentenced for the original offence as well as the new offence; and the *fine*, still much used for summary offences (the least serious) but declining in use for other offences.

Courts are required to take account of the means of the offender when calculating a fine, but there has been resistance to the adoption of the kind of 'day fine' system operating in many other European countries. The day fine permits courts to ensure that the magnitude of the imposed fine reflects the offender's ability to pay (Ashworth 2015: 348–50). The Carter Review (2003: 27) argued that 'fines should replace community sentences for low-risk offenders', suggesting that some 30 per cent of community sentences ought to be replaced by fines, but no formal steps have been taken to bring that about.

The second tier of sentencing is occupied by *community sentences*. For the last 30 years in England and Wales it has been official policy that the courts should use community sentences instead of some shorter custodial sentences; in practice the use of community sentences has decreased over the past decade while the custodial rate has risen slightly. The 2003 Act retained the requirement that a court should not impose any community sentence unless satisfied that the offence is serious enough to warrant it; and also the requirement that, if the court decides that the case is serious enough, it should ensure that the community order (a) is the most suitable for the offender, and (b) imposes restrictions on liberty which are commensurate with the seriousness of the offence (Criminal Justice Act 2003, section 148(2)). In many such cases a 'pre-sentence report' will be prepared by the Probation Service to 'assist' the court. The theory and practice of community sentences are discussed by McNeill and Robinson in this volume, and the 15 possible requirements (including unpaid work, drug rehabilitation, and so on) are set out there, with the possibility of imprisonment on breach as a 'last resort' (Sentencing Guidelines Council 2004: para. 1.1.47).[7]

Finally, there are 'third tier' sentences. Within England and Wales, a *suspended sentence order* is a term of imprisonment which is suspended. This order should only be imposed when the court is satisfied that a custodial sentence is unavoidable, and that the court would have imposed imprisonment if the power to suspend had not been available. A court is empowered to suspend a sentence of imprisonment of up to two years for a period of up to two years, and the court may add to the order one or more of the same 15 requirements that apply to community sentences (see earlier). On breach of a suspended sentence order the court must activate the prison sentence unless it would be unjust to do so. The other third tier sentence is *immediate imprisonment*,

[7] Available at: http://www.sentencingcouncil.org.uk, accessed 1 September 2016.

and this will be discussed in detail below. At all three tiers there are separate orders for young offenders (and also for mentally disordered offenders (see Peay, this volume)).

In all cases involving death or injury, loss, or damage, the court must consider making a *compensation order*, requiring the offender to make compensatory payments to the victim according to the offender's ability to pay. The court may also, where appropriate, impose one of several preventive orders—for example, a criminal behaviour order, a sexual harm prevention order, a serious crime prevention order, and so on. In drug trafficking cases there are mandatory provisions requiring the judge to consider making a *confiscation order*, requiring the offender to yield certain assets to the court, and the Proceeds of Crime Act 2002 (UK) makes confiscation orders available in other serious cases too.

Scotland too has different 'tiers' or levels of sentence ranging from absolute discharge and admonition (essentially a warning but one which remains on a criminal record), to restriction of liberty orders (electronic tagging) and other community sentences, to life imprisonment and orders for life-long restriction. Arguably, however, the Scottish approach has been more innovative than that of England and Wales in its preference for community sentences over short periods of imprisonment. The Criminal Justice and Licensing (Scotland) Act came into force in 2011, and provides for the Community Payback Order (replacing provisions for Community Service Orders, Probation Orders, and Supervised Attendance Orders). The legislation also contains a presumption against short periods of imprisonment of three months or less. In 2015, the Cabinet Secretary for Justice reaffirmed the Scottish commitment to 'robust' and consistently delivered community penalties as a means by which 'to actively address the underlying causes of offending behaviour' (Matheson 2015).

SENTENCING PATTERNS

ENGLAND AND WALES

Figures 37.1 and 37.2 reveal sentencing patterns for indictable offences in the magistrates' and Crown Courts in 2014. As can be seen, fines are the most frequent disposal for indictable offences in the magistrates' courts (accounting for 26 per cent of all cases), followed by community orders (25 per cent), custody (15 per cent), and suspended sentences (8 per cent). Reflecting their more serious caseload, in the Crown Court immediate custody was imposed in over half the cases (56 per cent), followed in frequency by suspended sentences (27 per cent) and community orders (12 per cent). Fines accounted for only 2 per cent of cases (see Figure 37.2).

Table 37.1 summarizes trends for the principal sentences imposed for indictable offences over the period 2000–14. Several important trends are worth noting. First, the volume of indictable cases sentenced declined by 14 per cent during this time. This reflects the fall in the volume of police recorded crime in England and Wales which in turn reduced the number of cases appearing for sentencing (see Ministry of Justice 2016a: Figure 6; and Maguire and McVie, this volume). Second, following

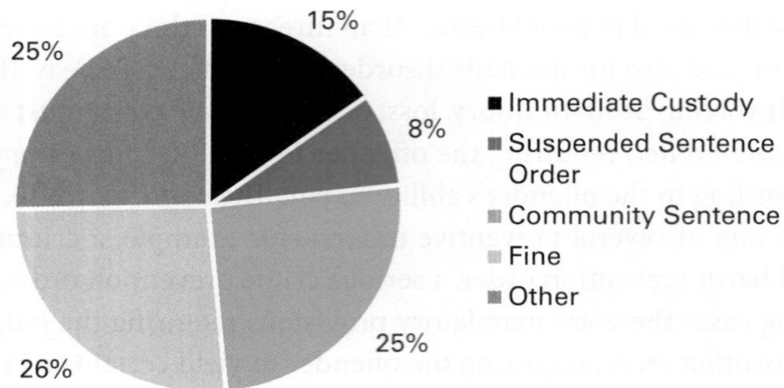

Figure 37.1 Sentences imposed, indictable offences, magistrates' courts, 2014
Source: Adapted from Ministry of Justice, Sentencing Statistics.

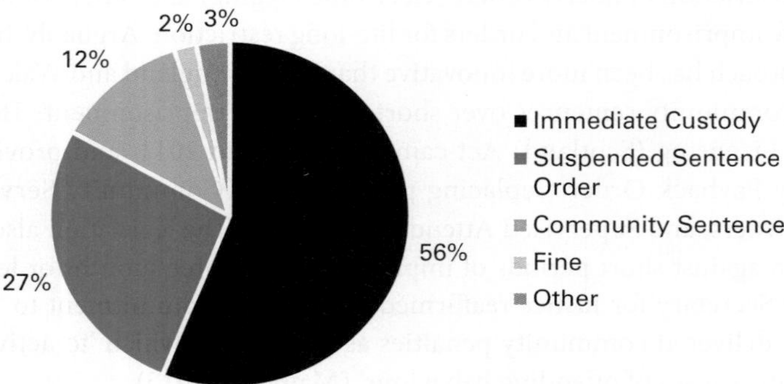

Figure 37.2 Sentences imposed, indictable offences, Crown Court, 2014
Source: Adapted from Ministry of Justice, Sentencing Statistics.

the re-introduction of the suspended sentence in 2005, the use of this order increased dramatically, from 2,143 indictable cases in 2004 to 38,928 a decade later (Table 37.1). Even more surprising is the fact that the use of immediate custody actually rose over the same period (from 25 per cent to 27 per cent of all indictable cases, see Table 37.1). This suggests that courts sometimes use suspended sentences where they would otherwise impose a community sentence, not an immediate custodial sentence—a clear example of net-widening and of the law being misapplied in the courts.

Third, the proportionate use of fines declined—from 25 per cent to 19 per cent of all cases from the beginning to the end of the period. A fine was the most severe sanction in 82,110 cases in 2000, declining to 53,571 in 2014. Where did these cases which previously resulted in a fine go? As can be seen in Table 37.1, the decline in fines was accompanied by a dramatic increase in the use of suspended sentences of imprisonment due to their revival in 2005 (see earlier). This may be described as 'up-tariffing'—by which we mean the increasing tendency to impose a more severe sanction. Finally, the use of community orders declined over this period to account for only 21 per cent of cases in 2014 from 30 per cent in 2000 (see Table 37.1).

Table 37.1 demonstrates the enduring appeal of imprisonment as a sanction in this jurisdiction, and shows that the spread of sentencing guidelines (discussed later) has not led to any discernible reduction in the use of imprisonment. As can be seen in

Table 37.1, the number of immediate terms of custody rose from 74,037 in 2007 to 87,558 in 2011, an increase of almost 20 per cent in four years. Finally, Table 37.2 places the English trends in a comparative European perspective, summarizing prison population statistics for a range of countries. As can be seen, England and Wales has one of the highest rates of prisoners per 100,000 population.

It is hard to make more detailed comparisons between sentencing practices in the United Kingdom jurisdictions since the databases are not comparable, and Northern Ireland in particular lacks comprehensive sentencing statistics. A study of sentencing in England and Wales and Northern Ireland noted that 2006 was the most recent year for which comparable data were available (O'Connell 2012). This study found that for many common offences (e.g. robbery, theft, burglary, fraud and forgery, criminal

Table 37.1 Sentences imposed in England and Wales, all indictable offences, 2000–2014[1]

	Immediate Custody	Suspended Sentence	Community Order	Fine	Other Disposals	Total cases sentenced
2000	80,784 *25%*	2,453 *<1%*	97,948 *30%*	82,110 *25%*	65,368 *20%*	326,210 *(100%)*
2001	80,273	2,139	102,063	77,466	63,401	323,203
2002	85,151	1,963	110,768	78,470	62,355	336,744
2003	80,794	2,055	109,648	78,250	65,238	333,930
2004	79,938	2,143	111,784	65,095	60,120	316,937
2005	76,291	5,610	111,724	58,433	60,150	306,598
2006	73,532	20,799	102,971	51,628	53,607	302,537
2007	74,037	27,254	105,142	49,463	56,362	312,258
2008	79,058	28,455	102,782	49,646	55,959	315,900
2009	80,265	31,131	107,924	55,351	51,921	326,592
2010	82,939	34,176	108,495	59,437	62,375	347,422
2011	87,558	34,422	100,286	58,288	61,304	341,858
2012	81,082	31,883	82,815	53,667	56,669	306,116
2013	77,843	35,429	66,487	53,159	57,981	290,899
2014	75,770 *27%*	38,928 *14%*	58,879 *21%*	53,571 *19%*	53,661 *19%*	280,809 *(100%)*
change 2000–2014	*+6%*	*+1,200%*	*−40%*	*−35%*	*−18%*	*−14%*

[1] *Notes*: row percentages rounded.

Source: Ministry of Justice (2015) Contains public sector information licensed under the Open Government Licence v3.0.

Table 37.2 Prison Population Totals, EU Countries, 2015

Ranking	Country	Prison Population Total	Prisoners per 100,000 population
1	United Kingdom: England & Wales	85,982	148
2	Poland	72,609	191
3	France	66,864	100
4	Spain	63,025	136
5	Germany	61,906	76
6	Italy	52,434	86
7	Romania	28,355	143
8	Czech Republic	20,628	195
9	Hungary	18,424	187
10	Portugal	14,238	138
11	Greece	11,798	109
12	Belgium	11,769	105
13	Netherlands	11,603	69
14	Slovakia	9,991	184
15	Bulgaria	9,028	125

Source: Institute for Criminal Policy Research (2015) World Prison Brief: Prison Population totals. Available at: http://www.prisonstudies.org/world-prison-brief-data. Across the UK, the number of people in prison increased significantly over the period 1990–2015, although there was significant regional variation. The prison population in England and Wales rose by over 90 per cent in this period, an average rise of 3.6 per cent per annum. The increase was more modest in both Scotland (64 per cent) and Northern Ireland (68 per cent; see Allen and Dempsey 2016).

damage, violent offences) courts in Northern Ireland imposed longer custodial sentences than courts in England (O'Connell 2012). Differences in the use of different disposals also emerged. For several categories of offending, courts in England and Wales used community sentences to a greater extent than did courts in Northern Ireland. On the other hand, Northern Ireland courts made greater use of suspended sentences and fines.

SCOTLAND

Consistent with the historical trends, with respect to Scotland, the latest statistics show that the use of custody as a sanction is somewhat lower than in England (National Statistics 2015). Of all those convicted in 2014–15 in Scotland, 53 per cent received financial penalties; 17 per cent received community sentences and 13 per cent received custodial sentences. A further 16 per cent were issued other sentences, which were mostly admonishments. Of note are the recent reductions in the use of custody and a concomitant rise in the use of community alternatives in Scotland, indicating that the net-widening that has occurred in England and Wales has been avoided north of the border. Custodial sentences have declined since they peaked at 16,944 in 2008–09, and are now 18 per cent below that peak (National Statistics 2016). Community sentences now account for a higher proportion of total court sentences than 10 years ago, having increased by 5 percentage points from 12 per cent of all sentences in 2005–06 (ibid).

VARIATION IN SENTENCING OUTCOMES

Alleged inconsistencies in sentencing have been a cause for concern the world over—ever since the first scientific analysis was published in 1932 using data from the US (Gaudet, Harris, and St. John 1932). Since then, empirical research in the United States, Canada, and other countries has repeatedly demonstrated variability in sentencing, across a range of different methodologies.[8]

In the magistrates' courts, where, as noted, most sentencing in England and Wales takes place, local variation is a longstanding phenomenon (e.g. Tarling *et al.* 1985). Recent statistics show that the immediate custody rate for indictable offences in the magistrates' courts varied from a low of 14 per cent in Surrey to 21 per cent in the West Midlands (Ministry of Justice 2015a). Variations are also to be found in the Crown Court. In 2014 the custody rate for indictable offences in the Crown Court varied from 52 per cent in Surrey to 65 per cent in Kent (ibid.). The average custodial sentence imposed also varied significantly—from a low of 20 months in Norfolk to a high of 31 months in Sussex (Ministry of Justice 2015a: Table 5.2). Mason *et al.* (2007) attempted to explain variation in sentencing practices by differences in the seriousness of cases and characteristics of offenders appearing for sentence but concluded that these factors were insufficient. They note that 'some kind of local "court culture" is at work which perpetuates differences in sentencing outcomes for comparable cases' (2007: 26).

THE EVOLUTION OF A CUSTODIAL 'TARIFF'

Apart from the few mandatory and minimum sentences, discussed below, the general approach to sentencing in the UK jurisdictions is to set a fairly high maximum sentence for each offence. One consequence is that most day-to-day sentencing practices are little affected by legislative constraints.

For Crown Court sentencing in England and Wales, some normal ranges or starting points have developed over the years, often termed 'the going rate' by judges and 'the tariff' by others. The evolution of the custodial tariff was largely driven by the judges, and in the 1980s the Court of Appeal began to issue a few 'guideline judgments' which

[8] Where there are fairly high maximum penalties and a wide range of available sentences, inconsistency might appear to be an obvious consequence. Yet even before there were many statutory restrictions and guidelines, judges expressed themselves as having little choice in the sentences they passed: 'I have no alternative but to...' (Ashworth *et al.* 1984: 53–4). 20 years later the sentencers interviewed by Hough *et al.* (2003: 38) expressed themselves similarly.

formalized the 'going rate' for certain offences. Lord Lane, the then Lord Chief Justice, would occasionally take a particular case and, rather than giving a judgment on the facts alone, would construct a judgment dealing with sentencing for all the main varieties of that particular crime. The first of these was in the case of *Aramah*,[9] where guidance was given on sentencing levels for the whole range of drugs offences.

In Scotland, guideline judgments can be issued by both the High Court (when sitting as the appeal court) and by the Sheriff Appeal Court. In recent years, they have included *Lin*, which addressed sentencing levels for those who play a minor role in large-scale drug operations,[10] and *Gemmell*, which provided guidance on sentencing after a plea of guilty.[11]

SENTENCING GUIDELINES

Sentencing guidelines of one kind or another now exist in several jurisdictions including the US, South Korea, Uganda, and China. The oldest —and the most researched — are found in the United States, where guidelines originated in the 1970s. Many US states use two-dimensional sentencing grids. One dimension is the seriousness of the crime and the other the offender's criminal history. For any given offence, the guidelines specify a sentence length range for each of a number of categories of criminal history (see Frase 2005 for discussion). The US-style guidelines have been rejected by other jurisdictions. The guideline system in England and Wales structures sentencers' discretion yet allows more flexibility than the US grid-based schemes. Other countries such as Sweden and Israel have developed what may be described as 'guidance by words'. In most other countries courts continue to sentence as they have for decades, enjoying wide discretion and guided only by appellate review (see von Hirsch *et al.* 2009: ch. 6).

EVOLUTION OF STRUCTURED SENTENCING IN THE UK

England and Wales

In 2010, the Coroners and Justice Act 2009 introduced a number of changes to the sentencing guidelines in England and Wales (for a history of the guidelines to that point, see Ashworth and Wasik 2010). Section 125 of the new Act states that:

(1) Every court—

(a) must, in sentencing an offender, follow any sentencing guidelines which are relevant to the offender's case, and

[9] *R v Aramah* (1982) 4 Cr App R (S) 407.

[10] *Lin v HM Advocate* [2007] HCJAC 62.

[11] *Gemmell v HM Advocate* [2012] HCJAC 36. For the current list of guideline judgments in Scotland, see Scottish Sentencing Council, Guideline Judgments, available at: https://www.scottishsentencingcouncil.org.uk/about-sentencing/guideline-judgments/, accessed 1 September 2016.

(b) must, in exercising any other function relating to the sentencing of offenders, follow any sentencing guidelines which are relevant to the exercise of that function,

unless the court is satisfied that it would be contrary to the interests of justice to do so.

Second, previous statutory bodies were replaced by a single authority, the *Sentencing Council of England and Wales*, which since then has issued a number of guidelines. The first new guideline—which came into effect in June 2011—relates to the assault offences.[12]

The new format of guideline requires a sentencing court to follow an explicit methodology in determining sentence (Roberts and Rafferty 2011). For example, the guideline for causing grievous bodily harm (Offences Against the Person Act 1861, section 18) identifies three overlapping ranges of sentence length, each range relating to a separate category of seriousness. The ranges are: 9–16 years' custody for the most serious assaults; 5–9 years' custody for cases of intermediate seriousness, and a 3–5 years' custody for the least serious cases.

In order to decide on the sentence the court should follow the guideline, which identifies a series of nine steps. The first task is to determine which of the three categories of seriousness is appropriate for the case. The most serious cases which involve a high level of harm and a high level of culpability on the part of the offender will fall into the category with the longest sentence length range (9–16 years). Once a court has determined which category range is appropriate, it should use the starting point sentence within the range as a point of departure. For the most serious category the starting point—from which a court should calculate a provisional sentence—is 12 years' custody. The second step is to 'fine tune' the sentence within the chosen range by considering other factors relating to the seriousness of the crime as well as personal mitigation. Having completed this, the court should then follow seven other steps to determine the final sentence.

The English sentencing guidelines allow courts considerable latitude within which to determine sentence and are more flexible than the sentencing grids found in states such as Minnesota. What effect have they had in terms of promoting greater consistency in sentencing—one of the primary objectives of any sentencing guidelines system? Although the Council has a statutory duty to 'monitor the operation and effect of its sentencing guidelines' and to 'consider what conclusions can be drawn' from this monitoring,[13] this statutory obligation has been rather narrowly interpreted. The Council publishes annual 'departure' rates for offences covered by its guidelines, but since the statutory definition of a departure sentence rests upon the total offence range—rather than the more limited guideline category range—the departure rates are for this reason alone very low. For example, data from 2014 show that fully 97 per cent of assault and burglary offences fell within the overall guidelines range (Sentencing Council 2015: Tables 6.1 and 6.3).

Academic analyses published to date suggest a positive impact on consistency across courts and the application of the offence specific guidelines. Pina-Sanchez and Linacre (2013, 2014) demonstrated that for a number of high volume offences, the guideline

[12] See https://www.sentencingcouncil.org.uk, accessed 1 September 2016.

[13] Section 128(1)(a) and (b).

factors were being applied in a consistent way across courts. Pina-Sanchez (2015) evaluated the impact of the new assault guideline on variability in sentencing. He conducted a pre-post analysis using the Council's dataset and concluded that 'consistency improved in all the offences studied after the new guideline came into force' (2015: 87). Irwin-Rogers and Perry (2015) explored sentencing for domestic burglary and their analyses 'provided a strong indication that the courts were sentencing in a manner that was consistent with the domestic burglary guideline and in particular the principle that that the factors in step one of the guideline should have more of an influence on sentence severity than the factors in step two' (2015: 210). These studies, while limited in scope, suggest the English guidelines have had a positive effect on promoting consistency. More research is clearly needed, however. The guidelines have attracted critics. For example, Padfield (2013) has questioned whether the guidelines have successfully ensured fairer, more consistent outcomes, while a recurrent critique is that the guidelines permit too much discretion at sentencing (e.g. Ashworth 2011; Young and King 2013; and Hutton 2013).

Scotland

A Scottish Sentencing Council was created in 2015 and it has a duty to prepare sentencing guidelines for the consideration of the High Court of Justiciary, Scotland's highest criminal court, which may approve them in whole or in part, and with or without modifications. The Council is also tasked to: conduct research into sentencing practices; help develop sentencing policy; publish information on sentencing; provide general advice on sentencing, and publish guideline judgments (court opinions which provide guidance on sentences in similar cases).[14] In addition the Council must consider the likely costs and benefits of implementing guidelines, in the form of impact assessments, and critically assess their wider effects on the criminal justice system more generally. Although still in development, the Scottish guidelines are more likely to resemble the English rather than the US format.

KEY ISSUES IN SENTENCING

We turn now to examine the key issues of sentencing policy and practice identified in the introduction, and assess them in terms of fairness and consistency.

NET-WIDENING

A common problem in sentencing that has arisen repeatedly over time and in many jurisdictions is referred to as 'net-widening'. This occurs when a sanction is introduced or amended with the explicit purpose of reducing the use of imprisonment. For example, a new, tough community penalty such as house arrest with electronic monitoring may be introduced to reduce the number of people being sent to prison. Net-widening

[14] See https://www.scottishsentencingcouncil.org.uk, accessed 1 September 2016.

occurs when the courts use the new (or amended) disposal in ways not intended by the legislature which was responsible for the reform.

The suspended sentence order (SSO) in England and Wales is a good example of this penal phenomenon. Until 2005, courts could only impose an SSO in exceptional circumstances. The consequence was that it was rarely imposed, accounting for less than 1 per cent of all sentences in 2004 (Roberts and Ashworth 2016). In 2005 this restriction was lifted and the total number of SSOs rose from 2,855 in 2004 to 52,979 in 2014. If some or most of these orders had been imposed in cases which previously would have been sent to prison, we would expect the immediate custody rate to have fallen as the rate of SSOs rose. No such pattern emerges from the data. In fact, the rate of immediate custody actually increased slightly from 2004 to 2014. Where did the SSOs come from then? It seems clear that they came from cases previously receiving a community penalty. While the volume of SSOs rose steadily, the volume of community orders fell, from 201,503 across all courts in 2004 to 112,638 in 2014. This constitutes a classic case of penal net-widening, and has been noted repeatedly by scholars (e.g. Bottoms 1981; Hedderman and Barnes 2015). In effect, sentencers have failed to apply the law faithfully, leading to unfairness in terms of people being sent to prison when they should not be. The Scottish statistics suggest that similar net-widening has not taken place, since community sentences have increased and custodial sentences decreased (see earlier).

RACE AND SENTENCING

For many years there has been an over-representation of non-white people in prison. In 2014, there were approximately 10 white people per 10,000 population in the prison population, compared to 55 per 10,000 for black persons aged 15 or more (Ministry of Justice 2015b: Figure 7.1). However, this finding should not be taken as conclusive evidence of racial discrimination at sentencing. As noted earlier in this chapter, the people sentenced by the courts are a quantitatively and qualitatively selected group. For example, the stop-and-search rate of black people is many times higher than that of whites; black people plead not guilty more often than others (and are acquitted at a higher rate than others), and thus if convicted they forfeit the guilty plea discount (see Ministry of Justice 2015b).

The most detailed academic study of race and sentencing in England and Wales found that the largest difference (70 per cent) was that many more black people were committed to the Crown Court and sentenced there; the offences for which they were convicted were more serious (10 per cent); sentences were longer, chiefly because black people often forfeited the guilty plea discount (13 per cent); and the remaining 7 per cent of the difference was unexplained, and presumed to be some kind of 'race effect' (see Hood 1992). This raises concerns about possible discrimination, and also raises broader questions about criminal justice policy (e.g. in the US the 'war on drugs' has been identified as a major factor in the imprisonment of young black males (Tonry 2011: ch 3)) and about the under-representation of non-white personnel in the criminal justice system.[15]

[15] In England and Wales, the latest (2016) statistics show that 5 per cent of court judges self-identify as BAME (Judicial Office Statistics Bulletin 2016: 4).

The Ministry of Justice conducted a detailed analysis which controlled for the influence of a range of variables, including offence of conviction and, number of prior convictions. The report concluded that being from a black, Asian, or minority ethnic (BAME) background raised the probability of being sentenced to prison. In the author's words, 'the effect was small, but statistically significant' (Hopkins 2015: 4). However, even this study, the most sophisticated to date, was unable to control for some important case factors which may have influenced the court's decision to imprison. For example, the analysis did not include plea, the timing of the plea, whether the offender had multiple current convictions, or any other mitigating and aggravating factors. Until a more definitive study, conducted perhaps with a wider range of variables, is available, conclusions about the fairness of racial differences in sentencing will remain tentative.

SENTENCING FEMALE OFFENDERS

Another important demographic variable at sentencing is gender (see also Burman and Gelsthorpe, this volume). The sentencing of women has long been, and still remains a problematic area (see Player 2012). On the one hand, female offenders are more likely than men to receive a discharge and more likely to receive a community sentence, while they are also less likely to receive a custodial sentence. On the other hand, the number of women in prison in England and Wales almost trebled between 1992 and 2002, and has remained around the 4,000 mark since then. Alongside England and Wales, Scotland has one of the highest female prison populations in Northern Europe. Scotland has an average daily female prison population of 404: 318 sentenced women, 85 women on remand (untried or awaiting sentence), and 1 woman awaiting deportation, accounting for approximately 5 per cent of the total prison population. Every year in Scotland, approximately 3,000 women are imprisoned, compared to approximately 34,000 men. The number of women in Scottish prisons is increasing at a faster rate than their male counterparts, having practically doubled over the past decade, despite no corresponding increase in the seriousness of their offending. This has been attributed in part to the use of short sentences, particularly for women with mental health problems (Wilson 2015; Scottish Centre for Crime and Justice Research 2015).

Major enquiries into the imprisonment of women have confirmed that many of them receive short custodial sentences, which disrupt their lives, fail to address their offending behaviour, and have little impact on reoffending (Corston 2007: 5; Angiolini 2012: 3). These reports emphasized that most of these women pose no threat to society: many have convictions for small-scale property offending, and some (particularly non-British female prisoners) have convictions for drug trafficking. Imprisonment may be harder for women because of separation from children for whom they have been the primary carer, and because women tend to be imprisoned further from their home than men. Moreover, 'women offenders experience high rates of mental health disorder, victimization abuse, and substance abuse, and have low skills and rates of employment. Their specific needs are distinct from those of male offenders' (Social Exclusion Task Force 2009). Yet, despite government acceptance of the Corston recommendations in England and Wales, a House of Commons committee found that progress in implementing them had been patchy and lacking in commitment (Justice Committee 2013), leading to continuing unfairness in practice.

GUILTY PLEA REDUCTIONS

All common law jurisdictions offer sentence reductions to offenders who plead guilty. A guilty plea spares victims and witnesses from having to testify in court, and saves the criminal justice system (especially courts, prosecutors, and the police) the expense of mounting a prosecution and running a trial. Plea-based 'discounts' are a controversial element of the sentencing process, however. If the reduction is too significant, there is a strong possibility that some defendants who are not guilty, or not guilty of the charge laid, will enter a plea simply to secure the 'discount'. In addition, since plea is considered unrelated to the harm or culpability of the offender, a substantial discount will undermine the principle of proportionality. If a crime attracts a six-year sentence, and the offender benefits from, say a 50 per cent discount for pleading guilty, he may end up serving less time in prison than someone convicted of a less serious crime, but who is convicted only after a trial. This would violate the principle of proportionality. For this reason, most jurisdictions limit the reductions offered to defendants who plead guilty to one third or less, but even this level of reduction is regarded as too high by many scholars (see, e.g., Darbyshire 2000 and for discussion Leverick 2014).

Substantial discounts create considerable pressure on defendants to forgo the right to trial which goes with the presumption of innocence. Where defendants are advised that the discount may make the difference between a custodial and a non-custodial sentence, the risk of innocent people pleading guilty is particularly high.

In England and Wales, the statutory foundation for sentence reductions is set out in section 144 of the Criminal Justice Act 2003. The guilty plea rate has steadily increased from 63 per cent in 2005 to 71 per cent in 2009 (Ministry of Justice 2010b: 98). The Sentencing Guidelines Council issued a definitive guideline on *Reduction of Sentence for a Guilty Plea* (2007), which recognizes various pragmatic reasons for the discount—saving cost, avoiding trials, reducing anxiety among victims and witnesses.[16] The guideline establishes a sliding scale, with a maximum reduction of one-third for a guilty plea indicated at the earliest opportunity, reducing to one-tenth if the guilty plea is tendered 'at the door of the court'. The guideline also states that 'the reduction principle may properly form the basis for imposing . . . an alternative to an immediate custodial sentence'. Thus the guilty plea discount may well make the difference between community and custody. The guideline was based on judicial practice at the time, and therefore it is not surprising that in practice the sentence reductions awarded by courts track the guidelines recommended reductions fairly closely. For example, in 2014, 89 per cent of defendants who entered their guilty plea at the 'first reasonable opportunity' to do so received the full one-third reduction recommended by the guideline (Sentencing Council 2015: Figure 5.2; see also Roberts and Bradford 2015).

In contrast, the Scottish High Court has turned away from the 'sliding scale' and, recognizing the dangers of encouraging the innocent to plead guilty, has insisted that there should be no automatic reduction in sentence but only a reduction based on the public benefit in each case (Leverick 2014). Whether the English or the Scottish approach achieves greater fairness is open to considerable debate.

[16] At the time of writing (August 2016), the Sentencing Council is in the process of issuing a revised guideline.

INDETERMINATE SENTENCES

Despite the poor prospects of accurate prediction, governments in many countries regard it as politically necessary to have some kind of 'dangerousness' statute, proclaiming greater public protection from sexual and violent predators. In England and Wales the Criminal Justice Act 2003 adopted this approach and introduced a three-pronged strategy against 'dangerous' offenders. Thus, where the offence had a maximum of life imprisonment, the court was required to impose life imprisonment if the court found that the current offence was serious enough to justify a life sentence, and if the offender was 'dangerous'. If the offence was 'serious' but either did not carry life imprisonment or was not sufficiently serious, the court was required to impose a sentence of imprisonment for public protection (IPP).

The IPP sentence was hardly less constraining than life imprisonment, in the sense that the court set a minimum term, after which release is only when the Parole Board thinks the risk to the public no longer justifies imprisonment, and release is on licence indefinitely. Then there is the third form of sentence, the extended sentence, composed of the proportionate sentence for the offence, plus an extension period (on licence with conditions) for a violent offence or a sexual offence. The condition that must be fulfilled before a court imposes any of these sentences is a finding that 'there is a significant risk to members of the public of serious harm occasioned by the commission by him of further specified offences'.

The 'dangerousness' provisions in the 2003 Act were a penological disaster. They were mandatory, and they spread the net so widely as to perpetrate real injustice by subjecting relatively low-level offenders to indefinite imprisonment. Moreover, the planning was so poor that the prisons were unable to provide sufficient courses for IPP prisoners to complete in order to secure their release (see, e.g., House of Commons 2008: paras 39–85). The government recognized some of these criticisms, and in 2008 the mandatory element of the 'dangerousness' sentences described above was removed, and the threshold for imposing such a sentence was increased to crimes 'worth' four years' imprisonment. The coalition government went further, declaring that 'the limitations in our ability to predict future serious offending call into question the whole basis on which many offenders are sentenced to IPP' (Ministry of Justice 2010a: para. 186). In 2012, IPP sentences were abolished in favour of automatic life imprisonment for the second serious offence, provided that the offences reach a high threshold of seriousness. This sentence will catch only the most serious offenders. However, this does not remove the unfairness and scandal of IPP sentences, since there remains an urgent need to reconsider the cases of some 4,000 people subjected to IPP sentences between 2003 and 2012 and still imprisoned. Moreover, some 19 per cent of the prison population of England and Wales are now serving indeterminate or life sentences, vastly more than our Western European neighbours. Is this really justified by the nature of the crimes committed?

MANDATORY MINIMUM SENTENCES

The UK has long experience of mandatory sentences, in the form of the life sentence for murder and mandatory disqualification from driving for drunk drivers. However, in the 1980s and 1990s so-called 'three strikes and you're out' sentences were introduced in many US jurisdictions, mandating very long sentences on the third felony conviction. These attracted the attention of English politicians, and in 1997 two minimum sentences were introduced in England and Wales—a three-year minimum for the third domestic burglary, and a seven-year minimum for the third drug trafficking offence. Later statutes have introduced a five-year minimum for offences of firearms possession, and a six-month minimum for the second offence of carrying a knife.

What is the theory behind minimum sentences? The main purpose is to reduce or eliminate the sentencing discretion of the court, in the hope that this will increase deterrence and (by leading to longer sentences) increase public protection. However, a study of the US evidence by Tonry (2009) found no proven deterrent effects, and did not find increases in consistency in sentencing because the deals struck by prosecutors meant that not all cases were prosecuted under the same provision. The main objection to minimum and mandatory sentences is that they produce unfairness, by requiring the courts to sentence unalike cases as if they were alike. Many matters of personal mitigation, which would normally lead to sentence reduction, have to be ignored by the courts if the sentence is mandatory. In the US case of *Lockyer v Andrade*,[17] where the offender was mandatorily sentenced to twice life with a minimum of 50 years' imprisonment for two thefts involving a total of 11 blank video-tapes, it was claimed that 'three strikes' sentence was so grossly disproportionate as to amount to 'cruel and unusual punishment'; but a majority of the US Supreme Court held that the sentences were not grossly disproportionate.

THE ROLE OF THE VICTIM

The role of the victim at sentencing has long been controversial. In many US jurisdictions, crime victims have the right to complete a Victim Impact Statement (VIS) in which they both describe the effects of the crime, and if they so desire, make a specific recommendation for sentence. Other countries have also adopted a victim input scheme, but victims are not permitted to suggest a particular sentence. In England and Wales, victims have been allowed to depose a Victim Personal Statement (VPS) since 2001 and a similar scheme was introduced in Scotland by the Criminal Justice (Scotland) Act 2003. The VPS allows the victim to describe the impact of the crime, and is then used by the criminal justice system at different stages of the criminal process. If the case results in a conviction, the VPS will be considered by the court at sentencing.

There is now a significant literature on the effects of victim impact statements on victims and the sentencing process (Roberts 2012). The general conclusion that may be drawn is that many victims report having benefitted from deposing an impact statement. In addition, research on the VPS scheme in England and Wales revealed that the vast majority of victims who submitted a statement expressed the view that they would do so again if victimized in the future. On the other hand, there is still debate as to whether these statements improve or impair the fairness of sentencing. Advocates

[17] *Lockyer v Andrade* 538 US 63 (2003). See also *Ewing v California* 538 US 11 (2003), which involved the theft of three golf clubs, and with the same result.

argue that the use of victim statements promotes victim welfare and may also assist courts in calibrating the seriousness of offences. Critics suggest that the statements introduce extraneous variation into the sentencing equation and may result in harsher sentencing. The use of statements does not seem to have resulted in the uplift in severity that some critics feared, although some scholars still regard the statements as increasing the degree of variability or subjectivity in sentencing outcomes (for research into the VPS, see Chalmers *et al.* 2007 and Roberts and Manikis 2013; for discussion of the normative issues, see Ashworth 2015).

CONCLUSION

The subject matter of this chapter has been sentencing, that is, the imposition of punitive sanctions on offenders. In whose hands does the power to punish reside? The simple model is that Parliament lays down the structure and the sentencing options, and the courts apply them in individual cases. That simple model has been amended by the arrival of definitive sentencing guidelines: the Sentencing Council lays down guidelines that shape and constrain judicial discretion. But even that does not tell the whole story. The police may impose a Penalty Notice for Disorder, a simple caution, or some other out-of-court penalty; the Crown Prosecution Service (in England and Wales) may offer a conditional caution; a regulatory agency or Her Majesty's Revenue and Customs may issue a warning notice or a financial penalty; a Procurator-Fiscal (in Scotland) may impose a fine, etc. None of these is compulsory—the individual may refuse the offer and challenge the agency to bring a prosecution in court—but in practice there are strong incentives (quicker, cheaper, 'less hassle') to accept the offer to divert the case from court.

Thus the power to punish moves, in effect, away from the courts and away from due process and transparency. If a prosecution is brought, the prosecutor may enter into a charge bargain or plea bargain, which again effectively takes power away from the court (e.g. if some charges are reduced or dropped). Where the court imposes a sentence, other agencies have the discretion to determine its precise contents. The probation service may determine the kind of unpaid work to be performed as part of a community sentence or community payback. The prison allocation system determines where the offender will serve a prison sentence. And, most powerfully, the Parole Boards of England and Wales and of Scotland have the task of deciding the release date of those prisoners on indeterminate sentences, extended sentences, and some other very long sentences. Thus the power to punish in individual cases has moved away from the courts to a significant extent, with the consequent dilution of due process and transparency.

For those who are sentenced in court, the most significant development would appear to be the introduction of sentencing guidelines. Sentencers in England and Wales now have more structure and guidance than at any previous time. Within a couple of years Scottish courts should also have guidelines as a result of the creation of the

Scottish Sentencing Council. Although there are benefits in terms of more consistent sentencing, the failure to use the power of guidelines to reduce the use of imprisonment is to be regretted. Whilst the prison population in England and Wales has stabilized in the period 2010–15 (Allen and Dempsey 2016), it remains much higher than many other Western nations. Indeed, the collective failure of the legislature and the courts to implement a more parsimonious approach to the use of custody as a sanction constitutes the most important shortcoming of sentencing in this, and indeed many other Western jurisdictions.

SELECTED FURTHER READING

Readings on rationales for sentencing and related issues may be found in von Hirsch *et al.*'s *Principled Sentencing: Readings on Theory and Policy* (2009) and Frase's *Just Sentencing* (2013). Sentencing texts include Ashworth's *Sentencing and Criminal Justice* (2015) and Easton and Piper's *Sentencing and Punishment* (2016). Essays on the English sentencing practice and guidelines can be found in Ashworth and Roberts' *Sentencing Guidelines: Exploring the English Model* (2013) and Roberts' *Exploring Sentencing Practice in England and Wales* (2015). For international sentencing, see Tonry's *Sentencing Policies and Practices in Western Countries* (2016). For discussion of sentencing developments in Scotland, see Tata's 'The Struggle for Sentencing Reform: Will the English model spread?' (2013). The websites of the English and Welsh and Scottish Sentencing Councils contain information about sentencing and guidelines; see https://www.sentencingcouncil.co.uk and https://www.scottishsentencingcouncil.org.uk. Overviews of trends in the prison population can be found in the Ministry of Justice's *Story of the Prison Population: 1993-2016, England and Wales* (2016b) and Allen and Dempsey's *Prison Population Statistics* (2016).

REFERENCES

Allen, G. and Dempsey, N. (2016), *Prison Population Statistics*, Briefing Paper, Number SN/SG/04334, House of Commons Library.

Angiolini, E. (2012), *Report of the Commission on Women Offenders*, Edinburgh: Scottish Executive.

Ashworth, A. (2010), 'Coroners and Justice Act 2009: Sentencing Guidelines and the Sentencing Council,' *Criminal Law Review*, 5: 389–401.

Ashworth, A. (2015), *Sentencing and Criminal Justice*, 6th edn, Cambridge: Cambridge University Press.

Ashworth, A. *et al.* (1984), *Sentencing in the Crown Court*, Oxford: Centre for Criminology, University of Oxford.

Ashworth, A. and Redmayne, M. (2010), *The Criminal Process*, 4th edn, Oxford: Oxford University Press.

Ashworth, A. and Roberts, J. V. (eds) (2013), *Sentencing Guidelines: Exploring the English Model*, Oxford: Oxford University Press.

Ashworth, A. and Wasik, M. (2010), 'Ten years of the Sentencing Advisory Panel', in Sentencing Guidelines Council and Sentencing Advisory Panel, Annual Report, available at: http://www.sentencing-council.org.uk, accessed 1 September 2016.

Bottoms, A. (1981), 'The Suspended Sentence in England, 1967-1978,' *British Journal of Criminology*, 21(1): 1–26.

Carter Review (2003), *Managing Offenders, Reducing Crime*, London: The Strategy Unit.

Chalmers, J., Duff, P., and Leverick, F. (2007), 'Victim impact statements: can work, do work (for those who bother to make them)', *Criminal Law Review*, 360–79.

Corston, Baroness (2007), *Review of Women with particular vulnerabilities in the Criminal Justice System*, London: Home Office.

Crown Office and Procurator Fiscal Service (2015), 'Statistics on Case Processing: Last Five Years', available at: http://www.crownoffice.gov.uk/images/Documents/Statistics/Statistics%20on%20Case%20Processing%20Last%205%20Years%202010-15.pdf, accessed 1 September 2016.

Courts and Tribunals Judiciary (2015), 'Magistrates: Who are they?', available at: https://www.judiciary.gov.uk, accessed 1 September 2016.

Darbyshire, P. (2000), 'The Mischief of Plea Bargaining and Sentencing Rewards', *Criminal Law Review*, 895–910.

EASTON, S. AND PIPER, C. (2016), *Sentencing and Punishment: The Quest for Justice*, 4th edn, Oxford: Oxford University Press.

FRASE, R. (2005), 'Sentencing Guidelines in Minnesota, 1978–2003', in M. Tonry (ed.), *Crime and Justice: A Review of Research, vol. 32*, Chicago: University of Chicago Press.

FRASE, R. (2013), *Just Sentencing*, New York: Oxford University Press.

GAUDET, F., HARRIS, G., and ST. JOHN, C. (1932), 'Individual Differences in the Sentencing Tendencies of Judges', *International Journal of Criminal Law, Criminology and Political Science*, 23: 811–18.

HEDDERMAN, C. AND BARNES, R. (2015), 'Sentencing Women: An Analysis of Recent Trends,' in J. V. Roberts (ed.), *Exploring Sentencing Practice in England and Wales*, London: Palgrave Macmillan.

HOME OFFICE (1999), 'Digest 4: Information on the Criminal Justice System', London: Home Office.

HOME OFFICE (2015), 'Crime Outcomes in England and Wales 2014/2015: Statistical Bulletin, 01/15', available at: https://www.gov.uk/government/uploads/system/uploads/attachment_data/file/445753/hosb0115.pdf, accessed 1 September 2016.

HOOD, R. (1992), *Race and Sentencing*, Oxford: Oxford University Press.

HOPKINS, K. (2015), 'Associations between police-recorded ethnic background and being sentenced to prison in England and Wales', London: Ministry of Justice.

HOUGH, M., JACOBSON, J., and MILLIE, A. (2003), *The Decision to Imprison*, London: Prison Reform Trust.

HOUGH, M., BRADFORD, B., JACKSON. J., and ROBERTS, J. V., (2013), 'Attitudes to Sentencing and Trust in Justice: Exploring Recent Trends from the Crime Survey of England and Wales', London: Ministry of Justice.

HOUSE OF COMMONS (2008), *Toward Effective Sentencing. Report of the Justice Committee*, London: The Stationery Office.

HOUSE OF COMMONS JUSTICE COMMITTEE (2013), *Women Offenders: After the Corston Report*, HC 92, London: The Stationery Office.

HUTTON, N. (2013), 'The Definitive Guideline on Assault Offences', in A. Ashworth and J. V. Roberts, (eds), *Sentencing Guidelines: Exploring the English Model*, Oxford: Oxford University Press.

IRWIN-ROGERS, K. and PERRY, T. (2015), 'Exploring the Impact of Sentencing Factors on Sentencing Domestic Burglary', in J. V. Roberts (ed.), *Exploring Sentencing Practice in England and Wales*, London: Palgrave Macmillan.

JUDICIAL OFFICE (2016), *Judicial Office Statistics Bulletin*. London: Judicial Office.

JUDICIARY OF SCOTLAND (2015), Court Structure, available at: http://www.scotland-judiciary.org.uk/16/0/Court-Structure, accessed 1 September 2016.

LEVERICK, F. (2014), 'Sentence Discounting for Guilty Pleas: An Argument for Certainty over Discretion', *Criminal Law Review*, 5: 338–49.

MASON, T., DE SILVA, N., SHARMA, N., BROWN, D., and HARPER, G. (2007), *Local Variation in Sentencing in England and Wales*, London: Ministry of Justice.

MATHESON, M. (2015), *Apex Scotland Annual Lecture. Fairer Justice: A Vision for Scotland*, available at: http://www.apexscotland.org.uk/wp-content/uploads/2015/09/apex_annual_lecture_2015_LoRes.pdf, accessed 1 September 2016.

MINISTRY OF JUSTICE (2010a), *Breaking the Cycle: Effective Punishment, Rehabilitation and Sentencing of Offenders*, available at: https://www.gov.uk/government/uploads/system/uploads/attachment_data/file/185936/breaking-the-cycle.pdf, accessed 1 September 2016.

MINISTRY OF JUSTICE (2010b), Judicial and Court Statistics 2009, available at: http://www.justice.gov.uk/downloads/statistics/mojstats/jcs-stats-2009-211010.pdf, accessed 1 September 2016.

MINISTRY OF JUSTICE (2014), *Court Statistics Quarterly: January to March 2014*, available at: https://www.gov.uk/government/uploads/system/uploads/attachment_data/file/321352/court-statistics-jan-mar-2014.pdf, accessed 1 September 2016.

MINISTRY OF JUSTICE (2015a), *Criminal Justice System Statistics Quarterly December 2014*, available at: https://www.gov.uk/government/uploads/system/uploads/attachment_data/file/428932/criminal-justice-statistics-december-2014.pdf, accessed 1 September 2016.

MINISTRY OF JUSTICE (2015b), *Statistics on Race and the Criminal Justice System 2014*, available at: https://www.gov.uk/government/uploads/system/uploads/attachment_data/file/480250/bulletin.pdf, accessed 1 September 2016, London: Ministry of Justice.

MINISTRY OF JUSTICE (2016a), *Crime in England and Wales. Bulletin Tables*, London: Ministry of Justice.

MINISTRY OF JUSTICE (2016b), *Story of the Prison Population: 1993-2016*, available at: https://www.gov.uk/government/uploads/system/uploads/attachment_data/file/541667/prison-population-story-1993-2016.pdf, accessed 1 September 2016, London: Ministry of Justice.

NATIONAL STATISTICS (2015), *Criminal Proceedings in Scotland, 2013-2014. Statistcal Bulletin Series, Crime and Justice*, available at: http://www.gov.scot/Publications/2014/12/1343, accessed 1 September 2016.

NATIONAL STATISTICS (2016), *Criminal Proceedings in Scotland, 2014-2015. Statistical Bulletin Series, Crime and Justice*, available at: <http://www.gov.scot/Resource/0049/00494474.pdf>. Accessed 1st September 2016.

O'CONNELL, F. (2012), *Sentencing Comparisons in Northern Ireland and England and Wales*, Belfast: Northern Ireland Assembly.

OFFICE FOR NATIONAL STATISTICS (2015), *Crime in England and Wales, Year Ending March 2015*, available at: http://www.ons.gov.uk/peoplepopulationandcommunity/crimeandjustice/bulletins/crimeinenglandandwales/2015-07-16, accessed 1 September 2016.

PADFIELD, N. (2013), 'Exploring the Success of Sentencing Guidelines', in A. Ashworth and J. V. Roberts (eds), *Sentencing Guidelines: Exploring the English Model*, Oxford: Oxford University Press.

PINA-SANCHEZ, J. (2015), 'Defining and measuring Consistency in Sentencing', in J. Roberts (ed.), *Exploring Sentencing Practice in England and Wales*, London: Palgrave.

PINA-SANCHEZ and LINACRE, R. (2013), 'Sentence Consistency in England and Wales', *British Journal of Criminology*, 53(6): 1118–35.

PINA-SANCHEZ and LINACRE, R. (2014), 'Enhancing Consistency in Sentencing: Exploring the Effects of Guidelines in England and Wales', *Journal of Quantitative Criminology*, 30(4): 731–48.

PLAYER, E. (2012), 'Sentencing Women: Toward Gender Equality', in L. Zedner and J. V. Roberts (eds), *Principles and Values in Criminal Law and Criminal Justice: Essays in Honour of Andrew Ashworth*, Oxford: Oxford University Press.

RADZINOWICZ, L. and HOOD, R. (1990), *The Emergence of Penal Policy in Victorian and Edwardian England*, Oxford: Oxford University Press.

ROBERTS, J. V. (2012), 'Crime Victims, Sentencing and Release from Prison', in K. Reitz and J. Petersilia (eds), *The Oxford Handbook of Sentencing and Corrections*, New York: Oxford University Press.

ROBERTS, J. V. (ed.) (2015), *Exploring Sentencing Practice in England and Wales*, London: Palgrave.

ROBERTS, J. V. and ASHWORTH, A. (2016), 'The Evolution of Sentencing Policy and Practice in England and Wales, 1996-2015,' in M. Tonry (ed.), *Crime and Justice: A Review of Research, vol. 45*, Chicago: University of Chicago Press.

ROBERTS, J. V. and BRADFORD B. (2015), 'Sentence Reductions for a Guilty Plea: New Empirical Evidence from England and Wales', *Journal of Empirical Legal Studies*, 12(2): 187–210.

ROBERTS, J. V. and MANIKIS, M. (2013), 'Victim Personal Statements: Latest (and last) Trends from the Witnesses and Victims Experience Survey in England and Wales', *Criminology and Criminal Justice*, 13(3): 245–61.

ROBERTS, J. V. and RAFFERTY, A. (2011), 'Sentencing Guidelines in England and Wales: Exploring the new Format', *Criminal Law Review*, 9: 680–9.

SCOTTISH CENTRE FOR CRIME AND JUSTICE RESEARCH (2015), 'Who's in prison? A snapshot of Scotland's prison population', available at: http://www.sccjr.ac.uk/wp-content/uploads/2015/10/SCCJR-Whos-in-prison.pdf, accessed 1 September 2016.

SENTENCING COUNCIL FOR ENGLAND AND WALES (2015), *Crown Court Sentencing Survey. 2014. Annual Publication*, London: Sentencing Council, available at: https://www.sentencingcouncil.org.uk/publications/item/crown-court-sentencing-survey-annual-publication-2014-full-report-2/, accessed 1 September 2016.

SENTENCING GUIDELINES COUNCIL (2004), *Overarching Principles: Seriousness. Definitive Guideline*, London: Sentencing Guidelines Council.

SENTENCING GUIDELINES COUNCIL (2007), *Sentence Reductions for a Guilty Plea. Definitive Guideline*, London: Sentencing Guidelines Council.

SOCIAL EXCLUSION TASK FORCE (2009), *Reaching Out: An Action Plan on Social Exclusion*, London: Cabinet Office.

TARLING, R., MOXON, D., and JONES, P. (1985), 'Sentencing of Adults and Juveniles in Magistrates' Courts', in D. Moxon (ed.), *Managing Criminal Justice*, London: HMSO.

TATA, C. (2013), 'The Struggle for Sentencing Reform: Will the English Model Spread?', in A. Ashworth and J. V. Roberts (eds), *Sentencing Guidelines: Exploring the English Model*, Oxford: Oxford University Press.

TONRY, M. (2009), 'The Mostly Unintended Consequences of Mandatory Penalties: Two Centuries of Consistent Findings', in M. Tonry (ed.), *Crime and Justice, A Review of Research, vol. 38*, Chicago: University of Chicago Press.

TONRY, M. (2011), *Punishing Race*, New York: Oxford University Press.

TONRY, M. (2016), 'Sentencing Policies and Practices in Western Countries: Comparative and Cross-National Perspectives', in M. Tonry (ed.), *Crime and Justice: A Review of Research, vol. 45*, Chicago: University of Chicago Press.

VON HIRSCH, A. (1976), *Doing Justice*, New York: Hill and Wang.

VON HIRSCH, A., ASHWORTH, A., and ROBERTS, J. V. (eds) (2009), *Principled Sentencing: Readings in Theory and Policy*, 3rd edn, Oxford: Hart.

WILSON, T. L. (2015), *International Review of Custodial Models for Women: Key Messages from Scotland*, Scottish Government Social Research, available at: http://www.gov.scot/Resource/0048/00487211.pdf, accessed 30 July 2016.

YOUNG, W. and KING, A. (2013), 'The Origins and Evolution of Sentencing Guidelines: A Comparison of England and Wales and New Zealand', in A. Ashworth and J. V. Roberts (eds), *Sentencing Guidelines: Exploring the English Model*, Oxford: Oxford University Press.

38

PUNISHMENT IN THE COMMUNITY: EVOLUTION, EXPANSION, AND MODERATION

Gwen Robinson and Fergus McNeill

INTRODUCTION

Many jurisdictions have, in recent years, seen the diversification of forms of punishment in the community, as well as their expansion, such that increasing numbers of offenders are subject to these forms of punishment. Yet, despite their development and growth, community sanctions have attracted little serious scholarly attention, particularly when compared with imprisonment (Robinson 2016a; Heard 2015). Indeed, it may be surprising to some that in many jurisdictions there are far more people subject to forms of punishment in the community than are currently in custody. In March 2014 in England and Wales, 218,671 people were under probation service supervision; the prison population that month averaged 84,443.[1] Following more recent reforms, this number is expected to increase by at least 45,000 due to the extension of post-release supervision to those completing a prison sentence of under 12 months.[2] In Scotland, in 2013–14, 20,363 new community sentences were commenced alongside a further 1,025 new cases of mandatory post-release supervision. In addition, a further 2,489 people began some form of 'voluntary throughcare' (most of these being short-sentence prisoners not subject to mandatory post-release supervision).[3] In the same period, the average daily prison population was 7,851.[4,5] In other words, in both jurisdictions there are about three times more people under supervision than in custody.

[1] See https://www.gov.uk/government/statistics/prison-population-figures-2014, accessed 21 September 2015.

[2] See https://www.gov.uk/government/uploads/system/uploads/attachment_data/file/305741/offender-management-statistics-october-december-2013.pdf, accessed 24 October 2015.

[3] See http://www.gov.scot/Resource/0047/00474323.pdf, accessed 21 September 2015.

[4] See https://www.holyrood.com/articles/news/scotlands-prison-population-seven-year-low, accessed 21 September 2015.

[5] Even in the land of 'mass incarceration' (the USA), the number of people subject to probation or parole dwarfs the number imprisoned; of the near 7 million people under some form of correctional supervision in 2013 in the USA, 4,751,400 were being supervised in the community (Glaze and Kaeble 2014).

In this chapter we set out to explore the changing contours of these forms of punishment with particular reference to these two UK jurisdictions (England and Wales and Scotland) and with more limited attention to Northern Ireland. That relative neglect reflects our recognition that we know just enough about Northern Ireland to realize that we know too little to do justice either to its complexities or to its importance. In particular, the history of punishment in the community in Northern Ireland, especially throughout the period of conflict referred to as 'the Troubles' and since devolution and power-sharing, represents a uniquely instructive example of the importance of the relationships between a state with disputed legitimacy, a divided civil society, and a probation service carefully navigating its way both through these conflicts and through the communities it served (see Carr and Maruna 2012; Carr 2016). Although these three jurisdictions remain (for now at least) neighbours in a single United Kingdom, they present a very varied set of arrangements for, and developments of, community punishment (Robinson and McNeill 2016).

One of the particular challenges faced by researchers in our field concerns terminology: finding a label on which all can agree and which captures an increasingly diverse range of sanctions and other disposals is an ongoing problem (Robinson *et al.* 2013; Raynor 2012). As we acknowledged in our recent book (Robinson and McNeill 2016), our choice of *punishment in the community* has no more universal appeal than the alternatives, but for us it has two principal advantages. The first lies in its explicit reference to the *penal* character of a wide range of sanctions and measures which share in common a restriction on the offender's liberty through the imposition of behavioural conditions and/or obligations. Whilst other scholars may prefer the more neutral, legally oriented terminology of *community sanctions and measures* (CSM)[6] adopted by the Council of Europe (1992), we maintain that it is important to acknowledge the fact that CSM—even when intended to be constructive—are always underwritten by the threat of other (typically more punitive) sanctions in the event of non-compliance. We shall also argue (see later) that the *penalization* of community sanctions and measures—that is, the bolstering of their punitive credentials—is one of the most important developments in the field in the last 25 years or so.

A further strength of our chosen terminology (which it shares with the term CSM) is that it captures periods of supervision which are properly conceived as elements of custodial sentences: that is, in conjunction with a suspended sentence, or a period 'on licence' in the latter part of or in addition to a custodial term. Several alternative labels—such as *probation, alternatives to custody*, and *community penalties* fail in those terms and arguably begin to look all the more limited considering the growing use of supervision as an adjunct to imprisonment. This is particularly the case in England and Wales since the implementation of the 2014 Offender Rehabilitation Act which has extended mandatory post-custodial supervision to short prison sentences of under 12 months (Tomczak 2015). We therefore defend our choice of terminology, whilst

[6] *Community sanctions and measures* are defined by the Council of Europe (1992) as those 'which maintain the offender in the community and involve some restriction of his liberty through the imposition of conditions and/or obligations'. In this chapter we restrict our focus to those sanctions and measures which are imposed by the criminal courts upon conviction, either as a sanction or in lieu of one: thus we do not consider those community-based *measures* that may be imposed prior to a conviction, such as supervised alternatives to pre-trial detention, which are included in the Council of Europe's definition of CSM.

accepting that it is not the preferred one among scholars or practitioners internationally, or even—as will become clear—in all parts of the UK.

To date, much research in this area has tended to be preoccupied with questions of effectiveness or utility, even when laudably directed at normative ends such as minimizing the harms of imprisonment through developing suitable alternatives. In this chapter, while still addressing these important questions, we want to delve a little more deeply into punishment in the community. Our primary intention is not to explore whether or not these sanctions 'work' towards particular formal goals; rather, we aim to explore why punishment in the community has evolved in the ways that it has. Effectiveness and utility are a part of that story, but only a part.

In this chapter, we adopt a broadly social constructionist approach, proceeding from the basic idea that the part of the penal field which interests us is neither an inevitable nor a necessarily static entity. Rather, it is one which has emerged in specific contexts and has subsequently been vulnerable to a range of influences which have shaped its evolution. It should be no surprise then that when we consider punishment in the community across jurisdictions, we see both similarities and stark contrasts. Across time and space, forms of punishment in the community have faced challenges to their legitimacy, and have strived to adapt accordingly (see Robinson and McNeill (2016) for a more developed discussion of our broad approach).

TYPES OF PUNISHMENT IN THE COMMUNITY IN HISTORICAL PERSPECTIVE

The history of punishment in the community is, in part, a history of penal innovation. In the UK, inspiration for innovative approaches for dealing with offenders in the community has tended to be found in the USA and brought to England and Wales and (sometimes separately) to Scotland (see McNeill and Whyte 2007). The available types of punishment in the community have proliferated significantly in recent years, culminating in a complex range of options which can be combined in different ways by sentencers. For example, in England and Wales, the first statutory community-based measure made available to the courts—the probation order—remained the sole option for several decades after its introduction in 1907. In the early twenty-first century it has been displaced by a community order which consists of 12 possible requirements[7] that can be used in various combinations. Probation emerged and developed a little more slowly in Northern Ireland, where the foundational Probation Act (Northern Ireland) was passed in 1950. Community service legislation followed in 1976, a few

[7] For a full list of requirements see http://www.sentencingcouncil.org.uk/about-sentencing/types-of-sentence/community-sentences/, accessed 29 March 2016. Scotland's community payback order (despite sounding as though it may be focused on community service or unpaid work) takes a broadly similar form, with sentencers choosing from nine possible requirements. See http://www.gov.scot/Resource/Doc/925/0110081.pdf, accessed 6 January 2016.

years after England and Wales (Carr 2016). Although new legal arrangements for post-release supervision have been developed recently, the two traditional community sanctions remain in place. In addition, the Criminal Justice (Northern Ireland) Order 1996 introduced both the combination order (combining probation and community service) and the custody probation order, which allows the imposition of a period of imprisonment followed by probation supervision.

SUPERVISION

The probation order was the first example of a statutory measure enabling the offender to remain in the community but nonetheless requiring him or her to submit to supervision by a court-appointed probation officer for a specified period of time, under threat of returning to court for sentencing in the event of further offending or failure to comply with supervision. Conceived as an alternative to a formal sanction, the probation order involved a voluntary agreement between the court, the offender, and a court-appointed probation officer, whose role was to provide guidance and practical assistance aimed at preventing recidivism. The origins of contemporary forms of punishment in the community are thus, somewhat paradoxically, found in a system which was established explicitly as an *alternative to punishment,* inspired at least in part by a desire to save those individuals thought to be deserving of a second chance from the harms of imprisonment (Robinson 2016b). Partly inspired by a system of probation established in Boston in the late nineteenth century, probation in UK jurisdictions consolidated the ad-hoc practices of 'reformative diversion' which some sentencers had been using since the 1820s, initially with juveniles. In his influential study of *Punishment and Welfare,* Garland (1985) argued that the establishment of probation at the turn of the twentieth century was evidence of a penal system that was newly alive to ideas about the possibility of reforming offenders through a combination of practical help and moral influence. However, Garland also observed that the new regime of probation represented not just a more humane response to crime, but also a more extensive and subtle network of control.

The practice of offender supervision also has a long history in relation to released prisoners: the earliest incarnation of a system of conditional release or parole in England and Wales dates back to the 1850s, when imprisonment had become the sanction of first resort for the majority of major crimes, and released prisoners were subject to a 'ticket-of-leave' system which required them to report to the police at regular intervals, maintain a steady job, and avoid association with other offenders (Klingele 2013; Shute 2003). Subsequently, forms of conditional release from prison have developed and expanded, and are often characterized as the 'safety valve' of penal systems needing to relieve the pressures associated with high rates of imprisonment (Cavadino *et al.* 2013).

UNPAID WORK IN THE COMMUNITY

Following on from the development of supervisory measures, the next innovation in the community context was unpaid work or community service, again based on experience in America (Advisory Council on the Penal System 1970; Harding

2013). Introduced in England and Wales in the mid-1970s and in Northern Ireland and Scotland a few years later, community service was the first explicit form of *punishment* in the community. Retributive, reparative, and rehabilitative qualities have been claimed for this type of sanction, rendering it an attractive option for sentencers and politicians with divergent views about the 'proper' purposes of punishment.

In some respects, the CSO marked a radical departure from probation, not only in that it was constructed explicitly as a sanction (i.e. as a form of punishment rather than a suspension of it), but also because it was conceived as a direct alternative to custody. This was certainly not the first time that policy-makers had sought to use community sanctions to reduce the use of imprisonment; that had been part of their logic since their inception. But it was the first time in the UK jurisdictions that, in theory if not always in practice, sentencers were asked explicitly to divert to community sentences those whose offences were seen as meriting custodial sentences. It also differed in its explicit connection with a reparative penal philosophy: that is, the idea that offenders should make amends for the harms caused by their offending not by deprivation of liberty but rather in the form of unpaid work for the benefit of the community. Prior to the revival of rehabilitation later in the decade, Bottoms (1980) suggested that penal systems were likely to take a 'reparative turn', not least because of a growing victims' movement which was raising consciousness about victim-oriented solutions to harmful actions in both civil and criminal spheres.

COMPULSORY TREATMENT AND OTHER REQUIRED ACTIVITIES

More recently, the UK has seen a proliferation of types of punishment in the community, which Bottoms *et al.* (2004) characterize as a 'new generation' of options situated on the ladder (or tariff) of penal severity between custodial and financial penalties. These include, firstly, forms of compulsory treatment that can be prescribed as part of a community-based sanction or measure. Typically tailored to an assessment of offending-related needs, packages of treatment may target drug or alcohol misuse; mental health problems; or specific types or patterns of offending, such as sexual offending or domestic violence. They may comprise psychological and/or medical interventions, and may in some cases involve residence at a treatment facility. Among the range of types of punishment in the community, it is these treatment options which most often raise questions about the importance of the offender's consent and cooperation, which are not necessarily easy to resolve (Canton 2014). Other requirements or activities which offenders can be compelled or encouraged to undertake include testing for alcohol or illicit substances, and residence at a specific address, such as a hostel, with its own regime of surveillance and/or support (Reeves 2011).

RESTRICTIONS AND PROHIBITIONS

When thinking of the forms that punishment in the community can take, it is easiest perhaps to think about things offenders are required to do, such as attending supervision appointments, doing unpaid work in the community, and so on; and, traditionally, this has been the dominant model. However, in recent decades many jurisdictions have also begun to introduce restrictions and prohibitions to the arsenal of community-based options: that is, things that offenders are required *not* to do (in addition, of course, to not reoffending). These may be spatial: that is, places or areas which the individual may not enter ('exclusion zones'); or they may combine spatial and temporal elements, as in a curfew which requires an individual to stay at home or in another specified place for specific periods of the day or night. Spatial restrictions are increasingly reinforced with electronic monitoring devices that can track movements or otherwise detect non-compliance (Nellis *et al.* 2012). All three UK jurisdictions now have legislation that permits electronic monitoring as part of community sentences in certain circumstances, and all three have contracted with private sector organizations to provide and deploy the technology. Other developing technologies allow for the monitoring of abstinence from alcohol. Although no requirement to submit to such monitoring has yet been made lawful in England and Wales or Scotland, in some pilot projects supervisees have been invited to 'volunteer' for such monitoring. Finally, offenders may be subject to prohibited activities that include foreign travel, attending football matches, and entering licensed premises.

EVOLVING RATIONALES FOR PUNISHMENT IN THE COMMUNITY

It is a relatively easy task to chart the development of types or forms of punishment in the community, but it is rather more challenging to elucidate their rationales or justifications in such a neat, chronological order. Particularly in looking to the recent past, the canvass becomes rather crowded, such that rationales overlap and jostle for position, and it becomes more difficult to 'periodize' such developments (Robinson *et al.* 2013). In this section we consider four contemporary rationales or narratives for punishment in the community in UK jurisdictions, and some of the tensions between them.

REHABILITATION

Ever since the emergence of probation at the turn of the twentieth century, the rehabilitation of offenders has formed part of the narrative scaffold around community-based punishment, but its importance has fluctuated, as have its various meanings and the practices associated with it. Historical accounts of probation as a penal innovation (e.g. Vanstone 2004; Garland 1985) have emphasized the particular social, political, and cultural shifts which coalesced at that time and brought the welfare or reform of the individual—formerly the preserve of philanthropists and charitable bodies—into the domain of state responsibility. Subsequently, the early decades of the twentieth century witnessed the transformation of probation practice as ideas about moral reformation gave way to a more pseudo-scientific discourse centred on diagnosis, treatment, and rehabilitation (Bottoms 1980; Garland 1985, 2001).

Rehabilitation continued to be the dominant rationale for probation until the 1970s. At that time, the collapse of the so-called 'rehabilitative ideal' (Allen 1981) in America and in England and Wales reflected a crisis of legitimacy which was the outcome of a three-pronged attack exposing serious weaknesses in rehabilitation's theoretical base, its ethical credentials, and its effectiveness in terms of reducing reoffending (Raynor and Robinson 2009). Some commentators forecast the death of rehabilitation and/or the institution of probation which had been founded on rehabilitative zeal, but such forecasts have proved to be overly pessimistic. Not only did probation find new rationales to support it (considered later in the chapter), but there also followed, in the 1990s, a revival and reformation of correctional rehabilitation, in the form of a 'What Works?' movement led mainly by North American correctional psychologists. This movement gradually gained momentum among British researchers and senior practitioners, and later won government support with its promise of programmes (informed by cognitive-behavioural psychology) capable of delivering significant reductions in recidivism (see Raynor 2012).

However, the so-called 'new rehabilitation' had to adapt to a changed social and political context which meant de-emphasizing the welfarist and humanitarian rationales of the past, in favour of an emphasis on the 'responsibilization' of offenders and the utilitarian value of rehabilitative interventions as crime reducing measures. David Garland (1997: 6) was among the first to observe this important realignment of rehabilitation in England and Wales with the needs and interests of victims and the protection of the public, when he stated that 'It is future victims who are now "rescued" by rehabilitative work, rather than the offenders themselves'. Rehabilitation in and after the 1990s also came to be seen less as a generic prescription for individuals subject to supervision, and instead as an expensive resource, to be carefully rationed in line with new evidence about its impact on offenders with different profiles of risk and 'criminogenic needs' (Robinson 2008).

In this context, attention to broader understandings of rehabilitation—as a process of social reintegration into the community or as the removal of criminal labels—have tended to disappear from official discourse, except where these other aspirations could be justified as being inextricably linked to the more politically acceptable ends of reducing reoffending and protecting the public. Good examples of this in England and Wales are the current emphasis on the resettlement of ex-prisoners, and the recent reform of the 1974 Rehabilitation of Offenders Act. In Scotland, reintegration (sometimes cast as 'social inclusion') has endured as a formal priority of policy and practice. Even if the last two decades have witnessed the emergence of a much sharper focus on reducing reoffending and public protection, Scottish policy and practice discourse has tended to link these objectives, arguing that reintegration is necessary in order to secure reduced reoffending (see McNeill 2016).

REPARATION

Rehabilitation's crisis in the 1970s coincided with growing concern among policy-makers about the problem of a growing prison population (Home Office 1977), and this was to provide fertile ground both for the development of new community-based sanctions and measures and new rationales for the existing 'probation' apparatus. The community service order (CSO) was an innovation which encapsulated both such developments. Reparation ('making amends') has continued to feature as a rationale for punishment in the community, most obviously within the context of community service. However, the prominence of reparation as a rationale varies greatly across jurisdictions. Scotland has recently stressed the reparative dimension of community punishment, passing legislation in 2010 which attempted to enshrine a reparative logic for almost all types of community punishment, rebranding them as 'community payback orders' (McNeill 2011, 2016). Meanwhile, in England and Wales, reparative activities have come to be rebranded in more punitive terms: a Cabinet Office report published in 2008 suggested that unpaid work performed by offenders should be unfulfilling and unpleasant, and that individuals should wear high-visibility vests identifying them as offenders (Casey 2008; Harding 2013). Whilst the latter development was ostensibly in the interests of building public confidence in community punishment by enhancing its visibility, it has also been interpreted as an exercise in stigmatizing and shaming offenders (Maruna and King 2008).

More recently however, England and Wales has seen something of a reparative turn in the form of strong government support for restorative justice interventions which involve direct or indirect communication between offenders and their victims. This has included funding for the experimental use of restorative justice between conviction and sentence (Kirby and Jacobson 2015). Like community service, however, restorative justice is consistent with penal philosophies besides reparation (including rehabilitation), hence its potential appeal to a variety of audiences (Robinson and Shapland 2008). In Northern Ireland, restorative justice has been thoroughly integrated in the development of youth justice, and has played an important part in the wider dynamics of the peace process, but its adoption and development within the statutory system for adults has been much more limited (Eriksson 2009).

MANAGEMENT

A managerial rationale underpins a number of inter-related developments that have affected punishment in the community since the 1980s. Among these has been a growing emphasis on the *systemization* of criminal justice and the contributions of each of the system's parts to the cost-effective management of risks posed by offenders (Bottoms 1995; Garland 1996). In the community punishment context, this first became evident in the language of *alternatives to custody* which emerged in the 1980s to justify the continuing provision of probation and community service following the crisis of rehabilitation, and signalled a lowering of expectations about the impacts of penal sanctions of all kinds. At a time of rising imprisonment rates, the promotion of community-based sanctions and measures as credible alternatives to custody afforded them systemic legitimacy: that is, it emphasized their value in serving the needs of a penal system which was under strain (Raynor 1988). Subsequently, the gradual extension of post-custodial supervision in conjunction with early release from prison has performed the same legitimizing function for community punishment.

Meanwhile, some of the features of the 'new penology' described by Feeley and Simon (1992) in the American context have become evident in the UK—most notably in the development and spread of sophisticated assessment tools for the classification of offenders according to profiles of risk. Recent decades have also witnessed the growing popularity of other technologies associated with what Feeley and Simon call 'management in place', such as electronic monitoring and drug testing. These are forms of surveillance that are less oriented toward rehabilitation than to the management or containment of risks, and as such are examples of a general lowering of expectations about the propensity of any form of punishment to change people. Rather, the aim is to deliver cost-effective external control.

More generally, 'management' has become an established part of the discourse of community punishment, especially in England and Wales. For example, 2005 saw the introduction of an Offender Management Model (OMM) which was accompanied by a rebranding of probation staff as offender managers. Another recent innovation is Integrated Offender Management (IOM), a model in which teams comprising police and probation staff work together to manage the risks posed to communities by prolific offenders (Wong 2013). IOM teams also exemplify a move toward increasing partnership working across statutory criminal justice agencies and with third sector providers, particularly in respect of high risk groups of offenders, in the pursuit of shared goals centred on public protection. The most prominent example of this is the formal Multi-Agency Public Protection Arrangements (MAPPA) (Kemshall and Maguire 2001) which have developed to deal with high risk violent and sexual offenders. Both MAPPA and variants of IOM schemes have spread from England and Wales to Scotland and to Northern Ireland.

PUNITIVENESS

As we have already noted, early community-based disposals enjoyed the legal status of alternatives to punishment and were justified by concern with the welfare and reform of the offender and the well-being of the community in mind. However, particularly in England and Wales, there has been a growing tendency to emphasize and enhance the punitive credentials of community sanctions and measures. There are several explanations for this, beginning with the introduction of a desert-based sentencing framework in the early 1990s, once again mirroring developments in the USA. Although driven by liberal intentions to encourage sentencers to use custody less, this policy development necessitated presenting all penalties with reference to their retributive qualities, and it was in this context (following the 1991 Criminal Justice Act) that probation and the community service order came to be rebranded as forms of 'punishment in the community': that is, 'middle range' sanctions offering restrictions on offenders' liberty (alongside their other, more constructive qualities) (Worrall 1997).

The other important driver of a punitive rationale for community punishment has been the politicization of crime and criminal justice—again, especially in England and Wales—and the increasing resort on the part of policy-makers and politicians to what Bottoms (1995) has called 'populist punitiveness' (see also Newburn 2007). In this context, punishment in the community has suffered relentless criticism for being too 'soft' or closely aligned with the needs and/or interests of offenders, to the alleged detriment of victims and the so-called 'law abiding majority' (Home Office 2006). As a consequence, there have been numerous attempts to 'toughen up' such sanctions, which have included abolishing the requirement for probation officers to hold a social work qualification; the abolition of the traditional requirement of offender consent to supervision (Raynor 2014); the rebranding of specific sanctions to emphasize their punitive credentials (e.g. see Harding 2013 on the case of community service); the creation of more 'intensive' and surveillant types of sanction (e.g. see Mews and Coxon 2014 for a recent example); and a less tolerant approach to the enforcement of punishment in the community (Robinson and Ugwudike 2012). Most recently, in 2013, legislation was introduced in England and Wales requiring courts to include a 'punitive requirement' in all community sentences for adult offenders, or combining such an order with a financial penalty. A press release announcing this development described it as 'a move to improve public confidence in community sentences' (Ministry of Justice 2013), although no evidence was produced to show that public confidence in such sentences was low (Maruna and King 2008). Drawing in part on such evidence, in the Scottish context, recent attempts to enhance the credibility of community punishment have focused more on enhancing their effectiveness (in terms of reducing reoffending) or on highlighting their reparative possibilities (Scottish Prisons Commission 2008; McNeill 2016).

PUNISHMENT (IN THE COMMUNITY) AND SOCIETY

Analysis of these various adaptations of punishment in the community, which we have cast here and elsewhere (Robinson *et al.* 2013) as related to a struggle for the legitimacy of related institutions and practices, speaks to the question of the broader relationships between punishment (in the community) and society. In the last 30 years or so, scholarship on the relationships between punishment and society has expanded rapidly. The early 1980s brought the publication both of *The Power to Punish* (Garland and Young 1983) and of *Punishment and Welfare* (Garland 1985). Although both of these books paid significant attention to probation and other forms of community punishment, the subsequent development of the academic field of 'punishment and society' has focused mainly on prisons and imprisonment. Yet, some scholars now argue that this is an era not just of 'mass incarceration' but also of 'mass probation' (Phelps 2013a) or 'mass supervision' (McNeill 2013; McNeill and Beyens 2013). Neglect of these developments in favour of a focus on incarceration means that the evolution of punishment in the community has been relatively under-theorized. In consequence, not only is punishment in the community poorly understood in and of itself, but also wider theses about 'punishment and society' will remain incomplete until this neglect is remedied (see Robinson 2016a).

Of course, there is a great deal of extant scholarship on punishment and society that can help to analyse punishment in the community, and we have referred to some of this literature in the previous section. For example, Garland's (2001) influential account of the emergence of a late-modern *Culture of Control*, despite discussing probation and parole only in passing, has much to offer and has been much cited by probation scholars. Garland (2001) develops what he calls a 'conjunctural account' of late-modern penality that takes account both of constraining social structures and of the choices and contingencies that nonetheless shape penal adaptation. Summing up his work, he explains:

> I have tried to show how the field of crime control and criminal justice has been affected by changes in the social organization of the societies in which it functions, by the distinctive problems of social order characteristic of that form of social organization, and by the political, cultural and criminological adaptations that have emerged in response to these distinctive problems. (Garland 2001: 193)

The resources for this kind of conjunctural explanation of penal evolution were reviewed in Garland's (1990) earlier work *Punishment and Modern Society*, which considered the contributions of Marx, Durkheim, Weber, and Foucault (among others) to the sociology of punishment. In a recent book chapter (McNeill and Robinson 2016), we attempted to follow Garland's lead in sketching out how these thinkers might account for punishment in the community's emergence and development as a penal institution and as a set of connected penal discourses and practices. Centrally, we were concerned to understand the social, cultural, and political conditions that gave rise to and subsequently have shaped the development of community punishment.

We began with Foucault's work because it has undoubtedly been most influential amongst those seeking to understand punishment in the community as a social and a penal institution. Foucault's work exposes the spread of a particular mode of power—*disciplinary power*—throughout the social body. At the core of disciplinary power are the principles of individualization and constant visibility (famously characterized by Bentham's eighteenth-century 'Panopticon' prison design) which work in tandem to produce compliant subjects who habitually behave in the required manner. In the context of punishment, discipline is a way of exercising penal power and control which is less punitive than it is corrective: its primary objective is 'normalization'—that is, a re-adjustment of the individual toward the 'norm' of what Foucault terms 'docility-utility' (1977: 137), but which today might be called habitual compliance (see Bottoms 2001).

Foucault's concept and characterization of 'discipline' has proven to be useful for probation scholars, both in analysing the origins of probation as a mode of regulation, and in making sense of more recent developments. For example, Garland's (1985) *Punishment and Welfare* draws heavily on Foucault's notion of disciplinary penality in analysing the birth of the modern penal complex in Britain. Jonathan Simon's (1993) study of the development of parole in California similarly locates the formal/legal origins of parole in the context of the social, political, and cultural shifts which coalesced around the turn of the twentieth century to inaugurate a specifically *modern* form of penality: one that brought the welfare/reform of the individual into the domain of state responsibility and, in that process, extended the reach of disciplinary power. Both scholars show how the pursuit of 'normalization' (or correction) was transformed in the early decades of the twentieth century as ideas about moral reformation gave way to a more 'scientific' discourse centred on diagnosis, treatment, and 'rehabilitation'.

The collapse of confidence in rehabilitation in Britain and the USA ignited intense debate among scholars working within a primarily Foucauldian framework. The early

1980s saw some British scholars predicting the demise of disciplinary power, and with it traditional probation supervision, in favour of an expansion of 'non-disciplinary' disposals which did not aim to correct or transform their subjects, such as the (then relatively new) sanction of community service (Bottoms 1980). These analyses however went against the grain of other accounts that emphasized an *extension* of discipline in the context of both formal and informal domains of social control. The so-called 'dispersal of discipline' thesis was elaborated in Cohen's (1985) seminal book *Visions of Social Control,* in which the focus was the gap between, on the one hand, the rhetoric of decarceration and diversion and, on the other, the reality of an expanding deviance-control system which Cohen thought was emerging at that time. He utilized a much-cited 'fishing net' analogy (in which 'deviants are the fish' (1985: 42)) to describe the increasing extension, widening, dispersal, and invisibility of the (non-carceral) social control apparatus as he observed it. It is from this source that scholars adopted the concepts of 'new widening' and 'mesh thinning', metaphors that have become staples in analyses of community punishment—and sentencing trends more generally—over the last 30 years.

The idea that the proliferation of forms of social control beyond the prison should be seen as an inherently positive development was heavily criticized by Cohen, who was quick to point out that more and different community-based sanctions and measures did not necessarily imply *less* (or less intensive) control; nor did they inevitably lead to a reduction in the use of imprisonment. Indeed, this argument has received support recently from empirical analyses of rates of punishment in the community in Europe which provide, for the first time, convincing evidence both of significant growth in such sanctions and measures *and* of their failure to displace imprisonment (Aebi *et al.* 2015). Likewise, some scholars have criticized the drift away from the use of 'simple' suspended sentences to suspended sentences with conditions, partly driven by renewed confidence about 'what works' in rehabilitation. Typically the additional conditions have a disciplinary character and their imposition increases the penal demands on their subjects and thereby the risks of breach and incarceration (van Zyl Smit *et al.* 2015).

The fate of disciplinary power in the wake of the collapse of the 'rehabilitative ideal' (Allen 1981) was also the subject of the highly influential 'new penology' thesis which has been hotly contested over the last 20 years across a number of jurisdictions (Simon 1993; Feeley and Simon 1992). The new penology thesis essentially contends that late modern societies have moved on from the dominant disciplinary modes of control described by Foucault, in favour of managerial, risk-based strategies. Jonathan Simon has described a decisive shift, starting in the mid-1970s, from a 'clinical' model of practice (centred on the normalization of ex-prisoners) to a 'managerial' model, characterized by significantly lowered expectations and functioning as a mechanism for securing the borders of communities by channelling their least stable members back to prison. We have already discussed the related 'management' adaptation of community punishment above, noting the development of the preoccupation with risk management that is now part of both criminological and correctional common sense. That said, whether the dominance of risk discourses and practices has been at the expense of more ambitious objectives of reform and rehabilitation continues to be the subject of much debate (e.g. Hannah-Moffat 1999; Garland 2001; McNeill *et al.* 2009;

Robinson 2002, 2008; Robinson and McNeill 2016). Foucauldian concepts have also informed some recent studies of the rise and proliferation of surveillance technologies, including the electronic monitoring of offenders which is an increasingly significant element of community sanctions and measures throughout and beyond Europe (Nellis *et al.* 2012).

Foucault's influence on probation and parole scholarship has been so great that it seems fair to say that the potential contributions of other social theorists have been relatively neglected. Thus, it is only very recently that McNeill and Dawson (2014) offered an initial and speculative Durkheimian reading of probation's evolution. Durkheim's influential account of penal evolution placed its emphasis on the *cultural* contexts of penal change. His analysis of the transition in more complex societies to more *organic* forms of social solidarity based on *moral individualism* (Durkheim 1958) suggested a shift in modern punishment towards more humane and restitutive approaches and away from the punitive and repressive measures associated with mechanical solidarity in less developed societies (Durkheim 1973). Nonetheless, Durkheim argued that, at the turn of the twentieth century, the institutionalized forms of restitutive (rather than repressive) punishment appropriate to organic solidarity had failed to emerge, meaning that punishment was failing to fulfill its cultural functions in expressing and reinforcing shared beliefs around moral individualism.

Given that this was the historical moment of probation's emergence in the UK, it seems odd that probation's historians have not looked to Durkheim for inspiration. After all, probation's legal architecture (in the UK at least) was a contract or bond between offender and court that allowed the offender to avoid repressive punishment if she or he proved worthy of the trust that the bond implied. This was to be demonstrated through good conduct and (sometimes) temperance in which the offender made restitution through self-improvement.

In examining punishment in the community today, McNeill and Dawson (2014) argue that a Durkheimian analysis might serve to clarify how and why:

> probation's future development—like punishment's—may depend less on evidence of its 'effectiveness' or 'quality' and more on shifting forms of social organization; on their expression in terms of changing moral sensibilities; and on the changing dynamics of political or governmental authority . . . (McNeill and Dawson 2014: 12)

Such an analysis of community punishment could perhaps help us to understand the limits of 'evidence-based' reform in the field that often vex probation scholars. It can also help to make sense of the development of the punitive adaptations of community punishment referred to above.

That said, though Durkheim's ideas might enable scholars to add a cultural account to Foucauldian reading of punishment in the community as an exercise of disciplinary power, neither elucidates probation and parole's relationships to political economy. In essence, Marxist historians and sociologists of punishment have analysed penal systems as social institutions of capitalist societies; rigged in favour of the property owners and against the dispossessed. As De Giorgi suggests, such analyses

> . . . contend that penal politics plays a very different role than defending society from crime: both the historical emergence of specific penal practices and their persistence in

> contemporary societies are structurally linked to the dominant relations of production and to the hegemonic forms of work organization. In a society divided into classes, criminal law cannot reflect any 'general interest'. (De Giorgi 2013: 41)

Despite the potency and popularity of Marxist critiques of punishment, they have been used only very rarely in making sense of the evolution of probation. Although far from being a Marxist analysis, Maurice Vanstone's work, focusing on practice-related discourses, has significantly challenged and revised the traditional story of probation's origins as an essentially altruistic endeavour, characterized by humanitarian impulses linked to religious ideals. As Vanstone (2004) notes, Young's (1976) earlier account of the history of probation stressed the role of charity in maintaining the position of the middle classes. Woven into the supposed benevolence (and beneficence) of these activities was implicit confirmation that, where 'unfortunates' failed to capitalize on the opportunities that charitable endeavours provided, this was the result of intractable *individual* degeneracy, deflecting attention from broader economic or political analyses of social problems. Amongst a broader range of philanthropic activities, probation emerges in this account as a class-based activity that justifies the existing social order and defends it through its mechanisms of persuasion, supervision, and control (see also Mahood 1991; Garland 1985).

This brief resume of just three critical perspectives on the evolution of punishment in the community only begins to reveal some of the inter-relationships between structure, culture, and power in that evolution but, returning to the inspiration Garland (2001) provides, it does perhaps suggest both the viability and the necessity of developing such an analysis of that evolution.

COMPARATIVE PERSPECTIVES AND CONTEMPORARY CHALLENGES

The development of comparative perspectives on criminal justice has emerged as one important means of refining the sort of conjunctural account of the emergence of the 'Culture of Control' that Garland (2001) offers. Some suggest, for example, that his analysis over-states, over-generalizes, and sometimes under-evidences the changes he identifies within the USA and the UK. In particular, it has been suggested that many of the social and cultural changes he relies upon to explain how penality has evolved in these two countries have also occurred in many other jurisdictions where a 'culture of control' has *not* emerged, or not to the same extent (e.g. Snacken 2009). Thus some scholars have stressed the importance of re-examining differences in political systems (Gottschalk 2013) and in 'varieties of capitalism' (Hall and Soskice 2001) in order to explain differences between states subject to broadly similar social and cultural pressures (Lacey 2008).

For these reasons, the development of comparative analyses of criminal justice—and of community punishment—has become increasingly important. In some recent work with European colleagues in a COST Action (research network) on Offender

Supervision in Europe[8] spanning 23 countries, we have begun to develop new methods for comparative research on offender supervision. This work has been informed by dialogue with colleagues doing similar work in the USA and elsewhere (see Page 2013; Phelps 2013a, 2013b; Miller 2014). For example, in a recent book (Robinson and McNeill 2016), we worked with colleagues to explore the adequacy of the four narratives discussed earlier (rehabilitative, reparative, managerial, and punitive) as a means of explaining the evolution of community punishment in 11 jurisdictions. We found that while these four narrative adaptations had significant value in making sense of developments across these jurisdictions, specific social, cultural, and political contexts affected their relative importance; and, in some places, suggested the need for other adaptations to be added to our explanatory frameworks. For example, in Northern Ireland and Scotland, changing constitutional arrangements required us to consider the role of punishment in the community in two quite different projects of 'state-building' (see Carr 2016; McNeill 2016), and in Romania pressures for 'Europeanization' (from both within and outside the country) were of critical importance (Durnescu 2015). Across all of the jurisdictions, we noted that the ideas and practices that seemed to travel best (like community service and electronic monitoring) did so because they offered putative solutions to systemic and political problems rather than because they promised 'effectiveness' in rehabilitative terms (McNeill and Robinson 2016).

Other European colleagues have recently produced statistical analyses that tend to confirm the importance of studying the evolution of 'mass supervision' in comparative terms. Aebi *et al.* (2015) have shown that the numbers of people subject to offender supervision have grown significantly (if unevenly) in almost all European jurisdictions in recent years. Of the 29 countries in their review, 17 now have more people under supervision than in prison. Perhaps more importantly, this expansion of supervision cannot be explained by crime rates and, crucially, it has *not* led to a reduction in the use of imprisonment, despite the hopes of probation advocates. Indeed, seven of the countries with the highest probation rates are simultaneously among the top ten in terms of rates of imprisonment. Aebi *et al.*'s (2015) work therefore suggests that the expansion of these forms of sanction has led to widening of the net, sweeping more European citizens into diversifying forms of penal control (Cohen 1985).

Looking beyond Europe, similar work by Michelle Phelps (2013a) has explored the relationships between mass incarceration and what she terms 'mass probation' across the 50 states of the USA, between 1980 and 2010. Using regression modelling and state-level case studies, she examined whether probation acted as a driver of or brake upon the build-up in prison populations in this period. She found that two main features determine the nature and impact of the probation–prison link. The first is the extent to which probation diverts individuals from imprisonment or draws cases under greater supervision. The second is the extent to which probation really provides opportunities for rehabilitation that succeed in reducing future imprisonment, or merely acts as a pathway to deeper entrenchment in the penal system. These two features are shaped by three institutional practices: sentencing processes, the effectiveness and quality of supervision and services, and policies and procedures around enforcement (Phelps 2013a).

[8] See http://www.offendersupervision.eu, accessed 25 March 2016.

In the COST Action, as well as examining different institutional-historical contexts (Robinson and McNeill 2016) we sought to develop new ways of exploring variations in supervision as a lived experience, as a socially constructed set of practices, and as a key site of penal decision-making (McNeill and Beyens 2013, 2016). Though reporting on the outcomes of the COST Action is beyond the scope of this chapter, it is perhaps useful to conclude this section by balancing the foregoing discussion of contexts and institutional adaptations of community punishment with some discussion of its impacts. But rather than following the conventional approach of examining the effectiveness of community punishment in formal terms (whether as diversion from custody, as rehabilitation, as reparation, or as retribution), we focus here on evidence about the lived experience of being supervised.

Our initial review of existing research concluded, perhaps unsurprisingly, that the nature of such experiences, though quite often positive, is also highly variable and contingent upon the nature and quality of relationships between supervisor and supervisee (Durnescu *et al.* 2013). Moreover, we found that such research is bedeviled by methodological weaknesses associated with its typical routes of access, with associated selection effects (leading to the probable over-sampling of people with positive experiences) and with its reliance on *accounts* rather than *observations* of supervision.

These weaknesses in the research base are concerning in the light of other evidence that paints a much less benign picture of supervision. In the USA for example, some studies suggest that there are intermediate sanctions that surveyed prisoners equate with prison in terms of punitiveness. For some individuals, intensive forms of probation 'may actually be the more dreaded penalty' (Petersilia and Deschenes 1994: 306; see also Payne and Gainey 1998; May and Wood 2010). More recently, Durnescu (2011) has specifically explored the 'pains of probation' as experienced in Romania. Alongside deprivations of time and the other practical and financial costs of compliance, and limitations on their autonomy and privacy, probationers also reported the pain of the 'forced return to the offence' and the pain of a life lived 'under a constant threat'. The threat in question in Durnescu's (2011) study was that of breach or revocation and with it further punishment.

In broad terms, in the USA a number of rich ethnographic studies have begun to provide compelling evidence of the dominating, intrusive, and sometimes capricious power of supervisory authorities, and of the (perceived) illegitimacy of their 'responsibilizing' practices, as well as of how supervisees often try to subvert and resist their subjugation (see Cox 2011, 2013; Miller 2014; Werth 2011, 2013). In similar vein, Digard's (2010, 2014) English study of the experiences of post-release supervision (and recall to custody) for people convicted of sexual offences suggests that their required submission to disciplinary processes continued long after release and that such forms of supposedly rehabilitative supervision have significant penal bite and are often experienced as illegitimate and procedurally unfair.

Hayes' (2015) recent study of 20 supervisees and supervisors in an English probation trust revealed six types of 'pains of (supervised) community penalties': pains of rehabilitation (related to shame and to the efforts associated with changing one's life); pains of liberty deprivation (loss of time, money, and freedom); pains associated with penal welfare issues (accommodation, finance, employment, etc.); pains associated with external agencies' involvement in supervision (related to the intensification and sometimes hostile nature of their interventions); process pains (linked to the legitimacy or illegitimacy of actions by police, courts, and probation services); and pains associated with stigma (from family members, friends, strangers, and in job-seeking processes). Hayes' painstaking analysis shows that the pains of stigma, of criminal justice processing, and of external agency involvement are usually *unaffected* by the supervisory relationship. While that relationship often serves to ameliorate the pains of penal welfare issues, it tends to *exacerbate* the pains of rehabilitation and liberty deprivation.

One of the pilot studies undertaken within the COST Action explored similar issues using visual methods; we asked people with experience of supervision in England, Germany, and Scotland to take photographs representing their experiences (see Fitzgibbon *et al.*, forthcoming). These photographs were then discussed in interviews and focus groups. The resulting analysis is complex but, as in Hayes' (2015) study, the findings underline the possibility that supervision can be productive *at the same time as* being painful (see also McNeill 2009). The analysis also suggests that both legitimacy (in the exercise of authority) and utility (in the provision of meaningful help) may allow supervision to become more productive. But it is important to acknowledge that even when probation is productive, it still hurts. As Fitzgibbon *et al*, (forthcoming) conclude:

> To paraphrase the common misreporting of supervisory sentences in the British press; people do not 'walk free from court' when such sanctions are imposed. They walk away under judgment, under constraint, under threat and into a situation where their time is no longer their own. They enter a liminal position as 'half-citizens'; their liberty has been preserved, but their autonomy and status are significantly compromised.

CONCLUSION: PENAL MODERATION IN THE COMMUNITY

In this chapter, we have tried to explain the expanding range of forms of punishment in the community and to account for their evolution and development in the UK. In the preceding section, we looked beyond these borders both to mainland Europe and to the USA in order to suggest the importance of comparative work on community punishment. By expanding our gaze we brought two key issues into sharper focus. Firstly, there now seems to be compelling evidence that punishment in the community, for the most part, has failed to deliver the reductions in the use of the imprisonment that have been one of its key rationales in most jurisdictions. The numbers of people subject to these diversifying forms of punishment have expanded rapidly but this has produced little appreciable positive effect on prison populations. Secondly, and equally importantly, recent research tends to confirm the penal (i.e. painful) character of punishment in the community, even when cast in rehabilitative terms. As Hayes argues:

> . . . this is not to say that efforts at promoting rehabilitation [through supervision] are any less desirable (much less effective). Rather, it is to note that, whether at the level of policy or of individual practise, we must recognise supervised community penalties as systems of 'pain delivery', however benevolent the intention (Christie, 1981: 18–19). Whether one is concerned with calibrating the pains of (supervised, community-based) punishment or with minimising them, and whether at the level of policy or practice, we should recall Christie's (1981: 11) admonition that we should 'look for alternatives to punishment, not only alternative punishments'. (Hayes 2015: 99–100)

We argue therefore that the case for penal moderation, both in the volume and intensity of punishment (Snacken 2015; Loader 2010), must extend to punishment in the community as well as imprisonment. The final report of the COST Action on *Offender Supervision in Europe* sums up this argument in calling for adherence to two core principles in the future development of probation and parole systems:

1. Since supervision hurts, decisions about imposing and revoking supervision must be bound by considerations of proportionality. No one should be subject to more demanding or intrusive supervision than their offending deserves.
2. Supervision must be delivered in ways that actively minimize unintended and unnecessary pains both for those subject to supervision and for others affected by it (e.g. family members) (McNeill and Beyens 2016: 9).

In relation to the second principle, the report also suggests that efforts to improve the practice of supervision should attend carefully to its legitimacy and helpfulness in the light of strong evidence that these qualities support engagement, minimize pains, address needs, and thereby support desistance and reintegration.

Of course, the uptake of these principles depends in large part on the sorts of social, cultural and political conditions that we discussed in the middle of this chapter. Nonetheless, our view is that the ethical and effective development of punishment in the community—like the ethical development of imprisonment—depends at least as much on confronting the need for restraint as it does on improving the contexts and contents of the sanctions themselves.

SELECTED FURTHER READING

For those interested in the emergence of probation in England and Wales, we recommend Vanstone's *Supervising Offenders in the Community* (2004), or, for a more wide-ranging historical account of the changing contours of penality around the turn of the twentieth century, Garland's *Punishment & Welfare* (1985) is excellent. Garland's *The Culture of Control* (2001) is also indispensable for those who wish to understand developments in community punishment in the context of more recent shifts in the social and penal landscapes. On the history and development of parole in the USA, Simon's (1993) *Poor Discipline* (1993) is not to be missed, and Cohen's *Visions of Social Control* (1985) is also highly recommended as a classic Foucauldian analysis of the dispersal of punishment (including punishment in the community). For those wishing to explore punishment in the community in other jurisdictions, Robinson and McNeill's *Community Punishment: European Perspectives* (2016) includes essays from 11 European jurisdictions. McNeill and Beyens' *Offender Supervision in*

Europe (2013) is also useful in that it provides overviews of European research on a number of themes relevant to offender supervision. For insights into the use of electronic monitoring in a variety of jurisdictions, Nellis *et al*.'s *Electronically Monitored Punishment: International and Critical Perspectives* (2012) is also excellent. For a recent discussion of the use of probation in the USA, we recommend Phelps' article 'The Paradox of Probation: Community Supervision in the Age of Mass Incarceration' (2013a). Finally, both *The Probation Journal* and the *European Journal of Probation* are great sources for articles on a range of topics in this field.

REFERENCES

Advisory Council on the Penal System (1970), 'Non-Custodial and Semi-Custodial Penalties', London: HMSO.

Aebi, M., Delgrance, N., and Marguet, Y. (2015), 'Have community sanctions and measures widened the net of the European criminal justice systems?', *Punishment & Society*, 17(5): 575–97.

Allen, F. A. (1981), *The Decline of the Rehabilitative Ideal: Penal Policy and Social Purpose*, New Haven: Yale University Press.

Bottoms, A. (1980), 'An introduction to "the coming crisis"', in A. E. Bottoms and R. H. Preston (eds), *The Coming Penal Crisis*, Edinburgh: Scottish Academic Press.

Bottoms, A. (1995), 'The philosophy and politics of punishment and sentencing', in C. Clarkson and R. Morgan (eds), *The Politics of Sentencing Reform*, Oxford: Clarendon Press.

Bottoms, A. (2001), 'Compliance with community penalties', in A. Bottoms, L. Gelsthorpe, and S. Rex (eds), *Community Penalties: Change and Challenges*, Cullompton: Willan.

Bottoms, A., Rex, S., and Robinson, G. (2004), 'How did we get here?', in A. Bottoms, S. Rex, and G. Robinson (eds), *Alternatives to Prison: Options For an Insecure Society*, Cullompton: Willan.

Canton, R. (2014), 'Yes, no, possibly, maybe: Community sanctions, consent and cooperation', *European Journal of Probation*, 6(3): 209–24.

Carr, N. (2016), 'Contingent legitimacy: Community sanctions in Northern Ireland', in G. Robinson and F. McNeill (eds), *Community Punishment: European Perspectives*, Abingdon: Routledge.

Carr, N. and Maruna, S. (2012), 'Legitimacy Through Neutrality: Probation and Conflict in Northern Ireland', *Howard Journal of Criminal Justice*, 51(5): 474–87.

Casey, L. (2008), *Engaging Communities in Fighting Crime: A Review (Casey Report)*, London: Cabinet Office.

Cavadino, M., Dignan, J., and Mair, G. (2013), *The Penal System: An Introduction*, 5th edn, London: Sage.

Christie, N. (1981), *Limits to Pain: The Role of Punishment in Penal Policy*, Oslo: Universitetforslaget.

Cohen, S. (1985), *Visions of Social Control*, Cambridge: Polity.

Council of Europe (1992), 'Recommendation No. R (92) 16 of the Committee of Ministers to member states on the European rules on community sanctions and measures', Council of Europe: Strasbourg.

Cox, A. (2011), 'Doing the programme or doing me? The pains of youth imprisonment', *Punishment & Society*, 13(5): 592–610.

Cox, A. (2013), 'New visions of social control? Young peoples' perceptions of community penalties', *Journal of Youth Studies* 16(1): 135–50.

De Giorgi, A. (2013), 'Punishment and Political Economy', in J. Simon and R. Sparks (eds), *The Sage Handbook of Punishment and Society*, London and New York: Sage.

Digard, L. (2010), 'When legitimacy is denied: Sex offenders' perceptions and experiences of prison recall', *Probation Journal*, 57(1): 1–19.

Digard, L. (2014), 'Encoding risk: Probation work and sex offenders' narrative identities', *Punishment & Society*, 16(4): 428–47.

Durkheim, E. (1958), 'The State', in E. Durkheim (1986), *Durkheim on Politics and the State*, Stanford: Stanford University Press.

Durkheim, E. (1973), 'Two Laws of Penal Evolution', *Economy and Society*, 2(3): 285–308.

Durnescu, I. (2011), 'Pains of probation: Effective practice and human rights', *International Journal of Offender Therapy and Comparative Criminology*, 55(4): 530–45.

Durnescu, I. (2015), 'Romania: Empty shells, emulation and Europeanisation', in G. Robinson and F. McNeill (eds), *Community Punishment: European Perspectives*, Abingdon: Routledge.

Durnescu, I., Enengl, C., and Grafl, G. (2013), 'Experiencing supervision', in F. McNeill and K. Beyens (eds), *Offender Supervision in Europe*. Basingstoke: Palgrave.

Eriksson, A. (2009), *Justice in Transition: Community Restorative Justice in Northern Ireland*, Cullompton: Willan.

Feeley, M. and Simon, J. (1992), 'The new penology: notes on the emerging strategy of corrections and its implications', *Criminology*, 30(4): 449–74.

Fitzgibbon, D., Graebsch, C., and McNeill, F. (forthcoming), 'Pervasive Punishment: Experiencing Supervision', in M. Brown and E. Carrabine (eds),

The Routledge International Handbook of Visual Criminology, London: Routledge.

Foucault, M. (1977), *Discipline & Punish*, London: Allen Lane.

Garland, D. (1985), *Punishment and Welfare*, Aldershot: Gower.

Garland, D. (1996), 'The limits of the sovereign state: strategies of crime control in contemporary society', *British Journal of Criminology*, 36(4): 445–71.

Garland, D. (1997), 'Probation and the reconfiguration of crime control', in R. Burnett (ed.), *The Probation Service: Responding to Change (Proceedings of the Probation Studies Unit First Colloquium)*, Oxford: University of Oxford Centre for Criminological Research.

Garland, D. (2001), *The Culture of Control*, Oxford: Oxford University Press.

Garland, D. and Young, P. (eds) (1983), *The Power to Punish*, Aldershot: Gower.

Glaze, L. and Kaeble, D. (2014), *Correctional Populations in the United States, 2013*, Washington, DC: Bureau of Justice Statistics, Office of Justice Programs, US Department of Justice, available at: http://www.bjs.gov/content/pub/pdf/cpus13.pdf, accessed 28 July 2016.

Gottschalk, M. (2013), 'The Carceral State and the Politics of Punishment', in J. Simon and R. Sparks (eds), *The Sage Handbook of Punishment and Society*, London and New York: Sage.

Hall, P. and Soskice, D. (2001), *Varieties of Capitalism: The Institutional Foundations of Comparative Advantage*, Oxford: Oxford University Press.

Hannah-Moffat, K. (1999), 'Moral agent or actuarial subject: risk and Canadian women's imprisonment', *Theoretical Criminology*, 3(1): 1, 71–94.

Harding, J. (2013), 'Forty years of community service', *The Guardian*, 8 January.

Hayes, D. (2015), 'The impact of supervision on the pains of community penalties in England & Wales: An exploratory study', *European Journal of Probation*, 7(2): 85–102.

Heard, C. (2015), 'Community Sentences Since 2000: How they work—and why they have not cut prisoner numbers', London: Centre for Crime and Justice Studies, available at: http://www.crimeandjustice.org.uk/publications/community-sentences-2000, accessed 10 January 2017.

Home Office (1977), *A Review of Criminal Justice Policy 1976*, London: HMSO.

Home Office (2006), *Rebalancing the Criminal Justice System in Favour of the Law-Abiding Majority: Cutting Crime, Reducing Re-offending and Protecting the Public*, London: Home Office.

Kemshall, H. and Maguire, M. (2001), 'Public protection, partnership and risk penality: the multi-agency risk management of sexual and dangerous offenders', *Punishment & Society*, 3(2): 237–64.

Kirby, A. and Jacobson, J. (2015), *Evaluation of the Pre-Sentence RJ Pathfinder*, London: ICPR.

Klingele, C. (2013), 'Rethinking the use of community supervision', *Journal of Criminal Law and Criminology*, 103(4): 1015–69.

Lacey, N. (2008), *The Prisoner's Dilemma: Political Economy and Punishment in Contemporary Democracies*, Cambridge: Cambridge University Press.

Loader, I. (2010), 'For penal moderation: Notes towards a public philosophy of punishment', *Theoretical Criminology*, 14(3): 349–67.

McNeill, F. (2009), 'Helping, Holding, Hurting: Recalling and reforming punishment', the 6th annual Apex Lecture, at the Signet Library, Parliament Square, Edinburgh, 8 September 2009, available at: https://pure.strath.ac.uk/portal/files/521675/strathprints026701.pdf, accessed 27 July 2016.

McNeill, F. (2011), 'Determined to Punish? Scotland's Choice', in G. Hassan and R. Ilett (eds), *Radical Scotland: Arguments for Self-Determination*, Edinburgh: Luath Press.

McNeill, F. (2013), 'Community Sanctions and European Penology', in T. Daems, S. Snacken, and D. Van Zyl Smit (eds), *European Penology*, London: Hart.

McNeill, F. (2016), 'Reductionism, rehabilitation and reparation: Community punishment in Scotland', in G. Robinson and F. McNeill (eds), *Community Punishment: European Perspectives*, Abingdon, Routledge.

McNeill, F. and Beyens, K. (eds) (2013), *Offender Supervision in Europe*, Basingstoke: Palgrave Macmillan.

McNeill, F. and Beyens, K. (2016), 'COST Action IS1106: Final Report', available at: http://www.offendersupervision.eu/wp-content/uploads/2016/03/Final-Report.pdf, accessed 27 July 2016.

McNeill, F., Burns, N., Halliday, S., Hutton, N., and Tata, C. (2009), 'Risk, responsibility and reconfiguration: Penal adaptation and misadaptation', *Punishment & Society*, 11(4): 419–42.

McNeill, F. and Dawson, M. (2014), 'Social Solidarity, Penal Evolution and Probation', *British Journal of Criminology*, 54(5): 892–907.

McNeill, F. and Whyte, B. (2007), *Reducing Reoffending: Social Work and Community Justice in Scotland*, Cullompton: Willan.

Mahood, L. (1991), *Policing Gender, Class and Family in Britain, 1950-1940*, London: UCL Press.

Maruna, S. and King, A. (2008) 'Selling the public on probation: beyond the bib', *Probation Journal*, 55(4): 337–51.

May, D. and Wood, P. (2010), *Ranking Correctional Punishments: Views from Offenders, Practitioners and the Public*, Durham, NC: Carolina Academic Press.

Mews, A. and Coxon, C. (2014), *Updated analysis of the impact of the Intensive Alternatives to Custody pilots on re-offending rates (Ministry of Justice Analytical Summary)*, London: Ministry of Justice.

Miller, R. (2014), 'Devolving the Carceral State: Race, Prisoner Reentry, and the Micro Politics of Urban

Poverty Management', *Punishment & Society*, 16(3): 305–35.

Ministry of Justice (2013), 'Radical overhaul of sentencing continues', Press Release, 2 December 2013, available at: https://www.gov.uk/government/news/radical-overhaul-of-sentencing-continues, accessed 6 July 2016.

Nellis, M., Beyens, K., and Kaminski, D. (eds) (2012), *Electronically Monitored Punishment: International and Critical Perspectives*, London: Routledge.

Newburn, T. (2007), '"Toughon crime": Penal policy in England & Wales', *Crime and Justice*, 36(1): 425–70.

Page, J. (2013), 'Punishment and the Penal Field' in J. Simon and R. Sparks (eds), *The Sage Handbook of Punishment and Society*, London and New York: Sage.

Payne, B. and Gainey, R. (1998), 'A Qualitative Assessment of the Pains Experienced on Electronic Monitoring', *International Journal of Offender Therapy and Comparative Criminology*, 42(2): 149–63.

Petersilia, J. and Deschenes, E. (1994), 'Perceptions of punishment: Inmates and staff rank the severity of prison versus intermediate sanctions', *The Prison Journal*, 74(3): 306–28.

Phelps, M. (2013a), 'The Paradox of Probation: Community Supervision in the Age of Mass Incarceration', *Law and Policy*, 35(1–2): 55–80.

Phelps, M. (2013b), 'The Paradox of Probation: Understanding the Expansion of an "Alternative" to Incarceration during the Prison Boom', PhD thesis, Princeton: University of Princeton.

Raynor, P. (1988), *Probation as an Alternative to Custody*, Aldershot: Avebury.

Raynor, P. (2012), 'Community penalties, probation, and offender management', in M. Maguire, R. Morgan, and R. Reiner (eds), *The Oxford Handbook of Criminology*, 5th edn, Oxford: Oxford University Press.

Raynor, P. (2014), 'Consent to probation in England & Wales: How it was abolished, and why it matters', *European Journal of Probation*, 6(3): 296–307.

Raynor, P. and Robinson, G. (2009), *Rehabilitation, Crime and Justice*, Basingstoke: Palgrave Macmillan.

Reeves, C. (2011), 'The changing role of probation hostels: Voices from the inside', *British Journal of Community Justice*, 9(3): 51–64.

Robinson, G. (2002), 'Exploring risk management in the probation service: contemporary developments in England and Wales', *Punishment & Society*, 4(1): 5–25.

Robinson, G. (2008), 'Late-modern Rehabilitation: The Evolution of a Penal Strategy', *Punishment & Society*, 10(4): 429–45.

Robinson, G. (2016a), 'The Cinderella Complex: Punishment, society and community sanctions', *Punishment & Society*, 18(1): 95–112.

Robinson, G. (2016b), 'Three narratives and a funeral: Community punishment in England & Wales', in G. Robinson and F. McNeill (eds), *Community Punishment: European Perspectives*, Abingdon: Routledge.

Robinson, G. and McNeill, F. (2016), *Community Punishment: European Perspectives*, Abingdon: Routledge.

Robinson, G., McNeill, F., and Maruna, S. (2013), 'Punishment in society: The improbable persistence of probation and other community sanctions and measures', in J. Simon and R. Sparks (eds), *The Sage Handbook of Punishment and Society*, London: Sage.

Robinson, G. and Shapland, J. (2008), 'Reducing recidivism: A task for restorative justice?', *British Journal of Criminology*, 48(3): 337–58.

Robinson, G. and Ugwudike, P. (2012), 'Investing in toughness: Probation, enforcement and legitimacy', *Howard Journal of Criminal Justice*, 51(3): 300–16.

Scottish Prisons Commission (2008), *Scotland's Choice*, Edinburgh: Scottish Prisons Commission.

Shute, S. (2003), 'The development of parole and the role of research in its reform', in L. Zedner and A. Ashworth (eds), *The Criminological Foundations of Penal Policy: Essays in Honour of Roger Hood*, Oxford: Oxford University Press.

Simon, J. (1993), *Poor Discipline: Parole and the Social Control of the Underclass 1890-1990*, London: University of Chicago Press.

Snacken, S. (2015), 'Punishment, legitimate policies and values: Penal moderation, dignity and human rights', *Punishment & Society*, 17(3): 397–423.

Tomczak, P. (2015), 'The voluntary sector and the mandatory statutory supervision requirement: Expanding the carceral net', *British Journal of Criminology*, doi: 10.1093/bjc/azv091.

van Zyl Smit, D., Snacken, S., and Hayes, D. (2015), '"One cannot legislate kindness": Ambiguities in European legal instruments on non-custodial sanctions', *Punishment & Society*, 17(1): 3–26.

Vanstone, M. (2004), *Supervising Offenders in the Community*, Aldershot: Ashgate.

Werth, R. (2011), 'I do what I'm told, sort of: Reformed subjects, unruly citizens, and parole', *Theoretical Criminology*, 16(3): 329–46.

Werth, R. (2013), 'The construction and stewardship of responsible yet precarious subjects: Punitive ideology, rehabilitation, and "tough love" among parole personnel', *Punishment & Society*, 15(3): 219–46.

Wong, K. (2013), 'Integrated offender management: assessing the impacts and benefits—holy grail or fool's errand?', *British Journal of Community Justice*, 11(2/3): 59–81.

Worrall, A. (1997), *Punishment in the Community*, Harlow: Longman..

Young, P. (1976), 'A Sociological Analysis of the Early History of Probation', *British Journal of Law and Society*, 3(1): 44–58.

39

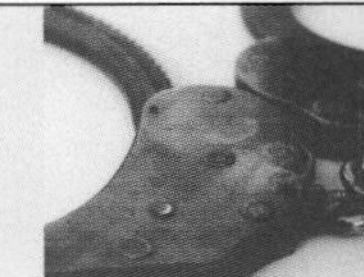

RECONFIGURING PENAL POWER

Ben Crewe and Alison Liebling

> We do not dissent from the plain truth that incarceration implies force, at least in 'the last instance'. Prisons are dominative institutions. [But] we would also argue that an account that places its whole emphasis on the imposition of order by relentless force glosses over many important complexities of prison life and effaces some significant variations in the social organization of different prisons. One aspect of such difference . . . concerns the extent to which the staff of different prisons succeed or fail in legitimating their deployment of power and authority and the techniques and strategies which they deploy in seeking to secure such legitimacy. (Sparks *et al.* 1996: 35)

INTRODUCTION

In their book on legitimacy in high-security prisons, *Prisons and the Problem of Order*, Sparks *et al.* (1996) sought to counter the view shared by 'radical pessimist' and 'conservative pragmatist' penal scholars that prisons were entirely non-legitimate institutions. For the radical pessimists, whose writings had highlighted blatant abuses of power in British prisons in the 1970s and 80s (Fitzgerald 1987; Scraton *et al.* 1991), the essence of imprisonment was coercive, and its characteristic features were conflict and antagonism. For 'conservative pragmatists', such as the American scholar John Dilulio, the non-legitimate nature of prisons was such that they required firm control to inhibit their in-built tendency towards disorder (Dilulio 1987).

As the quote above makes clear, Sparks and colleagues did not dispute that all forms of incarceration were founded, in some sense, on the use of force, and that 'the social order of the prison is imposed and enforced' (1996: 300). However, in noting that some prisons generated more conflict and resentment than others, they sought to emphasize that some were more successful in legitimating their own practices and generating some level of consent among the governed. As they noted, prison staff operated with an acute—if often tacit—understanding that they needed to 'tailor their actions, demeanour, and demands in recognition of prisoners' customary expectations' (Sparks *et al.* 1996: 303). To focus solely on power's most coercive forms was to ignore the possibility that different institutions met these expectations to a greater degree than others, on the basis of modes of authority that went beyond force and threat. As their analysis proceeded to demonstrate, within high-security prisons in England and Wales in the late 1980s, there was considerable divergence in the strategies adopted to generate order, in the degree to which prisoners assented to these regimes, and in the social consequences of these different models of order.

Sparks and colleagues' call for 'more nuanced and appropriate conceptions of the links between order, power and legitimacy in penal relations' (Sparks and Bottoms 1995: 52) changed the terms of penal scholarship significantly, but has been met only partially. Few penal scholars have sought to conceptualize or evaluate differing forms of penal power and order (although see Kruttschnitt and Gartner 2005). In part, this reflects an enduring tendency to regard power as inherently damaging, and therefore not to look beyond its more egregious features. Young (cited in McMahon 1992: 215) summarized this stance as follows: 'beware of power, distrust those who hold it, resist its exercise, attack its institutions'. As McMahon (1992) argues, this position sees the exercise of penal power 'as always, and everywhere, involving only more social control, repression, domination, and subjection' (1992: 218). This orientation often finds its expression in descriptions of prison officers as agents of state power, or as brutal thugs (e.g. Cohen and Taylor 1972; Sim 2008). While such descriptions are not always unjustified, they are highly reductive, overlooking the range of attitudes and behaviours that prison officers express and exhibit, and the full range of functions they perform. Most problematically, absolutist cynicism about the nature of penal power and order makes it impossible to identify which forms of penal authority are more oppressive, destructive, or unreasonable than others, with what consequences for the daily lives and well-being of prisoners. This is surprising, given that prisoners are sensitive and well-informed evaluators of their own predicament. Even a brief conversation on a prison wing reveals that prisoners are able to identify regimes that are more respectful, fairer, and safer than others, to articulate how power 'feels' in such establishments, and to describe the impact of different regimes on their psychological security and well-being, their opportunities for self-determination, and their everyday behaviour.

Our aim in this chapter is to describe changing forms of power in contemporary prisons in England and Wales, and the impact of these changes on staff culture, staff–prisoner relationships, and prison order. How are recent changes in the organization and balance of penal power manifested, with what consequences? How can they be conceptualized? In addressing these questions, we re-visit an earlier attempt to characterize the texture of penal authority, before describing how, even in the last few years, this texture has been reconfigured, as cuts to prison staffing levels have radically reshaped how prison officers use, and are able to use, their power on the landings.

PENAL POWER

It is clear from the literature that prisons can have different configurations of power and there there is usually a gap between the 'official' intended model and what happens in practice. The balance of power between prisoners, staff (and unions), governors or managers, headquarters, and increasingly, politicians, alters as policy intentions and the ideologies to which these are linked, shift. Different configurations of power are regarded by prisoners as more or less legitimate, and these evaluations have a direct impact on their behaviour, attitudes, and well-being.

The assumption that prison staff are all-powerful is questionable. In this regard, there is considerable divergence between two of the classic studies of prison life (Sykes 1958 and Mathiesen 1965), although this might be explained by their distinct geographical locations (as well as by each prison's distinct function). Sykes (1958) highlighted the 'defects in total power' and 'cracks in the [institutional] monolith', in his study of a US maximum security prison, emphasizing the various ways in which the seemingly total power of prison officers was, in practice, compromised. Any recourse to force was highly hazardous. Officers were outnumbered, and were dependent on prisoners (to appear competent, and to discharge a range of daily tasks). Some subsequent studies, such as McEvoy's (2001) account of paramilitary imprisonment in Northern Ireland, are consistent with Sykes' portrayal of the power balance between staff and prisoners. In McEvoy's study, the latter were cohesive, organized, and ideologically hostile to their captors, regarding themselves as political prisoners and questioning the legitimacy of the state that held them. Able to communicate with organizations outside the prison, and highly disciplined within it, they were able to exert exceptional levels of pressure on prison staff, to the extent that the wings were in effect run by prisoners themselves.

In contrast, Mathiesen (1965) described prisoners within a medium-security, treatment-oriented correctional institution in Norway as feeling highly dependent on prison staff. Atomized and divided, from their position of weakness, they engaged in a form of 'censoriousness', in which they challenged prison staff not on the basis of an alternative value system, but for failing to correctly implement the rules of the institution. Studies of imprisoned sex offenders have generally reported similar findings: such prisoners exhibit little collective solidarity and challenge staff authority mainly through recourse to institutional norms and regulations, and legal challenge (Sparks *et al.* 1996). As Bottoms (2005) notes, these divergent descriptions in part reflect the lens through which power is observed. Sykes' account in effect assumes the perspective of prison officers. Mathiesen writes from the position of the atomized and dependent prisoner. Other studies (e.g. Ben-David 1992 in Israel) have described both political and even romantic affiliations between staff and prisoners and the risks these affiliations pose to the presumed basic split between staff and prisoners (see also Ben-David and Silfen 1994). The types of power that prison officers can use (e.g. coercive, expert, referent or personal, legal, and reward), or are regarded as acceptable, vary and are linked (in both directions) to the kinds of relationships they have with prisoners (see Hepburn 1985 and Liebling *et al.* 2011) as well as to the kinds of social relationships and hierarchies that develop as a result (Street 1965). Very little research in recent years has sought to trace this chain of authority, either empirically or theoretically.

PENAL POWER AND THE WEIGHT OF IMPRISONMENT

In a recent article (Crewe *et al.* 2014a), we argued that the concept of the 'weight' of imprisonment had been under-theorized within penological research. First conceptualized by David Downes (1988) (although initially labelled 'depth') to convey the degree to which imprisonment was 'damaging and repressive', the term was subsequently reframed by King and McDermott (1995) to convey the burden of the sentence: the pressure that it brought down upon the prisoner, according to such matters as how staff used their power, relations with other prisoners, the material conditions in which prisoners lived, the rights and privileges afforded to them, and the nature of the regime (including access to work and education).

The terminology and connotations of weight, alongside the tendency among penologists to see power as inherently suppressive and preventative, meant that little attention had been given to the ways in which different formations of penal power might be damaging or dangerous or, conversely, reasonable and supportive. *Prisons and the Problem of Order* was thus a notable exception. Of the two high-security prisons featured in this analysis, Albany was more controlled and oppressive, delivering a predictable regime, but at the expense of what we would call 'harmony' values and outcomes, such as humanity and respect. In the other prison, Long Lartin, staff used their discretion to provide a more flexible and 'open' regime, which was in some ways more relaxed than Albany, and provided prisoners with more autonomy. Compared to Albany, Long Lartin exhibited a lower level of protest, disobedience, and non-compliance among its prisoners, and it generated fewer disciplinary infractions. However, higher levels of self-determination and freedom of movement among prisoners enabled a greater and more severe degree of 'backstage violence' arising from deep and extensive conflicts brewing between prisoners over time: 'the regime gave rise to opportunities for trouble and predation on fellow inmates, . . . and hence to some risks in day-to-day inmate life' (Sparks *et al.* 1996: 318). Long Lartin's fewer incidents of violence were more serious and protracted.

Sparks *et al.*'s analysis brought to light a number of issues. First, even within a single prison system, the means of accomplishing order varied considerably between prisons of the same type. Second, legitimacy was complex and multi-dimensional. Securing the approval of prisoners with regard to some of its most important aspects could diminish their approval in relation to others. So while Sparks *et al.* asserted that Long Lartin's 'more "social" crime prevention style gave its captive population cause to confer greater *legitimacy* on the prison' (ibid.: 322), they did not downplay the fact that 'some aspects of Albany's "situational control" genuinely reduced opportunities for trouble' (ibid.: 322). Third, then, there were negative consequences for prisoners both when power was asserted upon prisoners too rigidly and forcefully, and when it was asserted too lightly. Fourth, even generalizations of this kind were too broad, since there was not a complete consensus among prisoners as to which establishment was preferable: as Sparks *et al.* noted, some older prisoners preferred Albany's austere stability to Long Lartin's risky autonomy.

Our previous contribution to debate about such issues stems from a comparative study of quality of life and culture in a range of public and private prisons, in which we sought to conceptualize and evaluate different forms of authority within the two sectors (see Crewe *et al.* 2014a, 2014b, 2015). All of the five private sector prisons within our study were described by prisoners in terms that we summarized as 'light'. For example, custody officers in the private sector were more likely to call prisoners by their preferred names and less often judged them negatively than their counterparts in public sector prisons, who tended to be more punitive and morally judgmental. However, prisoners in the public sector prisons evaluated their overall quality of life more positively than those in three of the private sector prisons, in domains such as interpersonal treatment, as well as in relation to safety, policing, and staff professionalism. In other words—we argued—prisons that were somewhat heavy were in some ways deemed preferable to those that were unduly light.

In the less good private sector prisons, prisoners complained that interpersonal courtesy was less important to them than the forms of staff experience in the public sector that enabled their questions to be answered and their requests to be met. Private sector custody officers were described as 'nice' but rather ineffective, while public sector prison officers were considered less pleasant, but more knowledgeable, and better able to run a safe and predictable regime. In the less good private prisons, weaknesses in the use of authority, and the inconsistent use of power, created regimes that felt rather under-controlled—'like a council estate' (prisoner, private sector). Prisoners wanted uniformed staff to exude authority, and to use it judiciously and consistently, so that they 'knew where they stood' and could be confident that incidents would be handled quickly and confidently. They also wanted these staff to provide a form of 'supportive limit setting' (Wachtel and McCold 2001)—a combination of boundaries, clarity, and care—that protected them not only from other prisoners but from environmental temptations, such as drugs and violence, to which they recognized they could be attracted (discussed later in the chapter).

The study helped us to describe some characteristic differences between the sectors. While the very good private sector prisons were better than the public sector establishments in terms of overall quality of life for prisoners, they too exhibited some weaknesses with regard to matters such as policing and security. The public sector prisons delivered a well-oiled regime, in which prisoners generally felt safe, but did so without a great deal of care. Many of these differences reflected different levels of staff experience: in the private sector prisons, turnover was higher, and a greater proportion of frontline staff had worked in prisons for less than three years, meaning that experience and 'jailcraft' on the prison landings were lacking. In the public sector prisons, low turnover created a different set of problems: many experienced staff were 'trapped' in a job that they did not enjoy, and which had made them cynical, but which paid them reasonably well, generating attitudes that were jaded and self-interested. Cultures and practices were different in each.

Our conclusion was that, to account for our findings, an axis ranging from 'heavy' to 'light' needed to be combined with one ranging from 'absence' to 'presence' (see Figure 39.1, in which we have included prisons from a range of studies, including three that we refer to later). Absence and presence denoted the *availability* of uniformed staff on the prison landings, their *depth and quality of engagement* with prisoners, and

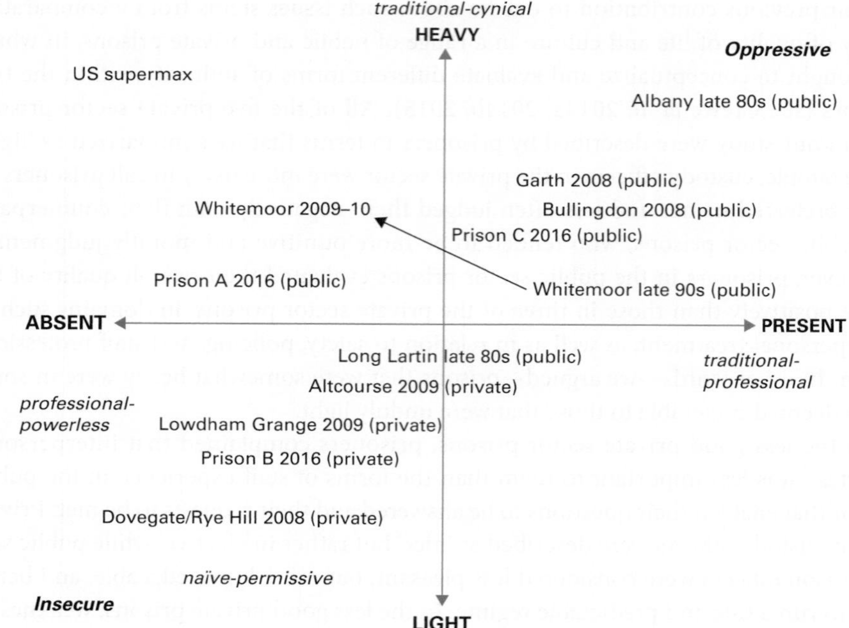

Figure 39.1 Heavy-light, absent-present

the degree to which they *imprinted their authority* on the environment, through action (such as policing) and competence (using authority well). Lightness was desirable only when combined with staff *presence* (a precise term we will return to later). When combined with an absence of authority, it was highly undesirable, creating an environment that was under-policed, unsafe, and unpredictable. The private sector prisons were located within this quadrant, with those that were particularly poor-performing in its far corner. In such establishments, deficits in the exercise of confident authority meant that the wings were chaotic, 'run' as much by prisoners as by staff, with power flowing from 'below' from prisoners onto staff, and from prisoner to prisoner, in relatively unregulated ways. Prisoners lived in a state of considerable insecurity, in part due to inconsistencies in the use of staff authority (sometimes excessive, sometimes insufficient, and often unpredictable) alongside disorganized regimes. These feelings of insecurity were exacerbated by the forms of drug dealing and predation that were allowed to prosper in the absence of adequate policing and supervision.

In contrast, the public sector prisons in our study sat in the 'heavy-present' quadrant. Power was imposed onto prisoners by uniformed staff, often based on attitudes that were punitive or regressive, creating an atmosphere that was somewhat austere and oppressive. At the same time, the availability of staff, their confidence and experience, and their ability to maintain a predictable regime, gave prisoners a degree of security and certainty about rules and boundaries, about their own safety, and about their routes to release. At its best, this confident position was combined with a problem-solving orientation and more benign and constructive attitudes towards prisoners—this was 'traditional-professional' authority: less heavy but clearly present.

The two remaining positions within the diagram also require description. *Heavy-absent* is most starkly embodied by supermax prisons in North America, in which order is achieved through extreme situational control measures and the use of technology, where the primary role of staff is to manage prisoners at a distance and implement control and restraint procedures rather than form relationships of any meaning (King 1999; Rhodes 2004).

Supermax prisons deliberately eliminate the need for relational dynamics in establishing order and control. Interactions between prisoners and staff are discouraged; staff discretion is minimized in favour of the strict application of rules (Haney 2008). Prisoners are, in effect, entombed. Their almost total social segregation means that they are relatively safe from their peers, but the corollary of their isolation is profound relational and sensual deprivation (Haney 2006). Physical security is assured at the expense of psychological health.

A less acute version of heavy-absent has been found recently within some high-security and other prisons in England and Wales, in contrast to a more professionally confident 'heavy-present' form of power found in the same establishments in 1998–9 (see Liebling and Price 2001; Liebling *et al.* 2011). In such prisons, the oppressiveness of the environment results from restrictive security measures combined with a culture in which uniformed staff have retreated from prisoner engagement, due to a lack of cultural affinity with young, ethnic minority prisoner groups, anxieties about how to respect prisoners' claims to religious expression while also policing their riskier manifestations (Liebling *et al.* 2012; Liebling and Arnold 2012), or disillusionment with the job. Staff–prisoner relationships in these establishments are characterized by mutual mistrust and cultural distance. Staff carry out their security tasks, but without the cordial relations that make them less aggravating to prisoners. Such features are mirrored within an increasingly violent and fractured prisoner subculture, in which prisoners are left to negotiate life on the landings with each other, with tensions resulting from competing assertions of cultural practices (often between an increasingly visible and assertive Muslim sub-group and a resistant or resentful sub-group of non-Muslim prisoners). Prisoners describe being in this social world as like 'swimming in a shark tank' (Liebling and Arnold 2012: 420). There is, we have found in subsequent research, still considerable variation in the balance of power and the shape that staff–prisoner relationships take between high security prisons (Liebling *et al.* 2015). These differences have underlying them very different conceptions of the moral status of the prisoner, which can range from *I-It* relations, in which prisoners are regarded as 'experienced objects' to *I-Thou* relations in which they are approached as 'experiencing subjects' (see further Liebling 2015). We reintroduce these terms when we summarize our findings in three contemporary prisons at the end of our chapter.

Forms of imprisonment that combine heaviness with *absence* are arguably its least legitimate variety. Whereas establishments that are heavy-present provide prisoners with a level of support and protection, and those that are light-absent offer some degree of humanity and autonomy, prisons that are 'heavy-absent' combine the oppressiveness of weight with the insecurity of absence. Power is imposed overbearingly without enhancing any aspects of prisoner well-being. In contrast, prisons that are 'light' but 'present' represent the most legitimate quadrant within our diagram. In such establishments, power undoubtedly flows, but it does so almost imperceptibly, because of the relational manner in which it operates. Staff 'know their prisoners': they understand their moods and preoccupations, allowing them to use their discretion effectively. They generate compliance through practices that are procedurally fair, or via normative commitment, and produce safety through a form of 'dynamic authority'—based on being visible, interactive, and quietly authoritative—that rarely requires power to be deployed in its coercive mode (see Liebling *et al.* 2010; Liebling 2011). They are challenging without being antagonistic, are supportive without being over-directive, and convey confidence without being domineering.

The prisons that most resemble this model tend to be well-staffed small units or prisons with a formal, therapeutic orientation. As described in a range of literature (Fitzgerald 1987; Cooke 1989; Bottomley 1990, 1994; Bottomley and Hay 1991; Bottomley *et al.* 1994; Genders and Player 1995; Stevens 2013), such places exhibit staff–prisoner relationships whose density and intensity represents a positive fusion of care and control. In a recent study of HMP Grendon—a prison run as a democratic therapeutic community—Stevens (2013), for example, documents the quality of trust and support that runs both through staff–prisoner and prisoner–prisoner relationships, including the 'open-door' policy which gives prisoners 'constant, "legitimate", informal access' (ibid.: 93) to officers throughout the day, and practices such as communal dining, which provide 'opportunities for gaining social confidence and for expressing responsibility and care' (ibid.: 95). At the same time, prisoners are made to take considerable responsibility for their daily conduct, in relation to matters such as punctuality, but also through public challenges at small group and community meetings which force prisoners to account for their behaviour. The description of such meetings as 'gruelling' (ibid.: 116) is telling, for while they are far more democratic, supportive, and transparent than disciplinary mechanisms in most prison establishments, the term points to the ways that power is exercised upon prisoners through psycho-therapeutic discourse and the norms of the prison 'community'. This form of power can still operate coercively, but on balance, prisoners both prefer and choose to engage with it. Indeed, as Stevens explains, normative bonds to the therapeutic community, and 'social, informal controls' (ibid.: 119), form the basis for prisoner compliance and the prison's model of crime prevention. To put this another way, authority is (overall) exercised relationally, in a form that generates normative commitment and comparatively high levels of legitimacy. Despite the risks of 'therapeutic ideology acting as power', prisoners rate the 'moral quality of life' at Grendon higher than almost any other establishment (see NOMS 2014; Liebling assisted by Arnold 2004; and Table 39.1, below).

IMPLICATIONS

Our analysis developed beyond an attempt to characterize differences between public and private sector prisons, to make some empirically derived inferences about prison culture, authority and the prisoner experience. First, then, our findings indicated the need to revisit the idea of 'respect' within prisons, and to broaden its definition beyond conventional understandings (Hulley *et al.* 2012). In all of the prisons within our study, the majority of prisoners (around two-thirds) reported that they 'got on well' with the officers on their wings. However, as an indicator of 'respect', such statements were relatively un-discriminating—'getting on well' was the least strong test of this construct. In explaining what they meant by 'respectful treatment', prisoners identified the meeting of their needs to be just as important as 'politeness' or interpersonal 'niceness'. The nature of prison life (the ways in which it deprives prisoners of autonomy, information, goods, and services) is such that, while such behaviours are a necessary condition of respectful treatment, their value is diminished if prisoners are unable to find out answers to questions about their entitlements, or about how they can progress through their sentence and the system. Indeed, when staff are careless with their power or incapable of meeting prisoners' needs, their friendliness is perceived as 'fake' or superficial.

A more suitable definition of respect might therefore comprise having one's emotional, practical, and interpersonal needs taken seriously, or having staff who are reliably responsive. Such a concept is similar to Richard Sennett's notion of respect as 'taking the needs of others seriously' (Sennett 1993: 52). In our analysis, we formed two 'respect' dimensions: 'interpersonal respect', comprising honesty, trust, and fairness as well as courtesy, and 'organizational respect', which reflected levels of organizational competence and collective professionalism. All of the prisons in our study scored more highly on the former measure than the latter, indicating that it is easier to achieve a 'thin' form of respect than to establish an organization that is responsive, fair in its expectations, and transparent in its decisions. The provision of this kind of 'respect-plus' regime, which marries respectful treatment with staff professionalism and bureaucratic decency, constitutes a much stronger test of legitimacy. The same can be said of the concept of 'humanity' which has strong and weak forms (see Liebling, assisted by Arnold 2004: 214–28).[1] Most of the dimensions of prison quality we have developed in our research, via extensive conversations with prisoners about what matters most to them, are about the ways in which staff behave, shaped by their attitudes and orientation. In this sense, professional *action* clearly matters.

A second contribution of our analysis—which follows from the first—was to emphasize the centrality of staff professionalism in shaping prisoner outcomes. Here, a key distinction is between staff *attitudes* and staff *behaviour*. In the private sector prisons in the study, the attitudes of uniformed staff were progressive, humane, and relatively rehabilitative (if sometimes naïve). However, deficiencies in staff competence, confidence, knowledge, and experience—what we would summarize as 'basic professionalism'—meant that frontline staff were unable to deliver the kinds of outcomes for prisoners that reflected their positive sentiments. A lack of basic professionalism functioned as an *inhibitor*. Conversely, in the public sector prisons, the attitudes of staff towards prisoners were less caring, trusting, and rehabilitative, on the whole. In one of the public sector prisons, of the uniformed staff who returned surveys to us, none agreed or strongly agreed with the statement 'most prisoners are decent people'

[1] The strongest tests are arguably the items, 'I am treated as a person of value in this prison' and 'Staff here treat me with kindness'. Fewer prisons score positively on these items than on the more general items, such as, 'I am being looked after with humanity in here'.

(compared to 19 per cent in the private sector comparator). As in many other public sector establishments, staff subscribed to a 'safety plus entitlements' philosophy, in which the model of safety was rather defensive, based on maintaining control and discipline, rather than relational or dynamic, while the vision of decency was narrow and austere, based on a view of prisoners as undeserving:

> They're not in here because they're good boys and sometimes they don't do as they're told and unfortunately if you've got to stand up and be a little bit physical with them and aggressive in return, that has to happen otherwise it would just be chaos. (Officer, public sector prison)

> [We're being] pushed to say 'Mr', which has no bearing whatsoever in my book on treating them decently. If you give them exactly what they're entitled to . . . and as safe an environment as you can, that's being decent. (Officer, public sector prison)

However, high levels of basic professionalism in this sector—the ability of staff to deliver this rather no-frills version of imprisonment, their knowledgability, and a contractual or paternalistic provision of care (see Tait 2011)—protected prisoners somewhat from these 'edgy' dispositions, and ensured that their quality of life was reasonable. Basic professionalism served as an *insulator*. While private sector staff could not fully deliver on their attitudes, public sector staff delivered to some extent despite theirs. We have tried to capture this meaning of the term professionalism in a single dimension, 'staff professionalism' ('staff competence and confidence in the use of authority') as well as in a cluster of dimensions (including 'staff professionalism', 'organization and consistency', 'fairness', and 'bureaucratic legitimacy') in our ongoing work on conceptualizing and measuring the moral quality of prison life (see further Liebling *et al.* 2011).

Looking across the seven establishments in the study, levels of staff professionalism, as rated by prisoners, varied more than levels of such matters as respect and safety, not least because prisoners' feelings of respect, safety, fairness, and other such issues were determined by the ways in which staff wielded their authority and how confident they felt in their roles. Indeed, the professionalism cluster of dimensions within our survey together contributed significantly to variations in outcomes such as prisoners' personal development ('an environment that helps prisoners with offending behavior, preparation for release and the development of their potential') and overall quality of life. Where such factors are lacking—that is, in prisons where staff are 'absent'—prisoners either have insufficient 'headspace' to engage in change (Blagden *et al.* 2014) because life is too chaotic, or—that is, in prisons that are 'heavy'—they feel too defiant in the face of unfairness and indecency to do so. To summarize, then, staff professionalism both varies and matters.

Third, our findings resonated considerably with the emerging literature on self-legitimacy—power-holders' recognition of, or confidence in, their own entitlement to power (Tankebe 2016). Staff in the private sector were much more likely to express reservations about how to deploy their power than those in the public sector. Prisoners were sensitive to these anxieties, reading them in the ways that staff carried themselves, and making fine distinctions between times when the under-use of power reflected the 'skilled use of discretion' (Liebling and Price 2001: 124) rather than a form of 'avoidance' (Gilbert 1997). In the following quotation, for example, a prisoner contrasts the ability of staff in both sectors to gauge when to exercise power and when to hold back:

> I noticed at [a public sector prison], staff were better at taking the abuse and leaving it, not saying anything back, not trying to antagonise you in any way and not trying to upset you in any way. They're not so good at that here . . . like I say, sometimes they bite back and then you'll get threats 'if you carry on like that you won't get anything', kind of things . . . but I think HMP staff . . . they sit back and let you do your screaming and shouting, and let you get it all out, and because they know that once you've got it all out and you walk out the office, you automatically feel better and you automatically calm down. (Prisoner, private sector prison)

It is significant that what is referred to here is the deliberate and well-informed under-use of power. While staff in Long Lartin were confident in their use of power, but were making a moral decision to exercise it lightly, based on a clear philosophy of practice, in some private sector prisons, lenience is the outcome of weakness or necessity: either because there are insufficient staff, or because staff lack confidence and self-legitimacy. Certainly, staff in Long Lartin were rarely 'absent' in anything like the sense of the poorly performing private prisons that we have described, and, when incidents occurred, their interventions were swift and committed (Sparks, personal communication). It is important to distinguish, then, between forms of 'lightness' that are imbued with professionalism ('presence'), and forms of 'lightness' that have more to do with its absence. Where staff inhabit their role fully (a state of mind rather than a set of specific practices) they can be 'present' in a way that prisoners feel, but that remains 'light' and therefore more legitimate.

Fourth, our analysis was an attempt to think through the different ways in which authority could be organized and experienced in general in contemporary prisons, and to reconsider the terms of penal power itself. As implied in Sparks *et al.*'s elaboration of Albany's strengths, power in prisons can be protective as well as repressive. The majority of prisoners do not desire an absence of power any more than do staff (Liebling assisted by Arnold 2004). Insufficient attention has been given to the potentially positive consequences of the use of 'good' power in prison and the negative consequences of its under-use, even though it should be clear that there is a threshold point at both ends of the staff culture spectrum: not just when staff are resistant and cynical, and too eager to use their power, but also when they are powerless or naïve, and are too reluctant to employ it. Prisoners recognize that the use of power in prison is necessary, desirable, and can be legitimate, even when it is used 'against' them:

> You always need . . . it might well be unpleasant to say if you have been treated badly by authority, but you need authority in life. (Prisoner, public sector prison)

> I think for everything to run properly there has to be rules, and those rules to a certain degree have to be kept, right? If somebody asks you to do something here and you say 'no I'm not doing it', . . . then they should be able to have the power and weight behind them to actually to enforce it. (Prisoner, private sector prison)

Comments of this kind draw our attention to the benefits that prisoners recognize in being protected from some of their own inclinations. Under-policed environments offer temptations that many are keen, but unable, to resist (see Shapland and Bottoms 2011):

> It's too easy to get in trouble in here. I've kicked [drugs] before when inside and I thought, yeah, I'm going to do that again once I was in. It barely lasted 12 hours. I couldn't believe

> how easy it was to get drugs in here. I've never seen it like this before. (Prisoner, public sector prison)

> My life is worse in here. There's no structure. There's no rules. It's a free-for-all and staff barely exist . . . I'm involved in more criminal activity in here than I was on the out. That's not good, is it? I don't think that's what prison should be for. (Prisoner, public sector prison)

As suggested here, structure, boundaries and the imposition of certain types of authority could all have positive functions and effects. This was not frequent, but it was striking when we saw, or prisoners described, it.

PENAL POWER IN TRANSITION

In the years since we undertook fieldwork for the study that informed this argument, prisons have undergone significant transition. Much of this transformation has been driven by the combination of resource reductions and the spectre of private sector competition. Whereas an earlier phase of private sector competition was partly motivated by an ambition to accelerate progressive culture change in public sector prisons, this aim has been superseded by a requirement to reduce the costs of imprisonment overall: an almost purely economic rationality (Liebling and Crewe 2012). The drive to privatize high numbers of prisons has been halted, but on the basis of promises made by senior managers in the public sector to emulate private sector costs (which have also been reduced). Budget cuts have been savage, and have inevitably been felt most keenly in relation to staffing levels. Since 2010–11, the National Offender Management Service has reduced its costs by nearly a quarter (NOMS 2015), resulting in a 30 per cent reduction in the number of public sector prison staff (Prison Reform Trust 2016), during which time the prison population has been relatively stable. Prisons have moved from high-resource to low-resource institutions; public sector prisons increasingly resemble their private sector counterparts; and the terms and conditions of work within the two sectors are more closely aligned than ever. There was arguably waste and management laxity in an earlier era (see Liebling and Crewe 2012) but now there is 'grip', accountability, and austerity. The key administrative changes have been reductions in the regime (in particular the number of hours per day, and especially evening, that prisoners are unlocked), a benchmarking exercise reducing staff (including senior manager grades) to a minimum, reductions in the availability of work, education and courses, and new restrictions on the availability of temporary release.

These changes have reconfigured penal power in significant ways. In what remains of this chapter, then, we want to reflect on these transitions, including the ways in which they are being manifested in staff–prisoner relationships, matters of penal order and legitimacy, and the prisoner experience. We do this by drawing on findings from three recent 'MQPL +' research exercises in prisons in England and Wales, where we have spent time, as a team, researching staff and prisoner quality of life through survey methods, informal conversations, interviews, and focused observations (on methods and an example of recent findings, see Liebling *et al.* 2015).[2] While not necessarily representative (they were all prisons of some 'operational concern'), we are confident that these establishments provide insights into some of the general changes in prison life in England and Wales over recent years. All three research exercises took place in 2015–16.

In Prison A—a public sector, category C training prison—we found both staff and prisoners in despair. Many prisoners were too fearful, despondent, or frustrated with regime inconsistencies to leave the wings, in order to attend training or education. Staff had 'checked out' psychologically, in a manner that reflected an indifference towards their duty of care towards prisoners. On one wing, prisoners pointed to a sign quoting the Prison Service's statement of purpose and spoke indignantly about the gap between its modest aspirations and their treatment. Uniformed staff were frequently heard shouting and swearing at prisoners, and responding aggressively to reasonable complaints and requests. In ways that were resonant of prisons three decades ago, officers—albeit, fewer of them than in the past—were often found drinking tea together in offices rather than unlocking ('once I've finished this . . .') and engaging with prisoners. With regard to staff culture and attitudes, then, the prison was 'heavy'. There were few indications of violence, but a negative and unsympathetic attitude towards prisoners, and a cynical view about the possibility of rehabilitation ('they're never going to change—we'll see 'em back here in a few months'; 'most don't want to be rehabilitated—this is fun to them'), gave the prison an oppressive feel.

At the same time, power was largely 'absent', both in terms of a lack of interactive engagement with prisoners, and an under-use of authority, with staff preferring to stay in and around wing offices (where they felt safe) rather than patrol and police the wings (where they felt vulnerable, and were bombarded with prisoner requests, partly as a result of the longer hours spent locked up). To quote one officer, 'On the big wings there's one member of staff during "feeding time" and the other is around. You don't police, because you daren't'. While some prisoners expressed a preference for this laissez-faire model of authority ('staff are good as gold. They leave you alone'), they welcomed this 'hands off' style of policing mainly because it enabled them to engage in illicit behavior (drug use, drug dealing, exploitation of other prisoners, and so on). Prisoners who were less able to cope, who were vulnerable, and who did not carry power, were left feeling helpless and fearful. This state of affairs is not dissimilar to the 'liberal' regime at Long Lartin described by Sparks *et al.* (see Sparks *et al.* 1996), but its causes and consequences, as well as the precise form this under-policed form of (dis) order takes, are quite different. It had more of the character of Northern Ireland in the 1970s: staff were demoralized, and felt vulnerable and powerless. This left prisoners with considerable unchecked power.

Prison B—a modern local prison, run by a private company, mainly holding prisoners on remand or serving short sentences—exhibited different characteristics. Staff were very rarely to be found hiding in wing offices. Instead, they were engaging with prisoners constantly in an attempt to meet their needs, albeit in a rather disorganized and haphazard

[2] Here, we wish to thank Katherine Auty, Aiden Cope, Alice Ievins, Deborah Kant, Amy Ludlow, Martha Morey, Anna Schliehe, Bethany Schmidt, and Ezgi Taboglu, for their assistance in undertaking these exercises with us.

manner. The orientation of uniformed staff to prisoners was relatively benign ('I'm not here to make their lives a misery'), although levels of violence, disorder, and mundane demands that staff were encountering were putting these positive attitudes under strain. Such problems reflected the relative inexperience of uniformed staff, their low numbers, and their lack of confident authority. The environment was chaotic and insecure, relationships were lax and sometimes neglectful, and prisoners were able to swear at staff or push past them at prison gates without being challenged. Staff were therefore 'absent' in terms of their use of authority, but the staff culture was not 'heavy' as such.

Indeed, the nature of staff interaction with prisoners was such that the culture felt less absent than in Prison A, and considerably lighter. Prisoners felt angry, frustrated, and neglected, but noticed that staff were attempting to do their best for them, and did not act in a way that reflected moral disregard: 'They treat us like we're human and we're in their care. They treat us like we're here as punishment, not for—that gives you hope'. Staff and prisoners expressed mutual sympathy for each other's plight: 'They're run off their feet—we can see that' (prisoner) . . . 'I wish we could offer more. They should have courses and purpose. We used to have lots of activities' (officer). Overall, then, this prison was 'light-absent'—light because staff were not 'pressing' negative attitudes on prisoners, and tried hard to respond to their many requests, but 'absent' because there were simply too few of them—two on a wing for 60, with little experience between them, and the second often disappearing off the wing to escort prisoners or carry out other tasks.

Prison C, a Category B local prison was the best performing prison of the three. Discipline staff complained that they were too busy delivering the basic regime to do person-based work (they were 'chasing the day'; and it was 'hard to find time to do a favour for a prisoner'). Frequent cross-deployment to cover shortfalls on other units compounded this problem: staff felt 'like musical chairs'. Some stark differences were found in the quality of life experienced by different groups of prisoners—a common characteristic of a 'traditional culture'. Some staff had unhelpful and negative attitudes towards prisoners and their work. However, on the whole, prisoners evaluated their treatment considerably more positively than in Prisons A and B. Compared to these establishments, it had a greater proportion of experienced and knowledeable staff, in part because its geographic location meant that its pay was competitive within the local jobs market but also because the prison had served many distinct and specialist functions in its past, and the long-serving officer body had worked in many of these units or areas.

With regard to staff authority, the establishment was very 'present'. Staff–prisoner engagement on the landings was limited, and prisoners perceived some staff as rather distant, but experienced staff got out among prisoners, and sought to engage them in banter and conversation. Staff displayed considerable pride in, and strong loyalty to, the prison and each other. They felt duty-bound to make the 'bare-bones' benchmark settlement work and were committed to the preservation of their role in the public sector (which had been threatened). As in the public sector prisons that formed part of our earlier study, although the prison had some heavy cultural habits, including some uniformed staff who over-used their power somewhat, staff were delivering a reliable and reasonably safe regime to prisoners, which was improving steadily, and many prisoners were able to find ways of spending their time constructively.

Table 39.1 shows the means scores on all of our Measuring the Quality of Prison Life dimensions for each of these prisons. It also includes an establishment that we

Table 39.1 Mean quality of prison life scores for each prison

	Prison A Heavy-absent	Prison B Light-absent	Prison C Heavy-present	Prison D Light-present
Harmony Dimensions				
Entry into custody	2.72	2.69	2.85	**3.74**
Respect/courtesy	2.99	**3.21**	**3.23**	**3.99**
Staff–prisoner relationships	2.80	**3.07**	**3.20**	**3.93**
Humanity	2.74	2.93	**3.01**	**3.86**
Decency	2.60	2.80	2.83	**3.90**
Care for the vulnerable	2.84	2.87	**3.13**	**3.80**
Help and assistance	2.83	2.97	**3.15**	**3.73**
Professionalism Dimensions				
Staff professionalism	2.81	2.99	**3.37**	**3.79**
Bureaucratic legitimacy	2.30	2.53	2.77	**3.26**
Fairness	2.46	2.65	2.86	**3.53**
Organization and consistency	2.14	2.31	2.89	**3.60**
Security Dimensions				
Policing and security	2.51	2.57	**3.26**	**3.45**
Prisoner safety	2.91	**3.06**	**3.45**	**3.69**
Prisoner adaptation	2.88	**3.17**	**3.41**	**4.07**
Drugs and exploitation	2.05	2.14	2.70	**3.33**
Conditions and Family Contact Dimensions				
Conditions	**3.45**	**3.48**	**3.48**	**4.20**
Family contact	**3.33**	**3.23**	**3.35**	**3.71**
Wellbeing and Development Dimensions				
Personal development	2.60	2.76	2.97	**4.11**
Personal autonomy	2.75	2.76	2.97	**3.78**
Wellbeing	2.34	2.54	2.83	**3.17**
Distress	**3.19**	**3.16**	**3.45**	**3.60**

have previously characterized as 'light-present' (Prison D), which routinely scores extremely well on the MQPL survey. Scores of 3 and above (on a 5-point scale) are positive and are highlighted in the Table. All dimensions are scored positively, so a 2.05 on drugs and exploitation mean that prisoners are strongly agreeing that there are major problems of drug availability and exploitation among prisoners in the prison.

These scores vary significantly between the prisons, in ways that reflect our qualitative characterizations. First, it is telling that Prison B outperforms Prison A on 'harmony dimensions': here, heaviness, is manifested in lower scores for dimensions such as 'respect/courtesy', 'staff–prisoner relationships' and 'humanity'. But it is also striking—and consistent with our theorization—that Prison C outscores Prison B on these dimensions. That is to say, even when staff attitudes are somewhat 'heavy', the presence and professionalism of experienced officers mean that prisoners experience a greater level of respect and care than in an establishment in which frontline staff are benign but professionally ineffective. Second, the 'absence' of power is reflected in lower scores for the security dimensions, particularly 'policing and security', which manifests most directly the outcome of staff under-using their power, whether through fear, inexperience, or indifference. As Table 39.2 shows, well over 50 per cent of prisoners in Prisons A and B agreed with the item 'Supervision of prisoners is poor in this prison', compared to 29 per cent in Prison C and 19 per cent in Prison D. Third, the clear step-change in scores within the table, from left to right, confirms our overall argument about the relative legitimacy of different modes of penal authority. We return to this argument at the end of the chapter.

THE OUTCOMES OF PENAL POWER

The primary consequences of the changes we have observed (especially in prisons A and B, but also to some extent in C) are threefold. First, environmental conditions are reshaping prisoner behaviour in ways that are mainly undesirable. With regard to regime engagement, chaotic, unpredictable and indifferent regimes mean that feelings of resignation and demoralization predominate ('I've given up—this prison has beaten me'; 'I don't try to do anything anymore—it's pointless'; 'there's no consistency, so people just give up'). Many staff use the same language of apathy and de-motivation ('I've given up trying—I just show up for the pay cheque'). Yet prisoners also report that, in their daily interactions with prison staff, the most successful means of gaining attention involve drastic action, because more measured approaches can be overlooked or ignored by staff, whether they are overwhelmed or apathetic: 'The only way to get attention from the screws is to kick off or slice up'; 'you have to make a protest to even get a TV'. 'It seems like the lads who are disruptive get more than the lads who are complying'. The suggestion in the last quote that non-compliance is (in the short term) beneficial, and is encouraged by the daily climate, is significant. Prisoners consistently point to the impact of the regime not only on their behaviour and compliance with the regime, but also on the kind of person they are inclined to be:

> Yeah, the rules are clear on paper, but not in practice. It can drive you crazy. You do what you're told, you follow the rules, and you don't get anywhere. You see others swear, kick off, and then get Enhanced or moved on . . . You don't know what to do. I actually want to progress and follow the rules, but this is a game. Rules don't matter. It makes me not want to comply. It makes me angry. (Prisoner)

> I was Enhanced before I came here. I was the second servery worker on my wing. But there's no reason to apply yourself here, no motivation, no payoff. (Prisoner)

In many respects, such establishments feel like custodial warehouses, with very little sense of purpose beyond containing prisoners in the present ('We're left to rot. We're just vegetating'). However, such terminology underplays the degree to which these establishments cause prisoners damage, rather than simply hold them in stasis. To quote one prisoner:

> They say I'm supposed to be addressing my 'offending behaviour' in here, right? How I am supposed to do that when the prison is providing me with all things that get me into trouble? I'm using [drugs] more in here. I'm selling more. I'm fighting more . . . They've set me up to fail. They're making all my problems worse, actually.' (Prisoner)

Second, because of cuts to staffing levels, there is an increasing degree of power-sharing between staff and prisoners (see Liebling *et al.* 2015, where we first began to witness this development in a longitudinal study of the privatization of Birmingham prison). In some establishments, such as Prison C, authority is actively and carefully *delegated* to trusted prisoners, who work in roles (such as providing information to new arrivals, or distributing application and complaint forms) that free up staff to focus on other duties. In such arrangements, prisoners are integrated into the wing management structure, and are carefully overseen. In other establishments, such as Prison A, power is handed to selective prisoners in more informal, collusive, and unaccountable ways. Officers are overt in using powerful prisoners to 'sort out trouble', in return for significant perks. Alternatively, as in Prison C, power-sharing is more haphazard. Prisoners claim power from staff, rather than having it delegated to them, as a way of managing the chaos they see around them. On some wings, prisoners volunteer to help staff persuade other prisoners to go to their cells at times of 'lock-up', and assist new staff by telling them how the regime functions.

Here, then, we find three differing outcomes of a low-cost model of penal provision, each reflecting a particular configuration of authority. In prisoners' language, Prison C was 'a screws' nick', and this was reflected in the manner in which power-sharing was carefully controlled and overseen. Staff contracted out aspects of their own influence, but did not relinquish it. By contrast, in both Prisons A and B, new and inexperienced staff reported feeling 'overwhelmed' on the prison wings, and unsure of how best to use their power. In both, staff consistently overlooked rule infractions, from low-level infringements, such as smoking on the landings or walking around wings semi-naked, to more serious violations, such as the open use of mobile phones, cell robberies, and abusive behaviour towards other prisoners and staff. However, the distributions of power in these establishments differed. Prison B was a 'cons' nick', that is, a place where power was in the hands of the prisoners, and where staff had little control over this arrangement. Meanwhile, Prison A was summarized as 'a screws' prison, but prisoners run it', a phrase which signalled the way that staff were competent and authoritative in terms of capability, but were choosing to contract out their authority to prisoners rather than activate it themselves. As the results for the MQPL item 'this prison is run by prisoners rather than staff' demonstrate (see Table 39.2), these differences in the ways that power-sharing was managed were extremely significant. In Prison C, under 12 per cent of prisoners agreed or strongly agreed with the item 'this prison is run by prisoners rather than staff', compared to around 50 per cent in prisons A and B. In all three establishments, and in Prison D, the regime functioned only because of the involvement, in some form, of the captives, but the overall balance of power between prisoners and staff varied considerably across these different models.[3]

Power-sharing was the basis of prison order described by Sykes, in his classic (1958) study of Trenton maximum-security prison, New Jersey. It was a model that Sykes appeared to think was inevitable, given the 'defects in total power', including the lack of a 'duty of compliance' among prisoners. Staff were required to accommodate prisoner power, and to overlook certain kinds of rule infringements, because they were outnumbered by them and were in many ways reliant on them. Order was accomplished *via* the prisoner hierarchy, so that men who had credibility both with staff and their peers were given influential work assignments, and allowed or allocated perks, which enabled them to exert influence over the rest of the prisoner population. In the years that followed Sykes' study, other scholars disputed what appeared to be a rather romantic view of power-sharing and challenged the idea that it was the only means of effective governance: Crouch and Marquant (1989) described a semi-formalized system in the Texas prison system whereby control was maintained through some prisoners being sanctioned by the administration to commit brutality against others; Jacobs (1977) detailed how the emergence of a more politicized prisoner culture led to a breakdown of 'accommodations' between prison guards and prisoner leaders, with prison gangs replacing the prisoner elite as the source of material and psychological 'buffering' from institutional deprivation. That is, gang membership became a more effective way of obtaining a reasonable quality of life than seeking out a position of power within an administratively-sanctioned hierarchy. DiIulio (1987) described power-sharing as a 'corrupt alliance' (ibid.: 2), which effectively authorized violence and exploitation, and could be avoided through a mode of governance based on assertive authority, regime delivery and due process.

For our purposes, the return of power-sharing to prisons in England and Wales is significant chiefly because it represents a reconfiguration of penal order. Prisoners and prison staff often refer to the sociological cliché that order in prisons relies on the consent of prisoners, in the sense that prisoners could almost always take control of a wing temporarily given their numerical advantage over staff. However, the active incorporation of prisoners into aspects of administrative delivery and (most significantly) control represents a considerable re-setting of the balance of power within prisons from

[3] An important question here is, what makes the difference in Prison D (and the few other prisons we know to be like it)? We have not evaluated this prison, but prisoners evaluate it very highly on MQPL surveys conducted by NOMS. It remains of interest to us as prison scholars that even in times of austerity and turbulence, some prisons manage to be outstanding in the eyes of prisoners.

a period, from 1994 onwards, in which control was very deliberately returned to staff (following an earlier period of welcome liberalization after the Woolf inquiry) through a range of policies and practices (such as the incentives and earned privileges scheme, increased situational control, and sanctions for inciting trouble; see Liebling, assisted by Arnold, 2004), to one in which prison managers and administrators recognize the virtual impossibility of running their establishments without the need for prisoners to assist them. But the current 'shared powers' model is rather different in practice, and reasoning, than the model that Lord Woolf, User Voice, staff in special units, and other proponents of 'democratic deliberation' would advocate.

Such a return to a shared powers model (by accident rather than design) means that the experience of staff authority varies a great deal between prisoners, with some having their needs met much more actively than others (to quote one officer, 'all we have time for are the naughty boys, and not the good lads who want to change'). The quality of the prisoner experience is increasingly dependent on the prisoner's position in the prisoner hierarchy, and this hierarchy is reinforced by the ways that staff distribute their attention and authority. In some establishments, influential prisoners are granted much greater time out of cell, freedom of movement, and access to staff than their peers, while prisoners who are weaker, more vulnerable, and less vocal are scared to circulate on or beyond the wings, or are left neglected in their cells ('The only thing they do for you if you're vulnerable is lock you behind your door. I don't think anyone noticed when I harmed myself recently'). Some prisoners exist on the wings with very little interaction with or care from staff, as prisoners often point out: 'staff here have got too much to do. They're concerned about the day to day running of the prison, not about our individual needs'. Although staff cultures of this kind can be described in quite general terms (ranging from 'custodial-apathetic' through 'benign-ineffective' to 'lean but innovative' at best), the experience of these cultures among prisoners is highly differential, ranging from highly present to almost completely absent. Such differences in the prisoner experience make it harder to plot establishments on the diagram we presented earlier. They are also reflected in the scores for the items 'In this prison, things only happen for you if your face fits' and 'In this prison, there is a real "pecking order" between prisoners' (see Table 39.2). Here, the marked differences between Prisons A and B and Prisons C and D emphasize the outcomes of deficiencies in staff authority: a steeper prisoner hierarchy, and a less fair distribution of staff attention.

Meanwhile, recent shifts in staff behaviour problematize the way that we have conceptualized 'heaviness' and 'lightness', and 'absence' and 'presence'. In our initial description, we emphasized that presence was only partially literal, that is, to do with staff 'being there'. It now seems more obvious that there is an important difference between officers being physically present but un-engaged relationally (due to demoralization or indifference), as in Prison A (occupying space, but doing little, or using their authority reactively rather than dynamically), and being largely absent but highly active when available (i.e. willing to engage, but overwhelmed). In some public sector prisoners, a threshold has been breached, so that uniformed staff have retreated physically and stopped using (or found themselves unable to use) their professional competence productively. They are present in person but absent in practice. In these contexts, 'getting through the day', which Liebling and Price (2001) described as an active process of using and under-using power to 'keep the peace', comes to mean 'fire-fighting'

Table 39.2 MQPL item results

This prison is run by prisoners rather than staff.

	Mean	% SA/A	% SD/D	% SA	% A	% N	% D	% SD
Prison A—Heavy-absent	2.61	50.7	23.2	17.4	33.3	26.1	17.4	5.8
Prison B—Light-absent	2.67	46.0	26.7	20.0	26.0	27.3	20.7	6.0
Prison C—Heavy-present	**3.85**	11.7	67.6	4.8	6.9	20.7	33.8	33.8
Prison D—Light-present	**3.23**	29.9	46.7	10.3	19.6	23.4	29.9	16.8

In this prison things only happen for you if your face fits.

	Mean	% SA/A	% SD/D	% SA	% A	% N	% D	% SD
Prison A—Heavy-absent	2.23	61.3	10.2	25.5	35.8	28.5	10.2	0.0
Prison B—Light-absent	2.28	63.8	13.4	24.2	39.6	22.8	11.4	2.0
Prison C—Heavy-present	2.74	41.7	23.6	13.2	28.5	34.7	18.1	5.6
Prison D—Light-present	**3.36**	24.8	56.2	8.6	16.2	19.0	42.9	13.3

Supervision of prisoners is poor in this prison.

	Mean	% SA/A	% SD/D	% SA	% A	% N	% D	% SD
Prison A—Heavy-absent	2.30	57.7	13.1	26.3	31.4	29.2	12.4	0.7
Prison B—Light-absent	2.45	54.4	16.8	20.8	33.6	28.9	13.4	3.4
Prison C—Heavy-present	**3.03**	28.8	35.6	11.0	17.8	35.6	28.1	7.5
Prison D—Light-present	**3.50**	18.6	65.4	6.5	12.1	15.9	55.1	10.3

In this prison, there is a real 'pecking order' between prisoners.

	Mean	% SA/A	% SD/D	% SA	% A	% N	% D	% SD
Prison A—Heavy-absent	2.16	65.9	4.3	23.2	42.8	29.7	3.6	0.7
Prison B—Light-absent	2.36	55.7	8.1	20.1	35.6	36.2	4.7	3.4
Prison C—Heavy-present	2.70	35.2	16.2	11.3	23.9	48.6	15.5	0.7
Prison D—Light-present	**3.31**	26.9	52.9	9.6	17.3	20.2	38.5	14.4

Note: Bold and shading indicate a 'score of 3 or above', that is, a positive evaluation (on a 5-point scale).

and 'survival'. The difference here lies, first, in the way that authority and jailcraft are either *activated* or, in effect, *withdrawn*. A second difference relates to the orientation to time. When officers work hard to enable the day to pass peacefully, they do so in a way that provides a foundation for prisoners to 'work on themselves', their lives, and their futures. If their mode of activity is instead passive—muddling through the day, merely containing prisoners—the institution loses any sense of being oriented beyond the present.

CONCLUSION: RE-THINKING PENAL POWER

Our attempt to describe the ways in which power is being reconfigured in contemporary prisons is informed by our continuing research presence throughout the 1990s and 2000s, during which we were able to observe, over some periods in particular, significant improvements to penal order and practices motivated by genuine concerns to make prisons 'decent' and to improve outcomes (e.g. in relation to suicide prevention, safety and decency, and education provision). The current era is troubling, because some of these priorities have been subsumed (as they have in many public services) by a need to make savings, and to deliver more 'efficient' and less visionary models of imprisonment. The alternative method of cost-cutting—reducing the size of the prison population, whilst holding on to (or improving) moral quality (and therefore outcomes)—has not been seriously considered for political reasons. As we write, a new emphasis on 'rehabilitation', whilst welcome, looks wholly aspirational.

We are starting to understand 'staff professionalism'—a 'light-present' model of competent authority—and its links to order and legitimacy at a time when both are getting harder to achieve in practice. There are different degrees of legitimacy, and different legitimacy deficits in prisons, linked to different models of order, different modes of authority, and different views about the moral status of prisoners. Table 39.3 sketches these differences out tentatively, drawing on our heavy-light conceptualization and also on the earlier work by Sparks *et al.* (1996). The table shows that legitimate authority lies along a continuum, with 'absence' appearing at the far end of each. The tendency in prisons is for forms of order to veer towards the far ends of the continuum rather than find the 'stable point' between repression (or over-use) and laxity (or under-use). In our most recent research we have seen the extremes at both ends in single prisons. In light-absent prisons, we find a 'stand back/ jump forwards' use of authority, as inexperienced and under-resourced staff struggle to enforce their power for the majority of the time, and then go overboard in doing so *because of* their lack of confidence, or the knowledge that they have 'let power go'. In many such establishments, the solution to the problem of order is for prisoners to be provided with incentives that commit them to the institution in a non-relational bind. In others, order is maintained through the coercive edges of the regime, such as highly restrictive units for prisoners deemed to be non-compliant or—as in Long Lartin in the late 1980s—the threat of being 'ghosted out' (i.e. transferred) to more oppressive prisons (Sparks *et al.* 1996). Some prisons attempt both. In 'heavy-absent' prisons, staff 'stand back' not because they cannot use their authority, but because they choose not to mobilize their relational power, either because of a lack of motivation, or because situational and coercive measures do much of their 'control work' for them. When they jump forwards, they do so with excessive zeal and confidence. In both types of establishment—absent-light and heavy-present—prisoner compliance rests less on the legitimacy of the regime, and more on feelings of despondency, helplessness, and resigned fatalism.

An underlying feature of these 'ideal types' is that officers hold either a 'tragic' or cynical perspective on prisoners. Staff come to resolve the problem of holding

Table 39.3 Authority, order, safety, and legitimacy in prison.

Mode of authority	Light-absent	Light-present	Heavy-present	Heavy-absent
Mode of order	Disorder	Good order	Firm order	Excess order
Feel	Normless	Relaxed, purposeful	Heavy	Oppressive
Model of safety	*Disregard for safety* 'corrupted authority' Avoidance, indifference Non-observation	*Relational* 'dynamic', interactive Proactive, Informal conflict resolution Intelligent trust Specialists as support	*'Reassurance/ defensive'/fragile* Vigilant/ Suspicious Risk-oriented distant, edgy controlled unlock Use of force Low-trust Specialists as risk	*Situational* Hyper-vigilant, Risk-oriented No trust
Professional confidence	*Low* Uncertainty, fear	*High* Comfort, assurance, courage	*Excessive* Intimidation, bluntness	*Excessive* Intimidation. bluntness
Moral position of officers	Some tragic 'reciprocators', some cynical 'avoiders'	Tragic (professionals)	Cynical (enforcers and professionals)	Cynical (enforcers), plus 'avoiders'
Use of authority	Under-enforcement and over-enforcement	Selective, judicious	'By the book', exacting	Under- and over-enforcement (stand-back, jump forwards)
Moral status of prisoners	Prisoners as 'irrelevant' or 'indulged'	Prisoners as 'experiencing subject-agents'	Prisoners as dangerous 'experienced subject-objects'	Prisoners as 'dangerous objects'
Degree of legitimacy	Low	High ++	Moderate - (+)	Very low --

authority, which brings danger, in two distinct ways. One is cynical—they simplify the world, insulating themselves from moral conflict. They become either 'enforcers' (over enthusiastic rule followers) or 'avoiders' (reluctant rule followers). The other is tragic—the recognition that we are all flawed, and that any of us, or our families, could end up in prison (see Muir 1977). In one of the forms this perspective takes these officers become 'reciprocators', or only helpers, who cannot reconcile themselves to the use of power. At their best, officers become 'professionals', living with the moral complexity of using coercion, knowing that it is an imperfect tool, being *prepared* to use it rather than reluctant or over eager. The 'professional' prison officer does not expect perfection from prisoners or from him or herself, but is *reconciled to* rather than over-enthusiastic or conflicted about the use of coercion. Muir's work focused on individual officer trajectories. Our interest is in whole prisons and their cultures, so when we add Muir's typology (developed by Gilbert 1977; and Liebling 2011) to our prison models, we see that these 'types' are distributed differently in each prison. The new low-resource model may turn professionals into avoiders (see Lerman and Page 2016), or it may, on lower pay scales and with an incomplete understanding of what makes a good prison officer, recruit naive reciprocators who lack sufficient training or experience to combine their helpful orientation with the 'dynamic use of authority'. As we have shown in this chapter, the consequences of these configurations are highly significant in the lives and experiences of prisoners.

SELECTED FURTHER READING

The best starting points for almost any sociological study of prison life is Sykes' *Society of Captives* (1958) and Goffman's *Asylums* (1961), which explore the deprivations of imprisonment and the ways that prisoners adapt to the pains and problems of prison life. Liebling's *Prisons and their Moral Performance* (2004) and Crewe's *The Prisoner Society* (2009) provide contemporary accounts of many of the issues that were of concern to earlier theorists. For a good overview of debates about prison privatization, and for an earlier elaboration of the argument made in this chapter, see Crewe *et al.*'s 'Heavy-light, absent-present: rethinking the weight of imprisonment' (2014) in the *British Journal of Sociology*. Three good first-hand introductions to life in prison are James' *A Life Inside* (2005), Shannon and Morgan's *The Invisible Crying Tree* (1996) (letters between a life-sentence prisoner and his penfriend), and Crewe and Bennett's *The Prisoner* (2011). Ramsbotham's *Prisongate* (2003) gives a perspective on the prison system from the point of view of a former Chief Inspector of Prisons. The journal *Punishment & Society* publishes high-quality articles on prisons and punishment, while Jewkes *et al.*'s, *The Handbook on Prisons* (2016), contains chapters by a range of scholars and practitioners on various aspects of penality and prison life.

REFERENCES

Ben-David, S. (1992), 'Staff-to-Inmates Relations in a Total Institution: A Model of Five Modes of Association', *International Journal of Offender Therapy and Comparative Criminology*, 36(3): 209–19.

Ben-David, S. and Silfen, P. (1994), 'In Quest of a Lost Father? Inmates' Preferences of Staff Relation in a Psychiatric Prison Ward', *International Journal of Offender Therapy and Comparative Criminology*, 38(2): 131–9.

Blagden, N., Winder, B., and Hames, C. (2014), '"They Treat Us Like Human Beings"- Experiencing a Therapeutic Sex Offenders Prison', *International Journal of Offender Therapy and Comparative Criminology*, 60(4): 371–96.

Bottomley, A. K. (1994), 'Long-term prisoners', in E. Player and M. Jenkins (eds), *Prisons After Woolf*, London: Routledge.

Bottomley, A. K. and Hay, W. (1991), *Special Units for Difficult Prisoners*, Hull: University Of Hull.

Bottomley, A. K., Liebling, A., and Sparks, R. (1994), *Barlinnie Special Unit and Shotts Unit: An Assessment*, Scottish Prison Service Occasional Paper (7), Edinburgh: Scottish Prison Service.

Bottoms, A. (2005), 'Power in prisons', presentation Barcelona 2005.

Cohen, S. and Taylor, L. (1972), *Psychological Survival: The Experience of Long-Term Imprisonment*, Harmondsworth: Penguin.

Cooke, D. J. (1989), 'Containing Violent Prisoners: An Analysis of the Barlinnie Special Unit', *British Journal of Criminology*, 29(2): 129–43.

Crewe, B. (2009), *The Prisoner Society: Power, Adaptation and Social Life in an English Prison*, Oxford: Oxford University Press.

Crewe, B. and Bennett, J. (2011), *The Prisoner*, Cullompton: Willan.

Crewe, B., Liebling, A., and Hulley, S. (2011), 'Staff culture, the use of authority, and prisoner outcomes in public and private prisons', *Australia and New Zealand Journal of Criminology*, 44(1): 94–115.

Crewe, B., Liebling, A., and Hulley, S. (2014a), 'Heavy-light, absent-present: Re-thinking the "weight" of imprisonment', *British Journal of Sociology*, 65(3): 387–410.

Crewe, B., Liebling, A., and Hulley, S. (2014b), 'Staff-prisoner relationships, staff professionalism and the use of authority in public and private sector prisons', *Law and Social Inquiry*, 40(2): 309–44.

Crouch, B. and Marquart, J. (1989), *An Appeal to Justice*, Austin: University of Texas Press.

DiLulio, J. (1987), *Governing Prisons*, New York: Free Press.

Downes, D. (1988), *Contrasts in Tolerance: Post-War Penal Policy in the Netherlands and England and Wales*, Oxford: Clarendon.

Fitzgerald, M. (1987), 'The telephone rings: long term imprisonment', in A. E. Bottoms and R. Light (eds), *Problems of Long-Term Imprisonment*, Aldershot: Gower.

Genders, E. and Player, E. (1995), *Grendon: A Study of a Therapeutic Prison*, Oxford: Clarendon.

Gilbert, M. (1997), 'The Illusion of Structure: A Critique of the Classical Model of Organisation and the Discretionary Power of Correctional Officers', *Criminal Justice Review*, 22(1): 49–64.

Goffman, E. (1961), *Asylums: Essays on the Social Situation of Mental Patients and Other Inmates*, London: Penguin.

Haney, C. (2006), *Reforming Punishment: Psychological Limits to the Pains of Imprisonment*, Washington: American Psychological Association Books.

Haney, C. (2008), 'A culture of harm: taming the dynamics of cruelty in supermac prisons', *Criminal Justice and Behavior*, 35(8): 956–84.

Hepburn, J. (1985), 'The Exercise of Power in Coercive Organizations: A Study of Prison Guards', *Criminology*, 23(1):145–64.

Hulley, S., Liebling, A., and Crewe, B. (2012), 'Respect in prisons: Prisoners' experiences of respect in public and private sector prisons', *Criminology and Criminal Justice*, 12: 3–23.

Jacobs, J. (1977), *Stateville: The Penitentiary in Mass Society*, Chicago: University of Chicago Press.

James, E. (2005), *A Life Inside: A Prisoner's Notebook*, London: Atlantic Books.

Jewkes, Y., Bennett., J., and Crewe, B (2016), *The Handbook on Prisons*, London: Routledge.

King, R. (1999), 'The Rise and Rise of *Supermax*. An American Solution in Search of a Problem?', *Punishment & Society*, 1(2): 163–86.

King, R. D. and McDermott, K. (1995), *The State of Our Prisons*, Oxford: Clarendon Press.

Kruttschnitt, C. and Gartner, R. (2005), *Marking Time in the Golden State: Women's Imprisonment in California*, Cambridge: Cambridge University Press.

Lerman, A. and Page, J. (2016), 'Does the Front Line Reflect the Party Line? The Politicization of Punishment and Prison Officers' Perspectives Toward Incarceration', *British Journal of Criminology*, 56(3): 578–601.

Liebling, A. (2011), 'Distinctions and Distinctiveness in the Work of Prison Officers: Legitimacy and Authority Revisited', *European Journal of Criminology*, 8(6): 484–99.

Liebling, A. assisted by Arnold, H. (2004), *Prisons and Their Moral Performance: A Study of Values, Quality, and Prison Life*, Oxford: Clarendon.

Liebling, A. and Arnold, H. (2012), 'Social relationships between prisoners in a maximum security prison: Violence, faith, and the declining nature of trust', *Journal of Criminal Justice*, 40(5): 413–24.

Liebling, A., Arnold, H., and Straub, C. (2012), *An Exploration of Staff–Prisoner Relationships at HMP Whitemoor: Twelve Years On*, London: National Offender Management Service.

Liebling, A. and Crewe, B. (2012), 'Prisons beyond the new penology: the shifting moral foundations of prison management', in J. Simon and R. Sparks (eds), *The Sage Handbook of Punishment and Society*, London: Sage.

Liebling, A. and Price, D. (2001), *The Prison Officer*, Winchester: Waterside Press.

Liebling, A., Price, D., and Shefer, G. (2011), *The Prison Officer*, 2nd edn, Cullompton: Willan.

Liebling, A., Armstrong, R., Bramwell, R., and Williams, R. (2015), 'Locating trust in a climate of fear: religion, moral status, prisoner leadership, and risk in maximum security prisons: key findings', ESRC Transforming Social Science Scheme, available at: http://www.prc.crim.cam.ac.uk/publications/trust-report, accessed 23 January 2017.

Mathiesen, T. (1965), *The Defences of the Weak*, London: Tavistock.

McEvoy, K. (2001), *Paramilitary Imprisonment in Northern Ireland: Resistance, Management and Release*, Oxford: Oxford University Press.

McMahon, M. (1992), *The Persistent Prison? Rethinking Decarceration and Penal Reform*, Toronto: University of Toronto Press.

NOMS (2014), 'Results from an MQPL Survey at HMP Grendon', Audit and Assurance: National Offender Management Service.

NOMS (2015), *Annual Report and Accounts 2014/15*, London: The Stationery Office.

Prison Reform Trust (2016), *The Bromley Briefings*, London: Prison Reform Trust.

Rhodes, L. (2004), *Total Confinement: Madness and Reason in the Maximum Security Prison*, Berkeley, Los Angeles and London: University of California Press.

Scraton, P., Sim, J., and Skidmore, P. (1991), *Prisons Under Protest*, Buckingham: Open University Press.

Sennett, R. (1993), *Authority*, New York: Norton.

Shannon, T. and Morgan, C. (1995), *The Invisible Crying Tree*, Worcestershire: Polperro Heritage Press.

Shapland, J. and Bottoms, A. (2011), 'Reflections on Social Values, Offending and Desistance Among Young Adult Recidivists', *Punishment & Society*, 13(3): 256–82.

Sim, J. (2008), 'An Inconvenient Criminological Truth: Pain, Punishment and Prison Officers', in J. Bennett, B. Crewe, and A. Wahidin, *Understanding Prison Staff*, Cullompton: Willan.

Sparks, R. and Bottoms, A. (1995), 'Legitimacy and Order in Prisons', *The British Journal of Sociology*, 46(1): 45–62.

Sparks, R., Bottoms, A., and Hay, W. (1996), *Prisons and the Problem of Order*, Oxford: Clarendon.

Stevens, A. (2013), *Offender Rehabilitation and Therapeutic Communities: Enabling Change the TC Way*, Abingdon: Routledge.

Street, D. (1965), 'The inmate group in custodial and treatment settings', *American Sociological Review*, 30(1): 40–55.

Sykes, G. (1958), *The Society of Captives: A Study of a Maximum-Security Prison*, Princeton: Princeton University Press.

Tait, S. (2011), 'A typology of prison officer approaches to care', *European Journal of Criminology*, 8(6): 440–54.

Tankebe, J. (2016), 'Rightful authority: exploring the structure of police self-legitiamcy', in A. Liebling, J. Shapland, and J. Tankebe (eds), *Crime, Justice and Social Order: Essays in Honour of A.E. Bottoms*, forthcoming.

Wachtel, T. and McCold, P. (2001), 'Restorative Justice in Everyday Life', in H. Strang and J. Braithwaite (eds), *Restorative Justice and Civil Society*, Cambridge: Cambridge University Press.

40

MARKETIZING CRIMINAL JUSTICE

Amy Ludlow

> Government is clearly failing to manage performance across the board, and to achieve the best for citizens out of the contracts into which they have entered.
>
> (House of Commons Public Accounts Committee 2014)

> Narey describes the moment his views changed, at a contracted prison, watching new prisoners arriving 'being called "Mr Brown", and being offered a cup of tea and being treated with dignity which I knew was beyond the public sector... It wasn't about efficiency... it was just about humanity'.
>
> (personal communication with Martin Narey, former Chief Executive of the National Offender Management Service, quoted in Le Vay 2016: 26)

INTRODUCTION

A now considerable body of work describes the political, economic, and sociological circumstances in which many governments have, since the 1960s, reimagined and reconfigured how their citizens access public services (e.g. Sennett 2006; Sandel 2013; Stuckler and Basu 2013). This includes criminal justice. Provision through government bureaucracy has been replaced widely by 'delivery' through 'service providers' who compete against each other in markets for public sector business. Manifestations of market thinking include privatized ownership and management, private sector design, finance, construction, and management of whole institutions, outsourcing or contracting out of core or ancillary functions, and competition or market testing processes in which public and private service providers are compared and Service Level Agreements introduced to govern provision. The language with which these varied processes of marketization are described is often imprecise and ideologically charged (Harding 1997: 1; Johnston 1992: 214–20).

Marketization promises to 'liberate' governments from public sector monopoly and enable them to provide lower cost, higher quality and better managed public services; they can do more, and better, for less (Le Grand 2007). The market is said to offer an 'all-purpose key to better provision of public services': a means to solve 'management ills' in many different contexts and an 'apolitical framework within which many different values could be pursued effectively' (Hood 1991: 8; Pollitt and Bouckaert 2011). Yet, evidence about the efficiency and effectiveness of marketized public services is limited, and outcomes between sectors vary. Contracting out has been found to work best in 'simpler, more transactional services like waste management'. The impact of competition in complex services, like health or education, is less clear (Institute for Government 2013: 4). Crouch has described the unshaken, yet mostly empirically unsubstantiated, faith in free markets to deliver economic and social prosperity as 'the strange non-death of neo-liberalism' (Crouch 2011).

Private actors have long been involved in the delivery of law enforcement and public order (D'Amico 2010; Nemeth 1989). However, many contemporary governments moved away from this and chose to deliver criminal justice services directly, through state employees. Direct state delivery was linked to the search for consistency and improved standards, through centralization and nationalization. Where the private sector was involved in delivering criminal justice, as was the case for example in labour leasing arrangements in the USA in the late nineteenth and early twentieth century, activities became notorious for their exploitation and brutality (Ryan and Ward 1989; Hallett 2006).

Since the late twentieth century, many governments have returned, at least in part, to non-direct provision of criminal justice services, including through private companies. Though the 'deep structures' of political decision-making vary between countries (Jones and Newburn 2005), problems of prison overcrowding, and desires to reduce cost and improve standards have been common motivators in favour of (re-)diversified provision (Harding 2001: 269). Internationally, the USA led the way from the 1960s onwards; Australia soon followed. Private delivery of criminal justice has since expanded exponentially in the USA, encompassing probation (especially in many southern states) and policing (Pastor 2003). Serious concerns have been raised about the private sector's involvement in US probation (Human Rights Watch 2014; Georgia Department of Audits and Accounts Performance 2014).[1] Although the USA has more privately managed prisons, internationally, Australia imprisons the highest proportion of its prisoners in privately managed facilities (18.5 per cent overall in 2016: Australian Productivity Commission 2016: Table 8A.2). In August 2016, US Deputy Attorney General Sally Yates announced a goal of 'reducing—and ultimately ending—our use of privately operated prisons' on the grounds that private sector providers offer poorer services and do not save substantially on costs.[2] The announcement signals an important change in policy direction, but its practical impacts are yet to be seen and are, in any case, limited to federal US prisons.

Within Europe, the UK has been at the forefront of marketizing criminal justice. The key private players are: Global Solutions Limited (GSL); Premier Detention Services (PDS), which is owned by Serco; UK Detention Services (UKDS), which is owned by

[1] In 2012, an Alabama County judge shut down a private probation company that he described in his Order as 'a judicially sanctioned extortion racket': see http://media.al.com/spotnews/other/Judge%20Hub%20Harrington%20order%20to%20Harpersville.pdf, accessed 11 January 2017.

[2] http://apps.washingtonpost.com/g/documents/national/justice-department-memo-announcing-announcing-the-end-of-its-use-of-private-prisons/2127/, accessed 10 January 2017.

Sodexo; and Group 4 Securicor. Between them, these companies operate seven out of the UK's ten main immigration removal centres. They manage a small, but culturally significant, proportion of prisons (14 out of a total of 123), housing men and women. Private companies operate prisons of all levels of security save for the most secure. They also run prisoner and immigration detainee escorting and court services. Management of Lincolnshire Police's custody suite is fully privatized, though privatization and marketization in policing have generally been more limited than in other criminal justice sectors (White 2015). Following the government's Transforming Rehabilitation reform agenda of September 2013, probation services for low- and medium-risk offenders have been largely privatized, operated by complex consortia that raise serious challenges for transparency and good governance (Padfield 2016).

The marketization agenda, and the dominance of competition and economic rationality paradigms, have attracted considerable criticism in criminal justice. Particular concerns include democratic accountability, neglect of the expressive moral functions of state penal power, legitimacy, and social equity in the distribution of security as a social good (e.g. Loader and Walker 2006; Padfield 2006; Zedner 2006). Feeley and Simon (1992) theorized the application of new public management to criminal justice as the emergence of a 'new penology': a conception and practice of criminal justice that is actuarial, 'aggregate, risk-focused, distant, quantitative, rational, [and] control-oriented', and that treats offenders 'as units to be managed rather than moral agents with futures' (Liebling and Crewe 2013: 284). The new penology is said to have converted the central task of imprisonment from social or personal transformation to human containment and risk management 'at reasonable fiscal, political and legal costs' (Simon 2007: 153; Sparks 2003). This has brought with it instrumental, rather than normative, ordering practices. Hierarchical and state-driven governance has been displaced in favour of a plural, polycentric, and network model of governance. The new penology has prioritized 'practices and values of efficiency, targets and comparison, along with the vague new concept of performance'. 'Old concerns with justice and individuality' are said to be displaced, and the moral life of criminal justice institutions corroded (Liebling 2004: 4; see also Garland 2002; Young 2007).

While the new penology literature provides a persuasive lens through which to understand contemporary penal policy and practice, Feeley and Simon's thesis has been criticized. Coleman and Sim provide a useful overview of some key criticisms (2005: 102–5). Building upon this literature, Liebling and Crewe have argued that the new penology overstates the degree to which the old penology 'was ever as humane and rehabilitative as its advocates may have wanted to claim, while overlooking the institutional chaos and abuse that help explain the shift towards a more managerialist era' (Liebling and Crewe 2013: 284). They also highlight how new penology thinking has been applied in different ways within institutions in ways that lead to sociologically and morally significant variations. They argue that these variations can be disguised (and are therefore unrecognized) by the blanket approach taken in the new penology literature, which defines several decades of penality using one term.

This chapter builds upon the second aspect of Liebling and Crewe's critique, arguing that there are subtle, but significant, differences between mechanisms and processes of marketization, which are not always attended to in analyses of the re-emergence of privatization and competition policies in criminal justice. Research has focused upon the public/private distinction rather than considered the effects of ownership and service management transfers between sectors, and less still has explored criminal justice in the context of many, varied and hyper-mobile service providers that are now operating within and across criminal justice services and institutions. Departing from this tendency to consider marketization at an abstract and general level, this chapter describes and explores the substance and detail of how market mechanisms are used in the commissioning of criminal justice services in England and Wales, focusing especially upon the prison sector. By tracing how marketization processes have been mobilized over time, including within the current context of fiscal restraint, a more nuanced account of marketization is articulated, which positions market mechanisms as malleable, instrumental rather than mechanical, and varied, both in their design and impacts. The implications of these changes in marketization policy and practice are explored, reflecting especially upon consequences for strategic direction within the sector, service quality, and the professional and moral identities and practices of criminal justice practitioners. A central argument is that there has been too little reflection upon the penological significance, or moral sustainability, of the 'bigger and cheaper' model of criminal justice that is currently being pursued. In the current context, marketization processes are being used in ways that are disabling, rather than enabling, legitimate penal order. They are contributing to deteriorations in staff and prisoner safety and well-being and further eroding organizational hopes that imprisonment might do more good than damage to peoples' ambitions to live law-abiding lives (Liebling and Crewe, this volume; Liebling and Ludlow 2016).

MARKETIZING PRISONS IN ENGLAND AND WALES—NEW LANDSCAPES

TRANSITIONS IN PRISON COMMISSIONING

The private sector established itself within the UK criminal justice system in the operation of immigration removal centres (Bacon 2005). The depth and breadth of the private sector's penetration into immigration detention has not, until recently, attracted the attention it deserves (though see e.g. Bosworth 2014; Uglevik 2014). Most academic and public debate has focused instead upon the involvement of the private sector in prisons. In the 1980s, aged buildings, overcrowding, hostile industrial relations, and poor management were said to be holding back much needed improvement (King and McDermott 1989). This prompted a recommendation from the House of Commons Home Affairs Committee in 1987 to use the private sector 'as an experiment' to construct and manage new prisons (House of Commons Home Affairs Committee 1987a; House of Commons Home Affairs Committee 1987b). Seven years later, in 1994, the first privately managed prison opened (HMP Wolds). The experimental involvement of the private sector in prisons quickly developed to include longer contracts (of 15 years and more), and to incorporate the private financing and construction of prisons, as well as their management (Ludlow 2012). In the years that followed, 11 new-build prisons were opened under private management. Scotland and Northern Ireland did not follow suit.

In time, the experiment developed a stage further, moving away from pure private management of new-build prisons, towards the construction of a market in which the public sector became both commissioner and bidder in competitions for the management of existing operational prisons. Inspired by Lord Carter's 2003 report, the National Offender Management Service (NOMS) was created, hurriedly and imperfectly, to provide a new organizational framework to support these new ways of operating (Ludlow 2015: 67; Padfield 2006). Some suspected that the amalgamation of probation and prison services through NOMS was 'simply a Trojan horse for smuggling in "contestability" to yet another public sector body' (Stelman 2007). The Transforming Rehabilitation agenda has proved this to be an accurate prediction.

In the first round of competition the public sector retained one contested prison (HMP Manchester), and won one back from the private sector (HMP Buckley Hall). During this period, competition and marketization were predominantly motivated by improvement. Debate continued about how much 'better' privately managed prisons were performing compared to their publicly managed counterparts, and concerns began to be raised about some of the negative consequences of 'robust' private sector management models but, as Liebling and Crewe have argued, the marketization agenda during this period was tied explicitly and strenuously to 'moral ends': this was an era of 'managerialism-plus' (Liebling and Crewe 2013: 292) or 'neo-liberalism with a guilty conscience' (Liebling 2004: 4).

July 2008 signalled a new era in prison marketization policy, with a more far-reaching and routine commitment to competition in the sector. This coincided with the onset of the financial crisis and the need for the Prison Service to make challenging budget cuts. Ministerial approval was given for a Prison Competition Strategy, consisting of three strands: (1) the re-competition of all contracted (public and private) prisons; (2) new build prisons in which only the private and third sectors could participate; and (3) continued performance management and benchmarking to identify 'poor' performance against private sector costings. By 2010, the Ministry of Justice was subject to a 23 per cent budget cut to be achieved by 2014–15 (HM Treasury 2010: 55–6). In this context, in 2011, Justice Secretary Ken Clarke re-committed to competition as a mechanism by which to achieve general improvement, rather than merely to manage poor performance. He said:

> For offender services, I intend to employ the principle that competition will apply at some stage to all those services not currently bound to public sector delivery by statute. This will mean the benefits of competition can be felt much more widely, contrasting with the previous approach of only using competition when procuring new services or as a way of managing poor performance.' (HC Written Ministerial Statements 13 July 2011, vol 531, cols 31–33WS)

These political commitments were implemented by two phases of market testing, known as 'Prison Competitions Programme' phases 1 and 2 (PCP1 and PCP2). PCP1 began in 2009: five prisons were put out to tender, including a new-build prison (Featherstone II, now HMP Oakwood), the re-competition of two contracted prisons (one public sector, HMP Buckley Hall, and one private sector, HMP and YOI Doncaster), and two non-contracted 'poor performing' public sector prisons (HMPs Birmingham and Wellingborough). The inclusion of HMPs Birmingham and Wellingborough raised, for the first time, the prospect of a management transfer of an operational public sector prison to the private sector (aside from a failed attempt at HMP Brixton in 2001, which stalled for want of interest from the private sector). PCP2 began in 2013: nine prisons were put out to tender, including eight public prisons (HMPs Acklington and Castington (merged to form HMP Northumberland), Durham, Hatfield, Lindholme, Moorland, Onley, and Coldingley) and the re-competition of one private prison, HMP Wolds (the first privately managed prison , which was opened in 1994).[3] The prospect of an operational public sector prison transferring to private sector management was realized in PCP1 and PCP2: first in October 2011, when management of HMP Birmingham was transferred to G4S, and secondly in December 2013, with the transfer of HMP Northumberland to Sodexo. The competition for Wellingborough was aborted because the prison was judged to require too much capital investment to make its future viable.

PCP2 did not result in any further transfers beyond HMP Northumberland. This was because the public sector bid for HMP Durham was considered to provide best value for money and a decision was taken to use the Durham model as a 'benchmark' to be implemented in all Category B local and Category C training prisons from October 2013 (NOMS 2013: 11). This was intended to speed up cost-saving (rather than service improvement) across the estate by importing private sector cost and staffing models without the time, cost, and political and legal risks of competitive tendering exercises (Secretary of State for Justice Q 12, HC (Session 2012–13) 741-i.). Further benchmarks have been developed for the high security and women's estates, and young offender institutions as part of what is now NOMS' Prison Unit Cost programme. Implementation of these further benchmarks began in March 2014. The new benchmarks have demanded 'new ways of working'; reduced staffing levels, delayered staffing structures, and more flexible staff deployment to deliver reduced daily prison regimes. Implementation of benchmarking has led to a 30 per cent reduction in the public sector prison workforce (Prison Reform Trust 2016: 5).

Liebling and Crewe describe the period from 2007 onwards as 'managerialism-minus' coupled with 'punitive austerity': 'economy and efficiency are prioritized above any moral mission'. '"Old penology" values of decency and relationships are transformed into "new penology" language of cost-savings and effectiveness' (Liebling and Crewe 2013: 294–5). Yet marketization policy and practice during this period are not as uniform or unidirectional as the new penology account might suggest. Julian Le Vay accurately characterizes markestization policy in prisons as 'stop/start' (Le Vay 2006: 33). Alongside the withdrawal of HMP Wellingborough from PCP1 and the demise of PCP2 in favour of internally generated efficiencies through benchmarking, competitions for clusters of prisons were cancelled, including in Kent and South Yorkshire. Plans for three new-build 2500 bed 'titan' prisons and new-for-old replacement prisons did not come to fruition, with one exception, eventually, in Wrexham (HMP Berwyn) which is presently under construction, and for which no private sector

[3] http://ted.europa.eu/udl?uri=TED:NOTICE:336076-2011:TEXT:EN:HTML, accessed 11 January 2017.

bids were invited. Ken Clarke's 2011 competition strategy, which subjected prisons that were not poorly performing to competition, was cancelled by incoming Secretary of State, Chris Grayling, in favour of benchmarking and, under Michael Gove, in 2016, in favour of the creation of six 'reform prisons' (HMPs Wandsworth, Holme House, Kirklevington Grange, Coldingley, High Down, and Ranby). Reform prisons are a central pillar of what the government has described as the 'biggest shakeup of prisons since Victorian times'. Governors at these prisons have been given increased legal and financial freedoms. Former Secretary of State for Justice, Michael Gove, promised to legislate to extend these freedoms 'much further—enabling prisons to be established as independent legal entities with the power to enter into contracts; generate and retain income; and establish their own boards with external expertise.'[4] The legal form in which these reforms will be embodied is unclear, as is ongoing political commitment to them under incoming Secretary of State for Justice, Liz Truss.

What further emerges from this account of prison marketization is that the commissioning of prison services in England and Wales has moved away from the contracting out of whole, new-build prisons to private companies, in return for a simple operating fee, towards a more complex and hybrid position in which the private sector occupies a more limited and contingent position. Through benchmarking, private sector models of efficiency have been distilled and applied across the prison estate without the need for competition or transfer of prisons from public to private sector management. Internal reorganization has also been prioritized over outsourcing through restructuring exercises, such as the merger of HMPs Everthorpe and Wolds, which were previously separately publicly and privately managed respectively, to form HMP Humber in 2015, and through the introduction of reform prisons.

Where contracting out is pursued, it is being used in a more targeted way, for specific services, with greater focus on outcomes, through results based payment mechanisms. Greater use is being made of horizontal commissioning whereby services that span multiple prisons are contracted out as a package. These contract packages are managed centrally by NOMS, outside of an individual establishment's control. The hope is that contracting in this way will enable economies of scale to be harnessed. An important example of this is the contracting out of facilities management at 50 prisons to Carillion, which happened in 2014. Some evidence suggests that the horizontal contracting out of facilities management has led to a deterioration rather than an improvement in the upkeep of prison infrastructure (e.g. HMP Ford Independent Monitoring Board 2015: 5). Rather than simple operating fees, NOMS has also increased its use of results based payment mechanisms, tying payment to reduced reconviction rates. Key examples are the Social Impact Bond that has been piloted at HMP Peterborough and the payment by results mechanism used at HMP Doncaster. A mixed picture has emerged from re-conviction data (Ministry of Justice 2014) and evaluations of these initiatives, with some reported successes at HMP Peterborough (RAND Europe 2014, 2015), but fewer at HMP Doncaster (GVA 2012; GVA and Carney Green 2015). Fox and Albertson have argued that payment by results brings with it high levels of uncertainty, and 'the associated risk to investors will lead to a

[4] https://www.gov.uk/government/news/biggest-shake-up-of-prison-system-announced-as-part-of-queens-speech, accessed 11 January 2017.

sub-optimal provision of interventions in the criminal justice sector' (2011: 410). In May 2012, the Ministry of Justice tendered contracts for a pilot rehabilitation programme at HMP Leeds using payment by results. The National Audit Office reported that the competition closed 'without a successful bid after all but 1 of the 6 potential providers decided not to compete. The firms reported that the model for the pilot was unworkable' (NAO 2015: 24).

HOW COMMISSIONING LANDSCAPES SHAPE PRISON POLICY AND PRACTICE

These new ways of doing business have important implications for the public and private sectors, as well as for theoretical understandings about the nature and role of marketization in criminal justice. First, decisions about how to deliver criminal justice services and by whom are now taking place in a more mature and fluid market, with increased interaction and cross-fertilization between public and private sector providers. We know, especially from the work of Crewe *et al.* (2011, 2014) that there is no straightforward relationship between which sector manages a prison and its staff culture and quality of life. As the market has matured, some of the cultural challenges in public sector prisons have emerged in longer-term privately managed establishments. The culture of public sector prisons is also changing as many have been forced, through benchmarking, to adapt to significantly leaner staffing models, which previously have characterized private sector management. Greater fluidity between sectors, and 'the revolving door of knowledge' (Podmore 2015), increasingly pose questions about fair play and competitive advantage among the small group of competitors within the market. One example that gave rise to such questions was former NOMS Director General, Phil Wheatley's, move to work for G4S in January 2011. His move to G4S came shortly before the announcement that G4S had succeeded in the competition to manage HMP Birmingham, displacing the incumbent public sector.

Secondly, though commissioning lessons have been learned, learning has been incremental, and old decisions and 'start/stop' misfires linger in ways that make marketization policy and practice more partial, unwieldy, and limited than a new penological theoretical account might suggest. Some contracts, for example, are too long to reap the refresher benefits of competition, and some have too great a focus on process measures at the expense of outcome delivery. As Le Vay recounts, prisons financed under the Private Finance Initiative 'were spared closure, even though some appeared high cost and not very well performing, because the contracts were unfeasibly costly to end' (Le Vay 2016: 37). The result is a cumbersome and, at times, prohibitive contractual legacy, which requires sophisticated management and can be difficult to alter quickly in response to changing political ambitions. It seems likely that the manpower and resource implications of the complex task of market and contract management have some restraining influence upon the nature and scale of further marketization processes. This is partly because major failings in the design and management of some criminal justice contracts, such as the electronic monitoring contracts between the Ministry of Justice and G4S and Serco, have increased political pressure to ensure that sufficient expertise is invested in the commissioning cycle as a whole. This includes planning, procuring, monitoring, managing, and reviewing, rather than merely delivering (HM Government 2013; NAO 2013; NAO 2014a, 2014b).

The use and scale of marketization may also be inhibited by uncertainty generated by start/stop misfires, such as the decision not to take forward the South Yorkshire prison cluster competition. Decisions of this sort can erode confidence among private sector providers about the state's competence and the viability of future business in the sector. They can also lead to negative operational consequences, including at prisons that are managed by the private sector. For example, in HMP Doncaster, which is operated by Serco, staff vacancies were left deliberately unfilled in order to absorb staff from other prisons in the South Yorkshire cluster who otherwise would have been made redundant. The decision not to continue with the cluster competition led, in part, to serious staffing difficulties at HMP Doncaster, which have contributed to the prison receiving negative reports from HM Inspectorate of Prisons and the Committee for the Prevention of Torture. Doncaster has been given until November 2016 to improve under threat of the contract being terminated. Serco may feel deterred from participating in future competitive processes because of the reputational and financial risks of the current situation at HMP Doncaster and the contributory role that NOMS played in this.

Thirdly, management transfers within and between sectors have given rise to new challenges about mobilization, transition, and transformation. Transfers in prison management, such as that which occurred at HMP Birmingham in October 2011, have proven to be highly complex processes that have exposed shortcomings in expertise and capacity and wide gaps and conflicts between policy aspirations and what can be achieved in practice. Competitive tendering processes, which have been imagined as tools to bring about rapid and dramatic cultural improvement, have proved to be less straightforwardly or immediately revolutionary. Significantly, employment regulation in this field, which means that, as a starting point, all existing staff transfer over to the employ of the new operator on their existing terms and conditions of employment, results in management transfers being less of a 'big bang' and more of a subtle and gradual signalling and processing of cultural continuities and discontinuities, working with broadly the same group of managers and staff as was previously employed (Ludlow 2015; Robinson *et al.* 2015). These experiences may partially account for NOMS' current preference for reform through internal reorganization rather than through competitive tendering exercises.

Finally, benchmarking has narrowed the cost differential between publicly and privately managed prisons in ways that ostensibly radically alter the marketization landscape. Le Vay argues that benchmarking is the death knell of prison competition as we have known it: 'there is so little difference private and public sector costs that competition is now pretty much an irrelevancy, at most a theoretical sanction against some future failure by the public sector.' (Le Vay 2016: 42). One potentially positive effect of this may be to shift the focus of future commissioning attention onto quality improvement, rather than predominantly cost saving. However, a less positive effect for those who have argued in favour of a mixed prison provide economy is that benchmarking, coupled with pressures to 'play contracts by the letter' since the electronic monitoring contract scandal (Le Vay 2016: 68), cast doubt on the likelihood of sufficiently profitable and certain future business for private providers. This may mean that there will be no feasible competitive market in the future. There are already concerns that the dominance of Serco and G4S means that, in practice, one (public sector) monopoly is merely being swapped for another sort of (private sector) monopoly.

The new approach of disaggregating and horizontally commissioning non-core custodial services (e.g. facilities management, healthcare, resettlement, industries, and resettlement) may further disincentivize private sector participation in the market. If private sector prison directors do not have control over many of the services that are provided in their prisons, it becomes difficult to maintain high quality regimes, and thereby safeguard corporate reputation. The pre-existing contracting out of education and healthcare in prisons has not been altogether successful. In the context of prison education, Gerry Czerniawski has argued that 'neo-liberal logic that alleges that competitive tendering and performance outcomes are the best drivers to improve prison education has culminated in a race-to-the-bottom in the standards of educational provision for prisoners' (Czerniawski 2016: 208). The extension of horizontal commissioning to other prison services gives rise to further broader questions about accountability and effective management. In evidence before the House of Commons Justice Select Committee, the former Chief Inspector of Prisons, Nick Hardwick, former Director of NOMS, Phil Wheatley, and some private prison contractors raised concerns that 'having too many separate contracts operating in prisons could fragment and therefore compromise the integration of the system' (House of Commons Justice Committee 2015: 53). One effect of horizontal commissioning is to open up a gap between people who interact with services on a daily basis, and so understand their shortcomings and have incentives to improve them, and people who are responsible for managing the contracts, who are located remotely within NOMS and whose abilities to contract manage have been criticized (Ministry of Justice 2013; NAO 2014b).

MARKETIZATION EXPERIENCES AND OUTCOMES: QUALITY, IDENTITY, AND CULTURE

In the second quote that introduced this chapter, former Chief Executive of the Prison Service, Martin Narey, placed humanity at the heart of his motivations for opening up prisons to competitive tendering processes: 'It wasn't about efficiency . . . it was just about humanity.' In 2001, when Martin Narey addressed prison governors at a conference shortly before the first private prison was due to open, he highlighted the many well-documented failings of the public sector, describing them as a 'litany of failure and moral neglect' (Narey 2001: 3).

Competition policy in prisons has been criticized for its 'curious imprecision about what competition was for—why it was a good idea' (Le Vay 2016: 10; Ludlow 2015). Few, however, would argue against improved (or sustained) quality being important among its ambitions. The experiences of staff and prisoners, caught within the net of marketization processes, must be central to any enquiry about the effects and significance of market-making in the prison sector. Alongside understanding how marketization policy and practice shape high level strategy and governance, we ought to explore, and empirically probe, their effects on daily prison life, and consider what this might tell us about the nature of the contemporary penal state (Garland 2013; Liebling and Ludlow, forthcoming).

There is good evidence to suggest that the introduction of private sector management to a small number of prisons in the early 1990s in England and Wales acted as a catalyst for some improvements to public sector prisons that have made meaningful differences to the quality of life of people in prison. These included standardized improvements to daily prison regimes, increasing time out of cells, and access to a wider range of purposeful activities. The private sector has also been at the forefront of using technology in prisons, including CCTV, biometric technology, on-wing kiosks through which prisoners can order canteen (food, drinks, cosmetics, etc.) and book appointments, and in-cell telephones. Some of this technology can increase transparency, and enable prisoners to exercise greater personal autonomy and keep in better contact with family and friends. More significantly, perhaps, it reduces operating costs by decreasing the involvement of prison staff in routine prison processes. According to evidence presented to the House of Commons Justice Committee, for every prison custody officer saved, an estimated £750,000 is saved over the lifetime of a 25-year contract (House of Commons Justice Committee 2015: 9). Some public sector prisons have introduced kiosks to reap similar cost savings. The use of technology to replace staff is not without its risks. Legitimate order, safety, and well-being are largely relationally and dynamically produced, through interactions and relationships between staff and prisoners (Liebling *et al.* 2011). A kiosk with which prisoners transact is no substitute for skilled staff who are able to deliver safe and purposeful regimes through their relational use of power, experience, and skills. As Liebling and Crewe have noted, improvements in conditions have not ameliorated prisoner complaints about 'the administration of punishment, the lack of empathy for their predicament, and limited opportunities for growth and development' (Liebling and Crewe 2013: 301).

The introduction of privately managed prisons also generated leverage to push through broader changes to how all public sector prison staff are remunerated and deployed; flattening management structures, reducing staffing levels, and increasing levels of flexibility for managers within the contracts of employment of uniformed staff. Some of the government's difficulties in implementing prison reforms had arisen from the intransigence of the Prison Officers' Association (POA), the trade union that represents most prison officers in the UK. In 1997, former Director General of the Prison Service, Derek Lewis, described the POA as the 'principal obstacle to progress' (Lewis 1997: 137) and in 2004 Alison Liebling described the union as 'placing constraints on modernisation' (Liebling with Arnold 2004: 402). In a study of UK prison governors' views and experiences of privatization, Crewe and Liebling found that even those governors who objected ideologically to the introduction of private prison management, accepted that public sector prisons had improved 'enormously' because of competition, which had rebalanced industrial power away from staff and in favour of management. As governors put it 'the inside story of prison privatisation in the UK was principally the story of finally controlling or cubing union power.' Directors of privately managed prisons 'talked with enthusiasm about the relief of managing cooperative staff, and the benefits this brought' (Liebling and Crewe 2013: 293; Crewe and Liebling 2012). Government policy has been accused of lacking honesty about the extent to which reforming employment and industrial relationships with prison staff have been central concerns of those driving prison privatization (Taylor and Cooper 2008: 4), but the practically limiting effects of marketization upon public sector terms and conditions of employment are undeniable. Benchmarking has taken maximum advantage of leverage generated by public/private staffing model comparisons and applied it in a systematic way across the estate This is discussed further later in the chapter.

The presence of a private sector prison employment model has challenged public sector staffing culture more broadly, beyond terms and conditions of employment, by highlighting (positive and negative) differences in working practices between and within sectors. There are important differences between how staff in public and private prisons exercise their authority and these differences cause variation in prisoner quality of life between prisons. Public sector prisons tend to be 'heavier', infused with authority which, when exercised poorly, feels oppressive, unfair, and uncaring. Private sector prisons tend to be 'light', in ways that can feel less inhibiting, more caring, but also less safe, because prison staff are sometimes 'absent' or insufficiently active in managing trouble (Crewe *et al.* 2011, 2014; and Liebling and Crewe, this volume). Better quality of life experiences in prison are related to better outcomes post release (Auty and Liebling, submitted). The emergence of private sector 'lightness' has helped the public sector's 'heaviness' to be articulated and challenged. With regained power, through privatization, it became possible to manage out some of the abusive ways in which some public sector prison staff exercised power in their relationships with prisoners, and to demand more decent and progressive staff–prisoner interactions. There was an operational vision of better (more humane but also leaner and cheaper) practice to which managers could refer, both as a source of inspiration for improvement but also as a threat for what might happen to staff that were impervious or obstructive to reform. The private sector's 'lightness' has also highlighted, albeit perhaps inadequately, the public sector's strengths in the confident and 'present' use of authority, by a stable and experienced group of loyal and vocationally oriented staff. These strengths are under considerable pressure because of the importation of leaner and cheaper staffing models from the private sector into the public sector, through benchmarking. There are significant obstacles to comparing cost alongside quality between the sectors (Le Vay 2016: 159–96; Rynne and Harding 2016: 155–7).

Although the presence of the private sector has brought with it some direct and referred benefits, private prison management has not been a guarantee of high or improved performance. Just as with the public sector, some of the 'best' and 'worst' performing prisons are privately managed (Rynne and Harding 2016: 158–9). Evidence of children being physically and emotionally abused by staff in G4S operated Medway Secure Training Centre (a prison for 12–17 year olds) provides a high profile recent example of some of the poorest private sector practice. Following the broadcast of evidence of abuse obtained through undercover journalists working at Medway, the Justice Secretary formed an Independent Improvement Board, which reported in March 2016. The Board's wide-ranging review highlighted deficiencies in the commissioning, contracting, management, and monitoring of Medway. In the Board's view, these deficiencies had contributed to Medway's poor culture and the abusive practices of some of its staff. The Board reported that it 'felt that G4S had a much better understanding of the terms of the contract than the Youth Justice Board, and that they may be using this knowledge to interpret the contract in terms more favourable to them'; that 'there was a risk that G4S would deliver "what is in the contract" rather than deliver what was in the wider interests of young people'; that G4S was 'penalised for incidents that do not necessarily improve safeguarding or rehabilitation and that avoiding contractual penalties has become more important than considering what purpose the provisions behind the penalty serves for the young people'; that 'the Youth Justice Board has not articulated the contract in terms that enables effective and nurturing care and rehabilitation of young people'; and that 'there is an over-reliance in the Youth Justice Board on the views and opinions of other organisations rather than developing contract management and monitoring arrangements that are robust enough' (Medway Improvement Board 2016: 52–3). Medway is a long way from Martin Narey's aspiration of increasing humanity through privatization. G4S has decided to leave the Secure Training Centre market.

Competitive tendering exercises, in which the public sector is permitted to compete against private sector bidders, have raised the enticing possibility that they might, at best, combine the strengths of public and private prison cultures and simultaneously challenge and counteract both sectors' weaknesses. As outlined above, this possibility was raised in two competitive tendering exercises for prisons in England and Wales, PCP1 in 2009 and PCP2 in 2013. Both processes resulted in the transfer of operational public sector prisons into private sector management: HMP Birmingham to G4S in 2011, and HMP Northumberland to Sodexo in 2013. The inclusion of HMP Birmingham in PCP1 was motivated principally by poor performance and obstructive local industrial relations which were thought to have held back much needed improvement (Ludlow 2015: 27). Internationally, the leading example of a similar transfer was of Parklea Correctional Centre, near Sydney, from public sector management to GEO in 2009. In the UK, there have been some private to public transfers, such as G4S managed HMP Wolds to the public sector in 2012, but fluidity between sectors is generally low. Within the broader criminal justice system there have been transfers between different private sector providers, but there are no examples of whole prisons transfers. Private to private transfers generally do not raise prospects for cultural change of the same magnitude as public to private or private to public transfers. The transfer of Acacia prison, in Western Australia, is among the few international examples where a whole prison has been transferred from one private operator (AIMS) to another (Serco). The decision to transfer Acacia in 2006 was motivated by AIMS' failure 'to make significant improvements'. 'The first contract period [under AIMS] was affected by a number of issues due to inaccurate staffing level estimates, poor accountability structures within the contracting company, and poorly defined corporate decision-making structures.' Acacia experienced problems with staff retention post-transfer, but the prison's overall performance has since improved (Andrew *et al.* 2016: 50).

Just as with outsourced private sector delivery without competition, private sector management following a competitive tendering exercise has not proved to be a straightforward, cost free, or panacea solution to resolve all of the ills of public sector prisons. This is contrary to its presentation in government policy, which has generally positioned markets in public life as natural and the private sector as a self-evident source of improvement. Empirical evidence about the nature and effects of these competitive tendering processes points towards a more nuanced and limited account of the improvement outcomes that marketization processes can deliver. In practice, competitive tendering exercises have proven complex, with questions about whether the public sector has adequate expertise. They have proven time-consuming and expensive and can risk order and safety for both staff and prisoners.[5] They have lacked clarity of vision and purpose, and arguably they have been driven by procurement processes that are more readily focused on cost reduction than quality improvement. The competitive process for HMP Birmingham has been described thus: 'Following a process that cost £5.84 million, the Birmingham competition produced a contract between the Government and G4S with a value of £316.5 million that is impenetrable to all but lawyers in its length and language, which is more focused upon NOMS' needs than prisoner needs, and which lacks vision and ambition for future service improvement and the important role of the workforce in delivering it' (Ludlow 2015: 194).

The competition for HMP Birmingham provides a useful case study for reflecting upon the nature, effects and significance of competitive tendering exercises as processes of marketization, particularly in light of the new penology thesis. Ethnographic research during the competitive tendering exercise and mixed method studies during the three years following Birmingham's privatization, document a two-year competitive tendering process at Birmingham (originally forecast to take only nine months) that was experienced by staff as demoralizing and disempowering (Ludlow 2015; Liebling *et al.* 2012, 2013, 2015). During the competition, staff reported that nobody communicated with them in a language that they could understand and NOMS' responsibilities as an employer were broadly neglected. There were six self-inflicted deaths in HMP Birmingham during the height of the competition in 2010 compared with none in 2009, two in 2007 and 2008, and one in 2005 and 2006. Some staff attributed these deaths to the destabilization and uncertainty created by the competition process (Ludlow 2015: 172). The procurement process was approached as a transactional task, administered from afar, with apparently little understanding of Birmingham's enduring problems and how competition (and the particular form of competition that was used) would address those problems. A traumatized institution and staff group transferred to G4S in October 2011.

Rather than enabling reform, the early principal effect of competition was to create negativity, hostility, and anxiety among staff, which constrained improvement at Birmingham, especially in the early days after G4S had taken over the prison's management. Staff and managers felt devalued, alienated, and 'tarred' by working for a 'failing' public sector institution. This added to the commercial challenges of an already high risk commercial venture. As Le Vay has argued, the use of competition to 'punish' the public sector carries with it risks that the commercial perspective (the interests and perspectives of the private sector) will not be properly understood, with inadequately considered consequences for the future of the market (Le Vay 2016: 26). Staff were preoccupied by their own 'private troubles'. They retreated from wings and the confident and professional use of authority, with consequent adverse impacts upon safety and order for prisoners (Liebling *et al.* 2012; Liebling *et al.* 2014; Zacka 2014; Lipsky 1980). Anxiety paralysed progress. Staff lacked the security that they needed to adapt to the future and sought security in trying to preserve the past. Staff described facing a crisis

[5] The military were involved in contingency planning following the decision to privatize HMP Birmingham: see http://www.bbc.co.uk/news/uk-politics-12920843, accessed 11 January 2017.

of self-legitimacy, many having linked 'wearing the Crown on their shoulder', which had now been removed, to their sense of 'rightful authority' and moral and professional purpose (Tankebe 2014). In policing, a greater sense of self-legitimacy has been shown to be linked to greater commitment to democratic modes of criminal justice practice (Bradford and Quinton 2014).

Since privatization, quality of life for prisoners at HMP Birmingham has improved, significantly and across almost all dimension measures (e.g. decency, humanity, and fairness), albeit against a low quality baseline. In a survey conducted by NOMS' Audit and Corporate Assurance team in May 2009, 83.8 per cent of prisoners at Birmingham scored their overall quality of life negatively. By 2013, two years after privatization, 'prisoners and staff rated their quality of life and treatment significantly better than in 2011 and 2012, and were feeling as though their prison "was finally settling down". Staff views of senior management were positive, and feelings of safety, control and security were positive, for the first time. Professional orientations towards prisoners were improved. Prisoners noticed and appreciated these changes' (Liebling *et al.* 2014). Ironically, since benchmarking, operational staff at HMP Birmingham are among the best paid prison officers in the country.

Notwithstanding these improvements, evidence about the experience and impacts of the competitive process at Birmingham begs questions about the costs, losses, and risks entailed by these processes, as much as their potential gains. Some of the damaging consequences and experiences of competition at Birmingham were avoidable and might have set the prison on a more positive course for improvement with fewer 'casualties'. It is possible to imagine a less brutalizing process, based on greater transparency and information sharing, careful advance planning, clearer vision and, perhaps above all, an explicit articulation of, and therefore preservation of, the strengths of the public sector, in order to combine these strengths with those of the private sector. As Liebling and Ludlow have argued, 'To construct a process from an unstated but powerful set of assumptions about how the "public sector has failed", and the "private sector has the answers" omits to carry with it the significant strengths visible in public sector prison work (pride, loyalty, public service, experience and the competent use of authority). It underestimates some of the weaknesses inherent in private sector operations (cheap staff, high turnover, lack of loyalty, inexperience, and a drift into criminal justice work rather than a vocation)' (Liebling and Ludlow, forthcoming).

Although NOMS has not initiated further competitive tendering exercises for whole prisons since PCP2, there is evidence that some of the processual and conceptual errors that were observed at HMP Birmingham are being repeated elsewhere (Ludlow 2014; see also Liebling 2006). There are significant parallels between findings from HMP Birmingham's privatization and the Transforming Rehabilitation probation reform process in which supervision for all low- and medium-risk offenders has been contracted out to mixed consortia of private, quasi-public, and third sector bodies (Community Rehabilitation Companies: CRCs). Robinson *et al.* (2015) have described probation workers as deprived of information and opportunities for agency during the competitive process, and bereft of any rationale for why radical privatization was thought to be necessary or beneficial and any consideration of what might be lost through such a process. They describe probation staff, who now find themselves working within newly privatized Community Rehabilitation Companies, as inhabiting liminal spaces 'betwixt and between' socially constructed identities, which has generated feelings of anxiety, disempowerment, and de-professionalization. Further themes include separation, grief, and loss, powerlessness, status anxiety, new challenges to loyalty and trust, and processes of dis-identification and re-identification (Robinson *et al.* 2015; see also Deering and Feilzer 2015).

The effects that these transformations in probation will have upon service quality and the experiences of people under supervision are still unfolding. Early indications are mostly inconclusive or somewhat negative (NAO 2016; HM Inspectorate of Probation 2016; Burke and Collett 2016). The National Audit Office has praised the Ministry of Justice's success in sustaining services throughout a period of major change but has highlighted shortcomings in how new services were procured (in five of 21 CRCs only one compliant bid was received) and has raised concerns about the increased workloads of all probation staff following the reforms, and the adverse impacts that this is having upon staff supervision and training and service provision to offenders (see also Dominey 2016). NOMS has invested significantly in the contract management of CRCs, reporting that 151 full-time equivalent staff have been employed at a cost of 2.1 per cent of the total contract value. The National Audit Office has raised concerns about deficiencies in monitoring the National Probation Service and 'the extent and trajectory of contract management and operational assurance activity' as CRC contracts mature (NAO 2016: 7).

The same critiques of competitive tendering processes, of underestimating the weaknesses inherent in the private sector operating model, and of avoiding more fundamental questions about the right cost/quality/prison population size thresholds, can be levelled at the benchmarking processes in prisons. Imposing private sector cost models upon all public sector prisons has imposed efficiencies across the estate in a systematic way, without the cost and risk of running individual competitive processes. However, the effects of benchmarking are deeply contested. As Le Vay puts it, 'The Cost and Benchmarking Programme, completed across the public prison system by April 2015, has driven down staffing levels across the prison system much further than previously thought possible—or safe' (Le Vay 2016: 37). The House of Commons Justice Select Committee described the situation as:

> All available indicators, including those recorded by HM Inspectorate of Prisons and NOMS itself, are pointing towards a rapid deterioration in standards of safety and levels of performance over the last year or so. Most concerning to us is that since 2012 there has been a 38% rise in self-inflicted deaths, a 9% rise in self-harm, a 7% rise in assaults, and 100% rise in incidents of concerted indiscipline. Complaints to the Prisons and Probation Ombudsman and other sources have risen. There are fewer opportunities for rehabilitation, including diminished access to education, training, libraries, religious leaders, and offending behaviour courses. (House of Commons Justice Committee 2015: 33)

The Committee also received evidence of 'low staff morale and higher sickness rates, partially explained by work-related stress' since benchmarking (House of Commons Justice Committee 2015: 37). In 2015, more prison staff resigned from their posts than were made redundant. The Committee felt that it 'is not possible to avoid the conclusion that the confluence of estate modernization and re-configuration, efficiency savings, staffing shortages, and changes in operational policy, including to the Incentives and Earned Privileges scheme, have made a significant contribution to the deterioration in safety' (House of Commons Justice Committee 2015: 43; see also Liebling and Ludlow 2016).

Crewe and Liebling (this volume) have described how benchmarking is reconfiguring penal power with three main outcomes: (1) producing environmental conditions that are reshaping prisoner behaviour in ways that are mainly undesirable; (2) increasing power-sharing between staff and prisoners in ways that can be compatible with legitimate penal order when authority is 'actively and carefully delegated to trusted prisoners', but can also be problematic when power is 'handed over in more informal, collusive and unaccountable ways'; and (3) causing some staff to feel so overwhelmed that they retreat and, though they are 'physically present', they are 'un-engaged relationally'—'present in person but absent in practice'. Getting through the day has come to mean 'fire-fighting' and 'survival'; a poor foundation 'for prisoners to "work on themselves", their lives and their futures' (see also Maguire and Raynor 2016). These important penological and sociological changes do not appear to have been considered in the political decision-making processes that have led to the pursuit of a cheaper and bigger prison system. Some of the negative effects of benchmarking might have been predicted from evidence about the experience of imprisonment and models of order in US prisons from which the turn to larger, cheaper prisons appears to have been inspired (see, e.g., Petersilia 2008). This form of marketization in prisons—the universal and uncritical adoption of private sector staffing and operating practices—does not appear to be achieving Martin Narey's original aspirations for maximizing humanity. It is not clear that the maximization of humanity is now even part of the political discourse that is shaping decisions about whether and how to apply market mechanisms to prisons. Perhaps this should not come as a surprise. As Simon and Feeley put it, the new penology 'has trouble with the concept of humanity' (Simon and Feeley 1995: 173).

CONCLUSIONS AND A LOOK TO THE FUTURE

This chapter has sought to demonstrate how processes of marketization vary significantly over time, between jurisdiction, and within criminal justice services. Different forms of marketization and differences in how marketization processes are operated meaningfully affect the sorts of service that result and the quality of life for people who live and work within criminal justice institutions. As David Faulkner put it, in *Servant of the Crown*:

> The mechanisms of 'contestability' . . . can be used in different ways, with different underlying objectives. . .. They can be used competitively, to save costs, impose standardisation and uniformity, and punish or threaten punishment for failure. Or they can be used co-operatively to encourage innovative and experiment. They can be rigid and 'top-down', requiring compliance with a centrally-imposed specification, or they can be flexible and help to promote local creativity. The process can be complex, time-consuming and

> bureaucratic, encouraging artificial devices to gain favour or win contracts, or it can be open and accessible to new ideas from old or new sources. Commissioners can concentrate on getting best value from whatever competing sources are already available, or they can accept a public responsibility to use the process of commissioning in ways that will 'grow' the skills and capacity, and the values and relationships, that will be needed for the future.... The outcomes of commissioning could be beneficial or disastrous, depending on the choices that are made. (Faulkner 2014: 194)

The picture of commissioning that emerges from the discussion above has most in common with the competitive, top-down approach that Faulkner describes. The driving aim, and principal effect, of marketization in the prisons sector in England and Wales has been to save cost more than to improve quality. This is most apparent in the importation of standardized private sector cost models to all public prisons, through benchmarking, which has caused significant deterioration in quality of life for staff and prisoners in many prisons and is fundamentally reconfiguring penal power. As John Podmore has argued, 'There is a real danger ... that benchmarking not only generates a whole new bureaucracy of its own but that the costs of it do not feature in any financial analysis. There is a further danger that it develops and promotes the mediocre rather than develop the exceptional. There is certainly no evidence of the transfer of best practice in such an approach rather a culture of self-protection in the world of tick-box and league table comparisons' (Podmore 2015). Some prisons have been more successful than others at navigating these changes and maintaining forms of legitimate penal order that nurture personal development within new and challenging financial and institutional circumstances. From a new penology perspective, benchmarking provides an example, alongside others in this chapter, of where the experiences and outcomes of marketization processes have not been as homogenous or universal as theory describes. It seems important to probe these empirical differences and account, theoretically, for their presence, causes, and effects, not least to learn more about how we might nurture institutional resilience to some of the damage caused by reforms such as benchmarking.

Shortly after he took office as Secretary of State for Justice in 2012, Chris Grayling outlined to the House of Commons Justice Committee his desire to 'develop a penal system that was cheaper, not smaller' (House of Commons Justice Committee 2015: 9). This vision of penal policy has substantially persisted notwithstanding ministerial changes. Insights from comparative penology are a helpful reminder that this model is a policy choice, and is only one 'proposition for change which, like any proposition, should be subject to rigorous critique' (Sennett 2006: 10). We know that big prisons, that house men and women a long way away from their families and communities, are less safe and inflict more harm than smaller, local prisons (House of Commons Justice Committee 2015: 17). Big, cheap custody makes society less, rather than more, safe and does not bring with it the economic advantages that are claimed (Armstrong and Maruna 2016). As Alison Liebling has argued, drawing on David Garland's work, many of the conditions that do most to support people to live law-abiding lives lie outside the prison. '[I]n opting for larger, cheaper prisons and more clusters we are privileging a certain economic kind of understanding of the problems faced. We risk forgetting that there are other shared aims (such as social justice, crime prevention and inclusion, or legitimate prison communities) and there is a moral language which has been excluded from this debate' (Liebling 2011: 11; Liebling 2008; Maguire and Raynor 2016: 16).

Following the competitions for HMPs Birmingham and Northumberland, prison commissioning in England and Wales had shown signs of moving away from bare competition that is about punishing or threatening punishment for failure. There were elements of the Transforming Rehabilitation probation restructuring programme that reflected a potentially more innovative, flexible, inclusive, and locally grounded vision of commissioning. Greater care than has been seen previously was given to thinking about how the design of the procurement process enabled or disabled the participation of small and medium sized enterprises (SMEs). Collaborations with SMEs and third sector bidders were encouraged to promote greater market diversity and innovation. The extent to which this has translated into practical service improvements remains unclear and further research is needed to explore relationships between public, private, and third sector partners, and their service users (Mills *et al.* 2012; Tomczak and Albertson 2016). Nevertheless, procuring services in these more ambitious ways is a complex task, demanding high levels of skill, vision, purpose, judgement, and joined-up-thinking, which may exceed existing public sector capabilities and resources. This difficult work must be conducted within a model of government that compartmentalises the state into arbitrary departments for the purposes of funding and service delivery. The best judgement of commissioning teams can be constrained and compromised by political mandates that impose unrealistic or imprudent demands about scale, pace, and purpose.

The introduction of reform prisons, with increased freedoms for their Executive Governors, may pull prison commissioning practice in a more cooperative, localized, and improvement-driven direction; but these are unchartered waters. Unlike all previous forms of marketization, Executive Governors do not have complete, newly designed visions for their prisons embodied in Service Level Agreements. The parameters of their powers and expectations about what they must deliver are undefined. They will require tenacity and new skills. As the House of Commons Justice Committee put it, 'the evolving nature of the role of governors has implications both for models of procurement and for models of leadership, with more emphasis required on influencing and relationship management skills' (House of Commons Justice Committee 2015: 54). The new Secretary of State's commitment to reform prisons is not clear. The language she has adopted to describe them has already softened; 'enabled prisons' seem less radical than how they were presented by their brainchild, former Secretary of State, Michael Gove. Leaders of enabled prisons will require courage, as much as skill. The dismissal of Derek Lewis in 1995, as former Director General of the Prison Service, by the then Home Secretary, is a reminder of the ease with which civil servants can become political scapegoats (Lewis 1997).

It is, of course, essential that taxpayers' money is spent wisely within the criminal justice system. What appears to be lacking, in thinking about how to deliver and commission criminal justice services, is how to strike the right balance between cost and quality and the role that marketization policies can, or ought to, play in getting this balance right. The private sector does not have all of the 'answers'—'surrendering' a public service to the market will not necessarily improve it. There is a tipping point beyond which order and decency are lost in favour of a system of mass warehousing that brutalizes and ceases to aspire to play a positive role in supporting people towards better futures. At this point, imprisonment becomes a bare expression of state power; so lacking in legitimacy that it is unable to engage those who have breached the law in moral conversation. Disorder and violence often result (Carrabine 2005; Sparks and Bottoms 1995; Rynne *et al.* 2008). There has been too little reflection upon the penological significance or moral sustainability of this model of bigger, cheaper criminal justice.

Within this context it seems essential to recognize that commissioning and contracting processes do not play merely purposive, mechanical, or technical functions. Perhaps the most important lesson to be learned is that privatization is not an end in itself (Van der Hoeven and Sziraczki 1997: 16). Market mechanisms are not benign tools or tools of inherent improvement. To be used appropriately, in ways that maximize humanity, they need to be designed and operationalized with clear vision and moral values, rather than mere economic rationality. Just as economies that are more open to foreign trade have been found to have larger governments (Rodrik 1998), so more open markets in public services require greater proactive governance and regulation.

Market mechanisms have, embedded within them, a complexity that, without masterful management, can become self-fulfilling, divorced from what it was hoped the process would achieve. Market mechanisms also have embedded within them what Philip Bobbitt has described as a 'market state' orientation; a drive to maximize individual opportunities through commercial means over the well-being of the nation as a whole (Bobbitt 2002). As David Faulkner reports, 'Commenting on Bobbit's book, while David Blunkett as Home Secretary welcomed the market state as being more democratic than a state dominated by a metropolitan elite; the former Archbishop of Canterbury, Dr Rowan Williams, criticized it as lacking a sense of moral values.' In Faulkner's view, the market state is 'an abdication of political leadership'. For Faulkner, the market state context makes 'it more than ever necessary to reaffirm and hold on to the values of fairness and justice, and of humanity and compassion, and to ensure that public services and the institutions of state are working together to protect them' (Faulkner 2014: 179). It might prove beneficial to think more often about commissioning, contracting, and marketization processes through this lens. More important than polarizing questions about which sector is 'better' (public or private), may be the question of whether or not processes and outcomes of marketization, as they are unfolding in their variously nuanced forms, strengthen and protect, or undermine and erode, fairness, justice, compassion, and humanity.

SELECTED FURTHER READING

For those interested in exploring policy responses of austerity to the global financial crisis and thinking about how these have shaped marketization decisions in criminal justice, Blyth's *Austerity: the History of a Dangerous Idea* (2013) provides an engaging and powerful critique. In thinking more broadly about how economic and social policy reforms are reframing conceptions and experiences of work and the workplace, Lipsky's *Street Level Bureaucracy: Dilemmas of the Individual in Public Service* (1980) is an important starting point, developed in interesting ways by Zacka in his doctoral thesis at Harvard University 'When the State meets the Street: Moral Agency and Discretionary Power at the Frontlines of Public Service' (2014). Hepple's article in the *Industrial Law Journal* 'Back to the Future: Employment Law under the Coalition Government' (2013) offers a lively account of policy-making in the employment law field, which is highly accessible for non-lawyers. A wealth of commissioning and contracting material can also be found on the government's Contracts Finder website (https://www.gov.uk/contracts-finder).

REFERENCES

ANDREW, J., BAKER, M., and ROBERTS, P. (2016), *Prison Privatisation in Australia: The State of the Nation. Accountability, Costs, Performance and Efficiency*, Sydney: University of Sydney Business School.

ARMSTRONG, R. and MARUNA, S. (2016), 'Examining imprisonment through a social justice lens', in S. Farrall, B. Goldson, I. Loader, and A. Dockley (eds), *Justice and Penal Reform: Reshaping the Penal Landscape*, Oxford: Routledge.

AUSTRALIAN PRODUCTIVITY COMMISSION (2016), Report on Government Services 2016, ch. 8, vol. C, attachment tables, available at: http://www.pc.gov.au/research/ongoing/report-on-government-services/2016/justice/corrective-services, accessed 11 January 2017.

AUTY, K. and LIEBLING, A. (submitted), 'Exploring the relationship between prison social climate and reoffending'.

BACON, C. (2005), 'The evolution of immigration detention in the UK: the involvement of private sector companies' Refugee Studies Centre working paper no.27, Oxford: University of Oxford.

BLYTH, M. (2013), *Austerity: the History of a Dangerous Idea*, Oxford: Oxford University Press.

BOBBITT, P. (2002), *The Shield of Achilles: War, Peace and the Course of History*, London: Penguin.

BOSWORTH, M. (2014), *Inside Immigration Detention*, Oxford: Oxford University Press.

BRADFORD, B. and QUINTON, P. (2014), 'Self-legitimacy, police culture and support for democratic policing in an English constabulary', *British Journal of Criminology*, 54(6): 1023–46.

BURKE, L. and COLLETT, S. (2016), 'Transforming rehabilitation: organizational bifurcation and the end of probation as we knew it?', *Probation Journal*, 63(2): 120–35.

CARRABINE, E. (2005), 'Prison riots, social order and the problem of legitimacy', *British Journal of Criminology*, 45(6): 896–913.

CARTER, P. (2003), *Managing Offenders, Reducing Crime: A New Approach*, London: The Stationery Office.

COLEMAN, R. and SIM, J. (2005), 'Contemporary statecraft and the punitive obsession: a critique of the new penology thesis', in J. Pratt, D. Brown, S. Hallsworth, M. Brown, and W. Morrison (eds), *The New Punitiveness: Current Trends, Theories and Perspectives*, Cullompton: Willan.

CREWE, B. and LIEBLING, A. (2012), 'Insider views of private sector competition', in Helyar-Cardwell (ed.), *Delivering Justice: the Role of the Public, Private and Voluntary Sectors in the Prison System*, London: Criminal Justice Alliance Publications.

CREWE, B., LIEBLING, A., and HULLEY, S. (2011), 'Staff culture, use of authority and prisoner quality of life in public and private sector prisons', *Australian & New Zealand Journal of Criminology*, 44(1): 94–115.

CREWE, B., LIEBLING, A., and HULLEY, S. (2014), 'Heavy-light, absent-present: rethinking the "weight" of imprisonment', *British Journal of Sociology*, 65(3): 387–410.

CROUCH, C. (2011), *The Strange Non-Death of Neoliberalism*, Cambridge: Polity.

CZERNIAWSKI, G. (2016), 'A race to the bottom—prison education and the English and Welsh policy context', *Journal of Education Policy*, 31(2): 198–212.

D'AMICO, D. (2010), 'The prison in economics: private and public incarceration in Ancient Greece', *Public Choice*, 145(3–4): 461–82.

DEERING, J. and FEILZER, M. (2015), *Privatising Probation: is Transforming Rehabilitation the end of the Probation Ideal?*, Bristol: Policy.

DOMINEY, J. (2016), 'Fragmenting probation: recommendations from research', *Probation Journal*, 63(2): 136–43.

FAULKNER, D. (2014), *Servant of the Crown: A Civil Servant's Story of Criminal Justice and Public Service Reform*, Hampshire: Waterside.

FEELEY, M. and SIMON, J. (1992), 'The new penology: notes on the emerging strategy of corrections and its implications', *Criminology*, 30(4): 449–74.

FOX, C. and ALBERTSON, K. (2011), 'Payment by results and social impact bonds in the criminal justice sector: new challenges for the concept of evidence-based policy?', *Criminology & Criminal Justice*, 11(5): 395–413.

GARLAND, D. (2002), *The Culture of Control*, Chicago: University of Chicago Press,

GARLAND, D. (2013), 'Penality and the penal state', *Criminology*, 51(3): 475–517.

GEORGIA DEPARTMENT OF AUDITS AND ACCOUNTS PERFORMANCE AUDIT DIVISION (2014), 'Misdemeanour Probation Operations, performance audit report no. 12-06, April 2014.

GVA (2012), 'Findings and lessons learned from the early implementation of the HMP Doncaster payment by results pilot', Ministry of Justice Research Series 18/12, November 2012, available at: https://www.gov.uk/government/uploads/system/uploads/attachment_data/file/217388/hmp-doncaster-payment-by-results-pilot.pdf, accessed 11 January 2017.

GVA and Carney Green (2015), 'HMP Doncaster Payment by Results pilot: final process evaluation report', Ministry of Justice Analytical Series, available at: https://www.gov.uk/government/uploads/system/uploads/attachment_data/file/449494/hmp-doncaster-pbr-final-evaluation.pdf, accessed 11 January 2017.

Hallett, M. (2006), *Private Prisons in America: A Critical Race Perspective*, Chicago, Ill: University of Illinois Press.

Harding, R. (1997), *Private Prisons and Public Accountability*, Buckingham: Open University Press.

Harding, R. (2001), 'Private prisons', in M. Tonry and J. Petersilia (eds), *Crime and Justice: A Review of Research*, vol. 28, Chicago: University of Chicago Press.

Hepple, B. (2013), 'Back to the Future: Employment Law under the Coalition Government', *Industrial Law Journal*, 42(3): 203–23.

Hood, C. (1991), 'A public management for all seasons?', *Public Administration*, 69(1): 3–19.

House of Commons Home Affairs Committee (1987a), 'Third Report of the Home Affairs Committee: State and Use of Prisons, 1986-87, HC 35', London: House of Commons.

House of Commons Home Affairs Committee (1987b), 'Fourth Report of the Home Affairs Committee: Contract Provision of Prisons, 1986-87, HC 291', London: House of Commons.

House of Commons Justice Committee (2015), 'Prisons: Planning and Policies, ninth report of session 2014–15, HC 309', London: The Stationery Office.

House of Commons Public Accounts Committee (2014), 'Contracting Out Public Services to the Private Sector, 47th report of session 2013–14, HC 777', London: The Stationery Office.

HM Government (2013), 'Cross Government Review of Major Contracts: Summary of Findings and Recommendations Endorsed by the Oversight Group', available at: https://www.gov.uk/government/uploads/system/uploads/attachment_data/file/268800/Cross_Government_Review_of_Major_Contracts_Summary_Report.pdf, accessed 11 January 2017.

HM Inspection of Probation (2016), 'A Thematic Inspection of the Delivery of Unpaid Work', available at: https://www.justiceinspectorates.gov.uk/hmiprobation/wp-content/uploads/sites/5/2016/01/Unpaid-Work-Thematic-report.pdf, accessed 11 January 2017.

HM Treasury (2010), 'Spending Review 2010', Cm 7942, available at: https://www.gov.uk/government/uploads/system/uploads/attachment_data/file/203826/Spending_review_2010.pdf, accessed 11 January 2017.

HMP Ford Independent Monitoring Board (2015), Annual Report November 2014 to October 2015, available at: http://www.imb.org.uk/wp-content/uploads/2016/02/Ford-2014-15.pdf, accessed 11 January 2017.

Human Rights Watch (2014) 'Profiting from Probation: America's "Offender-Funded" Probation Industry', available at: https://www.hrw.org/sites/default/files/reports/us0214_ForUpload_0.pdf, accessed 11 January 2017.

Institute for Government (2013), 'Making Public Service Markets Work: Professionalising Government's Approach to Commissioning and Market Stewardship', London: Institute for Government, available at: http://www.instituteforgovernment.org.uk/sites/default/files/publications/Making_public_service_markets_work_final_0.pdf, accessed 11 January 2017.

Johnston, L. (1992), *The Rebirth of Private Policing*, London: Routledge.

Jones, T. and Newburn, T. (2005), 'Comparative criminal justice policy-making in the US and the UK: the case of private prisons', *British Journal of Criminology*, 45(1): 58–80.

King, R. and McDermott, K. (1989), 'British prisons 1970-1987: the ever-deepening crisis', *British Journal of Criminology*, 29(2): 107–28.

Le Grand (2007), *The Other Invisible Hand: Delivering Public Services through Choice and Competition*, Princeton: Princeton University Press.

Le Vay, J. (2016), *Competition for Prisons: Public or Private?*, Bristol: Policy.

Lewis, D. (1997), *Hidden Agendas: Politics, Law and Disorder*, London: Hamish Hamilton.

Liebling A. (2004), 'The late modern prison and the question of values', *Current Issues in Criminal Justice*, 16(2): 202–19.

Liebling, A. (2006), 'Lessons from prison privatization for probation', in M. Hough, R. Allen, and U. Padel, *Reshaping Probation and Prisons: The New Offender Management Framework*, Bristol: Policy.

Liebling, A. (2008), 'Titan prisons: do size, efficiency and legitimacy matter?', in M. Hough, R. Allen, and E. Soloman (eds), *Tackling Prison Overcrowding: Build More Prisons? Sentence Fewer Offenders?*, Bristol: Policy.

Liebling, A. (2011), 'The cost to prison legitimacy of cuts', *Prison Service Journal*, 198: 3–11.

Liebling, A. with Arnold, H. (2004), *Prisons and their Moral Performance: A Study of Values, Quality and Prison Life*, Oxford: Clarendon Studies in Criminology, Oxford University Press.

Liebling, A. and Crewe, B. (2013), 'Prisons beyond the new penology: the shifting moral foundations of prison management', in J. Simon and R. Sparks (eds), *The Sage Handbook of Punishment and Society*, London: Sage.

Liebling, A., Crewe, B., Hulley, S., Hutton, M., Clay, N., and Kant, D. (2012), 'Understanding prisons: extended MQPL and SQL exercises: HMP Birmingham', unpublished Prisons

Research Centre report, Institute of Criminology, Cambridge: University of Cambridge.

Liebling, A., Hulley, S., Clay, N., Hutton, M., Kant, D., and Ludlow, A. (2013), 'Birmingham prison: a benchmark study, one year on', unpublished Prisons Research Centre report, Institute of Criminology, Cambridge: University of Cambridge.

Liebling, A. and Ludlow, A. (2016), 'Suicide, distress and the quality of prison life', in Y. Jewkes, B. Crewe, and J. Bennett (eds), *Handbook on Prisons*, Oxford: Routledge.

Liebling, A. and Ludlow, A. (forthcoming), 'Privatising public prisons: penality, law and practice', *Australia & New Zealand Journal of Criminology*, Online First, doi/full/10.1177/0004865816671380.

Liebling, A., Price, D., and Shefer, G. (2011), *The Prison Officer*, Oxford: Willan Publishing.

Liebling. A., Schmidt, B., Crewe, B., Auty, K., Armstrong, R., Akoensi, T., Kant, D., Ludlow, A., and Ievins, A. (2015), 'Birmingham prison: the transition from public to private sector and its impact on staff and prisoner quality of life—a three year study', NOMS Analytical Summary.

Lipsky, M. (1980), *Street-level Bureaucracy: Dilemmas of the Individual in Public Services*, New York: Russell Sage Foundation.

Loader, I. and Walker, N. (2006), 'Necessary virtues: the legitimate place of the state in the production of security', in J. Wood and B. Dupont (eds), *Democracy, Society and the Governance of Security*, Cambridge: Cambridge University Press.

Ludlow, A. (2012), 'Competition and contestability in action: restructuring the prison sector to achieve workforce and industrial change', *Public Law*, 3: 508–26.

Ludlow, A. (2014), 'Transforming Rehabilitation: what lessons might be learned from prison privatization?', *European Journal of Probation*, 6(1): 67–81.

Ludlow, A. (2015), *Privatising Public Prisons: Labour Law and the Public Procurement Process*, Oxford: Bloomsbury.

Maguire, M. and Raynor, P. (2016), 'Offender management in and after prison: the end of "end to end"?', *Criminology & Criminal* Justice, 1–20.

Medway Improvement Board (2016), 'Final Report of the Board's Advice to Secretary of State for Justice', available at: https://www.gov.uk/government/uploads/system/uploads/attachment_data/file/523167/medway-report.pdf, accessed 11 January 2017.

Mills, A., Meek, R., and Gojkovic, D. (2012), 'Partners, guests or competitors: relationships between criminal justice and third sector staff in prisons', *Probation Journal*, 59(4): 391–405.

Ministry of Justice (2013), 'Contract Management Review', London: MoJ, available at: https://www.gov.uk/government/publications/contract-management-review, accessed 11 January 2017.

Ministry of Justice (2014), 'Peterborough Social Impact Bond, HMP Doncaster, Payment by Results pilots: final re-conviction results for cohorts 1', available at: https://www.gov.uk/government/uploads/system/uploads/attachment_data/file/341682/pbr-pilots-cohort-1-results.pdf, accessed 11 January 2017.

Narey, M. (2001), Speech to the Prison Service Conference, Nottingham, Feb 2001.

NAO (2013), 'The Ministry of Justice's Electronic Monitoring Contracts, HC 737', London: National Audit Office.

NAO (2014a), 'Transforming Government's Contract Management, HC 269', London: National Audit Office.

NAO (2014b), 'Home Office/Ministry of Justice: Transforming Contract Management, HC 268', National Audit Office.

NAO (2015), 'Outcome-based Payment Schemes: Government's Use of Payment by Results, HC 86', London: National Audit Office.

NAO (2016), 'Transforming Rehabilitation, HC 951', London: National Audit Office.

NOMS (2013), Business Plan 2013–2014, available at: http://www.no-offence.org/pdfs/22.pdf, accessed 11 January 2017.

Nemeth, C. (1989), *Private Security and the Law*, Cincinnati: Anderson.

Padfield, N. (2006), 'A critical perspective on private prisons in England and Wales', in N. Capus *et al.* (eds), *Public–Privé: Vers un nouveau partage du contrôle de la criminalité*, Chur: Verlag Rüegger.

Padfield, N. (2016), 'The magnitude of the offender rehabilitation and "through the gate" resettlement revolution', *Criminal Law Review*, 2: 98–114.

Pastor, J. (2003), *The Privatization of Police in America*, London: McFarland and Company.

Petersilia, J. (2008), 'California's correctional paradox of excess and deprivation', *Crime and Justice: A Review of Research*, 37(1): 207–78.

Podmore, J. (2015), Submission to the Economic Regulation Authority, Inquiry into the Efficiency and Performance of Western Australian Prisons, unpublished report, August 2015.

Pollitt, C. and Bouckaert, G. (2011), *Public Management Reform: A Comparative Analysis—New Public Management, Governance, and the Neo-Weberian State*, 3rd edn, Oxford: Oxford University Press.

Prison Reform Trust (2016), 'Bromley Briefings—Prison: the facts', Summer 2016, available at: http://www.prisonreformtrust.org.uk/Publications/Factfile, accessed 17 January 2017.

RAND Europe (2014), 'Phase 2 report from the payment by results Social Impact Bond pilot at HMP Peterborough', Ministry of Justice Analytical Series, available at: https://www.gov.uk/government/uploads/system/uploads/attachment_data/file/325738/peterborough-phase-2-pilot-report.pdf, accessed 11 January 2017.

RAND Europe (2015), 'The payment by results Social Impact Bond pilot at HMP Peterborough: final process evaluation report', Ministry of Justice Analytical Series, available at: https://www.gov.uk/government/uploads/system/uploads/attachment_data/file/486512/social-impact-bond-pilot-peterborough-report.pdf, accessed 11 January 2017.

ROBINSON, G., BURKE, L., and MILLINGS, M. (2015), 'Criminal justice identities in transition: the case of devolved probation services in England and Wales', *British Journal of Criminology*, 56(1): 161–78.

RODRIK, D. (1998), 'Why do more open governments have bigger governments?', *Journal of Political Economy*, 106(5): 997–1032.

RYAN, M. and WARD, T. (1989), *Privatization and the Penal System: The American Experience and the Debate in Britain*, Milton Keynes: Open University Press.

RYNNE, J. and HARDING, R. (2016), 'Private prisons', in Y. Jewkes, B. Crewe, and J. Bennett (eds), *Handbook on Prisons*, Oxford: Routledge.

RYNNE, J., HARDING, R., and WORTLEY, R. (2008), 'Market testing and prison riots: how public-sector commercialization contributed to a prison riot', *Criminology & Public Policy*, 7(1): 117–42.

SANDEL, M. (2013), *What Money Can't Buy: The Moral Limits of Markets*, London: Penguin.

SENNETT, R. (2006), *The Culture of the New Capitalism*, New Haven: Yale University Press.

SIMON, J. (2007), *Governing through Crime: How the War on Crime Transformed American Democracy and Created a Culture of Fear*, Oxford: Oxford University Press.

SIMON, J. and FEELEY, M. (1995), 'True crime: the new penology and public discourse on crime', in T. Blomberg and S. Cohen (eds), *Punishment and Social Control*, New York: Aldine de Gruyter.

SPARKS, R. (2003), 'Punishment, populism and political culture in late modernity', in S. McConville (ed.), *The Use of Punishment*, Oxford: Willan.

SPARKS, R. and BOTTOMS, A. (1995), 'Legitimacy and order in prisons', *British Journal of Sociology*, 46(1): 45–62.

STELMAN, A. (2007), 'From probation to the National Offender Management Service: issues of contestability, culture and community involvement', *Probation Journal*, 54(1): 91–2.

STUCKLER, D. and BASU, S. (2013), *The Body Economic: Why Austerity Kills*, London: Allen Lane.

TANKEBE, J. (2014), 'Rightful authority: exploring the structure of police self-legitimacy', available at: http://dx.doi.org/10.2139/ssrn.2499717, accessed 11 January 2017.

TAYLOR, P. and COOPER, C. (2008), '"It was absolute hell": inside the private prison', *Capital & Class*, 32(3): 3–30.

TOMCZAK, P. and ALBERTSON, K. (2016), 'Prisoner relationships with voluntary sector practitioners', *The Howard Journal of Crime and Justice*, 55(1–2): 57–72.

UGLEVIK, T. (2014), 'The incarceration of foreigners in European prisons', in S. Pickering and J. Ham (eds), *The Routledge Handbook on Crime and International Migration*, Oxford: Routledge.

VAN DER HOEVEN, R. and SZIRACZKI, G. (eds) (1997), *Lessons from Privatization: Labour Issues in Developing and Transitional Countries*, Geneva: International Labour Office.

WHITE, A. (2015), 'The politics of police "privatization": a multiple streams approach', *Criminology & Criminal Justice*, 15(3): 283–99.

YOUNG, J. (2007), *The Vertigo of Late Modernity*, London: Sage.

ZACKA, B. (2014), 'When the state meets the street: moral agency and discretionary power at the frontlines of public service', unpublished dissertation submitted in partial fulfilment of the requirements for the degree of Doctor of Philosophy in Political Science, Cambridge, MA: Harvard University.

ZEDNER, L. (2006), 'Liquid security: managing the market for crime control', *Criminology & Criminal Justice*, 6(3): 267–88.

CHAPTER ACKNOWLEDGEMENTS

I am grateful for colleagues' helpful comments on earlier drafts of this chapter, especially Alison Liebling, John Rynne, and Gareth Evans. All errors are my own.

41

YOUTH JUSTICE

Lesley McAra

> In all actions concerning children, whether undertaken by public or private social welfare institutions, courts of law, administrative authorities or legislative bodies, the best interests of the child shall be a primary consideration.
>
> (Article 3: United Nations Convention on the Rights of the Child)

> Penal discourse is as much concerned with its projected image, public representation and legitimacy, as it is with organising the practice of regulation.
>
> (David Garland, Punishment and Welfare, 1985)

> Just because they're young doesn't mean they're not human beings—they're still people and they still have rights.
>
> (Cohort Member aged 18, Edinburgh Study of Youth Transitions and Crime)

INTRODUCTION

This chapter explores the founding principles, operational functioning and impact of the institutions which have evolved across the four nations in the United Kingdom to deal with children and young people who come into conflict with the law. Its principal empirical focus will be the shifting patterns of control which have emerged over the past 20 years: a period defined by major transformations in the architecture of youth justice in a wider context of rapid social, political, and economic change. As I aim to demonstrate, this recent history has been characterized by a persistent disjuncture between: (1) normative claims about youth justice (as exemplified by the best interests principle of the United Nations Convention on the Rights of the Child, cited above); (2) the ways in which policy discourse on youth justice has been utilized as part of an on-going legitimation (statecraft) project in response to a range of global and sub-state dynamics; and (3) the impact of youth justice practice on the lives of the young people who are made subject to its tutelage, with research indicating that, despite a welcome reduction in the number of young people entering the youth justice system, interventions are often experienced as dehumanizing and undermining of basic entitlements (McAra 2016; McAlister and Carr 2014; Webster 2015; Goldson 2013). My overall argument will be that, unless there is better alignment between these three dimensions—the normative, the political, and the experiential—justice for children and young people cannot and will never be delivered.

As highlighted in the editors' introduction to this volume, the *Oxford Handbook of Criminology* should be regarded as a living archive. Each of the past five editions has included a chapter on youth justice, and whilst the overall structure and content of these chapters has changed over time (as has the authorship), together they provide a weighty and authoritative body of knowledge about the history and development of youth justice (especially in England and Wales). In this new chapter, I do not intend to replicate this history but rather to explore its legacies with regard to the nature and function of youth justice as it has evolved into the second decade of the twenty-first century.

The chapter begins with an exploration of the normative framings of youth justice as found in the raft of international conventions to which the UK is currently signatory, and the dominant paradigms which have come to shape both criminological and political debate. It then tracks in more detail the changes made to youth justice policy across the four nations and interrogates the drivers of these variant transformations. This is followed by a review of recent research on young people's experience of contact with systems of justice. The chapter concludes with some reflections on the future of youth justice in these uncertain and somewhat turbulent times.

KEY PARADIGMS AND NORMATIVE FRAMINGS

The categories of childhood, adolescence, and youth are highly contested and their deployment in policy debate is often closely tied to particular ideological visions for society: as Sukarieh (2012) reminds us, we always need to pay critical attention to '[who is doing] the talking, in what contexts and to what political and economic ends' (2012: 427–8).

At the global level normative framings of youth justice in late modernity have been characterized by the search for a universe of discourse—a shared set of narratives with which to promote a sense of common purpose amongst a community of states and to enable judgements to be made about the moral efficacy of particular systems of justice. International rights conventions and associated protocols are of course exemplars of this cosmopolitan dynamic. By contrast at the state or sub-state level, framings have been characterized by greater complexity and contingency, with the ebb and flow of paradigms being more overtly bound up with the politics of place. I'm going to begin this section of the chapter with a critical review of human rights conventions and identification of some of the conceptual and practical limitations of this global project. This will be followed by a review of the more localized paradigms which have been evoked in youth justice policy as it has evolved within the UK. Rather than exploring the contexts of their deployment (picked up in the second section of this chapter), I am going to treat them as ideal types, offering a deconstruction of their ontological assumptions including the nature of personhood and model of social relations which underpin their core maxims. In doing so the aim is to reconnect the reader with first principles about justice for children.

INTERNATIONAL CONVENTIONS AND THE RIGHTS OF THE CHILD

A range of international rights conventions and protocols offer protections to children who come into conflict with the law, and these form a touchstone against which the precepts, processes, and impacts of youth justice systems worldwide can be assessed. These conventions include: the UN Convention on the Rights of the Child (UNCRC) (1989); the UN Standard Minimum Rules for the Administration of Juvenile Justice (the Beijing Rules, 1985); the UN Guidelines for the Prevention of Juvenile Delinquency (the Riyadh Guidelines, 1990); and the UN Rules for the Protection of Juveniles Deprived on their Liberty (the Havana Rules 1990). In addition, the European Convention on Human Rights (1950) contains general provisions which also apply to children within signatory states and the more recent European Charter of Fundamental Rights (2000) also gives explicit protections to children in EU member states only.

A close reading of these conventions reveals a range of conflicting imperatives, not least the way in which childhood is invoked as a universal category whilst at the same time cultural norms and political specificity are utilized as delimiting criteria (see, e.g., Harris-Short 2003, McAra 2010; Put and Walgrave 2006). The search for a global narrative, acceptable to all signatories, has, arguably, resulted in a degree of vagueness in terms of drafting, leaving some articles open to wide interpretation. International conventions, for example, define a child as someone below the age of 18 (UNCRC, Article 1; Havana Rules, Article 11a) but do not specify a minimum limit for the age of criminal responsibility, with the Beijing rules (Article 4.1.) stating that it should not 'be fixed at too low a level bearing in mind the facts of emotional, mental and intellectual maturity' —which of course may differ from child to child and be judged differently according to political and cultural context. The Havana Rules state that there should be an age limit below which it is not permitted to deprive a child of liberty, but again do not specify what this should be (other than it must be 'determined by law', Rule 11a).

The Beijing Rules, in particular, contain competing imperatives as between the rights of the child and the needs of society (Rule 2.3); and highlight at one and the same time the need for interventions to be parsimonious (emphasizing prevention, diversion, and community-based programmes with custody as a last resort—Rules 1.1, 1.2, 1.3, 11.1 to 11.4, and 19.1) and proportionate both to the seriousness of the offence and the circumstances of the offender (emphasizing here the provision of care, protection, educational, and vocational skills, Rule 5.1). There is no consideration as to how these imperatives can be balanced. Indeed the rules acknowledge that, in terms of implementation, cognizance needs to be paid to the 'economic, social and cultural conditions prevailing in each Member state' (Rule 1.5), with the implication that there may be widespread variation as to interpretation of need or parsimony. Similarly, Article 40, 4 of the UNCRC states that children must be dealt with in a manner appropriate to their well-being and proportionate both to their circumstances and the offence. While the UNCRC foregrounds the 'best interests of the child' as the core principle in decision-making, again there is no clear definition as to what best interests might constitute.

Taken together these conventions and protocols straddle uneasily the precepts of justice and welfare (see Table 41.1, p. 942)—a conceptual mash-up of responsibilization and child protection—eloquent testimony to some of the ambiguities in contemporary theorizing about child development (see Tisdale and Punch 2012 for an overview). The danger in the lack of specificity is that it potentially enables state actors to find ways of finessing shortcomings in protections offered to children without seeming to flout particular articles. As evidence, witness the major variation across signatory states with regard to the age of criminal responsibility: at the time of writing, age 8 in Scotland (although this is currently under review); age 10 across the rest of the UK; contrasted with age 15 in Finland and Sweden and age 18 in Belgium (for most offences) (Goldson 2013).

Aside from these ambiguities the UN conventions and protocols have been criticized because they lack teeth. The principles of the UNCRC are intended to become legally binding norms and the UN has constructed a system for monitoring implementation, which includes periodic reporting by state signatories to which a specially designated UN committee responds (see http://www.ohchr.org/EN/HRBodies/CRC/Pages/CRCIntro.aspx). However countries are enabled to place reservations on whether they take up particular dimensions of the conventions and the monitoring committee is considered by some to be weak in term of the powers at its disposal to hold states to account. While the monitoring committee can investigate individual complaints, it relies for the most part on shaming or chastizing states in its published responses.

At the time of writing (summer 2016), the efficacy of the rights framework is currently under scrutiny by the UK Conservative government. It was elected on a mandate to abolish the Human Rights Act 1998 (which integrated the European Convention on Human Rights into UK law), with proposals to create a British Bill of Rights. Human rights groups have expressed concerns about the potential for weakened protection that such a development may bring. However, even more pressingly, the result of the EU referendum within the UK (for 'Brexit'), if implemented, will mean that the stronger legal protections for children that currently exist via the European Charter of Human Rights will be lost[1] (see Locke 2016).

DOMINANT PARADIGMS IN UK POLICY

The conceptual mix of justice and welfare, highlighted above, also inheres in the dominant framings of youth justice which have evolved across the UK over the past 150 years, since the first specialist institutions were developed, to deal with the problems posed

[1] Regarding children, the Charter states that the best interests principle, the promotion of well-being, and the views of children must inform decision-making. As Locke argues: if an Act of Parliament contradicts the Charter rights 'any UK court [is] obliged not to apply that Act in the case before it. By contrast, under the Human Rights Act [it is only the] senior courts that make a declaration of incompatibility . . . and this does not change the outcome of the case—the Act [in question will] remain applicable—[it] merely opens up an expedited route for amending the Act'.

Table 41.1 Juvenile justice paradigms

	Just deserts	Welfare	Restorative	Actuarial	Desistance	Diversionary
Personhood	Child as rights bearer Individuals constitutionally self-interested	Child as bearer of entitlements Individuals a product of experience	Child as bearer of entitlements and rights Individuals constitutionally 'good'	Child qualified bearer of rights Individuals potentially 'bad'	Child as bearer of rights Individual identity product of interplay between structure and agency	Child as bearer of rights Individuals product of social encounters
	Offender as rational and responsible The rational man	Offender as non-rational, irresponsible The patient	Offender as rational and responsible The penitent	Offender as dangerous The commodity	Offender as self-determining The flawed identity	Offender adapts to ascribed identities The deviant status
Social relations	Core relationships: Contractual-state vs. individual citizen	Core relationships: Nested model of state, community family, child	Core relationships: Inclusive-child, victim and community	Core relationships: Adversarial-community vs. potential offender	Core relationship: Inclusive: child and community	Core relationship: reflexive regulatory practices shaping individual sense of self
	Didactic	Transformative	Integrationist	Protective	Redemption	Preventative
	Audience: Citizens	Audience: Offender and family	Audience: Community and victims	Audience: Public	Audience: Offender and community	Audience: The child
	Sensibility: Retribution (Vengeance)	Sensibility: Philanthropy (Paternalism)	Sensibility: Connection (Infliction of shame)	Sensibility: Fear (Hate)	Sensibility: Connection (Exclusion)	Sensibility: Rational calculus (Managerialist)
Intervention	Deter and punish	Diagnose and to rescue	Support victims, restore harm, reconnect child to community, build more cohesive peaceful community	Diminish current and future risk, safeguard victims and wider community	Support recovery and establishment of 'real me' identity, build effective practitioner-child relationships, asset based	Diminish negative effects of regulatory practices and support inclusion
	Proportionality to deeds, parsimony	Proportionality to needs	Proportionality to harm caused	Proportionality to risk	Proportionality to need for value change and agentic rediscovery in context of wider opportunity	Proportionality to pernicious consequences of agency impact

Source: Adapted from McAra (2010) and McAra and McVie (2015).

by troublesome children. Indeed the youth justice institutional complex arose out of impulsions both to rescue children but also to punish them (Gelsthorpe and Kemp 2013). Children were simultaneously conceived as being vulnerable, lacking in full capacity, requiring intervention to address their needs, and as rationally calculating individuals whose transgressions deserved swift and proportionate sanctioning. The reformatory movement in the nineteenth century exemplifies this somewhat internally conflicted approach (see McAra and McVie 2015).

The 20-year period from the mid 1990s to the present day, which forms the central focus of this chapter, has been characterized by increased complexity in institutional understandings of youth offending and the types of intervention which constitute an appropriate response. Indeed it is possible to identify four key paradigms which have now been grafted onto youth justice systems across the UK: restorative, actuarial, diversionary, and desistance. Here I deconstruct their core precepts.

As shown in Table 41.1, the *restorative paradigm* conceives children as having both positive entitlements and rights, with personhood understood as being shaped directly by the community and cultural context (Zehr and Mika 1998). As with the 'just deserts' paradigm, offenders are considered to be rational, with the capacity to take responsibility for their behaviour but crucially also acknowledge the suffering which they have caused. The key problematic for this paradigm is to determine the age at which young people can be said to have evolved the capacity to understand the consequences of action, but also its effect on others so that meaningful apology can be made. Victims are a key audience within this paradigm, and intervention is aimed at restoring the harm caused and reconnecting the child with the community.

The *actuarial model* frames the child primarily in terms of his or her capacity or potential for wrong doing with needs constructed as evidence of risk. The nature of intervention deemed suitable in particular cases is calibrated according to the level of risk posed (in extreme cases such interventions may require to be indeterminate in nature), with the objective of protecting society and preventing future victimization. Expert input to risk assessment is needed, to ensure that early intervention is targeted appropriately. As I have argued elsewhere (McAra 2010), offenders within this paradigm become a commodity to be assessed, with the principal audience for intervention being the wider public. By viewing the child's behaviour and their immediate family and social context as signifiers of risk, this paradigm provides a justification for intervention even before the child is born and also far beyond the transition into adulthood (should risk be assessed as high): a life-course approach to offender management.

The *diversionary paradigm* stems primarily from the work of Smith and colleagues at Lancaster (see Smith 2010), and has been further developed as an ideal type by McAra and McVie (2015). This paradigm is predicated on labelling theory. Whilst the child is conceived as a rights bearer, their identity and sense of self is predominantly a product of social encounters. Where such encounters produce negative or 'spoiled' versions of selfhood, then this undermines the child's right to develop in dignity. The deviant status is a conferred identity, which can be exacerbated by interactions with authority. Regulatory practices always have consequences in terms of shaping the child's sense of self, and in evolving a diversionary practice, the aim is to prevent the emergence and reproduction of deviance as an identity. This involves careful systems management and rational calculation of the potential for harm in terms of intervention.

The key problematic for the diversionary paradigm is to ensure that both the age of criminal responsibility and the period of transition to adulthood are managed in non-stigmatizing and non-criminalizing ways: and this is suggestive of greater alignment between these ages than in other paradigms (the abolition of criminalization of children until they reach the age of majority).

Finally the *desistance paradigm* (as exemplified in the work of McNeill 2006, see also Shapland and Bottoms this volume), views identity as a product of soft-determinism. The emphasis of intervention is to support the construction of a non-offender identity, to enable redemption (through 'making good', Maruna 2001), with relationships between the practitioner and the child key to personal transformation. However opportunities have to be consciously constructed, so that asset-based approaches to intervention, which build social capital, can be turned into practical action. A key aim of the desistance paradigm is to promote social inclusion and connection. In contradistinction to the diversionary paradigm, the nature of identity does not become stuck or transposed by external labelling processes. It is a more fluid conception, underpinned by a strong sense of self-determination. Intervention is not inherently criminogenic, to the extent that it can facilitate the process of positive change—enabling offenders to reconstruct flawed identities, and overcome the exclusionary dynamics which may inhere within wider society. As applied to youth justice, the key problematic for this paradigm is to gauge the age at which the capacity for self-determination, for understanding the impact of behaviours on others, and to atone for wrong-doing, is reached.

The point of deconstructing the above paradigms is to emphasize the major differences between their imperatives and demonstrate the potential for tension and contradiction when they are invoked simultaneously in policy debate. Indeed, as will be demonstrated later in the chapter, young people today have to actively negotiate their way through a tutelary complex which simultaneously holds them to account for their actions (as per the justice, restorative, and desistance paradigms), whilst acknowledging that their age, stage, and circumstance render them vulnerable and lacking in full capacity (as per the welfarist and diversionary paradigms). Such ambiguity has the potential to undermine the legitimacy of youth justice interventions in the eyes of the young people who become the object of regulation.

Nonetheless, ambiguity in normative framings may endure as a political strategy—not least because the young people who come within the purview of youth justice are very rarely (if ever) conceived as a core group to whom governments look, to shore up support. History shows us that conflicted narratives can sometimes attain a degree of hegemony, as witness the longevity of penal-welfarism in the early to mid-twentieth century (see Garland, this volume). Indeed, there is evidence from a range of jurisdictions that the law and regulatory orders of late modernity seek to establish authority by deploying narratives of fear and risk at the same time as narratives of intimacy and connectedness, as states grapple with the complexities of 'belongings and otherings' against a backdrop of global and more localized transformations and pressures (McAra 2010). Importantly, there can be a degree of political pragmatism in the selection and deployment of the variant paradigms within the tutelary complex, as much as ideological commitment to their normative underpinnings, and governments often play on the sensibilities (both negative and positive, see Table 41.1) that inhere within core paradigms as a means of asserting the right to rule. What then have been the contexts in which the above paradigms have been invoked across the UK over the past two decades? How has youth justice in practice been utilized as an element of political strategy and with what effects? It is to these questions that the next section of the chapter turns.

YOUTH JUSTICE IN THESE ISLES

In his seminal 1996 article 'The Limits of the Sovereign State', David Garland reviewed the variant penal strategies deployed by governments in so-called high crime societies (including the UK and USA). According to Garland, high crime rates undermined one of the nation-state's foundational claims to legitimacy—namely to provide security for its citizens within its own territorial boundaries. In adaptation to this challenging environment, governments evolved new modes of governing crime, through the promulgation of two distinctive narratives: (1) the criminology of everyday life in which the criminal was constructed as a flawed consumer rather than a pathological misfit, and crime control strategies focused on empowering citizens and communities to inhibit crime opportunities; (2) the criminology of the other, which played on popular fears and insecurities by constructing the criminal as an outsider, differentiated from 'us' by labels such as 'sex beasts' or 'yobs', thereby justifying a more punitive and authoritarian response.

Some 20 years later we have come to a new crossroads. Far from remaining a high crime society, recorded crime rates in the UK (and other western jurisdictions) are at their lowest for many decades (see Maguire and McVie, this volume). As part of the UK national governments' on-going quests for legitimacy they have had to adapt to a number of critical junctures: the terrorist attacks in New York (9/11), London (7/7), and Glasgow (6/30) with ongoing implications for national and international security, including the so-called war on terror; the global economic crash in 2008 and its continuing fallout; the constitutional transformations precipitated by devolution across Scotland, Northern Ireland, and Wales; and even the more recent turmoil caused by the United Kingdom's referendum on membership of the European Union (which has highlighted populist anxieties around the themes of immigration, asylum, and race). Taken together these critical junctures highlight the significance of both globalized and more localized (sub-state) dynamics for understanding the ways in which the power to punish is currently exercised, justified, and reproduced. In contrast to the world described by Garland in 1996, youth justice has adapted to these dynamics by the appropriation and deployment of a more complex set of penal discourses than hitherto (as set out in the previous section of the chapter), discourses which have become instruments within the broader polity building and democratizing projects across the four nations which make up the United Kingdom. As I aim to demonstrate these discourses have come to play more of a role in the construction of a legitimate image for the 'penal state' (Garland 2013), than they have in transforming the organizational practices of youth justice in ways that are experienced as empowering by those who become subject to their tutelage (a theme to which I will return in the third section of the chapter). I take each nation in turn.

ENGLAND

The recent history of youth justice in England has been characterized by massive upheaval and change, particularly over the New Labour years from 1997 to 2010 (in which a range of new initiatives was introduced in every single year in the form of programmes, pilot initiatives, action plans, green papers, and statutes). In the more recent era of coalition and then Conservative-led government in the UK, youth justice has become less of a priority, but the turbulence in the system has continued.

1997–2010: The reforming zeal

The New Labour government made 'youth justice' a centre piece of its emergent strategy of governance, framed by the mantra 'tough on crime, tough on the causes of crime'. In doing so it demonstrated a number of stochastic[2] features of 'statecraft' which were also reflected in the devolved nations within the UK as they sought to establish their right to rule. These features were: *differentiation* from the past; construction of new or revised institutional *architecture*; selection and nurturing of new *audiences* (groups to whom policy 'speaks'); and, as has already been foregrounded, introducing greater *complexity* into policy discourse.

In terms of differentiation, the New Labour government sought to distinguish itself from the previous extremely punitive conservative administration, by declaring that the principal aim of youth justice was to prevent offending by children and young people, with system development predicated on the three Rs: Restoration, Responsibility, and Reintegration. In order to deliver the new youth justice, the Labour government grafted onto the existing framework of youth courts, a innovative institutional architecture including the development of a new Youth Justice Board, with statutory authority to monitor, advise on standards, and disseminate good practice in youth justice. Additionally, local authority youth offending teams (YOTs), multi-disciplinary in orientation (with representatives from probation, social work, police, health, and education) were conceived to coordinate provision of youth justice services (enabled by the Crime and Disorder Act 1998). Finally, youth offender panels were established (by the Youth Justice and Criminal Evidence Act 1999). The latter comprised two lay members from the local community and a YOT member and dealt with first time offenders under the age of 16 appearing before the courts and who had pled guilty (a contract was to be agreed with the young person which might include reparation or restitution to the victim).

The evolving statutory framework introduced a raft of new orders and schemes (examples are set out in Table 41.2), widening the reach of youth justice to include the troublesome behaviour of those below the age of criminal responsibility (via child safety orders) and taking a more structured approach to police discretion (with the new reprimand and final warning scheme). Controversially the rebuttal presumption

[2] By stochastic, I mean exhibiting a pattern of behaviour but one which is not always substantively predictable.

Table 41.2 Examples of new 'orders' and schemes

	Statute
Anti-social behaviour order (for anyone age 10+ acting in a manner likely to cause harassment, alarm, stress to one or more persons)	Crime and Disorder Act 1998
Parenting orders	
Child safety order (for under-10s where behaviour would constitute crime if age 10+)	
Local child curfew	
Reparation order	
Reprimand and final warning scheme	
Detention and Training Order (comprises period in custody and supervision in the community)	
Referral orders Youth offender contracts	The Youth Justice and Criminal Evidence Act 1999
Attachment of electronic monitoring or curfew condition to any community order	Criminal Justice and Court Services Act 2000
New sentences for under-18s including public protection sentence for serious violent or sexual offences	Criminal Justice Act 2003
Drug Testing and Treatment Order as part of supervision order or action plan order	
Extension of police powers to disperse groups of young people	Anti-social Behaviour Act 2003
Parenting contracts where children excluded from school, truanting or antisocial behaviour	

of *doli incapax* was abolished—meaning that for children between the ages of 10 and 14, the prosecution no longer had to prove that the young person was capable of forming the intent to commit a crime, separate from the fact that a crime had been committed (the so-called 'adulterization' of children, Goldson and Muncie 2006).

Importantly, the preventative orientation of youth justice drove an institutional architecture in which risk management narratives could thrive. Access to services was predicated on risk assessment (using tools such as ASSET). The actuarial imperative also extended to the more rehabilitative dimensions of emergent policy such as *Youth Inclusion Programmes* for 13 to 16 year olds (implemented in 2000) or *Positive Action Programmes* for those aged between 8 and 19 (implemented from 2003). These were targeted at young people who had been assessed as being at risk of offending, truancy, or school exclusion. A government review in 2007 entitled *Building on Progress Security and Justice,* placed further emphasis on prevention, with YOTs being required to intervene in children's lives at the earliest possible point on the basis of a range of triggering risk factors.

This complex range of orders was rationalized somewhat by the *Criminal Justice and Immigration Act* 2008 which introduced the Youth Rehabilitation Order as a replacement for other court based orders, but this was an order which had 18 different potential requirements! In addition the *Youth Crime Action Plan* of 2008 set out a target of reducing the number of first-time entrants to the youth justice system below the age of 18 by one fifth by 2020, accompanied by a triple strategy of 'non-negotiable' support and targeted interventions for the 110,000 so-called 'high risk families' whose children were identified as being most likely to become prolific offenders. And finally a scaled approach to risk management was operationalized by the Youth Justice Board from 2009, with the aim of finessing the relationship between risk, the sentence of the court, and the nature of intervention.

As this overview indicates, the normative framing of youth justice brought together a constellation of different paradigms: justice, welfare, actuarialism, and restoration, and generated a new set of audiences including victims and communities. Taken as a whole the new youth justice was underscored by a series of tensions—the promotion of social inclusion and citizenship at the same time as developing exclusionary and incapacitative intervention; increased responsibilization at the same time as increasing the tutelage of children and their families in every aspect of their lives and at each stage of the youth justice process. Moreover the costs of youth justice programmes increased massively over this period—with a 102 per cent increase in expenditure between 2001 and 2009 (the peak year of expenditure) (see Youth Justice Annual Accounts for the relevant years).

(ii) 2010 to Present: Austerity, diversion, and localism

From the reforming zeal of the new labour administrations, the new Conservative/Liberal Democrat coalition government which was elected in May 2010 instituted a change of direction, as the stochastic model of statecraft would anticipate. Greater emphasis was placed on diversion (adding it to the panoply of extant paradigms), and there was a loosening of controls on decision-making practices. For example the police were given greater discretion, with proposals to replace the reprimand and final warning scheme with a system of cautioning (as set out in the Legal Aid, Sentencing and Punishment of Offenders Bill 2012, now enacted). At the same time however proposals were also made to extend curfew hours and the maximum duration of Youth Rehabilitation Orders.

In keeping with the rules of statecraft, the immediate response of the coalition government was also to move the furniture around, with plans to abolish the Youth Justice Board and absorb its functions more centrally into a new youth justice division of the Ministry of Justice as part of a broader rationalization of non-departmental public bodies (although this was never implemented, see Souhami 2015).

The coalition government also published a green paper in 2010 *Breaking the Cycle: Effective Punishment, Rehabilitation and Sentencing of Offenders*, with a new emphasis on payment by results (to be measured principally by reductions in reoffending) and proposals for 'reinvestment grants' to be given to consortia of local authorities to achieve targeted reductions in the use of custody, and to widen the use of restorative justice. Through such measures the government aimed to install what it termed a 'rehabilitation revolution'. However the admixture of rationales in the title of the paper was not suggestive of simplification in the paradigmatic framing of youth justice, with the document also containing the familiar refrains of parental responsibilization, early intervention, and prevention for those at risk. Somewhat ominously, the extremely punitive reaction to the London Riots of 2011 indicated that the veneer of rehabilitation was extremely thin (Bateman 2012a).

The trialling of new national standards in 2012 was interpreted by some commentators as heralding a less prescriptive era, with the easing of some timescales and what Bateman (2012b) has termed the 'less mechanistic' use of risk and needs assessment tools. From 2013 there have been plans to alter dramatically the youth custodial estate, by decommissioning all custodial units for young women—and a consultation was set in motion (Transforming Youth Custody) with proposals to develop a new secure estate predicated on education (via secure colleges), with some residual secure home capacity for those under the age of 12. However, some elements of the reform programme were halted because of budgetary pressures, with the need to make major savings in the overall running costs: indeed the period of the coalition government was characterized by a major shrinking in total expenditure on programmes (with the annual accounts of the Youth Justice Board showing a reduction of around 50 per cent in total programme expenditure between 2010 and 2014).

Since the election of a majority conservative government in 2015, the future of youth justice has become somewhat uncertain, not least because political debates about youth justice have been notable by their absence. However a review of the youth justice system led by Charlie Taylor and put in place by the former Secretary of State for Justice (Michael Gove), produced its interim report in early 2016. Among the Report's key arguments included a call for educational inclusion and the need for greater devolution of youth justice to local areas (Ministry of Justice 2016a). This more rehabilitative ethos is also reflected in the four new resettlement consortia pilots, established in 2015–16 by the Youth Justice Board to support young people leaving custody, by linking them with educational or employment opportunities, ensuring availability of appropriate accommodation and access to coaching and life-skills training. It also infuses the more holistic approach to risk assessment being pioneered through AssetPlus (deployed from 2015). Were the May government to embrace the Taylor recommendations and roll out these pilot schemes more widely, then we should expect to see a new set of players and audiences emerge, as more localized agencies and institutions grapple for resources.

WALES

In Wales, devolution was enabled with the passage of the Government of Wales Act 1998. Initially the Welsh Assembly did not have primary law-making powers and youth justice was not (and, at the time of writing, is not yet) a devolved matter, nor were other aspects of policing and criminal justice. As such the new Welsh Assembly inherited the architecture of youth justice that was evolving across England and Wales (described above). However the New Assembly did have responsibility for the range of services which would normally partner with youth offending teams in delivering services including: children's services, health, social services, education, and housing.

In an effort to establish authority, the Welsh Assembly made a conscious effort to differentiate itself from what had gone before: in the words of Rhodri Morgan, to put 'clear red water' between Wales and England. This included the so-called 'dragonisation'

(Edwards and Hughes 2009) of much social policy. In doing so the Assembly embraced more explicitly a child rights perspective, focusing children's services on delivering a series of 'entitlements', which were universal (rather than targeted) and free at the point of need (Haines *et al.* 2013). '*Extending Entitlement*' was published in 2000 and was followed up in 2004 by a commitment to integrate the precepts of the UNCRC into policy-making for children and young people, and the publication of the *All Wales Youth Offending Strategy*. The latter marked a major step away from the hyper-intensive policy activity in England in terms of ethos, underscoring a more holistic (welfarist) approach to dealing with young people who come into conflict with the law, based on the mantra 'children first offenders second'. For the first time concerns were also expressed about the cultural and resettlement needs of young people from Wales who were remanded or served custodial sentences across the border in England. This theme was taken up by the Howard League in Wales in their report *Thinking Beyond Prison* Bars (2009), which stated that Welsh children imprisoned in England was 'the worst possible option' (2009: 6).

The holistic approach gained further purchase as the devolved arrangements grew in maturity. The Wales Act 2006 gave the Assembly primary law-making powers over 20 areas of policy. Importantly this included legislative competence for social services, health and education, which, under the terms of the Crime and Disorder Act 1998, were required to contribute staffing and resources to Youth Offending Teams. Indeed, Drakeford (2010) has estimated that up to 70 per cent of the total budgets for youth offending teams in Wales has come from agencies which are not under the control of the Youth Justice Board and UK central government.

While the Youth Justice Committee for Wales has worked closely with the Youth Justice Board to build a distinctive policy framework for the devolved nation, interrogation of joint documents highlights some of the difficulties in attempting to follow a more progressive agenda within the architecture of a broader system. For example Haines (2009) has pointed to the potential for conflict between different dimensions of the *All Wales Youth Offending Strategy*. Although the Strategy emphasizes more welfarist imperatives, it also states a need for balance between the interests of the child and the community, with restorative and punitive measures being highlighted as core components of that balance alongside 'supported rehabilitation'. Such tensions continue to beset the delivery plan for the strategy (published in 2009).

Since 2008, there has been a gradual but marked grafting of the diversionary paradigm onto the wider child rights ethos (as exemplified by the multi-agency Swansea Bureau Model, see Haines *et al.* 2013), along with early intervention programmes (such as *Families First*) aimed at reducing the numbers of young people coming into the youth justice system. These developments have been followed up by the Welsh government *Youth Crime Prevention Fund* (delivered since April 2013), to resource diversion schemes based, *inter alia*, on education, training, sports, and the arts, and have culminated in the publication of *Children and Young People First* (2014). The latter is a joint initiative of the Welsh Government and the Youth Justice Board and pulls together and re-emphasizes commitments to: the needs of the child, holistic and multi-agency services, as well as early intervention and diversion. It also highlights the importance of reducing the harm that may be caused by criminal justice contacts, with further emphasis on the needs of victims and their capacity to participate in restorative processes. This links too to the enhanced case management approach piloted from 2013–14, predicated on trauma informed practice.

Within Wales, the grafting of new paradigms onto the youth justice complex and the consistent attempts to differentiate approaches from those in England (especially with regard to overall ethos), has been the result of a creative and negotiated set of practices, improvising within the delimits of the devolutionary infrastructure. Following the recommendations of the Welsh government commissioned Morgan Report on devolution and youth justice (2010), and the findings of the Silk commission on devolution (2011), proposals have been made to devolve youth justice fully to Wales, with a longer term commitment to devolve policing and criminal justice.

NORTHERN IRELAND

In Northern Ireland, a devolved Assembly was established as result of the Belfast/Good Friday Agreement 1998 although it has had a somewhat turbulent history and has had various periods of suspension. As with the other jurisdictions, developments relating to youth justice have followed a similar pattern (differentiation, construction of new architecture and new audiences, and added complexity in paradigmatic framings), but one adapted to the political and cultural dynamics of a post-conflict and traumatized civic society.

Prior to the Belfast Agreement, youth justice in Northern Ireland was broadly shaped by the same legislative and policy developments as in England (McVie 2011). It was primarily a court-based model (see McAra 2010) with a dedicated youth court for children aged between 10 and 17, although children, under certain circumstances could be tried in the adult courts. However, under the terms of the Agreement, a criminal justice review was set up, and this included a review of arrangements for children who come into conflict with the law. A particular ambition was to ensure that human rights infused any emergent institutional frameworks. The recommendations of the review were given statutory footing with the passage of the Justice (Northern Ireland) Act 2002. This included a set of specified aims for youth justice, the primary ones being to protect the public and (similar to England) to prevent offending, but a key objective of the system was also to secure the welfare of the child—a somewhat conflicted framework. The Youth Justice Agency was set up in 2003 to oversee developments. (Initially linked to the Northern Ireland Office, the Agency is now based in the Justice Department following the formal devolution of criminal justice in 2010).

A particularly distinctive feature of youth justice in Northern Ireland since the turn of the century, has been the major focus on restorative justice. This focus on mediation and negotiation was partially a result of Northern Ireland's distinctive history of conflict and peace-making. The first conferencing service was introduced in Belfast in 2003 and conferencing was rolled out nationally in 2006. Conferences can be held at different stages of the youth justice process, for example, prosecutors are empowered to use conferencing as an alternative to prosecution and the courts can issue a conferencing order as disposal on conviction.

Further innovations introduced by the 2002 Act, but which were linked more closely to the public protection and welfare components of the youth justice policy frame, were community responsibility orders (for low level offenders which would involve instruction in citizenship and practical activities, followed in 2004 with an anti-social behaviour agenda) and a custody care order to accommodate young people aged between 10 and 13 in the child care system rather than being held in custody with older children (see O'Mahoney and Campbell 2004 for further discussion). Diversion also came to the fore with a formal Youth Diversion Scheme implemented in 2003 as a replacement for the juvenile justice liaison scheme (which had been in operation since 1975), with specialist officers triaging cases.

From the mid-2000s onwards a particular trend has been increased emphasis on the more welfarist dimensions of the policy frame. The Office of the First Minister and the Deputy First Minister published a 10-year strategy for children and young people in 2006 which was predicated on a holistic approach to supporting the well-being of children. Both the *Strategic Framework for Reducing Offending* (Department of Justice 2013) and the *Delivering Social Change document* (Northern Ireland Executive), developed these themes with recognition, respectively, that the root causes of offending generally require interventions that are beyond the reach of the criminal justice system (e.g. improving the well-being and life chances of vulnerable individuals), with explicit commitments to tackle poverty, improve health, and install the UNCRC obligations into frameworks for action. Importantly the demands of the UK government Northern Ireland Office to implement similar arrangements to England for non-negotiable support for at risk children and families, were rejected, with a focus instead on the provision of intergenerational support to build trust and more positive relationships with young people. Following the Youth Justice Review 2011 (see also the third section of this chapter below), there has been a rationalization of youth custody with all young prisoners now being held in Woodlands Secure Centre. Lastly, a more recent emphasis has been placed on desistance, with a commitment in 2015 by the Justice Minister to embed desistance theory into criminal justice policy and practice, including youth justice. A further paradigm grafted onto an already somewhat complex conceptual mix.

SCOTLAND

Since the Act of Union in 1707, Scotland has always had a separate legal and educational system and the quasi-state which evolved in the form of the Scottish Office enabled a somewhat autonomous approach to matters of justice to flourish. Prior to devolution juvenile justice was characterized by a strong commitment to welfarism, enshrined in the Social Work (Scotland) Act 1968 which set in train the children's hearing system and turned over to social work the former remit of the probation service, with a statutory commitment to promote social welfare. The children's hearing (lay tribunal) system is aimed at early and minimal intervention focused on the needs of the child, and avoiding criminalization and stigma (see Kilbrandon 1964). Cases are referred to the Reporter who assesses whether there is a *prima facie* case that at least one ground for referral to a hearing has been met and that the child is in need of compulsory measures of care. Scotland has always been in an anomalous position by dealing with 16 and 17 year olds mostly in the adult criminal justice system (although supervision requirements can be extended up to the age of 18 and the courts can refer young people back to the hearings). Importantly, prior to devolution the children's hearing system became caught up with identity politics, symbolic of difference between Scotland and

England (particularly when there was a retreat from welfarism in England from the 1970s onwards, and where such signifiers of divergence within Scotland became part of a constitutional claim of right for self-determination) (McAra 2011, 2016).

Somewhat paradoxically the early years after devolution were accompanied by greater convergence in youth justice, with the new labour/liberal democratic coalition government looking south of the border for inspiration. As with the other devolved jurisdictions, this stemmed from a mode of polity building predicated on *differentiation*. The new era was characterized by major architectural expansion: over a 100 new institutions were created along with the introduction of national standards and fast tracking procedures. Youth courts were piloted, with the then Cabinet Secretary for Justice stating that 'punishment' was a key part of the youth justice process (a statement unthinkable 10 years previously). Whilst the children's hearing system remained at the heart of youth justice, a range of competing rationales were imported into policy including restorative measures (police restorative cautioning), actuarialism, as well as just deserts. Victims too became an important audience for youth justice, highlighted as a discrete and morally deserving group. Families of young offenders also began to be the object of regulation. Specific examples of borrowings include the antisocial behaviour agenda from 2004 which introduced anti-social behaviour orders for under 16 year olds, (only around 15 were ever made); parenting orders (none of which were ever made), and curfews. Stringent targets were set for reduction in the number of persistent offenders by 10 per cent in two years (from a curiously specified base-line of 1201!).

From 2007 there has been a Scottish National Party (SNP) administration in Scotland, elected (first as a minority government) on a more progressive social democratic and preventative agenda. This heralded a period of further transformation in youth justice (in accordance with the precepts of statecraft). Existing targets were scrapped, and the overtly tough rhetoric about youth crime was replaced by a more nuanced discourse. The publication of the policy document *Preventing Offending by Young People: A Framework for Action* marked the first major statement of intent. This contained a multiplicity of conflicted ambitions, including a return to a more welfarist approach with an emphasis on health and education and a more holistic approach to child development. Victims and the wider community too were highlighted as key audiences. The document also contained elements of a 'just deserts' paradigm, foregrounding proportionality and responsibilization. Whilst multi-agency partnership working and early intervention were flagged as key to service delivery, emphasis was placed on the need to build individual, family and community capacities to address barriers faced. This was somewhat akin to the desistance paradigm's asset based approach, but crucially highlighting individual responsibilities and duties. Once the SNP became a majority administration (from 2011–16) and following the stochastic dynamic of governance, it made further changes to the architecture of justice, with some degree of centralization, including the construction of a national children's panel (previously this was locally based), and most notorious of all, the construction of a single national police force. With this rationalization has come a greater focus on diversion, as exemplified by the Whole System Approach (set out in *Preventing Offending: Getting it Right for Children and Young People*, Scottish Government 2015).

In Scotland the age of prosecution has been raised to 12 (with the implementation of the Criminal Justice and Licensing [Scotland] Act 2010), and serious consideration is being given to raising the age of criminal responsibility from 8 to 12. There has also been legislative change to ensure that offences admitted during children's hearings could be classified as alternatives to prosecution rather than convictions, to remove stigma (see Children's Hearing [Scotland] Act 2011). The wider justice strategy for Scotland is predicated on an inclusive approach—with an overt commitment to the production of a flourishing society. This has made incursions into policies for young people in custody, with Polmont Young Offenders Institution implementing an educational regime, one of great ambition but somewhat challenging to implement (see HMIPS 2016). Taken together these more recent developments highlight greater commonalities with the other devolved nations than hitherto, with a degree of convergence between Wales and Northern Ireland in terms of overall ethos and approach.

FINAL REFLECTIONS

This short history, has shown how youth justice discourse has been shaped by the imperatives of statecraft and polity building not only across the newly devolved nations but also in England from 1997 onwards. Much political effort has been expended to highlight differences from previous modes of governance, and to create a new architecture for a more complex set of paradigmatic framings and audiences. As the quotation from Garland at the head of this chapter states, representation, projected image, and search for legitimacy have each underscored key developments. While particular policy narratives come to 'make sense' at key stages (thus restorative imperatives make sense in the context of post-conflict societies, and rights-based child-centred approaches make sense in the context of the more progressive and creative policy-making context in Wales), governments display a high level of pragmatism when grafting new sets of paradigms onto extant frameworks. Thus it is unsurprising that actuarialism was embraced by the government in England (and Wales) in the late 1990s as a means of demonstrating its capacity for control and that diversion has been embraced at a time of economic uncertainty, given that it may reduce reliance on more expensive disposals and help cut the number of young people entering the justice system (see Drakeford 2010). In adapting to these sub-state and more globalized dynamics, systems have transcended the bifurcated strategies described by Garland in 1996, and embraced a multiplicity of 'criminologies' linked to versions of the child offender as: penitent; commodity; flawed identity; and deviant status (see Table 41.1).

How then are these complex framings translated into the day-to-day practice of institutions delivering services, and how are they experienced by the children and young people who become subject to their tutelage? These are subjects of the third and final section of the chapter.

IMPACTS OF YOUTH JUSTICE

At the start of the chapter I included a rather heartfelt quotation from a cohort member of the Edinburgh Study of Youth Transitions and Crime, reflecting on his treatment at the hands of the police and the justice system in Scotland. His negative perception, arguably,contrasts quite sharply with what might be seen as the major success story of youth justice in recent years: the sustained reductions (across all UK jursdictions) in the number of young people coming within the ambit of youth justice. Framed by these twin positionings, this final section offers some reflections on the efficacy of youth justice systems, with regard to their capacity to deliver justice to children and young people. It touches on the following three questions: is there any evidence that the activity of youth justice systems across the UK has led to reductions in youth crime; are these systems operating in accordance with the international human rights standards to which the UK is signatory; and how far and in what ways have institutions of youth justice contributed to the well-being and flourishing (best interests) of the young people who become subject to their tutelage?

HAVE YOUTH JUSTICE SYSTEMS REDUCED YOUTH CRIME?

The relationship between crime and punishment has always been a vexed one. As David J. Smith has observed, fluctuations in the crime rate are more likely to have been impacted by social and economic changes, than the influence of the criminal justice system (Smith, D. J. 1999). Research has consistently shown that rule-breaking is widespread in the teenage years, but that only a small proportion of rule-breakers are caught and processed by institutions of youth justice. For example the Edinburgh Study of Youth Transitions and Crime found that over 96 per cent of its cohort of 4,300 young people admitted to at least one of the offences included in the questionnaire during their teenage years, whereas only around 12 per cent were ever referred to the Reporter on offence grounds. Research and official statistics also consistently show that the 'captive' population tends to be drawn from the most poor and dispossessed families and neighbourhoods (across all UK jurisdictions), and contains disproportionately high numbers of young people from ethnic minority groups (especially in England and Wales) (McAra 2016; YJB 2016, see also Bowling and Phillips, this volume).

Given these selection effects, the relationship between system intervention and crime reduction is likely to be more complex and contingent than policy documents and statements of national standards might suggest. Indeed a linear relationship is often assumed in these documents between interventions and outcomes; by contrast research studies have shown that youth justice outcomes are often confounded by broader contextual factors beyond the control of either the individual child or the deliverers of intervention (Gray 2013). Moreover official targets for crime reduction generally focus on reconviction rather than reoffending rates, and the former are arguably a better measure of institutional activity than they are of individual behaviour.

Much of the knowledge-base about the impact of system contact on behaviour at the individual level comes from research evaluating specialist programmes (as for example the 'what works' literature, see McGuire 1995) and/or exploring the nature and quality of relationships built up between the practitioner and the young person (as found in some variants of desistance research, see also Shapland and Bottoms, this volume). Only rarely does research take a more holistic approach to analysis, examining the cumulative effects of systemic processing on young people over time and critically engaging with the wider contexts (social, cultural, political) within which such processing takes place (Smith 2010;

McAra and McVie 2007; Gray 2013). Two (potentially interrelated) phenomena might, however, be taken as evidence of system impact: firstly (as noted above) the major reductions which have occurred over the past decade in the numbers of young people who are caught up and processed by youth justice institutions and secondly the so-called 'crime drop'. I will offer some comments on each in turn.

The shrinking client group

Recent trends suggest that the 'captive' population is in decline across all jurisdictions which make up the UK.[3] Whilst the UK does have an aging population and the number of young people in the general population has correspondingly reduced, this does not in itself explain the shrinking client group of youth justice. As shown in Figures 41.1 to 41.3, pp 957 and 958, when statistics on youth justice activity are expressed as a rate per 1000 population rather than a raw number, the reductions are (with only a few exceptions) both marked and sustained. Thus within Scotland there have been major reductions in the rate of offence referrals to the Reporter since 2005–06 (by 83 per cent). In England and Wales over the same time frame there has been a reduction of 78 per cent in the rate of first time entrants to youth justice,[4] with a 21 per cent reduction in first-time entrants also evident in Northern Ireland since 2011–12 (analysis is limited here because of data availability). Custody rates too have dramatically declined across the jurisdictions, with a 60 per cent reduction in both the rate per 1000 population of 16 and 17 year olds in custody[5] (Scotland), and 10 to 17 year olds held in the secure estate (England and Wales). Whilst Northern Ireland too has experienced a long-term reduction in the use of custody for children, rates have been more stable in years since the new Woodlands Juvenile Justice Centre has been open (since 2007).

Part of the decline in the youth justice client group may be attributable to a greater emphasis on diversion within the youth justice policy frames across the four nations (Bateman 2012a). However, it is important not to overstate the impact of diversionary policies, as there is evidence of major local variations in terms of youth justice practice within each jurisdiction, at odds with the aggregate national level rates, and some of the reductions highlighted above predate the implementation of diversionary policies (Muncie 2011; Haines and Case 2015; Kelly and Armitage 2015). For example, within Northern Ireland, custody rates were already in decline at the point at which restorative diversionary initiatives were implemented (see Goldson 2011), and within Scotland referrals to the Reporter were on a similarly downward trajectory well before the implementation of the Whole System Approach.

More significantly there is evidence that some systems are rather less successful than others at reducing reconviction rates for those young people who do become sucked

[3] Comparative data are difficult to generate, because of differences in institutional architecture, the age range and scope of youth justice across each of the four nations, and changes in the law and recording procedures which render time trend data somewhat problematic. Gaining access to historical data, including disaggregated data from Wales and England, and clear and consistent data from Northern Ireland has presented some challenges. Scotland has the most comprehensive and accessible statistical resources.

[4] The rate of first-time entrants in England and Wales has been calculated from Youth Justice Board statistics and population data from the Office for National Statistics (ONS).

[5] Rate calculated from Scottish Prison Statistics and population data from the National Records of Scotland. Young people under 16 can be held in secure care for offending and for care and protection: these groups are not disaggregated in published data.

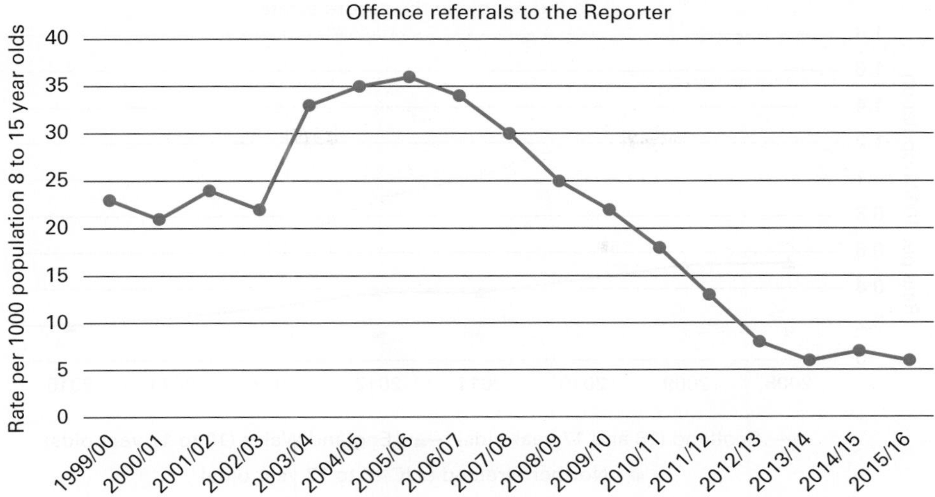

Figure 41.1 Scotland
Source: Scottish Children's Reporter Administration statistics and population data from the National Records of Scotland.

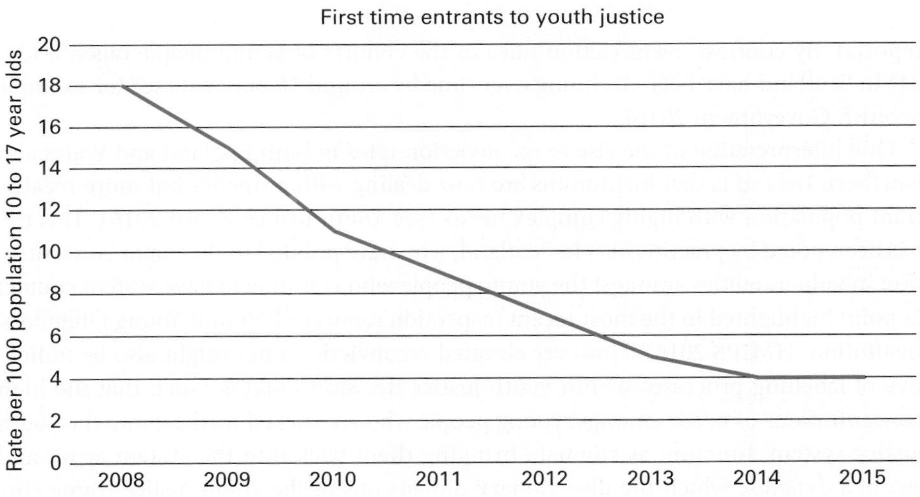

Figure 41.2 England and Wales
Source: Youth Justice Board statistics and population data from the Office for National Statistics (ONS).

into the system. Each jurisdiction publishes data which tracks the subsequent conviction histories of cohorts of young people who have had system contact (although the data are not generated in exactly the same way across the jurisdictions, so extreme caution is required in interpreting trends). The latest figures for England and Wales suggest that reconviction rates amongst recent cohorts have risen by 10 per cent (since 2003) to a peak of 38 per cent for the most recently followed up cohort (Ministry of Justice 2016b). For Northern Ireland, only very short-term data are accessible but they too mirror the pattern in England and Wales, with reconviction rates rising by around 18 per cent in the cohorts between 2010–11 and 2013–14 (Youth Justice Agency

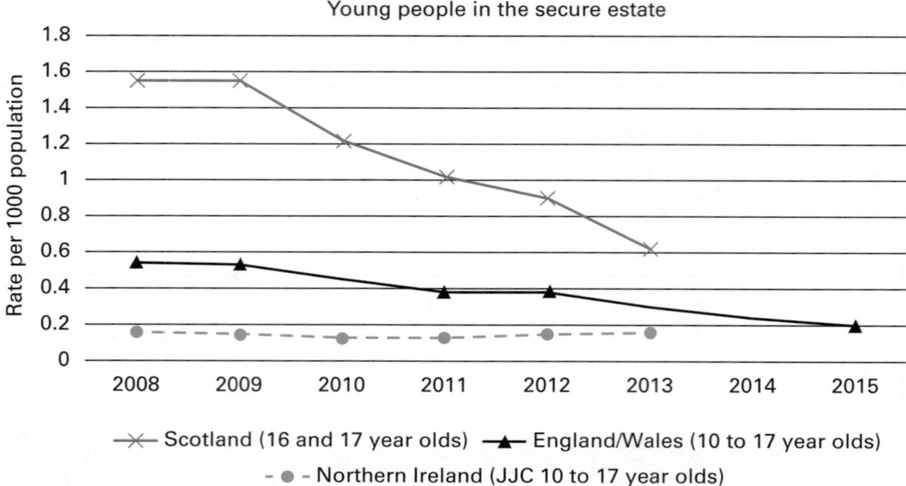

Figure 41.3 Comparative custody rates

Source: Scottish Prison Statistics and population data from the National Records of Scotland, Youth Justice Board statistics and population data from the Office for National Statistics, and Northern Ireland Youth Justice Agency annual workload statistics.

reports). By contrast, reconviction rates in the cohorts of young people (aged under 21) in Scotland have been declining over time by around 16 per cent (see for example Scottish Government 2016).

One interpretation of the rise in reconviction rates in both England and Wales and Northern Ireland is that institutions are now dealing with a smaller but more recalcitrant population with highly complex needs (see Youth Justice Board 2016). This too has been noted by practitioners in Scotland, who have pointed to the major concentration in vulnerabilities amongst the young people who continue to have system contact (a point highlighted in the most recent inspection report of Polmont Young Offenders' Institution, HMIPS 2016). However elevated reconviction rates might also be indicative of labelling processes within youth justice decision-making (such that the high concentrations of needs amongst young people who are sucked furthest into the youth justice system, function as stigmata bringing them back into the system again and again, a dynamic which the diversionary dimensions of the youth justice frame currently leave unchallenged, see later in the chapter).

The 'crime drop'

As noted, the UK (along with many other western jurisdictions) is said to have experienced an overall drop in crime from around the mid-1990s, with youth crime showing a particularly sharp downward trend (see Maguire and McVie, this volume). Somewhat ironically much of the evidence mustered by theorists of the crime drop, to demonstrate that such a drop has in fact occurred, comes from official statistics of criminal convictions and police-recorded crime (rather than from self-reports). So the 'crime drop' may well be the result of transformations in youth justice activity rather than actual reductions in criminal behaviour.

Potential explanations for the crime drop have focused on a diverse range of factors from the growth of target hardening and other crime prevention measures which have inhibited property crime, to the declining use of lead in petrol (with presumed behavioural impacts) and even the legalization of abortion (leading to reductions in the population) (see McAra and McVie, this volume for further critical discussion). An alternative hypothesis, however, might be that youth crime has not really declined very much, but that traditional modes of counting and recording are not simply agile enough to keep pace with transformations in sites of youthful transgression (see, e.g., Cesaroni *et al.* 2012).

Many young people are not 'available' for policing in ways that marked institutional activity in past decades—a shift from hanging around the streets to embracing mobile technologies and the wider digital world somewhere 'indoors'. Here offending might take the form of online bullying, sexual harassment, extreme pornography, trolling, skimming, and scamming, to name but a few. Arguably, the fluid nature of youth cultures, the changing modalities of urban governance (see Bannister and Flint, this volume), and shifts in patterns of consumption, open up new crime opportunities and new possibilities for the criminal imagination. Moreover the splintering of the borders between the public and private spheres which digital technology brings, may result in new and more intensive forms of vulnerability for those who become the victims of exclusionary practices, not always within the reach of youth justice institutions as currently constituted.

In sum, the answer to the question posed about the relationship between youth justice policy and youth crime reduction is that we do not know with any certainty the causal direction (if any) of the relationship, not least because of the paucity of self-reported offending data, the shifting situational contexts of crime, and the lack of information about emergent forms of digital and online crime. Whilst the shrinking number of young people caught up in formal measures and the reductions in youth custody are very welcome, without more detailed understanding about the drivers of such processes, the sustainability of these downward trajectories is somewhat open to question.

DO YOUTH JUSTICE SYSTEMS COMPLY WITH INTERNATIONAL HUMAN RIGHTS STANDARDS?

There is evidence that the jurisdictions across the UK have systematically flouted aspects of international norms over many years. As highlighted in the first section of this chapter, the United Nations routinely monitors the progress which signatory states have made in promoting the rights of the child. The most recent UN response was published in July 2016 and highlighted a number of aspects of institutional arrangements and functioning in all four nations which were of major concern. I pick out here some of the core thematics linked to the situation of children who come into conflict with the law.

Firstly, all UK jurisdictions were chided about the age of criminal responsibility, which was considered to be far too low. The use of custody too came under critical scrutiny. Whilst the declining numbers of young people in custody was praised, nonetheless the committee was of the view that they were still disproportionately high. Critical comments were also made about the nature of life sentences for children convicted of murder and the Committee also felt more could be done to make custody a disposal of last resort—with a recommendation to ensure that this was enshrined in statute across all four nations. Linked to this, concerns were expressed about the continued use of solitary confinement and inappropriate use of restraint within secure institutions, as well as lack of access to education and to health services. The Committee's findings in this regard find some support in the recent Panorama programme (January 2016) on Medway Secure Training Centre which uncovered major mistreatment of children, and in the Howard League's review of restraint, solitary confinement, and strip-searching of children 10 years on from the Carlile Inquiry (Howard League 2016). This latter review found that the rate of restraint had more than doubled over the past five years in England and Wales, that pain was still being used illegally to ensure compliance, and that children were often locked in their cells for 23 hours a day. While a review into conditions at Medway has recently reported, the Howard League's conclusions make for bleak reading.

The UN monitoring committee also made critical comments about police stop and search powers, with concerns expressed about discriminatory practices and the need to end all non-statutory stops. Tasering or use of 'energy projectiles' against children was highlighted as a key problem as was concern about the use of acoustic devices (such as 'mosquitos) to disperse children from public places. Again these findings are reflected in research. For example, within Scotland, Murray (2015) has highlighted the massive increase in police stops over recent years and the ways in which these fall disproportionately on young people from poor neighbourhoods, and in England and Wales the Equality and Human Rights Commission (2013) has reported that young people from ethnic minorities are six times more likely to be stopped than other young people.

A further concern identified by the Committee relates to the 'best interests' principle. Here the UK was criticized for failing to install this principle in all decision-making practices relating to children. Linked to this, serious concerns were also expressed about levels of child poverty across the UK, the high levels of inequality, as well as discriminatory use of school exclusion. And finally the UN monitoring report noted that the state parties had made insufficient efforts to counter negative public attitudes towards children and in particular older children and those from minority groups, including ethnic minorities and faith groups, travellers, children of asylum seekers and migrants, those with disabilities, and LGBT groups. These comments touch on major concerns (alluded to earlier) regarding the disproportionate number of Black and Minority Ethnic young people within the youth justice system in England and Wales and particularly within the secure estate. For example, Youth Justice Board figures show that in 2014–15, 40 per cent of prisoners under the age of 18 were from ethnic minority backgrounds. Whilst efforts are being made to develop diversity toolkits (see Youth Justice Board report 2016), and there has been a joint commitment by the Department for Education and the Youth Justice Board to tackle issues of diversity and equality within the care system, more work is urgently needed to address these issues.

Taken together, a reading of the monitoring reports produced since the UK became signatory to the UNCRC, indicates that most of the above issues are longstanding in nature, with seeming recalcitrance exhibited by both the UK national government and the devolved nations in embracing *fully* the child rights framework (as evidence see the similarity between issues raised in the July 2016 monitoring report and the committee's response to the UK and NI period report of 1999, (United Nations 2002), in terms of age of criminal responsibility, nature and use of custody, poverty and inequality, and discrimination). This is a troubling indictment of institutional practices across England and the devolved nations.

DO YOUTH JUSTICE SYSTEMS CONTRIBUTE TO THE WELL-BEING OF YOUNG PEOPLE?

Finally, how far do youth justice systems contribute in practice to the flourishing of the young people who come within their ambit? Whilst there is evidence that committed and highly trained practitioners, well-resourced programmes, and carefully managed diversionary initiatives can make a major difference to the lives of young people (see McNeill and Weaver 2010; Smith 2010), there is a growing body of evidence which points to major shortcomings in the capacity of youth justice systems to deliver some of their fundamental objectives.

Each of the youth justice systems across the four nations does emphasize child well-being and highlights the need to partner with other agencies (health, education, social work). However, youth justice is, in itself, a somewhat blunt instrument for the coordination and delivery of holistic services. With greater devolution and an emphasis on localism, there is potential for an uneven spread of services across each jurisdiction and consequently geographic variation in the experience of young people (see Kelly and Armitage 2015). Additionally, payment by results within England and Wales runs the risk of skewing outcome measures, with further reification of reconviction rates as the principal metric of success. Local level (especially third sector) institutions are likely to become embroiled in a battle for survival, with pressures to deliver results to retain precious short-term funding: a commodification of justice in response to economic pressures to drive cost down (Yates 2012).

Many research projects from across the four nations have found a disjuncture between policy claims, the performance of institutions (in terms of their day to day cultural practices), and the impact on the young people who come under the criminal justice gaze, (McAra 2016; McAlister and Carr 2014). Gray (2013), for example, in her research on YOT partnerships in action in England, has highlighted the ways in which the fusion between needs and risk discourse in contemporary policy framings, means that the wider structural environment in which intervention takes place can never be fully challenged (thus reinforcing and reproducing extant inequalities).

Within Northern Ireland, although the restorative justice interventions here have been highlighted as exemplars of best practice, there is a cumulative body of evidence which suggests that young people often have very negative experiences of conferencing, with lack of participation from young people (including also victims), demeaning modes of questioning and discussions at conferences, exposure to multiple conferences, and disproportionality in terms of outcome agreements (McAlister and Carr 2014; Maruna *et al.* 2007). As Convery *et al.* (2008) have argued conferencing requires individuals to take responsibility for their behaviour but does not take account of the damaging and harmful structural contexts of their lives, nor does it afford in practice the active participation anticipated by human rights standards. Moreover whilst restorative justice may come to make sense as a political narrative in the post-conflict world, Harland and McCready (2014), have also highlighted the continued negative impact of paramilitary punishments and alternative community codes of justice on young men in Northern Ireland, as a profoundly negative backdrop to their involvement with the formal youth justice system.

(As was noted) just over 10 years after the new governance of Northern Ireland was instituted, a major review of youth justice (2011), found that there was still a need to build further trust between children and the police and that young people felt disrespected. While the review was complimentary about restorative processes it made some hard hitting comments about delays in the system, the need for greater involvement of victims, better training for lawyers representing children in the courts, better interagency working and more early intervention. The review also highlighted shortcomings in relations to rights protection. Although the Youth Justice Agency has taken formal steps to address the recommendations of the review, it is acknowledged that this may take many years, with critics noting that some of the more challenging recommendations have met with a 'lukewarm' response (Hamilton *et al.* 2016: 9).

Within Scotland a similar disjuncture between policy and practice has been found. The Edinburgh Study of Youth Transitions and Crime, for example, has strong evidence that the youth justice system consistently recycles a group of young people—the usual suspects—mostly drawn from the most impoverished communities, whilst the deeds of their more affluent counterparts are often overlooked. In modelling youth justice decision-making both cross-sectionally and longitudinally, the findings show how the working cultures of key institutions focus on poverty, and previous form (namely warning or charges, referrals to the children's hearing system, referrals to court in the previous year) as key markers for action and/or intervention. These cultures seem impervious to the changing political mores within which they are situated, highlighting a degree of institutional inertia over time in a context of more rapid discursive transformation at the level of policy debate (McAra 2016). The findings also demonstrate that the impact of contacts with the system have deleterious consequences for young people, by entrenching them in poverty and hence reproducing the conditions in which violence has been found to flourish (McAra and McVie 2015). These are the unintended effects of the tendency of governments to deliver policy change by focusing on institutional structures (architecture, as discussed in the second section of this chapter) rather than/or in addition to, the day-to-day practices or cultures of those who work within the system. While Study findings are supportive of a maximum diversionary approach to dealing with young people in conflict with the law, to diminish the criminogenic effects of agency contact, they also highlight the importance of tackling poverty and promoting a wide social justice agenda as being key to crime reduction and safer communities (McAra and McVie 2015). As the findings from research across the four nations can testify, youth justice systems by themselves cannot deliver on this agenda.

CONCLUSION

In this chapter I have explored the philosophical framings of debates on youth justice and deconstructed the complex set of discourses which have been deployed across the four nations in the UK over recent decades. Competing versions of childhood, the relationship between citizen and state, and the appropriate modes of intervention, have been grafted onto systems, with limited critical oversight of how contradictions will be negotiated by the practitioners in their day-to-day encounters with young people nor by the children and young people made subject to their tutelage.

Taken together the sections in this chapter highlight the ways in which youth justice systems are shaped by the evolving social, political, and economic contexts in which they are situated, but also can play a crucial role in the reproduction of political power. As I have argued, conflicted narratives come to 'make sense' to policy-makers and politicians in a context of localized pressures to establish the right to govern and more globalized pressures linked to economic crisis, and the anxieties and insecurities provoked by the war on terror; pressures which are more multi-layered than those described by Garland in 1996 when setting out the then limits of the sovereign state.

The drivers of polity building across the devolved nations, the impulsion for differentiation, the tendencies to deliver this via architectural transformation, and to introduce greater complexity in the narratives around youth crime and punishment, inevitably mean that governments have focused as much attention on their projected images and public representation as they do on making meaningful change to organizational cultures and their real world impacts on young people. These narratives are also being deployed against a backdrop of systematic violation of core components of international human rights standards, including and especially the age of criminal responsibility.

Youth justice systems are increasingly required to leverage resource and broker relationships between other agencies in order to support the young people in their care. That such activity fails to tackle the structural disadvantages faced by these young people and indeed sometimes serves to reproduce those disadvantages, reinforces the tragic qualities of justice, and creates a legitimation gap with profound consequences for the citizenship and inclusion of young people.

Fundamentally, to deliver justice for children who come into conflict with the law we need to reconcile the tensions between normative framings, their political deployment, and their impact on the lived experience of the young people themselves. As research shows, those who become the object of regulation are amongst the most vulnerable and dispossessed groups in our society. Recognizing the fragility and sometime skewed nature of the philosophical and institutional complex of youth justice is a first, but much needed, step towards real world transformation.

SELECTED FURTHER READING

As was noted, the *Oxford Handbook of Criminology* series constitutes a major archive of research on youth justice in its own right, with important essays by: Geoff Pearson, *Youth, Crime and Society* (1st edn, 1994); Tim Newburn, *Youth Crime and Youth Culture* (4th edn, 2007); Rod Morgan and Tim Newburn, *Youth Justice* (4th edn, 2007) and *Youth Crime and Justice: Rediscovering Devolution, Discretion and Diversion* (5th edn, 2012).

The specialist journal *Youth Justice: An International Journal* (Sage publishing), contains a wealth of articles based on original research on aspects of youth crime and justice across the UK jurisdictions and internationally. More particularly each edition contains an overview of policy, research, and practice developments curated by Tim Bateman, and commentary on legal developments in youth justice by Nigel Stone. Together these contributions form a rich set of resources for researchers.

Recommended specialist books on youth crime and justice are: Muncie's, *Youth and Crime* (2014); and Goldson and Muncie's edited collection *Youth Crime and Justice* (2015). For readers interested in the philosophy of punishment and critical analysis of paradigmatic framings a useful introduction is provided by Duff and Garland's *A Reader on Punishment* (1994).

Finally, readers should always be encouraged to go back to classic texts on crime and punishment. Particular recommendations are: Cohen's *Visions of Social Control: Crime, Punishment and Classification* (1985); Matza's *Delinquency and Drift* (1964), Pearson's *Hooligan: A History of Respectable Fears* (1983); *and Thorpe and colleagues'* key text on diversion, *Out of Care: The Community Support of Juvenile Offenders* (1980).

REFERENCES

Bateman, T. (2012a), 'Who Pulled the Plug? Towards an Explanation of the Fall in Child Imprisonment in England and Wales', *Youth Justice*, 12(1): 36–52.

Bateman, T. (2012b), 'Youth Justice News', *Youth Justice*, 12(2): 144–55.

Cesaroni, C., Downing, S., and Alvi, S. (2012), 'Bullying Enters the 21st Century? Turning a Critical Eye to Cyber-bullying Research', *Youth Justice*, 12(3): 199–211.

Cohen, S. (1985), *Visions of Social Control: Crime, Punishment and Classification*, Cambridge: Polity in Association with Basil Blackwell.

Convery, U., Haydon, D., Moore, L., and Scraton, P. (2008), 'Children, Rights and Justice in Northern Ireland', *Youth Justice*, 8(3): 245–63.

Drakeford, M. (2010), 'Devolution and Youth Justice in Wales', *Criminology and Criminal Justice*, 10(2): 137–54.

Duff, A. and Garland, G. A. (eds) (1994), *A Reader on Punishment*, Oxford: Oxford University Press.

Edwards, A. and Hughes, G. (2009), 'The Preventive Turn and the Promotion of Safer Communities In England and Wales: Political Inventiveness and Governmental Instabilities', *Criminology & Criminal Justice*, 9(1): 433–58.

Garland, D. (1985), *Punishment and Welfare: A History of Penal Strategies*, Aldershot, Gower.

Garland, D. (1996), 'The Limits of the Sovereign State', *British Journal of Criminology*, 26(94): 445–71.

Garland, D. (2013), 'Penality and the Penal State: 2012 Sutherland Address', *Criminology*, 51(3): 475–517.

Gelsthorpe, L. and Kemp, V. (2013), 'Juvenile Justice: England and Wales', in J. Winterdyk (ed.), *Comparative Juvenile Justice*, Toronto: Canadian Scholars' Press.

Goldson, B. (2011), 'Time for a Fresh Start, But is This It? A Critical Assessment of the Report of the Independent Commission on Youth Crime and Antisocial Behaviour', *Youth Justice*, 11(1): 3–27.

Goldson, B. (2013), 'Unsafe, Unjust and Harmful to Wider Society: Grounds for Raising the Minimum Age of Criminal Responsibility in England and Wales', *Youth Justice*, 13(2): 111–30.

Goldson, B. and Muncie, J. (2006), 'Critical Anatomy: Towards a Principled Youth Justice', in B. Goldson and J. Muncie (eds), *Youth Crime and Justice: Critical Issues*, London: Sage.

Goldson, B. and Muncie, J. (2015) (eds), *Youth Crime and Justice*, 2nd edn, London: Sage.

Gray, P. (2013), 'Assemblages of Penal Governance, Social Justice and Youth Justice Partnerships', *Theoretical Criminology*, 17 (November): 517–34.

Haines, K. (2009), 'Putting Children First in Wales: The Evaluation of Extending Entitlement', *Social Work Review*, 3(4): 22–30.

Haines, K. and Case, S. (2015), 'Children First, Offenders Second: the Centrality of Engagement in Positive Youth Justice', *The Howard Journal of Criminal Justice*, 54(2): 157–75.

Haines, K., Case, S., Davies, K., and Charles, A. (2013), 'The Swansea Bureau: A Model of Diversion from the Youth Justice System', *International Journal of Law, Crime and Justice*, 41(2): 167–97.

Hamilton, C., Fitzgibbon, W., and Carr, N. (2016), 'Punishment, Youth Justice and Cultural Contingency: Towards a Balanced Approach, Youth Justice?', *Youth Justice*, doi: 10.1177/1473225415619500.

Harland, K. and McCready, S. (2014), 'Rough Justice: Considerations on the Role of Violence, Masculinity, and the Alienation of Young Men in Communities and Peacebuilding Processes in Northern Ireland', *Youth Justice*, 14(3): 269–83.

Harris-Short, S. (2003), 'International Human Rights Law: Imperialist, Inept and Ineffective? Cultural Relativism and the UN Convention on the Rights of the Child', *Human Rights Quarterly*, 25(1): 130–81.

HMIPS (2016), 'Longitudinal Inspection HMYOI Polmont 19-21 April 2016', available at: https://www.prisonsinspectoratescotland.gov.uk/publications/longitudinal-inspection-hmyoi-polmont-19-21-april-2016, accessed 26 January 2017.

Howard League in Wales (2009), *Thinking Beyond Bars*, Howard League for Penal Reform.

Kelly, L. and Armitage, V. (2015), 'Diverse Diversions: Youth Justice Reform, Localised

Practices and a "New Interventionist Diversion"?', *Youth Justice*, 15(2): 117–33.

Kilbrandon Committee (1964), *Report on Children and Young Persons, Scotland*, Edinburgh, HMSO.

Locke T. (2016), 'What does Brexit have to do with Human Rights?', available at: http://blog.oup.com/2016/06/brexit-human-rights-law/, accessed 12 January 2017.

Maruna, S. (2001), *Making Good: How Ex-Convicts Reform and Build Their Lives*, Washington, DC: American Psychological Association.

Maruna, S., Wright, S., Brown, J., van Marle, F., Devlin, R., and Liddle, M. (2007), *Youth Conferencing as Shame Management: Results of a Long-term Follow-up Study*, submitted to the Youth Conference Service, Youth Justice Agency, by ARCS (UK) Ltd.

Matza, D. (1964), *Deliquency and Drift*, New York: John Wiley.

McAlister, S. and Carr, N. (2014), 'Experiences of Youth Justice: Youth Justice Discourses and their Multiple Effects, *Youth Justice*, 14(3): 241–54.

McAra, L. (2010), 'Models of Youth Justice', in D. Smith (ed.), *A New Response to Youth Crime*, Cullompton: Willan.

McAra, L. (2011) 'The Impact of Multi-Level Governance on Crime Control and Punishment', in A. Crawford, *International and Comparative Criminal Justice and Urban Governance: Convergence and Divergence in Global, National and Local Settings*, Cambridge: Cambridge University Press.

McAra, L. (2016), 'Can Criminologists Change the World? Critical Reflections on the Politics, Performance and Effects of Criminal Justice', *British Journal of Criminology*, advance access: doi: 10.1093/bjc/azw015.

McAra, L. and McVie, S. (2007), 'Youth Justice? The Impact of Agency Contact on Desistance from Offending', *European Journal of Criminology*, 4(3): 315–45.

McAra, L. and McVie, S. (2015), 'The Case for Diversion and Minimum Necessary Intervention', in B. Goldson and J. Muncie (eds), *Youth Crime and Justice*, 2nd edn, London: Sage.

McGuire, J. (ed.) (1995), *What Works Reducing Offending: Guidelines from Research and Practice*, Chichester: Wiley.

McNeill, F. (2006), 'A Desistance Paradigm for Offender Management', *Criminology and Criminal Justice*, 6(1): 39–62.

McNeill, F. and Weaver, B. (2010), 'Changing Lives? Desistance Research and Offender Management. SCCJR Project Report; No.03/2010', available at: http://www.sccjr.ac.uk/publications/changing-lives-desistance-research-and-offender-management/, accessed 26 January 2017.

McVie S. (2011), 'Alternative models of youth justice: lessons from Scotland and Northern Ireland', *Journal of Children's Services*, 6(2): 106–14.

Ministry of Justice (2016a), *Review of the Youth Justice System: Interim Report*, available at: https://www.gov.uk/government/uploads/system/uploads/attachment_data/file/498736/youth-justice-review.pdf, accessed 12 January 2017.

Ministry of Justice (2016b), Proven Reoffending Statistics Quarterly Bulletin January to December 2014, England and Wales, https://www.gov.uk/government/uploads/system/uploads/attachm.

Morgan, R. and Newburn, T. (2007), 'Youth Justice', in M. Maguire, R. Morgan, and R. Reiner, *The Oxford Handbook of Criminology*, 4th edn, Oxford: Oxford University Press.

Morgan, R. and Newburn, T. (2012), 'Youth Crime and Justice, Rediscovering Devolution, Discretion and Diversion?', in M. Maguire, R. Morgan, and R. Reiner, *The Oxford Handbook of Criminology*, 5th edn, Oxford: Oxford University Press.

Muncie, J. (2011), 'Illusions of Difference: Comparative Youth justice in Devolved United Kingdom', *British Journal of Criminology*, 51: 40–57.

Muncie, J. (2014), *Youth and Crime*, 4th edn, London: Sage.

Murray, K. (2015), 'Policing, Prevention and the Rise of Stop and Search in Scotland', *Scottish Justice Matters*, 3(2): 5–6.

Newburn, T. (2007), *Youth Crime and Youth Culture*, in M. Maguire, R. Morgan, and R. Reiner, *The Oxford Handbook of Criminology*, 4th edn, Oxford: Oxford University Press.

O'Mahoney, D. and Campbell, C. (2004), 'Mainstreaming Restorative Justice for Young Offenders through Youth Conferencing: The Experience of Northern Ireland', in J. Junger-Tas and S. Decker (eds), *The International Handbook of Juvenile Justice*, New York: Springer.

Pearson, G. (1983), *Hooligan: A History of Respectable Fears*, Basingstoke: Macmillan.

Pearson, G. (1994), 'Youth, Crime and Society', in M. Maguire, R. Morgan, and R. Reiner, *The Oxford Handbook of Criminology*, 1st edn, Oxford: Oxford University Press.

Put, J. and Walgrave, L. (2006), 'Belgium: From Protection towards Accountability', in J. Muncie and B. Goldson (eds), *Comparative Youth Justice*, London: Sage.

Scottish Government (2015), *Preventing Offending: Getting it Right for Children and Young People*, available at: http://www.gov.scot/Resource/0047/00479251.pdf, accessed 26 January 2017.

Scottish Government (2016), *Reconviction Rates in Scotland: 2013-14 Offender Cohort*, available at: http://www.gov.scot/Publications/2016/05/2243, accessed 26 January 2017.

Thorpe, D. H., Smith, D., Green, C. J., and Paley, J. H. (1980), *Out of Care: The Community Support of Juvenile Offenders*, London: George Allen & Unwin.

Tisdale, E. and Punch, S. (2012), 'Not So New? Looking Critically at Childhood Studies, *Children's Geographies*, 10(3): 249–64.

Smith, D. (2010), 'Out of Care 30 Years On', *Criminology & Criminal Justice*, 10(2): 119–35.

Smith, D. J. (1999), 'Less Crime without more Punishment', *Edinburgh Law Review*, 3(3): 1–20.

Souhami, A. (2015), 'The Central Institutions of Youth Justice: Government Bureaucracy and the Importance of the Youth Justice Board for England and Wales', *Youth Justice*, 15(3): 209–25.

SUKARIEH, M. (2012), 'From Terrorists to Revolutionaries: The Emergence of "Youth" in the Arab World and the Discourse of Globalisation', *Interface*, 4(2): 424–37.

UNITED NATIONS (2002), 'Committee on the Rights of the Child, Thirty-First Session, Consideration of Reports Submitted by States Parties, under Article 44 of The Convention, Concluding observations: United Kingdom of Great Britain and Northern Ireland', available at: http://www.togetherscotland.org.uk/pdfs/uncrc%20%20%20uk%20second%20concluding%20observations%202002.pdf, accessed 26 January 2017.

WEBSTER, C. (2015), 'The Undeserving?', *Scottish Justice Matters*, 3(3): 12–14.

YATES, J. (2012), 'What Prospects Youth Justice? Children in Trouble in the Age of Austerity', *Social Policy and Administration*, 46(4): 432–47.

YOUTH JUSTICE BOARD and WELSH GOVERNMENT (2014), *Youth Justice Strategy for Wales: Children and Young People First*, available at: https://www.gov.uk/government/publications/youth-justice-strategy-for-wales-children-and-young-people-first, accessed 26 January 2017.

YOUTH JUSTICE BOARD (2016), *Youth Justice Board for England and Wales Business Plan 2016/17*, available at: https://www.gov.uk/government/uploads/system/uploads/attachment_data/file/567003/yjb-business-plan-2016-17.pdf, accessed 26 January 2017.

ZEHR, H. and MIKA, H. (1998), 'Fundamental Concepts of Restorative Justice', *Contemporary Justice Review*, 1(1): 47–55.

42

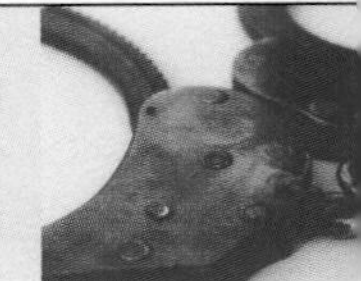

RESTORATIVE JUSTICE IN THE TWENTY-FIRST CENTURY: MAKING EMOTIONS MAINSTREAM

Meredith Rossner

INTRODUCTION

Although we are fed a steady diet of 'courtroom drama' in popular culture, the reality of court is more banal. Jury trials are rare, most offenders plead guilty, and cases are routinely processed with bureaucratic and administrative gusto. If emotions are expressed, they generally take the form of seemingly contrived indignation of judges and lawyers during a sentencing hearing. Victims are sometimes invited to give impact statements in select cases, offenders rarely speak at all.

This chapter will explore a very different type of justice encounter, one that puts the emotional expressions of victims, offenders, and community members at the centre of the interaction. Restorative justice involves bringing together people who have been affected by a crime to take part in a discussion around what happened, how people were affected, and how to make things better. Implicit in this approach is a model of justice that reconceptualizes crime as an offence against a particular person or community, rather than simply a violation of state law (Christie 1977). If crime is about people as well as law, then justice should be about repairing relationships between those people in addition to more abstract notions of criminalization and desert.

Restorative justice has been around since at least the 1970s in Western justice systems, though it arguably has roots in more ancient forms of dispute resolution (Braithwaite 2002a). Once conceived of as a 'new lens' through which to view justice (Zehr 1990), it is increasingly seen as a complementary part of wider criminal justice (Hoyle 2012; Shapland *et al.* 2006). Today restorative justice practices can be found across most of the world. In England and Wales, the 2014 Restorative Justice Action Plan sets out an ambitious vision for the expansion of restorative justice, with the goal of ensuring restorative justice is available to victims of crime and at all stages of the criminal justice process, irrespective of the case, the offence, the offender's age, or the location of the crime (Ministry of Justice 2014). Scotland also has a robust approach to restorative justice, with options available to victims of youth crime (Scottish Executive 2005) and limited diversion schemes for adults (Kirkwood 2010). Northern Ireland has perhaps the most integrated and entrenched system for restorative justice, with the 2002 Justice (Northern Ireland) Act providing a statutory basis for the use of restorative justice for nearly all types of youth offences (Jacobson and Gibbs 2009; Payne *et al.* 2010). Elsewhere around the world restorative justice has gained momentum with legislation, government initiatives, and NGOs providing some form of restorative justice across Australia and New Zealand, Europe, and North America (Galaway and Hudson 1996; Larsen 2014, Maxwell and Liu 2007). Promising restorative justice initiatives also lie outside the Western world, most notably the various peace-building activities in the Pacific Islands, the Middle East, and parts of Africa (Braithwaite 2002a; Braithwaite and Gohar 2014).

It can be said with some confidence that restorative justice has now emerged as a mainstream option for victims and offenders for a range of offences and contexts across the world (London 2011; Shapland 2014). This is perhaps why of all the editions of the *Handbook*, this is the first to include a full chapter on restorative justice.[1] On the other hand, it can also be seen as one of the more over-hyped criminal justice initiatives in modern times. Even with significant investment in restorative justice schemes around the world, case flow remains relatively low and support can be lukewarm (Rossner *et al.* 2013; Shapland *et al.* 2011; Wigzell and Hough 2015).

And yet restorative justice has proven enormously compelling to both criminologists and politicians (even Oprah Winfrey is an advocate, see Richards 2005). A particular strength is that it can appeal to both the political Right and Left, to victims' organizations and to prison activists. This is perhaps because it can suit various, and at times conflicting, justice and political objectives: to empower victims, to reduce offending, to include communities in the justice process, to save money, and to reduce incarceration. It also stands out as a process that focuses on emotions and building social bonds in a criminal justice system that is increasingly bureaucratized and depersonalized (Garland 2001). Indeed, its popularity may stem from the fact that it provides a veneer of social cohesion that masks more oppressive criminal justice practices (Bottoms 2003).

The rise of restorative justice in different contexts to suit different issues and ideologies has led to a significant amount of confusion and debate about what it actually is, and what it purports to do. One source of this confusion is that at times restorative justice is conceived of as a normative theory of how justice ought to be and at other times it is limited to an explanatory account of a specific process (Braithwaite and Pettit 2000). This chapter seeks to clarify the normative and explanatory aspects of restorative justice as a social movement, practice, and criminological theory. This chapter examines competing definitions of restorative justice, the principles and goals that underlie it, the empirical research surrounding it, and the explanatory theories that seek to account for its successes and failures. It concludes by surveying the current

[1] Restorative Justice was discussed in previous editions of the Oxford Handbook, in both Carolyn Hoyle's and Lucia Zedner's chapters on victims and the criminal justice process.

sites of debate and tension within the restorative justice community, and the relationships between theory, research, policy, and practice.

WHAT IS RESTORATIVE JUSTICE?

Defining a concept that has captured the imaginations of criminal justice practitioners and criminologists for many decades should be a relatively straightforward task. The term restorative justice has been used countless times as something of an omnibus term to describe various innovations in criminal justice. Practices include activities such as victim–offender mediation, family group conferences, restorative conferences, restorative cautions, sentencing circles, and community reparation boards. Given this diversity, it is not surprising that it has proved difficult to reach a consensus about its definition. This has resulted in significant confusion, obfuscation, and contestation (Doolin 2007; McCold 1998; Johnstone and Van Ness 2007).[2]

One source of confusion is that restorative justice has been defined at times as a set of values and other times as a practice (Braithwaite 2002b; Marshall 1999; Wright 1991). It has been referred to by some scholars as 'more of an idea, philosophy, set of values, or sensibility than a single and uniform set of practices of processes' (Menkel-Meadow 2007: 179). This approach is attractive in that it creates a wide umbrella for restorative practices. For this reason, Johnstone (2011) argues that those who seek to define restorative justice should focus on 'the range of goals and values embodied in the practice of restorative justice' rather than viewing restorative justice 'simply as a new technique for controlling crime' (2011: 5). From this perspective, the goal for the future of restorative justice is to 'cement a common core of values and ethics' (Shapland 2014: 124).

Other scholars seek to define restorative justice as a specific practice or a procedure (McCold 2000). They argue that while it is important to articulate its underlying values and aspirations, restorative justice needs to be defined in concrete terms and 'not [as] an alternative to retributive justice, not a new way of thinking about crime and justice, and not a set of aspirations for social change' (Daly 2016: 5). One reason for this approach, most relevant to criminologists, is that defining it as a practice allows it to be subject to empirical inquiry.

This approach is taken in the widely used definition by the Home Office researcher Tony Marshall:

[2] This debate goes well beyond the scope of this chapter. I am taking the relatively narrow conception of restorative justice as it is used in domestic criminal justice contexts. There are also restorative justice agendas in other organizational settings, most notably schools and workplaces (Johnstone 2008). Restorative justice is also a concept associated with political reconciliation in post conflict societies, such as truth commissions and other peace building programmes. Restorative justice in domestic criminal justice may well be a different animal approaches taken in schools, workplaces, and in international human rights/transitional justice.

> Restorative justice is a process whereby all the parties with a stake in a particular offence come together to resolve collectively how to deal with the aftermath of the offence and its implications for the future. (Marshall 1999: 5)

This definition has proliferated across the restorative justice world, and appears in most books and articles on the subject. The key element of this definition is that it is a practice (people 'come together' to 'deal' with something). This definition also includes a forward-looking element (dealing with 'implications for the future').[3] However, Marshall prefaces his definition by stating that restorative justice 'is not any particular practice, but a set of principles which may orientate the general practice of any agency of group in relation to crime' (1999: 5). This conflation of practice and principle has confused many.

Embedded in Marshall's definition is a second source of confusion about restorative justice. It has been variously defined as a process or an outcome (or both). A process-based definition stresses dialogue and cooperation. While most definitions include some description of a process, many also incorporate an emphasis on future outcomes. This is hinted at in the Marshall definition but not elaborated on. This can include a focus on 'repairing the harm' through apology, forgiveness, repayment, or some other symbolic or material reparation (Retzinger and Scheff 1996).

For instance, the Ministry of Justice 2014 Action Plan for Restorative justice expands upon Marshall's definition:

> The MoJ defines [restorative justice] as the process that brings those harmed by crime, and those responsible for the harm, into communication, enabling everyone affected by a particular incident to play a part in repairing the harm and finding a positive way forward (2014: 3).

This definition incorporates elements of both process and outcomes. 'Repairing the harm' may include apology/forgiveness, symbolic or material reparation, or some other form. 'A positive way forward' likely refers to a commitment on the part of the individual to stop offending. This is made more explicit in the definition given by the New South Wales adult restorative justice programme, where participants 'work together to find ways that can help heal the harm and help prevent the offender engaging in offending behaviour in the future'. (New South Wales Department of Justice). An outcomes-based definition is perhaps more inclusive, as it could include cases where victims are not willing to consent to a restorative justice process (Dignan 2003).

It is certainly expected that positive outcomes will result from a restorative justice process. But a danger of including outcomes in a definition of restorative justice is that there is no clear reason why certain outcomes will be reached in all cases, particularly when the process is dominated by the unique needs and desires of different people in specific contexts. As restorative justice is mainstreamed there is a danger that a focus on on outcomes will come to dominate (Shapland 2014), and lead to a one-size-fits-all model. For instance, offenders could be compelled to apologize, or victims to forgive, presenting a danger to the integrity of the practice.

Recently, Daly has suggested that restorative justice is best defined as a justice mechanism (2016):

[3] For a thorough critique of this definition, see Dignan (2005).

> Restorative justice is a contemporary justice mechanism to address crime, disputes, and bounded community conflict. The mechanism is a meeting (or several meetings) of affected individuals, facilitated by one or more impartial people. Meetings can take place at all phases of the criminal process, pre-arrest, diversion from court, pre-sentence, and post-sentence, as well as for offending or conflicts not reported to the police. Specific practices will vary, depending on context, but are guided by rules and procedures that align with what is appropriate in the context of the crime, dispute, or bounded conflict (Daly 2016: 14).

This is a rather useful definition, as it avoids the imprecision and confusion of alternative approaches.[4] It is also a criminological definition, in that it can be used to develop an empirical agenda. In this definition, restorative justice is a *practice* and a *process*, not a *value* or an *outcome*. Certain values underpin the practice, and those values can and should be debated and adjusted in different contexts. Similarly, restorative justice processes are likely to have some kind of an outcome, but this will depend on the legal, procedural, and cultural context in which it takes place. Potential values and outcomes expand and contract in different situations; elements of the process remain the same.[5]

Furthermore, one can identify the core elements of the restorative justice mechanism. These core elements are: lay encounters, expressive narratives, and ritual dynamics.

LAY ENCOUNTERS

A unique element of restorative justice practices is that they empower lay people—victims, offenders, families, friends, and community members—to actively participate in some kind of deliberative forum. In a well-known and enduring critique of contemporary criminal justice, Christie (1977) famously pointed out that criminal law and criminal procedure 'steals' conflict, and the power to deal with conflict, from those most affected by it. A criminal justice system that is dominated by professionalization and bureaucratization is less able to address the direct needs of victims, offenders, and communities (Garland 2001).[6] Restorative justice, on the other hand, is expressly designed to be a bottom-up encounter, where lay people interact with each other to address the specific impacts of a particular criminal offence or conflict. The main forms that this encounter can take include victim–offender mediation, family group conferencing, restorative justice conferencing, and circle sentencing.

[4] Note that this definition excludes practices that are sometimes included under the restorative justice umbrella, such as indigenous courts, problem solving courts, and truth commissions. It also presents a challenge to contemporary practices that might have been termed 'partly restorative' by McCold and Wachtel (2003), such as some forms of restorative cautioning and community justice panels. See Paterson and Clamp (2012) for more on this. Strang *et al.* (2013) similarly excludes these types of practices in their systematic review of restorative justice, as very few of them have undergone rigorous evaluations.

[5] An important caveat is that this process does not replace adversarial fact-finding. Some threshold of responsibility is a prerequisite to all restorative justice. This can mean that an offender pleads guilty or is found guilty in court, or in diversionary schemes it can mean that they admit responsibility prior to the restorative justice encounter (in New Zealand, the offender must 'decline to deny' the offence in order to be eligible). The starting point of restorative justice is a discussion of what happened, the details of which may or may not be contested, but this is substantively different from an examination/cross examination to determine 'the facts'.

[6] Alternatively, one can interpret this 'theft' as relieving a burden. Victims are a diverse group, and some may not want the responsibility of dealing with the conflict or may be relieved that the state has stepped in.

Victim–offender mediation involves an encounter between victim and offender, convened by a neutral third party facilitator. This model has evolved from various approaches mainly conentrated in North America and Europe. Family group conferencing and restorative justice conferencing arose out of practices developed in New Zealand and Australia and involve meetings between victims, offenders, and direct stakeholders such as family, friends, and respected community members. Circle sentencing, generally found in indigenous communities across North America, involves an encounter between a number of different stakeholders, including judges and other criminal justice officials, in a particular conflict (Johnstone 2011).[7]

While lay people are at the centre of the restorative justice encounter, professionals always have, and will continue to have, an important role in the process. Restorative justice processes can include roles for facilitators, service providers, social workers, probation officers, and police. Professionals also participate 'outside the circle' with a complex web of criminal justice staff supporting the integration of restorative justice into the courts or other institutions. A burgeoning literature on 'democratic professionalism' suggest that professionals serve a vital role in meeting the needs of lay participants, but that effective collaboration requires a clear delineation of roles and tasks as well as an explicit set of shared goals (Dzur 2008; Rossner and Bruce 2016).

NARRATIVE/EXPRESSIVE ELEMENTS

The second defining element of a restorative justice mechanism is that it involves the creation and development of a narrative that articulates the voices of lay people. Indeed, restorative justice encounters are carefully designed and managed so that specific types of narratives emerge. Most processes rely on a variation of a 'script' where a facilitator first asks the offender to describe the events leading up to the offence and the details of the offence. Then the victim and other participants speak about how they have been affected by the offence. After a dialogue, the facilitator will often return to the offender and ask how they have been affected by the offence and by what they have heard.

This structure allows for intertwining narratives of accountability and harm to develop (Rossner *et al.* 2013). A narrative of harm allows the victim and other stakeholders to articulate the impact of an offence in their own words. A narrative of accountability allows the offender to acknowledge the harm that has been caused, accept responsibility, and express remorse. In these narratives, a range of emotions can be expressed, including anger, fear, anxiety, shame, guilt, remorse, and hope. This expressive dimension, expressed through these narratives, is a particularly compelling part of restorative justice (Freiberg 2001; Sherman 2003). Indeed, the emotional element of restorative justice may be its defining characteristic.

[7] Note here the distinction between circle sentencing and the broader concept of 'indigenous courts' or 'indigenous justice'. Circle sentencing is a particular justice practice arising from North American indigenous communities that involves community members, victims, and offenders into a deliberative forum about how to address the harm of a particular offence or set of offences. This is outcomes focused, surely, but the unique justice mechanism is the restorative process. The larger concept of indigenous justice may contain elements of restorative justice but is not itself restorative. See Daly and Marchetti (2012) for more on this.

The types of narratives found in restorative justice encounters are rather different from the 'hegemonic tales' that dominate courtroom interactions (Ewick and Silbey 1995). While victims may be allowed to speak in court when providing a victim impact statement, this is not the same as a narrative that is co-produced, challenged, and negotiated over the course of an interaction, and reports of these events suggest that they may prove to be unsatisfactory encounters (Rock 2010). Offenders and community members are largely excluded from courtroom narratives. When they do speak, they are obliged to use words and phrases foreign and unfamiliar to them (Carlen 1974; Ericson and Baranek 1982). In restorative justice everybody speaks, and facilitators are trained to encourage the expression of emotion.

RITUAL

A final distinguishing feature of restorative justice concerns its ritual dynamics. It is widely acknowledged by sociologists and anthropologists that ritual plays an important role in social life (Durkheim 1995; Douglas 1984). As Durkheim pointed out over a century ago, rituals are important because they help one to make sense of a society's collective values, morals, and symbols, and give structure, order, and dignity to otherwise shapeless social events. They also produce 'collective effervescence' or feelings of solidarity with others. In other words, rituals can help to create and sustain belief in a moral order (Collins 2004).

Criminologists have noted that most criminal justice systems have developed increasingly sophisticated 'degradation rituals' to mark the guilt and punishment of an offender (Garfinkel 1956). However, unlike in other social institutions (such as education, the family, the military), criminal justice fails to provide corresponding 'reintegration rituals' that welcome an offender back into a moral community (Maruna 2011; also Llewellyn and Hoebel 1941). Restorative justice scholars have long suggested that it is a unique form of ritual that runs counter to the dynamics of other criminal justice interventions (Braithwaite and Mugford 1994; Zehr 1990).

Theoretical perspectives on why ritual dynamics can account for success in restorative justice will be discussed later in this chapter. For now, it is useful to identify some elements of a restorative justice ritual that make it unique. This includes its staging, choreography, casting, scripting, and symbols. Dramaturgical metaphors abound in restorative justice, and provide a useful way of articulating the ritual elements. First, restorative justice has physical boundaries: participants usually sit in a circle, with no hierarchy and with clear delineations between who is part of the circle and who is an outsider. This sets it apart from an adversarial staging of a court. Second, facilitators make an effort to design a seating arrangement that both supports vulnerable parties and maximizes interaction (Rossner 2013). Third, in many forms of restorative justice, particularly conferencing models, much effort goes into identifying and encouraging a 'community of care' (McCold 2004). Facilitators are tasked with identifying the 'right people', a particularly challenging job in urban anomic environments (Shapland *et al.* 2011). The scripted nature of the practice, discussed in the previous section, means that most encounters follow roughly similar trajectories. Finally, the process usually results in some kind of agreement. These 'outcome agreements', reflect the consensus of the participants and detail steps the offender will take to 'repair the harm'. They are usually written down and signed by all present.

When restorative justice is viewed as a justice mechanism marked by lay encounters, narratives, and ritual, this can allow for both consistency and variations within the process, to suit the needs and the contexts of particular conflicts and particular people (Shapland 2014). For instance, a restorative justice conference between the offender and victim of serious sexual assault (Miller and Iovanni 2013) or homicide (Walters 2015) may look and feel very different from a conference between a juvenile offender and a local shop owner in a theft case. There will be variation in the process in terms of the amount and type of preparation, the staging, and the way that risk is assessed. But the emphasis on lay people speaking, room for emotional expression, and ritual dynamics remain the same.

RESTORATIVE VALUES, PRINCIPLES, AND STANDARDS

While restorative justice may be defined as a justice mechanism, it is clear that certain values, principles, and standards underpin the process (Braithwaite 2002b; Johnstone 2011; Roche 2003; Van Ness 2003).[8] Braithwaite supplies a comprehensive framework for identifying different types of standards and principles that ought to permeate a restorative justice practice (2002b), distinguishing between procedural standards and standards that are an outcome or an end state (Strang and Braithwaite 2000). This distinction between procedural and outcome standards is particularly useful when it comes time to evaluate the success of restorative justice.

First, Braithwaite identifies *constraining* standards, such as empowerment, non-domination, and accountability.[9] These standards form the basis of any restorative practice and must be honoured and enforced as 'fundamental procedural safeguards' (Braithwaite 2003: 8). These are procedural standards: their violation becomes immediately apparent during a restorative justice encounter and should not be tolerated.

The second category consists of *maximizing* standards, including restoration of relationships, emotional restoration, and the prevention of future injustice, often interpreted as the reduction of offending.[10] These are end-state standards, and they are consistent with what victims and offenders say they want out of such a practice (Strang 2002). While constraining standards must always be honoured, achievement of maximizing standards is conditional on the contexts, desires, and capabilities of the

[8] Although a value, a principle, and a standard are all slightly different concepts, they tend to be used interchangeably in the restorative justice literature.

[9] The full list of constraining standards includes: non domination; empowerment; honouring upper limits on sanctions; respectful listening; equal concern for all stakeholders; accountability; appealability; and respect for fundamental human rights as outlined in international declarations and conventions.

[10] The full list of maximizing standards includes: restoration of human dignity; property loss, safety, damaged relationships, communities, the environment, freedom, compassion or caring, peace, a sense of duty as a citizen; emotional restoration; provision of social support to develop human capabilities; and the prevention of future injustice.

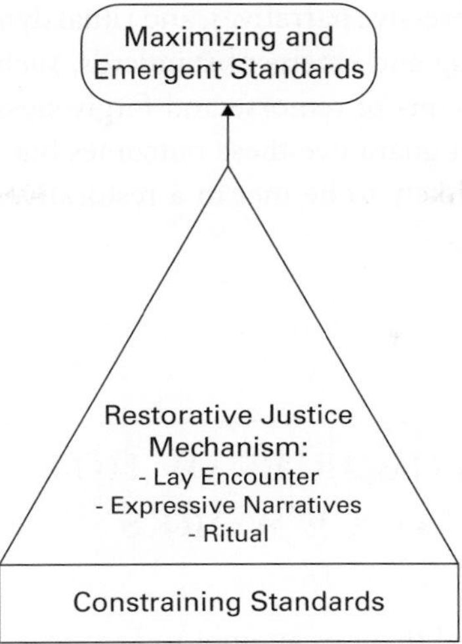

Figure 42.1 Defining restorative justice

parties. If appropriate they should be encouraged, but not mandated. This list provides useful metrics by which to evaluate the success of restorative justice, working with the hypothesis that restorative justice processes are more likely to achieve these standards than traditional court practices.

The final category consists of *emergent* standards, including remorse, apology, censure of the act, and forgiveness.[11] These principles are no less important than the maximizing standards, but they differ in key conceptual ways. While maximizing standards can be actively encouraged during a restorative justice encounter, emergent standards should only arise organically. For instance, a victim of crime should never be required to express forgiveness just as an offender should never be compelled to show remorse, as this would violate the constraining standards of non-domination and empowerment. Like maximizing standards, emergent standards provide metrics by which one can evaluate restorative justice processes.

Taken together, these restorative justice principles complement a republican theory of justice stressing non-domination and freedom (Braithwaite and Petit 1990). They articulate certain normative principles about how justice ought to be done. Explanatory theories of how restorative justice works in practice gives credence to the normative assertions. In this way, normative and explanatory theories are integrated: we progressively refine restorative justice values as we do more empirical research (Braithwaite 2003). Republicanism sets out a vision for justice, and the growing empirical research base helps to refine the practice to meet that vision, however imperfectly.

Figure 42.1 demonstrates the relationship between the restorative justice mechanism and restorative justice standards. Constraining standards are at the base of the pyramid and they are what every restorative justice encounter is built upon. The restorative justice mechanism is a specific practice and its key elements are encounters between lay

[11] The full list of emergent standards includes: remorse over injustice; apology; censure of the act; forgiveness; and mercy.

people, an emphasis on expressive narratives, and ritual dynamics. Outcomes of restorative justice are maximizing and emergent standards, such as restoration, prevention of future injustice, expressions of remorse and forgiveness, and others. A restorative justice mechanism will not guarantee these outcomes but advocates hypothesize that such standards are more likely to be met in a restorative justice process than other criminal justice processes.

EXPLANATORY THEORIES OF HOW RESTORATIVE JUSTICE WORKS

A number of criminological theories attempt to account for some of the claims made by restorative justice advocates. The three main approaches include: shame theories, procedural justice theories, and interaction ritual theory.

SHAME THEORIES

As explored earlier, one of the key elements of the restorative justice mechanism is the expression of emotion in narrative form. While a range of emotions are relevant to restorative justice theory, such as guilt, remorse, and empathy (Harris 2003; Harris *et al.* 2004; Van Stokkom 2002), shame is the central emotion around which most theory is built. Braithwaite's reintegrative shaming theory is the most well-known theoretical foundation for restorative justice. Though mention of restorative justice does not appear in Braithwaite's ground-breaking *Crime, Shame, and Reintegration* (1989), practitioners, advocates, and scholars quickly embraced the book's central concepts, such as the now-classic distinction between stigmatic and reintegrative shaming. Braithwaite demonstrates how most criminal justice processes and sanctions shame an offender in a way that is stigmatizing, condemning not just the wrongdoing but the individual herself. Reintegrative shaming, on the other hand, is a respectful process where disapproval of the criminal act is expressed but offenders are given a chance to express remorse and can then be welcomed back into a moral community. While stigmatic shaming can have long-term negative impacts on an individual, reintegrative shaming will theoretically strengthen social bonds and internally build a conscience that prevents future wrongdoing. This theory has been widely used by academics and practitioners to explain the mechanisms of restorative justice. In later works, Braithwaite connects reintegrative shaming theory to a restorative normative framework, identifying reintegrative shaming as an explanatory dynamic that can explain how remorse, apology, forgiveness, censure, mercy and other values may arise in restorative justice (2002a).

Other scholars shift the focus from the external act of shaming to the internal process of *feeling* ashamed. Scheff and Retzinger (2001) argue that shame is a repressed emotion in contemporary society and can often go unacknowledged. This leads to further shame about feeling ashamed, resulting in a cycle of aggression, anger, dysfunctional patterns of communication, and violence. According to Sheff and Retzinger, these negative consequences can simply be avoided if shame is acknowledged. A restorative justice conference, for example, can theoretically bring shame to the surface in a way that redirects aggressive emotions. When offenders and victims are both able to acknowledge any shame they might feel, this can lead to some kind of symbolic reparation and reintegration, usually through the expression of remorse and forgiveness (Retzinger and Scheff 1996). In later works, Braithwaite and colleagues incorporate elements of unacknowledged shame into a broader theory of restorative justice, shaming, and shame management, suggesting that in addition to making sure restorative justice encounters are reintegrative and not stigmatizing, one must bring shame to the surface in a positive way (Ahmed *et al.* 2001; Harris and Maruna 2006).

PROCEDURAL JUSTICE THEORY

Reintegrative shaming theory implies that shame needs to be coupled with respectful treatment. This is the heart of procedural justice theory, which asserts that if citizens feel that their treatment at the hands of authority figures is fair, inclusive, and respectful, they are more likely to obey the law (Tyler 1990; Tyler and Huo 2002).

Defiance theory incorporates elements of reintegrative shaming, unacknowledged shame, and procedural justice to argue that similar criminal sanctions have different effects for offenders in different social situations (Sherman 1993). Defiance, which can result in a rejection of the law and future offending, occurs when an offender views a sanction as illegitimate, has weak bonds to the sanctioning agent, or denies his or her shame in the offence. Deterrence, on the other hand, can result if the sanctions are regarded as legitimate, offenders express shame for their actions, and they have strong bonds with mainstream society.

The voluntary nature, deliberative structure, and encouragement of stakeholder participation can lead to increased perceptions of fairness, legitimacy, and social bonding. If restorative justice is perceived to be fairer than going to court, then it theoretically follows that restorative justice will encourage compliance with the law, thus preventing future injustices.

INTERACTION RITUAL THEORY

Procedural justice and shame theories make claims about how the process of restorative justice will lead to desired outcomes. However they don't specify precisely how feeling shame, fairness, or trust brings about such outcomes. A final theoretical perspective focuses on the micro-level elements of producing a successful ritual. Interaction ritual theory draw on a long tradition in sociology and anthropology arguing that one's sense of morals, community bonds, and the self are a function of the rituals in which one partakes, both sacred and profane (Collins 2004; Durkheim 1912).

The restorative justice ritual brings together victims and offenders, their emotions, and their stories to produce solidarity and other conciliatory emotions (Rossner 2013). In particular, ritual theory posits that by bringing people together in a face-to-face encounter with clear barriers to outsiders and a shared focus of attention, a certain rhythm will build up between participants as they become more in sync with each other's emotions and perspectives. This rhythm will lead to people feeling connected to each other, in a kind of Durkheimian 'collective effervescence' (Collins 2004). Solidarity and shared emotion may then be demonstrated through expressions of apology and forgiveness, and symbolic integration through handshakes, eye contact, and hugs (Rossner 2011). This is a particularly striking type of ritual when one considers the asymmetrical degradation rituals of court (Carlen 1976; Rock 1993). In theory, the micro-level production of solidarity and shared emotion provides restorative justice with the unique power to achieve its standards and goals.

While these theories can help explain why restorative justice might achieve successful outcomes, they can also account for its failures. A worry is that restorative justice can become another form of degradation ritual, marked by stigmatic shaming, unfair processes, and coercion (Braithwaite and Mugford 1994). As theoretical, empirical, and normative accounts of restorative justice develop, an examination of both what works and what does not can help to clarify theory, improve standards, and enhance practice.

EMPIRICAL RESEARCH

Restorative justice has been subject to an enormous amount of empirical research, perhaps more than any other criminal justice innovation in recent history (Strang and Sherman 2015). Much of the research examines restorative justice as a diversion or a supplement to court and focuses on outcomes such as restoration, fairness, legitimacy, and future offending, largely mapping onto the maximizing and emergent principles articulated by Braithwaite. Whereas early research tended not to include a control group or to utilize matched controls, a growing body of research now draws on randomized controlled trials (Sherman *et al.* 2015b). Responding to calls for more in-depth analysis of the process and dynamics of restorative justice (Braithwaite 2002a), there is also a sizable qualitative literature drawing on observations and interviews that looks more closely at the actual practices of restorative justice. This research includes a focus on facilitation and staging (Bruce 2013; Bolitho 2015), power (Cook 2006), emotions (Rossner 2011), language (Hayes and Snow 2013), and others. A small number of studies have examined how the dynamics of conferences influence outcomes (Hayes and Daly 2003; Hipple *et al.* 2014, 2015; Rossner 2013).

PARTICIPANT EXPERIENCES WITH RESTORATIVE JUSTICE

Braithwaite's constraining standards include respect, accountability, empowerment, and non domination. His maximizing and emergent standards include concepts such as restoration, apology, and forgiveness. Extant research suggests that all of these are experienced, on average, in greater quantities by participants in restorative justice conferences compared to those whose cases end up in traditional courts.

Research from the US, Britain, Australia, New Zealand, and Canada suggests that both offenders and victims perceive restorative justice as fairer, more satisfying, and more legitimate than that which is offered in the courtroom. Offenders who participate in restorative justice have a better understanding of what is happening, are more actively involved in their case, and are more likely to report that they are treated with respect and fairness (Barnes *et al.* 2015; Morris and Maxwell 1998; Tyler *et al.* 2007; Umbreit *et al.* 1994). Restorative justice conferences can also result in a higher frequency—and larger amounts—of restitution paid to victims (Strang 2002; Umbreit *et al.* 2004).

In a comprehensive study of restorative justice for British offenders, Shapland and colleagues (2007) reported that the large majority of victims and offenders found their conferences to be useful, felt a sense of closure, and were more satisfied with their procedures than those who went to court. Notably, those whose offences were most serious were significantly more likely to find their conference useful compared to those who committed less serious offences.

Research from Australia examining the role of shame in restorative justice reports that offenders who participate in restorative justice conferences experience both reintegrative and stigmatic shame in higher quantities than offenders who go to court (Ahmed *et al.* 2001). This suggests that while restorative justice can maximize positive emotions, it can also provide a space for more harmful processes. All emotions, both positive and negative, have the potential to be amped up in such intensive encounters.

HEALING VICTIMS

There is clear evidence that restorative justice is beneficial to victims of crime. Symbolic reparation, generally in the form of an apology, is often important to victims' satisfaction levels. Victims who meet their offender and receive an apology are more forgiving, feel more sympathetic towards the offender, and are less likely to desire physical revenge (Sherman and Strang 2011). Similarly, Poulson's (2003) review of restorative justice evaluations illustrates a range of positive psychological outcomes for victims.

Randomized trials in Great Britain which built on Strang's (2002) work provide strong evidence of increased well-being for victims who meet with their offender, compared with victims who do not (Shapland *et al.* 2007; Strang *et al.* 2006). This is confirmed by Angel *et al.* (2014) who analyse Post Traumatic Stress (PTS) symptoms in victims of crime randomly assigned to a restorative justice conference or a control and find significantly reduced levels of PTS symptoms immediately following a conference. The authors also report that women suffer more post-traumatic stress symptoms after a crime, but also benefit more from restorative justice than men.

A minority of victims and offenders feel worse after a conference, specifically when they reported not being involved or disrespected when reaching an outcome (Morris and Maxwell 1993; Strang 2002). Similarly, Shapland *et al.* (2007) found that the minority of participants that were unhappy with their conference pointed to instances where they felt they were not being taken seriously, or that they felt uninformed or not included in a follow-up after the conference. Finally, Choi *et al.* (2012) point out that when victims are unhappy with their experience of restorative justice it is often when they feel little attention has been paid to the process and most of the focus is on developing suitable outcomes for the offender. Although such cases are greatly outnumbered by those with positive outcomes, they do highlight the links between the conference dynamics and subsequent satisfaction. Victims and offenders do not always feel that they can tell their story, develop rapport, or achieve solidarity. When elements of the process go wrong, participants can leave the interaction leaving worse.

REDUCING REOFFENDING

The best research on restorative justice and reoffending shows a modest but consistent positive effect on recidivism reduction. Due to the many challenges of adequate implementation and evaluation, much research on restorative justice and recidivism has been hindered by the lack of an adequate comparison group, little statistical power, or other methodological issues (Weatherburn and Macadam 2013). The most rigorous evaluations of restorative justice employ either a randomized or matched control group for comparison and suggests that restorative justice can reduce future injustices by both reducing reoffending and saving money.

A thorough review of the early evidence on restorative justice appeared in Braithwaite (2002a), with cautiously optimistic conclusions about its effectiveness. Since then, a number of meta-analyses and systematic reviews have attempted to address some of the methodological limitations of previous research by pooling data to look at trends in results (Bonta *et al.* 2006; Bradshaw and Roseborough 2005; Bradshaw *et al.* 2006; Latimer *et al.* 2005). Though the impact of restorative justice on recidivism varies by degree, all studies conclude that restorative justice, compared to court, results in a modest reduction in offending. There is also evidence of secondary deterrence in a reduced desire for revenge by victims, thus potentially preventing future retaliatory crimes (Strang 2002). Most recently, Strang *et al.* (2013) report on a systematic review of the most rigorous randomized controlled trials of restorative justice. Across 10 experiments, they found an overall positive impact on the frequency recidivism. Furthermore, the analysis shows some support for the argument that restorative justice is more effective for violent crime than it is for property crime, and for adult offenders over young offenders. While the effect sizes of these analyses are not large, they are contrary to conventional wisdom and standard practice, which frames restorative justice as most suitable for low-level, juvenile property crimes (Sherman *et al.* 2015a, see also Wood and Suzuki 2016). This finding is supported by Rossner (2013) who finds that individuals with more, and more serious, previous convictions are more likely to benefit from restorative justice conferences than first time offenders.

There is also strong evidence to suggest that restorative justice conferencing is a cost-effective approach to reducing crime. Shapland and colleagues (2008) utilize innovative measures to examine the cost of crime and the impact of restorative justice, finding significant savings (in terms both of criminal justice processing costs and of the costs of reconvictions) for every £1 spent on delivering restorative justice conferences.

Like most criminal justice innovations, restorative justice suffers from a 'heterogeneity problem' (Braithwaite 2014), as not all restorative justice processes can be guaranteed to meet the high bar of maximizing and emergent standards. Indeed, a major flaw in much of the thinking around restorative justice is that it 'holds out the promise that these things *should happen most of the time* when research suggests that these things can occur *some of the time*' (Daly 2003: 234). As such, it is useful to compare not only restorative justice to court, but to examine variations within restorative justice conferences. An analysis of within-conference variations shows that offending is less likely when offenders were remorseful and the outcome agreement was decided by general consensus (Hayes and Daly 2003). Similarly, Shapland and colleagues (2008) report that decreases in offending are most likely when offenders reported that the conference helped them realize the harm done, that they found it was useful, that they wanted to meet the victim, and when they were observed to be actively participating in the conference. Hipple *et al.* (2014, 2015) report similar results: conferences that observers reported to be 'restorative' resulted in less offending, both in the short and long term. Rossner (2013) analyses the ritual dynamics of restorative justice conferences, comparing the reoffending frequencies for offenders who participated in emotionally intense and high solidarity conferences with offenders who participated in less intense conferences, finding that offenders in the former category offended at a much lower frequency, even five years after their conference (see also Sherman *et al.* 2015b).

To conclude, the research on restorative justice conferencing and reoffending suggests that it is right to be optimistic about this process. However, there are important caveats to be made. First, restorative justice seems to be most effective when it meets constraining, maximizing, and emergent standards. Not all conferences achieve restoration, reparation, or reductions in offending and we should not expect them to. Second, these principles are most likely to be met in cases with more serious crime, with adult offenders, and where the emotional intensity is high. Such conferences are harder to organize, more time consuming, more politically risky, and more expensive, but may be the most effective.[12] Third, the evidence base is largely limited to tests of the conferencing model, including face-to-face meetings between victims, offenders, and other stakeholders (Sherman *et al.* 2015a). One should be cautious about generalizing these findings to less intensive interventions. For instance, a common practice for police in the UK is to deliver a 'street level restorative justice', where a person might be cautioned in a restorative matter by a police officer on the spot after being apprehended. The offender might be asked to think about harm and making amends, but victims and other stakeholders are not usually involved (Hoyle *et al.* 2002; Paterson and Clamp 2012). While practices such as restorative cautioning might meet the standards and values set out by Braithwaite (2002b), their effects have not been rigorously measured. There is a danger that research about restorative conferencing is being used as an evidence base for related but fundamentally different models operating under the same 'restorative' banner.

RESTORATIVE JUSTICE AS PUNISHMENT

Beyond the many empirical questions about the effects of restorative justice, there are also a great many normative debates about the value of restorative practices for society.

[12] Maxwell and Morris (2001) have similarly argued that since high quality restorative justice is so resource-intensive, practices should focus on persistent serious offenders.

One current debate of relevance to criminologists and criminal law scholars centres on whether restorative justice can meet the punitive aims of criminal justice. This is particularly important in the current political context, where restorative justice is positioned as a mainstream option for offenders and victims.

Early advocates of restorative practices, often connected to prison abolition movements, argued that restorative justice was a new paradigm of justice that could entirely replace contemporary adversarial and retributivist criminal justice practices (Zehr 1990). Restorative justice was asserted to be the opposite of 'punitive justice' or 'retributive justice'. Such radical claims helped to articulate restorative values, distinguish it from 'business as usual', and publicize the concept. But there was significant disagreement about this, including critiques from criminal justice practitioners who sought to incorporate restorative justice into their existing practice and from criminal law theorists who challenged the retributive–restorative dichotomy (Daly 2002; Duff 2003; Zedner 1994). Indeed, Daly (2012) has suggested that 'the retributive-restorative oppositional contrast stalled a more sophisticated conceptual development of restorative justice in its formative years' (2012: 358). Rather than simply dismiss punishment as an illegitimate goal of criminal justice, punishment needs to be taken seriously, both as a theoretical construct and a social institution (see Garland 1990).

Instead of an alternative to punishment, restorative justice can be seen as an 'alternative punishment' (Duff 1992). One reason for this that it places certain obligations, and some pains, upon offenders (Daly 2002). However, Walgrave (2008) has argued that such pain cannot be punitive, as it is not inflicted to meet retributive goals. Retributive punishment is the intentional infliction of pain, whereas in a restorative justice context pain is merely a byproduct, such as the pain resulting from feelings of remorse. Duff (2003), critiques restorative justice scholars for their myopic focus on the harm of crime, arguing that in order to meet the standard of criminal responsibility, an offence must also be seen as morally wrong. While harm can be repaired through symbolic or material reparation, in Duff's view a wrong must be addressed retributively, through acts of censure. Restorative justice may be an ideal outlet for such censure, and can therefore satisfy retributive aims. Similarly, London (2011) argues that restorative justice should have a retributive element in order to promote trust and legitimacy. This view is also reflected in social psychological experiments, where participants preferred restorative processes that contained retributive elements, particularly for serious crime (Gromet and Darley 2006).

Whether or not the infliction of pain is intentional, and therefore punitive, many offenders report the experience of restorative justice as painful. Indeed, many say that apologizing to one's victims is harder than going to court. Its proponents often emphasize that it is not a 'soft option' and is therefore a legitimate element of criminal justice (Johnstone 2011). There is also a growing jurisprudence of restorative justice, with courts in Canada and New Zealand concluding that restorative justice can meet retributivist aims through denunciation and censure (Foley 2014).

Other areas of debate include whether restorative justice should be a diversion or supplement to prosecution (Gavrielides 2008), where it belongs in the criminal justice system (Shapland *et al.* 2011), its use for prisoners serving long sentences for serious crime (Bolitho 2015; Miller 2011), its use in cases of sexual violence and family violence (Daly and Stubbs 2006; Ptacek 2009), and its relationship to indigenous justice (Daly 2002). While each of these areas merits a longer discussion, the constraints of this chapter prevent this.

CONCLUSION: THE FUTURE OF RESTORATIVE JUSTICE

Restorative justice has been a part of criminal justice in England and Wales for a number of years, with provisions set out for youth justice, probation, and prisons (Crawford and Newburn 2003; Hoyle 2012). In recent years, it seems that restorative justice may be having another revival. There has been a flurry of statements, action plans, and legislation indicating that the 2010 Coalition government, and likely the 2015 Conservative government, supports the integration of restorative justice in all stages of the criminal justice system (Collins 2015). A restorative justice action plan was published by the Ministry of Justice in 2012 and again in 2014 asserting the government's commitment to the practice. Other notable milestones include the 2013 Code of Practice for Victims, stating that all victims of young offenders have a right to restorative justice, and victims of adult offenders have the right to learn about restorative justice and assess its appropriateness. These were not empty promises either; they were paired with a commitment to invest £29 million, channelled through local Police and Crime Commissioners, into the provision of restorative justice at the local level. At the same time, the Crime and Courts Act 2013 provides statutory support for restorative justice at the pre-sentence stage, allowing courts to defer sentence to allow restorative justice to take place. There is also recent investment in Neighborhood Justice Panels to tackle low-level crime, a new Rehabilitation Activity Requirement introduced in community and suspended sentences with restorative justice as an option, and a pathfinder programme investigating the use of restorative justice at the pre-sentence stage in select crown courts. While this ambitious set of strategies is promising, its current implementation has been more piecemeal (Wright 2015). In an effort to bring some structure to a disparate set of practices and policies, the Restorative Justice Council, an independent third sector membership body advocating for restorative practice, has developed its own statement of principles and a Restorative Service Quality Mark which restorative justice programmes nationwide can seek to obtain.

Elsewhere around the world restorative justice has continued to benefit from continued investment. The jurisdictions with the most coordinated and successful efforts are New Zealand and Northern Ireland. New Zealand has completely transformed its juvenile justice system over 25 years to one where every effort is made to divert cases out of the courts into restorative justice conferencing, regardless of the seriousness of the offence or the history of the offender. There is less support however for restorative justice in adult cases. One reason for this is the different way restorative justice is incorporated into legislation. The 1989 Children, Young Persons, and Their Families Act effectively mandates restorative justice as a first option of all young offenders. In the case of adults, support for restorative justice appears in three different acts (the Sentencing Act 2002, Parole Act 2002, and the Victims' Rights Act 2002), but only encourages its use in vague terms. The story is similar in Northern Ireland. Originating out of community restorative justice schemes developed to deal with paramilitary violence, the Justice (Northern Ireland) Act 2002 legislated restorative justice conferences for all young offenders, either as a diversion or as part of a court order. There is no legislative basis for adult restorative justice in Northern Ireland, but there are a growing number of schemes run through probation and victims' services.

There are three observations to be made about this recent upswing. First, the current mood is one in a long cycle that sees the popularity of, and the resources for, restorative justice ebb and flow in many jurisdictions. Restorative justice has been on the verge of 'taking off' since at least the 1980s and needs sustained support in order for this to be achieved.

Second, as restorative justice practices expand, attention should be paid to the empirical base, which suggests that restorative justice conferences are more effective when they are emotionally intense encounters, with victims and stakeholders present, and for more serious crimes with adult offenders. The best research to date has focused on the conferencing model, and caution should be advised when generalizing from this model to different restorative practices. Marshall warned of this, with much foresight, when he concluded:

> It is its ability to absorb many different concerns that gives it appeal, and it is its grounding in successful practice that gives it persuasive justification. In this lies its strength and weakness. There is a grave danger that Restorative Justice may end up being all things to all men and women, concealing important divergences of practice and aim. (1999: 30).

Third, research into restorative justice has shown that it can be a success, but significant hurdles first need to be overcome. These include: maintaining referrals and case flow, ensuring cooperation between services (especially when it comes to data sharing), and upholding standards for training and practice to ensure high quality and consistent service. At the same time, a strength of restorative justice is its neutrality—too much integration within criminal justice can undermine this, as well as leading to net-widening, abuse, and unaccountability. Many of these issues have been addressed by providing a statutory basis for restorative justice. The experiences of Northern Ireland and New Zealand, where restorative justice has been formally incorporated into the youth justice system, are particularly illustrative in this regard (for a more thorough discussion, see Shapland *et al.* 2008, 2011). Without a legislative basis the implementation and development of restorative justice relies on the leadership of local judges, legal professionals, and community activists. This is not enough to sustain its growth. In both New Zealand and Ireland, restorative justice has experienced significant support and success when it has a statutory basis. When it does not, as is the case for adults in both countries, its implementation is less impressive. In the face of growing evidence that restorative justice is most effective for adults and serious crime, its future as a mainstream component of the criminal justice system depends on statutory support.

SELECTED FURTHER READING

The best readings that provide comprehensive analysis of theory, research, and debates in restorative justice include Braithwaite's *Restorative Justice and Responsive Regulation* (2002a); Johnstone's *Restorative Justice: Ideas, Values, and Debates* (2011); Cunneen and Hoyle's, *Debating Restorative Justice* (2010); Von Hirsh *et al.*'s *Restorative Justice and Criminal Justice: Competing or Reconcilable Paradigms* (2003); Johnstone and Van Ness' *Handbook of Restorative Justice* (2007); Dignan's *Understanding Victims and Restorative Justice* (2005); and the 2002 special issue on restorative justice in the *British Journal of Criminology*. Readings that include original empirical research on restorative justice can be found in Strang's *Repair or Revenge: Victims and Restorative Justice* (2002); Shapland *et al.*'s *Restorative Justice in Practice* (2011); Rossner's, *Just Emotions: Rituals of Restorative Justice* (2013); Ahmed *et al.*'s, *Shame Management Through Reintegration* (2001), Roche's, *Accountability in Restorative Justice* (2003); and Miller's, *After the Crime: The Power of Restorative Justice Dialogues Between Victims and Violent Offenders* (2011).

REFERENCES

AHMED, E., HARRIS, N., BRAITHWAITE, J. and BRAITHWAITE, V. (2001), *Shame Management Through Reintegration*, Cambridge: Cambridge University Press.

ANGEL, C. M., SHERMAN, L. W., STRANG, H., ARIEL, B., BENNETT, S., INKPEN, N., KEANE, A., and RICHMOND, T. S. (2014), 'Short-term effects of restorative justice conferences on post-traumatic stress symptoms among robbery and burglary victims: a randomized controlled trial', *Journal of Experimental Criminology*, 10(3): 291–307.

BARNES, G. C., HYATT, J. M., ANGEL, C. M., STRANG, H., and SHERMAN, L. W. (2015), 'Are restorative justice conferences more fair than criminal courts? Comparing levels of observed procedural justice in the reintegrative shaming experiments (RISE)', *Criminal Justice Policy Review*, 26(2): 103–30.

BOLITHO, J. (2015), 'Putting justice needs first: a case study of best practice in restorative justice', *Restorative Justice*, 3(2): 256–81.

BONTA, J., JESSEMAN, R., RUGGE, T., and CORMIER, R. (2006), 'Restorative justice and recidivism: Promises made, promises kept', in D. Sullivan and L. Tifft (eds), *Handbook of Restorative Justice: A Global Perspective*, London: Routledge.

BOTTOMS, A. (2003), 'Some sociological reflections on restorative justice', in A. von Hirsch, J. V. Roberts, A. E. Bottoms, K. Roach, and M. Schiff (eds), *Restorative Justice and Criminal Justice: Competing or Reconcilable Paradigms*, Oxford: Hart.

BRADSHAW, W. and ROSEBOROUGH, D. (2005), 'Restorative justice dialogue: The impact of mediation and conferencing on juvenile recidivism', *Federal Probation*, 69(2): 15–21.

BRADSHAW, W., ROSEBOROUGH, D., and UMBREIT, M. S. (2006), 'The effect of victim offender mediation on juvenile offender recidivism: A meta-analysis', *Conflict Resolution Quarterly*, 24(1): 87–98.

BRAITHWAITE, J. (1989), *Crime, Shame and Reintegration*, Cambridge: Cambridge University Press.

BRAITHWAITE, J. (2002a), *Restorative Justice and Responsive Regulation*, Oxford: Oxford University Press.

BRAITHWAITE, J. (2002b), 'Setting standards for restorative justice', *British Journal of Criminology*, 42(3): 563–77.

BRAITHWAITE, J. (2003), 'Principles of restorative justice', in A. von Hirsch, J. V. Roberts, A. E. Bottoms, K. Roach, and M. Schiff (eds), *Restorative Justice and Criminal Justice: Competing or Reconcilable Paradigms*, Oxford: Hart.

BRAITHWAITE, J. (2014), 'Evidence for Restorative Justice', *Vermont Bar Journal*, 40(2): 18–27.

BRAITHWAITE, J. and GOHAR, A. (2014), 'Restorative justice, policing and insurgency: Learning from Pakistan', *Law & Society Review*, 48(3): 531–61.

BRAITHWAITE, J. and MUGFORD, S. (1994), 'Conditions of successful reintegration ceremonies: Dealing with juvenile offenders', *British Journal of Criminology*, 34(2): 139–71.

BRAITHWAITE, J. and PETTIT, P. (1990), *Not Just Deserts: A Republican Theory of Criminal justice*, Oxford: Clarendon.

BRAITHWAITE, J. and PETTIT, P. (2000), 'Republicanism and restorative justice: an explanatory and normative connection', in H. Strang and J. Braithwaite (eds), *Restorative Justice: From Philosophy to Practice*, Burlington: Ashgate.

BRUCE, J. (2013), 'Understanding Back Stage and Front Stage Work in Restorative Justice Conferences: The Benefits of Using Ethnographic Techniques', *Current Issues in Criminal Justice*, 25(1): 517–27.

CARLEN, P. (1974), 'Remedial routines for the maintenance of control in magistrates' courts', *British Journal of Law and Soceity*, 1(2): 101–17.

Carlen, P. (1976), *Magistrates' Justice*, London: Martin Robinson and Co.

Choi, J. J., Bazemore, G., and Gilbert, M. J. (2012), 'Review of research on victims' experiences in restorative justice: Implications for youth justice', *Children and Youth Services Review*, 34(1): 35–42.

Christie, N. (1977), 'Conflicts as property', *British Journal of Criminology*, 17(1): 1–15.

Collins, J. (2015), 'Restorative Justice in England and Wales: from the margins to the mainstream', *Restorative Justice*, 3(1): 129–34.

Collins, R. (2004), *Interaction Ritual Chains*, Princeton: Princeton University Press.

Crawford, A. and Newburn, T. (2003), *Youth Offending and Restorative Justice: Implementing Reform in Youth Justice*, London: Routledge.

Cunneen, C. and Hoyle, C. (2010), *Debating Restorative Justice*, Oxford: Hart.

Daly, K. (2002), 'Restorative justice: The real story', *Punishment & Society*, 4(1): 55–79.

Daly, K. (2003), 'Mind the gap: Restorative justice in theory and practice', in A. von Hirsch, J. V. Roberts, A. E. Bottoms, K. Roach, and M. Schiff (eds), *Restorative justice and criminal justice: Competing or reconcilable paradigms*, Oxford: Hart.

Daly, K., (2012), 'The Punishment Debate in Restorative Justice', in J. Simon and R. Sparks (eds), *The Handbook of Punishment and Society*, London: Sage.

Daly, K. (2016), 'What is restorative justice? Fresh answers to a vexed question', *Victims & Offenders*, 11(1): 9–29.

Daly, K. and Marchetti, E. (2012), 'Innovative justice processes: Restorative justice, indigenous justice, and therapeutic jurisprudence', in M. Marmo, W. de Lint, and D. Palmer (eds), *Crime and Justice: A Guide to Criminology*, 4th edn, Sydney, Australia: Lawbook Company.

Daly, K. and Stubbs, J. (2006), 'Feminist engagement with restorative justice', *Theoretical Criminology*, 10(1): 9–28.

Dignan, J. (2003), 'Towards a Systematic Model of Restorative Justice', in A. von Hirsch, J. V. Roberts, A. E. Bottoms, K. Roach, and M. Schiff (eds), *Restorative Justice and Criminal Justice: Competing or Reconcilable Paradigms*, Oxford: Hart.

Dignan, J. (2005), *Understanding Victims and Restorative Justice*, London: Open University.

Doolin, K. (2007), 'But what does it mean? Seeking definitional clarity in restorative justice', *The Journal of Criminal Law*, 71(5): 427–40.

Douglas, M. (1984 [1966]), *Purity and Danger: An Analysis of the Concepts of Pollution and Taboo*, New York: Routledge.

Duff, R. A. (1992), 'Alternatives to punishment—or alternative punishments?', in W. Cragg (ed.), *Retributivism and Its Critics*, Stuttgart: Franz Steiner.

Duff, R. A. (2003), 'Restoration and retribution', in A. von Hirsch, J. V. Roberts, A. E. Bottoms, K. Roach, and M. Schiff (eds), *Restorative Justice and Criminal Justice: Competing or Reconcilable Paradigms*, Oxford: Hart.

Durkheim, E (1995 [1912]), *Elementary Forms of Religious Life*, New York: Free Press.

Dzur, A. W. (2008), *Democratic Professionalism: Citizen Participation and the Reconstruction of Professional Ethics, Identity, and Practice*, University Park: Penn State Press.

Ericson, R. V. and Baranek, P. M. (1982), *The Ordering of Justice: A Study of Accused Persons as Dependants in the Criminal Process*, Toronto: University of Toronto Press.

Ewick, P. and Silbey, S. S. (1995), 'Subversive stories and hegemonic tales: Toward a sociology of narrative', *Law and Society Review*, 29(2): 197–226.

Foley, T. (2014), *Developing Restorative Justice Jurisprudence: Rethinking Responses to Criminal Wrongdoing*, Farnham: Ashgate.

Freiberg, A. (2001), 'Affective Versus Effective Justice: Instrumentalism and Emotionalism in Criminal Justice', *Punishment & Society*, 3(2): 265–78.

Galaway, B. and Hudson, J. (eds) (1996), *Restorative Justice: International Perspectives*, Monsey, NY: Criminal Justice Press.

Garfinkel, H. (1956), 'Conditions of successful degradation ceremonies', *American Journal of Sociology*, 61(5): 420–4.

Garland, D. (1990), *Punishment and Modern Society: A Study in Social Theory*, Chicago: University of Chicago Press.

Garland, D. (2001), *The Culture of Control: Crime and Social Order in Contemporary Society*, Chicago: University of Chicago Press.

Gavrielides, T. (2008), 'Restorative justice—the perplexing concept: Conceptual fault-lines and power battles within the restorative justice movement', *Criminology and Criminal Justice*, 8(2): 165–83.

Gromet, D. M. and Darley, J. M. (2006), 'Restoration and retribution: How including retributive components affects the acceptability of restorative justice procedures', *Social Justice Research*, 19(4): 395–432.

Harris, N. (2003), 'Reassessing the dimensionality of the moral emotions', *British Journal of Psychology*, 94(4): 457–73.

Harris, N., Walgrave, L., and Braithwaite, J. (2004), 'Emotional dynamics in restorative conferences', *Theoretical Criminology*, 8(2): 191–210.

Harris, N. and Maruna, S. (2006), 'Shame, Shaming and Restorative Justice', in D. T. Sullivan, L. Tifft (ed.), *Handbook of Restorative Justice*, Abingdon: Routledge.

Hayes, H. and Daly, K. (2003), 'Youth justice conferencing and reoffending', *Justice Quarterly*, 20(4): 725–64.

Hayes, H. and Snow, P. (2013), 'Oral language competence and restorative justice processes: Refining preparation and the measurement of conference outcomes', *Trends and Issues in Crime and Criminal Justice*, 463: 1–7.

Hipple, N. K., Gruenewald, J., and McGarrell, E. F. (2014), 'Restorativeness, procedural justice, and defiance as predictors of reoffending of participants in family group conferences', *Crime & Delinquency*, 60(8): 1131–57.

HIPPLE, N. K., GRUENEWALD, J., and MCGARRELL, E. F. (2015), 'Restorativeness, procedural justice, and defiance as long-term predictors of reoffending of participants in family group conferences', *Criminal justice and behavior*, 42(11): 1110–27.

HOYLE, C., YOUNG, R., and HILL, R. (2002), *Proceed with Caution: An Evaluation of the Thames Valley Police Initiative in Restorative Cautioning*, York: Joseph Rowntree Foundation.

HOYLE, C. (2012), 'Victims, the criminal process, and restorative justice', in R. Morgan, M. Maguire, and R. Reiner (eds), *The Oxford Handbook of Criminology*, 5th edn, Oxford: Oxford University Press.

JACOBSON, J. and GIBBS, P. (2009), *Making Amends: Restorative Youth Justice in Northern Ireland*, London: The Prison Reform Trust.

JOHNSTONE, G. (2008), 'The agendas of the restorative justice movement', in H. Ventura Miller (ed.), *Restorative Justice: From Theory to Practice*, Bingley: Emerald Group.

JOHNSTONE, G. (2011), *Restorative Justice: Ideas, Values, Debates*, 2nd edn, Cullompton: Willan.

JOHNSTONE, G. and VAN NESS, D. W. (2007), *Handbook of Restorative Justice*, Cullompton: Willan.

KIRKWOOD, S. (2010), 'Restorative justice cases in Scotland: Factors related to participation, the restorative process, agreement rates and forms of reparation', *European Journal of Criminology*, 7(2): 107–22.

LARSEN, J. J. (2014), *Restorative Justice in the Australian Criminal Justice System*, Canberra: Australian Institute of Criminology.

LATIMER, J., DOWDEN, C., and MUISE, D. (2005), 'The effectiveness of restorative justice practices: A meta-analysis', *The Prison Journal*, 85(2): 127–44.

LLEWELLYN, K. N. and HOEBEL, E. A. (1941), *The Cheyenne Way: Conflict and Case Law in Primitive Jurisprudence*, Norman: University of Oklahoma Press.

LONDON, R. (2011), *Crime, Punishment, and Restorative Justice: From the Margins to the Mainstream*, Boulder: First Forum Press.

MARSHALL, T. (1999), *Restorative Justice: An Overview*, A report by the Home Office Research Development and Statistics Directorate.

MARUNA, S. (2011), 'Reentry as a rite of passage', *Punishment & Society*, 13(1): 3–28.

MAXWELL, G. A. and MORRIS, A. (2001), 'Family group conferences and re-offending', in A. Morris and G. Maxwell (eds), *Restorative Justice for Juveniles: Conferencing, Mediation and Circles*, Oxford: Hart.

MAXWELL, G. M. and LIU, J. H. F. (eds) (2007), *Restorative Justice and Practices in New Zealand: Towards a Restorative Society*, Victoria University of Wellington-Institute of Policy Studies.

MCCOLD, P. (1998), 'Restorative justice: variations on a theme', in L. Walgrave (ed.), *Restorative Justice for Juveniles: Potentialities, Risks and Problems for Research*, Leuven: Leuven University Press.

MCCOLD, P. (2000), 'Toward a holistic vision of restorative juvenile justice: a reply to the maximalist model', *Contemporary Justice Review*, 3(4): 357–414.

MCCOLD, P. (2004), 'What is the role of community in restorative justice theory and practice', in H. Zehr and B. Towes (eds), *Critical Issues in Restorative Justice*, Cullompton: Willan.

MCCOLD, P. and WACHTEL, T. (2003), 'In pursuit of paradigm: A theory of restorative justice', Paper presented at 13th World Congress of Criminology, International Institute for Restorative Practices, Rio de Janeiro, Brazil.

MENKEL-MEADOW, C. (2007), 'Restorative justice: What is it and does it work?', *Annual Review of Law and Social Science*, 10(1): 161–87.

MILLER, S. L. (2011), *After the Crime: The Power of Restorative Justice Dialogues Between Victims and Violent Offenders*, New York: NYU Press.

MILLER, S. L. and IOVANNI, L. (2013), 'Using restorative justice for gendered violence: Success with a postconviction model', *Feminist Criminology*, 8(4): 247–68.

MINISTRY OF JUSTICE (2014), *Restorative Justice Action Plan for the Criminal Justice System*, London: Ministry of Justice.

MORRIS, A. and MAXWELL, G. M. (1993), 'Juvenile justice in New Zealand: A new paradigm', *Australian & New Zealand Journal of Criminology*, 26(1): 72–90.

MORRIS, A. and MAXWELL, G. (1998), 'Restorative Justice in New Zealand: Family Group Conferences as a Case Study', *Western Criminology Review*, 1(1): 1–19.

NEW SOUTH WALES DEPARTMENT OF JUSTICE, Forum Sentencing website, http://www.forumsentencing.justice.nsw.gov.au/, accessed 17 January 2017.

PATERSON, C. and CLAMP, K. (2012), 'Exploring recent developments in restorative policing in England and Wales', *Criminology & Criminal Justice*, 12(5): 593–611.

PAYNE, B., CONWAY, V., BELL, C., FALK, A., FLYNN, H., MCNEIL, C., and RICE, F. (2010), *Restorative Practices in Northern Ireland: A Mapping Exercise*, School of Law, Queen's University, Belfast.

POULSON, B. (2003), 'A Third Voice: A Review of Empirical Research on the Psychological Outcomes of Restorative Justice', *Utah Law Review*, 2003(1): 167–204.

PTACEK, J. (ed.) (2009), *Restorative Justice and Violence Against Women*, Oxford: Oxford University Press.

RETZINGER, S. M. and SCHEFF, T. J. (1996), 'Strategy for community conferences: Emotions and social bonds', in B. Galaway and J. Hudson (eds), *Restorative Justice: International Perspectives*, Monsey, NY: Criminal Justice Press.

RICHARDS, K. M. (2005), 'Unlikely friends? Oprah Winfrey and restorative justice', *Australian & New Zealand Journal of Criminology*, 38(3): 381–99.

ROCHE, D. (2003), *Accountability in Restorative Justice*, Oxford: Oxford University Press.

ROBINSON, G. and SHAPLAND, J. (2008), 'Reducing Recidivism: A Task for Restorative Justice?', *British Journal of Criminology*, 48(3): 337–58.

Rock, P. E. (1993), *The Social World of an English Crown Court: Witness and Professionals in the Crown Court Centre at Wood Green*, Oxford: Clarendon.

Rock, P. (2010), 'Hearing victims of crime': The delivery of impact statements as ritual behaviour in four London trials for murder and manslaughter', in A. Bottoms and J. Roberts (eds), *Victims in the Criminal Justice System*, London: Routledge.

Rossner, M. (2011), 'Emotions and interaction ritual: A micro analysis of restorative justice', *British Journal of Criminology*, 51(1): 95–119.

Rossner, M. (2013), *Just Emotions: Rituals of Restorative Justice*, Oxford: Oxford University Press.

Rossner, M., Bruce, J., and Meher, M. (2013), *The Process and Dynamics of Restorative Justice: Research on Forum Sentencing*, Report to the New South Wales Department of Justice and Attorney General, Sydney: University of Western Sydney.

Rossner, M., and Bruce, J. (2016), 'Community participation in restorative justice: Rituals, reintegration, and quasi-professionalization', *Victims & Offenders*, 11(1): 107–25.

Scottish Executive (2005), *Restorative Justice Services in the Children's Hearings System*, Edinburgh: Scottish Executive.

Scheff, T. and Retzinger, S. (1991), *Emotions and Violence: Shame and Rage in Destructive Conflicts*, Lanham: Lexington.

Shapland, J. (2014), 'Implications of growth: Challenges for restorative justice', *International Review of Victimology*, 20(1): 111–27.

Shapland, J., Robinson, G., and Sorsby, A. (2011), *Restorative Justice in Practice: Evaluating What Works for Victims and Offenders*, Abingdon: Routledge.

Shapland, J., Atkinson, A., Atkinson, H., Colledge, E., Dignan, J., Howes, M., Johnstone, J., Robinson, G., and Sorsby, A. (2006), 'Situating restorative justice within criminal justice', *Theoretical Criminology*, 10(4): 505–32.

Shapland, J., Atkinson, A., Atkinson, H., Chapman, B., Dignan, J., Howes, M., Johnstone, J., Robinson, G., and Sorsby, A. (2007), *Restorative Justice: The Views of Victims and Offenders*, Ministry of Justice Research Series, 3(07).

Shapland, J., Atkinson, A., Atkinson, H., Dignan, J., Edwards, L., Hibbert, J., Howes, M., Johnstone, J., Robinson, G., and Sorsby, A. (2008), *Does Restorative Justice Affect Reconviction? The Fourth Report from the Evaluation of Three Schemes*, Ministry of Justice Research Series, 10(08).

Sherman, L. W. (1993), 'Defiance, deterrence, and irrelevance: A theory of the criminal sanction', *Journal of Research in Crime and Delinquency*, 30(4): 445–73.

Sherman, L. W. (2003), 'Reason for emotion: Reinventing justice with theories, innovations, and research—The American Society of Criminology 2002 Presidential Address', *Criminology*, 41(1): 1–38.

Sherman, L. and Strang, H. (2011), 'Empathy for the devil: the nature and nurture of revenge', in S. Karstedt, I. Loader, and H. Strang, *Emotions, Crime and Justice*, Oxford: Hart.

Sherman, L. W., Strang, H., Mayo-Wilson, E., Woods, D. J., and Ariel, B. (2015a), 'Are restorative justice conferences effective in reducing repeat offending? Findings from a Campbell systematic review', *Journal of Quantitative Criminology*, 31(1): 1–24.

Sherman, L. W., Strang, H., Barnes, G., Woods, D. J., Bennett, S., Inkpen, N., Newbury-Birch, D., Rossner, M., Angel, C., Mearns, M., and Slothower, M. (2015b), 'Twelve experiments in restorative justice: the Jerry Lee program of randomized trials of restorative justice conferences', *Journal of Experimental Criminology*, 11(4): 501–40.

Strang, H. (2002), *Repair or Revenge: Victims and Restorative Justice*, Oxford: Clarendon.

Strang, H. and Braithawaite, J. (2000), 'Introduction', in H. Strang and J. Braithawaite (eds), *Restorative Justice: Philosophy to Practice*, Aldershot: Dartmouth.

Strang, H. and Sherman, L. (2015), 'The morality of evidence: the second annual lecture for Restorative Justice: An International Journal', *Restorative Justice*, 3(1): 6–27.

Strang, H., Sherman, L. W., Mayo-Wilson, E., Woods, D., and Ariel, B. (2013), 'Restorative justice conferencing (RJC) using face-to-face meetings of offenders and victims: Effects on offender recidivism and victim satisfaction. A systematic review', *Campbell Systematic Reviews*, 9(12).

Strang, H., Sherman, L., Angel, C. M., Woods, D. J., Bennett, S., Newbury-Birch, D., and Inkpen, N. (2006), 'Victim evaluations of face-to-face restorative justice conferences: A quasi-experimental analysis', *Journal of Social Issues*, 62(2): 281–306.

Tyler, T. (1990), *Why People Obey the Law: Procedural Justice, Legitimacy, and Compliance*, New Haven: Yale University Press.

Tyler, T. and Huo, Y. (2002), *Trust in the Law: Encouraging Public Cooperation with the Police and Courts*, New York: Russell Sage Foundation.

Tyler, T., Sherman, L., Strang, H., Barnes, G., and Woods, D. (2007), 'Reintegrative Shaming, Procedural Justice and Recidivism: The Engagement of Offenders' Psychological Mechanisms in the Canberra RISE Drinking-and-Driving Experiment', *Law and Society Review*, 41(3): 553–86.

Umbreit, M. S., Coates, R. B., and Kalanj, B. (1994), *Victim Meets Offender: The Impact of Restorative Justice and Mediation*, Monsey, NY: Criminal Justice Press.

Umbreit, M. S., Coates, R. B., and Vos, B. (2004), 'Victim-offender mediation: Three decades of practice and research', *Conflict Resolution Quarterly*, 22(1–2): 279–303.

Van Ness, D. (2003), 'Proposed basic principles on the use of restorative justice: Recognising the aims and limits of restorative justice', in A. von Hirsch, J. V. Roberts, A. E. Bottoms, K. Roach, and M. Schiff (eds), *Restorative Justice and Criminal justice: Competing or Reconcilable Paradigms*, Oxford: Hart.

Van Stokkom, B. (2002), 'Moral emotions in restorative justice conferences: Managing shame, designing empathy', *Theoretical Criminology*, 6(3): 339–60.

Von Hirsch, A., Roberts, J. V., Bottoms, A. E., Roach, K., and Schiff, M. (eds) (2003), *Restorative Justice and Criminal Justice: Competing or Reconcilable Paradigms*, Oxford: Hart.

Walters, M. (2015), 'I Thought "He's a Monster"... [But] He Was Just ... Normal": Examining the Therapeutic Benefits of Restorative Justice for Homicide', *British Journal of Criminology*, 55(6): 1207–25.

Walgrave, L. (2008), *Restorative Justice, Self Interest and Responsible Citizenship*, Cullompton: Willan.

Weatherburn, D. and Macadam, M. (2013), 'A review of restorative justice responses to offending', *Evidence Base*, 1: 1–20.

Wigzell, A. and Hough, M. (2015), *The NOMS RJ Capacity Building Programme: A Study of the Quality of Participant and Implementation Experiences*, London: Institute for Criminal Policy Research.

Wood, W. R. and Suzuki, M. (2016), 'Four challenges in the future of restorative justice', *Victims & Offenders*, 11(1): 149–72.

Wright, M. (1991), *Justice for Victims and Offenders*, Milton Keynes: Open University Press.

Wright, M. (2015), 'Making it happen or letting it happen', *Restorative Justice*, 3(1): 119–28.

Zehr, H. (1990), *Changing Lenses: A New Focus for Crime and Justice*, Scottdale: Herald.

Zedner, L. (1994), 'Reparation and retribution: are they reconcilable?', *Modern Law Review*, 57(2): 228–50.

43

CRIMINOLOGICAL ENGAGEMENTS

Alison Liebling, Fergus McNeill, and Bethany E. Schmidt

INTRODUCTION

This chapter considers the relationships between criminology and the worlds of penal policy and practice. We deliberately focus less on the standard questions of how, why, and when research informs policy, and more on the day-to-day interactions we have experienced and reflected upon throughout our research endeavours and encounters, and on their implications for theory, research, practice, and policy development. We draw substantially on our own work and on some specific examples, but also on the work of those around us and elsewhere, and we take stock of our intentions, our aspirations, and frustrations, and our 'effects' and failures as 'engaged criminologists'. Since our work is mainly at the penal end of the criminal justice process, that will be the main locus of our discussion, but much of what we have to say has broader relevance for those interested in the role of criminological research in crime prevention, community safety, policing, and the courts.

Two of us are well-established academics of relatively long-standing, with reputations (whether good or bad) for high levels of engagement with practitioners and policy-makers, mainly in two different jurisdictions (England and Wales, and Scotland). Sometimes we work with official sources of funding and/or by invitation from within the penal systems we seek to influence. At other times, we do work that is separate, externally funded or unfunded and theoretical. Borrowing Aristotle's distinction between constitutive and productive ends (or goods), we believe in the generation of knowledge as a constitutive end; as something that we can and should pursue for its own sake, but we also see social scientific knowledge as a productive end. In other words, we think that the knowledge we strive (with others) to create can and should contribute to 'the good society'. More specifically, we think that criminological knowledge can play a part in supporting the development of a more legitimate and effective penal system, where the term effective means functioning in ways that might support rather than damage the development of a just social order. But, of course, for knowledge to do good, it needs to *be* (qualitatively) 'good'—in the sense that it should be produced through the patient, honest, rigorous, and disciplined forms of enquiry that research requires.

The third voice in our chapter is a 'new generation' criminologist-in-the making who faces all the familiar early-career stage problems of gaining access to and establishing credentials in the field, sometimes with our help, but who (like many of her generation) is already a master at it, and has also taught us much about the possibilities of establishing an influential research presence in formerly unchartered territories for criminology (e.g. in Tunisia). She has fewer taken-for-granted orientations towards the status quo, and our conversations on this topic have benefitted significantly from her different (and sometimes less habituated or tolerant) experiences and insights. Whatever our career stages, we three are all still learning our craft, and about the ways in which an authentic and connected analysis of our social world might help in the search for justice.

In this chapter, we consider our hopes for, and articulate some fears about, the research life and living it well. We reject both the 'radical critical' (or wholly oppositional) and the 'detached theoretical' positions, arguing for forms of criminological engagement that are often subtle, long term and relational (even if often also opportunistic) rather than occasional, mechanical, linear, or instrumental. Our use of the term 'critical' in relation to social science means (drawing on the New Shorter Oxford English Dictionary) not 'judging unfavourably' but 'the art of examination', involving a thorough and balanced interpretive analysis of the qualities and character of a setting or practice; a 'correct reading', where the term 'correct' means the best reading we can manage. We argue that engagement improves understanding, even if it also creates risks of collusion or co-option. Together, we take issue *both* with arguments that 'relevance' must mean 'subordination' *and* also with current narrow conceptions of 'impact'. We argue that a variety of 'criminological engagements' is desirable and possible, but that some of our best experiences of engagement have been rooted in or begin with particular epistemological and methodological positions and commitments. Our model suggests that 'influence' can be accomplished, sometimes unintentionally or unplanned, at *every* stage of the research process, including several years after particular studies have ended, and away from the political life cycle.

THE ORIGINS AND HISTORY OF BRITISH CRIMINOLOGY: ENGAGED PROFESSIONALS AND SOCIAL REFORM

British criminology's origins lie in the action-oriented disciplines of psychiatry, psychoanalysis, medicine, and the law (see Garland 1988 and Rock, this volume). The clinical exploration of the individual personality (or—following the Lombrosian tradition—the body) and the search for better forensic treatment, often in prison and by medical officers, aligned the subject with government institutions, but also institutional reform, from the outset. 'Engaged professionals' offered both systematic investigation and (sometimes) radical critique (Garland 1988: 136). The Reverend W. Douglas Morrison, for example, a 'pioneer in criminology' (Robin 1964), became a prison chaplain at Wandsworth prison in the 1890s. His 'radical criticisms of the system helped provoke the appointment of the Gladstone Committee in 1984' (Garland 1988: 136-7; Housden 2006). Morrison argued, among his many published accounts of the failings of late Victorian prisons in *The Daily Chronicle* and elsewhere:

> [I]mprisonment so far from serving the purpose of protecting society adds considerably to its dangers. The casual offender is the person to whom crime is merely an isolated incident in an otherwise law-abiding life. The habitual criminal is a person to whom crime has become a trade; he is a person who makes his living by preying on the community. The prison is the breeding ground of the habitual criminal. The habitual offender is the casual offender to begin with. But the prison deteriorates him, debases him mentally and morally, reduces him to a condition of apathy, unfits and indisposes him for the tasks and duties of life; and when liberated he is infinitely more dangerous to society than when he entered it. It is not sufficiently recognized that punishment may be of a character which defeats the ends of justice. (Morrison 1898: 69)

His critique in a series of articles ('Our Dark Places') was particularly savage. Morrison spoke of a 'slow torture' which made the prison 'a machine for State-produced murder and insanity' (Housden 2006: 12). The official response to his writings by the then Commissioner Du Cane was hostile and defensive, but following an unsatisfactory rebuttal of his critique, Home Secretary Herbert Asquith set up a departmental committee of inquiry under Herbert John Gladstone MP. The Report of that Inquiry was to become a landmark in British penal policy and would 'play a vital role' in the future development of the British penal system (Radzinowicz 1939):

> We think that the system should be made more elastic, more capable of being adapted to the special cases of individual prisoners; that prison discipline and treatment should be more effectually designed to maintain, stimulate, or awaken the higher susceptibilities of prisoners, to develop their moral instincts, to train them in orderly and industrial habits, and whenever possible to turn them out of the prison better men and women, both physically and morally, than when they came in. (Prisons Committee [Gladstone Report] 1895: 7)

Growing statistical and methodological expertise, clinical experience and the engaged practical concerns of insiders working in criminal justice lent criminology an 'administrative' role for which critics have admonished it throughout its development as a discipline. Radical criminology of the 1970s and 80s attempted to challenge this disposition. But as Rock argues (this volume), even radical criminologists had to eventually engage in the empirical exploration of real crimes of violence—in the home and among the impoverished—as well as showing links between and challenging these forms of violence and state power.

Our point is that criminology simultaneously has conservative, liberal, *and* radical lineage and that there is nothing inherently 'legitimating' for the state about empirical criminological research. There are many ways of conducting and engaging in empirical research which usefully contribute to the larger project of developing knowledge. There are always important questions to be asked about 'the nature of a knowledge which is linked so closely to forms of institutional power and policy' (Garland 1988: 144) and we should be appropriately self-critical about this. On the other hand, sometimes engaging with those forms of institutional power strengthens our independent and critical theorizing and the prospects of change. Research done well can make 'facile gestures' from any political perspective more difficult and less defensible (Rock 2014). Whilst acknowledging the many political choices we make in selecting subjects, methodologies, and audiences, we remain firmly of the view that we can change the world by 'right description', partly because radical critique is implicit and immanent in right description (Liebling 2015).

FORMS OF ENGAGEMENT

We noted above that we have chosen in this chapter deliberately to focus less on the 'standard questions' of how, why, and when criminological research might inform criminal justice *policy*. It is perhaps worth beginning this section by elaborating some of the problems of assuming that criminology (or indeed any social science) should seek to exercise influence, or to generate 'impact' at all, or principally by this route. Figure 43.1 seeks to illustrate the much more complex set of relationships, engagements, and directions of influence that exist.

If, for example, we examine the typology of forms of criminological engagements discussed by Loader and Sparks (2011), we find the research–policy relationship implicitly prioritized in the first three forms. Thus, the 'scientific expert', who might be associated mostly with notions of evidence-based policy, takes no normative position (beyond a commitment to empiricism) but aims to use scientific findings to shape more adaptive policy (and thereby practice) responses to crime-related problems. The 'policy advisor' and the 'observer-turned-player' work to bring a somewhat wider range of criminological and criminal justice knowledge to bear on how executives and parliaments develop and change law and policy (and thereby practice). The 'social movement theorist/activist' works differently—perhaps with users, stakeholders, and communities of interest—to generate more collective pressures on political processes.

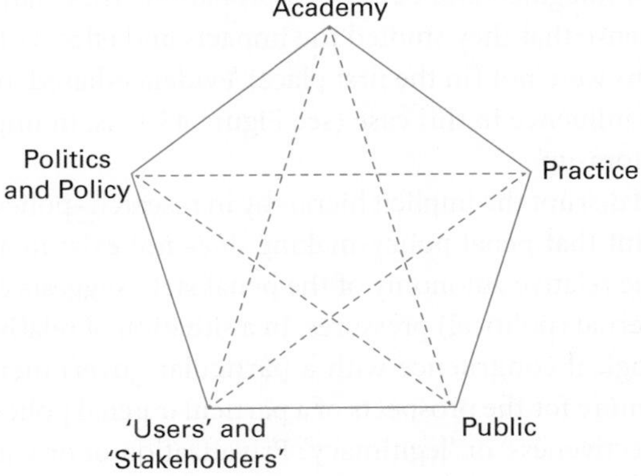

Figure 43.1 Criminological engagements

The 'lonely prophet' is cast as a somewhat disengaged but nonetheless important voice, berating the abuses and failings of the system and of those in power. She/he shouts because her commitment and vocation demands it, not because she expects anyone in power to listen. If she/he has influence, it will not usually be with policy-makers; rather, it will rest in removing scales from our eyes, arousing our resistance to or revolt against an unjust status quo.

From our perspective, none of these forms of engagement seems an accurate or satisfying description of what we think we do or how we try to do it. Moreover, we think that there are flaws in the assumptions that lie behind each of them. Exploring these flaws may help to clarify our position.

The first problem is one of *implicit hierarchy*. By this we mean that it is assumed in most (if not all) of these positions that to secure change criminologists should seek to influence those 'at the top'—the politicians, senior civil servants, and executives that make up what Garland (2013) refers to as 'the penal state'—those who have the power to change how the system is constituted, resourced, governed, and regulated. While we do not dismiss the importance of these forms of penal power, it is wrong to assume that the penal state *determines* the nature and impact of the penal system. An analysis of penal change (or stability) that privileges 'policy-makers' within the penal state neglects, for example, the ways in which power, authority, and influence are *distributed* within penal systems. In particular, it underestimates the extent to which practitioners (at all levels) instantiate and constitute penality. As one of us has argued elsewhere, governmental rationalities and technologies exercise powerful but indirect effects on penality as practised and experienced. The 'governmentality gap' in our analyses of penal change and stability is an important one (McNeill *et al.* 2009). For present purposes, we suggest that direct criminological engagements with *practice* (as well as with or through policy) may be of critical value.

Consider the role of practitioners in penal innovation. The progenitors of probation, for example, both in the USA and in the UK, were neither policy-makers nor researchers (at least understood in the usual senses); they were judges who developed imaginative responses to practical problems. They may have thus *become* policy-makers—first locally, then nationally and internationally—but they were not insiders in the penal state when they first imagined and developed probation. They may also have become researchers in the sense that they studied the impacts and effects of their innovations, but their innovations were not (in the first place) 'evidence-based' or 'research-driven'. So, the direction of influence in this case (see Figure 43.1) is, in important ways, non-hierarchical or 'bottom-up'.

Equally, we could disrupt the implicit hierarchy in research–policy thinking by making the obvious point that penal policy-making does not exist in a vacuum. Garland (2013) notes that the relative autonomy of the penal state suggests different degrees of insulation from external (political) pressures. In a situation of relatively low autonomy, for example, ideological congruence with a particular government's wider political agenda will matter more for the prospects of a particular penal policy than criminological evidence of 'effectiveness' or 'legitimacy'. Privatization of or within penal systems is an obvious example here since the enthusiasm of its advocates both precedes and exceeds any empirical case that can be made for its effectiveness in improving penal outcomes (see Hedderman 2013). Equally, privatization might be successfully resisted 'from below' through public, professional, or union opposition, at least where privatization advocates find themselves in a weak position in the penal field (Page 2011).

Recognizing the exposure of (some) penal states to ideological and political forces therefore suggests that criminological engagements *beyond* the penal state—with civil society and with the wider polity—may have the potential to be as influential as penal policy engagements, particularly in democratic societies. Although some scholars have argued for the development of mechanisms to protect penal policy from party and electoral politics (Lacey 2008), we agree with Loader and Sparks (2011: 117) that the path to a 'better politics of crime and its regulation' lies through criminological engagements that improve the quality of democratic debate. It is perhaps here that the 'social movement theorist/activist' and the 'lonely prophet' do their work.

However, even if we challenge the hierarchical assumptions that lend priority to engagement with policy-makers, and stress instead the significance of engagements with practitioners, users, stakeholders, and civil society, a second problem relates to implicit assumptions about 'who knows best' about punishment and penal reform. We might term this a problem of *epistemic privilege*. In different ways and for different reasons, all five of Loader and Sparks' (2011) characters seem to think that they know best how to change the penal system.

The 'scientific expert' who thinks she/he knows 'what works', perhaps on the basis of randomized control trials or meta-analyses, roots their privilege in a particular set of claims about methodological rigour. Through the appliance of science, a 'solution' to the policy challenge has been designed, engineered, and tested; the problem is now one of 'technology transfer' (Bourgon *et al.* 2010) or implementation—and we now have a 'science' specifically for implementation too. The 'policy advisor' and the 'observer turned player', as we have seen, draw on a wider range of forms of evidence, and may sometimes integrate normative analyses and arguments into their prescriptions—but implicitly they claim an epistemic privilege based on their criminological expertise. Rather than offering 'expert solutions', the 'social movement theorist' and the 'lonely prophet' are perhaps more likely to present analyses of the failures and injustices that the current system creates or exacerbates through its institutional forms, cultures, and practices; they will certainly weave normative claims into these analyses. But, even if they reject selling criminological remedies for social problems, they nonetheless trade on their own cultural capital (as scholars) to endow their critique with a particular status.

In different ways then, these various dispositions might sometimes quieten or silence other knowledge claims rooted, for example, in experience of, and reflection upon, being a penal subject, a penal practitioner, a penal policy-maker, or a politician. Of course, researchers often amplify certain of these voices but, to extend the metaphor, sometimes amplification can cause distortion. The question of which voices academics choose to quieten and which to amplify often reflects our own commitments, partialities, and interests. Indeed, even the notion that we make choices about quietening and amplifying reflects the epistemic privilege and social position that (some) academics (sometimes) occupy. We do not wish to overstate this, but sometimes authoritative academic contributions to public debate become difficult to ignore, especially when these contributions reinforce or are reinforced by other forms of expertise.

Raising this issue throws into sharp relief the need for criminologists to clarify the *particular* value of *their* knowledge. Conventionally, academics tend to defend the value of research and scholarship in two ways; one related to method and one related to theory. In relation to methods, we argue that the disciplined nature of our inquiry leads to the production of knowledge of special standing; knowledge that is qualitatively different from reflection on 'lay' experience, for example. In relation to theory, we argue that our ability to observe, analyse, and interpret the social worlds we study, and to synthesize scholarship or to refine arguments about them, is based on an unusual (and hard-won) command of cognate ideas, or of methods of reasoning-with-evidence. To summarize, we are able to see better because we look harder and because we have a body of knowledge that enables us to make better sense of what we see.

As committed social scientists, it is hardly surprising that we have much sympathy with these claims. But our experience of criminological engagements suggests we moderate them significantly. Our preferred position might be better summed up thus: We are able to see things with a certain sort of clarity because we have specific skills that enable us look at social problems or phenomena in particular ways and because our knowledge, values and skills enable or require us to *work with others* in making sense of what we see—and then in figuring out (together) what to do about it. No certainties are possible even in the best kinds of social science; only the gradual development of better accounts of social phenomena, and corrections of misunderstandings about them. Smith (2010) calls this perspective 'epistemological humility'.

We will say more about this position later in the chapter, and illustrate it, but we recognize that for some colleagues our account so far may raise questions about *independence*. For some scholars, academic freedom requires independence from non-academic 'interference' in research. While submission to academic peer review and to professional-collegial self-regulation is necessary, any external influence upon knowledge production is viewed with suspicion, since it risks importing biases and interests that might distort research processes, thus tainting the knowledge produced.

We have some sympathy with this position too, not least because we have at times suffered the subtle and sometimes overt forms of political interference in the conduct and dissemination of research against which defenders of academic freedom protest. However, some claims about academic independence are themselves problematic. For example, it is almost impossible to imagine *any* form of empirical research that can be conducted without establishing some degree of *interdependence*. Negotiating funding and access both entail the creation of relationships of reciprocal exchange; securing the data typically depends at the very least on promising to meet the requirements of funders and showing some sensitivity to the legitimate interests and needs of the research site. For us, this does not inherently compromise the independence of our *analyses*, but it does compel us to act ethically in honouring the terms of engagement that all parties agree. This is not to cede control of the research agenda. Indeed, in our experience, we have usually been able to build our own research questions around the (sometimes) more narrowly conceived questions our funders or gatekeepers started out with. In practice, they have most often welcomed the additional insights these 'extra-curricular' or more theoretically informed questions bring (see Bottoms 2003).

More significantly, some visions or versions of academic independence come close to setting up exploitation of research 'subjects'. Such exploitation is implicit in a model of independence that treats 'the field' as a place we visit merely in order to extract data with which we hasten back to our 'ivory towers' in order to expertly conduct analyses. Indeed, the metaphors of 'tower' and 'field' are interesting (and mutually insulting) ones. The tower is pristine, safe, and defended; it offers a privileged view of the landscape and its lofty construction implies esteem. The field is messy and dirty. Those in it lack both perspective and status. At the same time, it is impossible to see, hear, smell, taste, touch, and *feel* what is going on in the field from the tower. Perhaps most relevant to this chapter, the perspective that the tower allows might help us to see things differently—and to notice things that can't easily be seen from within the field. But the opposite is also true: to try to reform the field without being in it would be foolhardy and probably dangerous, unless one's intention is simply to fire projectiles from the tower to reshape the field. That would be 'impact' to be sure, but not of the sort we would seek or endorse.

Instead, criminological engagement for us implies constant movement between the 'tower' and the 'field'. While we recognize the privilege and the value of having a place for refuge and reflection—a site where independence of mind can be developed and refreshed, or the wisdom of colleagues can be sought—we also recognize that reflection and analysis happens continuously in the field. Knowledge production and exchange is going on all the time in the penal sites we visit. Our distinctive contribution is not to trump or displace these processes, disrespecting our non-academic partners' skills, capacities, or ethics en masse. However, it *is* our task to bring *our* methodological and theoretical knowledge and skills to bear in respectfully challenging, developing, supplementing, or re-imagining knowledge and its uses in penal policy and practice. It follows that, paradoxically, we must maintain *critical* perspective *at the same time as* narrowing the gaps between theory, research, policy, and practice. Put another way, we need independence of mind and thought, as free as possible from the influence of 'interests' that might distort research processes and findings, but we also need to respect, recognize, and manage the practical interdependencies and existing expertise that meaningful engagement requires.

To flesh out the discussion of ways of conceptualizing and negotiating criminological engagements, we provide some illustrations and reflect on what they taught us.

THREE (POSITIVE) EXPERIENCES OF ENGAGEMENT

TRUST AND RELATIONSHIPS IN HIGH SECURITY PRISONS

Two examples arose in two 'accidental-longitudinal' studies of high security prisons by the first author, with others (Liebling *et al.* 2015a, 2015b). The first is the use of a Dialogue group in the early stages of ethnographic work in prison: a weekly afternoon-long session with a regular group of prisoners to discuss matters of mutual interest, sometimes with literature distributed in advance, to stimulate discussion. The sessions were difficult and time-consuming to arrange in a high security prison, and took up a full day of our research week, but it had no other purpose than to 'get to know you and the prison', and 'for you to get to know us'. It transformed our project. Time spent talking, meeting, discussing ideas, and being present, brought an authenticity and degree of insight to the research we did not anticipate. It made our project more 'collaborative'. We had requested the Dialogue group as a way of 're-entering' the field after a long gap between ethnographic projects in Whitemoor prison, and because there had once been a Dialogue group in the prison, which we had been invited to attend, the first time around (Price and Liebling 1999). Running it ourselves was challenging (Liebling *et al.* 2015b). But it was so valuable, and so much appreciated, that when the third ethnography came around—in a different high security prison altogether, two prisoners who had participated in our Whitemoor Dialogue group came to welcome us in the prison's library asking, 'are we going to have a Dialogue group, then?' So we did. These groups became places of deep conversation and relationship building, as Cohen and Taylor powerfully demonstrate in their 1970s version of collaborative research with long-term prisoners, published as 'Psychological Survival' (1972). There was scope for emotional content, critique of us and of research (lively conversations which always lead to greater understanding and commitment to research among our participants, despite the clear limitations in 'helping them now' that we always acknowledge), and for deep understandings to develop. These relationships got us invited into some of the 'darkest corners' of the prison, but also made us more aware of how far prison life was also infused by trust, love, and constructive survival strategies as well as anger and power. Our Dialogue participants eventually became our first interviewees, and the meaning-making that went on in these interviews was deeply satisfying, to us as researchers and to our participants. These criminological engagements felt insightful, respectful and 'right'. Such forms of engagement can equally be created with prison staff (see, e.g. Arnold 2005) or with those in higher positions of power (see, e.g. Liebling and Crewe 2012, 2016). They can be 'appreciative' (see Liebling *et al.* 1999) and 'generative' (see Liebling 2015). This does not make them inherently uncritical or one-sided.

The 'return to Whitemoor' study led to a follow up project funded by the Economic and Social Research Council (ESRC) on the location and building of trust in two other high security prisons, selected for contrast (see Liebling *et al.* 2015a). As we had anticipated (given the experience above), studying trust took us further than studying the 'presenting problem' of risk; because exploring trust *built* trust. We were painfully aware of the centrality of risk in such deep end penal settings, but we needed to penetrate the 'distrust paralysis' framing life in prison, in order to find out what was 'really going on' in each prison. As a result of our slow and trust-oriented methodology, we were able to describe some important differences in the shape and tone of prisoner social organization in these prisons. We found a link between our methodological approach and our emerging data. Where trust in the prison in general was lowest, and staff kept a distance from prisoners, the prisoners organized themselves hierarchically, asserted narrow, polarized, and politically charged identities, and sometimes appointed religious leaders on their wings. In other words, faith and power were more likely to coexist in low-trust climates, and faith identities were more inclined to be adopted, or used strategically to gain advantage or intimidate staff and other prisoners. Where trust was higher (albeit still 'guarded'), and prisoners were approached as 'experiencing subjects', rather than 'experienced objects' (see Liebling 2015), the social organization of prisoners was flatter and more fluid, growth and change was more likely, faith practices and explorations had more to do with meaning, religious doubt was permissible, and risks were contained, managed, and reduced as a dialogue took place about how to reduce or give up violence. On the wings where trust was 'placed intelligently', whatever identity mattered most (e.g. faith, ethnicity, or geographical location)—Muslim prisoners, Christians, Mancunians, or Scousers, interacted. They were on food boats together, they learned things from one another, and they invited each other to festivals or ceremonies. Some described an 'uneasy' truce, but it was more of a norm to cooperate rather than to compete or struggle for power (see Liebling *et al.* 2015a). We learned that recognition and misrecognition, ways of knowing and not knowing, of understanding or misunderstanding others, were *processes* with *outcomes*. This is an important lesson for us as research scholars.

Prisoners in both of our main research sites decided that it was so important to talk about trust that they decided to carry on doing it without us after we left. They described 'awakenings' in letters to us, as they created a mood in which it was possible to ask questions about faith, faith practices, cultural practices, and individual experience. They invited staff to attend. An incoming Governor supported them in their trust-building work. We were invited back for meetings, as well as onto various local and national working parties to help transform practice in this area of work. Methods, findings, theory, and developing practice became interconnected. Our growing confidence that we understood some of the problems of high security prisons made us credible and better informed critics of its current use and form.

DESISTANCE, REINTEGRATION, AND CHANGE

Similar processes (and outcomes) have been experienced in quite different settings by the second author of this chapter. Between 2011–12, he worked with several academic colleagues (Steve Farrall, Claire Lightowler, and Shadd Maruna) to develop and coordinate the ESRC-funded project Desistance Knowledge Exchange (RES-189-25-0258). The project was conceived in response to demands from policy-makers, practitioners, and others for a clearer articulation of the implications of desistance research for probation practice or (more broadly) 'offender management'. Responding to these demands represented a problem for the academics involved, who had all been critical of the highly prescriptive and managerialized misuses of 'what works?' scholarship in the 1990s. Moreover, desistance research itself suggested that supporting the process required a much more complex and reflexive dialogue between those involved (policy-makers, practitioners, people with, convictions, etc.). It followed that we could not and should not seek to develop the manual or programme or practice protocols for which some were asking.

Instead, the 'investigators' tried to design a process of 'knowledge exchange' that would offer a forum for the kind of reflexive dialogue that seemed necessary. To that end, we brought people together who had different forms of knowledge about desistance, rehabilitation, and reintegration (academic, professional, and personal). We did this in several ways, setting up a blog site (as a forum and repository for the dialogue[1]), making a film together, and then using the film to stimulate dialogue in 'appreciative inquiry' workshops to generate propositions for changes in the penal system.

Unsurprisingly, these propositions ranged far beyond the focus on practices of supervision with which we began. In many respects, they underlined and focused on the importance of work not to change 'offenders' through such practices but rather to better engage civil society in re/integration.[2] Studies of re-entry and desistance have increasingly suggested that securing and maintaining a place of belonging is often extremely difficult and that this undermines rehabilitative efforts and investments (Miller 2014; Nugent and Schinkel 2016). It is increasingly clear that shifting and reforming social relations lie at the heart of desistance processes (Weaver 2015). But it was primarily through the dialogue that the DesKE project created that the full import of this dawned on the second author. In simple terms, it led him to realize (and to argue) that re/integration is profoundly affected by the reception of the returning citizen and that, since the development of rehabilitation has focused so much on developing methods for changing individuals, it has been seriously underdeveloped in both theory and practice (McNeill 2012, 2014; Kirkwood and McNeill 2015).

That realization necessarily prompted a change in the second author's research agenda and in his approach to engagements with penal reform. Rather than focusing primarily on work to develop better adapted supervisory practices, his efforts have shifted towards efforts to ensure that people with convictions are better heard and heeded in debates about reform, for example, through helping to establish an organization of and for people with convictions.[3] He has also begun to work with others to explore the role of creative practices and cultural processes in developing both a richer dialogue about punishment and new practices and processes of reintegration, by helping to establish an organization that brings academics, artists, practitioners, and people with convictions and others together to share their stories creatively and to build community in the process.[4] In both of these activities, the focus and locus of change efforts has shifted from individuals to institutions, systems, communities, civil society, and the state itself. In this case therefore, criminological engagement has changed (or impacted upon) the criminologist involved; his agenda, practices, approaches, and concerns.

RESEARCH AND REFORM IN TUNISIAN PRISONS

The third author of this chapter recently completed a pilot study of the quality of life in Tunisian prisons, which inadvertently explored some of the political and professional complexities we raise in this chapter. Since its revolution in 2011, Tunisia has been transitioning from decades of authoritarian rule to the Arab world's only democracy. Social, cultural, and institutional paradigms have been shifting alongside the nation's political transformation, including reform efforts within the criminal justice system.

[1] See http://blogs.iriss.org.uk/discoveringdesistance/, accessed 29 June 2016.

[2] See http://blogs.iriss.org.uk/discoveringdesistance/files/2013/08/DesKE-Propositions.pdf, accessed 8 February 2016.

[3] See http://www.positiveprison.org, accessed 29 June 2016.

[4] http://www.voxliminis.co.uk, accessed 29 June 2016.

Prisons have recently become more porous here, as civil society has gained (limited) access in order to monitor conditions, investigate allegations of torture or abuse, and assess compliance with international human rights standards. However, the saturation of Non Governmental Organizations, their narrow or incomplete understanding of 'what matters most' to prison occupants, and a deficit-oriented approach to evaluation has arguably impeded reform efforts by alienating and shaming prison authorities. Methodologically rigorous, empirical research (in nearly every discipline) is all but absent in Tunisia. Being granted access to such a closed-off world was nothing short of remarkable. Persistent, yet patient, negotiations with Tunisian prison authorities over many months and several visits eventually opened doors that had previously been closed to researchers, and most of society. 'Selling' knowledge and academic expertise to curious, though sceptical, authorities took considerable time and engagement. They posed practical, but difficult questions: 'What good is knowledge?' 'We need money and resources to reform—what will research do for us?'

Tunisia, much like prison services and universities in the UK, sought policy-oriented outputs to justify the research (and exposure). But there, the research terrain was a blank canvas. Once we were inside the prison walls, we were given unprecedented access. We—two foreign and experienced field researchers, with two local and inexperienced assistants—were novel.[5] We built rapport, gained trust, and eventually became 'children of the house', rather than 'guests'. Prisoners and staff alike were enthusiastic to engage, have their voices heard, and be recognized. The authorities were eager to understand how our foreign lens could illuminate life within their prisons. We were appreciative in our approach, intentionally setting our orientation and methods apart from civil society monitors, towards whom the prisons felt a deep distrust. We sought to understand their world on their terms, and from the perspective of all prison occupants. We were not there to judge or simply to criticize. We were there to understand and authentically describe life as it unfolded.

'PRESENCE', RECOGNITION, AND BEARING WITNESS

All actual life is encounter (Buber 2010: 62).

Between us, we have learned that knowledge-generation is slow and cumulative, that it takes time to 'read a situation' in complex human and social environments, precisely because knowledge is 'situated'. It is, and should be, an iterative process, with the research community and the world of practice teaching and learning from each other at every step of the way. We have learned that humility is an important and valued quality that researchers must cultivate and that research participants welcome a research presence of the kinds we outline above. They often know nothing about the

[5] Bethany Schmidt would like to thank her colleague in this study, Andrew M. Jefferson, and their two research assistants, Yasmin Haloui and Souhir Châari.

research 'gatekeeping' processes that are intended to protect them. The question of when or whether research can harm or, conversely, support participants is more complex and nuanced than our research frameworks typically acknowledge. Sometimes, politically driven, overtly critical, or abolitionist research agendas can inadvertently close doors or alienate those they claim to support. In the same way, 'protections' that limit the kinds of questions that can be asked, or the length and nature of the contact permitted, can impose inappropriate constraints on ordinary human interactions which are both ethically and methodologically defensible. Whilst our methodologies sometimes break the rules of (non) engagement we are often required to follow, we can do worse than 'being a Thou' (a whole person, with no 'reduction of the *I* or of the *Thou*'; Buber 2010) in the field for others.[6]

A rarely acknowledged counterweight to the emphasis on access, and the policing of it, and on the protection of 'human subjects' from interference or harm, is the value of an appropriate and interested 'research presence' to people being punished and those who work in the penal system. Being in the field, listening, observing, and noticing cultures, practices and decisions, can validate 'champions' of good practice, keep good work aflame when it seems barely alight, and can bring hope to a population who feel otherwise forgotten. Research can, however fleetingly, capture and tell 'stories without an audience', reducing dehumanizing feelings of 'ethical loneliness' or the sense of injustice at not being heard (Stauffer 2015). Once agreed, research can reach into places where power is flowing unobserved, except by those who experience or wield it. Asking questions in such unreachable places can change situations, in the short and longer term. One prisoner still insists that we (Liebling *et al.* 2015a) were 'sent by God', because he had lost all hope of ever making any progress out of the prison he felt 'buried in'. We 'simply' (it was not so simple) asked questions, until senior staff working in the institution came to realize that the circumstances of his confinement (e.g. on an administrative 'no one-to-one contact' procedure) were illegitimate. The encounter between researchers, partners, and participants can (at its most 'mundane') temporarily alleviate loneliness and despair, or it can reframe a life or a practice: prisoners, staff, and senior managers have often reflected that an extended conversation about their experience or working life has enabled an important (and usually helpful) shift in understanding and perspective. Some prepare for a second stage interview by writing notes, keeping a diary, or talking with friends about what the interview revealed. So many prisoners have said, 'you know what, miss (or often, our names), that's the most I've talked since I've been in here!'. Practitioners often make similar comments about the opportunities for deep reflection on practice that research engagements create.

Increasingly, as we have learned to be more self-consciously appreciative and person-centred, partners and participants have expressed enthusiasm for or meaning in research encounters. They shake our hands, use our names, and tell us that our presence in their world gives them hope, and makes them feel 'seen': not just understood, but acknowledged as people with potential, who matter ('Do you ever think about us

[6] Buber's analysis of I-Thou encounters proposes that a *meeting* between embedded, experiencing persons should occur, with 'no system of ideas, no foreknowledge, and no fancy' intervening between 'I and Thou'. When we impose such constraints, we force others to 'appear as an *It*': as experienced, projected, alienated objects. Conversely, we can bring forth or meet a Thou in careful and curious dialogue. This is not easy: 'How powerful is the unbroken world of *It*, and how delicate are the appearances of the *Thou*' (Buber 2010: 98).

when you are not here?' The answer is 'Yes'). The building of trust, and the feeling of recognition, generates deep and authentic conversation, allows space for reflection, and provides an atmosphere in which both of us in the encounter are learning about who our participants are, and may want to be in the future. An absence of cynicism, the avoidance of labels and diagnoses, and care to check powerful or institutionalized assumptions, permit the meaning of action to be worked out afresh.

This is not collusion, as under these conditions, and with sufficient time, participants (both penal subjects and penal practitioners) may acknowledge parts of their nature, past, or behaviour that they regret, and have been struggling to understand. There is, and should be, a link between our efforts at criminological *verstehen* (an understanding of the intention, meaning, context, and emotional content of action) and the feeling of recognition reported by our research participants (Berlin 2013: 44). They become, as we suggested above, a *Thou* (a 'distinct personal being' with moral commitments and complex capacities) and not an *It* (the projection of others' assumptions) in the research journey (see Smith 2010: 61; Buber 2010; Liebling 2015). We claim no exclusive expertise in using this approach, and we have seen it in action in other work, but we attempt to describe it here in order to defend and encourage it, to challenge some of the official frameworks that seek to 'protect research participants' from such encounters, and to propose strong links between this person-centred approach and the quality of our data. There are always day-to-day constraints of time, funding, job security, and other restrictions on research practice, and we have inherent limitations as people, but our practices should aim to be acceptable to research participants 'in real time' as well as to remote or politically configured committees.

This basic orientation to participants is made complex by the attention we pay to all of those with whom we engage in our work—prisoners/offenders, staff and senior managers or policy-makers—but these tensions and conflicts between the worldviews or frameworks of power holders, and those who are its subjects, constitute the very penal field we are seeking to understand. The form that power takes, its distribution, and how it is experienced, differ over time as well as between penal sites (and jurisdictions). Diagnosing and describing these distinct formations and their underlying cultural conditions has become an important dimension of our work in this area. Of course, we hold, have collected, or grown, powers and privileges of our own over the course of our research lives, or we would not be in a position to write this account or carry out our work. Our powers are mainly (but not exclusively), and certainly feel, soft, fragile, and contingent, and they are subject to many constraints. We consider some of the challenges we have faced, and continue to face, below.

SOME PROBLEMS AND CHALLENGES OF ENGAGEMENT

Despite all that we have said above, and our willingness to do it, one of the less visible but extraordinary difficulties of engaged research is fielding, or navigating, 'interests'—academic, political, professional, and personal—and (in all four spheres) power/ambition. These intersecting interests shape and constrain us, those with whom we engage, and responses to our research. Doing policy-relevant research means there are high stakes for all concerned. The process, of (for example) managing (or being managed by) Steering Groups, negotiating detail, discussing drafts of reports, and in the end, taking a 'line', can be emotionally fraught, and personally testing. Reconciling honesty with diplomacy and tact, often on the spot at tense meetings, can be a serious challenge. Getting this wrong, or losing the argument, can result in delays to publication, declined access, changes in the tone of reports, and the loss of valued relationships. Keeping both integrity and relationships intact requires fine judgement, some courage, faith in the data, and thorough understanding of the field. This is one of the reasons why management-at-a-distance research leadership models do not work. Acquiring research grants commits us to being in the field, not to transferring data collection to cheaper and less experienced others. An apprenticeship model, involving Principal Investigators and research teams working side by side for long periods, produces better outcomes (including the training and development of less experienced research personnel, and the challenge they provide to our established practices) than other approaches, but is not systematically built in to our professional infrastructure. Responsible research requires an intensity of focus and presence that funders and university managers routinely underestimate.

We are acutely aware that there are some special problems of carrying out research in an adverse policy climate. This is a very different experience, with its own implications, from doing so in a more liberal, enlightened climate (e.g. in the years post-Woolf, 1991–3) or when policy and practice, for example in the prevention of prison suicides, is improving. There are times when we have found doing research in the 'wrong policy climate' deeply uncomfortable (e.g. Liebling 1999) or when we have not responded to invitations to apply for research funding because it is too obvious that the research question is futile, insincerely asked, or sets the wrong agenda.

For those entering the field or in the early stages of building a career (though some of these problems are shared whatever the career stage), there are special difficulties of power, standing, and climate. Criminology as a 'moral enterprise' often conflicts with a wary, defensive political penal climate in which austerity and punitive policy-driven agendas dominate the discourse. The changing landscape of criminal justice, fuelled by an escalating trend to govern through crime, has led to an institutional culture dominated by fear, security, and control. Many penological researchers are denied access, or face significant constraints determined by distant panels of decision-makers. The evolving landscape of academic life, too, has changed the nature of funded research. As research has become more aggressively market driven, demonstrating 'impact' or 'producing deliverables' often trumps the deep, sustained, and slow forms of engagement required for critical reflection. Criminologists find themselves working in environments that demand greater efficiency and output, and a dependency on 'income generation'. The contractual arrangements between funding bodies and academics set a variety of boundaries around the research to be completed. These arrangements regulate the nature of information to be gathered, the way the research will be reported, and sometimes the form of dissemination. In this context, the concept of 'academic freedom' is under considerable threat.

Changes in the 'research field' have created a precarious and complicated terrain. Some of the current challenges in research methodology and practice have been borne out of institutional-reputational fears, or aversion to an evidence-base that may run contrary to current policy. These perceived risks of exposure often lead to publication delays, rigid and over bureaucratic contractual negotiations, censorship, barriers to access, or the withholding of findings from the public. Conducting academically rigorous, meaningful research, and reflecting openly on its moral and theoretical implications within a fear-infused political context is not easily negotiated. Whilst many of these challenges are not new, the constraints have arguably become tighter and more prevalent in some jurisdictions. In England and Wales in particular, some of the 'hostilities' of an earlier era (see, e.g., Cohen and Taylor 1977) have returned, in an even heavier guise. Gaining access to prisons in England and Wales, for example, requires applicants to identify which of the prison service's priorities the research is most relevant to: 'delivering the punishment and orders of the court'; 'security, safety and public protection'; 'reducing reoffending'; or 'improving efficiency and reducing costs'. Finding space within these narrowly conceived priorities to argue for curiosity-driven, exploratory, or unconventional studies can result in denial due to 'resource constraints' or 'security concerns'.

For many of the growing penal research community, there remains a determination and obligation to conduct meaningful and thoughtful, high quality empirical research despite the many institutional limitations and changing political priorities. At times this requires creative or unorthodox, but always careful and respectful, modes of engagement with those who hold the keys to access or funding. Navigating the way is not easy or comfortable. Some colleagues have given up the fight after finding the power and politics of penological research too oppositional. Others have written insightfully about the struggle and the moral complications of conducting such research.

Nearly 20 years ago, Mike Presdee and Reece Walters recounted their experience of research(er) suppression. In 1996, the Australian government attempted to censor their presentation entitled 'Mixing Policy and Practice with Politics' at the Australian and New Zealand Society of Criminology conference. The paper related to an evaluation of a crime prevention strategy that was critical of state policy. The conference convenors refused to accept this censorship, despite the threat of legal action, and instead created a special plenary session on academic freedom. The debate at this session was unanimously in support of academic freedom and the condemnation of the state in its efforts to suppress the dissemination of independent research. However, there was some dissention; some of the academics present argued that criminologists needed to exert better diligence in safeguarding against the loss of copyright and intellectual property by carefully negotiating these matters prior to signing contractual agreements. John Braithwaite argued that social science researchers were constantly faced with governments having 'carte blanche over intellectual property' and that criminologists needed to be 'buccaneers' when it comes to publishing their research. He went on to say, 'You can try and stop me and you can probably take away the report, but that would be foolish because I will go to the press and get the report out in a much better way' (Presdee and Walters 1998). Braithwaite continues to research, write, and publish: we know of no criminologists who have been formally sanctioned for their work, but perhaps repressive self-governance is a significant risk in all of our lives.

This brief case (there are many others like it that we know of—but few appear in published form) raises several important questions about the current and future role of criminology. What does 'academic freedom' mean in a changing, increasingly legalistic and managerial research environment? Do we have an ethical obligation to disseminate findings? Does this obligation transcend contractual agreements, as it does in other fields? How do we balance relationships when objectives or values are in conflict with each other? Haskell (1996) argues that academic research must reflect a commitment to intellectual authority and to our obligation as 'critic and conscience of society'. Presdee and Walters warned that the increase in contract research, which legally binds academics to provide information to clients or stakeholders, is capable of restricting academic freedom, not only in terms of dissemination but in terms of scope and as a curiosity-driven exercise. Loader and Sparks (2011: 55), drawing on Wilsdon and colleagues (2005: 47), pose an urgent question for social science policy: 'how do we best strengthen the contribution that scientists and research can make to the health and robustness of our shared public realm?' Fostering a sense of 'scientific citizenship' is founded on methods of 'upstream public engagement' that are critical and valuable to academic life, and to building an informed public.

Brusten (1981) has written about the 'policing of knowledge' through government acts of intimidation or research suppression, and its more subtle forms, like limiting field access, or prescribing/proscribing methodologies in practice. Policing of knowledge also comes from the market-driven trend of contractual work. Radzinowicz (1994: 101) described this as governmental tampering with research by 'setting the agenda . . . in relation to the administrator's conception of what kind of knowledge is needed', and therefore, what kind of knowledge is produced and disseminated. It has often been the case that administrators find the research they could not conceive of highest value in developing better practice. Sometimes loosening the control on research can lead to better outcomes for all.

Presdee and Walters (1998) note that criminology 'is a sensitive enterprise, which often questions the role of the 'state' and its relationships to its citizenry' (156). David Garland has argued that research may provide unwelcome views to governments who seek confirmation of their political agenda (1997). Foucault (1977) warned that it is through these forms of regulation, censorship, or suppression of information that power is exerted to control or regulate the production of knowledge. The policy/impact-driven research agenda, favoured by government funding bodies in particular, can create precarious research relationships in which neither government nor the public have much to gain. Researchers have had to adapt their diplomatic and methodological prowess in order to coexist or survive within the current and changing penal climate. There are risks of this to scholarship and the trajectory of knowledge generation within our field.

By contrast, gaining and sustaining prison access in the Tunisian context was an ongoing 'dance' involving long and careful negotiations. But there were no contracts or forms, limitations on dissemination, or research panels to determine the 'value' of such work. Access was achieved dialogically and through mutual regard. There were some compromises and occasional pushback. The third author, her colleagues, and prison officials tested each other's boundaries, as this was uncharted and unfamiliar territory for them all. There was reciprocated respect and recognition of professional competence: the authorities knew their prisons from an operational and local perspective, and the research team were 'prison experts' in other international domains. They trusted the team to do our jobs. Positive risks were taken, which were never taken for granted. Sometimes the unbureaucratized newcomer to prisons research is allowed freedoms to explore and learn that have been legislated away in more 'developed' but risk averse economies. 'Professionalisation' of process does not always bring about higher quality research.

CONCLUSION

There are risks that as criminologists working in an increasingly commodified 'knowledge industry' we will follow rather than inform policy (as Paul Rock suggests in his chapter, this volume)—perhaps especially when we engage in specific, government funded, and often politically constrained policy evaluation. We should resist this, and encourage our partners to be literate and enlightened users of, commissioners of, and partners in meaningful research. This has worked, to a considerable extent, in our collective experiences here and abroad.

Our work, collectively and cumulatively, is about whether and with what consequences the state can, and to what extent it does, use its penal power legitimately and in the way in which penality is conceived and organized. This changes over time, as do the numbers and types of people subjected to penal sanctions of different sorts and, different lengths of time. From this, we learn much about how organizations think, and operate, from our own encounters with them. If we emerge brutalized and reeling from an attempt to organize access, or from a period of fieldwork, this tells us something important about what is going on around us. Penal practice has a way of communicating its motives and values beyond those who are its principal subjects. Engaged criminological research is both a challenge and a privilege. We do not deny that there is a politics of knowledge-building. Our reflections in this chapter are intended as a gathering together of our own experience and a stimulus to more open discussion and careful reflection on these important questions of knowledge, power, and reform.

SELECTED FURTHER READING

The best introduction to sociological research of the kind we describe is C. Wright Mills' *The Sociological Imagination* (1959). There are many helpful recent collections on the politics, methods, and emotional effects of engaged criminological research, including special editions of *Qualitative Inquiry* ('Doing Prison Research Differently', edited by Yvonne Jewkes (2014)), the *International Journal for Crime, Justice and Social Democracy*, edited by Hilde Tubex (2015), and *Qualitative Research in Criminology: Advances in Criminological Theory*, edited by J. Miller and W. Palacios (2015). See also McAra's 'Can Criminologists Change The World? Critical Reflections On The Politics, Performance And Effects Of Criminal Justice' (2016).

REFERENCES

ARNOLD, H. (2005), 'The effects of prison work', in A. Liebling and S. Maruna (eds) (2005), *The Effects of Imprisonment*, Cullompton: Willan.

BERLIN, I. (2013), *The Proper Study of Mankind: An Anthology of Essays*, London: Vintage.

BOTTOMS, A. E. (2003), 'Theoretical Reflections on the Evaluations of a Penal Policy Initiative', in L. Zedner and A. Ashworth (eds), *The Criminological Foundations of Penal Policy: Essays in Honour of Roger Hood*, Oxford: Oxford University Press.

BOURGON, G., BONTA, J., RUGGE, T., and GUTTIEREZ, L. (2010), 'Technology transfer: the importance of ongoing clinical supervision in translating "what works" to everyday community supervision', in F. McNeill, P. Raynor, and C. Trotter (eds), *Offender Supervision: New Directions in Theory, Research and Practice*, Cullompton: Willan.

BRUSTEN, M. (1981), 'State control of information in the field of deviance and social control', *Working Papers in European Criminology*, 2.

BUBER, M. (2010), *I and Thou* (trans. R. G. Smith), CT: Martino Publishers.

COHEN, S. and TAYLOR, L. (1977), 'Talking about Prison Blues', in C. Bell and H. Newby (eds), *Doing Sociological Research*, London: George Allen and Unwin.

COHEN, S. and TAYLOR, L. (1972), *Psychological Survival: The Experience of Long-Term Imprisonment*, Middlesex: Penguin.

FOUCAULT, M. (1977), *Discipline and Punish: The Birth of the Prison*, London: Allen Lane.

GARLAND, D. (1988), 'British criminology before 1935', *British Journal of Criminology*, 28(1): 1–17.

GARLAND, D. (1997), 'Of Crimes and Criminals: The Development of Criminology in Britain', in M. Maguire, R. Morgan, and R. Reiner (eds), *The Oxford Handbook of Criminology*, 2nd edn, Oxford: Oxford University Press.

GARLAND, D. (2013), 'Penality and the Penal State', *Criminology*, 51(3): 475–517.

HASKELL, T. (1996), 'Justifying the Rights of Academic Freedom in the era of 'Power/Knowledge', in L. Menand (ed.), *The Future of Academic Freedom*, Chicago: University of Chicago Press.

HEDDERMAN, C. (2013), 'Payment By Results: Hopes, Fears and Evidence', *British Journal of Community Justice*, 11(2–3): 43–58.

HOUSDEN, M. (2006), 'Oscar Wilde's imprisonment and an early idea of "Banal Evil"' or 'Two "wasps" in the system. How Reverend W.D. Morrison and Oscar Wilde challenged penal policy in late Victorian England', (25 October 2006), *forum historiae iuris*, available at: http://www.forhistiur.de/2006-10-housden/, accessed 4 August 2016.

KIRKWOOD, S. and MCNEILL, F. (2015), 'Integration and Reintegration: Comparing pathways to citizenship through asylum and criminal justice', *Criminology & Criminal Justice*, 15(5): 511–26.

LACEY, N. (2008), *The Prisoners' Dilemma: Political Economy and Punishment in Contemporary Democracies*, Cambridge: Cambridge University Press.

LIEBLING, A. (1999), 'Doing research in prison: Breaking the silence?', *Theoretical Criminology*, 3(2): 147–73.

LIEBLING, A. (2015), 'Description at the Edge? I-It/I-Thou Relations and Action in Prisons Research', *International Journal for Crime, Justice and Social Democracy*, 4(1): 18–32.

LIEBLING, A., ARMSTRONG, R., BRAMWELL, R., and WILLIAMS, R. (2015a), 'Locating trust in a climate of fear: religion, moral status, prisoner leadership, and risk in maximum security prisons—key findings from an innovative study', ESRC Report: Key Research Findings ES/L003120/1, available at: http://www.prc.crim.cam.ac.uk/publications/trust-report, accessed 4 August 2016.

LIEBLING, A., ARNOLD, H., and STRAUB, C. (2015b), 'Prisons Research beyond the Conventional: Dialogue, "Creating Miracles" and Staying Sane in a Maximum-Security Prison', in D. Drake, R. Earle, and J. Sloan (eds), *The Palgrave Handbook of Prison Ethnography*, Basingstoke: Palgrave Macmillan.

LIEBLING, A., PRICE, D., and ELLIOTT, C. (1999), 'Appreciative inquiry and relationships in prison', *Punishment & Society*, 1(1): 71–98.

LIEBLING, A., PRICE, D., and HM PRISON SERVICE (1999), *An Exploration of Staff Prisoner Relationships at HMP Whitemoor*, London: HM Prison Service.

LIEBLING, A. and CREWE, B. (2012), 'Prisons beyond the new penology: the shifting moral foundations of prison management', in R. Sparks and J. Simon (eds), *The Sage Handbook of Punishment and Society*, London: Sage.

LIEBLING, A and CREWE, B (2016, forthcoming), 'Prison Governance: Why Moral Values Matter', *For Justice and Mercy: International Reflections on Prison Chaplaincy*, Nijmegen: Wolf Legal Publishers.

LOADER, I. and SPARKS, R. (2011), *Public Criminology?*, New York: Routledge.

MCNEILL, F. (2012), 'Four forms of "offender" rehabilitation: Towards an interdisciplinary perspective', *Legal and Criminological Psychology*, 17(1): 18–36.

MCNEILL, F. (2014), 'Punishment as Rehabilitation', in G. Bruinsma and D. Weisburd (eds), *Encyclopedia of Criminology and Criminal Justice*, New York: Springer. [A final draft version of this paper is available open access online at: http://blogs.iriss.org.uk/discoveringdesistance/files/2012/06/McNeill-When-PisR.pdf, accessed 13 January 2017.]

MCNEILL, F., BURNS, N., HALLIDAY, S., HUTTON, N., and TATA, C. (2009), 'Risk, responsibility and reconfiguration: Penal adaptation and misadaptation', *Punishment & Society*, 11(4): 419–42.

MILLER, R. (2014), 'Devolving the Carceral State: Race, Prisoner Re-entry, and the Micro Politics of Urban Poverty Management', *Punishment & Society*, 16(3): 305–35.

Morrison, W. D. (1898), 'Letter to the Editor', *The Times* (London), 8 January 1898.

Nugent, B. and Schinkel, M. (2016), 'The pains of desistance', *Criminology & Criminal Justice*, 16(5): 568–84, doi: 10.1177/1748895816634812.

Page, J. (2011), *The Toughest Beat: Politics, Punishment and the Prison Officers Union in California*, Oxford: Oxford University Press.

Presdee, M. and Walters, R. (1998), 'The Perils and Politics of Criminological Research and the Threat to Academic Freedom', *Current Issues in Criminal Justice*, 10(2): 156–67.

Prisons Committee (The Gladstone Report) (1895), *Report from the Departmental Committee on Prisons*, London: HMSO.

Radzinowicz, L. (1939), 'The Evolution of the Modern Penal System', *The Modern Law Review*, 3(2): 121–35.

Radzinowicz, L. (1994), 'Reflections on the state of criminology', *British Journal of Criminology*, 34(2): 99–104.

Robin, G. D. (1964), 'Pioneers in Criminology: William Douglas Morrison (1852-1943)', *Journal of Criminal Law and Criminology*, 55(1): 48–58.

Rock, P. (2014), 'The public faces of public criminology', *Criminology & Criminal Justice*, 14(4): 412–33.

Smith, C. (2010). *What is a person?: Rethinking Humanity, Social Life, and the Moral Good from the Person Up*, Chicago: University of Chicago Press.

Stauffer, J. (2015), *Ethical Loneliness: The Injustice of Not Being Heard*, New York: Columbia University Press.

Weaver, B. (2015), *Offending and Desistance: The Importance of Social Relations*, (vol. 8), London: Routledge.

Wilsdon, J., Wynne, B., and Stilgoe, J. (2005), *The Public Value of Science*, London: Demos.

INDEX

A

B

E

F

G

H

N

O

P

R

S

U

V